W9-CMO-760

VATICAN II
WEEKDAY
MISSAL

VATICAN II
WEEKDAY
MISSAL

Prepared
by the Daughters of St. Paul

Seasonal Themes
by Bruce T. Morrill, S.J.
Professor of Theology, Boston College

Biblical Commentaries
for the Scripture Readings
by Celia Sirois, MA
Instructor in Sacred Scripture

With the *New American Bible* Text
from the **Revised Weekday Lectionary**

Pauline
BOOKS & MEDIA
BOSTON

The Daughters of St. Paul
of the U.S. Province
dedicate the revised edition of the

VATICAN II WEEKDAY MISSAL

to Mary, Queen of the Apostles,
who always gives to us
Jesus her Son—
suffering, glorified, eucharistic,
the Way, the Truth, and the Life of humanity.

GENERAL CONTENTS

PROPER OF SEASONS

THE ORDER OF MASS

How to Use
The Vatican II Weekday Missal

The Vatican II Weekday Missal, companion volume to *The Vatican II Sunday Missal*, presents the inexhaustible riches of the liturgical and biblical texts from the official Sacramentary and the revised Lectionary of the *New Roman Missal*.

The **calendars** on pages 12–41 provide the dates of celebrations through the years 2015.

For the parts of the Eucharistic Celebration used every day, turn to the **Order of Mass** (pp. 884–977).

For the changeable parts of the Eucharistic Celebration, that is, the Proper of the day,* check the following sources:

1) The **liturgical calendar** (pp. 26–41) gives the page number for the current week of the current year, referring to the Propers for that particular week.

2) The **general calendar** (pp. 12–25) gives the page number for the feasts of Jesus Christ, the Blessed Virgin Mary, and the saints that occur throughout the year.

---

* The Proper of the day or the changeable parts of the Mass include both Antiphons and Prayers and the Liturgy of the Word or biblical readings. These occur in this order: Entrance Antiphon, Opening Prayer, First Reading, Responsorial Psalm, Second Reading (if designated), Alleluia Verse or Verse before the Gospel, Gospel, Prayer over the Gifts, Communion Antiphon, Prayer after Communion.

IMPORTANT—The following Masses are found in **The Vatican II Sunday Missal:**

ALL SUNDAY MASSES

HOLY DAYS OF OBLIGATION:

Mary, Mother of God—January 1

Ascension—Thursday after the Sixth Sunday of Easter or Seventh Sunday of Easter

Assumption of the Blessed Virgin Mary—August 15

All Saints—November 1

Immaculate Conception—December 8

Christmas—December 25

HOLY WEEK SERVICES:

Holy Thursday—Evening Mass of the Lord's Supper

Good Friday— Celebration of the Lord's Passion

The Easter Vigil

THE FOLLOWING SOLEMNITIES AND FEASTS:

Baptism of the Lord—Sunday after January 6 or sometimes transferred to a Monday

Presentation of the Lord—February 2

Joseph, Husband of Mary—March 19

Annunciation of the Lord—March 25

Nativity of John the Baptist—June 24

Transfiguration of the Lord—August 6

Exaltation of the Holy Cross—September 14

All Souls—November 2

Dedication of the Lateran Basilica in Rome—November 9

General Calendar

* indicates celebrations proper to the dioceses of the United States

January

Solemnity	1.	MARY, MOTHER OF GOD	Sun. M.
Memorial	2.	Basil the Great and Gregory Nazianzen, bishops and doctors	1774
	3.		
Memorial	4.	*Elizabeth Ann Seton, religious	1775
Memorial	5.	*John Neumann, bishop	1776
Optional M.	6.	*Blessed André Bessette, religious*	1778
Optional M.	7.	*Raymond of Peñafort, priest*	1779
	8.		
	9.		
	10.		
	11.		
	12.		
Optional M.	13.	*Hilary, bishop and doctor*	1780
	14.		
	15.		
	16.		
Memorial	17.	Anthony, abbot	1781
	18.		
	19.		
Optional M.	20.	*Fabian, pope and martyr*	1784
		or *Sebastian, martyr*	1785
Memorial	21.	Agnes, virgin and martyr	1786
Optional M.	22.	*Vincent, deacon and martyr*	1786
	23.		
Memorial	24.	Francis de Sales, bishop and doctor	1787
Feast	25.	CONVERSION OF PAUL, APOSTLE	1789

Memorial	26. Timothy and Titus, bishops	1794
Optional M.	27. *Angela Merici, virgin*	1796
Memorial	28. Thomas Aquinas, priest and doctor	1797
	29.	
	30.	
Memorial	31. John Bosco, priest	1798
Solemnity	Sunday between Jan 2 and Jan 8: EPIPHANY	Sun. M.
Feast	Sunday after Jan 6: BAPTISM OF THE LORD	Sun. M.

February

	1.	
Feast	2. PRESENTATION OF THE LORD	Sun. M.
Optional M.	3. *Blase, bishop and martyr* or *Ansgar, bishop*	1799 1800
	4.	
Memorial	5. Agatha, virgin and martyr	1800
Memorial	6. Paul Miki, priest and martyr, and Companions, martyrs	1801
	7.	
Optional M.	8. *Jerome Emiliani, priest*	1802
	9.	
Memorial	10. Scholastica, virgin	1803
Optional M.	11. *Our Lady of Lourdes*	1804
	12.	
	13.	
Memorial	14. Cyril, monk, and Methodius, bishop	1805
	15.	
	16.	
Optional M.	17. *Seven Founders of the Order of* *Servites, religious*	1806

	18.	
	19.	
	20.	
Optional M.	21. *Peter Damian, bishop and doctor*	1807
Feast	22. CHAIR OF PETER, APOSTLE	1808
Memorial	23. Polycarp, bishop and martyr	1810
	24.	
	25.	
	26.	
	27.	
	28.	

March

	1.	
	2.	
Optional M.	3. **Katharine Drexel, virgin*	1811
Optional M.	4. *Casimir, prince*	1812
	5.	
	6.	
Memorial	7. Perpetua and Felicity, martyrs	1813
Optional M.	8. *John of God, religious*	1814
Optional M.	9. *Frances of Rome, religious*	1815
	10.	
	11.	
	12.	
	13.	
	14.	
	15.	
	16.	
Optional M.	17. *Patrick, bishop*	1815
Optional M.	18. *Cyril of Jerusalem, bishop and doctor*	1817
Solemnity	19. JOSEPH, HUSBAND OF MARY	Sun. M.
	20.	

	21.		
	22.		
Optional M.	23.	*Toribio de Mogrovejo, bishop*	1818
	24.		
Solemnity	25.	ANNUNCIATION OF THE LORD	Sun. M.
	26.		
	27.		
	28.		
	29.		
	30.		
	31.		

April

	1.		
Optional M.	2.	*Francis of Paola, hermit*	1819
	3.		
Optional M.	4.	*Isidore, bishop and doctor*	1820
Optional M.	5.	*Vincent Ferrer, priest*	1821
	6.		
Memorial	7.	John Baptist de la Salle, priest	1821
	8.		
	9.		
	10.		
Memorial	11.	Stanislaus, bishop and martyr	1822
	12.		
Optional M.	13.	*Martin I, pope and martyr*	1823
	14.		
	15.		
	16.		
	17.		
	18.		
	19.		
	20.		

Optional M.	21. *Anselm, bishop and doctor*	1824
	22.	
Optional M.	23. *George, martyr*	1825
	or *Adalbert, bishop and martyr*	1825
Optional M.	24. *Fidelis of Sigmaringen, priest and martyr*	1826
Feast	25. MARK, EVANGELIST	1827
	26.	
	27.	
Optional M.	28. *Peter Chanel, priest and martyr*	1830
	or *Louis Mary de Montfort, priest*	1831
Memorial	29. Catherine of Siena, virgin and doctor	1831
Optional M.	30. *Pius V, pope*	1833

May

Feast	1. JOSEPH THE WORKER	1834
Memorial	2. Athanasius, bishop and doctor	1839
Feast	3. PHILIP AND JAMES, APOSTLES	1841
	4.	
	5.	
	6.	
	7.	
	8.	
	9.	
Optional M.	10. *Blessed Damien Joseph de Veuster of Moloka'i, priest*	1844
	11.	
Optional M.	12. *Nereus and Achilleus, martyrs*	1845
	or *Pancras, martyr*	1845
	13.	
Feast	14. MATTHIAS, APOSTLE	1846
Optional M.	15. *Isidore, farmer*	1850
	16.	
	17.	

Optional M.	18. *John I, pope and martyr*	1851
	19.	
Optional M.	20. *Bernardine of Siena, priest*	1852
	21.	
	22.	
	23.	
	24.	
Optional M.	25. *Venerable Bede, priest and doctor*	1854
	or *Gregory VII, pope*	1855
	or *Mary Magdalene de' Pazzi, virgin*	1856
Memorial	26. Philip Neri, priest	1857
Optional M.	27. *Augustine of Canterbury, bishop*	1858
	28.	
	29.	
	30.	
Feast	31. VISITATION OF THE BLESSED VIRGIN MARY	1859
Solemnity	First Sunday after Pentecost: HOLY TRINITY	Sun. M.
Solemnity	Sunday after Trinity Sunday: CORPUS CHRISTI	Sun. M.
Solemnity	Friday following Second Sunday after Pentecost: SACRED HEART OF JESUS	983
Memorial	Saturday following Second Sunday after Pentecost: Immaculate Heart of Mary	1864

June

Memorial	1. Justin, martyr	1866
Optional M.	2. *Marcellinus and Peter, martyrs*	1868
Memorial	3. Charles Lwanga and Companions, martyrs	1869
	4.	
Memorial	5. Boniface, bishop and martyr	1870
Optional M.	6. *Norbert, bishop*	1871
	7.	

	8.		
Optional M.	9.	*Ephrem, deacon and doctor*	1872
	10.		
Memorial	11.	Barnabas, apostle	1873
	12.		
Memorial	13.	Anthony of Padua, priest and doctor	1876
	14.		
	15.		
	16.		
	17.		
	18.		
Optional M.	19.	*Romuald, abbot*	1877
	20.		
Memorial	21.	Aloysius Gonzaga, religious	1878
Optional M.	22.	*Paulinus of Nola, bishop*	1880
		or *John Fisher, bishop and martyr,*	
		and Thomas More, martyr	1882
	23.		
Solemnity	24.	BIRTH OF JOHN THE BAPTIST	Sun. M.
	25.		
	26.		
Optional M.	27.	*Cyril of Alexandria, bishop and doctor*	1883
Memorial	28.	Irenaeus, bishop and martyr	1883
Solemnity	29.	PETER AND PAUL, APOSTLES	Sun. M.
Optional M.	30.	*First Martyrs of the Church*	
		of Rome	1886

July

Optional M.	1.	**Blessed Junipero Serra, priest*	1887
	2.		
Feast	3.	THOMAS, APOSTLE	1888
Optional M.	4.	*Elizabeth of Portugal, queen*	1890
		or **Independence Day*	1891

Optional M.	5. *Anthony Mary Zaccaria, priest*	1895
Optional M.	6. *Maria Goretti, virgin and martyr*	1895
	7.	
	8.	
	9.	
	10.	
Memorial	11. Benedict, abbot	1897
	12.	
Optional M.	13. *Henry, king*	1899
Memorial	14. *Blessed Kateri Tekakwitha, virgin	1900
Memorial	15. Bonaventure, bishop and doctor	1901
Optional M.	16. *Our Lady of Mount Carmel*	1902
	17.	
Optional M.	18. *Camillus de Lellis, priest*	1903
	19.	
	20.	
Optional M.	21. *Lawrence of Brindisi, priest and doctor*	1904
Memorial	22. Mary Magdalene	1907
Optional M.	23. *Bridget of Sweden, religious*	1912
	24.	
Feast	25. JAMES, APOSTLE	1912
Memorial	26. Joachim and Ann, parents of Mary	1915
	27.	
	28.	
Memorial	29. Martha	1918
Optional M.	30. *Peter Chrysologus, bishop and doctor*	1921
Memorial	31. Ignatius of Loyola, priest	1922

August

Memorial	1. Alphonsus Liguori, bishop and doctor	1925
Optional M.	2. *Eusebius of Vercelli, bishop*	1927
	or *Peter Julian Eymard, priest*	1927
	3.	

Memorial	4. John Mary Vianney, priest	1928
Optional M.	5. *Dedication of the Basilica of Saint Mary Major*	1930
Feast	6. TRANSFIGURATION OF THE LORD	Sun. M.
Optional M.	7. *Sixtus II, pope and martyr, and Companions, martyrs* or *Cajetan, priest*	1931 1932
Memorial	8. Dominic, priest	1933
	9.	
Feast	10. LAWRENCE, DEACON AND MARTYR	1934
Memorial	11. Clare, virgin	1936
	12.	
Optional M.	13. *Pontian, pope and martyr, and Hippolytus, priest and martyr*	1938
Memorial	14. Maximilian Mary Kolbe, priest and martyr	1939
Solemnity	15. ASSUMPTION OF THE BLESSED VIRGIN MARY	Sun. M.
Optional M.	16. *Stephen of Hungary, king*	1942
	17.	
Optional M.	18. *°Jane Frances de Chantal, religious*	1943
Optional M.	19. *John Eudes, priest*	1944
Memorial	20. Bernard, abbot and doctor	1944
Memorial	21. Pius X, pope	1946
Memorial	22. Queenship of Mary	1947
Optional M.	23. *Rose of Lima, virgin*	1949
Feast	24. BARTHOLOMEW, APOSTLE	1950
Optional M.	25. *Louis, king* or *Joseph Calasanz, priest*	1954 1954
	26.	
Memorial	27. Monica	1955
Memorial	28. Augustine, bishop and doctor	1957
Memorial	29. Beheading of John the Baptist, martyr	1959

30.

31.

September

		First Monday of September: Labor Day	1963
	1.		
	2.		
Memorial	3.	Gregory the Great, pope and doctor	1963
	4.		
	5.		
	6.		
	7.		
Feast	8.	BIRTH OF MARY	1965
Memorial	9.	*Peter Claver, priest	1969
	10.		
	11.		
	12.		
Memorial	13.	John Chrysostom, bishop and doctor	1969
Feast	14.	EXALTATION OF THE HOLY CROSS	Sun. M.
Memorial	15.	Our Lady of Sorrows	1971
Memorial	16.	Cornelius, pope and marty, and Cyprian, bishop and martyr	1977
Optional M.	17.	*Robert Bellarmine, bishop and doctor*	1978
	18.		
Optional M.	19.	*Januarius, bishop and martyr*	1979
Memorial	20.	Andrew Kim Taegon, priest and martyr, and Paul Chong Hasang, catechist and martyr, and Companions, martyrs	1980
Feast	21.	MATTHEW, APOSTLE AND EVANGELIST	1982
	22.		
	23.		
	24.		

	25.	
Optional M.	26. *Cosmas and Damian, martyrs*	1985
Memorial	27. Vincent de Paul, priest	1986
Optional M.	28. *Wenceslaus, king and martyr*	1988
	or *Lawrence Ruiz, martyr,*	
	and Companions, martyrs	1989
Feast	29. MICHAEL, GABRIEL, AND RAPHAEL,	
	ARCHANGELS	1990
Memorial	30. Jerome, priest and doctor	1994

October

Memorial	1. Thérèse of the Child Jesus, virgin	
	and doctor	1997
Memorial	2. Guardian Angels	2000
	3.	
Memorial	4. Francis of Assisi, religious	2004
	5.	
Optional M.	6. *Bruno, priest*	2006
	or **Blessed Marie-Rose Durocher, virgin*	2007
Memorial	7. Our Lady of the Rosary	2008
	8.	
Optional M.	9. *Denis, bishop and martyr,*	
	and Companions, martyrs	2009
	or *John Leonardi, priest*	2010
	10.	
	11.	
	12.	
	13.	
Optional M.	14. *Callistus I, pope and martyr*	2011
Memorial	15. Teresa of Jesus, virgin and doctor	2012
Optional M.	16. *Hedwig, religious*	2014
	or *Margaret Mary Alacoque, virgin*	2015
Memorial	17. Ignatius of Antioch, bishop and martyr	2016

Feast	18. LUKE, EVANGELIST	2018
Memorial	19. *Isaac Jogues and John de Brébeuf, priests and martyrs, and Companions, martyrs	2022
	or *Paul of the Cross, priest	2023
	20.	
	21.	
	22.	
Optional M.	23. *John of Capistrano, priest*	2024
Optional M.	24. *Anthony Mary Claret, bishop*	2025
	25.	
	26.	
	27.	
Feast	28. SIMON AND JUDE, APOSTLES	2026
	29.	
	30.	
	31.	

November

Solemnity	1. ALL SAINTS	Sun. M.
	2. ALL SOULS	Sun. M.
Optional M.	3. *Martin de Porres, religious*	2029
Memorial	4. Charles Borromeo, bishop	2030
	5.	
	6.	
	7.	
	8.	
Feast	9. DEDICATION OF THE LATERAN BASILICA	Sun. M.
Memorial	10. Leo the Great, pope and doctor	2032
Memorial	11. Martin of Tours, bishop	2033
Memorial	12. Josaphat, bishop and martyr	2036
Memorial	13. *Frances Xavier Cabrini, virgin and religious	2037

	14.	
Optional M.	15. *Albert the Great, bishop and doctor*	2038
Optional M.	16. *Margaret of Scotland, queen*	2039
	or *Gertrude, virgin*	2040
Memorial	17. Elizabeth of Hungary, religious	2041
Optional M.	18. *Dedication of the Basilicas of Peter and Paul, apostles*	2042
	or **Rose Philippine Duchesne, virgin*	2046
	19.	
	20.	
Memorial	21. Presentation of Mary	2046
Memorial	22. Cecilia, virgin and martyr	2047
Optional M.	23. *Clement I, pope and martyr*	2048
	or *Columban, abbot*	2048
	or *Blessed Miguel Agustin Pro, priest and martyr*	2049
Optional M.	24. *Andrew Dung-Lac, priest and martyr, and Companions, martyrs*	2050
	25.	
	26.	
	27.	
	28.	
	29.	
Feast	30. ANDREW, APOSTLE	2050
	Fourth Thursday: **Thanksgiving Day*	2054
Solemnity	Last Sunday in Ordinary Time: CHRIST THE KING	Sun. M.

December

	1.	
	2.	
Memorial	3. Francis Xavier, priest	2056

Optional M.	4. *John of Damascus, priest, religious, and doctor*	2057
	5.	
Optional M.	6. *Nicholas, bishop*	2058
Memorial	7. *Ambrose, bishop and doctor*	2059
Solemnity	8. IMMACULATE CONCEPTION OF THE BLESSED VIRGIN MARY	Sun. M.
Optional M.	9. **Juan Diego, hermit*	2060
	10.	
Optional M.	11. *Damasus I, pope*	2061
Feast	12. OUR LADY OF GUADALUPE	2062
Memorial	13. Lucy, virgin and martyr	2062
Memorial	14. John of the Cross, priest and doctor	2063
	15.	
	16.	
	17.	
	18.	
	19.	
	20.	
Optional M.	21. *Peter Canisius, priest and doctor*	2065
	22.	
Optional M.	23. *John of Kanty, priest*	2066
	24.	
	25.	
Feast	26. STEPHEN, FIRST MARTYR	159
Feast	27. JOHN, APOSTLE AND EVANGELIST	163
Feast	28. THE HOLY INNOCENTS, MARTYRS	167
Optional M.	29. *Thomas Becket, bishop and martyr*	2067
	30.	
Optional M.	31. *Sylvester I, pope*	2068

LITURGICAL CALENDAR

This **Liturgical Calendar** is to be used in conjunction with the **General Calendar** (pp. 12–25).

Page number refers only to the beginning of the week or to a specific day.

S.M. refers to **Vatican II Sunday Missal.**

Year I and **Year II** designate the Series of Readings only for the 34 Weeks in Ordinary Time, which are arranged in a two-year cycle: **Year I** is for the odd years (2001, 2003, etc.), and **Year II** is for the even years (2002, 2004, etc.). Please note that the liturgical year begins with advent.

In some dioceses of the United States the **Solemnity of the Ascension** is celebrated on the Seventh Sunday of Easter.

Lectionary Cycle	Page	2001 — II	2002 — I	2003 — II
1st Week of Advent	49	3–8 Dec	2–7 Dec	1–6 Dec
Immaculate Conception	*S.M.*	*8 Dec*	*9 Dec*	*8 Dec*
2nd Week of Advent	75	10–15 Dec	9–14 Dec	8–13 Dec
3rd Week of Advent	99	———	16 Dec	15–16 Dec
December 17–24	123	17–24 Dec	17–24 Dec	17–24 Dec
Christmas	*S.M.*	*25 Dec*	*25 Dec*	*25 Dec*
Octave of Christmas	159	26–31 Dec	26–31 Dec	26–31 Dec
Holy Family	*S.M.*	*30 Dec*	*29 Dec*	*28 Dec*
		2002 — II	**2003 — I**	**2004 — II**
Mary, Mother of God	*S.M.*	*1 Jan*	*1 Jan*	*1 Jan*
If before Epiphany Jan 2–7	183	2–5 Jan	2–4 Jan	2–3 Jan
Epiphany of the Lord	*S.M.*	*6 Jan*	*5 Jan*	*4 Jan*
After Epiphany Mon–Sat (or Jan 7–12)	210	7–12 Jan	6–11 Jan	5–10 Jan
Baptism of the Lord	*S.M.*	*13 Jan*	*12 Jan*	*11 Jan*
1st in Ordinary Time	235	14–19 Jan	13–18 Jan	12–17 Jan
2nd in Ordinary Time	265	21–26 Jan	20–25 Jan	19–24 Jan
3rd in Ordinary Time	296	28 Jan–2 Feb	27 Jan–1 Feb	26–31 Jan
4th in Ordinary Time	327	4–9 Feb	3–8 Feb	2–7 Feb
Presentation of the Lord	*S.M.*	*2 Feb*	*2 Feb*	*2 Feb*
5th in Ordinary Time	360	11–12 Feb	10–15 Feb	9–14 Feb
If before Lent 6th in Ordinary Time	392	———	17–22 Feb	16–21 Feb
7th in Ordinary Time	421	———	24 Feb–1 Mar	23–24 Feb
8th in Ordinary Time	452	———	3–4 Mar	———
9th in Ordinary Time	482	———		
Ash Wednesday	523	*13 Feb*	*5 Mar*	*25 Feb*
After Ash Wednesday	531	14–16 Feb	6–8 Mar	26–28 Feb
1st Week of Lent	543	18–23 Feb	10–15 Mar	1–6 Mar
2nd Week of Lent	567	25 Feb–2 Mar	17–22 Mar	8–13 Mar

Lectionary Cycle	Page	2002 — II	2003 — I	2004 — II
3rd Week of Lent	597	4–9 Mar	24–29 Mar	15–20 Mar
Joseph, Husband of Mary	*S.M.*	*19 Mar*	*19 Mar*	*19 Mar*
Annunciation	*S.M.*	*8 Apr*	*25 Mar*	*25 Mar*
4th Week of Lent	622	11–16 Mar	31 Mar–5 Apr	22–27 Mar
5th Week of Lent	652	18–23 Mar	7–12 Apr	29 Mar–3 Apr
Holy Week Mon–Wed	686	25–27 Mar	14–16 Apr	5–7 Apr
Chrism Mass	699	28 Mar	17 Apr	8 Apr
Easter Triduum	*S.M.*	*28–30 Mar*	*17–19 Apr*	*8–10 Apr*
Easter	*S.M.*	*31 Mar*	*20 Apr*	*11 Apr*
Octave of Easter	710	1–6 Apr	21–26 Apr	12–17 Apr
2nd Week of Easter	738	8–13 Apr	28 Apr–3 May	19–24 Apr
3rd Week of Easter	762	15–20 Apr	5–10 May	26 Apr–1 May
4th Week of Easter	786	22–27 Apr	12–17 May	3–8 May
5th Week of Easter	811	29 Apr–4 May	19–24 May	10–15 May
6th Week of Easter	835	6–11 May	26–31 May	17–22 May
Ascension	*S.M.*	*9 May*	*29 May*	*20 May*
7th Week of Easter	859	13–18 May	2–7 June	24–29 May
Pentecost	*S.M.*	*19 May*	*8 June*	*30 May*
Trinity Sunday	*S.M.*	*26 May*	*15 June*	*6 June*
Corpus Christi	*S.M.*	*2 June*	*22 June*	*13 June*
If after Pentecost 6th in Ordinary Time	392	—	—	
7th in Ordinary Time	421	20–25 May	—	
8th in Ordinary Time	452	27 May–1 June	—	
9th in Ordinary Time	482	3–8 June	—	31 May–5 June
Always after Pentecost 10th in Ordinary Time	995	10–15 June	9–14 June	7–12 June
Sacred Heart of Jesus	983	7 June	27 June	18 June
11th in Ordinary Time	1024	17–22 June	16–21 June	14–19 June
12th in Ordinary Time	1056	24–29 June	23–28 June	21–26 June

Lectionary Cycle	Page	2002 — II	2003 — I	2004 — II
Birth of John the Baptist	**S.M.**	24 June	24 June	24 June
Peter and Paul, Apostles	**S.M.**	29 June	29 June	29 June
13th in Ordinary Time	**1091**	1–6 July	30 June–5 July	28 June–3 July
14th in Ordinary Time	**1126**	8–13 July	7–12 July	5–10 July
15th in Ordinary Time	**1158**	15–20 July	14–19 July	12–17 July
16th in Ordinary Time	**1191**	22–27 July	21–26 July	19–24 July
17th in Ordinary Time	**1223**	29 July–3 Aug	28 July–Aug 2	26–31 July
18th in Ordinary Time	**1254**	5–10 Aug	4–9 Aug	2–7 Aug
Transfiguration	**S.M.**	6 Aug	6 Aug	6 Aug
19th in Ordinary Time	**1289**	12–17 Aug	11–16 Aug	9–14 Aug
Assumption	**S.M.**	15 Aug	15 Aug	15 Aug
20th in Ordinary Time	**1323**	19–24 Aug	18–23 Aug	16–21 Aug
21st in Ordinary Time	**1356**	26–31 Aug	25–30 Aug	23–28 Aug
22nd in Ordinary Time	**1383**	2–7 Sept	1–6 Sept	30 Aug–4 Sept
23rd in Ordinary Time	**1411**	9–14 Sept	8–13 Sept	6–11 Sept
24th in Ordinary Time	**1440**	16–21 Sept	15–20 Sept	13–18 Sept
Triumph of the Cross	**S.M.**	14 Sept	14 Sept	14 Sept
25th in Ordinary Time	**1469**	23–28 Sept	22–27 Sept	20–25 Sept
26th in Ordinary Time	**1499**	30 Sept–5 Oct	29 Sept–4 Oct	27 Sept–2 Oct
27th in Ordinary Time	**1531**	7–12 Oct	6–11 Oct	4–9 Oct
28th in Ordinary Time	**1562**	14–19 Oct	13–18 Oct	11–16 Oct
29th in Ordinary Time	**1589**	21–26 Oct	20–25 Oct	18–23 Oct
30th in Ordinary Time	**1617**	28 Oct–2 Nov	27 Oct–1 Nov	25–30 Oct
All Saints	**S.M.**	1 Nov	1 Nov	1 Nov
All Souls	**S.M.**	2 Nov	2 Nov	2 Nov
31st in Ordinary Time	**1645**	4–9 Nov	3–8 Nov	1–6 Nov
32nd in Ordinary Time	**1674**	11–16 Nov	10–15 Nov	8–13 Nov
Dedication of St. John Lateran	**S.M.**	9 Nov	9 Nov	9 Nov
33rd in Ordinary Time	**1703**	18–23 Nov	17–22 Nov	15–20 Nov
34th in Ordinary Time	**1737**	25–30 Nov	24–29 Nov	22–27 Nov

Lectionary Cycle	Page	2004 — I	2005 — II	2006 — I
1st Week of Advent	49	29 Nov–4 Dec	28 Nov–3 Dec	4–9 Dec
Immaculate Conception	*S.M.*	*8 Dec*	*8 Dec*	*8 Dec*
2nd Week of Advent	75	6–11 Dec	5–10 Dec	11–16 Dec
3rd Week of Advent	99	13–16 Dec	12–16 Dec	——
December 17–24	123	17–24 Dec	17–24 Dec	18–24 Dec
Christmas	*S.M.*	*25 Dec*	*25 Dec*	*25 Dec*
Octave of Christmas	159	27–31 Dec	26–31 Dec	26–30 Dec
Holy Family	*S.M.*	*26 Dec*	*30 Dec*	*31 Dec*
		2005 — I	**2006 — II**	**2007 — I**
Mary, Mother of God	*S.M.*	*1 Jan*	*1 Jan*	*1 Jan*
If before Epiphany Jan 2–7	183	——	2–7 Jan	2–6 Jan
Epiphany of the Lord	*S.M.*	*2 Jan*	*8 Jan*	*7 Jan*
After Epiphany Mon–Sat (or Jan 7–12)	210	3–8 Jan	——	——
Baptism of the Lord	*S.M.*	*9 Jan*	*9 Jan*	*8 Jan*
1st in Ordinary Time	235	10–15 Jan	9–14 Jan	8–13 Jan
2nd in Ordinary Time	265	17–22 Jan	16–21 Jan	15–20 Jan
3rd in Ordinary Time	296	24–29 Jan	23–28 Jan	22–27 Jan
4th in Ordinary Time	327	31 Jan–5 Feb	30 Jan–4 Feb	29 Jan–3 Feb
Presentation of the Lord	*S.M.*	*2 Feb*	*2 Feb*	*2 Feb*
5th in Ordinary Time	360	7–8Feb	6–11 Feb	5–10 Feb
If before Lent 6th in Ordinary Time	392	——	13–18 Feb	12–17 Feb
7th in Ordinary Time	421	——	20–25 Feb	19–20 Feb
8th in Ordinary Time	452	——	27–28 Feb	——
9th in Ordinary Time	482	——	——	——
Ash Wednesday	523	9 Feb	1 Mar	21 Feb
After Ash Wednesday	531	22–24 Feb	10–12 Feb	2–4 Mar
1st Week of Lent	543	14–19 Feb	6–11 Mar	26 Feb–3 Mar
2nd Week of Lent	567	21–26 Feb	13–18 Mar	5–10 Mar

Lectionary Cycle	Page	2005 — I	2006 — II	2007 — I
3rd Week of Lent	597	28 Feb–5 Mar	20–25 Mar	12–17 Mar
Joseph, Husband of Mary	*S.M.*	*19 Mar*	*20 Mar*	*19 Mar*
Annunciation	*S.M.*	*4 Apr*	*25 Mar*	*26 Mar*
4th Week of Lent	622	7–12 Mar	27 Mar–1 Apr	19–24 Mar
5th Week of Lent	652	14–19 Mar	3–8 Apr	26–31 Mar
Holy Week Mon–Wed	686	21–23 Mar	10–12 Apr	2–4 Apr
Chrism Mass	699	24 Mar	13 Apr	5 Apr
Easter Triduum	*S.M.*	*24–26 Mar*	*13–15 Apr*	*5–7 Apr*
Easter	*S.M.*	*27 Mar*	*16 Apr*	*8 Apr*
Octave of Easter	710	28 Mar–2 Apr	17–22 Apr	9–14 Apr
2nd Week of Easter	738	4–9 Apr	24–29 Apr	16–21 Apr
3rd Week of Easter	762	11–16 Apr	1–6 May	23–28 Apr
4th Week of Easter	786	18–23 Apr	8–13 May	30 Apr–5 May
5th Week of Easter	811	25–30 Apr	15–20 May	7–12 May
6th Week of Easter	835	2–7 May	22–27 May	14–19 May
Ascension	*S.M.*	*5 May*	*25 May*	*17 May*
7th Week of Easter	859	9–14 May	29 May–3 June	21–26 May
Pentecost	*S.M.*	*15 May*	*4 June*	*27 May*
Trinity Sunday	*S.M.*	*22 May*	*11 June*	*3 June*
Corpus Christi	*S.M.*	*29 May*	*18 June*	*10 June*
If after Pentecost 6th in Ordinary Time	392	——	——	——
7th in Ordinary Time	421	16–21 May	——	——
8th in Ordinary Time	452	23–28 May	——	28 May–2 June
9th in Ordinary Time	482	30 May–4 June	5–10 June	4–9 June
Always after Pentecost 10th in Ordinary Time	995	6–11 June	12–17 June	11–16 June
Sacred Heart of Jesus	983	3 June	23 June	15 June
11th in Ordinary Time	1024	13–18 June	19–24 June	18–23 June
12th in Ordinary Time	1056	20–25 June	26 June–1 July	25–30 June

Lectionary Cycle	Page	2005 — I	2006 — II	2007 — I
Birth of John the Baptist	**S.M.**	*24 June*	*24 June*	*24 June*
Peter and Paul, Apostles	**S.M.**	*29 June*	*29 June*	*29 June*
13th in Ordinary Time	**1091**	27 June–2 July	3–8 July	2–7 July
14th in Ordinary Time	**1126**	4–9 July	10–15 July	9–14 July
15th in Ordinary Time	**1158**	11–16 July	17–22 July	16–21 July
16th in Ordinary Time	**1191**	18–23 July	24–29 July	23–28 July
17th in Ordinary Time	**1223**	25–30 July	31 July–5 Aug	30 July–4 Aug
18th in Ordinary Time	**1254**	1–6 Aug	7–12 Aug	6–11 Aug
Transfiguration	**S.M.**	*6 Aug*	*6 Aug*	*6 Aug*
19th in Ordinary Time	**1289**	8–13 Aug	14–19 Aug	13–18 Aug
Assumption	**S.M.**	*15 Aug*	*15 Aug*	*15 Aug*
20th in Ordinary Time	**1323**	15–20 Aug	21–26 Aug	20–25 Aug
21st in Ordinary Time	**1356**	22–27 Aug	28 Aug–2 Sept	27 Aug–1 Sept
22nd in Ordinary Time	**1383**	29 Aug–3 Sept	4–9 Sept	3–8 Sept
23rd in Ordinary Time	**1411**	5–10 Sept	11–16 Sept	10–15 Sept
24th in Ordinary Time	**1440**	12–17 Sept	18–23 Sept	17–22 Sept
Triumph of the Cross	**S.M.**	*14 Sept*	*14 Sept*	*14 Sept*
25th in Ordinary Time	**1469**	19–24 Sept	25–30 Sept	24–29 Sept
26th in Ordinary Time	**1499**	26 Sept–1 Oct	2–7 Oct	1–6 Oct
27th in Ordinary Time	**1531**	3–8 Oct	9–14 Oct	8–13 Oct
28th in Ordinary Time	**1562**	10–15 Oct	16–21 Oct	15–20 Oct
29th in Ordinary Time	**1589**	17–22 Oct	23–28 Oct	22–27 Oct
30th in Ordinary Time	**1617**	24–29 Oct	30 Oct–4 Nov	29 Oct–3 Nov
All Saints	**S.M.**	*1 Nov*	*1 Nov*	*1 Nov*
All Souls	**S.M.**	*2 Nov*	*2 Nov*	*2 Nov*
31st in Ordinary Time	**1645**	31 Oct–5 Nov	6–11 Nov	5–10 Nov
32nd in Ordinary Time	**1674**	7–12 Nov	13–18 Nov	12–17 Nov5
Dedication of St. John Lateran	**S.M.**	*9 Nov*	*9 Nov*	*9 Nov*
33rd in Ordinary Time	**1703**	14–19 Nov	20–25 Nov	19–24 Nov
34th in Ordinary Time	**1737**	21–26 Nov	27 Nov–2 Dec	26 Nov–1 Dec

Lectionary Cycle	Page	2007 — II	2008 — I	2009 — II
1st Week of Advent	49	3–8 Dec	1–6 Dec	30 Nov–5 Dec
Immaculate Conception	*S.M.*	*8 Dec*	*8 Dec*	*8 Dec*
2nd Week of Advent	75	10–15 Dec	8–13 Dec	7–12 Dec
3rd Week of Advent	99	——	15–16 Dec	14–16 Dec
December 17–24	123	17–24 Dec	17–24 Dec	17–24 Dec
Christmas	*S.M.*	*25 Dec*	*25 Dec*	*25 Dec*
Octave of Christmas	159	26–31 Dec	26–31 Dec	26–31 Dec
Holy Family	*S.M.*	*30 Dec*	*28 Dec*	*27 Dec*
		2008 — II	**2009 — I**	**2010 — II**
Mary, Mother of God	*S.M.*	*1 Jan*	*1 Jan*	*1 Jan*
If before Epiphany Jan 2–7	183	2–5 Jan	2–3 Jan	2 Jan
Epiphany of the Lord	*S.M.*	*6 Jan*	*4 Jan*	*3 Jan*
After Epiphany Mon–Sat (or Jan 7–12)	210	7–12 Jan	5–10 Jan	4–9 Jan
Baptism of the Lord	*S.M.*	*13 Jan*	*11 Jan*	*10 Jan*
1st in Ordinary Time	235	14–19 Jan	12–17 Jan	11–16 Jan
2nd in Ordinary Time	265	21–26 Jan	19–24 Jan	18–23 Jan
3rd in Ordinary Time	296	28 Jan–2 Feb	26–31 Jan	25–30 Jan
4th in Ordinary Time	327	4–5 Feb	2–7 Feb	1–6 Feb
Presentation of the Lord	*S.M.*	*2 Feb*	*2 Feb*	*2 Feb*
5th in Ordinary Time	360	——	9–14 Feb	8–13 Feb
If before Lent 6th in Ordinary Time	392	——	16–21 Feb	15–16 Feb
7th in Ordinary Time	421	——	23–24 Feb	
8th in Ordinary Time	452	——	——	
9th in Ordinary Time	482	——	——	
Ash Wednesday	523	6 Feb	25 Feb	**17 Feb**
After Ash Wednesday	531	7–9 Feb	26–28 Feb	18–20 Feb
1st Week of Lent	543	11–16 Feb	2–7 Mar	22–27 Feb
2nd Week of Lent	567	18–23 Feb	9–14 Mar	1–6 Mar

Lectionary Cycle	Page	2008 — II	2009 — I	2010 — II
3rd Week of Lent	597	25 Feb–1 Mar	16–21 Mar	8–13 Mar
Joseph, Husband of Mary	*S.M.*	*31 Mar*	*19 Mar*	*19 Mar*
Annunciation	*S.M.*	*1 Apr*	*25 Mar*	*25 Mar*
4th Week of Lent	622	3–8 Mar	23–28 Mar	15–20 Mar
5th Week of Lent	652	10–15 Mar	30 Mar–4 Apr	22–27 Mar
Holy Week Mon–Wed	686	17–19 Mar	6–8 Apr	29–31 Mar
Chrism Mass	699	20 Mar	9 Apr	1 Apr
Easter Triduum	*S.M.*	*20–22 Mar*	*9–11 Apr*	*1–3 Apr*
Easter	*S.M.*	*23 Mar*	*12 Apr*	*4 Apr*
Octave of Easter	710	24–29 Mar	13–18 Apr	5–10 Apr
2nd Week of Easter	738	31 Mar–5 Apr	20–25 Apr	12–17 Apr
3rd Week of Easter	762	7–12 Apr	27 Apr–2 May	19–24 Apr
4th Week of Easter	786	14–19 Apr	4–9 May	26 Apr–1 May
5th Week of Easter	811	21–26 Apr	11–16 May	3–8 May
6th Week of Easter	835	28 Apr–3 May	18–23 May	10–15 May
Ascension	*S.M.*	*1 May*	*21 May*	*13 May*
7th Week of Easter	859	5–10 May	25–30 May	17–22 May
Pentecost	*S.M.*	*11 May*	*31 May*	*23 May*
Trinity Sunday	*S.M.*	*18 May*	*7 June*	*30 May*
Corpus Christi	*S.M.*	*25 May*	*14 June*	*6 June*
If after Pentecost				
6th in Ordinary Time	392	12–17 May	——	
7th in Ordinary Time	421	19–24 May	——	——
8th in Ordinary Time	452	26–31 May		24–29 May
9th in Ordinary Time	482	2–7 June	1–6 June	31 May–5 June
Always after Pentecost				
10th in Ordinary Time	995	9–14 June	8–13 June	7–12 June
Sacred Heart of Jesus	983	30 May	19 June	11 June
11th in Ordinary Time	1024	16–21 June	15–20 June	14–19 June
12th in Ordinary Time	1056	23–28 June	22–27 June	21–26 June

Lectionary Cycle	Page	2008 — II	2009 — I	2010 — II
Birth of John the Baptist	**S.M.**	*24 June*	*24 June*	*24 June*
Peter and Paul, Apostles	**S.M.**	*29 June*	*29 June*	*29 June*
13th in Ordinary Time	**1091**	30 June–5 July	29 June–4 July	28 June–3 July
14th in Ordinary Time	**1126**	7–12 July	6–11 July	5–10 July
15th in Ordinary Time	**1158**	14–19 July	13–18 July	12–17 July
16th in Ordinary Time	**1191**	21–26 July	20–25 July	19–24 July
17th in Ordinary Time	**1223**	28 July–2 Aug	27 July–1 Aug	26–31 July
18th in Ordinary Time	**1254**	4–9 Aug	3–8 Aug	2–7 Aug
Transfiguration	**S.M.**	*6 Aug*	*6 Aug*	*6 Aug*
19th in Ordinary Time	**1289**	11–16 Aug	10–15 Aug	9–14 Aug
Assumption	**S.M.**	*15 Aug*	*15 Aug*	*15 Aug*
20th in Ordinary Time	**1323**	18–23 Aug	17–22 Aug	16–21 Aug
21st in Ordinary Time	**1356**	25–30 Aug	24–29 Aug	23–28 Aug
22nd in Ordinary Time	**1383**	1–6 Sept	31 Aug–5 Sept	30 Aug–4 Sept
23rd in Ordinary Time	**1411**	8–13 Sept	7–12 Sept	6–11 Sept
24th in Ordinary Time	**1440**	15–20 Sept	14–19 Sept	13–18 Sept
Triumph of the Cross	**S.M.**	*14 Sept*	*14 Sept*	*14 Sept*
25th in Ordinary Time	**1469**	22–27 Sept	21–26 Sept	20–25 Sept
26th in Ordinary Time	**1499**	29 Sept–4 Oct	28 Sept–3 Oct	27 Sept–2 Oct
27th in Ordinary Time	**1531**	6–11 Oct	5–10 Oct	4–9 Oct
28th in Ordinary Time	**1562**	13–18 Oct	12–17 Oct	11–16 Oct
29th in Ordinary Time	**1589**	20–25 Oct	19–24 Oct	18–23 Oct
30th in Ordinary Time	**1617**	27 Oct–1 Nov	26–31 Oct	25–30 Oct
All Saints	**S.M.**	*1 Nov*	*1 Nov*	*1 Nov*
All Souls	**S.M.**	*2 Nov*	*2 Nov*	*2 Nov*
31st in Ordinary Time	**1645**	3–8 Nov	2–7 Nov	1–6 Nov
32nd in Ordinary Time	**1674**	10–15 Nov	9–14 Nov	8–13 Nov
Dedication of St. John Lateran	**S.M.**	*9 Nov*	*9 Nov*	*9 Nov*
33rd in Ordinary Time	**1703**	17–22 Nov	16–21 Nov	15–20 Nov
34th in Ordinary Time	**1737**	24–29 Nov	23–28 Nov	22–27 Nov

Lectionary Cycle	Page	2010 — I	2011 — II	2012 — I
1st Week of Advent	49	29 Nov–4 Dec	28 Nov–3 Dec	3–8 Dec
Immaculate Conception	*S.M.*	*8 Dec*	*8 Dec*	*8 Dec*
2nd Week of Advent	75	6–11 Dec	5–10 Dec	10–15 Dec
3rd Week of Advent	99	13–16 Dec	12–16 Dec	——
December 17–24	123	17–24 Dec	17–24 Dec	17–24 Dec
Christmas	*S.M.*	*25 Dec*	*25 Dec*	*25 Dec*
Octave of Christmas	159	27–31 Dec	26–31 Dec	26–31 Dec
Holy Family	*S.M.*	*26 Dec*	*30 Dec*	*30 Dec*
		2011 — I	2012 — II	2013 — I
Mary, Mother of God	*S.M.*	*1 Jan*	*1 Jan*	*1 Jan*
If before Epiphany Jan 2–7	183	——	2–7 Jan	2–5 Jan
Epiphany of the Lord	*S.M.*	*2 Jan*	*8 Jan*	*6 Jan*
After Epiphany Mon–Sat (or Jan 7–12)	210	3–8 Jan	——	7–12 Jan
Baptism of the Lord	*S.M.*	*9 Jan*	*9 Jan*	*13 Jan*
1st in Ordinary Time	235	10–15 Jan	9–14 Jan	14–19 Jan
2nd in Ordinary Time	265	17–22 Jan	16–21 Jan	21–26 Jan
3rd in Ordinary Time	296	24–29 Jan	23–28 Jan	28 Jan–2 Feb
4th in Ordinary Time	327	31 Jan–5 Feb	30 Jan–4 Feb	4–9 Feb
Presentation of the Lord	*S.M.*	*2 Feb*	*2 Feb*	*2 Feb*
5th in Ordinary Time	360	7–12 Feb	6–11 Feb	11–12 Feb
If before Lent 6th in Ordinary Time	392	14–19 Feb	13–18 Feb	——
7th in Ordinary Time	421	21–26 Feb	20–21 Feb	——
8th in Ordinary Time	452	28 Feb–5 Mar	——	——
9th in Ordinary Time	482	7–8 Mar	——	——
Ash Wednesday	*523*	*9 Mar*	*22 Feb*	*13 Feb*
After Ash Wednesday	531	10–12 Mar	23–25 Feb	14–16 Feb
1st Week of Lent	543	14–19 Mar	27 Feb–3 Mar	18–23 Feb
2nd Week of Lent	567	21–26 Mar	5–10 Mar	25 Feb–2 Mar

Lectionary Cycle	Page	2011 — I	2012 — II	2013 — I
3rd Week of Lent	597	28 Mar–2 Apr	12–17 Mar	4–9 Mar
Joseph, Husband of Mary	*S.M.*	*19 Mar*	*19 Mar*	*19 Mar*
Annunciation	*S.M.*	*25 Mar*	*26 Mar*	*8 Apr*
4th Week of Lent	622	4–9 Apr	19–24 Mar	11–16 Mar
5th Week of Lent	652	11–16 Apr	26–31 Mar	18–23 Mar
Holy Week Mon–Wed	686	18–20 Apr	2–4 Apr	25–27 Mar
Chrism Mass	699	21 Apr	5 Apr	28 Mar
Easter Triduum	*S.M.*	*21–23 Apr*	*5–7 Apr*	*28–30 Mar*
Easter	*S.M.*	*24 Apr*	*8 Apr*	*31 Mar*
Octave of Easter	710	25–30 Apr	9–14 Apr	1–6 Apr
2nd Week of Easter	738	2–7 May	16–21 Apr	8–13 Apr
3rd Week of Easter	762	9–14 May	23–28 Apr	15–20 Apr
4th Week of Easter	786	16–21 May	30 Apr–5 May	22–27 Apr
5th Week of Easter	811	23–28 May	7–12 May	29 Apr–4 May
6th Week of Easter	835	30 May–4 June	14–19 May	6–11 May
Ascension	*S.M.*	*2 June*	*17 May*	*9 May*
7th Week of Easter	859	6–11 June	21–26 May	13–18 May
Pentecost	*S.M.*	*12 June*	*27 May*	*19 May*
Trinity Sunday	*S.M.*	*19 June*	*3 June*	*26 May*
Corpus Christi	*S.M.*	*26 June*	*10 June*	*2 June*
If after Pentecost 6th in Ordinary Time	392	—	—	—
7th in Ordinary Time	421	—	—	20–25 May
8th in Ordinary Time	452	—	28 May–2 June	27 May–1 June
9th in Ordinary Time	482	—	4–9 June	3–8 June
Always after Pentecost 10th in Ordinary Time	995	—	11–16 June	10–15 June
Sacred Heart of Jesus	983	1 July	15 June	7 June
11th in Ordinary Time	1024	13–18 June	18–23 June	17–22 June
12th in Ordinary Time	1056	20–25 June	25–30 June	24–29 June

Lectionary Cycle	Page	2011 — I	2012 — II	2013 — I
Birth of John the Baptist	**S.M.**	*24 June*	*24 June*	*24 June*
Peter and Paul, Apostles	**S.M.**	*29 June*	*29 June*	*29 June*
13th in Ordinary Time	**1091**	27 June–2 July	2–7 July	1–6 July
14th in Ordinary Time	**1126**	4–9 July	9–14 July	8–13 July
15th in Ordinary Time	**1158**	11–16 July	16–21 July	15–20 July
16th in Ordinary Time	**1191**	18–23 July	23–28 July	22–27 July
17th in Ordinary Time	**1223**	25–30 July	30 July–4 Aug	29 July–3 Aug
18th in Ordinary Time	**1254**	1–6 Aug	6–11 Aug	5–10 Aug
Transfiguration	**S.M.**	*6 Aug*	*6 Aug*	*6 Aug*
19th in Ordinary Time	**1289**	8–13 Aug	13–18 Aug	12–17 Aug
Assumption	**S.M.**	*15 Aug*	*15 Aug*	*15 Aug*
20th in Ordinary Time	**1323**	15–20 Aug	20–25 Aug	19–24 Aug
21st in Ordinary Time	**1356**	22–27 Aug	27 Aug–1 Sept	26–31 Aug
22nd in Ordinary Time	**1383**	29 Aug–3 Sept	3–8 Sept	2–7 Sept
23rd in Ordinary Time	**1411**	5–10 Sept	10–15 Sept	9–14 Sept
24th in Ordinary Time	**1440**	12–17 Sept	17–22 Sept	16–21 Sept
Triumph of the Cross	**S.M.**	*14 Sept*	*14 Sept*	*14 Sept*
25th in Ordinary Time	**1469**	19–24 Sept	24–29 Sept	23–28 Sept
26th in Ordinary Time	**1499**	26 Sept–1 Oct	1–6 Oct	30 Sept–5 Oct
27th in Ordinary Time	**1531**	3–8 Oct	8–13 Oct	7–12 Oct
28th in Ordinary Time	**1562**	10–15 Oct	15–20 Oct	14–19 Oct
29th in Ordinary Time	**1589**	17–22 Oct	22–27 Oct	21–26 Oct
30th in Ordinary Time	**1617**	24–29 Oct	29 Oct–3 Nov	28 Oct–2 Nov
All Saints	**S.M.**	*1 Nov*	*1 Nov*	*1 Nov*
All Souls	**S.M.**	*2 Nov*	*2 Nov*	*2 Nov*
31st in Ordinary Time	**1645**	31 Oct–5 Nov	5–10 Nov	4–9 Nov
32nd in Ordinary Time	**1674**	7–12 Nov	12–17 Nov	11–16 Nov
Dedication of St. John Lateran	**S.M.**	*9 Nov*	*9 Nov*	*9 Nov*
33rd in Ordinary Time	**1703**	14–19 Nov	19–24 Nov	18–23 Nov
34th in Ordinary Time	**1737**	21–26 Nov	26 Nov–1 Dec	25–30 Nov

Lectionary Cycle	Page	2013 — II	2014 — I	2015 — II
1st Week of Advent	49	2–7 Dec	1–6 Dec	30 Nov–5 Dec
Immaculate Conception	*S.M.*	*9 Dec*	*8 Dec*	*8 Dec*
2nd Week of Advent	75	9–14 Dec	8–13 Dec	7–12 Dec
3rd Week of Advent	99	16 Dec	15–16 Dec	14–16 Dec
December 17–24	123	17–24 Dec	17–24 Dec	17–24 Dec
Christmas	*S.M.*	*25 Dec*	*25 Dec*	*25 Dec*
Octave of Christmas	159	26–31 Dec	26–31 Dec	26–31 Dec
Holy Family	*S.M.*	*29 Dec*	*28 Dec*	*27 Dec*
		2014 — II	**2015 — I**	**2016 — II**
Mary, Mother of God	*S.M.*	*1 Jan*	*1 Jan*	*1 Jan*
If before Epiphany Jan 2–7	183	2–4 Jan	2–3 Jan	2 Jan
Epiphany of the Lord	*S.M.*	*5 Jan*	*4 Jan*	*3 Jan*
After Epiphany Mon–Sat (or Jan 7–12)	210	6–11 Jan	5–10 Jan	4–9 Jan
Baptism of the Lord	*S.M.*	*12 Jan*	*11 Jan*	*10 Jan*
1st in Ordinary Time	235	13–18 Jan	12–17 Jan	11–16 Jan
2nd in Ordinary Time	265	20–25 Jan	19–24 Jan	18–23 Jan
3rd in Ordinary Time	296	27 Jan–1 Feb	26–31 Jan	25–30 Jan
4th in Ordinary Time	327	3–8 Feb	2–7 Feb	1–6 Feb
Presentation of the Lord	*S.M.*	*2 Feb*	*2 Feb*	*2 Feb*
5th in Ordinary Time	360	10–15 Feb	9–14 Feb	8–9 Feb
If before Lent 6th in Ordinary Time	392	17–22 Feb	16–17 Feb	——
7th in Ordinary Time	421	24 Feb–1 Mar	——	——
8th in Ordinary Time	452	3–4 Mar	——	——
9th in Ordinary Time	482	——		
Ash Wednesday	523	*5 Mar*	*18 Feb*	*10 Feb*
After Ash Wednesday	531	6–8 Mar	19–21 Feb	11–13 Feb
1st Week of Lent	543	10–15 Mar	23–28 Feb	15–20 Feb
2nd Week of Lent	567	17–22 Mar	2–7 Mar	22–27 Feb

Lectionary Cycle	Page	2014 — II	2015 — I	2016 — II
3rd Week of Lent	597	24–29 Mar	9–14 Mar	29 Feb–5 Mar
Joseph, Husband of Mary	*S.M.*	19 Mar	19 Mar	19 Mar
Annunciation	*S.M.*	25 Mar	25 Mar	4 Apr
4th Week of Lent	622	31 Mar–5 Apr	16–21 Mar	7–12 Mar
5th Week of Lent	652	7–12 Apr	23–28 Mar	14–19 Mar
Holy Week Mon–Wed	686	14–16 Apr	30 Mar–1 Apr	21–23 Mar
Chrism Mass	699	17 Apr	2 Apr	24 Mar
Easter Triduum	*S.M.*	17–19 Apr	2–4 Apr	24–26 Mar
Easter	*S.M.*	20 Apr	5 Apr	27 Mar
Octave of Easter	710	21–26 Apr	6–11 Apr	28 Mar–2 Apr
2nd Week of Easter	738	28 Apr–3 May	13–18 Apr	4–9 Apr
3rd Week of Easter	762	5–10 May	20–25 Apr	11–16 Apr
4th Week of Easter	786	12–17 May	27 Apr–2 May	18–23 Apr
5th Week of Easter	811	19–24 May	4–9 May	25–30 Apr
6th Week of Easter	835	26–31 May	11–16 May	2–7 May
Ascension	*S.M.*	29 May	14 May	5 May
7th Week of Easter	859	2–7 June	18–23 May	9–14 May
Pentecost	*S.M.*	8 June	24 May	15 May
Trinity Sunday	*S.M.*	15 June	31 May	22 May
Corpus Christi	*S.M.*	22 June	7 June	29 May
If after Pentecost 6th in Ordinary Time	392	—	—	
7th in Ordinary Time	421	—	—	16–21 May
8th in Ordinary Time	452	—	25–30 May	23–28 May
9th in Ordinary Time	482	—	1–6 June	30 May–4 June
Always after Pentecost 10th in Ordinary Time	995	9–14 June	8–13 June	6–11 June
Sacred Heart of Jesus	983	27 June	12 June	3 June
11th in Ordinary Time	1024	16–21 June	15–20 June	13–18 June
12th in Ordinary Time	1056	23–28 June	22–27 June	20–25 June

Lectionary Cycle	Page	2014 — II	2015 — I	2016 — II
Birth of John the Baptist	*S.M.*	*24 June*	*24 June*	*24 June*
Peter and Paul, Apostles	*S.M.*	*29 June*	*29 June*	*29 June*
13th in Ordinary Time	1091	30 June–5 July	29 June–4 July	27 June–2 July
14th in Ordinary Time	1126	7–12 July	6–11 July	4–9 July
15th in Ordinary Time	1158	14–19 July	13–18 July	11–16 July
16th in Ordinary Time	1191	21–26 July	20–25 July	18–23 July
17th in Ordinary Time	1223	28 July–2 Aug	27 July–1 Aug	25–30 July
18th in Ordinary Time	1254	4–9 Aug	3–8 Aug	1–6 Aug
Transfiguration	*S.M.*	*6 Aug*	*6 Aug*	*6 Aug*
19th in Ordinary Time	1289	11–16 Aug	10–15 Aug	8–13 Aug
Assumption	*S.M.*	*15 Aug*	*15 Aug*	*15 Aug*
20th in Ordinary Time	1323	18–23 Aug	17–22 Aug	15–20 Aug
21st in Ordinary Time	1356	25–30 Aug	24–29 Aug	22–27 Aug
22nd in Ordinary Time	1383	1–6 Sept	31 Aug–5 Sept	29 Aug–3 Sept
23rd in Ordinary Time	1411	8–13 Sept	7–12 Sept	5–10 Sept
24th in Ordinary Time	1440	15–20 Sept	14–19 Sept	12–17 Sept
Triumph of the Cross	*S.M.*	*14 Sept*	*14 Sept*	*14 Sept*
25th in Ordinary Time	1469	22–27 Sept	21–26 Sept	19–24 Sept
26th in Ordinary Time	1499	29 Sept–4 Oct	28 Sept–3 Oct	26 Sept–1 Oct
27th in Ordinary Time	1531	6–11 Oct	5–10 Oct	3–8 Oct
28th in Ordinary Time	1562	13–18 Oct	12–17 Oct	10–15 Oct
29th in Ordinary Time	1589	20–25 Oct	19–24 Oct	17–22 Oct
30th in Ordinary Time	1617	27 Oct–1 Nov	26–31 Oct	24–29 Oct
All Saints	*S.M.*	*1 Nov*	*1 Nov*	*1 Nov*
All Souls	*S.M.*	*2 Nov*	*2 Nov*	*2 Nov*
31st in Ordinary Time	1645	3–8 Nov	2–7 Nov	31 Oct–5 Nov
32nd in Ordinary Time	1674	10–15 Nov	9–14 Nov	7–12 Nov
Dedication of St. John Lateran	*S.M.*	*9 Nov*	*9 Nov*	*9 Nov*
33rd in Ordinary Time	1703	17–22 Nov	16–21 Nov	14–19 Nov
34th in Ordinary Time	1737	24–29 Nov	23–28 Nov	21–26 Nov

PROPER OF SEASONS

Advent and Christmas
Seeking the Spirituality of the Seasons

Perhaps contemporary Roman Catholics experience the greatest dissonance between keeping the seasons of the Church year and living in our commercially driven society during the Christmas cycle, beginning with Advent. While the feasts of Christmas and Epiphany comprise the climax and conclusion, respectively, of this season of the Church year, the market cycle brings Christmas decorations and music to stores by mid-November at the latest. As Christmas parties are scheduled into the weekends of December, we walk on those same weekends into churches that are marked by some plain boughs, an Advent wreath, and purple vestments.

We feel the dissonance no less at the other end of the Christmas liturgical season. The worked-up hype for Christmas ends on December 24, not only with the closing of stores but also, for so many Roman Catholics, with the celebration of the vigil Mass, late that afternoon or early evening, and then the opening of presents and so forth. Time then emerges for the invaluable gift of sharing our lives, of visiting relatives and friends as well as, hopefully, the lonely or neglected, and of sitting for an extended time around dinner tables to feel the unique bond known only in a festive meal. And then, isn't Christmas over?

Those who continue to celebrate the Christmas season liturgically through the following two Sundays return to churches still decked with poinsettias and wreathes, nativity scenes and candles. Christmas hymns and carols abound, and Scripture readings recount wise men and the flight to Egypt or the presentation of the infant Jesus in the Temple. But the liturgy can feel a bit odd if our homes are already stripped of Christmas decorations. Doesn't it sometimes feel like the Church has put its red-ribboned wreathes and lighted trees up too late and left them around too long?

This symbolic dissonance causes varied reactions among believers. Many people take consolation in the subdued liturgical space of the Advent season as a prayerful get-away from frenetic Christmas preparations. Others revel in the counter-cultural message of the Advent and Christmas season, although its precise message may vary. Some might fall in line with a contemporary adage: "Christ is the reason for the season." A more negatively critical version of this approach is the call by some that "we need to get the 'Christ' back into 'Christmas.'" Still others might counter that Christ has been there all along in countless quiet ways, in every gesture of reunion, every sign of love shared, every act of charity.

How can we celebrate the Advent and Christmas season more fully, consciously, and actively? We can look to the Church's liturgy for a spirituality of Advent and Christmas that will nourish our faith.

Watching for Christ's Second Coming, Remembering His First

The key to unlocking the spirituality of Christmas lies in recognizing that this feast is a liturgical tradition in Roman Catholicism (and also in the Eastern and Orthodox churches). As a liturgical celebration, Christmas reveals and invites us into the paschal mystery, God's ongoing redemption of humanity and all creation through the birth, life, death, and glorification of Christ. Sunday, the day of the resurrection, is the original Christian feast. For over a century it was the only feast of the Church, celebrated weekly with the word of God and the eucharistic body and blood of Christ. Only in the later second and third centuries did churches expand their liturgy into annual cycles, first and widely with the development of Easter, but also in scattered places with an anniversary-commemoration of Jesus' birth, coinciding with the winter solstice festivals of the Mediterranean world.

The celebrations of Christmas (the anniversary of Jesus' birth) and Epiphany (the appearance of God's Son) spread across the churches, East and West, in the fourth century. In Rome the December 25 celebration of Jesus' birth included recollection of the shepherds' adoration, while the "Epiphany" (manifestation) commemorated on January 6 was that of Christ to the nations, as represented by the adoring Magi. Other churches, however, associated Epiphany with the manifestation of Jesus as God's beloved Son at his baptism in the Jordan. These churches baptized people on this feast and a period of baptismal preparation, marked by prayer, ascetical practices, and more frequent (even daily) liturgy developed. By the turn of the fifth century in Spain and Gaul the start of this preparatory period for Christmas and Epiphany was set at December 17, exactly three weeks before January 6, the day on which the baptisms would take place. Only in the sixth century did the Church in Rome begin to celebrate Advent in preparation for Christmas and Epiphany, gradually arriving at a four week period. In the seventh century, the primary meaning of the season emerged as the preparation for the coming of the Lord, but in a twofold sense: remembering his nativity so as to contemplate his glorious second coming at the end of time.

Today the Roman Catholic celebration of Advent is as much about watching for the day when Christ will come again in glory as it is about preparing for the annual feast of Jesus' birth. The Gospel reading on the First Sunday in Advent is from the same chapters proclaimed on the last Sundays of the liturgical year each November (Matthew 24, Mark 13, Luke 21). The Church begins its year on the same note on which it ended: watch for the day of the Lord's coming, live lives of gospel faith, for you know not the day or the hour! This is the theme through December 16, with John the Baptist sounding the apocalyptic cry in the Gospel readings of the second and third Sundays. On the December 17 the focus shifts to commemorating Christ's first coming as the child born of Mary.

How might Advent's hope for the Lord's second coming and reflection back on his birth long ago shape the way we practice our faith today? During the first phase of Advent the liturgy invites us to embrace and proclaim our troubled world's longing for the final, definitive inbreaking of the kingdom of God, Christ's creation of a new heavens and a new earth whereon the Sun of Justice will never set. We join our hearts and voices, our bodies and spirits, with all of creation—so riddled by war, poverty, disease, and pollution—in the groaning appeal for salvation. But therein lies the gift of the season. If we enter into the liturgical tradition, the groan becomes an expectant cry, a confident assurance that the Lord, who will one day make all things new, renews our strength and grants us peace as we join in his mission of compassion, mercy, and forgiveness. The second and final phase of Advent grounds this confidence in the quiet joy of remembering the Lord's humble birth, the awesome mystery of God's love emptied out in the life of a child, Emmanuel, God with us now.

BRUCE T. MORRILL, S.J.

FIRST WEEK OF ADVENT

Monday

Entrance Antiphon

Nations, hear the message of the Lord, and make it known to the ends of the earth: Our Savior is coming. Have no more fear.
(See Jer 31:10; Is 35:4)

Opening Prayer

Lord our God,
help us to prepare
for the coming of Christ your Son.
May he find us waiting,
eager in joyful prayer.
We ask this through our Lord Jesus Christ, your Son,
who lives and reigns with you and the Holy Spirit,
one God, for ever and ever.

TODAY'S LIVING WORD

The readings for today look to the future, to the "days to come" when all nations shall make their way to "the house of the God of Jacob." As the Gospel puts it, many will come from east and west to find a place "with Abraham, Isaac, and Jacob at the banquet in the kingdom of heaven." Both Isaiah, in the selection for years B and C, and Matthew's Jesus proclaim that the God of Israel wills the salvation of all, not just of Jews.

Yet both recognize the privilege of Israel in God's saving plan. So in Isaiah, the house of Jacob must itself "walk in the light" before it can light the way for others. This is why Jesus, who expresses amazement at the centurion's faith, is likewise amazed at the lack of faith of so many in Israel.

The selection from Isaiah for year A is also future oriented, but it looks to the more immediate future, when a remnant will be purified and protected by the glory of God, "a smoking cloud by day and a light of flaming fire by night." Thus will the house of Jacob come to walk in the light of the Lord and so be light for all nations.

FIRST READING   (Cycles B and C)   Is 2:1–5

The LORD will gather all nations
into the eternal peace of the Kingdom of God.

A reading from the Book of the Prophet Isaiah

This is what Isaiah, son of Amoz,
  saw concerning Judah and Jerusalem.

  In days to come,
The mountain of the LORD's house
  shall be established as the highest mountain
  and raised above the hills.
All nations shall stream toward it;
  many peoples shall come and say:
"Come, let us climb the LORD's mountain,
  to the house of the God of Jacob,
That he may instruct us in his ways,
  and we may walk in his paths."
For from Zion shall go forth instruction,
  and the word of the LORD from Jerusalem.
He shall judge between the nations,
  and impose terms on many peoples.
They shall beat their swords into plowshares
  and their spears into pruning hooks;
One nation shall not raise the sword against another,
  nor shall they train for war again.

O house of Jacob, come,
  let us walk in the light of the LORD!
The word of the Lord.

In A cycle, when this reading is used on the **First Sunday of Advent,** the following reading replaces it.

FIRST READING

Is 4:2–6

There will be splendor for the survivors.

A reading from the Book of the Prophet Isaiah

On that day,
The branch of the LORD will be luster and glory,
 and the fruit of the earth will be honor and splendor
  for the survivors of Israel.
He who remains in Zion
 and he who is left in Jerusalem
Will be called holy:
 every one marked down for life in Jerusalem.
When the LORD washes away
 the filth of the daughters of Zion,
And purges Jerusalem's blood from her midst
 with a blast of searing judgment,
Then will the LORD create,
 over the whole site of Mount Zion
 and over her place of assembly,
A smoking cloud by day
 and a light of flaming fire by night.
For over all, the LORD's glory will be shelter and protection:
 shade from the parching heat of day,
 refuge and cover from storm and rain.

The word of the Lord.

Responsorial Psalm

Ps 122:1–2, 3–4b, 4cd–5, 6–7, 8–9

R. **Let us go rejoicing to the house of the Lord.**

I rejoiced because they said to me,
 "We will go up to the house of the LORD."

And now we have set foot
 within your gates, O Jerusalem.

 R. Let us go rejoicing to the house of the Lord.

Jerusalem, built as a city
 with compact unity.
To it the tribes go up,
 the tribes of the Lord.

 R. Let us go rejoicing to the house of the Lord.

According to the decree for Israel,
 to give thanks to the name of the Lord.
In it are set up judgment seats,
 seats for the house of David.

 R. Let us go rejoicing to the house of the Lord.

Pray for the peace of Jerusalem!
 May those who love you prosper!
May peace be within your walls,
 prosperity in your buildings.

 R. Let us go rejoicing to the house of the Lord.

Because of my relatives and friends
 I will say, "Peace be within you!"
Because of the house of the Lord, our God,
 I will pray for your good.

 R. Let us go rejoicing to the house of the Lord.

 Alleluia, alleluia   See Ps 80:4
 Come and save us, Lord our God;
 let your face shine upon us, that we may be saved.
 Alleluia, alleluia

GOSPEL   Mt 8:5–11
 *Many will come from the east and the west
 into the Kingdom of heaven.*

A reading from the holy Gospel according to Matthew

When Jesus entered Capernaum, a centurion approached him
and appealed to him, saying, "Lord, my servant is lying at

home paralyzed, suffering dreadfully." He said to him, "I will come and cure him." The centurion said in reply, "Lord, I am not worthy to have you enter under my roof; only say the word and my servant will be healed. For I too am a man subject to authority, with soldiers subject to me. And I say to one, 'Go,' and he goes; and to another, 'Come here,' and he comes; and to my slave, 'Do this,' and he does it." When Jesus heard this, he was amazed and said to those following him, "Amen, I say to you, in no one in Israel have I found such faith. I say to you, many will come from the east and the west, and will recline with Abraham, Isaac, and Jacob at the banquet in the Kingdom of heaven."

The Gospel of the Lord.

Liturgy of the Eucharist, *p. 897.*

Prayer over the Gifts

Pray, brethren...

Father,
from all you give us
we present this bread and wine.
As we serve you now,
accept our offering
and sustain us with your promise of eternal life.

Grant this through Christ our Lord.

Preface of Advent I, *p. 937.*

Communion Antiphon

Come to us, Lord, and bring us peace. We will rejoice in your presence and serve you with all our heart.

(See Ps 105:4 – 5; Is 38:3)

Prayer after Communion

Let us pray.

Pause for silent prayer, if this has not preceded.

Father,
may our communion
teach us to love heaven.
May its promise and hope
guide our way on earth.
We ask this through Christ our Lord.

Tuesday

Entrance Antiphon

See, the Lord is coming and with him all his saints. Then there will be endless day.   (See Zec 14:5, 7)

Opening Prayer

God of mercy and consolation,
help us in our weakness and free us from sin.
Hear our prayers
that we may rejoice at the coming of your Son,
who lives and reigns with you and the Holy Spirit,
one God, for ever and ever.

TODAY'S LIVING WORD

In the Hebrew Bible the Spirit of God *(ruach elohim)* denotes Israel's lived experience of God's powerful presence. As "breath" or "wind," God's *ruach* is a driving, divine force, known chiefly by its effects, particularly in Israel's history. The gift of God's Spirit enabled an individual, however insignificant or uncredentialed, to be God's agent. Such was the case of Moses, Joshua, the judges, Saul, David, and the ideal king Isaiah foresees in today's reading. God's Spirit would equip this royal shoot from the stump of Jesse with the qualities needed to do God's work—to "judge the poor with justice, and decide aright for the land's afflicted."

The Gospel depicts Jesus too as impelled by God's Spirit. Seized by the Spirit, he celebrates God's choice of "the childlike," a preferential option for the powerless and the poor that he continues in his own ministry. We must situate ourselves among these for, by the advent and the activity of the Holy Spirit, we now enjoy the revelation that prophets and kings wished to see and to hear, but never did.

FIRST READING
Is 11:1–10

The Spirit of the LORD God shall rest upon him.

A reading from the Book of the Prophet Isaiah

On that day,
A shoot shall sprout from the stump of Jesse,
      and from his roots a bud shall blossom.
The Spirit of the LORD shall rest upon him:
      a Spirit of wisdom and of understanding,
A Spirit of counsel and of strength,
      a Spirit of knowledge and of fear of the LORD,
      and his delight shall be the fear of the LORD.
Not by appearance shall he judge,
      nor by hearsay shall he decide,
But he shall judge the poor with justice,
      and decide aright for the land's afflicted.
He shall strike the ruthless with the rod of his mouth,
      and with the breath of his lips he shall slay the wicked.
Justice shall be the band around his waist,
      and faithfulness a belt upon his hips.

Then the wolf shall be a guest of the lamb,
      and the leopard shall lie down with the kid;
The calf and the young lion shall browse together,
      with a little child to guide them.

The cow and the bear shall be neighbors,
    together their young shall rest;
    the lion shall eat hay like the ox.
The baby shall play by the cobra's den,
    and the child lay his hand on the adder's lair.
There shall be no harm or ruin on all my holy mountain;
    for the earth shall be filled with knowledge of the Lord,
    as water covers the sea.

    On that day,
The root of Jesse,
    set up as a signal for the nations,
The Gentiles shall seek out,
    for his dwelling shall be glorious.

The word of the Lord.

Responsorial Psalm

Ps 72:1–2, 7–8, 12–13, 17

**R. Justice shall flourish in his time, and fullness of peace
for ever.**

O God, with your judgment endow the king,
  and with your justice, the king's son;
He shall govern your people with justice
  and your afflicted ones with judgment.

**R. Justice shall flourish in his time, and fullness of peace
for ever.**

Justice shall flower in his days,
  and profound peace, till the moon be no more.
May he rule from sea to sea,
  and from the River to the ends of the earth.

**R. Justice shall flourish in his time, and fullness of peace
for ever.**

He shall rescue the poor when he cries out,
  and the afflicted when he has no one to help him.

He shall have pity for the lowly and the poor;
  the lives of the poor he shall save.

> **R. Justice shall flourish in his time, and fullness of peace
> for ever.**

May his name be blessed forever;
  as long as the sun his name shall remain.
In him shall all the tribes of the earth be blessed;
  all the nations shall proclaim his happiness.

> **R. Justice shall flourish in his time, and fullness of peace
> for ever.**

> **Alleluia, alleluia**
> Behold, our Lord shall come with power;
>   he will enlighten the eyes of his servants.
> **Alleluia, alleluia**

GOSPEL   Lk 10:21–24

Jesus rejoices in the Holy Spirit.

A reading from the holy Gospel according to Luke

Jesus rejoiced in the Holy Spirit and said, "I give you praise,
Father, Lord of heaven and earth, for although you have hidden
these things from the wise and the learned you have revealed
them to the childlike. Yes, Father, such has been your gracious
will. All things have been handed over to me by my Father. No
one knows who the Son is except the Father, and who the Father
is except the Son and anyone to whom the Son wishes to reveal
him."

   Turning to the disciples in private he said, "Blessed are the
eyes that see what you see. For I say to you, many prophets
and kings desired to see what you see, but did not see it, and to
hear what you hear, but did not hear it."

The Gospel of the Lord.

Liturgy of the Eucharist, *p. 897.*

Prayer over the Gifts

Pray, brethren...

Lord,
we are nothing without you.
As you sustain us with your mercy,
receive our prayers and offerings.
We ask this through Christ our Lord.

Preface of Advent I, *p. 937.*

Communion Antiphon

The Lord is just; he will award the crown of justice to all who
have longed for his coming.   (2 Tm 4:8)

Prayer after Communion

Let us pray.

Pause for silent prayer, if this has not preceded.

Father,
you give us food from heaven.
By our sharing in this mystery,
teach us to judge wisely the things of earth
and to love the things of heaven.
Grant this through Christ our Lord.

Wednesday

Entrance Antiphon

The Lord is coming and will not delay; he will bring every
hidden thing to light and reveal himself to every nation.
                                    (See Hab 2:3; 1 Cor 4:5)

Opening Prayer

Lord our God,
grant that we may be ready

to receive Christ when he comes in glory
and to share in the banquet of heaven,
where he lives and reigns with you and the Holy Spirit,
one God, for ever and ever.

TODAY'S LIVING WORD

In both of today's readings the hand of the Lord comes to rest on a mountain. In the passage from Isaiah, the mountain is Zion, the site of the city of Jerusalem. "On this mountain," the prophet says, God will rescue a hungry, hurting, humiliated people—by providing a feast of rich food, wiping the tears from their eyes and removing the stigma of exile. On that day, the people will rejoice in the God who has acted to save them.

In the selection from Matthew, the mountain is symbolic but no less significant. Here again God acts to feed the hungry crowd, having first made the mute speak, the deformed sound, the cripples walk, and the blind see. And "they glorified the God of Israel."

For Isaiah, "that day" is the beginning of the end time. But for Matthew, as for us, "that day" has arrived with the coming of Jesus. With the rising of Jesus, death is destroyed forever, and every Eucharist is a foretaste of the feast God has prepared "on this mountain."

FIRST READING

Is 25:6–10a

*The LORD invites us to his feast
and will wipe away the tears from all faces.*

A reading from the Book of the Prophet Isaiah

On this mountain the LORD of hosts
    will provide for all peoples
A feast of rich food and choice wines,
    juicy, rich food and pure, choice wines.
On this mountain he will destroy
    the veil that veils all peoples,
The web that is woven over all nations;
    he will destroy death forever.

The Lord GOD will wipe away
  the tears from all faces;
The reproach of his people he will remove
  from the whole earth; for the LORD has spoken.

  On that day it will be said:
"Behold our God, to whom we looked to save us!
  This is the LORD for whom we looked;
  let us rejoice and be glad that he has saved us!"
For the hand of the LORD will rest on this mountain.
The word of the Lord.

Responsorial Psalm
Ps 23:1–3a, 3b–4, 5, 6

R. I shall live in the house of the Lord all the days of my life.

The LORD is my shepherd; I shall not want.
  In verdant pastures he gives me repose;
Beside restful waters he leads me;
  he refreshes my soul.

R. I shall live in the house of the Lord all the days of my life.

He guides me in right paths
  for his name's sake.
Even though I walk in the dark valley
  I fear no evil; for you are at my side
With your rod and your staff
  that give me courage.

R. I shall live in the house of the Lord all the days of my life.

You spread the table before me
  in the sight of my foes;
You anoint my head with oil;
  my cup overflows.

R. I shall live in the house of the Lord all the days of my life.

Only goodness and kindness follow me
  all the days of my life;

And I shall dwell in the house of the LORD
  for years to come.

R. I shall live in the house of the Lord all the days of my life.

Alleluia, alleluia
Behold, the Lord comes to save his people;
blessed are those prepared to meet him.
Alleluia, alleluia

GOSPEL

Mt 15:29–37

Jesus heals many and multiplies the bread.

A reading from the holy Gospel according to Matthew

At that time: Jesus walked by the Sea of Galilee, went up on the mountain, and sat down there. Great crowds came to him, having with them the lame, the blind, the deformed, the mute, and many others. They placed them at his feet, and he cured them. The crowds were amazed when they saw the mute speaking, the deformed made whole, the lame walking, and the blind able to see, and they glorified the God of Israel.

Jesus summoned his disciples and said, "My heart is moved with pity for the crowd, for they have been with me now for three days and have nothing to eat. I do not want to send them away hungry, for fear they may collapse on the way." The disciples said to him, "Where could we ever get enough bread in this deserted place to satisfy such a crowd?" Jesus said to them, "How many loaves do you have?" "Seven," they replied, "and a few fish." He ordered the crowd to sit down on the ground. Then he took the seven loaves and the fish, gave thanks, broke the loaves, and gave them to the disciples, who in turn gave them to the crowds. They all ate and were satisfied. They picked up the fragments left over—seven baskets full.

The Gospel of the Lord.

Liturgy of the Eucharist, *p. 897.*

Prayer over the Gifts

Pray, brethren...

Lord,
may the gift we offer in faith and love
be a continual sacrifice in your honor
and truly become our eucharist and our salvation.

Grant this through Christ our Lord.

Preface of Advent I, *p. 937.*

Communion Antiphon

The Lord our God comes in strength and will fill his servants
with joy.   (Is 40:10; see 34:5)

Prayer after Communion

Let us pray.

Pause for silent prayer, if this has not preceded.

God of mercy,
may this eucharist bring us your divine help,
free us from our sins,
and prepare us for the birthday of our Savior,
who is Lord for ever and ever.

Thursday

Entrance Antiphon

Lord, you are near, and all your commandments are just; long
have I known that you decreed them for ever.

(See Ps 118:151–152)

Opening Prayer

Father,
we need your help.

Free us from sin and bring us to life.
Support us by your power.

Grant this through our Lord Jesus Christ, your Son,
who lives and reigns with you and the Holy Spirit,
one God, for ever and ever.

TODAY'S LIVING WORD

In today's Gospel, an excerpt from the Sermon on the Mount, Jesus tells his disciples that his words are the firm foundation on which they must build their lives. The words of Jesus the Jew are undergirded by the words of the Hebrew Bible, such as the words of the prophet Isaiah in today's first reading. Isaiah not only urges his people to build on solid rock; he also insists that a sturdy house, a strong city is one "that is just, one that keeps faith." Similarly, Jesus teaches that it is not enough to cry out "Lord, Lord"; one must do the will of the heavenly Father by putting the words of Jesus into practice.

Jesus comes. But it is not enough for us to give him a home in our lives. As today's readings tell us, we must build those homes on rock—"the eternal Rock"—the God who alone is the stronghold of our city.

FIRST READING   Is 26:1–6

Let in a nation that is just, one that keeps faith.

A reading from the Book of the Prophet Isaiah

On that day they will sing this song in the land of Judah:

"A strong city have we;
      he sets up walls and ramparts to protect us.
Open up the gates
      to let in a nation that is just,
      one that keeps faith.
A nation of firm purpose you keep in peace;
      in peace, for its trust in you."

Trust in the LORD forever!
    For the LORD is an eternal Rock.
He humbles those in high places,
    and the lofty city he brings down;
He tumbles it to the ground,
    levels it with the dust.
It is trampled underfoot by the needy,
    by the footsteps of the poor.

The word of the Lord.

Responsorial Psalm   Ps 118:1 and 8–9, 19–21, 25–27a

R. Blessed is he who comes in the name of the Lord.

Give thanks to the LORD, for he is good,
    for his mercy endures forever.
It is better to take refuge in the LORD
    than to trust in man.
It is better to take refuge in the LORD
    than to trust in princes.

R. Blessed is he who comes in the name of the Lord.

Open to me the gates of justice;
    I will enter them and give thanks to the LORD.
This gate is the LORD's;
    the just shall enter it.
I will give thanks to you, for you have answered me
    and have been my savior.

R. Blessed is he who comes in the name of the Lord.

O LORD, grant salvation!
    O LORD, grant prosperity!
Blessed is he who comes in the name of the LORD;
    we bless you from the house of the LORD.
    The LORD is God, and he has given us light.

R. Blessed is he who comes in the name of the Lord.

Or: **R. Alleluia.**

Alleluia, alleluia   Is 55:6
Seek the LORD while he may be found;
call him while he is near.
Alleluia, alleluia

GOSPEL   Mt 7:21, 24–27

*Whoever does the will of my Father
will enter the Kingdom of heaven.*

A reading from the holy Gospel according to Matthew

Jesus said to his disciples: "Not everyone who says to me, 'Lord, Lord,' will enter the Kingdom of heaven, but only the one who does the will of my Father in heaven.

"Everyone who listens to these words of mine and acts on them will be like a wise man who built his house on rock. The rain fell, the floods came, and the winds blew and buffeted the house. But it did not collapse; it had been set solidly on rock. And everyone who listens to these words of mine but does not act on them will be like a fool who built his house on sand. The rain fell, the floods came, and the winds blew and buffeted the house. And it collapsed and was completely ruined."

The Gospel of the Lord.

Liturgy of the Eucharist, *p. 897.*

Prayer over the Gifts

Pray, brethren...

Father,
from all you give us
we present this bread and wine.
As we serve you now,
accept our offering
and sustain us with your promise of eternal life.

Grant this through Christ our Lord.

Preface of Advent I, *p. 937.*

Communion Antiphon

Let our lives be honest and holy in this present age, as we wait for the happiness to come when our great God reveals himself in glory. (Ti 2:12–13)

Prayer after Communion

Let us pray.

Pause for silent prayer, if this has not preceded.

Father,
may our communion
teach us to love heaven.
May its promise and hope
guide our way on earth.
We ask this through Christ our Lord.

Friday

Entrance Antiphon

The Lord is coming from heaven in splendor to visit his people, and bring them peace and eternal life.

Opening Prayer

Jesus, our Lord,
save us from our sins.
Come, protect us from all dangers
and lead us to salvation,
for you live and reign with the Father and the Holy Spirit,
one God, for ever and ever.

TODAY'S LIVING WORD

In literature, blindness is often a metaphor for lack of knowledge, and it seems to function this way in today's two readings. Clearly, the eyes of the two blind men in the Gospel have already been opened by faith. Already they know Jesus as Son of David and trust in his power to save. The miracle that restores their physical sight is only an outward sign of their spiritual status: "Let it be done for you according to your faith." The passage from Isaiah metaphorically uses both blindness and deafness to describe the divine reversal that God is about to work in Judah: "The lowly will ever find joy in the Lord.... For the tyrant will be no more." Thus will knowledge of God return to the land. "On that day the deaf shall hear the words of a book; and out of gloom and darkness the eyes of the blind shall see."

In Advent we wait once again for what God will surely do in "a very little while," not the birth of Jesus, an unrepeatable event, but our own rebirth "out of gloom and darkness" into the light of the knowledge of God. Again we hope to see the work of God's hands in our midst and to sanctify God's holy name.

FIRST READING   Is 29:17–24

On that day, the eyes of the blind shall see.

A reading from the Book of the Prophet Isaiah

Thus says the Lord GOD:
But a very little while,
    and Lebanon shall be changed into an orchard,
    and the orchard be regarded as a forest!
On that day the deaf shall hear
    the words of a book;
And out of gloom and darkness,
    the eyes of the blind shall see.
The lowly will ever find joy in the LORD,
    and the poor rejoice in the Holy One of Israel.
For the tyrant will be no more
    and the arrogant will have gone;
All who are alert to do evil will be cut off,

those whose mere word condemns a man,
Who ensnare his defender at the gate,
    and leave the just man with an empty claim.
Therefore thus says the LORD,
    the God of the house of Jacob,
    who redeemed Abraham:
Now Jacob shall have nothing to be ashamed of,
    nor shall his face grow pale.
When his children see
    the work of my hands in his midst,
They shall keep my name holy;
    they shall reverence the Holy One of Jacob,
    and be in awe of the God of Israel.
Those who err in spirit shall acquire understanding,
    and those who find fault shall receive instruction.

The word of the Lord.

Responsorial Psalm

Ps 27:1, 4, 13–14

R. The Lord is my light and my salvation.

The LORD is my light and my salvation;
    whom should I fear?
The LORD is my life's refuge;
    of whom should I be afraid?

R. The Lord is my light and my salvation.

One thing I ask of the LORD;
    this I seek:
To dwell in the house of the LORD
    all the days of my life,
That I may gaze on the loveliness of the LORD
    and contemplate his temple.

R. The Lord is my light and my salvation.

I believe that I shall see the bounty of the LORD
   in the land of the living.
Wait for the LORD with courage;
   be stouthearted, and wait for the LORD.

   R. The Lord is my light and my salvation.

   Alleluia, alleluia
   Behold, our Lord shall come with power;
   he will enlighten the eyes of his servants.
   Alleluia, alleluia

GOSPEL

Mt 9:27–31

Believing in Jesus, two who were blind are cured.

A reading from the holy Gospel according to Matthew

As Jesus passed by, two blind men followed him, crying out,
"Son of David, have pity on us!" When he entered the house,
the blind men approached him and Jesus said to them, "Do
you believe that I can do this?" "Yes, Lord," they said to him.
Then he touched their eyes and said, "Let it be done for you
according to your faith." And their eyes were opened. Jesus
warned them sternly, "See that no one knows about this." But
they went out and spread word of him through all that land.
The Gospel of the Lord.

   Liturgy of the Eucharist, *p. 897.*

Prayer over the Gifts

Pray, brethren...

Lord,
we are nothing without you.
As you sustain us with your mercy,
receive our prayers and offerings.
We ask this through Christ our Lord.

Preface of Advent I, *p. 937.*

Communion Antiphon

We are waiting for our Savior, the Lord Jesus Christ; he will transfigure our lowly bodies into copies of his own glorious body.

(Phil 3:20 – 21)

Prayer after Communion

Let us pray.

Pause for silent prayer, if this has not preceded.

Father,
you give us food from heaven.
By our sharing in this mystery,
teach us to judge wisely the things of earth
and to love the things of heaven.
Grant this through Christ our Lord.

Saturday

Entrance Antiphon

Come, Lord, from your cherubim throne; let us see your face, and we shall be saved.

(Ps 79:4, 2)

Opening Prayer

God our Father,
you loved the world so much
you gave your only Son to free us
from the ancient power of sin and death.
Help us who wait for his coming,
and lead us to true liberty.

We ask this through our Lord Jesus Christ, your Son,
who lives and reigns with you and the Holy Spirit,
one God, for ever and ever.

TODAY'S LIVING WORD

Both of today's readings attest to God's compassion. In the text from Isaiah, God, who was made to punish Israel for their sin, is moved to pity by their wounds. So the prophet says, "[God] will heal the bruises left by his blows." Isaiah depicts the Holy One of Israel as a healer, binding up the people's wounds, blessing them with abundant life, signified by the recurring images of bread and water. Because the Holy One is also their teacher, with abundant life will come brilliant light, "like the light of seven days."

In today's Gospel, Matthew's Jesus too is both teacher and healer. "Jesus went around to all the towns and villages, teaching in their synagogues…and curing every disease and illness." He too is moved with pity for the lost, "because they were troubled and abandoned." This motivates him to dispatch his disciples—and all the others whom the Lord of the harvest will send—to prepare people for the coming judgment. This is an Advent mission: sharing the good news of God's reign, giving as a gift the gift we have received.

FIRST READING
Is 30:19–21, 23–26

The Merciful One will show you mercy when you cry out.

A reading from the Book of the Prophet Isaiah

Thus says the Lord GOD,
    the Holy One of Israel:
O people of Zion, who dwell in Jerusalem,
    no more will you weep;
He will be gracious to you when you cry out,
    as soon as he hears he will answer you.
The Lord will give you the bread you need
    and the water for which you thirst.
No longer will your Teacher hide himself,
    but with your own eyes you shall see your Teacher,
While from behind, a voice shall sound in your ears:
    "This is the way; walk in it,"
    when you would turn to the right or to the left.

He will give rain for the seed
    that you sow in the ground,
And the wheat that the soil produces
    will be rich and abundant.
On that day your flock will be given pasture
    and the lamb will graze in spacious meadows;
The oxen and the asses that till the ground
    will eat silage tossed to them
    with shovel and pitchfork.
Upon every high mountain and lofty hill
    there will be streams of running water.
On the day of the great slaughter,
    when the towers fall,
The light of the moon will be like that of the sun
    and the light of the sun will be seven times greater
    like the light of seven days.
On the day the LORD binds up the wounds of his people,
    he will heal the bruises left by his blows.

The word of the Lord.

Responsorial Psalm

Ps 147:1–2, 3–4, 5–6

R. Blessed are all who wait for the Lord.

Praise the LORD, for he is good;
    sing praise to our God, for he is gracious;
    it is fitting to praise him.
The LORD rebuilds Jerusalem;
    the dispersed of Israel he gathers.

R. Blessed are all who wait for the Lord.

He heals the brokenhearted
    and binds up their wounds.

He tells the number of the stars;
  he calls each by name.

  R. Blessed are all who wait for the Lord.

Great is our LORD and mighty in power:
  to his wisdom there is no limit.
The LORD sustains the lowly;
  the wicked he casts to the ground.

  R. Blessed are all who wait for the Lord.

  Alleluia, alleluia   Is 33:22
  The LORD is our Judge, our Lawgiver, our King;
  he it is who will save us.
  Alleluia, alleluia

GOSPEL   Mt 9:35 — 10:1, 5a, 6 – 8

At the sight of the crowds,
Jesus' heart was moved with pity for them.

A reading from the holy Gospel according to Matthew

Jesus went around to all the towns and villages, teaching in their synagogues, proclaiming the Gospel of the Kingdom, and curing every disease and illness. At the sight of the crowds, his heart was moved with pity for them because they were troubled and abandoned, like sheep without a shepherd. Then he said to his disciples, "The harvest is abundant but the laborers are few; so ask the master of the harvest to send out laborers for his harvest."

  Then he summoned his Twelve disciples and gave them authority over unclean spirits to drive them out and to cure every disease and every illness.

  Jesus sent out these Twelve after instructing them thus, "Go to the lost sheep of the house of Israel. As you go, make this proclamation: 'The Kingdom of heaven is at hand.' Cure the sick, raise the dead, cleanse lepers, drive out demons. Without cost you have received; without cost you are to give."

The Gospel of the Lord.

Liturgy of the Eucharist, *p. 897.*

Prayer over the Gifts

Pray, brethren...

Lord,
may the gift we offer in faith and love
be a continual sacrifice in your honor
and truly become our eucharist and our salvation.

We ask this through Christ our Lord.

Preface of Advent I, *p. 937.*

Communion Antiphon

I am coming quickly, says the Lord, and will repay each man according to his deeds.   (Rv 22:12)

Prayer after Communion

Let us pray.

Pause for silent prayer, if this has not preceded.

God of mercy,
may this eucharist bring us your divine help,
free us from our sins,
and prepare us for the birthday of our Savior,
who is Lord for ever and ever.

SECOND WEEK OF ADVENT

Monday

Entrance Antiphon

Nations, hear the message of the Lord, and make it known to the ends of the earth: Our Savior is coming. Have no more fear.
(See Jer 31:10; Is 35:4)

Opening Prayer

Lord,
free us from our sins and make us whole.
Hear our prayer,
and prepare us to celebrate the incarnation of your Son,
who lives and reigns with you and the Holy Spirit,
one God, for ever and ever.

TODAY'S LIVING WORD

Today's Gospel, the Lucan version of a familiar story adapted from Mark, introduces an element of conflict in the cure of the paralytic. For our purposes, the controversy establishes that the authority of Jesus is indeed the authority of the one God. The good news dramatized by the story concerns the incredible things that the authority of God effects: forgiveness of sins, fullness of life. This is Isaiah's theme as well.

In today's reading, the prophet Isaiah issues an Advent message. He announces that God is coming "with vindication" (to judge) and "with divine recompense" (to save). This divine visitation will cause barren places to bloom and broken people to burst into song. For God comes to open a highway, a holy way, "for those with a journey to make." On it the redeemed and the ransomed will walk, like the paralytic in the Gospel, returning home with joy.

FIRST READING

God himself will come and save you.

A reading from the Book of the Prophet Isaiah

> The desert and the parched land will exult;
>> the steppe will rejoice and bloom.
> They will bloom with abundant flowers,
>> and rejoice with joyful song.
> The glory of Lebanon will be given to them,
>> the splendor of Carmel and Sharon;
> They will see the glory of the Lord,
>> the splendor of our God.
> Strengthen the hands that are feeble,
>> make firm the knees that are weak,
> Say to those whose hearts are frightened:
>> Be strong, fear not!
> Here is your God,
>> he comes with vindication;
> With divine recompense
>> he comes to save you.
> Then will the eyes of the blind be opened,
>> the ears of the deaf be cleared;
> Then will the lame leap like a stag,
>> then the tongue of the mute will sing.
>
> Streams will burst forth in the desert,
>> and rivers in the steppe.
> The burning sands will become pools,
>> and the thirsty ground, springs of water;
> The abode where jackals lurk
>> will be a marsh for the reed and papyrus.

A highway will be there,
  called the holy way;
No one unclean may pass over it,
  nor fools go astray on it.
No lion will be there,
  nor beast of prey go up to be met upon it.
It is for those with a journey to make,
  and on it the redeemed will walk.
Those whom the LORD has ransomed will return
  and enter Zion singing,
  crowned with everlasting joy;
They will meet with joy and gladness,
  sorrow and mourning will flee.

The word of the Lord.

Responsorial Psalm

Ps 85:9ab and 10, 11–12, 13–14

R. Our God will come to save us!

I will hear what God proclaims;
  the LORD—for he proclaims peace to his people.
Near indeed is his salvation to those who fear him,
  glory dwelling in our land.

R. Our God will come to save us!

Kindness and truth shall meet;
  justice and peace shall kiss.
Truth shall spring out of the earth,
  and justice shall look down from heaven.

R. Our God will come to save us!

The LORD himself will give his benefits;
  our land shall yield its increase.
Justice shall walk before him,
  and salvation, along the way of his steps.

R. Our God will come to save us!

Alleluia, alleluia
Behold the king will come, the Lord of the earth,
and he himself will lift the yoke of our captivity.
Alleluia, alleluia

GOSPEL

Lk 5:17–26

We have seen incredible things today.

A reading from the holy Gospel according to Luke

One day as Jesus was teaching, Pharisees and teachers of the law, who had come from every village of Galilee and Judea and Jerusalem, were sitting there, and the power of the Lord was with him for healing. And some men brought on a stretcher a man who was paralyzed; they were trying to bring him in and set him in his presence. But not finding a way to bring him in because of the crowd, they went up on the roof and lowered him on the stretcher through the tiles into the middle in front of Jesus. When Jesus saw their faith, he said, "As for you, your sins are forgiven."

Then the scribes and Pharisees began to ask themselves, "Who is this who speaks blasphemies? Who but God alone can forgive sins?" Jesus knew their thoughts and said to them in reply, "What are you thinking in your hearts? Which is easier, to say, 'Your sins are forgiven,' or to say, 'Rise and walk'? But that you may know that the Son of Man has authority on earth to forgive sins"—he said to the one who was paralyzed, "I say to you, rise, pick up your stretcher, and go home."

He stood up immediately before them, picked up what he had been lying on, and went home, glorifying God. Then astonishment seized them all and they glorified God, and, struck with awe, they said, "We have seen incredible things today."

The Gospel of the Lord.

Liturgy of the Eucharist, *p. 897.*

Prayer over the Gifts

Pray, brethren...

Father,
from all you give us
we present this bread and wine.
As we serve you now,
accept our offering
and sustain us with your promise of eternal life.

Grant this through Christ our Lord.

Preface of Advent I, *p. 937.*

Communion Antiphon

Come to us, Lord, and bring us peace. We will rejoice in your presence and serve you with all our heart.

(See Ps 105:4–5; Is 38:3)

Prayer after Communion

Let us pray.

Pause for silent prayer, if this has not preceded.

Father,
may our communion
teach us to love heaven.
May its promise and hope
guide our way on earth.

We ask this through Christ our Lord.

Tuesday

Entrance Antiphon

See, the Lord is coming and with him all his saints. Then there will be endless day.

(See Zec 14:5, 7)

Opening Prayer

Almighty God,
help us to look forward
to the glory of the birth of Christ our Savior:
his coming is proclaimed joyfully
to the ends of the earth,
for he lives and reigns with you and the Holy Spirit,
one God, for ever and ever.

TODAY'S LIVING WORD

The image of God as shepherd informs both of today's readings. The prophet Isaiah depicts the Lord God coming in power, like a shepherd who feeds his flock and gathers the lambs in his arms, "carrying them in his bosom." In Matthew Jesus describes the heavenly Father in the same way, as a shepherd who leaves the ninety-nine out on the hills to search for the sheep that has strayed. But Matthew's version of this favorite parable injects a note of caution that is missing in Luke's account: "If he finds it...." Matthew thus warns us that the Good Shepherd's search is not always successful, but depends on the lost sheep's readiness to be found. In Advent the Church plies us with images of salvation in order to prepare in the wasteland the way of the Lord. We the lost sheep hang on every word, straining to hear the herald's cry, the good news that "the mouth of the Lord has spoken."

FIRST READING

Is 40:1–11

God consoles his people.

A reading from the Book of the Prophet Isaiah

Comfort, give comfort to my people,
    says your God.
Speak tenderly to Jerusalem, and proclaim to her
    that her service is at an end,
    her guilt is expiated;

Indeed, she has received from the hand of the LORD
  double for all her sins.

A voice cries out:
In the desert prepare the way of the LORD!
  Make straight in the wasteland a highway for our God!
Every valley shall be filled in,
  every mountain and hill shall be made low;
The rugged land shall be made a plain,
  the rough country, a broad valley.
Then the glory of the LORD shall be revealed,
  and all people shall see it together;
  for the mouth of the LORD has spoken.

A voice says, "Cry out!"
  I answer, "What shall I cry out?"
"All flesh is grass,
  and all their glory like the flower of the field.
The grass withers, the flower wilts,
  when the breath of the LORD blows upon it.
  So then, the people is the grass.
Though the grass withers and the flower wilts,
  the word of our God stands forever."

Go up onto a high mountain,
  Zion, herald of glad tidings;
Cry out at the top of your voice,
  Jerusalem, herald of good news!
Fear not to cry out
  and say to the cities of Judah:
  Here is your God!
Here comes with power

the Lord God,
    who rules by his strong arm;
Here is his reward with him,
    his recompense before him.
Like a shepherd he feeds his flock;
    in his arms he gathers the lambs,
Carrying them in his bosom,
    and leading the ewes with care.

The word of the Lord.

Responsorial Psalm

Ps 96:1–2, 3 and 10ac, 11–12, 13

R. **The Lord our God comes with power.**

Sing to the LORD a new song;
    sing to the LORD, all you lands.
Sing to the LORD; bless his name;
    announce his salvation, day after day.

R. **The Lord our God comes with power.**

Tell his glory among the nations;
    among all peoples, his wondrous deeds.
Say among the nations: The LORD is king;
    he governs the peoples with equity.

R. **The Lord our God comes with power.**

Let the heavens be glad and the earth rejoice;
    let the sea and what fills it resound;
    let the plains be joyful and all that is in them!
Then let all the trees of the forest rejoice.

R. **The Lord our God comes with power.**

They shall exult before the LORD, for he comes;
    for he comes to rule the earth.
He shall rule the world with justice
    and the peoples with his constancy.

R. The Lord our God comes with power.

Alleluia, alleluia
The day of the Lord is near:
Behold, he comes to save us.
Alleluia, alleluia

GOSPEL   Mt 18:12–14

God does not will that the little ones be lost.

A reading from the holy Gospel according to Matthew

Jesus said to his disciples: "What is your opinion? If a man has a hundred sheep and one of them goes astray, will he not leave the ninety-nine in the hills and go in search of the stray? And if he finds it, amen, I say to you, he rejoices more over it than over the ninety-nine that did not stray. In just the same way, it is not the will of your heavenly Father that one of these little ones be lost."

The Gospel of the Lord.

Liturgy of the Eucharist, *p. 897.*

Prayer over the Gifts

Pray, brethren...

Lord,
we are nothing without you.
As you sustain us with your mercy,
receive our prayers and offerings.
We ask this through Christ our Lord.

Preface of Advent I, *p. 937.*

Communion Antiphon

   The Lord is just; he will award the crown of justice to all who have longed for his coming.   (2 Tm 4:8)

Prayer after Communion

Let us pray.

Pause for silent prayer, if this has not preceded.

Father,
You give us food from heaven.
By our sharing in this mystery,
teach us to judge wisely the things of earth
and to love the things of heaven.

Grant this through Christ our Lord.

Wednesday

Entrance Antiphon

**The Lord is coming and will not delay; he will bring every
hidden thing to light and reveal himself to every nation.**

(See Hab 2:3; 1 Cor 4:5)

Opening Prayer

All-powerful Father,
we await the healing power of Christ your Son.
Let us not be discouraged by our weaknesses
as we prepare for his coming.
Keep us steadfast in your love.

We ask this through our Lord Jesus Christ, your Son,
who lives and reigns with you and the Holy Spirit,
one God, for ever and ever.

TODAY'S LIVING WORD

Today's first reading centers on a poignant reproach God addresses to the exiles in Babylon: "Why, O Jacob, do you say, and
declare, O Israel, 'My way is hidden from the Lord, and my right is
disregarded by my God?'" Discouraged, the exiles doubt the care of

their Creator. Isaiah's task is to reassure them: "The Lord is the eternal God…. He does not faint nor grow weary." And more: "They that hope in the Lord will renew their strength, they will soar as with eagles' wings." In today's Gospel Jesus also extends a poignant invitation, addressed to "exiles"—to those in Israel who were marginalized for not keeping the Law. To them Jesus offers another way: "Take my yoke upon you and learn from me."

The season of Advent can be for all of us a great weariness. Life does become burdensome beneath the Christmas crush. Only the yoke of Jesus is easy; only his burden is light.

FIRST READING   Is 40:25–31

The Lord God is almighty and gives strength to the fainting.

A reading from the Book of the Prophet Isaiah

To whom can you liken me as an equal?
      says the Holy One.
Lift up your eyes on high
      and see who has created these things:
He leads out their army and numbers them,
      calling them all by name.
By his great might and the strength of his power
      not one of them is missing!
Why, O Jacob, do you say,
      and declare, O Israel,
"My way is hidden from the LORD,
      and my right is disregarded by my God"?

Do you not know
      or have you not heard?
The LORD is the eternal God,
      creator of the ends of the earth.
He does not faint nor grow weary,
      and his knowledge is beyond scrutiny.

He gives strength to the fainting;
  for the weak he makes vigor abound.
Though young men faint and grow weary,
  and youths stagger and fall,
They that hope in the LORD will renew their strength,
  they will soar as with eagles' wings;
They will run and not grow weary,
  walk and not grow faint.

The word of the Lord.

Responsorial Psalm

Ps 103:1–2, 3–4, 8 and 10

R. O bless the Lord, my soul!

Bless the LORD, O my soul;
  and all my being, bless his holy name.
Bless the LORD, O my soul,
  and forget not all his benefits.

R. O bless the Lord, my soul!

He pardons all your iniquities,
  he heals all your ills.
He redeems your life from destruction,
  he crowns you with kindness and compassion.

R. O bless the Lord, my soul!

Merciful and gracious is the LORD,
  slow to anger and abounding in kindness.
Not according to our sins does he deal with us,
  nor does he requite us according to our crimes.

R. O bless the Lord, my soul!

Alleluia, alleluia
Behold, the Lord comes to save his people;
blessed are those prepared to meet him.
Alleluia, alleluia

GOSPEL

Mt 11:28–30

Come to me, all you who labor.

A reading from the holy Gospel according to Matthew

Jesus said to the crowds: "Come to me, all you who labor and are burdened, and I will give you rest. Take my yoke upon you and learn from me, for I am meek and humble of heart; and you will find rest for yourselves. For my yoke is easy, and my burden light."

The Gospel of the Lord.

Liturgy of the Eucharist, *p. 897.*

Prayer over the Gifts

Pray, brethren...

Lord,
may the gift we offer in faith and love
be a continual sacrifice in your honor
and truly become our eucharist and our salvation.

Grant this through Christ our Lord.

Preface of Advent I, *p. 937.*

Communion Antiphon

The Lord our God comes in strength and will fill his servants with joy.   (Is 40:10; see 34:5)

Prayer after Communion

Let us pray.

Pause for silent prayer, if this has not preceded.

God of mercy,
may this eucharist bring us your divine help,
free us from our sins,
and prepare us for the birthday of our Savior,
who is Lord for ever and ever.

Thursday

Entrance Antiphon

Lord, you are near, and all your commandments are just; long have I known that you decreed them for ever.

(See Ps 118:151–152)

Opening Prayer

Almighty Father,
give us the joy of your love
to prepare the way for Christ our Lord.
Help us to serve you and one another.

We ask this through our Lord Jesus Christ, your Son,
who lives and reigns with you and the Holy Spirit,
one God, for ever and ever.

TODAY'S LIVING WORD

Today's Gospel introduces the great Advent figure, John the Baptist. But the text is puzzling. To say as Jesus does that "the least in the Kingdom of heaven is greater than he" is to exclude John from God's kingdom. Scholars such as Daniel Harrington take this to mean that, with Jesus, "a wholly new period of salvation history has begun."*

The prophet Isaiah suggests that anything "the hand of the Lord" does is always wholly new. In today's reading, God's intervention on behalf of the exiles in Babylon is described, not just as a new Exodus, but also as a whole new creation. The newest feature of this text is the use of the word "redeemer" *(go'el)* as a title for God. The term denotes one's next of kin, who, according to the law of Israel, was obligated to come to one's aid (cf. Lv 25:25). This, the prophet dares to say, is the relationship God has with Israel! "Your *go'el* is the Holy One of Israel."

* *The Gospel of Matthew,* Sacra Pagina 1 (Collegeville: Liturgical Press, 1991), p. 160.

FIRST READING
Is 41:13-20

I am your redeemer, the Holy One of Israel.

A reading from the Book of the Prophet Isaiah

I am the LORD, your God,
    who grasp your right hand;
It is I who say to you, "Fear not,
    I will help you."
Fear not, O worm Jacob,
    O maggot Israel;
I will help you, says the LORD;
    your redeemer is the Holy One of Israel.
I will make of you a threshing sledge,
    sharp, new, and double-edged,
To thresh the mountains and crush them,
    to make the hills like chaff.
When you winnow them, the wind shall carry them off
    and the storm shall scatter them.
But you shall rejoice in the LORD,
    and glory in the Holy One of Israel.

The afflicted and the needy seek water in vain,
    their tongues are parched with thirst.
I, the LORD, will answer them;
    I, the God of Israel, will not forsake them.
I will open up rivers on the bare heights,
    and fountains in the broad valleys;
I will turn the desert into a marshland,
    and the dry ground into springs of water.
I will plant in the desert the cedar,
    acacia, myrtle, and olive;
I will set in the wasteland the cypress,

together with the plane tree and the pine,
That all may see and know,
observe and understand,
That the hand of the LORD has done this,
the Holy One of Israel has created it.

The word of the Lord.

Responsorial Psalm

Ps 145:1 and 9, 10–11, 12–13ab

R. The Lord is gracious and merciful; slow to anger, and
of great kindness.

I will extol you, O my God and King,
and I will bless your name forever and ever.
The LORD is good to all
and compassionate toward all his works.

R. The Lord is gracious and merciful; slow to anger, and
of great kindness.

Let all your works give you thanks, O LORD,
and let your faithful ones bless you.
Let them discourse of the glory of your Kingdom
and speak of your might.

R. The Lord is gracious and merciful; slow to anger, and
of great kindness.

Let them make known to men your might
and the glorious splendor of your Kingdom.
Your Kingdom is a Kingdom for all ages,
and your dominion endures through all generations.

R. The Lord is gracious and merciful; slow to anger, and
of great kindness.

Alleluia, alleluia   See Is 45:8
Let the clouds rain down the Just One,
and the earth bring forth a Savior.
Alleluia, alleluia

GOSPEL

Mt 11:11–15

None greater than John the Baptist has been born.

A reading from the holy Gospel according to Matthew

Jesus said to the crowds: "Amen, I say to you, among those born of women there has been none greater than John the Baptist; yet the least in the Kingdom of heaven is greater than he. From the days of John the Baptist until now, the Kingdom of heaven suffers violence, and the violent are taking it by force. All the prophets and the law prophesied up to the time of John. And if you are willing to accept it, he is Elijah, the one who is to come. Whoever has ears ought to hear."

The Gospel of the Lord.

Liturgy of the Eucharist, *p. 897.*

Prayer over the Gifts

Pray, brethren...

Father,
from all you give us
we present this bread and wine.
As we serve you now,
accept our offering
and sustain us with your promise of eternal life.

Preface of Advent I, *p. 937.*

Communion Antiphon

Let our lives be honest and holy in this present age, as we wait for the happiness to come when our great God reveals himself in glory.   (Ti 2:12 –13)

Prayer after Communion

Let us pray.

Pause for silent prayer, if this has not preceded.

Father,
may our communion
teach us to love heaven.
May its promise and hope
guide our way on earth.
We ask this through Christ our Lord.

Friday

Entrance Antiphon

The Lord is coming from heaven in splendor to visit his people, and bring them peace and eternal life.

Opening Prayer

All-powerful God,
help us to look forward in hope
to the coming of our Savior.
May we live as he has taught,
ready to welcome him with burning love and faith.

We ask this through our Lord Jesus Christ, your Son,
who lives and reigns with you and the Holy Spirit,
one God, for ever and ever.

TODAY'S LIVING WORD

Both of today's readings convey a sense of frustration. Isaiah's oracle depicts God as Israel's teacher, who leads them on the way they should go—morally (by giving them commandments) and materially (by bringing home from exile). The conditional: "If you would…" implies that they are reluctant learners. Similarly in today's brief excerpt from Matthew, Jesus uses an analogy to describe his contemporaries' refusal to receive the good news of God's kingdom, either from John the Baptist or from him.

Taken together, the two readings present us with a challenge. The Holy One of Israel would teach us too what is for our good. But we are as reluctant to hearken to God's way as was ancient Israel. We vacillate, as Jesus' contemporaries did, between one religious style and another, looking for loopholes. "But wisdom is vindicated by her works." May our good works this Advent prove the wisdom of God's way.

FIRST READING

Is 48:17–19

If only you would hearken to my commandments.

A reading from the Book of the Prophet Isaiah

Thus says the Lord, your redeemer,
    the Holy One of Israel:
I, the Lord, your God,
    teach you what is for your good,
    and lead you on the way you should go.
If you would hearken to my commandments,
    your prosperity would be like a river,
    and your vindication like the waves of the sea;
Your descendants would be like the sand,
    and those born of your stock like its grains,
Their name never cut off
    or blotted out from my presence.

The word of the Lord.

Responsorial Psalm

Ps 1:1– 2, 3, 4 and 6

R. **Those who follow you, Lord, will have the light of life.**

Blessed the man who follows not
    the counsel of the wicked
Nor walks in the way of sinners,
    nor sits in the company of the insolent,

But delights in the law of the LORD
  and meditates on his law day and night.

   R. Those who follow you, Lord, will have the light of life.

He is like a tree
  planted near running water,
That yields its fruit in due season,
  and whose leaves never fade.
  Whatever he does, prospers.

   R. Those who follow you, Lord, will have the light of life.

Not so the wicked, not so;
  they are like chaff which the wind drives away.
For the LORD watches over the way of the just,
  but the way of the wicked vanishes.

   R. Those who follow you, Lord, will have the light of life.

   Alleluia, alleluia
   The Lord will come; go out to meet him!
   He is the prince of peace.
   Alleluia, alleluia

GOSPEL

Mt 11:16–19

They listened to neither John nor to the Son of Man.

A reading from the holy Gospel according to Matthew

Jesus said to the crowds: "To what shall I compare this generation? It is like children who sit in marketplaces and call to one another, 'We played the flute for you, but you did not dance, we sang a dirge but you did not mourn.' For John came neither eating nor drinking, and they said, 'He is possessed by a demon.' The Son of Man came eating and drinking and they said, 'Look, he is a glutton and a drunkard, a friend of tax collectors and sinners.' But wisdom is vindicated by her works."

The Gospel of the Lord.

   Liturgy of the Eucharist, *p. 897.*

Prayer over the Gifts

Pray, brethren...

Lord,
we are nothing without you.
As you sustain us with your mercy,
receive our prayers and offerings.
We ask this through Christ our Lord.

Preface of Advent I, *p. 937.*

Communion Antiphon

**We are waiting for our Savior, the Lord Jesus Christ; he will
transfigure our lowly bodies into copies of his own glorious body.**

(Phil 3:20 – 21)

Prayer after Communion

Let us pray.

Pause for silent prayer, if this has not preceded.

Father,
you give us food from heaven.
By our sharing in this mystery,
teach us to judge wisely the things of earth
and to love the things of heaven.

Saturday

Entrance Antiphon

**Come, Lord, from your cherubim throne; let us see your face,
and we shall be saved.**   (Ps 79:4, 2)

Opening Prayer

Lord,
let your glory dawn to take away our darkness.
May we be revealed as the children of light

at the coming of your Son,
who lives and reigns with you and the Holy Spirit,
one God, for ever and ever.

TODAY'S LIVING WORD

Today's Gospel presents a distinctly Christian reading of the Hebrew Scriptures. According to the prophet Malachi, Elijah would return to usher in the "great and terrible" day of the Lord (3:23–24). Today's reading from Sirach also echoes this idea. In the Gospel, Matthew's Jesus identifies John the Baptist as Elijah, and this has become the standard Christian designation of John. In fact, in Luke the angel Gabriel announces the role John is to play in God's saving plan with an allusion to the words of Malachi, saying that God himself "will go before him in the spirit and power of Elijah—to turn the hearts of fathers toward children..." (1:17; cf. Sir 48:10). Elijah's main task, anticipating the coming day of the Lord, is to establish peace within the family by reconciling parents and children. This might be a good resolution for the Advent season.

FIRST READING

Sir 48:1–4, 9–11

Elijah was enveloped in a whirlwind.

A reading from the Book of Sirach

In those days,
like a fire there appeared the prophet Elijah
    whose words were as a flaming furnace.
Their staff of bread he shattered,
    in his zeal he reduced them to straits;
By the Lord's word he shut up the heavens
    and three times brought down fire.
How awesome are you, Elijah, in your wondrous deeds!
    Whose glory is equal to yours?
You were taken aloft in a whirlwind of fire,
    in a chariot with fiery horses.

You were destined, it is written, in time to come
  to put an end to wrath before the day of the LORD,
To turn back the hearts of fathers toward their sons,
  and to re-establish the tribes of Jacob.
  Blessed is he who shall have seen you
  and who falls asleep in your friendship.
The word of the Lord.

Responsorial Psalm
Ps 80:2ac and 3b, 15–16, 18–19

**R. Lord, make us turn to you; let us see your face and we
  shall be saved.**

O shepherd of Israel, hearken,
From your throne upon the cherubim, shine forth.
Rouse your power.

**R. Lord, make us turn to you; let us see your face and we
  shall be saved.**

Once again, O LORD of hosts,
  look down from heaven, and see;
Take care of this vine,
  and protect what your right hand has planted,
  the son of man whom you yourself made strong.

**R. Lord, make us turn to you; let us see your face and we
  shall be saved.**

May your help be with the man of your right hand,
  with the son of man whom you yourself made strong.
Then we will no more withdraw from you;
  give us new life, and we will call upon your name.

**R. Lord, make us turn to you; let us see your face and we
  shall be saved.**

> **Alleluia, alleluia** Lk 3:4, 6
> Prepare the way of the Lord, make straight his paths:
> All flesh shall see the salvation of God.
> **Alleluia, alleluia**

GOSPEL

Mt 17:9a, 10–13

Elijah has already come, and they did not recognize him.

A reading from the holy Gospel according to Matthew

As they were coming down from the mountain, the disciples asked Jesus, "Why do the scribes say that Elijah must come first?" He said in reply, "Elijah will indeed come and restore all things; but I tell you that Elijah has already come, and they did not recognize him but did to him whatever they pleased. So also will the Son of Man suffer at their hands." Then the disciples understood that he was speaking to them of John the Baptist.

The Gospel of the Lord.

Liturgy of the Eucharist, *p. 897.*

Prayer over the Gifts

Pray, brethren...

Lord,
may the gift we offer in faith and love
be a continual sacrifice in your honor
and truly become our eucharist and our salvation.
Grant this through Christ our Lord.

Preface of Advent I, *p. 937.*

Communion Antiphon

I am coming quickly, says the Lord, and will repay each man according to his deeds.   (Rv 22:12)

Prayer after Communion

Let us pray.

Pause for silent prayer, if this has not preceded.

God of mercy,
may this eucharist bring us your divine help,

free us from our sins,
and prepare us for the birthday of our Savior,
who is Lord for ever and ever.

THIRD WEEK OF ADVENT

Monday

*For the **Advent weekday Masses** from December 17 to December 24, see*
pp. 123–158.

Entrance Antiphon

Nations, hear the message of the Lord, and make it known to the ends of the earth: Our Savior is coming. Have no more fear.

(See Jer 31:10; Is 35:4)

Opening Prayer

Lord,
hear our voices raised in prayer.
Let the light of the coming of your Son
free us from the darkness of sin.

We ask this through our Lord Jesus Christ, your Son,
who lives and reigns with you and the Holy Spirit,
one God, for ever and ever.

TODAY'S LIVING WORD

Both readings today are concerned with legitimizing authority. Both want to establish whether certain individuals or events are "of heavenly or of human origin." The oracle of Balaam reported in the Book of Numbers legitimizes the rise of David and his conquest of Moab. Foreseen by a prophet, "one who sees what the Almighty sees," David's accession is surely of God. Similarly, in today's Gospel, the opponents of Jesus want to know the origin of his authority. If Jesus simply were to say that his power is from God, that would be construed as blasphemy. So he avoids answering by asking a question about the authority of John the Baptist.

It is important to note that it was not his opponents' question but their hidden agenda that caused Jesus to demur. The question, in fact, is one that we must often ask as we seek to discern what in our experience is of God and what is not. Let us ask it seriously and sincerely, ready to hear and to heed the answer.

FIRST READING

Nm 24:2–7, 15–17a

A star shall advance from Jacob.

A reading from the Book of Numbers

When Balaam raised his eyes and saw Israel encamped, tribe by tribe, the spirit of God came upon him, and he gave voice to his oracle:

> The utterance of Balaam, son of Beor,
>> the utterance of a man whose eye is true,
> The utterance of one who hears what God says,
>> and knows what the Most High knows,
> Of one who sees what the Almighty sees,
>> enraptured, and with eyes unveiled:
> How goodly are your tents, O Jacob;
>> your encampments, O Israel!
> They are like gardens beside a stream,
>> like the cedars planted by the LORD.
> His wells shall yield free-flowing waters,
>> he shall have the sea within reach;
> His king shall rise higher,
>> and his royalty shall be exalted.

Then Balaam gave voice to his oracle:

> The utterance of Balaam, son of Beor,
>> the utterance of the man whose eye is true,

The utterance of one who hears what God says,
  and knows what the Most High knows,
Of one who sees what the Almighty sees,
  enraptured, and with eyes unveiled.
I see him, though not now;
  I behold him, though not near:
A star shall advance from Jacob,
  and a staff shall rise from Israel.

The word of the Lord.

Responsorial Psalm

Ps 25:4–5ab, 6 and 7bc, 8–9

R. Teach me your ways, O Lord.

Your ways, O Lord, make known to me;
  teach me your paths,
Guide me in your truth and teach me,
  for you are God my savior.

R. Teach me your ways, O Lord.

Remember that your compassion, O Lord,
  and your kindness are from of old.
In your kindness remember me,
  because of your goodness, O Lord.

R. Teach me your ways, O Lord.

Good and upright is the Lord;
  thus he shows sinners the way.
He guides the humble to justice,
  he teaches the humble his way.

R. Teach me your ways, O Lord.

Alleluia, alleluia   Ps 85:8
Show us, Lord, your love,
and grant us your salvation.
Alleluia, alleluia

GOSPEL

Mt 21:23–27

John's baptism: where did it come from?

A reading from the holy Gospel according to Matthew

When Jesus had come into the temple area, the chief priests and the elders of the people approached him as he was teaching and said, "By what authority are you doing these things? And who gave you this authority?" Jesus said to them in reply, "I shall ask you one question, and if you answer it for me, then I shall tell you by what authority I do these things. Where was John's baptism from? Was it of heavenly or of human origin?" They discussed this among themselves and said, "If we say 'Of heavenly origin,' he will say to us, 'Then why did you not believe him?' But if we say, 'Of human origin,' we fear the crowd, for they all regard John as a prophet." So they said to Jesus in reply, "We do not know." He himself said to them, "Neither shall I tell you by what authority I do these things."

The Gospel of the Lord.

Liturgy of the Eucharist, *p. 897.*

Prayer over the Gifts

Pray, brethren...

Father,
from all you give us
we present this bread and wine.
As we serve you now,
accept our offering
and sustain us with your promise of eternal life.

Grant this through Christ our Lord.

Preface of Advent I, *p. 937.*

Communion Antiphon

Come to us, Lord, and bring us peace. We will rejoice in your presence and serve you with all our heart.

(See Ps 105:4–5; Is 38:3)

Prayer after Communion

Let us pray.

Pause for silent prayer, if this has not preceded.

Father,
may our communion
teach us to love heaven.
May its promise and hope
guide our way on earth.

We ask this through Christ our Lord.

Tuesday

*For the **Advent weekday Masses** from December 17 to December 24, see pp. 123–158.*

Entrance Antiphon

See, the Lord is coming and with him all his saints. Then there will be endless day.   (See Zec 14:5, 7)

Opening Prayer

Father of love,
you made a new creation
through Jesus Christ your Son.
May his coming free us from sin
and renew his life within us,
for he lives and reigns with you and the Holy Spirit,
one God, for ever and ever.

Today's Living Word

Today's Gospel continues the standoff begun in yesterday's reading between Jesus and his opponents, the chief priests and elders. The parable of the two sons likens them to the elder son who, when told to go and work in the vineyard, agrees to go but never does. The tax collectors and prostitutes, on the other hand, are like the second son who at first refuses, but repents and does what his father wanted. Therefore, Jesus says, they are streaming into the kingdom of God ahead of their more reputable religious leaders. The excerpt from Zephaniah draws a similar distinction. Here "the proud braggarts" who exalt themselves on the temple mount are cast as the elder son, while the remnant, "a people humble and lowly," play the part of the repentant second son. They "take refuge in the name of the Lord."

The message is obvious. What matters in the end is conversion and concrete action, the obedience of faith.

FIRST READING

Zep 3:1–2, 9–13

Messianic salvation is promised to all of the poor.

A reading from the Book of the Prophet Zephaniah

Thus says the LORD:
Woe to the city, rebellious and polluted,
　　to the tyrannical city!
She hears no voice,
　　accepts no correction;
In the LORD she has not trusted,
　　to her God she has not drawn near.

For then I will change and purify
　　the lips of the peoples,
That they all may call upon the name of the LORD,
　　to serve him with one accord;
From beyond the rivers of Ethiopia
　　and as far as the recesses of the North,
　　they shall bring me offerings.

On that day
You need not be ashamed
   of all your deeds,
   your rebellious actions against me;
For then will I remove from your midst
   the proud braggarts,
And you shall no longer exalt yourself
   on my holy mountain.
But I will leave as a remnant in your midst
   a people humble and lowly,
Who shall take refuge in the name of the LORD:
   the remnant of Israel.
They shall do no wrong
   and speak no lies;
Nor shall there be found in their mouths
   a deceitful tongue;
They shall pasture and couch their flocks
   with none to disturb them.

The word of the Lord.

Responsorial Psalm

Ps 34:2–3, 6–7, 17–18, 19 and 23

   R. **The Lord hears the cry of the poor.**

I will bless the LORD at all times;
   his praise shall be ever in my mouth.
Let my soul glory in the LORD;
   the lowly will hear me and be glad.

   R. **The Lord hears the cry of the poor.**

Look to him that you may be radiant with joy,
   and your faces may not blush with shame.
When the poor one called out, the LORD heard,
   and from all his distress he saved him.

   R. **The Lord hears the cry of the poor.**

The LORD confronts the evildoers,
　to destroy remembrance of them from the earth.
When the just cry out, the LORD hears them,
　and from all their distress he rescues them.

R. The Lord hears the cry of the poor.

The LORD is close to the brokenhearted;
　and those who are crushed in spirit he saves.
The LORD redeems the lives of his servants;
　no one incurs guilt who takes refuge in him.

R. The Lord hears the cry of the poor.

Alleluia, alleluia
Come, O Lord, do not delay;
forgive the sins of your people.
Alleluia, alleluia

GOSPEL
Mt 21:28–32

John came and sinners believed in him.

A reading from the holy Gospel according to Matthew

Jesus said to the chief priests and the elders of the people: "What is your opinion? A man had two sons. He came to the first and said, 'Son, go out and work in the vineyard today.' The son said in reply, 'I will not,' but afterwards he changed his mind and went. The man came to the other son and gave the same order. He said in reply, 'Yes, sir,' but did not go. Which of the two did his father's will?" They answered, "The first." Jesus said to them, "Amen, I say to you, tax collectors and prostitutes are entering the Kingdom of God before you. When John came to you in the way of righteousness, you did not believe him; but tax collectors and prostitutes did. Yet even when you saw that, you did not later change your minds and believe him."

The Gospel of the Lord.

Liturgy of the Eucharist, *p. 897.*

Prayer over the Gifts

Pray, brethren...

Lord,
we are nothing without you.
As you sustain us with your mercy,
receive our prayers and offerings.

We ask this through Christ our Lord.

Preface of Advent I, *p. 937.*

Communion Antiphon

The Lord is just; he will award the crown of justice to all who have longed for his coming.   (2 Tm 4:8)

Prayer after Communion

Let us pray.

Pause for silent prayer, if this has not preceded.

Father,
you give us food from heaven.
By our sharing in this mystery,
teach us to judge wisely the things of earth
and to love the things of heaven.

Grant this through Christ our Lord.

Wednesday

Entrance Antiphon

The Lord is coming and will not delay; he will bring every hidden thing to light and reveal himself to every nation.
(See Hab 2:3; 1 Cor 4:5)

*For the **Advent weekday Masses** from December 17 to December 24, see pp. 123–158.*

Opening Prayer

Father,
may the coming celebration of the birth of your Son
bring us your saving help
and prepare us for eternal life.

Grant this through our Lord Jesus Christ, your Son,
who lives and reigns with you and the Holy Spirit,
one God, for ever and ever.

TODAY'S LIVING WORD

The juxtaposition of today's two readings helps us to appreciate the "scandal" Jesus caused. The passage from Isaiah is a magnificent profession of faith in one, and only one, God. This God and no other is the Lord, the Creator and Savior of all, to whom every knee must bend and by whom every tongue must swear. In the Gospel, Jesus responds to the query of John's disciples. The summary of his ministry—"The blind regain their sight, the lame walk, lepers are cleansed, the deaf hear, the dead are raised, the poor have the good news proclaimed to them"—is a summons to believe that, in him and through him, the Lord and no other is acting to save. Then, as though acknowledging the leap of faith this massive claim requires, Jesus adds, "Blessed is the one who takes no offense *(skandalizo)* at me."

In Advent we prepare ourselves to revisit the jarring juxtaposition of today's readings in the mystery of the Incarnation. "So great a God, so tiny an infant!" exclaimed St. Francis of Assisi. Blessed is the one who can hold both in one thought.

FIRST READING

Is 45:6c–8, 18, 21c–25

Let the clouds rain down.

A reading from the Book of the Prophet Isaiah

I am the LORD, there is no other;
    I form the light, and create the darkness,

I make well-being and create woe;
    I, the LORD, do all these things.
Let justice descend, O heavens, like dew from above,
    like gentle rain let the skies drop it down.
Let the earth open and salvation bud forth;
    let justice also spring up!
    I, the LORD, have created this.

    For thus says the LORD,
The creator of the heavens,
    who is God,
The designer and maker of the earth
    who established it,
Not creating it to be a waste,
    but designing it to be lived in:
I am the LORD, and there is no other.

Who announced this from the beginning
    and foretold it from of old?
Was it not I, the LORD,
    besides whom there is no other God?
    There is no just and saving God but me.

Turn to me and be safe,
    all you ends of the earth,
    for I am God; there is no other!
By myself I swear,
    uttering my just decree
    and my unalterable word:
To me every knee shall bend;
    by me every tongue shall swear,
Saying, "Only in the LORD

are just deeds and power.
Before him in shame shall come
    all who vent their anger against him.
In the LORD shall be the vindication and the glory
    of all the descendants of Israel."
The word of the Lord.

Responsorial Psalm

Ps 85:9ab and 10, 11–12, 13–14

**R. Let the clouds rain down the Just One, and the earth
    bring forth a Savior.**

I will hear what God proclaims;
    the LORD—for he proclaims peace to his people.
Near indeed is his salvation to those who fear him,
    glory dwelling in our land.

**R. Let the clouds rain down the Just One, and the earth
    bring forth a Savior.**

Kindness and truth shall meet;
    justice and peace shall kiss.
Truth shall spring out of the earth,
    and justice shall look down from heaven.

**R. Let the clouds rain down the Just One, and the earth
    bring forth a Savior.**

The LORD himself will give his benefits;
    our land shall yield its increase.
Justice shall walk before him,
    and salvation, along the way of his steps.

**R. Let the clouds rain down the Just One, and the earth
    bring forth a Savior.**

Alleluia, alleluia   See Is 40:9–10
Raise your voice and tell the Good News:
Behold, the Lord GOD comes with power.
Alleluia, alleluia

GOSPEL

Go back and tell John what you have seen and heard.

A reading from the holy Gospel according to Luke

At that time, John summoned two of his disciples and sent them to the Lord to ask, "Are you the one who is to come, or should we look for another?" When the men came to the Lord, they said, "John the Baptist has sent us to you to ask, 'Are you the one who is to come, or should we look for another?'" At that time Jesus cured many of their diseases, sufferings, and evil spirits; he also granted sight to many who were blind. And Jesus said to them in reply, "Go and tell John what you have seen and heard: the blind regain their sight, the lame walk, lepers are cleansed, the deaf hear, the dead are raised, the poor have the good news proclaimed to them. And blessed is the one who takes no offense at me."

The Gospel of the Lord.

Liturgy of the Eucharist, *p. 897.*

Prayer over the Gifts

Pray, brethren...

Lord,
may the gift we offer in faith and love
be a continual sacrifice in your honor
and truly become our eucharist and our salvation.

Grant this through Christ our Lord.

Preface of Advent I, *p. 937.*

Communion Antiphon

The Lord our God comes in strength and will fill his servants with joy.   (Is 40:10; see 34:5)

Prayer after Communion

Let us pray.

Pause for silent prayer, if this has not preceded.

God of mercy,
may this eucharist bring us your divine help,
free us from our sins,
and prepare us for the birthday of our Savior,
who is Lord for ever and ever.

Thursday

*For the **Advent weekday Masses** from December 17 to December 24, see pp. 123–158.*

Entrance Antiphon

Lord, you are near, and all your commandments are just; long have I known that you decreed them for ever.

(See Ps 118:151–152)

Opening Prayer

Lord,
our sins bring us unhappiness.
Hear our prayer for courage and strength.
May the coming of your Son
bring us the joy of salvation.

We ask this through our Lord Jesus Christ, your Son,
who lives and reigns with you and the Holy Spirit,
one God, for ever and ever.

TODAY'S LIVING WORD

Today's readings announce the new future God creates for exiles and outcasts. The poem from Isaiah is addressed to exiled Israel. Powerful primal images of hopelessness—the barren womb, the broken marriage, the flood in Noah's days—are enlisted to convey the reversal that the "enduring love" of God will bring: "For a brief moment I abandoned you, but with great tenderness I will take you back...says the Lord, your redeemer." The Gospel too draws on powerful images to make its point. "What did you go out to the desert to see?" asks Jesus. The baptism of John is an oasis in the desert for all the people, even for tax collectors, priming them for the good news of Jesus. The citation from Scripture, combining Exodus (23:20) and Malachi (3:1), reiterates: "I am sending my messenger ahead of you, he will prepare your way before you."

Like exiled Israel and the eager audience of John, may we this Advent be filled with anticipation at the new future God continues to create for us in Jesus the Christ.

FIRST READING

Is 54:1–10

Like a forsaken wife, the Lord has called you back.

A reading from the Book of the Prophet Isaiah

Raise a glad cry, you barren one who did not bear,
    break forth in jubilant song, you who were not in labor,
For more numerous are the children of the deserted wife
    than the children of her who has a husband,
        says the Lord.
Enlarge the space for your tent,
    spread out your tent cloths unsparingly;
    lengthen your ropes and make firm your stakes.
For you shall spread abroad to the right and to the left;
    your descendants shall dispossess the nations
    and shall people the desolate cities.

Fear not, you shall not be put to shame;
    you need not blush, for you shall not be disgraced.
The shame of your youth you shall forget,
    the reproach of your widowhood no longer remember.
For he who has become your husband is your Maker;
    his name is the Lord of hosts;

Your redeemer is the Holy One of Israel,
  called God of all the earth.
The LORD calls you back,
  like a wife forsaken and grieved in spirit,
A wife married in youth and then cast off,
  says your God.
For a brief moment I abandoned you,
  but with great tenderness I will take you back.
In an outburst of wrath, for a moment
  I hid my face from you;
But with enduring love I take pity on you,
  says the LORD, your redeemer.

This is for me like the days of Noah,
  when I swore that the waters of Noah
  should never again deluge the earth;
So I have sworn not to be angry with you,
  or to rebuke you.
Though the mountains leave their place
  and the hills be shaken,
My love shall never leave you
  nor my covenant of peace be shaken,
  says the LORD, who has mercy on you.

The word of the Lord.

Responsorial Psalm

Ps 30:2 and 4, 5–6, 11–12a and 13b

R. I will praise you, Lord, for you have rescued me.

I will extol you, O LORD, for you drew me clear
  and did not let my enemies rejoice over me.
O LORD, you brought me up from the nether world;
  you preserved me from among those going down into the pit.

R. I will praise you, Lord, for you have rescued me.

Sing praise to the Lord, you his faithful ones,
  and give thanks to his holy name.
For his anger lasts but a moment;
  a lifetime, his good will.
At nightfall, weeping enters in,
  but with the dawn, rejoicing.

R. I will praise you, Lord, for you have rescued me.

"Hear, O Lord, and have pity on me;
  O Lord, be my helper."
You changed my mourning into dancing;
  O Lord, my God, forever will I give you thanks.

R. I will praise you, Lord, for you have rescued me.

Alleluia, alleluia   Lk 3:4, 6
Prepare the way of the Lord, make straight his paths:
All flesh shall see the salvation of God.
Alleluia, alleluia

GOSPEL   Lk 7:24 – 30
  John is the messenger who prepares the way of the Lord.

A reading from the holy Gospel according to Luke

When the messengers of John the Baptist had left, Jesus began
to speak to the crowds about John. "What did you go out to the
desert to see—a reed swayed by the wind? Then what did you
go out to see? Someone dressed in fine garments? Those who
dress luxuriously and live sumptuously are found in royal
palaces. Then what did you go out to see? A prophet? Yes, I
tell you, and more than a prophet. This is the one about whom
Scripture says:

Behold, I am sending my messenger ahead of you,
he will prepare your way before you.

I tell you, among those born of women, no one is greater than
John; yet the least in the Kingdom of God is greater than he."

(All the people who listened, including the tax collectors, who were baptized with the baptism of John, acknowledged the righteousness of God; but the Pharisees and scholars of the law, who were not baptized by him, rejected the plan of God for themselves.)

The Gospel of the Lord.

Liturgy of the Eucharist, *p. 897.*

Prayer over the Gifts

Pray, brethren...

Father,
from all you give us
we present this bread and wine.
As we serve you now,
accept our offering
and sustain us with your promise of eternal life.

Grant this through Christ our Lord.

Preface of Advent I, *p. 937.*

Communion Antiphon

Let our lives be honest and holy in this present age, as we wait for the happiness to come when our great God reveals himself in glory.   (Ti 2:12–13)

Prayer after Communion

Let us pray.

Pause for silent prayer, if this has not preceded.

Father,
may our communion
teach us to love heaven.
May its promise and hope
guide our way on earth.

We ask this through Christ our Lord.

Friday

*For the **Advent weekday Masses** from December 17 to December 24, see pp. 123–158.*

Entrance Antiphon

The Lord is coming from heaven in splendor to visit his people, and bring them peace and eternal life.

Opening Prayer

All-powerful Father,
guide us with your love
as we await the coming of your Son.
Keep us faithful
that we may be helped through life
and brought to salvation.

We ask this through our Lord Jesus Christ, your Son,
who lives and reigns with you and the Holy Spirit,
one God, for ever and ever.

TODAY'S LIVING WORD

Although the brevity of today's Gospel excerpt from John makes it difficult to see, there are points of contact between the two readings. As Isaiah insists that God is the source of his words—"Thus says the Lord"—Jesus presents witnesses in defense of his ministry. Both of his witnesses come from God: John was sent by God, and the works of Jesus have been given to him by the Father. Isaiah's concern in today's oracle is to say that God welcomes and wills to save not just Jerusalem Jews but all people "who join themselves to the Lord, ministering to him, loving the name of the Lord, and becoming his servants." Thus, the religious ritual of God's house is open to others besides the dispersed of Israel. Similarly the Gospel of John, more boldly than the other three, attests to the universality of God's saving will revealed in Jesus, and reinterprets the religious feasts of Judaism accordingly.

In its Advent liturgy, the Church also calls John the Baptist and the works of Jesus to testify that the Father has sent Jesus to us and that he is "truly the Savior of the world" (Jn 4:42).

FIRST READING
Is 56:1–3a, 6–8

My house shall be called a house of prayer for all peoples.

A reading from the Book of the Prophet Isaiah

Thus says the LORD:
Observe what is right, do what is just;
    for my salvation is about to come,
      my justice, about to be revealed.
Blessed is the man who does this,
    the son of man who holds to it;
Who keeps the sabbath free from profanation,
    and his hand from any evildoing.
Let not the foreigner say,
    when he would join himself to the LORD,
    "The LORD will surely exclude me from his people."

The foreigners who join themselves to the LORD,
    ministering to him,
Loving the name of the LORD,
    and becoming his servants—
All who keep the sabbath free from profanation
    and hold to my covenant,
Them I will bring to my holy mountain
    and make joyful in my house of prayer;
Their burnt offerings and sacrifices
    will be acceptable on my altar,
For my house shall be called
    a house of prayer for all peoples.

Thus says the Lord GOD,
  who gathers the dispersed of Israel:
Others will I gather to him
  besides those already gathered.
The word of the Lord.

Responsorial Psalm

Ps 67:2–3, 5, 7–8

R. O God, let all the nations praise you!

May God have pity on us and bless us;
  may he let his face shine upon us.
So may your way be known upon earth;
  among all nations, your salvation.

R. O God, let all the nations praise you!

May the nations be glad and exult
  because you rule the peoples in equity;
  the nations on the earth you guide.

R. O God, let all the nations praise you!

The earth has yielded its fruits;
  God, our God, has blessed us.
May God bless us,
  and may all the ends of the earth fear him!

R. O God, let all the nations praise you!

> **Alleluia, alleluia**
> Come, Lord, bring us your peace
> that we may rejoice before you with a perfect heart.
> **Alleluia, alleluia**

GOSPEL

Jn 5:33–36

John was a burning and shining lamp.

A reading from the holy Gospel according to John

Jesus said to the Jews: "You sent emissaries to John, and he
testified to the truth. I do not accept testimony from a human

being, but I say this so that you may be saved. John was a burning and shining lamp, and for a while you were content to rejoice in his light. But I have testimony greater than John's. The works that the Father gave me to accomplish, these works that I perform testify on my behalf that the Father has sent me."

The Gospel of the Lord.

Liturgy of the Eucharist, *p. 897.*

Prayer over the Gifts

Pray, brethren...

Lord,
we are nothing without you.
As you sustain us with your mercy,
receive our prayers and offerings.
We ask this through Christ our Lord.

Preface of Advent I, *p. 937.*

Communion Antiphon

We are waiting for our Savior, the Lord Jesus Christ; he will transfigure our lowly bodies into copies of his own glorious body.
(Phil 3:20–21)

Prayer after Communion

Let us pray.

Pause for silent prayer, if this has not preceded.

Father,
you give us food from heaven.
By our sharing in this mystery,
teach us to judge wisely the things of earth
and to love the things of heaven.
Grant this through Christ our Lord.

From Advent into Christmas
O Emmanuel, Come

The "O" Antiphons

By the ninth century the Church at Rome, as well as throughout Charlemagne's dominion, adopted a series of seven special antiphons to accompany the singing of the Magnificat during Vespers (evening prayer) in the final week before Christmas. Called the "Great O Antiphons," because each begins with the acclamation "O," these verses both signal the shift in the thematic focus of Advent on December 17 and function as a countdown to the Feast of the Lord's Nativity. The structure and content of the antiphons, nonetheless, continue to proclaim the fundamental truth we celebrate throughout the Advent-Christmas season: we are called to live our lives now in the practical hope of Christ's second, definitive coming, the promise of which was begun in his first coming among us as a man. The Great O Antiphons are poetic meditations on the qualities that characterize the life that God has given us through the life, death, and resurrection of the Messiah.

The seven antiphons share a common pattern. They begin with the cry, "O," address the Messiah according to a specific biblical title, and then recount the salvific will and action of God that each title recalls. On the basis of this divine name and memory follows the human plea,

"Come," accompanied by the request that God act now, again, according to the same saving pattern, hoping that God will finally bring the pattern to completion. With the first antiphon, sung on the evening of December 17, we pray: "O Wisdom, O holy Word of God, you govern all creation with your strong yet tender care. Come and show your people the way to salvation."

Over the ensuing nights the Christ of God is acclaimed Lord of Israel, Flower of Jesse's Stem, Key of David, Radiant Dawn, King of All Nations, Keystone of the Church, and, finally, Emmanuel. Those titles remind us of God as the One who gives the law, raises up Israel as a sign to the nations, delivers his people from death's captivity, reveals justice for the oppressed, gives true joy and peace to every human heart, and promises freedom from sin to every creature he has created from the dust.

BRUCE T. MORRILL, S.J.

WEEKDAYS OF ADVENT FROM DECEMBER 17 TO DECEMBER 24

The following readings are used from December 17 to 24. If a Sunday occurs during this time, the weekday readings for that day are omitted, but they may be anticipated or used on another day during the week, especially to avoid duplicating the Sunday readings.

December 17

Entrance Antiphon

You heavens, sing for joy, and earth exult! Our Lord is coming; he will take pity on those in distress.   (See Is 49:13)

Opening Prayer

Father,
creator and redeemer of mankind,
you decreed, and your Word became man,
born of the Virgin Mary.
May we come to share the divinity of Christ,
who humbled himself to share our human nature,
for he lives and reigns with you and the Holy Spirit,
one God, for ever and ever.

TODAY'S LIVING WORD

Today's readings both serve to announce and in some sense divinely authorize coming events in God's unfolding plan. In the reading from Genesis, taken from the farewell address of the dying Jacob, the patriarch pronounces blessings (or curses) on each of his twelve sons. Today's text is his blessing of Judah which, with poetic imagery, foreshadows the prominence the tribe of Judah will enjoy when David comes to power. The Gospel is Matthew's version of

Jesus' family record. Matthew has imposed a pattern on this gene-alogy—three sets of fourteen generations. Since fourteen is a multiple of the perfect number seven, this may be his way of telling us that Jesus comes in "the fullness of time." The most striking feature of Matthew's genealogy is the presence of four women, whose unconventional marital histories furthered the unfolding plan of God. They prepare us for Mary's role in the birth of Jesus.

In the Bible, farewell addresses and family records serve to demonstrate the continuity of God's saving plan. All the readings of Advent invite us to appreciate how the wisdom of God faithfully guides all things.

FIRST READING

Gn 49:2, 8–10

The scepter shall not depart from Judah.

A reading from the Book of Genesis

Jacob called his sons and said to them:
"Assemble and listen, sons of Jacob,
    listen to Israel, your father.

"You, Judah, shall your brothers praise
    —your hand on the neck of your enemies;
    the sons of your father shall bow down to you.
Judah, like a lion's whelp,
    you have grown up on prey, my son.
He crouches like a lion recumbent,
    the king of beasts—who would dare rouse him?
The scepter shall never depart from Judah,
    or the mace from between his legs,
While tribute is brought to him,
    and he receives the people's homage."
The word of the Lord.

Responsorial Psalm

Ps 72:1–2, 3–4ab, 7–8, 17

R. **Justice shall flourish in his time, and fullness of peace for ever.**

O God, with your judgment endow the king,
  and with your justice, the king's son;
He shall govern your people with justice
  and your afflicted ones with judgment.

R. **Justice shall flourish in his time, and fullness of peace for ever.**

The mountains shall yield peace for the people,
  and the hills justice.
He shall defend the afflicted among the people,
  save the children of the poor.

R. **Justice shall flourish in his time, and fullness of peace for ever.**

Justice shall flower in his days,
  and profound peace, till the moon be no more.
May he rule from sea to sea,
  and from the River to the ends of the earth.

R. **Justice shall flourish in his time, and fullness of peace for ever.**

May his name be blessed forever;
  as long as the sun his name shall remain.
In him shall all the tribes of the earth be blessed;
  all the nations shall proclaim his happiness.

R. **Justice shall flourish in his time, and fullness of peace for ever.**

Alleluia, alleluia
  O Wisdom of our God Most High,
  guiding creation with power and love:
  come to teach us the path of knowledge!
Alleluia, alleluia

GOSPEL Mt 1:1–17

The genealogy of Jesus Christ, the son of David.

A reading from the beginning of the holy Gospel according to Matthew

The book of the genealogy of Jesus Christ, the son of David, the son of Abraham.

Abraham became the father of Isaac, Isaac the father of Jacob, Jacob the father of Judah and his brothers. Judah became the father of Perez and Zerah, whose mother was Tamar. Perez became the father of Hezron, Hezron the father of Ram, Ram the father of Amminadab. Amminadab became the father of Nahshon, Nahshon the father of Salmon, Salmon the father of Boaz, whose mother was Rahab. Boaz became the father of Obed, whose mother was Ruth. Obed became the father of Jesse, Jesse the father of David the king.

David became the father of Solomon, whose mother had been the wife of Uriah. Solomon became the father of Rehoboam, Rehoboam the father of Abijah, Abijah the father of Asaph. Asaph became the father of Jehoshaphat, Jehoshaphat the father of Joram, Joram the father of Uzziah. Uzziah became the father of Jotham, Jotham the father of Ahaz, Ahaz the father of Hezekiah. Hezekiah became the father of Manasseh, Manasseh the father of Amos, Amos the father of Josiah. Josiah became the father of Jechoniah and his brothers at the time of the Babylonian exile.

After the Babylonian exile, Jechoniah became the father of Shealtiel, Shealtiel the father of Zerubbabel, Zerubbabel the father of Abiud. Abiud became the father of Eliakim, Eliakim the father of Azor, Azor the father of Zadok. Zadok became the father of Achim, Achim the father of Eliud, Eliud the father of Eleazar. Eleazar became the father of Matthan, Matthan the father of Jacob, Jacob the father of Joseph, the husband of Mary. Of her was born Jesus who is called the Christ.

Thus the total number of generations from Abraham to David is fourteen generations; from David to the Babylonian exile, fourteen generations; from the Babylonian exile to the Christ, fourteen generations.

The Gospel of the Lord.

Liturgy of the Eucharist, *p. 897.*

Prayer over the Gifts

Pray, brethren...

Lord,
bless these gifts of your Church
and by this eucharist
renew us with the bread from heaven.
We ask this in the name of Jesus the Lord.

Preface of Advent II, *p. 937.*

Communion Antiphon

The Desired of all nations is coming, and the house of the Lord will be filled with his glory.   (See Hg 2:8)

Prayer after Communion

Let us pray.

Pause for silent prayer, if this has not preceded.

God our Father,
as you nourish us with the food of life,
give us also your Spirit,

so that we may be radiant with his light
at the coming of Christ your Son,
who is Lord for ever and ever.

December 18

Entrance Antiphon

Christ our King is coming, the Lamb whom John proclaimed.

Opening Prayer

All-powerful God,
renew us by the coming feast of your Son
and free us from our slavery to sin.

Grant this through our Lord Jesus Christ, your Son,
who lives and reigns with you and the Holy Spirit,
one God, for ever and ever.

TODAY'S LIVING WORD

The prophecy of Jeremiah, in the dark days preceding the fall of
Judah, foresees the restoration of the ideal of kingship among God's
people. The future king announced in today's reading will be God's
agent, governing wisely and doing what is right and just in the land.
Therefore, he will deserve the title, "The Lord our justice." Today's
Gospel gives the same title to Joseph. He is a just ("righteous") man,
says Matthew. His justice is demonstrated first of all in his decision
not to expose Mary to the law, which would have permitted him
some personal satisfaction. Rather, he determines to act in the spirit
and not in the letter of the law. His justice is further proven when he
becomes the agent of God's justice (God's saving work) by his
unquestioning obedience to God's command.

Joseph was a just man whose righteousness made him not rigid,
but ready at a moment's notice to act on the new word of God that
was revealed to him. In Advent the Church gives him to us as an
example of how obedience to God's law can open us to the revelation of Emmanuel, "God is with us."

FIRST READING

Jer 23:5–8

I will raise up a righteous shoot to David.

A reading from the Book of the Prophet Jeremiah

> Behold, the days are coming, says the LORD,
>> when I will raise up a righteous shoot to David;
> As king he shall reign and govern wisely,
>> he shall do what is just and right in the land.
> In his days Judah shall be saved,
>> Israel shall dwell in security.
> This is the name they give him:
>> "The LORD our justice."

Therefore, the days will come, says the LORD when they shall no longer say, "As the LORD lives, who brought the children of Israel out of the land of Egypt"; but rather, "As the LORD lives, who brought the descendants of the house of Israel up from the land of the north"—and from all the lands to which I banished them; they shall again live on their own land.

The word of the Lord.

Responsorial Psalm

Ps 72:1–2, 12–13, 18–19

**R.   Justice shall flourish in his time, and fullness of peace
    for ever.**

O God, with your judgment endow the king,
    and with your justice, the king's son;
He shall govern your people with justice
    and your afflicted ones with judgment.

**R.   Justice shall flourish in his time, and fullness of peace
    for ever.**

For he shall rescue the poor when he cries out,
    and the afflicted when he has no one to help him.

He shall have pity for the lowly and the poor;
  the lives of the poor he shall save.

**R. Justice shall flourish in his time, and fullness of peace
for ever.**

Blessed be the LORD, the God of Israel,
  who alone does wondrous deeds.
And blessed forever be his glorious name;
  may the whole earth be filled with his glory.

**R. Justice shall flourish in his time, and fullness of peace
for ever.**

Alleluia, alleluia
O Leader of the House of Israel,
  giver of the Law to Moses on Sinai:
come to rescue us with your mighty power!
Alleluia, alleluia

GOSPEL   Mt 1:18–25

Jesus was born of Mary, the betrothed of Joseph, a son of David.

A reading from the holy Gospel according to Matthew

This is how the birth of Jesus Christ came about. When his
mother Mary was betrothed to Joseph, but before they lived
together, she was found with child through the Holy Spirit.
Joseph her husband, since he was a righteous man, yet unwilling
to expose her to shame, decided to divorce her quietly. Such
was his intention when, behold, the angel of the Lord appeared
to him in a dream and said, "Joseph, son of David, do not be
afraid to take Mary your wife into your home. For it is through
the Holy Spirit that this child has been conceived in her. She
will bear a son and you are to name him Jesus, because he will
save his people from their sins." All this took place to fulfill
what the Lord had said through the prophet:

Behold, the virgin shall be with child and bear a son,
and they shall name him Emmanuel,

which means "God is with us." When Joseph awoke, he did as the angel of the Lord had commanded him and took his wife into his home. He had no relations with her until she bore a son, and he named him Jesus.

The Gospel of the Lord.

Liturgy of the Eucharist, *p. 897.*

Prayer over the Gifts

Pray, brethren...

Lord,
may this sacrifice
bring us into the eternal life of your Son,
who died to save us from death,
for he is Lord for ever and ever.

Preface of Advent II, *p. 937.*

Communion Antiphon

His name will be called Emmanuel, which means God is with us.
(Mt 1:23)

Prayer after Communion

Let us pray.

Pause for silent prayer, if this has not preceded.

Lord,
we receive mercy in your Church.
Prepare us to celebrate with fitting honor
the coming feast of our redemption.

We ask this in the name of Jesus the Lord.

December 19

Entrance Antiphon

He who is to come will not delay; and then there will be no fear in our lands, because he is our Savior.   (See Heb 10:37)

Opening Prayer

Father,
you show the world the splendor of your glory
in the coming of Christ, born of the Virgin.
Give to us true faith and love
to celebrate the mystery of God made man.

We ask this through our Lord Jesus Christ, your Son,
who lives and reigns with you and the Holy Spirit,
one God, for ever and ever.

TODAY'S LIVING WORD

Today's Gospel, the announcement of the birth of John the Baptist, makes several allusions to the announcement of the birth of Samson in the Book of Judges. In both accounts an angel appears to one of a barren couple to announce that, by the power of God, they will be enabled to conceive and bear a son. According to the angel, both sons will be Nazirites, never drinking wine or strong drink (cf. Nm 6:1–21), and both will be consecrated to God from the womb—in John's case, "filled with the Holy Spirit." Finally, both Samson and John will usher in the deliverance of their people.

Luke's infancy narrative is full of allusions like this. It is his way of demonstrating the consistency of God's activity in every generation. Luke's allusive style is characteristic of Advent too. In Advent we contemplate God's activity in previous generations, the better to appreciate God's activity in our own.

FIRST READING   Jgs 13:2–7, 24–25a

The birth of Samson is announced by an angel.

A reading from the Book of Judges

There was a certain man from Zorah, of the clan of the Danites, whose name was Manoah. His wife was barren and had borne no children. An angel of the LORD appeared to the woman and said to her, "Though you are barren and have had no children, yet you will conceive and bear a son. Now, then, be careful to take no wine or strong drink and to eat nothing unclean. As for the son you will conceive and bear, no razor shall touch his head, for this boy is to be consecrated to God from the womb. It is he who will begin the deliverance of Israel from the power of the Philistines."

The woman went and told her husband, "A man of God came to me; he had the appearance of an angel of God, terrible indeed. I did not ask him where he came from, nor did he tell me his name. But he said to me, 'You will be with child and will bear a son. So take neither wine nor strong drink, and eat nothing unclean. For the boy shall be consecrated to God from the womb, until the day of his death.'"

The woman bore a son and named him Samson. The boy grew up and the LORD blessed him; the Spirit of the LORD stirred him.

The word of the Lord.

Responsorial Psalm
Ps 71:3–4a, 5–6ab, 16–17

R. My mouth shall be filled with your praise, and I will sing your glory!

Be my rock of refuge,
  a stronghold to give me safety,
  for you are my rock and my fortress.
O my God, rescue me from the hand of the wicked.

**R. My mouth shall be filled with your praise, and I will
sing your glory!**

For you are my hope, O LORD;
  my trust, O God, from my youth.
On you I depend from birth;
  from my mother's womb you are my strength.

**R. My mouth shall be filled with your praise, and I will
sing your glory!**

I will treat of the mighty works of the LORD;
  O God, I will tell of your singular justice.
O God, you have taught me from my youth,
  and till the present I proclaim your wondrous deeds.

**R. My mouth shall be filled with your praise, and I will
sing your glory!**

Alleluia, alleluia
O Root of Jesse's stem,
sign of God's love for all his people:
come to save us without delay!
Alleluia, alleluia

GOSPEL
Lk 1:5 – 25

The birth of John the Baptist is announced by Gabriel.

A reading from the holy Gospel according to Luke

In the days of Herod, King of Judea, there was a priest named
Zechariah of the priestly division of Abijah; his wife was
from the daughters of Aaron, and her name was Elizabeth.
Both were righteous in the eyes of God, observing all the
commandments and ordinances of the Lord blamelessly. But
they had no child, because Elizabeth was barren and both
were advanced in years.

Once when he was serving as priest in his division's turn
before God, according to the practice of the priestly service,

he was chosen by lot to enter the sanctuary of the Lord to burn incense. Then, when the whole assembly of the people was praying outside at the hour of the incense offering, the angel of the Lord appeared to him, standing at the right of the altar of incense. Zechariah was troubled by what he saw, and fear came upon him.

But the angel said to him, "Do not be afraid, Zechariah, because your prayer has been heard. Your wife Elizabeth will bear you a son, and you shall name him John. And you will have joy and gladness, and many will rejoice at his birth, for he will be great in the sight of the Lord. He will drink neither wine nor strong drink. He will be filled with the Holy Spirit even from his mother's womb, and he will turn many of the children of Israel to the Lord their God. He will go before him in the spirit and power of Elijah to turn the hearts of fathers toward children and the disobedient to the understanding of the righteous, to prepare a people fit for the Lord."

Then Zechariah said to the angel, "How shall I know this? For I am an old man, and my wife is advanced in years." And the angel said to him in reply, "I am Gabriel, who stand before God. I was sent to speak to you and to announce to you this good news. But now you will be speechless and unable to talk until the day these things take place, because you did not believe my words, which will be fulfilled at their proper time."

Meanwhile the people were waiting for Zechariah and were amazed that he stayed so long in the sanctuary. But when he came out, he was unable to speak to them, and they realized that he had seen a vision in the sanctuary. He was gesturing to them but remained mute.

Then, when his days of ministry were completed, he went home.

After this time his wife Elizabeth conceived, and she went into seclusion for five months, saying, "So has the Lord done for me at a time when he has seen fit to take away my disgrace before others."

The Gospel of the Lord.

Liturgy of the Eucharist, *p. 897.*

Prayer over the Gifts

Pray, brethren...
Lord of mercy,
receive the gifts we bring to your altar.
Let your power take away our weakness
and make our offerings holy.

We ask this in the name of Jesus the Lord.

Preface of Advent II, *p. 937.*

Communion Antiphon

The dawn from on high shall break upon us, to guide our feet on the road to peace.   (Lk 1:78–79)

Prayer after Communion

Let us pray.

Pause for silent prayer, if this has not preceded.

Father,
we give you thanks for the bread of life.
Open our hearts in welcome
to prepare for the coming of our Savior,
who is Lord for ever and ever.

December 20

Entrance Antiphon

A shoot will spring from Jesse's stock, and all mankind will see the saving power of God.   (See Is 11:1; 40:5; Lk 3:6)

Opening Prayer

God of love and mercy,
help us to follow the example of Mary,
always ready to do your will.
At the message of an angel
she welcomed your eternal Son
and, filled with the light of your Spirit,
she became the temple of your Word,
who lives and reigns with you and the Holy Spirit,
one God, for ever and ever.

TODAY'S LIVING WORD

Catholic scholars today agree that, in its historical context, today's prophecy from Isaiah cannot be read as a prediction of the birth of Jesus. Joseph Jensen sums up the reasons this way: (1) the Hebrew *'almah* is not the technical term for virgin; (2) an event that would take place seven centuries later could not be a sign for King Ahaz; and (3) the virginal conception of Jesus is in no sense a visible sign confirming Isaiah's words. Better to "understand the *'almah* to be a wife of Ahaz and the child to be a son born to Ahaz himself."* The child will be a visible sign that God has not abandoned David's house, indeed, that "God is with us."

The Gospel announces the birth of another child, also of David's line, who will be called Son of God and whose reign will be without end. This *'almah*, however, *is* a virgin. As the *Catechism of the Catholic Church* tells us, only "the eyes of faith can discover...the mysterious reasons why God in his saving plan wanted his Son to be born of a virgin." It goes on, "Mary's virginity manifests God's absolute initiative in the Incarnation" (nn. 502, 503).

Formerly known as the "Golden Mass," today's liturgy has special Marian importance and was historically celebrated with special ceremonies and beauty. With its attention to Mary, this Mass influenced the development of the Hail Mary and the Angelus.

* *Isaiah 1–39*, Old Testament Message 8, 2nd ed. (Wilmington: Michael Glazier, Inc., 1989), p. 96.

FIRST READING
Is 7:10 –14

Behold, the virgin shall be with child.

A reading from the Book of the Prophet Isaiah

The Lord spoke to Ahaz:
Ask for a sign from the Lord, your God;
    let it be deep as the nether world, or high as the sky!
But Ahaz answered,
    "I will not ask! I will not tempt the Lord!"
Then Isaiah said:
    Listen, O house of David!
Is it not enough for you to weary men,
    must you also weary my God?
Therefore the Lord himself will give you this sign:
    the virgin shall conceive and bear a son,
    and shall name him Emmanuel.
The word of the Lord.

Responsorial Psalm
Ps 24:1–2, 3 – 4ab, 5 – 6

R. Let the Lord enter; he is the king of glory.

The Lord's are the earth and its fullness;
  the world and those who dwell in it.
For he founded it upon the seas
  and established it upon the rivers.

R. Let the Lord enter; he is the king of glory.

Who can ascend the mountain of the LORD?
  or who may stand in his holy place?
He whose hands are sinless, whose heart is clean,
  who desires not what is vain.

R. Let the Lord enter; he is the king of glory.

He shall receive a blessing from the LORD,
  a reward from God his savior.
Such is the race that seeks for him,
  that seeks the face of the God of Jacob.

R. Let the Lord enter; he is the king of glory.

> **Alleluia, alleluia**
> O Key of David,
> opening the gates of God's eternal Kingdom:
> come and free the prisoners of darkness!
> **Alleluia, alleluia**

GOSPEL   Lk 1:26–38

You will conceive in your womb and bear a son.

A reading from the holy Gospel according to Luke

In the sixth month, the angel Gabriel was sent from God to a town of Galilee called Nazareth, to a virgin betrothed to a man named Joseph, of the house of David, and the virgin's name was Mary. And coming to her, he said, "Hail, full of grace! The Lord is with you." But she was greatly troubled at what was said and pondered what sort of greeting this might be. Then the angel said to her, "Do not be afraid, Mary, for you have found favor with God. Behold, you will conceive in your womb and bear a son, and you shall name him Jesus. He will be great and will be called Son of the Most High, and the Lord God will give him the throne of David his father, and he will rule over the house of Jacob forever, and of his Kingdom there will be no end."

But Mary said to the angel, "How can this be, since I have no relations with a man?" And the angel said to her in reply, "The Holy Spirit will come upon you, and the power of the Most High will overshadow you. Therefore the child to be born will be called holy, the Son of God. And behold, Elizabeth, your relative, has also conceived a son in her old age, and this is the sixth month for her who was called barren; for nothing will be impossible for God."

Mary said, "Behold, I am the handmaid of the Lord. May it be done to me according to your word." Then the angel departed from her.

The Gospel of the Lord.

Liturgy of the Eucharist, *p. 897.*

Prayer over the Gifts

Pray, brethren...

Lord,
accept this sacrificial gift.
May the eucharist we share
bring us to the eternal life
we seek in faith and hope.

Grant this through Christ our Lord.

Preface of Advent II, *p. 937.*

Communion Antiphon

The angel said to Mary: you shall conceive and bear a son, and you shall call him Jesus. (Lk 1:31)

Prayer after Communion

Let us pray.

Pause for silent prayer, if this has not preceded.

Lord,
watch over the people you nourish with this eucharist.
Lead them to rejoice in true peace.

We ask this in the name of Jesus the Lord.

December 21

Entrance Antiphon

Soon the Lord God will come, and you will call him Emmanuel, for God is with us. (See Is 7:14; 8:10)

Opening Prayer

Lord,
hear the prayers of your people.
May we who celebrate the birth of your Son as man
rejoice in the gift of eternal life when he comes in glory,
for he lives and reigns with you and the Holy Spirit,
one God, for ever and ever.

TODAY'S LIVING WORD

A visitation theme binds today's readings together. In the Song of Songs, a young woman celebrates a springtime visit by her lover. The Gospel is Luke's account of Mary's visit to her cousin Elizabeth. Both visits are joyful occasions: the lover springs gazelle-like across the hills, and John *in utero* leaps for joy. Here again Luke's allusive style is evident. The leaping of the baby in Elizabeth's womb recalls the jostling of Esau and Jacob in Rebecca's womb (Gn 25:22) and points to the future roles of John and Jesus. As in the Genesis story, the firstborn (John) will in God's plan be surpassed by the one who comes after him (Jesus). The leaping of the baby also recalls David's joyful dance before the ark (2 Sm 6:5). Here Mary herself is the ark, the new Jerusalem, in whom the presence of God now dwells.

The alternate first reading from Zephaniah invites Jerusalem to rejoice and sing joyfully, for God is in their midst. But even more, it says this "mighty savior" is glad to be there with them: "He will rejoice over you…. He will sing joyfully because of you."

FIRST OPTION

FIRST READING

Sg 2:8–14

> *Hark! my lover comes, springing across the mountains.*

A reading from the Song of Songs

> Hark! my lover—here he comes
> springing across the mountains,
> leaping across the hills.
> My lover is like a gazelle
> or a young stag.
> Here he stands behind our wall,
> gazing through the windows,
> peering through the lattices.
> My lover speaks; he says to me,
> "Arise, my beloved, my dove, my beautiful one,
> and come!
>
> "For see, the winter is past,
> the rains are over and gone.
> The flowers appear on the earth,
> the time of pruning the vines has come,
> and the song of the dove is heard in our land.
> The fig tree puts forth its figs,
> and the vines, in bloom, give forth fragrance.
> Arise, my beloved, my beautiful one,
> and come!
>
> "O my dove in the clefts of the rock,
> in the secret recesses of the cliff,

Let me see you,
> let me hear your voice,

For your voice is sweet,
> and you are lovely."

The word of the Lord.

Or:

SECOND OPTION

FIRST READING

Zep 3:14–18a

The King of Israel, the LORD, is in your midst.

A reading from the Book of the Prophet Zephaniah

Shout for joy, O daughter Zion!
> Sing joyfully, O Israel!

Be glad and exult with all your heart,
> O daughter Jerusalem!

The LORD has removed the judgment against you,
> he has turned away your enemies;

The King of Israel, the LORD, is in your midst,
> you have no further misfortune to fear.

On that day, it shall be said to Jerusalem:
> Fear not, O Zion, be not discouraged!

The LORD, your God, is in your midst,
> a mighty savior;

He will rejoice over you with gladness,
> and renew you in his love,

He will sing joyfully because of you,
> as one sings at festivals.

The word of the Lord.

Responsorial Psalm

Ps 33:2–3, 11–12, 20–21

R. Exult, you just, in the Lord! Sing to him a new song.

Give thanks to the LORD on the harp;
  with the ten-stringed lyre chant his praises.
Sing to him a new song;
  pluck the strings skillfully, with shouts of gladness.

R. Exult, you just, in the Lord! Sing to him a new song.

But the plan of the LORD stands forever;
  the design of his heart, through all generations.
Blessed the nation whose God is the LORD,
  the people he has chosen for his own inheritance.

R. Exult, you just, in the Lord! Sing to him a new song.

Our soul waits for the LORD,
  who is our help and our shield,
For in him our hearts rejoice;
  in his holy name we trust.

R. Exult, you just, in the Lord! Sing to him a new song.

Alleluia, alleluia
O Emmanuel, our King and Giver of Law:
come to save us, Lord our God!
Alleluia, alleluia

GOSPEL

Lk 1:39–45

And how does this happen to me,
that the mother of my Lord should come to me?

A reading from the holy Gospel according to Luke

Mary set out in those days and traveled to the hill country in haste to a town of Judah, where she entered the house of Zechariah and greeted Elizabeth. When Elizabeth heard Mary's greeting, the infant leaped in her womb, and Elizabeth, filled with the Holy Spirit, cried out in a loud voice and said, "Most blessed are you among women, and blessed is the fruit of your womb. And how does this happen to me, that the mother of my Lord should come to me? For at the moment the sound of your greeting reached my ears, the infant in my womb leaped for joy. Blessed are you who believed that what was spoken to you by the Lord would be fulfilled."

The Gospel of the Lord.

Liturgy of the Eucharist, *p. 897.*

Prayer over the Gifts

Pray, brethren...

Lord of love,
receive these gifts
which you have given to your Church.
Let them become for us
the means of our salvation.

We ask this through Christ our Lord.

Preface of Advent II, *p. 937.*

Communion Antiphon

Blessed are you for your firm believing, that the promises of the Lord would be fulfilled.   (Lk 1:45)

Prayer after Communion

Let us pray.

Pause for silent prayer, if this has not preceded.

Lord,
help us to serve you
that we may be brought to salvation.
May this eucharist be our constant protection.

Grant this in the name of Jesus the Lord.

December 22

Entrance Antiphon

Gates, lift up your heads! Stand erect, ancient doors, and let in the King of glory. (Ps 23:7)

Opening Prayer

God our Father,
you sent your Son
to free mankind from the power of death.
May we who celebrate the coming of Christ as man
share more fully in his divine life,
for he lives and reigns with you and the Holy Spirit,
one God, for ever and ever.

TODAY'S LIVING WORD

In a way today's first reading simply provides a setting for the responsorial psalm, which is the canticle of Hannah, the mother of Samuel. The reading describes Hannah bringing her young son to the sanctuary in Shiloh to dedicate him to the Lord. She reminds us of another young Jewish mother who will one day present her firstborn son in the temple in Jerusalem. Today's Gospel records that young woman's canticle, which bears a striking resemblance to Hannah's. Both of these songs, on the lips of women, mothers, anticipate what God will do through the agency of their sons. Both image God's saving activity concretely as toppling unjust structures and disarming oppressive regimes.

"The bows of the mighty are broken," declares Hannah, and Mary echoes, "He has cast down the mighty from their thrones." "The well-fed hire themselves out for bread," Hannah says, and Mary answers, "He has filled the hungry with good things."

These are songs of the *anawim,* the poor who have no recourse or resource of their own and must wait for God to save them. They capture the true spirit of Advent.

FIRST READING

1 Sm 1:24–28

Hannah gives thanks for the birth of Samuel.

A reading from the first Book of Samuel

In those days, Hannah brought Samuel with her, along with a three-year-old bull, an ephah of flour, and a skin of wine, and presented him at the temple of the LORD in Shiloh. After the boy's father had sacrificed the young bull, Hannah, his mother, approached Eli and said: "Pardon, my lord! As you live, my lord, I am the woman who stood near you here, praying to the LORD. I prayed for this child, and the LORD granted my request. Now I, in turn, give him to the LORD; as long as he lives, he shall be dedicated to the LORD." She left Samuel there.

The word of the Lord.

Responsorial Psalm

1 Sm 2:1, 4–5, 6–7, 8abcd

R. My heart exults in the Lord, my Savior.

"My heart exults in the LORD,
  my horn is exalted in my God.
I have swallowed up my enemies;
  I rejoice in my victory."

R. My heart exults in the Lord, my Savior.

"The bows of the mighty are broken,
  while the tottering gird on strength.
The well-fed hire themselves out for bread,
  while the hungry batten on spoil.
The barren wife bears seven sons,
  while the mother of many languishes."

R. My heart exults in the Lord, my Savior.

"The LORD puts to death and gives life;
  he casts down to the nether world;
  he raises up again.

The LORD makes poor and makes rich,
  he humbles, he also exalts."

R. My heart exults in the Lord, my Savior.

"He raises the needy from the dust;
  from the dung heap he lifts up the poor,
To seat them with nobles
  and make a glorious throne their heritage."

R. My heart exults in the Lord, my Savior.

Alleluia, alleluia
O King of all nations and keystone of the Church:
come and save man, whom you formed from the dust!
Alleluia, alleluia

GOSPEL   Lk 1:46–56

The Mighty One has done great things for me.

A reading from the holy Gospel according to Luke

Mary said:

"My soul proclaims the greatness of the Lord;
  my spirit rejoices in God my savior.
  for he has looked upon his lowly servant.
From this day all generations will call me blessed:
  the Almighty has done great things for me,
  and holy is his Name.
  He has mercy on those who fear him
  in every generation.
He has shown the strength of his arm,
  and has scattered the proud in their conceit.
He has cast down the mighty from their thrones
  and has lifted up the lowly.
He has filled the hungry with good things,
  and the rich he has sent away empty.
He has come to the help of his servant Israel

> for he remembered his promise of mercy,
> the promise he made to our fathers,
> to Abraham and his children for ever."

Mary remained with Elizabeth about three months and then returned to her home.

The Gospel of the Lord.

Liturgy of the Eucharist, *p. 897.*

Prayer over the Gifts

Pray, brethren...

Lord God,
with confidence in your love
we come with gifts to worship at your altar.
By the mystery of this eucharist
purify us and renew your life within us.

We ask this through Christ our Lord.

Preface of Advent II, *p. 937.*

Communion Antiphon

My soul proclaims the greatness of the Lord, for the Almighty has done great things for me.   (Lk 1:46, 49)

Prayer after Communion

Let us pray.

Pause for silent prayer, if this has not preceded.

Lord,
strengthen us by the sacrament we have received.
Help us to go out to meet our Savior
and to merit eternal life
with lives that witness to our faith.

We ask this in the name of Jesus the Lord.

December 23

Entrance Antiphon

A little child is born for us, and he shall be called the mighty God; every race on earth shall be blessed in him.

(See Is 9:6; Ps 71:17)

Opening Prayer

Father,
we contemplate the birth of your Son.
He was born of the Virgin Mary
and came to live among us.
May we receive forgiveness and mercy
through our Lord Jesus Christ, your Son,
who lives and reigns with you and the Holy Spirit,
one God, for ever and ever.

TODAY'S LIVING WORD

The prophecy of Malachi in today's first reading shaped the Gospel portrait of John the Baptist in many ways. It is given to us today as an aid to interpreting Luke's account of the Baptist's birth. The Gospel scene is homey, even humorous. Elizabeth and Zechariah must insist, over the protests of family and friends, that the child's name is John. With that, Zechariah's "mouth was opened, his tongue freed, and he spoke blessing God." All are astonished and, although the fear that descends on all in the environs is really awe, it is colored to some extent by the words of the first reading. In Christian tradition, John the Baptist is the messenger sent to prepare the way of the Lord. He is the Elijah who will announce that "great and terrible" day.

The Gospel concludes by saying that all who heard of these happenings in the hill country of Judea "took them to heart." Similarly, in Advent we store in our hearts the signs and wonders the Church proclaims, asking ourselves once again, "What, then, will this child be?"

FIRST READING

Mal 3:1–4, 23–24

*I will send you Elijah, the prophet, before
the day of the LORD comes.*

A reading from the Book of the Prophet Malachi

Thus says the Lord GOD:
Lo, I am sending my messenger
   to prepare the way before me;
And suddenly there will come to the temple
   the LORD whom you seek,
And the messenger of the covenant whom you desire.
   Yes, he is coming, says the LORD of hosts.
But who will endure the day of his coming?
   And who can stand when he appears?
For he is like the refiner's fire,
   or like the fuller's lye.
He will sit refining and purifying silver,
   and he will purify the sons of Levi,
Refining them like gold or like silver
   that they may offer due sacrifice to the LORD.
Then the sacrifice of Judah and Jerusalem
   will please the LORD,
   as in the days of old, as in years gone by.

Lo, I will send you
   Elijah, the prophet,
Before the day of the LORD comes,
   the great and terrible day,
To turn the hearts of the fathers to their children,
   and the hearts of the children to their fathers,
Lest I come and strike
   the land with doom.
The word of the Lord.

Responsional Psalm

Ps 25:4–5ab, 8–9, 10 and 14

R. Lift up your heads and see; your redemption is near at hand.

Your ways, O LORD, make known to me;
  teach me your paths,
Guide me in your truth and teach me,
  for you are God my savior.

R. Lift up your heads and see; your redemption is near at hand.

Good and upright is the LORD;
  thus he shows sinners the way.
He guides the humble to justice,
  he teaches the humble his way.

R. Lift up your heads and see; your redemption is near at hand.

All the paths of the LORD are kindness and constancy
  toward those who keep his covenant and his decrees.
The friendship of the LORD is with those who fear him,
  and his covenant, for their instruction.

R. Lift up your heads and see; your redemption is near at hand.

Alleluia, alleluia
O King of all nations and keystone of the Church:
come and save man, whom you formed from the dust!
Alleluia, alleluia

GOSPEL

Lk 1:57–66

The birth of John the Baptist.

A reading from the holy Gospel according to Luke

When the time arrived for Elizabeth to have her child she gave birth to a son. Her neighbors and relatives heard that the Lord had shown his great mercy toward her, and they rejoiced with her. When they came on the eighth day to circumcise the child, they were going to call him Zechariah after his father, but his mother said in reply, "No. He will be called John." But they answered her, "There is no one among your relatives who has this name." So they made signs, asking his father what he wished him to be called. He asked for a tablet and wrote, "John is his name," and all were amazed. Immediately his mouth was opened, his tongue freed, and he spoke blessing God. Then fear came upon all their neighbors, and all these matters were discussed throughout the hill country of Judea. All who heard these things took them to heart, saying, "What, then, will this child be?" For surely the hand of the Lord was with him.

The Gospel of the Lord.

Liturgy of the Eucharist, *p. 897.*

Prayer over the Gifts

Pray, brethren...

Lord,
you have given us this memorial
as the perfect form of worship.
Restore us to your peace
and prepare us to celebrate the coming of our Savior,
for he is Lord for ever and ever.

Preface of Advent II, *p. 937.*

Communion Antiphon

I stand at the door and knock, says the Lord. If anyone hears my voice and opens the door, I will come in and sit down to supper with him and he with me. (Rv 3:20)

Prayer after Communion

Let us pray.

Pause for silent prayer, if this has not preceded.

Lord,
as you nourish us with the bread of life,
give peace to our spirits
and prepare us to welcome your Son with ardent faith.

We ask this through Christ our Lord.

December 24
Mass in the Morning

Entrance Antiphon

The appointed time has come; God has sent his Son into the world.   (See Gal 4:4)

Opening Prayer

Come, Lord Jesus,
do not delay;
give new courage to your people who trust in your love.
By your coming, raise us to the joy of your kingdom,
where you live and reign with the Father and the Holy Spirit,
one God, for ever and ever.

TODAY'S LIVING WORD

In today's two readings, the oracle of Nathan and the canticle of Zechariah, God's covenant fidelity comes to the fore. Nathan's dream thwarts David's ambition to build a house for God. Then, playing on the word for house *(bayit)*, the oracle goes on to say that God will build a house (a dynasty) for David—a house and a kingdom that will stand firm forever. These words signal a dramatic departure from the old covenant theology that taught that Israel must have no king but God. This divine promise is the essence of God's covenant with David. The canticle of Zechariah picks up this new covenant theology and announces a still newer divine initiative. The emphasis falls on God as covenant maker, moved and motivated by kindness and mercy.

The new initiative of God is, of course, the coming of Jesus that John will herald. But even as it proclaims this great good news the Church never forgets, to paraphrase James Sanders, that "God is the subject of all the verbs" in the Christmas story.*

* *Canon and Community* (Philadelphia: Fortress Press, 1984), p. 59.

FIRST READING
2 Sm 7:1– 5, 8b –12, 14a, 16

*The Kingdom of David shall endure forever
in the sight of the LORD.*

A reading from the second Book of Samuel

When King David was settled in his palace, and the LORD had given him rest from his enemies on every side, he said to Nathan the prophet, "Here I am living in a house of cedar, while the ark of God dwells in a tent!" Nathan answered the king, "Go, do whatever you have in mind, for the LORD is with you." But that night the LORD spoke to Nathan and said: "Go, tell my servant David, 'Thus says the LORD: Should you build me a house to dwell in?

"'It was I who took you from the pasture and from the care of the flock to be commander of my people Israel. I have been with you wherever you went, and I have destroyed all your enemies before you. And I will make you famous like the great ones of the earth. I will fix a place for my people Israel; I will plant them so that they may dwell in their place without further disturbance. Neither shall the wicked continue to afflict them as they did of old, since the time I first appointed judges over my people Israel. I will give you rest from all your enemies. The LORD also reveals to you that he will establish a house for you. And when your time comes and you rest with your ancestors, I will raise up your heir after you, sprung from your loins, and I will make his Kingdom firm. I will be a father to him, and he shall be a son to me. Your house and your Kingdom shall endure forever before me; your throne shall stand firm forever.'"

The word of the Lord.

Responsorial Psalm

Ps 89:2–3, 4–5, 27 and 29

R. For ever I will sing the goodness of the Lord.

The favors of the Lord I will sing forever;
  through all generations my mouth shall proclaim your
    faithfulness.
For you have said, "My kindness is established forever";
  in heaven you have confirmed your faithfulness.

R. For ever I will sing the goodness of the Lord.

"I have made a covenant with my chosen one,
  I have sworn to David my servant:
Forever will I confirm your posterity
  and establish your throne for all generations."

R. For ever I will sing the goodness of the Lord.

"He shall say of me, 'You are my father,
  my God, the rock, my savior.'
Forever I will maintain my kindness toward him,
  and my covenant with him stands firm."

R. For ever I will sing the goodness of the Lord.

Alleluia, alleluia
O Radiant Dawn,
splendor of eternal light, sun of justice:
come and shine on those who dwell in darkness
  and in the shadow of death.
Alleluia, alleluia

GOSPEL

Lk 1:67–79

The daybreak from on high has visited us.

A reading from the holy Gospel according to Luke

Zechariah his father, filled with the Holy Spirit, prophesied, saying:

"Blessed be the Lord, the God of Israel;
    for he has come to his people and set them free.
He has raised up for us a mighty Savior,
    born of the house of his servant David.
Through his prophets he promised of old
    that he would save us from our enemies,
    from the hands of all who hate us.
He promised to show mercy to our fathers
    and to remember his holy covenant.
This was the oath he swore to our father Abraham:
    to set us free from the hand of our enemies,
    free to worship him without fear,
    holy and righteous in his sight
        all the days of our life.
You, my child, shall be called the prophet of the Most High,
    for you will go before the Lord to prepare his way,
    to give his people knowledge of salvation
    by the forgiveness of their sins.
In the tender compassion of our God
    the dawn from on high shall break upon us,
    to shine on those who dwell in darkness and the
        shadow of death,
    and to guide our feet into the way of peace."

The Gospel of the Lord.

Liturgy of the Eucharist, *p. 897.*

Prayer over the Gifts

Pray, brethren...

Father,
accept the gifts we offer.
By our sharing in this eucharist
free us from sin
and help us to look forward in faith
to the glorious coming of your Son,
who is Lord for ever and ever.

Preface of Advent II, *p. 937.*

Communion Antiphon

Blessed be the Lord God of Israel, for he has visited and redeemed his people.
(Lk 1:68)

Prayer after Communion

Let us pray.

Pause for silent prayer, if this has not preceded.

Lord,
your gift of the eucharist has renewed our lives.
May we who look forward to the feast of Christ's birth
rejoice for ever in the wonder of his love,
for he is Lord for ever and ever.

Christmas Season

WEEKDAYS OF THE CHRISTMAS SEASON

For CHRISTMAS (Vigil Mass, Mass at Midnight, Mass at Dawn, Mass During the Day), *see* **Vatican II Sunday Missal,** *pp. 66–89.*

December 26
Saint Stephen, first martyr

Feast

The Acts of the Apostles describes the death of St. Stephen, the first Christian martyr (Acts 6 and 7). He was one of the first deacons appointed by the apostles. In his death, Stephen imitated Jesus by forgiving his persecutors. The mention of Saul, who will become Paul, reminds us that the blood of martyrs is the seed of the faith.

Entrance Antiphon

The gates of heaven opened for Stephen, the first of the martyrs; in heaven, he wears the crown of victory.

Opening Prayer

Lord,
today we celebrate the entrance of St. Stephen
into eternal glory.
He died praying for those who killed him.
Help us to imitate his goodness
and to love our enemies.
We ask this through our Lord Jesus Christ, your Son,
who lives and reigns with you and the Holy Spirit,
one God, for ever and ever.

TODAY'S LIVING WORD

In today's Gospel, Jesus warns his disciples that they will suffer persecution at the hands of both religious and civil authorities, just as he did. But he reassures them that the Holy Spirit will be available to them, telling them how to respond. Jesus' words are dramatized in the account from Acts of Stephen's martyrdom. It is particularly striking how closely Stephen resembles Jesus in this story. Like Luke's Jesus, he is a prophet who works "great wonders and signs among the people." Like Jesus, he often debates his opponents. Like Jesus, he is executed outside the city of Jerusalem and he dies praying, "Receive my spirit."

On December 25 we remember Jesus' coming *to* us. On December 26, the feast of St. Stephen, we are reminded of Jesus' coming *through* us—and of what a costly grace bearing witness to Jesus can be.

FIRST READING   Acts 6:8–10; 7:54–59
I see the heavens opened.

A reading from the Acts of the Apostles

Stephen, filled with grace and power, was working great wonders and signs among the people. Certain members of the so-called Synagogue of Freedmen, Cyrenians, and Alexandrians, and people from Cilicia and Asia, came forward and debated with Stephen, but they could not withstand the wisdom and the spirit with which he spoke.

When they heard this, they were infuriated, and they ground their teeth at him. But he, filled with the Holy Spirit, looked up intently to heaven and saw the glory of God and Jesus standing at the right hand of God, and he said, "Behold, I see the heavens opened and the Son of Man standing at the right hand of God." But they cried out in a loud voice, covered their ears, and rushed upon him together. They threw him out of the city, and began to stone him. The witnesses laid down their cloaks at the feet of a young man named Saul. As they were stoning Stephen, he called out, "Lord Jesus, receive my spirit."

The word of the Lord.

Responsorial Psalm
Ps 31:3cd–4, 6 and 8ab, 16bc and 17

R. Into your hands, O Lord, I commend my spirit.

Be my rock of refuge,
  a stronghold to give me safety.
You are my rock and my fortress;
  for your name's sake you will lead and guide me.

R. Into your hands, O Lord, I commend my spirit.

Into your hands I commend my spirit;
  you will redeem me, O LORD, O faithful God.
I will rejoice and be glad because of your mercy.

R. Into your hands, O Lord, I commend my spirit.

Rescue me from the clutches of my enemies and my persecutors.
Let your face shine upon your servant;
  save me in your kindness.

R. Into your hands, O Lord, I commend my spirit.

Alleluia, alleluia Ps 118:26a, 27a
Blessed is he who comes in the name of the LORD:
the LORD is God and has given us light.
Alleluia, alleluia

GOSPEL
Mt 10:17–22

For it will not be you who speak but the Spirit of your Father.

A reading from the holy Gospel according to Matthew

Jesus said to his disciples: "Beware of men, for they will hand you over to courts and scourge you in their synagogues, and you will be led before governors and kings for my sake as a witness before them and the pagans. When they hand you over, do not worry about how you are to speak or what you are to say. You will be given at that moment what you are to say. For it will not be you who speak but the Spirit of your Father speaking through you. Brother will hand over brother to death, and the father his child; children will rise up against parents and have them put to death. You will be hated by all because of my name, but whoever endures to the end will be saved."

The Gospel of the Lord.

Liturgy of the Eucharist, *p. 897.*

Prayer over the Gifts

Pray, brethren...

Father,
be pleased with the gifts we bring in your honor
as we celebrate the feast of St. Stephen.
Grant this through Christ our Lord.

Preface of Christmas I–III, *pp. 938–939.*

Communion Antiphon

As they stoned him, Stephen prayed aloud: Lord Jesus, receive my spirit.   (Acts 7:58)

Prayer after Communion

Let us pray.

Pause for silent prayer, if this has not preceded.

Lord,
we thank you for the many signs of your love for us.
Save us by the birth of your Son
and give us joy in honoring St. Stephen the martyr.

We ask this through Christ our Lord.

December 27
Saint John, apostle and evangelist

Feast

Along with Peter and James, John was one in the inner group of apostles who were especially close to Jesus. John and his brother James earned the title "Sons of Thunder." John is traditionally regarded as the author of the fourth Gospel and the apostle of love. Tradition also holds that he is the only one of the apostles who was not martyred.

Entrance Antiphon

The Lord opened his mouth in the assembly, and filled him with the spirit of wisdom and understanding, and clothed him in a robe of glory.   (Sir 15:5)

Opening Prayer

God our Father,
you have revealed the mysteries of your Word
through St. John the apostle.
By prayer and reflection
may we come to understand the wisdom he taught.

Grant this through our Lord Jesus Christ, your Son,
who lives and reigns with you and the Holy Spirit,
one God, for ever and ever.

TODAY'S LIVING WORD

Many modern Catholic scholars question whether the beloved disciple, who figures so prominently in the second half of the Fourth Gospel, is in fact John the son of Zebedee, whose feast we celebrate today. Be that as it may, what today's Gospel says of the disciple Jesus loved applies to John and to all who, like him, "saw and believed." Saw what? Not the cave of Bethlehem, but the empty tomb. Not swaddling clothes, but burial cloths first spoke of the word of life, revealed in Jesus the Christ. As today's first reading tells us, the apostles in turn proclaimed this life to us, so that we might share life with them. That is why we profess that our community is indeed "apostolic." It is based on the faithful witness of those who heard, saw, and touched the word of life.

In poem number 906, Emily Dickinson observes that we see most clearly "through an Open Tomb."* So it was for the early Church. In that "Light—enabling Light," they came at last to understand the significance of the crib as well as of the cross.

* *The Complete Poems*, Thomas Johnson, ed., 13th ed. (Boston: Little, Brown and Company, 1960), p. 428.

FIRST READING   1 Jn 1:1–4

What we have seen and heard we proclaim now to you.

A reading from the beginning of the first Letter of Saint John

Beloved:

> What was from the beginning,
> what we have heard,
> what we have seen with our eyes,
> what we looked upon
> and touched with our hands
> concerns the Word of life—
> for the life was made visible;
> we have seen it and testify to it
> and proclaim to you the eternal life
> that was with the Father and was made visible to us—
> what we have seen and heard
> we proclaim now to you,
> so that you too may have fellowship with us;
> for our fellowship is with the Father
> and with his Son, Jesus Christ.

We are writing this that our joy may be complete.

The word of the Lord.

Responsorial Psalm
Ps 97:1–2, 5–6, 11–12

R. Rejoice in the Lord, you just!

The LORD is king; let the earth rejoice;
  let the many isles be glad.
Clouds and darkness are around him,
  justice and judgment are the foundation of his throne.

R. Rejoice in the Lord, you just!

The mountains melt like wax before the LORD,
  before the LORD of all the earth.
The heavens proclaim his justice,
  and all peoples see his glory.

R. Rejoice in the Lord, you just!

Light dawns for the just;
  and gladness, for the upright of heart.
Be glad in the LORD, you just,
  and give thanks to his holy name.

R. Rejoice in the Lord, you just!

Alleluia, alleluia   See *Te Deum*
We praise you, O God,
we acclaim you as Lord;
the glorious company of Apostles praise you.
Alleluia, alleluia

GOSPEL
Jn 20:1a and 2–8

*The other disciple ran faster than Peter
and arrived at the tomb first.*

A reading from the holy Gospel according to John

On the first day of the week, Mary Magdalene ran and went to Simon Peter and to the other disciple whom Jesus loved, and told them, "They have taken the Lord from the tomb, and we do not know where they put him." So Peter and the other disciple went out and came to the tomb. They both ran, but the other disciple ran faster than Peter and arrived at the tomb first; he bent down and saw the burial cloths there, but did not go in. When Simon Peter arrived after him, he went into the tomb and saw the burial cloths there, and the cloth that had covered his head, not with the burial cloths but rolled up in a separate place. Then the other disciple also went in, the one who had arrived at the tomb first, and he saw and believed.

The Gospel of the Lord.

Liturgy of the Eucharist, *p. 897.*

Prayer over the Gifts

Pray, brethren...

Lord,
bless these gifts we present to you.
With St. John may we share
in the hidden wisdom of your eternal Word
which you reveal at this eucharistic table.
We ask this in the name of Jesus the Lord.

Preface of Christmas I–III, *pp. 938–939.*

Communion Antiphon

The Word of God became man, and lived among us. Of his riches we have all received.   (Jn 1:14, 16)

Prayer after Communion

Let us pray.

Pause for silent prayer, if this has not preceded.

Almighty Father,
St. John proclaimed
that your Word became flesh for our salvation.
Through this eucharist may your Son always live in us,
for he is Lord for ever and ever.

December 28
The Holy Innocents, martyrs

Feast

The Holy Innocents are the infant boys who were slain by the jealous Herod the Great. How many were there? If the population of Bethlehem is estimated as around 1,000, perhaps about 20 boys were slain. Today their feast reminds us to pray for the protection of all human life, including the unborn.

Entrance Antiphon

These innocent children were slain for Christ. They follow the spotless Lamb, and proclaim for ever: Glory to you, Lord.

Opening Prayer

Father,
the Holy Innocents offered you praise
by the death they suffered for Christ.
May our lives bear witness
to the faith we profess with our lips.
We ask this through our Lord Jesus Christ, your Son,
who lives and reigns with you and the Holy Spirit,
one God, for ever and ever.

TODAY'S LIVING WORD

Today's Gospel reports the massacre of the holy innocents at the command of Herod, the king of the Jews. Told only by Matthew, the story looks backward to the birth of Moses and forward to the death of Jesus. Moses was born in similar circumstances, when Pharaoh, the king of the Egyptians, had ordered the massacre of all Hebrew boys (cf. Ex 1:16). The Gospel story also announces the death of Jesus, when another threatened client of Rome—not Herod this time, but Pilate—will determine to destroy the "King of the Jews." In Matthew's scheme, history repeats itself.

Not only in the world of Matthew's Gospel, but in our own world too, history seems to repeat itself with depressing regularity. The massacre of innocent children continues, and Rachel weeps inconsolably. "If we say, 'We are without sin,'" the letter of John warns us, "we deceive ourselves." Our only hope is to acknowledge our sin and ask forgiveness of the wholly innocent One, who was offered for our sins, "and not for our sins only but for those of the whole world."

FIRST READING   1 Jn 1:5—2:2

The Blood of his Son Jesus Christ cleanses us from all sin.

A reading from the first Letter of Saint John

Beloved:

This is the message that we have heard from Jesus Christ and proclaim to you: God is light, and in him there is no darkness at all. If we say, "We have fellowship with him," while we continue to walk in darkness, we lie and do not act in truth. But if we walk in the light as he is in the light, then we have fellowship with one another, and the Blood of his Son Jesus cleanses us from all sin. If we say, "We are without sin," we deceive ourselves, and the truth is not in us. If we acknowledge our sins, he is faithful and just and will forgive our sins and cleanse us from every wrongdoing. If we say, "We have not sinned," we make him a liar, and his word is not in us.

My children, I am writing this to you so that you may not commit sin. But if anyone does sin, we have an Advocate with the Father, Jesus Christ the righteous one. He is expiation for our sins, and not for our sins only but for those of the whole world.

The word of the Lord.

Responsorial Psalm   Ps 124:2–3, 4–5, 7cd–8

R. **Our soul has been rescued like a bird**
   from the fowler's snare.

Had not the Lord been with us—
When men rose up against us,

then would they have swallowed us alive,
When their fury was inflamed against us.

> **R. Our soul has been rescued like a bird
> from the fowler's snare.**

Then would the waters have overwhelmed us;
The torrent would have swept over us;
 over us then would have swept the raging waters.

> **R. Our soul has been rescued like a bird
> from the fowler's snare.**

Broken was the snare,
 and we were freed.
Our help is in the name of the LORD,
 who made heaven and earth.

> **R. Our soul has been rescued like a bird
> from the fowler's snare.**

> **Alleluia, alleluia**   See *Te Deum*
> We praise you, O God,
> we acclaim you as Lord;
> the white-robed army of martyrs praise you.
> **Alleluia, alleluia**

GOSPEL

Mt 2:13 –18

He ordered the massacre of all boys in Bethlehem.

A reading from the holy Gospel according to Matthew

When the magi had departed, behold, the angel of the Lord
appeared to Joseph in a dream and said, "Rise, take the child
and his mother, flee to Egypt, and stay there until I tell you.
Herod is going to search for the child to destroy him." Joseph
rose and took the child and his mother by night and departed
for Egypt. He stayed there until the death of Herod, that what
the Lord had said through the prophet might be fulfilled,

Out of Egypt I called my son.

When Herod realized that he had been deceived by the magi,

he became furious. He ordered the massacre of all the boys in Bethlehem and its vicinity two years old and under, in accordance with the time he had ascertained from the magi. Then was fulfilled what had been said through Jeremiah the prophet:

> *A voice was heard in Ramah,*
>> *sobbing and loud lamentation;*
> *Rachel weeping for her children,*
>> *and she would not be consoled,*
>> *since they were no more.*

The Gospel of the Lord.

Liturgy of the Eucharist, *p. 897.*

Prayer over the Gifts

Pray, brethren...

Lord,
you give us your life even before we understand.
Receive the offerings we bring in love,
and free us from sin.

We ask this in the name of Jesus the Lord.

Preface of Christmas I–III, *pp. 938–939.*

Communion Antiphon

These have been ransomed for God and the Lamb as the first-fruits of mankind; they follow the Lamb wherever he goes.

(Rv 14:4)

Prayer after Communion

Let us pray.

Pause for silent prayer, if this has not preceded.

Lord,
by a wordless profession of faith in your Son,

the innocents were crowned with life at his birth.
May all people who receive your holy gifts today
come to share in the fullness of salvation.

We ask this through Christ the Lord.

December 29
Fifth Day in the Octave of Christmas

Entrance Antiphon

**God loved the world so much, he gave his only Son, that all
who believe in him might not perish, but might have eternal life.**

(Jn 3:16)

Opening Prayer

All-powerful and unseen God,
the coming of your light into our world
has made the darkness vanish.
Teach us to proclaim the birth of your Son Jesus Christ,
who lives and reigns with you and the Holy Spirit,
one God, for ever and ever.

TODAY'S LIVING WORD

Today's selection from 1 John could be a commentary on Simeon,
the prophet who appears in today's excerpt from the Gospel of Luke.
What 1 John says of the man who claims to know God—that he
keeps God's commandments—can certainly be said of Simeon. His
credentials are that he is "righteous and devout," which means that
he keeps the law of God. In John's view, this explains Simeon's
knowledge of Jesus when he comes into the temple.

But there is more. With the help of the Holy Spirit, Simeon is
given to see, as 1 John puts it, that "darkness is passing away, and
the true light is already shining." So he greets the arrival of Jesus as
"a light for revelation to the Gentiles, and glory for your people

Israel." May keeping God's word equip us, as it did Simeon, to continue in the light, until that day when the Master dispels all our darkness and dismisses us in peace.

FIRST READING

1 Jn 2:3–11

Those who love their brother remain in the light.

A reading from the first Letter of Saint John

Beloved:

The way we may be sure that we know Jesus is to keep his commandments. Whoever says, "I know him," but does not keep his commandments is a liar, and the truth is not in him. But whoever keeps his word, the love of God is truly perfected in him. This is the way we may know that we are in union with him: whoever claims to abide in him ought to walk just as he walked.

Beloved, I am writing no new commandment to you but an old commandment that you had from the beginning. The old commandment is the word that you have heard. And yet I do write a new commandment to you, which holds true in him and among you, for the darkness is passing away, and the true light is already shining. Whoever says he is in the light, yet hates his brother, is still in the darkness. Whoever loves his brother remains in the light, and there is nothing in him to cause a fall. Whoever hates his brother is in darkness; he walks in darkness and does not know where he is going because the darkness has blinded his eyes.

The word of the Lord.

Responsorial Psalm

Ps 96:1–2a, 2b–3, 5b–6

R. Let the heavens be glad and the earth rejoice!

Sing to the LORD a new song;
  sing to the LORD, all you lands.
Sing to the LORD; bless his name.

R. Let the heavens be glad and the earth rejoice!

Announce his salvation, day after day.
Tell his glory among the nations;
  among all peoples, his wondrous deeds.

R. Let the heavens be glad and the earth rejoice!

The LORD made the heavens.
Splendor and majesty go before him;
  praise and grandeur are in his sanctuary.

R. Let the heavens be glad and the earth rejoice!

Alleluia, alleluia Lk 2:32
A light of revelation to the Gentiles
and glory for your people Israel.
Alleluia, alleluia

GOSPEL   Lk 2:22–35

This is the light of revelation to the Gentiles.

A reading from the holy Gospel according to Luke

When the days were completed for their purification according
to the law of Moses, the parents of Jesus took him up to
Jerusalem to present him to the Lord, just as it is written in the
law of the Lord, *Every male that opens the womb shall be
consecrated to the Lord,* and to offer the sacrifice of *a pair of
turtledoves or two young pigeons,* in accordance with the dictate
in the law of the Lord.

  Now there was a man in Jerusalem whose name was Simeon.
This man was righteous and devout, awaiting the consolation
of Israel, and the Holy Spirit was upon him. It had been revealed
to him by the Holy Spirit that he should not see death before

he had seen the Christ of the Lord. He came in the Spirit into the temple; and when the parents brought in the child Jesus to perform the custom of the law in regard to him, he took him into his arms and blessed God, saying:

"Lord, now let your servant go in peace;
    your word has been fulfilled:
my own eyes have seen the salvation
    which you prepared in the sight of every people,
a light to reveal you to the nations
    and the glory of your people Israel."

The child's father and mother were amazed at what was said about him; and Simeon blessed them and said to Mary his mother, "Behold, this child is destined for the fall and rise of many in Israel, and to be a sign that will be contradicted (and you yourself a sword will pierce) so that the thoughts of many hearts may be revealed."

The Gospel of the Lord.

Liturgy of the Eucharist, *p. 897.*

Prayer over the Gifts

Pray, brethren...

Lord,
receive our gifts in this wonderful exchange:
from all you have given us
we bring you these gifts,
and in return, you give us yourself.
We ask this through Christ our Lord.

Preface of Christmas I–III, *pp. 938–939.*

When Eucharistic Prayer I is used, the special Christmas form of IN UNION WITH THE WHOLE CHURCH is said.

Communion Antiphon

Through the tender compassion of our God, the dawn from on high shall break upon us. (Lk 1:78)

Prayer after Communion

Let us pray.

Pause for silent prayer, if this has not preceded.

Father of love and mercy,
grant that our lives may always be founded
on the power of this holy mystery.
We ask this in the name of Jesus the Lord.

December 30
Sixth Day in the Octave of Christmas

When there is no Sunday within the octave of Christmas, the feast of the Holy Family is celebrated today (*see* **Vatican II Sunday Missal,** *p. 89*).

Entrance Antiphon

When peaceful silence lay over all, and night had run half of her swift course, your all-powerful word, O Lord, leaped down from heaven, from the royal throne. (Wis 18:14–15)

Opening Prayer

All-powerful God,
may the human birth of your Son
free us from our former slavery to sin
and bring us new life.

We ask this through our Lord Jesus Christ, your Son,
who lives and reigns with you and the Holy Spirit,
one God, for ever and ever.

TODAY'S LIVING WORD

The elderly woman Anna who appears in today's Gospel illustrates the teaching of the second part of today's first reading from 1 John. She is a woman who, in the words of John's letter, does "not love the world or the things of the world." Widowed after seven years of marriage, she spent all her days in the temple, and "worshiped night and day with fasting and prayer." Coming on the scene of the presentation of Jesus, she is instantly able to see what, in him, has come from the Father. "She gave thanks to God."

The first part of the first reading is an awkward literary construction that addresses three age groups—people in three different stages of Christian life—children, youth, and parents or elders. The task of each stage is succinctly suggested. Christian life begins in baptism with the forgiveness of sin. Next Christian formation requires the strength, derived from the power of God's word, to conquer evil inside and outside oneself. Then Christian maturity makes one, like Anna, able to see the gift of God "from the beginning."

FIRST READING

1 Jn 2:12–17

Those who do the will of God remain forever.

A reading from the first Letter of Saint John

I am writing to you, children, because your sins have been forgiven for his name's sake.

I am writing to you, fathers, because you know him who is from the beginning.

I am writing to you, young men, because you have conquered the Evil One.

I write to you, children, because you know the Father.

I write to you, fathers, because you know him who is from the beginning.

I write to you, young men, because you are strong and the word of God remains in you, and you have conquered the Evil One.

Do not love the world or the things of the world. If anyone loves the world, the love of the Father is not in him. For all that is in the world, sensual lust, enticement for the eyes, and a pretentious life, is not from the Father but is from the world. Yet the world and its enticement are passing away. But whoever does the will of God remains forever.

The word of the Lord.

Responsorial Psalm

Ps 96:7–8a, 8b–9, 10

R. Let the heavens be glad and the earth rejoice!

Give to the LORD, you families of nations,
  give to the LORD glory and praise;
  give to the LORD the glory due his name!

R. Let the heavens be glad and the earth rejoice!

Bring gifts, and enter his courts;
  worship the LORD in holy attire.
Tremble before him, all the earth.

R. Let the heavens be glad and the earth rejoice!

Say among the nations: The LORD is king.
He has made the world firm, not to be moved;
  he governs the peoples with equity.

R. Let the heavens be glad and the earth rejoice!

> **Alleluia, alleluia**
> A holy day has dawned upon us.
> Come, you nations, and adore the Lord.
> Today a great light has come upon the earth.
> **Alleluia, alleluia**

GOSPEL

Lk 2:36–40

*She spoke about the child to all who were
awaiting the redemption of Jerusalem.*

A reading from the holy Gospel according to Luke

There was a prophetess, Anna, the daughter of Phanuel, of the tribe of Asher. She was advanced in years, having lived seven years with her husband after her marriage, and then as a widow until she was eighty-four. She never left the temple, but worshiped night and day with fasting and prayer. And coming forward at that very time, she gave thanks to God and spoke about the child to all who were awaiting the redemption of Jerusalem.

When they had fulfilled all the prescriptions of the law of the Lord, they returned to Galilee, to their own town of Nazareth. The child grew and became strong, filled with wisdom; and the favor of God was upon him.

The Gospel of the Lord.

Liturgy of the Eucharist, *p. 897.*

Prayer over the Gifts

Pray, brethren...

Father,
in your mercy accept our gifts.
By sharing in this eucharist
may we come to live more fully the love we profess.

Grant this through Christ our Lord.

Preface of Christmas I–III, *pp. 938–939.*

Communion Antiphon

From his riches we have all received, grace for grace.

(Jn 1:16)

Prayer after Communion

Let us pray.

Pause for silent prayer, if this has not preceded.

God our Father,
in this eucharist you touch our lives.

Keep your love alive in our hearts
that we may become worthy of you.
We ask this through Christ our Lord.

December 31
Seventh Day in the Octave of Christmas

Entrance Antiphon

A child is born for us, a son given to us; dominion is laid on his shoulder, and he shall be called Wonderful-Counselor.

(Is 9:6)

Opening Prayer

Ever-living God,
in the birth of your Son
our religion has its origin and its perfect fulfillment.
Help us to share in the life of Christ
for he is the salvation of mankind,
who lives and reigns with you and the Holy Spirit,
one God, for ever and ever.

TODAY'S LIVING WORD

Today's Gospel is the prologue of the Gospel according to John. It is a Christological hymn, summarizing the whole theology of the Fourth Gospel. Raymond Brown describes the movement of the prologue as "a great cycle," and Neal Flanagan says that it "swings like the arm of a mighty pendulum."* It has the literary form of a chain with a suspended pendant. This form, called a *chiasm,* traces the mission of the Word: his descent from God to this world of ours, where he "became flesh and made his dwelling," and his ascent, mission accomplished, back to the Father's side. The "pendant" that hangs on the chain consists of those verses that tell us why the Word was sent to us: "To those who did accept him he gave power to become children of God."

Having come to believe and be baptized in his name, we count ourselves among God's children. But the reading from 1 John warns us against complacency. He writes about "antichrists," defectors from the believing community, and urges true believers to hold fast to the grace and truth that came through Jesus Christ.

* Brown, *The Gospel and Epistle of John* (Collegeville: Liturgical Press, 1988) 21; Flanagan, "John," *The Collegeville Bible Commentary,* New Testament (Collegeville: Liturgical Press, 1992), p. 982.

FIRST READING

1 Jn 2:18–21

You have the anointing that comes from the Holy One,
and you have all knowledge.

A reading from the first Letter of Saint John

Children, it is the last hour; and just as you heard that the antichrist was coming, so now many antichrists have appeared. Thus we know this is the last hour. They went out from us, but they were not really of our number; if they had been, they would have remained with us. Their desertion shows that none of them was of our number. But you have the anointing that comes from the Holy One, and you all have knowledge. I write to you not because you do not know the truth but because you do, and because every lie is alien to the truth.

The word of the Lord.

Responsorial Psalm

Ps 96:1–2, 11–12, 13

R. Let the heavens be glad and the earth rejoice!

Sing to the LORD a new song;
  sing to the LORD, all you lands.
Sing to the LORD; bless his name;
  announce his salvation, day after day.

R. Let the heavens be glad and the earth rejoice!

Let the heavens be glad and the earth rejoice;
  let the sea and what fills it resound;

let the plains be joyful and all that is in them!
Then shall all the trees of the forest exult before the LORD.

R. Let the heavens be glad and the earth rejoice!

The LORD comes,
  he comes to rule the earth.
He shall rule the world with justice
  and the peoples with his constancy.

R. Let the heavens be glad and the earth rejoice!

> **Alleluia, alleluia**   Jn 1:14a, 12a
> The Word of God became flesh and dwelt among us.
> To those who accepted him
> he gave power to become the children of God.
> **Alleluia, alleluia**

GOSPEL   Jn 1:1–18

The Word became flesh.

A reading from the beginning of the holy Gospel according to John

In the beginning was the Word,
    and the Word was with God,
    and the Word was God.
He was in the beginning with God.
All things came to be through him,
    and without him nothing came to be.
What came to be through him was life,
    and this life was the light of the human race;
      the light shines in the darkness,
      and the darkness has not overcome it.

A man named John was sent from God. He came for testimony,
to testify to the light, so that all might believe through him. He
was not the light, but came to testify to the light. The true
light, which enlightens everyone, was coming into the world.

He was in the world,
> and the world came to be through him,
> but the world did not know him.

He came to what was his own,
> but his own people did not accept him.

But to those who did accept him he gave power to become children of God, to those who believe in his name, who were born not by natural generation nor by human choice nor by a man's decision but of God.

And the Word became flesh
> and made his dwelling among us,
> and we saw his glory,
> the glory as of the Father's only-begotten Son,
> full of grace and truth.

John testified to him and cried out, saying, "This was he of whom I said, 'The one who is coming after me ranks ahead of me because he existed before me.'" From his fullness we have all received, grace in place of grace, because while the law was given through Moses, grace and truth came through Jesus Christ. No one has ever seen God. The only-begotten Son, God, who is at the Father's side, has revealed him.

The Gospel of the Lord.

Liturgy of the Eucharist, *p. 897.*

When Eucharistic Prayer I is used, the special Christmas form of IN UNION WITH THE WHOLE CHURCH is said.

Prayer over the Gifts

Pray, brethren...

Father of peace,
accept our devotion and sincerity,

and by our sharing in this mystery
draw us closer to each other and to you.
We ask this in the name of Jesus the Lord.

Preface of Christmas I–III, *pp. 938–939.*

Communion Antiphon

**God's love for us was revealed when he sent his only Son into
the world, so that we could have life through him.** (1 Jn 4:9)

Prayer after Communion

Let us pray.

Pause for silent prayer, if this has not preceded.

Lord,
may this sacrament be our strength.
Teach us to value all the good you give us
and help us to strive for eternal life.

Grant this through Christ our Lord.

For **January 1,** *Octave of Christmas:* SOLEMNITY OF MARY, MOTHER
OF GOD, *see* **Vatican II Sunday Missal,** *p. 103.*

From January 2 to Epiphany (Liturgy of the Word)

January 2   (if before Epiphany)

Antiphons and Prayers, *pp. 201–209.*

TODAY'S LIVING WORD

First John was written in the heat of dissension within the
Johannine community. Members of the community were denying
"Jesus Christ come in the flesh" (4:2). These dissidents are the liars,
the antichrists of today's reading. Throughout this passage the author
appeals to the indwelling of the Holy Spirit (the Paraclete) whom
the Father has sent to guide Christians to all truth (Jn 16:13). He

argues that their anointing with the Holy Spirit at baptism will enable them to stand firm in the present crisis as well as on the last day, when Christ will reveal himself for all to see. Today's Gospel presents John the Baptist as an example of one who, filled with the Holy Spirit, allows what he heard from the beginning to remain in his heart, even in the heat of confrontation.

The Gospel suggests that John the Baptist is able to know who Jesus is because he knows so well whom he himself is not—not the Messiah, not Elijah, not the Prophet. We must take our cue from him and learn to recognize and revere the humanity of Jesus by reckoning honestly with our own.

FIRST READING

1 Jn 2:22–28

Let what you heard from the beginning remain in you.

A reading from the first Letter of Saint John

Beloved:

Who is the liar? Whoever denies that Jesus is the Christ. Whoever denies the Father and the Son, this is the antichrist. Anyone who denies the Son does not have the Father, but whoever confesses the Son has the Father as well.

Let what you heard from the beginning remain in you. If what you heard from the beginning remains in you, then you will remain in the Son and in the Father. And this is the promise that he made us: eternal life. I write you these things about those who would deceive you. As for you, the anointing that you received from him remains in you, so that you do not need anyone to teach you. But his anointing teaches you about everything and is true and not false; just as it taught you, remain in him.

And now, children, remain in him, so that when he appears we may have confidence and not be put to shame by him at his coming.

The word of the Lord.

Responsorial Psalm

Ps 98:1, 2–3ab, 3cd–4

R. All the ends of the earth have seen the saving power of God.

Sing to the LORD a new song,
 for he has done wondrous deeds;
His right hand has won victory for him,
 his holy arm.

R. All the ends of the earth have seen the saving power of God.

The LORD has made his salvation known:
 in the sight of the nations he has revealed his justice.
He has remembered his kindness and his faithfulness
 toward the house of Israel.

R. All the ends of the earth have seen the saving power of God.

All the ends of the earth have seen
 the salvation by our God.
Sing joyfully to the LORD, all you lands;
 break into song; sing praise.

R. All the ends of the earth have seen the saving power of God.

Alleluia, alleluia   Heb 1:1–2
In times past, God spoke to our ancestors through the prophets:
in these last days, he has spoken to us through his Son.
Alleluia, alleluia

GOSPEL

Jn 1:19–28

There is one who is coming after me.

A reading from the holy Gospel according to John

This is the testimony of John. When the Jews from Jerusalem sent priests and Levites to him to ask him, "Who are you?" He admitted and did not deny it, but admitted, "I am not the Christ." So they asked him, "What are you then? Are you Elijah?" And he said, "I am not." "Are you the Prophet?" He answered, "No." So they said to him, "Who are you, so we can give an answer to those who sent us? What do you have to say for yourself?" He said:

"I am *the voice of one crying out in the desert,*
'*Make straight the way of the Lord,*'

as Isaiah the prophet said." Some Pharisees were also sent. They asked him, "Why then do you baptize if you are not the Christ or Elijah or the Prophet?" John answered them, "I baptize with water; but there is one among you whom you do not recognize, the one who is coming after me, whose sandal strap I am not worthy to untie." This happened in Bethany across the Jordan, where John was baptizing.

The Gospel of the Lord.

Liturgy of the Eucharist, *p. 897.*

January 3   (if before Epiphany)

Antiphons and Prayers, *pp. 201–209.*

TODAY'S LIVING WORD

The prologue of John's Gospel declares of Jesus: "To those who did accept him he gave power to become children of God" (1:12). Today's reading from the Letter of John explores what it means to be God's children. Children of God, born of God by water and the Spirit (Jn 1:13, 3:5), share God's life which is holy. Therefore, first and foremost, holiness must characterize their lives. Furthermore, although children of God already have eternal life, they await an even greater share of God's life in the future when, says 1 John, "we shall be like him, for we shall see him as he is." In today's Gospel, John the Baptist bears double witness to this great good news when he identifies Jesus as "the Lamb of God, who takes away the sin of the world," and the one "who will baptize with the Holy Spirit."

In this season of grace, may we come more and more to appreciate "what love the Father has bestowed on us that we may be called the children of God."

FIRST READING

1 Jn 2:29 — 3:6

No one who remains in him sins.

A reading from the first Letter of Saint John

If you consider that God is righteous, you also know that everyone who acts in righteousness is begotten by him.

See what love the Father has bestowed on us that we may be called the children of God. Yet so we are. The reason the world does not know us is that it did not know him. Beloved, we are God's children now; what we shall be has not yet been revealed. We do know that when it is revealed we shall be like him, for we shall see him as he is. Everyone who has this hope based on him makes himself pure, as he is pure.

Everyone who commits sin commits lawlessness, for sin is lawlessness. You know that he was revealed to take away sins, and in him there is no sin. No one who remains in him sins; no one who sins has seen him or known him.

The word of the Lord.

Responsional Psalm

Ps 98:1, 3cd–4, 5–6

R. All the ends of the earth have seen the saving power of God.

Sing to the LORD a new song,
  for he has done wondrous deeds;
His right hand has won victory for him,
  his holy arm.

R. All the ends of the earth have seen the saving power of God.

All the ends of the earth have seen
  the salvation by our God.
Sing joyfully to the LORD, all you lands;
  break into song; sing praise.

> **R. All the ends of the earth have seen the saving power
>   of God.**

Sing praise to the LORD with the harp,
  with the harp and melodious song.
With trumpets and the sound of the horn
  sing joyfully before the King, the LORD.

> **R. All the ends of the earth have seen the saving power
>   of God.**

> **Alleluia, alleluia**   Jn 1:14a, 12a
> The Word of God became flesh and dwelt among us.
> To those who accepted him
>   he gave power to become the children of God.
> **Alleluia, alleluia**

GOSPEL   Jn 1:29–34

Behold the Lamb of God.

A reading from the holy Gospel according to John

John the Baptist saw Jesus coming toward him and said,
"Behold, the Lamb of God, who takes away the sin of the world.
He is the one of whom I said, 'A man is coming after me who
ranks ahead of me because he existed before me.' I did not
know him, but the reason why I came baptizing with water
was that he might be made known to Israel." John testified
further, saying, "I saw the Spirit come down like a dove from
the sky and remain upon him. I did not know him, but the one
who sent me to baptize with water told me, 'On whomever
you see the Spirit come down and remain, he is the one who

will baptize with the Holy Spirit.' Now I have seen and testified that he is the Son of God."

The Gospel of the Lord.

Liturgy of the Eucharist, *p. 897.*

January 4   (if before Epiphany)

Antiphons and Prayers, *pp. 201–209.*

TODAY'S LIVING WORD

Today's first reading from 1 John reiterates that children of God must be holy as God is holy. They cannot sin because they are begotten of God. And to be holy, he concludes, is to "love [one's] brother." Today's Gospel also reiterates: "Behold, the Lamb of God," and the first followers of Jesus respond. The passage is punctuated with John's special vocabulary. Jesus asks, "What are you looking for?" The disciples reply, "Rabbi…where are you staying?" In John, a disciple is one who looks for Jesus, seeking him in faith, wanting above all to stay with him. The Greek word for stay here is *menein,* sometimes translated "abide" or "remain." In this Gospel, it describes a permanent relationship.

In a way, the Gospel reading ends by dramatizing the conclusion of the first reading. Andrew teaches us that the best way to love our brothers and sisters is to seek them out and bring them to Jesus.

FIRST READING   1 Jn 3:7–10

Those who are begotten by God commit no sin.

A reading from the first Letter of Saint John

Children, let no one deceive you. The person who acts in righteousness is righteous, just as he is righteous. Whoever sins belongs to the Devil, because the Devil has sinned from the beginning. Indeed, the Son of God was revealed to destroy the works of the Devil. No one who is begotten by God commits sin, because God's seed remains in him; he cannot sin because he is begotten by God. In this way, the children of God and the children of the Devil are made plain; no one who fails to act in righteousness belongs to God, nor anyone who does not love his brother.

The word of the Lord.

Responsorial Psalm

Ps 98:1, 7–8, 9

R. All the ends of the earth have seen the saving power of God.

Sing to the LORD a new song,
  for he has done wondrous deeds;
His right hand has won victory for him,
  his holy arm.

R. All the ends of the earth have seen the saving power of God.

Let the sea and what fills it resound,
  the world and those who dwell in it;
Let the rivers clap their hands,
  the mountains shout with them for joy before the LORD.

R. All the ends of the earth have seen the saving power of God.

The LORD comes;
  he comes to rule the earth;
He will rule the world with justice
  and the peoples with equity.

R. All the ends of the earth have seen the saving power of God.

Alleluia, alleluia   Heb 1:1–2
In the past God spoke to our ancestors through the prophets;
  in these last days, he has spoken to us through the Son.
Alleluia, alleluia

GOSPEL

Jn 1:35–42

We have found the Messiah.

A reading from the holy Gospel according to John

John was standing with two of his disciples, and as he watched Jesus walk by, he said, "Behold, the Lamb of God." The two disciples heard what he said and followed Jesus. Jesus turned and saw them following him and said to them, "What are you looking for?" They said to him, "Rabbi" (which translated means Teacher), "where are you staying?" He said to them, "Come, and you will see." So they went and saw where he was staying, and they stayed with him that day. It was about four in the afternoon. Andrew, the brother of Simon Peter, was one of the two who heard John and followed Jesus. He first found his own brother Simon and told him, "We have found the Messiah," which is translated Christ. Then he brought him to Jesus. Jesus looked at him and said, "You are Simon the son of John; you will be called Cephas," which is translated Peter. The Gospel of the Lord.

Liturgy of the Eucharist, *p. 897.*

January 5   (if before Epiphany)

Antiphons and Prayers, *pp. 201–209.*

TODAY'S LIVING WORD

It is instructive to watch Jesus gathering his disciples in today's Gospel. The call of each is individual, distinctive. First Andrew and an unnamed disciple were led to Jesus by the preaching of the Baptist. Then Andrew brought his brother Simon. In today's reading, Jesus addresses Philip directly, but Nathanael is harder to persuade. They are simple men, conditioned as we are by the biases of their time and place. "Can anything good come from Nazareth?" Nathanael retorts, needing to see for himself. Yet these simple men of Israel, having come in time to see the much greater things that Jesus had promised, laid the firm foundation on which the Church is built.

According to today's first reading, the firmness of that foundation would be shown, then and now, by the love of Christians for one another. Eternal life is most truly expressed in corporal works of mercy. This is how we know "that we have passed from death to life."

FIRST READING   1 Jn 3:11–21

We have passed from death to life
because we love our brothers.

A reading from the first Letter of Saint John

Beloved:

This is the message you have heard from the beginning: we should love one another, unlike Cain who belonged to the Evil One and slaughtered his brother. Why did he slaughter him? Because his own works were evil, and those of his brother righteous. Do not be amazed, then, brothers and sisters, if the world hates you. We know that we have passed from death to life because we love our brothers. Whoever does not love remains in death. Everyone who hates his brother is a murderer, and you know that no murderer has eternal life remaining in him. The way we came to know love was that he laid down his life for us; so we ought to lay down our lives for our brothers. If someone who has worldly means sees a brother in need and refuses him compassion, how can the love of God remain in him? Children, let us love not in word or speech but in deed and truth.

Now this is how we shall know that we belong to the truth and reassure our hearts before him in whatever our hearts condemn, for God is greater than our hearts and knows everything. Beloved, if our hearts do not condemn us, we have confidence in God.

The word of the Lord.

Responsorial Psalm

Ps 100:1b–2, 3, 4, 5

R. Let all the earth cry out to God with joy.

Sing joyfully to the LORD, all you lands;
  serve the LORD with gladness;
  come before him with joyful song.

R. Let all the earth cry out to God with joy.

Know that the LORD is God;
  he made us, his we are;
  his people, the flock he tends.

R. Let all the earth cry out to God with joy.

Enter his gates with thanksgiving,
  his courts with praise;
Give thanks to him; bless his name.

R. Let all the earth cry out to God with joy.

The LORD is good:
  the LORD, whose kindness endures forever,
  and his faithfulness, to all generations.

R. Let all the earth cry out to God with joy.

> **Alleluia, alleluia**
> A holy day has dawned upon us.
> Come, you nations, and adore the Lord.
> Today a great light has come upon the earth.
> **Alleluia, alleluia**

GOSPEL

Jn 1:43 – 51

You are the Son of God; you are the King of Israel.

A reading from the holy Gospel according to John

Jesus decided to go to Galilee, and he found Philip. And Jesus said to him, "Follow me." Now Philip was from Bethsaida, the town of Andrew and Peter. Philip found Nathanael and told him, "We have found the one about whom Moses wrote in the law, and also the prophets, Jesus, son of Joseph, from Nazareth."

But Nathanael said to him, "Can anything good come from Nazareth?" Philip said to him, "Come and see." Jesus saw Nathanael coming toward him and said of him, "Here is a true child of Israel. There is no duplicity in him." Nathanael said to him, "How do you know me?" Jesus answered and said to him, "Before Philip called you, I saw you under the fig tree." Nathanael answered him, "Rabbi, you are the Son of God; you are the King of Israel." Jesus answered and said to him, "Do you believe because I told you that I saw you under the fig tree? You will see greater things than this." And he said to him, "Amen, amen, I say to you, you will see the sky opened and the angels of God ascending and descending on the Son of Man." The Gospel of the Lord.

Liturgy of the Eucharist, *p. 897.*

January 6   (if before Epiphany)

If the Epiphany is celebrated on Sunday, January 7 or 8, the following readings are used for the Mass on January 6.

Antiphons and Prayers, *pp. 201–209.*

TODAY'S LIVING WORD

Both of today's readings are concerned with testimony. Together they span Jesus' entire public life. The Gospel selection begins with the testimony of John the Baptist, who announces the coming of one more powerful than himself. Then follows the baptism of Jesus, which signals the start of Jesus' ministry. In Mark, Jesus' baptism itself bears witness, assuring the reader that Jesus of Nazareth is indeed the beloved Son of God. As Raymond Brown explains, the conclusion of 1 John, today's first reading, takes us back to John's account of the death of Jesus. "Before dying, Jesus handed over the Spirit. After his death, water (the symbol of the Spirit) flowed from his side, mingled with the blood he had shed salvifically"* (19:30,

34). Dissidents in the Johannine community who denied the role of Jesus' humanity in salvation may have been passing over his bloody death. So 1 John insists, "there are three that testify, the Spirit, the water, and the blood."

The point of all this for us is well put by Brown, who suggests that 1 John reminds Christians that Baptism and Eucharist "testify to their faith in Jesus, as well as nourish it."

* *The Gospel and Epistles of John* (Collegeville: Liturgical Press, 1988), p. 120.

FIRST READING
1 Jn 5:5 –13

The Spirit, the water, and the Blood.

A reading from the first Letter of Saint John

Beloved:

Who indeed is the victor over the world but the one who believes that Jesus is the Son of God?

This is the one who came through water and Blood, Jesus Christ, not by water alone, but by water and Blood. The Spirit is the one who testifies, and the Spirit is truth. So there are three that testify, the Spirit, the water, and the Blood, and the three are of one accord. If we accept human testimony, the testimony of God is surely greater. Now the testimony of God is this, that he has testified on behalf of his Son. Whoever believes in the Son of God has this testimony within himself. Whoever does not believe God has made him a liar by not believing the testimony God has given about his Son. And this is the testimony: God gave us eternal life, and this life is in his Son. Whoever possesses the Son has life; whoever does not possess the Son of God does not have life.

I write these things to you so that you may know that you have eternal life, you who believe in the name of the Son of God.

The word of the Lord.

Responsorial Psalm

Ps 147:12–13, 14–15, 19–20

R. Praise the Lord, Jerusalem.

Glorify the LORD, O Jerusalem;
   praise your God, O Zion.
For he has strengthened the bars of your gates;
   he has blessed your children within you.

R. Praise the Lord, Jerusalem.

He has granted peace in your borders;
   with the best of wheat he fills you.
He sends forth his command to the earth;
   swiftly runs his word!

R. Praise the Lord, Jerusalem.

He has proclaimed his word to Jacob,
   his statutes and his ordinances to Israel.
He has not done thus for any other nation;
   his ordinances he has not made known to them. Alleluia.

R. Praise the Lord, Jerusalem.

Or: **R. Alleluia.**

> **Alleluia, alleluia**   See Mk 9:6
> The heavens were opened and the voice of the Father thundered:
> This is my beloved Son. Listen to him.
> **Alleluia, alleluia**

FIRST OPTION

GOSPEL

Mk 1:7–11

You are my beloved Son; with you I am well pleased.

A reading from the holy Gospel according to Mark

This is what John the Baptist proclaimed: "One mightier than I is coming after me. I am not worthy to stoop and loosen the thongs of his sandals. I have baptized you with water; he will baptize you with the Holy Spirit."

It happened in those days that Jesus came from Nazareth of Galilee and was baptized in the Jordan by John. On coming up out of the water he saw the heavens being torn open and the Spirit, like a dove, descending upon him. And a voice came from the heavens, "You are my beloved Son; with you I am well pleased."

The Gospel of the Lord.

Or:

SECOND OPTION

GOSPEL   Lk 3:23 – 38 or 3:23, 31– 34, 36, 38

The genealogy of Jesus Christ, the son of Adam, the son of God.

A reading from the holy Gospel according to Luke
Long form follows; for short form omit what is in brackets.

When Jesus began his ministry he was about thirty years of age. He was the son, as was thought, of Joseph, the son of Heli, [the son of Matthat, the son of Levi, the son of Melchi, the son of Jannai, the son of Joseph, the son of Mattathias, the son of Amos, the son of Nahum, the son of Esli, the son of Naggai, the son of Maath, the son of Mattathias, the son of Semein, the son of Josech, the son of Joda, the son of Joanan, the son of Rhesa, the son of Zerubbabel, the son of Shealtiel, the son of Neri, the son of Melchi, the son of Addi, the son of Cosam, the son of Elmadam, the son of Er, the son of Joshua, the son of Eliezer, the son of Jorim, the son of Matthat, the son of Levi, the son of Simeon, the son of Judah, the son of Joseph, the son of Jonam, the son of Eliakim,] the son of Melea, the son of Menna, the son of Mattatha, the son of Nathan, the son of David, the son of Jesse, the son of Obed, the son of Boaz, the son of Sala, the son of Nahshon, the son of Amminadab, the son of Admin, the son of Arni, the son of Hezron, the son of Perez, the son of Judah, the son of Jacob, the son of Isaac, the son of Abraham, the son of Terah, the son of Nahor, [the son of Serug, the son of Reu, the son of Peleg, the son of Eber, the son of Shelah,] the son of Cainan, the son of Arphaxad, the son of Shem, the son of Noah, the son of Lamech, [the son of Methuselah, the son of Enoch, the son of Jared, the son of Mahalaleel, the son of Cainan,] the son of Enos, the son of Seth, the son of Adam, the son of God.

The Gospel of the Lord.

Liturgy of the Eucharist, *p. 897.*

January 7   (if before Epiphany)

If the Epiphany is celebrated on Sunday, January 8, the following readings are used for the Mass on January 7.

Antiphons and Prayers, *pp. 201–209.*

TODAY'S LIVING WORD

The ending of 1 John, today's first reading, is a profession of confidence in God: "If we ask anything according to his will, he hears us." At first glance today's Gospel, Jesus' first miracle or "sign," seems to illustrate the point exactly. In this story the mother of Jesus is cast as the persistent petitioner whose prayer is finally answered. On taking a closer look, the exchange that takes place between Jesus and his mother puzzles us. Jesus' reply to his mother's request— literally, "What to me and to you?"—sounds like a refusal. Yet he proceeds to change the water into wine.

The seeming reluctance of Jesus in this story does two things. It shows his mother to be one of those who truly believe in Jesus without having seen miraculous signs. With utter confidence, she says to the stewards, "Do whatever he tells you." At the same time, by raising the question of Jesus' "hour," it also makes clear that Jesus acts here, as he will in his "hour," only to do the will of the Father, whose glory he has come to reveal.

FIRST READING   1 Jn 5:14 – 21

God hears us in regard to whatever we ask.

A reading from the first Letter of Saint John

Beloved:

We have this confidence in God, that if we ask anything according to his will, he hears us. And if we know that he hears us in regard to whatever we ask, we know that what we have asked him for is ours. If anyone sees his brother sinning, if the sin is not deadly, he should pray to God and he will give him life. This is only for those whose sin is not deadly. There is such a thing as deadly sin, about which I do not say that you should pray. All wrongdoing is sin, but there is sin that is not deadly.

We know that no one begotten by God sins; but the one begotten by God he protects, and the Evil One cannot touch him. We know that we belong to God, and the whole world is under the power of the Evil One. We also know that the Son of God has come and has given us discernment to know the one who is true. And we are in the one who is true, in his Son Jesus Christ. He is the true God and eternal life. Children, be on your guard against idols.

The word of the Lord.

Responsorial Psalm   Ps 149:1– 2, 3 – 4, 5 and 6a and 9b

R. The Lord takes delight in his people.

Sing to the LORD a new song
  of praise in the assembly of the faithful.

Let Israel be glad in their maker,
  let the children of Zion rejoice in their king.

R. The Lord takes delight in his people.

Let them praise his name in the festive dance,
  let them sing praise to him with timbrel and harp.
For the LORD loves his people,
  and he adorns the lowly with victory.

R. The Lord takes delight in his people.

Let the faithful exult in glory;
  let them sing for joy upon their couches;
Let the high praises of God be in their throats.
  This is the glory of all his faithful. Alleluia.

R. The Lord takes delight in his people.

Or: **R. Alleluia.**

Alleluia, alleluia Lk 7:16
A great prophet has arisen in our midst
and God has visited his people.
Alleluia, alleluia

GOSPEL   Jn 2:1–11

Jesus did this as the beginning of his signs at Cana in Galilee.

A reading from the holy Gospel according to John

There was a wedding at Cana in Galilee, and the mother of
Jesus was there. Jesus and his disciples were also invited to
the wedding. When the wine ran short, the mother of Jesus
said to him, "They have no wine." And Jesus said to her,
"Woman, how does your concern affect me? My hour has not
yet come." His mother said to the servers, "Do whatever he
tells you." Now there were six stone water jars there for Jewish
ceremonial washings, each holding twenty to thirty gallons.
Jesus told them, "Fill the jars with water." So they filled them
to the brim. Then he told them, "Draw some out now and take

it to the headwaiter." So they took it. And when the headwaiter tasted the water that had become wine, without knowing where it came from (although the servers who had drawn the water knew), the headwaiter called the bridegroom and said to him, "Everyone serves good wine first, and then when people have drunk freely, an inferior one; but you have kept the good wine until now." Jesus did this as the beginning of his signs at Cana in Galilee and so revealed his glory, and his disciples began to believe in him.

The Gospel of the Lord.

Liturgy of the Eucharist, *p. 897.*

From January 2 to Epiphany

(Antiphons and Prayers)

Before the Epiphany—

From January 2 to Epiphany, the *antiphons and prayers* are designated for Monday through Saturday as follows below (pp. 201–209), whereas the *Liturgy of the Word* is designated for specific dates: January 2, etc. (pp. 183–201).

After the Epiphany—

For the propers of the days following the Epiphany, turn to pp. 210–232.

From January 2 to Epiphany

Monday

Entrance Antiphon

A holy day has dawned upon us. Come, you nations, and adore the Lord. Today a great light has come upon the earth.

Opening Prayer

Lord,
keep us true in the faith,
proclaiming that Christ your Son,
who is one with you in eternal glory,
became man and was born of a virgin mother.
Free us from all evil
and lead us to the joy of eternal life.

We ask this through our Lord Jesus Christ, your Son,
who lives and reigns with you and the Holy Spirit,
one God, for ever and ever.

Liturgy of the Word: *for Jan. 2, see p. 183; Jan. 3, p. 186; Jan. 4, p. 189; Jan. 5, p. 191; Jan. 6, p. 194; Jan. 7, p. 198.*

Prayer over the Gifts

Pray, brethren...

Lord,
receive our gifts in this wonderful exchange:
from all you have given us
we bring you these gifts,
and in return, you give us yourself.

We ask this through Christ our Lord.

Preface of Christmas I–III, *pp. 938–939*

Communion Antiphon

We have seen his glory the glory of the Father's only Son, full of grace and truth.   (Jn 1:14)

Prayer after Communion

Let us pray.
Pause for silent prayer, if this has not preceded.

Father of love and mercy,
grant that our lives may always be founded
on the power of this holy mystery.
We ask this in the name of Jesus the Lord.

From January 2 to Epiphany

Tuesday

Entrance Antiphon

Blessed is he who comes in the name of the Lord; the Lord God shines upon us. (Ps 117:26–27)

Opening Prayer

God our Father,
when your Son was born of the Virgin Mary
he became like us in all things but sin.
May we who have been reborn in him
be free from our sinful ways.
We ask this through our Lord Jesus Christ, your Son,
who lives and reigns with you and the Holy Spirit,
one God, for ever and ever.

Liturgy of the Word: *for Jan. 2, see p. 183; Jan. 3, p. 186; Jan. 4, p. 189; Jan. 5, p. 191; Jan. 6, p. 194; Jan. 7, p. 198.*

Prayer over the Gifts

Pray, brethren...
Father,
in your mercy accept our gifts.
By sharing in this eucharist
may we come to live more fully the love we profess.

Grant this through Christ our Lord.

Preface of Christmas I–III, *pp. 938–939.*

Communion Antiphon

God loved us so much that he sent his own Son in the likeness of sinful flesh.   (Eph 2:4; Rom 8:3)

Prayer after Communion

Let us pray.

Pause for silent prayer, if this has not preceded.

God our Father,
in this eucharist you touch our lives.
Keep your love alive in our hearts
that we may become worthy of you.
We ask this through Christ our Lord.

From January 2 to Epiphany

Wednesday

Entrance Antiphon

The people who walked in darkness have seen a great light; on those who lived in the shadow of death, light has shone. (Is 9:2)

Opening Prayer

All-powerful Father,
you sent your Son Jesus Christ
to bring the new light of salvation to the world.
May he enlighten us with his radiance,
who lives and reigns with you and the Holy Spirit,
one God, for ever and ever.

Liturgy of the Word: *for Jan. 2, see p. 183; Jan. 3, p. 186; Jan. 4, p. 189; Jan. 5, p. 191; Jan. 6, p. 194; Jan. 7, p. 198.*

Prayer over the Gifts

Pray, brethren...

Father of peace,
accept our devotion and sincerity,
and by our sharing in this mystery
draw us closer to each other and to you.

We ask this in the name of Jesus the Lord.

Preface of Christmas I–III, *pp. 938–939.*

Communion Antiphon

The eternal life which was with the Father has been revealed to us. (1 Jn 1:2)

Prayer after Communion

Let us pray.

Pause for silent prayer, if this has not preceded.

Lord,
may this sacrament be our strength.
Teach us to value all the good you give us
and help us to strive for eternal life.

Grant this through Christ our Lord.

From January 2 to Epiphany

Thursday

Entrance Antiphon

In the beginning, before all ages, the Word was God; that Word was born a man to save the world. (See Jn 1:1)

Opening Prayer

Father,
you make known the salvation of mankind
at the birth of your Son.
Make us strong in faith
and bring us to the glory you promise.

We ask this through our Lord Jesus Christ, your Son,
who lives and reigns with you and the Holy Spirit,
one God, for ever and ever.

Liturgy of the Word: *for Jan. 2, see p. 183; Jan. 3, p. 186; Jan. 4, p. 189; Jan. 5, p. 191; Jan. 6, p. 194; Jan. 7, p. 198.*

Prayer over the Gifts

Pray, brethren...

Lord,
receive our gifts in this wonderful exchange:
from all you have given us
we bring you these gifts,
and in return, you give us yourself.

We ask this through Christ our Lord.

Preface of Christmas I–III, *pp. 938–939.*

Communion Antiphon

God loved the world so much, he gave his only Son, that all who believe in him might not perish, but might have eternal life.

(Jn 3:16)

Prayer after Communion

Let us pray.

Pause for silent prayer, if this has not preceded.

Father of love and mercy,

grant that our lives may always be founded
on the power of this holy mystery.
We ask this in the name of Jesus the Lord.

From January 2 to Epiphany

Friday

Entrance Antiphon

The Lord is a light in darkness to the upright; he is gracious, merciful, and just.   (Ps 111:4)

Opening Prayer

Lord,
fill our hearts with your light.
May we always acknowledge Christ as our Savior
and be more faithful to his gospel,
for he lives and reigns with you and the Holy Spirit,
one God, for ever and ever.

Liturgy of the Word: *for Jan. 2, see p. 183; Jan. 3, p. 186; Jan. 4, p. 189; Jan. 5, p. 191; Jan. 6, p. 194; Jan. 7, p. 198.*

Prayer over the Gifts

Pray, brethren...

Father,
in your mercy accept our gifts.
By sharing in this eucharist
may we come to live more fully the love we profess.

Grant this through Christ our Lord.

Preface of Christmas I–III, *pp. 938–939.*

Communion Antiphon

God's love for us was revealed when he sent his only Son into the world, so that we could have life through him.   (1 Jn 4:9)

Prayer after Communion

Let us pray.

Pause for silent prayer, if this has not preceded.

God our Father,
in this eucharist you touch our lives.
Keep your love alive in our hearts
that we may become worthy of you.

We ask this through Christ our Lord.

___

From January 2 to Epiphany

Saturday

Entrance Antiphon

God sent his own Son, born of a woman, so that we could be adopted as his sons.   (Gal 4:4–5)

Opening Prayer

All-powerful and ever-living God,
you give us a new vision of your glory
in the coming of Christ your Son.
He was born of the Virgin Mary
and came to share our life.
May we come to share his eternal life
in the glory of your kingdom,
where he lives and reigns with you and the Holy Spirit,
one God, for ever and ever.

Liturgy of the Word: *for Jan. 2, see p. 183; Jan. 3, p. 186; Jan. 4, p. 189; Jan. 5, p. 191; Jan. 6, p. 194; Jan. 7, p. 198.*

Prayer over the Gifts

Pray, brethren...

Father of peace,
accept our devotion and sincerity,
and by our sharing in this mystery
draw us closer to each other and to you.

We ask this in the name of Jesus the Lord.

Preface of Christmas I–III, *pp. 938–939.*

Communion Antiphon

From his riches we have all received, grace for grace.

(Jn 1:16)

Prayer after Communion

Let us pray.

Pause for silent prayer, if this has not preceded.

Lord,
may this sacrament be our strength.
Teach us to value all the good you give us
and help us to strive for eternal life.

We ask this in the name of Jesus the Lord.

For EPIPHANY, *see* **Vatican II Sunday Missal,** *p. 114.*

In the dioceses of the United States of America, where Epiphany is celebrated on the Sunday between January 2 and January 8, the following readings are used on the days that follow Epiphany up to the following Saturday. Nevertheless, on Monday after the Sunday on which the Baptism of the Lord is celebrated (that is, the Sunday after January 6), the readings of Ordinary Time begin, and any readings left over from those assigned for January 7 to January 12 are omitted.

Monday after Epiphany
or January 7

Entrance Antiphon

A holy day has dawned upon us. Come, you nations, and adore the Lord. Today a great light has come upon the earth.

Opening Prayer

Lord,
let the light of your glory shine within us,
and lead us through the darkness of this world
to the radiant joy of our eternal home.

We ask this through our Lord Jesus Christ, your Son,
who lives and reigns with you and the Holy Spirit,
one God, for ever and ever.

TODAY'S LIVING WORD

Today's first reading from 1 John continues the condemnation of the world begun in John's Gospel. The world is a dangerous place. The spirit of the antichrist "is already in the world," he says. Therefore, to be popular in the world—as are his opponents, who do not acknowledge "Jesus Christ come in the flesh"—is itself proof that one does not belong to God but to the world that does not accept Jesus. In today's Gospel, however, Jesus himself seems to be enjoying a certain popularity in the world. As he tours all of Galilee, he is followed by "great crowds...from Galilee, the Decapolis, Jerusalem, and Judea, and from beyond the Jordan." His reputation reaches even into Syria.

Yet Matthew is aware of the world's eventual rejection of Jesus, and begins his account of Jesus' ministry by noting that "John had been arrested." Jesus, as it were, takes up where John left off. His message—"The kingdom of heaven is at hand"—is John's message. His fate will be the same as John's: rejection by the world.

FIRST READING

Test the spirits to see whether they belong to God.

A reading from the first Letter of Saint John

Beloved:

We receive from him whatever we ask, because we keep his commandments and do what pleases him. And his commandment is this: we should believe in the name of his Son, Jesus Christ, and love one another just as he commanded us. Those who keep his commandments remain in him, and he in them, and the way we know that he remains in us is from the Spirit whom he gave us.

Beloved, do not trust every spirit but test the spirits to see whether they belong to God, because many false prophets have gone out into the world. This is how you can know the Spirit of God: every spirit that acknowledges Jesus Christ come in the flesh belongs to God, and every spirit that does not acknowledge Jesus does not belong to God. This is the spirit of the antichrist who, as you heard, is to come, but in fact is already in the world. You belong to God, children, and you have conquered them, for the one who is in you is greater than the one who is in the world. They belong to the world; accordingly, their teaching belongs to the world, and the world listens to them. We belong to God, and anyone who knows God listens to us, while anyone who does not belong to God refuses to hear us. This is how we know the spirit of truth and the spirit of deceit.

The word of the Lord.

Responsorial Psalm

R. **I will give you all the nations for an inheritance.**

The LORD said to me, "You are my Son;
   this day I have begotten you.
Ask of me and I will give you
   the nations for an inheritance
   and the ends of the earth for your possession."

R. I will give you all the nations for an inheritance.

And now, O kings, give heed;
   take warning, you rulers of the earth.
Serve the LORD with fear, and rejoice before him;
   with trembling rejoice.

R. I will give you all the nations for an inheritance.

Alleluia, alleluia   See Mt 4:23
Jesus proclaimed the Gospel of the Kingdom
and cured every disease among the people.
Alleluia, alleluia

GOSPEL   Mt 4:12–17, 23–25
            The Kingdom of heaven is at hand.

A reading from the holy Gospel according to Matthew

When Jesus heard that John had been arrested, he withdrew to
Galilee. He left Nazareth and went to live in Capernaum by
the sea, in the region of Zebulun and Naphtali, that what had
been said through Isaiah the prophet might be fulfilled:

   Land of Zebulun and land of Naphtali,
      the way to the sea, beyond the Jordan,
      Galilee of the Gentiles,
   the people who sit in darkness
      have seen a great light,
   on those dwelling in a land overshadowed by death
      light has arisen.

From that time on, Jesus began to preach and say, "Repent, for
the Kingdom of heaven is at hand."

He went around all of Galilee, teaching in their synagogues, proclaiming the Gospel of the Kingdom, and curing every disease and illness among the people. His fame spread to all of Syria, and they brought to him all who were sick with various diseases and racked with pain, those who were possessed, lunatics, and paralytics, and he cured them. And great crowds from Galilee, the Decapolis, Jerusalem, and Judea, and from beyond the Jordan followed him.

The Gospel of the Lord.

Liturgy of the Eucharist, *p. 897.*

Prayer over the Gifts

Pray, brethren...

Lord,
receive our gifts in this wonderful exchange:
from all you have give us
we bring you these gifts,
and in return, you give us yourself.

We ask this through Christ our Lord.

Preface of Epiphany, *p. 940.*

Communion Antiphon

We have seen his glory, the glory of the Father's only Son, full of grace and truth.   (Jn 1:14)

Prayer after Communion

Let us pray.

Pause for silent prayer, if this has not preceded.

Father of love and mercy,
grant that our lives may always be founded
on the power of this holy mystery.

We ask this in the name of Jesus the Lord.

Tuesday after Epiphany
or January 8

Entrance Antiphon

Blessed is he who comes in the name of the Lord; the Lord God shines upon us.   (Ps 117:26 – 27)

Opening Prayer

Father,
your Son became like us
when he revealed himself in our nature:
help us to become more like him,
who lives and reigns with you and the Holy Spirit,
one God, for ever and ever.

TODAY'S LIVING WORD

Today's brief selection from 1 John contains one of the central insights of that letter: "In this is love: not that we have loved God, but that he loved us." First John teaches that the love of God was revealed by Jesus, who was sent to the world "that we might have life through him." In today's Gospel, the love of God is revealed in a number of biblical images that are taken up and "translated" into the words and actions of Jesus. In the prophecy of Ezekiel, God's love had been depicted as the compassionate care of a shepherd; here Jesus is moved with pity for the people who are "like sheep without a shepherd." On the desert journey to the promised land, God had fed the Israelites with manna; here in a deserted place, Jesus gives the hungry crowd bread and fish. Elisha had once multiplied twenty barley loaves to feed a hundred men; here Jesus multiplies five loaves to feed five thousand.

Jesus' revelation of God's love in human words and human gestures informs and enlivens the sacraments. No less than the hungry crowd in that deserted place, in the Eucharist we are also fed—and so "have life through him."

FIRST READING

1 Jn 4:7–10

God is love.

A reading from the first Letter of Saint John

Beloved, let us love one another, because love is of God; everyone who loves is begotten by God and knows God. Whoever is without love does not know God, for God is love. In this way the love of God was revealed to us: God sent his only-begotten Son into the world so that we might have life through him. In this is love: not that we have loved God, but that he loved us and sent his Son as expiation for our sins.

The word of the Lord.

Responsorial Psalm

Ps 72:1–2, 3–4, 7–8

R. Lord, every nation on earth will adore you.

O God, with your judgment endow the king,
  and with your justice, the king's son;
He shall govern your people with justice
  and your afflicted ones with judgment.

R. Lord, every nation on earth will adore you.

The mountains shall yield peace for the people,
  and the hills justice.
He shall defend the afflicted among the people,
  save the children of the poor.

R. Lord, every nation on earth will adore you.

Justice shall flower in his days,
  and profound peace, till the moon be no more.
May he rule from sea to sea,
  and from the River to the ends of the earth.

R. Lord, every nation on earth will adore you.

> **Alleluia, alleluia** Lk 4:18
> The Lord has sent me to bring glad tidings to the poor
> and to proclaim liberty to captives.
> **Alleluia, alleluia**

GOSPEL

Mk 6:34 – 44

Multiplying the loaves, Jesus shows himself as a prophet.

A reading from the holy Gospel according to Mark

When Jesus saw the vast crowd, his heart was moved with pity for them, for they were like sheep without a shepherd; and he began to teach them many things. By now it was already late and his disciples approached him and said, "This is a deserted place and it is already very late. Dismiss them so that they can go to the surrounding farms and villages and buy themselves something to eat." He said to them in reply, "Give them some food yourselves." But they said to him, "Are we to buy two hundred days' wages worth of food and give it to them to eat?" He asked them, "How many loaves do you have? Go and see." And when they had found out they said, "Five loaves and two fish." So he gave orders to have them sit down in groups on the green grass. The people took their places in rows by hundreds and by fifties. Then, taking the five loaves and the two fish and looking up to heaven, he said the blessing, broke the loaves, and gave them to his disciples to set before the people; he also divided the two fish among them all. They all ate and were satisfied. And they picked up twelve wicker baskets full of fragments and what was left of the fish. Those who ate of the loaves were five thousand men.

The Gospel of the Lord.

Liturgy of the Eucharist, *p. 897.*

Prayer over the Gifts

Pray, brethren...

Father,
in your mercy accept our gifts.

By sharing in this eucharist
may we come to live more fully the love we profess.

Grant this through Christ our Lord.

   Preface of Epiphany, *p. 940.*

Communion Antiphon

   God loved us so much that he sent his own Son in the likeness of sinful flesh.   (Eph 2:4; Rom 8:3)

Prayer after Communion

Let us pray.

   Pause for silent prayer, if this has not preceded.

God our Father,
in this eucharist you touch our lives.
Keep your love alive in our hearts
that we may become worthy of you.

We ask this through Christ our Lord.

Wednesday after Epiphany
or January 9

Entrance Antiphon

   The people who walked in darkness have seen a great light; on those who lived in the shadow of death, light has shone. (Is 9:2)

Opening Prayer

God, light of all nations,
give us the joy of lasting peace,
and fill us with your radiance
as you filled the hearts of our fathers.

We ask this through our Lord Jesus Christ, your Son,
who lives and reigns with you and the Holy Spirit,
one God, for ever and ever.

TODAY'S LIVING WORD

Today's two readings are both about seeing God. John's first letter begins with a statement also found in John's Gospel: "No one has ever seen God" (cf. Jn 1:18, 6:46). The point is that only the Son has seen the Father; therefore, only the Son can show us the Father. But today's selection says more: the love of God that Jesus revealed *to* us is also revealed *through* us, when God's love, dwelling in us, "is brought to perfection." Others do see God in us, "if we love one another."

The Gospel recounts how Jesus' disciples, in a boat far out on the lake, are given a manifestation of God, a "theophany." Several biblical allusions make Mark's intention clear. In the Psalms, God's path is "through the mighty waters" (77:20) and in Job, God "treads upon the crests of the sea," passing by the one who does not see (9:8, 11). Finally, Jesus' "It is I" echoes the divine name "I AM" (cf. Ex 3:14). But because the disciples of Jesus are as yet unable, in the words of 1 John, to acknowledge "that Jesus is the Son of God," the ability to see God eludes them. They are blinded by fear.

FIRST READING   1 Jn 4:11–18

If we love one another, God remains in us.

A reading from the first Letter of John

Beloved, if God so loved us, we also must love one another. No one has ever seen God. Yet, if we love one another, God remains in us, and his love is brought to perfection in us.

This is how we know that we remain in him and he in us, that he has given us of his Spirit. Moreover, we have seen and testify that the Father sent his Son as savior of the world. Whoever acknowledges that Jesus is the Son of God, God remains in him and he in God. We have come to know and to believe in the love God has for us.

God is love, and whoever remains in love remains in God and God in him. In this is love brought to perfection among us, that we have confidence on the day of judgment because as he is, so are we in this world. There is no fear in love, but perfect love drives out fear because fear has to do with punishment, and so one who fears is not yet perfect in love.

The word of the Lord.

Responsorial Psalm   Ps 72:1–2, 10, 12–13

R. Lord, every nation on earth will adore you.

O God, with your judgment endow the king,
  and with your justice, the king's son;
He shall govern your people with justice
  and your afflicted ones with judgment.

R. Lord, every nation on earth will adore you.

The kings of Tarshish and the Isles shall offer gifts;
  the kings of Arabia and Seba shall bring tribute.

R. Lord, every nation on earth will adore you.

For he shall rescue the poor when he cries out,
  and the afflicted when he has no one to help him.
He shall have pity for the lowly and the poor;
  the lives of the poor he shall save.

R. Lord, every nation on earth will adore you.

Alleluia, alleluia   See 1 Tm 3:16
Glory to you, O Christ, proclaimed to the Gentiles.
Glory to you, O Christ, believed in throughout the world.
Alleluia, alleluia

GOSPEL   Mk 6:45 – 52

They saw Jesus walking on the sea.

A reading from the holy Gospel according to Mark

After the five thousand had eaten and were satisfied, Jesus made his disciples get into the boat and precede him to the other side toward Bethsaida, while he dismissed the crowd. And when he had taken leave of them, he went off to the mountain to pray. When it was evening, the boat was far out on the sea and he was alone on shore. Then he saw that they were tossed about while rowing, for the wind was against them. About the fourth watch of the night, he came toward them walking on the sea. He meant to pass by them. But when they saw him walking on the sea, they thought it was a ghost and cried out. They had all seen him and were terrified. But at once he spoke with them, "Take courage, it is I, do not be afraid!" He got into the boat with them and the wind died down. They were completely astounded. They had not understood the incident of the loaves. On the contrary, their hearts were hardened.

The Gospel of the Lord.

Liturgy of the Eucharist, *p. 897.*

Prayer over the Gifts

Pray, brethren...

Father of peace,
accept our devotion and sincerity,
and by our sharing in this mystery
draw us closer to each other and to you.

We ask this in the name of Jesus the Lord.

Preface of Epiphany, *p. 940.*

Communion Antiphon

The eternal life which was with the Father has been revealed to us.   (1 Jn 1:2)

Prayer after Communion

Let us pray.

Pause for silent prayer, if this has not preceded.

Lord,
may this sacrament be our strength.
Teach us to value all the good you give us
and help us to strive for eternal life.
Grant this through Christ our Lord.

Thursday after Epiphany
or January 10

Entrance Antiphon

**In the beginning, before all ages, the Word was God: that Word
was born a man to save the world.**   (See Jn 1:1)

Opening Prayer

God our Father,
through Christ your Son
the hope of eternal life dawned on our world.
Give to us the light of faith
that we may always acknowledge him as our Redeemer
and come to the glory of his kingdom,
where he lives and reigns with you and the Holy Spirit,
one God, for ever and ever.

TODAY'S LIVING WORD

"Whoever is begotten by God conquers the world," declares 1
John in today's first reading. "The victory that conquers the world is
our faith." Faith gives us a share in Jesus' victory over sin and death,
the "world" of 1 John. In the Gospel for today, Jesus proclaims his

victory in Isaiah's words. Anointed by the Spirit, he is sent "to bring glad tidings to the poor...to proclaim liberty to captives and recovery of sight to the blind, to let the oppressed go free." The Greek word used to describe Jesus liberating captives and releasing prisoners is *aphesis,* the word also used for forgiveness of sins (cf. Lk 1:77). Above all, Jesus has overcome the world by freeing us from the power of the evil one.

The Gospel tells us too that the victory of Jesus is more than a promise; it is a present reality. The words of Isaiah are actualized in the works of Jesus "today." So the victory of Jesus is accessible to us in the liturgy of the Church, the "today" of the living, liberating God, revealed in Jesus the Christ (cf. *Catechism of the Catholic Church,* n. 1165).

FIRST READING   1 Jn 4:19 —5:4

Those who love God must also love their brother and sister.

A reading from the first Letter of Saint John

Beloved, we love God because he first loved us. If anyone says, "I love God," but hates his brother, he is a liar; for whoever does not love a brother whom he has seen cannot love God whom he has not seen. This is the commandment we have from him: Whoever loves God must also love his brother.

Everyone who believes that Jesus is the Christ is begotten by God, and everyone who loves the Father loves also the one begotten by him. In this way we know that we love the children of God when we love God and obey his commandments. For the love of God is this, that we keep his commandments. And his commandments are not burdensome, for whoever is begotten by God conquers the world. And the victory that conquers the world is our faith.

The word of the Lord.

Responsorial Psalm

Ps 72:1–2, 14 and 15bc, 17

R. Lord, every nation on earth will adore you.

O God, with your judgment endow the king,
   and with your justice, the king's son;
He shall govern your people with justice
   and your afflicted ones with judgment.

R. Lord, every nation on earth will adore you.

From fraud and violence he shall redeem them,
   and precious shall their blood be in his sight.
May they be prayed for continually;
   day by day shall they bless him.

R. Lord, every nation on earth will adore you.

May his name be blessed forever;
   as long as the sun his name shall remain.
In him shall all the tribes of the earth be blessed;
   all the nations shall proclaim his happiness.

R. Lord, every nation on earth will adore you.

> **Alleluia, alleluia** Lk 4:18
> The Lord has sent me to bring glad tidings to the poor
> and to proclaim liberty to captives.
> **Alleluia, alleluia**

GOSPEL   Lk 4:14 – 22

Today this Scripture passage is fulfilled.

A reading from the holy Gospel according to Luke

Jesus returned to Galilee in the power of the Spirit, and news
of him spread throughout the whole region. He taught in their
synagogues and was praised by all.

   He came to Nazareth, where he had grown up, and went
according to his custom into the synagogue on the sabbath
day. He stood up to read and was handed a scroll of the prophet

Isaiah. He unrolled the scroll and found the passage where it was written:

> The Spirit of the Lord is upon me,
>> because he has anointed me
>>> to bring glad tidings to the poor.
> He has sent me to proclaim liberty to captives
>> and recovery of sight to the blind,
>>> to let the oppressed go free,
> and to proclaim a year acceptable to the Lord.

Rolling up the scroll, he handed it back to the attendant and sat down, and the eyes of all in the synagogue looked intently at him. He said to them, "Today this Scripture passage is fulfilled in your hearing." And all spoke highly of him and were amazed at the gracious words that came from his mouth.

The Gospel of the Lord.

Liturgy of the Eucharist, *p. 897.*

Prayer over the Gifts

Pray, brethren...

Lord,
receive our gifts in this wonderful exchange:
from all you have given us
we bring you these gifts,
and in return, you give us yourself.

We ask this through Christ our Lord.

Preface of Epiphany, *p. 940.*

Communion Antiphon

   God loved the world so much, he gave his only Son, that all who believe in him might not perish, but might have eternal life.

(Jn 3:16)

Prayer after Communion

Let us pray.

Pause for silent prayer, if this has not preceded.

Father of love and mercy,
grant that our lives may always be founded
on the power of this holy mystery.

We ask this in the name of Jesus the Lord.

Friday after Epiphany
or January 11

Entrance Antiphon

The Lord is a light in darkness to the upright; he is gracious, merciful, and just.   (Ps 111:4)

Opening Prayer

All-powerful Father,
you have made known the birth of the Savior
by the light of a star.
May he continue to guide us with his light,
for he lives and reigns with you and the Holy Spirit,
one God, for ever and ever.

TODAY'S LIVING WORD

In today's Gospel Jesus cures a leper and sends him to the priest as the law required (cf. Lv 13—14). Then he adds, "that will be proof [testimony, *martyrion* in Greek] for them." Scholars are unsure as to whether this testimony is intended for the priest or for Jesus' opponents. What matters for our purposes is that this puzzling remark of Jesus' introduces the idea of testimony. Already Jesus is on trial.

This notion stands behind today's first reading too. In John, Jesus is on trial throughout his entire ministry. Witnesses testify on his

behalf, among them the Baptist, Scripture, Jesus' works, believers and the beloved disciple. But as James McPolin explains, ultimately in John all testimony to Jesus is the work of the Father, Son, and Spirit. It derives from the Father, "the source of all revelation"; it has Jesus as its "sole object," and is enabled by the indwelling Spirit.*
Not surprisingly, a Latin version of this text of 1 John expands the threefold witness of Spirit, blood and water to reflect as well the "Father, Word, and Holy Spirit."

* *John*, New Testament Message 6, 4th ed. (Wilmington: Michael Glazier, Inc., 1986), pp. 97–98.

FIRST READING
1 Jn 5:5–13

The Spirit, the water, and the Blood.

A reading from the first Letter of Saint John

Beloved:

Who indeed is the victor over the world but the one who believes that Jesus is the Son of God?

This is the one who came through water and Blood, Jesus Christ, not by water alone, but by water and Blood. The Spirit is the one who testifies, and the Spirit is truth. So there are three who testify, the Spirit, the water, and the Blood, and the three are of one accord. If we accept human testimony, the testimony of God is surely greater. Now the testimony of God is this, that he has testified on behalf of his Son. Whoever believes in the Son of God has this testimony within himself. Whoever does not believe God has made him a liar by not believing the testimony God has given about his Son. And this is the testimony: God gave us eternal life, and this life is in his Son. Whoever possesses the Son has life; whoever does not possess the Son of God does not have life.

I write these things to you so that you may know that you have eternal life, you who believe in the name of the Son of God.

The word of the Lord.

Responsorial Psalm   Ps 147:12–13, 14–15, 19–20

R. Praise the Lord, Jerusalem.

Glorify the LORD, O Jerusalem;
  praise your God, O Zion.
For he has strengthened the bars of your gates;
  he has blessed your children within you.

R. Praise the Lord, Jerusalem.

He has granted peace in your borders;
  with the best of wheat he fills you.
He sends forth his command to the earth;
  swiftly runs his word!

R. Praise the Lord, Jerusalem.

He has proclaimed his word to Jacob,
  his statutes and his ordinances to Israel.
He has not done thus for any other nation;
  his ordinances he has not made known to them. Alleluia.

R. Praise the Lord, Jerusalem.

Alleluia, alleluia   See Mt 4:23
Jesus proclaimed the Gospel of the Kingdom
and cured every disease among the people.
Alleluia, alleluia

GOSPEL   Lk 5:12–16

The leprosy left him immediately.

A reading from the holy Gospel according to Luke

It happened that there was a man full of leprosy in one of the towns where Jesus was; and when he saw Jesus, he fell prostrate, pleaded with him, and said, "Lord, if you wish, you can make me clean." Jesus stretched out his hand, touched him, and said, "I do will it. Be made clean." And the leprosy left him immediately. Then he ordered him not to tell anyone, but "Go, show yourself to the priest and offer for your cleansing what Moses prescribed; that will be proof for them." The report about him spread all the more, and great crowds assembled to listen to him and to be cured of their ailments, but he would withdraw to deserted places to pray.

The Gospel of the Lord.

Liturgy of the Eucharist, *p. 897.*

Prayer over the Gifts

Pray, brethren...

Father,
in your mercy accept our gifts.
By sharing in this eucharist
may we come to live more fully the love we profess.

Grant this through Christ our Lord.

Preface of Epiphany, *p. 940.*

Communion Antiphon

God's love for us was revealed when he sent his only Son into the world, so that we could have life through him.   (1 Jn 4:9)

Prayer after Communion

Let us pray.

Pause for silent prayer, if this has not preceded.

God our Father,
in this eucharist you touch our lives.
Keep your love alive in our hearts
that we may become worthy of you.

We ask this through Christ our Lord.

Saturday after Epiphany
or January 12

Entrance Antiphon

God sent his own Son, born of a woman, so that we could be adopted as his sons.   (Gal 4:4–5)

Opening Prayer

God our Father,
through your Son you made us a new creation.
He shared our nature and became one of us;
with his help, may we become more like him,
who lives and reigns with you and the Holy Spirit,
one God, for ever and ever.

TODAY'S LIVING WORD

Today's readings use two different images to affirm the same reality: that the one true God is revealed in Jesus the Christ. The first reading, from 1 John, takes its lead from the prologue of the Fourth Gospel. That text says of Jesus, "to those who did accept him he gave power to become children of God," adding, "to those who believe in his name, who were born not by natural generation nor by human choice nor by a man's decision but of God" (1:12–13). Therefore, 1 John speaks of Christians as being God's children, begotten of God. The Gospel turns instead to the Hebrew Bible where Israel is portrayed as God's bride, betrothed to God. In this scheme, Jesus is the bridegroom who comes to claim the bride, and John the Baptist is his best man.

Begotten of God, betrothed to God—however we think of ourselves as believers baptized in Jesus' name—our joy, like John's, is completed by Christ's coming. Like John, we want to decrease, not to lose but to find ourselves in him and in "the One who is true."

FIRST READING

1 Jn 5:14 – 21

God hears us in regard to whatever we ask.

A reading from the first Letter of Saint John

Beloved:

We have this confidence in him that if we ask anything according to his will, he hears us. And if we know that he hears us in regard to whatever we ask, we know that what we have asked him for is ours. If anyone sees his brother sinning, if the sin is not deadly, he should pray to God and he will give him life. This is only for those whose sin is not deadly. There is such a thing as deadly sin, about which I do not say that you should pray. All wrongdoing is sin, but there is sin that is not deadly.

We know that anyone begotten by God does not sin; but the one begotten by God he protects, and the Evil One cannot touch him. We know that we belong to God, and the whole world is under the power of the Evil One. We also know that the Son of God has come and has given us discernment to know the one who is true. And we are in the one who is true, in his Son Jesus Christ. He is the true God and eternal life. Children, be on your guard against idols.

The word of the Lord.

Responsorial Psalm

149:1–2, 3–4, 5–6a and 9b

R. **The Lord takes delight in his people.**

Sing to the Lord a new song
   of praise in the assembly of the faithful.
Let Israel be glad in their maker,
   let the children of Zion rejoice in their king.

R. **The Lord takes delight in his people.**

Let them praise his name in the festive dance,
   let them sing praise to him with timbrel and harp.

For the LORD loves his people,
  and he adorns the lowly with victory.

R. The Lord takes delight in his people.

Let the faithful exult in glory;
  let them sing for joy upon their couches;
Let the high praises of God be in their throats.
  This is the glory of all his faithful. Alleluia.

R. The Lord takes delight in his people.

> **Alleluia, alleluia**   Mt 4:16
> The people who sit in darkness have seen a great light,
> on those dwelling in a land overshadowed by death
> light has arisen.
> **Alleluia, alleluia**

GOSPEL   Jn 3:22–30

The friend of the bridegroom rejoices at the bridegroom's voice.

A reading from the holy Gospel according to John

Jesus and his disciples went into the region of Judea, where he
spent some time with them baptizing. John was also baptizing
in Aenon near Salim, because there was an abundance of water
there, and people came to be baptized, for John had not yet
been imprisoned. Now a dispute arose between the disciples
of John and a Jew about ceremonial washings. So they came
to John and said to him, "Rabbi, the one who was with you
across the Jordan, to whom you testified, here he is baptizing
and everyone is coming to him." John answered and said, "No
one can receive anything except what has been given from
heaven. You yourselves can testify that I said that I am not the
Christ, but that I was sent before him. The one who has the
bride is the bridegroom; the best man, who stands and listens
for him, rejoices greatly at the bridegroom's voice. So this joy

of mine has been made complete. He must increase; I must decrease."

The Gospel of the Lord.

Liturgy of the Eucharist, *p. 897.*

Prayer over the Gifts

Pray, brethren...

Father of peace,
accept our devotion and sincerity,
and by our sharing in this mystery
draw us closer to each other and to you.

We ask this in the name of Jesus the Lord.

Preface of Epiphany, *p. 940.*

Communion Antiphon

From his riches we have all received, grace for grace. (Jn 1:16)

Prayer after Communion

Let us pray.

Pause for silent prayer, if this has not preceded.

Lord,
may this sacrament be our strength.
Teach us to value all the good you give us
and help us to strive for eternal life.

Grant this through Christ our Lord.

Ordinary Time

Ordinary time includes thirty-three or thirty-four weeks. It begins on Monday after the Sunday which follows January 6 and continues until the beginning of Lent; it begins again on Monday after Pentecost Sunday and ends on Saturday before the first Sunday of Advent.

The missal thus has thirty-four Masses for the Sundays and weekdays of this time. They are used as follows:

a) On Sundays the Mass corresponding to the number of that ordinary Sunday is used, unless there is a solemnity or a feast which replaces the Sunday.

b) On weekdays any of the thirty-four Masses may be celebrated, according to the pastoral needs of the people.

The ordinary Sundays and weekdays are computed in this way:

a) The Sunday when the feast of the Baptism of the Lord is celebrated replaces the first ordinary Sunday, but the week that follows is counted as the first ordinary week. The other Sundays and weeks are numbered in order until the beginning of Lent.

b) If the number of ordinary weeks is thirty-four, after Pentecost the series is resumed with the week which follows immediately the last week celebrated before Lent.

The Masses of Pentecost, Trinity, (and in countries where Corpus Christi is not observed as a holy day of obligation and is therefore celebrated on the following Sunday) and Corpus Christi replace the Sunday Masses in these weeks. If the number of ordinary weeks is thirty-three, the first week which would otherwise follow Pentecost is omitted.

The Gloria and the Profession of faith are sung or said on Sundays; they are omitted on weekdays.

On Sundays one of the prefaces for Sundays in ordinary time is sung or said.

Two antiphons are given for communion, the first from the psalms, the second for the most part from the Gospel. Either one may be selected, but preference should be given to the antiphon which may happen to come from the gospel of the Mass.

FIRST WEEK IN ORDINARY TIME

The feast of the BAPTISM OF THE LORD *(see* **Vatican II Sunday Missal,** *p. 119) takes the place of the First Sunday in Ordinary Time.*

The **Antiphons and Prayers** *may be the following, or may be chosen from any of the other 33 weeks in Ordinary Time (refer to Liturgical Calendar, pp. 26–41).*

The **Liturgy of the Word** *varies: for Monday, see p. 236; Tuesday, p. 241; Wednesday, p. 246; Thursday, p. 250; Friday, p. 255; Saturday, p. 260.*

Entrance Antiphon

I saw a man sitting on a high throne, being worshiped by a great number of angels who were singing together: This is he whose kingdom will last for ever.

Opening Prayer

Let us pray

[that we will know and do what God wills]

Pause for silent prayer.

Father of love,
hear our prayers.
Help us to know your will
and to do it with courage and faith.

Grant this through our Lord Jesus Christ, your Son,
who lives and reigns with you and the Holy Spirit,
one God, for ever and ever.

Prayer over the Gifts

Pray, brethren...

Lord,
accept our offering.
Make us grow in holiness
and grant what we ask you in faith.

We ask this in the name of Jesus the Lord.

Preface of Weekdays in Ordinary Time I–VI, *pp. 948–950.*

Communion Antiphon

Lord, you are the source of life, and in the light of your glory we find happiness.   (Ps 35:10)

Or:

I came that men may have life, and have it to the full, says the Lord.   (Jn 10:10)

Prayer after Communion

Let us pray.
Pause for silent prayer, if this has not preceded.

All-powerful God,
you renew us with your sacraments.

Help us to thank you by lives of faithful service.

We ask this through Christ our Lord.

When the BAPTISM OF THE LORD *occurs on Monday of the First Week in Ordinary Time, the readings assigned to Monday may be joined to those of Tuesday so that the opening of each book will be read.*

Monday

Antiphons and Prayers, *p. 235;* **Liturgy of the Word** *for Year I (odd years) follows; Year II (even years), p. 238.*

TODAY'S LIVING WORD

"The Kingdom of God is at hand!" With these words Jesus begins his public ministry. The phrase he chooses to sum up his message is rooted in the Judaism of his day. In the Hebrew Scriptures, the reign or Kingdom of God is a symbol, a way of speaking about God's powerful rule over all creation. Acknowledging God's kingly rule is good news, as Psalm 97 proclaims: "The Lord is king; let the earth rejoice." Behind the symbol of God's reign lies the rich, rambling story of God's activity in the world. This story reaches back to creation itself and retells all the words God spoke through the prophets "in times past" and all the wonders God worked on behalf of the poor, of people like Hannah in the first reading. At the time of Jesus, the reign of God was awaited as a dynamic event, God's coming to rule as king. Jesus announces the nearness of that coming.

The message of Jesus demands a radical reordering of one's whole life. Today's Gospel shows us just how radical this can be, as Jesus' first disciples abandon financial security and family ties to follow Jesus literally. Such literal following may not be required of us, but our response to Jesus' call must be just as immediate and total.

Year I

FIRST READING

Heb 1:1–6

God spoke to us through the Son.

A reading from the beginning of the Letter to the Hebrews

Brothers and sisters:

In times past, God spoke in partial and various ways to our ancestors through the prophets; in these last days, he spoke to us through the Son, whom he made heir of all things and through whom he created the universe,

> *who is the refulgence of his glory,*
> *the very imprint of his being,*
> *and who sustains all things by his mighty word.*
> *When he had accomplished purification from sins,*
> *he took his seat at the right hand of the Majesty on high,*
> *as far superior to the angels*
> *as the name he has inherited is more excellent than theirs.*

For to which of the angels did God ever say:

> *You are my Son; this day I have begotten you?*

Or again:

>   *I will be a father to him, and he shall be a Son to me?*

And again, when he leads the first born into the world, he says:

>   *Let all the angels of God worship him.*

The word of the Lord.

Responsial Psalm

Ps 97:1 and 2b, 6 and 7c, 9

R. Let all his angels worship him.

The LORD is king; let the earth rejoice;
  let the many isles be glad.
  Justice and judgment are the foundation of his throne.

R. Let all his angels worship him.

The heavens proclaim his justice,
  and all peoples see his glory.
Let all his angels worship him.

R. Let all his angels worship him.

Because you, O LORD, are the Most High over all the earth,
  exalted far above all gods.

R. Let all his angels worship him.

Alleluia Verse *and* **Gospel,** *p. 240.*

Year II

FIRST READING

1 Sm 1:1–8

>   *Hannah's rival turned it into a constant reproach
>   to her that the LORD had left her barren.*

A reading from the beginning of the first Book of Samuel

There was a certain man from Ramathaim, Elkanah by name,
a Zuphite from the hill country of Ephraim. He was the son of
Jeroham, son of Elihu, son of Tohu, son of Zuph, an Ephraimite.

He had two wives, one named Hannah, the other Peninnah;
Peninnah had children, but Hannah was childless. This man
regularly went on pilgrimage from his city to worship the Lord
of hosts and to sacrifice to him at Shiloh, where the two sons
of Eli, Hophni and Phinehas, were ministering as priests of the
Lord. When the day came for Elkanah to offer sacrifice, he
used to give a portion each to his wife Peninnah and to all her
sons and daughters, but a double portion to Hannah because
he loved her, though the Lord had made her barren. Her rival,
to upset her, turned it into a constant reproach to her that the
Lord had left her barren. This went on year after year; each
time they made their pilgrimage to the sanctuary of the Lord,
Peninnah would approach her, and Hannah would weep and
refuse to eat. Her husband Elkanah used to ask her: "Hannah,
why do you weep, and why do you refuse to eat? Why do you
grieve? Am I not more to you than ten sons?"

The word of the Lord.

Responsorial Psalm   Ps 116:12–13, 14–17, 18–19

R. To you, Lord, I will offer a sacrifice of praise.

How shall I make a return to the Lord
  for all the good he has done for me?
The cup of salvation I will take up,
  and I will call upon the name of the Lord.

R. To you, Lord, I will offer a sacrifice of praise.

My vows to the Lord I will pay
  in the presence of all his people.
Precious in the eyes of the Lord
  is the death of his faithful ones.
O Lord, I am your servant;
  I am your servant, the son of your handmaid;
  you have loosed my bonds.

R. To you, Lord, I will offer a sacrifice of praise.

My vows to the LORD I will pay
 in the presence of all his people,
In the courts of the house of the LORD,
 in your midst, O Jerusalem.

R. To you, Lord, I will offer a sacrifice of praise.

Or: **R. Alleluia.**

> **Alleluia, alleluia** Mk 1:15
> The Kingdom of God is at hand;
> repent and believe in the Gospel.
> **Alleluia, alleluia**

Years I and II

GOSPEL   Mk 1:14–20

Repent, and believe in the Gospel.

A reading from the holy Gospel according to Mark

After John had been arrested, Jesus came to Galilee proclaiming the Gospel of God: "This is the time of fulfillment. The Kingdom of God is at hand. Repent, and believe in the Gospel."

As he passed by the Sea of Galilee, he saw Simon and his brother Andrew casting their nets into the sea; they were fishermen. Jesus said to them, "Come after me, and I will make you fishers of men." Then they left their nets and followed him. He walked along a little farther and saw James, the son of Zebedee, and his brother John. They too were in a boat mending their nets. Then he called them. So they left their father Zebedee in the boat along with the hired men and followed him.

The Gospel of the Lord.

Liturgy of the Eucharist, *p. 897;* **Prayer over the Gifts,** *p. 235.*

Tuesday

Antiphons and Prayers, *p. 235;* **Liturgy of the Word** *for Year I (odd years) follows; Year II (even years), p. 243.*

TODAY'S LIVING WORD

In his Gospel, Mark presents Jesus as the agent of God's reign, the one who in his words and deeds not only announced but actualized the kingly power of God. So it was that Jesus astonished the crowds, for he both taught and acted with unparalleled authority.

But creation had rebelled, rejecting God's rule and subjecting itself instead to the rule of God's enemy. So the ministry of Jesus was a power struggle, most dramatically enacted in his exorcisms. Invariably the demons recognized the Holy One of God who had come to destroy them, and Jesus cast them out with one word of command.

Mark notes the amazement of the people but he does not invite us to share it. He knows that the loud cry, which here signals Jesus' power over the unclean spirit, will one day be torn from Jesus himself as he breathes his last on the cross. This fullest revelation of God's power will be met not with amazement but with abandonment. As the author of Hebrews taught, "We...see Jesus 'crowned with glory and honor' because he suffered death." As Hannah learned, humiliation precedes exaltation.

Year I

FIRST READING
Heb 2:5–12

*He made the one who leads them to their salvation
perfect through suffering.*

A reading from the Letter to the Hebrews

It was not to angels that God subjected the world to come, of which we are speaking. Instead, someone has testified somewhere:

What is man that you are mindful of him,

> *or the son of man that you care for him?*
> *You made him for a little while lower than the angels;*
>   *you crowned him with glory and honor,*
>   *subjecting all things under his feet.*

In "subjecting" all things to him, he left nothing not "subject to him." Yet at present we do not see "all things subject to him," but we do see Jesus "crowned with glory and honor" because he suffered death, he who "for a little while" was made "lower than the angels," that by the grace of God he might taste death for everyone.

For it was fitting that he, for whom and through whom all things exist, in bringing many children to glory, should make the leader to their salvation perfect through suffering. He who consecrates and those who are being consecrated all have one origin. Therefore, he is not ashamed to call them "brothers" saying:

> *I will proclaim your name to my brethren,*
> *in the midst of the assembly I will praise you.*

The word of the Lord.

Responsorial Psalm

Ps 8:2ab and 5, 6–7, 8–9

R. You have given your Son rule over the works of your hands

O LORD, our Lord,
  how glorious is your name over all the earth!
What is man that you should be mindful of him,
  or the son of man that you should care for him?

R. You have given your Son rule over the works of your hands

You have made him little less than the angels,
  and crowned him with glory and honor.

You have given him rule over the works of your hands,
  putting all things under his feet.

> **R. You have given your Son rule over the works of
>   your hands**

All sheep and oxen,
  yes, and the beasts of the field,
The birds of the air, the fishes of the sea,
  and whatever swims the paths of the seas.

> **R. You have given your Son rule over the works of
>   your hands.**

Alleluia Verse *and* **Gospel,** *p. 245.*

Year II

FIRST READING
1 Sm 1:9–20

*The L*ORD* God remembered Hannah, and she gave birth to Samuel.*

A reading from the first Book of Samuel

Hannah rose after a meal at Shiloh, and presented herself before
the LORD; at the time, Eli the priest was sitting on a chair near
the doorpost of the LORD's temple. In her bitterness she prayed
to the LORD, weeping copiously, and she made a vow, promising: "O LORD of hosts, if you look with pity on the misery of
your handmaid, if you remember me and do not forget me, if
you give your handmaid a male child, I will give him to the
LORD for as long as he lives; neither wine nor liquor shall he
drink, and no razor shall ever touch his head." As she remained
long at prayer before the LORD, Eli watched her mouth, for
Hannah was praying silently; though her lips were moving,
her voice could not be heard. Eli, thinking her drunk, said to
her, "How long will you make a drunken show of yourself?

Sober up from your wine!" "It isn't that, my lord," Hannah answered. "I am an unhappy woman. I have had neither wine nor liquor; I was only pouring out my troubles to the LORD. Do not think your handmaid a ne'er-do-well; my prayer has been prompted by my deep sorrow and misery." Eli said, "Go in peace, and may the God of Israel grant you what you have asked of him." She replied, "Think kindly of your maidservant," and left. She went to her quarters, ate and drank with her husband, and no longer appeared downcast. Early the next morning they worshiped before the LORD, and then returned to their home in Ramah.

When Elkanah had relations with his wife Hannah, the LORD remembered her. She conceived, and at the end of her term bore a son whom she called Samuel, since she had asked the LORD for him.

The word of the Lord.

Responsorial Psalm

1 Sm 2:1, 4–5, 6–7, 8abcd

R. My heart exults in the Lord, my Savior.

"My heart exults in the LORD,
  my horn is exalted in my God.
I have swallowed up my enemies;
  I rejoice in my victory."

R. My heart exults in the Lord, my Savior.

"The bows of the mighty are broken,
  while the tottering gird on strength.
The well-fed hire themselves out for bread,
  while the hungry batten on spoil.
The barren wife bears seven sons,
  while the mother of many languishes."

R. My heart exults in the Lord, my Savior.

"The LORD puts to death and gives life;
  he casts down to the nether world;
  he raises up again.
The LORD makes poor and makes rich;
  he humbles, he also exalts."

R. My heart exults in the Lord, my Savior.

"He raises the needy from the dust;
  from the dung heap he lifts up the poor,
To seat them with nobles
  and make a glorious throne their heritage."

R. My heart exults in the Lord, my Savior.

> **Alleluia, alleluia**   See 1 Thes 2:13
> Receive the word of God, not as the word of men,
> but as it truly is, the word of God.
> **Alleluia, alleluia**

Years I and II

GOSPEL   Mk 1:21–28

Jesus taught them as one having authority.

A reading from the holy Gospel according to Mark

Jesus came to Capernaum with his followers, and on the sabbath
he entered the synagogue and taught. The people were astonished at his teaching, for he taught them as one having authority
and not as the scribes. In their synagogue was a man with an
unclean spirit; he cried out, "What have you to do with us,
Jesus of Nazareth? Have you come to destroy us? I know who
you are—the Holy One of God!" Jesus rebuked him and said,
"Quiet! Come out of him!" The unclean spirit convulsed him
and with a loud cry came out of him. All were amazed and
asked one another, "What is this? A new teaching with authority.
He commands even the unclean spirits and they obey him."

His fame spread everywhere throughout the whole region of Galilee.

The Gospel of the Lord.

Liturgy of the Eucharist, *p. 897;* **Prayer over the Gifts,** *p. 235.*

Wednesday

Antiphons and Prayers, *p. 235;* **Liturgy of the Word** *for Year I (odd years) follows; Year II (even years), p. 248.*

TODAY'S LIVING WORD

Most of Mark's first chapter describes a day in the ministry of Jesus. Throughout that day Jesus repeatedly acts so as to "destroy the one who has the power of death, that is, the devil," as Hebrews puts it, by casting out demons and curing the sick. The next morning finds him rising early and going off to a lonely place to pray.

Mark's Gospel shows Jesus at prayer on three separate occasions. Each time his ministry is being misunderstood. Clearly, Mark wants us to recognize that Jesus was tempted, as we may be at times, by the siren song of popular demand. "Everyone is looking for you!" says Peter. Jesus prayed at those times. Like Samuel, he turned an attentive ear to God's word, and in communion with God he found his true purpose. The Letter to the Hebrews places Psalm 40 on the lips of Jesus: "Behold, I come to do your will, O God."

Year I

FIRST READING   Heb 2:14–18

*He had to become like his brothers and sisters
in every way, that he might be merciful.*

A reading from the Letter to the Hebrews

Since the children share in blood and Flesh, Jesus likewise shared in them, that through death he might destroy the one who has the power of death, that is, the Devil, and free those who through fear of death had been subject to slavery all their life. Surely he did not help angels but rather the descendants of Abraham; therefore, he had to become like his brothers and sisters in every way, that he might be a merciful and faithful high priest before God to expiate the sins of the people. Because he himself was tested through what he suffered, he is able to help those who are being tested.

The word of the Lord.

Responsorial Psalm

Ps 105:1–2, 3–4, 6–7, 8–9

R. The Lord remembers his covenant for ever.

Give thanks to the LORD, invoke his name;
  make known among the nations his deeds.
Sing to him, sing his praise,
  proclaim all his wondrous deeds.

R. The Lord remembers his covenant for ever.

Glory in his holy name;
  rejoice, O hearts that seek the LORD!
Look to the LORD in his strength;
  seek to serve him constantly.

R. The Lord remembers his covenant for ever.

You descendants of Abraham, his servants,
  sons of Jacob, his chosen ones!
He, the LORD, is our God;
  throughout the earth his judgments prevail.

R. The Lord remembers his covenant for ever.

He remembers forever his covenant
  which he made binding for a thousand generations—
Which he entered into with Abraham
  and by his oath to Isaac.

R. The Lord remembers his covenant for ever.

Or: **R. Alleluia.**

Alleluia Verse *and* **Gospel,** *p. 249f.*

Year II

FIRST READING   1 Sm 3:1–10, 19–20

Speak, O LORD, for your servant is listening.

A reading from the first Book of Samuel

During the time young Samuel was minister to the LORD under Eli, a revelation of the LORD was uncommon and vision infrequent. One day Eli was asleep in his usual place. His eyes had lately grown so weak that he could not see. The lamp of God was not yet extinguished, and Samuel was sleeping in the temple of the LORD where the ark of God was. The LORD called to Samuel, who answered, "Here I am."

Samuel ran to Eli and said, "Here I am. You called me." "I did not call you," Eli said. "Go back to sleep." So he went back to sleep. Again the LORD called Samuel, who rose and went to Eli. "Here I am," he said. "You called me." But Eli answered, "I did not call you, my son. Go back to sleep." At that time Samuel was not familiar with the LORD, because the LORD had not revealed anything to him as yet. The LORD called Samuel again, for the third time. Getting up and going to Eli, he said, "Here I am. You called me." Then Eli understood that the LORD was calling the youth. So Eli said to Samuel, "Go to sleep, and if you are called, reply, 'Speak, LORD, for your servant is listening.'" When Samuel went to sleep in his place, the LORD came and revealed his presence, calling out as before, "Samuel, Samuel!" Samuel answered, "Speak, for your servant is listening."

Samuel grew up, and the LORD was with him, not permitting any word of his to be without effect. Thus all Israel from Dan to Beersheba came to know that Samuel was an accredited prophet of the LORD.

The word of the Lord.

Responsorial Psalm

Ps 40:2 and 5, 7–8a, 8b–9, 10

R. **Here am I, Lord; I come to do your will.**

I have waited, waited for the LORD,
  and he stooped toward me and heard my cry.
Blessed the man who makes the LORD his trust;
  who turns not to idolatry
  or to those who stray after falsehood.

R. **Here am I, Lord; I come to do your will.**

Sacrifice or oblation you wished not,
  but ears open to obedience you gave me.
Burnt offerings or sin-offerings you sought not;
  then said I, "Behold I come."

R. **Here am I, Lord; I come to do your will.**

"In the written scroll it is prescribed for me.
To do your will, O my God, is my delight,
  and your law is within my heart!"

R. **Here am I, Lord; I come to do your will.**

I announced your justice in the vast assembly;
  I did not restrain my lips, as you, O LORD, know.

R. **Here am I, Lord; I come to do your will.**

Alleluia, alleluia   Jn 10:27
My sheep hear my voice, says the Lord.
I know them, and they follow me.
Alleluia, alleluia

Years I and II

GOSPEL   Mk 1:29–39

Jesus cured many who were sick with various diseases.

A reading from the holy Gospel according to Mark

On leaving the synagogue Jesus entered the house of Simon and Andrew with James and John. Simon's mother-in-law lay sick with a fever. They immediately told him about her. He approached, grasped her hand, and helped her up. Then the fever left her and she waited on them.

When it was evening, after sunset, they brought to him all who were ill or possessed by demons. The whole town was gathered at the door. He cured many who were sick with various diseases, and he drove out many demons, not permitting them to speak because they knew him.

Rising very early before dawn, he left and went off to a deserted place, where he prayed. Simon and those who were with him pursued him and on finding him said, "Everyone is looking for you." He told them, "Let us go on to the nearby villages that I may preach there also. For this purpose have I come." So he went into their synagogues, preaching and driving out demons throughout the whole of Galilee.

The Gospel of the Lord.

Liturgy of the Eucharist, *p. 897;* **Prayer over the Gifts,** *p. 235.*

Thursday

Antiphons and Prayers, *p. 235;* **Liturgy of the Word** *for Year I (odd years) follows; Year II (even years), p. 253.*

Today's Living Word

The episode that concludes Mark's first chapter is riddled with textual problems and scholars disagree on how to resolve them. To name a few: some manuscripts say that Jesus was moved with anger rather than with pity, and the change of tone in the story is puzzling, as Jesus sends the man away with a rebuke.

The two readings that the Church has attached to this one both shed light on one aspect of this text. The selection from the Book of Samuel demonstrates divine anger: the disastrous defeat of Israel is punishment for the wickedness of Eli's house. The passage from the Letter to the Hebrews sternly warns: "Take care…that none of you may have an evil and unfaithful heart." However, the Gospel makes indisputably clear that Jesus has the will and the power to save, whether he is moved by human pity or by divine anger. Because of that, for us it is always "today"—always the day of salvation—if we but hear his voice.

Year I

FIRST READING

Heb 3:7–14

Encourage yourselves daily while it is still "today."

A reading from the Letter to the Hebrews

The Holy Spirit says:

Oh, that today you would hear his voice,
   "Harden not your hearts as at the rebellion
   in the day of testing in the desert,
where your ancestors tested and tried me
   and saw my works for forty years.
Because of this I was provoked with that generation
   and I said, 'They have always been of erring heart,
   and they do not know my ways.'

> *As I swore in my wrath,*
>   *'They shall not enter into my rest.'"*

Take care, brothers and sisters, that none of you may have an evil and unfaithful heart, so as to forsake the living God. Encourage yourselves daily while it is still "today," so that none of you may grow hardened by the deceit of sin. We have become partners of Christ if only we hold the beginning of the reality firm until the end.

The word of the Lord.

Responsial Psalm

Ps 95:6–7c, 8–9, 10–11

R. If today you hear his voice, harden not your hearts.

Come, let us bow down in worship;
  let us kneel before the LORD who made us.
For he is our God,
  and we are the people he shepherds, the flock he guides.

R. If today you hear his voice, harden not your hearts.

Oh, that today you would hear his voice:
  "Harden not your hearts as at Meribah,
  as in the day of Massah in the desert,
Where your fathers tempted me;
  they tested me though they had seen my works."

R. If today you hear his voice, harden not your hearts.

Forty years I was wearied of that generation;
  I said: "This people's heart goes astray,
  they do not know my ways."
Therefore I swore in my anger:
  "They shall never enter my rest."

R. If today you hear his voice, harden not your hearts.

Alleluia Verse *and* **Gospel,** *p. 254.*

Year II

FIRST READING

1 Sm 4:1–11

Israel was defeated and the ark of God was captured.

A reading from the first Book of Samuel

The Philistines gathered for an attack on Israel. Israel went out to engage them in battle and camped at Ebenezer, while the Philistines camped at Aphek. The Philistines then drew up in battle formation against Israel. After a fierce struggle Israel was defeated by the Philistines, who slew about four thousand men on the battlefield. When the troops retired to the camp, the elders of Israel said, "Why has the LORD permitted us to be defeated today by the Philistines? Let us fetch the ark of the LORD from Shiloh that it may go into battle among us and save us from the grasp of our enemies."

So the people sent to Shiloh and brought from there the ark of the LORD of hosts, who is enthroned upon the cherubim. The two sons of Eli, Hophni and Phinehas, were with the ark of God. When the ark of the LORD arrived in the camp, all Israel shouted so loudly that the earth resounded. The Philistines, hearing the noise of shouting, asked, "What can this loud shouting in the camp of the Hebrews mean?" On learning that the ark of the LORD had come into the camp, the Philistines were frightened. They said, "Gods have come to their camp." They said also, "Woe to us! This has never happened before. Woe to us! Who can deliver us from the power of these mighty gods? These are the gods that struck the Egyptians with various plagues and with pestilence. Take courage and be manly, Philistines; otherwise you will become slaves to the Hebrews, as they were your slaves. So fight manfully!" The Philistines fought and Israel was defeated; every man fled to his own tent. It was a disastrous defeat, in which Israel lost thirty thousand foot soldiers. The ark of God was captured, and Eli's two sons, Hophni and Phinehas, were among the dead.

The word of the Lord.

Responsorial Psalm
Ps 44:10–11, 14–15, 24–25

R. Redeem us, Lord, because of your mercy.

Yet now you have cast us off and put us in disgrace,
  and you go not forth with our armies.
You have let us be driven back by our foes;
  those who hated us plundered us at will.

R. Redeem us, Lord, because of your mercy.

You made us the reproach of our neighbors,
  the mockery and the scorn of those around us.
You made us a byword among the nations,
  a laughingstock among the peoples.

R. Redeem us, Lord, because of your mercy.

Why do you hide your face,
  forgetting our woe and our oppression?
For our souls are bowed down to the dust,
  our bodies are pressed to the earth.

R. Redeem us, Lord, because of your mercy.

Alleluia, alleluia   See Mt 4:23
Jesus preached the Gospel of the Kingdom
and cured every disease among the people.
Alleluia, alleluia

Years I and II

GOSPEL
Mk 1:40–45

The leprosy left him, and he was made clean.

A reading from the holy Gospel according to Mark

A leper came to him and kneeling down begged him and said, "If you wish, you can make me clean." Moved with pity, he stretched out his hand, touched the leper, and said to him, "I do will it. Be made clean." The leprosy left him immediately, and he was made clean. Then, warning him sternly, he dismissed him at once. Then he said to him, "See that you tell no one anything, but go, show yourself to the priest and offer for your cleansing what Moses prescribed; that will be proof for them." The man went away and began to publicize the whole matter. He spread the report abroad so that it was impossible for Jesus to enter a town openly. He remained outside in deserted places, and people kept coming to him from everywhere.

The Gospel of the Lord.

Liturgy of the Eucharist, *p. 897;* **Prayer over the Gifts,** *p. 235.*

Friday

Antiphons and Prayers, *p. 235;* **Liturgy of the Word** *for Year I (odd years) follows; Year II (even years), p. 257.*

TODAY'S LIVING WORD

The story of Jesus healing the paralytic is sometimes misread, casting Jews and Judaism in a negative light. Parts of the Letter to the Hebrews may be read this way as well, so let the reader beware.

The scribes in Mark's story objected to Jesus' words, "your sins are forgiven," but not because forgiveness of sins was foreign to Judaism. Judaism is a religion of forgiveness. The very words that Jesus spoke were the words the priests in the temple would say to any sinner who brought a sin-offering. What the scribes found blasphemous was Jesus' declaring sins forgiven outside the temple ritual that God had provided for the forgiveness of sins. Just as in the days of Samuel, when the establishment of the kingship had seemed to some like a usurping of God's rule, so it was at the time of Jesus. To some people, the authority Jesus claimed seemed to usurp the role God had given to the priests of the temple. But God is not bound by roles or rituals. Where there is faith, like that of the friends of the paralytic, miracles happen and they fill us with praise.

Year I

FIRST READING

Heb 4:1–5, 11

Let us strive to enter into that rest.

A reading from the Letter to the Hebrews

Let us be on our guard while the promise of entering into his rest remains, that none of you seem to have failed. For in fact we have received the Good News just as our ancestors did. But the word that they heard did not profit them, for they were not united in faith with those who listened. For we who believed enter into that rest, just as he has said:

> *As I swore in my wrath,*
> *"They shall not enter into my rest,"*

and yet his works were accomplished at the foundation of the world. For he has spoken somewhere about the seventh day in this manner, *And God rested on the seventh day from all his works;* and again, in the previously mentioned place, *They shall not enter into my rest.*

Therefore, let us strive to enter into that rest, so that no one may fall after the same example of disobedience.

The word of the Lord.

Responsorial Psalm

Ps 78:3 and 4bc, 6c–7, 8

R. **Do not forget the works of the Lord!**

What we have heard and know,
  and what our fathers have declared to us,
  we will declare to the generation to come
The glorious deeds of the Lord and his strength.

> **R. Do not forget the works of the Lord!**

That they too may rise and declare to their sons
  that they should put their hope in God,
And not forget the deeds of God
  but keep his commands.

> **R. Do not forget the works of the Lord!**

And not be like their fathers,
  a generation wayward and rebellious,
A generation that kept not its heart steadfast
  nor its spirit faithful toward God.

> **R. Do not forget the works of the Lord!**

Alleluia Verse *and* **Gospel,** *p. 259.*

Year II

FIRST READING   1 Sm 8:4–7, 10–22a

*You will complain against the king whom you have chosen,
    but on that day the Lord will not answer you.*

A reading from the first Book of Samuel

All the elders of Israel came in a body to Samuel at Ramah
and said to him, "Now that you are old, and your sons do not
follow your example, appoint a king over us, as other nations
have, to judge us."

Samuel was displeased when they asked for a king to judge
them. He prayed to the Lord, however, who said in answer:
"Grant the people's every request. It is not you they reject,
they are rejecting me as their king."

Samuel delivered the message of the LORD in full to those who were asking him for a king. He told them: "The rights of the king who will rule you will be as follows: He will take your sons and assign them to his chariots and horses, and they will run before his chariot. He will also appoint from among them his commanders of groups of a thousand and of a hundred soldiers. He will set them to do his plowing and his harvesting, and to make his implements of war and the equipment of his chariots. He will use your daughters as ointment makers, as cooks, and as bakers. He will take the best of your fields, vineyards, and olive groves, and give them to his officials. He will tithe your crops and your vineyards, and give the revenue to his eunuchs and his slaves. He will take your male and female servants, as well as your best oxen and your asses, and use them to do his work. He will tithe your flocks and you yourselves will become his slaves. When this takes place, you will complain against the king whom you have chosen, but on that day the LORD will not answer you."

The people, however, refused to listen to Samuel's warning and said, "Not so! There must be a king over us. We too must be like other nations, with a king to rule us and to lead us in warfare and fight our battles." When Samuel had listened to all the people had to say, he repeated it to the LORD, who then said to him, "Grant their request and appoint a king to rule them."

The word of the Lord.

Responsorial Psalm

Ps 89:16–17, 18–19

R. For ever I will sing the goodness of the Lord.

Blessed the people who know the joyful shout;

in the light of your countenance, O LORD, they walk.
At your name they rejoice all the day,
  and through your justice they are exalted.

R. For ever I will sing the goodness of the Lord.

For you are the splendor of their strength,
  and by your favor our horn is exalted.
For to the LORD belongs our shield,
  and to the Holy One of Israel, our King.

R. For ever I will sing the goodness of the Lord.

Alleluia, alleluia Lk 7:16
A great prophet has arisen in our midst
and God has visited his people.
Alleluia, alleluia

Years I and II

GOSPEL   Mk 2:1–12

The Son of Man has authority to forgive sins on earth.

A reading from the holy Gospel according to Mark

When Jesus returned to Capernaum after some days, it became known that he was at home. Many gathered together so that there was no longer room for them, not even around the door, and he preached the word to them. They came bringing to him a paralytic carried by four men. Unable to get near Jesus because of the crowd, they opened up the roof above him. After they had broken through, they let down the mat on which the paralytic was lying. When Jesus saw their faith, he said to him, "Child, your sins are forgiven." Now some of the scribes were sitting there asking themselves, "Why does this man speak that way? He is blaspheming. Who but God alone can forgive sins?" Jesus immediately knew in his mind what they were thinking to themselves, so he said, "Why are you thinking such things in your hearts? Which is easier, to say to the paralytic, 'Your sins are forgiven,' or to say, 'Rise, pick up your mat and walk'? But that you may know that the Son of Man has authority to forgive sins on earth"—he said to the paralytic, "I say to you, rise, pick up your mat, and go home." He rose, picked up his mat at once, and went away in the sight of everyone. They were all astounded and glorified God, saying, "We have never seen anything like this."

The Gospel of the Lord.

Liturgy of the Eucharist, *p. 897;* **Prayer over the Gifts,** *p. 235.*

Saturday

Antiphons and Prayers, *p. 235;* **Liturgy of the Word** *for Year I (odd years) follows; Year II (even years), p. 262.*

TODAY'S LIVING WORD

In order to understand why Jesus' table-fellowship so often drew the criticism of the Pharisees, it is necessary to know something about the Pharisees and something about Jesus. The Pharisees were an association of laymen whose aim was to extend the holiness of the temple into everyday life. One way they did this was by insisting in their daily meals on a degree of purity that, in fact, was required only for the temple. For some Pharisees this strict observance worked as a boundary, separating them from other Jews whom they judged to be "sinners." Although he agreed with the Pharisees on many points, Jesus' mission was to restore the wholeness of Israel. So by eating with tax collectors and sinners, he challenged one of the many boundaries that divided his people.

God's grace cannot be measured, managed, or monopolized, but many good people try to do so, counting themselves among God's chosen. The tragic story of Saul is a case in point. As the passage from Hebrews suggests, the surest way to guard against self-righteousness is to submit oneself regularly to the penetrating judgment of God's word.

Year I

FIRST READING

Heb 4:12–16

Let us confidently approach the throne of grace.

A reading from the Letter to the Hebrews

The word of God is living and effective, sharper than any two-edged sword, penetrating even between soul and spirit, joints and marrow, and able to discern reflections and thoughts of the heart. No creature is concealed from him, but everything is naked and exposed to the eyes of him to whom we must render an account.

Since we have a great high priest who has passed through the heavens, Jesus, the Son of God, let us hold fast to our confession. For we do not have a high priest who is unable to sympathize with our weaknesses, but one who has similarly been tested in every way, yet without sin. So let us confidently approach the throne of grace to receive mercy and to find grace for timely help.

The word of the Lord.

Responsorial Psalm

Ps 19:8, 9, 10, 15

R. **Your words, Lord, are Spirit and life.**

The law of the LORD is perfect,
   refreshing the soul;
The decree of the LORD is trustworthy,
   giving wisdom to the simple.

R. **Your words, Lord, are Spirit and life.**

The precepts of the LORD are right,
  rejoicing the heart;
The command of the LORD is clear,
  enlightening the eye.

   R. Your words, Lord, are Spirit and life.

The fear of the LORD is pure,
  enduring forever;
The ordinances of the LORD are true,
  all of them just.

   R. Your words, Lord, are Spirit and life.

Let the words of my mouth and the thought of my heart
  find favor before you,
  O LORD, my rock and my redeemer.

   R. Your words, Lord, are Spirit and life.

   Alleluia Verse *and* **Gospel,** *p. 264.*

Year II

FIRST READING   1 Sm 9:1–4, 17–19; 10:1

This is the man of whom the LORD God spoke,
Saul who will rule his people.

A reading from the first Book of Samuel

There was a stalwart man from Benjamin named Kish, who was
the son of Abiel, son of Zeror, son of Becorath, son of Aphiah, a
Benjaminite. He had a son named Saul, who was a handsome
young man. There was no other child of Israel more handsome
than Saul; he stood head and shoulders above the people.

    Now the asses of Saul's father, Kish, had wandered off. Kish
said to his son Saul, "Take one of the servants with you and go
out and hunt for the asses." Accordingly they went through
the hill country of Ephraim, and through the land of Shalishah.

Not finding them there, they continued through the land of Shaalim without success. They also went through the land of Benjamin, but they failed to find the animals.

When Samuel caught sight of Saul, the LORD assured him, "This is the man of whom I told you; he is to govern my people."

Saul met Samuel in the gateway and said, "Please tell me where the seer lives." Samuel answered Saul: "I am the seer. Go up ahead of me to the high place and eat with me today. In the morning, before dismissing you, I will tell you whatever you wish."

Then, from a flask he had with him, Samuel poured oil on Saul's head; he also kissed him, saying: "The LORD anoints you commander over his heritage. You are to govern the LORD's people Israel, and to save them from the grasp of their enemies roundabout.

"This will be the sign for you that the LORD has anointed you commander over his heritage."

The word of the Lord.

Responsorial Psalm

Ps 21:2–3, 4–5, 6–7

R. Lord, in your strength the king is glad.

O LORD, in your strength the king is glad;
  in your victory how greatly he rejoices!
You have granted him his heart's desire;
  you refused not the wish of his lips.

R. Lord, in your strength the king is glad.

For you welcomed him with goodly blessings,
  you placed on his head a crown of pure gold.
He asked life of you: you gave him
  length of days forever and ever.

R. Lord, in your strength the king is glad.

Great is his glory in your victory;
  majesty and splendor you conferred upon him.
For you made him a blessing forever;
  you gladdened him with the joy of your face.

R. Lord, in your strength the king is glad.

> **Alleluia, alleluia**   Lk 4:18
> The Lord sent me to bring glad tidings to the poor
> and to proclaim liberty to captives.
> **Alleluia, alleluia**

Years I and II

GOSPEL   Mk 2:13–17

I did not come to call the righteous but sinners.

A reading from the holy Gospel according to Mark

Jesus went out along the sea. All the crowd came to him and
he taught them. As he passed by, he saw Levi, son of Alphaeus,
sitting at the customs post. Jesus said to him, "Follow me."
And he got up and followed Jesus. While he was at table in his
house, many tax collectors and sinners sat with Jesus and his
disciples; for there were many who followed him. Some scribes
who were Pharisees saw that Jesus was eating with sinners
and tax collectors and said to his disciples, "Why does he eat
with tax collectors and sinners?" Jesus heard this and said to
them, "Those who are well do not need a physician, but the
sick do. I did not come to call the righteous but sinners."

The Gospel of the Lord.

Liturgy of the Eucharist, *p. 897;* **Prayer over the Gifts,** *p. 235.*

SECOND WEEK IN ORDINARY TIME

The **Antiphons and Prayers** *may be the following, or may be chosen from any of the other 33 weeks in Ordinary Time (refer to Liturgical Calendar, pp. 26–41).*

The **Liturgy of the Word** *varies: for Monday, see p. 267; Tuesday, p. 271; Wednesday, p. 276; Thursday, p. 281; Friday, p. 286; Saturday, p. 292.*

Entrance Antiphon

May all the earth give you worship and praise, and break into song to your name, O God, Most High.   (Ps 66:4)

Opening Prayer

Let us pray
  [to our Father for the gift of peace]
    Pause for silent prayer.

Father of heaven and earth,
hear our prayers,
and show us the way to peace in the world.

Grant this through our Lord Jesus Christ, your Son,
who lives and reigns with you and the Holy Spirit,
one God, for ever and ever.

Alternative Opening Prayer

Let us pray
  [for the gift of peace]
    Pause for silent prayer.

Almighty and ever-present Father,
your watchful care reaches from end to end
and orders all things in such power
that even the tensions and the tragedies of sin
cannot frustrate your loving plans.

Help us to embrace your will,
give us the strength to follow your call,
so that your truth may live in our hearts
and reflect peace to those who believe in your love.

We ask this in the name of Jesus the Lord.

Prayer over the Gifts

Pray, brethren...

Father,
may we celebrate the eucharist
with reverence and love,
for when we proclaim the death of the Lord
you continue the work of his redemption,
who is Lord for ever and ever.

Preface of Weekdays in Ordinary Time I–VI, *pp. 948–950.*

Communion Antiphon

**The Lord has prepared a feast for me: given wine in plenty for
me to drink.** (Ps 23:5)

Or:

We know and believe in God's love for us. (1 Jn 4:16)

Prayer after Communion

Let us pray.

Pause for silent prayer, if this has not preceded.

Lord,
you have nourished us with bread from heaven.
Fill us with your Spirit,
and make us one in peace and love.
We ask this through Christ our Lord.

Monday

Antiphons and Prayers, *p. 265;* **Liturgy of the Word** *for Year I (odd years) follows; Year II (even years), p. 269.*

TODAY'S LIVING WORD

Today's readings mine the Hebrew Scriptures for ways of talking about Jesus. The author of the Letter to the Hebrews depicts Jesus in the language of the temple as a high priest "according to the order of Melchizedek." New Testament writers often quote Psalm 110, which follows the reading; it places Jesus in the royal line of David whose scepter "the Lord will extend from Zion." The selection from Mark's Gospel identifies Jesus as the bridegroom, a startling designation. In the Hebrew Scriptures and in other Jewish writings, the image of the bridegroom never refers to the Messiah, but only to God.

The presence of the bridegroom in this Gospel is another way of signifying that the reign of God was present in the ministry of Jesus. That powerful presence, the startling new thing that God was doing in and through Jesus, then as now demanded a brand new response. The old forms, the old ways would not do. New wine must have new skins.

Year I

FIRST READING

Heb 5:1–10

Son though he was, he learned obedience from what he suffered.

A reading from the Letter to the Hebrews

Brothers and sisters:

Every high priest is taken from among men and made their representative before God, to offer gifts and sacrifices for sins. He is able to deal patiently with the ignorant and erring, for he himself is beset by weakness and so, for this reason, must make sin offerings for himself as well as for the people. No one takes this honor upon himself but only when called by God, just as Aaron was. In the same way, it was not Christ who glorified himself in becoming high priest, but rather the one who said to him:

>   *You are my Son:*
>   *this day I have begotten you;*

just as he says in another place,

>   *You are a priest forever*
>   *according to the order of Melchizedek.*

In the days when he was in the Flesh, he offered prayers and supplications with loud cries and tears to the one who was able to save him from death, and he was heard because of his reverence. Son though he was, he learned obedience from what he suffered; and when he was made perfect, he became the source of eternal salvation for all who obey him.

The word of the Lord.

Responsorial Psalm   Ps 110:1, 2, 3, 4

R. You are a priest for ever, in the line of Melchizedek.

The LORD said to my Lord: "Sit at my right hand
  till I make your enemies your footstool."

R. You are a priest for ever, in the line of Melchizedek.

The scepter of your power the LORD will stretch forth from Zion:
  "Rule in the midst of your enemies."

R. You are a priest for ever, in the line of Melchizedek.

"Yours is princely power in the day of your birth, in holy splendor;
  before the daystar, like the dew, I have begotten you."

R. You are a priest for ever, in the line of Melchizedek.

The Lord has sworn, and he will not repent:
"You are a priest forever, according to the order of Melchizedek."

R. You are a priest for ever, in the line of Melchizedek.

Alleluia Verse *and* **Gospel,** *p. 270.*

Year II

FIRST READING   1 Sm 15:16–23

Obedience is better than sacrifice.
Because you have rejected the command of the Lord,
he, too, has rejected you as ruler.

A reading from the first Book of Samuel

Samuel said to Saul: "Stop! Let me tell you what the Lord said to me last night." Saul replied, "Speak!" Samuel then said: "Though little in your own esteem, are you not leader of the tribes of Israel? The Lord anointed you king of Israel and sent you on a mission, saying, 'Go and put the sinful Amalekites under a ban of destruction. Fight against them until you have exterminated them.' Why then have you disobeyed the Lord? You have pounced on the spoil, thus displeasing the Lord." Saul answered Samuel: "I did indeed obey the Lord and fulfill the mission on which the Lord sent me. I have brought back Agag, and I have destroyed Amalek under the ban. But from the spoil the men took sheep and oxen, the best of what had been banned, to sacrifice to the Lord their God in Gilgal." But Samuel said:

"Does the Lord so delight in burnt offerings and sacrifices
    as in obedience to the command of the Lord?
Obedience is better than sacrifice,
    and submission than the fat of rams.

For a sin like divination is rebellion,
and presumption is the crime of idolatry.
Because you have rejected the command of the LORD,
he, too, has rejected you as ruler."

The word of the Lord.

Responsorial Psalm
Ps 50:8–9, 16bc–17, 21 and 23

R. To the upright I will show the saving power of God.

"Not for your sacrifices do I rebuke you,
for your burnt offerings are before me always.
I take from your house no bullock,
no goats out of your fold."

R. To the upright I will show the saving power of God.

"Why do you recite my statutes,
and profess my covenant with your mouth,
Though you hate discipline
and cast my words behind you?"

R. To the upright I will show the saving power of God.

"When you do these things, shall I be deaf to it?
Or do you think that I am like yourself?
I will correct you by drawing them up before your eyes.
He that offers praise as a sacrifice glorifies me;
and to him that goes the right way I will show the salvation of God."

R. To the upright I will show the saving power of God.

Alleluia, alleluia   Heb 4:12
The word of God is living and effective,
able to discern reflections and thoughts of the heart.
Alleluia, alleluia

Years I and II

GOSPEL
Mk 2:18–22

The bridegroom is with them.

A reading from the holy Gospel according to Mark

The disciples of John and of the Pharisees were accustomed to fast. People came to Jesus and objected, "Why do the disciples of John and the disciples of the Pharisees fast, but your disciples do not fast?" Jesus answered them, "Can the wedding guests fast while the bridegroom is with them? As long as they have the bridegroom with them they cannot fast. But the days will come when the bridegroom is taken away from them, and then they will fast on that day. No one sews a piece of unshrunken cloth on an old cloak. If he does, its fullness pulls away, the new from the old, and the tear gets worse. Likewise, no one pours new wine into old wineskins. Otherwise, the wine will burst the skins, and both the wine and the skins are ruined. Rather, new wine is poured into fresh wineskins."

The Gospel of the Lord.

Liturgy of the Eucharist, *p. 897;* **Prayer over the Gifts,** *p. 266.*

Tuesday

Antiphons and Prayers, *p. 265;* **Liturgy of the Word** *for Year I (odd years) follows; Year II (even years), p. 273.*

TODAY'S LIVING WORD

In fairness to the Pharisees and the religious tradition they represent, it should be noted that the saying of Jesus—"The sabbath was made for man, not man for the sabbath"—has parallels in the writings of the rabbis. The Pharisees themselves subordinated sabbath law to human need. As Mark tells it, the purpose of this story is not to contrast Jesus and the Pharisees, but to compare him to David. Jesus responds to the Pharisees' protests by citing an episode from the story of David in 1 Samuel 21. There David disregarded the sanctity of the tabernacle in order to feed his men. Mark implies that Jesus enjoyed the same freedom David did.

John Shea, among others, has observed that the freedom of David and Jesus was rooted in their sense that God trusted them.* The same may be said of Abraham. For us who are their heirs, the creative fidelity of God on their behalf is, as Hebrews says, a firm anchor, a sure hope. "The Lord will remember his covenant forever."

* *Stories of God*, 6th ed. (Chicago: Thomas More Press, 1978), p. 133.

Year I

FIRST READING   Heb 6:10–20

This hope we have as an anchor sure and firm.

A reading from the Letter to the Hebrews

Brothers and sisters:

God is not unjust so as to overlook your work and the love you have demonstrated for his name by having served and continuing to serve the holy ones. We earnestly desire each of you to demonstrate the same eagerness for the fulfillment of hope until the end, so that you may not become sluggish, but imitators of those who, through faith and patience, are inheriting the promises.

When God made the promise to Abraham, since he had no one greater by whom to swear, *he swore by himself*, and said, *I will indeed bless you and multiply* you. And so, after patient waiting, Abraham obtained the promise. Now, men swear by someone greater than themselves; for them an oath serves as a guarantee and puts an end to all argument. So when God wanted to give the heirs of his promise an even clearer demonstration of the immutability of his purpose, he intervened with an oath, so that by two immutable things, in which it was impossible for God to lie, we who have taken refuge might be strongly encouraged to hold fast to the hope that lies before us. This we have as an anchor of the soul, sure and firm, which reaches into the interior behind the veil, where Jesus has entered on our behalf as forerunner, becoming high priest forever according to the order of Melchizedek.

The word of the Lord.

Responsorial Psalm

Ps 111:1–2, 4 – 5, 9 and 10c

R. The Lord will remember his covenant for ever.

I will give thanks to the LORD with all my heart
  in the company and assembly of the just.
Great are the works of the LORD,
  exquisite in all their delights.

R. The Lord will remember his covenant for ever.

He has won renown for his wondrous deeds;
  gracious and merciful is the LORD.
He has given food to those who fear him;
  he will forever be mindful of his covenant.

R. The Lord will remember his covenant for ever.

He has sent deliverance to his people;
  he has ratified his covenant forever;
holy and awesome is his name.
His praise endures forever.

R. The Lord will remember his covenant for ever.

Or: **R. Alleluia.**

Alleluia Verse *and* **Gospel,** *p. 275f.*

Year II

FIRST READING

1 Sm 16:1–13

*Samuel anointed David in the presence of his brothers,
and the Spirit of the LORD God rushed upon him.*

A reading from the first Book of Samuel

The LORD said to Samuel: "How long will you grieve for Saul, whom I have rejected as king of Israel? Fill your horn with oil, and be on your way. I am sending you to Jesse of Bethlehem, for I have chosen my king from among his sons." But Samuel replied: "How can I go? Saul will hear of it and kill me." To this the LORD answered: "Take a heifer along and say, 'I have come to sacrifice to the LORD.' Invite Jesse to the sacrifice, and I myself will tell you what to do; you are to anoint for me the one I point out to you."

Samuel did as the LORD had commanded him. When he entered Bethlehem, the elders of the city came trembling to meet him and inquired, "Is your visit peaceful, O seer?" He replied: "Yes! I have come to sacrifice to the LORD. So cleanse yourselves and join me today for the banquet." He also had Jesse and his sons cleanse themselves and invited them to the sacrifice. As they came, he looked at Eliab and thought, "Surely the LORD's anointed is here before him." But the LORD said to Samuel: "Do not judge from his appearance or from his lofty stature, because I have rejected him. Not as man sees does God see, because he sees the appearance but the LORD looks into the heart." Then Jesse called Abinadab and presented him before Samuel, who said, "The LORD has not chosen him." Next Jesse presented Shammah, but Samuel said, "The LORD has not chosen this one either." In the same way Jesse presented seven sons before Samuel, but Samuel said to Jesse, "The LORD has not chosen any one of these." Then Samuel asked Jesse, "Are these all the sons you have?" Jesse replied, "There is still the youngest, who is tending the sheep." Samuel said to Jesse, "Send for him; we will not begin the sacrificial banquet until he arrives here." Jesse sent and had the young man brought to them. He was ruddy, a youth handsome to behold and making a splendid appearance. The LORD said, "There—anoint him, for this is he!" Then Samuel, with the horn of oil in hand, anointed him in the midst of his brothers; and from that day on, the Spirit of the LORD rushed upon David. When Samuel took his leave, he went to Ramah.

The word of the Lord.

Responsorial Psalm
Ps 89:20, 21–22, 27–28

> **R. I have found David, my servant.**

Once you spoke in a vision,
  and to your faithful ones you said:
"On a champion I have placed a crown;
  over the people I have set a youth."

> **R. I have found David, my servant.**

"I have found David, my servant;
  with my holy oil I have anointed him,
That my hand may be always with him,
  and that my arm may make him strong."

> **R. I have found David, my servant.**

"He shall say of me, 'You are my father,
  my God, the Rock, my savior.'
And I will make him the first-born,
  highest of the kings of the earth."

> **R. I have found David, my servant.**

> **Alleluia, alleluia**   See Eph 1:17–18
> May the Father of our Lord Jesus Christ
> enlighten the eyes of our hearts,
> that we may know what is the hope
> that belongs to our call.
> **Alleluia, alleluia**

Years I and II

GOSPEL   Mk 2:23–28

The sabbath was made for people, not people for the sabbath.

A reading from the holy Gospel according to Mark

As Jesus was passing through a field of grain on the sabbath, his disciples began to make a path while picking the heads of grain. At this the Pharisees said to him, "Look, why are they doing what is unlawful on the sabbath?" He said to them, "Have you never read what David did when he was in need and he and his companions were hungry? How he went into the house of God when Abiathar was high priest and ate the bread of offering that only the priests could lawfully eat, and shared it with his companions?" Then he said to them, "The sabbath was made for man, not man for the sabbath. That is why the Son of Man is lord even of the sabbath."

The Gospel of the Lord.

Liturgy of the Eucharist, *p. 897;* **Prayer over the Gifts,** *p. 266.*

Wednesday

Antiphons and Prayers, *p. 265;* **Liturgy of the Word** *for Year I (odd years) follows; Year II (even years), p. 278.*

TODAY'S LIVING WORD

Here again is a Gospel story that, taken out of context, may misrepresent the Jews of Jesus' day as hard of heart. At the time of Jesus, Judaism contained a number of religious groups, like the Pharisees and the Sadducees, who disagreed with one another and among themselves as to how God's law should be lived. Sabbath observance was one issue these groups hotly debated. Although all Jews, including Jesus, agreed *that* the Sabbath must be kept holy, there were different opinions about *how*. It was understood among the rabbis that when life was at risk, sabbath observance was superseded. But this was clearly not the case with the man with the shriveled hand. It seems that Jesus was liberal in his view of what could be done on the sabbath.

But what does this story say to us, who are no longer embroiled in such debates? Like all the miracles of Jesus, this one too bears witness to the kingly power of God. As all the readings tell us, that power is often revealed in the most unlikely places—in the priesthood of Melchizedek, in the victory of David, and in the ministry of Jesus the Jew.

Year I

FIRST READING
Heb 7:1–3, 15–17

You are a priest forever according to the order of Melchizedek.

A reading from the Letter to the Hebrews

Melchizedek, king of Salem and priest of God Most High, met Abraham as he returned from his defeat of the kings and *blessed him*. And Abraham apportioned to him *a tenth of everything*. His name first means righteous king, and he was also "king of Salem," that is, king of peace. Without father, mother, or ancestry, without beginning of days or end of life, thus made to resemble the Son of God, he remains a priest forever.

It is even more obvious if another priest is raised up after the likeness of Melchizedek, who has become so, not by a law expressed in a commandment concerning physical descent but by the power of a life that cannot be destroyed. For it is testified:

You are a priest forever according to the order of Mel-chizedek.

The word of the Lord.

Responsorial Psalm

Ps 110:1, 2, 3, 4

R. You are a priest for ever, in the line of Melchizedek.

The LORD said to my Lord: "Sit at my right hand
till I make your enemies your footstool."

R. You are a priest for ever, in the line of Melchizedek.

The scepter of your power the LORD will stretch forth from Zion:
"Rule in the midst of your enemies."

R. You are a priest for ever, in the line of Melchizedek.

"Yours is princely power in the day of your birth, in holy splendor;
before the daystar, like the dew, I have begotten you."

R. You are a priest for ever, in the line of Melchizedek.

The LORD has sworn, and he will not repent:
"You are a priest forever, according to the order of Melchizedek."

R. You are a priest for ever, in the line of Melchizedek.

Alleluia Verse *and* **Gospel,** *p. 280.*

Year II

FIRST READING

1 Sm 17:32–33, 37, 40–51

David overcame the Philistine with sling and stone.

A reading from the first Book of Samuel

David spoke to Saul: "Let your majesty not lose courage. I am
at your service to go and fight this Philistine." But Saul
answered David, "You cannot go up against this Philistine and
fight with him, for you are only a youth, while he has been a
warrior from his youth."

David continued: "The LORD, who delivered me from the
claws of the lion and the bear, will also keep me safe from the
clutches of this Philistine." Saul answered David, "Go! the
LORD will be with you."

Then, staff in hand, David selected five smooth stones from

the wadi and put them in the pocket of his shepherd's bag. With his sling also ready to hand, he approached the Philistine.

With his shield bearer marching before him, the Philistine also advanced closer and closer to David. When he had sized David up, and seen that he was youthful, and ruddy, and handsome in appearance, the Philistine held David in contempt. The Philistine said to David, "Am I a dog that you come against me with a staff?" Then the Philistine cursed David by his gods and said to him, "Come here to me, and I will leave your flesh for the birds of the air and the beasts of the field." David answered him: "You come against me with sword and spear and scimitar, but I come against you in the name of the LORD of hosts, the God of the armies of Israel that you have insulted. Today the LORD shall deliver you into my hand; I will strike you down and cut off your head. This very day I will leave your corpse and the corpses of the Philistine army for the birds of the air and the beasts of the field; thus the whole land shall learn that Israel has a God. All this multitude, too, shall learn that it is not by sword or spear that the LORD saves. For the battle is the LORD's and he shall deliver you into our hands."

The Philistine then moved to meet David at close quarters, while David ran quickly toward the battle line in the direction of the Philistine. David put his hand into the bag and took out a stone, hurled it with the sling, and struck the Philistine on the forehead. The stone embedded itself in his brow, and he fell prostrate on the ground. Thus David overcame the Philistine with sling and stone; he struck the Philistine mortally, and did it without a sword. Then David ran and stood over him; with the Philistine's own sword which he drew from its sheath he dispatched him and cut off his head.

The word of the Lord.

Responsorial Psalm

Ps 144:1b, 2, 9–10

R. Blessed be the Lord, my Rock!

Blessed be the LORD, my rock,
 who trains my hands for battle, my fingers for war.

R. Blessed be the Lord, my Rock!

My refuge and my fortress,
 my stronghold, my deliverer,
My shield, in whom I trust,
 who subdues my people under me.

R. Blessed be the Lord, my Rock!

O God, I will sing a new song to you;
 with a ten-stringed lyre I will chant your praise,
You who give victory to kings,
 and deliver David, your servant from the evil sword.

R. Blessed be the Lord, my Rock!

Alleluia, alleluia   See Mt 4:23
 Jesus preached the Gospel of the Kingdom
 and cured every disease among the people.
Alleluia, alleluia

Years I and II

GOSPEL

Mk 3:1–6

Is it lawful on the sabbath to save life rather than to destroy it?

A reading from the holy Gospel according to Mark

Jesus entered the synagogue. There was a man there who had a withered hand. They watched Jesus closely to see if he would cure him on the sabbath so that they might accuse him. He said to the man with the withered hand, "Come up here before us." Then he said to the Pharisees, "Is it lawful to do good on the sabbath rather than to do evil, to save life rather than to destroy it?" But they remained silent. Looking around at them with anger and grieved at their hardness of heart, Jesus said to the man, "Stretch out your hand." He stretched it out and his hand was restored. The Pharisees went out and immediately took counsel with the Herodians against him to put him to death.

The Gospel of the Lord.

Liturgy of the Eucharist, *p. 897;* **Prayer over the Gifts,** *p. 266.*

Thursday

Antiphons and Prayers, *p. 265;* **Liturgy of the Word** *for Year I (odd years) follows; Year II (even years), p. 283.*

TODAY'S LIVING WORD

Scholars refer to these verses as a transitional summary. Mark here recapitulates the ministry of Jesus, mentioning his healing miracles and exorcisms, and noting the vast numbers who followed him. He also refers to Jesus commanding the unclean spirits "not to make him known." This is the "messianic secret."

Throughout the first part of Mark's Gospel, Jesus' miracles are routinely followed by an injunction to silence. As students of Mark have come to understand, there is more here than an attempt at crowd control—although for Jesus, as for David, the enthusiasm of the crowds will incite rival powers to jealousy. Rather, the messianic secret is Mark's way of forestalling a premature proclamation of Jesus' messiahship. The messiahship of Jesus is most fully revealed not in his miracles but in his suffering and death. So for Mark, as for us, there can be no true proclamation of Jesus as Messiah that does not embrace his cross.

Year I

FIRST READING   Heb 7:25—8:6

He offered sacrifice once for all when he offered himself.

A reading from the Letter to the Hebrews

Jesus is always able to save those who approach God through him, since he lives forever to make intercession for them.

It was fitting that we should have such a high priest: holy, innocent, undefiled, separated from sinners, higher than the heavens. He has no need, as did the high priests, to offer sacrifice day after day, first for his own sins and then for those of the people; he did that once for all when he offered himself. For the law appoints men subject to weakness to be high priests, but the word of the oath, which was taken after the law, appoints a son, who has been made perfect forever.

The main point of what has been said is this: we have such a high priest, who has taken his seat at the right hand of the throne of the Majesty in heaven, a minister of the sanctuary and of the true tabernacle that the Lord, not man, set up. Now every high priest is appointed to offer gifts and sacrifices; thus the necessity for this one also to have something to offer. If then he were on earth, he would not be a priest, since there are those who offer gifts according to the law. They worship in a copy and shadow of the heavenly sanctuary, as Moses was warned when he was about to erect the tabernacle. For God says, "See that you make everything according to the pattern shown you on the mountain." Now he has obtained so much more excellent a ministry as he is mediator of a better covenant, enacted on better promises.

The word of the Lord.

Responsorial Psalm
Ps 40:7–8a, 8b–9, 10, 17

R. Here am I, Lord; I come to do your will.

Sacrifice or oblation you wished not,

but ears open to obedience you gave me.
Burnt offerings or sin-offerings you sought not;
    then said I, "Behold I come."

R. Here am I, Lord; I come to do your will.

"In the written scroll it is prescribed for me,
To do your will, O my God, is my delight,
    and your law is within my heart!"

R. Here am I, Lord; I come to do your will.

I announced your justice in the vast assembly;
    I did not restrain my lips, as you, O LORD, know.

R. Here am I, Lord; I come to do your will.

May all who seek you
    exult and be glad in you,
And may those who love your salvation
    say ever, "The LORD be glorified."

R. Here am I, Lord; I come to do your will.

Alleluia Verse *and* **Gospel,** *p. 285.*

___

Year II

FIRST READING   1 Sm 18:6–9; 19:1–7

My father Saul is trying to kill you.

A reading from the first Book of Samuel

When David and Saul approached (on David's return after slaying the Philistine), women came out from each of the cities of Israel to meet King Saul, singing and dancing, with tambourines, joyful songs, and sistrums. The women played and sang:

    "Saul has slain his thousands,
    and David his ten thousands."

Saul was very angry and resentful of the song, for he thought: "They give David ten thousands, but only thousands to me. All that remains for him is the kingship." And from that day on, Saul was jealous of David.

Saul discussed his intention of killing David with his son Jonathan and with all his servants. But Saul's son Jonathan, who was very fond of David, told him: "My father Saul is trying to kill you. Therefore, please be on your guard tomorrow morning; get out of sight and remain in hiding. I, however, will go out and stand beside my father in the countryside where you are, and will speak to him about you. If I learn anything, I will let you know."

Jonathan then spoke well of David to his father Saul, saying to him: "Let not your majesty sin against his servant David, for he has committed no offense against you, but has helped you very much by his deeds. When he took his life in his hands and slew the Philistine, and the LORD brought about a great victory for all Israel through him, you were glad to see it. Why, then, should you become guilty of shedding innocent blood by killing David without cause?" Saul heeded Jonathan's plea and swore, "As the LORD lives, he shall not be killed." So Jonathan summoned David and repeated the whole conversation to him. Jonathan then brought David to Saul, and David served him as before.

The word of the Lord.

Responsorial Psalm

Ps 56:2–3, 9–10a, 10b–11, 12–13

R. In God I trust; I shall not fear.

Have mercy on me, O God, for men trample upon me;
    all the day they press their attack against me.

My adversaries trample upon me all the day;
  yes, many fight against me.

R. In God I trust; I shall not fear.

My wanderings you have counted;
  my tears are stored in your flask;
  are they not recorded in your book?
Then do my enemies turn back,
  when I call upon you.

R. In God I trust; I shall not fear.

Now I know that God is with me.
  In God, in whose promise I glory,
  in God I trust without fear;
  what can flesh do against me?

R. In God I trust; I shall not fear.

I am bound, O God, by vows to you;
  your thank offerings I will fulfill.
For you have rescued me from death,
  my feet, too, from stumbling;
  that I may walk before God in the light of the living.

R. In God I trust; I shall not fear.

> **Alleluia, alleluia** See 2 Tm 1:10
> Our Savior Jesus Christ has destroyed death
> and brought life to light through the Gospel.
> **Alleluia, alleluia**

Years I and II

GOSPEL   Mk 3:7–12

*The unclean spirits shouted, "You are the Son of God,"
but Jesus warned them sternly not to make him known.*

A reading from the holy Gospel according to Mark

Jesus withdrew toward the sea with his disciples. A large number of people followed from Galilee and from Judea. Hearing what he was doing, a large number of people came to him also from Jerusalem, from Idumea, from beyond the Jordan, and from the neighborhood of Tyre and Sidon. He told his disciples to have a boat ready for him because of the crowd, so that they would not crush him. He had cured many and, as a result, those who had diseases were pressing upon him to touch him. And whenever unclean spirits saw him they would fall down before him and shout, "You are the Son of God." He warned them sternly not to make him known.

The Gospel of the Lord.

Liturgy of the Eucharist, *p. 897;* **Prayer over the Gifts,** *p. 266.*

Friday

Antiphons and Prayers, *p. 265;* **Liturgy of the Word** *for Year I (odd years) follows; Year II (even years), p. 289.*

TODAY'S LIVING WORD

Mark describes Jesus' choice of the Twelve as a decisive moment in his ministry: "he appointed Twelve." The word "appointed" is weak; the Greek says, "he *made* the Twelve" *(εποιησεν=epoiesen).* This action of Jesus is a clue to the intent and purpose of his earthly mission. For Jesus and his fellow Jews, the number twelve could only refer to the twelve tribes of Israel. Although in Jesus' time only two and a half tribes remained, ever since the time of the prophet Ezekiel the people had hoped that all Israel, all twelve tribes, would be restored in the last days. Against this background, Jesus' creation of the Twelve was a sign that the last days were dawning and the reign of God was at hand.

Like David who refused to seize power on his own terms by killing Saul, Jesus always remained firmly and faithfully within the way that God had traced for his people. Only later did Christians and Jews go their separate ways. Hebrews reflects the tension of that time when it speaks of the new covenant negating the old. Our own times, however, invite us to rediscover our common heritage with the Jews.

Year I

FIRST READING   Heb 8:6–13

He is mediator of a better covenant.

A reading from the Letter to the Hebrews

Brothers and sisters:

Now our high priest has obtained so much more excellent a ministry as he is mediator of a better covenant, enacted on better promises.

For if that first covenant had been faultless, no place would have been sought for a second one. But he finds fault with them and says:

> *Behold, the days are coming, says the Lord,*
>> *when I will conclude a new covenant with the house of*
>> *Israel and the house of Judah.*
> *It will not be like the covenant I made with their fathers*
>> *the day I took them by the hand to lead*
>> *them forth from the land of Egypt;*
>> *for they did not stand by my covenant*
>> *and I ignored them, says the Lord.*
> *But this is the covenant I will establish with the house of*
>> *Israel*
>> *after those days, says the Lord:*
> *I will put my laws in their minds*
>> *and I will write them upon their hearts.*
> *I will be their God,*

and they shall be my people.
  And they shall not teach, each one his fellow citizen and
      kin, saying,
  "Know the Lord,"
    for all shall know me, from least to greatest.
  For I will forgive their evildoing
    and remember their sins no more.

When he speaks of a "new" covenant, he declares the first one obsolete. And what has become obsolete and has grown old is close to disappearing.

The word of the Lord.

Responsorial Psalm   Ps 85:8 and 10, 11–12, 13–14

R. Kindness and truth shall meet.

Show us, O LORD, your mercy,
  and grant us your salvation.
Near indeed is his salvation to those who fear him,
  glory dwelling in our land.

R. Kindness and truth shall meet.

Kindness and truth shall meet;
  justice and peace shall kiss.
Truth shall spring out of the earth,
  and justice shall look down from heaven.

R. Kindness and truth shall meet.

The LORD himself will give his benefits;
  our land shall yield its increase.
Justice shall walk before him,
  and salvation, along the way of his steps.

R. Kindness and truth shall meet.

Alleluia Verse *and* **Gospel,** *p. 291.*

Year II

FIRST READING
1 Sm 24:3–21

I will not raise a hand against my lord,
for he is the LORD's anointed.

A reading from the first Book of Samuel

Saul took three thousand picked men from all Israel and went in search of David and his men in the direction of the wild goat crags. When he came to the sheepfolds along the way, he found a cave, which he entered to relieve himself. David and his men were occupying the inmost recesses of the cave.

David's servants said to him, "This is the day of which the LORD said to you, 'I will deliver your enemy into your grasp; do with him as you see fit.'" So David moved up and stealthily cut off an end of Saul's mantle. Afterward, however, David regretted that he had cut off an end of Saul's mantle. He said to his men, "The LORD forbid that I should do such a thing to my master, the LORD's anointed, as to lay a hand on him, for he is the LORD's anointed." With these words David restrained his men and would not permit them to attack Saul. Saul then left the cave and went on his way. David also stepped out of the cave, calling to Saul, "My lord the king!" When Saul looked back, David bowed to the ground in homage and asked Saul: "Why do you listen to those who say, 'David is trying to harm you'? You see for yourself today that the LORD just now delivered you into my grasp in the cave. I had some thought of killing you, but I took pity on you instead. I decided, 'I will not raise a hand against my lord, for he is the LORD's anointed and a father to me.' Look here at this end of your mantle which I hold. Since I cut off an end of your mantle and did not kill

you, see and be convinced that I plan no harm and no rebellion.
I have done you no wrong, though you are hunting me down
to take my life. The LORD will judge between me and you, and
the LORD will exact justice from you in my case. I shall not
touch you. The old proverb says, 'From the wicked comes forth
wickedness.' So I will take no action against you. Against whom
are you on campaign, O king of Israel? Whom are you pur-
suing? A dead dog, or a single flea! The LORD will be the judge;
he will decide between me and you. May he see this, and take
my part, and grant me justice beyond your reach!"

When David finished saying these things to Saul, Saul
answered, "Is that your voice, my son David?" And Saul wept
aloud. Saul then said to David: "You are in the right rather
than I; you have treated me generously, while I have done you
harm. Great is the generosity you showed me today, when the
LORD delivered me into your grasp and you did not kill me.
For if a man meets his enemy, does he send him away
unharmed? May the LORD reward you generously for what you
have done this day. And now, I know that you shall surely be
king and that sovereignty over Israel shall come into your
possession."

The word of the Lord.

Responsional Psalm   Ps 57:2, 3–4, 6 and 11

R. Have mercy on me, God, have mercy.

Have mercy on me, O God; have mercy on me,
  for in you I take refuge.
In the shadow of your wings I take refuge,
  till harm pass by.

R. Have mercy on me, God, have mercy.

I call to God the Most High,
  to God, my benefactor.

May he send from heaven and save me;
  may he make those a reproach who trample upon me;
  may God send his mercy and his faithfulness.

  R. Have mercy on me, God, have mercy.

Be exalted above the heavens, O God;
  above all the earth be your glory!
For your mercy towers to the heavens,
  and your faithfulness to the skies.

  R. Have mercy on me, God, have mercy.

  Alleluia, alleluia   2 Cor 5:19
  God was reconciling the world to himself in Christ,
  and entrusting to us the message of reconciliation.
  Alleluia, alleluia

Years I and II

GOSPEL   Mk 3:13–19
Jesus summoned those whom he wanted and they came to him.

A reading from the holy Gospel according to Mark

Jesus went up the mountain and summoned those whom he
wanted and they came to him. He appointed Twelve, whom he
also named Apostles, that they might be with him and he might
send them forth to preach and to have authority to drive out
demons: He appointed the Twelve: Simon, whom he named
Peter; James, son of Zebedee, and John the brother of James,
whom he named Boanerges, that is, sons of thunder; Andrew,
Philip, Bartholomew, Matthew, Thomas, James the son of
Alphaeus; Thaddeus, Simon the Cananean, and Judas Iscariot
who betrayed him.

The Gospel of the Lord.

  Liturgy of the Eucharist, *p. 897;* **Prayer over the Gifts,** *p. 266.*

Saturday

Antiphons and Prayers, *p. 265;* **Liturgy of the Word** *for Year I (odd years) follows; Year II (even years), p. 294.*

TODAY'S LIVING WORD

Two of the three readings for today present us with poignant personal moments. In 2 Samuel, David learns of the defeat of the Israelites and of the death of Saul and Jonathan. In the short passage from Mark, Jesus discovers that members of his own extended family do not understand him or even believe in him. "They set out to seize him, for they said, 'He is out of his mind.'" Both David's grief and Jesus' disappointment are emotionally charged moments. Having known bereavement and betrayal in our own lives, we can empathize.

For us, the Letter to the Hebrews holds good news—or better, hides it in the elaborate comparison it makes between the temple priesthood and the priesthood of Christ. It says that as high priest, Christ "entered once for all into the sanctuary, not with the blood of goats and calves but with his own blood, thus obtaining eternal redemption." The good news is that where he has entered, we may follow, bringing our battered, broken hearts into the sanctuary, the one safe place, that is the presence of the living God.

Year I

FIRST READING   Heb 9:2–3, 11–14

He entered once for all into the Sanctuary with his own Blood.

A reading from the Letter to the Hebrews

A tabernacle was constructed, the outer one, in which were the lampstand, the table, and the bread of offering; this is called the Holy Place. Behind the second veil was the tabernacle called the Holy of Holies.

But when Christ came as high priest of the good things that have come to be, passing through the greater and more perfect tabernacle not made by hands, that is, not belonging to this creation, he entered once for all into the sanctuary, not with the blood of goats and calves but with his own Blood, thus obtaining eternal redemption. For if the blood of goats and bulls and the sprinkling of a heifer's ashes can sanctify those who are defiled so that their flesh is cleansed, how much more will the Blood of Christ, who through the eternal spirit offered himself unblemished to God, cleanse our consciences from dead works to worship the living God.

The word of the Lord.

Responsorial Psalm
Ps 47:2–3, 6–7, 8–9

R. God mounts his throne to shouts of joy: a blare of trumpets for the Lord.

All you peoples, clap your hands,
  shout to God with cries of gladness,
For the LORD, the Most High, the awesome,
  is the great king over all the earth.

R. God mounts his throne to shouts of joy: a blare of trumpets for the Lord.

God mounts his throne amid shouts of joy;
  the LORD, amid trumpet blasts.
Sing praise to God, sing praise;
  sing praise to our king, sing praise.

R. God mounts his throne to shouts of joy: a blare of trumpets for the Lord.

For king of all the earth is God:
  sing hymns of praise.
God reigns over the nations,
  God sits upon his holy throne.

R. God mounts his throne to shouts of joy: a blare of trumpets for the Lord.

Alleluia Verse *and* **Gospel,** *p. 295f.*

FIRST READING   2 Sm 1:1–4, 11–12, 19, 23–27

How can the warriors have fallen in battle!

A reading from the second Book of Samuel

David returned from his defeat of the Amalekites and spent
two days in Ziklag. On the third day a man came from Saul's
camp, with his clothes torn and dirt on his head. Going to David,
he fell to the ground in homage. David asked him, "Where do
you come from?" He replied, "I have escaped from the camp
of the children of Israel." "Tell me what happened," David
bade him. He answered that many of the soldiers had fled the
battle and that many of them had fallen and were dead, among
them Saul and his son Jonathan.

David seized his garments and rent them, and all the men
who were with him did likewise. They mourned and wept and
fasted until evening for Saul and his son Jonathan, and for the
soldiers of the LORD of the clans of Israel, because they had
fallen by the sword.

"Alas! the glory of Israel, Saul,
    slain upon your heights;
    how can the warriors have fallen!

"Saul and Jonathan, beloved and cherished,
    separated neither in life nor in death,
    swifter than eagles, stronger than lions!
Women of Israel, weep over Saul,
    who clothed you in scarlet and in finery,
    who decked your attire with ornaments of gold.

"How can the warriors have fallen—
in the thick of the battle,
slain upon your heights!

"I grieve for you, Jonathan my brother!
most dear have you been to me;
more precious have I held love for you than love for
women.

"How can the warriors have fallen,
the weapons of war have perished!"

The word of the Lord.

Responsorial Psalm

Ps 80:2 – 3, 5 – 7

R. Let us see your face, Lord, and we shall be saved.

O shepherd of Israel, hearken,
O guide of the flock of Joseph!
From your throne upon the cherubim, shine forth
before Ephraim, Benjamin and Manasseh.
Rouse your power,
and come to save us.

R. Let us see your face, Lord, and we shall be saved.

O Lord of hosts, how long will you burn with anger
while your people pray?
You have fed them with the bread of tears
and given them tears to drink in ample measure.
You have left us to be fought over by our neighbors,
and our enemies mock us.

R. Let us see your face, Lord, and we shall be saved.

Alleluia, alleluia   See Acts 16:14b
Open our hearts, O Lord,
to listen to the words of your Son.
Alleluia, alleluia

Years I and II

GOSPEL   Mk 3:20–21

They said, "He is out of his mind."

A reading from the holy Gospel according to Mark

Jesus came with his disciples into the house. Again the crowd gathered, making it impossible for them even to eat. When his relatives heard of this they set out to seize him, for they said, "He is out of his mind."

The Gospel of the Lord.

Liturgy of the Eucharist, *p. 897;* **Prayer over the Gifts,** *p. 266.*

THIRD WEEK IN ORDINARY TIME

The **Antiphons and Prayers** *may be the following, or may be chosen from any of the other 33 weeks in Ordinary Time (refer to Liturgical Calendar, pp. 26–41).*

The **Liturgy of the Word** *varies: for Monday, see p. 298; Tuesday, p. 303; Wednesday, p. 307; Thursday, p. 312; Friday, p. 317; Saturday, p. 322.*

Entrance Antiphon

Sing a new song to the Lord! Sing to the Lord, all the earth. Truth and beauty surround him, he lives in holiness and glory.

(Ps 96:1, 6)

Opening Prayer

Let us pray

   [for unity and peace]

      Pause for silent prayer.

All-powerful and ever-living God,
direct your love that is within us,
that our efforts in the name of your Son
may bring mankind to unity and peace.

We ask this through our Lord Jesus Christ, your Son,
who lives and reigns with you and the Holy Spirit,
one God, for ever and ever.

Alternative Opening Prayer

Let us pray
  [pleading that our vision
  may overcome our weakness]
    Pause for silent prayer.

Almighty Father,
the love you offer
always exceeds the furthest expression
of our human longing,
for you are greater than the human heart.
Direct each thought, each effort of our life,
so that the limits of our faults and weaknesses
may not obscure the vision of your glory
or keep us from the peace you have promised.
We ask this through Christ our Lord.

Prayer over the Gifts

Pray, brethren...
Lord,
receive our gifts.
Let our offerings make us holy
and bring us salvation.

Grant this through Christ our Lord.

Preface of Weekdays in Ordinary Time I–VI, *pp. 948–950.*

Communion Antiphon

  **Look up at the Lord with gladness and smile; your face will
never be ashamed.**

(Ps 34:6)

Or:

I am the light of the world, says the Lord; the man who follows me will have the light of life.   (Jn 8:12)

Prayer after Communion

Let us pray.

   Pause for silent prayer, if this has not preceded.

God, all-powerful Father,
may the new life you give us increase our love
and keep us in the joy of your kingdom.

We ask this in the name of Jesus the Lord.

Monday

Antiphons and Prayers, *p. 296;* **Liturgy of the Word** *for Year I (odd years) follows; Year II (even years), p. 300.*

TODAY'S LIVING WORD

Jesus' exorcisms caused some people to question the source of his power over Satan. In this story, two related charges are brought against him: that he is possessed and that he casts out demons with the help of the prince of demons. Jesus answers by drawing two analogies that point out the illogic of the charge. Then he adds: "No one can enter a strong man's house…unless he first ties up the strong man." In this parable, Satan is the strong man and Jesus the robber who overpowers Satan and plunders his house. It is typical of Jesus to refer to himself indirectly, for example, as bridegroom or bandit. But massive claims are often implicit in such metaphors. Behind this image is a passage from Isaiah 49, where God is the robber who takes booty from a warrior and captives from a tyrant. Without using the phrase "reign of God," Jesus proclaims that in his exorcisms God's kingly power is already breaking the power of Satan.

The unstoppable power of God that made David strong against his enemies makes Jesus strong against all the enemies of God's people. So it was, as Hebrews says, that he was able "to take away sin by his sacrifice."

Year I

FIRST READING Heb 9:15, 24–28

*Christ who offered once to take away the sins of many,
will appear a second time to those who eagerly await him.*

A reading from the Letter to the Hebrews

Christ is mediator of a new covenant: since a death has taken place for deliverance from transgressions under the first covenant, those who are called may receive the promised eternal inheritance.

For Christ did not enter into a sanctuary made by hands, a copy of the true one, but heaven itself, that he might now appear before God on our behalf. Not that he might offer himself repeatedly, as the high priest enters each year into the sanctuary with blood that is not his own; if that were so, he would have had to suffer repeatedly from the foundation of the world. But now once for all he has appeared at the end of the ages to take away sin by his sacrifice. Just as it is appointed that human beings die once, and after this the judgment, so also Christ, offered once to take away the sins of many, will appear a second time, not to take away sin but to bring salvation to those who eagerly await him.

The word of the Lord.

Responsorial Psalm Ps 98:1, 2–3ab, 3cd–4, 5–6

**R. Sing to the Lord a new song, for he has done
marvelous deeds.**

Sing to the LORD a new song,
  for he has done wondrous deeds;
His right hand has won victory for him,
  his holy arm.

R. Sing to the Lord a new song, for he has done marvelous deeds.

The LORD has made his salvation known:
  in the sight of the nations he has revealed his justice.
He has remembered his kindness and his faithfulness
  toward the house of Israel.

R. Sing to the Lord a new song, for he has done marvelous deeds.

All the ends of the earth have seen
  the salvation by our God.
Sing joyfully to the LORD, all you lands;
  break into song; sing praise.

R. Sing to the Lord a new song, for he has done marvelous deeds.

Sing praise to the LORD with the harp,
  with the harp and melodious song.
With trumpets and the sound of the horn
  sing joyfully before the King, the LORD.

R. Sing to the Lord a new song, for he has done marvelous deeds.

Alleluia Verse *and* **Gospel,** *p. 302.*

Year II

FIRST READING   2 Sm 5:1–7, 10

You shall shepherd my people Israel.

A reading from the second Book of Samuel

All the tribes of Israel came to David in Hebron and said: "Here we are, your bone and your flesh. In days past, when Saul was our king, it was you who led the children of Israel out and brought them back. And the LORD said to you, 'You shall shepherd my people Israel and shall be commander of Israel.'"

When all the elders of Israel came to David in Hebron, King
David made an agreement with them there before the LORD,
and they anointed him king of Israel. David was thirty years
old when he became king, and he reigned for forty years: seven
years and six months in Hebron over Judah, and thirty-three
years in Jerusalem over all Israel and Judah.

Then the king and his men set out for Jerusalem against the
Jebusites who inhabited the region. David was told, "You
cannot enter here: the blind and the lame will drive you away!"
which was their way of saying, "David cannot enter here."
But David did take the stronghold of Zion, which is the City
of David.

David grew steadily more powerful, for the LORD of hosts
was with him.

The word of the Lord.

Responsorial Psalm
Ps 89:20, 21–22, 25–26

R. My faithfulness and my mercy shall be with him.

Once you spoke in a vision,
  and to your faithful ones you said:
"On a champion I have placed a crown;
  over the people I have set a youth."

R. My faithfulness and my mercy shall be with him.

"I have found David, my servant;
  with my holy oil I have anointed him,
That my hand may be always with him,
  and that my arm may make him strong."

R. My faithfulness and my mercy shall be with him.

"My faithfulness and my mercy shall be with him,
  and through my name shall his horn be exalted.
I will set his hand upon the sea,
  his right hand upon the rivers."

R. My faithfulness and my mercy shall be with him.

Alleluia, alleluia   See 2 Tm 1:10
Our Savior Jesus Christ has destroyed death
and brought life to light through the Gospel.
Alleluia, alleluia

Years I and II

GOSPEL   Mk 3:22–30

It is the end of Satan.

A reading from the holy Gospel according to Mark

The scribes who had come from Jerusalem said of Jesus, "He
is possessed by Beelzebul," and "By the prince of demons he
drives out demons."

Summoning them, he began to speak to them in parables,
"How can Satan drive out Satan? If a kingdom is divided against
itself, that kingdom cannot stand. And if a house is divided
against itself, that house will not be able to stand. And if Satan
has risen up against himself and is divided, he cannot stand;
that is the end of him. But no one can enter a strong man's
house to plunder his property unless he first ties up the strong
man. Then he can plunder his house. Amen, I say to you, all
sins and all blasphemies that people utter will be forgiven them.
But whoever blasphemes against the Holy Spirit will never
have forgiveness, but is guilty of an everlasting sin." For they
had said, "He has an unclean spirit."

The Gospel of the Lord.

Liturgy of the Eucharist, *p. 897;* **Prayer over the Gifts,** *p. 297.*

Tuesday

Antiphons and Prayers, p. 296; **Liturgy of the Word** for Year I (odd years) follows; Year II (even years), p. 305.

TODAY'S LIVING WORD

All four Gospels preserve an episode early in Jesus' ministry in which he distances himself from his natural family—his mother and his brothers and sisters—and redefines family on the basis of the obedience of faith. "Whoever does the will of God is my brother and sister and mother." This is Mark's version of that episode. Because Mark's Gospel begins with Jesus' baptism, not with his birth, even Mary is counted among those "outside."

The public ministry of Jesus was guided solely by the will of God. In fact, the author of the Letter to the Hebrews sums up Jesus' whole redemptive mission in one verse from Psalm 40: "I come to do your will." To do God's will, as Jesus did, may require us at times to reassess our family ties. The sequel of the story of David dancing before the ark is a case in point. The text goes on to say that when David returned to his own family, his wife Michal rebuked him sharply for embarrassing himself and his family by dancing with abandon before the Lord.

Year I

FIRST READING   Heb 10:1–10

Behold, I come to do your will, O God.

A reading from the Letter to the Hebrews

Brothers and sisters:

Since the law has only a shadow of the good things to come, and not the very image of them, it can never make perfect those who come to worship by the same sacrifices that they offer continually each year. Otherwise, would not the sacrifices have ceased to be offered, since the worshipers, once cleansed, would no longer have had any consciousness of sins? But in those sacrifices there is only a yearly remembrance of sins, for it is impossible that the blood of bulls and goats take away sins. For this reason, when he came into the world, he said:

> *Sacrifice and offering you did not desire,*
>> *but a body you prepared for me;*
> *in burnt offerings and sin offerings you took no delight.*
> *Then I said, As is written of me in the scroll,*
>> *Behold, I come to do your will, O God.*

First he says, *Sacrifices and offerings, burnt offerings and sin offerings, you neither desired nor delighted in*. These are offered according to the law. Then he says, *Behold, I come to do your will*. He takes away the first to establish the second. By this "will," we have been consecrated through the offering of the Body of Jesus Christ once for all.

The word of the Lord.

Responsorial Psalm

Ps 40:2 and 4ab, 7–8a, 10, 11

R. Here am I, Lord; I come to do your will.

I have waited, waited for the LORD,
  and he stooped toward me.
And he put a new song into my mouth,
  a hymn to our God.

R. Here am I, Lord; I come to do your will.

Sacrifice or oblation you wished not,
  but ears open to obedience you gave me.
Burnt offerings or sin-offerings you sought not;
  then said I, "Behold I come."

R. Here am I, Lord; I come to do your will.

I announced your justice in the vast assembly;
  I did not restrain my lips, as you, O LORD, know.

R. Here am I, Lord; I come to do your will.

Your justice I kept not hid within my heart;
  faithfulness and your salvation I have spoken of;
I have made no secret of your kindness and your truth
  in the vast assembly.

R. Here am I, Lord; I come to do your will.

Alleluia Verse *and* **Gospel,** *p. 306.*

Year II

FIRST READING

2 Sm 6:12b–15, 17–19

David and all the children of Israel were bringing up the ark
of the LORD with shouts of joy.

A reading from the second Book of Samuel

David went to bring up the ark of God from the house of Obed-edom into the City of David amid festivities. As soon as the bearers of the ark of the LORD had advanced six steps, he sacrificed an ox and a fatling. Then David, girt with a linen apron, came dancing before the LORD with abandon, as he and all the house of Israel were bringing up the ark of the LORD with shouts of joy and to the sound of the horn. The ark of the LORD was brought in and set in its place within the tent David had pitched for it. Then David offered burnt offerings and peace offerings before the LORD. When he finished making these offerings, he blessed the people in the name of the LORD of hosts. He then distributed among all the people, to each man and each woman in the entire multitude of Israel, a loaf of bread, a cut of roast meat, and a raisin cake. With this, all the people left for their homes.

The word of the Lord.

Responsorial Psalm

Ps 24:7, 8, 9, 10

R. Who is this king of glory? It is the Lord!

Lift up, O gates, your lintels;
  reach up, you ancient portals,
  that the king of glory may come in!

R. Who is this king of glory? It is the Lord!

Who is this king of glory?
  The LORD, strong and mighty,
  the LORD, mighty in battle.

R. Who is this king of glory? It is the Lord!

Lift up, O gates, your lintels;
  reach up, you ancient portals,
  that the king of glory may come in!

R. Who is this king of glory? It is the Lord!

Who is this king of glory?
  The LORD of hosts; he is the king of glory.

R. Who is this king of glory? It is the Lord!

Alleluia, alleluia   See Mt 11:25
Blessed are you, Father, Lord of heaven and earth;
  you have revealed to little ones the mysteries of the Kingdom.
Alleluia, alleluia

Years I and II

GOSPEL

Mk 3:31–35

Whoever does the will of God is my brother and sister and mother.

A reading from the holy Gospel according to Mark

The mother of Jesus and his brothers arrived at the house. Standing outside, they sent word to Jesus and called him. A crowd seated around him told him, "Your mother and your brothers and your sisters are outside asking for you." But he said to them in reply, "Who are my mother and my brothers?"

And looking around at those seated in the circle he said, "Here are my mother and my brothers. For whoever does the will of God is my brother and sister and mother."

The Gospel of the Lord.

Liturgy of the Eucharist, *p. 897;* **Prayer over the Gifts,** *p. 297.*

Wednesday

Antiphons and Prayers, *p. 296;* **Liturgy of the Word** *for Year I (odd years) follows; Year II (even years), p. 309.*

TODAY'S LIVING WORD

All three of today's readings attest to the power of God's word. In the Letter to the Hebrews as a whole, as well as in today's selection, the author explores the mystery of Jesus with constant reference to the inspired word of God, the Hebrew Scriptures. In 2 Samuel the word of God, spoken to David through the prophet Nathan, will shape the messianic hope of Jews and Christians for ages to come. But of the three, the parable of the sower is the most compelling.

Scholars often observe that the parable is more concerned with the seed than with the sower. In the Bible, seed is an image for the word of God. Jesus seems to be responding to those among his followers—people like us, perhaps—who are impatient for signs of his mission's success. In the story he tells, the seed undergoes every possible reversal and still yields a rich harvest in the end. Such is the resilience of God's word.

Year I

FIRST READING   Heb 10:11–18

He has made perfect forever those who are being consecrated.

A reading from the Letter to the Hebrews

Every priest stands daily at his ministry, offering frequently those same sacrifices that can never take away sins. But this one offered one sacrifice for sins, and took his seat forever at the right hand of God; now he waits until his enemies are made his footstool. For by one offering he has made perfect forever those who are being consecrated. The Holy Spirit also testifies to us, for after saying:

> *This is the covenant I will establish with them*
> *after those days, says the Lord:*
> *"I will put my laws in their hearts,*
> *and I will write them upon their minds,"*

he also says:

> *Their sins and their evildoing*
> *I will remember no more.*

Where there is forgiveness of these, there is no longer offering for sin.

The word of the Lord.

Responsorial Psalm   Ps 110:1, 2, 3, 4

R. You are a priest for ever, in the line of Melchizedek.

The LORD said to my Lord: "Sit at my right hand
  till I make your enemies your footstool."

R. You are a priest for ever, in the line of Melchizedek.

The scepter of your power the LORD will stretch forth from Zion:
  "Rule in the midst of your enemies."

R. You are a priest for ever, in the line of Melchizedek.

"Yours is princely power in the day of your birth, in holy splendor;
  before the daystar, like the dew, I have begotten you."

R. You are a priest for ever, in the line of Melchizedek.

The LORD has sworn, and he will not repent:
  "You are a priest forever, according to the order of
  Melchizedek."

R. You are a priest for ever, in the line of Melchizedek.

Alleluia Verse *and* **Gospel,** *p. 310f.*

Year II

FIRST READING   2 Sm 7:4–17

I will raise up your heir after you and
I will make his Kingdom firm.

A reading from the second Book of Samuel

That night the LORD spoke to Nathan and said: "Go, tell my servant David, 'Thus says the LORD: Should you build me a house to dwell in? I have not dwelt in a house from the day on which I led the children of Israel out of Egypt to the present, but I have been going about in a tent under cloth. In all my wanderings everywhere among the children of Israel, did I ever utter a word to any one of the judges whom I charged to tend my people Israel, to ask: Why have you not built me a house of cedar?'

"Now then, speak thus to my servant David, 'The LORD of hosts has this to say: It was I who took you from the pasture and from the care of the flock to be commander of my people Israel. I have been with you wherever you went, and I have destroyed all your enemies before you. And I will make you famous like the great ones of the earth. I will fix a place for my people Israel; I will plant them so that they may dwell in their place without further disturbance. Neither shall the wicked continue to afflict them as they did of old, since the time I first appointed judges over my people Israel. I will give you rest from all your enemies. The LORD also reveals to you that he will establish a house for you. And when your time comes and you rest with your ancestors, I will raise up your heir after you, sprung from your loins, and I will make his Kingdom firm. It is he who shall build a house for my name. And I will make his royal throne firm forever. I will be a father to him, and he shall be a son to me. And if he does wrong, I will correct him with the rod of men and with human chastisements; but I will not withdraw my favor from him as I withdrew it from your predecessor Saul, whom I removed from my presence. Your house and your kingdom shall endure forever before me; your throne shall stand firm forever.'" Nathan reported all these words and this entire vision to David.

The word of the Lord.

Responsorial Psalm

Ps 89:4 – 5, 27 – 28, 29 – 30

R. For ever I will maintain my love for my servant.

"I have made a covenant with my chosen one;
  I have sworn to David my servant:
I will make your dynasty stand forever
  and establish your throne through all ages."

R. For ever I will maintain my love for my servant.

"He shall cry to me, 'You are my father,
  my God, the Rock that brings me victory!'
I myself make him firstborn,
  Most High over the kings of the earth."

R. For ever I will maintain my love for my servant.

"Forever I will maintain my love for him;
  my covenant with him stands firm.
I will establish his dynasty forever,
  his throne as the days of the heavens."

R. For ever I will maintain my love for my servant.

Alleluia, alleluia
The seed is the word of God, Christ is the sower;
all who come to him will live for ever.
Alleluia, alleluia

Years I and II

GOSPEL   Mk 4:1–20

A sower went out to sow.

A reading from the holy Gospel according to Mark

On another occasion, Jesus began to teach by the sea. A very large crowd gathered around him so that he got into a boat on the sea and sat down. And the whole crowd was beside the sea on land. And he taught them at length in parables, and in the course of his instruction he said to them, "Hear this! A sower went out to sow. And as he sowed, some seed fell on the path, and the birds came and ate it up. Other seed fell on rocky ground where it had little soil. It sprang up at once because the soil was not deep. And when the sun rose, it was scorched and it withered for lack of roots. Some seed fell among thorns, and the thorns grew up and choked it and it produced no grain. And some seed fell on rich soil and produced fruit. It came up and grew and yielded thirty, sixty, and a hundredfold." He added, "Whoever has ears to hear ought to hear."

And when he was alone, those present along with the Twelve questioned him about the parables. He answered them, "The mystery of the Kingdom of God has been granted to you. But to those outside everything comes in parables, so that

they may look and see but not perceive,
    and hear and listen but not understand,
        in order that they may not be converted and be
            forgiven."

Jesus said to them, "Do you not understand this parable? Then how will you understand any of the parables? The sower sows the word. These are the ones on the path where the word is sown. As soon as they hear, Satan comes at once and takes away the word sown in them. And these are the ones sown on rocky ground who, when they hear the word, receive it at once with joy. But they have no roots; they last only for a time. Then when tribulation or persecution comes because of the word, they quickly fall away. Those sown among thorns are another sort. They are the people who hear the word, but worldly anxiety, the lure of riches, and the craving for other things intrude and choke the word, and it bears no fruit. But those sown on rich soil are the ones who hear the word and accept it and bear fruit thirty and sixty and a hundredfold." The Gospel of the Lord.

Liturgy of the Eucharist, *p. 897;* **Prayer over the Gifts,** *p. 297.*

Thursday

Antiphons and Prayers, *p. 296;* **Liturgy of the Word** *for Year I (odd years) follows; Year II (even years), p. 314.*

TODAY'S LIVING WORD

In chapter 4 Mark explores the purpose of Jesus' parables. Earlier in the chapter, following the parable of the sower, he seemed to suggest that Jesus spoke in parables in order to conceal the mystery of the reign of God from those "outside," that the mystery Jesus revealed was the private property of an in-group. Today's reading corrects that perception. The saying about the lamp is a proverb. It tells us that concealment was not why Jesus used parables.

The parables of Jesus were not compact stories with a moral but puzzles intended to tease the mind into active thought, to use the words of C. H. Dodd.* The element of mystery in Jesus' parables was not meant to conceal the good news of God's rule, but to confront his hearers with the challenge of conversion and faith. Jesus came to issue an invitation, not a command. Having heard it, we have only, like David, to find the courage to turn in prayer to the God whose generosity compels us. Or as Hebrews would say, "let us approach [God] with a sincere heart and in absolute trust."

* *Parables of the Kingdom* (New York: Scribner's, 1961), p. 5.

Year I

FIRST READING

Heb 10:19–25

Let us hold unwaveringly to our confession that gives us hope and consider how to raise one another to love.

A reading from the Letter to the Hebrews

Brothers and sisters:

Since through the Blood of Jesus we have confidence of entrance into the sanctuary by the new and living way he opened for us through the veil, that is, his flesh, and since we have "a great priest over the house of God," let us approach with a sincere heart and in absolute trust, with our hearts sprinkled clean from an evil conscience and our bodies washed in pure water. Let us hold unwaveringly to our confession that gives us hope, for he who made the promise is trustworthy. We must consider how to rouse one another to love and good works. We should not stay away from our assembly, as is the custom of some, but encourage one another, and this all the more as you see the day drawing near.

The word of the Lord.

Responsorial Psalm

Ps 24:1–2, 3–4ab, 5–6

R. Lord, this is the people that longs to see your face.

The LORD's are the earth and its fullness;
  the world and those who dwell in it.
For he founded it upon the seas
  and established it upon the rivers.

R. Lord, this is the people that longs to see your face.

Who can ascend the mountain of the LORD?
  or who may stand in his holy place?
He whose hands are sinless, whose heart is clean,
  who desires not what is vain.

R. Lord, this is the people that longs to see your face.

He shall receive a blessing from the LORD,
  a reward from God his savior.
Such is the race that seeks for him,
  that seeks the face of the God of Jacob.

R. Lord, this is the people that longs to see your face.

Alleluia Verse *and* **Gospel,** *p. 316.*

Year II

FIRST READING   2 Sm 7:18–19, 24–29

Who am I, Lord GOD, and who are the members of my house?

A reading from the second Book of Samuel

After Nathan had spoken to King David, the king went in and sat before the LORD and said, "Who am I, Lord GOD, and who are the members of my house, that you have brought me to this point? Yet even this you see as too little, Lord GOD; you have also spoken of the house of your servant for a long time to come: this too you have shown to man, Lord GOD!

"You have established for yourself your people Israel as yours forever, and you, LORD, have become their God. And now, LORD God, confirm for all time the prophecy you have made concerning your servant and his house, and do as you have promised. Your name will be forever great, when men say, 'The LORD of hosts is God of Israel,' and the house of your servant David stands firm before you. It is you, LORD of hosts, God of Israel, who said in a revelation to your servant, 'I will build a house for you.' Therefore your servant now finds the courage to make this prayer to you. And now, Lord GOD, you are God and your words are truth; you have made this generous promise to your servant. Do, then, bless the house of your servant that it may be before you forever; for you, Lord GOD, have promised, and by your blessing the house of your servant shall be blessed forever."

The word of the Lord.

Responsorial Psalm   Ps 132:1–2, 3–5, 11, 12, 13–14

R. The Lord God will give him the throne of David, his father.

LORD, remember David
  and all his anxious care;
How he swore an oath to the LORD,
  vowed to the Mighty One of Jacob.

R. The Lord God will give him the throne of David, his father.

"I will not enter the house where I live,
  nor lie on the couch where I sleep;
I will give my eyes no sleep,
  my eyelids no rest,
Till I find a home for the LORD,
  a dwelling for the Mighty One of Jacob."

R. The Lord God will give him the throne of David, his father.

The LORD swore an oath to David
  a firm promise from which he will not withdraw:
"Your own offspring
  I will set upon your throne."

**R. The Lord God will give him the throne of David,
his father.**

"If your sons keep my covenant,
  and the decrees which I shall teach them,
Their sons, too, forever
  shall sit upon your throne."

**R. The Lord God will give him the throne of David,
his father.**

For the LORD has chosen Zion,
  he prefers her for his dwelling:
"Zion is my resting place forever;
  in her I will dwell, for I prefer her."

**R. The Lord God will give him the throne of David,
his father.**

> **Alleluia, alleluia**   Ps 119:105
> A lamp to my feet is your word,
> a light to my path.
> **Alleluia, alleluia**

Years I and II

GOSPEL   Mk 4:21–25

A lamp is to be placed on a lampstand.
The measure with which you measure will be measured out to you.

A reading from the holy Gospel according to Mark

Jesus said to his disciples, "Is a lamp brought in to be placed under a bushel basket or under a bed, and not to be placed on a lampstand? For there is nothing hidden except to be made visible; nothing is secret except to come to light. Anyone who has ears to hear ought to hear." He also told them, "Take care what you hear. The measure with which you measure will be measured out to you, and still more will be given to you. To the one who has, more will be given; from the one who has not, even what he has will be taken away."

The Gospel of the Lord.

Liturgy of the Eucharist, *p. 897;* **Prayer over the Gifts,** *p. 297.*

Friday

Antiphons and Prayers, *p. 296;* **Liturgy of the Word** *for Year I (odd years) follows; Year II (even years), p. 319.*

TODAY'S LIVING WORD

"You need endurance to do the will of God and receive what he has promised," declares the Letter to the Hebrews. This is the point of the first parable in today's Gospel reading. The seed of God's word, the power of God's rule, grows slowly, secretly. Living in the time between sowing and harvesting demands patient endurance.

The second parable contains a comic twist that is easy to miss. In telling the story of the mustard seed, Jesus had in mind two texts from the Hebrew Scriptures. Ezekiel 17 and Daniel 4 both describe Israel in its future glory as a great tree, a noble cedar, in whose ample branches the birds of the air will nest. Jesus announced the dawning of that future glory in words that recalled the grandeur of the prophets' vision only to deflate it. Israel in glory would be a shrub, not a tree. In this way Jesus challenged illusions of grandeur, Israel's and ours. Similarly, David's sin shattered any illusions he may have had about himself as God's anointed. But for us as for David there is always hope, for God is not taken in by our posturing. With grace and humor, God saves us from ourselves.

Year I

FIRST READING   Heb 10:32–39

Do not throw away your confidence.
It will have a great reward.

A reading from the Letter to the Hebrews

Remember the days past when, after you had been enlightened, you endured a great contest of suffering. At times you were publicly exposed to abuse and affliction; at other times you associated yourselves with those so treated. You even joined in the sufferings of those in prison and joyfully accepted the confiscation of your property, knowing that you had a better and lasting possession. Therefore, do not throw away your confidence; it will have great recompense. You need endurance to do the will of God and receive what he has promised.

> *For, after just a brief moment,*
>   *he who is to come shall come;*
>   *he shall not delay.*
> *But my just one shall live by faith,*
>   *and if he draws back I take no pleasure in him.*

We are not among those who draw back and perish, but among those who have faith and will possess life.

The word of the Lord.

Responsorial Psalm   Ps 37:3–4, 5–6, 23–24, 39–40

R. The salvation of the just comes from the Lord.

Trust in the LORD and do good,
    that you may dwell in the land and be fed in security.
Take delight in the LORD,
    and he will grant you your heart's requests.

R. The salvation of the just comes from the Lord.

Commit to the LORD your way;
    trust in him, and he will act.
He will make justice dawn for you like the light;
    bright as the noonday shall be your vindication.

R. The salvation of the just comes from the Lord.

By the LORD are the steps of a man made firm,
  and he approves his way.
Though he fall, he does not lie prostrate,
  for the hand of the LORD sustains him.

R. The salvation of the just comes from the Lord.

The salvation of the just is from the LORD;
  he is their refuge in time of distress.
And the LORD helps them and delivers them;
  he delivers them from the wicked and saves them,
  because they take refuge in him.

R. The salvation of the just comes from the Lord.

Alleluia Verse *and* **Gospel,** *p. 321.*

Year II

FIRST READING   2 Sm 11:1–4a, 5–10a, 13–17

You have despised me and have taken the wife
of Uriah to be your wife (see 2 Sm 12:10).

A reading from the second Book of Samuel

At the turn of the year, when kings go out on campaign, David sent out Joab along with his officers and the army of Israel, and they ravaged the Ammonites and besieged Rabbah. David, however, remained in Jerusalem. One evening David rose from his siesta and strolled about on the roof of the palace. From the roof he saw a woman bathing, who was very beautiful. David had inquiries made about the woman and was told, "She is Bathsheba, daughter of Eliam, and wife of Joab's armor bearer Uriah the Hittite." Then David sent messengers and took her. When she came to him, he had relations with her. She then returned to her house. But the woman had conceived, and sent the information to David, "I am with child."

David therefore sent a message to Joab, "Send me Uriah the Hittite." So Joab sent Uriah to David. When he came, David questioned him about Joab, the soldiers, and how the war was going, and Uriah answered that all was well. David then said to Uriah, "Go down to your house and bathe your feet." Uriah left the palace, and a portion was sent out after him from the king's table. But Uriah slept at the entrance of the royal palace with the other officers of his lord, and did not go down to his own house. David was told that Uriah had not gone home. On the day following, David summoned him, and he ate and drank with David, who made him drunk. But in the evening Uriah went out to sleep on his bed among his lord's servants, and did not go down to his home. The next morning David wrote a letter to Joab which he sent by Uriah. In it he directed: "Place Uriah up front, where the fighting is fierce. Then pull back and leave him to be struck down dead." So while Joab was besieging the city, he assigned Uriah to a place where he knew the defenders were strong. When the men of the city made a sortie against Joab, some officers of David's army fell, and among them Uriah the Hittite died.

The word of the Lord.

Responsorial Psalm   Ps 51:3–4, 5–6a, 6bcd–7, 10–11

R. Be merciful, O Lord, for we have sinned.

Have mercy on me, O God, in your goodness;
   in the greatness of your compassion wipe out my offense.
Thoroughly wash me from my guilt
   and of my sin cleanse me.

R. Be merciful, O Lord, for we have sinned.

For I acknowledge my offense,
   and my sin is before me always:

"Against you only have I sinned,
and done what is evil in your sight."

R. Be merciful, O Lord, for we have sinned.

I have done such evil in your sight
that you are just in your sentence,
blameless when you condemn.
True, I was born guilty,
a sinner, even as my mother conceived me.

R. Be merciful, O Lord, for we have sinned.

Let me hear the sounds of joy and gladness;
the bones you have crushed shall rejoice.
Turn away your face from my sins,
and blot out all my guilt.

R. Be merciful, O Lord, for we have sinned.

> **Alleluia, alleluia**   See Mt 11:25
> Blessed are you, Father, Lord of heaven and earth;
> you have revealed to little ones the mysteries of the Kingdom.
> **Alleluia, alleluia**

Years I and II

GOSPEL   Mk 4:26–34

A man scatters seed on the land and would sleep and the
seed would sprout and grow, he knows not how.

A reading from the holy Gospel according to Mark

Jesus said to the crowds: "This is how it is with the Kingdom
of God; it is as if a man were to scatter seed on the land and
would sleep and rise night and day and the seed would sprout
and grow, he knows not how. Of its own accord the land yields
fruit, first the blade, then the ear, then the full grain in the ear.
And when the grain is ripe, he wields the sickle at once, for the
harvest has come."

He said, "To what shall we compare the Kingdom of God, or what parable can we use for it? It is like a mustard seed that, when it is sown in the ground, is the smallest of all the seeds on the earth. But once it is sown, it springs up and becomes the largest of plants and puts forth large branches, so that the birds of the sky can dwell in its shade." With many such parables he spoke the word to them as they were able to understand it. Without parables he did not speak to them, but to his own disciples he explained everything in private.

The Gospel of the Lord.

Liturgy of the Eucharist, *p. 897;* **Prayer over the Gifts,** *p. 297.*

Saturday

Antiphons and Prayers, *p. 296;* **Liturgy of the Word** *for Year I (odd years) follows; Year II (even years), p. 325.*

TODAY'S LIVING WORD

In the two first readings given to us today, we meet two of those men of old who were approved by God because of their faith—Abraham in the Letter to the Hebrews and David in 2 Samuel. Set side by side as they are here, they present the light and the dark side of the life of faith. Abraham's faith is proven in his readiness to sacrifice Isaac; not only is his son spared, but his descendants will be as numerous as the stars. David's faith falters in his sin against Bathsheba and Uriah; not only is he bereft of his son, but the sword will never depart from his house. Although his sin is forgiven, the consequences of that sin remain.

These stories tell us that it is indeed "a fearful thing to fall into the hands of the living God" (Heb 10:31). Yet our only safety lies within those hands. That is the message of today's Gospel. In the Bible, the sea symbolizes chaos. In Psalm 107, for example, God's power is revealed as God quiets the wind and calms the waters of the sea. In this Gospel story, Jesus does what God does—and asks us, "Why are you terrified?"

Year I

FIRST READING

Heb 11:1–2, 8–19

He was looking forward to the city
whose architect and maker is God.

A reading from the Letter to the Hebrews

Brothers and sisters:

Faith is the realization of what is hoped for and evidence of things not seen. Because of it the ancients were well attested.

By faith Abraham obeyed when he was called to go out to a place that he was to receive as an inheritance; he went out, not knowing where he was to go. By faith he sojourned in the promised land as in a foreign country, dwelling in tents with Isaac and Jacob, heirs of the same promise; for he was looking forward to the city with foundations, whose architect and maker is God. By faith he received power to generate, even though he was past the normal age—and Sarah herself was sterile—for he thought that the one who had made the promise was trustworthy. So it was that there came forth from one man, himself as good as dead, descendants as numerous as the stars in the sky and as countless as the sands on the seashore.

All these died in faith. They did not receive what had been promised but saw it and greeted it from afar and acknowledged themselves to be strangers and aliens on earth, for those who speak thus show that they are seeking a homeland. If they had been thinking of the land from which they had come, they would have had opportunity to return. But now they desire a better homeland, a heavenly one. Therefore, God is not ashamed to be called their God, for he has prepared a city for them.

By faith Abraham, when put to the test, offered up Isaac, and he who had received the promises was ready to offer his only son, of whom it was said, *Through Isaac descendants shall bear your name.* He reasoned that God was able to raise even from the dead, and he received Isaac back as a symbol.

The word of the Lord.

Responsorial Psalm   Lk 1:69–70, 71–72, 73–75

R. Blessed be the Lord the God of Israel; he has come to his people.

He has raised up for us a mighty savior,
  born of the house of his servant David.

R. Blessed be the Lord the God of Israel; he has come to his people.

Through his holy prophets he promised of old
  that he would save us from our sins,
  from the hands of all who hate us.
He promised to show mercy to our fathers
  and to remember his holy covenant.

R. Blessed be the Lord the God of Israel; he has come to his people.

This was the oath he swore to our father Abraham:
  to set us free from the bonds of our enemies,
  free to worship him without fear,
  holy and righteous in his sight
  all the days of our life.

R. Blessed be the Lord the God of Israel; he has come to his people.

Alleluia Verse *and* **Gospel,** *p. 326f.*

Year II

FIRST READING   2 Sm 12:1–7a, 10–17

I have sinned against the Lord.

A reading from the second Book of Samuel

The Lord sent Nathan to David, and when he came to him, Nathan said: "Judge this case for me! In a certain town there were two men, one rich, the other poor. The rich man had flocks and herds in great numbers. But the poor man had nothing at all except one little ewe lamb that he had bought. He nourished her, and she grew up with him and his children. She shared the little food he had and drank from his cup and slept in his bosom. She was like a daughter to him. Now, the rich man received a visitor, but he would not take from his own flocks and herds to prepare a meal for the wayfarer who had come to him. Instead he took the poor man's ewe lamb and made a meal of it for his visitor." David grew very angry with that man and said to him: "As the Lord lives, the man who has done this merits death! He shall restore the ewe lamb fourfold because he has done this and has had no pity."

Then Nathan said to David: "You are the man! Thus says the Lord God of Israel: 'The sword shall never depart from your house, because you have despised me and have taken the wife of Uriah to be your wife.' Thus says the Lord: 'I will bring evil upon you out of your own house. I will take your wives while you live to see it, and will give them to your neighbor. He shall lie with your wives in broad daylight. You have done this deed in secret, but I will bring it about in the presence of all Israel, and with the sun looking down.'"

Then David said to Nathan, "I have sinned against the Lord."

Nathan answered David: "The Lord on his part has forgiven your sin: you shall not die. But since you have utterly spurned the Lord by this deed, the child born to you must surely die." Then Nathan returned to his house.

The Lord struck the child that the wife of Uriah had borne to David, and it became desperately ill. David besought God for the child. He kept a fast, retiring for the night to lie on the ground clothed in sackcloth. The elders of his house stood beside him urging him to rise from the ground; but he would not, nor would he take food with them.

The word of the Lord.

Responsorial Psalm   Ps 51:12–13, 14–15, 16–17

R. Create a clean heart in me, O God.

A clean heart create for me, O God,
  and a steadfast spirit renew within me.
Cast me not out from your presence,
  and your Holy Spirit take not from me.

R. Create a clean heart in me, O God.

Give me back the joy of your salvation,
  and a willing spirit sustain in me.
I will teach transgressors your ways,
  and sinners shall return to you.

R. Create a clean heart in me, O God.

Free me from blood guilt, O God, my saving God;
  then my tongue shall revel in your justice.
O Lord, open my lips,
  and my mouth shall proclaim your praise.

R. Create a clean heart in me, O God.

Alleluia, alleluia   Jn 3:16
God so loved the world that he gave his only-begotten Son,
so that everyone who believes in him might have eternal life.
Alleluia, alleluia

Years I and II

GOSPEL   Mk 4:35–41

Who then is this whom even wind and sea obey?

A reading from the holy Gospel according to Mark

On that day, as evening drew on, Jesus said to his disciples: "Let us cross to the other side." Leaving the crowd, they took Jesus with them in the boat just as he was. And other boats were with him. A violent squall came up and waves were breakingover the boat, so that it was already filling up. Jesus was in the stern, asleep on a cushion. They woke him and said to him, "Teacher, do you not care that we are perishing?" He woke up, rebuked the wind, and said to the sea, "Quiet! Be still!" The wind ceased and there was great calm. Then he asked them, "Why are you terrified? Do you not yet have faith?" They were filled with great awe and said to one another, "Who then is this whom even wind and sea obey?"

The Gospel of the Lord.

Liturgy of the Eucharist, *p. 897;* **Prayer over the Gifts,** *p. 297.*

FOURTH WEEK IN ORDINARY TIME

The **Antiphons and Prayers** *may be the following, or may be chosen from any of the other 33 weeks in Ordinary Time (refer to Liturgical Calendar, pp. 26–41).*

The **Liturgy of the Word** *varies: for Monday, see p. 329; Tuesday, p. 335; Wednesday, p. 341; Thursday, p. 346; Friday, p. 350; Saturday, p. 355.*

Entrance Antiphon

Save us, Lord our God, and gather us together from the nations, that we may proclaim your holy name and glory in your praise.

Opening Prayer

Let us pray
    [for a greater love of God
    and of our fellow men]
        Pause for silent prayer.

Lord our God,
help us to love you with all our hearts
and to love all men as you love them.

Grant this through our Lord Jesus Christ, your Son,
who lives and reigns with you and the Holy Spirit,
one God, for ever and ever.

Alternative Opening Prayer

Let us pray
    [joining in the praise of the living God
    for we are his people]
        Pause for silent prayer.

Father in heaven,
from the days of Abraham and Moses
until this gathering of your Church in prayer,
you have formed a people in the image of your Son.
Bless this people with the gift of your kingdom.
May we serve you with our every desire
and show love for one another
even as you have loved us.

Grant this through Christ our Lord.

Prayer over the Gifts

Pray, brethren...

Lord,
be pleased with the gifts we bring to your altar,

and make them the sacrament of our salvation.

We ask this through Christ our Lord.

Preface of Weekdays in Ordinary Time I–VI, *pp. 948–950.*

Communion Antiphon

Let your face shine on your servant, and save me by your love.
Lord, keep me from shame, for I have called to you.

(Ps 30:17–18)

Or:

Happy are the poor in spirit; the kingdom of heaven is theirs!
Happy are the lowly; they shall inherit the land.   (Mt 5:3–4)

Prayer after Communion

Let us pray.

Pause for silent prayer, if this has not preceded.

Lord,
you invigorate us with this help to our salvation.
By this eucharist give the true faith continued growth
throughout the world.

We ask this in the name of Jesus the Lord.

Monday

Antiphons and Prayers, *p. 327;* **Liturgy of the Word** *for Year I (odd years) follows; Year II (even years), p. 332.*

TODAY'S LIVING WORD

Today's Gospel is the story of an exorcism that betrays the raw humor of a folk tale, the episode of the pigs stampeding to their deaths. The description of the demoniac is horrifying and repulsive. Only in the light of the other two readings does the message of this one come into focus.

The rebellion of Absalom reduced David to a shadow of himself.

He made his way weeping up the Mount of Olives, head covered and feet bare, while Shimei cursed him and threw stones at him. David here was not so different than the Gerasene demoniac. David too was tragically alienated—from his son, his subjects, and his royal self. The plight of God's people as described in Hebrews—"they went about...needy, afflicted, tormented," wandering in deserts, dwelling in caves—is also reminiscent of the Gerasene. Each of these desperate human situations cries out for God to see and to save. The Gospel tells us that in Jesus, God does just that.

Year I

FIRST READING   Heb 11:32–40

By faith they conquered kingdoms.
God had foreseen something better for us.

A reading from the Letter to the Hebrews

Brothers and sisters:

What more shall I say? I have not time to tell of Gideon, Barak, Samson, Jephthah, of David and Samuel and the prophets, who by faith conquered kingdoms, did what was righteous, obtained the promises; they closed the mouths of lions, put out raging fires, escaped the devouring sword; out of weakness they were made powerful, became strong in battle, and turned back foreign invaders. Women received back their dead through resurrection. Some were tortured and would not accept deliverance, in order to obtain a better resurrection. Others endured mockery, scourging, even chains and imprisonment. They were stoned, sawed in two, put to death at sword's point; they went about in skins of sheep or goats, needy, afflicted, tormented. The world was not worthy of them. They wandered about in deserts and on mountains, in caves and in crevices in the earth.

Yet all these, though approved because of their faith, did not receive what had been promised. God had foreseen something better for us, so that without us they should not be made perfect.

The word of the Lord.

Responsorial Psalm

Ps 31:20, 21, 22, 23, 24

> **R. Let your hearts take comfort, all who hope in the Lord.**

How great is the goodness, O LORD,
  which you have in store for those who fear you,
And which, toward those who take refuge in you,
  you show in the sight of the children of men.

> **R. Let your hearts take comfort, all who hope in the Lord.**

You hide them in the shelter of your presence
  from the plottings of men;
You screen them within your abode
  from the strife of tongues.

> **R. Let your hearts take comfort, all who hope in the Lord.**

Blessed be the LORD whose wondrous mercy
  he has shown me in a fortified city.

> **R. Let your hearts take comfort, all who hope in the Lord.**

Once I said in my anguish,
  "I am cut off from your sight";
Yet you heard the sound of my pleading
  when I cried out to you.

> **R. Let your hearts take comfort, all who hope in the Lord.**

Love the LORD, all you his faithful ones!
  The LORD keeps those who are constant,
  but more than requites those who act proudly.

R. Let your hearts take comfort, all who hope in the Lord.

Alleluia Verse *and* **Gospel,** *p. 334.*

Year II

FIRST READING   2 Sm 15:13–14, 30; 16:5–13

Let us take flight, or none of us will escape from Absalom.
Let Shimei alone and let him curse, for the LORD has told him to.

A reading from the second Book of Samuel

An informant came to David with the report, "The children of Israel have transferred their loyalty to Absalom." At this, David said to all his servants who were with him in Jerusalem: "Up! Let us take flight, or none of us will escape from Absalom. Leave quickly, lest he hurry and overtake us, then visit disaster upon us and put the city to the sword."

As David went up the Mount of Olives, he wept without ceasing. His head was covered, and he was walking barefoot. All those who were with him also had their heads covered and were weeping as they went.

As David was approaching Bahurim, a man named Shimei, the son of Gera of the same clan as Saul's family, was coming out of the place, cursing as he came. He threw stones at David and at all the king's officers, even though all the soldiers, including the royal guard, were on David's right and on his left. Shimei was saying as he cursed: "Away, away, you murderous and wicked man! The LORD has requited you for all the bloodshed in the family of Saul, in whose stead you became king, and the LORD has given over the kingdom to your son Absalom. And now you suffer ruin because you are a murderer." Abishai, son of Zeruiah, said to the king: "Why should this dead dog curse my lord the king? Let me go over, please, and lop off his head." But the king replied: "What business is it of mine or of yours, sons of Zeruiah, that he curses? Suppose the LORD has told him to curse David; who then will dare to say, 'Why are you doing this?'" Then the king said to Abishai and to all his servants: "If my own son, who came forth from my loins, is seeking my life, how much more might this Benjaminite do so? Let him alone and let him curse, for the LORD has told him to. Perhaps the LORD will look upon my affliction and make it up to me with benefits for the curses he is uttering this day." David and his men continued on the road, while Shimei kept abreast of them on the hillside, all the while cursing and throwing stones and dirt as he went.

The word of the Lord.

Responsorial Psalm   Ps 3:2–3, 4–5, 6–7

R. Lord, rise up and save me.

O LORD, how many are my adversaries!
    Many rise up against me!
Many are saying of me,
    "There is no salvation for him in God."

R. Lord, rise up and save me.

But you, O LORD, are my shield;
    my glory, you lift up my head!
When I call out to the LORD,
    he answers me from his holy mountain.

R. Lord, rise up and save me.

When I lie down in sleep,
    I wake again, for the LORD sustains me.
I fear not the myriads of people
    arrayed against me on every side.

R. Lord, rise up and save me.

Alleluia, alleluia   Lk 7:16
A great prophet has arisen in our midst
and God has visited his people.
Alleluia, alleluia

Years I and II

GOSPEL   Mk 5:1–20

Unclean spirit, come out of the man!

A reading from the holy Gospel according to Mark

Jesus and his disciples came to the other side of the sea, to the territory of the Gerasenes. When he got out of the boat, at once a man from the tombs who had an unclean spirit met him. The man had been dwelling among the tombs, and no one could restrain him any longer, even with a chain. In fact, he had frequently been bound with shackles and chains, but the chains had been pulled apart by him and the shackles smashed, and no one was strong enough to subdue him. Night and day among the tombs and on the hillsides he was always crying out and bruising himself with stones. Catching sight of Jesus from a distance, he ran up and prostrated himself before him, crying out in a loud voice, "What have you to do with me, Jesus, Son of the Most High God? I adjure you by God, do not torment me!" (He had been saying to him, "Unclean spirit, come out of the man!") He asked him, "What is your name?" He replied, "Legion is my name. There are many of us." And he pleaded earnestly with him not to drive them away from that territory.

Now a large herd of swine was feeding there on the hillside. And they pleaded with him, "Send us into the swine. Let us enter them." And he let them, and the unclean spirits came out and entered the swine. The herd of about two thousand rushed down a steep bank into the sea, where they were drowned. The swineherds ran away and reported the incident in the town and throughout the countryside. And people came out to see what had happened. As they approached Jesus, they caught sight of the man who had been possessed by Legion, sitting there clothed and in his right mind. And they were seized with fear. Those who witnessed the incident explained to them what had happened to the possessed man and to the swine. Then they began to beg him to leave their district. As he was getting into the boat, the man who had been possessed pleaded to remain with him. But Jesus would not permit him but told him instead, "Go home to your family and announce to them all that the Lord in his pity has done for you." Then the man went off and began to proclaim in the Decapolis what Jesus had done for him; and all were amazed.

The Gospel of the Lord.

Liturgy of the Eucharist, *p. 897;* **Prayer over the Gifts,** *p. 328.*

Tuesday

Antiphons and Prayers, *p. 327;* **Liturgy of the Word** *for Year I (odd years) follows; Year II (even years), p. 337.*

TODAY'S LIVING WORD

The two miracle stories in today's reading from Mark present us with "a cloud of witnesses," as Hebrews would say. There is Jairus, the synagogue official whose daughter is near death; the desperate woman afflicted with a hemorrhage for a dozen years; and, of course, Peter, James, and John, the privileged witnesses of Jesus' saving work. The first story is begun, interrupted by the second story, and then finally completed, creating what scholars describe as a "sand-wiching" effect. Mark intends that we read one story in light of the other. Doing so, we discover that the salvation from death that Jairus sought for his daughter is accessible only to those who have faith, like the woman with the hemorrhage.

If there is a point of contact between this Gospel and the selection from 2 Samuel, it lies in the anguish of the two fathers, Jairus and David. More often than not our lived experience is like David's rather than that of Jairus. At these times, above all, we must keep "our eyes fixed on Jesus, the leader and perfecter of faith."

Year I

FIRST READING
Heb 12:1–4

Let us persevere in running the race that lies before us.

A reading from the Letter to the Hebrews

Brothers and sisters:
Since we are surrounded by so great a cloud of witnesses, let us rid ourselves of every burden and sin that clings to us and persevere in running the race that lies before us while keeping our eyes fixed on Jesus, the leader and perfecter of faith. For the sake of the joy that lay before him Jesus endured the cross, despising its shame, and has taken his seat at the right of the throne of God. Consider how he endured such opposition from sinners, in order that you may not grow weary and lose heart. In your struggle against sin you have not yet resisted to the point of shedding blood.

The word of the Lord.

Responsorial Psalm
Ps 22:26b–27, 28 and 30, 31–32

R. **They will praise you, Lord, who long for you.**

I will fulfill my vows before those who fear him.
The lowly shall eat their fill;
    they who seek the LORD shall praise him:
    "May your hearts be ever merry!"

R. They will praise you, Lord, who long for you.

All the ends of the earth
  shall remember and turn to the LORD;
All the families of the nations
  shall bow down before him.
To him alone shall bow down
  all who sleep in the earth;
Before him shall bend
  all who go down into the dust.

R. They will praise you, Lord, who long for you.

And to him my soul shall live;
  my descendants shall serve him.
Let the coming generation be told of the LORD
  that they may proclaim to a people yet to be born
  the justice he has shown.

R. They will praise you, Lord, who long for you.

Alleluia Verse *and* **Gospel**, *p. 339.*

Year II

FIRST READING   2 Sm 18:9–10, 14b, 24–25a, 30–19:3

My son Absalom, if only I had died instead of you.

A reading from the second Book of Samuel

Absalom unexpectedly came up against David's servants. He was mounted on a mule, and, as the mule passed under the branches of a large terebinth, his hair caught fast in the tree. He hung between heaven and earth while the mule he had been riding ran off. Someone saw this and reported to Joab that he had seen Absalom hanging from a terebinth. And taking three pikes in hand, he thrust for the heart of Absalom, still hanging from the tree alive.

Now David was sitting between the two gates, and a lookout went up to the roof of the gate above the city wall, where he looked about and saw a man running all alone. The lookout shouted to inform the king, who said, "If he is alone, he has good news to report." The king said, "Step aside and remain in attendance here." So he stepped aside and remained there. When the Cushite messenger came in, he said, "Let my lord the king receive the good news that this day the LORD has taken your part, freeing you from the grasp of all who rebelled against you." But the king asked the Cushite, "Is young Absalom safe?" The Cushite replied, "May the enemies of my lord the king and all who rebel against you with evil intent be as that young man!"

The king was shaken, and went up to the room over the city gate to weep. He said as he wept, "My son Absalom! My son, my son Absalom! If only I had died instead of you, Absalom, my son, my son!"

Joab was told that the king was weeping and mourning for Absalom; and that day's victory was turned into mourning for the whole army when they heard that the king was grieving for his son.

The word of the Lord.

Responsorial Psalm   Ps 86:1–2, 3–4, 5–6

R. **Listen, Lord, and answer me.**

Incline your ear, O LORD; answer me,
    for I am afflicted and poor.
Keep my life, for I am devoted to you;
    save your servant who trusts in you.
    You are my God.

R. **Listen, Lord, and answer me.**

Have mercy on me, O Lord,
    for to you I call all the day.

Gladden the soul of your servant,
  for to you, O Lord, I lift up my soul.

R. Listen, Lord, and answer me.

For you, O Lord, are good and forgiving,
  abounding in kindness to all who call upon you.
Hearken, O LORD, to my prayer
  and attend to the sound of my pleading.

R. Listen, Lord, and answer me.

  Alleluia, alleluia   Mt 8:17
  Christ took away our infirmities
  and bore our diseases.
  Alleluia, alleluia

Years I and II

GOSPEL   Mk 5:21–43

Little girl, I say to you, arise!

A reading from the holy Gospel according to Mark

When Jesus had crossed again in the boat to the other side, a large crowd gathered around him, and he stayed close to the sea. One of the synagogue officials, named Jairus, came forward. Seeing him he fell at his feet and pleaded earnestly with him, saying, "My daughter is at the point of death. Please, come lay your hands on her that she may get well and live." He went off with him and a large crowd followed him.

    There was a woman afflicted with hemorrhages for twelve years. She had suffered greatly at the hands of many doctors and had spent all that she had. Yet she was not helped but only grew worse. She had heard about Jesus and came up behind him in the crowd and touched his cloak. She said, "If I but touch his clothes, I shall be cured." Immediately her flow of blood dried up. She felt in her body that she was healed of her affliction. Jesus, aware at once that power had gone out from him, turned around in the crowd and asked, "Who has touched my clothes?" But his disciples said to him, "You see how the crowd is pressing upon you, and yet you ask, Who touched me?" And he looked around to see who had done it. The woman, realizing what had happened to her, approached in fear and trembling. She fell down before Jesus and told him the whole truth. He said to her, "Daughter, your faith has saved you. Go in peace and be cured of your affliction."

While he was still speaking, people from the synagogue official's house arrived and said, "Your daughter has died; why trouble the teacher any longer?" Disregarding the message that was reported, Jesus said to the synagogue official, "Do not be afraid; just have faith." He did not allow anyone to accompany him inside except Peter, James, and John, the brother of James. When they arrived at the house of the synagogue official, he caught sight of a commotion, people weeping and wailing loudly. So he went in and said to them, "Why this commotion and weeping? The child is not dead but asleep." And they ridiculed him. Then he put them all out. He took along the child's father and mother and those who were with him and entered the room where the child was. He took the child by the hand and said to her, *"Talitha koum,"* which means, "Little girl, I say to you, arise!" The girl, a child of twelve, arose immediately and walked around. At that they were utterly astounded. He gave strict orders that no one should know this and said that she should be given something to eat.

The Gospel of the Lord.

Liturgy of the Eucharist, *p. 897;* **Prayer over the Gifts,** *p. 328.*

Wednesday

Antiphons and Prayers, *p. 327;* **Liturgy of the Word** *for Year I (odd years) follows; Year II (even years), p. 343.*

TODAY'S LIVING WORD

In a way the story of David in 2 Samuel inverts this Gospel story. By ordering a census of all the tribes of Israel, David was in effect setting himself over and against his people. As Walter Brueggemann explains, "a royal census was not a neutral tool of policy." Rather, it served one of two purposes, both oppressive: taxation or military draft.* In the Gospel story, his people set themselves over and against Jesus. Because of their lack of faith, he could work no miracle there.

The whole dynamic of Mark's Gospel is summed up in this one brief episode. The wisdom and miraculous deeds of Jesus are greeted with amazement, which soon gives way to suspicion and scandal. "They took offense at him." At times all of us find Jesus and his Gospel too much for us too. That is when Hebrews is most persuasive: "Strengthen your drooping hands and your weak knees. Make straight paths for your feet, that what is lame may not be dislocated but healed."

* *Power, Providence & Personality* (Louisville: Westminster/John Knox Press, 1990), p. 103.

Year I

FIRST READING

Heb 12:4–7, 11–15

The Lord disciplines those he loves.

A reading from the Letter to the Hebrews

Brothers and sisters:

In your struggle against sin you have not yet resisted to the point of shedding blood. You have also forgotten the exhortation addressed to you as children:

> My son, do not disdain the discipline of the Lord

or lose heart when reproved by him;
   for whom the Lord loves, he disciplines;
      he scourges every son he acknowledges.

Endure your trials as "discipline"; God treats you as his sons. For what "son" is there whom his father does not discipline? At the time, all discipline seems a cause not for joy but for pain, yet later it brings the peaceful fruit of righteousness to those who are trained by it.

So strengthen your drooping hands and your weak knees. Make straight paths for your feet, that what is lame may not be dislocated but healed.

Strive for peace with everyone, and for that holiness without which no one will see the Lord. See to it that no one be deprived of the grace of God, that no bitter root spring up and cause trouble, through which many may become defiled.

The word of the Lord.

Responsorial Psalm   Ps 103:1–2, 13–14, 17–18a

R. The Lord's kindness is everlasting to those who fear him.

Bless the LORD, O my soul;
   and all my being, bless his holy name.
Bless the LORD, O my soul,
   and forget not all his benefits.

R. The Lord's kindness is everlasting to those who fear him.

As a father has compassion on his children,
   so the LORD has compassion on those who fear him,
For he knows how we are formed;
   he remembers that we are dust.

R. The Lord's kindness is everlasting to those who fear him.

But the kindness of the LORD is from eternity
   to eternity toward those who fear him,

And his justice toward children's children
  among those who keep his covenant.

R. The Lord's kindness is everlasting to those who fear him.

Alleluia Verse *and* **Gospel,** *p. 345.*

Year II

FIRST READING   2 Sm 24:2, 9–17

It is I who have sinned; but these are sheep; what have they done?

A reading from the second Book of Samuel

King David said to Joab and the leaders of the army who were
with him, "Tour all the tribes in Israel from Dan to Beer-sheba
and register the people, that I may know their number." Joab
then reported to the king the number of people registered: in
Israel, eight hundred thousand men fit for military service; in
Judah, five hundred thousand.

    Afterward, however, David regretted having numbered the
people, and said to the LORD: "I have sinned grievously in what
I have done. But now, LORD, forgive the guilt of your servant,
for I have been very foolish." When David rose in the morning,
the LORD had spoken to the prophet Gad, David's seer, saying:
"Go and say to David, 'This is what the LORD says: I offer you
three alternatives; choose one of them, and I will inflict it on
you.'" Gad then went to David to inform him. He asked: "Do
you want a three years' famine to come upon your land, or to
flee from your enemy three months while he pursues you, or
to have a three days' pestilence in your land? Now consider
and decide what I must reply to him who sent me." David
answered Gad: "I am in very serious difficulty. Let us fall by
the hand of God, for he is most merciful; but let me not fall by

344   ORDINARY TIME

the hand of man." Thus David chose the pestilence. Now it was the time of the wheat harvest when the plague broke out among the people. The Lord then sent a pestilence over Israel from morning until the time appointed, and seventy thousand of the people from Dan to Beer-sheba died. But when the angel stretched forth his hand toward Jerusalem to destroy it, the Lord regretted the calamity and said to the angel causing the destruction among the people, "Enough now! Stay your hand." The angel of the Lord was then standing at the threshing floor of Araunah the Jebusite. When David saw the angel who was striking the people, he said to the Lord: "It is I who have sinned; it is I, the shepherd, who have done wrong. But these are sheep; what have they done? Punish me and my kindred."

The word of the Lord.

Responsorial Psalm   Ps 32:1–2, 5, 6, 7

R. Lord, forgive the wrong I have done.

Blessed is he whose fault is taken away,
  whose sin is covered.
Blessed the man to whom the Lord imputes not guilt,
  in whose spirit there is no guile.

R. Lord, forgive the wrong I have done.

Then I acknowledged my sin to you,
  my guilt I covered not.
I said, "I confess my faults to the Lord,"
  and you took away the guilt of my sin.

R. Lord, forgive the wrong I have done.

For this shall every faithful man pray to you
  in time of stress.
Though deep waters overflow,
  they shall not reach him.

R. Lord, forgive the wrong I have done.

You are my shelter; from distress you will preserve me;
  with glad cries of freedom you will ring me round.

R. Lord, forgive the wrong I have done.

> **Alleluia, alleluia**   Jn 10:27
> My sheep hear my voice, says the Lord;
> I know them, and they follow me.
> **Alleluia, alleluia**

Years I and II

GOSPEL   Mk 6:1– 6

A prophet is not without honor except in his native place.

A reading from the holy Gospel according to Mark

Jesus departed from there and came to his native place, accompanied by his disciples. When the sabbath came he began to teach in the synagogue, and many who heard him were astonished. They said, "Where did this man get all this? What kind of wisdom has been given him? What mighty deeds are wrought by his hands! Is he not the carpenter, the son of Mary, and the brother of James and Joseph and Judas and Simon? And are not his sisters here with us?" And they took offense at him. Jesus said to them, "A prophet is not without honor except in his native place and among his own kin and in his own house." So he was not able to perform any mighty deed there, apart from curing a few sick people by laying his hands on them. He was amazed at their lack of faith.

The Gospel of the Lord.

Liturgy of the Eucharist, *p. 897;* **Prayer over the Gifts,** *p. 328.*

Thursday

Antiphons and Prayers, *p. 327;* **Liturgy of the Word** *for Year I (odd years) follows; Year II (even years), p. 348.*

TODAY'S LIVING WORD

As David counseled Solomon, so Jesus counsels the Twelve. They are to continue his ministry in word and deed. Mark makes this clear by the words he chooses to describe their commission. Like Jesus, they are to preach "repentance," expel demons, and heal the sick. The instructions Jesus gives are the rules of the road for traveling missionaries. As an itinerant teacher, Jesus depended on the hospitality of those to whom he ministered, and so would his disciples. Their dependence on the generosity of others would be absolute and practical; they were to take "no food, no sack, no money in their belts." They were to receive graciously whatever hospitality was offered. The instruction to stay in one house "until you leave from there" was meant to keep missionaries from shopping for better accommodations.

If we have "approached...the city of the living God," as Hebrews says, it is only because God has drawn near to us, through the mission of Jesus continued by his Church.

Year I

FIRST READING   Heb 12:18–19, 21–24

You have approached Mount Zion and the city of the living God.

A reading from the Letter to the Hebrews

Brothers and sisters:

You have not approached that which could be touched and a blazing fire and gloomy darkness and storm and a trumpet blast and a voice speaking words such that those who heard begged that no message be further addressed to them. Indeed, so fearful was the spectacle that Moses said, "I am terrified and trembling." No, you have approached Mount Zion and the city of the living God, the heavenly Jerusalem, and countless angels in festal gathering, and the assembly of the firstborn enrolled in heaven, and God the judge of all, and the spirits of the just made perfect, and Jesus, the mediator of a new covenant, and the sprinkled Blood that speaks more eloquently than that of Abel.

The word of the Lord.

Responsorial Psalm
Ps 48:2 – 3ab, 3cd – 4, 9, 10 – 11

R. O God, we ponder your mercy within your temple.

Great is the LORD and wholly to be praised
  in the city of our God.
His holy mountain, fairest of heights,
  is the joy of all the earth.

R. O God, we ponder your mercy within your temple.

Mount Zion, "the recesses of the North,"
  the city of the great King.
God is with her castles;
  renowned is he as a stronghold.

R. O God, we ponder your mercy within your temple.

As we had heard, so have we seen
  in the city of the LORD of hosts,
In the city of our God;
  God makes it firm forever.

R. O God, we ponder your mercy within your temple.

O God, we ponder your mercy
  within your temple.
As your name, O God, so also your praise
  reaches to the ends of the earth.
Of justice your right hand is full.

R. O God, we ponder your mercy within your temple.

Alleluia Verse *and* **Gospel,** *p. 349.*

FIRST READING   1 Kgs 2:1–4, 10–12

I am going the way of all flesh.
Take courage and be a man.

A reading from the first Book of Kings

When the time of David's death drew near, he gave these instructions to his son Solomon: "I am going the way of all flesh. Take courage and be a man. Keep the mandate of the LORD, your God, following his ways and observing his statutes, commands, ordinances, and decrees as they are written in the law of Moses, that you may succeed in whatever you do, wherever you turn, and the LORD may fulfill the promise he made on my behalf when he said, 'If your sons so conduct themselves that they remain faithful to me with their whole heart and with their whole soul, you shall always have someone of your line on the throne of Israel.'"

David rested with his ancestors and was buried in the City of David. The length of David's reign over Israel was forty years: he reigned seven years in Hebron and thirty-three years in Jerusalem.

Solomon was seated on the throne of his father David, with his sovereignty firmly established.

The word of the Lord.

Responsorial Psalm   1 Chr 29:10, 11ab, 11d–12a, 12bcd

   R. Lord, you are exalted over all.

"Blessed may you be, O LORD,
   God of Israel our father,
   from eternity to eternity."

R. Lord, you are exalted over all.

"Yours, O Lᴏʀᴅ, are grandeur and power,
  majesty, splendor, and glory."

R. Lord, you are exalted over all.

"Lᴏʀᴅ, you are exalted over all.
  Yours, O Lᴏʀᴅ, is the sovereignty;
  you are exalted as head over all.
Riches and honor are from you."

R. Lord, you are exalted over all.

"In your hand are power and might;
  it is yours to give grandeur and strength to all."

R. Lord, you are exalted over all.

Alleluia, alleluia   Mk 1:15
The Kingdom of God is at hand;
repent and believe in the Gospel.
Alleluia, alleluia

Years I and II

GOSPEL   Mk 6:7–13

Jesus summoned the Twelve and began to send them out.

A reading from the holy Gospel according to Mark

Jesus summoned the Twelve and began to send them out two
by two and gave them authority over unclean spirits. He
instructed them to take nothing for the journey but a walking
stick—no food, no sack, no money in their belts. They were,
however, to wear sandals but not a second tunic. He said to
them, "Wherever you enter a house, stay there until you leave
from there. Whatever place does not welcome you or listen to
you, leave there and shake the dust off your feet in testimony
against them." So they went off and preached repentance. The

Twelve drove out many demons, and they anointed with oil
many who were sick and cured them.

The Gospel of the Lord.

Liturgy of the Eucharist, *p. 897;* **Prayer over the Gifts,** *p. 328.*

Friday

Antiphons and Prayers, *p. 327;* **Liturgy of the Word** *for Year I (odd
years) follows; Year II (even years), p. 352.*

TODAY'S LIVING WORD

The selection from Hebrews urges us: "Remember your leaders
who spoke the word of God to you." The reading from the Old
Testament Book of Sirach and the passage from Mark's Gospel present
us with two great men whose lives speak to us of God—one a
messiah, the other a martyr. In the life and death of each, the early
Church found resonance with the life and death of Jesus. Sirach's
praise of David is poetic and prayerful. He is the Lord's "anointed"
(messiah) and his whole life rises like a sacred offering before God.
Mark's account of the martyrdom of John the Baptist, on the other
hand, is pointedly prosaic. He is the Lord's prophet, and his life is
sacrificed to ensure the political survival of a corrupt client-king.
Both converge in the experience of Jesus.

And in ours? The martyrdom of John is "sandwiched" between
Jesus' sending out his disciples and their returning to him. This is
Mark's way of telling us that disciples of Jesus may expect to share
John's fate, like Jesus himself. "Consider the outcome of their way
of life," says Hebrews, "and imitate their faith."

Year I

FIRST READING
Heb 13:1–8

Jesus Christ is the same yesterday, today, and forever.

A reading from the Letter to the Hebrews

Let brotherly love continue. Do not neglect hospitality, for through it some have unknowingly entertained angels. Be mindful of prisoners as if sharing their imprisonment, and of the ill-treated as of yourselves, for you also are in the body. Let marriage be honored among all and the marriage bed be kept undefiled, for God will judge the immoral and adulterers. Let your life be free from love of money but be content with what you have, for he has said, *I will never forsake you or abandon you.* Thus we may say with confidence:

> *The Lord is my helper,*
> *and I will not be afraid.*
> *What can anyone do to me?*

Remember your leaders who spoke the word of God to you. Consider the outcome of their way of life and imitate their faith. Jesus Christ is the same yesterday, today, and forever.

The word of the Lord.

Responsorial Psalm
Ps 27:1, 3, 5, 8b–9abc

R. The Lord is my light and my salvation.

The LORD is my light and my salvation;
  whom should I fear?
The LORD is my life's refuge;
  of whom should I be afraid?

R. The Lord is my light and my salvation.

Though an army encamp against me,
  my heart will not fear;
Though war be waged upon me,
  even then will I trust.

R. The Lord is my light and my salvation.

For he will hide me in his abode
  in the day of trouble;

He will conceal me in the shelter of his tent,
  he will set me high upon a rock.

R. The Lord is my light and my salvation.

Your presence, O Lord, I seek.
Hide not your face from me;
  do not in anger repel your servant.
You are my helper: cast me not off.

R. The Lord is my light and my salvation.

Alleluia Verse and **Gospel**, p. 354.

Year II

FIRST READING

Sir 47:2–11

With his every deed David offered thanks to God Most High;
in words of praise he loved his Maker.

A reading from the Book of Sirach

Like the choice fat of the sacred offerings,
    so was David in Israel.
He made sport of lions as though they were kids,
    and of bears, like lambs of the flock.
As a youth he slew the giant
    and wiped out the people's disgrace,
When his hand let fly the slingstone
    that crushed the pride of Goliath.
Since he called upon the Most High God,
    who gave strength to his right arm
To defeat the skilled warrior
    and raise up the might of his people,
Therefore the women sang his praises,
    and ascribed to him tens of thousands

and praised him when they blessed the Lord.
When he assumed the royal crown, he battled
 and subdued the enemy on every side.
He destroyed the hostile Philistines
 and shattered their power till our own day.
With his every deed he offered thanks
 to God Most High, in words of praise.
With his whole being he loved his Maker
 and daily had his praises sung;
 He set singers before the altar and by their voices
  he made sweet melodies,
He added beauty to the feasts
 and solemnized the seasons of each year
So that when the Holy Name was praised,
 before daybreak the sanctuary would resound.
The LORD forgave him his sins
 and exalted his strength forever;
He conferred on him the rights of royalty
 and established his throne in Israel.
The word of the Lord.

Responsorial Psalm

Ps 18:31, 47 and 50, 51

 R. Blessed be God my salvation!

God's way is unerring,
 the promise of the LORD is fire-tried;
 he is a shield to all who take refuge in him.

 R. Blessed be God my salvation!

The LORD live! And blessed be my Rock!
 Extolled be God my savior.
Therefore will I proclaim you, O LORD, among the nations,
 and I will sing praise to your name.

R. Blessed be God my salvation!

You who gave great victories to your king
  and showed kindness to your anointed,
  to David and his posterity forever.

R. Blessed be God my salvation!

> **Alleluia, alleluia** See Lk 8:15
> Blessed are they who have kept the word with a generous heart,
> and yield a harvest through perseverance.
> **Alleluia, alleluia**

Years I and II

GOSPEL   Mk 6:14 – 29

It is John whom I beheaded. He has been raised up.

A reading from the holy Gospel according to Mark

King Herod heard about Jesus, for his fame had become widespread, and people were saying, "John the Baptist has been raised from the dead; that is why mighty powers are at work in him." Others were saying, "He is Elijah"; still others, "He is a prophet like any of the prophets." But when Herod learned of it, he said, "It is John whom I beheaded. He has been raised up."

Herod was the one who had John arrested and bound in prison on account of Herodias, the wife of his brother Philip, whom he had married. John had said to Herod, "It is not lawful for you to have your brother's wife." Herodias harbored a grudge against him and wanted to kill him but was unable to do so. Herod feared John, knowing him to be a righteous and holy man, and kept him in custody. When he heard him speak he was very much perplexed, yet he liked to listen to him.

Herodias had an opportunity one day when Herod, on his birthday, gave a banquet for his courtiers, his military officers, and the leading men of Galilee. His own daughter came in and performed a dance that delighted Herod and his guests. The king said to the girl, "Ask of me whatever you wish and I will grant it to you." He even swore many things to her, "I will grant you whatever you ask of me, even to half of my kingdom." She went out and said to her mother, "What shall I ask for?" Her mother replied, "The head of John the Baptist." The girl hurried back to the king's presence and made her request, "I want you to give me at once on a platter the head of John the Baptist." The king was deeply distressed, but because of his oaths and the guests he did not wish to break his word to her. So he promptly dispatched an executioner with orders to bring back his head. He went off and beheaded him in the prison. He brought in the head on a platter and gave it to the girl. The girl in turn gave it to her mother. When his disciples heard about it, they came and took his body and laid it in a tomb.

The Gospel of the Lord.

Liturgy of the Eucharist, *p. 897;* **Prayer over the Gifts,** *p. 328.*

Saturday

Antiphons and Prayers, *p. 327;* **Liturgy of the Word** *for Year I (odd years) follows; Year II (even years), p. 358.*

TODAY'S LIVING WORD

The three readings for today invite us to reflect on pastoral leadership. The author of the Letter to the Hebrews exhorts his readers to obey their leaders and to submit to them, mindful of the responsibility they bear. The excerpt from 1 Kings contains the prayer of a young king who, wanting to be a good leader, asks only for "an understanding heart." The brief episode from Mark vividly describes the tireless service that will be required of the apostles of Jesus. Solomon's question seems to lie just under the surface of all three readings: "Who is able to govern this vast people of yours?"

Each reading suggests the same answer. Mark shows the apostles simply participating in Jesus' pastoral ministry to the vast crowd, who are "like sheep without a shepherd." In the reading from Kings, it is clearly by God's favor that Solomon rules with a wise and understanding heart. But the prayer in Hebrews says it best: it asks that through Jesus, "the great shepherd of the sheep," God may "carry out in you what is pleasing to him." In short, the answer to Solomon's question is: not you, but God in you.

Year I

FIRST READING

Heb 13:15–17, 20–21

May the God of peace, who brought up from the dead
the great shepherd, furnish you with all that is good.

A reading from the Letter to the Hebrews

Brothers and sisters:

Through Jesus, let us continually offer God a sacrifice of praise, that is, the fruit of lips that confess his name. Do not neglect to do good and to share what you have; God is pleased by sacrifices of that kind.

Obey your leaders and defer to them, for they keep watch over you and will have to give an account, that they may fulfill their task with joy and not with sorrow, for that would be of no advantage to you.

May the God of peace, who brought up from the dead the great shepherd of the sheep by the Blood of the eternal covenant, furnish you with all that is good, that you may do his will. May he carry out in you what is pleasing to him through Jesus Christ, to whom be glory forever and ever. Amen.

The word of the Lord.

Responsorial Psalm

Ps 23:1–3a, 3b–4, 5, 6

R. The Lord is my shepherd; there is nothing I shall want.

The LORD is my shepherd; I shall not want.
  In verdant pastures he gives me repose.
Beside restful waters he leads me;
  he refreshes my soul.

R. The Lord is my shepherd; there is nothing I shall want.

He guides me in right paths
  for his name's sake.
Even though I walk in the dark valley
  I fear no evil; for you are at my side
With your rod and your staff
  that give me courage.

R. The Lord is my shepherd; there is nothing I shall want.

You spread the table before me
  in the sight of my foes;
You anoint my head with oil;
  my cup overflows.

R. The Lord is my shepherd; there is nothing I shall want.

Only goodness and kindness follow me
  all the days of my life;
And I shall dwell in the house of the LORD
  for years to come.

R. The Lord is my shepherd; there is nothing I shall want.

Alleluia Verse *and* **Gospel,** *p. 359.*

FIRST READING   1 Kgs 3:4–13

Give your servant an understanding heart to judge your people.

A reading from the first Book of Kings

Solomon went to Gibeon to sacrifice there, because that was the most renowned high place. Upon its altar Solomon offered a thousand burnt offerings. In Gibeon the LORD appeared to Solomon in a dream at night. God said, "Ask something of me and I will give it to you." Solomon answered: "You have shown great favor to your servant, my father David, because he behaved faithfully toward you, with justice and an upright heart; and you have continued this great favor toward him, even today, seating a son of his on his throne. O LORD, my God, you have made me, your servant, king to succeed my father David; but I am a mere youth, not knowing at all how to act. I serve you in the midst of the people whom you have chosen, a people so vast that it cannot be numbered or counted. Give your servant, therefore, an understanding heart to judge your people and to distinguish right from wrong. For who is able to govern this vast people of yours?"

The LORD was pleased that Solomon made this request. So God said to him: "Because you have asked for this—not for a long life for yourself, nor for riches, nor for the life of your enemies, but for understanding so that you may know what is right—I do as you requested. I give you a heart so wise and understanding that there has never been anyone like you up to now, and after you there will come no one to equal you. In addition, I give you what you have not asked for, such riches and glory that among kings there is not your like."

The word of the Lord.

Responsorial Psalm

Ps 119:9, 10, 11, 12, 13, 14

R. Lord, teach me your statutes.

How shall a young man be faultless in his way?
  By keeping to your words.

R. Lord, teach me your statutes.

With all my heart I seek you;
  let me not stray from your commands.

R. Lord, teach me your statutes.

Within my heart I treasure your promise,
  that I may not sin against you.

R. Lord, teach me your statutes.

Blessed are you, O LORD;
  teach me your statutes.

R. Lord, teach me your statutes.

With my lips I declare
  all the ordinances of your mouth.

R. Lord, teach me your statutes.

In the way of your decrees I rejoice,
  as much as in all riches.

R. Lord, teach me your statutes.

Alleluia, alleluia Jn 10:27
  My sheep hear my voice, says the Lord;
  I know them, and they follow me.
Alleluia, alleluia

Years I and II

GOSPEL   Mk 6:30–34

They were like sheep without a shepherd.

A reading from the holy Gospel according to Mark

The Apostles gathered together with Jesus and reported all they
had done and taught. He said to them, "Come away by

yourselves to a deserted place and rest a while." People were coming and going in great numbers, and they had no opportunity even to eat. So they went off in the boat by themselves to a deserted place. People saw them leaving and many came to know about it. They hastened there on foot from all the towns and arrived at the place before them.

When Jesus disembarked and saw the vast crowd, his heart was moved with pity for them, for they were like sheep without a shepherd; and he began to teach them many things.

The Gospel of the Lord.

Liturgy of the Eucharist, *p. 897;* **Prayer over the Gifts,** *p. 328.*

FIFTH WEEK IN ORDINARY TIME

The **Antiphons and Prayers** *may be the following, or may be chosen from any of the other 33 weeks in Ordinary Time (refer to Liturgical Calendar, pp. 26–41).*

The **Liturgy of the Word** *varies: for Monday, see p. 362; Tuesday, p. 367; Wednesday, p. 373; Thursday, p. 377; Friday, p. 382; Saturday, p. 386.*

Entrance Antiphon

Come, let us worship the Lord. Let us bow down in the presence of our maker, for he is the Lord our God.   (Ps 95:6 –7)

Opening Prayer

Let us pray
  [that God will watch over us and protect us]

   Pause for silent prayer.

Father,
watch over your family
and keep us safe in your care,
for all our hope is in you.

Grant this through our Lord Jesus Christ, your Son,
who lives and reigns with you and the Holy Spirit,
one God, for ever and ever.

Alternative Opening Prayer

Let us pray
  [with reverence in the presence of the living God]
    Pause for silent prayer.

In faith and love we ask you, Father,
to watch over your family gathered here.
In your mercy and loving kindness
no thought of ours is left unguarded,
no tear unheeded, no joy unnoticed.
Through the prayer of Jesus
may the blessings promised to the poor in spirit
lead us to the treasures of your heavenly kingdom.

We ask this in the name of Jesus the Lord.

Prayer over the Gifts

Pray, brethren...

Lord our God,
may the bread and wine
you give us for our nourishment on earth
become the sacrament of our eternal life.

We ask this through Christ our Lord.

Preface of Weekdays in Ordinary Time I–VI, *pp. 948–950.*

Communion Antiphon

Give praise to the Lord for his kindness, for his wonderful deeds toward men. He has filled the hungry with good things, he has satisfied the thirsty.
                (Ps 107:8–9)

Or:

Happy are the sorrowing; they shall be consoled. Happy those who hunger and thirst for what is right; they shall be satisfied.

(Mt 5:5 – 6)

Prayer after Communion

Let us pray.

Pause for silent prayer, if this has not preceded.

God our Father,
you give us a share in the one bread and the one cup
and make us one in Christ.
Help us to bring your salvation and joy
to all the world.
We ask this through Christ our Lord.

Monday

Antiphons and Prayers, *p. 360;* **Liturgy of the Word** *for Year I (odd years) follows; Year II (even years), p. 365.*

TODAY'S LIVING WORD

Today's three readings deal with the theme of home-making. Describing the first three days of creation, the Book of Genesis shows God overcoming the deep and the dark in order to make the earth a habitable, hospitable place for human beings—a home. In the first Book of Kings, the priests of Israel carry the ark of the covenant into the holy of holies. The dark cloud symbolizes the presence of God, who takes up residence in the princely house—the home—that Solomon has built. Finally, the Gospel of Mark suggests that the powerful presence of God has found a new home in the ministry of Jesus. Mark says that the crowds "began to bring in the sick on mats to wherever they heard he was," and all who touched the "tassel on his cloak...were healed."

Mark's meaning is only fully disclosed in the Greek verb translated here as "were healed." That word *(esozonto)* connotes more than mere physical healing. In the vocabulary of the early Church, it described the total experience of salvation: not just wellness, but wholeness—in other words, coming home.

Year I

FIRST READING

Gn 1:1–19

God spoke, and it was done.

A reading from the beginning of the Book of Genesis

In the beginning, when God created the heavens and the earth, the earth was a formless wasteland, and darkness covered the abyss, while a mighty wind swept over the waters.

Then God said, "Let there be light," and there was light. God saw how good the light was. God then separated the light from the darkness. God called the light "day," and the darkness he called "night." Thus evening came, and morning followed—the first day.

Then God said, "Let there be a dome in the middle of the waters, to separate one body of water from the other." And so it happened: God made the dome, and it separated the water above the dome from the water below it. God called the dome "the sky." Evening came, and morning followed—the second day.

Then God said, "Let the water under the sky be gathered into a single basin, so that the dry land may appear." And so it happened: the water under the sky was gathered into its basin, and the dry land appeared. God called the dry land "the earth," and the basin of the water he called "the sea." God saw how good it was. Then God said, "Let the earth bring forth vege-tation: every kind of plant that bears seed and every kind of fruit tree on earth that bears fruit with its seed in it." And so it happened: the earth brought forth every kind of plant that bears seed and every kind of fruit tree on earth that bears fruit with its seed in it. God saw how good it was. Evening came, and morning followed—the third day.

Then God said: "Let there be lights in the dome of the sky, to separate day from night. Let them mark the fixed times, the days and the years, and serve as luminaries in the dome of the sky, to shed light upon the earth." And so it happened: God made the two great lights, the greater one to govern the day, and the lesser one to govern the night; and he made the stars. God set them in the dome of the sky, to shed light upon the earth, to govern the day and the night, and to separate the light from the darkness. God saw how good it was. Evening came, and morning followed—the fourth day.

The word of the Lord.

Responsorial Psalm   Ps 104:1–2a, 5–6, 10 and 12, 24 and 35c

R. **May the Lord be glad in his works.**

Bless the LORD, O my soul!
  O LORD, my God, you are great indeed!
You are clothed with majesty and glory,
  robed in light as with a cloak.

R. **May the Lord be glad in his works.**

You fixed the earth upon its foundation,
  not to be moved forever;
With the ocean, as with a garment, you covered it;
  above the mountains the waters stood.

R. **May the Lord be glad in his works.**

You send forth springs into the watercourses
  that wind among the mountains.

Beside them the birds of heaven dwell;
  from among the branches they send forth their song.

R. May the Lord be glad in his works.

How manifold are your works, O LORD!
  In wisdom you have wrought them all—
  the earth is full of your creatures;
Bless the LORD, O my soul! Alleluia.

R. May the Lord be glad in his works.

Alleluia Verse *and* **Gospel**, *p. 366f.*

Year II

FIRST READING

1 Kgs 8:1–7, 9–13

*They brought the ark of the covenant into the holy of holies,
and a cloud filled the temple of the LORD.*

A reading from the first Book of Kings

The elders of Israel and all the leaders of the tribes, the princes
in the ancestral houses of the children of Israel, came to King
Solomon in Jerusalem, to bring up the ark of the LORD's
covenant from the City of David, which is Zion. All the people
of Israel assembled before King Solomon during the festival
in the month of Ethanim (the seventh month). When all the
elders of Israel had arrived, the priests took up the ark; they
carried the ark of the LORD and the meeting tent with all the
sacred vessels that were in the tent. (The priests and Levites
carried them.)

  King Solomon and the entire community of Israel present
for the occasion sacrificed before the ark sheep and oxen too
many to number or count. The priests brought the ark of the
covenant of the LORD to its place beneath the wings of the

cherubim in the sanctuary, the holy of holies of the temple. The cherubim had their wings spread out over the place of the ark, sheltering the ark and its poles from above. There was nothing in the ark but the two stone tablets which Moses had put there at Horeb, when the LORD made a covenant with the children of Israel at their departure from the land of Egypt.

When the priests left the holy place, the cloud filled the temple of the LORD so that the priests could no longer minister because of the cloud, since the LORD's glory had filled the temple of the LORD. Then Solomon said, "The LORD intends to dwell in the dark cloud; I have truly built you a princely house, a dwelling where you may abide forever."

The word of the Lord.

Responsorial Psalm

Ps 132:6–7, 8–10

R. Lord, go up to the place of your rest!

Behold, we heard of it in Ephrathah;
  we found it in the fields of Jaar.
Let us enter into his dwelling,
  let us worship at his footstool.

R. Lord, go up to the place of your rest!

Advance, O LORD, to your resting place,
  you and the ark of your majesty.
May your priests be clothed with justice;
  let your faithful ones shout merrily for joy.
For the sake of David your servant,
  reject not the plea of your anointed.

R. Lord, go up to the place of your rest!

Alleluia, alleluia   See Mt 4:23
Jesus preached the Gospel of the Kingdom
and cured every disease among the people.
Alleluia, alleluia

Years I and II

GOSPEL   Mk 6:53–56

As many as touched it were healed.

A reading from the holy Gospel according to Mark

After making the crossing to the other side of the sea, Jesus and his disciples came to land at Gennesaret and tied up there. As they were leaving the boat, people immediately recognized him. They scurried about the surrounding country and began to bring in the sick on mats to wherever they heard he was. Whatever villages or towns or countryside he entered, they laid the sick in the marketplaces and begged him that they might touch only the tassel on his cloak; and as many as touched it were healed.

The Gospel of the Lord.

Liturgy of the Eucharist, *p. 897;* **Prayer over the Gifts,** *p. 361.*

Tuesday

Antiphons and Prayers, *p. 360;* **Liturgy of the Word** *for Year I (odd years) follows; Year II (even years), p. 370.*

TODAY'S LIVING WORD

Mark is not entirely accurate in his presentation of the issue under discussion in this Gospel story. In Jesus' time, there were as many as seven types of Pharisees. Not all of them, and certainly not all Jews, practiced the ritual handwashing described in this passage. This was one way that one group sought to live God's law. Jesus' concern was that too much attention to such human customs could lead to the neglect of God's commandments. One example was the practice of korban, which involved declaring something "sacred" and thereby removing it from the claims of others.

In his prayer found in 1 Kings, Solomon asks: "Can it indeed be that God dwells on earth?" Genesis answers with a resounding YES!

Having created men and women "in the divine image," God dwells with us, within us. Sacred places like the temple of Solomon and sacred practices like the handwashing of some Pharisees all pale in comparison to the sacred dignity of the human person, which the law of God proclaims and protects.

Year I

FIRST READING

Gn 1:20—2:4a

Let us make man in our own image, after our likeness.

A reading from the Book of Genesis

God said, "Let the water teem with an abundance of living creatures, and on the earth let birds fly beneath the dome of the sky." And so it happened: God created the great sea monsters and all kinds of swimming creatures with which the water teems, and all kinds of winged birds. God saw how good it was, and God blessed them, saying, "Be fertile, multiply, and fill the water of the seas; and let the birds multiply on the earth." Evening came, and morning followed—the fifth day.

Then God said, "Let the earth bring forth all kinds of living creatures: cattle, creeping things, and wild animals of all kinds." And so it happened: God made all kinds of wild animals, all kinds of cattle, and all kinds of creeping things of the earth. God saw how good it was. Then God said: "Let us make man in our image, after our likeness. Let them have dominion over the fish of the sea, the birds of the air, and the cattle, and over all the wild animals and all the creatures that crawl on the ground."

God created man in his image;

in the divine image he created him;
male and female he created them.

God blessed them, saying: "Be fertile and multiply; fill the earth and subdue it. Have dominion over the fish of the sea, the birds of the air, and all the living things that move on the earth." God also said: "See, I give you every seed-bearing plant all over the earth and every tree that has seed-bearing fruit on it to be your food; and to all the animals of the land, all the birds of the air, and all the living creatures that crawl on the ground, I give all the green plants for food." And so it happened. God looked at everything he had made, and he found it very good. Evening came, and morning followed—the sixth day.

Thus the heavens and the earth and all their array were completed. Since on the seventh day God was finished with the work he had been doing, he rested on the seventh day from all the work he had undertaken. So God blessed the seventh day and made it holy, because on it he rested from all the work he had done in creation.

Such is the story of the heavens and the earth at their creation.

The word of the Lord.

Responsional Psalm

Ps 8:4–5, 6–7, 8–9

**R. O Lord, our God, how wonderful your name in all
  the earth!**

When I behold your heavens, the work of your fingers,
  the moon and the stars which you set in place—
What is man that you should be mindful of him,
  or the son of man that you should care for him?

**R. O Lord, our God, how wonderful your name in all
  the earth!**

You have made him little less than the angels,

and crowned him with glory and honor.
You have given him rule over the works of your hands,
  putting all things under his feet.

**R. O Lord, our God, how wonderful your name in all
  the earth!**

All sheep and oxen,
  yes, and the beasts of the field,
The birds of the air, the fishes of the sea,
  and whatever swims the paths of the seas.

**R. O Lord, our God, how wonderful your name in all
  the earth!**

Alleluia Verse *and* **Gospel,** *p. 371f.*

Year II

FIRST READING

1 Kgs 8:22–23, 27–30

*You have said: My name shall be there,
to hear the prayers of your people Israel.*

A reading from the first Book of Kings

Solomon stood before the altar of the LORD in the presence of
the whole community of Israel, and stretching forth his hands
toward heaven, he said, "LORD, God of Israel, there is no God
like you in heaven above or on earth below; you keep your
covenant of mercy with your servants who are faithful to you
with their whole heart.

"Can it indeed be that God dwells on earth? If the heavens
and the highest heavens cannot contain you, how much less
this temple which I have built! Look kindly on the prayer and
petition of your servant, O LORD, my God, and listen to the cry
of supplication which I, your servant, utter before you this day.
May your eyes watch night and day over this temple, the place
where you have decreed you shall be honored; may you heed

the prayer which I, your servant, offer in this place. Listen to the petitions of your servant and of your people Israel which they offer in this place. Listen from your heavenly dwelling and grant pardon."

The word of the Lord.

Responsorial Psalm
Ps 84:3, 4, 5 and 10, 11

R. How lovely is your dwelling place, Lord, mighty God!

My soul yearns and pines
  for the courts of the LORD.
My heart and my flesh
  cry out for the living God.

R. How lovely is your dwelling place, Lord, mighty God!

Even the sparrow finds a home,
  and the swallow a nest
  in which she puts her young—
Your altars, O LORD of hosts,
  my king and my God!

R. How lovely is your dwelling place, Lord, mighty God!

Blessed they who dwell in your house!
  continually they praise you.
O God, behold our shield,
  and look upon the face of your anointed.

R. How lovely is your dwelling place, Lord, mighty God!

I had rather one day in your courts
  than a thousand elsewhere;
I had rather lie at the threshold of the house of my God
  than dwell in the tents of the wicked.

R. How lovely is your dwelling place, Lord, mighty God!

Alleluia, alleluia Ps 119:36, 29b
Incline my heart, O God, to your decrees;
and favor me with your law.
Alleluia, alleluia

GOSPEL   Mk 7:1-13

You disregard God's commandment but cling to human tradition.

A reading from the holy Gospel according to Mark

When the Pharisees with some scribes who had come from Jerusalem gathered around Jesus, they observed that some of his disciples ate their meals with unclean, that is, unwashed, hands. (For the Pharisees and, in fact, all Jews, do not eat without carefully washing their hands, keeping the tradition of the elders. And on coming from the marketplace they do not eat without purifying themselves. And there are many other things that they have traditionally observed, the purification of cups and jugs and kettles and beds.) So the Pharisees and scribes questioned him, "Why do your disciples not follow the tradition of the elders but instead eat a meal with unclean hands?" He responded, "Well did Isaiah prophesy about you hypocrites, as it is written:

> *This people honors me with their lips,*
>> *but their hearts are far from me;*
> *in vain do they worship me,*
>> *teaching as doctrines human precepts.*

You disregard God's commandment but cling to human tradition." He went on to say, "How well you have set aside the commandment of God in order to uphold your tradition! For Moses said, *Honor your father and your mother,* and *Whoever curses father or mother shall die.* Yet you say, 'If someone says to father or mother, "Any support you might have had from me is *qorban*" ' (meaning, dedicated to God), you allow him to do nothing more for his father or mother. You nullify the word of God in favor of your tradition that you have handed on. And you do many such things."

The Gospel of the Lord.

Liturgy of the Eucharist, *p. 897;* **Prayer over the Gifts,** *p. 361.*

Wednesday

Antiphons and Prayers, *p. 360;* **Liturgy of the Word** *for Year I (odd years) follows; Year II (even years), p. 375.*

TODAY'S LIVING WORD

In Mark's version, Jesus' debate with some Pharisees on the issue of ritual purity leads him to make a striking public statement, which Mark sums up in an editorial comment: "Thus he declared all foods clean." Many scholars doubt that Jesus, the observant Jew, did in fact abolish the Jewish food laws. If he did, why did the earliest Christians continue to keep them, as Acts says they did? Rather, the words of Jesus make an important distinction between ritual purity and moral purity.

In the Gospel Jesus offers a catalog of the wickedness that may come "from within people, from their hearts" to render a person impure. Psalm 37 takes a more positive approach. It says that wisdom comes out of the just man, because the law of God is in his heart. Such was the case of Solomon, as long as his heart was with his God. Such was the condition of all humanity—in the beginning.

Year I

FIRST READING   Gn 2:4b–9, 15–17

The LORD God planted a garden in Eden
and placed there the man whom he had formed.

A reading from the Book of Genesis

At the time when the LORD God made the earth and the

heavens—while as yet there was no field shrub on earth and no grass of the field had sprouted, for the LORD God had sent no rain upon the earth and there was no man to till the soil, but a stream was welling up out of the earth and was watering all the surface of the ground—the LORD God formed man out of the clay of the ground and blew into his nostrils the breath of life, and so man became a living being.

Then the LORD God planted a garden in Eden, in the east, and he placed there the man whom he had formed. Out of the ground the LORD God made various trees grow that were delightful to look at and good for food, with the tree of life in the middle of the garden and the tree of the knowledge of good and evil.

The LORD God then took the man and settled him in the garden of Eden, to cultivate and care for it. The LORD God gave man this order: "You are free to eat from any of the trees of the garden except the tree of knowledge of good and evil. From that tree you shall not eat; the moment you eat from it you are surely doomed to die."

The word of the Lord.

Responsorial Psalm   Ps 104:1–2a, 27–28, 29bc–30

R. O bless the Lord, my soul!

Bless the LORD, O my soul!
  O LORD, my God, you are great indeed!
You are clothed with majesty and glory,
  robed in light as with a cloak.

R. O bless the Lord, my soul!

All creatures look to you
  to give them food in due time.
When you give it to them, they gather it;
  when you open your hand, they are filled with good things.

R. O bless the Lord, my soul!

If you take away their breath, they perish
 and return to their dust.
When you send forth your spirit, they are created,
 and you renew the face of the earth.

R. O bless the Lord, my soul!

Alleluia Verse *and* **Gospel,** *p. 376f.*

Year II

FIRST READING

1 Kgs 10:1–10

The Queen of Sheba saw all the wisdom of Solomon.

A reading from the first Book of Kings

The queen of Sheba, having heard of Solomon's fame, came to test him with subtle questions. She arrived in Jerusalem with a very numerous retinue, and with camels bearing spices, a large amount of gold, and precious stones. She came to Solomon and questioned him on every subject in which she was interested. King Solomon explained everything she asked about, and there remained nothing hidden from him that he could not explain to her.

When the queen of Sheba witnessed Solomon's great wisdom, the palace he had built, the food at his table, the seating of his ministers, the attendance and garb of his waiters, his banquet service, and the burnt offerings he offered in the temple of the LORD, she was breathless. "The report I heard in my country about your deeds and your wisdom is true," she told the king. "Though I did not believe the report until I came and saw with my own eyes, I have discovered that they were not telling me the half. Your wisdom and prosperity surpass the report I heard. Blessed are your men, blessed these servants of yours, who stand before you always and listen to your wisdom. Blessed be the LORD, your God, whom it has pleased to place you on the throne of Israel. In his enduring love for Israel, the LORD has made you king to carry out judgment and justice." Then she gave the king one hundred and twenty gold talents, a very large quantity of spices, and precious stones. Never again did anyone bring such an abundance of spices as the queen of Sheba gave to King Solomon.

The word of the Lord.

Responsorial Psalm

Ps 37:5-6, 30-31, 39-40

R. The mouth of the just murmurs wisdom.

Commit to the LORD your way;
  trust in him, and he will act.
He will make justice dawn for you like the light;
  right as the noonday shall be your vindication.

R. The mouth of the just murmurs wisdom.

The mouth of the just man tells of wisdom
  and his tongue utters what is right.
The law of his God is in his heart,
  and his steps do not falter.

R. The mouth of the just murmurs wisdom.

The salvation of the just is from the LORD;
  he is their refuge in time of distress.
And the LORD helps them and delivers them;
  he delivers them from the wicked and saves them,
  because they take refuge in him.

R. The mouth of the just murmurs wisdom.

Alleluia, alleluia   See Jn 17:17b, 17a
Your word, O Lord, is truth:
consecrate us in the truth.
Alleluia, alleluia

Years I and II

GOSPEL   Mk 7:14–23

What comes out of the man, that is what defiles him.

A reading from the holy Gospel according to Mark

Jesus summoned the crowd again and said to them, "Hear me, all of you, and understand. Nothing that enters one from outside can defile that person; but the things that come out from within are what defile."

When he got home away from the crowd his disciples questioned him about the parable. He said to them, "Are even you likewise without understanding? Do you not realize that everything that goes into a person from outside cannot defile, since it enters not the heart but the stomach and passes out into the latrine?" (Thus he declared all foods clean.) "But what comes out of the man, that is what defiles him. From within the man, from his heart, come evil thoughts, unchastity, theft, murder, adultery, greed, malice, deceit, licentiousness, envy, blasphemy, arrogance, folly. All these evils come from within and they defile."

The Gospel of the Lord.

Liturgy of the Eucharist, *p. 897;* **Prayer over the Gifts,** *p. 361.*

Thursday

Antiphons and Prayers, *p. 360;* **Liturgy of the Word** *for Year I (odd years) follows; Year II (even years), p. 380.*

TODAY'S LIVING WORD

Women are prominent in all three of today's readings. In the passage from Genesis, God makes "a suitable partner" for the man.

Interestingly, the Hebrew word *ezer*, rendered here as "partner," is routinely used in the Psalms to refer to God who is Israel's covenant partner. This choice of words is one way in which the author of this story points to the dignity of woman. The author of 1 Kings, however, blames the wives of Solomon for turning his heart away from the Lord, thus making these foreign women ultimately responsible for the schism soon to follow. In the selection from Mark, Jesus himself is confronted by a foreign woman.

Jesus in this story seems strangely out of character. He answers the pleading woman with an awkward rebuff; he seems reluctant to heal. On the other hand, she is every woman who loves her child. She will not be put off. At that moment, she is a "suitable partner" for Jesus: they match wits and Jesus yields, turning his face to the Gentile world.

Year I

FIRST READING

Gn 2:18 – 25

*The LORD God brought her to Adam,
and the two of them became one flesh.*

A reading from the Book of Genesis

The LORD God said: "It is not good for the man to be alone. I will make a suitable partner for him." So the LORD God formed out of the ground various wild animals and various birds of the air, and he brought them to the man to see what he would call them; whatever the man called each of them would be its name. The man gave names to all the cattle, all the birds of the air, and all the wild animals; but none proved to be the suitable partner for the man.

So the LORD God cast a deep sleep on the man, and while he was asleep, he took out one of his ribs and closed up its place with flesh. The LORD God then built up into a woman the rib that he had taken from the man. When he brought her to the man, the man said:

> "This one, at last, is bone of my bones
>   and flesh of my flesh;
> this one shall be called 'woman,'
>   for out of 'her man' this one has been taken."

That is why a man leaves his father and mother and clings to his wife, and the two of them become one flesh.

The man and his wife were both naked, yet they felt no shame.

The word of the Lord.

Responsorial Psalm   Ps 128:1–2, 3, 4–5

R. Blessed are those who fear the Lord.

Blessed are you who fear the LORD,
    who walk in his ways!
For you shall eat the fruit of your handiwork;
    blessed shall you be, and favored.

R. Blessed are those who fear the Lord.

Your wife shall be like a fruitful vine
    in the recesses of your home;
Your children like olive plants
    around your table.

R. Blessed are those who fear the Lord.

Behold, thus is the man blessed
    who fears the LORD.
The LORD bless you from Zion:
    may you see the prosperity of Jerusalem
    all the days of your life.

R. Blessed are those who fear the Lord.

Alleluia Verse *and* **Gospel,** *p.* 381.

Year II

FIRST READING

1 Kgs 11:4–13

Since you have not kept my covenant, I will deprive you of the kingdom, but I will leave your son one tribe for the sake of my servant David.

A reading from the first Book of Kings

When Solomon was old his wives had turned his heart to strange gods, and his heart was not entirely with the LORD, his God, as the heart of his father David had been. By adoring Astarte, the goddess of the Sidonians, and Milcom, the idol of the Ammonites, Solomon did evil in the sight of the LORD; he did not follow him unreservedly as his father David had done. Solomon then built a high place to Chemosh, the idol of Moab, and to Molech, the idol of the Ammonites, on the hill opposite Jerusalem. He did the same for all his foreign wives who burned incense and sacrificed to their gods. The LORD, therefore, became angry with Solomon, because his heart was turned away from the LORD, the God of Israel, who had appeared to him twice (for though the LORD had forbidden him this very act of following strange gods, Solomon had not obeyed him).

So the LORD said to Solomon: "Since this is what you want, and you have not kept my covenant and my statutes which I enjoined on you, I will deprive you of the kingdom and give it to your servant. I will not do this during your lifetime, however, for the sake of your father David; it is your son whom I will deprive. Nor will I take away the whole kingdom. I will leave your son one tribe for the sake of my servant David and of Jerusalem, which I have chosen."

The word of the Lord.

Responsorial Psalm
Ps 106:3–4, 35–36, 37 and 40

R. Remember us, O Lord, as you favor your people.

Blessed are they who observe what is right,
  who do always what is just.
Remember us, O Lord, as you favor your people;
  visit us with your saving help.

R. Remember us, O Lord, as you favor your people.

But they mingled with the nations
  and learned their works.
They served their idols,
  which became a snare for them.

R. Remember us, O Lord, as you favor your people.

They sacrificed their sons
  and their daughters to demons.
And the Lord grew angry with his people,
  and abhorred his inheritance.

R. Remember us, O Lord, as you favor your people.

Alleluia, alleluia   Jas 1:21bc
Humbly welcome the word that has been planted in you
and is able to save your souls.
Alleluia, alleluia

Years I and II

GOSPEL
Mk 7:24–30

The dogs under the table eat the children's scraps.

A reading from the holy Gospel according to Mark

Jesus went to the district of Tyre. He entered a house and wanted
no one to know about it, but he could not escape notice. Soon
a woman whose daughter had an unclean spirit heard about
him. She came and fell at his feet. The woman was a Greek, a
Syrophoenician by birth, and she begged him to drive the

demon out of her daughter. He said to her, "Let the children be fed first. For it is not right to take the food of the children and throw it to the dogs." She replied and said to him, "Lord, even the dogs under the table eat the children's scraps." Then he said to her, "For saying this, you may go. The demon has gone out of your daughter." When the woman went home, she found the child lying in bed and the demon gone.

The Gospel of the Lord.

Liturgy of the Eucharist, *p. 897;* **Prayer over the Gifts,** *p. 361.*

Friday

Antiphons and Prayers, *p. 360;* **Liturgy of the Word** *for Year I (odd years) follows; Year II (even years), p. 384.*

TODAY'S LIVING WORD

Commenting on the Genesis account of the fall, the *Catechism of the Catholic Church* attributes the first sin to the fact that the man and the woman let their trust in their Creator die in their hearts (n. 397). As a result, they hide in shame from God as well as from each other. In the first Book of Kings, Solomon is deprived of his kingdom, having turned his heart away from the Lord, the God of Israel. The prophet Ahijah therefore gives ten tribes to Jeroboam. Alienation and division are the consequences of sin.

If the two first readings underscore the tragic effects of sin, the reading from Mark declares the joyous event of the dawn of salvation. The last verse is an allusion to Isaiah 35. It is Mark's way of indicating that God's glorious future, which the prophet had announced as a time when the deaf would hear and the speechless sing, was already present in the ministry of Jesus. Therefore, all of us who have been baptized in his name must listen to his word with open ears, and proclaim it with clear voices.

Year I

FIRST READING

Gn 3:1–8

You will be like gods, knowing what is good and what is evil.

A reading from the Book of Genesis

Now the serpent was the most cunning of all the animals that the LORD God had made. The serpent asked the woman, "Did God really tell you not to eat from any of the trees in the garden?" The woman answered the serpent: "We may eat of the fruit of the trees in the garden; it is only about the fruit of the tree in the middle of the garden that God said, 'You shall not eat it or even touch it, lest you die.'" But the serpent said to the woman: "You certainly will not die! No, God knows well that the moment you eat of it your eyes will be opened and you will be like gods who know what is good and what is evil." The woman saw that the tree was good for food, pleasing to the eyes, and desirable for gaining wisdom. So she took some of its fruit and ate it; and she also gave some to her husband, who was with her, and he ate it. Then the eyes of both of them were opened, and they realized that they were naked; so they sewed fig leaves together and made loincloths for themselves.

When they heard the sound of the LORD God moving about in the garden at the breezy time of the day, the man and his wife hid themselves from the LORD God among the trees of the garden.

The word of the Lord.

Responsorial Psalm

Ps 32:1–2, 5, 6, 7

R. Blessed are those whose sins are forgiven.

Blessed is he whose fault is taken away,
  whose sin is covered.
Blessed the man to whom the LORD imputes not guilt,
  in whose spirit there is no guile.

   R. Blessed are those whose sins are forgiven.

Then I acknowledged my sin to you,
  my guilt I covered not.
I said, "I confess my faults to the LORD,"
  and you took away the guilt of my sin.

   R. Blessed are those whose sins are forgiven.

For this shall every faithful man pray to you
  in time of stress.
Though deep waters overflow,
  they shall not reach him.

   R. Blessed are those whose sins are forgiven.

You are my shelter; from distress you will preserve me;
  with glad cries of freedom you will ring me round.

   R. Blessed are those whose sins are forgiven.

   Alleluia Verse *and* **Gospel,** *p. 000.*

Year II

FIRST READING   1 Kgs 11:29 – 32; 12:19

   Israel went into rebellion against David's house to this day.

A reading from the first Book of Kings

Jeroboam left Jerusalem, and the prophet Ahijah the Shilonite
met him on the road. The two were alone in the area, and the
prophet was wearing a new cloak. Ahijah took off his new
cloak, tore it into twelve pieces, and said to Jeroboam:

   "Take ten pieces for yourself; the LORD, the God of Israel,
says: 'I will tear away the kingdom from Solomon's grasp and

will give you ten of the tribes. One tribe shall remain to him for the sake of David my servant, and of Jerusalem, the city I have chosen out of all the tribes of Israel.' "

Israel went into rebellion against David's house to this day.

The word of the Lord.

Responsorial Psalm
Ps 81:10–11ab, 12–13, 14–15

R. I am the Lord, your God: hear my voice.

"There shall be no strange god among you
  nor shall you worship any alien god.
I, the LORD, am your God
  who led you forth from the land of Egypt."

R. I am the Lord, your God: hear my voice.

"My people heard not my voice,
  and Israel obeyed me not;
So I gave them up to the hardness of their hearts;
  they walked according to their own counsels."

R. I am the Lord, your God: hear my voice.

"If only my people would hear me,
  and Israel walk in my ways,
Quickly would I humble their enemies;
  against their foes I would turn my hand."

R. I am the Lord, your God: hear my voice.

Alleluia, alleluia   See Acts 16:14b
Open our hearts, O Lord,
to listen to the words of your Son.
Alleluia, alleluia

Years I and II

GOSPEL
Mk 7:31–37

He makes the deaf hear and the mute speak.

A reading from the holy Gospel according to Mark

Jesus left the district of Tyre and went by way of Sidon to the Sea of Galilee, into the district of the Decapolis. And people brought to him a deaf man who had a speech impediment and begged him to lay his hand on him. He took him off by himself away from the crowd. He put his finger into the man's ears and, spitting, touched his tongue; then he looked up to heaven and groaned, and said to him, *"Ephphatha!"* (that is, "Be opened!") And immediately the man's ears were opened, his speech impediment was removed, and he spoke plainly. He ordered them not to tell anyone. But the more he ordered them not to, the more they proclaimed it. They were exceedingly astonished and they said, "He has done all things well. He makes the deaf hear and the mute speak."

The Gospel of the Lord.

Liturgy of the Eucharist, *p. 897;* **Prayer over the Gifts,** *p. 361.*

Saturday

Antiphons and Prayers, *p. 360;* **Liturgy of the Word** *for Year I (odd years) follows; Year II (even years), p. 389.*

TODAY'S LIVING WORD

Adam's overreaching will be punished: he will eke out a meager living from the hard ground to which he will finally return. Similarly, Jeroboam's overreaching will also be punished: his house will be "cut off and destroyed from the earth." Such is the lot of those who grasp at God's gifts.

In contrast, the Gospel story of the multiplication of the loaves signifies and celebrates the bounty of God's kingdom. The miracle points in three directions: past, present and future. The setting in a "deserted place" recalls God's goodness in the past, the gift of manna in the wilderness. That the people in the story "ate and were satisfied" and that seven baskets were left over looks to the future, to the abundance of the messianic age. According to Isaiah 25, God will then set before all peoples a feast. Finally, the verbs used to describe the actions of Jesus—he took, he gave thanks, he broke, he gave—bring us back to the present, to the Eucharist where, already though not yet, we "taste and see the goodness of the Lord."

Year I

FIRST READING

Gn 3:9 – 24

God banished him from the garden of Eden to till the ground.

A reading from the Book of Genesis

The LORD God called to Adam and asked him, "Where are you?" He answered, "I heard you in the garden; but I was afraid, because I was naked, so I hid myself." Then he asked, "Who told you that you were naked? You have eaten, then, from the tree of which I had forbidden you to eat!" The man replied, "The woman whom you put here with me—she gave me fruit from the tree, and so I ate it." The LORD God then asked the woman, "Why did you do such a thing?" The woman answered, "The serpent tricked me into it, so I ate it."

Then the LORD God said to the serpent:

"Because you have done this, you shall be banned
   from all the animals
   and from all the wild creatures;
On your belly shall you crawl,
   and dirt shall you eat
   all the days of your life.
I will put enmity between you and the woman,
   and between your offspring and hers;
He will strike at your head,
   while you strike at his heel."

To the woman he said:

"I will intensify the pangs of your childbearing;
    in pain shall you bring forth children.
Yet your urge shall be for your husband,
    and he shall be your master."

To the man he said: "Because you listened to your wifeand
ate from the tree of which I had forbidden you to eat,

"Cursed be the ground because of you!
    In toil shall you eat its yield
    all the days of your life.
Thorns and thistles shall it bring forth to you,
    as you eat of the plants of the field.
By the sweat of your face
    shall you get bread to eat,
Until you return to the ground,
    from which you were taken;
For you are dirt,
    and to dirt you shall return."

The man called his wife Eve, because she became the mother
of all the living.

For the man and his wife the LORD God made leather
garments, with which he clothed them. Then the LORD God
said: "See! The man has become like one of us, knowing what
is good and what is evil! Therefore, he must not be allowed to
put out his hand to take fruit from the tree of life also, and thus
eat of it and live forever." The LORD God therefore banished
him from the garden of Eden, to till the ground from which he
had been taken. When he expelled the man, he settled him east
of the garden of Eden; and he stationed the cherubim and the
fiery revolving sword, to guard the way to the tree of life.

The word of the Lord.

Responsorial Psalm

Ps 90:2, 3 – 4abc, 5 – 6, 12 – 13

R. In every age, O Lord, you have been our refuge.

Before the mountains were begotten
  and the earth and the world were brought forth,
    from everlasting to everlasting you are God.

R. In every age, O Lord, you have been our refuge.

You turn man back to dust,
  saying, "Return, O children of men."
For a thousand years in your sight
  are as yesterday, now that it is past,
    or as a watch of the night.

R. In every age, O Lord, you have been our refuge.

You make an end of them in their sleep;
  the next morning they are like the changing grass,
Which at dawn springs up anew,
  but by evening wilts and fades.

R. In every age, O Lord, you have been our refuge.

Teach us to number our days aright,
  that we may gain wisdom of heart.
Return, O LORD! How long?
  Have pity on your servants!

R. In every age, O Lord, you have been our refuge.

Alleluia Verse *and* **Gospel,** *p. 391.*

Year II

FIRST READING

1 Kgs 12:26 – 32; 13:33 – 34

Jeroboam made two golden calves.

A reading from the first Book of Kings

Jeroboam thought to himself: "The kingdom will return to David's house. If now this people go up to offer sacrifices in the temple of the LORD in Jerusalem, the hearts of this people will return to their master, Rehoboam, king of Judah, and they will kill me." After taking counsel, the king made two calves of gold and said to the people: "You have been going up to Jerusalem long enough. Here is your God, O Israel, who brought you up from the land of Egypt." And he put one in Bethel, the other in Dan. This led to sin, because the people frequented those calves in Bethel and in Dan. He also built temples on the high places and made priests from among the people who were not Levites. Jeroboam established a feast in the eighth month on the fifteenth day of the month to duplicate in Bethel the pilgrimage feast of Judah, with sacrifices to the calves he had made; and he stationed in Bethel priests of the high places he had built.

Jeroboam did not give up his evil ways after this, but again made priests for the high places from among the common people. Whoever desired it was consecrated and became a priest of the high places. This was a sin on the part of the house of Jeroboam for which it was to be cut off and destroyed from the earth.

The word of the Lord.

Responsorial Psalm   Ps 106:6–7ab, 19–20, 21–22

R. **Remember us, O Lord, as you favor your people.**

We have sinned, we and our fathers;
  we have committed crimes; we have done wrong.
Our fathers in Egypt
  considered not your wonders.

R. **Remember us, O Lord, as you favor your people.**

They made a calf in Horeb
  and adored a molten image;

They exchanged their glory
  for the image of a grass-eating bullock.

R. Remember us, O Lord, as you favor your people.

They forgot the God who had saved them,
  who had done great deeds in Egypt,
Wondrous deeds in the land of Ham,
  terrible things at the Red Sea.

R. Remember us, O Lord, as you favor your people.

> **Alleluia, alleluia**   Mt 4:4b
> One does not live on bread alone,
>   but on every word that comes forth from the mouth of God.
> **Alleluia, alleluia**

Years I and II

GOSPEL   Mk 8:1–10

They ate and were satisfied.

A reading from the holy Gospel according to Mark

In those days when there again was a great crowd without anything to eat, Jesus summoned the disciples and said, "My heart is moved with pity for the crowd, because they have been with me now for three days and have nothing to eat. If I send them away hungry to their homes, they will collapse on the way, and some of them have come a great distance." His disciples answered him, "Where can anyone get enough bread to satisfy them here in this deserted place?" Still he asked them, "How many loaves do you have?" They replied, "Seven." He ordered the crowd to sit down on the ground. Then, taking the seven loaves he gave thanks, broke them, and gave them to his disciples to distribute, and they distributed them to the crowd. They also had a few fish. He said the blessing over them and ordered them distributed also. They ate and were satisfied. They picked up the fragments left over—seven baskets. There were about four thousand people.

He dismissed the crowd and got into the boat with his disciples and came to the region of Dalmanutha.

The Gospel of the Lord.

Liturgy of the Eucharist, *p. 897;* **Prayer over the Gifts,** *p. 361.*

SIXTH WEEK IN ORDINARY TIME

The **Antiphons and Prayers** *may be the following, or may be chosen from any of the other 33 weeks in Ordinary Time (refer to Liturgical Calendar, pp. 26–41).*

The **Liturgy of the Word** *varies: for Monday, see p. 394; Tuesday, p. 398; Wednesday, p. 403; Thursday, p. 407; Friday, p. 412; Saturday, p. 416.*

Entrance Antiphon

Lord, be my rock of safety, the stronghold that saves me. For the honor of your name, lead me and guide me.   (Ps 31:3–4)

Opening Prayer

Let us pray
  [that everything we do
  will be guided by God's law of love]

Pause for silent prayer.

God our Father,
you have promised to remain for ever
with those who do what is just and right.
Help us to live in your presence.

We ask this through our Lord Jesus Christ, your Son,
who lives and reigns with you and the Holy Spirit,
one God, for ever and ever.

Alternative Opening Prayer

Let us pray
[for the wisdom that is greater than human words]
Pause for silent prayer.

Father in heaven,
the loving plan of your wisdom took flesh in Jesus Christ,
and changed mankind's history
by his command of perfect love.
May our fulfillment of his command reflect your wisdom
and bring your salvation to the ends of the earth.

We ask this through Christ our Lord.

Prayer over the Gifts

Pray, brethren...
Lord,
we make this offering in obedience to your word.
May it cleanse and renew us,
and lead us to our eternal reward.

We ask this in the name of Jesus the Lord.

Preface of Weekdays in Ordinary Time I–VI, *pp. 948–950.*

Communion Antiphon

**They ate and were filled; the Lord gave them what they wanted:
they were not deprived of their desire.**   (Ps 78:29 – 30)

Or:

**God loved the world so much, he gave his only Son, that all
who believe in him might not perish, but might have eternal life.**

(Jn 3:16)

Prayer after Communion

Let us pray.
Pause for silent prayer, if this has not preceded.

Lord,
you give us food from heaven.
May we always hunger
for the bread of life.
Grant this through Christ our Lord.

Monday

Antiphons and Prayers, *p. 392;* **Liturgy of the Word** *for Year I (odd years) follows; Year II (even years), p. 396.*

TODAY'S LIVING WORD

The mysterious story of Cain and Abel offers no explanation why God accepts Abel's sacrifice and rejects Cain's. "Nor should one be sought," says Wilfrid Harrington. "The acceptance of the sacrifice is placed completely within God's free will."* This inequality, originating in the free will of God, gives rise to Cain's resentment. Yet God makes it clear to Cain that his resentment need not control him, understandable though it may be. He can master it and live in dignity with the tension of divine freedom. A similar tension underlies the Gospel story. Jesus' opponents want to solve the mystery of his claims with a sign from heaven. They would force God's hand, as it were. But Jesus says that no such sign will be given.

The Letter of James calls us to full maturity in the Christian life and says that this requires endurance among other things. Endurance is not passivity but patience. It is the ability to live in dignity with the tension of God's freedom and the mystery of God's ways.

* *In the Beginning God...* (Manchester: Koinonia Press, 1976), p. 64.

Year I

FIRST READING

Gn 4:1–15, 25

Cain attacked his brother Abel and killed him.

A reading from the Book of Genesis

The man had relations with his wife Eve, and she conceived and bore Cain, saying, "I have produced a man with the help of the LORD." Next she bore his brother Abel. Abel became a keeper of flocks, and Cain a tiller of the soil. In the course of time Cain brought an offering to the LORD from the fruit of the soil, while Abel, for his part, brought one of the best firstlings of his flock. The LORD looked with favor on Abel and his offering, but on Cain and his offering he did not. Cain greatly resented this and was crestfallen. So the LORD said to Cain: "Why are you so resentful and crestfallen. If you do well, you can hold up your head; but if not, sin is a demon lurking at the door: his urge is toward you, yet you can be his master."

Cain said to his brother Abel, "Let us go out in the field." When they were in the field, Cain attacked his brother Abel and killed him. Then the LORD asked Cain, "Where is your brother Abel?" He answered, "I do not know. Am I my brother's keeper?" The LORD then said: "What have you done! Listen: your brother's blood cries out to me from the soil! Therefore you shall be banned from the soil that opened its mouth to receive your brother's blood from your hand. If you till the soil, it shall no longer give you its produce. You shall become a restless wanderer on the earth." Cain said to the LORD: "My punishment is too great to bear. Since you have now banished me from the soil, and I must avoid your presence and become a restless wanderer on the earth, anyone may kill me at sight." "Not so!" the LORD said to him. "If anyone kills Cain, Cain shall be avenged sevenfold." So the LORD put a mark on Cain, lest anyone should kill him at sight.

Adam again had relations with his wife, and she gave birth to a son whom she called Seth. "God has granted me more

offspring in place of Abel," she said, "because Cain slew him."
The word of the Lord.

Responsorial Psalm
Ps 50:1 and 8, 16bc–17, 20–21

R. Offer to God a sacrifice of praise.

God the LORD has spoken and summoned the earth,
  from the rising of the sun to its setting.
"Not for your sacrifices do I rebuke you,
  for your burnt offerings are before me always."

R. Offer to God a sacrifice of praise.

"Why do you recite my statutes,
  and profess my covenant with your mouth
Though you hate discipline
  and cast my words behind you?"

R. Offer to God a sacrifice of praise.

"You sit speaking against your brother;
  against your mother's son you spread rumors.
When you do these things, shall I be deaf to it?
  Or do you think that I am like yourself?
  I will correct you by drawing them up before your eyes."

R. Offer to God a sacrifice of praise.

Alleluia Verse *and* **Gospel,** *p. 398.*

Year II

FIRST READING
Jas 1:1–11

*The testing of your faith produces perseverance
so that you may be perfect and complete.*

A reading from the beginning of the Letter of Saint James

James, a servant of God and of the Lord Jesus Christ, to the
twelve tribes in the dispersion, greetings.

Consider it all joy, my brothers and sisters, when you encounter various trials, for you know that the testing of your faith produces perseverance. And let perseverance be perfect, so that you may be perfect and complete, lacking in nothing. But if any of you lacks wisdom, he should ask God who gives to all generously and ungrudgingly, and he will be given it. But he should ask in faith, not doubting, for the one who doubts is like a wave of the sea that is driven and tossed about by the wind. For that person must not suppose that he will receive anything from the Lord, since he is a man of two minds, unstable in all his ways.

The brother in lowly circumstances should take pride in high standing, and the rich one in his lowliness, for he will pass away "like the flower of the field." For the sun comes up with its scorching heat and dries up the grass, its flower droops, and the beauty of its appearance vanishes. So will the rich person fade away in the midst of his pursuits.

The word of the Lord.

Responsorial Psalm

Ps 119:67, 68, 71, 72, 75, 76

R. Be kind to me, Lord, and I shall live.

Before I was afflicted I went astray,
  but now I hold to your promise.

R. Be kind to me, Lord, and I shall live.

You are good and bountiful;
  teach me your statutes.

R. Be kind to me, Lord, and I shall live.

It is good for me that I have been afflicted,
  that I may learn your statutes.

R. Be kind to me, Lord, and I shall live.

The law of your mouth is to me more precious
   than thousands of gold and silver pieces.

R. Be kind to me, Lord, and I shall live.

I know, O LORD, that your ordinances are just,
   and in your faithfulness you have afflicted me.

R. Be kind to me, Lord, and I shall live.

Let your kindness comfort me
   according to your promise to your servants.

R. Be kind to me, Lord, and I shall live.

> **Alleluia, alleluia**   Jn 14:6
> I am the way and the truth and the life, says the Lord;
> no one comes to the Father except through me.
> **Alleluia, alleluia**

Years I and II

GOSPEL   Mk 8:11–13

Why does this generation seek a sign?

A reading from the holy Gospel according to Mark

The Pharisees came forward and began to argue with Jesus,
seeking from him a sign from heaven to test him. He sighed
from the depth of his spirit and said, "Why does this generation
seek a sign? Amen, I say to you, no sign will be given to this
generation." Then he left them, got into the boat again, and
went off to the other shore.

The Gospel of the Lord.

Liturgy of the Eucharist, *p. 897;* **Prayer over the Gifts,** *p. 393.*

Tuesday

Antiphons and Prayers, *p. 392;* **Liturgy of the Word** *for Year I (odd years) follows; Year II (even years), p. 401.*

TODAY'S LIVING WORD

In the Gospel story, Jesus experiences the same frustration that God expresses in the reading from Genesis. Leading into the story of Noah, the author of Genesis writes that God "regretted that he had made man on the earth, and his heart was grieved," seeing how evil were the desires of the human heart. Jesus too is grieved to discover that his disciples have closed their minds and still do not understand, even after the miracle of the loaves.

Closer to home, the Letter of James may cause us to wonder how often we ourselves must grieve the heart of God. James suggests, for example, that when the tug of our passions tempts us, we say, "I am being tempted by God." Or when we blame God for the blindness of our minds and the bankruptcy of our hearts, must not God be grieved—the God who wills only to bless us with every worthwhile gift and to bestow on us the crown of life?

Year I

FIRST READING
Gn 6:5–8; 7:1–5, 10

I will wipe out from the earth the men whom I have created.

A reading from the Book of Genesis

When the LORD saw how great was man's wickedness on earth, and how no desire that his heart conceived was ever anything but evil, he regretted that he had made man on the earth, and his heart was grieved.

So the LORD said: "I will wipe out from the earth the men whom I have created, and not only the men, but also the beasts and the creeping things and the birds of the air, for I am sorry that I made them." But Noah found favor with the LORD.

Then the LORD said to Noah: "Go into the ark, you and all your household, for you alone in this age have I found to be truly just. Of every clean animal, take with you seven pairs, a male and its mate; and of the unclean animals, one pair, a male and its mate; likewise, of every clean bird of the air, seven pairs, a male and a female, and of all the unclean birds, one pair, a male and a female. Thus you will keep their issue alive over all the earth. Seven days from now I will bring rain down on the earth for forty days and forty nights, and so I will wipe out from the surface of the earth every moving creature that I have made." Noah did just as the Lord had commanded him.

As soon as the seven days were over, the waters of the flood came upon the earth.

The word of the Lord.

Responsorial Psalm

Ps 29:1a and 2, 3ac–4, 3b and 9c–10

R. The Lord will bless his people with peace.

Give to the Lord, you sons of God,
  give to the Lord glory and praise,
Give to the Lord the glory due his name;
  adore the Lord in holy attire.

R. The Lord will bless his people with peace.

The voice of the Lord is over the waters,
  the Lord, over vast waters.
The voice of the Lord is mighty;
  the voice of the Lord is majestic.

R. The Lord will bless his people with peace.

The God of glory thunders,
  and in his temple all say, "Glory!"
The Lord is enthroned above the flood;
  the Lord is enthroned as king forever.

R. The Lord will bless his people with peace.

Alleluia Verse *and* **Gospel,** *p. 402.*

Year II

FIRST READING

Jas 1:12–18

God himself tempts no one.

A reading from the Letter of Saint James

Blessed is he who perseveres in temptation, for when he has been proven he will receive the crown of life that he promised to those who love him. No one experiencing temptation should say, "I am being tempted by God"; for God is not subject to temptation to evil, and he himself tempts no one. Rather, each person is tempted when lured and enticed by his desire. Then desire conceives and brings forth sin, and when sin reaches maturity it gives birth to death.

Do not be deceived, my beloved brothers and sisters: all good giving and every perfect gift is from above, coming down from the Father of lights, with whom there is no alteration or shadow caused by change. He willed to give us birth by the word of truth that we may be a kind of firstfruits of his creatures.

The word of the Lord.

Responsorial Psalm

Ps 94:12–13a, 14–15, 18–19

R. **Blessed the man you instruct, O Lord.**

Blessed the man whom you instruct, O LORD,
  whom by your law you teach,
Giving him rest from evil days.

R. **Blessed the man you instruct, O Lord.**

For the LORD will not cast off his people,
  nor abandon his inheritance;
But judgment shall again be with justice,
  and all the upright of heart shall follow it.

R. **Blessed the man you instruct, O Lord.**

When I say, "My foot is slipping,"
  your mercy, O LORD, sustains me;
When cares abound within me,
  your comfort gladdens my soul.

R. Blessed the man you instruct, O Lord.

Alleluia, alleluia   Jn 14:23
Whoever loves me will keep my word, says the Lord;
and my Father will love him
and we will come to him.
Alleluia, alleluia

Years I and II

GOSPEL   Mk 8:14 – 21

*Watch out, guard against the leaven of the Pharisees
and the leaven of Herod.*

A reading from the holy Gospel according to Mark

The disciples had forgotten to bring bread, and they had only
one loaf with them in the boat. Jesus enjoined them, "Watch
out, guard against the leaven of the Pharisees and the leaven
of Herod." They concluded among themselves that it was
because they had no bread. When he became aware of this he
said to them, "Why do you conclude that it is because you
have no bread? Do you not yet understand or comprehend?
Are your hearts hardened? Do you have eyes and not see, ears
and not hear? And do you not remember, when I broke the five
loaves for the five thousand, how many wicker baskets full of
fragments you picked up?" They answered him, "Twelve."
"When I broke the seven loaves for the four thousand, how
many full baskets of fragments did you pick up?" They
answered him, "Seven." He said to them, "Do you still not
understand?"

The Gospel of the Lord.

Liturgy of the Eucharist, *p. 897;* **Prayer over the Gifts,** *p. 393.*

Wednesday

Antiphons and Prayers, *p. 392;* **Liturgy of the Word** *for Year I (odd years) follows; Year II (even years), p. 405.*

TODAY'S LIVING WORD

Throughout his Gospel Mark describes Jesus' ministry as one in which demons are cast out immediately and the sick are cured immediately. The miracle recounted in today's Gospel does not fit that pattern. Perhaps in this story Mark is more interested in describing the progress of recovery than the pattern of Jesus' power. In the early Church, Jesus' healing of the blind was a symbol of baptism. In the life of faith there are no quick lessons. Sight comes gradually for us, as it did for the man in the story. To change the metaphor, that is why James tells us to "welcome the word that has been planted in you and is able to save your souls." We are not just to listen to it, but also to "be doers of the word," which is the only way that faith can grow.

The story of Noah was also a symbol of baptism in the early Church. Saved by water in the ark, Noah could not immediately walk out onto the surface of the earth. Saved by the waters of baptism, it takes time for us too to walk with confidence into the dawning light of the new day God has made.

Year I

FIRST READING

Gn 8:6–13, 20–22

Noah saw that the surface of the ground was drying up.

A reading from the Book of Genesis

At the end of forty days Noah opened the hatch he had made in the ark, and he sent out a raven, to see if the waters had lessened on the earth. It flew back and forth until the waters dried off from the earth. Then he sent out a dove, to see if the waters had lessened on the earth. But the dove could find no place to alight and perch, and it returned to him in the ark, for there was water all over the earth. Putting out his hand, he caught the dove and drew it back to him inside the ark. He waited seven days more and again sent the dove out from the ark. In the evening the dove came back to him, and there in its bill was a plucked-off olive leaf! So Noah knew that the waters had lessened on the earth. He waited still another seven days and then released the dove once more; and this time it did not come back.

In the six hundred and first year of Noah's life, in the first month, on the first day of the month, the water began to dry up on the earth. Noah then removed the covering of the ark and saw that the surface of the ground was drying up.

Noah built an altar to the LORD, and choosing from every clean animal and every clean bird, he offered burnt offerings on the altar. When the LORD smelled the sweet odor, he said to himself: "Never again will I doom the earth because of man since the desires of man's heart are evil from the start; nor will I ever again strike down all living beings, as I have done.

As long as the earth lasts,
    seedtime and harvest,
    cold and heat,
Summer and winter,
    and day and night
    shall not cease."

The word of the Lord.

Responsorial Psalm
Ps 116:12–13, 14–15, 18–19

R. To you, Lord, I will offer a sacrifice of praise.

How shall I make a return to the LORD

for all the good he has done for me?
The cup of salvation I will take up,
  and I will call upon the name of the LORD.

R. To you, Lord, I will offer a sacrifice of praise.

My vows to the LORD I will pay
  in the presence of all his people.
Precious in the eyes of the LORD
  is the death of his faithful ones.

R. To you, Lord, I will offer a sacrifice of praise.

My vows to the LORD I will pay
  in the presence of all his people,
In the courts of the house of the LORD,
  in your midst, O Jerusalem.

R. To you, Lord, I will offer a sacrifice of praise.

Or: **R. Alleluia.**

Alleluia Verse *and* **Gospel,** *p. 406f.*

Year II

FIRST READING

Jas 1:19–27

Be doers of the word and not hearers only.

A reading from the Letter of Saint James

Know this, my dear brothers and sisters: everyone should be quick to hear, slow to speak, slow to anger for anger does not accomplish the righteousness of God. Therefore, put away all filth and evil excess and humbly welcome the word that has been planted in you and is able to save your souls.

Be doers of the word and not hearers only, deluding yourselves. For if anyone is a hearer of the word and not a doer, he is like a man who looks at his own face in a mirror. He sees himself, then goes off and promptly forgets what he looked like. But the one who peers into the perfect law of freedom and perseveres, and is not a hearer who forgets but a doer who acts; such a one shall be blessed in what he does.

If anyone thinks he is religious and does not bridle his tongue but deceives his heart, his religion is vain. Religion that is pure and undefiled before God and the Father is this: to care for orphans and widows in their affliction and to keep oneself unstained by the world.

The word of the Lord.

Responsorial Psalm

Ps 15:2–3a, 3bc–4ab, 5

R. Who shall live on your holy mountain, O Lord?

He who walks blamelessly and does justice;
  who thinks the truth in his heart
  and slanders not with his tongue.

R. Who shall live on your holy mountain, O Lord?

Who harms not his fellow man,
  nor takes up a reproach against his neighbor;
By whom the reprobate is despised,
  while he honors those who fear the LORD.

R. Who shall live on your holy mountain, O Lord?

Who lends not his money at usury
  and accepts no bribe against the innocent.
He who does these things
  shall never be disturbed.

R. Who shall live on your holy mountain, O Lord?

Alleluia, alleluia   See Eph 1:17–18
May the Father of our Lord Jesus Christ
enlighten the eyes of our hearts,
  that we may know what is the hope
  that belongs to his call.
Alleluia, alleluia

Years I and II

GOSPEL
Mk 8:22 – 26

His sight was restored and he could see everything distinctly.

A reading from the holy Gospel according to Mark

When Jesus and his disciples arrived at Bethsaida, people brought to him a blind man and begged Jesus to touch him. He took the blind man by the hand and led him outside the village. Putting spittle on his eyes he laid his hands on the man and asked, "Do you see anything?" Looking up the man replied, "I see people looking like trees and walking." Then he laid hands on the man's eyes a second time and he saw clearly; his sight was restored and he could see everything distinctly. Then he sent him home and said, "Do not even go into the village."

The Gospel of the Lord.

Liturgy of the Eucharist, *p. 897;* **Prayer over the Gifts,** *p. 393.*

Thursday

Antiphons and Prayers, *p. 392;* **Liturgy of the Word** *for Year I (odd years) follows; Year II (even years), p. 410.*

TODAY'S LIVING WORD

Today's reading from Genesis describes the covenant God made with Noah and his descendants under the sign of the rainbow. In the view of Judaism, the covenant with Noah reveals God's will for the salvation of all human beings without distinction. The author of the Letter of James also underscores God's impartiality. After all, he asks, "Did not God choose those who are poor in the world to be rich in faith and heirs of the Kingdom?" So he warns, "show no partiality as you adhere to the faith in our glorious Lord Jesus Christ."

In today's Gospel, Jesus also shows himself impartial. Peter's

profession of faith in Jesus as the Messiah is incomplete, for Peter
has not yet recognized or reckoned with the true nature of Jesus'
messiahship. This is made dramatically clear when he adamantly
refuses to accept Jesus' prediction of the passion. Jesus responds
with his eyes on his disciples—those there present and those still to
come, like us. "Get behind me, Satan!" His point is inescapable:
any disciple, even Peter, who denies the cross stands on the side of
Satan.

Year I

FIRST READING

Gn 9:1–13

I set my bow in the clouds to serve as a sign
of the covenant between me and the earth.

A reading from the Book of Genesis

God blessed Noah and his sons and said to them: "Be fertile
and multiply and fill the earth. Dread fear of you shall come
upon all the animals of the earth and all the birds of the air,
upon all the creatures that move about on the ground and all
the fishes of the sea; into your power they are delivered. Every
creature that is alive shall be yours to eat; I give them all to
you as I did the green plants. Only flesh with its lifeblood still
in it you shall not eat. For your own lifeblood, too, I will demand
an accounting: from every animal I will demand it, and from
one man in regard to his fellow man I will demand an accounting for human life.

If anyone sheds the blood of man,
by man shall his blood be shed;
For in the image of God
has man been made.

Be fertile, then, and multiply; abound on earth and subdue it."

God said to Noah and to his sons with him: "See, I am now establishing my covenant with you and your descendants after you and with every living creature that was with you: all the birds, and the various tame and wild animals that were with you and came out of the ark. I will establish my covenant with you, that never again shall all bodily creatures be destroyed by the waters of a flood; there shall not be another flood to devastate the earth." God added: "This is the sign that I am giving for all ages to come, of the covenant between me and you and every living creature with you: I set my bow in the clouds to serve as a sign of the covenant between me and the earth."

The word of the Lord.

Responsorial Psalm
Ps 102:16–18, 19–21, 29 and 22–23

R. From heaven the Lord looks down on the earth.

The nations shall revere your name, O LORD,
  and all the kings of the earth your glory,
When the LORD has rebuilt Zion
  and appeared in his glory;
When he has regarded the prayer of the destitute,
  and not despised their prayer.

R. From heaven the Lord looks down on the earth.

Let this be written for the generation to come,
  and let his future creatures praise the LORD:
"The LORD looked down from his holy height,
  from heaven he beheld the earth,
To hear the groaning of the prisoners,
  to release those doomed to die."

R. From heaven the Lord looks down on the earth.

The children of your servants shall abide,
  and their posterity shall continue in your presence,

That the name of the LORD may be declared in Zion,
  and his praise, in Jerusalem,
When the peoples gather together,
  and the kingdoms, to serve the LORD.

R. From heaven the Lord looks down on the earth.

Alleluia Verse *and* **Gospel,** *p. 411.*

Alleluia Verse *and* **Gospel,** *p. 411.*

Year II

FIRST READING

Jas 2:1–9

Did not God choose those who are poor in the world?
You, however, dishonored the person who is poor.

A reading from the Letter of Saint James

My brothers and sisters, show no partiality as you adhere to
the faith in our glorious Lord Jesus Christ. For if a man with
gold rings and fine clothes comes into your assembly, and a
poor person with shabby clothes also comes in, and you pay
attention to the one wearing the fine clothes and say, "Sit here,
please," while you say to the poor one, "Stand there," or "Sit
at my feet," have you not made distinctions among yourselves
and become judges with evil designs?

Listen, my beloved brothers and sisters. Did not God choose
those who are poor in the world to be rich in faith and heirs of
the Kingdom that he promised to those who love him? But
you dishonored the poor. Are not the rich oppressing you? And
do they themselves not haul you off to court? Is it not they
who blaspheme the noble name that was invoked over you?
However, if you fulfill the royal law according to the Scripture,
You shall love your neighbor as yourself, you are doing well.
But if you show partiality, you commit sin, and are convicted
by the law as transgressors.

The word of the Lord.

Responsorial Psalm
Ps 34:2–3, 4–5, 6–7

R. The Lord hears the cry of the poor.

I will bless the LORD at all times;
  his praise shall be ever in my mouth.
Let my soul glory in the LORD;
  the lowly will hear me and be glad.

R. The Lord hears the cry of the poor.

Glorify the LORD with me,
  let us together extol his name.
I sought the LORD, and he answered me
  and delivered me from all my fears.

R. The Lord hears the cry of the poor.

Look to him that you may be radiant with joy,
  and your faces may not blush with shame.
When the poor one called out, the LORD heard,
  and from all his distress he saved him.

R. The Lord hears the cry of the poor.

Alleluia, alleluia   See Jn 6:63c, 68c
Your words, Lord, are Spirit and life;
you have the words of everlasting life.
Alleluia, alleluia

Years I and II

GOSPEL
Mk 8:27–33

You are the Christ. The Son of Man must suffer much.

A reading from the holy Gospel according to Mark

Jesus and his disciples set out for the villages of Caesarea Philippi. Along the way he asked his disciples, "Who do people say that I am?" They said in reply, "John the Baptist, others Elijah, still others one of the prophets." And he asked them, "But who do you say that I am?" Peter said to him in reply,

"You are the Christ." Then he warned them not to tell anyone about him.

He began to teach them that the Son of Man must suffer greatly and be rejected by the elders, the chief priests, and the scribes, and be killed, and rise after three days. He spoke this openly. Then Peter took him aside and began to rebuke him. At this he turned around and, looking at his disciples, rebuked Peter and said, "Get behind me, Satan. You are thinking not as God does, but as human beings do."

The Gospel of the Lord.

Liturgy of the Eucharist, *p. 897;* **Prayer over the Gifts,** *p. 393.*

Friday

Antiphons and Prayers, *p. 392;* **Liturgy of the Word** *for Year I (odd years) follows; Year II (even years), p. 414.*

TODAY'S LIVING WORD

In Genesis, the central problem of the story of Babel is answered in the story of Abraham. In the story of Babel, the people of the land of Shinar decide to secure their own existence. "Come, let us build ourselves a city and a tower with its top in the sky," they say, "and so make a name for ourselves." But their efforts end in disaster and they are scattered all over the earth, just as they feared. In the language of today's Gospel, they sought to save their life but lost it. Abraham, on the other hand, surrendered his life in faith and saved it.

The Letter of James goes on to show that Abraham's faith was proven in his works, specifically in his readiness to sacrifice Isaac. In offering his only son, Abraham was surrendering his own future as well. James says that for such faith in action, "he was called 'the friend of God.'" What God asked of Abraham, Jesus asks of all his disciples. Faithful following of Jesus entails self-denial and self-sacrifice. There is no other way.

Year I

FIRST READING   Gn 11:1–9

Let us go down and there confuse their language.

A reading from the Book of Genesis

The whole world spoke the same language, using the same words. While the people were migrating in the east, they came upon a valley in the land of Shinar and settled there. They said to one another, "Come, let us mold bricks and harden them with fire." They used bricks for stone, and bitumen for mortar. Then they said, "Come, let us build ourselves a city and a tower with its top in the sky, and so make a name for ourselves; otherwise we shall be scattered all over the earth."

The LORD came down to see the city and the tower that they had built. Then the LORD said: "If now, while they are one people, all speaking the same language, they have started to do this, nothing will later stop them from doing whatever they presume to do. Let us then go down and there confuse their language, so that one will not understand what another says." Thus the LORD scattered them from there all over the earth, and they stopped building the city. That is why it was called Babel, because there the LORD confused the speech of all the world. It was from that place that he scattered them all over the earth.

The word of the Lord.

Responsional Psalm   Ps 33:10–11, 12–13, 14–15

R. **Blessed the people the Lord has chosen to be his own.**

The LORD brings to nought the plans of nations;
  he foils the designs of peoples.

But the plan of the LORD stands forever;
  the design of his heart, through all generations.

   R. Blessed the people the Lord has chosen to be his own.

Blessed the nation whose God is the LORD,
  the people he has chosen for his own inheritance.
From heaven the LORD looks down;
  he sees all mankind.

   R. Blessed the people the Lord has chosen to be his own.

From his fixed throne he beholds
  all who dwell on the earth,
He who fashioned the heart of each,
  he who knows all their works.

   R. Blessed the people the Lord has chosen to be his own.

   Alleluia Verse *and* Gospel, *p. 416.*

Year II

FIRST READING   Jas 2:14–24, 26

   For just as a body without a spirit is dead,
   so also faith without works is dead.

A reading from the Letter of Saint James

What good is it, my brothers and sisters, if someone says he
has faith but does not have works? Can that faith save him? If
a brother or sister has nothing to wear and has no food for the
day, and one of you says to them, "Go in peace, keep warm,
and eat well," but you do not give them the necessities of the
body, what good is it? So also faith of itself, if it does not have
works, is dead.

   Indeed someone might say, "You have faith and I have
works." Demonstrate your faith to me without works, and I
will demonstrate my faith to you from my works. You believe

that God is one. You do well. Even the demons believe that and tremble. Do you want proof, you ignoramus, that faith without works is useless? Was not Abraham our father justified by works when he offered his son Isaac upon the altar? You see that faith was active along with his works, and faith was completed by the works. Thus the Scripture was fulfilled that says, *Abraham believed God, and it was credited to him as righteousness,* and he was called *the friend of God.* See how a person is justified by works and not by faith alone. For just as a body without a spirit is dead, so also faith without works is dead.

The word of the Lord.

Responsorial Psalm

Ps 112:1–2, 3–4, 5–6

R. Blessed the man who greatly delights in the Lord's commands.

Blessed the man who fears the LORD,
  who greatly delights in his commands.
His posterity shall be mighty upon the earth;
  the upright generation shall be blessed.

R. Blessed the man who greatly delights in the Lord's commands.

Wealth and riches shall be in his house;
  his generosity shall endure forever.
Light shines through the darkness for the upright;
  he is gracious and merciful and just.

R. Blessed the man who greatly delights in the Lord's commands.

Well for the man who is gracious and lends,
  who conducts his affairs with justice;
He shall never be moved;
  the just man shall be in everlasting remembrance.

R. Blessed the man who greatly delights in the Lord's commands.

Alleluia, alleluia   Jn 15:15b
I call you my friends, says the Lord,
for I have made known to you all that the Father has told me.
Alleluia, alleluia

Years I and II

GOSPEL   Mk 8:34 —9:1

*Those who lose their lives for my sake
and that of the Gospel, will save them.*

A reading from the holy Gospel according to Mark

Jesus summoned the crowd with his disciples and said to them, "Whoever wishes to come after me must deny himself, take up his cross, and follow me. For whoever wishes to save his life will lose it, but whoever loses his life for my sake and that of the Gospel will save it. What profit is there for one to gain the whole world and forfeit his life? What could one give in exchange for his life? Whoever is ashamed of me and of my words in this faithless and sinful generation, the Son of Man will be ashamed of when he comes in his Father's glory with the holy angels."

He also said to them, "Amen, I say to you, there are some standing here who will not taste death until they see that the Kingdom of God has come in power."

The Gospel of the Lord.

Liturgy of the Eucharist, *p. 897;* **Prayer over the Gifts,** *p. 393.*

Saturday

Antiphons *and* **Prayers,** *p. 392;* **Liturgy of the Word** *for Year I (odd years) follows; Year II (even years), p. 419.*

Today's Living Word

The Letter to the Hebrews defines faith as "the realization of what is hoped for and evidence of things not seen." In the transfiguration, Peter, James, and John are given a glimpse of what all Christians hope for and long to see: Christ in glory. The vision overwhelms Peter, who exclaims, "It is good that we are here." Then as he tries to capture the moment by suggesting that they build tents on the site, the heavenly voice speaks: "This is my beloved Son." These words, confided to Jesus at his baptism, are addressed now to his disciples. With this, the vision ends.

The selection from James is addressed to Christian teachers. The author, himself a teacher, realizes that teaching is an awesome ministry. The conclusion of the transfiguration story depicts Peter, James, and John, future Christian teachers, puzzling over what they have just seen and heard. They struggle to reconcile their lived experience with what they have previously learned from scribes and from Scripture about resurrection. As they do so, the voice from heaven insists: "Listen to him."

Year I

FIRST READING
Heb 11:1–7

*By faith we understand that the universe was
ordered by the word of God.*

A reading from the Letter to the Hebrews

Brothers and sisters:

Faith is the realization of what is hoped for and evidence of things not seen. Because of it the ancients were well attested. By faith we understand that the universe was ordered by the word of God, so that what is visible came into being through the invisible. By faith Abel offered to God a sacrifice greater than Cain's. Through this, he was attested to be righteous, God bearing witness to his gifts, and through this, though dead, he still speaks. By faith Enoch was taken up so that he should not see death, and *he was found no more because God had taken him.* Before he was taken up, he was attested to have pleased God. But without faith it is impossible to please him, for anyone who approaches God must believe that he exists and that he rewards those who seek him. By faith Noah, warned about what was not yet seen, with reverence built an ark for the salvation of his household. Through this, he condemned the world and inherited the righteousness that comes through faith.

The word of the Lord.

Responsorial Psalm   Ps 145:2–3, 4–5, 10–11

R. I will praise your name for ever, Lord.

Every day will I bless you,
   and I will praise your name forever and ever.
Great is the LORD and highly to be praised;
   his greatness is unsearchable.

R. I will praise your name for ever, Lord.

Generation after generation praises your works
   and proclaims your might.
They speak of the splendor of your glorious majesty
   and tell of your wondrous works.

R. I will praise your name for ever, Lord.

Let all your works give you thanks, O LORD,
   and let your faithful ones bless you.
Let them discourse of the glory of your Kingdom
   and speak of your might.

R. I will praise your name for ever, Lord.

Alleluia Verse *and* **Gospel,** p. 420.

Year II

FIRST READING

Jas 3:1–10

No human being can tame the tongue.

A reading from the Letter of Saint James

Not many of you should become teachers, my brothers and sisters, for you realize that we will be judged more strictly, for we all fall short in many respects. If anyone does not fall short in speech, he is a perfect man, able to bridle the whole body also. If we put bits into the mouths of horses to make them obey us, we also guide their whole bodies. It is the same with ships: even though they are so large and driven by fierce winds, they are steered by a very small rudder wherever the pilot's inclination wishes. In the same way the tongue is a small member and yet has great pretensions.

Consider how small a fire can set a huge forest ablaze. The tongue is also a fire. It exists among our members as a world of malice, defiling the whole body and setting the entire course of our lives on fire, itself set on fire by Gehenna. For every kind of beast and bird, of reptile and sea creature, can be tamed and has been tamed by the human species, but no man can tame the tongue. It is a restless evil, full of deadly poison. With it we bless the Lord and Father, and with it we curse men who are made in the likeness of God. From the same mouth come blessing and cursing. My brothers and sisters, this need not be so.

The word of the Lord.

Responsorial Psalm

Ps 12:2–3, 4–5, 7–8

R. You will protect us, Lord.

Help, O LORD! for no one now is dutiful;
  faithfulness has vanished from among the children of men.
Everyone speaks falsehood to his neighbor;
  with smooth lips they speak, and double heart.

R. You will protect us, Lord.

May the LORD destroy all smooth lips,
  every boastful tongue,
Those who say, "We are heroes with our tongues;
  our lips are our own; who is lord over us?"

R. You will protect us, Lord.

The promises of the LORD are sure,
  like tried silver, freed from dross, sevenfold refined.
You, O LORD, will keep us
  and preserve us always from this generation.

R. You will protect us, Lord.

Alleluia, alleluia See Mk 9:6
The heavens were opened and the voice of the Father thundered:
This is my beloved Son. Listen to him.
Alleluia, alleluia

Years I and II

GOSPEL   Mk 9:2–13
Jesus was transfigured before them.

A reading from the holy Gospel according to Mark

Jesus took Peter, James, and John and led them up a high
mountain apart by themselves. And he was transfigured before
them, and his clothes became dazzling white, such as no fuller
on earth could bleach them. Then Elijah appeared to them along
with Moses, and they were conversing with Jesus. Then Peter
said to Jesus in reply, "Rabbi, it is good that we are here! Let
us make three tents: one for you, one for Moses, and one for

Elijah." He hardly knew what to say, they were so terrified. Then a cloud came, casting a shadow over them; then from the cloud came a voice, "This is my beloved Son. Listen to him." Suddenly, looking around, the disciples no longer saw anyone but Jesus alone with them.

As they were coming down from the mountain, he charged them not to relate what they had seen to anyone, except when the Son of Man had risen from the dead. So they kept the matter to themselves, questioning what rising from the dead meant. Then they asked him, "Why do the scribes say that Elijah must come first?" He told them, "Elijah will indeed come first and restore all things, yet how is it written regarding the Son of Man that he must suffer greatly and be treated with contempt? But I tell you that Elijah has come and they did to him whatever they pleased, as it is written of him."

The Gospel of the Lord

Liturgy of the Eucharist, *p. 897;* **Prayer over the Gifts**, *p. 393.*

SEVENTH WEEK IN ORDINARY TIME

The **Antiphons and Prayers** *may be the following, or may be chosen from any of the other 33 weeks in Ordinary Time (refer to Liturgical Calendar, pp. 26–41).*

The **Liturgy of the Word** *varies: for Monday, see p. 423; Tuesday, p. 428; Wednesday, p. 433; Thursday, p. 438; Friday, p. 442; Saturday, p. 447.*

Entrance Antiphon

Lord, your mercy is my hope, my heart rejoices in your saving power. I will sing to the Lord for his goodness to me.   (Ps 13:6)

Opening Prayer

Let us pray

[that God will make us more like Christ, his Son]

Pause for silent prayer.

Father,
keep before us the wisdom and love
you have revealed in your Son.
Help us to be like him
in word and deed,
for he lives and reigns with you and the Holy Spirit,
one God, for ever and ever.

Alternative Opening Prayer

Let us pray
　　[to the God of power and might,
　　for his mercy is our hope]

Pause for silent prayer.

Almighty God,
Father of our Lord Jesus Christ,
faith in your word is the way to wisdom,
and to ponder your divine plan is to grow in the truth.
Open our eyes to your deeds,
our ears to the sound of your call,
so that our every act may increase our sharing
in the life you have offered us.

Grant this through Christ our Lord.

Prayer over the Gifts

Pray, brethren...

Lord,
as we make this offering,
may our worship in Spirit and truth
bring us salvation.

We ask this in the name of Jesus the Lord.

Preface of Weekdays in Ordinary Time I–VI, *pp. 948–950.*

Communion Antiphon

I will tell all your marvelous works. I will rejoice and be glad in you, and sing to your name, Most High. (Ps 9:2–3)

Or:

Lord, I believe that you are the Christ, the Son of God, who was to come into this world. (Jn 11:27)

Prayer after Communion

Let us pray.

Pause for silent prayer, if this has not preceded.

Almighty God,
help us to live the example of love
we celebrate in this eucharist,
that we may come to its fulfillment in your presence.

We ask this through Christ our Lord.

Monday

Antiphons and Prayers, *p. 421;* **Liturgy of the Word** *for Year I (odd years) follows; Year II (even years), p. 425.*

TODAY'S LIVING WORD

As the story of the transfiguration was a preview of Jesus' risen glory, so this story is a preview too. Here we see the disciples without Jesus, attempting in his absence to carry on his work—driving out demons and debating with scribes. It is a glimpse into the future of the Church. Although Jesus gave them authority over unclean spirits, the disciples cannot expel the demon that torments the boy. No doubt the scribes have outclassed them in discussion as well. The answer to their predicament lies in the miracle story sandwiched between two references to the disciples' powerlessness. They must admit their lack of faith in Jesus and make the prayer of the desperate father their own: "Help my unbelief!"

Called to share his wisdom and power, the followers of Jesus can only do so through faith. "Everything is possible to one who has faith." This is not to say that faith can do anything, but that faith does not put limits on what God can do. James calls such faith "wisdom from above"; as Sirach says, it is a gift lavished on God's friends.

Year I

FIRST READING   Sir 1:1–10

Before all things else wisdom was created.

A reading from the beginning of the Book of Sirach

All wisdom comes from the LORD
    and with him it remains forever, and is before all time
The sand of the seashore, the drops of rain,
    the days of eternity: who can number these?
Heaven's height, earth's breadth,
    the depths of the abyss: who can explore these?
Before all things else wisdom was created;
    and prudent understanding, from eternity.
The word of God on high is the fountain of wisdom
    and her ways are everlasting.
To whom has wisdom's root been revealed?
    Who knows her subtleties?
To whom has the discipline of wisdom been revealed?
    And who has understood the multiplicity of her ways ?
There is but one, wise and truly awe-inspiring,
    seated upon his throne:
There is but one, Most High
    all-powerful creator-king and truly awe-inspiring one,
    seated upon his throne and he is the God of dominion.

It is the LORD; he created her through the Holy Spirit,
has seen her and taken note of her.
He has poured her forth upon all his works,
upon every living thing according to his bounty;
he has lavished her upon his friends.
The word of the Lord.

Responsorial Psalm

Ps 93:1ab, 1cd – 2, 5

R. **The Lord is king; he is robed in majesty.**

The LORD is king, in splendor robed;
robed is the LORD and girt about with strength.

R. **The Lord is king; he is robed in majesty.**

And he has made the world firm,
not to be moved.
Your throne stands firm from of old;
from everlasting you are, O LORD.

R. **The Lord is king; he is robed in majesty.**

Your decrees are worthy of trust indeed:
holiness befits your house,
O LORD, for length of days.

R. **The Lord is king; he is robed in majesty.**

Alleluia Verse and **Gospel**, p. 427.

Year II

FIRST READING

Jas 3:13 –18

*If you have bitter jealousy and selfish ambition
in your hearts, do not boast.*

A reading from the Letter of Saint James

Beloved:
Who among you is wise and understanding? Let him show his

works by a good life in the humility that comes from wisdom. But if you have bitter jealousy and selfish ambition in your hearts, do not boast and be false to the truth. Wisdom of this kind does not come down from above but is earthly, unspiritual, demonic. For where jealousy and selfish ambition exist, there is disorder and every foul practice. But the wisdom from above is first of all pure, then peaceable, gentle, compliant, full of mercy and good fruits, without inconstancy or insincerity. And the fruit of righteousness is sown in peace for those who cultivate peace.

The word of the Lord.

Responsorial Psalm

Ps 19:8, 9, 10, 15

R. The precepts of the Lord give joy to the heart.

The law of the LORD is perfect,
  refreshing the soul;
The decree of the LORD is trustworthy,
  giving wisdom to the simple.

R. The precepts of the Lord give joy to the heart.

The precepts of the LORD are right,
  rejoicing the heart;
The command of the LORD is clear,
  enlightening the eye.

R. The precepts of the Lord give joy to the heart.

The fear of the LORD is pure,
  enduring forever;
The ordinances of the LORD are true,
  all of them just.

R. The precepts of the Lord give joy to the heart.

Let the words of my mouth and the thought of my heart
  find favor before you,
O LORD, my rock and my redeemer.

R. The precepts of the Lord give joy to the heart.

Alleluia, alleluia   See 2 Tm 1:10
Our Savior Jesus Christ has destroyed death
and brought life to light through the Gospel.
Alleluia, alleluia

Years I and II

GOSPEL   Mk 9:14–29

I do believe, help my unbelief!

A reading from the holy Gospel according to Mark

As Jesus came down from the mountain with Peter, James,
John and approached the other disciples, they saw a large crowd
around them and scribes arguing with them. Immediately on
seeing him, the whole crowd was utterly amazed. They ran up
to him and greeted him. He asked them, "What are you arguing
about with them?" Someone from the crowd answered him,
"Teacher, I have brought to you my son possessed by a mute
spirit. Wherever it seizes him, it throws him down; he foams
at the mouth, grinds his teeth, and becomes rigid. I asked your
disciples to drive it out, but they were unable to do so." He
said to them in reply, "O faithless generation, how long will I
be with you? How long will I endure you? Bring him to me."
They brought the boy to him. And when he saw him, the spirit
immediately threw the boy into convulsions. As he fell to the
ground, he began to roll around and foam at the mouth. Then
he questioned his father, "How long has this been happening
to him?" He replied, "Since childhood. It has often thrown
him into fire and into water to kill him. But if you can do
anything, have compassion on us and help us." Jesus said to
him, "'If you can!' Everything is possible to one who has faith."

Then the boy's father cried out, "I do believe, help my unbelief!" Jesus, on seeing a crowd rapidly gathering, rebuked the unclean spirit and said to it, "Mute and deaf spirit, I command you: come out of him and never enter him again!" Shouting and throwing the boy into convulsions, it came out. He became like a corpse, which caused many to say, "He is dead!" But Jesus took him by the hand, raised him, and he stood up. When he entered the house, his disciples asked him in private, "Why could we not drive the spirit out?" He said to them, "This kind can only come out through prayer."

The Gospel of the Lord.

Liturgy of the Eucharist, *p. 897;* **Prayer over the Gifts,** *p. 422.*

Tuesday

Antiphons and Prayers, *p. 421;* **Liturgy of the Word** *for Year I (odd years) follows; Year II (even years), p. 431.*

TODAY'S LIVING WORD

The two first readings highlight different aspects of today's Gospel story. Predicting his passion, Jesus shows himself to be well-schooled in the way of wisdom. He knows that God's servants are often tried by adversity and crushed by misfortune, as Sirach teaches. Having studied "the generations long past," he knows too that God saves in time of trouble.

The argument that preoccupies Jesus' disciples in the same Gospel story deserves the stern warning of James: "Where do the conflicts among you come from?… Humble yourselves before the Lord and he will exalt you." More gently, Jesus tells them the same thing. In Jesus' day, the child that he set before the Twelve was not a symbol of innocence, but of poverty and powerlessness. Children in that world were vulnerable and voiceless, as they are today. Jesus was telling the Twelve—and us—that true greatness consists in extending a warm welcome to the least of his brothers and sisters.

Year I

FIRST READING   Sir 2:1–11

Prepare yourself for trials.

A reading from the Book of Sirach

My son, when you come to serve the LORD,
    stand in justice and fear,
    prepare yourself for trials.
Be sincere of heart and steadfast,
    incline your ear and receive the word of understanding,
    undisturbed in time of adversity.
Wait on God, with patience, cling to him, forsake him not;
    thus will you be wise in all your ways.
Accept whatever befalls you,
    when sorrowful, be steadfast,
    and in crushing misfortune be patient;
For in fire gold and silver are tested,
    and worthy people in the crucible of humiliation.
Trust God and God will help you;
    trust in him, and he will direct your way;
    keep his fear and grow old therein.
You who fear the LORD, wait for his mercy,
    turn not away lest you fall.
You who fear the LORD, trust him,
    and your reward will not be lost.
You who fear the LORD, hope for good things,
    for lasting joy and mercy.
You who fear the LORD, love him,
    and your hearts will be enlightened.
Study the generations long past and understand;

has anyone hoped in the LORD and been disappointed?
Has anyone persevered in his commandments and been forsaken?
has anyone called upon him and been rebuffed?
Compassionate and merciful is the LORD;
he forgives sins, he saves in time of trouble
and he is a protector to all who seek him in truth.

The word of the Lord.

Responsorial Psalm   Ps 37:3 – 4, 18 – 19, 27 – 28, 39 – 40

R. Commit your life to the Lord, and he will help you.

Trust in the LORD and do good,
that you may dwell in the land and be fed in security.
Take delight in the LORD,
and he will grant you your heart's requests.

R. Commit your life to the Lord, and he will help you.

The LORD watches over the lives of the wholehearted;
their inheritance lasts forever.
They are not put to shame in an evil time;
in days of famine they have plenty.

R. Commit your life to the Lord, and he will help you.

Turn from evil and do good,
that you may abide forever;
For the LORD loves what is right,
and forsakes not his faithful ones.

R. Commit your life to the Lord, and he will help you.

The salvation of the just is from the LORD;
he is their refuge in time of distress.
And the LORD helps them and delivers them;
he delivers them from the wicked and saves them,
because they take refuge in him.

R. Commit your life to the Lord, and he will help you.

Alleluia Verse *and* **Gospel,** *p. 432.*

Year II

FIRST READING   Jas 4:1–10

You ask but you do not receive, because you ask wrongly.

A reading from the Letter of Saint James

Beloved:

Where do the wars and where do the conflicts among you come from? Is it not from your passions that make war within your members? You covet but do not possess. You kill and envy but you cannot obtain; you fight and wage war. You do not possess because you do not ask. You ask but do not receive, because you ask wrongly, to spend it on your passions. Adulterers! Do you not know that to be a lover of the world means enmity with God? Therefore, whoever wants to be a lover of the world makes himself an enemy of God. Or do you suppose that the Scripture speaks without meaning when it says, *The spirit that he has made to dwell in us tends toward jealousy?* But he bestows a greater grace; therefore, it says:

> God resists the proud,
>   but gives grace to the humble.

So submit yourselves to God. Resist the Devil, and he will flee from you. Draw near to God, and he will draw near to you. Cleanse your hands, you sinners, and purify your hearts, you of two minds. Begin to lament, to mourn, to weep. Let your laughter be turned into mourning and your joy into dejection. Humble yourselves before the Lord and he will exalt you.

The word of the Lord.

Responsorial Psalm   Ps 55:7 – 8, 9 –10a, 10b –11a, 23

R. Throw your cares on the Lord, and he will support you.

And I say, "Had I but wings like a dove,
  I would fly away and be at rest.
Far away I would flee;
  I would lodge in the wilderness."

> **R. Throw your cares on the Lord, and he will support you.**

"I would wait for him who saves me
  from the violent storm and the tempest."
Engulf them, O Lord; divide their counsels.

> **R. Throw your cares on the Lord, and he will support you.**

In the city I see violence and strife,
  day and night they prowl about upon its walls.

> **R. Throw your cares on the Lord, and he will support you.**

Cast your care upon the LORD,
  and he will support you;
  never will he permit the just man to be disturbed.

> **R. Throw your cares on the Lord, and he will support you.**

> **Alleluia, alleluia**   Gal 6:14
> May I never boast except in the Cross of our Lord Jesus Christ,
> through which the world has been crucified to me and I to the
>   world.
> **Alleluia, alleluia**

Years I and II

GOSPEL   Mk 9:30–37

The Son of Man is to be handed over.
Whoever wishes to be first, shall be last of all.

A reading from the holy Gospel according to Mark

Jesus and his disciples left from there and began a journey
through Galilee, but he did not wish anyone to know about it.
He was teaching his disciples and telling them, "The Son of
Man is to be handed over to men and they will kill him, and

three days after his death the Son of Man will rise." But they did not understand the saying, and they were afraid to question him.

They came to Capernaum and, once inside the house, he began to ask them, "What were you arguing about on the way?" But they remained silent. For they had been discussing among themselves on the way who was the greatest. Then he sat down, called the Twelve, and said to them, "If anyone wishes to be first, he shall be the last of all and the servant of all." Taking a child, he placed it in their midst, and putting his arms around it, he said to them, "Whoever receives one child such as this in my name, receives me; and whoever receives me, receives not me but the One who sent me."

The Gospel of the Lord.

Liturgy of the Eucharist, *p. 897;* **Prayer over the Gifts,** *p. 422.*

Wednesday

Antiphons and Prayers, *p. 421;* **Liturgy of the Word** *for Year I (odd years) follows; Year II (even years), p. 436.*

Today's Living Word

In today's reading, James warns against "boasting in your arrogance." John's words to Jesus in the Gospel story show more than a little arrogance and pretension: "We saw someone driving out demons in your name, and we tried to prevent him because he does not follow us"—that is, he is not one of us. In answer, Jesus the teacher takes his cue from Moses, that other great teacher. Numbers 11 recounts how Joshua wanted to stop Eldad and Medad from prophesying because they had not gone as commanded to the tent of meeting. But Moses answered, "Are you jealous for my sake? Would that all the people of the Lord were prophets!" In a similar situation, Jesus also counsels tolerance: "Whoever is not against us is for us."

As Christians, we have been baptized in Jesus' name, but that name does not belong to us. We do not have exclusive rights to the wisdom and power of God revealed in Jesus. Being wise men, Moses and Jesus both recognized that wisdom, the power of God, often walks with us "as a stranger," as Sirach puts it.

Year I

FIRST READING   Sir 4:11–19

Those who love her the Lord loves.

A reading from the Book of Sirach

Wisdom breathes life into her children
    and admonishes those who seek her.
He who loves her loves life;
    those who seek her will be embraced by the Lord.
He who holds her fast inherits glory;
    wherever he dwells, the LORD bestows blessings.
Those who serve her serve the Holy One;
    those who love her the LORD loves.
He who obeys her judges nations;
    he who hearkens to her dwells in her inmost chambers.
If one trusts her, he will possess her;
    his descendants too will inherit her.
She walks with him as a stranger
    and at first she puts him to the test;
Fear and dread she brings upon him
    and tries him with her discipline
      until she try him by her laws and trust his soul.

Then she comes back to bring him happiness
    and reveal her secrets to them
    and she will heap upon him
    treasures of knowledge and an understanding of justice.
But if he fails her, she will abandon him
    and deliver him into the hands of despoilers.

The word of the Lord.

Responsorial Psalm   <small>Ps 119:165, 168, 171, 172, 174, 175</small>

R. O Lord, great peace have they who love your law.

Those who love your law have great peace,
  and for them there is no stumbling block.

R. O Lord, great peace have they who love your law.

I keep your precepts and your decrees,
  for all my ways are before you.

R. O Lord, great peace have they who love your law.

My lips pour forth your praise,
  because you teach me your statutes.

R. O Lord, great peace have they who love your law.

May my tongue sing of your promise,
  for all your commands are just.

R. O Lord, great peace have they who love your law.

I long for your salvation, O LORD,
  and your law is my delight.

R. O Lord, great peace have they who love your law.

Let my soul live to praise you,
  and may your ordinances help me.

R. O Lord, great peace have they who love your law.

Alleluia Verse *and* **Gospel,** *p.* 437.

FIRST READING

Jas 4:13–17

You have no idea what your life will be like.
Instead you should say: If the Lord wills it.

A reading from the Letter of Saint James

Beloved:

Come now, you who say, "Today or tomorrow we shall go into such and such a town, spend a year there doing business, and make a profit"— you have no idea what your life will be like tomorrow. You are a puff of smoke that appears briefly and then disappears. Instead you should say, "If the Lord wills it, we shall live to do this or that." But now you are boasting in your arrogance. All such boasting is evil. So for one who knows the right thing to do and does not do it, it is a sin.

The word of the Lord.

Responsorial Psalm

Ps 49:2–3, 6–7, 8–10, 11

R. Blessed are the poor in spirit; the Kingdom of heaven
is theirs!

Hear this, all you peoples;
   hearken, all who dwell in the world,
Of lowly birth or high degree,
   rich and poor alike.

R. Blessed are the poor in spirit; the Kingdom of heaven
is theirs!

Why should I fear in evil days
   when my wicked ensnarers ring me round?
They trust in their wealth;
   the abundance of their riches is their boast.

R. Blessed are the poor in spirit; the Kingdom of heaven
is theirs!

Yet in no way can a man redeem himself,
  or pay his own ransom to God;
Too high is the price to redeem one's life; he would never have
      enough
  to remain alive always and not see destruction.

> **R. Blessed are the poor in spirit; the Kingdom of heaven
>   is theirs!**

For he can see that wise men die,
  and likewise the senseless and the stupid pass away,
  leaving to others their wealth.

> **R. Blessed are the poor in spirit; the Kingdom of heaven
>   is theirs!**

> **Alleluia, alleluia**   Jn 14:6
> I am the way and the truth and the life, says the Lord;
> no one comes to the Father except through me.
> **Alleluia, alleluia**

Years I and II

GOSPEL   Mk 9:38 – 40

Whoever is not against us is for us.

A reading from the holy Gospel according to Mark

John said to Jesus, "Teacher, we saw someone driving out
demons in your name, and we tried to prevent him because he
does not follow us." Jesus replied, "Do not prevent him. There
is no one who performs a mighty deed in my name who can at
the same time speak ill of me. For whoever is not against us is
for us."

The Gospel of the Lord.

Liturgy of the Eucharist, *p. 897;* **Prayer over the Gifts,** *p. 422.*

Thursday

Antiphons and Prayers, *p. 421;* **Liturgy of the Word** *for Year I (odd years) follows; Year II (even years), p. 440.*

TODAY'S LIVING WORD

All three readings for today sound an alarm. "Delay not your conversion to the Lord," Sirach insists. "Weep and wail over your impending miseries," cries James. "If your hand causes you to sin, cut it off!" commands Jesus. These hard sayings relentlessly force us to acknowledge that one day God will judge all of us. In these verses, Mark again shows Jesus' concern for the little ones, those "little ones" so easily led astray. But Jesus knows too that we are often our own worst enemies. Occasions of sin arise from within ourselves, as well as from outside. Borrowing the vivid imagery of Isaiah 66, he says in no uncertain terms: whatever in you causes sin must be rooted out at all cost, so that you may enter life and avoid the fires of hell.

Such hard sayings are rarely heard in our day. But the truth they convey is as essential as salt: "If salt becomes insipid, with what will you restore its flavor?"

Year I

FIRST READING   Sir 5:1–8

Delay not your conversion to the LORD.

A reading from the Book of Sirach

Rely not on your wealth;
    say not: "I have the power."
Rely not on your strength
    in following the desires of your heart.
Say not: "Who can prevail against me?"
    or, "Who will subdue me for my deeds?"
    for God will surely exact the punishment.

Say not: "I have sinned, yet what has befallen me?"
>   for the Most High bides his time.
Of forgiveness be not overconfident,
>   adding sin upon sin.
Say not: "Great is his mercy;
>   my many sins he will forgive."
For mercy and anger alike are with him;
>   upon the wicked alights his wrath.
Delay not your conversion to the LORD,
>   put it not off from day to day.
For suddenly his wrath flames forth;
>   at the time of vengeance you will be destroyed.
Rely not upon deceitful wrath,
>   for it will be no help on the day of wrath.

The word of the Lord.

Responsorial Psalm

Ps 1:1–2, 3, 4 and 6

> **R. Blessed are they who hope in the Lord.**

Blessed the man who follows not
>   the counsel of the wicked
Nor walks in the way of sinners,
>   nor sits in the company of the insolent,
But delights in the law of the LORD
>   and meditates on his law day and night.

> **R. Blessed are they who hope in the Lord.**

He is like a tree
>   planted near running water,
That yields its fruit in due season,
>   and whose leaves never fade.
>   Whatever he does, prospers.

> **R. Blessed are they who hope in the Lord.**

Not so the wicked, not so;
   they are like chaff which the wind drives away.
For the LORD watches over the way of the just,
   but the way of the wicked vanishes.

R. Blessed are they who hope in the Lord.

Alleluia Verse *and* **Gospel,** *p. 441.*

Year II

FIRST READING
Jas 5:1–6

The workers from whom you withheld the wages, are crying aloud;
   their cries have reached the ears of the Lord of hosts.

A reading from the Letter of Saint James

Come now, you rich, weep and wail over your impending miseries. Your wealth has rotted away, your clothes have become moth-eaten, your gold and silver have corroded, and that corrosion will be a testimony against you; it will devour your flesh like a fire. You have stored up treasure for the last days. Behold, the wages you withheld from the workers who harvested your fields are crying aloud; and the cries of the harvesters have reached the ears of the Lord of hosts. You have lived on earth in luxury and pleasure; you have fattened your hearts for the day of slaughter. You have condemned; you have murdered the righteous one; he offers you no resistance.

The word of the Lord.

Responsorial Psalm
Ps 49:14–15ab, 15cd–16, 17–18, 19–20

R. Blessed are the poor in spirit; the Kingdom of heaven
   is theirs!

This is the way of those whose trust is folly,

the end of those contented with their lot:
Like sheep they are herded into the nether world;
   death is their shepherd and the upright rule over them.

**R. Blessed are the poor in spirit; the Kingdom of heaven
     is theirs!**

Quickly their form is consumed;
   the nether world is their palace.
But God will redeem me
   from the power of the nether world by receiving me.

**R. Blessed are the poor in spirit; the Kingdom of heaven
     is theirs!**

Fear not when a man grows rich,
   when the wealth of his house becomes great,
For when he dies, he shall take none of it;
   his wealth shall not follow him down.

**R. Blessed are the poor in spirit; the Kingdom of heaven
     is theirs!**

Though in his lifetime he counted himself blessed,
   "They will praise you for doing well for yourself,"
He shall join the circle of his forebears
   who shall never more see light.

**R. Blessed are the poor in spirit; the Kingdom of heaven
     is theirs!**

Alleluia, alleluia   See 1 Thes 2:13
Receive the word of God, not as the word of men,
but as it truly is, the word of God.
Alleluia, alleluia

Years I and II

GOSPEL   Mk 9:41–50

*It is better for you to enter into life with one hand,
than with two hands to go into Gehenna.*

A reading from the holy Gospel according to Mark

Jesus said to his disciples: "Anyone who gives you a cup of water to drink because you belong to Christ, amen, I say to you, will surely not lose his reward.

"Whoever causes one of these little ones who believe in me to sin, it would be better for him if a great millstone were put around his neck and he were thrown into the sea. If your hand causes you to sin, cut it off. It is better for you to enter into life maimed than with two hands to go into Gehenna, into the unquenchable fire. And if your foot causes you to sin, cut if off. It is better for you to enter into life crippled than with two feet to be thrown into Gehenna. And if your eye causes you to sin, pluck it out. Better for you to enter into the Kingdom of God with one eye than with two eyes to be thrown into Gehenna, where *their worm does not die, and the fire is not quenched.*

"Everyone will be salted with fire. Salt is good, but if salt becomes insipid, with what will you restore its flavor? Keep salt in yourselves and you will have peace with one another."

The Gospel of the Lord.

Liturgy of the Eucharist, *p. 897;* **Prayer over the Gifts,** *p. 422.*

Friday

Antiphons and Prayers, *p. 421;* **Liturgy of the Word** *for Year I (odd years) follows; Year II (even years), p. 445.*

TODAY'S LIVING WORD

Divorce was as live an issue in Jesus' day as it is in ours. Mark's account preserves the earliest memory of Jesus' teaching on this painful human dilemma. The question is put to him as a test: Is divorce legal? Jesus answers with a question of his own: "What did Moses command you?" It is important to note how vague Moses' teaching is on this point. No law in the written Torah—the first five books of the Hebrew Scriptures—clearly states the grounds for divorce. Deuteronomy 24, however, does assume the practice of divorce, and on that basis the opponents of Jesus respond that Moses permitted it. Jesus' teaching is also based on Torah. Turning to Genesis, he declares that God intended "from the beginning of creation" that marriage be indissoluble.

The teaching of Jesus is as important for what it says about marriage as for what it says about divorce. Clearly he honors the union of two people whose "yes" means "yes," as James might put it. And surely all that Sirach says of the "faithful friend" is true of the faithful spouse as well.

Year I

FIRST READING   Sir 6:5–17

Faithful friends are beyond price.

A reading from the Book of Sirach

A kind mouth multiplies friends and appeases enemies,
    and gracious lips prompt friendly greetings.
Let your acquaintances be many,
    but one in a thousand your confidant.
When you gain a friend, first test him,
    and be not too ready to trust him.
For one sort is a friend when it suits him,
    but he will not be with you in time of distress.
Another is a friend who becomes an enemy,
    and tells of the quarrel to your shame.
Another is a friend, a boon companion,
    who will not be with you when sorrow comes.

When things go well, he is your other self,
  and lords it over your servants;
But if you are brought low, he turns against you
  and avoids meeting you.
Keep away from your enemies;
  be on your guard with your friends.
A faithful friend is a sturdy shelter;
  he who finds one finds a treasure.
A faithful friend is beyond price,
  no sum can balance his worth.
A faithful friend is a life-saving remedy,
  such as he who fears God finds;
For he who fears God behaves accordingly,
  and his friend will be like himself.

The word of the Lord.

Responsorial Psalm   Ps 119:12, 16, 18, 27, 34, 35

  R. Guide me, Lord, in the way of your commands.

Blessed are you, O LORD;
  teach me your statutes.

  R. Guide me, Lord, in the way of your commands.

In your statutes I will delight;
  I will not forget your words.

  R. Guide me, Lord, in the way of your commands.

Open my eyes, that I may consider
  the wonders of your law.

  R. Guide me, Lord, in the way of your commands.

Make me understand the way of your precepts,
  and I will meditate on your wondrous deeds.

  R. Guide me, Lord, in the way of your commands.

Give me discernment, that I may observe your law
  and keep it with all my heart.

R. Guide me, Lord, in the way of your commands.

Lead me in the path of your commands,
  in it I delight.

R. Guide me, Lord, in the way of your commands.

Alleluia Verse *and* **Gospel,** *p. 446.*

Year II

FIRST READING   Jas 5:9–12

The Judge is standing before the gates.

A reading from the Letter of Saint James

Do not complain, brothers and sisters, about one another, that
you may not be judged. Behold, the Judge is standing before
the gates. Take as an example of hardship and patience, brothers
and sisters, the prophets who spoke in the name of the Lord.
Indeed we call blessed those who have persevered. You have
heard of the perseverance of Job, and you have seen the purpose
of the Lord, because *the Lord is compassionate and merciful.*

But above all, my brothers and sisters, do not swear, either
by heaven or by earth or with any other oath, but let your "Yes"
mean "Yes" and your "No" mean "No," that you may not incur
condemnation.

The word of the Lord.

Responsorial Psalm   Ps 103:1–2, 3–4, 8–9, 11–12

R. The Lord is kind and merciful.

Bless the LORD, O my soul;
  and all my being, bless his holy name.

Bless the LORD, O my soul,
   and forget not all his benefits.

R. The Lord is kind and merciful.

He pardons all your iniquities,
   he heals all your ills.
He redeems your life from destruction,
   he crowns you with kindness and compassion.

R. The Lord is kind and merciful.

Merciful and gracious is the LORD,
   slow to anger and abounding in kindness.
He will not always chide,
   nor does he keep his wrath forever.

R. The Lord is kind and merciful.

For as the heavens are high above the earth,
   so surpassing is his kindness toward those who fear him.
As far as the east is from the west,
   so far has he put our transgressions from us.

R. The Lord is kind and merciful.

Alleluia, alleluia   See Jn 17:17b, 17a
Your word, O Lord, is truth;
consecrate us in the truth.
Alleluia, alleluia

Years I and II

GOSPEL   Mk 10:1–12

What God has joined together, no human being must separate.

A reading from the holy Gospel according to Mark

Jesus came into the district of Judea and across the Jordan.
Again crowds gathered around him and, as was his custom,
he again taught them. The Pharisees approached him and
asked, "Is it lawful for a husband to divorce his wife?" They

were testing him. He said to them in reply, "What did Moses command you?" They replied, "Moses permitted a husband to write a bill of divorce and dismiss her." But Jesus told them, "Because of the hardness of your hearts he wrote you this commandment. But from the beginning of creation, *God made them male and female. For this reason a man shall leave his father and mother and be joined to his wife, and the two shall become one flesh.* So they are no longer two but one flesh. Therefore what God has joined together, no human being must separate." In the house the disciples again questioned Jesus about this. He said to them, "Whoever divorces his wife and marries another commits adultery against her; and if she divorces her husband and marries another, she commits adultery."

The Gospel of the Lord.

Liturgy of the Eucharist, *p. 897;* **Prayer over the Gifts,** *p. 422.*

Saturday

Antiphons and Prayers, *p. 421;* **Liturgy of the Word** *for Year I (odd years) follows; Year II (even years), p. 450.*

TODAY'S LIVING WORD

These three readings have a sacramental quality. The Council of Trent found scriptural evidence in this passage from James for the practice of anointing the sick. According to Tertullian, some early Christians used this selection from Mark as scriptural justification for infant baptism. Commenting on these verses, Wilfrid Harrington goes so far as to suggest that there may be "a gleam of a baptismal formula"* in the words of Jesus: "Let the children come to me; do not prevent them, for the kingdom of God belongs to such as these." In both cases, the Church discovered in the human words and

gestures of Jesus—his healing the sick and welcoming the children—
a precedent and a pattern for its own sacramental ministry.

The reading from Sirach uncovers the anthropology—the understanding of the human person—on which sacramental theology is
built. Made in God's image, human beings are uniquely equipped
to discover and "describe the wonders of his deeds and praise his
holy name."

* Mark, New Testament Message 4 (Wilmington: Michael Glazier, Inc., 1979),
p. 158.

Year I

FIRST READING

Sir 17:1–15

In his own image the Lord made them.

A reading from the Book of Sirach

God from the earth created man,
   and in his own image he made him.
He makes man return to earth again,
   and endows him with a strength of his own.
Limited days of life he gives him,
   with power over all things else on earth.
He puts the fear of him in all flesh,
   and gives him rule over beasts and birds.
He created for them counsel, and a tongue and eyes and ears,
   and an inventive heart,
      and filled them with the discipline of understanding.
He created in them knowledge of the spirit;
With wisdom he fills their heart;
   good and evil he shows them.
He put the fear of himself upon their hearts,
   and showed them his mighty works,

That they might glory in the wonder of his deeds
  and praise his holy name.
He has set before them knowledge,
  a law of life as their inheritance;
An everlasting covenant he has made with them,
  his justice and his judgments he has revealed to them.
His majestic glory their eyes beheld,
  his glorious voice their ears heard.
He says to them, "Avoid all evil";
  each of them he gives precepts about his fellow men.
Their ways are ever known to him,
  they cannot be hidden from his eyes.
Over every nation he places a ruler,
  but God's own portion is Israel.
All their actions are clear as the sun to him,
  his eyes are ever upon their ways.

The word of the Lord.

Responsorial Psalm   Ps 103:13 –14, 15 –16, 17 –18

  **R. The Lord's kindness is everlasting to those who fear
    him.**

As a father has compassion on his children,
  so the LORD has compassion on those who fear him,
For he knows how we are formed;
  he remembers that we are dust.

  **R. The Lord's kindness is everlasting to those who fear
    him.**

Man's days are like those of grass;
  like a flower of the field he blooms;
The wind sweeps over him and he is gone,
  and his place knows him no more.

R. **The Lord's kindness is everlasting to those who fear him.**

But the kindness of the LORD is from eternity
to eternity toward those who fear him,
And his justice toward children's children
among those who keep his covenant.

R. **The Lord's kindness is everlasting to those who fear him.**

Alleluia Verse *and* **Gospel,** *p. 451.*

Year II

FIRST READING

Jas 5:13 – 20

The fervent prayer of a righteous person is very powerful.

A reading from the Letter of Saint James

Beloved:

Is anyone among you suffering? He should pray. Is anyone in good spirits? He should sing a song of praise. Is anyone among you sick? He should summon the presbyters of the Church, and they should pray over him and anoint him with oil in the name of the Lord. The prayer of faith will save the sick person, and the Lord will raise him up. If he has committed any sins, he will be forgiven.

Therefore, confess your sins to one another and pray for one another, that you may be healed. The fervent prayer of a righteous person is very powerful. Elijah was a man like us; yet he prayed earnestly that it might not rain, and for three years and six months it did not rain upon the land. Then Elijah prayed again, and the sky gave rain and the earth produced its fruit.

My brothers and sisters, if anyone among you should stray from the truth and someone bring him back, he should know that whoever brings back a sinner from the error of his way will save his soul from death and will cover a multitude of sins. The word of the Lord.

Responsorial Psalm

Ps 141:1–2, 3 and 8

R. Let my prayer come like incense before you.

O LORD, to you I call; hasten to me;
 hearken to my voice when I call upon you.
Let my prayer come like incense before you;
 the lifting up of my hands, like the evening sacrifice.

R. Let my prayer come like incense before you.

O LORD, set a watch before my mouth,
 a guard at the door of my lips.
For toward you, O God, my LORD, my eyes are turned;
 in you I take refuge; strip me not of life.

R. Let my prayer come like incense before you.

> **Alleluia, alleluia**   See Mt 11:25
> Blessed are you, Father, Lord of heaven and earth;
> you have revealed to little ones the mysteries of the Kingdom.
> **Alleluia, alleluia**

Years I and II

GOSPEL

Mk 10:13–16

*Whoever does not accept the Kingdom of God
like a child will not enter it.*

A reading from the holy Gospel according to Mark

People were bringing children to Jesus that he might touch them, but the disciples rebuked them. When Jesus saw this he became indignant and said to them, "Let the children come to me; do not prevent them, for the Kingdom of God belongs to such as these. Amen, I say to you, whoever does not accept the Kingdom of God like a child will not enter it." Then he embraced the children and blessed them, placing his hands on them.

The Gospel of the Lord.

Liturgy of the Eucharist, *p. 897;* **Prayer over the Gifts,** *p. 422.*

EIGHTH WEEK IN ORDINARY TIME

The **Antiphons and Prayers** *may be the following, or may be chosen from any of the other 33 weeks in Ordinary Time (refer to Liturgical Calendar, pp. 26–41).*

The **Liturgy of the Word** *varies: for Monday, see p. 454; Tuesday, p. 459; Wednesday, p. 463; Thursday, p. 468; Friday, p. 473; Saturday, p. 478.*

Entrance Antiphon

The Lord has been my strength; he has led me into freedom. He saved me because he loves me.   (Ps 18:19 – 20)

Opening Prayer

Let us pray
    [that God will bring peace to the world
    and freedom to his Church]

> *Pause for silent prayer.*

Lord,
guide the course of world events
and give your Church the joy and peace
of serving you in freedom.

We ask this through our Lord Jesus Christ, your Son,
who lives and reigns with you and the Holy Spirit,
one God, for ever and ever.

Alternative Opening Prayer

Let us pray
   [that the peace of Christ
   may find welcome in the world]

Pause for silent prayer.

Father in heaven,
form in us the likeness of your Son
and deepen his life within us.
Send us as witnesses of gospel joy
into a world of fragile peace and broken promises.
Touch the hearts of all men with your love
that they in turn may love one another.
We ask this through Christ our Lord.

Prayer over the Gifts

Pray, brethren...
God our Creator,
may this bread and wine we offer
as a sign of our love and worship
lead us to salvation.
Grant this through Christ our Lord.

Preface of Weekdays in Ordinary Time I–VI, *pp. 948–950.*

Communion Antiphon

I will sing to the Lord for his goodness to me, I will sing the
name of the Lord, Most High.
(Ps 13:6)

Or:

I, the Lord, am with you always, until the end of the world.
(Mt 28:20)

Prayer after Communion

Let us pray.

Pause for silent prayer, if this has not preceded.

God of salvation,
may this sacrament
which strengthens us here on earth
bring us to eternal life.

We ask this in the name of Jesus the Lord.

Monday

Antiphons and Prayers, *p. 452;* **Liturgy of the Word** *for Year I (odd years) follows; Year II (even years), p. 456.*

TODAY'S LIVING WORD

Today's Gospel is a story of missed opportunity. A man approaches Jesus with the question: "What must I do to inherit eternal life?" Jesus' answer is thoroughly Jewish, "You know the commandments." "All of these I have observed from my youth," the man replies. Moved, Jesus invites him to do one thing more. In Judaism, the word *zekhut* describes the hundredfold to which Jesus is calling the rich man. As Jacob Neusner explains, it is gained "by an act of renunciation...which heaven cannot compel but highly prizes."* For the man in the Gospel story to give all he had to the poor and to throw in his lot with Jesus would have been such an act. But he "had many possessions."

Although his age is never mentioned, Christians have traditionally depicted the man in this Gospel as young, as though such opportunities are only offered to the young. But Jesus repeats his invitation throughout our lives. To accept it is to gain the "inheritance that is imperishable" which Peter so joyfully announced. To refuse it is to go away sad, like one of "those who have never lived" (Sirach).

* Neusner and Bruce D. Chilton, *Revelation: The Torah and the Bible* (Valley Forge: Trinity Press International, 1995), p. 77.

Year I

FIRST READING

Sir 17:20 – 24

Turn again to the Most High,
and learn the judgments of God.

A reading from the Book of Sirach

To the penitent God provides a way back,
  he encourages those who are losing hope
  and has chosen for them the lot of truth.
Return to him and give up sin,
  pray to the Lord and make your offenses few.
Turn again to the Most High and away from your sin,
  hate intensely what he loathes,
  and know the justice and judgments of God,
Stand firm in the way set before you,
  in prayer to the Most High God.

Who in the nether world can glorify the Most High
  in place of the living who offer their praise?
Dwell no longer in the error of the ungodly,
  but offer your praise before death.
No more can the dead give praise
  than those who have never lived;
You who are alive and well
  shall praise and glorify God in his mercies.
How great the mercy of the Lord,
  his forgiveness of those who return to him!
The word of the Lord.

Responsorial Psalm

Ps 32:1–2, 5, 6, 7

  R. Let the just exult and rejoice in the Lord.

Blessed is he whose fault is taken away,
  whose sin is covered.
Blessed the man to whom the LORD imputes not guilt,
  in whose spirit there is no guile.

R. Let the just exult and rejoice in the Lord.

Then I acknowledged my sin to you,
  my guilt I covered not.
I said, "I confess my faults to the LORD,"
  and you took away the guilt of my sin.

R. Let the just exult and rejoice in the Lord.

For this shall every faithful man pray to you
  in time of stress.
Though deep waters overflow,
  they shall not reach him.

R. Let the just exult and rejoice in the Lord.

You are my shelter; from distress you will preserve me;
  with glad cries of freedom you will ring me round.

R. Let the just exult and rejoice in the Lord.

Alleluia Verse and **Gospel**, p. 458.

Year II

FIRST READING   1 Pt 1:3–9

> *Although you have not seen him, you love him;*
> *you rejoice with an indescribable and glorious joy.*

A reading from the first Letter of Saint Peter

Blessed be the God and Father of our Lord Jesus Christ, who
in his great mercy gave us a new birth to a living hope through
the resurrection of Jesus Christ from the dead, to an inheritance
that is imperishable, undefiled, and unfading, kept in heaven
for you who by the power of God are safeguarded through

faith, to a salvation that is ready to be revealed in the final time. In this you rejoice, although now for a little while you may have to suffer through various trials, so that the genuineness of your faith, more precious than gold that is perishable even though tested by fire, may prove to be for praise, glory, and honor at the revelation of Jesus Christ. Although you have not seen him you love him; even though you do not see him now yet you believe in him, you rejoice with an indescribable and glorious joy, as you attain the goal of faith, the salvation of your souls.

The word of the Lord.

Responsorial Psalm

Ps 111:1–2, 5–6, 9 and 10c

R. The Lord will remember his covenant for ever.

I will give thanks to the LORD with all my heart
  in the company and assembly of the just.
Great are the works of the LORD,
  exquisite in all their delights.

R. The Lord will remember his covenant for ever.

He has given food to those who fear him;
  he will forever be mindful of his covenant.
He has made known to his people the power of his works,
  giving them the inheritance of the nations.

R. The Lord will remember his covenant for ever.

He has sent deliverance to his people;
  he has ratified his covenant forever;
holy and awesome is his name.
His praise endures forever.

R. The Lord will remember his covenant for ever.

Or: **R. Alleluia.**

Alleluia, alleluia   2 Cor 8:9
Jesus Christ became poor although he was rich,
so that by his poverty you might become rich.
Alleluia, alleluia

Years I and II

GOSPEL   Mk 10:17–27

Go, sell what you have, and give to the poor.

A reading from the holy Gospel according to Mark

As Jesus was setting out on a journey, a man ran up, knelt down before him, and asked him, "Good teacher, what must I do to inherit eternal life?" Jesus answered him, "Why do you call me good? No one is good but God alone. You know the commandments: *You shall not kill; you shall not commit adultery; you shall not steal; you shall not bear false witness; you shall not defraud; honor your father and your mother."* He replied and said to him, "Teacher, all of these I have observed from my youth." Jesus, looking at him, loved him and said to him, "You are lacking in one thing. Go, sell what you have, and give to the poor and you will have treasure in heaven; then come, follow me." At that statement, his face fell, and he went away sad, for he had many possessions.

Jesus looked around and said to his disciples, "How hard it is for those who have wealth to enter the Kingdom of God!" The disciples were amazed at his words. So Jesus again said to them in reply, "Children, how hard it is to enter the Kingdom of God! It is easier for a camel to pass through the eye of a needle than for one who is rich to enter the Kingdom of God." They were exceedingly astonished and said among themselves, "Then who can be saved?" Jesus looked at them and said, "For men it is impossible, but not for God. All things are possible for God."

The Gospel of the Lord.

Liturgy of the Eucharist, *p. 897;* **Prayer over the Gifts,** *p. 453.*

Tuesday

Antiphons and Prayers, *p. 452;* **Liturgy of the Word** *for Year I (odd years) follows; Year II (even years), p. 461.*

TODAY'S LIVING WORD

In today's Gospel, Jesus promises the hundredfold to all who have left everything to follow him. Such total renunciation and reliance on God goes beyond the rules and rituals of religious observance. This is the sense of Sirach's words, when he says that the worship most pleasing to God consists in justice and generosity.

Jesus assures Peter that God's response to such total self-giving is made "in this present age" as well as "in the age to come." In the present, the disciples are given back everything they thought they had left—with one exception. Jesus says they will receive "a hundred times more now in this present age: houses and brothers and sisters and mothers and children and lands"—but not fathers. This is not to exclude male parents from the community of Jesus. It is rather to ensure that that community remains free of male domination. In the community of Jesus' disciples there is one Father, only one—and that is the Holy One who, as Peter writes, calls us to be holy.

Year I

FIRST READING   Sir 35:1–12

To keep the law is a great oblation.

A reading from the Book of Sirach

To keep the law is a great oblation,
    and he who observes the

commandments sacrifices a peace offering.
In works of charity one offers fine flour,
    and when he gives alms he presents his sacrifice of
        praise.
To refrain from evil pleases the LORD,
    and to avoid injustice is an atonement.
Appear not before the LORD empty-handed,
    for all that you offer is in fulfillment of the precepts.
The just one's offering enriches the altar
    and rises as a sweet odor before the Most High.
The just one's sacrifice is most pleasing,
    nor will it ever be forgotten.
In a generous spirit pay homage to the LORD,
    be not sparing of freewill gifts.
With each contribution show a cheerful countenance,
    and pay your tithes in a spirit of joy.
Give to the Most High as he has given to you,
    generously, according to your means.

For the LORD is one who always repays,
    and he will give back to you sevenfold.
But offer no bribes, these he does not accept!
    Trust not in sacrifice of the fruits of extortion.
For he is a God of justice,
    who knows no favorites.

The word of the Lord.

Responsorial Psalm   Ps 50:5–6, 7–8, 14 and 23

   R. To the upright I will show the saving power of God.

"Gather my faithful ones before me,
    those who have made a covenant with me by sacrifice."

And the heavens proclaim his justice;
  for God himself is the judge.

  R. To the upright I will show the saving power of God.

"Hear, my people, and I will speak;
  Israel, I will testify against you;
  God, your God, am I.
Not for your sacrifices do I rebuke you,
  for your burnt offerings are before me always.

  R. To the upright I will show the saving power of God.

"Offer to God praise as your sacrifice
  and fulfill your vows to the Most High.
He that offers praise as a sacrifice glorifies me;
  and to him that goes the right way I will show the salvation of God."

  R. To the upright I will show the saving power of God.

  Alleluia Verse *and* **Gospel,** *p. 462f.*

_____

Year II

FIRST READING

1 Pt 1:10–16

They prophesied about the grace that was to be yours;
therefore, live soberly and set your hopes completely
on the grace to be brought to you.

A reading from the first Letter of Saint Peter

Beloved:

Concerning the salvation of your souls the prophets who
prophesied about the grace that was to be yours searched and
investigated it investigating the time and circumstances that
the Spirit of Christ within them indicated when it testified in
advance to the sufferings destined for Christ and the glories to
follow them. It was revealed to them that they were serving
not themselves but you with regard to the things that have now

been announced to you by those who preached the Good News to you through the Holy Spirit sent from heaven, things into which angels longed to look.

Therefore, gird up the loins of your mind, live soberly, and set your hopes completely on the grace to be brought to you at the revelation of Jesus Christ. Like obedient children, do not act in compliance with the desires of your former ignorance but, as he who called you is holy, be holy yourselves in every aspect of your conduct, for it is written, *Be holy because I am holy.*

The word of the Lord.

Responsorial Psalm   Ps 98:1, 2 – 3ab, 3cd – 4

R. The Lord has made known his salvation.

Sing to the LORD a new song,
  for he has done wondrous deeds;
His right hand has won victory for him,
  his holy arm.

R. The Lord has made known his salvation.

The LORD has made his salvation known:
  in the sight of the nations he has revealed his justice.
He has remembered his kindness and his faithfulness
  toward the house of Israel.

R. The Lord has made known his salvation.

All the ends of the earth have seen
  the salvation by our God.
Sing joyfully to the LORD, all you lands;
  break into song; sing praise.

R. The Lord has made known his salvation.

Alleluia, alleluia   See Mt 11:25
Blessed are you, Father, Lord of heaven and earth;
  you have revealed to little ones the mysteries of the Kingdom.
Alleluia, alleluia

Years I and II

GOSPEL   Mk 10:28–31

You will receive a hundred times as much persecution in this present age, and eternal life in the age to come.

A reading from the holy Gospel according to Mark

Peter began to say to Jesus, "We have given up everything and followed you." Jesus said, "Amen, I say to you, there is no one who has given up house or brothers or sisters or mother or father or children or lands for my sake and for the sake of the Gospel who will not receive a hundred times more now in this present age: houses and brothers and sisters and mothers and children and lands, with persecutions, and eternal life in the age to come. But many that are first will be last, and the last will be first."

The Gospel of the Lord.

Liturgy of the Eucharist, *p. 897;* **Prayer over the Gifts,** *p. 453.*

Wednesday

Antiphons and Prayers, *p. 452;* **Liturgy of the Word** *for Year I (odd years) follows; Year II (even years), p. 465.*

TODAY'S LIVING WORD

In Mark's Gospel, each prediction of the passion is followed by a dramatic example of the disciples' failure to grasp what Jesus is telling them. Today's selection is a case in point. Following the third prediction of his passion, the sons of Zebedee ask Jesus to give them places of honor when he comes into his glory. Jesus couches his answer in biblical imagery—the cup and the bath of pain. Both symbolize suffering and death, but James and John do not understand that. Neither do the other ten, who are indignant at the two brothers for trying to gain an edge on the rest of them. One more time Jesus must explain: "It shall not be so among you."

In the failure of the disciples Mark holds up a mirror and invites us to see ourselves. Like James and John, how often do we make requests of Jesus without knowing what we are asking? "Give new signs and work new wonders," we pray, unmindful of the cup and the bath of pain. How slow are we to realize that we were ransomed, "not with perishable things like silver or gold but with the precious blood of Christ as of a spotless unblemished lamb"?

Year I

FIRST READING   Sir 36:1, 4–5a, 10–17

The nations will know that there is no God but you.

A reading from the Book of Sirach

Come to our aid, O God of the universe,
> look upon us, show us the light of your mercies,
> and put all the nations in dread of you!

Thus they will know, as we know,
> that there is no God but you, O Lord.

Give new signs and work new wonders.

Gather all the tribes of Jacob,
> that they may inherit the land as of old,
Show mercy to the people called by your name;
> Israel, whom you named your firstborn.

Take pity on your holy city,
> Jerusalem, your dwelling place.
Fill Zion with your majesty,
> your temple with your glory.

Give evidence of your deeds of old;
> fulfill the prophecies spoken in your name,
Reward those who have hoped in you,

and let your prophets be proved true.
Hear the prayer of your servants,
for you are ever gracious to your people;
and lead us in the way of justice.
Thus it will be known to the very ends of the earth
that you are the eternal God.
The word of the Lord.

Responsorial Psalm
Ps 79:8, 9, 11 and 13

R. Show us, O Lord, the light of your kindness.

Remember not against us the iniquities of the past;
may your compassion quickly come to us,
for we are brought very low.

R. Show us, O Lord, the light of your kindness.

Help us, O God our savior,
because of the glory of your name;
Deliver us and pardon our sins
for your name's sake.

R. Show us, O Lord, the light of your kindness.

Let the prisoners' sighing come before you;
with your great power free those doomed to death.
Then we, your people and the sheep of your pasture,
will give thanks to you forever;
through all generations we will declare your praise.

R. Show us, O Lord, the light of your kindness.

Alleluia Verse *and* **Gospel,** *p. 467.*

Year II

FIRST READING
1 Pt 1:18–25

*You were ransomed with the precious Blood of Christ,
as of a spotless unblemished Lamb.*

A reading from the first Letter of Saint Peter

Beloved:

Realize that you were ransomed from your futile conduct, handed on by your ancestors, not with perishable things like silver or gold but with the precious Blood of Christ as of a spotless unblemished Lamb. He was known before the foundation of the world but revealed in the final time for you, who through him believe in God who raised him from the dead and gave him glory, so that your faith and hope are in God.

Since you have purified yourselves by obedience to the truth for sincere brotherly love, love one another intensely from a pure heart. You have been born anew, not from perishable but from imperishable seed, through the living and abiding word of God, for:

> "All flesh is like grass,
>   and all its glory like the flower of the field;
> the grass withers,
>   and the flower wilts;
> but the word of the Lord remains forever."

This is the word that has been proclaimed to you.

The word of the Lord.

Responsorial Psalm

Ps 147:12–13, 14–15, 19–20

R. Praise the Lord, Jerusalem.

Glorify the LORD, O Jerusalem;
  praise your God, O Zion.
For he has strengthened the bars of your gates;
  he has blessed your children within you.

R. Praise the Lord, Jerusalem.

He has granted peace in your borders;
  with the best of wheat he fills you.
He sends forth his command to the earth;
  swiftly runs his word!

R. Praise the Lord, Jerusalem.

He has proclaimed his word to Jacob,
  his statutes and his ordinances to Israel.
He has not done thus for any other nation;
  his ordinances he has not made known to them. Alleluia.

R. Praise the Lord, Jerusalem.

Or: **R. Alleluia.**

Alleluia, alleluia Mk 10:45
The Son of Man came to serve,
  and to give his life as a ransom for many.
Alleluia, alleluia

Years I and II

GOSPEL Mk 10:32 – 45

*Behold, we are going up to Jerusalem
and the Son of Man will be handed over.*

A reading from the holy Gospel according to Mark

The disciples were on the way, going up to Jerusalem, and
Jesus went ahead of them. They were amazed, and those who
followed were afraid. Taking the Twelve aside again, he began
to tell them what was going to happen to him. "Behold, we are
going up to Jerusalem, and the Son of Man will be handed
over to the chief priests and the scribes, and they will condemn
him to death and hand him over to the Gentiles who will mock
him, spit upon him, scourge him, and put him to death, but
after three days he will rise."

Then James and John, the sons of Zebedee, came to Jesus

and said to him, "Teacher, we want you to do for us whatever we ask of you." He replied, "What do you wish me to do for you?" They answered him, "Grant that in your glory we may sit one at your right and the other at your left." Jesus said to them, "You do not know what you are asking. Can you drink the chalice that I drink or be baptized with the baptism with which I am baptized?" They said to him, "We can." Jesus said to them, "The chalice that I drink, you will drink, and with the baptism with which I am baptized, you will be baptized; but to sit at my right or at my left is not mine to give but is for those for whom it has been prepared." When the ten heard this, they became indignant at James and John. Jesus summoned them and said to them, "You know that those who are recognized as rulers over the Gentiles lord it over them, and their great ones make their authority over them felt. But it shall not be so among you. Rather, whoever wishes to be great among you will be your servant; whoever wishes to be first among you will be the slave of all. For the Son of Man did not come to be served but to serve and to give his life as a ransom for many."

The Gospel of the Lord.

Liturgy of the Eucharist, *p. 897;* **Prayer over the Gifts,** *p. 453.*

Thursday

Antiphons and Prayers, *p. 452;* **Liturgy of the Word** *for Year I (odd years) follows; Year II (even years), p. 471.*

TODAY'S LIVING WORD

"I want to see," says blind Bartimaeus in today's reading from Mark. In the Gospels to believe is to have one's eyes opened to the revelation of God in nature and in history. "How beautiful are all his works!" exclaims Sirach, awestruck at the glory of God that fills all creation. Peter's letter is crowded with colorful images as he invites the newly baptized to see themselves now as God's own people—"newborn infants...living stones...a chosen race, a royal priesthood, a holy nation."

The story of Bartimaeus is the story of a call as well as of a cure. When Jesus summons, the blind beggar throws off his cloak and comes. This gesture recalls the response of the first disciples who immediately left their nets when Jesus called. The beggar's cloak is the "tool of his trade," the net in which he catches the alms on which he lives. He abandons all this for the chance to see, and seeing, he "followed him on the way." "I want to see," we cry too. And to us Mark says, "Get up! Jesus is calling you!"

Year I

FIRST READING

Sir 42:15–25

The glory of the LORD fills all his works.

A reading from the Book of Sirach

Now will I recall God's works;
> what I have seen, I will describe.
At God's word were his works brought into being;
> they do his will as he has ordained for them.
As the rising sun is clear to all,
> so the glory of the LORD fills all his works;
Yet even God's holy ones must fail
> in recounting the wonders of the LORD,
Though God has given these, his hosts, the strength
> to stand firm before his glory.
He plumbs the depths and penetrates the heart;
> their innermost being he understands.
The Most High possesses all knowledge,

and sees from of old the things that are to come:
He makes known the past and the future,
    and reveals the deepest secrets.
No understanding does he lack;
    no single thing escapes him.
Perennial is his almighty wisdom;
    he is from all eternity one and the same,
With nothing added, nothing taken away;
    no need of a counselor for him!
How beautiful are all his works!
    even to the spark and fleeting vision!
The universe lives and abides forever;
    to meet each need, each creature is preserved.
All of them differ, one from another,
    yet none of them has he made in vain,
For each in turn, as it comes, is good;
    can one ever see enough of their splendor?

The word of the Lord.

Responsorial Psalm   Ps 33:2–3, 4–5, 6–7, 8–9

R. By the word of the Lord the heavens were made.

Give thanks to the LORD on the harp;
    with the ten-stringed lyre chant his praises.
Sing to him a new song;
    pluck the strings skillfully, with shouts of gladness.

R. By the word of the Lord the heavens were made.

For upright is the word of the LORD,
    and all his works are trustworthy.
He loves justice and right;
    of the kindness of the LORD the earth is full.

R. By the word of the Lord the heavens were made.

By the word of the Lord the heavens were made;
  by the breath of his mouth all their host.
He gathers the waters of the sea as in a flask;
  in cellars he confines the deep.

R. By the word of the Lord the heavens were made.

Let all the earth fear the Lord;
  let all who dwell in the world revere him.
For he spoke, and it was made;
  he commanded, and it stood forth.

R. By the word of the Lord the heavens were made.

Alleluia Verse *and* **Gospel,** *p. 472f.*

Year II

FIRST READING   1 Pt 2:2–5, 9–12

You are a chosen race, a royal priesthood,
so that you may announce the praises of him who called you.

A reading from the first Letter of Saint Peter

Beloved:

Like newborn infants, long for pure spiritual milk so that
through it you may grow into salvation, for you have tasted
that the Lord is good. Come to him, a living stone, rejected by
human beings but chosen and precious in the sight of God,
and, like living stones, let yourselves be built into a spiritual
house to be a holy priesthood to offer spiritual sacrifices
acceptable to God through Jesus Christ.

You are *a chosen race, a royal priesthood, a holy nation, a*
people of his own, so that you may announce the praises of
him who called you out of darkness into his wonderful light.

Once you were *no people*
  but now you are God's people;

you *had not received mercy*
but now you have received mercy.

Beloved, I urge you as aliens and sojourners to keep away from worldly desires that wage war against the soul. Maintain good conduct among the Gentiles, so that if they speak of you as evildoers, they may observe your good works and glorify God on the day of visitation.

The word of the Lord.

Responsorial Psalm

Ps 100:2, 3, 4, 5

R. Come with joy into the presence of the Lord.

Sing joyfully to the LORD, all you lands;
  serve the LORD with gladness;
  come before him with joyful song.

R. Come with joy into the presence of the Lord.

Know that the LORD is God;
  he made us, his we are;
  his people, the flock he tends.

R. Come with joy into the presence of the Lord.

Enter his gates with thanksgiving,
  his courts with praise;
Give thanks to him;
  bless his name.

R. Come with joy into the presence of the Lord.

The LORD is good:
  his kindness endures forever,
  and his faithfulness, to all generations.

R. Come with joy into the presence of the Lord.

Alleluia, alleluia   Jn 8:12
  I am the light of the world, says the Lord;
  whoever follows me will have the light of life.
Alleluia, alleluia

Years I and II

GOSPEL   Mk 10:46–52

Master, I want to see.

A reading from the holy Gospel according to Mark

As Jesus was leaving Jericho with his disciples and a sizable crowd, Bartimaeus, a blind man, the son of Timaeus, sat by the roadside begging. On hearing that it was Jesus of Nazareth, he began to cry out and say, "Jesus, son of David, have pity on me." And many rebuked him, telling him to be silent. But he kept calling out all the more, "Son of David, have pity on me." Jesus stopped and said, "Call him." So they called the blind man, saying to him, "Take courage; get up, Jesus is calling you." He threw aside his cloak, sprang up, and came to Jesus. Jesus said to him in reply, "What do you want me to do for you?" The blind man replied to him, "Master, I want to see." Jesus told him, "Go your way; your faith has saved you." Immediately he received his sight and followed him on the way.

The Gospel of the Lord.

Liturgy of the Eucharist, *p. 897;* **Prayer over the Gifts,** *p. 453.*

Friday

Antiphons and Prayers, *p. 452;* **Liturgy of the Word** *for Year I (odd years) follows; Year II (even years), p. 475.*

TODAY'S LIVING WORD

In today's Gospel, Mark has combined two symbolic actions of Jesus—cursing the fig tree and cleansing the temple—with a group of Jesus' sayings on prayer. The two symbolic acts must be understood against the background of Jesus' conviction that, in the words of Peter, "The end of all things is at hand." With the end always in view, Jesus dramatically demanded that the temple be purified and prepared to be the focal point of the new thing God would do in the last days, when all the nations would come to Jerusalem to pray, as Isaiah had promised. By sandwiching this action of Jesus within the strange story of the cursing of the fig tree, Mark underlines the critical nature of Jesus' action. Like those other "godly men," the prophets before him, Jesus too condemned the corruption that had stripped temple worship of its good fruit.

The Letter of Peter urges us to take Jesus at his word—"all that you ask for in prayer, believe that you will receive it and it shall be yours"—by remaining calm and always able to pray.

Year I

FIRST READING   Sir 44:1, 9–13

Our ancestors were merciful,
and their name will live for generations.

A reading from the Book of Sirach

Now will I praise those godly men,
   our ancestors, each in his own time.
But of others there is no memory,
   for when they ceased, they ceased.
And they are as though they had not lived,
   they and their children after them.
Yet these also were godly men
   whose virtues have not been forgotten;
Their wealth remains in their families,
   their heritage with their descendants;
Through God's covenant with them their family endures,
   their posterity, for their sake.
And for all time their progeny will endure,
   their glory will never be blotted out.
The word of the Lord.

Responsorial Psalm   Ps 149:1b–2, 3–4, 5–6a and 9b

   R. The Lord takes delight in his people.

Sing to the LORD a new song
   of praise in the assembly of the faithful.
Let Israel be glad in their maker,
   let the children of Zion rejoice in their king.

   R. The Lord takes delight in his people.

Let them praise his name in the festive dance,
   let them sing praise to him with timbrel and harp.
For the LORD loves his people,
   and he adorns the lowly with victory.

   R. The Lord takes delight in his people.

Let the faithful exult in glory;
   let them sing for joy upon their couches;
Let the high praises of God be in their throats.
   This is the glory of all his faithful. Alleluia.

   R. The Lord takes delight in his people.

   Or: **R. Alleluia.**

   Alleluia Verse *and* **Gospel,** *p. 476f.*

_____

Year II

FIRST READING   1 Pt 4:7–13

   Be good stewards of God's varied grace.

A reading from the first Letter of Saint Peter

Beloved:
The end of all things is at hand. Therefore be serious and sober-minded so that you will be able to pray. Above all, let your love for one another be intense, because love covers a multitude of sins. Be hospitable to one another without complaining. As each one has received a gift, use it to serve one another as good stewards of God's varied grace. Whoever preaches, let it

be with the words of God; whoever serves, let it be with the strength that God supplies, so that in all things God may be glorified through Jesus Christ, to whom belong glory and dominion forever and ever. Amen.

Beloved, do not be surprised that a trial by fire is occurring among you, as if something strange were happening to you. But rejoice to the extent that you share in the sufferings of Christ, so that when his glory is revealed you may also rejoice exultantly.

The word of the Lord.

Responsorial Psalm

Ps 96:10, 11–12, 13

R. The Lord comes to judge the earth.

Say among the nations: The LORD is king.
He has made the world firm, not to be moved;
  he governs the peoples with equity.

R. The Lord comes to judge the earth.

Let the heavens be glad and the earth rejoice;
  let the sea and what fills it resound;
  let the plains be joyful and all that is in them!
Then shall all the trees of the forest exult.

R. The Lord comes to judge the earth.

Before the LORD, for he comes;
  for he comes to rule the earth.
He shall rule the world with justice
  and the peoples with his constancy.

R. The Lord comes to judge the earth.

Alleluia, alleluia   See Jn 15:16
  I chose you from the world,
    to go and bear fruit that will last, says the Lord.
  Alleluia, alleluia

Years I and II

GOSPEL   Mk 11:11–26

My house will be called a house of prayer for all peoples.
Have faith in God.

A reading from the holy Gospel according to Mark

Jesus entered Jerusalem and went into the temple area. He looked around at everything and, since it was already late, went out to Bethany with the Twelve.

The next day as they were leaving Bethany he was hungry. Seeing from a distance a fig tree in leaf, he went over to see if he could find anything on it. When he reached it he found nothing but leaves; it was not the time for figs. And he said to it in reply, "May no one ever eat of your fruit again!" And his disciples heard it.

They came to Jerusalem, and on entering the temple area he began to drive out those selling and buying there. He overturned the tables of the money changers and the seats of those who were selling doves. He did not permit anyone to carry anything through the temple area. Then he taught them saying, "Is it not written:

My house shall be called a house of prayer for all peoples?
But you have made it a den of thieves."

The chief priests and the scribes came to hear of it and were seeking a way to put him to death, yet they feared him because the whole crowd was astonished at his teaching. When evening came, they went out of the city.

Early in the morning, as they were walking along, they saw the fig tree withered to its roots. Peter remembered and said to him, "Rabbi, look! The fig tree that you cursed has withered."

Jesus said to them in reply, "Have faith in God. Amen, I say to you, whoever says to this mountain, 'Be lifted up and thrown into the sea,' and does not doubt in his heart but believes that what he says will happen, it shall be done for him. Therefore I tell you, all that you ask for in prayer, believe that you will receive it and it shall be yours. When you stand to pray, forgive anyone against whom you have a grievance, so that your heavenly Father may in turn forgive you your transgressions." The Gospel of the Lord.

Liturgy of the Eucharist, *p. 897;* **Prayer over the Gifts,** *p. 453.*

Saturday

Antiphons and Prayers, *p. 452;* **Liturgy of the Word** *for Year I (odd years) follows; Year II (even years), p. 480.*

TODAY'S LIVING WORD

The Old Testament Book of Sirach concludes with a canticle on wisdom. Clearly the wisdom Sirach celebrates is not esoteric knowledge but ethical instruction. He says that from his youth it has kept his feet on the level path. Such wisdom is practical; it issues in praise of God, its author. In today's Gospel, Jesus also demonstrates practical wisdom. His enemies want to trap him into making a public claim that he acts with God's authority. This would set him up for the charge of blasphemy. So Jesus evades their question with a question of his own.

The Letter of Jude contains practical wisdom as well. Jude offers a program for Christian life, counseling prayer "in the Holy Spirit" and perseverance "in the love of God." He also gives sound advice on how to deal with those who have gone astray. "On those who waver, have mercy," he says, but be realistic in rescuing the others. He urges his readers to recognize their limitations and not to associate with those who have succumbed to false teaching, confiding them instead to the mercy of the one, the only God who saves.

Year I

FIRST READING   Sir 51:12cd–20

Give me wisdom and I will give you glory.

A reading from the Book of Sirach

I thank the LORD and I praise him;
   I bless the name of the LORD.
When I was young and innocent,
   I sought wisdom openly in my prayer
I prayed for her before the temple,
   and I will seek her until the end,
   and she flourished as a grape soon ripe.
My heart delighted in her,
My feet kept to the level path
   because from earliest youth I was familiar with her.
In the short time I paid heed,
   I met with great instruction.
Since in this way I have profited,
   I will give my teacher grateful praise.
I became resolutely devoted to her—
   the good I persistently strove for.
My soul was tormented in seeking her,
My hand opened her gate
   and I came to know her secrets.
I directed my soul to her,
   and in cleanness I attained to her.

The word of the Lord.

Responsorial Psalm   Ps 19:8, 9, 10, 11

   R. The precepts of the Lord give joy to the heart.

The law of the LORD is perfect,
　refreshing the soul.
The decree of the LORD is trustworthy,
　giving wisdom to the simple.

R. The precepts of the Lord give joy to the heart.

The precepts of the LORD are right,
　rejoicing the heart.
The command of the LORD is clear,
　enlightening the eye.

R. The precepts of the Lord give joy to the heart.

The fear of the LORD is pure,
　enduring forever;
The ordinances of the LORD are true,
　all of them just.

R. The precepts of the Lord give joy to the heart.

They are more precious than gold,
　than a heap of purest gold;
Sweeter also than syrup
　or honey from the comb.

R. The precepts of the Lord give joy to the heart.

Alleluia Verse *and* **Gospel**, *p. 481f.*

Year II

FIRST READING

Jud 17, 20b–25

*To the one who is able to keep you from stumbling and to present
you unblemished and exultant in the presence of his glory.*

A reading from the Letter of Saint Jude

Beloved, remember the words spoken beforehand by the
Apostles of our Lord Jesus Christ. Build yourselves up in your
most holy faith; pray in the Holy Spirit. Keep yourselves in

the love of God and wait for the mercy of our Lord Jesus Christ that leads to eternal life. On those who waver, have mercy; save others by snatching them out of the fire; on others have mercy with fear, abhorring even the outer garment stained by the flesh.

To the one who is able to keep you from stumbling and to present you unblemished and exultant, in the presence of his glory, to the only God, our savior, through Jesus Christ our Lord be glory, majesty, power, and authority from ages past, now, and for ages to come. Amen.

The word of the Lord.

Responsorial Psalm   Ps 63:2, 3–4, 5–6

R. My soul is thirsting for you, O Lord my God.

O God, you are my God whom I seek;
  for you my flesh pines and my soul thirsts
    like the earth, parched, lifeless and without water.

R. My soul is thirsting for you, O Lord my God.

Thus have I gazed toward you in the sanctuary
  to see your power and your glory,
For your kindness is a greater good than life;
  my lips shall glorify you.

R. My soul is thirsting for you, O Lord my God.

Thus will I bless you while I live;
  lifting up my hands, I will call upon your name.
As with the riches of a banquet shall my soul be satisfied,
  and with exultant lips my mouth shall praise you.

R. My soul is thirsting for you, O Lord my God.

Alleluia, alleluia   See Col 3:16a, 17c
Let the word of Christ dwell in you richly;
  giving thanks to God the Father through him.
Alleluia, alleluia

Years I and II

GOSPEL   Mk 11:27–33

By what authority are you doing these things?

A reading from the holy Gospel according to Mark

Jesus and his disciples returned once more to Jerusalem. As he was walking in the temple area, the chief priests, the scribes, and the elders approached him and said to him, "By what authority are you doing these things? Or who gave you this authority to do them?" Jesus said to them, "I shall ask you one question. Answer me, and I will tell you by what authority I do these things. Was John's baptism of heavenly or of human origin? Answer me." They discussed this among themselves and said, "If we say, 'Of heavenly origin,' he will say, 'Then why did you not believe him?' But shall we say, 'Of human origin'?"—they feared the crowd, for they all thought John really was a prophet. So they said to Jesus in reply, "We do not know." Then Jesus said to them, "Neither shall I tell you by what authority I do these things."

The Gospel of the Lord.

Liturgy of the Eucharist, *p. 897;* **Prayer over the Gifts,** *p. 453.*

NINTH WEEK IN ORDINARY TIME

The **Antiphons and Prayers** *may be the following, or may be chosen from any of the other 33 weeks in Ordinary Time (refer to Liturgical Calendar, pp. 26–41).*

The **Liturgy of the Word** *varies: for Monday, see p. 484; Tuesday, p. 489; Wednesday, p. 494; Thursday, p. 500; Friday, p. 506; Saturday, p. 511.*

Entrance Antiphon

O look at me and be merciful, for I am wretched and alone. See my hardship and my poverty, and pardon all my sins.

(Ps 25:16, 18)

Opening Prayer

Let us pray
[for God's care and protection]

Pause for silent prayer.

Father,
your love never fails.
Hear our call.
Keep us from danger
and provide for all our needs.

Grant this through our Lord Jesus Christ, your Son,
who lives and reigns with you and the Holy Spirit,
one God, for ever and ever.

Alternative Opening Prayer

Let us pray
[for the confidence born of faith]

Pause for silent prayer.

God our Father,
teach us to cherish the gifts that surround us.
Increase our faith in you
and bring our trust to its promised fulfillment
in the joy of your kingdom.

Grant this through Christ our Lord.

Prayer over the Gifts

Pray, brethren...

Lord,
as we gather to offer our gifts
confident in your love,
make us holy by sharing your life with us
and by this eucharist forgive our sins.

We ask this through Christ our Lord.

Preface of Weekdays in Ordinary Time I–VI, *pp. 948–950.*

Communion Antiphon

I call upon you, God, for you will answer me; bend your ear and hear my prayer.
(Ps 17:6)

Or:

I tell you solemnly, whatever you ask for in prayer, believe that you have received it, and it will be yours, says the Lord.
(Mk 11:23–24)

Prayer after Communion

Let us pray.
Pause for silent prayer, if this has not preceded.

Lord,
as you give us the body and blood of your Son,
guide us with your Spirit
that we may honor you
not only with our lips,
but also with the lives we lead,
and so enter your kingdom.
We ask this in the name of Jesus the Lord.

Monday

Antiphons and Prayers, *p. 482;* **Liturgy of the Word** *for Year I (odd years) follows; Year II (even years), p. 487.*

Today's Living Word

The parables of Jesus that the Gospel writers recount naturally reflect their respective concerns. Here Mark has expanded Jesus' parable of the vineyard and appended to it two verses from Psalm 118 in order to drive his point home: the rejection of Jesus by some of the leaders of Israel was a tragic mistake. To discover the original meaning of the parable as Jesus told it is more difficult. Pheme Perkins suggests that we consider the owner of the vineyard and the manner in which he deals with the tenants.* In a way he is like Tobit, a good man who does not conform to the logic of the world, but who conducts himself by another law. So he appeals repeatedly to the tenants and even sends his son, while his neighbors and perhaps even we wonder, "Will this man never learn!"

Jesus seems to say: such is the power of God. Peter adds that this is the divine power that has "bestowed on us everything that makes for life and devotion." This is the divine nature we are called to share.

* *Hearing the Parables of Jesus* (New York: Paulist Press, 1981), pp. 191–92.

Year I

FIRST READING
Tb 1:3; 2:1a–8

Tobit walked on the paths of truth and righteousness.

A reading from the Book of Tobit

I, Tobit, have walked all the days of my life on the paths of truth and righteousness. I performed many charitable works for my kinsmen and my people who had been deported with me to Nineveh, in Assyria.

On our festival of Pentecost, the feast of Weeks, a fine dinner was prepared for me, and I reclined to eat. The table was set for me, and when many different dishes were placed before me, I said to my son Tobiah: "My son, go out and try to find a poor man from among our kinsmen exiled here in Nineveh. If he is a sincere worshiper of God, bring him back with you, so that he can share this meal with me. Indeed, son, I shall wait for you to come back."

Tobiah went out to look for some poor kinsman of ours. When he returned he exclaimed, "Father!" I said to him, "What is it, son?" He answered, "Father, one of our people has been murdered! His body lies in the market place where he was just strangled!" I sprang to my feet, leaving the dinner untouched; and I carried the dead man from the street and put him in one of the rooms, so that I might bury him after sunset. Returning to my own quarters, I washed myself and ate my food in sorrow. I was reminded of the oracle pronounced by the prophet Amos against Bethel:

> "All your festivals shall be turned into mourning,
>   and all your songs into lamentation."

And I wept. Then at sunset I went out, dug a grave, and buried him.

The neighbors mocked me, saying to one another: "He is still not afraid! Once before he was hunted down for execution because of this very thing; yet now that he has scarcely escaped, here he is again burying the dead!"

The word of the Lord.

Responsorial Psalm
Ps 112:1b–2, 3b–4, 5–6

R. Blessed the man who fears the Lord.

Blessed the man who fears the LORD,
    who greatly delights in his commands.
His posterity shall be mighty upon the earth;
    the upright generation shall be blessed.

R. Blessed the man who fears the Lord.

His generosity shall endure forever.
Light shines through the darkness for the upright;
    he is gracious and merciful and just.

R. Blessed the man who fears the Lord.

Well for the man who is gracious and lends,
    who conducts his affairs with justice;
He shall never be moved;
    the just man shall be in everlasting remembrance.

R. Blessed the man who fears the Lord.

Or: **R. Alleluia.**

Alleluia Verse *and* **Gospel,** *p. 488.*

Year II

FIRST READING

2 Pt 1:2–7

God has bestowed on us the precious and very great promises,
so that through them you may come to share in the divine nature.

A reading from the second Letter of Saint Peter

Beloved:

May grace and peace be yours in abundance through knowledge of God and of Jesus our Lord.

His divine power has bestowed on us everything that makes for life and devotion, through the knowledge of him who called us by his own glory and power. Through these, he has bestowed on us the precious and very great promises, so that through them you may come to share in the divine nature, after escaping from the corruption that is in the world because of evil desire. For this very reason, make every effort to supplement your faith with virtue, virtue with knowledge, knowledge with self-control, self-control with endurance, endurance with devotion, devotion with mutual affection, mutual affection with love.
The word of the Lord.

Responsorial Psalm

Ps 91:1–2, 14–15b, 15c–16

R. In you, my God, I place my trust.

You who dwell in the shelter of the Most High,
  who abide in the shadow of the Almighty,
Say to the LORD, "My refuge and my fortress,
  my God, in whom I trust."

R. In you, my God, I place my trust.

Because he clings to me, I will deliver him;
  I will set him on high because he acknowledges my name.
He shall call upon me, and I will answer him;
  I will be with him in distress.

  R. In you, my God, I place my trust.

I will deliver him and glorify him;
  with length of days I will gratify him
  and will show him my salvation.

  R. In you, my God, I place my trust.

  Alleluia, alleluia   See Rv 1:5ab
  Jesus Christ, you are the faithful witness,
  the firstborn of the dead;
  you have loved us and freed us from our sins by your Blood.
  Alleluia, alleluia

Years I and II

GOSPEL   Mk 12:1–12
They seized the beloved son, killed him,
and threw him out of the vineyard.

A reading from the holy Gospel according to Mark

Jesus began to speak to the chief priests, the scribes, and the
elders in parables. "A man planted a vineyard, put a hedge
around it, dug a wine press, and built a tower. Then he leased
it to tenant farmers and left on a journey. At the proper time he
sent a servant to the tenants to obtain from them some of the
produce of the vineyard. But they seized him, beat him, and
sent him away empty-handed. Again he sent them another
servant. And that one they beat over the head and treated
shamefully. He sent yet another whom they killed. So, too,
many others; some they beat, others they killed. He had one

other to send, a beloved son. He sent him to them last of all, thinking, 'They will respect my son.' But those tenants said to one another, 'This is the heir. Come, let us kill him, and the inheritance will be ours.' So they seized him and killed him, and threw him out of the vineyard. What then will the owner of the vineyard do? He will come, put the tenants to death, and give the vineyard to others. Have you not read this Scripture passage:

> *The stone that the builders rejected*
> *   has become the cornerstone;*
> *by the Lord has this been done,*
> *   and it is wonderful in our eyes?"*

They were seeking to arrest him, but they feared the crowd, for they realized that he had addressed the parable to them. So they left him and went away.

The Gospel of the Lord.

Liturgy of the Eucharist, *p. 897;* **Prayer over the Gifts,** *p. 483.*

Tuesday

Antiphons and Prayers, *p. 482;* **Liturgy of the Word** *for Year I (odd years) follows; Year II (even years), p. 492.*

TODAY'S LIVING WORD

The tax this Gospel story mentions was a poll tax the Romans levied on all the people of Judea. It caused controversy among the Jews because of its political and religious implications. Paying the tax would seem to support the political claim of Rome. Because it had to be paid in Roman currency the tax also carried the implication of idolatry, for the coin was inscribed with the words "Tiberius Caesar, august son of the divine Augustus." Jesus' answer spoke to both levels of the debate. His "Repay to Caesar what belongs to Caesar" allowed for limited cooperation with Rome, which was the position of the Pharisees as well. His reference to "what belongs to God" (in Greek, "the things of God") made a subtle but significant religious distinction. Since all things belong to God, all things are owed God.

This story is often used to define Christian duty to God and nation—as if the two were on a par. This is not the meaning of Jesus' answer. Since as Peter says we "await new heavens and a new earth," we must, with the conscientiousness of Tobit, continually assess where our allegiance to the state must yield to the absolute claim of God.

Year I

FIRST READING

Tb 2:9–14

I was deprived of eyesight.

A reading from the Book of Tobit

On the night of Pentecost, after I had buried the dead, I, Tobit, went into my courtyard to sleep next to the courtyard wall. My face was uncovered because of the heat. I did not know there were birds perched on the wall above me, till their warm droppings settled in my eyes, causing cataracts. I went to see some doctors for a cure but the more they anointed my eyes with various salves, the worse the cataracts became, until I could see no more. For four years I was deprived of eyesight, and all my kinsmen were grieved at my condition. Ahiqar, however, took care of me for two years, until he left for Elymais.

At that time, my wife Anna worked for hire at weaving cloth, the kind of work women do. When she sent back the goods to their owners, they would pay her. Late in winter on the seventh of Dystrus, she finished the cloth and sent it back to the owners. They paid her the full salary and also gave her a young goat for the table. On entering my house the goat began to bleat.

I called to my wife and said: "Where did this goat come from? Perhaps it was stolen! Give it back to its owners; we have no right to eat stolen food!" She said to me, "It was given to me as a bonus over and above my wages." Yet I would not believe her, and told her to give it back to its owners. I became very angry with her over this. So she retorted: "Where are your charitable deeds now? Where are your virtuous acts? See! Your true character is finally showing itself!"

The word of the Lord.

Responsorial Psalm
Ps 112:1–2, 7–8, 9

R. The heart of the just one is firm, trusting in the Lord.

Blessed the man who fears the LORD,
  who greatly delights in his commands.
His posterity shall be mighty upon the earth;
  the upright generation shall be blessed.

R. The heart of the just one is firm, trusting in the Lord.

An evil report he shall not fear;
  his heart is firm, trusting in the LORD.
His heart is steadfast; he shall not fear
  till he looks down upon his foes.

R. The heart of the just one is firm, trusting in the Lord.

Lavishly he gives to the poor;
  his generosity shall endure forever;
  his horn shall be exalted in glory.

R. The heart of the just one is firm, trusting in the Lord.

Or: **R. Alleluia.**

Alleluia Verse *and* **Gospel,** *p. 493.*

Year II

FIRST READING

2 Pt 3:12–15a, 17–18

We await new heavens and a new earth.

A reading from the second Letter of Saint Peter

Beloved:

Wait for and hasten the coming of the day of God, because of which the heavens will be dissolved in flames and the elements melted by fire. But according to his promise we await new heavens and a new earth in which righteousness dwells.

Therefore, beloved, since you await these things, be eager to be found without spot or blemish before him, at peace. And consider the patience of our Lord as salvation.

Therefore, beloved, since you are forewarned, be on your guard not to be led into the error of the unprincipled and to fall from your own stability. But grow in grace and in the knowledge of our Lord and savior Jesus Christ. To him be glory now and to the day of eternity. Amen.

The word of the Lord.

Responsorial Psalm

Ps 90:2, 3–4, 10, 14 and 16

R. **In every age, O Lord, you have been our refuge.**

Before the mountains were begotten
    and the earth and the world were brought forth,
    from everlasting to everlasting you are God.

R. **In every age, O Lord, you have been our refuge.**

You turn man back to dust,
    saying, "Return, O children of men."
For a thousand years in your sight

are as yesterday, now that it is past,
  or as a watch of the night.

R. In every age, O Lord, you have been our refuge.

Seventy is the sum of our years,
  or eighty, if we are strong,
And most of them are fruitless toil,
  for they pass quickly and we drift away.

R. In every age, O Lord, you have been our refuge.

Fill us at daybreak with your kindness,
  that we may shout for joy and gladness all our days.
Let your work be seen by your servants
  and your glory by their children.

R. In every age, O Lord, you have been our refuge.

> **Alleluia, alleluia**   See Eph 1:17–18
> May the Father of our Lord Jesus Christ
> enlighten the eyes of our hearts,
> that we may know what is the hope
> that belongs to his call.
> **Alleluia, alleluia**

Years I and II

GOSPEL   Mk 12:13–17

*Repay to Caesar what belongs to Caesar and
to God what belongs to God.*

A reading from the holy Gospel according to Mark

Some Pharisees and Herodians were sent to Jesus to ensnare
him in his speech. They came and said to him, "Teacher, we
know that you are a truthful man and that you are not concerned
with anyone's opinion. You do not regard a person's status
but teach the way of God in accordance with the truth. Is it

lawful to pay the census tax to Caesar or not? Should we pay or should we not pay?" Knowing their hypocrisy he said to them, "Why are you testing me? Bring me a denarius to look at." They brought one to him and he said to them, "Whose image and inscription is this?" They replied to him, "Caesar's." So Jesus said to them, "Repay to Caesar what belongs to Caesar and to God what belongs to God." They were utterly amazed at him.

The Gospel of the Lord.

Liturgy of the Eucharist, *p. 897;* **Prayer over the Gifts,** *p. 483.*

Wednesday

Antiphons and Prayers, *p. 482;* **Liturgy of the Word** *for Year I (odd years) follows; Year II (even years), p. 498.*

TODAY'S LIVING WORD

Today's selection from Tobit presents us with parallel lives. Tobit and Sarah both suffer and in their suffering are verbally abused by those closest to them—Tobit by his wife, Sarah by her maid—and both contemplate death as release from suffering. But God heard their prayer. And that God is "not God of the dead but of the living," as Jesus will demonstrate in the Gospel. The Sadducees accepted as authoritative only the first five books of the Bible; therefore, they rejected the Pharisees' and Jesus' teaching on resurrection. The hypothetical case they put to Jesus was an attempt to reduce that teaching to absurdity. In answer, Jesus showed that they did not understand either the true nature of resurrected life or their own Scriptures.

Our hope in resurrection rests on the power of the living God revealed in Christ Jesus. As 2 Timothy declares, "Christ Jesus... destroyed death and brought life and immortality to light through the Gospel." A highly scientific age may not easily accept this good news, but we must proclaim it boldly, knowing in whom we have trusted.

Year I

FIRST READING   Tb 3:1–11a, 16 –17a

The prayer of these two petitioners was heard in the
glorious presence of Almighty God.

A reading from the Book of Tobit

Grief-stricken in spirit, I, Tobit, groaned and wept aloud.
Then with sobs I began to pray:

"You are righteous, O Lord,
    and all your deeds are just;
All your ways are mercy and truth;
    you are the judge of the world.
And now, O Lord, may you be mindful of me,
    and look with favor upon me.
Punish me not for my sins,
    nor for my inadvertent offenses,
    nor for those of my ancestors.

"We sinned against you,
    and disobeyed your commandments.
So you handed us over to plundering, exile, and death,
    till you made us the talk and reproach of all the nations
    among whom you had dispersed us.

"Yes, your judgments are many and true
    in dealing with me as my sins
    and those of my ancestors deserve.
For we have not kept your commandments,
    nor have we trodden the paths of truth before you.
"So now, deal with me as you please,
    and command my life breath to be taken from me,

that I may go from the face of the earth into dust.
It is better for me to die than to live,
  because I have heard insulting calumnies,
  and I am overwhelmed with grief.

"Lord, command me to be delivered from such anguish;
  let me go to the everlasting abode;
  Lord, refuse me not.
For it is better for me to die
  than to endure so much misery in life,
  and to hear these insults!"

On the same day, at Ecbatana in Media, it so happened that Raguel's daughter Sarah also had to listen to abuse, from one of her father's maids. For she had been married to seven husbands, but the wicked demon Asmodeus killed them off before they could have intercourse with her, as it is prescribed for wives. So the maid said to her: "You are the one who strangles your husbands! Look at you! You have already been married seven times, but you have had no joy with any one of your husbands. Why do you beat us? Is it on account of your seven husbands, Because they are dead? May we never see a son or daughter of yours!"

The girl was deeply saddened that day, and she went into an upper chamber of her house, where she planned to hang herself.

But she reconsidered, saying to herself: "No! People would level this insult against my father: 'You had only one beloved daughter, but she hanged herself because of ill fortune!' And thus would I cause my father in his old age to go down to the nether world laden with sorrow. It is far better for me not to hang myself, but to beg the Lord to have me die, so that I need no longer live to hear such insults."

At that time, then, she spread out her hands, and facing the window, poured out her prayer:

"Blessed are you, O Lord, merciful God,
and blessed is your holy and honorable name.
Blessed are you in all your works for ever!"

At that very time, the prayer of these two suppliants was heard in the glorious presence of Almighty God. So Raphael was sent to heal them both: to remove the cataracts from Tobit's eyes, so that he might again see God's sunlight; and to marry Raguel's daughter Sarah to Tobit's son Tobiah, and then drive the wicked demon Asmodeus from her.

The word of the Lord.

Responsorial Psalm
Ps 25:2–3, 4–5ab, 6 and 7bc, 8–9

R. To you, O Lord, I lift my soul.

In you I trust; let me not be put to shame,
  let not my enemies exult over me.
No one who waits for you shall be put to shame;
  those shall be put to shame who heedlessly break faith.

R. To you, O Lord, I lift my soul.

Your ways, O LORD, make known to me;
  teach me your paths,
Guide me in your truth and teach me,
  for you are God my savior.

R. To you, O Lord, I lift my soul.

Remember that your compassion, O LORD,
  and your kindness are from of old.
In your kindness remember me,
  because of your goodness, O LORD.

R. To you, O Lord, I lift my soul.

Good and upright is the LORD;
  thus he shows sinners the way.

He guides the humble to justice,
   he teaches the humble his way.

R. To you, O Lord, I lift my soul.

Alleluia Verse *and* **Gospel,** *p. 499.*

Year II

FIRST READING   2 Tm 1:1–3, 6–12

*Stir into flame the gift of God that you have
through the laying on of my hands.*

A reading from the beginning of the second Letter of Saint Paul
to Timothy

Paul, an Apostle of Christ Jesus by the will of God for the promise
of life in Christ Jesus, to Timothy, my dear child: grace, mercy,
and peace from God the Father and Christ Jesus our Lord.

   I am grateful to God, whom I worship with a clear conscience as my ancestors did, as I remember you constantly in
my prayers, night and day.

   For this reason, I remind you to stir into flame the gift of
God that you have through the imposition of my hands. For
God did not give us a spirit of cowardice but rather of power
and love and self-control. So do not be ashamed of your
testimony to our Lord, nor of me, a prisoner for his sake; but
bear your share of hardship for the Gospel with the strength
that comes from God.

   He saved us and called us to a holy life, not according to
our works but according to his own design and the grace
bestowed on us in Christ Jesus before time began, but now
made manifest through the appearance of our savior Christ
Jesus, who destroyed death and brought life and immortality

to light through the Gospel, for which I was appointed preacher and Apostle and teacher. On this account I am suffering these things; but I am not ashamed, for I know him in whom I have believed and am confident that he is able to guard what has been entrusted to me until that day.

The word of the Lord.

Responsorial Psalm
Ps 123:1b–2ab, 2cdef

R. To you, O Lord, I lift up my eyes.

To you I lift up my eyes
  who are enthroned in heaven.
Behold, as the eyes of servants
  are on the hands of their masters.

R. To you, O Lord, I lift up my eyes.

As the eyes of a maid
  are on the hands of her mistress,
So are our eyes on the LORD, our God,
  till he have pity on us.

R. To you, O Lord, I lift up my eyes.

> **Alleluia, alleluia**   Jn 11:25a, 26
> I am the resurrection and the life, says the Lord;
> whoever believes in me will never die.
> **Alleluia, alleluia**

Years I and II

GOSPEL
Mk 12:18–27

He is not God of the dead but of the living.

A reading from the holy Gospel according to Mark

Some Sadducees, who say there is no resurrection, came to Jesus and put this question to him, saying, "Teacher, Moses wrote for us, *If someone's brother dies, leaving a wife but no child, his brother must take the wife and raise up descendants for his brother.* Now there were seven brothers. The first married a woman and died, leaving no descendants. So the second brother married her and died, leaving no descendants, and the third likewise. And the seven left no descendants. Last of all the woman also died. At the resurrection when they arise whose wife will she be? For all seven had been married to her." Jesus said to them, "Are you not misled because you do not know the Scriptures or the power of God? When they rise from the dead, they neither marry nor are given in marriage, but they are like the angels in heaven. As for the dead being raised, have you not read in the Book of Moses, in the passage about the bush, how God told him, *I am the God of Abraham, the God of Isaac, and the God of Jacob?* He is not God of the dead but of the living. You are greatly misled."

The Gospel of the Lord.

Liturgy of the Eucharist, *p. 897;* **Prayer over the Gifts,** *p. 483.*

Thursday

Antiphons and Prayers, *p. 482;* **Liturgy of the Word** *for Year I (odd years) follows; Year II (even years), p. 504.*

TODAY'S LIVING WORD

Since the written Torah has 613 commandments, Jewish teachers were routinely asked, "Which is the first?" Jesus' answer combines two commandments: the first concerns loving God (from Deuteronomy 6), and the second concerns loving others (from Leviticus 19). This exchange with a scribe provides a pleasant interlude in a phase of Jesus' ministry that is riddled with controversy. Since his arrival in Jerusalem, Jesus has been challenged by the chief priests and leading men of the city, by a coalition of Pharisees and Herodians, and by some Sadducees. In contrast, this conversation is open and honest. The scribe's study of Torah has made him ready to receive the reign of God.

The same may be said of Tobiah and Paul. Like his father, Tobiah has taken to heart the words of Torah. His prayer makes that clear. So accompanied by an angel, he too is not far from God's reign. Finally Paul, the zealous Jew formed in the way of Torah and never far from God's reign, preaches even in chains. He is completely convinced of the faithfulness of God, who remains ever faithful, "for he cannot deny himself."

Year I

FIRST READING
Tb 6:10–11; 7:1bcde, 9–17; 8:4–9a

Call down your mercy on me and her
and allow us to live together to a happy old age.

A reading from the Book of Tobit

When the angel Raphael and Tobiah had entered Media and were getting close to Ecbatana, Raphael said to the boy, "Tobiah, my brother!" He replied: "Here I am!" He said: "Tonight we must stay with Raguel, who is a relative of yours. He has a daughter named Sarah."

So he brought him to the house of Raguel, whom they found seated by his courtyard gate. They greeted him first. He said to them, "Greetings to you too, brothers! Good health to you, and welcome!" And he brought them into his home.

Raguel slaughtered a ram from the flock and gave them a cordial reception. When they had bathed and reclined to eat, Tobiah said to Raphael, "Brother Azariah, ask Raguel to let me marry my kinswoman Sarah." Raguel overheard the words; so he said to the boy: "Eat and drink and be merry tonight, for no man is more entitled to marry my daughter Sarah than you, brother. Besides, not even I have the right to give her to anyone but you, because you are my closest relative. But I will explain the situation to you very frankly. I have given her in marriage to seven men, all of whom were kinsmen of ours, and all died on the very night they approached her. But now, son, eat and drink. I am sure the Lord will look after you both." Tobiah answered, "I will eat or drink nothing until you set aside what belongs to me."

Raguel said to him: "I will do it. She is yours according to the decree of the Book of Moses. Your marriage to her has been decided in heaven! Take your kinswoman; from now on you are her love, and she is your beloved. She is yours today and ever after. And tonight, son, may the Lord of heaven prosper you both. May he grant you mercy and peace." Then Raguel called his daughter Sarah, and she came to him. He took her by the hand and gave her to Tobiah with the words: "Take her according to the law. According to the decree written in the Book of Moses she is your wife. Take her and bring her back safely to your father. And may the God of heaven grant both of you peace and prosperity." Raguel then called Sarah's mother and told her to bring a scroll, so that he might draw up a marriage contract stating that he gave Sarah to Tobiah as his wife according to the decree of the Mosaic law. Her mother brought the scroll, and Raguel drew up the contract, to which they affixed their seals.

Afterward they began to eat and drink. Later Raguel called his wife Edna and said, "My love, prepare the other bedroom and bring the girl there." She went and made the bed in the room, as she was told, and brought the girl there. After she had cried over her, she wiped away the tears and said: "Be brave, my daughter. May the Lord grant you joy in place of your grief. Courage, my daughter." Then she left.

When the girl's parents left the bedroom and closed the door behind them, Tobiah arose from bed and said to his wife, "My love, get up. Let us pray and beg our Lord to have mercy on us and to grant us deliverance." She got up, and they started to pray and beg that deliverance might be theirs. And they began to say:

"Blessed are you, O God of our fathers,
   praised be your name forever and ever.
Let the heavens and all your creation
   praise you forever.
You made Adam and you gave him his wife Eve
   to be his help and support;
   and from these two the human race descended.
You said, 'It is not good for the man to be alone;
   let us make him a partner like himself.'
Now, Lord, you know that I take this wife of mine
   not because of lust,
   but for a noble purpose.
Call down your mercy on me and on her,
   and allow us to live together to a happy old age."

They said together, "Amen, amen," and went to bed for the night.

The word of the Lord.

Responsorial Psalm

Ps 128:1–2, 3, 4 – 5

R. Blessed are those who fear the Lord.

Blessed are you who fear the LORD,
   who walk in his ways!
For you shall eat the fruit of your handiwork;
   Blessed shall you be, and favored.

R. Blessed are those who fear the Lord.

Your wife shall be like a fruitful vine
 in the recesses of your home;
Your children like olive plants
 around your table.

R. Blessed are those who fear the Lord.

Behold, thus is the man blessed
 who fears the LORD.
The LORD bless you from Zion:
 may you see the prosperity of Jerusalem
 all the days of your life.

R. Blessed are those who fear the Lord.

Alleluia Verse *and* **Gospel,** *p. 505f.*

Year II

FIRST READING

2 Tm 2:8–15

The word of God is not chained.
If we have died with Christ, we shall also live with him.

A reading from the second Letter of Saint Paul to Timothy

Beloved:

Remember Jesus Christ, raised from the dead, a descendant of David: such is my Gospel, for which I am suffering, even to the point of chains, like a criminal. But the word of God is not chained. Therefore, I bear with everything for the sake of those who are chosen, so that they too may obtain the salvation that is in Christ Jesus, together with eternal glory. This saying is trustworthy:

   If we have died with him
      we shall also live with him;
   if we persevere
      we shall also reign with him.

But if we deny him
    he will deny us.
If we are unfaithful
    he remains faithful,
        for he cannot deny himself.

Remind people of these things and charge them before God to stop disputing about words. This serves no useful purpose since it harms those who listen. Be eager to present yourself as acceptable to God, a workman who causes no disgrace, imparting the word of truth without deviation.

The word of the Lord.

Responsorial Psalm

Ps 25:4–5ab, 8–9, 10 and 14

R. Teach me your ways, O Lord.

Your ways, O Lord, make known to me;
    teach me your paths,
Guide me in your truth and teach me,
    for you are God my savior.

R. Teach me your ways, O Lord.

Good and upright is the Lord;
    thus he shows sinners the way.
He guides the humble to justice,
    he teaches the humble his way.

R. Teach me your ways, O Lord.

All the paths of the Lord are kindness and constancy
    toward those who keep his covenant and his decrees.
The friendship of the Lord is with those who fear him,
    and his covenant, for their instruction.

R. Teach me your ways, O Lord.

Alleluia, alleluia See 2 Tm 1:10
Our Savior Jesus Christ has destroyed death
and brought life to light through the Gospel.
Alleluia, alleluia

Years I and II

GOSPEL   Mk 12:28–34

There is no commandment greater than these.

A reading from the holy Gospel according to Mark

One of the scribes came to Jesus and asked him, "Which is the first of all the commandments?" Jesus replied, "The first is this: *Hear, O Israel! The Lord our God is Lord alone! You shall love the Lord your God with all your heart, with all your soul, with all your mind, and with all your strength.* The second is this: *You shall love your neighbor as yourself.* There is no other commandment greater than these." The scribe said to him, "Well said, teacher. You are right in saying, *He is One and there is no other than he.* And *to love him with all your heart, with all your understanding, with all your strength, and to love your neighbor as yourself* is worth more than all burnt offerings and sacrifices." And when Jesus saw that he answered with understanding, he said to him, "You are not far from the Kingdom of God." And no one dared to ask him any more questions.

The Gospel of the Lord.

Liturgy of the Eucharist, *p. 897;* **Prayer over the Gifts,** *p. 483.*

Friday

Antiphons and Prayers, *p. 482;* **Liturgy of the Word** *for Year I (odd years) follows; Year II (even years), p. 509.*

TODAY'S LIVING WORD

The two first readings for today deal with sight. Tobit is enabled to see his son Tobiah, the light of his eyes, and Paul encourages Timothy his "son" to see him—his "way of life, purpose, faith, patience, love, endurance." Both stories, Tobit's and Paul's, are for us Sacred Scripture. They are part of that library of inspired books that speak to the Christian community with the authority of God's own word. Jesus' Bible was the Jewish Scriptures—the Law (the written Torah), the Prophets, and the Writings. The creative fidelity with which he approached them, evident in today's Gospel, should be the model for our own biblical study. In this passage, for example, Jesus interprets Psalm 110 to expose the narrowness of the messianic expectations of some scribes.

Sacred Scripture was part of Jesus' "equipment" as a teacher in Israel, and the Letter to Timothy says it should be ours too. Although our methods of biblical interpretation will be different than those of Jesus' day, they must, as did his, always recognize and respect the word of God as a living word that demands a lived response.

Year I

FIRST READING
Tb 11:5–17

God himself scourged me and behold, I now see my son Tobiah!

A reading from the Book of Tobit

Anna sat watching the road by which her son was to come. When she saw him coming, she exclaimed to his father, "Tobit, your son is coming, and the man who traveled with him!"

Raphael said to Tobiah before he reached his father: "I am certain that his eyes will be opened. Smear the fish gall on them. This medicine will make the cataracts shrink and peel off from his eyes; then your father will again be able to see the light of day."

Then Anna ran up to her son, threw her arms around him, and said to him, "Now that I have seen you again, son, I am ready to die!" And she sobbed aloud.

Tobit got up and stumbled out through the courtyard gate. Tobiah went up to him with the fish gall in his hand, and holding him firmly, blew into his eyes. "Courage, father," he said. Next he smeared the medicine on his eyes, and it made them smart. Then, beginning at the corners of Tobit's eyes, Tobiah used both hands to peel off the cataracts.

When Tobit saw his son, he threw his arms around him and wept. He exclaimed, "I can see you, son, the light of my eyes!" Then he said:

"Blessed be God,
   and praised be his great name,
   and blessed be all his holy angels.
May his holy name be praised
   throughout all the ages,
Because it was he who scourged me,
   and it is he who has had mercy on me.
Behold, I now see my son Tobiah!"

Then Tobit went back in, rejoicing and praising God with full voice for everything that had happened. Tobiah told his father that the Lord God had granted him a successful journey; that he had brought back the money; and that he had married Raguel's daughter Sarah, who would arrive shortly, for she was approaching the gate of Nineveh.

Tobit and Anna rejoiced and went out to the gate of Nineveh to meet their daughter-in-law. When the people of Nineveh saw Tobit walking along briskly, with no one leading him by the hand, they were amazed. Before them all Tobit proclaimed how God had mercifully restored sight to his eyes. When Tobit reached Sarah, the wife of his son Tobiah, he greeted her: "Welcome, my daughter! Blessed be your God for bringing you to us, daughter! Blessed is your father, and blessed is my son Tobiah, and blessed are you, daughter! Welcome to your home with blessing and joy. Come in, daughter!" That day there was joy for all the Jews who lived in Nineveh.

The word of the Lord.

Responsorial Psalm Ps 146:1b–2, 6c–7, 8–9a, 9bc–10

R. Praise the Lord, my soul!

Praise the LORD, O my soul;
  I will praise the LORD all my life;
  I will sing praise to my God while I live.

R. Praise the Lord, my soul!

The LORD keeps faith forever,
  secures justice for the oppressed,
  gives food to the hungry.
The LORD sets captives free.

R. Praise the Lord, my soul!

The LORD gives sight to the blind.
The LORD raises up those who are bowed down;
  the LORD loves the just.
The LORD protects strangers.

R. Praise the Lord, my soul!

The fatherless and the widow he sustains,
  but the way of the wicked he thwarts
The LORD shall reign forever,
  your God, O Zion, through all generations! Alleluia.

R. Praise the Lord, my soul!

Or: **R. Alleluia.**

Alleluia Verse *and* **Gospel,** *p. 511.*

Year II

FIRST READING 2 Tm 3:10–17

All who want to live religiously in Christ Jesus will be persecuted.

A reading from the second Letter of Saint Paul to Timothy

You have followed my teaching, way of life, purpose, faith, patience, love, endurance, persecutions, and sufferings, such as happened to me in Antioch, Iconium, and Lystra, persecutions that I endured. Yet from all these things the Lord delivered me. In fact, all who want to live religiously in Christ Jesus will be persecuted. But wicked people and charlatans will go from bad to worse, deceivers and deceived. But you, remain faithful to what you have learned and believed, because you know from whom you learned it, and that from infancy you have known the sacred Scriptures, which are capable of giving you wisdom for salvation through faith in Christ Jesus. All Scripture is inspired by God and is useful for teaching, for refutation, for correction, and for training in righteousness, so that one who belongs to God may be competent, equipped for every good work.

The word of the Lord.

Responsorial Psalm

Ps 119:157, 160, 161, 165, 166, 168

R. O Lord, great peace have they who love your law.

Though my persecutors and my foes are many,
  I turn not away from your decrees.

R. O Lord, great peace have they who love your law.

Permanence is your word's chief trait;
  each of your just ordinances is everlasting.

R. O Lord, great peace have they who love your law.

Princes persecute me without cause
  but my heart stands in awe of your word.

R. O Lord, great peace have they who love your law.

Those who love your law have great peace,
  and for them there is no stumbling block.

R. O Lord, great peace have they who love your law.

I wait for your salvation, O LORD,
  and your commands I fulfill.

R. O Lord, great peace have they who love your law.

I keep your precepts and your decrees,
  for all my ways are before you.

R. O Lord, great peace have they who love your law.

Alleluia, alleluia   Jn 14:23
Whoever loves me will keep my word,
  and my Father will love him
  and we will come to him.
Alleluia, alleluia

Years I and II

GOSPEL   Mk 12:35–37

How do the scribes claim that the Christ is the son of David?

A reading from the holy Gospel according to Mark

As Jesus was teaching in the temple area he said, "How do the
scribes claim that the Christ is the son of David? David himself,
inspired by the Holy Spirit, said:

> *The Lord said to my lord,*
> *'Sit at my right hand*
>   *until I place your enemies under your feet.'*

David himself calls him 'lord'; so how is he his son?" The
great crowd heard this with delight.

The Gospel of the Lord.

Liturgy of the Eucharist, *p. 897;* **Prayer over the Gifts,** *p. 483.*

Saturday

Antiphons and Prayers, *p. 482;* **Liturgy of the Word** *for Year I (odd
years) follows; Year II (even years), p. 514.*

Today's Living Word

As Raphael exhorted Tobit and Tobias before his departure, so Paul exhorts Timothy before his death. Both Raphael and Paul, angel and apostle, counsel good works and promise "a full life," "a crown of righteousness" to those who endure. The Gospel story also contains exhortation. Observing the people putting money into the collection box opposite the temple treasury, Jesus seizes the opportunity to teach his disciples a lesson. He directs their attention to a poor widow and her two small copper coins. He tells them that hers is the greater gift, for "she, from her poverty, has contributed all she had, her whole livelihood."

Scholars often note that the widow is presented as a foil for those scribes whose piety is showy and self-serving. But she prepares us as well for the self-giving of Jesus. As she gave her livelihood, so he will give his life. Perhaps Mark is suggesting that almsgiving, so highly praised in the Book of Tobit, is one practical way for us to follow Christ.

Year I

FIRST READING
Tb 12:1, 5 –15, 20

So now praise God. Behold,
I am about to ascend to him who sent me.

A reading from the Book of Tobit

Tobit called his son Tobiah and said to him, "Son, see to it that you give what is due to the man who made the journey with you; give him a bonus too." So he called Raphael and said, "Take as your wages half of all that you have brought back, and go in peace."

Raphael called the two men aside privately and said to them: "Thank God! Give him the praise and the glory. Before all the living, acknowledge the many good things he has done for you, by blessing and extolling his name in song. Honor and proclaim God's deeds, and do not be slack in praising him. A king's secret it is prudent to keep, but the works of God are to be declared and made known. Praise them with due honor. Do good, and evil will not find its way to you. Prayer and fasting are good, but better than either is almsgiving accompanied by righteousness. A little with righteousness is better than abundance with wickedness. It is better to give alms than to store up gold; for almsgiving saves one from death and expiates every sin. Those who regularly give alms shall enjoy a full life; but those habitually guilty of sin are their own worst enemies.

"I will now tell you the whole truth; I will conceal nothing at all from you. I have already said to you, 'A king's secret it is prudent to keep, but the works of God are to be made known with due honor.' I can now tell you that when you, Tobit, and Sarah prayed, it was I who presented and read the record of your prayer before the Glory of the Lord; and I did the same thing when you used to bury the dead. When you did not hesitate to get up and leave your dinner in order to go and bury the dead, I was sent to put you to the test. At the same time, however, God commissioned me to heal you and your daughter-in-law Sarah. I am Raphael, one of the seven angels who enter and serve before the Glory of the Lord.

"So now get up from the ground and praise God. Behold, I am about to ascend to him who sent me; write down all these things that have happened to you."

The word of the Lord.

Responsorial Psalm

Tb 13:2, 6efgh, 7, 8

R. Blessed be God, who lives for ever.

He scourges and then has mercy;
  he casts down to the depths of the nether world,
  and he brings up from the great abyss.
No one can escape his hand.

R. Blessed be God, who lives for ever.

So now consider what he has done for you,
  and praise him with full voice.
Bless the Lord of righteousness,
  and exalt the King of ages.

R. Blessed be God, who lives for ever.

In the land of my exile I praise him
  and show his power and majesty to a sinful nation.

R. Blessed be God, who lives for ever.

Bless the Lord, all you his chosen ones,
  and may all of you praise his majesty.
Celebrate days of gladness, and give him praise.

R. Blessed be God, who lives for ever.

Alleluia Verse *and* **Gospel,** *p. 516.*

Year II

FIRST READING   2 Tm 4:1–8

*I am already being poured out and the crown of righteousness
awaits me which the Lord will award to me.*

A reading from the second Letter of Saint Paul to Timothy

Beloved:
I charge you in the presence of God and of Christ Jesus, who
will judge the living and the dead, and by his appearing and
his kingly power: proclaim the word; be persistent whether it
is convenient or inconvenient; convince, reprimand, encourage
through all patience and teaching. For the time will come when

people will not tolerate sound doctrine but, following their own desires and insatiable curiosity, will accumulate teachers and will stop listening to the truth and will be diverted to myths. But you, be self-possessed in all circumstances; put up with hardship; perform the work of an evangelist; fulfill your ministry.

For I am already being poured out like a libation, and the time of my departure is at hand. I have competed well; I have finished the race; I have kept the faith. From now on the crown of righteousness awaits me, which the Lord, the just judge, will award to me on that day, and not only to me, but to all who have longed for his appearance.

The word of the Lord.

Responsorial Psalm
Ps 71:8–9, 14–15ab, 16–17, 22

R. I will sing of your salvation.

My mouth shall be filled with your praise,
  with your glory day by day.
Cast me not off in my old age;
  as my strength fails, forsake me not.

R. I will sing of your salvation.

But I will always hope
  and praise you ever more and more.
My mouth shall declare your justice,
  day by day your salvation.

R. I will sing of your salvation.

I will treat of the mighty works of the Lord;
  O GOD, I will tell of your singular justice.
O God, you have taught me from my youth,
  and till the present I proclaim your wondrous deeds.

R. I will sing of your salvation.

So will I give you thanks with music on the lyre,
  for your faithfulness, O my God!
I will sing your praises with the harp,
  O Holy One of Israel!

R. I will sing of your salvation.

Alleluia, alleluia   Mt 5:3
Blessed are the poor in spirit;
  for theirs is the Kingdom of heaven.
Alleluia, alleluia

Years I and II

GOSPEL   Mk 12:38–44

This poor widow has given more than all others.

A reading from the holy Gospel according to Mark

In the course of his teaching Jesus said, "Beware of the scribes, who like to go around in long robes and accept greetings in the marketplaces, seats of honor in synagogues, and places of honor at banquets. They devour the houses of widows and, as a pretext, recite lengthy prayers. They will receive a very severe condemnation."

He sat down opposite the treasury and observed how the crowd put money into the treasury. Many rich people put in large sums. A poor widow also came and put in two small coins worth a few cents. Calling his disciples to himself, he said to them, "Amen, I say to you, this poor widow put in more than all the other contributors to the treasury. For they have all contributed from their surplus wealth, but she, from her poverty, has contributed all she had, her whole livelihood."

The Gospel of the Lord.

Liturgy of the Eucharist, *p. 897;* **Prayer over the Gifts,** *p. 483.*

Lent

A Renewed Season of Renewal

L ent is first and foremost a liturgical season. What does the Church mean by that? As an extended liturgical action—an entire season—Lent's meaning rests in the larger context of the entire liturgical renewal inaugurated by the Second Vatican Council. By briefly considering how the Council (1962–1965) returned the Church's liturgy to its deepest traditional roots, we can go on to appreciate why Lent so powerfully shapes our Catholic identity as Christians.

"It is the goal of this most sacred Council to intensify the daily growth of Catholics in Christian living; to make more responsive to the requirements of our times those Church observances which are open to adaptation; to nurture whatever can contribute to the unity of all who believe in Christ; and to strengthen those aspects of the Church which can summon all of humankind into her embrace" (*Sacrosanctum Concilium*, n. 1). With these opening words of its first document, the Council was proclaiming that the work of renewing the Church for service to the modern world was an invitation from God.

The Council discerned that the heart of the Holy Spirit's renewal of the Church lay in the reform of the sacred liturgy, "the summit toward which the activity of the Church is directed...the fountain from which all her power flows" (*SC*, n. 10). And the key to renewing the Church's rites, it taught, lay in recovering what is most sound in ancient tradition. This may seem ironic. To serve the modern world better, the Church must find ways to embrace authentically and creatively her deepest traditions. In one sense, this has amounted to Catholicism's getting back to basics. Although divinely empowered, liturgy is also a human act of ritual. Like all ritual, the Church's liturgy had tended to accumulate multiple practices. Ritual can collapse under such an excess, leaving the people who do it unable to recognize the forest for the trees. Isolated attention to rubrics or devotions tended to leave the faithful unable to enter into the larger mystery of salvation, which the liturgy celebrates: in the liturgy, Christ's dying and rising becomes our dying and rising. The Spirit of Christ gives us a share in the pattern and fabric of the divine life revealed in Jesus.

Newly restored, the season of Lent forms us in sharing the mystery of Christ's death and resurrection. For this reason, Lent has, according to the Council, "a twofold character" (*SC*, n. 109). First, Lent focuses every member of the Church on Baptism, the sacrament whereby believers are joined eternally to Christ's pattern of life and death. For those already baptized, Lent is a time for recalling their Baptism. For those who will be baptized at Easter ("the elect"), it is the time of final preparation for receiving the sacraments of initiation (Baptism, Confirmation, and Eucharist). This baptismal focus gives rise to the second aspect of Lent: a spirit of penitence. For the elect, Lent amounts to an intense retreat during which the Church shows them Christ's generous call away from the darkness of sin into his own marvelous light. For the full members of the Church, therefore, Lent is also a forty-day retreat. As they gather around the elect in prayer each Sunday, the liturgy reminds them of their own temptations away from the Light they received in Baptism.

Repent and believe the Good News. Turn away from sin and live the Gospel. Such are the basics of this season. Whatever practices of prayer, fasting, and almsgiving the faithful undertake during Lent, these need to be done with this liturgical focus in mind: together we are celebrating the remarkable truth that neither we nor our world are left to our own wilderness wanderings. The Spirit of Christ is leading us forward through the waters of death into life at Easter. Therein lies our Christian identity.

Baptism: The Living Sacrament of Lent

As part of the larger liturgical cycle of Easter, Lent prepares us for the celebration of the Easter Triduum (Holy Thursday through Easter Sunday evening). The sacramental key to Easter is the celebration of Christian Baptism (along with Confirmation and the Eucharist) at the Easter Vigil. As the highlight of the entire liturgical year, the Vigil includes the liturgy of Baptism, wherein new members of the Church are baptized and "old" members renew their baptismal promises of faith. Assembled together in this profound annual celebration, all the baptized share the joy of being members of the body of the risen Christ now in the world.

During Lent, those who will be fully initiated into the body of Christ at the Easter Vigil (through Baptism, Confirmation, and Eucharist) undergo their final, intensive preparation. The process they follow is called the Rite of

Christian Initiation of Adults (RCIA), which is comprised of four stages:

(1) a period of inquiry and evangelization;

(2) the catechumenate;

(3) the period of purification and enlightenment;

(4) and the season of mystagogy.

The third period of the RCIA directly coincides with Lent. With the Church having discerned their election to the Easter sacraments, the catechumens are now called the "elect." The Liturgy of the Word for the third, fourth, and fifth Sundays of Lent focuses on the elect. Special readings from the Gospel of John each week provide the source for the priest to preach homilies that help the elect to discern concretely how Christ is calling them from the darkness of sin into his marvelous light. The scrutiny then takes place in the form of intercessions with the assembly praying over the elect, who kneel or bow in the midst of the community. The priest then prays an exorcism, asking God to protect the elect from evil and the reign of sin. Finally, he dismisses them, telling them how much the community looks forward to their joining the assembly soon for the Liturgy of the Eucharist at the Easter Vigil.

As the priest (with the help of the sponsors and catechists) scrutinizes, exorcises, and exhorts the elect, all of the members of the assembled church are drawn into these spiritual exercises. Seeing how God is now intensely forming these new believers for fullness of life in Baptism, the faithful "in the pews" are led to scrutinize themselves in light of the Gospel, to realign their own lives with the Baptism they have already undergone. Lent thereby becomes a retreat for the entire local church, a time set aside for an ongoing conversion.

A Liturgical Season of Penance

Lent is emerging once again as a liturgical season. It is a time not so much of individual feats of self-abnegation as of working together to share with joy the boundless mercy, forgiveness, and grace that God continuously extends to us in Christ Jesus. The action of God's grace, however, constitutes a twofold movement in our lives: a movement toward God and away from sin. In this Gospel perspective activities of penitence and self-denial find life-giving meaning. Christian faith recognizes that the initiative for repentance always comes from God. The attractiveness of God's love, mercy, and forgiveness revealed in Jesus fosters in us the desire to be close to him, to walk near him and his disciples. Our world steadily markets so many false images of happiness, preying on our sense of emptiness and inadequacy, pressing on us products and activities that fail to satisfy us. The sad, even sinful, irony in our consumer culture is that it identifies in us the deep human hunger for fulfillment only to exploit it by promising that more goods will fully satisfy us. It never works. As St. Augustine so eloquently wrote in his *Confessions,* our hearts are restless until they rest in God.

God wants our hearts as well as our souls and bodies. For this to be Good News, and not merely another empty promise, we find ourselves turning again to the community of faith, which is the sacrament of Christ's body now in the world. Lent is God's invitation to us through the

Church, in the fellowship of this body of Christ, to know the peace of God. This peace, beyond our understanding, is found and shared in the communion of believers gathered around the tables of God's Word and Eucharist. Each Ash Wednesday we proclaim from the Gospel of Matthew Jesus' instructions about praying, fasting, and giving alms to the poor (Mt 6:1–6,16–18). We draw strength and encouragement from the community of faith in knowing that we undertake penitential practices not as rugged individualists, but as fellow disciples. We encourage one another to leave behind whatever burdens us with false promises, and to take up the search for Jesus waiting to meet us in the poor. As our communal act of worship in Lent, praying, fasting, and almsgiving are anything but a program in self-improvement. They are, rather, a loving service of mutual encouragement.

Whenever we turn to the people and places that our world condemns as godless and worthless, whenever we take up the Christ-like pattern of comforting the sorrowful, healing the sick, befriending the stranger, feeding the hungry, and visiting the prisoner, we discover the soul-satisfying grace of God. In sharing God's self-giving love with one another, our entire lives become the worship of God; the liturgy becomes a recasting of our world.

BRUCE T. MORRILL, S.J.

Ash Wednesday

The ashes used today come from the palm branches blessed the preceding year for Passion Sunday.

Entrance Antiphon

Lord, you are merciful to all, and hate nothing you have created. You overlook the sins of men to bring them to repentance. You are the Lord our God. (See Wis 11:24–25, 27)

The penitential rite and the Gloria are omitted.

Opening Prayer

Let us pray
    [for the grace to keep Lent faithfully]

Pause for silent prayer.

Lord,
protect us in our struggle against evil.
As we begin the discipline of Lent,
make this day holy by our self-denial.

Grant this through our Lord Jesus Christ, your Son,
who lives and reigns with you and the Holy Spirit,
one God, for ever and ever.

Alternative Opening Prayer

Let us pray
    [in quiet remembrance of our need for redemption]

Pause for silent prayer.

Father in heaven,
the light of your truth bestows sight
to the darkness of sinful eyes.
May this season of repentance

bring us the blessing of your forgiveness
and the gift of your light.

Grant this through Christ our Lord.

TODAY'S LIVING WORD

In many ways today's New Testament readings—from 2 Corinthians and from Matthew—echo the Old Testament reading from
the prophet Joel. The setting of Joel's words is a time of crisis, a
defining moment. In that critical moment, he summons the whole
people of God to gather in the liturgical assembly to pray and to
fast. Playing on the Hebrew word *sub*, which means "turn," he tells
the people to "return" (repent) to the Lord their God in the hope that
God may "turn" (relent) and take pity on them. This is Paul's message
as well. Like Joel, he too addresses people at a defining moment,
the "acceptable time." As Christ's ambassador, he implores the Corinthians to return and be reconciled to the God who has graciously
turned to them in Christ.

Joel also warns the people that the public character of their
gathering must not detract from the intimately personal nature of
true conversion. They must rend their hearts and not their garments.
In the same way, Matthew's Jesus warns all of us that our Lenten
practices—prayer, fasting, almsgiving—must be for God's eyes only.

*If the blessing and distribution of ashes take place outside Mass, it is
appropriate that the Liturgy of the Word precede it, using texts assigned to
the Mass of Ash Wednesday.*

FIRST READING

Jl 2:12–18

Rend your hearts, not your garments.

A reading from the Book of the Prophet Joel

Even now, says the LORD,
    return to me with your whole heart,
        with fasting, and weeping, and mourning;
Rend your hearts, not your garments,

and return to the LORD, your God.
For gracious and merciful is he,
    slow to anger, rich in kindness,
    and relenting in punishment.
Perhaps he will again relent
    and leave behind him a blessing,
Offerings and libations
    for the LORD, your God.

Blow the trumpet in Zion!
    proclaim a fast,
    call an assembly;
Gather the people,
    notify the congregation;
Assemble the elders,
    gather the children
    and the infants at the breast;
Let the bridegroom quit his room
    and the bride her chamber.
Between the porch and the altar
    let the priests, the ministers of the LORD, weep,
And say, "Spare, O LORD, your people,
    and make not your heritage a reproach,
    with the nations ruling over them!
Why should they say among the peoples,
    'Where is their God?' "

Then the LORD was stirred to concern for his land
    and took pity on his people.
The word of the Lord.

Responsorial Psalm

Ps 51:3–4, 5–6ab, 12–13, 14 and 17

R. Be merciful, O Lord, for we have sinned.

Have mercy on me, O God, in your goodness;
  in the greatness of your compassion wipe out my offense.
Thoroughly wash me from my guilt
  and of my sin cleanse me.

R. Be merciful, O Lord, for we have sinned.

For I acknowledge my offense,
  and my sin is before me always:
"Against you only have I sinned,
  and done what is evil in your sight."

R. Be merciful, O Lord, for we have sinned.

A clean heart create for me, O God,
  and a steadfast spirit renew within me.
Cast me not out from your presence,
  and your Holy Spirit take not from me.

R. Be merciful, O Lord, for we have sinned.

Give me back the joy of your salvation,
  and a willing spirit sustain in me.
O Lord, open my lips,
  and my mouth shall proclaim your praise.

R. Be merciful, O Lord, for we have sinned.

SECOND READING

2 Cor 5:20—6:2

Be reconciled to God. Behold, now is the acceptable time.

A reading from the second Letter of Saint Paul to the Corinthians

Brothers and sisters:

We are ambassadors for Christ, as if God were appealing through us. We implore you on behalf of Christ, be reconciled to God. For our sake he made him to be sin who did not know sin, so that we might become the righteousness of God in him.

Working together, then, we appeal to you not to receive the grace of God in vain. For he says:

In an acceptable time I heard you,
and on the day of salvation I helped you.

Behold, now is a very acceptable time; behold, now is the day of salvation.

The word of the Lord.

Verse Before the Gospel   See Ps 95:8
If today you hear his voice,
harden not your hearts.

GOSPEL
Mt 6:1–6, 16–18

Your Father who sees in secret will repay you.

A reading from the holy Gospel according to Matthew

Jesus said to his disciples: "Take care not to perform righteous deeds in order that people may see them; otherwise, you will have no recompense from your heavenly Father. When you give alms, do not blow a trumpet before you, as the hypocrites do in the synagogues and in the streets to win the praise of others. Amen, I say to you, they have received their reward. But when you give alms, do not let your left hand know what your right is doing, so that your almsgiving may be secret. And your Father who sees in secret will repay you.

"When you pray, do not be like the hypocrites, who love to stand and pray in the synagogues and on street corners so that others may see them. Amen, I say to you, they have received their reward. But when you pray, go to your inner room, close the door, and pray to your Father in secret. And your Father who sees in secret will repay you.

"When you fast, do not look gloomy like the hypocrites. They neglect their appearance, so that they may appear to others to be fasting. Amen, I say to you, they have received their reward. But when you fast, anoint your head and wash your face, so that you may not appear to be fasting, except to your Father who is hidden. And your Father who sees what is hidden will repay you."

The Gospel of the Lord.

Blessing and Giving of Ashes

After the homily the priest joins his hands and says:

Dear friends in Christ,
let us ask our Father
to bless these ashes
which we will use
as the mark of our repentance.

Pause for silent prayer.

Lord,
bless the sinner who asks for your forgiveness
and bless ✠ all those who receive these ashes.
May they keep this lenten season
in preparation for the joy of Easter.

We ask this through Christ our Lord.

Or:

Lord,
bless these ashes ✠
by which we show that we are dust.
Pardon our sins
and keep us faithful to the discipline of Lent,
for you do not want sinners to die

but to live with the risen Christ,
who reigns with you for ever and ever.

He sprinkles the ashes with holy water in silence.
The priest then places ashes on those who come forward, saying to each:

Turn away from sin and be faithful to the gospel.   (Mk 1:15)

Or:

Remember, man, you are dust
and to dust you will return.

(See Gn 3:19)

Meanwhile some of the following antiphons or other appropriate songs are sung.

Antiphon 1

Come back to the Lord with all your heart;
leave the past in ashes,
and turn to God with tears and fasting,
for he is slow to anger and ready to forgive.   (See Jl 2:13)

Antiphon 2

Let the priests and ministers of the Lord
lament before his altar, and say:
Spare us, Lord; spare your people!
Do not let us die for we are crying out to you.

(See Jl 2:17; Est 13:17)

Antiphon 3

Lord, take away our wickedness.   (Ps 50:3)

These may be repeated after each verse of Psalm 50, HAVE MERCY ON ME, O GOD.

Responsory

Direct our hearts to better things, O Lord;
heal our sin and ignorance.
Lord, do not face us suddenly with death,
but give us time to repent.   (See Bar 3:5)

R. Turn to us with mercy, Lord; we have sinned against you.

V. Help us, God our savior, rescue us for the honor of your
name.   (Ps 78:9)

R. Turn to us with mercy, Lord; we have sinned against you.

After the giving of the ashes the priest washes his hands; the rite concludes
with the general intercessions or prayer of the faithful.

The **Profession of Faith** is not said.

Liturgy of the Eucharist, *p. 897.*

Prayer over the Gifts

Pray, brethren...

Lord,
help us to resist temptation
by our lenten works of charity and penance.
By this sacrifice
may we be prepared to celebrate
the death and resurrection of Christ our Savior
and be cleansed from sin and renewed in spirit.

We ask this through Christ our Lord.

Preface of Lent IV, *p. 942.*

Communion Antiphon

The man who meditates day and night on the law of the Lord
will yield fruit in due season.   (Ps 1:2–3)

Prayer after Communion

Let us pray.

Pause for silent prayer, if this has not preceded.

Lord,
through this communion
may our lenten penance give you glory
and bring us your protection.

We ask this in the name of Jesus the Lord.

Thursday after Ash Wednesday

Entrance Antiphon

When I cry to the Lord, he hears my voice and saves me from the foes who threaten me. Unload your burden onto the Lord, and he will support you.   (See Ps 54:17–20, 23)

Opening Prayer

Lord,
may everything we do
begin with your inspiration,
continue with your help,
and reach perfection under your guidance.

We ask this through our Lord Jesus Christ, your Son,
who lives and reigns with you and the Holy Spirit,
one God, for ever and ever.

TODAY'S LIVING WORD

Today's two readings issue the same call but in different contexts. In the passage from Deuteronomy, Moses tells his people that they choose life by walking in God's ways. In the Gospel passage from Luke, Jesus tells his disciples that they choose life by following in his steps. For Moses, walking in God's ways is more than a metaphor; it is a mode of action that requires keeping God's commandments, statutes and decrees. Similarly, for Luke's Jesus, following in his steps is more than a figure of speech; it is a faithful, faith-filled way of life that demands taking up one's cross each day. Finally, each in his own way, both Moses and Jesus promise fullness of life—on God's terms.

During this season of Lent, the Church joins its voice to that of Moses and Jesus to invite us to walk in God's way by following in Jesus' steps each day—beginning now.

FIRST READING   Dt 30:15–20

Behold, I set before you the blessing and the curse (Dt 11:26).

A reading from the Book of Deuteronomy

Moses said to the people: "Today I have set before you life and prosperity, death and doom. If you obey the commandments of the LORD, your God, which I enjoin on you today, loving him, and walking in his ways, and keeping his commandments, statutes and decrees, you will live and grow numerous, and the LORD, your God, will bless you in the land you are entering to occupy. If, however, you turn away your hearts and will not listen, but are led astray and adore and serve other gods, I tell you now that you will certainly perish; you will not have a long life on the land that you are crossing the Jordan to enter and occupy. I call heaven and earth today to witness against you: I have set before you life and death, the blessing and the curse. Choose life, then, that you and your descendants may live, by loving the LORD, your God, heeding his voice, and holding fast to him. For that will mean life for you, a long life for you to live on the land that the LORD swore he would give to your fathers Abraham, Isaac and Jacob."

The word of the Lord.

Responsorial Psalm

Ps 1:1–2, 3, 4 and 6

R. Blessed are they who hope in the Lord.

Blessed the man who follows not
   the counsel of the wicked
Nor walks in the way of sinners,
   nor sits in the company of the insolent,
But delights in the law of the LORD
   and meditates on his law day and night.

R. Blessed are they who hope in the Lord.

He is like a tree
   planted near running water,

That yields its fruit in due season,
  and whose leaves never fade.
  Whatever he does, prospers.

R. Blessed are they who hope in the Lord.

Not so the wicked, not so;
  they are like chaff which the wind drives away.
For the LORD watches over the way of the just,
  but the way of the wicked vanishes.

R. Blessed are they who hope in the Lord.

> **Verse Before the Gospel** Mt 4:17
> Repent, says the Lord;
> the Kingdom of heaven is at hand.

GOSPEL   Lk 9:22–25

Whoever loses his life for my sake will save it.

A reading from the holy Gospel according to Luke

Jesus said to his disciples: "The Son of Man must suffer greatly and be rejected by the elders, the chief priests, and the scribes, and be killed and on the third day be raised."

Then he said to all, "If anyone wishes to come after me, he must deny himself and take up his cross daily and follow me. For whoever wishes to save his life will lose it, but whoever loses his life for my sake will save it. What profit is there for one to gain the whole world yet lose or forfeit himself?"

The Gospel of the Lord.

Liturgy of the Eucharist, *p. 897.*

Prayer over the Gifts

Pray, brethren...

Lord,
accept these gifts.

May they bring us your mercy
and give you honor and praise.

We ask this in the name of Jesus the Lord.

Preface of Lent I–IV, *pp. 940–942.*

Communion Antiphon

Create a clean heart in me, O God; give me a new and stead-fast spirit. (Ps 50:12)

Prayer after Communion

Let us pray.

Pause for silent prayer, if this has not preceded.

Merciful Father,
may the gifts and blessings we receive
bring us pardon and salvation.

Grant this through Christ our Lord.

Friday after Ash Wednesday

Entrance Antiphon

The Lord heard me and took pity on me. He came to my help.
(Ps 29:11)

Opening Prayer

Lord,
with your loving care
guide the penance we have begun.
Help us to persevere with love and sincerity.

Grant this through our Lord Jesus Christ, your Son,
who lives and reigns with you and the Holy Spirit,
one God, for ever and ever.

TODAY'S LIVING WORD

Lent is a penitential season and fasting a common penitential practice, among Jews as among Christians. Today's readings take up this timely theme. The judgment oracle from Isaiah clarifies the purpose of fasting. Fasting—abstaining from food—allows those who are usually well-fed to identify imaginatively with the hunger of the poor and so to learn compassion. The people to whom the prophet speaks have missed this point. Even as they fast, they continue to drive their laborers, as did the Egyptian taskmasters of another time. God says to them and to us: "This, rather, is the fasting that I wish… sharing your bread with the hungry, sheltering the oppressed and the homeless; clothing the naked when you see them, and not turning your back on your own."

In today's Gospel, Jesus' reply to the objection of John's disciples further situates the practice of fasting. He says there is a time for fasting, the time when the groom is taken away. Fasting at that time enables us to recognize him when he appears to us again in the plight of the hungry poor.

FIRST READING

Is 58:1–9a

Is this the manner of fasting I wish?

A reading from the Book of the Prophet Isaiah

Thus says the Lord GOD:

Cry out full-throated and unsparingly,
 lift up your voice like a trumpet blast;
Tell my people their wickedness,
 and the house of Jacob their sins.
They seek me day after day,
 and desire to know my ways,
Like a nation that has done what is just
 and not abandoned the law of their God;
They ask me to declare what is due them,
 pleased to gain access to God.

"Why do we fast, and you do not see it?
    afflict ourselves, and you take no note of it?"
Lo, on your fast day you carry out your own pursuits,
    and drive all your laborers.
Yes, your fast ends in quarreling and fighting,
    striking with wicked claw.
Would that today you might fast
    so as to make your voice heard on high!
Is this the manner of fasting I wish,
    of keeping a day of penance:
That a man bow his head like a reed
    and lie in sackcloth and ashes?
Do you call this a fast,
    a day acceptable to the LORD?
This, rather, is the fasting that I wish:
    releasing those bound unjustly,
    untying the thongs of the yoke;
Setting free the oppressed,
    breaking every yoke;
Sharing your bread with the hungry,
    sheltering the oppressed and the homeless;
Clothing the naked when you see them,
    and not turning your back on your own.
Then your light shall break forth like the dawn,
    and your wound shall quickly be healed;
Your vindication shall go before you,
    and the glory of the LORD shall be your rear guard.
Then you shall call, and the LORD will answer,
    you shall cry for help, and he will say: Here I am!
The word of the Lord.

Responsional Psalm

Ps 51:3–4, 5–6ab, 18–19

R. A heart contrite and humbled, O God, you will not spurn.

Have mercy on me, O God, in your goodness;
  in the greatness of your compassion wipe out my offense.
Thoroughly wash me from my guilt
  and of my sin cleanse me.

R. A heart contrite and humbled, O God, you will not spurn.

For I acknowledge my offense,
  and my sin is before me always:
"Against you only have° I sinned,
  and done what is evil in your sight."

R. A heart contrite and humbled, O God, you will not spurn.

For you are not pleased with sacrifices;
  should I offer a burnt offering, you would not accept it.
My sacrifice, O God, is a contrite spirit;
  a heart contrite and humbled, O God, you will not spurn.

R. A heart contrite and humbled, O God, you will not spurn.

Verse Before the Gospel   See Am 5:14
Seek good and not evil so that you may live,
  and the LORD will be with you.

GOSPEL

Mt 9:14–15

When the bridegroom is taken from them, then they will fast.

A reading from the holy Gospel according to Matthew

The disciples of John approached Jesus and said, "Why do we and the Pharisees fast much, but your disciples do not fast?" Jesus answered them, "Can the wedding guests mourn as long as the bridegroom is with them? The days will come when the bridegroom is taken away from them, and then they will fast."
The Gospel of the Lord.

Liturgy of the Eucharist, *p. 897.*

Prayer over the Gifts

Pray, brethren...

Lord,
through this lenten eucharist
may we grow in your love and service
and become an acceptable offering to you.

We ask this through Christ our Lord.

  Preface of Lent I–IV, *pp. 940–942.*

Communion Antiphon

  Teach us your ways, O Lord, and lead us in your paths.

(Ps 24:4)

Prayer after Communion

Let us pray.
    Pause for silent prayer, if this has not preceded.

Lord,
may our sharing in this mystery
free us from our sins
and make us worthy of your healing.

We ask this in the name of Jesus the Lord.

Saturday after Ash Wednesday

Entrance Antiphon

  **Answer us, Lord, with your loving kindness, turn to us in your
great mercy.** (Ps 68:17)

Opening Prayer

Father,
look upon our weakness
and reach out to help us with your loving power.

We ask this through our Lord Jesus Christ, your Son,
who lives and reigns with you and the Holy Spirit,
one God, for ever and ever.

TODAY'S LIVING WORD

Both of today's readings use striking imagery to announce salvation. The words of Isaiah were apparently written before the walls of Jerusalem were rebuilt, after the exile. Salvation, therefore, will not only bring light into the darkness and water to the parched land; it will also equip the returning exiles to rebuild the city of God. Thus will the people come to be called "repairer of the breach" and "restorer of ruined homesteads." These titles might be given to Jesus too in today's Gospel. By calling the hated toll collector Levi to join the community of his disciples, Jesus continues his mission of restoring *all* Israel, including "tax collectors and sinners." To describe his saving work as repairer and restorer he chooses a medical image, quite common in the ancient world. He is a doctor who comes to restore the sick and repair the human spirit.

The season of Lent gathers us in table fellowship with Jesus and with one another. May his saving work in us equip us, in turn, to be in our world repairers of the breach and restorers of ruined homesteads.

FIRST READING
Is 58:9b–14

If you bestow your bread on the hungry,
then light shall rise for you in the darkness.

A reading from the Book of the Prophet Isaiah

Thus says the LORD:

If you remove from your midst oppression,
    false accusation and malicious speech;
If you bestow your bread on the hungry
    and satisfy the afflicted;
Then light shall rise for you in the darkness,
    and the gloom shall become for you like midday;

Then the LORD will guide you always
   and give you plenty even on the parched land.
He will renew your strength,
   and you shall be like a watered garden,
   like a spring whose water never fails.
The ancient ruins shall be rebuilt for your sake,
   and the foundations from ages past you shall raise up;
"Repairer of the breach," they shall call you,
   "Restorer of ruined homesteads."
If you hold back your foot on the sabbath
   from following your own pursuits on my holy day;
If you call the sabbath a delight,
   and the LORD's holy day honorable;
If you honor it by not following your ways,
   seeking your own interests, or speaking with malice—
Then you shall delight in the LORD,
   and I will make you ride on the heights of the earth;
I will nourish you with the heritage of Jacob, your father,
   for the mouth of the LORD has spoken.

The word of the Lord.

Responsorial Psalm   Ps 86:1–2, 3–4, 5–6

> **R. Teach me your way, O Lord, that I may walk
>   in your truth.**

Incline your ear, O LORD; answer me,
   for I am afflicted and poor.
Keep my life, for I am devoted to you;
   save your servant who trusts in you.
   You are my God.

> **R. Teach me your way, O Lord, that I may walk
>   in your truth.**

Have mercy on me, O Lord,
  for to you I call all the day.
Gladden the soul of your servant,
  for to you, O Lord, I lift up my soul.

**R. Teach me your way, O Lord, that I may walk
in your truth.**

For you, O Lord, are good and forgiving,
  abounding in kindness to all who call upon you.
Hearken, O LORD, to my prayer
  and attend to the sound of my pleading.

**R. Teach me your way, O Lord, that I may walk
in your truth.**

Verse Before the Gospel   Ez 33:11
I take no pleasure in the death of the wicked man, says the Lord,
but rather in his conversion, that he may live.

GOSPEL
Lk 5:27–32

I have not come to call righteous to repentance but sinners.

A reading from the holy Gospel according to Luke

Jesus saw a tax collector named Levi sitting at the customs
post. He said to him, "Follow me." And leaving everything
behind, he got up and followed him. Then Levi gave a great
banquet for him in his house, and a large crowd of tax collectors
and others were at table with them. The Pharisees and their
scribes complained to his disciples, saying, "Why do you eat
and drink with tax collectors and sinners?" Jesus said to them
in reply, "Those who are healthy do not need a physician, but
the sick do. I have not come to call the righteous to repentance
but sinners."

The Gospel of the Lord.

Liturgy of the Eucharist, *p. 897.*

Prayer over the Gifts

Pray, brethren...

Lord,
receive our sacrifice of praise and reconciliation.
Let it free us from sin
and enable us to give you loving service.
We ask this in the name of Jesus the Lord.

Preface of Lent I–IV, *pp. 940–942.*

Communion Antiphon

It is mercy that I want, and not sacrifice, says the Lord; I did not come to call the virtuous, but sinners.   (Mt 9:13)

Prayer after Communion

Let us pray.

Pause for silent prayer, if this has not preceded.

Lord,
we are nourished by the bread of life you give us.
May this mystery we now celebrate
help us to reach eternal life with you.
Grant this through Christ our Lord.

GOSPEL ACCLAMATIONS FOR LENT

1. **Glory and praise to you,
   Lord Jesus Christ!**

2. **Glory to you, Lord Jesus Christ,
   Wisdom of God the Father!**

3. **Glory to you, Word of God, Lord Jesus Christ!**

4. **Glory to you, Lord Jesus Christ,
   Son of the living God!**

5. **Praise and honor to you, Lord Jesus Christ!**

6. **Praise to you, Lord Jesus Christ,**
   King of endless glory!

7. **Marvelous and great are your works, O Lord!**

8. **Salvation, glory, and power to the Lord Jesus Christ!**

FIRST WEEK OF LENT
Monday

Entrance Antiphon

As the eyes of servants are on the hands of their master, so our eyes are fixed on the Lord our God, pleading for his mercy. Have mercy on us, Lord, have mercy.   (Ps 122:2–3)

Opening Prayer

God our savior,
bring us back to you
and fill our minds with your wisdom.
May we be enriched by our observance of Lent.

Grant this through our Lord Jesus Christ, your Son,
who lives and reigns with you and the Holy Spirit,
one God, for ever and ever.

TODAY'S LIVING WORD

In his commentary on Matthew, Daniel Harrington proposes a different interpretation of today's familiar judgment scene. In his view the phrase *panta ta ethne,* usually translated "all the nations," should be read as "all the Gentiles," meaning non-Jews who are not Christian. Furthermore, he suggests that "my least brothers" refers here, as elsewhere in Matthew, to Jesus' followers. Thus, this passage attempts "to explain how and why such persons can be part of God's kingdom. How? By acts of mercy to Christians. Why? Because such acts are done to the Son of Man/King."

Harrington concludes his comments on today's Gospel by re-marking, "If good works to Christians are so important for non-Christians (and non-Jews) to perform, how much more are they to be expected from Christians (and Jews)!"* This is the burden of the first reading from Leviticus. Based on the Ten Commandments, it instructs God's holy ones—Jews and Christians—to act justly and mercifully in their dealings with one another. This is what it means to "love your neighbor as yourself."

* *The Gospel of Matthew,* Sacra Pagina 1 (Collegeville: Liturgical Press, 1991), pp. 358–360.

FIRST READING   Lv 19:1–2, 11–18

Judge your fellow man justly.

A reading from the Book of Leviticus

The LORD said to Moses, "Speak to the whole assembly of the children of Israel and tell them: Be holy, for I, the LORD, your God, am holy.

"You shall not steal. You shall not lie or speak falsely to one another. You shall not swear falsely by my name, thus profaning the name of your God. I am the LORD.

"You shall not defraud or rob your neighbor. You shall not withhold overnight the wages of your day laborer. You shall not curse the deaf, or put a stumbling block in front of the blind, but you shall fear your God. I am the LORD.

"You shall not act dishonestly in rendering judgment. Show neither partiality to the weak nor deference to the mighty, but judge your fellow men justly. You shall not go about spreading slander among your kin; nor shall you stand by idly when your neighbor's life is at stake. I am the LORD.

"You shall not bear hatred for your brother in your heart. Though you may have to reprove him, do not incur sin because of him. Take no revenge and cherish no grudge against your fellow countrymen. You shall love your neighbor as yourself. I am the LORD."

The word of the Lord.

Responsorial Psalm

Ps 19:8, 9, 10, 15

R. Your words, Lord, are Spirit and life.

The law of the LORD is perfect,
  refreshing the soul.
The decree of the LORD is trustworthy,
  giving wisdom to the simple.

R. Your words, Lord, are Spirit and life.

The precepts of the LORD are right,
  rejoicing the heart.
The command of the LORD is clear,
  enlightening the eye.

R. Your words, Lord, are Spirit and life.

The fear of the LORD is pure,
  enduring forever;
The ordinances of the LORD are true,
  all of them just.

R. Your words, Lord, are Spirit and life.

Let the words of my mouth and the thought of my heart
  find favor before you,
O LORD, my rock and my redeemer.

R. Your words, Lord, are Spirit and life.

Verse Before the Gospel   2 Cor 6:2b
  Behold, now is a very acceptable time;
  behold, now is the day of salvation.

GOSPEL

Mt 25:31–46

Whatever you have done to the very least of my brothers,
you have done to me.

A reading from the holy Gospel according to Matthew

Jesus said to his disciples: "When the Son of Man comes in his glory, and all the angels with him, he will sit upon his glorious throne, and all the nations will be assembled before him. And he will separate them one from another, as a shepherd separates the sheep from the goats. He will place the sheep on his right and the goats on his left. Then the king will say to those on his right, 'Come, you who are blessed by my Father. Inherit the kingdom prepared for you from the foundation of the world. For I was hungry and you gave me food, I was thirsty and you gave me drink, a stranger and you welcomed me, naked and you clothed me, ill and you cared for me, in prison and you visited me.' Then the righteous will answer him and say, 'Lord, when did we see you hungry and feed you, or thirsty and give you drink? When did we see you a stranger and welcome you, or naked and clothe you? When did we see you ill or in prison, and visit you?' And the king will say to them in reply, 'Amen, I say to you, whatever you did for one of these least brothers of mine, you did for me.' Then he will say to those on his left, 'Depart from me, you accursed, into the eternal fire prepared for the Devil and his angels. For I was hungry and you gave me no food, I was thirsty and you gave me no drink, a stranger and you gave me no welcome, naked and you gave me no clothing, ill and in prison, and you did not care for me.' Then they will answer and say, 'Lord, when did we see you hungry or thirsty or a stranger or naked or ill or in prison, and not minister to your needs?' He will answer them, 'Amen, I say to you, what you did not do for one of these least ones, you did not do for me.' And these will go off to eternal punishment, but the righteous to eternal life."

The Gospel of the Lord.

Liturgy of the Eucharist, *p. 897.*

Prayer over the Gifts

Pray, brethren...

Lord,
may this offering of our love
be acceptable to you.
Let it transform our lives
and bring us your mercy.

We ask this through Christ our Lord.

Preface of Lent I–IV, *pp. 940–942.*

Communion Antiphon

I tell you, anything you did for the least of my brothers,
you did for me, says the Lord. Come, you whom my Father
has blessed; inherit the kingdom prepared for you since the
foundation of the world.   (Mt 25:40, 34)

Prayer after Communion

Let us pray.

Pause for silent prayer, if this has not preceded.

Lord,
through this sacrament
may we rejoice in your healing power
and experience your saving love in mind and body.

We ask this in the name of Jesus the Lord.

Tuesday

Entrance Antiphon

In every age, O Lord, you have been our refuge. From all
eternity, you are God.   (Ps 89:1– 2)

Opening Prayer

Father,
look on us, your children.
Through the discipline of Lent
help us to grow in our desire for you.

We ask this through our Lord Jesus Christ, your Son,
who lives and reigns with you and the Holy Spirit,
one God, for ever and ever.

TODAY'S LIVING WORD

Today's first reading from the prophet Isaiah affirms the power of God's word. Like rain and snow, it descends to earth from heaven and does not return (ascend) to God until it has achieved the divine purpose for which it was sent.

Today's Gospel, Matthew's version of the Our Father, also affirms the power of words—words offered in prayer to the heavenly Father. Here too we discern a pattern as the words that Jesus teaches his disciples cut a path, covering the distance between earth and heaven. Inspired by his longing for the coming of God's kingdom, the first three petitions ascend into God's presence while the other four return (descend) to earth, weighted by the human concern for food, forgiveness, and freedom from evil in all its forms. Yet the power of this prayer does not lie in the multiplication of words, but in the fact that it is the prayer of Jesus, who is himself the Word. So as the Church teaches, when we pray the Lord's Prayer we invoke our heavenly Father "by the one Word he always hears" (*Catechism of the Catholic Church*, n. 2769).

FIRST READING   Is 55:10–11

My word will do whatever I will.

A reading from the Book of the Prophet Isaiah

Thus says the LORD:

Just as from the heavens
      the rain and snow come down

And do not return there
    till they have watered the earth,
    making it fertile and fruitful,
Giving seed to the one who sows
    and bread to the one who eats,
So shall my word be
    that goes forth from my mouth;
It shall not return to me void,
    but shall do my will,
    achieving the end for which I sent it.
The word of the Lord.

Responsorial Psalm

Ps 34:4–5, 6–7, 16–17, 18–19

R. From all their distress God rescues the just.

Glorify the LORD with me,
    let us together extol his name.
I sought the LORD, and he answered me
    and delivered me from all my fears.

R. From all their distress God rescues the just.

Look to him that you may be radiant with joy,
    and your faces may not blush with shame.
When the poor one called out, the LORD heard,
    and from all his distress he saved him.

R. From all their distress God rescues the just.

The LORD has eyes for the just,
    and ears for their cry.
The LORD confronts the evildoers,
    to destroy remembrance of them from the earth.

R. From all their distress God rescues the just.

When the just cry out, the LORD hears them,
    and from all their distress he rescues them.

The LORD is close to the brokenhearted;
  and those who are crushed in spirit he saves.

R. From all their distress God rescues the just.

Verse Before the Gospel Mt 4:4b
One does not live on bread alone,
  but on every word that comes forth from the mouth of God.

GOSPEL

Mt 6:7–15

This is how you are to pray.

A reading from the holy Gospel according to Matthew

Jesus said to his disciples: "In praying, do not babble like the pagans, who think that they will be heard because of their many words. Do not be like them. Your Father knows what you need before you ask him.

"This is how you are to pray:
  Our Father who art in heaven,
    hallowed be thy name,
    thy Kingdom come,
  thy will be done,
    on earth as it is in heaven.
  Give us this day our daily bread;
  and forgive us our trespasses,
    as we forgive those who trespass against us;
  and lead us not into temptation,
    but deliver us from evil.

"If you forgive men their transgressions, your heavenly Father will forgive you. But if you do not forgive men, neither will your Father forgive your transgressions."

The Gospel of the Lord.

Liturgy of the Eucharist, *p. 897.*

Prayer over the Gifts

Pray, brethren...

Father of creation,
from all you have given us
we bring you this bread and wine.
May it become for us the food of eternal life.

We ask this in the name of Jesus the Lord.

Preface of Lent I–IV, *pp. 940–942.*

Communion Antiphon

**My God of justice, you answer my cry; you come to my help
when I am in trouble. Take pity on me, Lord, and hear my prayer.**
(Ps 4:2)

Prayer after Communion

Let us pray.

Pause for silent prayer, if this has not preceded.

Lord,
may we who receive this sacrament
restrain our earthly desires
and grow in love for the things of heaven.

Grant this through Christ our Lord.

Wednesday

Entrance Antiphon

**Remember your mercies, Lord, your tenderness from ages past.
Do not let our enemies triumph over us; O God, deliver Israel
from all her distress.**
(Ps 24:6, 3, 22)

Opening Prayer

Lord,
look upon us and hear our prayer.
By the good works you inspire,
help us to discipline our bodies
and to be renewed in spirit.

Grant this through our Lord Jesus Christ, your Son,
who lives and reigns with you and the Holy Spirit,
one God, for ever and ever.

TODAY'S LIVING WORD

The story of Jonah links today's two readings. In the first reading the original call of Jonah is repeated. This time "Jonah made ready and went to Nineveh, according to the Lord's bidding." Much to his surprise, on hearing his warning the people of Nineveh responded immediately and all of them repented. In the Gospel, the preaching of Jonah becomes a sign, a standard by which another prophet assesses the response of his hearers. The people of Jesus' day are compared unfavorably to the Ninevites of Jonah's experience, "because at the preaching of Jonah they repented, and there is something greater than Jonah here," Jesus tells them.

Another point of contact links the two readings. The message of the Book of Jonah was partly to show that salvation is offered to all, even to Ninevites, whose wickedness was legendary in the ancient world. Similarly, the Gospel proclaims that salvation is offered even to pagans, whose immorality was well-known among the Jews. Such is the mystery of God.

FIRST READING

Jon 3:1–10

The Ninevites turned from their evil way.

A reading from the Book of the Prophet Jonah

The word of the LORD came to Jonah a second time: "Set out for the great city of Nineveh, and announce to it the message that I will tell you." So Jonah made ready and went to Nineveh, according to the LORD's bidding. Now Nineveh was an enormously large city; it took three days to go through it. Jonah began his journey through the city, and had gone but a single day's walk announcing, "Forty days more and Nineveh shall be destroyed," when the people of Nineveh believed God; they proclaimed a fast and all of them, great and small, put on sackcloth.

When the news reached the king of Nineveh, he rose from his throne, laid aside his robe, covered himself with sackcloth, and sat in the ashes. Then he had this proclaimed throughout Nineveh, by decree of the king and his nobles: "Neither man nor beast, neither cattle nor sheep, shall taste anything; they shall not eat, nor shall they drink water. Man and beast shall be covered with sackcloth and call loudly to God; every man shall turn from his evil way and from the violence he has in hand. Who knows, God may relent and forgive, and withhold his blazing wrath, so that we shall not perish." When God saw by their actions how they turned from their evil way, he repented of the evil that he had threatened to do to them; he did not carry it out.

The word of the Lord.

Responsorial Psalm

Ps 51:3–4, 12–13, 18–19

R. **A heart contrite and humbled, O God,
you will not spurn.**

Have mercy on me, O God, in your goodness;
    in the greatness of your compassion wipe out my offense.
Thoroughly wash me from my guilt
    and of my sin cleanse me.

R. **A heart contrite and humbled, O God,
you will not spurn.**

A clean heart create for me, O God,
  and a steadfast spirit renew within me.
Cast me not out from your presence,
  and your Holy Spirit take not from me.

  R. A heart contrite and humbled, O God,
      you will not spurn.

For you are not pleased with sacrifices;
  should I offer a burnt offering, you would not accept it.
My sacrifice, O God, is a contrite spirit;
  a heart contrite and humbled, O God, you will not spurn.

  R. A heart contrite and humbled, O God,
      you will not spurn.

  Verse Before the Gospel   Jl 2:12–13
  Even now, says the LORD,
  return to me with your whole heart
  for I am gracious and merciful.

GOSPEL   Lk 11:29–32

No sign will be given to this generation except the sign of Jonah.

A reading from the holy Gospel according to Luke

While still more people gathered in the crowd, Jesus said to them, "This generation is an evil generation; it seeks a sign, but no sign will be given it, except the sign of Jonah. Just as Jonah became a sign to the Ninevites, so will the Son of Man be to this generation. At the judgment the queen of the south will rise with the men of this generation and she will condemn them, because she came from the ends of the earth to hear the wisdom of Solomon, and there is something greater than Solomon here. At the judgment the men of Nineveh will arise with this generation and condemn it, because at the preaching of Jonah they repented, and there is something greater than Jonah here."

The Gospel of the Lord.

  Liturgy of the Eucharist, *p. 897.*

Prayer over the Gifts

Pray, brethren...

Lord,
from all you have given us,
we bring you these gifts in your honor.
Make them the sacrament of our salvation.
We ask this through Christ our Lord.

Preface of Lent I–IV, *pp. 940–942.*

Communion Antiphon

**Lord, give joy to all who trust in you; be their defender and
make them happy for ever.**   (Ps 5:12)

Prayer after Communion

Let us pray.

Pause for silent prayer, if this has not preceded.

Father,
you never fail to give us the food of life.
May this eucharist renew our strength
and bring us to salvation.
Grant this through Christ our Lord.

Thursday

Entrance Antiphon

**Let my words reach your ears, Lord; listen to my groaning,
and hear the cry of my prayer, O my King, my God.** (Ps 5:2–3)

Opening Prayer

Father,
without you we can do nothing.
By your Spirit help us to know what is right

and to be eager in doing your will.

We ask this through our Lord Jesus Christ, your Son,
who lives and reigns with you and the Holy Spirit,
one God, for ever and ever.

TODAY'S LIVING WORD

Today's Gospel brings us Jesus' teaching on prayer as found in
the Sermon on the Mount. Assuming that we are all children of the
same heavenly Father, Jesus urges us to ask, to seek, to knock,
confident that God will answer. The prayer of Esther found in today's
first reading is an example of prayer that asks, seeks, and knocks
with absolute confidence that God will hear. The story of Esther,
which provides the basis for the Jewish feast of Purim, is a work of
fiction that in the Hebrew makes no direct reference to God at all.
However, our text is taken from the Greek version (indicated by the
letter C), which interjects a religious note. Her prayer makes Esther's
religious faith explicit. The source of her courage is reliance on God.

Today's readings tell us that courage and confidence in prayer
are only possible in the context of a relationship with God. The
context of Esther's prayer is her membership in Israel, the people
chosen by God "from among all peoples…as a lasting heritage."
And Jesus urges his disciples to consider themselves children of the
heavenly Father who gives only "good things to those who ask him!"

FIRST READING   Est C:12, 14–16, 23–25

I have no protector other than you, LORD.

A reading from the Book of Esther

Queen Esther, seized with mortal anguish, had recourse to the
LORD. She lay prostrate upon the ground, together with her
handmaids, from morning until evening, and said: "God of
Abraham, God of Isaac, and God of Jacob, blessed are you.
Help me, who am alone and have no help but you, for I am
taking my life in my hand. As a child I used to hear from the

books of my forefathers that you, O LORD, always free those who are pleasing to you. Now help me, who am alone and have no one but you, O LORD, my God.

"And now, come to help me, an orphan. Put in my mouth persuasive words in the presence of the lion and turn his heart to hatred for our enemy, so that he and those who are in league with him may perish. Save us from the hand of our enemies; turn our mourning into gladness and our sorrows into wholeness."

The word of the Lord.

Responsorial Psalm   Ps 138:1–2ab, 2cde–3, 7c–8

R. Lord, on the day I called for help, you answered me.

I will give thanks to you, O LORD, with all my heart,
   for you have heard the words of my mouth;
   in the presence of the angels I will sing your praise;
I will worship at your holy temple
   and give thanks to your name.

R. Lord, on the day I called for help, you answered me.

Because of your kindness and your truth;
   for you have made great above all things
   your name and your promise.
When I called, you answered me;
   you built up strength within me.

R. Lord, on the day I called for help, you answered me.

Your right hand saves me.
The LORD will complete what he has done for me;
   your kindness, O LORD, endures forever;
   forsake not the work of your hands.

R. Lord, on the day I called for help, you answered me.

Verse Before the Gospel   Ps 51:12a, 14a
A clean heart create for me, God;
   give me back the joy of your salvation.

GOSPEL

Mt 7:7–12

Everyone who asks, receives.

A reading from the holy Gospel according to Matthew

Jesus said to his disciples: "Ask and it will be given to you; seek and you will find; knock and the door will be opened to you. For everyone who asks, receives; and the one who seeks, finds; and to the one who knocks, the door will be opened. Which one of you would hand his son a stone when he asked for a loaf of bread, or a snake when he asked for a fish? If you then, who are wicked, know how to give good gifts to your children, how much more will your heavenly Father give good things to those who ask him.

"Do to others whatever you would have them do to you. This is the law and the prophets."

The Gospel of the Lord.

Liturgy of the Eucharist, *p. 897.*

Prayer over the Gifts

Pray, brethren...

Lord,
be close to your people,
accept our prayers and offerings,
and let us turn to you with all our hearts.

We ask this in the name of Jesus the Lord.

Preface of Lent I–IV, *pp. 940–942.*

Communion Antiphon

Everyone who asks will receive; whoever seeks shall find, and to him who knocks it shall be opened.   (Mt 7:8)

Prayer after Communion

Let us pray.

> *Pause for silent prayer, if this has not preceded.*

Lord our God,
renew us by these mysteries.
May they heal us now
and bring us eternal salvation.

Grant this through Christ our Lord.

Friday

Entrance Antiphon

Lord, deliver me from my distress. See my hardship and my poverty, and pardon all my sins. (Ps 24:17–18)

Opening Prayer

Lord,
may our observance of Lent
help to renew us and prepare us
to celebrate the death and resurrection of Christ,
who lives and reigns with you and the Holy Spirit,
one God, for ever and ever.

TODAY'S LIVING WORD

In today's first reading the prophet Ezekiel sheds new light on the law of Israel, while in today's Gospel the prophet Jesus does the same. The law Ezekiel is concerned with is found in Deuteronomy and states that each individual is responsible for his or her own actions. "Only for his own guilt shall a man be put to death" (24:16). Ezekiel expands on this point of law and explores what happens when an individual repents. "If the wicked man turns away from all the sins he committed," he says, "he shall surely live, he shall not die." The law Jesus is concerned with is, of course, what we know as the fifth commandment (cf. Ex 20:13). Jesus expands the prohibition of murder to include anger, abusive language, and an attitude of contempt, all of which can lead to murder.

Neither Ezekiel nor Jesus is tampering with the law; rather each in his own way is taking the law to a greater depth. The only difference is that Ezekiel is doing so as God's agent, and Matthew's Jesus as himself the arbiter of God's law.

FIRST READING   Ez 18:21–28

Do I derive any pleasure from the death of the wicked
and not rejoice when he turns from his evil way that he may live?

A reading from the Book of the Prophet Ezekiel

Thus says the Lord GOD: If the wicked man turns away from all the sins he committed, if he keeps all my statutes and does what is right and just, he shall surely live, he shall not die. None of the crimes he committed shall be remembered against him; he shall live because of the virtue he has practiced. Do I indeed derive any pleasure from the death of the wicked? says the Lord GOD. Do I not rather rejoice when he turns from his evil way that he may live?

And if the virtuous man turns from the path of virtue to do evil, the same kind of abominable things that the wicked man does, can he do this and still live? None of his virtuous deeds shall be remembered, because he has broken faith and committed sin; because of this, he shall die. You say, "The LORD's way is not fair!" Hear now, house of Israel: Is it my way that is unfair, or rather, are not your ways unfair? When someone virtuous turns away from virtue to commit iniquity, and dies, it is because of the iniquity he committed that he must die. But if the wicked, turning from the wickedness he has committed, does what is right and just, he shall preserve his life; since he has turned away from all the sins that he committed, he shall surely live, he shall not die.

The word of the Lord.

Responsorial Psalm

Ps 130:1–2, 3–4, 5–7a, 7bc–8

R. If you, O Lord, mark iniquities, who can stand?

Out of the depths I cry to you, O LORD;
  LORD, hear my voice!
Let your ears be attentive
  to my voice in supplication.

R. If you, O Lord, mark iniquities, who can stand?

If you, O LORD, mark iniquities,
  LORD, who can stand?
But with you is forgiveness,
  that you may be revered.

R. If you, O Lord, mark iniquities, who can stand?

I trust in the LORD;
  my soul trusts in his word.
My soul waits for the LORD
  more than sentinels wait for the dawn.
  Let Israel wait for the LORD.

R. If you, O Lord, mark iniquities, who can stand?

For with the LORD is kindness
  and with him is plenteous redemption;
And he will redeem Israel
  from all their iniquities.

R. If you, O Lord, mark iniquities, who can stand?

Verse Before the Gospel   Ez 18:31

Cast away from you all the crimes
you have committed, says the Lord,
and make for yourselves a new heart and a new spirit.

GOSPEL

Go first and be reconciled with your brother.

A reading from the holy Gospel according to Matthew

Jesus said to his disciples: "I tell you, unless your righteousness surpasses that of the scribes and Pharisees, you will not enter into the Kingdom of heaven.

"You have heard that it was said to your ancestors, *You shall not kill; and whoever kills will be liable to judgment.* But I say to you, whoever is angry with his brother will be liable to judgment, and whoever says to his brother, *Raqa*, will be answerable to the Sanhedrin, and whoever says, 'You fool,' will be liable to fiery Gehenna. Therefore, if you bring your gift to the altar, and there recall that your brother has anything against you, leave your gift there at the altar, go first and be reconciled with your brother, and then come and offer your gift. Settle with your opponent quickly while on the way to court. Otherwise your opponent will hand you over to the judge, and the judge will hand you over to the guard, and you will be thrown into prison. Amen, I say to you, you will not be released until you have paid the last penny."

The Gospel of the Lord.

Liturgy of the Eucharist, *p. 897*.

Prayer over the Gifts

Pray, brethren...

Lord of mercy,
in your love accept these gifts.
May they bring us your saving power.
We ask this in the name of Jesus the Lord.

Preface of Lent I–IV, *pp. 940–942*.

Communion Antiphon

By my life, I do not wish the sinner to die, says the Lord, but to turn to me and live. (Ez 33:11)

Prayer after Communion

Let us pray.

Pause for silent prayer, if this has not preceded.

Lord,
may the sacrament you give us
free us from our sinful ways and bring us new life.
May this eucharist lead us to salvation.

Grant this through Christ our Lord.

Saturday

Entrance Antiphon

The law of the Lord is perfect, reviving the soul; his commandments are the wisdom of the simple. (Ps 18:8)

Opening Prayer

Eternal Father,
turn our hearts to you.
By seeking your kingdom
and loving one another,
may we become a people who worship you
in spirit and truth.

Grant this through our Lord Jesus Christ, your Son,
who lives and reigns with you and the Holy Spirit,
one God, for ever and ever.

TODAY'S LIVING WORD

In today's reading from Deuteronomy, Moses solemnly declares that the distinguishing mark of Israel's divine election as the cherished, chosen people of God is that they wholeheartedly observe God's commandments, statutes and decrees. In today's excerpt from the Sermon on the Mount, Jesus tells his disciples that the distinguishing mark of their divine sonship is that they love their enemies. In fact, his words echo the Book of Deuteronomy: "You are children of the Lord your God" (14:1).

Both readings tell us that to be chosen by God, to be children of God brings with it an awesome responsibility. It demands that we act accordingly. The holiness of our lives must show forth the wholeness (the "perfection") of God. Reflecting on this, Dag Hammarskjöld wrote, "Your responsibility is indeed terrifying…. You fancy you can be responsible *to* God; can you carry the responsibility *for* God?"*

* *Markings,* trans. Leif Sjoberg & W. H. Auden (New York: Ballantine Books, 1964), p. 135.

FIRST READING

Dt 26:16–19

You will be a people sacred to the LORD God.

A reading from the Book of Deuteronomy

Moses spoke to the people, saying: "This day the LORD, your God, commands you to observe these statutes and decrees. Be careful, then, to observe them with all your heart and with all your soul. Today you are making this agreement with the LORD: he is to be your God and you are to walk in his ways and observe his statutes, commandments and decrees, and to hearken to his voice. And today the LORD is making this agreement with you: you are to be a people peculiarly his own, as he promised you; and provided you keep all his commandments, he will then raise you high in praise and renown and glory above all other nations he has made, and you will be a people sacred to the LORD, your God, as he promised."

The word of the Lord.

Responsorial Psalm

Ps 119:1–2, 4–5, 7–8

R. Blessed are they who follow the law of the Lord!

Blessed are they whose way is blameless,
  who walk in the law of the LORD.
Blessed are they who observe his decrees,
  who seek him with all their heart.

R. Blessed are they who follow the law of the Lord!

You have commanded that your precepts
  be diligently kept.
Oh, that I might be firm in the ways
  of keeping your statutes!

R. Blessed are they who follow the law of the Lord!

I will give you thanks with an upright heart,
  when I have learned your just ordinances.
I will keep your statutes;
  do not utterly forsake me.

R. Blessed are they who follow the law of the Lord!

Verse Before the Gospel   2 Cor 6:2b
Behold, now is a very acceptable time;
behold, now is the day of salvation.

GOSPEL

Mt 5:43 – 48

Be perfect, just as your heavenly Father is perfect.

A reading from the holy Gospel according to Matthew

Jesus said to his disciples: "You have heard that it was said, *You shall love your neighbor and hate your enemy.* But I say to you, love your enemies, and pray for those who persecute you, that you may be children of your heavenly Father, for he makes his sun rise on the bad and the good, and causes rain to fall on the just and the unjust. For if you love those who love you, what recompense will you have? Do not the tax collectors do the same? And if you greet your brothers and sisters only, what is unusual about that? Do not the pagans do the same? So be perfect, just as your heavenly Father is perfect."

The Gospel of the Lord.

Liturgy of the Eucharist, *p. 897.*

Prayer over the Gifts

Pray, brethren...

Lord,
may we be renewed by this eucharist.
May we become more like Christ your Son,
who is Lord for ever and ever.

Preface of Lent I–IV, *pp. 940–942.*

Communion Antiphon

Be perfect, as your heavenly Father is perfect, says the Lord.
(Mt 5:48)

Prayer after Communion

Let us pray.

Pause for silent prayer, if this has not preceded.

Lord,
may the word we share
be our guide to peace in your kingdom.
May the food we receive
assure us of your constant love.
We ask this in the name of Jesus the Lord.

SECOND WEEK OF LENT
Monday

Entrance Antiphon

Redeem me, Lord, and have mercy on me; my foot is set on the right path, I worship you in the great assembly.

(Ps 25:11–12)

Opening Prayer

God our Father,
teach us to find new life through penance.
Keep us from sin,
and help us live by your commandment of love.

We ask this through our Lord Jesus Christ, your Son,
who lives and reigns with you and the Holy Spirit,
one God, for ever and ever.

TODAY'S LIVING WORD

Both of today's readings acknowledge the compassion of God. In the prayer from the Book of Daniel, an exiled people cry for mercy. They admit their guilt but dare to remind God: "Yours, O Lord, our God, are compassion and forgiveness!" The Gospel opens with a call to "Be merciful, just as your Father is merciful," that is, not to judge or condemn. But because this is Luke's version of this saying of Jesus, it has another meaning too.

For Luke sharing material possessions is a hallmark of true discipleship. Today's saying, which occurs in the Sermon on the Plain, carries this economic sense as well. In the verses immediately preceding today's, Luke indicates that loving enemies includes sharing one's goods with them. Similarly, these verses show that pardoning others involves canceling their debts. This concretizes the command of Jesus. Compassion costs, but it will also be richly rewarded with a "lapful" of good things.

FIRST READING

We have sinned, been wicked and done evil.

A reading from the Book of the Prophet Daniel

"Lord, great and awesome God, you who keep your merciful covenant toward those who love you and observe your commandments! We have sinned, been wicked and done evil; we have rebelled and departed from your commandments and your laws. We have not obeyed your servants the prophets, who spoke in your name to our kings, our princes, our fathers, and all the people of the land. Justice, O Lord, is on your side; we are shamefaced even to this day: we, the men of Judah, the residents of Jerusalem, and all Israel, near and far, in all the countries to which you have scattered them because of their treachery toward you. O Lord, we are shamefaced, like our kings, our princes, and our fathers, for having sinned against you. But yours, O Lord, our God, are compassion and forgiveness! Yet we rebelled against you and paid no heed to your command, O Lord, our God, to live by the law you gave us through your servants the prophets."

The word of the Lord.

Responsorial Psalm

R. Lord, do not deal with us according to our sins.

Remember not against us the iniquities of the past;
    may your compassion quickly come to us,
    for we are brought very low.

R. Lord, do not deal with us according to our sins.

Help us, O God our savior,
    because of the glory of your name;
Deliver us and pardon our sins
    for your name's sake.

R. Lord, do not deal with us according to our sins.

Let the prisoners' sighing come before you;
   with your great power free those doomed to death.
Then we, your people and the sheep of your pasture,
   will give thanks to you forever;
   through all generations we will declare your praise.

R. Lord, do not deal with us according to our sins.

Verse Before the Gospel See Jn 6:63c, 68c
Your words, Lord, are Spirit and life;
you have the words of everlasting life.

GOSPEL   Lk 6:36–38

Forgive and you will be forgiven.

A reading from the holy Gospel according to Luke

Jesus said to his disciples: "Be merciful, just as your Father is merciful.

   "Stop judging and you will not be judged. Stop condemning and you will not be condemned. Forgive and you will be forgiven. Give and gifts will be given to you; a good measure, packed together, shaken down, and overflowing, will be poured into your lap. For the measure with which you measure will in return be measured out to you."

The Gospel of the Lord.

Liturgy of the Eucharist, *p. 897.*

Prayer over the Gifts

Pray, brethren...

Father of mercy,
hear our prayer.
May the grace of this mystery
prevent us from becoming absorbed in material things.
Grant this through Christ our Lord.

Preface of Lent I–IV, *pp. 940–942.*

Communion Antiphon

Be merciful as your Father is merciful, says the Lord.

(Lk 6:36)

Prayer after Communion

Let us pray.

Pause for silent prayer, if this has not preceded.

Lord,
may this communion bring us pardon
and lead us to the joy of heaven.

We ask this in the name of Jesus the Lord.

Tuesday

Entrance Antiphon

Give light to my eyes, Lord, lest I sleep in death, and my enemy say: I have overcome him.

(Ps 12:4–5)

Opening Prayer

Lord,
watch over your Church,
and guide it with your unfailing love.
Protect us from what could harm us
and lead us to what will save us.
Help us always,
for without you we are bound to fail.

Grant this through our Lord Jesus Christ, your Son,
who lives and reigns with you and the Holy Spirit,
one God, for ever and ever.

Today's Living Word

Today's readings are aimed at rulers responsible for the administration of their respective communities. Isaiah has in mind the princes of Judah whom he urges to act with justice on behalf of the powerless and the poor. The Gospel seems to attack the scribes and Pharisees, but the real targets of Matthew's Jesus are Christian leaders who would imitate certain of the scribes and Pharisees of their day. "You have but one teacher," says Jesus, "you have but one master."

The second part of Isaiah's oracle, on the other hand, is a call to conversion that reaches beyond the ruling class to all God's people, then and now. The prophet says that they stand at a crossroad and must choose the path of salvation or of destruction, to "eat the good things of the land" or to be themselves eaten by the sword. At this critical juncture, God invites them to "set things right." Forgiveness is possible, but the choice is theirs—and ours.

FIRST READING

Is 1:10, 16–20

Learn to do good; make justice your aim.

A reading from the Book of the Prophet Isaiah

Hear the word of the LORD,
    princes of Sodom!
Listen to the instruction of our God,
    people of Gomorrah!
Wash yourselves clean!
Put away your misdeeds from before my eyes;
    cease doing evil; learn to do good.
Make justice your aim: redress the wronged,
    hear the orphan's plea, defend the widow.
Come now, let us set things right,
    says the LORD:
Though your sins be like scarlet,
    they may become white as snow;

Though they be crimson red,
  they may become white as wool.
If you are willing, and obey,
  you shall eat the good things of the land;
But if you refuse and resist,
  the sword shall consume you:
  for the mouth of the LORD has spoken!

The word of the Lord.

Responsorial Psalm
Ps 50:8–9, 16bc–17, 21 and 23

R. To the upright I will show the saving power of God.

"Not for your sacrifices do I rebuke you,
  for your burnt offerings are before me always.
I take from your house no bullock,
  no goats out of your fold."

R. To the upright I will show the saving power of God.

"Why do you recite my statutes,
  and profess my covenant with your mouth,
Though you hate discipline
  and cast my words behind you?"

R. To the upright I will show the saving power of God.

"When you do these things, shall I be deaf to it?
  Or do you think that I am like yourself?
  I will correct you by drawing them up before your eyes.
He that offers praise as a sacrifice glorifies me;
  and to him that goes the right way I will show the salvation of God."

R. To the upright I will show the saving power of God.

Verse Before the Gospel Ez 18:31
Cast away from you all the crimes
you have committed, says the Lord,
and make for yourselves a new heart and a new spirit.

GOSPEL

Mt 23:1–12

They preach but they do not practice.

A reading from the holy Gospel according to Matthew

Jesus spoke to the crowds and to his disciples, saying, "The scribes and the Pharisees have taken their seat on the chair of Moses. Therefore, do and observe all things whatsoever they tell you, but do not follow their example. For they preach but they do not practice. They tie up heavy burdens hard to carry and lay them on people's shoulders, but they will not lift a finger to move them. All their works are performed to be seen. They widen their phylacteries and lengthen their tassels. They love places of honor at banquets, seats of honor in synagogues, greetings in marketplaces, and the salutation 'Rabbi.' As for you, do not be called 'Rabbi.' You have but one teacher, and you are all brothers. Call no one on earth your father; you have but one Father in heaven. Do not be called 'Master'; you have but one master, the Christ. The greatest among you must be your servant. Whoever exalts himself will be humbled; but whoever humbles himself will be exalted."

The Gospel of the Lord.

Liturgy of the Eucharist, *p. 897.*

Prayer over the Gifts

Pray, brethren...

Lord,
bring us closer to you by this celebration.
May it cleanse us from our faults
and lead us to the gifts of heaven.
We ask this through Christ our Lord.

Preface of Lent I–IV, *pp. 940–942.*

Communion Antiphon

I will tell all your marvelous works. I will rejoice and be glad in you, and sing to your name, Most High.　　(Ps 9:2–3)

Prayer after Communion

Let us pray.

Pause for silent prayer, if this has not preceded.

Lord,
may the food we receive
bring us your constant assistance
that we may live better lives.

We ask this in the name of Jesus the Lord.

Wednesday

Entrance Antiphon

Do not abandon me, Lord. My God, do not go away from me! Hurry to help me, Lord, my Savior.　　(Ps 37:22–23)

Opening Prayer

Father,
teach us to live good lives,
encourage us with your support
and bring us to eternal life.

We ask this through our Lord Jesus Christ, your Son,
who lives and reigns with you and the Holy Spirit,
one God, for ever and ever.

TODAY'S LIVING WORD

The readings for today reveal the plotting of certain citizens of Jerusalem to kill Jeremiah and Jesus. This is the context of Jeremiah's prayer and the content of Jesus' third prediction of the passion. Both men are tragically misunderstood. Jeremiah's adversaries reason that they have nothing to lose by destroying Jeremiah—not instruction from the priests, nor counsel from the wise, nor messages from the prophets. They fail to appreciate how often the prayer of Jeremiah has averted God's wrath. In the Gospel, even Jesus' disciples fail to understand the significance of his words. This is made embarrassingly clear by the request of Zebedee's sons, which Matthew has put on the lips of their mother.

Without their knowing it, however, the request of Zebedee's sons and Jesus' reply implicate them in the suffering of Jesus. "My chalice you will indeed drink," he tells them. Like them, so must we be ready to give our lives as he did to serve the needs of all, we who in the Eucharist eat the bread and drink the cup of Jesus.

FIRST READING
Jer 18:18–20

Come, let us persecute him.

A reading from the Book of the Prophet Jeremiah

The people of Judah and the citizens of Jerusalem said, "Come, let us contrive a plot against Jeremiah. It will not mean the loss of instruction from the priests, nor of counsel from the wise, nor of messages from the prophets. And so, let us destroy him by his own tongue; let us carefully note his every word."

Heed me, O LORD,
    and listen to what my adversaries say.
Must good be repaid with evil
    that they should dig a pit to take my life?
Remember that I stood before you
    to speak in their behalf,
    to turn away your wrath from them.

The word of the Lord.

Responsorial Psalm
Ps 31:5–6, 14, 15–16

R. Save me, O Lord, in your kindness.

You will free me from the snare they set for me,
  for you are my refuge.
Into your hands I commend my spirit;
  you will redeem me, O Lord, O faithful God.

  R. Save me, O Lord, in your kindness.

I hear the whispers of the crowd, that frighten me from every side,
  as they consult together against me, plotting to take my life.

  R. Save me, O Lord, in your kindness.

But my trust is in you, O Lord;
  I say, "You are my God."
In your hands is my destiny; rescue me
  from the clutches of my enemies and my persecutors.

  R. Save me, O Lord, in your kindness.

Verse Before the Gospel Jn 8:12
  I am the light of the world, says the Lord;
  whoever follows me will have the light of life.

GOSPEL   Mt 20:17–28

They will condemn the Son of Man to death.

A reading from the holy Gospel according to Matthew

As Jesus was going up to Jerusalem, he took the Twelve disciples aside by themselves, and said to them on the way, "Behold, we are going up to Jerusalem, and the Son of Man will be handed over to the chief priests and the scribes, and they will condemn him to death, and hand him over to the Gentiles to be mocked and scourged and crucified, and he will be raised on the third day."

  Then the mother of the sons of Zebedee approached Jesus with her sons and did him homage, wishing to ask him for something. He said to her, "What do you wish?" She answered him, "Command that these two sons of mine sit, one at your right and the other at your left, in your kingdom." Jesus said in reply, "You do not know what you are asking. Can you drink the chalice that I am going to drink?" They said to him, "We can." He replied, "My chalice you will indeed drink, but to sit at my right and at my left, this is not mine to give but is for those for whom it has been prepared by my Father." When the ten heard this, they became indignant at the two brothers. But Jesus summoned them and said, "You know that the rulers of the Gentiles lord it over them, and the great ones make their authority over them felt. But it shall not be so among you. Rather, whoever wishes to be great among you shall be your servant; whoever wishes to be first among you shall be your slave. Just so, the Son of Man did not come to be served but to serve and to give his life as a ransom for many."

The Gospel of the Lord.

Liturgy of the Eucharist, *p. 897.*

Prayer over the Gifts

Pray, brethren...

Lord,
accept this sacrifice,
and through this holy exchange of gifts
free us from the sins that enslave us.

We ask this in the name of Jesus the Lord.

Preface of Lent I–IV, *pp. 940–942.*

Communion Antiphon

The Son of Man did not come to be served, but to serve, and to give his life as a ransom for many.   (Mt 20:28)

Prayer after Communion

Let us pray.

Pause for silent prayer, if this has not preceded.

Lord our God,
may the eucharist you give us
as a pledge of unending life
help us to salvation.

Grant this through Christ our Lord.

Thursday

Entrance Antiphon

Test me, O God, and know my thoughts; see whether I step in the wrong path, and guide me along the everlasting way.

(Ps 138:23 – 24)

Opening Prayer

God of love,
bring us back to you.
Send your Spirit to make us strong in faith
and active in good works.

Grant this through our Lord Jesus Christ, your Son,
who lives and reigns with you and the Holy Spirit,
one God, for ever and ever.

TODAY'S LIVING WORD

The words of Jeremiah in today's first reading sound a theme that reaches back to Genesis. "More tortuous than all else is the human heart, beyond remedy," the prophet declares. This was God's conclusion too in the aftermath of the flood: "The desires of man's heart are evil from the start" (Gn 9:21). Today's Gospel parable probes the mind and tests the heart of a rich man, for the instruction of Jesus' hearers. So deluded is this man that even in torment in "the netherworld," he cannot grasp the reality of his situation. Claiming Abraham as his father, he tries to commandeer the services of Lazarus to fetch him water and to warn his brothers. But his efforts are all in vain, for God gives to everyone "according to the merit of his deeds."

Typically, for Luke the perversity of the rich man's heart is revealed in his neglect of the poor man who lay at his door. This may be a clue for us too who have not only the words of Moses and the prophets to guide us, but the witness of Jesus who rose from the dead.

FIRST READING
Jer 17:5–10

A curse on those who trust in mortals;
a blessing on those who trust in the Lord God.

A reading from the Book of the Prophet Jeremiah

Thus says the LORD:

Cursed is the man who trusts in human beings,
    who seeks his strength in flesh,
    whose heart turns away from the LORD.
He is like a barren bush in the desert
    that enjoys no change of season,
But stands in a lava waste,
    a salt and empty earth.
Blessed is the man who trusts in the LORD,
    whose hope is the LORD.
He is like a tree planted beside the waters
    that stretches out its roots to the stream:
It fears not the heat when it comes,
    its leaves stay green;
In the year of drought it shows no distress,
    but still bears fruit.
More tortuous than all else is the human heart,
    beyond remedy; who can understand it?
I, the LORD, alone probe the mind

and test the heart,
To reward everyone according to his ways,
according to the merit of his deeds.

The word of the Lord.

Responsorial Psalm

Ps 1:1–2, 3, 4 and 6

R. **Blessed are they who hope in the Lord.**

Blessed the man who follows not
the counsel of the wicked
Nor walks in the way of sinners,
nor sits in the company of the insolent,
But delights in the law of the LORD
and meditates on his law day and night.

R. **Blessed are they who hope in the Lord.**

He is like a tree
planted near running water,
That yields its fruit in due season,
and whose leaves never fade.
Whatever he does, prospers.

R. **Blessed are they who hope in the Lord.**

Not so, the wicked, not so;
they are like chaff which the wind drives away.
For the LORD watches over the way of the just,
but the way of the wicked vanishes.

R. **Blessed are they who hope in the Lord.**

Verse Before the Gospel   See Lk 8:15
Blessed are they who have kept the word with a generous heart
and yield a harvest through perseverance.

GOSPEL

Lk 16:19–31

Good things came to you and bad things to Lazarus;
now he is comforted while you are in agony.

A reading from the holy Gospel according to Luke

Jesus said to the Pharisees: "There was a rich man who dressed in purple garments and fine linen and dined sumptuously each day. And lying at his door was a poor man named Lazarus, covered with sores, who would gladly have eaten his fill of the scraps that fell from the rich man's table. Dogs even used to come and lick his sores. When the poor man died, he was carried away by angels to the bosom of Abraham. The rich man also died and was buried, and from the netherworld, where he was in torment, he raised his eyes and saw Abraham far off and Lazarus at his side. And he cried out, 'Father Abraham, have pity on me. Send Lazarus to dip the tip of his finger in water and cool my tongue, for I am suffering torment in these flames.' Abraham replied, 'My child, remember that you received what was good during your lifetime while Lazarus likewise received what was bad; but now he is comforted here, whereas you are tormented. Moreover, between us and you a great chasm is established to prevent anyone from crossing who might wish to go from our side to yours or from your side to ours.' He said, 'Then I beg you, father, send him to my father's house, for I have five brothers, so that he may warn them, lest they too come to this place of torment.' But Abraham replied, 'They have Moses and the prophets. Let them listen to them.' He said, 'Oh no, father Abraham, but if someone from the dead goes to them, they will repent.' Then Abraham said, 'If they will not listen to Moses and the prophets, neither will they be persuaded if someone should rise from the dead.' "
The Gospel of the Lord.

Liturgy of the Eucharist, *p. 897.*

Prayer over the Gifts

Pray, brethren...

Lord,
may this sacrifice bless our lenten observance.
May it lead us to sincere repentance.
We ask this through Christ our Lord.

Preface of Lent I–IV, *pp. 940–942.*

Communion Antiphon

Happy are those of blameless life, who follow the law of the Lord.   (Ps 118:1)

Prayer after Communion

Let us pray.
Pause for silent prayer, if this has not preceded.
Lord,
may the sacrifice we have offered strengthen our faith
and be seen in our love for one another.
We ask this in the name of Jesus the Lord.

Friday

Entrance Antiphon

To you, Lord, I look for protection, never let me be disgraced. You are my refuge; save me from the trap they have laid for me.
(Ps 30:2, 5)

Opening Prayer

Merciful Father,
may our acts of penance bring us your forgiveness,
open our hearts to your love,
and prepare us for the coming feast of the resurrection.

We ask this through our Lord Jesus Christ, your Son,
who lives and reigns with you and the Holy Spirit,
one God, for ever and ever.

TODAY'S LIVING WORD

Joining the story of the betrayal of Joseph to the parable of the tenants sharpens the poignancy of the Gospel portrait of Jesus. The parable places Jesus in the long line of God's servants who, sent as messengers to Israel, were sometimes brutally rejected (cf. Neh 9:26). To this, the story of Joseph adds the theme of betrayal by one's own. Both texts, the story from Genesis and the parable in Matthew, have undergone revision. In the Genesis account, Reuben vies with Judah to be the hero of the story. In Matthew's version of the parable, the punishment of the tenants is meant to evoke the destruction of Jerusalem by the Romans in 70 C.E. For us, however, the interest lies in how these texts interpret the passion and death of Jesus.

The parable suggests that the death of Jesus will bring about a dramatic change in the leadership of Israel, God's vineyard (cf. Is 5:1–7). No doubt Matthew anticipates the claim of his community that the vineyard has been given to them. For Christians, the story of Joseph suggests how the Son of God, betrayed by his brothers, may in God's plan and purpose be their salvation.

FIRST READING

Gn 37:3–4, 12–13a, 17b–28a

Here comes the man of dreams; let us kill him.

A reading from the Book of Genesis

Israel loved Joseph best of all his sons, for he was the child of his old age; and he had made him a long tunic. When his brothers saw that their father loved him best of all his sons, they hated him so much that they would not even greet him.

One day, when his brothers had gone to pasture their father's flocks at Shechem, Israel said to Joseph, "Your brothers, you know, are tending our flocks at Shechem. Get ready; I will send you to them."

So Joseph went after his brothers and caught up with them in Dothan. They noticed him from a distance, and before he came up to them, they plotted to kill him. They said to one another: "Here comes that master dreamer! Come on, let us kill him and throw him into one of the cisterns here; we could say that a wild beast devoured him. We shall then see what comes of his dreams."

When Reuben heard this, he tried to save him from their hands, saying, "We must not take his life. Instead of shedding blood," he continued, "just throw him into that cistern there in the desert; but do not kill him outright." His purpose was to rescue him from their hands and return him to his father. So when Joseph came up to them, they stripped him of the long tunic he had on; then they took him and threw him into the cistern, which was empty and dry.

They then sat down to their meal. Looking up, they saw a caravan of Ishmaelites coming from Gilead, their camels laden with gum, balm and resin to be taken down to Egypt. Judah said to his brothers: "What is to be gained by killing our brother and concealing his blood? Rather, let us sell him to these Ishmaelites, instead of doing away with him ourselves. After all, he is our brother, our own flesh." His brothers agreed. They sold Joseph to the Ishmaelites for twenty pieces of silver.

The word of the Lord.

Responsorial Psalm   Ps 105:16–17, 18–19, 20–21

   R. **Remember the marvels the Lord has done.**

When the LORD called down a famine on the land
   and ruined the crop that sustained them,
He sent a man before them,
   Joseph, sold as a slave.

R. Remember the marvels the Lord has done.

They had weighed him down with fetters,
   and he was bound with chains,
Till his prediction came to pass
   and the word of the LORD proved him true.

R. Remember the marvels the Lord has done.

The king sent and released him,
   the ruler of the peoples set him free.
He made him lord of his house
   and ruler of all his possessions.

R. Remember the marvels the Lord has done.

Verse Before the Gospel   Jn 3:16
God so loved the world that he gave his only-begotten Son;
so that everyone who believes in him might have eternal life.

GOSPEL   Mt 21:33–43, 45–46

This is the heir; let us kill him.

A reading from the holy Gospel according to Matthew

Jesus said to the chief priests and the elders of the people:
"Hear another parable. There was a landowner who planted a
vineyard, put a hedge around it, dug a wine press in it, and
built a tower. Then he leased it to tenants and went on a journey.
When vintage time drew near, he sent his servants to the tenants
to obtain his produce. But the tenants seized the servants and
one they beat, another they killed, and a third they stoned.
Again he sent other servants, more numerous than the first
ones, but they treated them in the same way. Finally, he sent
his son to them, thinking, 'They will respect my son.' But when
the tenants saw the son, they said to one another, 'This is the
heir. Come, let us kill him and acquire his inheritance.' They
seized him, threw him out of the vineyard, and killed him.

What will the owner of the vineyard do to those tenants when he comes?" They answered him, "He will put those wretched men to a wretched death and lease his vineyard to other tenants who will give him the produce at the proper times." Jesus said to them, "Did you never read in the Scriptures:

> The stone that the builders rejected
>   has become the cornerstone;
> by the Lord has this been done,
>   and it is wonderful in our eyes?

Therefore, I say to you, the Kingdom of God will be taken away from you and given to a people that will produce its fruit." When the chief priests and the Pharisees heard his parables, they knew that he was speaking about them. And although they were attempting to arrest him, they feared the crowds, for they regarded him as a prophet.

The Gospel of the Lord.

Liturgy of the Eucharist, *p. 897.*

Prayer over the Gifts

Pray, brethren...

God of mercy,
prepare us to celebrate these mysteries.
Help us to live the love they proclaim.

We ask this in the name of Jesus the Lord.

Preface of Lent I–IV, *pp. 940–942.*

Communion Antiphon

God loved us and sent his Son to take away our sins.

(1 Jn 4:10)

Prayer after Communion

Let us pray.

Pause for silent prayer, if this has not preceded.

Lord,
may this communion so change our lives
that we may seek more faithfully
the salvation it promises.

Grant this through Christ our Lord.

Saturday

Entrance Antiphon

**The Lord is loving and merciful, to anger slow, and full of love;
the Lord is kind to all, and compassionate to all his creatures.**

(Ps 144:8–9)

Opening Prayer

God our Father,
by your gifts to us on earth
we already share in your life.
In all we do,
guide us to the light of your kingdom.

Grant this through our Lord Jesus Christ, your Son,
who lives and reigns with you and the Holy Spirit,
one God, for ever and ever.

TODAY'S LIVING WORD

The prophecy of Micah concludes with a prayer for forgiveness,
a prayer made possible by the image that introduces it. The Shepherd
of Israel, who performed wonderful signs in "days of old" when they
came home from the land of Egypt, is ready to act once more.

Therefore, Israel prays with confidence that all their sins will be "cast into the depths of the sea," utterly forgotten. The same image dominates the parable of the prodigal son. Here again, true repentance brings about a total reversal of the sinner's lot. The son is fully restored as a son in his father's house, not as a servant. As Luke Timothy Johnson puts it, "the first part of the story is pure Gospel."*

The second part of the story, however, may address us more directly. As often happens in Luke, the Gospel reveals the thoughts of many hearts (cf. 2:35). The father's graciousness to the prodigal son exposes the smoldering rage and resentment of the "good son." His fidelity, grudgingly given, has been a kind of slavery. "All these years I served you," he says. Luke does not tell us what the good son does in the end. But it is comforting to know that his father came out to him as well.

* The Gospel of Luke, Sacra Pagina 3 (Collegeville: Liturgical Press, 1991), p. 242.

FIRST READING   Mi 7:14–15, 18–20

God will cast our sins into the depths of the sea.

A reading from the Book of the Prophet Micah

Shepherd your people with your staff,
    the flock of your inheritance,
That dwells apart in a woodland,
    in the midst of Carmel.
Let them feed in Bashan and Gilead,
    as in the days of old;
As in the days when you came from the land of Egypt,
    show us wonderful signs.

Who is there like you, the God who removes guilt
    and pardons sin for the remnant of his inheritance;
Who does not persist in anger forever,
    but delights rather in clemency,
And will again have compassion on us,
    treading underfoot our guilt?

You will cast into the depths of the sea all our sins;
You will show faithfulness to Jacob,
>   and grace to Abraham,
As you have sworn to our fathers
>   from days of old.
The word of the Lord.

Responsorial Psalm

Ps 103:1–2, 3–4, 9–10, 11–12

R. The Lord is kind and merciful.

Bless the LORD, O my soul;
>   and all my being, bless his holy name.
Bless the LORD, O my soul,
>   and forget not all his benefits.

R. The Lord is kind and merciful.

He pardons all your iniquities,
>   he heals all your ills.
He redeems your life from destruction,
>   he crowns you with kindness and compassion.

R. The Lord is kind and merciful.

He will not always chide,
>   nor does he keep his wrath forever.
Not according to our sins does he deal with us,
>   nor does he requite us according to our crimes.

R. The Lord is kind and merciful.

For as the heavens are high above the earth,
>   so surpassing is his kindness toward those who fear him.
As far as the east is from the west,
>   so far has he put our transgressions from us.

R. The Lord is kind and merciful.

Verse Before the Gospel Lk 15:18
>   I will get up and go to my father and shall say to him,
>   Father, I have sinned against heaven and against you.

GOSPEL

Your brother was dead and has come to life.

A reading from the holy Gospel according to Luke

Tax collectors and sinners were all drawing near to listen to Jesus, but the Pharisees and scribes began to complain, saying, "This man welcomes sinners and eats with them." So to them Jesus addressed this parable. "A man had two sons, and the younger son said to his father, 'Father, give me the share of your estate that should come to me.' So the father divided the property between them. After a few days, the younger son collected all his belongings and set off to a distant country where he squandered his inheritance on a life of dissipation. When he had freely spent everything, a severe famine struck that country, and he found himself in dire need. So he hired himself out to one of the local citizens who sent him to his farm to tend the swine. And he longed to eat his fill of the pods on which the swine fed, but nobody gave him any. Coming to his senses he thought, 'How many of my father's hired workers have more than enough food to eat, but here am I, dying from hunger. I shall get up and go to my father and I shall say to him, "Father, I have sinned against heaven and against you. I no longer deserve to be called your son; treat me as you would treat one of your hired workers."' So he got up and went back to his father. While he was still a long way off, his father caught sight of him, and was filled with compassion. He ran to his son, embraced him and kissed him. His son said to him, 'Father, I have sinned against heaven and against you; I no longer deserve to be called your son.' But his father ordered his servants, 'Quickly, bring the finest robe and put it on him; put a ring on his finger and sandals on his

feet. Take the fattened calf and slaughter it. Then let us celebrate with a feast, because this son of mine was dead, and
has come to life again; he was lost, and has been found.' Then
the celebration began. Now the older son had been out in the
field and, on his way back, as he neared the house, he heard
the sound of music and dancing. He called one of the servants
and asked what this might mean. The servant said to him,
'Your brother has returned and your father has slaughtered
the fattened calf because he has him back safe and sound.' He
became angry, and when he refused to enter the house, his
father came out and pleaded with him. He said to his father in
reply, 'Look, all these years I served you and not once did I
disobey your orders; yet you never gave me even a young
goat to feast on with my friends. But when your son returns
who swallowed up your property with prostitutes, for him
you slaughter the fattened calf.' He said to him, 'My son, you
are here with me always; everything I have is yours. But now
we must celebrate and rejoice, because your brother was dead
and has come to life again; he was lost and has been found.' "

The Gospel of the Lord.

Liturgy of the Eucharist, *p. 897.*

Prayer over the Gifts

Pray, brethren...

Lord,
may the grace of these sacraments
help us to reject all harmful things
and lead us to your spiritual gifts.

We ask this through Christ our Lord.

Preface of Lent I–IV, *pp. 940–942.*

Communion Antiphon

**My son, you should rejoice, because your brother was dead
and has come back to life; he was lost and is found.**   (Lk 15:32)

Prayer after Communion

Let us pray.

Pause for silent prayer, if this has not preceded.

Lord,
give us the spirit of love
and lead us to share in your life.
We ask this in the name of Jesus the Lord.

OPTIONAL MASS FOR
THE THIRD WEEK OF LENT

*This Mass may be used on any day of this week, especially in Cycles B
and C when the Gospel of the Samaritan woman is not read on the Third
Sunday of Lent.*

TODAY'S LIVING WORD

The climate of Palestine made biblical people appreciate the
necessity of water for life. So it is not surprising that water became
in the Bible a symbol for life itself. In today's first reading, the people's
thirst is the occasion for a revelation of God's saving power, while
in the Gospel, the revelation of God in Jesus is described as "living
water." Jeremiah had talked of God as "the fountain of living water"
(2:13, 17:13), and the phrase was used as well of the Torah, God's
word revealed to Moses. So when Jesus tells the Samaritan woman
that he would give her "living water...a spring of water welling up
to eternal life," he makes a massive claim. "While the law was given
through Moses, grace and truth [the gift of God] came through Jesus
Christ" (Jn 1:17).

"If you knew the gift of God," says Jesus. In Lent, we revisit the desert to discover the gift of God once more, as did the wilderness community of the first reading. Meeting Jesus there, we learn that God thirsts too, thirsts "that we may thirst for him" (*Catechism of the Catholic Church,* n. 2561).

FIRST READING

Ex 17:1–7

The Lord showed Moses water, that the people might drink.

A reading from the Book of Exodus

From the desert of Sin the whole congregation of the children of Israel journeyed by stages, as the Lord directed, and encamped at Rephidim.

There was no water for the people to drink. They quarreled, therefore, with Moses and said, "Give us water to drink." Moses replied, "Why do you quarrel with me? Why do you put the Lord to a test?" Then, in their thirst for water, the people grumbled against Moses, saying, "Why did you ever make us leave Egypt? Was it just to have us die here of thirst with our children and our livestock?" So Moses cried out to the Lord, "What shall I do with this people? A little more and they will stone me!" The Lord answered Moses, "Go over there in front of the people, along with some of the elders of Israel, holding in your hand, as you go, the staff with which you struck the river. I will be standing there in front of you on the rock in Horeb. Strike the rock, and the water will flow from it for the people to drink." This Moses did, in the presence of the elders of Israel. The place was called Massah and Meribah, because the children of Israel quarreled there and tested the Lord, saying, "Is the Lord in our midst or not?"

The word of the Lord.

Responsorial Psalm

Ps 95:1–2, 6–7ab, 7c–9

R. If today you hear his voice, harden not your hearts.

Come, let us sing joyfully to the LORD;
  let us acclaim the Rock of our salvation.
Let us come into his presence with thanksgiving;
  let us joyfully sing psalms to him.

R. If today you hear his voice, harden not your hearts.

Come, let us bow down in worship;
  let us kneel before the LORD who made us.
For he is our God,
  and we are the people he shepherds, the flock he guides.

R. If today you hear his voice, harden not your hearts.

Oh, that today you would hear his voice:
  "Harden not your hearts as at Meribah,
  as in the day of Massah in the desert,
Where your fathers tempted me;
  they tested me though they had seen my works."

R. If today you hear his voice, harden not your hearts.

Verse Before the Gospel   See Jn 4:42, 15
Lord, you are truly the Savior of the world;
  give me living water, that I may never thirst again.

GOSPEL

Jn 4:5–42

The water that I shall give will become a spring of eternal life.

A reading from the holy Gospel according to John

At that time, Jesus came to a town of Samaria called Sychar, near the plot of land that Jacob had given to his son Joseph. Jacob's well was there. Jesus, tired from his journey, sat down there at the well. It was about noon.

A woman of Samaria came to draw water. Jesus said to her, "Give me a drink." His disciples had gone into the town to buy food. The Samaritan woman said to him, "How can you, a Jew, ask me, a Samaritan woman, for a drink?"—For Jews use nothing in common with Samaritans.—Jesus answered and said to her, "If you knew the gift of God and who is saying to you, 'Give me a drink,' you would have asked him and he would have given you living water." The woman said to him, "Sir, you do not even have a bucket and the cistern is deep; where then can you get this living water? Are you greater than our father Jacob, who gave us this cistern and drank from it himself with his children and his flocks?" Jesus answered and said to her, "Everyone who drinks this water will be thirsty again; but whoever drinks the water I shall give will never thirst; the water I shall give will become in him a spring of water welling up to eternal life." The woman said to him, "Sir, give me this water, so that I may not be thirsty or have to keep coming here to draw water."

Jesus said to her, "Go call your husband and come back." The woman answered and said to him, "I do not have a husband." Jesus answered her, "You are right in saying, 'I do not have a husband.' For you have had five husbands, and the one you have now is not your husband. What you have said is true." The woman said to him, "Sir, I can see that you are a prophet. Our ancestors worshiped on this mountain; but you people say that the place to worship is in Jerusalem." Jesus said to her, "Believe me, woman, the hour is coming when you will worship the Father neither on this mountain nor in Jerusalem. You people worship what you do not understand; we worship what we understand, because salvation is from the Jews. But the hour is coming, and is now here, when true worshipers will worship the Father in Spirit and truth; and indeed the Father seeks such people to worship him. God is

Spirit, and those who worship him must worship in Spirit and truth." The woman said to him, "I know that the Christ is coming, the one called the Anointed; when he comes, he will tell us everything." Jesus said to her, "I am he, the one speaking with you."

At that moment his disciples returned, and were amazed that he was talking with a woman, but still no one said, "What are you looking for?" or "Why are you talking with her?" The woman left her water jar and went into the town and said to the people, "Come see a man who told me everything I have done. Could he possibly be the Christ?" They went out of the town and came to him. Meanwhile, the disciples urged him, "Rabbi, eat." But he said to them, "I have food to eat of which you do not know." So the disciples said to one another, "Could someone have brought him something to eat?" Jesus said to them, "My food is to do the will of the one who sent me and to finish his work. Do you not say, 'In four months the harvest will be here'? I tell you, look up and see the fields ripe for the harvest. The reaper is already receiving payment and gathering crops for eternal life, so that the sower and reaper can rejoice together. For here the saying is verified that 'One sows and another reaps.' I sent you to reap what you have not worked for; others have done the work, and you are sharing the fruits of their work."

Many of the Samaritans of that town began to believe in him because of the word of the woman who testified, "He told me everything I have done." When the Samaritans came to him, they invited him to stay with them; and he stayed there two days. Many more began to believe in him because of his word, and they said to the woman, "We no longer believe because of your word; for we have heard for ourselves, and we know that this is truly the savior of the world."

The Gospel of the Lord.

Liturgy of the Eucharist, *p. 897.*

Monday

Entrance Antiphon

My soul is longing and pining for the courts of the Lord; my heart and my flesh sing for joy to the living God. (Ps 83:3)

Opening Prayer

God of mercy,
free your Church from sin
and protect it from evil.
Guide us, for we cannot be saved without you.

We ask this through our Lord Jesus Christ, your Son,
who lives and reigns with you and the Holy Spirit,
one God, for ever and ever.

Today's Living Word

The two readings for today warn against prejudice and pre-conception. In the Gospel, Luke's Jesus is expelled from his home-town of Nazareth because he challenges his people's preconception that God's visitation will be only for them. Alluding to the biblical stories of Elijah, who saved a widow of Zarephath and her son from starvation, and Elisha, who cured the leprosy of Naaman, a Gentile enemy of Israel, Jesus intimates that his own ministry as messianic prophet will extend beyond the boundaries of Israel. They reject him for this. The first reading is the story of Naaman's cure and it too shatters preconceptions, both Naaman's and the reader's. Who would have thought that a little slave girl could help the mighty Naaman? Or that he could be healed by doing something so ordinary as washing in the Jordan? In fact, his preconception of what a prophet should do almost led Naaman to reject the way to health and wholeness.

"There is no God in all the earth, except in Israel," Naaman learns. He teaches us that the God of Israel acts in unexpected ways that challenge our prejudices and shatter our preconceptions.

FIRST READING   2 Kgs 5:1–15ab

There were many people with leprosy in Israel,
but none were made clean, except Naaman the Syrian (Lk 4:27).

A reading from the second Book of Kings

Naaman, the army commander of the king of Aram, was highly esteemed and respected by his master, for through him the LORD had brought victory to Aram. But valiant as he was, the man was a leper. Now the Arameans had captured in a raid on the land of Israel a little girl, who became the servant of Naaman's wife. "If only my master would present himself to the prophet in Samaria," she said to her mistress, "he would cure him of his leprosy." Naaman went and told his lord just what the slave girl from the land of Israel had said. "Go," said the king of Aram. "I will send along a letter to the king of Israel." So Naaman set out, taking along ten silver talents, six thousand gold pieces, and ten festal garments. To the king of Israel he brought the letter, which read: "With this letter I am sending my servant Naaman to you, that you may cure him of his leprosy."

When he read the letter, the king of Israel tore his garments and exclaimed: "Am I a god with power over life and death, that this man should send someone to me to be cured of leprosy? Take note! You can see he is only looking for a quarrel with me!" When Elisha, the man of God, heard that the king of Israel had torn his garments, he sent word to the king: "Why

have you torn your garments? Let him come to me and find
out that there is a prophet in Israel."

Naaman came with his horses and chariots and stopped at
the door of Elisha's house. The prophet sent him the message:
"Go and wash seven times in the Jordan, and your flesh will
heal, and you will be clean." But Naaman went away angry,
saying, "I thought that he would surely come out and stand
there to invoke the LORD his God, and would move his hand
over the spot, and thus cure the leprosy. Are not the rivers of
Damascus, the Abana and the Pharpar, better than all the waters
of Israel? Could I not wash in them and be cleansed?" With
this, he turned about in anger and left.

But his servants came up and reasoned with him. "My
father," they said, "if the prophet had told you to do something
extraordinary, would you not have done it? All the more now,
since he said to you, 'Wash and be clean,' should you do as he
said." So Naaman went down and plunged into the Jordan seven
times at the word of the man of God. His flesh became again
like the flesh of a little child, and he was clean.

He returned with his whole retinue to the man of God. On
his arrival he stood before him and said, "Now I know that
there is no God in all the earth, except in Israel."
The word of the Lord.

Responsorial Psalm

Ps 42:2, 3; 43:3, 4

R. **Athirst is my soul for the living God.**
When shall I go and behold the face of God?

As the hind longs for the running waters,
  so my soul longs for you, O God.

R. **Athirst is my soul for the living God.**
When shall I go and behold the face of God?

Athirst is my soul for God, the living God.
  When shall I go and behold the face of God?

> **R. Athirst is my soul for the living God.**
> **When shall I go and behold the face of God?**

Send forth your light and your fidelity;
  they shall lead me on
And bring me to your holy mountain,
  to your dwelling-place.

> **R. Athirst is my soul for the living God.**
> **When shall I go and behold the face of God?**

Then will I go in to the altar of God,
  the God of my gladness and joy;
Then will I give you thanks upon the harp,
  O God, my God!

> **R. Athirst is my soul for the living God.**
> **When shall I go and behold the face of God?**

> **Verse Before the Gospel**   See Ps 130:5, 7
> I hope in the LORD, I trust in his word;
>   with him there is kindness and plenteous redemption.

GOSPEL   Lk 4:24–30

Like Elijah and Elisha, Jesus was sent not only to the Jews.

A reading from the holy Gospel according to Luke

Jesus said to the people in the synagogue at Nazareth: "Amen,
I say to you, no prophet is accepted in his own native place.
Indeed, I tell you, there were many widows in Israel in the
days of Elijah when the sky was closed for three and a half
years and a severe famine spread over the entire land. It was to
none of these that Elijah was sent, but only to a widow in
Zarephath in the land of Sidon. Again, there were many lepers
in Israel during the time of Elisha the prophet; yet not one of

them was cleansed, but only Naaman the Syrian." When the people in the synagogue heard this, they were all filled with fury. They rose up, drove him out of the town, and led him to he brow of the hill on which their town had been built, to hurl him down headlong. But he passed through the midst of them and went away.

The Gospel of the Lord.

Liturgy of the Eucharist, *p. 897.*

Prayer over the Gifts

Pray, brethren...

Father,
bless these gifts
that they may become the sacrament of our salvation.

We ask this in the name of Jesus the Lord.

Preface of Lent I–IV, *pp. 940–942.*

Communion Antiphon

All you nations, praise the Lord, for steadfast is his kindly mercy to us.   (Ps 116:1–2)

Prayer after Communion

Let us pray.

Pause for silent prayer, if this has not preceded.

Lord,
forgive the sins of those
who receive your sacrament,
and bring us together in unity and peace.

Grant this through Christ our Lord.

Tuesday

Entrance Antiphon

I call upon you, God, for you will answer me; bend your ear and hear my prayer. Guard me as the pupil of your eye; hide me in the shade of your wings.   (Ps 16:6, 8)

Opening Prayer

Lord,
you call us to your service
and continue your saving work among us.
May your love never abandon us.

We ask this through our Lord Jesus Christ, your Son,
who lives and reigns with you and the Holy Spirit,
one God, for ever and ever.

TODAY'S LIVING WORD

In the first reading, Azariah (his Babylonian name is Abednego) is one of Daniel's Jewish companions in the court of King Nebuchadnezzar. Although he and his friends have attained power in the province of Babylon, they refuse to worship the golden statue that the king had erected and are consigned to the fiery furnace (cf. Dn 3:1–23). There Azariah prays not for himself but for his people. He appeals to the "kindness and great mercy" of God, asking for wonders that will bring glory to God's name.

In today's Gospel, Jesus teaches his disciples that in their dealings with one another, they must imitate the great mercy of God to which Azariah appeals. The parable dramatizes God's mercy by the wonderful generosity of the king who writes off the official's large debt. The official fails to understand, however, that having received mercy from the king, he must in turn show mercy to his fellow servants. In fact, the great mercy of the king that delivers him from debt depends on it.

FIRST READING

Dn 3:25, 34 – 43

We ask you to receive us with humble and contrite hearts.

A reading from the Book of the Prophet Daniel

Azariah stood up in the fire and prayed aloud:

"For your name's sake, O Lord, do not deliver us up forever,
    or make void your covenant.
Do not take away your mercy from us,
    for the sake of Abraham, your beloved,
    Isaac your servant, and Israel your holy one,
To whom you promised to multiply their offspring
    like the stars of heaven,
    or the sand on the shore of the sea.
For we are reduced, O Lord, beyond any other nation,
    brought low everywhere in the world this day
    because of our sins.
We have in our day no prince, prophet, or leader,
    no burnt offering, sacrifice, oblation, or incense,
    no place to offer first fruits, to find favor with you.
But with contrite heart and humble spirit
    let us be received;
As though it were burnt offerings of rams and bullocks,
    or thousands of fat lambs,
So let our sacrifice be in your presence today
    as we follow you unreservedly;
    for those who trust in you cannot be put to shame.
And now we follow you with our whole heart,
    we fear you and we pray to you.
Do not let us be put to shame,
    but deal with us in your kindness and great mercy.

Deliver us by your wonders,
   and bring glory to your name, O Lord."

The word of the Lord.

Responsorial Psalm
Ps 25:4–5ab, 6 and 7bc, 8–9

R. Remember your mercies, O Lord.

Your ways, O LORD, make known to me;
   teach me your paths,
Guide me in your truth and teach me,
   for you are God my savior.

R. Remember your mercies, O Lord.

Remember that your compassion, O LORD,
   and your kindness are from of old.
In your kindness remember me,
   because of your goodness, O LORD.

R. Remember your mercies, O Lord.

Good and upright is the LORD;
   thus he shows sinners the way.
He guides the humble to justice,
   he teaches the humble his way.

R. Remember your mercies, O Lord.

Verse Before the Gospel   Jl 2:12–13
Even now, says the LORD,
return to me with your whole heart;
for I am gracious and merciful.

GOSPEL
Mt 18:21–35

Unless each of you forgives your brother and sister,
the Father will not forgive you.

A reading from the holy Gospel according to Matthew

Peter approached Jesus and asked him, "Lord, if my brother sins against me, how often must I forgive him? As many as

seven times?" Jesus answered, "I say to you, not seven times but seventy-seven times. That is why the Kingdom of heaven may be likened to a king who decided to settle accounts with his servants. When he began the accounting, a debtor was brought before him who owed him a huge amount. Since he had no way of paying it back, his master ordered him to be sold, along with his wife, his children, and all his property, in payment of the debt. At that, the servant fell down, did him homage, and said, 'Be patient with me, and I will pay you back in full.' Moved with compassion the master of that servant let him go and forgave him the loan. When that servant had left, he found one of his fellow servants who owed him a much smaller amount. He seized him and started to choke him, demanding, 'Pay back what you owe.' Falling to his knees, his fellow servant begged him, 'Be patient with me, and I will pay you back.' But he refused. Instead, he had him put in prison until he paid back the debt. Now when his fellow servants saw what had happened, they were deeply disturbed, and went to their master and reported the whole affair. His master summoned him and said to him, 'You wicked servant! I forgave you your entire debt because you begged me to. Should you not have had pity on your fellow servant, as I had pity on you?' Then in anger his master handed him over to the torturers until he should pay back the whole debt. So will my heavenly Father do to you, unless each of you forgives your brother from your heart."
The Gospel of the Lord.

Liturgy of the Eucharist, *p. 897.*

Prayer over the Gifts
Pray, brethren...

Lord,
may the saving sacrifice we offer
bring us your forgiveness,
so that freed from sin, we may always please you.

Grant this through Christ our Lord.

Preface of Lent I–IV, *pp. 940–942.*

Communion Antiphon

Lord, who may stay in your dwelling place? Who shall live on your holy mountain? He who walks without blame and does what is right. (Ps 14:1– 2)

Prayer after Communion

Let us pray.

Pause for silent prayer, if this has not preceded.

Lord,
may our sharing in this holy mystery
bring us your protection, forgiveness and life.
We ask this in the name of Jesus the Lord.

Wednesday

Entrance Antiphon

Lord, direct my steps as you have promised, and let no evil hold me in its power. (Ps 118:133)

Opening Prayer

Lord,
during this lenten season
nourish us with your word of life
and make us one in love and prayer.

Grant this through our Lord Jesus Christ, your Son,

who lives and reigns with you and the Holy Spirit,
one God, for ever and ever.

TODAY'S LIVING WORD

In the Church's ancient liturgy, this Wednesday was the first "scrutiny" or test of the catechumens preparing for baptism. The test was on the commandments, so both readings center on that theme. "Whoever obeys and teaches these commandments will be called greatest in the kingdom of heaven." With these words Matthew's Jesus tells his disciples that they must practice what they preach (or teach). Specifically, they are to preach and to practice the law of God confided to Israel in the Torah and the teaching of the prophets, that is, the Hebrew Bible. Jesus says that this law will remain in force, for Christians as for Jews, "until heaven and earth pass away"—until the kingdom of God is fully revealed.

In Deuteronomy, Moses tells the Israelites who are about to take possession of the promised land that they will preach (or teach) by practicing the statutes and decrees of the Lord, their God. "For thus," he says, "will you give evidence of your wisdom and intelligence to the nations." And more: thus will they bear witness to the closeness and compassion of God, as will we who have received from Jesus the wisdom of Israel.

FIRST READING

Dt 4:1, 5–9

Keep the commandments and your work will be complete.

A reading from the Book of Deuteronomy

Moses spoke to the people and said: "Now, Israel, hear the statutes and decrees which I am teaching you to observe, that you may live, and may enter in and take possession of the land which the LORD, the God of your fathers, is giving you. Therefore, I teach you the statutes and decrees as the LORD, my God, has commanded me, that you may observe them in the land you are entering to occupy. Observe them carefully, for thus will you give evidence of your wisdom and intelligence to the nations, who will hear of all these statutes and say, 'This great nation is truly a wise and intelligent people.' For what great nation is there that has gods so close to it as the LORD, our God, is to us whenever we call upon him? Or what great nation has statutes and decrees that are as just as this whole law which I am setting before you today?

"However, take care and be earnestly on your guard not to forget the things which your own eyes have seen, nor let them slip from your memory as long as you live, but teach them to your children and to your children's children."

The word of the Lord.

Responsorial Psalm
Ps 147:12–13, 15–16, 19–20

R. Praise the Lord, Jerusalem.

Glorify the LORD, O Jerusalem;
  praise your God, O Zion.
For he has strengthened the bars of your gates;
  he has blessed your children within you.

R. Praise the Lord, Jerusalem.

He sends forth his command to the earth;
  swiftly runs his word!
He spreads snow like wool;
  frost he strews like ashes.

R. Praise the Lord, Jerusalem.

He has proclaimed his word to Jacob,
  his statutes and his ordinances to Israel.
He has not done thus for any other nation;
  his ordinances he has not made known to them.

R. Praise the Lord, Jerusalem.

Verse Before the Gospel   See Jn 6:63c, 68c
Your words, Lord, are Spirit and life;
you have the words of everlasting life.

GOSPEL

Mt 5:17–19

Whoever keeps and teaches the law will be called great.

A reading from the holy Gospel according to Matthew

Jesus said to his disciples: "Do not think that I have come to abolish the law or the prophets. I have come not to abolish but to fulfill. Amen, I say to you, until heaven and earth pass away, not the smallest letter or the smallest part of a letter will pass from the law, until all things have taken place. Therefore, whoever breaks one of the least of these commandments and teaches others to do so will be called least in the Kingdom of heaven. But whoever obeys and teaches these commandments will be called greatest in the Kingdom of heaven."

The Gospel of the Lord.

Liturgy of the Eucharist, *p. 897.*

Prayer over the Gifts

Pray, brethren...

Lord,
receive our prayers and offerings.
In time of danger,
protect all who celebrate this sacrament.

We ask this in the name of Jesus the Lord.

Preface of Lent I–IV, *pp. 940–942.*

Communion Antiphon

Lord, you will show me the path of life and fill me with joy in your presence.
(Ps 15:11)

Prayer after Communion

Let us pray.

Pause for silent prayer, if this has not preceded.

Lord,
may this eucharist forgive our sins,
make us holy,
and prepare us for the eternal life you promise.
We ask this through Christ our Lord.

Thursday

Entrance Antiphon

I am the Savior of all people, says the Lord. Whatever their troubles, I will answer their cry, and I will always be their Lord.

Opening Prayer

Father,
help us to be ready
to celebrate the great paschal mystery.
Make our love grow each day
as we approach the feast of our salvation.

We ask this through our Lord Jesus Christ, your Son,
who lives and reigns with you and the Holy Spirit,
one God, for ever and ever.

TODAY'S LIVING WORD

In today's first reading, the prophet Jeremiah decries the persistent hardness of his people's hearts, the stiffness of their necks. Both expressions point beyond the symptoms of sin to its source in the very core of the self. As the prophet Jesus casts out demons in today's Gospel, he encounters the obduracy of some of his people. Some accuse him of being Satan's agent; others test him by asking for a sign. In answer, Jesus offers a pithy parable. If Satan is "a strong man fully armed" guarding his possessions, then Jesus is the stronger one (cf. Lk 3:16) who, "by the finger of God," strips Satan of his power and sets free those in his possession. In this way, the works no less than the words of Jesus announce that the reign of God is upon us.

Today's pithy parable tells us that there is hope for our hard hearts and stiff necks. There is Jesus, the stronger one, who by the power of God can take booty from a warrior and rescue captives from a tyrant's grasp (cf. Is 49:24–25).

FIRST READING
Jer 7:23 – 28

This is the nation that will not listen to the voice of the LORD God.

A reading from the Book of the Prophet Jeremiah

Thus says the LORD: This is what I commanded my people: Listen to my voice; then I will be your God and you shall be my people. Walk in all the ways that I command you, so that you may prosper.

But they obeyed not, nor did they pay heed. They walked in the hardness of their evil hearts and turned their backs, not their faces, to me. From the day that your fathers left the land of Egypt even to this day, I have sent you untiringly all my servants the prophets. Yet they have not obeyed me nor paid heed; they have stiffened their necks and done worse than their fathers. When you speak all these words to them, they will not listen to you either; when you call to them, they will not answer you. Say to them: This is the nation that does not listen to the voice of the LORD, its God, or take correction. Faithfulness has disappeared; the word itself is banished from their speech.

The word of the Lord.

Responsorial Psalm
Ps 95:1–2, 6–7, 8–9

R. If today you hear his voice, harden not your hearts.

Come, let us sing joyfully to the LORD;
   let us acclaim the Rock of our salvation.

Let us come into his presence with thanksgiving;
   let us joyfully sing psalms to him.

   R. If today you hear his voice, harden not your hearts.

Come, let us bow down in worship;
   let us kneel before the LORD who made us.
For he is our God,
   and we are the people he shepherds, the flock he guides.

   R. If today you hear his voice, harden not your hearts.

Oh, that today you would hear his voice:
   "Harden not your hearts as at Meribah,
   as in the day of Massah in the desert,
Where your fathers tempted me;
   they tested me though they had seen my works."

   R. If today you hear his voice, harden not your hearts.

   Verse Before the Gospel   Jl 2:12–13
      Even now, says the LORD,
      return to me with your whole heart,
      for I am gracious and merciful.

GOSPEL   Lk 11:14–23
Whoever is not with me is against me.

A reading from the holy Gospel according to Luke

Jesus was driving out a demon that was mute, and when the
demon had gone out, the mute man spoke and the crowds were
amazed. Some of them said, "By the power of Beelzebul, the
prince of demons, he drives out demons." Others, to test him,
asked him for a sign from heaven. But he knew their thoughts
and said to them, "Every kingdom divided against itself will
be laid waste and house will fall against house. And if Satan is
divided against himself, how will his kingdom stand? For you
say that it is by Beelzebul that I drive out demons. If I, then,

drive out demons by Beelzebul, by whom do your own people drive them out? Therefore they will be your judges. But if it is by the finger of God that I drive out demons, then the Kingdom of God has come upon you. When a strong man fully armed guards his palace, his possessions are safe. But when one stronger than he attacks and overcomes him, he takes away the armor on which he relied and distributes the spoils. Whoever is not with me is against me, and whoever does not gather with me scatters."

The Gospel of the Lord.

Liturgy of the Eucharist, *p. 897.*

Prayer over the Gifts

Pray, brethren...

Lord,
take away our sinfulness
and be pleased with our offerings.
Help us to pursue the true gifts you promise
and not become lost in false joys.

Grant this through Christ our Lord.

Preface of Lent I–IV, *pp. 940–942.*

Communion Antiphon

You have laid down your precepts to be faithfully kept. May my footsteps be firm in keeping your commands. (Ps 118:4–5)

Prayer after Communion

Let us pray.

Pause for silent prayer, if this has not preceded.

Lord,
may your sacrament of life

bring us the gift of salvation
and make our lives pleasing to you.
We ask this in the name of Jesus the Lord.

Friday

Entrance Antiphon

Lord, there is no god to compare with you; you are great and do wonderful things, you are the only God.   (Ps 85:8, 10)

Opening Prayer

Merciful Father,
fill our hearts with your love
and keep us faithful to the gospel of Christ.
Give us the grace to rise above our human weakness.

Grant this through our Lord Jesus Christ, your Son,
who lives and reigns with you and the Holy Spirit,
one God, for ever and ever.

TODAY'S LIVING WORD

The epilogue of Hosea, today's first reading, is structured as call and response. Hosea calls the people to return to the Lord, in whom "the orphan finds compassion." In response, God declares, "I will love them freely; for my wrath is turned away from them." Thus is the life-giving love of God—"a verdant cypress tree"—proven once more.

In the Gospel, a scribe calls on Jesus to tell him which is the first of all the commandments, and Jesus responds with not one but two commandments: "You shall love the Lord your God.... You shall love your neighbor as yourself." The scribe repeats Jesus' answer in his own words and, echoing Hosea (6:6), adds that such love "is worth more than all burnt offerings and sacrifices." This does not negate the need for formal liturgy; it simply affirms the dispositions that must inform true religion as well as true repentance, as in today's first reading.

FIRST READING

Hos 14:2–10

We will not say to the work of our hands: our god.

A reading from the Book of the Prophet Hosea

Thus says the LORD:
Return, O Israel, to the LORD, your God;
  you have collapsed through your guilt.
Take with you words,
  and return to the LORD;
Say to him, "Forgive all iniquity,
    and receive what is good, that we may render
    as offerings the bullocks from our stalls.
Assyria will not save us,
  nor shall we have horses to mount;
We shall say no more, 'Our god,'
    to the work of our hands;
    for in you the orphan finds compassion."
I will heal their defection, says the LORD,
  I will love them freely;
    for my wrath is turned away from them.
I will be like the dew for Israel:
  he shall blossom like the lily;
He shall strike root like the Lebanon cedar,
  and put forth his shoots.
His splendor shall be like the olive tree
  and his fragrance like the Lebanon cedar.
Again they shall dwell in his shade
  and raise grain;

They shall blossom like the vine,
    and his fame shall be like the wine of Lebanon.

Ephraim! What more has he to do with idols?
    I have humbled him, but I will prosper him.
"I am like a verdant cypress tree"—
    Because of me you bear fruit!

Let him who is wise understand these things;
    let him who is prudent know them.
Straight are the paths of the LORD,
    in them the just walk,
    but sinners stumble in them.

The word of the Lord.

Responsorial Psalm   Ps 81:6c – 8a, 8bc – 9, 10 – 11ab, 14 and 17

R. I am the Lord your God: hear my voice.

An unfamiliar speech I hear:
  "I relieved his shoulder of the burden;
  his hands were freed from the basket.
In distress you called, and I rescued you."

R. I am the Lord your God: hear my voice.

"Unseen, I answered you in thunder;
  I tested you at the waters of Meribah.
Hear, my people, and I will admonish you;
  O Israel, will you not hear me?"

R. I am the Lord your God: hear my voice.

"There shall be no strange god among you
  nor shall you worship any alien god.
I, the LORD, am your God
  who led you forth from the land of Egypt."

R. I am the Lord your God: hear my voice.

"If only my people would hear me,
  and Israel walk in my ways,

I would feed them with the best of wheat,
  and with honey from the rock I would fill them."

R. I am the Lord your God: hear my voice.

Verse Before the Gospel Mt 4:17
Repent, says the Lord;
the Kingdom of heaven is at hand.

GOSPEL

Mk 12:28–34

*The Lord our God is one Lord,
and you shall love the Lord your God.*

A reading from the holy Gospel according to Mark

One of the scribes came to Jesus and asked him, "Which is the
first of all the commandments?" Jesus replied, "The first is
this: *Hear, O Israel! The Lord our God is Lord alone! You shall
love the Lord your God with all your heart, with all your soul,
with all your mind, and with all your strength.* The second is
this: *You shall love your neighbor as yourself.* There is no other
commandment greater than these." The scribe said to him,
"Well said, teacher. You are right in saying, *He is One and
there is no other than he.* And *to love him with all your heart,
with all your understanding, with all your strength, and to love
your neighbor as yourself* is worth more than all burnt offerings and sacrifices." And when Jesus saw that he answered
with understanding, he said to him, "You are not far from the
Kingdom of God." And no one dared to ask him any more
questions.

The Gospel of the Lord.

Liturgy of the Eucharist, *p. 897.*

Prayer over the Gifts

Pray, brethren...

Lord,
bless the gifts we have prepared.
Make them acceptable to you
and a lasting source of salvation.

We ask this in the name of Jesus the Lord.

Preface of Lent I–IV, *pp. 940–942.*

Communion Antiphon

To love God with all your heart, and your neighbor as your-self, is a greater thing than all the temple sacrifices.

(See Mk 12:33)

Prayer after Communion

Let us pray.

Pause for silent prayer, if this has not preceded.

Lord,
fill us with the power of your love.
As we share in this eucharist,
may we come to know fully
the redemption we have received.

We ask this through Christ our Lord.

Saturday

Entrance Antiphon

Bless the Lord, my soul, and remember all his kindnesses, for he pardons all my faults.
(Ps 102:2 – 3)

Opening Prayer

Lord,
may this lenten observance
of the suffering, death and resurrection of Christ
bring us to the full joy of Easter.

We ask this through our Lord Jesus Christ, your Son,
who lives and reigns with you and the Holy Spirit,
one God, for ever and ever.

TODAY'S LIVING WORD

Like yesterday's, today's reading from Hosea is structured as call and response. Only here the call to "return to the Lord" is insincere, as insubstantial as a morning cloud or "the dew that early passes away." The Lucan parable assesses the piety of the Pharisee in much the same way. Therefore, he did not go home from the temple justified as the tax collector did.

For Luke, as for many Christians after 70 C.E., the Pharisee had become a stock character, a hypocrite, hard of heart. In reality, the piety of the Pharisees was not any more susceptible to self-righteousness than that of any other religious group. And Jesus knew it. He wanted only to urge on his disciples the true repentance of the tax collector. Like Hosea, he did not devalue pious practices like sacrifice and holocaust or fasting and tithing, but he never forgot what the Pharisees themselves believed, that God desires love above all.

FIRST READING

Hos 6:1–6

What I want is love, not sacrifice.

A reading from the Book of the Prophet Hosea

"Come, let us return to the LORD,
    it is he who has rent, but he will heal us;
    he has struck us, but he will bind our wounds.
He will revive us after two days;
    on the third day he will raise us up,
    to live in his presence.
Let us know, let us strive to know the LORD;
    as certain as the dawn is his coming,
    and his judgment shines forth like the light of day!

He will come to us like the rain,
  like spring rain that waters the earth."

What can I do with you, Ephraim?
What can I do with you, Judah?
Your piety is like a morning cloud,
  like the dew that early passes away.
For this reason I smote them through the prophets,
  I slew them by the words of my mouth;
For it is love that I desire, not sacrifice,
  and knowledge of God rather than burnt offerings.

The word of the Lord.

Responsorial Psalm

Ps 51:3–4, 18–19, 20–21ab

R. It is mercy I desire, and not sacrifice.

Have mercy on me, O God, in your goodness;
  in the greatness of your compassion wipe out my offense.
Thoroughly wash me from my guilt
  and of my sin cleanse me.

R. It is mercy I desire, and not sacrifice.

For you are not pleased with sacrifices;
  should I offer a burnt offering, you would not accept it.
My sacrifice, O God, is a contrite spirit;
  a heart contrite and humbled, O God, you will not spurn.

R. It is mercy I desire, and not sacrifice.

Be bountiful, O LORD, to Zion in your kindness
  by rebuilding the walls of Jerusalem;
Then shall you be pleased with due sacrifices,
  burnt offerings and holocausts.

R. It is mercy I desire, and not sacrifice.

Verse Before the Gospel   Ps 95:8
If today you hear his voice,
harden not your hearts.

GOSPEL

Lk 18:9–14

The tax collector went home justified, not the Pharisee.

A reading from the holy Gospel according to Luke

Jesus addressed this parable to those who were convinced of their own righteousness and despised everyone else. "Two people went up to the temple area to pray; one was a Pharisee and the other was a tax collector. The Pharisee took up his position and spoke this prayer to himself, 'O God, I thank you that I am not like the rest of humanity—greedy, dishonest, adulterous—or even like this tax collector. I fast twice a week, and I pay tithes on my whole income.' But the tax collector stood off at a distance and would not even raise his eyes to heaven but beat his breast and prayed, 'O God, be merciful to me a sinner.' I tell you, the latter went home justified, not the former; for everyone who exalts himself will be humbled, and the one who humbles himself will be exalted."

The Gospel of the Lord.

Liturgy of the Eucharist, *p. 897.*

Prayer over the Gifts

Pray, brethren...

Lord,
by your grace you enable us
to come to these mysteries with renewed lives.
May this eucharist give you worthy praise.
Grant this through Christ our Lord.

Preface of Lent I–IV, *pp. 940–942.*

Communion Antiphon

He stood at a distance and beat his breast, saying: O God, be merciful to me, a sinner. (Lk 18:13)

Prayer after Communion

Let us pray.

Pause for silent prayer, if this has not preceded.

God of mercy,
may the holy gifts we receive
help us to worship you in truth,
and to receive your sacraments with faith.
We ask this in the name of Jesus the Lord.

OPTIONAL MASS FOR
THE FOURTH WEEK OF LENT

This Mass may be used on any day of this week, especially in Cycles B and C when the Gospel of the man born blind is not read on the Fourth Sunday of Lent.

TODAY'S LIVING WORD

Today's Gospel was part of baptismal instruction in the early Church. The baptismal elements of the story are easy to see: to St. Augustine, the man's blindness from birth signified original sin; Jesus' smearing the man's eyes with mud could be taken as an "anointing" as in the rite of Baptism; the man is told to wash, an obvious baptismal symbol; the name of the pool is Siloam—"One who has been sent"—which in John is another name for Jesus; and finally, in the early Church Baptism was often described as "enlightenment." The story also depicts the "post-baptismal catechesis" of the man whose eyes Jesus opened. Gradually, the man learns to name Jesus more and more truly as a "prophet," as one who is "from God," and as the Lord whom he worships.

The story is also an object lesson on the need to courageously profess one's faith before hostile forces. The first reading teaches this too. Even before their enemy, the people of God are confident that the Savior whom they trust will bring them forth to the light.

FIRST READING

Mi 7:7–9

I will arise; though I sit in darkness, the Lord is my light.

A reading from the Book of the Prophet Micah

I will look to the Lord,
>   I will put my trust in God my savior;
>   my God will hear me!

Rejoice not over me, O my enemy!
>   though I have fallen, I will arise;
>   though I sit in darkness, the Lord is my light.

The wrath of the Lord I will endure
>   because I have sinned against him,

Until he takes up my cause,
>   and establishes my right.

He will bring me forth to the light;
>   I will see his justice.

The word of the Lord.

Responsorial Psalm

Ps 27:1, 7–8a, 8b–9abc, 13–14

R. The Lord is my light and my salvation.

The Lord is my light and my salvation;
  whom should I fear?
The Lord is my life's refuge;
  of whom should I be afraid?

R. The Lord is my light and my salvation.

Hear, O Lord, the sound of my call;
  have pity on me and answer me.
Of you my heart speaks; you my glance seeks.

R. The Lord is my light and my salvation.

Your presence, O Lord, I seek!
Hide not your face from me;

do not in anger repel your servant.
You are my helper; cast me not off.

R. The Lord is my light and my salvation.

I believe that I shall see the bounty of the LORD
in the land of the living.
Wait for the LORD with courage;
be stouthearted, and wait for the LORD!

R. The Lord is my light and my salvation.

Verse Before the Gospel Jn 8:12
I am the light of the world, says the Lord;
whoever follows me will have the light of life.

GOSPEL   Jn 9:1–41

He went, washed and came back able to see.

A reading from the holy Gospel according to John

As Jesus passed by he saw a man blind from birth. His disciples asked him, "Rabbi, who sinned, this man or his parents, that he was born blind?" Jesus answered, "Neither he nor his parents sinned; it is so that the works of God might be made visible through him. We have to do the works of the one who sent me while it is day. Night is coming when no one can work. While I am in the world, I am the light of the world." When he had said this, he spat on the ground and made clay with the saliva, and smeared the clay on his eyes, and said to him, "Go, wash in the Pool of Siloam"—which means Sent. So he went and washed, and came back able to see.

His neighbors and those who had seen him earlier as a beggar said, "Isn't this the one who used to sit and beg?" Some said, "It is," but others said, "No, he just looks like him." He said, "I am." So they said to him, "How were your eyes opened?" He replied, "The man called Jesus made clay and anointed my eyes and told me, 'Go to Siloam and wash.' So I went there and washed and was able to see." And they said to him, "Where is he?" He said, "I don't know."

They brought the one who was once blind to the Pharisees. Now Jesus had made clay and opened his eyes on a sabbath. So then the Pharisees also asked him how he was able to see. He said to them, "He put clay on my eyes, and I washed, and now I can see." So some of the Pharisees said, "This man is not from God, because he does not keep the sabbath." But others said, "How can a sinful man do such signs?" And there was a division among them. So they said to the blind man again, "What do you have to say about him, since he opened your eyes?" He said, "He is a prophet."

Now the Jews did not believe that he had been blind and gained his sight until they summoned the parents of the one who had gained his sight. They asked them, "Is this your son, who you say was born blind? How does he now see?" His parents answered and said, "We know that this is our son and that he was born blind. We do not know how he sees now, nor do we know who opened his eyes. Ask him, he is of age; he can speak for himself." His parents said this because they were afraid of the Jews, for the Jews had already agreed that if anyone acknowledged him as the Christ, he would be expelled from the synagogue. For this reason his parents said, "He is of age; question him."

So a second time they called the man who had been blind and said to him, "Give God the praise! We know that this man is a sinner." He replied, "If he is a sinner, I do not know. One thing I do know is that I was blind and now I see." So they said to him, "What did he do to you? How did he open your eyes?" He answered them, "I told you already and you did not listen. Why do you want to hear it again? Do you want to become his disciples, too?" They ridiculed him and said, "You are that man's disciple; we are disciples of Moses! We know that God spoke to Moses, but we do not know where this one is from." The man answered and said to them, "This is what is so amazing, that you do not know where he is from, yet he opened my eyes. We know that God does not listen to sinners, but if one is devout and does his will, he listens to him. It is unheard of that anyone ever opened the eyes of a person born blind. If this man were not from God, he would not be able to do anything." They answered and said to him, "You were born totally in sin, and are you trying to teach us?" Then they threw him out.

When Jesus heard that they had thrown him out, he found him and said, "Do you believe in the Son of Man?" He answered and said, "Who is he, sir, that I may believe in him?" Jesus said to him, "You have seen him, and the one speaking with you is he." He said, "I do believe, Lord," and he worshiped him. Then Jesus said, "I came into this world for judgment, so that those who do not see might see, and those who do see might become blind."

Some of the Pharisees who were with him heard this and said to him, "Surely we are not also blind, are we?" Jesus said to them, "If you were blind, you would have no sin; but now you are saying, 'We see,' so your sin remains."
The Gospel of the Lord.

Liturgy of the Eucharist, *p. 897.*

Monday

Entrance Antiphon

Lord, I put my trust in you; I shall be glad and rejoice in your mercy, because you have seen my affliction. (Ps 30:7– 8)

Opening Prayer

Father, creator,
you give the world new life by your sacraments.
May we, your Church, grow in your life
and continue to receive your help on earth.

Grant this through our Lord Jesus Christ, your Son,
who lives and reigns with you and the Holy Spirit,
one God, for ever and ever.

TODAY'S LIVING WORD

Today's first reading announces the restoration of Jerusalem as a new creation, using the verb "create" *(bara)* three times. The Bible reserves *bara* for the creative activity of God alone, and what God creates is fullness of life. "No longer shall there be in it an infant who lives but a few days, or an old man who does not round out his full lifetime." In today's Gospel the new creation asserts itself in the cure of the royal official's son. The emphasis in the story falls on the power of Jesus' word. Coupled with the emphatic repetition of the word "create" in the first reading, it tells us that in and through Jesus, God's word is once again calling new heavens and a new earth into being. In John's Gospel the miracles of Jesus signify this.

The total transformation announced by Isaiah and anticipated in the ministry of Jesus has not yet been fully realized. Reality for us is not always rejoicing and happiness. But like the royal official in the story, we must put our faith in the word of Jesus.

FIRST READING

Is 65:17– 21

*No longer shall the sound of weeping or
the sound of crying be heard.*

A reading from the Book of the Prophet Isaiah

Thus says the LORD:

Lo, I am about to create new heavens
    and a new earth;
The things of the past shall not be remembered
    or come to mind.
Instead, there shall always be rejoicing and happiness
    in what I create;
For I create Jerusalem to be a joy
    and its people to be a delight;
I will rejoice in Jerusalem
    and exult in my people.
No longer shall the sound of weeping be heard there,
    or the sound of crying;
No longer shall there be in it
    an infant who lives but a few days,
    or an old man who does not round out his full lifetime;
He dies a mere youth who reaches but a hundred years,
    and he who fails of a hundred shall be thought accursed.
They shall live in the houses they build,
    and eat the fruit of the vineyards they plant.

The word of the Lord.

Responsorial Psalm
Ps 30:2 and 4, 5–6, 11–12a and 13b

R. I will praise you, Lord, for you have rescued me.

I will extol you, O LORD, for you drew me clear
    and did not let my enemies rejoice over me.
O LORD, you brought me up from the nether world;
    you preserved me from among those going down into the pit.

R. I will praise you, Lord, for you have rescued me.

Sing praise to the LORD, you his faithful ones,
 and give thanks to his holy name.
For his anger lasts but a moment;
 a lifetime, his good will.
At nightfall, weeping enters in,
 but with the dawn, rejoicing.

R. I will praise you, Lord, for you have rescued me.

"Hear, O LORD, and have pity on me;
 O LORD, be my helper."
You changed my mourning into dancing;
 O LORD, my God, forever will I give you thanks.

R. I will praise you, Lord, for you have rescued me.

Verse Before the Gospel   Am 5:14
Seek good and not evil so that you may live,
and the LORD will be with you.

GOSPEL

Jn 4:43 – 54

Go, your son will live.

A reading from the holy Gospel according to John

At that time Jesus left [Samaria] for Galilee. For Jesus himself
testified that a prophet has no honor in his native place. When
he came into Galilee, the Galileans welcomed him, since they
had seen all he had done in Jerusalem at the feast; for they
themselves had gone to the feast.

Then he returned to Cana in Galilee, where he had made
the water wine. Now there was a royal official whose son was
ill in Capernaum. When he heard that Jesus had arrived in
Galilee from Judea, he went to him and asked him to come
down and heal his son, who was near death. Jesus said to him,
"Unless you people see signs and wonders, you will not
believe." The royal official said to him, "Sir, come down before
my child dies." Jesus said to him, "You may go; your son will

live." The man believed what Jesus said to him and left. While the man was on his way back, his slaves met him and told him that his boy would live. He asked them when he began to recover. They told him, "The fever left him yesterday, about one in the afternoon." The father realized that just at that time Jesus had said to him, "Your son will live," and he and his whole household came to believe. Now this was the second sign Jesus did when he came to Galilee from Judea.

The Gospel of the Lord.

Liturgy of the Eucharist, *p. 897.*

Prayer over the Gifts

Pray, brethren...

Lord,
through the gifts we present
may we receive the grace
to cast off the old ways of life
and to redirect our course toward the life of heaven.
We ask this in the name of Jesus the Lord.

Preface of Lent I–IV, *pp. 940–942.*

Communion Antiphon

I shall put my spirit within you, says the Lord; you will obey my laws and keep my decrees.   (Ez 36:27)

Prayer after Communion

Let us pray.

Pause for silent prayer, if this has not preceded.

Lord,
may your gifts bring us life and holiness
and lead us to the happiness of eternal life.
We ask this through Christ our Lord.

Tuesday

Entrance Antiphon

Come to the waters, all you who thirst; though you have no money, come and drink with joy.   (See Is 55:1)

Opening Prayer

Father,
may our lenten observance
prepare us to embrace the paschal mystery
and to proclaim your salvation with joyful praise.

We ask this through our Lord Jesus Christ, your Son,
who lives and reigns with you and the Holy Spirit,
one God, for ever and ever.

TODAY'S LIVING WORD

Both of today's readings attest to God's life-giving power. In a vision, the prophet Ezekiel sees from beneath the threshold of the temple a trickle of water that swells into a river, fresh water that brings life wherever it flows—fish and fruit trees, food and medicine. In the Gospel, Jesus stands by the Sheep Pool in the place called Bethesda and sees a man who needs healing. He has been sick for thirty-eight years. Without waiting for the movement of the water, which was thought to have curative power, Jesus restores the man to fullness of life. Ironically, this life-giving work will in the end cost Jesus his life, for they "began to persecute Jesus."

The healed man is not an attractive character. When Jesus asks if he wants to be healed, he whines self-pityingly. When he is stopped for carrying his mat on the Sabbath, he blames the man who cured him. When he learns who Jesus is, he reports him to the authorities. He never takes hold of the life that Jesus has restored to him. So Jesus says to him and to us, "You are well; do not sin any more."

FIRST READING

Ex 47:1–9, 12

I saw water flowing from the temple,
and all who were touched by it were saved (see Roman Missal).

A reading from the Book of the Prophet Ezekiel

The angel brought me, Ezekiel, back to the entrance of the temple of the LORD, and I saw water flowing out from beneath the threshold of the temple toward the east, for the façade of the temple was toward the east; the water flowed down from the right side of the temple, south of the altar. He led me outside by the north gate, and around to the outer gate facing the east, where I saw water trickling from the right side. Then when he had walked off to the east with a measuring cord in his hand, he measured off a thousand cubits and had me wade through the water, which was ankle-deep. He measured off another thousand and once more had me wade through the water, which was now knee-deep. Again he measured off a thousand and had me wade; the water was up to my waist. Once more he measured off a thousand, but there was now a river through which I could not wade; for the water had risen so high it had become a river that could not be crossed except by swimming. He asked me, "Have you seen this, son of man?" Then he brought me to the bank of the river, where he had me sit. Along the bank of the river I saw very many trees on both sides. He said to me, "This water flows into the eastern district down upon the Arabah, and empties into the sea, the salt waters, which it makes fresh. Wherever the river flows, every sort of living creature that can multiply shall live, and there shall be abundant fish, for wherever this water comes the sea shall be made fresh. Along both banks of the river, fruit trees of every kind shall grow; their leaves shall not fade, nor their fruit fail. Every month they shall bear fresh fruit, for they shall be watered by the flow from the sanctuary. Their fruit shall serve for food, and their leaves for medicine."

The word of the Lord.

Responsorial Psalm

Ps 46:2–3, 5–6, 8–9

**R. The Lord of hosts is with us; our stronghold
is the God of Jacob.**

God is our refuge and our strength,
  an ever-present help in distress.
Therefore we fear not, though the earth be shaken
  and mountains plunge into the depths of the sea.

**R. The Lord of hosts is with us; our stronghold
is the God of Jacob.**

There is a stream whose runlets gladden the city of God,
  the holy dwelling of the Most High.
God is in its midst; it shall not be disturbed;
  God will help it at the break of dawn.

**R. The Lord of hosts is with us; our stronghold
is the God of Jacob.**

The LORD of hosts is with us;
  our stronghold is the God of Jacob.
Come! behold the deeds of the LORD,
  the astounding things he has wrought on earth.

**R. The Lord of hosts is with us; our stronghold
is the God of Jacob.**

Verse Before the Gospel Ps 51:12a, 14a
A clean heart create for me, O God;
  give me back the joy of your salvation.

GOSPEL

Jn 5:1–16

Immediately the man became well.

A reading from the holy Gospel according to John

There was a feast of the Jews, and Jesus went up to Jerusalem.
Now there is in Jerusalem at the Sheep Gate a pool called in
Hebrew Bethesda, with five porticoes. In these lay a large
number of ill, blind, lame, and crippled. One man was there
who had been ill for thirty-eight years. When Jesus saw him

lying there and knew that he had been ill for a long time, he said to him, "Do you want to be well?" The sick man answered him, "Sir, I have no one to put me into the pool when the water is stirred up; while I am on my way, someone else gets down there before me." Jesus said to him, "Rise, take up your mat, and walk." Immediately the man became well, took up his mat, and walked.

Now that day was a sabbath. So the Jews said to the man who was cured, "It is the sabbath, and it is not lawful for you to carry your mat." He answered them, "The man who made me well told me, 'Take up your mat and walk.' " They asked him, "Who is the man who told you, 'Take it up and walk'?" The man who was healed did not know who it was, for Jesus had slipped away, since there was a crowd there. After this Jesus found him in the temple area and said to him, "Look, you are well; do not sin any more, so that nothing worse may happen to you." The man went and told the Jews that Jesus was the one who had made him well. Therefore, the Jews began to persecute Jesus because he did this on a sabbath.

The Gospel of the Lord.

Liturgy of the Eucharist, p. 897.

Prayer over the Gifts

Pray, brethren...

Lord,
may your gifts of bread and wine
which nourish us here on earth
become the food of our eternal life.

Grant this through Christ our Lord.

Preface of Lent I–IV, pp. 940–942.

Communion Antiphon

The Lord is my shepherd; there is nothing I shall want. In green pastures he gives me rest, he leads me beside the waters of peace.   (Ps 22:1–2)

Prayer after Communion

Let us pray.

Pause for silent prayer, if this has not preceded.

Lord,
may your holy sacraments cleanse and renew us;
may they bring us your help
and lead us to salvation.

We ask this in the name of Jesus the Lord.

Wednesday

Entrance Antiphon

I pray to you, O God, for the time of your favor. Lord, in your great love, answer me.   (Ps 68:14)

Opening Prayer

Lord,
you reward virtue
and forgive the repentant sinner.
Grant us your forgiveness
as we come before you confessing our guilt.

We ask this through our Lord Jesus Christ, your Son,
who lives and reigns with you and the Holy Spirit,
one God, for ever and ever.

TODAY'S LIVING WORD

The oracle of Isaiah in today's first reading celebrates the works of God the Father, who restores the land, releases prisoners, and returns home an exiled people. In the Gospel, the Father shows the Son these same works, raising the dead and granting life. And so the Son, who does "what he sees the Father doing…give[s] life to whomever he wishes." But whereas in Isaiah the announcement of salvation is greeted with joyful song in heaven and on earth, in John's Gospel the words and works of Jesus draw an angry response.

The juxtaposition of these two readings also invites us to recognize a mother's love in the works of the Father. "Can a mother forget her infant, be without tenderness for the child of her womb?" God asks. The words take on particular force when they are placed alongside the Gospel that affirms that believing in Jesus is the way to eternal life, that is, to becoming children of God. "Even should she forget, I will never forget you," says the Lord our God.

FIRST READING   Is 49:8–15

I have given you as a covenant to the people, to restore the land.

A reading from the Book of the Prophet Isaiah

Thus says the LORD:
In a time of favor I answer you,
    on the day of salvation I help you;
        and I have kept you and given you as a covenant to the
            people,
To restore the land
    and allot the desolate heritages,
Saying to the prisoners: Come out!
To those in darkness: Show yourselves!
Along the ways they shall find pasture,
    on every bare height shall their pastures be.
They shall not hunger or thirst,
    nor shall the scorching wind or the sun strike them;
For he who pities them leads them
    and guides them beside springs of water.
I will cut a road through all my mountains,

and make my highways level.
See, some shall come from afar,
   others from the north and the west,
   and some from the land of Syene.
Sing out, O heavens, and rejoice, O earth,
   break forth into song, you mountains.
For the LORD comforts his people
   and shows mercy to his afflicted.
But Zion said, "The LORD has forsaken me;
   Lord has forgotten me."
Can a mother forget her infant,
   be without tenderness for the child of her womb?
Even should she forget,
   I will never forget you.
The word of the Lord.

Responsorial Psalm

Ps 145:8–9, 13cd–14, 17–18

   R. The Lord is gracious and merciful.

The LORD is gracious and merciful,
   slow to anger and of great kindness.
The LORD is good to all
   and compassionate toward all his works.

   R. The Lord is gracious and merciful.

The LORD is faithful in all his words
   and holy in all his works.
The LORD lifts up all who are falling
   and raises up all who are bowed down.

   R. The Lord is gracious and merciful.

The LORD is just in all his ways
   and holy in all his works.
The LORD is near to all who call upon him,
   to all who call upon him in truth.

R. The Lord is gracious and merciful.

Verse Before the Gospel   Jn 11:25a, 26
I am the resurrection and the life, says the Lord;
whoever believes in me will never die.

GOSPEL   Jn 5:17–30

*As the Father raises the dead and gives them life,
so also does the Son give life to those whom he chooses.*

A reading from the holy Gospel according to John

Jesus answered the Jews: "My Father is at work until now, so
I am at work." For this reason they tried all the more to kill
him, because he not only broke the sabbath but he also called
God his own father, making himself equal to God.

Jesus answered and said to them, "Amen, amen, I say to
you, the Son cannot do anything on his own, but only what he
sees the Father doing; for what he does, the Son will do also.
For the Father loves the Son and shows him everything that he
himself does, and he will show him greater works than these,
so that you may be amazed. For just as the Father raises the
dead and gives life, so also does the Son give life to whomever
he wishes. Nor does the Father judge anyone, but he has given
all judgment to the Son, so that all may honor the Son just as
they honor the Father. Whoever does not honor the Son does
not honor the Father who sent him. Amen, amen, I say to you,
whoever hears my word and believes in the one who sent me
has eternal life and will not come to condemnation, but has
passed from death to life. Amen, amen, I say to you, the hour
is coming and is now here when the dead will hear the voice of
the Son of God, and those who hear will live. For just as the
Father has life in himself, so also he gave to the Son the
possession of life in himself. And he gave him power to exercise

judgment, because he is the Son of Man. Do not be amazed at this, because the hour is coming in which all who are in the tombs will hear his voice and will come out, those who have done good deeds to the resurrection of life, but those who have done wicked deeds to the resurrection of condemnation.

"I cannot do anything on my own; I judge as I hear, and my judgment is just, because I do not seek my own will but the will of the one who sent me."

The Gospel of the Lord.

Liturgy of the Eucharist, *p. 897.*

Prayer over the Gifts

Pray, brethren...

Lord God,
may the power of this sacrifice wash away our sins,
renew our lives and bring us to salvation.
We ask this in the name of Jesus the Lord.

Preface of Lent I–IV, *pp. 940–942.*

Communion Antiphon

God sent his Son into the world, not to condemn it, but so that the world might be saved through him.   (Jn 3:17)

Prayer after Communion

Let us pray.

Pause for silent prayer, if this has not preceded.

Lord,
may we never misuse your healing gifts,
but always find in them a source of life and salvation.
Grant this through Christ our Lord.

Thursday

Entrance Antiphon

Let hearts rejoice who search for the Lord. Seek the Lord and his strength, seek always the face of the Lord.   (Ps 104:3 – 4)

Opening Prayer

Merciful Father,
may the penance of our lenten observance
make us your obedient people.
May the love within us be seen in what we do
and lead us to the joy of Easter.

Grant this through our Lord Jesus Christ, your Son,
who lives and reigns with you and the Holy Spirit,
one God, for ever and ever.

TODAY'S LIVING WORD

In the selection from Exodus, Moses is Israel's intercessor; in the passage from John, he is their accuser. The episode of the golden calf is the occasion for Moses once again to step into the breach before God in order to save his people. "The arguments of his prayer," the *Catechism of the Catholic Church* says, "will inspire the boldness of the great intercessors among the Jewish people and in the Church: God is love; he is therefore righteous and faithful; he cannot contradict himself; he must remember his marvelous deeds, since his glory is at stake, and he cannot forsake this people that bears his name" (n. 2577).

It is often observed that the ministry of Jesus in John's Gospel is cast as a trial; in today's Gospel, court is in session. Arguing in his own defense, Jesus turns the tables on those who accuse him of breaking Mosaic law by curing the man at the pool of Bethesda on the Sabbath. He tells them that Moses, their intercessor on whom they set their hopes, will accuse them before the Father. In this courtroom drama, even Moses bears witness to Jesus.

FIRST READING

Ex 32:7–14

Relent in punishing your people.

A reading from the Book of Exodus

The LORD said to Moses, "Go down at once to your people whom you brought out of the land of Egypt, for they have become depraved. They have soon turned aside from the way I pointed out to them, making for themselves a molten calf and worshiping it, sacrificing to it and crying out, 'This is your God, O Israel, who brought you out of the land of Egypt!' The LORD said to Moses, "I see how stiff-necked this people is. Let me alone, then, that my wrath may blaze up against them to consume them. Then I will make of you a great nation."

But Moses implored the LORD, his God, saying, "Why, O LORD, should your wrath blaze up against your own people, whom you brought out of the land of Egypt with such great power and with so strong a hand? Why should the Egyptians say, 'With evil intent he brought them out, that he might kill them in the mountains and exterminate them from the face of the earth'? Let your blazing wrath die down; relent in punishing your people. Remember your servants Abraham, Isaac and Israel, and how you swore to them by your own self, saying, 'I will make your descendants as numerous as the stars in the sky; and all this land that I promised, I will give your descendants as their perpetual heritage.' " So the LORD relented in the punishment he had threatened to inflict on his people.

The word of the Lord.

Responsorial Psalm

Ps 106:19–20, 21–22, 23

R. **Remember us, O Lord, as you favor your people.**

Our fathers made a calf in Horeb

and adored a molten image;
They exchanged their glory
  for the image of a grass-eating bullock.

R. Remember us, O Lord, as you favor your people.

They forgot the God who had saved them,
  who had done great deeds in Egypt,
Wondrous deeds in the land of Ham,
  terrible things at the Red Sea.

R. Remember us, O Lord, as you favor your people.

Then he spoke of exterminating them,
  but Moses, his chosen one,
Withstood him in the breach
  to turn back his destructive wrath.

R. Remember us, O Lord, as you favor your people.

Verse Before the Gospel   Jn 3:16
  God so loved the world that he gave his only-begotten Son,
  so that everyone who believes in him might have eternal life.

GOSPEL
Jn 5:31–47

The one who will accuse you is Moses,
in whom you have placed your hope.

A reading from the holy Gospel according to John

Jesus said to the Jews: "If I testify on my own behalf, my testimony is not true. But there is another who testifies on my behalf, and I know that the testimony he gives on my behalf is true. You sent emissaries to John, and he testified to the truth. I do not accept human testimony, but I say this so that you may be saved. He was a burning and shining lamp, and for a while you were content to rejoice in his light. But I have testimony greater than John's. The works that the Father gave me to accomplish, these works that I perform testify on my behalf that the Father has sent me. Moreover, the Father who sent me has testified on my behalf. But you have never heard his voice nor seen his form, and you do not have his word remaining in you, because you do not believe in the one whom he has sent. You search the Scriptures, because you think you have eternal life through them; even they testify on my behalf. But you do not want to come to me to have life.

"I do not accept human praise; moreover, I know that you do not have the love of God in you. I came in the name of my Father, but you do not accept me; yet if another comes in his own name, you will accept him. How can you believe, when you accept praise from one another and do not seek the praise that comes from the only God? Do not think that I will accuse you before the Father: the one who will accuse you is Moses, in whom you have placed your hope. For if you had believed Moses, you would have believed me, because he wrote about me. But if you do not believe his writings, how will you believe my words?"

The Gospel of the Lord.

Liturgy of the Eucharist, *p. 897.*

Prayer over the Gifts

Pray, brethren...

All-powerful God,
look upon our weakness.
May the sacrifice we offer
bring us purity and strength.

We ask this in the name of Jesus the Lord.

Preface of Lent I–IV, *pp. 940–942.*

Communion Antiphon

I will put my law within them, I will write it on their hearts; then I shall be their God, and they will be my people.

(Jer 31:33)

Prayer after Communion

Let us pray.

Pause for silent prayer, if this has not preceded.

Lord,
may the sacraments we receive
cleanse us of sin and free us from guilt,
for our sins bring us sorrow
but your promise of salvation brings us joy.

We ask this through Christ our Lord.

Friday

Entrance Antiphon

Save me, O God, by your power, and grant me justice! God, hear my prayer; listen to my plea. (Ps 53:3–4)

Opening Prayer

Father,
our source of life,
you know our weakness.
May we reach out with joy to grasp your hand
and walk more readily in your ways.

We ask this through our Lord Jesus Christ, your Son,
who lives and reigns with you and the Holy Spirit,
one God, for ever and ever.

TODAY'S LIVING WORD

Again in a scene from John's Gospel, confusion among the people leads to confrontation with Jesus. Here the people wonder if Jesus might be the Messiah after all. Then they remember that they know where he comes from, and there is a tradition that no one is supposed to know the Messiah's origins. But Jesus tells them that they do *not* know where he comes from. Only believers, who are themselves "from God," recognize the divine origin of Jesus. Only they know the One whom God has sent.

The first reading from the Book of Wisdom is a meditation on the Fourth Servant Song of Isaiah (cf. Is 52:13—53:12). The anonymous just one of the song is here beset by the wicked because he "styles himself a child of the Lord" and "boasts that God is his Father." Clearly, as the author of Wisdom reflected on Isaiah, the author of John reflected on Wisdom in depicting the mission of Jesus, God's just one, and the motives of his opponents. As the Church has recognized, "later biblical writings often depend upon earlier ones" and develop from these fresh insights, "sometimes quite different from the original."*

* *The Interpretation of the Bible in the Church* (Boston: Pauline Books & Media, 1993), p. 90.

FIRST READING

Wis 2:1a, 12–22

Let us condemn him to a shameful death.

A reading from the Book of Wisdom

The wicked said among themselves,
    thinking not aright:
"Let us beset the just one, because he is obnoxious to us;
    he sets himself against our doings,
Reproaches us for transgressions of the law
    and charges us with violations of our training.
He professes to have knowledge of God
    and styles himself a child of the Lord.
To us he is the censure of our thoughts;
    merely to see him is a hardship for us,
Because his life is not like that of others,
    and different are his ways.

He judges us debased;
    he holds aloof from our paths as from things impure.
He calls blest the destiny of the just
    and boasts that God is his Father.
Let us see whether his words be true;
    let us find out what will happen to him.
For if the just one be the son of God, he will defend him
    and deliver him from the hand of his foes.
With revilement and torture let us put him to the test
    that we may have proof of his gentleness
    and try his patience.
Let us condemn him to a shameful death;
    for according to his own words, God will take care of him."
These were their thoughts, but they erred;
    for their wickedness blinded them,
and they knew not the hidden counsels of God;
    neither did they count on a recompense of holiness
    nor discern the innocent souls' reward.

The word of the Lord.

Responsorial Psalm   Ps 34:17–18, 19–20, 21 and 23

    R. The Lord is close to the brokenhearted.

The LORD confronts the evildoers,
  to destroy remembrance of them from the earth.
When the just cry out, the LORD hears them,
  and from all their distress he rescues them.

    R. The Lord is close to the brokenhearted.

The LORD is close to the brokenhearted;
  and those who are crushed in spirit he saves.
Many are the troubles of the just man,
  but out of them all the LORD delivers him.

R. The Lord is close to the brokenhearted.

He watches over all his bones;
  not one of them shall be broken.
The LORD redeems the lives of his servants;
  no one incurs guilt who takes refuge in him.

R. The Lord is close to the brokenhearted.

> **Verse Before the Gospel** Mt 4:4b
> One does not live on bread alone,
> but on every word that comes forth from the mouth of God.

GOSPEL   Jn 7:1–2, 10, 25–30

They tried to arrest him, but his hour had not yet come.

A reading from the holy Gospel according to John

Jesus moved about within Galilee; he did not wish to travel in
Judea, because the Jews were trying to kill him. But the Jewish
feast of Tabernacles was near.

But when his brothers had gone up to the feast, he himself
also went up, not openly but as it were in secret.

Some of the inhabitants of Jerusalem said, "Is he not the
one they are trying to kill? And look, he is speaking openly
and they say nothing to him. Could the authorities have realized
that he is the Christ? But we know where he is from. When the
Christ comes, no one will know where he is from." So Jesus
cried out in the temple area as he was teaching and said, "You
know me and also know where I am from. Yet I did not come
on my own, but the one who sent me, whom you do not know,
is true. I know him, because I am from him, and he sent me."
So they tried to arrest him, but no one laid a hand upon him,
because his hour had not yet come.

The Gospel of the Lord.

Liturgy of the Eucharist, *p. 897.*

Prayer over the Gifts

Pray, brethren...

All-powerful God,
may the healing power of this sacrifice
free us from sin
and help us to approach you with pure hearts.

Grant this through Christ our Lord.

Preface of Lent I–IV, *pp. 940–942.*

Communion Antiphon

In Christ, through the shedding of his blood, we have redemption and forgiveness of our sins by the abundance of his grace.

(Eph 1:7)

Prayer after Communion

Let us pray.

Pause for silent prayer, if this has not preceded.

Lord,
in this eucharist we pass from death to life.
Keep us from our old and sinful ways
and help us to continue in the new life.
We ask this in the name of Jesus the Lord.

Saturday

Entrance Antiphon

The snares of death overtook me, the ropes of hell tightened around me; in my distress I called upon the Lord, and he heard my voice.

(Ps 17:5–7)

Opening Prayer

Lord,
guide us in your gentle mercy,

for left to ourselves
we cannot do your will.

Grant this through our Lord Jesus Christ, your Son,
who lives and reigns with you and the Holy Spirit,
one God, for ever and ever.

TODAY'S LIVING WORD

The readings today depict Jeremiah and Jesus as rejected prophets. Controversy swirls around Jeremiah, who is shocked and shaken to discover that his opponents have been "hatching plots" against him while he has been totally unsuspecting, "like a trusting lamb led to slaughter." In the Gospel, controversy swirls around Jesus too. The crowd is divided over the question of his origins. The temple police are taken in by his teaching. There is even dissent within the Pharisees' ranks, as Nicodemus objects, "Does our law condemn a person before it first hears him and finds out what he is doing?"

The reappearance of Nicodemus, that "closet Christian" who came to Jesus under cover of night (cf. Jn 3:2), is an interesting development. His defense of Jesus is weak and ineffective. The sarcasm of his fellows easily dismisses him. He is not a hero, and sometimes defending one's faith in Jesus requires nothing less than heroism.

FIRST READING
Jer 11:18–20

I am like a trusting lamb led to slaughter.

A reading from the Book of the Prophet Jeremiah

I knew their plot because the LORD informed me; at that time you, O LORD, showed me their doings.

Yet I, like a trusting lamb led to slaughter, had not realized that they were hatching plots against me: "Let us destroy the tree in its vigor; let us cut him off from the land of the living, so that his name will be spoken no more."

But, you, O LORD of hosts, O just Judge,
    searcher of mind and heart,

Let me witness the vengeance you take on them,
for to you I have entrusted my cause!

The word of the Lord.

Responsorial Psalm

Ps 7:2–3, 9bc–10, 11–12

R. O Lord, my God, in you I take refuge.

O LORD, my God, in you I take refuge;
save me from all my pursuers and rescue me,
Lest I become like the lion's prey,
to be torn to pieces, with no one to rescue me.

R. O Lord, my God, in you I take refuge.

Do me justice, O LORD, because I am just,
and because of the innocence that is mine.
Let the malice of the wicked come to an end,
but sustain the just,
O searcher of heart and soul, O just God.

R. O Lord, my God, in you I take refuge.

A shield before me is God,
who saves the upright of heart;
A just judge is God,
a God who punishes day by day.

R. O Lord, my God, in you I take refuge.

Verse Before the Gospel   See Lk 8:15

Blessed are they who have kept the word with a generous heart
and yield a harvest through perseverance.

GOSPEL

Jn 7:40–53

The Christ will not come from Galilee, will he?

A reading from the holy Gospel according to John

Some in the crowd who heard these words of Jesus said, "This
is truly the Prophet." Others said, "This is the Christ." But
others said, "The Christ will not come from Galilee, will he?

Does not Scripture say that the Christ will be of David's family and come from Bethlehem, the village where David lived?" So a division occurred in the crowd because of him. Some of them even wanted to arrest him, but no one laid hands on him.

So the guards went to the chief priests and Pharisees, who asked them, "Why did you not bring him?" The guards answered, "Never before has anyone spoken like this man." So the Pharisees answered them, "Have you also been deceived? Have any of the authorities or the Pharisees believed in him? But this crowd, which does not know the law, is accursed." Nicodemus, one of their members who had come to him earlier, said to them, "Does our law condemn a man before it first hears him and finds out what he is doing?" They answered and said to him, "You are not from Galilee also, are you? Look and see that no prophet arises from Galilee."

Then each went to his own house.

The Gospel of the Lord.

Liturgy of the Eucharist, *p. 897.*

Prayer over the Gifts

Pray, brethren...

Father,
accept our gifts
and make our hearts obedient to your will.

We ask this in the name of Jesus the Lord.

Preface of Lent I–IV, *pp. 940–942.*

Communion Antiphon

We have been ransomed with the precious blood of Christ, as with the blood of a lamb without blemish or spot.   (1 Pt 1:19)

Prayer after Communion

Let us pray.

Pause for silent prayer, if this has not preceded.

Lord,
may the power of your holy gifts free us from sin
and help us to please you in our daily lives.

We ask this through Christ our Lord.

OPTIONAL MASS FOR
THE FIFTH WEEK OF LENT

This Mass may be used on any day of this week, especially in Cycles B and C when the Gospel of Lazarus is not read on the Fifth Sunday of Lent.

TODAY'S LIVING WORD

In John's Gospel, Jesus' miracles are signs *(semeia)* revealing the glory of God in and through the person of Jesus. Jesus, who came so that all who believe in him might have eternal life, in this last sign gives physical life to his beloved Lazarus. The significance of the miracle is stated at the beginning and the end of the story. To the disciples at the beginning and to Martha at the end, Jesus promises a revelation of God's glory. St. Irenaeus once remarked that "The glory of God is the human person fully alive." This is the point of John's story too.

Both the raising of Lazarus and the raising of the Shunammite woman's child, today's first reading, highlight the response of strong women to the death of those they love.

Both Martha and the Shunammite recognize the life-giving power of God in the ministries of Jesus and Elisha. They have welcomed these men into their homes and when death strikes, they turn to them expectantly. Miracles will follow. May we who have welcomed into our hearts Jesus, "the resurrection and the life," trust him with our lives and the lives of those we love.

FIRST READING

2 Kgs 4:18b–21, 32–37

The man of God stretched himself over the boy,
and the child's flesh grew warm.

A reading from the second Book of Kings

The day came when the child of the Shunammite woman was old enough to go out to his father among the reapers. "My head hurts!" he complained to his father. "Carry him to his mother," the father said to a servant. The servant picked him up and carried him to his mother; he stayed with her until noon, when he died in her lap. The mother took him upstairs and laid him on the bed of the man of God. Closing the door on him, she went out.

When Elisha reached the house, he found the boy lying dead. He went in, closed the door on them both, and prayed to the LORD. Then he lay upon the child on the bed, placing his mouth upon the child's mouth, his eyes upon the eyes, and his hands upon the hands. As Elisha stretched himself over the child, the body became warm. He arose, paced up and down the room, and then once more lay down upon the boy, who now sneezed seven times and opened his eyes. Elisha summoned Gehazi and said, "Call the Shunammite." She came at his call, and Elisha said to her, "Take your son." She came in and fell at his feet in gratitude; then she took her son and left the room.

The word of the Lord.

Responsorial Psalm

Ps 17:1, 6–7, 8b and 15

R. **Lord, when your glory appears, my joy will be full.**

Hear, O LORD, a just suit;
    attend to my outcry;
    hearken to my prayer from lips without deceit.

R. **Lord, when your glory appears, my joy will be full.**

I call upon you, for you will answer me, O God;
  incline your ear to me; hear my word.
Show your wondrous mercies,
  O savior of those who flee
  from their foes to refuge at your right hand.

R. Lord, when your glory appears, my joy will be full.

Hide me in the shadow of your wings.
But I in justice shall behold your face;
  on waking, I shall be content in your presence.

R. Lord, when your glory appears, my joy will be full.

Verse Before the Gospel   Jn 11:25a, 26
I am the resurrection and the life, says the Lord;
whoever believes in me will never die.

GOSPEL
Jn 11:1–45

I am the resurrection and the life.

A reading from the holy Gospel according to John

There was a man who was ill, Lazarus from Bethany, the village of Mary and her sister Martha. Mary was the one who had anointed the Lord with perfumed oil and dried his feet with her hair; it was her brother Lazarus who was ill. So the sisters sent word to Jesus saying, "Master, the one you love is ill." When Jesus heard this he said, "This illness is not to end in death, but is for the glory of God, that the Son of God may be glorified through it." Now Jesus loved Martha and her sister and Lazarus. So when he heard that he was ill, he remained for two days in the place where he was. Then after this he said to his disciples, "Let us go back to Judea." The disciples said to him, "Rabbi, the Jews were just trying to stone you, and you want to go back there?" Jesus answered, "Are there not twelve hours in a day? If one walks during the day, he does not stumble, because he sees the light of this world. But if one walks at night, he stumbles, because the light is not in him." He said this, and then told them, "Our friend Lazarus is asleep, but I am going to awaken him." So the disciples said to him, "Master, if he is asleep, he will be saved." But Jesus was talking about his death, while they thought that he meant ordinary sleep. So then Jesus said to them clearly, "Lazarus has died. And I am glad for you that I was not there, that you may believe. Let us go to him." So Thomas, called Didymus, said to his fellow disciples, "Let us also go to die with him."

When Jesus arrived, he found that Lazarus had already been in the tomb for four days. Now Bethany was near Jerusalem, only about two miles away. And many of the Jews had come to Martha and Mary to comfort them about their brother. When Martha heard that Jesus was coming, she went to meet him; but Mary sat at home. Martha said to Jesus, "Lord, if you had been here, my brother would not have died. But even now I know that whatever you ask of God, God will give you." Jesus said to her, "Your brother will rise." Martha said to him, "I know he will rise, in the resurrection on the last day." Jesus told her, "I am the resurrection and the life; whoever believes in me, even if he dies, will live, and everyone who lives and believes in me will never die. Do you believe this?" She said to him, "Yes, Lord. I have come to believe that you are the Christ, the Son of God, the one who is coming into the world."

When she had said this, she went and called her sister Mary secretly, saying, "The teacher is here and is asking for you." As soon as she heard this, she rose quickly and went to him. For Jesus had not yet come into the village, but was still where Martha had met him. So when the Jews who were with her in the house comforting her saw Mary get up quickly and go out, they followed her, presuming that she was going to the tomb to weep there. When Mary came to where Jesus was and saw him, she fell at his feet and said to him, "Lord, if you had been here, my brother would not have died." When Jesus saw her weeping and the Jews who had come with her weeping, he became perturbed and deeply troubled, and said, "Where have you laid him?" They said to him, "Sir, come and see." And Jesus wept. So the Jews said, "See how he loved him." But some of them said, "Could not the one who opened the eyes of the blind man have done something so that this man would not have died?"

So Jesus, perturbed again, came to the tomb. It was a cave, and a stone lay across it. Jesus said, "Take away the stone." Martha, the dead man's sister, said to him, "Lord, by now there will be a stench; he has been dead for four days." Jesus said to her, "Did I not tell you that if you believe you will see the glory of God?" So they took away the stone. And Jesus raised his eyes and said, "Father, I thank you for hearing me. I know that you always hear me; but because of the crowd here I have said this, that they may believe that you sent me." And when he had said this, he cried out in a loud voice, "Lazarus, come out!" The dead man came out, tied hand and foot with burial bands, and his face was wrapped in a cloth. So Jesus said to them, "Untie him and let him go."

Now many of the Jews who had come to Mary and seen what he had done began to believe in him.

The Gospel of the Lord.

Liturgy of the Eucharist, *p. 897.*

Monday

Entrance Antiphon

God, take pity on me! My enemies are crushing me; all day long they wage war on me.   (Ps 55:2)

Opening Prayer

Father of love, source of all blessings,
help us to pass from our old life of sin
to the new life of grace.
Prepare us for the glory of your kingdom.

We ask this through our Lord Jesus Christ, your Son,
who lives and reigns with you and the Holy Spirit,
one God, for ever and ever.

TODAY'S LIVING WORD

In today's first reading Daniel intervenes on behalf of the chaste Susannah who has been wrongly condemned for adultery, and in the Gospel Jesus intervenes on behalf of a woman "who had been caught in adultery." This Gospel story does not appear in the earliest manuscripts of John. A copyist may have thought it a good illustration of Jesus' words in today's alternate Gospel reading, "I do not judge anyone." If, as John says, the Jews of Jesus' day were not allowed to put anyone to death (18:31), then bringing the unfortunate woman to Jesus may have been an attempt to entrap him. Condemning her to death would violate Roman law; failing to condemn her would be a breach of Jewish law. Jesus avoids the trap by doodling in the sand (cf. Jer 17:13).

In this light, the story does not negate the need for judges. Although Jesus did not come to judge the world, even he must pass judgment. But his judgment is true. The scribes and Pharisees in the story, however, are corrupt judges, like the two elders who attack Susannah. They are using the woman for their own ends.

FIRST READING

Dn 13:1–9, 15–17, 19–30, 33–62 or 13:14c–62

*Here I am about to die, though I have done
none of the things charged against me.*

A reading from the Book of the Prophet Daniel

Long form follows; for short form omit what is in brackets.

[In Babylon there lived a man named Joakim, who married a
very beautiful and God-fearing woman, Susanna, the daughter
of Hilkiah; her pious parents had trained their daughter
according to the law of Moses. Joakim was very rich; he had a
garden near his house, and the Jews had recourse to him often
because he was the most respected of them all.

That year, two elders of the people were appointed judges,
of whom the Lord said, "Wickedness has come out of Babylon:
from the elders who were to govern the people as judges."
These men, to whom all brought their cases, frequented the
house of Joakim. When the people left at noon, Susanna used
to enter her husband's garden for a walk. When the old men
saw her enter every day for her walk, they began to lust for
her. They suppressed their consciences; they would not allow
their eyes to look to heaven, and did not keep in mind just
judgments.

One day, while they were waiting for the right moment, she
entered the garden as usual, with two maids only. She decided
to bathe, for the weather was warm. Nobody else was there
except the two elders, who had hidden themselves and were
watching her. "Bring me oil and soap," she said to the maids,
"and shut the garden doors while I bathe."

As soon as the maids had left, the two old men got up and
hurried to her. "Look," they said, "the garden doors are shut,
and no one can see us; give in to our desire, and lie with us. If

you refuse, we will testify against you that you dismissed your maids because a young man was here with you."

"I am completely trapped," Susanna groaned. "If I yield, it will be my death; if I refuse, I cannot escape your power. Yet it is better for me to fall into your power without guilt than to sin before the Lord." Then Susanna shrieked, and the old men also shouted at her, as one of them ran to open the garden doors. When the people in the house heard the cries from the garden, they rushed in by the side gate to see what had happened to her. At the accusations by the old men, the servants felt very much ashamed, for never had any such thing been said about Susanna.

When the people came to her husband Joakim the next day, the two wicked elders also came, fully determined to put Susanna to death. Before all the people they ordered: "Send for Susanna, the daughter of Hilkiah, the wife of Joakim." When she was sent for, she came with her parents, children and all her relatives. All her relatives and the onlookers were weeping.

In the midst of the people the two elders rose up and laid their hands on her head. Through tears she looked up to heaven, for she trusted in the Lord wholeheartedly. The elders made this accusation: "As we were walking in the garden alone, this woman entered with two girls and shut the doors of the garden, dismissing the girls. A young man, who was hidden there, came and lay with her. When we, in a corner of the garden, saw this crime, we ran toward them. We saw them lying together, but the man we could not hold, because he was stronger than we; he opened the doors and ran off. Then we seized her and asked who the young man was, but she refused to tell us. We testify to this."] The assembly [believed them, since they were elders and judges of the people, and they] condemned Susanna to death.

But Susanna cried aloud: "O eternal God, you know what is hidden and are aware of all things before they come to be: you know that they have testified falsely against me. Here I am about to die, though I have done none of the things with which these wicked men have charged me."

The Lord heard her prayer. As she was being led to execution, God stirred up the holy spirit of a young boy named Daniel, and he cried aloud: "I will have no part in the death of this woman." All the people turned and asked him, "What is this you are saying?" He stood in their midst and continued, "Are you such fools, O children of Israel! To condemn a woman of Israel without examination and without clear evidence? Return to court, for they have testified falsely against her."

Then all the people returned in haste. To Daniel the elders said, "Come, sit with us and inform us, since God has given you the prestige of old age." But he replied, "Separate these two far from each other that I may examine them."

After they were separated one from the other, he called one of them and said: "How you have grown evil with age! Now have your past sins come to term: passing unjust sentences, condemning the innocent, and freeing the guilty, although the Lord says, 'The innocent and the just you shall not put to death.' Now, then, if you were a witness, tell me under what tree you saw them together." "Under a mastic tree," he answered. Daniel replied, "Your fine lie has cost you your head, for the angel of God shall receive the sentence from him and split you in two." Putting him to one side, he ordered the other one to be brought. Daniel said to him, "Offspring of Canaan, not of Judah, beauty has seduced you, lust has subverted your conscience. This is how you acted with the daughters of Israel, and in their fear they yielded to you; but a daughter of Judah did not tolerate your wickedness. Now, then, tell me under what tree you surprised them together." "Under an oak," he said. Daniel replied, "Your fine lie has cost you also your head, for the angel of God waits with a sword to cut you in two so as to make an end of you both."

The whole assembly cried aloud, blessing God who saves those who hope in him. They rose up against the two elders, for by their own words Daniel had convicted them of perjury. According to the law of Moses, they inflicted on them the penalty they had plotted to impose on their neighbor: they put them to death. Thus was innocent blood spared that day.

The word of the Lord.

Responsorial Psalm

Ps 23:1–3a, 3b–4, 5, 6

R. Even though I walk in the dark valley I fear no evil; for you are at my side.

The LORD is my shepherd; I shall not want.
  In verdant pastures he gives me repose;
Beside restful waters he leads me;
  he refreshes my soul.

R. Even though I walk in the dark valley I fear no evil; for you are at my side.

He guides me in right paths
  for his name's sake.
Even though I walk in the dark valley
  I fear no evil; for you are at my side
With your rod and your staff
  that give me courage.

**R. Even though I walk in the dark valley I fear no evil;
for you are at my side.**

You spread the table before me
  in the sight of my foes;
You anoint my head with oil;
  my cup overflows.

**R. Even though I walk in the dark valley I fear no evil;
for you are at my side.**

Only goodness and kindness follow me
  all the days of my life;
And I shall dwell in the house of the LORD
  for years to come.

**R. Even though I walk in the dark valley I fear no evil;
for you are at my side.**

Verse Before the Gospel   Ez 33:11

I take no pleasure in the death
of the wicked man, says the Lord,
  but rather in his conversion, that he may live.

GOSPEL
Jn 8:1–11

Let the person without sin be the first to throw a stone.

A reading from the holy Gospel according to John

Jesus went to the Mount of Olives. But early in the morning
he arrived again in the temple area, and all the people started
coming to him, and he sat down and taught them. Then the
scribes and the Pharisees brought a woman who had been
caught in adultery and made her stand in the middle. They
said to him, "Teacher, this woman was caught in the very act
of committing adultery. Now in the law, Moses commanded
us to stone such women. So what do you say?" They said this
to test him, so that they could have some charge to bring against
him. Jesus bent down and began to write on the ground with

his finger. But when they continued asking him, he straightened up and said to them, "Let the one among you who is without sin be the first to throw a stone at her." Again he bent down and wrote on the ground. And in response, they went away one by one, beginning with the elders. So he was left alone with the woman before him. Then Jesus straightened up and said to her, "Woman, where are they? Has no one condemned you?" She replied, "No one, sir." Then Jesus said, "Neither do I condemn you. Go, and from now on do not sin any more."

The Gospel of the Lord.

In Cycle C, when this Gospel is read on the preceding Sunday, the following text is used.

GOSPEL   Jn 8:12–20

I am the light of the world.

A reading from the holy Gospel according to John

Jesus spoke to them again, saying, "I am the light of the world. Whoever follows me will not walk in darkness, but will have the light of life." So the Pharisees said to him, "You testify on your own behalf, so your testimony cannot be verified." Jesus answered and said to them, "Even if I do testify on my own behalf, my testimony can be verified, because I know where I came from and where I am going. But you do not know where I come from or where I am going. You judge by appearances, but I do not judge anyone. And even if I should judge, my judgment is valid, because I am not alone, but it is I and the Father who sent me. Even in your law it is written that the testimony of two men can be verified. I testify on my behalf and so does the Father who sent me." So they said to him,

"Where is your father?" Jesus answered, "You know neither me nor my Father. If you knew me, you would know my Father also." He spoke these words while teaching in the treasury in the temple area. But no one arrested him, because his hour had not yet come.

The Gospel of the Lord.

Liturgy of the Eucharist, *p. 897.*

Prayer over the Gifts

Pray, brethren...

Lord,
as we come with joy
to celebrate the mystery of the eucharist,
may we offer you hearts
purified by bodily penance.

Grant this through Christ our Lord.

Preface of the Passion of the Lord I, *p. 942.*

Communion Antiphon

When the Gospel of the adulteress is read (Cycle C):

Has no one condemned you? The woman answered: No one, Lord. Neither do I condemn you: go and do not sin again.

(Jn 8:10–11)

When other Gospels are read:

I am the light of the world, says the Lord; the man who follows me will have the light of life.

(Jn 8:12)

Prayer after Communion

Let us pray.

Pause for silent prayer, if this has not preceded.

Father,
through the grace of your sacraments

may we follow Christ more faithfully
and come to the joy of your kingdom,
where he is Lord for ever and ever.

Tuesday

Entrance Antiphon

Put your hope in the Lord. Take courage and be strong.
(Ps 26:14)

Opening Prayer

Lord,
help us to do your will
that your Church may grow
and become more faithful in your service.
Grant this through our Lord Jesus Christ, your Son,
who lives and reigns with you and the Holy Spirit,
one God, for ever and ever.

TODAY'S LIVING WORD

In John's Gospel, sin consists of not believing in Jesus, who was
sent by God to reveal God the Father, "the one who…is true." So in
today's reading Jesus tells his critics, "You will die in your sins." Similarly in Numbers, the people's sin, the reason for their punishment,
is their refusal to believe that God, who led them out of Egypt, can
bring them safely through the wilderness. They too will die in their
sins. In Numbers, salvation lies in looking at the bronze serpent
mounted on a pole. In John, it lies in looking at the Son of Man
"lifted up" on the cross.

Three times in John's Gospel, Jesus refers to the lifting up of the
Son of Man. The word for "lift up" is *hypsoun,* a word that is used in
the New Testament to describe both the crucifixion and the ascension

of Jesus. In this way John tells us that the cross is the crown of Jesus' mission—that the glory of God is most fully revealed in the death and rising of Jesus. In Lent, we train our eyes to look on him whom we have pierced (Jn 19:37), our hope of salvation.

FIRST READING   Nm 21:4–9

Whoever looks at the bronze serpent, shall live.

A reading from the Book of Numbers

From Mount Hor the children of Israel set out on the Red Sea road, to bypass the land of Edom. But with their patience worn out by the journey, the people complained against God and Moses, "Why have you brought us up from Egypt to die in this desert, where there is no food or water? We are disgusted with this wretched food!"

In punishment the LORD sent among the people saraph serpents, which bit the people so that many of them died. Then the people came to Moses and said, "We have sinned in complaining against the LORD and you. Pray the LORD to take the serpents away from us." So Moses prayed for the people, and the LORD said to Moses, "Make a saraph and mount it on a pole, and whoever looks at it after being bitten will live." Moses accordingly made a bronze serpent and mounted it on a pole, and whenever anyone who had been bitten by a serpent looked at the bronze serpent, he lived.

The word of the Lord.

Responsorial Psalm   Ps 102:2–3, 16–18, 19–21

R. O Lord, hear my prayer, and let my cry come to you.

O LORD, hear my prayer,
  and let my cry come to you.

Hide not your face from me
   in the day of my distress.
Incline your ear to me;
   in the day when I call, answer me speedily.

R. O Lord, hear my prayer, and let my cry come to you.

The nations shall revere your name, O Lord,
   and all the kings of the earth your glory,
When the Lord has rebuilt Zion
   and appeared in his glory;
When he has regarded the prayer of the destitute,
   and not despised their prayer.

R. O Lord, hear my prayer, and let my cry come to you.

Let this be written for the generation to come,
   and let his future creatures praise the Lord:
"The Lord looked down from his holy height,
   from heaven he beheld the earth,
To hear the groaning of the prisoners,
   to release those doomed to die."

R. O Lord, hear my prayer, and let my cry come to you.

Verse Before the Gospel
The seed is the word of God, Christ is the sower;
all who come to him will live for ever.

GOSPEL   Jn 8:21–30

When you have lifted up the Son of Man,
then you will know that I am he.

A reading from the holy Gospel according to John

Jesus said to the Pharisees: "I am going away and you will look
for me, but you will die in your sin. Where I am going you
cannot come." So the Jews said, "He is not going to kill himself,
is he, because he said, 'Where I am going you cannot come'?"
He said to them, "You belong to what is below, I belong to what
is above. You belong to this world, but I do not belong to this

world. That is why I told you that you will die in your sins. For if you do not believe that I AM, you will die in your sins." So they said to him, "Who are you?" Jesus said to them, "What I told you from the beginning. I have much to say about you in condemnation. But the one who sent me is true, and what I heard from him I tell the world." They did not realize that he was speaking to them of the Father. So Jesus said to them, "When you lift up the Son of Man, then you will realize that I AM, and that I do nothing on my own, but I say only what the Father taught me. The one who sent me is with me. He has not left me alone, because I always do what is pleasing to him." Because he spoke this way, many came to believe in him.

The Gospel of the Lord.

Liturgy of the Eucharist, *p. 897.*

Prayer over the Gifts

Pray, brethren...

Merciful Lord,
we offer this gift of reconciliation
so that you will forgive our sins
and guide our wayward hearts.

We ask this through Christ our Lord.

Preface of the Passion of the Lord I, *p. 942.*

Communion Antiphon

When I am lifted up from the earth, I will draw all men to myself, says the Lord. (Jn 12:32)

Prayer after Communion

Let us pray.

Pause for silent prayer, if this has not preceded.

All-powerful God,
may the holy mysteries we share in this eucharist
make us worthy to attain the gift of heaven.
We ask this in the name of Jesus the Lord.

Wednesday

Entrance Antiphon

**Lord, you rescue me from raging enemies, you lift me up above
my attackers, you deliver me from violent men.**   (Ps 17:48 – 49)

Opening Prayer

Father of mercy,
hear the prayers of your repentant children
who call on you in love.
Enlighten our minds and sanctify our hearts.

We ask this through our Lord Jesus Christ, your Son,
who lives and reigns with you and the Holy Spirit,
one God, for ever and ever.

Today's Living Word

Both readings today raise the issue of God's power to save. The
three young men in the reading from Daniel are confident that God
can save them. But they refuse to argue the point; instead they act,
staking their lives on it. In the end, the truth about God is not proven
in theological debate but in the white-hot furnace of daring, decisive
action. In the context of John's Gospel, the words of Jesus—"You
will know the truth, and the truth will set you free"—attest that the
saving power of God is enfleshed in Jesus. Living according to his
teaching, truly being his disciple, is the way to salvation.

Jesus goes on to indict those who claim that Abraham is their
father. In whatever way the passage has been colored by escalating
hostility between John's community and the Jewish leaders, Jesus is

saying here that a true son acts like his father. While Jesus acknowledges that his Jewish opponents are "descendants of Abraham," they
are not "doing the works of Abraham." They will not believe, as
Abraham did. So we who also claim God as our Father are warned:
we must love the Son and live according to his word.

FIRST READING   Dn 3:14–20, 91–92, 95

The Lord has sent his angel to deliver his servants.

A reading from the Book of the Prophet Daniel

King Nebuchadnezzar said: "Is it true, Shadrach, Meshach,
and Abednego, that you will not serve my god, or worship the
golden statue that I set up? Be ready now to fall down and
worship the statue I had made, whenever you hear the sound
of the trumpet, flute, lyre, harp, psaltery, bagpipe, and all the
other musical instruments; otherwise, you shall be instantly
cast into the white-hot furnace; and who is the God who can
deliver you out of my hands?" Shadrach, Meshach, and Abednego answered King Nebuchadnezzar, "There is no need for
us to defend ourselves before you in this matter. If our God,
whom we serve, can save us from the white-hot furnace and
from your hands, O king, may he save us! But even if he will
not, know, O king, that we will not serve your god or worship
the golden statue that you set up."

King Nebuchadnezzar's face became livid with utter rage
against Shadrach, Meshach, and Abednego. He ordered the
furnace to be heated seven times more than usual and had some
of the strongest men in his army bind Shadrach, Meshach, and
Abednego and cast them into the white-hot furnace.

Nebuchadnezzar rose in haste and asked his nobles, "Did
we not cast three men bound into the fire?" "Assuredly, O king,"
they answered. "But," he replied, "I see four men unfettered

and unhurt, walking in the fire, and the fourth looks like a son of God." Nebuchadnezzar exclaimed, "Blessed be the God of Shadrach, Meshach, and Abednego, who sent his angel to deliver the servants who trusted in him; they disobeyed the royal command and yielded their bodies rather than serve or worship any god except their own God."

The word of the Lord.

Responsorial Psalm   Dn 3:52, 53, 54, 55, 56

R. Glory and praise for ever!

"Blessed are you, O Lord, the God of our fathers,
  praiseworthy and exalted above all forever;
And blessed is your holy and glorious name,
  praiseworthy and exalted above all for all ages."

R. Glory and praise for ever!

"Blessed are you in the temple of your holy glory,
  praiseworthy and exalted above all forever."

R. Glory and praise for ever!

"Blessed are you on the throne of your kingdom,
  praiseworthy and exalted above all forever."

R. Glory and praise for ever!

"Blessed are you who look into the depths
  from your throne upon the cherubim;
  praiseworthy and exalted above all forever."

R. Glory and praise for ever!

"Blessed are you in the firmament of heaven,
  praiseworthy and glorious forever."

R. Glory and praise for ever!

Verse Before the Gospel See Lk 8:15
Blessed are they who have kept the word with a generous heart
and yield a harvest through perseverance.

GOSPEL

Jn 8:31–42

If the Son makes you free, you will be free indeed.

A reading from the holy Gospel according to John

Jesus said to those Jews who believed in him, "If you remain in my word, you will truly be my disciples, and you will know the truth, and the truth will set you free." They answered him, "We are descendants of Abraham and have never been enslaved to anyone. How can you say, 'You will become free'?" Jesus answered them, "Amen, amen, I say to you, everyone who commits sin is a slave of sin. A slave does not remain in a household forever, but a son always remains. So if the Son frees you, then you will truly be free. I know that you are descendants of Abraham. But you are trying to kill me, because my word has no room among you. I tell you what I have seen in the Father's presence; then do what you have heard from the Father."

They answered and said to him, "Our father is Abraham." Jesus said to them, "If you were Abraham's children, you would be doing the works of Abraham. But now you are trying to kill me, a man who has told you the truth that I heard from God; Abraham did not do this. You are doing the works of your father!" So they said to him, "We were not born of fornication. We have one Father, God." Jesus said to them, "If God were your Father, you would love me, for I came from God and am here; I did not come on my own, but he sent me."

The Gospel of the Lord.

Liturgy of the Eucharist, *p. 897.*

Prayer over the Gifts

Pray, brethren...

Lord.

you have given us these gifts
to honor your name.
Bless them,
and let them become a source of health and strength.

We ask this through Christ our Lord.

Preface of the Passion of the Lord I, *p. 942.*

Communion Antiphon

God has transferred us into the kingdom of the Son he loves;
in him we are redeemed, and find forgiveness of our sins.

(Col 1:13–14)

Prayer after Communion

Let us pray.

Pause for silent prayer, if this has not preceded.

Lord,
may the mysteries we receive heal us,
remove sin from our hearts,
and make us grow strong
under your constant protection.

Grant this through Christ our Lord.

Thursday

Entrance Antiphon

Christ is the mediator of a new covenant so that since he has
died, those who are called may receive the eternal inheritance
promised to them.

(Heb 9:15)

Opening Prayer

Lord,
come to us;
free us from the stain of our sins.

Help us to remain faithful to a holy way of life,
and guide us to the inheritance you have promised.

Grant this through our Lord Jesus Christ, your Son,
who lives and reigns with you and the Holy Spirit,
one God, for ever and ever.

TODAY'S LIVING WORD

Today's Gospel contains the boldest claim on the lips of Jesus in all of John: "Before Abraham came to be, I AM." Not only is Jesus greater than Abraham; he bears God's own name (cf. Is 43:10, 25; 48:12). No wonder his Jewish listeners "picked up stones to throw at him." Stoning was the penalty for blasphemy. Since most scholars agree that the issue of Jesus' divine status was only raised after the resurrection, today's text reflects the faith of John's community. No doubt this is why they were being expelled from the synagogues. Hence the unremittingly negative portrayal of "the Jews" in John.

"Abraham your father rejoiced to see my day," says Jesus. "He saw it and was glad." The context of these words is Genesis 17, from which today's first reading is taken. God makes an everlasting covenant with Abraham and his descendants, "a host of nations." Later, when God promises Abraham a son, Abraham laughs (17:17). The rabbis interpreted this as rejoicing over the birth of Isaac, the realization of God's promise. John and his community proclaim that God's promise is finally, fully realized in Jesus.

FIRST READING
Gn 17:3–9

You will be the father of a multitude of nations.

A reading from the Book of Genesis

When Abram prostrated himself, God spoke to him: "My covenant with you is this: you are to become the father of a host of nations. No longer shall you be called Abram; your name shall be Abraham, for I am making you the father of a host of nations. I will render you exceedingly fertile; I will make nations of you; kings shall stem from you. I will maintain my covenant with you and your descendants after you throughout the ages as an everlasting pact, to be your God and the God of your descendants after you. I will give to you and to your descendants after you the land in which you are now staying, the whole land of Canaan, as a permanent possession; and I will be their God."

God also said to Abraham: "On your part, you and your descendants after you must keep my covenant throughout the ages."

The word of the Lord.

Responsorial Psalm

Ps 105:4–5, 6–7, 8–9

R. The Lord remembers his covenant for ever.

Look to the LORD in his strength;
  seek to serve him constantly.
Recall the wondrous deeds that he has wrought,
  his portents, and the judgments he has uttered.

R. The Lord remembers his covenant for ever.

You descendants of Abraham, his servants,
  sons of Jacob, his chosen ones!
He, the LORD, is our God;
  throughout the earth his judgments prevail.

R. The Lord remembers his covenant for ever.

He remembers forever his covenant
  which he made binding for a thousand generations—
Which he entered into with Abraham
  and by his oath to Isaac.

R. The Lord remembers his covenant for ever.

Verse Before the Gospel Ps 95:8
If today you hear his voice,
harden not your hearts.

GOSPEL

Your father, Abraham, rejoiced because he saw my day.

A reading from the holy Gospel according to John

Jesus said to the Jews: "Amen, amen, I say to you, whoever keeps my word will never see death." So the Jews said to him, "Now we are sure that you are possessed. Abraham died, as did the prophets, yet you say, 'Whoever keeps my word will never taste death.' Are you greater than our father Abraham, who died? Or the prophets, who died? Who do you make yourself out to be?" Jesus answered, "If I glorify myself, my glory is worth nothing; but it is my Father who glorifies me, of whom you say, 'He is our God.' You do not know him, but I know him. And if I should say that I do not know him, I would be like you a liar. But I do know him and I keep his word. Abraham your father rejoiced to see my day; he saw it and was glad." So the Jews said to him, "You are not yet fifty years old and you have seen Abraham?" Jesus said to them, "Amen, amen, I say to you, before Abraham came to be, I AM." So they picked up stones to throw at him; but Jesus hid and went out of the temple area.

The Gospel of the Lord.

Liturgy of the Eucharist, *p. 897.*

Prayer over the Gifts

Pray, brethren...

Merciful Lord,
accept the sacrifice we offer you
that it may help us grow in holiness
and advance the salvation of the world.

We ask this in the name of Jesus the Lord.

Preface of the Passion of the Lord I, *p. 942.*

Communion Antiphon

God did not spare his own Son, but gave him up for us all: with Christ he will surely give us all things.   (Rom 8:32)

Prayer after Communion

Let us pray.

Pause for silent prayer, if this has not preceded.

Lord of mercy,
let the sacrament which renews us
bring us to eternal life.

We ask this through Christ our Lord.

Friday

Entrance Antiphon

Have mercy on me, Lord, for I am in distress; rescue me from the hands of my enemies. Lord, keep me from shame, for I have called to you.   (Ps 30:10, 16, 18)

Opening Prayer

Lord,
grant us your forgiveness,
and set us free from our enslavement to sin.

We ask this through our Lord Jesus Christ, your Son,
who lives and reigns with you and the Holy Spirit,
one God, for ever and ever.

TODAY'S LIVING WORD

The context of today's reading from John is the Jewish feast of *Hanukkah*. This winter feast, which John calls the feast of the Dedication (10:22), commemorated the reconsecration of the temple that the Greek King Antiochus IV had desecrated in 167 B.C.E. In today's Gospel Jesus, standing in the temple precincts, refers to himself as "the one whom the Father has consecrated." For John this means that the holiness of the temple is found now in Jesus, whom the Father has made holy.

If Jesus claims to be God's consecrated one, Jeremiah claims to be God's client. Today's first reading is an excerpt from a prayer of Jeremiah, who finds himself surrounded by trusted friends who have become treacherous enemies. "But the Lord is with me, like a mighty champion," he declares and knows it to be so, "for [God] has rescued the life of the poor from the power of the wicked." The word for "poor" here is *'ebyon;* it describes all those pious, power-less folk whose cause God champions. In the same spirit, Lent invites us to place our cause before God with confidence, for our champion is "the one whom the Father has consecrated and sent into the world."

FIRST READING   Jer 20:10–13

The Lord God is with me, a mighty hero.

A reading from the Book of the Prophet Jeremiah

I hear the whisperings of many:
 "Terror on every side!
 Denounce! let us denounce him!"
All those who were my friends
 are on the watch for any misstep of mine.
"Perhaps he will be trapped; then we can prevail,
 and take our vengeance on him."
But the Lord is with me, like a mighty champion:
 my persecutors will stumble, they will not triumph.
In their failure they will be put to utter shame,
 to lasting, unforgettable confusion.
O Lord of hosts, you who test the just,
 who probe mind and heart,
Let me witness the vengeance you take on them,

for to you I have entrusted my cause.
Sing to the LORD,
     praise the LORD,
For he has rescued the life of the poor
     from the power of the wicked!
The word of the Lord.

Responsorial Psalm

Ps 18:2 –3a, 3bc – 4, 5 –6, 7

R. **In my distress I called upon the Lord,**
     and he heard my voice.

I love you, O LORD, my strength,
     O LORD, my rock, my fortress, my deliverer.

R. **In my distress I called upon the Lord,**
     and he heard my voice.

My God, my rock of refuge,
     my shield, the horn of my salvation, my stronghold!
Praised be the LORD, I exclaim,
     and I am safe from my enemies.

R. **In my distress I called upon the Lord,**
     and he heard my voice.

The breakers of death surged round about me,
     the destroying floods overwhelmed me;
The cords of the nether world enmeshed me,
     the snares of death overtook me.

R. **In my distress I called upon the Lord,**
     and he heard my voice.

In my distress I called upon the LORD
     and cried out to my God;
From his temple he heard my voice,
     and my cry to him reached his ears.

R. **In my distress I called upon the Lord,**
     and he heard my voice.

Verse Before the Gospel   See Jn 6:63c, 68c
Your words, Lord, are Spirit and life;
you have the words of everlasting life.

GOSPEL
Jn 10:31–42

They wanted to arrest Jesus, but he eluded them.

A reading from the holy Gospel according to John

The Jews picked up rocks to stone Jesus. Jesus answered them,
"I have shown you many good works from my Father. For
which of these are you trying to stone me?" The Jews answered
him, "We are not stoning you for a good work but for blasphemy. You, a man, are making yourself God." Jesus answered
them, "Is it not written in your law, 'I said, "You are gods" '?
If it calls them gods to whom the word of God came, and
Scripture cannot be set aside, can you say that the one whom
the Father has consecrated and sent into the world blasphemes
because I said, 'I am the Son of God'? If I do not perform my
Father's works, do not believe me; but if I perform them, even
if you do not believe me, believe the works, so that you may
realize and understand that the Father is in me and I am in the
Father." Then they tried again to arrest him; but he escaped
from their power.

He went back across the Jordan to the place where John
first baptized, and there he remained. Many came to him and
said, "John performed no sign, but everything John said about
this man was true." And many there began to believe in him.

The Gospel of the Lord.

Liturgy of the Eucharist, *p. 897.*

Prayer over the Gifts

Pray, brethren...

God of mercy,

may the gifts we present at your altar
help us to achieve eternal salvation.

Grant this through Christ our Lord.

Preface of the Passion of the Lord I, *p. 942.*

Communion Antiphon

Jesus carried our sins in his own body on the cross so that we could die to sin and live in holiness; by his wounds we have been healed. (1 Pt 2:24)

Prayer after Communion

Let us pray.

Pause for silent prayer, if this has not preceded.

Lord,
may we always receive the protection of this sacrifice.
May it keep us safe from all harm.

We ask this in the name of Jesus the Lord.

Saturday

Entrance Antiphon

Lord, do not stay away; come quickly to help me! I am a worm and no man: men scorn me, people despise me. (Ps 21:20, 7)

Opening Prayer

God our Father,
you always work to save us,
and now we rejoice in the great love
you give to your chosen people.
Protect all who are about to become your children,
and continue to bless those who are already baptized.
Grant this through our Lord Jesus Christ, your Son,

who lives and reigns with you and the Holy Spirit,
one God, for ever and ever.

TODAY'S LIVING WORD

The prophecy of Ezekiel in today's first reading looks to the day
when God will bring Israel home from exile and "make them one
nation upon the land." On that day all twelve tribes of David's
kingdom, torn in two by schism after the death of Solomon, will be
reunited. "Never again shall they be two nations, and never again
shall they be divided into two kingdoms." Today's Gospel extends
Ezekiel's vision beyond the boundaries of Israel. Jesus will die not
for Israel only, but "to gather into one the dispersed children of God."

The words of Caiaphas in today's Gospel implicate the Jewish
Sanhedrin in the death of Jesus. But we who during Lent reflect on
the events that led to Jesus' death must never forget the teaching of
the Church since Vatican II: that we may not hold all Jews responsible for the death of Jesus, neither those of Jesus' day nor of ours.
As Mary Boys puts it, "The Church reads the passion of Jesus Christ
so as to remember the extent of his love...not for assigning blame
for his death."*

* "A More Faithful Portrait of Judaism: An Imperative for Christian Educators,"
Within Context, ed. David P. Efroymson, Eugene J. Fisher, Leon Klenicki (Collegeville:
Liturgical Press, 1993), p. 15.

FIRST READING
Ez 37:21–28

I will make them into one nation.

A reading from the Book of the Prophet Ezekiel

Thus says the Lord GOD: I will take the children of Israel from
among the nations to which they have come, and gather them
from all sides to bring them back to their land. I will make them
one nation upon the land, in the mountains of Israel, and there
shall be one prince for them all. Never again shall they be two
nations, and never again shall they be divided into two kingdoms.

No longer shall they defile themselves with their idols, their
abominations, and all their transgressions. I will deliver them

from all their sins of apostasy, and cleanse them so that they may be my people and I may be their God. My servant David shall be prince over them, and there shall be one shepherd for them all; they shall live by my statutes and carefully observe my decrees. They shall live on the land that I gave to my servant Jacob, the land where their fathers lived; they shall live on it forever, they, and their children, and their children's children, with my servant David their prince forever. I will make with them a covenant of peace; it shall be an everlasting covenant with them, and I will multiply them, and put my sanctuary among them forever. My dwelling shall be with them; I will be their God, and they shall be my people. Thus the nations shall know that it is I, the LORD, who make Israel holy, when my sanctuary shall be set up among them forever.

The word of the Lord.

Responsorial Psalm
Jer 31:10, 11–12abcd, 13

R. **The Lord will guard us, as a shepherd guards his flock.**

Hear the word of the LORD, O nations,
  proclaim it on distant isles, and say:
He who scattered Israel, now gathers them together,
  he guards them as a shepherd his flock.

R. **The Lord will guard us, as a shepherd guards his flock.**

The LORD shall ransom Jacob,
  he shall redeem him from the hand of his conqueror.
Shouting, they shall mount the heights of Zion,
  they shall come streaming to the LORD's blessings:
The grain, the wine, and the oil,
  the sheep and the oxen.

**R. The Lord will guard us, as a shepherd
guards his flock.**

Then the virgins shall make merry and dance,
   and young men and old as well.
I will turn their mourning into joy,
   I will console and gladden them after their sorrows.

**R. The Lord will guard us, as a shepherd
guards his flock.**

Verse Before the Gospel   Ez 18:31
Cast away from you all the crimes you have committed,
   says the Lord,
   and make for yourselves a new heart and a new spirit.

GOSPEL

Jn 11:45–56

To gather together in unity the scattered children of God.

A reading from the holy Gospel according to John

Many of the Jews who had come to Mary and seen what Jesus
had done began to believe in him. But some of them went to
the Pharisees and told them what Jesus had done. So the chief
priests and the Pharisees convened the Sanhedrin and said,
"What are we going to do? This man is performing many signs.
If we leave him alone, all will believe in him, and the Romans
will come and take away both our land and our nation." But
one of them, Caiaphas, who was high priest that year, said to
them, "You know nothing, nor do you consider that it is better
for you that one man should die instead of the people, so that
the whole nation may not perish." He did not say this on his
own, but since he was high priest for that year, he prophesied
that Jesus was going to die for the nation, and not only for the
nation, but also to gather into one the dispersed children of
God. So from that day on they planned to kill him.

So Jesus no longer walked about in public among the Jews, but he left for the region near the desert, to a town called Ephraim, and there he remained with his disciples.

Now the Passover of the Jews was near, and many went up from the country to Jerusalem before Passover to purify themselves. They looked for Jesus and said to one another as they were in the temple area, "What do you think? That he will not come to the feast?"

The Gospel of the Lord.

Liturgy of the Eucharist, *p. 897.*

Prayer over the Gifts

Pray, brethren...

Ever-living God,
in baptism, the sacrament of our faith,
you restore us to life.
Accept the prayers and gifts of your people:
forgive our sins and fulfill our hopes and desires.

We ask this in the name of Jesus the Lord.

Preface of the Passion of the Lord I, *p. 942.*

Communion Antiphon

Christ was sacrificed so that he could gather together the scattered children of God.

(Jn 11:52)

Prayer after Communion

Let us pray.

Pause for silent prayer, if this has not preceded.

Father of mercy and power,
we thank you for nourishing us
with the body and blood of Christ
and for calling us to share in his divine life,
for he is Lord for ever and ever.

HOLY WEEK

For PASSION SUNDAY *(Palm Sunday), see* **Vatican II Sunday Missal,** p. 322.

Monday

Entrance Antiphon

Defend me, Lord, from all my foes: take up your arms and come swiftly to my aid for you have the power to save me.

(Ps 34:1–2; 139:8)

Opening Prayer

All-powerful God,
by the suffering and death of your Son,
strengthen and protect us in our weakness.

We ask this through our Lord Jesus Christ, your Son,
who lives and reigns with you and the Holy Spirit,
one God, for ever and ever.

TODAY'S LIVING WORD

The second part of Isaiah (chapters 40–55) has four passages which scholars designate as the "Servant Songs."* These poems depict the call and career of Israel as God's servant. In the light of Jesus' death and rising, the early Christians reread these poems with reference to Jesus. Hence the Gospels often identify Jesus with ideal Israel, the true servant of God. Today's first reading is the first Servant Song of Isaiah, which describes the servant's mode of operation. He will serve the "victory of justice" not by clamoring in the marketplace nor by crushing his enemies on the battlefield, but by his constant, quiet witness before the nations.

Today's Gospel presents us with two contrasting images of servanthood. Both Mary and Judas are disciples of Jesus; both belong to Jesus' inner circle; both have sat at Jesus' feet. So the question arises: what moved one to splendid generosity and the other to betrayal? Though the story does not let us see into their hearts, it does invite us to search our own.

* Isaiah 42:1–7; 49:1–7; 50:4–9; 52:13—53:12.

FIRST READING

Is 42:1–7

*He will not cry out, nor make his voice heard in the street
(First oracle of the Servant of the LORD).*

A reading from the Book of the Prophet Isaiah

Here is my servant whom I uphold,
    my chosen one with whom I am pleased,
Upon whom I have put my Spirit;
    he shall bring forth justice to the nations,
Not crying out, not shouting,
    not making his voice heard in the street.
A bruised reed he shall not break,
    and a smoldering wick he shall not quench,
Until he establishes justice on the earth;
    the coastlands will wait for his teaching.

Thus says God, the LORD,
    who created the heavens and stretched them out,
    who spreads out the earth with its crops,
Who gives breath to its people
    and spirit to those who walk on it:
I, the LORD, have called you for the victory of justice,
    I have grasped you by the hand;
I formed you, and set you
    as a covenant of the people,
    a light for the nations,
To open the eyes of the blind,

to bring out prisoners from confinement,
and from the dungeon, those who live in darkness.

The word of the Lord.

Responsorial Psalm   Ps 27:1, 2, 3, 13–14

R. **The Lord is my light and my salvation.**

The LORD is my light and my salvation;
  whom should I fear?
The LORD is my life's refuge;
  of whom should I be afraid?

R. **The Lord is my light and my salvation.**

When evildoers come at me
  to devour my flesh,
My foes and my enemies
  themselves stumble and fall.

R. **The Lord is my light and my salvation.**

Though an army encamp against me,
  my heart will not fear;
Though war be waged upon me,
  even then will I trust.

R. **The Lord is my light and my salvation.**

I believe that I shall see the bounty of the LORD
  in the land of the living.
Wait for the LORD with courage;
  be stouthearted, and wait for the LORD.

R. **The Lord is my light and my salvation.**

Verse Before the Gospel
Hail to you, our King;
you alone are compassionate with our faults.

GOSPEL   Jn 12:1–11

Let her keep this for the day of my burial.

A reading from the holy Gospel according to John

Six days before Passover Jesus came to Bethany, where Lazarus was, whom Jesus had raised from the dead. They gave a dinner for him there, and Martha served, while Lazarus was one of those reclining at table with him. Mary took a liter of costly perfumed oil made from genuine aromatic nard and anointed the feet of Jesus and dried them with her hair; the house was filled with the fragrance of the oil. Then Judas the Iscariot, one of his disciples, and the one who would betray him, said, "Why was this oil not sold for three hundred days' wages and given to the poor?" He said this not because he cared about the poor but because he was a thief and held the money bag and used to steal the contributions. So Jesus said, "Leave her alone. Let her keep this for the day of my burial. You always have the poor with you, but you do not always have me."

The large crowd of the Jews found out that he was there and came, not only because of him, but also to see Lazarus, whom he had raised from the dead. And the chief priests plotted to kill Lazarus too, because many of the Jews were turning away and believing in Jesus because of him.

The Gospel of the Lord.

Liturgy of the Eucharist, *p. 897.*

Prayer over the Gifts

Pray, brethren...

Lord,
look with mercy on our offerings.
May the sacrifice of Christ, your Son,
bring us to eternal life,
for he is Lord for ever and ever.

Preface of the Passion of the Lord II, *p. 943.*

Communion Antiphon

When I am in trouble, Lord, do not hide your face from me; hear me when I call, and answer me quickly.   (Ps 101:3)

Prayer after Communion

Let us pray.

Pause for silent prayer, if this has not preceded.

God of mercy,
be close to your people.
Watch over us who receive this sacrament of salvation,
and keep us in your love.

We ask this in the name of Jesus the Lord.

Tuesday

Entrance Antiphon

False witnesses have stood up against me, and my enemies threaten violence; Lord, do not surrender me into their power!
(Ps 26:12)

Opening Prayer

Father,
may we receive your forgiveness and mercy
as we celebrate the passion and death of the Lord,
who lives and reigns with you and the Holy Spirit,
one God, for ever and ever.

TODAY'S LIVING WORD

The second Servant Song, today's first reading, hints at the ups and downs of servant Israel's mission. Armed only with God's word, "a sharp-edged sword," and assured of God's protection "in the shadow of his arm," Israel will be the one in whom God will be glorified before all the nations. At times the servant is troubled. "I thought I had toiled in vain," he says, "and for nothing, uselessly, spent my strength." Yet he knows that his reward is with the Lord; he is made glorious in God's sight.

Today's Gospel describes a critical moment in the mission of Jesus. He is troubled at the treachery of Judas, who coolly takes the morsel from his hand and goes out into the night. Once Judas has left, Jesus turns to the others and instructs them one last time. "Now is the Son of Man glorified," he says, "and God is glorified in him." But those words do not rouse them. It is only when he tells them that they cannot follow him now that panic sets in. Their servanthood is still self-motivated and self-interested. They have yet to learn, like Jesus and the servant of the song, to yield to the greater glory of God.

FIRST READING

Is 49:1–6

I will make you a light to the nations,
that my salvation may reach to the ends of the earth
(Second oracle of the Servant of the Lord).

A reading from the Book of the Prophet Isaiah

Hear me, O islands,
    listen, O distant peoples.
The Lord called me from birth,
    from my mother's womb he gave me my name.
He made of me a sharp-edged sword
    and concealed me in the shadow of his arm.
He made me a polished arrow,
    in his quiver he hid me.
You are my servant, he said to me,
    Israel, through whom I show my glory.

Though I thought I had toiled in vain,
    and for nothing, uselessly, spent my strength,
Yet my reward is with the Lord,
    my recompense is with my God.

For now the LORD has spoken
    who formed me as his servant from the womb,
That Jacob may be brought back to him
    and Israel gathered to him;
And I am made glorious in the sight of the LORD,
    and my God is now my strength!
It is too little, he says, for you to be my servant,
    to raise up the tribes of Jacob,
    and restore the survivors of Israel;
I will make you a light to the nations,
    that my salvation may reach to the ends of the earth.

The word of the Lord.

Responsorial Psalm   Ps 71:1–2, 3–4a, 5ab–6ab, 15 and 17

    R. I will sing of your salvation.

In you, O LORD, I take refuge;
    let me never be put to shame.
In your justice rescue me, and deliver me;
    incline your ear to me, and save me.

    R. I will sing of your salvation.

Be my rock of refuge,
    a stronghold to give me safety,
    for you are my rock and my fortress.
O my God, rescue me from the hand of the wicked.

    R. I will sing of your salvation.

For you are my hope, O LORD;
    my trust, O God, from my youth.
On you I depend from birth;
    from my mother's womb you are my strength.

    R. I will sing of your salvation.

My mouth shall declare your justice,
    day by day your salvation.

O God, you have taught me from my youth,
  and till the present I proclaim your wondrous deeds.

R. I will sing of your salvation.

Verse Before the Gospel
Hail to you, our King, obedient to the Father;
you were led to your crucifixion
  like a gentle lamb to the slaughter.

GOSPEL   Jn 13:21–33, 36–38

One of you will betray me; the cock will not crow
before you deny me three times.

A reading from the holy Gospel according to John

Reclining at table with his disciples, Jesus was deeply troubled
and testified, "Amen, amen, I say to you, one of you will betray
me." The disciples looked at one another, at a loss as to whom
he meant. One of his disciples, the one whom Jesus loved, was
reclining at Jesus' side. So Simon Peter nodded to him to find
out whom he meant. He leaned back against Jesus' chest and
said to him, "Master, who is it?" Jesus answered, "It is the one
to whom I hand the morsel after I have dipped it." So he dipped
the morsel and took it and handed it to Judas, son of Simon the
Iscariot. After Judas took the morsel, Satan entered him. So
Jesus said to him, "What you are going to do, do quickly."
Now none of those reclining at table realized why he said this
to him. Some thought that since Judas kept the money bag,
Jesus had told him, "Buy what we need for the feast," or to
give something to the poor. So Judas took the morsel and left
at once. And it was night.

  When he had left, Jesus said, "Now is the Son of Man
glorified, and God is glorified in him. If God is glorified in
him, God will also glorify him in himself, and he will glorify

him at once. My children, I will be with you only a little while longer. You will look for me, and as I told the Jews, 'Where I go you cannot come,' so now I say it to you."

Simon Peter said to him, "Master, where are you going?" Jesus answered him, "Where I am going, you cannot follow me now, though you will follow later." Peter said to him, "Master, why can I not follow you now? I will lay down my life for you." Jesus answered, "Will you lay down your life for me? Amen, amen, I say to you, the cock will not crow before you deny me three times."

The Gospel of the Lord.

Liturgy of the Eucharist, *p. 897.*

Prayer over the Gifts

Pray, brethren...

Lord,
look with mercy on our offerings.
May we who share the holy gifts
receive the life they promise.

We ask this in the name of Jesus the Lord.

Preface of the Passion of the Lord II, *p. 943.*

Communion Antiphon

God did not spare his own Son, but gave him up for us all.

(Rom 8:32)

Prayer after Communion

Let us pray.

Pause for silent prayer, if this has not preceded.

God of mercy,
may the sacrament of salvation

which now renews our strength
bring us a share in your life for ever.
Grant this through Christ our Lord.

Wednesday

Entrance Antiphon

At the name of Jesus every knee must bend, in heaven, on earth, and under the earth; Christ became obedient for us even to death, dying on the cross. Therefore, to the glory of God the Father: Jesus Christ is Lord.   (Phil 2:10, 8, 11)

Opening Prayer

Father,
in your plan of salvation
your Son Jesus Christ accepted the cross
and freed us from the power of the enemy.
May we come to share the glory of his resurrection,
for he lives and reigns with you and the Holy Spirit,
one God, for ever and ever.

TODAY'S LIVING WORD

In the third Servant Song of Isaiah, the servant is described as having the ear and the tongue of a disciple. In Hebrew, the word "disciple" is the passive form of the verb "to teach." A disciple is one who is taught, one whose ear is opened to hear the word of God that must be spoken to the weary. The servant of today's song knows the cost of discipleship too. "I gave my back to those who beat me," he says. "My face I did not shield from buffets and spitting."

Today's Gospel also brings the question of discipleship to the fore. The early Church never forgot that Jesus was betrayed by one of his own. Although Jesus' death was "according to the Scripture," his words—"Woe to that man by whom the Son of Man is betrayed"—imply that Judas was nonetheless responsible for his action. As the "appointed time" of Jesus again draws near, it is our turn to question ourselves in the presence of Jesus: "Surely it is not I," Lord?

FIRST READING

Is 50:4 –9a

My face I did not shield from buffets and spitting
(Third oracle of the Servant of the Lord).

A reading from the Book of the Prophet Isaiah

The Lord GOD has given me
    a well-trained tongue,
That I might know how to speak to the weary
    a word that will rouse them.
Morning after morning
    he opens my ear that I may hear;
And I have not rebelled,
    have not turned back.
I gave my back to those who beat me,
    my cheeks to those who plucked my beard;
My face I did not shield
    from buffets and spitting.

The Lord GOD is my help,
    therefore I am not disgraced;
I have set my face like flint,
    knowing that I shall not be put to shame.
He is near who upholds my right;
    if anyone wishes to oppose me,
    let us appear together.
Who disputes my right?
    Let him confront me.

See, the Lord GOD is my help;
     who will prove me wrong?
The word of the Lord.

Responsorial Psalm
Ps 69:8 –10, 21– 22, 31 and 33– 34

R. Lord, in your great love, answer me.

For your sake I bear insult,
    and shame covers my face.
I have become an outcast to my brothers,
    a stranger to my mother's sons,
because zeal for your house consumes me,
    and the insults of those who blaspheme you fall upon me.

R. Lord, in your great love, answer me.

Insult has broken my heart, and I am weak,
    I looked for sympathy, but there was none;
    for consolers, not one could I find.
Rather they put gall in my food,
    and in my thirst they gave me vinegar to drink.

R. Lord, in your great love, answer me.

I will praise the name of God in song,
    and I will glorify him with thanksgiving:
"See, you lowly ones, and be glad;
    you who seek God, may your hearts revive!
For the LORD hears the poor,
    and his own who are in bonds he spurns not."

R. Lord, in your great love, answer me.

Verse Before the Gospel
A Hail to you, our King;
     you alone are compassionate with our errors.

Or:

B Hail to you, our King, obedient to the Father;
     you were led to your crucifixion like a gentle lamb
          to the slaughter.

GOSPEL

*The Son of Man indeed goes, as it is written of him,
but woe to that man by whom the Son of Man is betrayed.*

A reading from the holy Gospel according to Matthew

One of the Twelve, who was called Judas Iscariot, went to the chief priests and said, "What are you willing to give me if I hand him over to you?" They paid him thirty pieces of silver, and from that time on he looked for an opportunity to hand him over.

On the first day of the Feast of Unleavened Bread, the disciples approached Jesus and said, "Where do you want us to prepare for you to eat the Passover?" He said, "Go into the city to a certain man and tell him, 'The teacher says, "My appointed time draws near; in your house I shall celebrate the Passover with my disciples."'" The disciples then did as Jesus had ordered, and prepared the Passover.

When it was evening, he reclined at table with the Twelve. And while they were eating, he said, "Amen, I say to you, one of you will betray me." Deeply distressed at this, they began to say to him one after another, "Surely it is not I, Lord?" He said in reply, "He who has dipped his hand into the dish with me is the one who will betray me. The Son of Man indeed goes, as it is written of him, but woe to that man by whom the Son of Man is betrayed. It would be better for that man if he had never been born." Then Judas, his betrayer, said in reply, "Surely it is not I, Rabbi?" He answered, "You have said so."

The Gospel of the Lord.

Liturgy of the Eucharist, *p. 897.*

Prayer over the Gifts

Pray, brethren...

Lord,
accept the gifts we present
as we celebrate this mystery
of the suffering and death of your Son.
May we share in the eternal life he won for us,
for he is Lord for ever and ever.

Preface of the Passion of the Lord II, *p. 943.*

Communion Antiphon

The Son of Man did not come to be served, but to serve, and to give his life as a ransom for many. (Mt 20:28)

Prayer after Communion

Let us pray.

Pause for silent prayer, if this has not preceded.

All-powerful God,
the eucharist proclaims the death of your Son.
Increase our faith in its saving power
and strengthen our hope in the life it promises.
We ask this in the name of Jesus the Lord.

HOLY THURSDAY—CHRISM MASS

The Chrism Mass, which the bishop concelebrates with his presbyterium and at which the holy chrism is consecrated and the oils blessed, manifests the communion of the priests with their bishop in the same priesthood and ministry of Christ. The priests who concelebrate with the bishop should come to this Mass from different parts of the diocese, thus showing in the consecration of the chrism to be his witnesses and cooperators, just as in their daily ministry they are his helpers and counselors.

The faithful are also to be encouraged to participate in this Mass, and to receive the sacrament of the Eucharist.

From *The Preparation and Celebration of the Easter Feasts.*

Entrance Antiphon

Jesus Christ has made us a kingdom of priests to serve his God and Father: glory and kingship be his for ever and ever. Amen.   (Rv 1:6)

Opening Prayer

Father,
by the power of the Holy Spirit
you anointed your only Son
Messiah and Lord of creation;
you have given us a share in his consecration
to priestly service in your Church.
Help us to be faithful witnesses in the world
to the salvation Christ won for all mankind.

We ask this through our Lord Jesus Christ, your Son,
who lives and reigns with you and the Holy Spirit,
one God, for ever and ever.

TODAY'S LIVING WORD

The familiar passage from the prophecy of Isaiah is extended in today's reading to include these words: "You yourselves shall be named priests of the Lord, ministers of our God shall you be called." They are addressed to the people of God, newly returned from exile, and announce God's intention to reconstitute Israel as "a kingdom of priests, a holy nation" (cf. Ex 19:6). The reading from Revelation uses the same language to talk about the saving work of the risen Jesus. Having "freed us from our sins by his blood," it says, he "has made us into a Kingdom, priests for his God and Father." The context of each reading indicates that both are speaking of the priesthood of the people and not the ordained priesthood. Even today's Gospel, depicting Jesus preaching in the synagogue of Nazareth, must not obscure his status as a layman.

Historically, the struggle that led to the death of Jesus was not between the Jews and the first Christians. It was a struggle between the priests of Jerusalem and a Jewish layman who called them to conversion. On this day, when men renew their commitment to priestly service, that is matter for meditation.

FIRST READING

Is 61:1–3a, 6a, 8b–9

The LORD anointed me and sent me to bring glad tidings to the lowly, and to give them oil of gladness.

A reading from the Book of the Prophet Isaiah

The Spirit of the Lord GOD is upon me,
    because the LORD has anointed me;
He has sent me to bring glad tidings to the lowly,
    to heal the brokenhearted,
To proclaim liberty to the captives
    and release to the prisoners,
To announce a year of favor from the LORD
    and a day of vindication by our God,
    to comfort all who mourn;
To place on those who mourn in Zion
    a diadem instead of ashes,
To give them oil of gladness in place of mourning,
    a glorious mantle instead of a listless spirit.

You yourselves shall be named priests of the LORD,
    ministers of our God shall you be called.

I will give them their recompense faithfully,
    a lasting covenant I will make with them.
Their descendants shall be renowned among the nations,

and their offspring among the peoples;
   All who see them shall acknowledge them
      as a race the LORD has blessed.

The word of the Lord.

Responsorial Psalm

Ps 89:21–22, 25 and 27

   R. For ever I will sing the goodness of the Lord.

"I have found David, my servant;
   with my holy oil I have anointed him.
That my hand may always be with him;
   and that my arm may make him strong."

   R. For ever I will sing the goodness of the Lord.

"My faithfulness and my mercy shall be with him;
   and through my name shall his horn be exalted.
He shall say of me, 'You are my father,
   my God, the Rock, my savior!' "

   R. For ever I will sing the goodness of the Lord.

SECOND READING

Rv 1:5–8

*Christ has made us into a Kingdom,
priests for his God and Father.*

A reading from the Book of Revelation

[Grace to you and peace] from Jesus Christ, who is the faithful witness, the firstborn of the dead and ruler of the kings of the earth. To him who loves us and has freed us from our sins by his Blood, who has made us into a Kingdom, priests for his God and Father, to him be glory and power forever and ever. Amen.

   Behold, he is coming amid the clouds,
      and every eye will see him,
         even those who pierced him.

All the peoples of the earth will lament him.
    Yes. Amen.

"I am the Alpha and the Omega," says the Lord God, "the one who is and who was and who is to come, the Almighty."

The word of the Lord.

Verse Before the Gospel   Is 61:1 (cited in Lk 4:18)
The Spirit of the LORD is upon me;
    for he has sent me to bring glad tidings to the poor.

GOSPEL
Lk 4:16–21

The Spirit of the Lord is upon me,
because of which he has anointed me.

A reading from the holy Gospel according to Luke

Jesus came to Nazareth, where he had grown up, and went according to his custom into the synagogue on the sabbath day. He stood up to read and was handed a scroll of the prophet Isaiah. He unrolled the scroll and found the passage where it was written:

The Spirit of the Lord is upon me,
because he has anointed me
    to bring glad tidings to the poor.
He has sent me to proclaim liberty to captives
    and recovery of sight to the blind,
    to let the oppressed go free,
and to proclaim a year acceptable to the Lord.

Rolling up the scroll, he handed it back to the attendant and sat down, and the eyes of all in the synagogue looked intently at him. He said to them, "Today this Scripture passage is fulfilled in your hearing."

The Gospel of the Lord.

In his homily the bishop should urge the priests to be faithful in fulfilling their office in the Church and should invite them to renew publicly their priestly promises.

RENEWAL OF COMMITMENT TO PRIESTLY SERVICE

After the homily the bishop speaks to the priests in these or similar words:

My brothers,
today we celebrate the memory of the first eucharist,
at which our Lord Jesus Christ
shared with his apostles and with us
his call to the priestly service of his Church.
Now, in the presence of your bishop and God's holy people,
are your ready to renew your own dedication to Christ
as priests of his new covenant?

PRIESTS: I am.

BISHOP: At your ordination
you accepted the responsibilities of the priest-
    hood
out of love for the Lord Jesus and his Church.
Are you resolved to unite yourselves more
    closely to Christ
and to try to become more like him
by joyfully sacrificing your own pleasure
    and ambition
to bring his peace and love to your brothers
    and sisters?

PRIESTS: I am.

BISHOP: Are you resolved
to be faithful ministers of the mysteries of God,
to celebrate the eucharist and the other
    liturgical services
with sincere devotion?

Are you resolved to imitate Jesus Christ,
the head and shepherd of the Church,
by teaching the Christian faith
without thinking of your own profit,
solely for the well-being of the people
you were sent to serve?

PRIESTS: I am.

Then the bishop addresses the people:

BISHOP: My brothers and sisters,
pray for your priests.
Ask the Lord to bless them with the fullness
    of his love,
to help them be faithful ministers of Christ the
    High Priest,
so that they will be able to lead you to him,
the fountain of your salvation.

PEOPLE: **Lord Jesus Christ, hear us and answer our
prayer.**

BISHOP: Pray also for me
that despite my own unworthiness
I may faithfully fulfill the office of apostle
which Jesus Christ has entrusted to me.
Pray that I may become more like
our High Priest and Good Shepherd,
the teacher and servant of all,
and so be a genuine sign
of Christ's loving presence among you.

PEOPLE: **Lord Jesus Christ, hear us and answer our
prayer.**

BISHOP: May the Lord in his love
keep you close to him always,
and may he bring all of us,

his priests and people,
to eternal life.

ALL: **Amen.**

The **Profession of faith** and **general intercessions** are omitted.

Liturgy of the Eucharist, *p. 897.*

Prayer over the Gifts

Pray, brethren...

Lord God,
may the power of this sacrifice
cleanse the old weakness of our human nature.
Give us a newness of life
and bring us to salvation.

Grant this through Christ our Lord.

Preface of the Priesthood (Chrism Mass), *p. 943.*

Communion Antiphon

For ever I will sing the goodness of the Lord; I will proclaim
your faithfulness to all generations.   (Ps 88:2)

Prayer after Communion

Let us pray.

Pause for silent prayer, if this has not preceded.

Lord God almighty,
you have given us fresh strength
in these sacramental gifts.
Renew in us the image of Christ's goodness.

We ask this in the name of Jesus the Lord.

For the remainder of Holy Week, see **Vatican II Sunday Missal,** *pp. 362–*
398: **Holy Thursday—Evening Mass of the Lord's Supper,** *p. 362;* **Good**
Friday—Celebration of the Lord's Passion, *p. 373;* **The Easter Vigil,**
p. 398.

Celebrating the Easter Sacraments

Recognizing the Body of Christ in Our Midst

To speak of the Spirit of God raising Jesus up (see Rom 8:11) and the Spirit of the risen Christ coming down to make the Church Christ's body in the world is to describe two aspects of one mysterious reality. The Church celebrates liturgically this great mystery through the fifty days of Easter, from Easter morning to Pentecost Sunday. The Easter season celebrates the sacramental presence of the risen Christ in our midst. We encounter Christ now in the living sacraments that are the Church, namely, the men and women, girls and boys, young and old, who altogether comprise the body of Christ now in the world.

Do you want to see the risen Christ? Go to the great Easter Vigil and see people profess their faith in him, descend into the baptismal waters that sacramentally represent his death, and rise up from those waters in a new birth that promises a share in his resurrection. The climax of the Vigil is the celebration of the Easter sacraments. Through Baptism, Confirmation, and first sharing in the Eucharist, women and men become living members of the body of Christ, his Church. Robed in white, anointed with the Spirit, feasted at the banquet table of the Lamb, the neophytes are God's precious gift to the assembled

Church community. They are living signs that Christ continues to live in our midst, even to the end of this age.

The Easter season flows from that most holy night into fifty days of sacramental revelation. For each of the consecutive Sundays of Easter, if parishes celebrate the liturgy well, the priest opens the Mass by drawing water from the Easter font and sprinkling the assembly, reminding them that they have been baptized. They need not look up toward heaven but, rather, look within and among themselves to see and remember that Christ is with them now. The Liturgy of the Word teaches us how this is so. The first reading includes accounts of the early Church in the Acts of the Apostles. The second reading, from either the Letters of John or Peter or the Book of Revelation, instructs us how we can *live as Church.* Finally, Christ himself reveals to us in the Gospel of John how he shares God's life now in and among us.

The truth of God's Word comes further to us in sacrament. In the Easter season the sacraments are to be celebrated robustly. Children who were baptized as infants and now have reached the age of reason are sealed by the Holy Spirit in the Sacrament of Confirmation and welcomed to share fully at the table of the Eucharist. Celebrations of Confirmation and First Communion are a great gift to local church communities. Far from being something given or done to children, these sacramental celebrations are living, bodily signs of the new form of life the risen Christ shares with us through the power of the Holy Spirit. For this reason, these events best take place during the great fifty days of Easter. In addition, pastors should encourage parents of new babies to share their joy by celebrating the Sacrament of Baptism during Mass on one of the seven Sundays of Easter.

Through this rich variety of sacramental signs we receive the grace of knowing that, despite any appearances to the contrary, the risen Christ continues to live in our midst. Yes, our faults and imperfections, our fears and failings are often all too evident to ourselves and one another. Easter, however, is the Holy Spirit's gift to us as Church to know that Christ is present in our midst. The same Spirit who formed Jesus in Mary's womb, commissioned him in his baptism, and raised him from the dead, now forms us in Baptism and feeds us in Eucharist. The Spirit of the Risen Christ is working powerfully through our lives, leading us to follow the pattern of Jesus' life of loving and selfless service so as finally to share fully in his resurrection from the dead.

BRUCE T. MORRILL, S.J.

OCTAVE OF EASTER

Monday

Entrance Antiphon

The Lord brought you to a land flowing with milk and honey, so that his law would always be given honor among you, alleluia.

(Ex 13:5, 9)

Or:

The Lord has risen from the dead, as he foretold. Let there be happiness and rejoicing for he is our King for ever, alleluia.

*The **Gloria** is said or sung, p. 892.*

Opening Prayer

Father,
you give your Church constant growth
by adding new members to your family.
Help us put into action in our lives
the baptism we have received with faith.

We ask this through our Lord Jesus Christ, your Son,
who lives and reigns with you and the Holy Spirit,
one God, for ever and ever.

*The **Profession of faith** is not said.*

TODAY'S LIVING WORD

The Easter proclamation begins at the empty tomb, which admits of several explanations. Today's Gospel presents us with two possibilities. One is the story that was apparently still circulating among the Jews of Matthew's day, that the disciples of Jesus stole his body. The other is the burden of Peter's sermon, the first reading for today. Standing with the Eleven, Peter declares that God has freed Jesus from death and "raised him up." Because he is addressing Jews like himself, Peter goes to some length to demonstrate that what God has done for Jesus is according to the Scriptures.

Peter's lengthy argument from the Scriptures is proclamation, not proof, of the resurrection. He is asking his fellow Jews to believe that Jesus, whom they once rejected, is the Messiah. And he is asking them to take his word for it. In faith, we are the heirs of those Jews who were persuaded by the witness of Peter and the Eleven and their successors. May we, like the women in the Gospel, run to carry the good news to others.

FIRST READING

Acts 2:14, 22–33

God raised this Jesus; of this we are all witnesses.

A reading from the Acts of the Apostles

On the day of Pentecost, Peter stood up with the Eleven, raised his voice, and proclaimed: "You who are Jews, indeed all of you staying in Jerusalem. Let this be known to you, and listen to my words.

"You who are children of Israel, hear these words. Jesus the Nazorean was a man commended to you by God with mighty deeds, wonders, and signs, which God worked through him in your midst, as you yourselves know. This man, delivered up by the set plan and foreknowledge of God, you killed, using lawless men to crucify him. But God raised him up, releasing him from the throes of death, because it was impossible for him to be held by it. For David says of him:

> *I saw the Lord ever before me,*
> *with him at my right hand I shall not be disturbed.*
> *Therefore my heart has been glad and my tongue has*
>   *exulted;*
>   *my flesh, too, will dwell in hope,*
> *because you will not abandon my soul to the nether*
>   *world,*
>   *nor will you suffer your holy one to see corruption.*

You have made known to me the paths of life;
you will fill me with joy in your presence.

"My brothers, one can confidently say to you about the patriarch David that he died and was buried, and his tomb is in our midst to this day. But since he was a prophet and knew that God had sworn an oath to him that he would set one of his descendants upon his throne, he foresaw and spoke of the resurrection of the Christ, that neither was he abandoned to the netherworld nor did his flesh see corruption. God raised this Jesus; of this we are all witnesses. Exalted at the right hand of God, he poured forth the promise of the Holy Spirit that he received from the Father, as you both see and hear."

The word of the Lord.

Responsorial Psalm   Ps 16:1–2a and 5, 7–8, 9–10, 11

   R. Keep me safe, O God; you are my hope.

Keep me, O God, for in you I take refuge;
   I say to the LORD, "My Lord are you."
O LORD, my allotted portion and my cup,
   you it is who hold fast my lot.

   R. Keep me safe, O God; you are my hope.

I bless the LORD who counsels me;
   even in the night my heart exhorts me.
I set the LORD ever before me;
   with him at my right hand I shall not be disturbed.

   R. Keep me safe, O God; you are my hope.

Therefore my heart is glad and my soul rejoices,
   my body, too, abides in confidence;
Because you will not abandon my soul to the nether world,
   nor will you suffer your faithful one to undergo corruption.

   R. Keep me safe, O God; you are my hope.

You will show me the path to life,
   fullness of joys in your presence,
   the delights at your right hand forever.

R. Keep me safe, O God; you are my hope.

Or: **R. Alleluia.**

Alleluia, alleluia   Ps 118:24
This is the day the LORD has made;
let us be glad and rejoice in it.
Alleluia, alleluia

GOSPEL

Mt 28:8 –15

Go tell my brothers to go to Galilee,
and there they will see me.

A reading from the holy Gospel according to Matthew

Mary Magdalene and the other Mary went away quickly from the tomb, fearful yet overjoyed, and ran to announce the news to his disciples. And behold, Jesus met them on their way and greeted them. They approached, embraced his feet, and did him homage. Then Jesus said to them, "Do not be afraid. Go tell my brothers to go to Galilee, and there they will see me."

   While they were going, some of the guard went into the city and told the chief priests all that had happened. The chief priests assembled with the elders and took counsel; then they gave a large sum of money to the soldiers, telling them, "You are to say, 'His disciples came by night and stole him while we were asleep.' And if this gets to the ears of the governor, we will satisfy him and keep you out of trouble." The soldiers took the money and did as they were instructed. And this story has circulated among the Jews to the present day.

The Gospel of the Lord.

Liturgy of the Eucharist, *p. 897.*

Prayer over the Gifts

Pray, brethren...

Father,
you have given us new light by baptism
and the profession of your name.
Accept the gifts of your children
and bring us to eternal joy in your presence.
We ask this in the name of Jesus the Lord.

Preface of Easter I, *p. 944.*

When Eucharistic Prayer I is used, the special Easter forms of IN UNION WITH THE WHOLE CHURCH and FATHER, ACCEPT THIS OFFERING are said.

Communion Antiphon

Christ now raised from the dead will never die again; death no longer has power over him, alleluia.   (Rom 6:9)

Prayer after Communion

Let us pray.

Pause for silent prayer, if this has not preceded.

Lord,
may the life we receive in these Easter sacraments
continue to grow in our hearts.
As you lead us along the way of eternal salvation,
make us worthy of your many gifts.
Grant this through Christ our Lord.

Tuesday

Entrance Antiphon

If men desire wisdom, she will give them the water of knowledge to drink. They will never waver from the truth; they will stand firm for ever, alleluia.   (Sir 15:3–4)

*The **Gloria** is said or sung, p. 892.*

Opening Prayer

Father,
by this Easter mystery you touch our lives
with the healing power of your love.
You have given us the freedom of the sons of God.
May we who now celebrate your gift
find joy in it for ever in heaven.

Grant this through our Lord Jesus Christ, your Son,
who lives and reigns with you and the Holy Spirit,
one God, for ever and ever.

*The **Profession of faith** is not said.*

TODAY'S LIVING WORD

In today's Gospel we see the process whereby Mary Magdalene came to believe in the risen Lord. On finding the tomb empty, she immediately concludes that someone has taken the body of Jesus, and she is devastated. Her tears so blur her vision that she does not recognize the person standing before her. He asks the question that, in John, defines discipleship, "Whom are you looking for?" She answers that she seeks the dead Jesus—and hears the living Christ call her by name.

The same process can be discerned in Peter's audience in today's first reading. Empowered by the Spirit, Peter calls them by name. They are Israel, the descendants of Abraham; the promise was made to them and to their children. He declares that the promise has been fulfilled in Jesus whom they crucified. Deeply shaken, they ask, "What are we to do?" Peter tells them they must repent, that is, turn (like Magdalene) to see in the risen Jesus their Messiah and Lord. This is the faith that baptism signifies and celebrates: not devotion to the dead Jesus, but discipleship of the risen Christ.

FIRST READING   Acts 2:36–41

Repent and be baptized, every one of you, in the name of Jesus Christ.

A reading from the Acts of the Apostles

On the day of Pentecost, Peter said to the Jewish people, "Let the whole house of Israel know for certain that God has made him both Lord and Christ, this Jesus whom you crucified."

Now when they heard this, they were cut to the heart, and they asked Peter and the other Apostles, "What are we to do, my brothers?" Peter said to them, "Repent and be baptized, every one of you, in the name of Jesus Christ, for the forgiveness of your sins; and you will receive the gift of the Holy Spirit. For the promise is made to you and to your children and to all those far off, whomever the Lord our God will call." He testified with many other arguments, and was exhorting them, "Save yourselves from this corrupt generation." Those who accepted his message were baptized, and about three thousand persons were added that day.

The word of the Lord.

Responsorial Psalm   Ps 33:4–5, 18–19, 20 and 22

R. The earth is full of the goodness of the Lord.

Upright is the word of the Lord,
  and all his works are trustworthy.
He loves justice and right;
  of the kindness of the Lord the earth is full.

R. The earth is full of the goodness of the Lord.

See, the eyes of the Lord are upon those who fear him,
  upon those who hope for his kindness,
To deliver them from death
  and preserve them in spite of famine.

R. The earth is full of the goodness of the Lord.

Our soul waits for the Lord,
  who is our help and our shield.

May your kindness, O LORD, be upon us
   who have put our hope in you.

   R. The earth is full of the goodness of the Lord.

   Or: **R. Alleluia.**

   Alleluia, alleluia   Ps 118:24
   This is the day the LORD has made;
   let us be glad and rejoice in it.
   Alleluia, alleluia

GOSPEL

Jn 20:11–18

   I have seen the Lord, and he said these things to me.

A reading from the holy Gospel according to John

Mary Magdalene stayed outside the tomb weeping. And as
she wept, she bent over into the tomb and saw two angels in
white sitting there, one at the head and one at the feet where
the Body of Jesus had been. And they said to her, "Woman,
why are you weeping?" She said to them, "They have taken
my Lord, and I don't know where they laid him." When she
had said this, she turned around and saw Jesus there, but did
not know it was Jesus. Jesus said to her, "Woman, why are you
weeping? Whom are you looking for?" She thought it was the
gardener and said to him, "Sir, if you carried him away, tell
me where you laid him, and I will take him." Jesus said to her,
"Mary!" She turned and said to him in Hebrew, "Rabbouni,"
which means Teacher. Jesus said to her, "Stop holding on to
me, for I have not yet ascended to the Father. But go to my
brothers and tell them, 'I am going to my Father and your
Father, to my God and your God.'" Mary went and announced
to the disciples, "I have seen the Lord," and then reported what
he had told her.

The Gospel of the Lord.

Liturgy of the Eucharist, *p. 897.*

Prayer over the Gifts

Pray, brethren...

Lord,
accept these gifts from your family.
May we hold fast to the life you have given us
and come to the eternal gifts you promise.

We ask this in the name of Jesus the Lord.

Preface of Easter I, *p. 944.*

When Eucharistic Prayer I is used, the special Easter forms of IN UNION WITH THE WHOLE CHURCH and FATHER, ACCEPT THIS OFFERING are said.

Communion Antiphon

If you have been raised with Christ, seek the things that are above, where Christ is seated at the right hand of God, alleluia.

(Col 3:1–2)

Prayer after Communion

Let us pray.

Pause for silent prayer, if this has not preceded.

All-powerful Father,
hear our prayers.
Prepare for eternal joy
the people you have renewed in baptism.

We ask this through Christ our Lord.

Wednesday

Entrance Antiphon

Come, you whom my Father has blessed; inherit the kingdom prepared for you since the foundation of the world, alleluia.

(Mt 25:34)

The **Gloria** *is said or sung, p. 892.*

Opening Prayer

God our Father,
on this solemn feast you give us the joy of recalling
the rising of Christ to new life.
May the joy of our annual celebration
bring us to the joy of eternal life.

We ask this through our Lord Jesus Christ, your Son,
who lives and reigns with you and the Holy Spirit,
one God, for ever and ever.

The **Profession of faith** *is not said.*

TODAY'S LIVING WORD

Raymond Brown suggests that today's Gospel may be Luke's answer to those folks in his community—and ours—who look back with nostalgia to the first generation of Jesus' followers. They imagine that their faith would be stronger had they seen the risen Lord with their own eyes. Luke's story aims to show them otherwise. The two disciples walk and talk with Jesus on the road to Emmaus. But reflecting on the Scriptures makes their hearts burn, and they only recognize the risen Jesus in the breaking of the bread. Luke's point is that those same means of knowing the Lord—the Scriptures and the breaking of bread—are available to Christians of every generation in the liturgy of the Church.*

The reading from Acts makes the same point. In the ministry of the apostles, "in the name of Jesus Christ the Nazorean," the powerful words and deeds of Jesus continue to be available to those in need, like the lame beggar in the story. Luke drives the point home by dwelling on the astonishing effect of Peter's words and deeds. Twice the lame man leaps about, as Isaiah had promised (35:6) and Jesus had proclaimed (Lk 7:22).

* *A Risen Christ in Eastertime* (Collegeville: Liturgical Press, 1991), p. 50.

FIRST READING

Acts 3:1–10

What I do have I give you:
in the name of the Lord Jesus, rise and walk.

A reading from the Acts of the Apostles

Peter and John were going up to the temple area for the three o'clock hour of prayer. And a man crippled from birth was carried and placed at the gate of the temple called "the Beautiful Gate" every day to beg for alms from the people who entered the temple. When he saw Peter and John about to go into the temple, he asked for alms. But Peter looked intently at him, as did John, and said, "Look at us." He paid attention to them, expecting to receive something from them. Peter said, "I have neither silver nor gold, but what I do have I give you: in the name of Jesus Christ the Nazorean, rise and walk." Then Peter took him by the right hand and raised him up, and immediately his feet and ankles grew strong. He leaped up, stood, and walked around, and went into the temple with them, walking and jumping and praising God. When all the people saw him walking and praising God, they recognized him as the one who used to sit begging at the Beautiful Gate of the temple, and they were filled with amazement and astonishment at what had happened to him.

The word of the Lord.

Responsorial Psalm

Ps 105:1–2, 3–4, 6–7, 8–9

R. Rejoice, O hearts that seek the Lord.

Give thanks to the LORD, invoke his name;
    make known among the nations his deeds.
Sing to him, sing his praise,
    proclaim all his wondrous deeds.

R. Rejoice, O hearts that seek the Lord.

Glory in his holy name;
    rejoice, O hearts that seek the LORD!

Look to the LORD in his strength;
  seek to serve him constantly.

R. Rejoice, O hearts that seek the Lord.

You descendants of Abraham, his servants,
  sons of Jacob, his chosen ones!
He, the LORD, is our God;
  throughout the earth his judgments prevail.

R. Rejoice, O hearts that seek the Lord.

He remembers forever his covenant
  which he made binding for a thousand generations—
Which he entered into with Abraham
  and by his oath to Isaac.

R. Rejoice, O hearts that seek the Lord.

Or: **R. Alleluia.**

> **Alleluia, alleluia** Ps 118:24
> This is the day the LORD has made;
>   let us be glad and rejoice in it.
> **Alleluia, alleluia**

GOSPEL   Lk 24:13–35
  They recognized Jesus in the breaking of the bread.

A reading from the holy Gospel according to Luke

That very day, the first day of the week, two of Jesus' disciples were going to a village seven miles from Jerusalem called Emmaus, and they were conversing about all the things that had occurred. And it happened that while they were conversing and debating, Jesus himself drew near and walked with them, but their eyes were prevented from recognizing him. He asked them, "What are you discussing as you walk along?" They stopped, looking downcast. One of them, named Cleopas, said to him in reply, "Are you the only visitor to Jerusalem who does not know of the things that have taken place there in these days?" And he replied to them, "What sort of things?" They said to him, "The things that happened to Jesus the Nazarene, who was a prophet mighty in deed and word before God and all the people, how our chief priests and rulers both handed him over to a sentence of death and crucified him. But we were hoping that he would be the one to redeem Israel; and besides all this, it is now the third day since this took place. Some women from our group, however, have astounded us: they were at the tomb early in the morning and did not find his Body; they came back and reported that they had indeed seen a vision of angels who announced that he was alive. Then some of those with us went to the tomb and found things just as the women had described, but him they did not see." And he said to them, "Oh, how foolish you are! How slow of heart to believe all that the prophets spoke! Was it not necessary that the Christ should suffer these things and enter into his glory?" Then beginning with Moses and all the prophets, he interpreted to them what referred to him in all the Scriptures. As they approached the village to which they were going, he gave the impression that he was going on farther. But they urged him, "Stay with us, for it is nearly evening and the day is almost over." So he went in to stay with them. And it happened that, while he was with them at table, he took bread, said the blessing, broke it, and gave it to them. With that their eyes were opened and they recognized him, but he vanished from their sight. Then they said to each other, "Were not our hearts burning within us while he spoke to us on the way and opened the Scriptures to us?" So they set out at once and returned to

Jerusalem where they found gathered together the Eleven and those with them who were saying, "The Lord has truly been raised and has appeared to Simon!" Then the two recounted what had taken place on the way and how he was made known to them in the breaking of the bread.

The Gospel of the Lord.

Liturgy of the Eucharist, *p. 897.*

Prayer over the Gifts

Pray, brethren...

Lord,
accept this sacrifice of our redemption
and accomplish in us salvation of mind and body.

Grant this through Christ our Lord.

Preface of Easter I, *p. 944.*

When Eucharistic Prayer I is used, the special Easter forms of IN UNION WITH THE WHOLE CHURCH and FATHER, ACCEPT THIS OFFERING are said.

Communion Antiphon

The disciples recognized the Lord Jesus in the breaking of the bread, alleluia.   (Lk 24:35)

Prayer after Communion

Let us pray.

Pause for silent prayer, if this has not preceded.

Lord,
may this sharing in the sacrament of your Son
free us from our old life of sin
and make us your new creation.

We ask this in the name of Jesus the Lord.

Thursday

Entrance Antiphon

Your people praised your great victory, O Lord. Wisdom opened the mouth that was dumb, and made the tongues of babies speak, alleluia.   (Wis 10:20 – 21)

The **Gloria** *is said or sung, p. 892.*

Opening Prayer

Father,
you gather the nations to praise your name.
May all who are reborn in baptism
be one in faith and love.

Grant this through our Lord Jesus Christ, your Son,
who lives and reigns with you and the Holy Spirit,
one God, for ever and ever.

The **Profession of faith** *is not said.*

TODAY'S LIVING WORD

In today's first reading, Peter and John act on the commission that Jesus gave them in today's Gospel. "Repentance, for the for-give-ness of sins, would be preached in his [the Christ's] name to all the nations, beginning from Jerusalem." So Peter preaches to his fellow Israelites in Solomon's Portico. His sermon is thoroughly "Jewish." He says that the God who raised Jesus is "the God of Abraham, the God of Isaac, and the God of Jacob, the God of our ancestors." He further claims that the suffering of the Messiah was "announced beforehand through the mouth of all the prophets." Jesus is the "prophet like Moses" to whom Moses himself bore wit-ness. But by citing the promise God made to Abraham—"In your offspring all the families of the earth shall be blessed"—Peter hints as well that the good news is meant for "all the nations."

Just as the miracles of Jesus were often misconstrued, the miracle that Peter and John work in Jesus' name is also misinterpreted. So

Peter hastens to explain that faith in the name of the risen Jesus has made the lame man whole. Such faith can do the same for us.

FIRST READING

Acts 3:11–26

The author of life you put to death,
but God raised him from the dead.

A reading from the Acts of the Apostles

As the crippled man who had been cured clung to Peter and John, all the people hurried in amazement toward them in the portico called "Solomon's Portico." When Peter saw this, he addressed the people, "You children of Israel, why are you amazed at this, and why do you look so intently at us as if we had made him walk by our own power or piety? The God of Abraham, the God of Isaac, and the God of Jacob, the God of our fathers, has glorified his servant Jesus whom you handed over and denied in Pilate's presence, when he had decided to release him. You denied the Holy and Righteous One and asked that a murderer be released to you. The author of life you put to death, but God raised him from the dead; of this we are witnesses. And by faith in his name, this man, whom you see and know, his name has made strong, and the faith that comes through it has given him this perfect health, in the presence of all of you. Now I know, brothers and sisters, that you acted out of ignorance, just as your leaders did; but God has thus brought to fulfillment what he had announced beforehand through the mouth of all the prophets, that his Christ would suffer. Repent, therefore, and be converted, that your sins may be wiped away, and that the Lord may grant you times of refreshment and send you the Christ already appointed for you, Jesus, whom heaven must receive until the times of universal restoration of which

God spoke through the mouth of his holy prophets from of old. For Moses said:

> *A prophet like me will the Lord, your God, raise up for you*
> *from among your own kin;*
> *to him you shall listen in all that he may say to you.*
> *Everyone who does not listen to that prophet*
> *will be cut off from the people.*

"Moreover, all the prophets who spoke, from Samuel and those afterwards, also announced these days. You are the children of the prophets and of the covenant that God made with your ancestors when he said to Abraham, *In your offspring all the families of the earth shall be blessed.* For you first, God raised up his servant and sent him to bless you by turning each of you from your evil ways."

The word of the Lord.

Responsional Psalm   Ps 8:2ab and 5, 6–7, 8–9

R. O Lord, our God, how wonderful your name
in all the earth!

O LORD, our Lord,
  how glorious is your name over all the earth!
What is man that you should be mindful of him,
  or the son of man that you should care for him?

R. O Lord, our God, how wonderful your name
in all the earth!

You have made him little less than the angels,
  and crowned him with glory and honor.
You have given him rule over the works of your hands,
  putting all things under his feet.

R. O Lord, our God, how wonderful your name
in all the earth!

All sheep and oxen,
  yes, and the beasts of the field,
The birds of the air, the fishes of the sea,
  and whatever swims the paths of the seas.

  R. O Lord, our God, how wonderful your name
    in all the earth!

  Or: **R. Alleluia.**

    Alleluia, alleluia Ps 118:24
    This is the day the LORD has made;
    let us be glad and rejoice in it.
    Alleluia, alleluia

GOSPEL

Lk 24:35–48

Thus it was written that the Christ would suffer
and rise from the dead on the third day.

A reading from the holy Gospel according to Luke

The disciples of Jesus recounted what had taken place along the way, and how they had come to recognize him in the breaking of bread.

    While they were still speaking about this, he stood in their midst and said to them, "Peace be with you." But they were startled and terrified and thought that they were seeing a ghost. Then he said to them, "Why are you troubled? And why do questions arise in your hearts? Look at my hands and my feet, that it is I myself. Touch me and see, because a ghost does not have flesh and bones as you can see I have." And as he said this, he showed them his hands and his feet. While they were still incredulous for joy and were amazed, he asked them, "Have you anything here to eat?" They gave him a piece of baked fish; he took it and ate it in front of them.

He said to them, "These are my words that I spoke to you while I was still with you, that everything written about me in the law of Moses and in the prophets and psalms must be fulfilled." Then he opened their minds to understand the Scriptures. And he said to them, "Thus it is written that the Christ would suffer and rise from the dead on the third day and that repentance, for the forgiveness of sins, would be preached in his name to all the nations, beginning from Jerusalem. You are witnesses of these things."

The Gospel of the Lord.

Liturgy of the Eucharist, *p. 897.*

Prayer over the Gifts

Pray, brethren...

Lord,
accept our gifts
and grant your continuing protection
to all who have received new life in baptism.

We ask this in the name of Jesus the Lord.

Preface of Easter I, *p. 944.*

When Eucharistic Prayer I is used, the special Easter forms of IN UNION WITH THE WHOLE CHURCH and FATHER, ACCEPT THIS OFFERING are said.

Communion Antiphon

You are a people God claims as his own, to praise him who called you out of darkness into his marvelous light, alleluia.
(1 Pt 2:9)

Prayer after Communion

Let us pray.

Pause for silent prayer, if this has not preceded.

Lord,
may this celebration of our redemption
help us in this life
and lead us to eternal happiness.

We ask this through Christ our Lord.

Friday

Entrance Antiphon

The Lord led his people out of slavery. He drowned their enemies in the sea, alleluia. (Ps 77:53)

*The **Gloria** is said or sung, p. 892.*

Opening Prayer

Eternal Father,
you gave us the Easter mystery
as our covenant of reconciliation.
May the new birth we celebrate
show its effects in the way we live.

We ask this through our Lord Jesus Christ, your Son,
who lives and reigns with you and the Holy Spirit,
one God, for ever and ever.

*The **Profession of faith** is not said.*

TODAY'S LIVING WORD

All four Gospels have a story of Jesus calling fishermen to be "fishers of men." In the first three Gospels, these stories take place early in Jesus' public ministry and point to a future still some time away. In John it is an Easter story, inaugurating the mission of the Church in the wake of Jesus' resurrection. The details convey the meaning of the story. In the Gospels, fishing symbolizes the missionary activity of the Church, in which Peter plays a central role. Here that role is dramatized when, in answer to Jesus' request, Peter single-handedly hauls the net ashore. The word for "haul" is the same Greek word that is used to describe the Father's "drawing" disciples to Jesus (cf. Jn 6:44). The significance of the number 153 has been the subject of much speculation; whatever else, it promises an abundant harvest—contained by one unbroken net.

In today's first reading Peter, "filled with the Holy Spirit," casts wide his net among the elders, the leaders of the people, who want to know in whose name he is acting. Peter tells them he acts in the only name "under heaven...by which we are to be saved."

FIRST READING   Acts 4:1–12

There is no salvation through anyone else.

A reading from the Acts of the Apostles

After the crippled man had been cured, while Peter and John were still speaking to the people, the priests, the captain of the temple guard, and the Sadducees confronted them, disturbed that they were teaching the people and proclaiming in Jesus the resurrection of the dead. They laid hands on Peter and John and put them in custody until the next day, since it was already evening. But many of those who heard the word came to believe and the number of men grew to about five thousand.

On the next day, their leaders, elders, and scribes were assembled in Jerusalem, with Annas the high priest, Caiaphas, John, Alexander, and all who were of the high-priestly class. They brought them into their presence and questioned them, "By what power or by what name have you done this?" Then Peter, filled with the Holy Spirit, answered them, "Leaders of the people and elders: If we are being examined today about a good deed done to a cripple, namely, by what means he was saved, then all of you and all the people of Israel should know that it was in the name of Jesus Christ the Nazorean whom you crucified, whom God raised from the dead; in his name this man stands before you healed. He is *the stone rejected by you, the builders, which has become the cornerstone.* There is no salvation through anyone else, nor is there any other name under heaven given to the human race by which we are to be saved."

The word of the Lord.

Responsorial Psalm

Ps 118:1–2 and 4, 22–24, 25–27a

R. **The stone rejected by the builders has become the cornerstone.**

Give thanks to the Lord, for he is good,
  for his mercy endures forever.
Let the house of Israel say,
  "His mercy endures forever."
Let those who fear the Lord say,
  "His mercy endures forever."

R. **The stone rejected by the builders has become the cornerstone.**

The stone which the builders rejected
  has become the cornerstone.
By the Lord has this been done;
  it is wonderful in our eyes.
This is the day the Lord has made;
  let us be glad and rejoice in it.

R. **The stone rejected by the builders has become the cornerstone.**

O Lord, grant salvation!
  O Lord, grant prosperity!
Blessed is he who comes in the name of the Lord;
  we bless you from the house of the Lord.
  The Lord is God, and he has given us light.

R. **The stone rejected by the builders has become the cornerstone.**

Or: R. **Alleluia.**

Alleluia, alleluia   Ps 118:24
This is the day the LORD has made;
let us be glad and rejoice in it.
Alleluia, alleluia

GOSPEL
Jn 21:1–14

*Jesus came over and took the bread and gave it to them,
and in like manner the fish.*

A reading from the holy Gospel according to John

Jesus revealed himself again to his disciples at the Sea of
Tiberias. He revealed himself in this way. Together were Simon
Peter, Thomas called Didymus, Nathanael from Cana in Galilee,
Zebedee's sons, and two others of his disciples. Simon Peter
said to them, "I am going fishing." They said to him, "We also
will come with you." So they went out and got into the boat,
but that night they caught nothing. When it was already dawn,
Jesus was standing on the shore; but the disciples did not realize
that it was Jesus. Jesus said to them, "Children, have you caught
anything to eat?" They answered him, "No." So he said to
them, "Cast the net over the right side of the boat and you will
find something." So they cast it, and were not able to pull it in
because of the number of fish. So the disciple whom Jesus
loved said to Peter, "It is the Lord." When Simon Peter heard
that it was the Lord, he tucked in his garment, for he was lightly
clad, and jumped into the sea. The other disciples came in the
boat, for they were not far from shore, only about a hundred
yards, dragging the net with the fish. When they climbed out
on shore, they saw a charcoal fire with fish on it and bread.
Jesus said to them, "Bring some of the fish you just caught."
So Simon Peter went over and dragged the net ashore full of
one hundred fifty-three large fish. Even though there were so
many, the net was not torn. Jesus said to them, "Come, have

breakfast." And none of the disciples dared to ask him, "Who are you?" because they realized it was the Lord. Jesus came over and took the bread and gave it to them, and in like manner the fish. This was now the third time Jesus was revealed to his disciples after being raised from the dead.

The Gospel of the Lord.

Liturgy of the Eucharist, *p. 897.*

Prayer over the Gifts

Pray, brethren...

Lord,
bring to perfection the spirit of life
we receive from these Easter gifts.
Free us from seeking after the passing things in life
and help us set our hearts on the kingdom of heaven.

Grant this through Christ our Lord.

Preface of Easter I, *p. 944.*

When Eucharistic Prayer I is used, the special Easter forms of IN UNION WITH THE WHOLE CHURCH AND FATHER, ACCEPT THIS OFFERING are said.

Communion Antiphon

Jesus said to his disciples: Come and eat. And he took the bread, and gave it to them, alleluia.   (See Jn 21:12 –13)

Prayer after Communion

Let us pray.

Pause for silent prayer, if this has not preceded.

Lord,
watch over those you have saved in Christ.
May we who are redeemed by his suffering and death
always rejoice in his resurrection,
for he is Lord for ever and ever.

Saturday

Entrance Antiphon

The Lord led his people to freedom and they shouted with joy and gladness, alleluia.   (Ps 104:43)

*The **Gloria** is said or sung, p. 892.*

Opening Prayer

Father of love,
by the outpouring of your grace
you increase the number of those who believe in you.
Watch over your chosen family.
Give undying life to all
who have been born again in baptism.

Grant this through our Lord Jesus Christ, your Son,
who lives and reigns with you and the Holy Spirit,
one God, for ever and ever.

*The **Profession of faith** is not said.*

TODAY'S LIVING WORD

In today's first reading, Peter and John continue to share the lived experience of Jesus in Luke's Gospel. While teaching in the temple, after healing the lame man they are arrested and interrogated by the leaders of the people, among them Annas and Caiaphas. These want to know by what authority men of their stripe have done this thing. Boldly, Peter answers that "it was in the name of Jesus Christ the Nazorean whom you crucified, whom God raised from the dead." Even at this, their accusers can find no way to punish them for fear of the people, "who were all praising God for what had happened."

Today's Gospel, known as the "longer ending" of Mark, depicts the disciples of Jesus as being as disbelieving and as stubborn as the leaders of the people in Acts. Only seeing the risen Lord himself brings them to faith. His reprimand of them must strengthen our resolve to put our faith in the witness of those "who saw him after he had been raised" and to proclaim that good news "to every creature."

FIRST READING

Acts 4:13 – 21

*It is impossible for us not to speak about
what we have seen and heard.*

A reading from the Acts of the Apostles

Observing the boldness of Peter and John and perceiving them to be uneducated, ordinary men, the leaders, elders, and scribes were amazed, and they recognized them as the companions of Jesus. Then when they saw the man who had been cured standing there with them, they could say nothing in reply. So they ordered them to leave the Sanhedrin, and conferred with one another, saying, "What are we to do with these men? Everyone living in Jerusalem knows that a remarkable sign was done through them, and we cannot deny it. But so that it may not be spread any further among the people, let us give them a stern warning never again to speak to anyone in this name."

So they called them back and ordered them not to speak or teach at all in the name of Jesus. Peter and John, however, said to them in reply, "Whether it is right in the sight of God for us to obey you rather than God, you be the judges. It is impossible for us not to speak about what we have seen and heard." After threatening them further, they released them, finding no way to punish them, on account of the people who were all praising God for what had happened.

The word of the Lord.

Responsorial Psalm

Ps 118:1 and 14 –15ab, 16 –18, 19 –21

R. **I will give thanks to you, for you have answered me.**

Give thanks to the LORD, for he is good,
  for his mercy endures forever.

My strength and my courage is the L ORD,
  and he has been my savior.
The joyful shout of victory
  in the tents of the just.

R. I will give thanks to you, for you have answered me.

"The right hand of the L ORD is exalted;
  the right hand of the L ORD has struck with power."
I shall not die, but live,
  and declare the works of the L ORD.
Though the L ORD has indeed chastised me,
  yet he has not delivered me to death.

R. I will give thanks to you, for you have answered me.

Open to me the gates of justice;
  I will enter them and give thanks to the L ORD.
This is the gate of the L ORD;
  the just shall enter it.
I will give thanks to you, for you have answered me
  and have been my savior.

R. I will give thanks to you, for you have answered me.

Or: **R. Alleluia.**

Alleluia, alleluia   Ps 118:24
This is the day the L ORD has made;
let us be glad and rejoice in it.
Alleluia, alleluia

GOSPEL   Mk 16:9–15
*Go into the whole world and proclaim
the Gospel to every creature.*

A reading from the holy Gospel according to Mark

When Jesus had risen, early on the first day of the week, he
appeared first to Mary Magdalene, out of whom he had driven
seven demons. She went and told his companions who were
mourning and weeping. When they heard that he was alive
and had been seen by her, they did not believe.

After this he appeared in another form to two of them walking along on their way to the country. They returned and told the others; but they did not believe them either.

But later, as the Eleven were at table, he appeared to them and rebuked them for their unbelief and hardness of heart because they had not believed those who saw him after he had been raised. He said to them, "Go into the whole world and proclaim the Gospel to every creature."

The Gospel of the Lord.

Liturgy of the Eucharist, *p. 897.*

Prayer over the Gifts

Pray, brethren...

Lord,
give us joy by these Easter mysteries.
Let the continuous offering of this sacrifice
by which we are renewed
bring us to eternal happiness.
We ask this in the name of Jesus the Lord.

Preface of Easter I, *p. 944.*

When Eucharistic Prayer I is used, the special Easter forms of IN UNION WITH THE WHOLE CHURCH and FATHER, ACCEPT THIS OFFERING are said.

Communion Antiphon

All you who have been baptized have been clothed in Christ, alleluia.   (Gal 3:27)

Prayer after Communion

Let us pray.

Pause for silent prayer, if this has not preceded.

Lord,

look on your people with kindness
and by these Easter mysteries
bring us to the glory of the resurrection.

We ask this in the name of Jesus the Lord.

SECOND WEEK OF EASTER

Monday

Entrance Antiphon

**Christ now raised from the dead will never die again; death
no longer has power over him, alleluia.**   (Rom 6:9)

Opening Prayer

Almighty and ever-living God,
your Spirit made us your children,
confident to call you Father.
Increase your Spirit of love within us
and bring us to our promised inheritance.

Grant this through our Lord Jesus Christ, your Son,
who lives and reigns with you and the Holy Spirit,
one God, for ever and ever.

TODAY'S LIVING WORD

Today's first reading from the Acts of the Apostles continues the
now familiar pattern that characterizes Luke's view of the emerging
Church. Having been detained for questioning by the Jewish authorities, Peter and John are released and return to the community, who
"raised their voices to God with one accord." As we have come to
expect, in their prayer as in their preaching they turn the light of the

risen Lord on the Hebrew Scriptures. Their prayer is answered by the gift of the Holy Spirit, as Luke's Jesus had promised (11:13). So "filled with the Holy Spirit," they find the courage to continue to speak God's word—boldly.

Such boldness is totally lacking in Nicodemus who comes to Jesus under cover of night. But then Nicodemus is not yet ready to be "born of water and Spirit." The Easter proclamation questions us: are we?

FIRST READING

Acts 4:23 – 31

As they prayed, they were all filled with the Holy Spirit
and continued to speak the word of God with boldness.

A reading from the Acts of the Apostles

After their release Peter and John went back to their own people and reported what the chief priests and elders had told them. And when they heard it, they raised their voices to God with one accord and said, "Sovereign Lord, maker of heaven and earth and the sea and all that is in them, you said by the Holy Spirit through the mouth of our father David, your servant:

Why did the Gentiles rage
and the peoples entertain folly?
The kings of the earth took their stand
and the princes gathered together
against the Lord and against his anointed.

"Indeed they gathered in this city against your holy servant Jesus whom you anointed, Herod and Pontius Pilate, together with the Gentiles and the peoples of Israel, to do what your hand and your will had long ago planned to take place. And now, Lord, take note of their threats, and enable your servants to speak your word with all boldness, as you stretch forth your hand to heal, and signs and wonders are done through the name of your holy servant Jesus." As they prayed, the place where they were gathered shook, and they were all filled with the Holy Spirit and continued to speak the word of God with boldness.

The word of the Lord.

Responsorial Psalm

R. **Blessed are all who take refuge in the Lord.**

Why do the nations rage
  and the peoples utter folly?
The kings of the earth rise up,
  and the princes conspire together
  against the LORD and against his anointed:
"Let us break their fetters
  and cast their bonds from us!"

R. **Blessed are all who take refuge in the Lord.**

He who is throned in heaven laughs;
  the LORD derides them.
Then in anger he speaks to them;
  he terrifies them in his wrath:
"I myself have set up my king
  on Zion, my holy mountain."
I will proclaim the decree of the LORD.

R. **Blessed are all who take refuge in the Lord.**

The LORD said to me, "You are my Son;
  this day I have begotten you.
Ask of me and I will give you
  the nations for an inheritance
  and the ends of the earth for your possession.
You shall rule them with an iron rod;
  you shall shatter them like an earthen dish."

R. **Blessed are all who take refuge in the Lord.**

Or: R. **Alleluia.**

Alleluia, alleluia   Col 3:1
If then you were raised with Christ,
seek what is above,
where Christ is seated at the right hand of God.
Alleluia, alleluia

GOSPEL   Jn 3:1–8

No one can enter the Kingdom of God
without being born of water and Spirit.

A reading from the holy Gospel according to John

There was a Pharisee named Nicodemus, a ruler of the Jews.
He came to Jesus at night and said to him, "Rabbi, we know
that you are a teacher who has come from God, for no one can
do these signs that you are doing unless God is with him."
Jesus answered and said to him, "Amen, amen, I say to you,
unless one is born from above, he cannot see the Kingdom of
God." Nicodemus said to him, "How can a man once grown
old be born again? Surely he cannot reenter his mother's womb
and be born again, can he?" Jesus answered, "Amen, amen, I
say to you, unless one is born of water and Spirit he cannot
enter the Kingdom of God. What is born of flesh is flesh and
what is born of spirit is spirit. Do not be amazed that I told
you, 'You must be born from above.' The wind blows where it
wills, and you can hear the sound it makes, but you do not
know where it comes from or where it goes; so it is with
everyone who is born of the Spirit."

The Gospel of the Lord.

Liturgy of the Eucharist, *p. 897.*

Prayer over the Gifts

Pray, brethren...
Lord,

receive these gifts from your Church.
May the great joy you give us
come to perfection in heaven.

Grant this through Christ our Lord.

Preface of Easter II–V, *pp. 945–946.*

Communion Antiphon

**Jesus came and stood among his disciples and said to them:
Peace be with you, alleluia.** (Jn 20:19)

Prayer after Communion

Let us pray.

Pause for silent prayer, if this has not preceded.

Lord,
look on your people with kindness
and by these Easter mysteries
bring us to the glory of the resurrection.

We ask this in the name of Jesus the Lord.

Tuesday

Entrance Antiphon

**Let us shout out our joy and happiness, and give glory to God,
the Lord of all, because he is our King, alleluia.** (Rv 19:7, 6)

Opening Prayer

All-powerful God,
help us to proclaim the power of the Lord's resurrection.
May we who accept this sign of the love of Christ
come to share the eternal life he reveals,
for he lives and reigns with you and the Holy Spirit,
one God, for ever and ever.

TODAY'S LIVING WORD

Today's Gospel passage from John repeats Jesus' analogy likening the Holy Spirit to the wind that "blows where it wills" and is only "seen" by its effects. Intent on solving the problem of Jesus' words, Nicodemus is impervious to their power. Jesus' analogy urges him to accept the Spirit as he does the wind, as an inscrutable mystery.

The reading from Acts, a Lucan summary of the communal life of the early Church, attests to the power of the Spirit. Like a gust of wind, the gift of God has made this gathering of Christian Jews into an icon of all that is right and good. Because Luke is the author-artist here, the image blends the best of all worlds. The Hellenistic (Greco-Roman) appreciation of friendship is evident in the believers being "of one heart and mind." The blessings God promised to Israel are found here as well, in that there is no one needy among them (Dt 15:4). But this is not utopia, a human achievement. This is the effect of the Spirit through the effort of the apostles who, at the heart of the community, "bore witness to the resurrection of the Lord Jesus."

FIRST READING

Acts 4:32–37

The community of believers was of one heart and mind.

A reading from the Acts of the Apostles

The community of believers was of one heart and mind, and no one claimed that any of his possessions was his own, but they had everything in common. With great power the Apostles bore witness to the resurrection of the Lord Jesus, and great favor was accorded them all. There was no needy person among them, for those who owned property or houses would sell them, bring the proceeds of the sale, and put them at the feet of the Apostles, and they were distributed to each according to need.

Thus Joseph, also named by the Apostles Barnabas (which is translated "son of encouragement"), a Levite, a Cypriot by birth, sold a piece of property that he owned, then brought the money and put it at the feet of the Apostles.

The word of the Lord.

Responsorial Psalm

Ps 93:1ab, 1cd – 2, 5

R. The Lord is king; he is robed in majesty.

The LORD is king, in splendor robed;
  robed is the LORD and girt about with strength.

R. The Lord is king; he is robed in majesty.

And he has made the world firm,
  not to be moved.
Your throne stands firm from of old;
  from everlasting you are, O LORD.

R. The Lord is king; he is robed in majesty.

Your decrees are worthy of trust indeed:
  holiness befits your house,
  O LORD, for length of days.

R. The Lord is king; he is robed in majesty.

Or: **R. Alleluia.**

> **Alleluia, alleluia**   Jn 3:14 – 15
> The Son of Man must be lifted up,
> so that everyone who believes in him
> may have eternal life.
> **Alleluia, alleluia**

GOSPEL

Jn 3:7b –15

*No one has gone up to heaven except the one who
has come down from heaven, the Son of Man.*

A reading from the holy Gospel according to John

Jesus said to Nicodemus: " 'You must be born from above.' The wind blows where it wills, and you can hear the sound it makes, but you do not know where it comes from or where it goes; so it is with everyone who is born of the Spirit." Nicodemus answered and said to him, "How can this happen?" Jesus answered and said to him, "You are the teacher of Israel and you do not understand this? Amen, amen, I say to you, we speak of what we know and we testify to what we have seen, but you people do not accept our testimony. If I tell you about earthly things and you do not believe, how will you believe if I tell you about heavenly things? No one has gone up to heaven except the one who has come down from heaven, the Son of Man. And just as Moses lifted up the serpent in the desert, so must the Son of Man be lifted up, so that everyone who believes in him may have eternal life."

The Gospel of the Lord.

Liturgy of the Eucharist, *p. 897.*

Prayer over the Gifts

Pray, brethren...

Lord,
give us joy by these Easter mysteries.
Let the continuous offering of this sacrifice
by which we are renewed
bring us to eternal happiness.

We ask this in the name of Jesus the Lord.

Preface of Easter II–V, *pp. 945–946.*

Communion Antiphon

Christ had to suffer and to rise from the dead, and so enter into his glory, alleluia. (See Lk 24:46, 26)

Prayer after Communion

Let us pray.

Pause for silent prayer, if this has not preceded.

Lord,
may this celebration of our redemption
help us in this life
and lead us to eternal happiness.
We ask this through Christ our Lord.

Wednesday

Entrance Antiphon

I will be a witness to you in the world, O Lord. I will spread
the knowledge of your name among my brothers, alleluia.

(Ps 17:50; 21:23)

Opening Prayer

God of mercy,
you have filled us with the hope of resurrection
by restoring man to his original dignity.
May we who relive this mystery each year
come to share it in perpetual love.

Grant this through our Lord Jesus Christ, your Son,
who lives and reigns with you and the Holy Spirit,
one God, for ever and ever.

TODAY'S LIVING WORD

In today's Gospel Jesus describes his earthly mission as a struggle
between light and darkness. In John, darkness is the world's sinful
state, while light is the gift of salvation. Jesus says that "God so
loved the world" that he sent his only Son to bring light into the
darkness. But the world "preferred darkness to light," passing judgment on itself. The reading from Acts provides a concrete example
of the world's refusal of the light. The high priest and all his

supporters, the same coalition that acted against Jesus, are assembled again to take action against his followers. The apostles are arrested and thrown into the public jail, only to be released and recommissioned by an angel of the Lord, for the darkness will not overcome the light (cf. Jn 1:5).

The story in Acts also provides comic relief from the mounting tension between the apostles and the Jewish authorities. The embarrassment to the Sanhedrin, that solemn assembly, caused by the angel releasing their prisoners, is truly funny. It is a rare glimpse of divine levity. As Madeleine L'Engle once observed, "It was by gravity that Satan fell."* The moral of both readings seems to be: lighten up!

* *The Rock That Is Higher* (Wheaton, IL: Harold Shaw Publishers, 1993), p. 248.

FIRST READING

Acts 5:17–26

The men whom you put in prison are in the temple area and are teaching the people.

A reading from the Acts of the Apostles

The high priest rose up and all his companions, that is, the party of the Sadducees, and, filled with jealousy, laid hands upon the Apostles and put them in the public jail. But during the night, the angel of the Lord opened the doors of the prison, led them out, and said, "Go and take your place in the temple area, and tell the people everything about this life." When they heard this, they went to the temple early in the morning and taught. When the high priest and his companions arrived, they convened the Sanhedrin, the full senate of the children of Israel, and sent to the jail to have them brought in. But the court officers who went did not find them in the prison, so they came back and reported, "We found the jail securely locked and the guards stationed outside the doors, but when we opened them, we found no one inside." When the captain of the temple guard and the chief priests heard this report, they were at a loss about them, as to what this would come to. Then someone came in and reported to them, "The men whom you put in prison are in the temple area and are teaching the people." Then the captain and the court officers went and brought them, but without force, because they were afraid of being stoned by the people.

The word of the Lord.

Responsorial Psalm

Ps 34:2–3, 4–5, 6–7, 8–9

R. The Lord hears the cry of the poor.

I will bless the LORD at all times;
  his praise shall be ever in my mouth.
Let my soul glory in the LORD;
  the lowly will hear me and be glad.

R. The Lord hears the cry of the poor.

Glorify the LORD with me,
  let us together extol his name.
I sought the LORD, and he answered me
  and delivered me from all my fears.

R. The Lord hears the cry of the poor.

Look to him that you may be radiant with joy,
  and your faces may not blush with shame.
When the poor one called out, the LORD heard,
  and from all his distress he saved him.

R. The Lord hears the cry of the poor.

The angel of the LORD encamps
  around those who fear him, and delivers them.
Taste and see how good the LORD is;
  blessed the man who takes refuge in him.

R. The Lord hears the cry of the poor.

Or: **R. Alleluia.**

Alleluia, alleluia Jn 3:16
God so loved the world that he gave his only-begotten Son,
so that everyone who believes in him might have eternal life.
Alleluia, alleluia

GOSPEL   Jn 3:16–21

God sent his Son that the world might be saved through him.

A reading from the holy Gospel according to John

God so loved the world that he gave his only-begotten Son, so that everyone who believes in him might not perish but might have eternal life. For God did not send his Son into the world to condemn the world, but that the world might be saved through him. Whoever believes in him will not be condemned, but whoever does not believe has already been condemned, because he has not believed in the name of the only-begotten Son of God. And this is the verdict, that the light came into the world, but people preferred darkness to light, because their works were evil. For everyone who does wicked things hates the light and does not come toward the light, so that his works might not be exposed. But whoever lives the truth comes to the light, so that his works may be clearly seen as done in God.

The Gospel of the Lord.

Liturgy of the Eucharist, *p. 897.*

Prayer over the Gifts

Pray, brethren...

Lord God,
by this holy exchange of gifts
you share with us your divine life.
Grant that everything we do
may be directed by the knowledge of your truth.
We ask this in the name of Jesus the Lord.

Preface of Easter II–V, *pp. 945–946.*

Communion Antiphon

The Lord says, I have chosen you from the world to go and bear fruit that will last, alleluia.   (See Jn 15:16, 19)

Prayer after Communion

Let us pray.

Pause for silent prayer, if this has not preceded.

Merciful Father,
may these mysteries give us new purpose
and bring us to a new life in you.

Grant this through Christ our Lord.

Thursday

Entrance Antiphon

When you walked at the head of your people, O God, and lived with them on their journey, the earth shook at your presence, and the skies poured forth their rain, alleluia.

(See Ps 67:8–9, 20)

Opening Prayer

God of mercy,
may the Easter mystery we celebrate
be effective throughout our lives.

Grant this through our Lord Jesus Christ, your Son,
who lives and reigns with you and the Holy Spirit,
one God, for ever and ever.

TODAY'S LIVING WORD

Both of today's readings suggest legal proceedings. The Gospel employs courtroom language to summarize the burden of Jesus' message to Nicodemus. Only the one who accepts the testimony of Jesus, who comes from above, has eternal life. Anyone who will not accept it must face divine judgment, for "the wrath of God remains upon him." In the first reading, the apostles must endure the wrath of the Sanhedrin for refusing to obey their orders that strictly forbid them to testify to the risen Jesus by teaching about the power of his name. But Peter appeals to a higher law, the heavenly tribunal of the One who "is above all." "We must obey God rather than men!" he says.

The Son does not ration the gift of the Spirit, says Jesus in the Gospel. So Peter, testifying to the resurrection of Jesus before the Sanhedrin, boldly calls upon the Holy Spirit to bear witness too. He takes Jesus at his word: "When they take you before synagogues and before rulers and authorities…the Holy Spirit will teach you at that moment what you should say" (Lk 12:11–12).

FIRST READING

Acts 5:27–33

We are witnesses of these words, as is the Holy Spirit.

A reading from the Acts of the Apostles

When the court officers had brought the Apostles in and made them stand before the Sanhedrin, the high priest questioned them, "We gave you strict orders did we not, to stop teaching in that name. Yet you have filled Jerusalem with your teaching and want to bring this man's blood upon us." But Peter and the Apostles said in reply, "We must obey God rather than men. The God of our ancestors raised Jesus, though you had him killed by hanging him on a tree. God exalted him at his right hand as leader and savior to grant Israel repentance and forgiveness of sins. We are witnesses of these things, as is the Holy Spirit whom God has given to those who obey him."

When they heard this, they became infuriated and wanted to put them to death.

The word of the Lord.

Responsorial Psalm

Ps 34:2 and 9, 17–18, 19–20

R. The Lord hears the cry of the poor.

I will bless the LORD at all times;
  his praise shall be ever in my mouth.
Taste and see how good the LORD is;
  blessed the man who takes refuge in him.

R. The Lord hears the cry of the poor.

The LORD confronts the evildoers,
  to destroy remembrance of them from the earth.
When the just cry out, the LORD hears them,
  and from all their distress he rescues them.

R. The Lord hears the cry of the poor.

The LORD is close to the brokenhearted;
  and those who are crushed in spirit he saves.
Many are the troubles of the just man,
  but out of them all the LORD delivers him.

R. The Lord hears the cry of the poor.

Or: **R. Alleluia.**

Alleluia, alleluia Jn 20:29
  You believe in me, Thomas, because you have seen me,
  says the Lord;
  blessed are those who have not seen, but still believe!
Alleluia, alleluia

GOSPEL

Jn 3:31–36

The Father loves the Son and has given everything over to him.

A reading from the holy Gospel according to John

The one who comes from above is above all. The one who is of the earth is earthly and speaks of earthly things. But the one who comes from heaven is above all. He testifies to what he has seen and heard, but no one accepts his testimony. Whoever does accept his testimony certifies that God is trustworthy. For the one whom God sent speaks the words of God. He does not ration his gift of the Spirit. The Father loves the Son and has given everything over to him. Whoever believes in the Son has eternal life, but whoever disobeys the Son will not see life, but the wrath of God remains upon him.

The Gospel of the Lord.

Liturgy of the Eucharist, *p. 897.*

Prayer over the Gifts

Pray, brethren...

Lord,
accept our prayers and offerings.
Make us worthy of your sacraments of love
by granting us your forgiveness.

We ask this in the name of Jesus the Lord.

Preface of Easter II–V, *pp. 945–946.*

Communion Antiphon

I, the Lord, am with you always, until the end of the world, alleluia.
(Mt 28:20)

Prayer after Communion

Let us pray.

Pause for silent prayer, if this has not preceded.

Almighty and ever-living Lord,
you restored us to life
by raising Christ from death.
Strengthen us by this Easter sacrament;
may we feel its saving power in our daily life.

We ask this through Christ our Lord.

Friday

Entrance Antiphon

By your blood, O Lord, you have redeemed us from every tribe and tongue, from every nation and people: you have made us into the Kingdom of God, alleluia.   (Rv 5:9–10)

Opening Prayer

Father,
in your plan of salvation
your Son Jesus Christ accepted the cross
and freed us from the power of the enemy.
May we come to share the glory of his resurrection,
for he lives and reigns with you and the Holy Spirit,
one God, for ever and ever.

TODAY'S LIVING WORD

For Christians the story of Jesus multiplying the loaves has unmistakable eucharistic overtones. Raymond Brown lists the details that in John's version (today's Gospel) are "intended to remind the Christian reader of the Eucharist." The word John uses for "gave thanks" is *eucharisteo.* "Jesus himself distributes the bread, as he will at the Last Supper.... The Greek word for 'fragments' [the crusts that are left over], *klasma,* appears in early Christian literature as a technical name for the host."* In the scheme of John's Gospel, however, this miracle functions as a "sign" revealing the glory of God, and the people's misinterpretation of the sign causes Jesus to remove himself from them.

Rightly reading the signs of God's glory in our midst demands discernment. In today's first reading, the eminently sane Sanhedrin member, Gamaliel, is a model of discernment. He advises the Sanhedrin to leave the apostles alone, saying that if their activity is human in its origins, it will self-destruct. But if "it comes from God, you will not be able to destroy them; you may even find yourselves fighting against God."

* *The Gospel and Epistles of John* (Collegeville: Liturgical Press, 1988), p. 43.

FIRST READING

Acts 5:34–42

The Apostles went out rejoicing that they had been found worthy
to suffer dishonor for the sake of the name.

A reading from the Acts of the Apostles

A Pharisee in the Sanhedrin named Gamaliel, a teacher of the law, respected by all the people, stood up, ordered the Apostles to be put outside for a short time, and said to the Sanhedrin, "Fellow children of Israel, be careful what you are about to do to these men. Some time ago, Theudas appeared, claiming to be someone important, and about four hundred men joined him, but he was killed, and all those who were loyal to him were disbanded and came to nothing. After him came Judas the Galilean at the time of the census. He also drew people after him, but he too perished and all who were loyal to him were scattered. So now I tell you, have nothing to do with these men, and let them go. For if this endeavor or this activity is of human origin, it will destroy itself. But if it comes from God, you will not be able to destroy them; you may even find yourselves fighting against God." They were persuaded by him. After recalling the Apostles, they had them flogged, ordered them to stop speaking in the name of Jesus, and dismissed them. So they left the presence of the Sanhedrin, rejoicing that they had been found worthy to suffer dishonor for the sake of the name. And all day long, both at the temple and in their homes, they did not stop teaching and proclaiming the Christ, Jesus.

The word of the Lord.

Responsorial Psalm

Ps 27:1, 4, 13–14

R. One thing I seek: to dwell in the house of the Lord.

The Lord is my light and my salvation;
  whom should I fear?

The Lord is my life's refuge;
  of whom should I be afraid?

R. One thing I seek: to dwell in the house of the Lord.

One thing I ask of the Lord
  this I seek:
To dwell in the house of the Lord
  all the days of my life,
That I may gaze on the loveliness of the Lord
  and contemplate his temple.

R. One thing I seek: to dwell in the house of the Lord.

I believe that I shall see the bounty of the Lord
  in the land of the living.
Wait for the Lord with courage;
  be stouthearted, and wait for the Lord.

R. One thing I seek: to dwell in the house of the Lord.

Or: **R. Alleluia.**

Alleluia, alleluia Mt 4:4b
One does not live on bread alone,
  but on every word that comes forth from the mouth of God.
Alleluia, alleluia

GOSPEL   Jn 6:1–15

*Jesus distributed to those who were
reclining as much as they wanted.*

A reading from the holy Gospel according to John

Jesus went across the Sea of Galilee. A large crowd followed
him, because they saw the signs he was performing on the
sick. Jesus went up on the mountain, and there he sat down
with his disciples. The Jewish feast of Passover was near. When
Jesus raised his eyes and saw that a large crowd was coming
to him, he said to Philip, "Where can we buy enough food for
them to eat?" He said this to test him, because he himself knew

what he was going to do. Philip answered him, "Two hundred days' wages worth of food would not be enough for each of them to have a little." One of his disciples, Andrew, the brother of Simon Peter, said to him, "There is a boy here who has five barley loaves and two fish; but what good are these for so many?" Jesus said, "Have the people recline." Now there was a great deal of grass in that place. So the men reclined, about five thousand in number. Then Jesus took the loaves, gave thanks, and distributed them to those who were reclining, and also as much of the fish as they wanted. When they had had their fill, he said to his disciples, "Gather the fragments left over, so that nothing will be wasted." So they collected them, and filled twelve wicker baskets with fragments from the five barley loaves that had been more than they could eat. When the people saw the sign he had done, they said, "This is truly the Prophet, the one who is to come into the world." Since Jesus knew that they were going to come and carry him off to make him king, he withdrew again to the mountain alone.

The Gospel of the Lord.

Liturgy of the Eucharist, *p. 897.*

Prayer over the Gifts

Pray, brethren...

Lord,
accept these gifts from your family.
May we hold fast to the life you have given us
and come to the eternal gifts you promise.

We ask this in the name of Jesus the Lord.

Preface of Easter II–V, *pp. 945–946.*

Communion Antiphon

Christ our Lord was put to death for our sins; and he rose again to make us worthy of life, alleluia. (Rom 4:25)

Prayer after Communion

Let us pray.

Pause for silent prayer, if this has not preceded.

Lord,
watch over those you have saved in Christ.
May we who are redeemed by his suffering and death
always rejoice in his resurrection,
for he is Lord for ever and ever.

Saturday

Entrance Antiphon

You are a people God claims as his own, to praise him who called you out of darkness into his marvelous light, alleluia. (1 Pt 2:9)

Opening Prayer

God our Father,
look upon us with love.
You redeem us and make us your children in Christ.
Give us true freedom
and bring us to the inheritance you promised.

We ask this through our Lord Jesus Christ, your Son,
who lives and reigns with you and the Holy Spirit,
one God, for ever and ever.

TODAY'S LIVING WORD

John's version of the multiplication of the loaves ends with Jesus fleeing to the mountain alone. Before he rejoins them, the disciples set out on the lake toward Capernaum. Without Jesus, they soon find themselves in the dark, their boat buffeted by the strong wind and rough seas. Finally they see him walking on the water. "It is I," he tells them, "do not be afraid." His "It is I" is more than reassurance; it is revelation, a manifestation of the saving power of God whose name means I AM, with you and for you (cf. Is 43:11). Before they know it, they are safely ashore.

In the reading from Acts, the still small boat, which is the early Church, weathers its first storm. The Greek-speaking Christian Jews complain that their widows are being neglected in the daily distribution of food. This is the first test of the apostles' leadership, and they meet it by sharing the authority Jesus gave them. The imposition of hands signals the transfer of power. As the subsequent stories of Stephen and Philip will show, the seven men will not be administrative assistants but partners with the Twelve, in prayer and the ministry of the word.

FIRST READING
Acts 6:1–7

They chose seven men filled with the Holy Spirit.

A reading from the Acts of the Apostles

As the number of disciples continued to grow, the Hellenists complained against the Hebrews because their widows were being neglected in the daily distribution. So the Twelve called together the community of the disciples and said, "It is not right for us to neglect the word of God to serve at table. Brothers, select from among you seven reputable men, filled with the Spirit and wisdom, whom we shall appoint to this task, whereas we shall devote ourselves to prayer and to the ministry of the word." The proposal was acceptable to the whole community, so they chose Stephen, a man filled with faith and the Holy Spirit, also Philip, Prochorus, Nicanor, Timon, Parmenas, and Nicholas of Antioch, a convert to Judaism. They presented these men to the Apostles who prayed and laid hands on them. The word of God continued to spread, and the number of the disciples in Jerusalem increased greatly; even a large group of priests were becoming obedient to the faith.

The word of the Lord.

Responsorial Psalm

Ps 33:1–2, 4–5, 18–19

**R. Lord, let your mercy be on us,
   as we place our trust in you.**

Exult, you just, in the LORD;
  praise from the upright is fitting.
Give thanks to the LORD on the harp;
  with the ten-stringed lyre chant his praises.

**R. Lord, let your mercy be on us,
   as we place our trust in you.**

Upright is the word of the LORD,
  and all his works are trustworthy.
He loves justice and right;
  of the kindness of the LORD the earth is full.

**R. Lord, let your mercy be on us,
   as we place our trust in you.**

See, the eyes of the LORD are upon those who fear him,
  upon those who hope for his kindness,
To deliver them from death
  and preserve them in spite of famine.

**R. Lord, let your mercy be on us,
   as we place our trust in you.**

Or: **R. Alleluia.**

> **Alleluia, alleluia**
> Christ is risen, who made all things;
> he has shown mercy on all people.
> **Alleluia, alleluia**

GOSPEL

Jn 6:16–21

They saw Jesus, walking on the sea.

A reading from the holy Gospel according to John

When it was evening, the disciples of Jesus went down to the sea, embarked in a boat, and went across the sea to Capernaum. It had already grown dark, and Jesus had not yet come to them. The sea was stirred up because a strong wind was blowing. When they had rowed about three or four miles, they saw Jesus walking on the sea and coming near the boat, and they began to be afraid. But he said to them, "It is I. Do not be afraid." They wanted to take him into the boat, but the boat immediately arrived at the shore to which they were heading.

The Gospel of the Lord.

Liturgy of the Eucharist, *p. 897.*

Prayer over the Gifts

Pray, brethren...

Merciful Lord,
make holy these gifts
and let our spiritual sacrifice
make us an everlasting gift to you.

We ask this in the name of Jesus the Lord.

Preface of Easter II–V, *pp. 945–946.*

Communion Antiphon

Father, I want the men you have given me to be with me where I am, so that they may see the glory you have given me, alleluia.

(Jn 17:24)

Prayer after Communion

Let us pray.

Pause for silent prayer, if this has not preceded.

Lord,
may this eucharist,

which we have celebrated in memory of your Son,
help us to grow in love.
We ask this in the name of Jesus the Lord.

THIRD WEEK OF EASTER

Monday

Entrance Antiphon

The Good Shepherd is risen! He who laid down his life for his sheep, who died for his flock, he is risen, alleluia.

Opening Prayer

God our Father,
your light of truth
guides us to the way of Christ.
May all who follow him
reject what is contrary to the gospel.

We ask this through our Lord Jesus Christ, your Son,
who lives and reigns with you and the Holy Spirit,
one God, for ever and ever.

TODAY'S LIVING WORD

To use Johannine language, in both readings today what is from above clashes with what is from below. In Acts Stephen stands up to his opponents with irrefutable wisdom, his face radiant "like the face of an angel." He is the disciple of Jesus, the One who was sent from above and assured his followers that he would give them "a wisdom in speaking that all your adversaries will be powerless to resist or refute" (Lk 21:15). His opponents are no match for such wisdom from above; theirs is the wisdom from below, narrowly focused on preserving the temple and the law. In the Gospel, Jesus is found by a crowd who seek him for all the wrong reasons. Their concerns, like those of Stephen's accusers, are clearly from below. "You are looking for me not because you saw signs," Jesus tells them, "but because you ate the loaves and were filled."

It is all too easy for us as well to look for Jesus to provide our daily bread and preserve our cherished institutions. But the earth-shattering events of Easter shift our focus from our small concerns below to the One sent to us from above.

FIRST READING

Acts 6:8–15

They could not withstand the wisdom and the Spirit with which he spoke.

A reading from the Acts of the Apostles

Stephen, filled with grace and power, was working great wonders and signs among the people. Certain members of the so-called Synagogue of Freedmen, Cyreneans, and Alexandrians, and people from Cilicia and Asia, came forward and debated with Stephen, but they could not withstand the wisdom and the Spirit with which he spoke. Then they instigated some men to say, "We have heard him speaking blasphemous words against Moses and God." They stirred up the people, the elders, and the scribes, accosted him, seized him, and brought him before the Sanhedrin. They presented false witnesses who testified, "This man never stops saying things against this holy place and the law. For we have heard him claim that this Jesus the Nazorean will destroy this place and change the customs that Moses handed down to us." All those who sat in the Sanhedrin looked intently at him and saw that his face was like the face of an angel.

The word of the Lord.

Responsorial Psalm
Ps 119:23–24, 26–27, 29–30

R. Blessed are they who follow the law of the Lord!

Though princes meet and talk against me,
  your servant meditates on your statutes.
Yes, your decrees are my delight;
  they are my counselors.

R. Blessed are they who follow the law of the Lord!

I declared my ways, and you answered me;
  teach me your statutes.
Make me understand the way of your precepts,
  and I will meditate on your wondrous deeds.

R. Blessed are they who follow the law of the Lord!

Remove from me the way of falsehood,
  and favor me with your law.
The way of truth I have chosen;
  I have set your ordinances before me.

R. Blessed are they who follow the law of the Lord!

Or: **R. Alleluia.**

Alleluia, alleluia Mt 4:4b
One does not live on bread alone
  but on every word that comes forth from the mouth of God.
Alleluia, alleluia

GOSPEL
Jn 6:22–29

*Do not work for food that perishes
but for food that endures for eternal life.*

A reading from the holy Gospel according to John

[After Jesus had fed the five thousand men, his disciples saw him walking on the sea.] The next day, the crowd that remained across the sea saw that there had been only one boat there, and that Jesus had not gone along with his disciples in the boat, but only his disciples had left. Other boats came from Tiberias near the place where they had eaten the bread when the Lord gave thanks. When the crowd saw that neither Jesus nor his disciples were there, they themselves got into boats and came to Capernaum looking for Jesus. And when they found him across the sea they said to him, "Rabbi, when did you get here?" Jesus answered them and said, "Amen, amen, I say to you, you are looking for me not because you saw signs but because you ate the loaves and were filled. Do not work for food that perishes but for the food that endures for eternal life, which the Son of Man will give you. For on him the Father, God, has set his seal." So they said to him, "What can we do to accomplish the works of God?" Jesus answered and said to them, "This is the work of God, that you believe in the one he sent."

The Gospel of the Lord.

Liturgy of the Eucharist, *p. 897.*

Prayer over the Gifts

Pray, brethren...

Lord,
accept our prayers and offerings.
Make us worthy of your sacraments of love
by granting us your forgiveness.
We ask this in the name of Jesus the Lord.

Preface of Easter II–V, *pp. 945–946.*

Communion Antiphon

The Lord says, peace I leave with you, my own peace I give you; not as the world gives do I give, alleluia.   (Jn 14:27)

Prayer after Communion

Let us pray.

Pause for silent prayer, if this has not preceded.

Almighty and ever-living Lord,
you restored us to life
by raising Christ from death.
Strengthen us by this Easter sacrament;
may we feel its saving power in our daily life.

We ask this through Christ our Lord.

Tuesday

Entrance Antiphon

**All you who fear God, both the great and the small, give praise
to him! For his salvation and strength have come, the power of
Christ, alleluia.** (Rv 19:5; 12:10)

Opening Prayer

Father,
you open the kingdom of heaven
to those born again by water and the Spirit.
Increase your gift of love in us.
May all who have been freed from sins in baptism
receive all that you have promised.

We ask this through our Lord Jesus Christ, your Son,
who lives and reigns with you and the Holy Spirit,
one God, for ever and ever.

TODAY'S LIVING WORD

Today's reading from Acts relies on body language to deliver its
message. Stephen looks up "intently to heaven" and proclaims that

the risen Jesus stands at God's right hand. In the vision Jesus is standing, not sitting, to welcome Stephen into God's presence. Meanwhile, Stephen's accusers grind their teeth in anger and rush at him with their hands over their ears. As Stephen said, they show themselves to be "uncircumcised in heart and ears"—not truly belonging to the people of God, not attentive to God's word. Finally Stephen falls to his knees, dying in a posture of prayerful submission, while Saul concurs in the act by doing nothing but watching the witnesses' cloaks piled at his feet.

The Gospel message on the other hand depends on Bible language. Alluding to the Exodus story, the crowd challenges Jesus to match the miracle of Moses, who gave their ancestors manna to eat. Jesus' answer is a "rereading" of the text. He tells them that God gave the manna, not Moses. The same God now gives them the true bread of eternal life—Jesus himself.

FIRST READING

Acts 7:51— 8:1a

Lord Jesus, receive my spirit.

A reading from the Acts of the Apostles

Stephen said to the people, the elders, and the scribes: "You stiff-necked people, uncircumcised in heart and ears, you always oppose the Holy Spirit; you are just like your ancestors. Which of the prophets did your ancestors not persecute? They put to death those who foretold the coming of the righteous one, whose betrayers and murderers you have now become. You received the law as transmitted by angels, but you did not observe it."

When they heard this, they were infuriated, and they ground their teeth at him. But Stephen, filled with the Holy Spirit, looked up intently to heaven and saw the glory of God and Jesus standing at the right hand of God, and Stephen said, "Behold, I see the heavens opened and the Son of Man standing at the right hand of God." But they cried out in a loud voice, covered their ears, and rushed upon him together. They threw him out of the city, and began to stone him. The witnesses laid down their cloaks at the feet of a young man named Saul. As they were stoning Stephen, he called out, "Lord Jesus, receive my spirit." Then he fell to his knees and cried out in a loud voice, "Lord, do not hold this sin against them"; and when he said this, he fell asleep.

Now Saul was consenting to his execution.

The word of the Lord.

Responsorial Psalm   Ps 31:3cd–4, 6 and 7b and 8a, 17 and 21ab

R. Into your hands, O Lord, I commend my spirit.

Be my rock of refuge,
  a stronghold to give me safety.
You are my rock and my fortress;
  for your name's sake you will lead and guide me.

R. Into your hands, O Lord, I commend my spirit.

Into your hands I commend my spirit;
  you will redeem me, O LORD, O faithful God.
My trust is in the LORD;
  I will rejoice and be glad of your mercy.

R. Into your hands, O Lord, I commend my spirit.

Let your face shine upon your servant;
  save me in your kindness.
You hide them in the shelter of your presence
  from the plottings of men.

R. Into your hands, O Lord, I commend my spirit.

Or: **R. Alleluia.**

Alleluia, alleluia   Jn 6:35ab
I am the bread of life, says the Lord;
  whoever comes to me will never hunger.
Alleluia, alleluia

GOSPEL

Jn 6:30 – 35

*It was not Moses, but my Father who gives you
the true bread from heaven.*

A reading from the holy Gospel according to John

The crowd said to Jesus: "What sign can you do, that we may see and believe in you? What can you do? Our ancestors ate manna in the desert, as it is written:

He gave them bread from heaven to eat."

So Jesus said to them, "Amen, amen, I say to you, it was not Moses who gave the bread from heaven; my Father gives you the true bread from heaven. For the bread of God is that which comes down from heaven and gives life to the world."

So they said to Jesus, "Sir, give us this bread always." Jesus said to them, "I am the bread of life; whoever comes to me will never hunger, and whoever believes in me will never thirst."

The Gospel of the Lord.

Liturgy of the Eucharist, *p. 897.*

Prayer over the Gifts

Pray, brethren...

Lord,
receive these gifts from your Church.
May the great joy you give us
come to perfection in heaven.

Grant this through Christ our Lord.

Preface of Easter II–V, *pp. 945–946.*

Communion Antiphon

Because we have died with Christ, we believe that we shall also come to life with him, alleluia.   (Rom 6:8)

Prayer after Communion

Let us pray.

Pause for silent prayer, if this has not preceded.

Lord,
look on your people with kindness
and by these Easter mysteries
bring us to the glory of the resurrection.

We ask this in the name of Jesus the Lord.

Wednesday

Entrance Antiphon

Fill me with your praise and I will sing your glory; songs of joy will be on my lips, alleluia.   (Ps 70:8, 23)

Opening Prayer

Merciful Lord,
hear the prayers of your people.
May we who have received your gift of faith
share for ever in the new life of Christ.

Grant this through our Lord Jesus Christ, your Son,
who lives and reigns with you and the Holy Spirit,
one God, for ever and ever.

TODAY'S LIVING WORD

In his commentary on Acts, Luke Timothy Johnson suggests the possibility that Saul may have instigated the action against Stephen. He offers three reasons to support his suggestion: Saul is from Cilicia, as are some of Stephen's accusers; for Luke, placing clothing at someone's feet, as the witnesses place their cloaks at Saul's, is to recognize that person's authority; and, as today's reading records, Saul leads the subsequent persecution.* Be that as it may, today's text proves the truth of the old saying, "The blood of the martyrs is the seed of the Church." Persecution, not Church policy, accounts for the spread of the Gospel beyond Jerusalem and Judea and even into Samaria.

Philip's conversion of the Samaritans will require the confirmation of the apostles in Jerusalem (cf. Acts 8:14–17). For the early Church, welcoming the Samaritans into the fellowship of Jesus' followers would give new meaning to the words of Jesus in today's Gospel: "I will not reject anyone who comes to me."

* *The Acts of the Apostles,* Sacra Pagina 5 (Collegeville: Liturgical Press, 1992), p. 141.

FIRST READING
Acts 8:1b–8

They went about preaching the word.

A reading from the Acts of the Apostles

There broke out a severe persecution of the Church in Jerusalem, and all were scattered throughout the countryside of Judea and Samaria, except the Apostles. Devout men buried Stephen and made a loud lament over him. Saul, meanwhile, was trying to destroy the Church; entering house after house and dragging out men and women, he handed them over for imprisonment.

Now those who had been scattered went about preaching the word. Thus Philip went down to the city of Samaria and proclaimed the Christ to them. With one accord, the crowds paid attention to what was said by Philip when they heard it and saw the signs he was doing. For unclean spirits, crying out in a loud voice, came out of many possessed people, and many paralyzed and crippled people were cured. There was great joy in that city.

The word of the Lord.

Responsorial Psalm
Ps 66:1–3a, 4–5, 6–7a

R. Let all the earth cry out to God with joy.

Shout joyfully to God, all the earth,
  sing praise to the glory of his name;
  proclaim his glorious praise.
Say to God, "How tremendous are your deeds!"

R. Let all the earth cry out to God with joy.

"Let all on earth worship and sing praise to you,
  sing praise to your name!"
Come and see the works of God,
  his tremendous deeds among the children of Adam.

R. Let all the earth cry out to God with joy.

He has changed the sea into dry land;
  through the river they passed on foot;
  therefore let us rejoice in him.
He rules by his might forever.

R. Let all the earth cry out to God with joy.

Or: **R. Alleluia.**

> **Alleluia, alleluia**   See Jn 6:40
> Everyone who believes in the Son has eternal life,
> and I shall raise him on the last day, says the Lord.
> **Alleluia, alleluia**

GOSPEL   Jn 6:35–40

This is the will of my Father,
that all who see the Son may have eternal life.

A reading from the holy Gospel according to John

Jesus said to the crowds, "I am the bread of life; whoever comes to me will never hunger, and whoever believes in me will never thirst. But I told you that although you have seen me, you do not believe. Everything that the Father gives me will come to me, and I will not reject anyone who comes to me, because I came down from heaven not to do my own will but the will of the one who sent me. And this is the will of the one who sent me, that I should not lose anything of what he gave me, but that I should raise it on the last day. For this is the will of my Father, that everyone who sees the Son and believes in him may have eternal life, and I shall raise him on the last day."

The Gospel of the Lord.

> **Liturgy of the Eucharist,** *p. 897.*

Prayer over the Gifts

Pray, brethren...

Lord,
restore us by these Easter mysteries.
May the continuing work of our Redeemer
bring us eternal joy.

We ask this through Christ our Lord.

> **Preface of Easter II–V,** *pp. 945–946.*

Communion Antiphon

Christ has risen and shines upon us, whom he has redeemed by his blood, alleluia.

Prayer after Communion

Let us pray.

> *Pause for silent prayer, if this has not preceded.*

Lord,
may this celebration of our redemption
help us in this life
and lead us to eternal happiness.

We ask this through Christ our Lord.

Thursday

Entrance Antiphon

Let us sing to the Lord, he has covered himself in glory! The Lord is my strength, and I praise him: he is the Savior of my life, alleluia.   (Ex 15:1–2)

Opening Prayer

Father,
in this holy season
we come to know the full depth of your love.
You have freed us from the darkness of error and sin.
Help us to cling to your truths with fidelity.

We ask this through our Lord Jesus Christ, your Son,
who lives and reigns with you and the Holy Spirit,
one God, for ever and ever.

TODAY'S LIVING WORD

In John, disciples are the Father's gift to Jesus. That is the sense of Jesus' words in today's Gospel, "No one can come to me unless the Father who sent me draw him." The Ethiopian eunuch in Acts is a good example of one whom the Father draws to Jesus through the study of the Scriptures.

That he is returning from a pilgrimage to Jerusalem is important. The law excluded eunuchs from membership in the community of the Lord (Dt 23:2). But Isaiah had prophesied that some day that would change (cf. 56:3–5). For the eunuch in the story, that day arrives with Philip. Not unlike Jesus on the road to Emmaus, Philip meets the eunuch on the road leaving Jerusalem, interrupts his reading of Isaiah, and converses with him in his carriage. Just as Jesus opened the Scriptures for the two men in the Emmaus story, Philip does so for the eunuch, who asks to be baptized. As Jesus says in today's Gospel: "Everyone who listens to my Father and learns from him comes to me."

FIRST READING

Acts 8:26–40

Look, there is water. What is to prevent my being baptized?

A reading from the Acts of the Apostles

The angel of the Lord spoke to Philip, "Get up and head south on the road that goes down from Jerusalem to Gaza, the desert route." So he got up and set out. Now there was an Ethiopian eunuch, a court official of the Candace, that is, the queen of the Ethiopians, in charge of her entire treasury, who had come to Jerusalem to worship, and was returning home. Seated in his chariot, he was reading the prophet Isaiah. The Spirit said to Philip, "Go and join up with that chariot." Philip ran up and heard him reading Isaiah the prophet and said, "Do you understand what you are reading?" He replied, "How can I, unless someone instructs me?" So he invited Philip to get in and sit with him. This was the Scripture passage he was reading:

> *Like a sheep he was led to the slaughter,*
> > *and as a lamb before its shearer is silent,*
> > > *so he opened not his mouth.*
> *In his humiliation justice was denied him.*
> > *Who will tell of his posterity?*
> > > *For his life is taken from the earth.*

Then the eunuch said to Philip in reply, "I beg you, about whom is the prophet saying this? About himself, or about someone else?" Then Philip opened his mouth and, beginning with this Scripture passage, he proclaimed Jesus to him. As they traveled along the road they came to some water, and the eunuch said, "Look, there is water. What is to prevent my being baptized?" Then he ordered the chariot to stop, and

Philip and the eunuch both went down into the water, and he baptized him. When they came out of the water, the Spirit of the Lord snatched Philip away, and the eunuch saw him no more, but continued on his way rejoicing. Philip came to Azotus, and went about proclaiming the good news to all the towns until he reached Caesarea.

The word of the Lord.

Responsorial Psalm   Ps 66:8–9, 16–17, 20

R. Let all the earth cry out to God with joy.

Bless our God, you peoples,
  loudly sound his praise;
He has given life to our souls,
  and has not let our feet slip.

R. Let all the earth cry out to God with joy.

Hear now, all you who fear God, while I declare
  what he has done for me.
When I appealed to him in words,
  praise was on the tip of my tongue.

R. Let all the earth cry out to God with joy.

Blessed be God who refused me not
  my prayer or his kindness!

R. Let all the earth cry out to God with joy.

Or: R. Alleluia.

Alleluia, alleluia   Jn 6:51
I am the living bread that came down from heaven,
says the Lord;
whoever eats this bread will live forever.
Alleluia, alleluia

GOSPEL   Jn 6:44–51

I am the living bread that came down from heaven.

A reading from the holy Gospel according to John

Jesus said to the crowds: "No one can come to me unless the Father who sent me draw him, and I will raise him on the last day. It is written in the prophets:

They shall all be taught by God.

Everyone who listens to my Father and learns from him comes to me. Not that anyone has seen the Father except the one who is from God; he has seen the Father. Amen, amen, I say to you, whoever believes has eternal life. I am the bread of life. Your ancestors ate the manna in the desert, but they died; this is the bread that comes down from heaven so that one may eat it and not die. I am the living bread that came down from heaven; whoever eats this bread will live forever; and the bread that I will give is my Flesh for the life of the world."

The Gospel of the Lord.

Liturgy of the Eucharist, *p. 897.*

Prayer over the Gifts

Pray, brethren...

Lord God,
by this holy exchange of gifts
you share with us your divine life.
Grant that everything we do
may be directed by the knowledge of your truth.
We ask this in the name of Jesus the Lord.

Preface of Easter II–V, *pp. 945–946.*

Communion Antiphon

Christ died for all, so that living men should not live for themselves, but for Christ who died and was raised to life for them, alleluia.   (2 Cor 5:15)

Prayer after Communion

Let us pray.

Pause for silent prayer, if this has not preceded.

Merciful Father,
may these mysteries give us new purpose
and bring us to a new life in you.
Grant this through Christ our Lord.

Friday

Entrance Antiphon

The Lamb who was slain is worthy to receive strength and divinity, wisdom and power and honor, alleluia.   (Rv 5:12)

Opening Prayer

Father,
by the love of your Spirit,
may we who have experienced
the grace of the Lord's resurrection
rise to the newness of life in joy.

Grant this through our Lord Jesus Christ, your Son,
who lives and reigns with you and the Holy Spirit,
one God, for ever and ever.

TODAY'S LIVING WORD

Today's first reading recounts the call of Saul, who saw the risen Lord with blinding clarity on the road to Damascus. When Ananias is told to go to Saul, his objection reminds us that this is the man who breathed "murderous threats against the disciples of the Lord" and had authorization from the chief priests to carry them out. But God has chosen this very man to bring his name "before Gentiles, kings, and children of Israel." So Ananias goes to welcome Saul now as a brother.

Ananias describes the effects of baptism in two phrases. He tells Saul that he has come to help him "regain [his] sight and be filled with the Holy Spirit," which brings us to today's Gospel. In his eucharistic discourse, Jesus, the Son who has life from the living Father, shares that life with those who feed on his flesh and drink his blood. This is a hard saying. Only those who through the grace of baptism have recovered their sight and have been filled with the Spirit can accept it.

FIRST READING

Acts 9:1–20

This man is a chosen instrument of mine
to carry my name before the Gentiles.

A reading from the Acts of the Apostles

Saul, still breathing murderous threats against the disciples of the Lord, went to the high priest and asked him for letters to the synagogues in Damascus, that, if he should find any men or women who belonged to the Way, he might bring them back to Jerusalem in chains. On his journey, as he was nearing Damascus, a light from the sky suddenly flashed around him. He fell to the ground and heard a voice saying to him, "Saul, Saul, why are you persecuting me?" He said, "Who are you, sir?" The reply came, "I am Jesus, whom you are persecuting. Now get up and go into the city and you will be told what you must do." The men who were traveling with him stood speechless, for they heard the voice but could see no one. Saul got up from the ground, but when he opened his eyes he could see nothing; so they led him by the hand and brought him to Damascus. For three days he was unable to see, and he neither ate nor drank.

There was a disciple in Damascus named Ananias, and the Lord said to him in a vision, "Ananias." He answered, "Here I am, Lord." The Lord said to him, "Get up and go to the street called Straight and ask at the house of Judas for a man from Tarsus named Saul. He is there praying, and in a vision he has seen a man named Ananias come in and lay his hands on him, that he may regain his sight." But Ananias replied, "Lord, I have heard from many sources about this man, what evil things he has done to your holy ones in Jerusalem. And here he has authority from the chief priests to imprison all who call upon your name." But the Lord said to him, "Go, for this man is a chosen instrument of mine to carry my name before Gentiles, kings, and children of Israel, and I will show him what he will have to suffer for my name." So Ananias went and entered the house; laying his hands on him, he said, "Saul, my brother, the Lord has sent me, Jesus who appeared to you on the way by which you came, that you may regain your sight and be filled with the Holy Spirit." Immediately things like scales fell from his eyes and he regained his sight. He got up and was baptized, and when he had eaten, he recovered his strength.

He stayed some days with the disciples in Damascus, and he began at once to proclaim Jesus in the synagogues, that he is the Son of God.

The word of the Lord.

Responsorial Psalm
Ps 117:1bc, 2

R. Go out to all the world and tell the Good News.

Praise the LORD, all you nations;
   glorify him, all you peoples!

R. Go out to all the world and tell the Good News.

For steadfast is his kindness toward us,
   and the fidelity of the LORD endures forever.

R. Go out to all the world and tell the Good News.

Or: **R. Alleluia.**

Alleluia, alleluia Jn 6:56
Whoever eats my Flesh and drinks my Blood,
remains in me and I in him, says the Lord.
Alleluia, alleluia

GOSPEL   Jn 6:52-59

My Flesh is true food, and my Blood is true drink.

A reading from the holy Gospel according to John

The Jews quarreled among themselves, saying, "How can this man give us his Flesh to eat?" Jesus said to them, "Amen, amen, I say to you, unless you eat the Flesh of the Son of Man and drink his Blood, you do not have life within you. Whoever eats my Flesh and drinks my Blood has eternal life, and I will raise him on the last day. For my Flesh is true food, and my Blood is true drink. Whoever eats my Flesh and drinks my Blood remains in me and I in him. Just as the living Father sent me and I have life because of the Father, so also the one who feeds on me will have life because of me. This is the bread that came down from heaven. Unlike your ancestors who ate and still died, whoever eats this bread will live forever." These things he said while teaching in the synagogue in Capernaum.

The Gospel of the Lord.

Liturgy of the Eucharist, *p. 897.*

Prayer over the Gifts

Pray, brethren...
Merciful Lord,
make holy these gifts
and let our spiritual sacrifice
make us an everlasting gift to you.

We ask this in the name of Jesus the Lord.

Preface of Easter II–V, *pp. 945–946.*

Communion Antiphon

The man who died on the cross has risen from the dead, and has won back our lives from death, alleluia.

Prayer after Communion

Let us pray.

Pause for silent prayer, if this has not preceded.

Lord,
may this eucharist,
which we have celebrated in memory of your Son,
help us to grow in love.
We ask this in the name of Jesus the Lord.

Saturday

Entrance Antiphon

In baptism we have died with Christ, and we have risen to new life in him, because we believed in the power of God who raised him from the dead, alleluia.   (Col 2:12)

Opening Prayer

God our Father,
by the waters of baptism
you give new life to the faithful.
May we not succumb to the influence of evil
but remain true to your gift of life.

We ask this through our Lord Jesus Christ, your Son,
who lives and reigns with you and the Holy Spirit,
one God, for ever and ever.

TODAY'S LIVING WORD

Today's Gospel reports that, in the wake of Jesus' eucharistic discourse, "many of his disciples returned to their former way of life and no longer walked with him." In a poignant scene that resembles the confession of Peter at Caesarea Philippi related by the Synoptics (cf. Mk 8:27–30 and par.), Jesus asks the Twelve, "Do you also want to leave?" Always the spokesman, Peter answers, "Master, to whom shall we go? You have the words of eternal life."

In the selection from Acts, Peter heals Aeneas and raises Tabitha in the name of the risen Jesus. Both miracles are intended to remind us of previous miracles of Jesus in Luke. The healing of Aeneas recalls the cure of the paralytic who, at Jesus' command, "Rise, pick up your stretcher, and go home," stands up at once (5:17–26). The raising of Tabitha is like the raising of Jairus' daughter: Jesus sends the mourners out of the room, takes the little girl's hand and says, "Child, arise!" (8:49–56). Thus, by restoring physical life, Peter, like Jesus, bears witness to the Spirit who gives life.

FIRST READING
Acts 9:31–42

The Church was being built up, and with the consolation of the Holy Spirit she grew in numbers.

A reading from the Acts of the Apostles

The Church throughout all Judea, Galilee, and Samaria was at peace. She was being built up and walked in the fear of the Lord, and with the consolation of the Holy Spirit she grew in numbers.

As Peter was passing through every region, he went down to the holy ones living in Lydda. There he found a man named Aeneas, who had been confined to bed for eight years, for he was paralyzed. Peter said to him, "Aeneas, Jesus Christ heals you. Get up and make your bed." He got up at once. And all the inhabitants of Lydda and Sharon saw him, and they turned to the Lord.

Now in Joppa there was a disciple named Tabitha (which translated is Dorcas). She was completely occupied with good deeds and almsgiving. Now during those days she fell sick and died, so after washing her, they laid her out in a room upstairs. Since Lydda was near Joppa, the disciples, hearing that Peter was there, sent two men to him with the request, "Please come to us without delay." So Peter got up and went with them. When he arrived, they took him to the room upstairs where all the widows came to him weeping and showing him the tunics and cloaks that Dorcas had made while she was with them. Peter sent them all out and knelt down and prayed. Then he turned to her body and said, "Tabitha, rise up." She opened her eyes, saw Peter, and sat up. He gave her his hand and raised her up, and when he had called the holy ones and the widows, he presented her alive. This became known all over Joppa, and many came to believe in the Lord.

The word of the Lord.

Responsorial Psalm   Ps 116:12–13, 14 –15, 16 –17

R. How shall I make a return to the Lord for all the good he has done for me?

How shall I make a return to the LORD
   for all the good he has done for me?
The cup of salvation I will take up,
   and I will call upon the name of the LORD.

R. How shall I make a return to the Lord for all the good he has done for me?

My vows to the LORD I will pay
   in the presence of all his people.
Precious in the eyes of the LORD
   is the death of his faithful ones.

R. How shall I make a return to the Lord for all the good he has done for me?

O LORD, I am your servant;
   I am your servant, the son of your handmaid;
   you have loosed my bonds.

To you will I offer sacrifice of thanksgiving,
and I will call upon the name of the LORD.

**R. How shall I make a return to the Lord for all the good
he has done for me?**

Or: **R. Alleluia.**

Alleluia, alleluia   See Jn 6:63c, 68c
Your words, Lord, are Spirit and life;
you have the words of everlasting life.
Alleluia, alleluia

GOSPEL   Jn 6:60–69

To whom shall we go? You have the words of eternal life.

A reading from the holy Gospel according to John

Many of the disciples of Jesus who were listening said, "This
saying is hard; who can accept it?" Since Jesus knew that his
disciples were murmuring about this, he said to them, "Does
this shock you? What if you were to see the Son of Man
ascending to where he was before? It is the Spirit that gives
life, while the flesh is of no avail. The words I have spoken to
you are Spirit and life. But there are some of you who do not
believe." Jesus knew from the beginning the ones who would
not believe and the one who would betray him. And he said,
"For this reason I have told you that no one can come to me
unless it is granted him by my Father."

As a result of this, many of his disciples returned to their
former way of life and no longer walked with him. Jesus then
said to the Twelve, "Do you also want to leave?" Simon Peter
answered him, "Master, to whom shall we go? You have the
words of eternal life. We have come to believe and are
convinced that you are the Holy One of God."

The Gospel of the Lord.

Liturgy of the Eucharist, *p. 897.*

Prayer over the Gifts

Pray, brethren...

Lord,
accept these gifts from your family.
May we hold fast to the life you have given us
and come to the eternal gifts you promised.

We ask this in the name of Jesus the Lord.

Preface of Easter II–V, *pp. 945–946.*

Communion Antiphon

Father, I pray for them: may they be one in us, so that the world may believe it was you who sent me, alleluia.

(Jn 17:20–21)

Prayer after Communion

Let us pray.

Pause for silent prayer, if this has not preceded.

Lord,
watch over those you have saved in Christ.
May we who are redeemed by his suffering and death
always rejoice in his resurrection,
for he is Lord for ever and ever.

FOURTH WEEK OF EASTER

Monday

Entrance Antiphon

Christ now raised from the dead will never die again; death no longer has power over him, alleluia.

(Rom 6:9)

Opening Prayer

Father,
through the obedience of Jesus,
your servant and your Son,
you raised a fallen world.
Free us from sin
and bring us the joy that lasts for ever.
We ask this through our Lord Jesus Christ, your Son,
who lives and reigns with you and the Holy Spirit,
one God, for ever and ever.

TODAY'S LIVING WORD

The two Gospel selections for today unpack two separate parables of Jesus, both derived from the biblical image of God as Shepherd of Israel (cf. Ez 34). The first parable discusses access to the sheepfold, which is only through Jesus, who is himself the sheep gate. The second parable describes the good shepherd who "lays down his life for the sheep" who know his voice and follow him. In their context in John, the parables are a critique of the Jewish leaders of the previous chapter. Following today's first reading, an example of Peter's leadership, they provide criteria for Church leaders.

In the first reading, Peter acts as gatekeeper and is criticized for it. Through his ministry those "other sheep" are led into the fold, who in this case are the Gentile Cornelius and his household. The boundaries of the sheepfold are being redefined—not at Peter's initiative but because, as he explains to the Christian Jews in Jerusalem, the gift of God who is the Holy Spirit presses irresistibly toward that day when there will be one flock, one shepherd. And who are we to interfere?

FIRST READING
Acts 11:1–18

*God has then granted life-giving repentance
to the Gentiles too.*

A reading from the Acts of the Apostles

The Apostles and the brothers who were in Judea heard that the Gentiles too had accepted the word of God. So when Peter went up to Jerusalem the circumcised believers confronted him, saying, "You entered the house of uncircumcised people and ate with them." Peter began and explained it to them step by step, saying, "I was at prayer in the city of Joppa when in a trance I had a vision, something resembling a large sheet coming down, lowered from the sky by its four corners, and it came to me. Looking intently into it, I observed and saw the four-legged animals of the earth, the wild beasts, the reptiles, and the birds of the sky. I also heard a voice say to me, 'Get up, Peter. Slaughter and eat.' But I said, 'Certainly not, sir, because nothing profane or unclean has ever entered my mouth.' But a second time a voice from heaven answered, 'What God has made clean, you are not to call profane.' This happened three times, and then everything was drawn up again into the sky. Just then three men appeared at the house where we were, who had been sent to me from Caesarea. The Spirit told me to accompany them without discriminating. These six brothers also went with me, and we entered the man's house. He related to us how he had seen the angel standing in his house, saying, 'Send someone to Joppa and summon Simon, who is called Peter, who will speak words to you by which you and all your household will be saved.' As I began to speak, the Holy Spirit fell upon them as it had upon us at the beginning, and I remembered the word of the Lord, how he had said, 'John baptized with water but you will be baptized with the Holy Spirit.' If then God gave them the same gift he gave to us when we came to believe in the Lord Jesus Christ, who was I to be able to hinder God?" When they heard this, they stopped objecting and glorified God, saying, "God has then granted life-giving repentance to the Gentiles too."

The word of the Lord.

Responsorial Psalm

Ps 42:2–3; 43:3, 4

R. Athirst is my soul for the living God.

As the hind longs for the running waters,
  so my soul longs for you, O God.
Athirst is my soul for God, the living God.
  When shall I go and behold the face of God?

R. Athirst is my soul for the living God.

Send forth your light and your fidelity;
  they shall lead me on
And bring me to your holy mountain,
  to your dwelling-place.

R. Athirst is my soul for the living God.

Then will I go in to the altar of God,
  the God of my gladness and joy;
Then will I give you thanks upon the harp,
  O God, my God!

R. Athirst is my soul for the living God.

Or: **R. Alleluia.**

   Alleluia, alleluia Jn 10:14
   I am the good shepherd, says the Lord;
   I know my sheep, and mine know me.
   Alleluia, alleluia

GOSPEL

Jn 10:1–10

I am the gate for the sheep.

A reading from the holy Gospel according to John

Jesus said: "Amen, amen, I say to you, whoever does not enter a sheepfold through the gate but climbs over elsewhere is a thief and a robber. But whoever enters through the gate is the shepherd of the sheep. The gatekeeper opens it for him, and the sheep hear his voice, as he calls his own sheep by name and leads them out. When he has driven out all his own, he walks ahead of them, and the sheep follow him, because they recognize his voice. But they will not follow a stranger; they will run away from him, because they do not recognize the voice of strangers." Although Jesus used this figure of speech, they did not realize what he was trying to tell them.

So Jesus said again, "Amen, amen, I say to you, I am the gate for the sheep. All who came before me are thieves and robbers, but the sheep did not listen to them. I am the gate. Whoever enters through me will be saved, and will come in and go out and find pasture. A thief comes only to steal and slaughter and destroy; I came so that they might have life and have it more abundantly."

The Gospel of the Lord.

Or: In Cycle A, when this Gospel is read on the preceding Sunday, the following text is used.

GOSPEL   Jn 10:11–18

A good shepherd lays down his life for the sheep.

A reading from the holy Gospel according to John

Jesus said: "I am the good shepherd. A good shepherd lays down his life for the sheep. A hired man, who is not a shepherd and whose sheep are not his own, sees a wolf coming and leaves the sheep and runs away, and the wolf catches and scatters them. This is because he works for pay and has no concern for the sheep. I am the good shepherd, and I know mine and mine know me, just as the Father knows me and I know the Father; and I will lay down my life for the sheep. I have other sheep that do not belong to this fold. These also I must lead, and they will hear my voice, and there will be one flock, one shepherd. This is why the Father loves me, because I lay down my life in order to take it up again. No one takes it from me, but I lay it down on my own. I have power to lay it down, and power to take it up again. This command I have received from my Father."

The Gospel of the Lord.

Liturgy of the Eucharist, p. 897.

Prayer over the Gifts

Pray, brethren...

Lord,
receive these gifts from your Church.
May the great joy you give us
come to perfection in heaven.

Grant this through Christ our Lord.

Preface of Easter II–V, pp. 945–946.

Communion Antiphon

Jesus came and stood among his disciples and said to them: Peace be with you, alleluia. (Jn 20:19)

Prayer after Communion

Let us pray.

Pause for silent prayer, if this has not preceded.

Lord,
look on your people with kindness
and by these Easter mysteries
bring us to the glory of the resurrection.

We ask this in the name of Jesus the Lord.

Tuesday

Entrance Antiphon

Let us shout out our joy and happiness, and give glory to God, the Lord of all, because he is our King, alleluia.   (Rv 19:7, 6)

Opening Prayer

Almighty God,
as we celebrate the resurrection,
may we share with each other
the joy the risen Christ has won for us.

We ask this through our Lord Jesus Christ, your Son,
who lives and reigns with you and the Holy Spirit,
one God, for ever and ever.

TODAY'S LIVING WORD

In today's first reading from Acts, the rush of the Spirit again shakes the church in Jerusalem. The Greek-speaking Christian Jews, who have been forced to flee Jerusalem because of "the persecution that arose because of Stephen," spread the Gospel among their fellow Jews "as far as Phoenicia, Cyprus, and Antioch." But soon, by "the hand of the Lord," the message reached non-Jews as well. Many believed and were baptized. When the news reached Jerusalem, that Church dispatched Barnabas to assess the situation in Antioch. There he saw for himself evidence of "the grace of God" and rejoiced.

In Acts, the growth of the Church is the work of God's hand, while the community's role is to witness and welcome it. This is John's view as well. The Father draws disciples to Jesus (cf. 6:44). Therefore, says Jesus in today's Gospel, "No one can take them out of my hand."

FIRST READING   Acts 11:19–26

They began speaking to the Greeks as well,
proclaiming the Good News of Jesus Christ.

A reading from the Acts of the Apostles

Those who had been scattered by the persecution that arose because of Stephen went as far as Phoenicia, Cyprus, and Antioch, preaching the word to no one but Jews. There were some Cypriots and Cyrenians among them, however, who came to Antioch and began to speak to the Greeks as well, proclaiming the Lord Jesus. The hand of the Lord was with them and a great number who believed turned to the Lord. The news about them reached the ears of the Church in Jerusalem, and they sent Barnabas to go to Antioch. When he arrived and saw the grace of God, he rejoiced and encouraged them all to remain faithful to the Lord in firmness of heart, for he was a good man, filled with the Holy Spirit and faith. And a large number of people was added to the Lord. Then he went to Tarsus to look for Saul, and when he had found him he brought him to Antioch. For a whole year they met with the Church and taught a large number of people, and it was in Antioch that the disciples were first called Christians.

The word of the Lord.

Responsorial Psalm

Ps 87:1b–3, 4–5, 6–7

R. All you nations, praise the Lord.

His foundation upon the holy mountains
  the LORD loves:
The gates of Zion,
  more than any dwelling of Jacob.
Glorious things are said of you,
  O city of God!

R. All you nations, praise the Lord.

I tell of Egypt and Babylon
  among those who know the LORD;

Of Philistia, Tyre, Ethiopia:
  "This man was born there."
And of Zion they shall say:
  "One and all were born in her;
And he who has established her
  is the Most High LORD."

R. All you nations, praise the Lord.

They shall note, when the peoples are enrolled:
  "This man was born there."
And all shall sing, in their festive dance:
  "My home is within you."

R. All you nations, praise the Lord.

Or: **R. Alleluia.**

Alleluia, alleluia Jn 10:27
My sheep hear my voice, says the Lord;
I know them, and they follow me.
Alleluia, alleluia

GOSPEL   Jn 10:22–30

The Father and I are one.

A reading from the holy Gospel according to John

The feast of the Dedication was taking place in Jerusalem. It was winter. And Jesus walked about in the temple area on the Portico of Solomon. So the Jews gathered around him and said to him, "How long are you going to keep us in suspense? If you are the Christ, tell us plainly." Jesus answered them, "I told you and you do not believe. The works I do in my Father's name testify to me. But you do not believe, because you are not among my sheep. My sheep hear my voice; I know them, and they follow me. I give them eternal life, and they shall never perish. No one can take them out of my hand. My Father, who has given them to me, is greater than all, and no one can take them out of the Father's hand. The Father and I are one."

The Gospel of the Lord.

Liturgy of the Eucharist, *p. 897.*

Prayer over the Gifts

Pray, brethren...

Lord,
give us joy by these Easter mysteries;
let the continuous offering of this sacrifice
by which we are renewed
bring us to eternal happiness.
We ask this in the name of Jesus the Lord.

Preface of Easter II–V, *pp. 945–946.*

Communion Antiphon

Christ had to suffer and to rise from the dead, and so enter into his glory, alleluia.   (See Lk 24:46, 26)

Prayer after Communion

Let us pray.

Pause for silent prayer, if this has not preceded.

Lord,
may this celebration of our redemption
help us in this life
and lead us to eternal happiness.
We ask this through Christ our Lord.

Wednesday

Entrance Antiphon

I will be a witness to you in the world, O Lord. I will spread the knowledge of your name among my brothers, alleluia.
(Ps 17:50; 21:23)

Opening Prayer

God our Father,
life of the faithful,
glory of the humble,
happiness of the just,
hear our prayer.
Fill our emptiness
with the blessing of this eucharist,
the foretaste of eternal joy.

We ask this through our Lord Jesus Christ, your Son,
who lives and reigns with you and the Holy Spirit,
one God, for ever and ever.

TODAY'S LIVING WORD

The juxtaposition of today's readings creates an interesting effect. In the Gospel Jesus concludes his public ministry, while in Acts, Saul begins his. One last time, Jesus proclaims that he has "not come to condemn the world but to save the world." Salvation—eternal life—lies in believing in him, whom the Father has sent. In the reading from Acts, Luke takes great pains to show that Saul and Barnabas are also sent. Once again the Holy Spirit directly intervenes in the life of the community. Saul and Barnabas are to be "set apart" (that is, consecrated). So Paul, "sent forth by the Holy Spirit," embarks on the first of many missionary journeys.

Luke's language is important here. He refers to Paul by his Jewish name, Saul. He describes Saul and Barnabas preparing themselves for their commissioning by fasting and prayer, the hallmarks of Jewish piety. He notes what will become Saul's mode of operation on all his missionary journeys: "They proclaimed the word of God in the Jewish synagogues." In this way, Luke reminds us of something we easily forget: like Jesus, Paul was a fervent, faithful Jew.

FIRST READING   Acts 12:24 —13:5a
Set apart for me Barnabas and Saul.

A reading from the Acts of the Apostles

The word of God continued to spread and grow.

After Barnabas and Saul completed their relief mission, they returned to Jerusalem, taking with them John, who is called Mark.

Now there were in the Church at Antioch prophets and teachers: Barnabas, Symeon who was called Niger, Lucius of Cyrene, Manaen who was a close friend of Herod the tetrarch, and Saul. While they were worshiping the Lord and fasting, the Holy Spirit said, "Set apart for me Barnabas and Saul for the work to which I have called them." Then, completing their fasting and prayer, they laid hands on them and sent them off.

So they, sent forth by the Holy Spirit, went down to Seleucia and from there sailed to Cyprus. When they arrived in Salamis, they proclaimed the word of God in the Jewish synagogues.

The word of the Lord.

Responsorial Psalm   Ps 67:2–3, 5, 6 and 8

R. O God, let all the nations praise you!

May God have pity on us and bless us;
   may he let his face shine upon us.
So may your way be known upon earth;
   among all nations, your salvation.

R. O God, let all the nations praise you!

May the nations be glad and exult
   because you rule the peoples in equity;
   the nations on the earth you guide.

R. O God, let all the nations praise you!

May the peoples praise you, O God;
   may all the peoples praise you!
May God bless us,
   and may all the ends of the earth fear him!

R. O God, let all the nations praise you!

Or: **R. Alleluia.**

> **Alleluia, alleluia**   Jn 8:12
> I am the light of the world, says the Lord;
> whoever follows me will have the light of life.
> **Alleluia, alleluia**

GOSPEL   Jn 12:44–50

I came into the world as light.

A reading from the holy Gospel according to John

Jesus cried out and said, "Whoever believes in me believes not only in me but also in the one who sent me, and whoever sees me sees the one who sent me. I came into the world as light, so that everyone who believes in me might not remain in darkness. And if anyone hears my words and does not observe them, I do not condemn him, for I did not come to condemn the world but to save the world. Whoever rejects me and does not accept my words has something to judge him: the word that I spoke, it will condemn him on the last day, because I did not speak on my own, but the Father who sent me commanded me what to say and speak. And I know that his commandment is eternal life. So what I say, I say as the Father told me."

The Gospel of the Lord.

Liturgy of the Eucharist, *p. 897.*

Prayer over the Gifts

Pray, brethren...

Lord God,
by this holy exchange of gifts
you share with us your divine life.

Grant that everything we do
may be directed by the knowledge of your truth.

We ask this in the name of Jesus the Lord.

Preface of Easter II–V, pp. 945–946.

Communion Antiphon

The Lord says, I have chosen you from the world to go and bear fruit that will last, alleluia.   (See Jn 15:16, 19)

Prayer after Communion

Let us pray.

Pause for silent prayer, if this has not preceded.

Merciful Father,
may these mysteries give us new purpose
and bring us to a new life in you.

Grant this through Christ our Lord.

Thursday

Entrance Antiphon

When you walked at the head of your people, O God, and lived with them on their journey, the earth shook at your presence and the skies poured forth their rain, alleluia.   (See Ps 67:8 – 9, 20)

Opening Prayer

Father,
in restoring human nature
you have given us a greater dignity
than we had in the beginning.
Keep us in your love
and continue to sustain those
who have received new life in baptism.

We ask this through our Lord Jesus Christ, your Son,
who lives and reigns with you and the Holy Spirit,
one God, for ever and ever.

TODAY'S LIVING WORD

The concluding verse of today's Gospel is John's version of the saying of Jesus, "Whoever receives you receives me, and whoever receives me receives the one who sent me" (Mt 10:40). It adapts the ancient principle that the one who is sent represents (makes present) the one who sent him, and makes it the foundation of missionary activity. This is Luke's understanding of Christian mission, which is why in today's reading he describes Paul as doing precisely what Jesus did when he undertook his mission: preaching in a synagogue on the sabbath day (cf. Lk 4:16–30).

Paul's "sermon" fast-forwards the tape of Israel's history, pausing only to mention God's testimony on behalf of David, "I have found David...a man after my own heart; he will carry out my every wish." His point, of course, is the good news that from David's descendants God has now "brought to Israel a savior, Jesus."

FIRST READING   13:13–25

*From this man's descendants God, according to his promise,
has brought to Israel a savior, Jesus.*

A reading from the Acts of Apostles

From Paphos, Paul and his companions set sail and arrived at Perga in Pamphylia. But John left them and returned to Jerusalem. They continued on from Perga and reached Antioch in Pisidia. On the sabbath they entered into the synagogue and took their seats. After the reading of the law and the prophets, the synagogue officials sent word to them, "My brothers, if one of you has a word of exhortation for the people, please speak."

So Paul got up, motioned with his hand, and said, "Fellow children of Israel and you others who are God-fearing, listen.

The God of this people Israel chose our ancestors and exalted the people during their sojourn in the land of Egypt. With uplifted arm he led them out, and for about forty years he put up with them in the desert. When he had destroyed seven nations in the land of Canaan, he gave them their land as an inheritance at the end of about four hundred and fifty years. After these things he provided judges up to Samuel the prophet. Then they asked for a king. God gave them Saul, son of Kish, a man from the tribe of Benjamin, for forty years. Then he removed him and raised up David as their king; of him he testified, *I have found David, son of Jesse, a man after my own heart; he will carry out my every wish.* From this man's descendants God, according to his promise, has brought to Israel a savior, Jesus. John heralded his coming by proclaiming a baptism of repentance to all the people of Israel; and as John was completing his course, he would say, 'What do you suppose that I am? I am not he. Behold, one is coming after me; I am not worthy to unfasten the sandals of his feet.'"

The word of the Lord.

Responsorial Psalm   Ps 89:2–3, 21–22, 25 and 27

R. For ever I will sing the goodness of the Lord.

The favors of the Lord I will sing forever;
  through all generations my mouth shall proclaim
    your faithfulness.
For you have said, "My kindness is established forever";
  in heaven you have confirmed your faithfulness.

R. For ever I will sing the goodness of the Lord.

"I have found David, my servant;
  with my holy oil I have anointed him,

That my hand may be always with him,
　and that my arm may make him strong."

　　R. For ever I will sing the goodness of the Lord.

"My faithfulness and my mercy shall be with him,
　and through my name shall his horn be exalted.
He shall say of me, 'You are my father,
　my God, the Rock, my savior.' "

　　R. For ever I will sing the goodness of the Lord.

　　Or: **R. Alleluia.**

> **Alleluia, alleluia**　See Rv 1:5ab
> Jesus Christ, you are the faithful witness,
> 　the firstborn of the dead,
> 　you have loved us and freed us from our sins by your Blood.
> **Alleluia, alleluia**

GOSPEL

Jn 13:16–20

Whoever receives the one I send receives me.

A reading from the holy Gospel according to John

When Jesus had washed the disciples' feet, he said to them:
"Amen, amen, I say to you, no slave is greater than his master
nor any messenger greater than the one who sent him. If you
understand this, blessed are you if you do it. I am not speaking
of all of you. I know those whom I have chosen. But so that
the Scripture might be fulfilled, *The one who ate my food has
raised his heel against me.* From now on I am telling you before
it happens, so that when it happens you may believe that I AM.
Amen, amen, I say to you, whoever receives the one I send
receives me, and whoever receives me receives the one who
sent me."

The Gospel of the Lord.

　　Liturgy of the Eucharist, *p. 897.*

Prayer over the Gifts

Pray, brethren...

Lord,
accept our prayers and offerings.
Make us worthy of your sacraments of love
by granting us your forgiveness.

We ask this in the name of Jesus the Lord.

Preface of Easter II–V, *pp. 945–946.*

Communion Antiphon

**I, the Lord, am with you always, until the end of the world,
alleluia.**   (Mt 28:20)

Prayer after Communion

Let us pray.

Pause for silent prayer, if this has not preceded.

Almighty and ever-living Lord,
you restored us to life
by raising Christ from death.
Strengthen us by this Easter sacrament;
may we feel its saving power in our daily life.

We ask this through Christ our Lord.

Friday

Entrance Antiphon

**By your blood, O Lord, you have redeemed us from every tribe
and tongue, from every nation and people: you have made us
into the Kingdom of God, alleluia.**   (Rv 5:9–10)

Opening Prayer

Father of our freedom and salvation,

hear the prayers of those redeemed by your Son's suffering.
Through you may we have life;
With you may we have eternal joy.

We ask this through our Lord Jesus Christ, your Son,
who lives and reigns with you and the Holy Spirit,
one God, for ever and ever.

TODAY'S LIVING WORD

In today's Gospel Jesus declares, "I am the way and the truth and the life." This eminently quotable verse succinctly summarizes the theology of the Fourth Gospel. As commentators often note, the words "truth" and "life" qualify the word "way." The Johannine Jesus is here making a massive claim: he is the one and only way to the Father. "No one comes to the Father except through me." He offers those who believe in him this unique access to the Father by sharing with them the truth and the life of the Father. As the Word of God incarnate, Jesus is the fullest expression of the living God available to us, "the fullness of revelation," as we say. But the revelation, accessible through Jesus, is not information about God, but intimate communion with God, a share in God's own eternal life.

Paul tells the synagogue in Antioch that the fullest meaning of the prophets and psalms is revealed in the light of this good news.

FIRST READING   Acts 13:26–33

God has fulfilled his promise by raising Jesus from the dead.

A reading from the Acts of the Apostles

When Paul came to Antioch in Pisidia, he said in the synagogue: "My brothers, children of the family of Abraham, and those others among you who are God-fearing, to us this word of salvation has been sent. The inhabitants of Jerusalem and their leaders failed to recognize him, and by condemning him they fulfilled the oracles of the prophets that are read sabbath after sabbath. For even though they found no grounds for a death sentence, they asked Pilate to have him put to death, and when they had accomplished all that was written about him, they took him down from the tree and placed him in a tomb. But God raised him from the dead, and for many days he appeared to those who had come up with him from Galilee to Jerusalem. These are now his witnesses before the people. We ourselves are proclaiming this good news to you that what God promised our fathers he has brought to fulfillment for us, their children, by raising up Jesus, as it is written in the second psalm, *You are my Son; this day I have begotten you.*"

The word of the Lord.

Responsial Psalm
Ps 2:6–7, 8–9, 10–11ab

R. You are my Son; this day I have begotten you.

"I myself have set up my king
 on Zion, my holy mountain."
I will proclaim the decree of the LORD:
 The LORD said to me, "You are my Son;
 this day I have begotten you."

R. You are my Son; this day I have begotten you.

"Ask of me and I will give you
 the nations for an inheritance
 and the ends of the earth for your possession.
You shall rule them with an iron rod;
 you shall shatter them like an earthen dish."

R. You are my Son; this day I have begotten you.

And now, O kings, give heed;
 take warning, you rulers of the earth.
Serve the LORD with fear, and rejoice before him;
 with trembling rejoice.

R. You are my Son; this day I have begotten you.

Or: **R. Alleluia.**

Alleluia, alleluia Jn 14:6
I am the way and the truth and the life, says the Lord;
no one comes to the Father except through me.
Alleluia, alleluia

GOSPEL   Jn 14:1–6

I am the way and the truth and the life.

A reading from the holy Gospel according to John

Jesus said to his disciples: "Do not let your hearts be troubled. You have faith in God; have faith also in me. In my Father's house there are many dwelling places. If there were not, would I have told you that I am going to prepare a place for you? And if I go and prepare a place for you, I will come back again and take you to myself, so that where I am you also may be. Where I am going you know the way." Thomas said to him, "Master, we do not know where you are going; how can we know the way?" Jesus said to him, "I am the way and the truth and the life. No one comes to the Father except through me."

The Gospel of the Lord.

Liturgy of the Eucharist, *p. 897.*

Prayer over the Gifts

Pray, brethren...

Lord,
accept these gifts from your family.
May we hold fast to the life you have given us
and come to the eternal gifts you promise.

We ask this in the name of Jesus the Lord.

Preface of Easter II–V, *pp. 945–946.*

Communion Antiphon

Christ our Lord was put to death for our sins; and he rose again to make us worthy of life, alleluia.   (Rom 4:25)

Prayer after Communion

Let us pray.

Pause for silent prayer, if this has not preceded.

Lord,
watch over those you have saved in Christ.
May we who are redeemed by his suffering and death
always rejoice in his resurrection,
for he is Lord for ever and ever.

Saturday

Entrance Antiphon

**You are a people God claims as his own, to praise him who
called you out of darkness into his marvelous light, alleluia.**

(1 Pt 2:9)

Opening Prayer

Father,
may we whom you renew in baptism
bear witness to our faith by the way we live.
By the suffering, death, and resurrection of your Son
may we come to eternal joy.

We ask this through our Lord Jesus Christ, your Son,
who lives and reigns with you and the Holy Spirit,
one God, for ever and ever.

TODAY'S LIVING WORD

In John's Gospel, Jesus is the one and only way to the Father.
Today's reading makes it clear that he is much more than a spiritual
guide. When Philip asks him, "Show us the Father," Jesus answers,
"Whoever has seen me has seen the Father." Jesus and the Father
are one.

Jesus goes on to say, "Whoever believes in me will do the works that I do." This is Paul in the first reading for today. Like the preaching of Jesus in the synagogue on the sabbath (Lk 4:16–30), Paul's preaching in the synagogue on the sabbath is greeted first with acceptance and then with rejection. Just as Jesus had indicated in his sabbath sermon that his mission would reach beyond the boundaries of Israel, so here Paul announces his intention to turn to the Gentiles, with the very words of Isaiah that Simeon used in his prophecy of Jesus (Lk 2:32). Finally, the same violent abuse that drove Jesus out of Nazareth drives Paul and Barnabas out of Pisidia— rejoicing. Jesus and his disciples are one.

FIRST READING   Acts 13:44–52

We now turn to the Gentiles.

A reading from the Acts of the Apostles

On the following sabbath almost the whole city gathered to hear the word of the Lord. When the Jews saw the crowds, they were filled with jealousy and with violent abuse contradicted what Paul said. Both Paul and Barnabas spoke out boldly and said, "It was necessary that the word of God be spoken to you first, but since you reject it and condemn yourselves as unworthy of eternal life, we now turn to the Gentiles. For so the Lord has commanded us, *I have made you a light to the Gentiles, that you may be an instrument of salvation to the ends of the earth.*"

The Gentiles were delighted when they heard this and glorified the word of the Lord. All who were destined for eternal life came to believe, and the word of the Lord continued to spread through the whole region. The Jews, however, incited the women of prominence who were worshipers and the leading men of the city, stirred up a persecution against Paul and Barnabas, and expelled them from their territory. So they shook

the dust from their feet in protest against them and went to
Iconium. The disciples were filled with joy and the Holy Spirit.

The word of the Lord.

Responsorial Psalm

Ps 98:1, 2–3ab, 3cd–4

**R. All the ends of the earth have seen
the saving power of God.**

Sing to the LORD a new song,
  for he has done wondrous deeds;
His right hand has won victory for him,
  his holy arm.

**R. All the ends of the earth have seen
the saving power of God.**

The LORD has made his salvation known:
  in the sight of the nations he has revealed his justice.
He has remembered his kindness and his faithfulness
  toward the house of Israel.

**R. All the ends of the earth have seen
the saving power of God.**

All the ends of the earth have seen
  the salvation by our God.
Sing joyfully to the LORD, all you lands;
  break into song; sing praise.

**R. All the ends of the earth have seen
the saving power of God.**

Or: **R. Alleluia.**

Alleluia, alleluia Jn 8:31b–32
If you remain in my word, you will truly be my disciples,
and you will know the truth, says the Lord.
Alleluia, alleluia

GOSPEL

Jn 14:7–14

Whoever has seen me has seen the Father.

A reading from the holy Gospel according to John

Jesus said to his disciples: "If you know me, then you will also know my Father. From now on you do know him and have seen him." Philip said to Jesus, "Master, show us the Father, and that will be enough for us." Jesus said to him, "Have I been with you for so long a time and you still do not know me, Philip? Whoever has seen me has seen the Father. How can you say, 'Show us the Father'? Do you not believe that I am in the Father and the Father is in me? The words that I speak to you I do not speak on my own. The Father who dwells in me is doing his works. Believe me that I am in the Father and the Father is in me, or else, believe because of the works themselves. Amen, amen, I say to you, whoever believes in me will do the works that I do, and will do greater ones than these, because I am going to the Father. And whatever you ask in my name, I will do, so that the Father may be glorified in the Son. If you ask anything of me in my name, I will do it."

The Gospel of the Lord.

Liturgy of the Eucharist, *p. 897.*

Prayer over the Gifts

Pray, brethren...

Merciful Lord,
make holy these gifts
and let our spiritual sacrifice
make us an everlasting gift to you.

We ask this in the name of Jesus the Lord.

Preface of Easter II–V, *pp. 945–946.*

Communion Antiphon

Father, I want the men you have given me to be with me where I am, so that they may see the glory you have given me, alleluia.
(Jn 17:24)

Prayer after Communion

Let us pray.

Pause for silent prayer, if this has not preceded.

Lord,
may this eucharist,
which we have celebrated in memory of your Son,
help us to grow in love.
We ask this in the name of Jesus the Lord.

FIFTH WEEK OF EASTER

Monday

Entrance Antiphon

The Good Shepherd is risen! He who laid down his life for his sheep, who died for his flock, he is risen, alleluia.

Opening Prayer

Father,
help us to seek the values
that will bring us eternal joy in this changing world.
In our desire for what you promise
make us one in mind and heart.

Grant this through our Lord Jesus Christ, your Son,
who lives and reigns with you and the Holy Spirit,
one God, for ever and ever.

TODAY'S LIVING WORD

In today's Gospel, a disciple's question again interrupts the farewell discourse of Jesus. This time Judas (not Judas Iscariot) asks, "What happened that you will reveal yourself to us and not to the world?" Jesus answers that the world does not love God because it does not keep the commandments of Jesus, which are from the Father who sent him.

In the account from Acts, however, Paul and Barnabas find the godless Gentile world welcoming the Gospel message, even too much so. Mistaking the two apostles for gods, they are not easily dissuaded "from offering sacrifice to them." Still, their enthusiasm bodes well for the Gentile mission. Although they are pagans not yet converted to the living God from their follies, they are not entirely "clueless." They have begun to know God through the benefits bestowed in and through the created order, like the rain and rich harvests God sends down from heaven. A small beginning perhaps, but who would dare despise it?

FIRST READING   Acts 14:5–18

We proclaim to you Good News that you should
turn from these idols to the living God.

A reading from the Acts of the Apostles

There was an attempt in Iconium by both the Gentiles and the Jews, together with their leaders, to attack and stone Paul and Barnabas. They realized it, and fled to the Lycaonian cities of Lystra and Derbe and to the surrounding countryside, where they continued to proclaim the Good News.

At Lystra there was a crippled man, lame from birth, who had never walked. He listened to Paul speaking, who looked intently at him, saw that he had the faith to be healed, and called out in a loud voice, "Stand up straight on your feet." He jumped up and began to walk about. When the crowds saw what Paul had done, they cried out in Lycaonian, "The gods have come down to us in human form." They called Barnabas "Zeus" and Paul "Hermes," because he was the chief speaker. And the priest of Zeus, whose temple was at the entrance to the city, brought oxen and garlands to the gates, for he together with the people intended to offer sacrifice.

The Apostles Barnabas and Paul tore their garments when they heard this and rushed out into the crowd, shouting, "Men, why are you doing this? We are of the same nature as you, human beings. We proclaim to you good news that you should turn from these idols to the living God, *who made heaven and earth and sea and all that is in them.* In past generations he allowed all Gentiles to go their own ways; yet, in bestowing his goodness, he did not leave himself without witness, for he gave you rains from heaven and fruitful seasons, and filled you with nourishment and gladness for your hearts." Even with these words, they scarcely restrained the crowds from offering sacrifice to them.

The word of the Lord.

Responsorial Psalm
Ps 115:1–2, 3–4, 15–16

R. Not to us, O Lord, but to your name give the glory.

Not to us, O Lord, not to us
  but to your name give glory
  because of your mercy, because of your truth.
Why should the pagans say,
  "Where is their God?"

R. Not to us, O Lord, but to your name give the glory.

Our God is in heaven;
  whatever he wills, he does.
Their idols are silver and gold,
  the handiwork of men.

R. Not to us, O Lord, but to your name give the glory.

May you be blessed by the Lord,
  who made heaven and earth.
Heaven is the heaven of the Lord,
  but the earth he has given to the children of men.

R. Not to us, O Lord, but to your name give the glory.

Or: **R. Alleluia.**

Alleluia, alleluia   Jn 14:26
The Holy Spirit will teach you everything
and remind you of all I told you.
Alleluia, alleluia

GOSPEL   Jn 14:21–26
The Advocate whom the Father will send will teach you everything.

A reading from the holy Gospel according to John

Jesus said to his disciples: "Whoever has my commandments
and observes them is the one who loves me. Whoever loves
me will be loved by my Father, and I will love him and reveal
myself to him." Judas, not the Iscariot, said to him, "Master,
then what happened that you will reveal yourself to us and not
to the world?" Jesus answered and said to him, "Whoever loves
me will keep my word, and my Father will love him, and we
will come to him and make our dwelling with him. Whoever
does not love me does not keep my words; yet the word you
hear is not mine but that of the Father who sent me.

"I have told you this while I am with you. The Advocate, the
Holy Spirit whom the Father will send in my name—he will
teach you everything and remind you of all that I told you."

The Gospel of the Lord.

Liturgy of the Eucharist, *p. 897.*

Prayer over the Gifts

Pray, brethren...

Lord,
accept our prayers and offerings.
Make us worthy of your sacraments of love
by granting us your forgiveness.
We ask this in the name of Jesus the Lord.

Preface of Easter II–V, *pp. 945–946.*

Communion Antiphon

The Lord says, peace I leave with you, my own peace I give you; not as the world gives do I give, alleluia. (Jn 14:27)

Prayer after Communion

Let us pray.

Pause for silent prayer, if this has not preceded.

Almighty and ever-living Lord,
you restored us to life
by raising Christ from death.
Strengthen us by this Easter sacrament.

We ask this through Christ our Lord.

Tuesday

Entrance Antiphon

All you who fear God, both the great and the small, give praise to him! For his salvation and strength have come, the power of Christ, alleluia. (Rv 19:5; 12:10)

Opening Prayer

Father,
you restored your people to eternal life
by raising Christ your Son from death.
Make our faith strong and our hope sure.
May we never doubt that you will fulfill
the promises you have made.

Grant this through our Lord Jesus Christ, your Son,
who lives and reigns with you and the Holy Spirit,
one God, for ever and ever.

Today's Living Word

Both readings today announce imminent departures. In Acts, Paul and Barnabas conclude their missionary journey by revisiting each of the churches they founded. They admonish the fledgling communities and appoint elders over them to continue the work they have begun. In the Gospel, Jesus again tells the still uncomprehending disciples that he is going away for a time. "Peace" *(shalom)* is his farewell gift to them. It is not so much a present as a promise that will be fulfilled on Easter Sunday night, when they will receive the Holy Spirit (cf. Jn 20:19–23). This peace is not what passes for peace in the world. Rather, it is the saving work of Jesus— his death and resurrection—that has made our peace with God.

This part of Jesus' valedictory concludes with a profession of love for the Father.

It teaches us never to forget that the death of Jesus was, above all, an act of love.

FIRST READING

Acts 14:19–28

They called the Church together and reported what God had done with them.

A reading from the Acts of the Apostles

In those days, some Jews from Antioch and Iconium arrived and won over the crowds. They stoned Paul and dragged him out of the city, supposing that he was dead. But when the disciples gathered around him, he got up and entered the city. On the following day he left with Barnabas for Derbe.

After they had proclaimed the good news to that city and made a considerable number of disciples, they returned to Lystra and to Iconium and to Antioch. They strengthened the spirits of the disciples and exhorted them to persevere in the faith, saying, "It is necessary for us to undergo many hardships to enter the Kingdom of God." They appointed presbyters for them in each Church and, with prayer and fasting, commended them to the Lord in whom they had put their faith. Then they traveled through Pisidia and reached Pamphylia. After proclaiming the word at Perga they went down to Attalia. From there they sailed to Antioch, where they had been commended to the grace of God for the work they had now accomplished. And when they arrived, they called the Church together and reported what God had done with them and how he had opened the door of faith to the Gentiles. Then they spent no little time with the disciples.

The word of the Lord.

Responsorial Psalm

Ps 145:10–11, 12–13ab, 21

R. **Your friends make known, O Lord,**
   the glorious splendor of your kingdom.

Let all your works give you thanks, O Lord,
   and let your faithful ones bless you.
Let them discourse of the glory of your kingdom
   and speak of your might.

R. **Your friends make known, O Lord,**
   the glorious splendor of your kingdom.

Making known to men your might
   and the glorious splendor of your kingdom.
Your kingdom is a kingdom for all ages,
   and your dominion endures through all generations.

R. **Your friends make known, O Lord,**
   the glorious splendor of your kingdom.

May my mouth speak the praise of the Lord,
   and may all flesh bless his holy name forever and ever.

R. **Your friends make known, O Lord,**
   the glorious splendor of your kingdom.

Or: R. **Alleluia.**

Alleluia, alleluia See Lk 24:46, 26
Christ had to suffer and to rise from the dead,
and so enter into his glory.
Alleluia, alleluia

GOSPEL

Jn 14:27–31a

My peace I give to you.

A reading from the holy Gospel according to John

Jesus said to his disciples: "Peace I leave with you; my peace I give to you. Not as the world gives do I give it to you. Do not let your hearts be troubled or afraid. You heard me tell you, 'I am going away and I will come back to you.' If you loved me, you would rejoice that I am going to the Father; for the Father is greater than I. And now I have told you this before it happens, so that when it happens you may believe. I will no longer speak much with you, for the ruler of the world is coming. He has no power over me, but the world must know that I love the Father and that I do just as the Father has commanded me."

The Gospel of the Lord.

Liturgy of the Eucharist, *p. 897.*

Prayer over the Gifts

Pray, brethren...

Lord,
receive these gifts from your Church.
May the great joy you give us
come to perfection in heaven.

Grant this through Christ our Lord.

Preface of Easter II–V, *pp. 945–946.*

Communion Antiphon

Because we have died with Christ, we believe that we shall also come to life with him, alleluia.   (Rom 6:8)

Prayer after Communion

Let us pray.

Pause for silent prayer, if this has not preceded.

Lord,
look on your people with kindness
and by these Easter mysteries
bring us to the glory of the resurrection.
We ask this in the name of Jesus the Lord.

Wednesday

Entrance Antiphon

**Fill me with your praise and I will sing your glory; songs of
joy will be on my lips, alleluia.** (Ps 70:8, 23)

Opening Prayer

Father of all holiness,
guide our hearts to you.
Keep in the light of your truth
all those you have freed from the darkness of unbelief.

We ask this through our Lord Jesus Christ, your Son,
who lives and reigns with you and the Holy Spirit,
one God, for ever and ever.

TODAY'S LIVING WORD

In today's selection from Acts, early Church leaders confront the
burning question of their day: what Jewish practice, if any, should
be required of Gentile converts? In their book *Antioch & Rome*,
Brown and Meier detect four different answers to that question among
Christians of the first century. These range on a spectrum from the
reactionary view of the "Judaizers," who "insisted on full observance
of the Mosaic Law, including circumcision" for Gentile converts, to

the radical view of the Hellenists. These not only "did not insist on circumcision or observance of Jewish food laws," but saw "no abiding significance in Jewish cult and feasts."*

The teaching of the Fourth Gospel would have placed that community on the more radical side of the spectrum. The image of the vine and branches in today's reading is another way of saying that Jesus (the vine) is the only source of life. "Anyone who does not remain in me will be thrown out like a branch and wither." For these Christians it was not the practice of Judaism but the person of Jesus who was the only access to God, the sole source of eternal life.

* Raymond Brown and John Meier, *Antioch & Rome* (New York: Paulist Press, 1983), pp. 2, 6.

FIRST READING   Acts 15:1–6

*They decided to go up to Jerusalem to the Apostles
and presbyters about this question.*

A reading from the Acts of the Apostles

Some who had come down from Judea were instructing the brothers, "Unless you are circumcised according to the Mosaic practice, you cannot be saved." Because there arose no little dissension and debate by Paul and Barnabas with them, it was decided that Paul, Barnabas, and some of the others should go up to Jerusalem to the Apostles and presbyters about this question. They were sent on their journey by the Church, and passed through Phoenicia and Samaria telling of the conversion of the Gentiles, and brought great joy to all the brethren. When they arrived in Jerusalem, they were welcomed by the Church, as well as by the Apostles and the presbyters, and they reported what God had done with them. But some from the party of the Pharisees who had become believers stood up and said, "It is necessary to circumcise them and direct them to observe the Mosaic law."

The Apostles and the presbyters met together to see about this matter.

The word of the Lord.

Responsorial Psalm
Ps 122:1–2, 3–4ab, 4cd–5

R. Let us go rejoicing to the house of the Lord.

I rejoiced because they said to me,
  "We will go up to the house of the LORD."
And now we have set foot
  within your gates, O Jerusalem.

R. Let us go rejoicing to the house of the Lord.

Jerusalem, built as a city
  with compact unity.
To it the tribes go up,
  the tribes of the LORD.

R. Let us go rejoicing to the house of the Lord.

According to the decree for Israel,
  to give thanks to the name of the LORD.
In it are set up judgment seats,
  seats for the house of David.

R. Let us go rejoicing to the house of the Lord.

Or: **R. Alleluia.**

Alleluia, alleluia Jn 15:4a, 5b
Remain in me, as I remain in you, says the Lord;
whoever remains in me will bear much fruit.
Alleluia, alleluia

GOSPEL
Jn 15:1–8

Whoever remains in me and I in him will bear much fruit.

A reading from the holy Gospel according to John

Jesus said to his disciples: "I am the true vine, and my Father is the vine grower. He takes away every branch in me that does not bear fruit, and everyone that does he prunes so that it bears more fruit. You are already pruned because of the word that I spoke to you. Remain in me, as I remain in you. Just as a branch cannot bear fruit on its own unless it remains on the vine, so neither can you unless you remain in me. I am the vine, you are the branches. Whoever remains in me and I in him will bear much fruit, because without me you can do nothing. Anyone who does not remain in me will be thrown out like a branch and wither; people will gather them and throw them into a fire and they will be burned. If you remain in me and my words remain in you, ask for whatever you want and it will be done for you. By this is my Father glorified, that you bear much fruit and become my disciples."

The Gospel of the Lord.

Liturgy of the Eucharist, *p. 897.*

Prayer over the Gifts

Pray, brethren...

Lord,
restore us by these Easter mysteries.
May the continuing work of our Redeemer
bring us eternal joy.

We ask this through Christ our Lord.

Preface of Easter II–V, *pp. 945–946.*

Communion Antiphon

Christ has risen and shines upon us, whom he has redeemed by his blood, alleluia.

Prayer after Communion

Let us pray.

Pause for silent prayer, if this has not preceded.

Lord,
may this celebration of our redemption
help us in this life
and lead us to eternal happiness.
We ask this through Christ our Lord.

Thursday

Entrance Antiphon

Let us sing to the Lord, he has covered himself in glory! The Lord is my strength, and I praise him: he is the Savior of my life, alleluia.
(Ex 15:1–2)

Opening Prayer

Father,
in your love you have brought us
from evil to good and from misery to happiness.
Through your blessings
give the courage of perseverance
to those you have called and justified by faith.

Grant this through our Lord Jesus Christ, your Son,
who lives and reigns with you and the Holy Spirit,
one God, for ever and ever.

TODAY'S LIVING WORD

In Luke's scheme the original apostle to the Gentiles is Peter, not Paul. Therefore, in today's reading Peter speaks on their behalf before the Church leaders assembled in Jerusalem. Referring to his experience in the household of Cornelius (cf. Acts 10:44–49), he argues that Christian Jews should not place the "yoke" of the Mosaic Law on the shoulders of Gentile converts. "We believe that we are

saved through the grace of the Lord Jesus, in the same way as they."
The decision of the assembly comes from James, the leader of the
church in Jerusalem. It represents the more moderate view that "did
not insist on circumcision but did require converted Gentiles to keep
some Jewish observances."*

When Peter argues that Gentile converts should not be made to
observe the Mosaic law, he is referring to those requirements like
circumcision and the food laws. All God's people must keep the
Ten Commandments. This is the message Jesus gives in today's
Gospel: "If you keep my commandments, you will remain in my
love."

* Raymond Brown and John Meier, *Antioch & Rome* (New York: Paulist Press,
1983), p. 3.

FIRST READING   Acts 15:7–21

*It is my judgment, therefore, that we ought to
stop troubling the Gentiles who turn to God.*

A reading from the Acts of the Apostles

After much debate had taken place, Peter got up and said to
the Apostles and the presbyters, "My brothers, you are well
aware that from early days God made his choice among you
that through my mouth the Gentiles would hear the word of
the Gospel and believe. And God, who knows the heart, bore
witness by granting them the Holy Spirit just as he did us. He
made no distinction between us and them, for by faith he
purified their hearts. Why, then, are you now putting God to
the test by placing on the shoulders of the disciples a yoke
that neither our ancestors nor we have been able to bear? On
the contrary, we believe that we are saved through the grace
of the Lord Jesus, in the same way as they." The whole assembly fell silent, and they listened while Paul and Barnabas
described the signs and wonders God had worked among the
Gentiles through them.

After they had fallen silent, James responded, "My brothers, listen to me. Symeon has described how God first concerned himself with acquiring from among the Gentiles a people for his name. The words of the prophets agree with this, as is written:

> *After this I shall return*
> > *and rebuild the fallen hut of David;*
> *from its ruins I shall rebuild it*
> > *and raise it up again,*
> *so that the rest of humanity may seek out the Lord,*
> > *even all the Gentiles on whom my name is invoked.*
> *Thus says the Lord who accomplishes these things,*
> > *known from of old.*

It is my judgment, therefore, that we ought to stop troubling the Gentiles who turn to God, but tell them by letter to avoid pollution from idols, unlawful marriage, the meat of strangled animals, and blood. For Moses, for generations now, has had those who proclaim him in every town, as he has been read in the synagogues every sabbath."

The word of the Lord.

Responsorial Psalm

Ps 96:1–2a, 2b–3, 10

R. Proclaim God's marvelous deeds to all the nations.

Sing to the LORD a new song;
  sing to the LORD, all you lands.
Sing to the LORD; bless his name.

R. Proclaim God's marvelous deeds to all the nations.

Announce his salvation, day after day.
Tell his glory among the nations;
  among all peoples, his wondrous deeds.

R. Proclaim God's marvelous deeds to all the nations.

Say among the nations: The LORD is king.
He has made the world firm, not to be moved;
  he governs the peoples with equity.

R. Proclaim God's marvelous deeds to all the nations.

Or: **R. Alleluia.**

> **Alleluia, alleluia** Jn 10:27
> My sheep hear my voice, says the Lord;
> I know them, and they follow me.
> **Alleluia, alleluia**

GOSPEL   Jn 15:9–11
Remain in my love, that your joy might be complete.

A reading from the holy Gospel according to John

Jesus said to his disciples: "As the Father loves me, so I also love you. Remain in my love. If you keep my commandments, you will remain in my love, just as I have kept my Father's commandments and remain in his love.

"I have told you this so that my joy might be in you and your joy might be complete."

The Gospel of the Lord.

Liturgy of the Eucharist, *p. 897.*

Prayer over the Gifts

Pray, brethren...

Lord God,
by this holy exchange of gifts
you share with us your divine life.
Grant that everything we do
may be directed by the knowledge of your truth.

We ask this in the name of Jesus the Lord.

Preface of Easter II–V, *pp. 945–946.*

Communion Antiphon

Christ died for all, so that living men should not live for themselves, but for Christ who died and was raised to life for them, alleluia.   (2 Cor 5:15)

Prayer after Communion

Let us pray.

Pause for silent prayer, if this has not preceded.

Merciful Father,
may these mysteries give us new purpose
and bring us to a new life in you.

Grant this through Christ our Lord.

Friday

Entrance Antiphon

The Lamb who was slain is worthy to receive strength and divinity, wisdom and power and honor, alleluia.   (Rv 5:12)

Opening Prayer

Lord,
by this Easter mystery
prepare us for eternal life.
May our celebration of Christ's death and resurrection
guide us to salvation.

We ask this through our Lord Jesus Christ, your Son,
who lives and reigns with you and the Holy Spirit,
one God, for ever and ever.

TODAY'S LIVING WORD

In today's first reading, Silas and Barsabbas carry to Antioch the resolution of the Jerusalem assembly concerning the Jewish practices required of Gentile converts. Thus does the early Church seek to act concretely and creatively on the love command that binds all the members of Christ as one.

Jesus' "new commandment" frames today's Gospel. This love command of the Johannine Jesus restates the original love command (cf. Lv 19:18) in light of the death and rising of Jesus. As the love command in Leviticus was a call to imitate God (to be holy as God is holy, 19:2), so this one is a call to imitate Jesus, who laid down his life for his friends. As Abraham and Moses were friends of God, so disciples are friends of Jesus. As God's friends dared speak boldly to God in prayer, so may Jesus' followers ask anything of the Father in Jesus' name. Finally, as God chose Israel to be a fruitful vine, so Jesus has chosen his disciples to bear lasting fruit.

FIRST READING

Acts 15:22–31

It is the decision of the Holy Spirit and of us
not to place on you any burden beyond these necessities.

A reading from the Acts of the Apostles

The Apostles and presbyters, in agreement with the whole Church, decided to choose representatives and to send them to Antioch with Paul and Barnabas. The ones chosen were Judas, who was called Barsabbas, and Silas, leaders among the brothers. This is the letter delivered by them: "The Apostles and the presbyters, your brothers, to the brothers in Antioch, Syria, and Cilicia of Gentile origin: greetings. Since we have heard that some of our number who went out without any mandate from us have upset you with their teachings and disturbed your peace of mind, we have with one accord decided to choose representatives and to send them to you along with our beloved Barnabas and Paul, who have dedicated their lives to the name of our Lord Jesus Christ. So we are sending Judas and Silas who will also convey this same message by word of mouth: 'It is the decision of the Holy Spirit and of us not to place on you any burden beyond these necessities, namely, to abstain from meat sacrificed to idols, from blood, from meats of strangled animals, and from unlawful marriage. If you keep free of these, you will be doing what is right. Farewell.' "

And so they were sent on their journey. Upon their arrival in Antioch they called the assembly together and delivered the letter. When the people read it, they were delighted with the exhortation.

The word of the Lord.

Responsorial Psalm   Ps 57:8 – 9, 10 and 12

R. I will give you thanks among the peoples, O Lord.

My heart is steadfast, O God; my heart is steadfast;
   I will sing and chant praise.
Awake, O my soul; awake, lyre and harp!
   I will wake the dawn.

R. I will give you thanks among the peoples, O Lord.

I will give thanks to you among the peoples, O LORD,
   I will chant your praise among the nations.
For your mercy towers to the heavens,
   and your faithfulness to the skies.
Be exalted above the heavens, O God;
   above all the earth be your glory!

R. I will give you thanks among the peoples, O Lord.

Or: **R. Alleluia.**

   Alleluia, alleluia Jn 15:15b
   I call you my friends, says the Lord,
      for I have made known to you all that the Father has told me.
   Alleluia, alleluia

GOSPEL   Jn 15:12–17

   This is my commandment: love one another.

A reading from the holy Gospel according to John

Jesus said to his disciples: "This is my commandment: love one another as I love you. No one has greater love than this, to lay down one's life for one's friends. You are my friends if you do what I command you. I no longer call you slaves, because a slave does not know what his master is doing. I have called you friends, because I have told you everything I have heard from my Father. It was not you who chose me, but I who chose you and appointed you to go and bear fruit that will remain, so that whatever you ask the Father in my name he may give you. This I command you: love one another."

The Gospel of the Lord.

Liturgy of the Eucharist, *p. 897.*

Prayer over the Gifts

Pray, brethren...

Merciful Lord,
make holy these gifts
and let our spiritual sacrifice
make us an everlasting gift to you.

We ask this in the name of Jesus the Lord.

Preface of Easter II–V, *pp. 945–946.*

Communion Antiphon

The man who died on the cross has risen from the dead, and has won back our lives from death, alleluia.

Prayer after Communion

Let us pray.

Pause for silent prayer, if this has not preceded.

Lord,
may this eucharist,

which we have celebrated in memory of your Son,
help us to grow in love.
We ask this in the name of Jesus the Lord.

Saturday

Entrance Antiphon

**In baptism we have died with Christ, and we have risen to new
life in him, because we believed in the power of God who raised
him from the dead, alleluia.** (Col 2:12)

Opening Prayer

Loving Father,
through our rebirth in baptism
you give us your life and promise immortality.
By your unceasing care,
guide our steps toward the life of glory.

Grant this through our Lord Jesus Christ, your Son,
who lives and reigns with you and the Holy Spirit,
one God, for ever and ever.

TODAY'S LIVING WORD

The Holy Spirit, the "Spirit of Jesus," continued to direct the Gentile
mission. By the end of today's reading from Acts, Paul is poised to
bring the Gospel to Europe on his second missionary journey.

Since "no slave is greater than his master," Paul will suffer in the
service of the Gospel. Already on his first missionary journey with
Barnabas, Paul was falsely accused by prominent women of Antioch
in Pisidia and expelled from that territory (Acts 13:50). In Iconium,
"disbelieving Jews stirred up and poisoned the minds of the Gentiles"
against them. When some of these tried to attack and stone Paul
and Barnabas, they fled to Lystra and Derbe (14:2, 5–6). At Lystra,

Paul was stoned, dragged out of the city and left for dead (14:19). In the words of today's Gospel, having been sent into the world as Jesus was sent into the world, Paul, like Jesus, will come to know the world's hatred.

FIRST READING

Acts 16:1–10

Come over to Macedonia and help us.

A reading from the Acts of the Apostles

Paul reached also Derbe and Lystra where there was a disciple named Timothy, the son of a Jewish woman who was a believer, but his father was a Greek. The brothers in Lystra and Iconium spoke highly of him, and Paul wanted him to come along with him. On account of the Jews of that region, Paul had him circumcised, for they all knew that his father was a Greek. As they traveled from city to city, they handed on to the people for observance the decisions reached by the Apostles and presbyters in Jerusalem. Day after day the churches grew stronger in faith and increased in number.

They traveled through the Phrygian and Galatian territory because they had been prevented by the Holy Spirit from preaching the message in the province of Asia. When they came to Mysia, they tried to go on into Bithynia, but the Spirit of Jesus did not allow them, so they crossed through Mysia and came down to Troas. During the night Paul had a vision. A Macedonian stood before him and implored him with these words, "Come over to Macedonia and help us." When he had seen the vision, we sought passage to Macedonia at once, concluding that God had called us to proclaim the Good News to them.

The word of the Lord.

Responsorial Psalm
Ps 100:1b–2, 3, 5

R. Let all the earth cry out to God with joy.

Sing joyfully to the LORD, all you lands;
  serve the LORD with gladness;
  come before him with joyful song.

R. Let all the earth cry out to God with joy.

Know that the LORD is God;
  he made us, his we are;
  his people, the flock he tends.

R. Let all the earth cry out to God with joy.

The LORD is good:
  his kindness endures forever,
  and his faithfulness, to all generations.

R. Let all the earth cry out to God with joy.

Or: **R. Alleluia.**

> **Alleluia, alleluia** Col 3:1
> If then you were raised with Christ,
> seek what is above,
> where Christ is seated at the right hand of God.
> **Alleluia, alleluia**

GOSPEL
Jn 15:18–21

You do not belong to the world, and I have chosen you out of the world.

A reading from the holy Gospel according to John

Jesus said to his disciples: "If the world hates you, realize that it hated me first. If you belonged to the world, the world would love its own; but because you do not belong to the world, and I have chosen you out of the world, the world hates you. Remember the word I spoke to you, 'No slave is greater than his master.' If they persecuted me, they will also persecute you. If they kept my word, they will also keep yours. And they will do all these things to you on account of my name, because they do not know the one who sent me."

The Gospel of the Lord.

Liturgy of the Eucharist, *p. 897.*

Prayer over the Gifts

Pray, brethren...

Lord,
accept these gifts from your family.
May we hold fast to the life you have given us
and come to the eternal gifts you promise.
We ask this in the name of Jesus the Lord.

Preface of Easter II–V, *pp. 945–946.*

Communion Antiphon

Father, I pray for them: may they be one in us, so that the world may believe it was you who sent me, alleluia.

(Jn 17:20–21)

Prayer after Communion

Let us pray.

Pause for silent prayer, if this has not preceded.

Lord,
watch over those you have saved in Christ.
May we who are redeemed by his suffering and death
always rejoice in his resurrection,
for he is Lord for ever and ever.

SIXTH WEEK OF EASTER

Monday

Entrance Antiphon

Christ now raised from the dead will never die again; death no longer has power over him, alleluia.   (Rom 6:9)

Opening Prayer

God of mercy,
may our celebration of your Son's resurrection
help us to experience its effect in our lives.

We ask this through our Lord Jesus Christ, your Son,
who lives and reigns with you and the Holy Spirit,
one God, for ever and ever.

TODAY'S LIVING WORD

Today's readings introduce two essentials of Christian missionary activity in the person of Lydia in Acts and of the Paraclete in John. On the one hand, missionaries like Paul depended on the hospitality of women like Lydia who, in today's reading, prevails on Paul and his companions to stay at her house. On the other hand, the world's hatred of Jesus' disciples required the constant help of the Paraclete, "the Spirit of truth who proceeds from the Father," promised in today's Gospel. The courtroom drama that described the ministry of Jesus in John would continue to unfold in the mission of the Church. The Spirit's testimony was still needed.

Lydia and the Paraclete have something else in common. Their respective roles in the life and work of the Church, essential but behind the scenes, are characterized by "self-effacement" (cf. *Catechism of the Catholic Church*, n. 687). But they must never fade from the mind or the memory of the Church.

FIRST READING   Acts 16:11–15

The Lord opened her heart to pay attention to what Paul taught.

A reading from the Acts of the Apostles

We set sail from Troas, making a straight run for Samothrace, and on the next day to Neapolis, and from there to Philippi, a leading city in that district of Macedonia and a Roman colony. We spent some time in that city. On the sabbath we went outside the city gate along the river where we thought there would be a place of prayer. We sat and spoke with the women who had gathered there. One of them, a woman named Lydia, a dealer in purple cloth, from the city of Thyatira, a worshiper of God, listened, and the Lord opened her heart to pay attention to what Paul was saying. After she and her household had been baptized, she offered us an invitation, "If you consider me a believer in the Lord, come and stay at my home," and she prevailed on us.

The word of the Lord.

Responsorial Psalm

Ps 149:1b–2, 3–4, 5–6a and 9b

R. The Lord takes delight in his people.

Sing to the LORD a new song
  of praise in the assembly of the faithful.
Let Israel be glad in their maker,
  let the children of Zion rejoice in their king.

R. The Lord takes delight in his people.

Let them praise his name in the festive dance,
  let them sing praise to him with timbrel and harp.
For the LORD loves his people,
  and he adorns the lowly with victory.

R. The Lord takes delight in his people.

Let the faithful exult in glory;
  let them sing for joy upon their couches.
Let the high praises of God be in their throats.
  This is the glory of all his faithful. Alleluia.

R. The Lord takes delight in his people.

Or: **R. Alleluia.**

Alleluia, alleluia   Jn 15:26b, 27a
The Spirit of truth will testify to me, says the Lord,
and you also will testify.
Alleluia, alleluia

GOSPEL

Jn 15:26—16:4a

The Spirit of truth will testify to me.

A reading from the holy Gospel according to John

Jesus said to his disciples: "When the Advocate comes whom
I will send you from the Father, the Spirit of truth who proceeds
from the Father, he will testify to me. And you also testify,
because you have been with me from the beginning.

"I have told you this so that you may not fall away. They
will expel you from the synagogues; in fact, the hour is coming
when everyone who kills you will think he is offering worship
to God. They will do this because they have not known either
the Father or me. I have told you this so that when their hour
comes you may remember that I told you."

The Gospel of the Lord.

Liturgy of the Eucharist, *p. 897.*

Prayer over the Gifts

Pray, brethren...

Lord,
receive these gifts from your Church.
May the great joy you give us
come to perfection in heaven.

Grant this through Christ our Lord.

Preface of Easter II–V, *pp. 945–946.*

Communion Antiphon

Jesus came and stood among his disciples and said to them: Peace be with you, alleluia.   (Jn 20:19)

Prayer after Communion

Let us pray.

Pause for silent prayer, if this has not preceded.

Lord,
look on your people with kindness
and by these Easter mysteries
bring us to the glory of the resurrection.

We ask this in the name of Jesus the Lord.

Tuesday

Entrance Antiphon

Let us shout out our joy and happiness, and give glory to God, the Lord of all, because he is our King, alleluia.   (Rv 19:7, 6)

Opening Prayer

God our Father,
may we look forward with hope to our resurrection,
for you have made us your sons and daughters,
and restored the joy of our youth.

We ask this through our Lord Jesus Christ, your Son,
who lives and reigns with you and the Holy Spirit,
one God, for ever and ever.

TODAY'S LIVING WORD

The criminal justice system forms the setting for both readings today. The Gospel uses courtroom language, suggested by the name "Paraclete," a term that describes a court official. The Paraclete is sent to "convict the world." In this passage, the attorney for the defense, the Paraclete's usual role, becomes the prosecutor. Thus the disciples can rest assured that ultimately Jesus will win his suit against the world.

In the story from Acts, Paul and Silas are flogged and jailed "in the innermost cell," their feet chained to a stake. There they pray and sing hymns until an act of God releases them and their jailer becomes their host. "He and all his family were baptized." Spreading a table before Paul and Silas, he and his family then joyfully celebrate their newfound faith. Thus is another legal battle won against the hostile world.

FIRST READING

Acts 16:22–34

Believe in the Lord Jesus and you and
your household will be saved.

A reading from the Acts of the Apostles

The crowd in Philippi joined in the attack on Paul and Silas, and the magistrates had them stripped and ordered them to be beaten with rods. After inflicting many blows on them, they threw them into prison and instructed the jailer to guard them securely. When he received these instructions, he put them in the innermost cell and secured their feet to a stake.

About midnight, while Paul and Silas were praying and singing hymns to God as the prisoners listened, there was suddenly such a severe earthquake that the foundations of the jail shook; all the doors flew open, and the chains of all were pulled loose. When the jailer woke up and saw the prison doors wide open, he drew his sword and was about to kill himself, thinking that the prisoners had escaped. But Paul shouted out in a loud voice, "Do no harm to yourself; we are all here." He asked for a light and rushed in and, trembling with fear, he fell down before Paul and Silas. Then he brought them out and said, "Sirs, what must I do to be saved?" And they said, "Believe in the Lord Jesus and you and your household will be saved."

So they spoke the word of the Lord to him and to everyone in his house. He took them in at that hour of the night and bathed their wounds; then he and all his family were baptized at once. He brought them up into his house and provided a meal and with his household rejoiced at having come to faith in God. The word of the Lord.

Responsorial Psalm   Ps 138:1–2ab, 2cde–3, 7c–8

R. Your right hand saves me, O Lord.

I will give thanks to you, O Lord, with all my heart,
  for you have heard the words of my mouth;
  in the presence of the angels I will sing your praise;
I will worship at your holy temple,
  and give thanks to your name.

R. Your right hand saves me, O Lord.

Because of your kindness and your truth,
  you have made great above all things
  your name and your promise.
When I called, you answered me;
  you built up strength within me.

R. Your right hand saves me, O Lord.

Your right hand saves me.
The Lord will complete what he has done for me;
  your kindness, O Lord, endures forever;
  forsake not the work of your hands.

R. Your right hand saves me, O Lord.

Or: **R. Alleluia.**

> **Alleluia, alleluia** See Jn 16:7, 13
> I will send to you the Spirit of truth, says the Lord;
> he will guide you to all truth.
> **Alleluia, alleluia**

GOSPEL

Jn 16:5–11

For if I do not go, the Advocate will not come to you.

A reading from the holy Gospel according to John

Jesus said to his disciples: "Now I am going to the one who sent me, and not one of you asks me, 'Where are you going?' But because I told you this, grief has filled your hearts. But I tell you the truth, it is better for you that I go. For if I do not go, the Advocate will not come to you. But if I go, I will send him to you. And when he comes he will convict the world in regard to sin and righteousness and condemnation: sin, because they do not believe in me; righteousness, because I am going to the Father and you will no longer see me; condemnation, because the ruler of this world has been condemned."

The Gospel of the Lord.

Liturgy of the Eucharist, *p. 897.*

Prayer over the Gifts

Pray, brethren...

Lord,
give us joy by these Easter mysteries;
let the continuous offering of this sacrifice
by which we are renewed
bring us to eternal happiness.

We ask this in the name of Jesus the Lord.

Preface of Easter II–V, *pp. 945–946.*

Communion Antiphon

Christ had to suffer and to rise from the dead, and so enter into his glory, alleluia.

(See Lk 24:46, 26)

Prayer after Communion

Let us pray.

> *Pause for silent prayer, if this has not preceded.*

Lord,
may this celebration of our redemption
help us in this life
and lead us to eternal happiness.
We ask this through Christ our Lord.

Wednesday

Entrance Antiphon

**I will be a witness to you in the world, O Lord. I will spread
the knowledge of your name among my brothers, alleluia.**

(Ps 17:50; 21:23)

Opening Prayer

Lord,
as we celebrate your Son's resurrection,
so may we rejoice with all the saints
when he returns in glory,
who lives and reigns with you and the Holy Spirit,
one God, for ever and ever.

TODAY'S LIVING WORD

Paul writes in 1 Corinthians, "For Jews demand signs and Greeks
look for wisdom, but we proclaim Christ crucified, a stumbling block
to Jews and foolishness to Gentiles" (1:22–23). To some extent this
observation may reflect Paul's experience in Athens, reported in today's first reading. In his speech in the Areopagus he presents a familiar argument, one cited in the new *Catechism*, which concludes
as Paul does that the religious beliefs and behaviors of human beings

throughout history indicate that they are by nature religious (n. 28). At the same time, Paul's very modest success among the Athenians shows how difficult it can be to touch and to transform the religious imagination of a people (n. 29).

Today's Gospel suggests that even people who have been initiated in the following of Christ continue to need the Paraclete's help to grow in their understanding of what Jesus taught. So the Spirit continues, to the present day, to be "the Church's living memory" and loving mentor (*Catechism of the Catholic Church,* n. 1099).

FIRST READING
Acts 17:15, 22 —18:1

What therefore you unknowingly worship, I proclaim to you.

A reading from the Acts of the Apostles

After Paul's escorts had taken him to Athens, they came away with instructions for Silas and Timothy to join him as soon as possible.

Then Paul stood up at the Areopagus and said: "You Athenians, I see that in every respect you are very religious. For as I walked around looking carefully at your shrines, I even discovered an altar inscribed, 'To an Unknown God.' What therefore you unknowingly worship, I proclaim to you. The God who made the world and all that is in it, the Lord of heaven and earth, does not dwell in sanctuaries made by human hands, nor is he served by human hands because he needs anything. Rather it is he who gives to everyone life and breath and everything. He made from one the whole human race to dwell on the entire surface of the earth, and he fixed the ordered seasons and the boundaries of their regions, so that people might seek God, even perhaps grope for him and find him, though indeed he is not far from any one of us. For 'In him we live and move and have our being,' as even some of your poets have said, 'For we too are his offspring.' Since therefore we are the offspring of God, we ought not to think that the divinity is like an image fashioned from gold, silver, or stone by human art and imagination. God has overlooked the times of ignorance, but now he demands that all people everywhere repent because he has established a day on which he will 'judge the world with justice' through a man he has appointed, and he has provided confirmation for all by raising him from the dead."

When they heard about resurrection of the dead, some began to scoff, but others said, "We should like to hear you on this some other time." And so Paul left them. But some did join him, and became believers. Among them were Dionysius, a member of the Court of the Areopagus, a woman named Damaris, and others with them.

After this he left Athens and went to Corinth.

The word of the Lord.

Responsorial Psalm   Ps 148:1–2, 11–12, 13, 14

R. Heaven and earth are full of your glory.

Praise the LORD from the heavens;
   praise him in the heights.
Praise him, all you his angels;
   praise him, all you his hosts.

R. Heaven and earth are full of your glory.

Let the kings of the earth and all peoples,
   the princes and all the judges of the earth,
Young men too, and maidens,
   old men and boys.

R. Heaven and earth are full of your glory.

Praise the name of the LORD,
   for his name alone is exalted;
His majesty is above earth and heaven.

R. Heaven and earth are full of your glory.

He has lifted up the horn of his people;
Be this his praise from all his faithful ones,
   from the children of Israel, the people close to him.
   Alleluia.

R. Heaven and earth are full of your glory.

Or: **R. Alleluia.**

> **Alleluia, alleluia**   Jn 14:16
> I will ask the Father
> and he will give you another Advocate
> to be with you always.
> **Alleluia, alleluia**

GOSPEL

Jn 16:12–15

When the Spirit of truth comes, he will guide you to all truth.

A reading from the holy Gospel according to John

Jesus said to his disciples: "I have much more to tell you, but you cannot bear it now. But when he comes, the Spirit of truth, he will guide you to all truth. He will not speak on his own, but he will speak what he hears, and will declare to you the things that are coming. He will glorify me, because he will take from what is mine and declare it to you. Everything that the Father has is mine; for this reason I told you that he will take from what is mine and declare it to you."

The Gospel of the Lord.

Liturgy of the Eucharist, *p. 897.*

Prayer over the Gifts

Pray, brethren...

Lord God,
by this holy exchange of gifts

you share with us your divine life.
Grant that everything we do
may be directed by the knowledge of your truth.
We ask this in the name of Jesus the Lord.

Preface of Easter II–V, *pp. 945–946.*

Communion Antiphon

The Lord says, I have chosen you from the world to go and bear fruit that will last, alleluia.   (See Jn 15:16, 19)

Prayer after Communion

Let us pray.

Pause for silent prayer, if this has not preceded.

Merciful Father,
may these mysteries give us new purpose
and bring us to a new life in you.

Grant this through Christ our Lord.

Thursday

For the ASCENSION, *see* **Vatican II Sunday Missal,** *p. 517.*

This Mass is celebrated in places where the celebration of the Ascension is transferred to the Seventh Sunday of Easter.

Entrance Antiphon

When you walked at the head of your people, O God, and lived with them on their journey, the earth shook at your presence, and the skies poured forth their rain, alleluia.

(See Ps 67:8–9, 20)

Opening Prayer

Father,
may we always give you thanks
for raising Christ our Lord to glory,

because we are his people
and share the salvation he won,
for he lives and reigns with you and the Holy Spirit,
one God, for ever and ever.

TODAY'S LIVING WORD

In today's Gospel, Jesus puts this riddle to his disciples: "A little while and you will no longer see me, and again a little while later and you will see me." The disciples, not for the first time, are completely baffled by Jesus' words. Even though they have all the pieces of the puzzle ("Because I am going to the Father"), they cannot put them together. It is as though grief at the impending death of Jesus has already overtaken them, and in that breathless "little while" between the departure of one Paraclete and the arrival of the other, they are incapable of understanding. Jesus responds to their perplexity not with a solution, but with a solemn promise. "Your grief will become joy," he tells them, because the Spirit of truth will come and will answer all their questions (Jn 16:13, 23).

Impelled by the same Spirit of truth, Paul in the first reading preaches the word to both Jews and Greeks in Corinth. This is Luke's account of Paul's work among the Corinthians. Although it is ostensibly Paul's story, the plot is distinctly Lucan. Luke's purpose in Acts is to show how the mission to the Gentiles emerged as a result of the Jews' refusal of the Gospel. This is the gist of today's reading. Yet, even here it is apparent that the Jewish mission was not a complete failure. Crispus, the synagogue official, and his entire household believe and are baptized, because the Spirit of truth "blows where it wills" (Jn 3:8).

FIRST READING
Acts 18:1–8

*Paul stayed with them and worked
and entered into discussions in the synagogue.*

A reading from the Acts of the Apostles

Paul left Athens and went to Corinth. There he met a Jew named Aquila, a native of Pontus, who had recently come from Italy with his wife Priscilla because Claudius had ordered all the Jews to leave Rome. He went to visit them and, because he practiced the same trade, stayed with them and worked, for they were tentmakers by trade. Every sabbath, he entered into discussions in the synagogue, attempting to convince both Jews and Greeks.

When Silas and Timothy came down from Macedonia, Paul began to occupy himself totally with preaching the word, testifying to the Jews that the Christ was Jesus. When they opposed him and reviled him, he shook out his garments and said to them, "Your blood be on your heads! I am clear of responsibility. From now on I will go to the Gentiles." So he left there and went to a house belonging to a man named Titus Justus, a worshiper of God; his house was next to a synagogue. Crispus, the synagogue official, came to believe in the Lord along with his entire household, and many of the Corinthians who heard believed and were baptized.

The word of the Lord.

Responsorial Psalm   Ps 98:1, 2–3ab, 3cd–4

R. The Lord has revealed to the nations his saving power.

Sing to the LORD a new song,
   for he has done wondrous deeds;
His right hand has won victory for him,
   his holy arm.

R. The Lord has revealed to the nations his saving power.

The LORD has made his salvation known:
   in the sight of the nations he has revealed his justice.
He has remembered his kindness and his faithfulness
   toward the house of Israel.

R. The Lord has revealed to the nations his saving power.

All the ends of the earth have seen
 the salvation by our God.
Sing joyfully to the LORD, all you lands;
 break into song; sing praise.

R. The Lord has revealed to the nations his saving power.

Or: **R. Alleluia.**

> **Alleluia, alleluia** See Jn 14:18
> I will not leave you orphans, says the Lord;
> I will come back to you, and your hearts will rejoice.
> **Alleluia, alleluia**

GOSPEL

Jn 16:16–20

You will grieve, but your grief will become joy.

A reading from the holy Gospel according to John

Jesus said to his disciples: "A little while and you will no longer see me, and again a little while later and you will see me." So some of his disciples said to one another, "What does this mean that he is saying to us, 'A little while and you will not see me, and again a little while and you will see me,' and 'Because I am going to the Father'?" So they said, "What is this 'little while' of which he speaks? We do not know what he means." Jesus knew that they wanted to ask him, so he said to them, "Are you discussing with one another what I said, 'A little while and you will not see me, and again a little while and you will see me'? Amen, amen, I say to you, you will weep and mourn, while the world rejoices; you will grieve, but your grief will become joy."

The Gospel of the Lord.

Liturgy of the Eucharist, *p. 897.*

Prayer over the Gifts

Pray, brethren...

Lord,
accept our prayers and offerings.
Make us worthy of your sacraments of love
by granting us your forgiveness.
We ask this in the name of Jesus the Lord.

Preface of Easter II–V, *pp. 945–946.*

Communion Antiphon

I, the Lord, am with you always, until the end of the world,
alleluia.   (Mt 28:20)

Prayer after Communion

Let us pray.
> *Pause for silent prayer, if this has not preceded.*

Almighty and ever-living Lord,
you restored us to life
by raising Christ from death.
Strengthen us by this Easter sacrament;
may we feel its saving power in our daily life.
We ask this through Christ our Lord.

Friday

Entrance Antiphon

By your blood, O Lord, you have redeemed us from every tribe
and tongue, from every nation and people: you have made us
into the Kingdom of God, alleluia.   (See Rv 5:9–10)

Opening Prayer

Father,
you have given us eternal life

through Christ your Son
who rose from the dead
and now sits at your right hand.
When he comes again in glory,
may he clothe with immortality
all who have been born again in baptism.

We ask this through our Lord Jesus Christ, your Son,
who lives and reigns with you and the Holy Spirit,
one God, for ever and ever.

In places where the Ascension is celebrated on the Seventh Sunday of Easter,
the following Opening Prayer is said:

Lord,
hear our prayer
that your gospel may reach all men
and that we who receive salvation through your Word
may be your children in deed as well as in name.

We ask this through our Lord Jesus Christ, your Son,
who lives and reigns with you and the Holy Spirit,
one God, for ever and ever.

TODAY'S LIVING WORD

Today's reading from Acts is rather strange. In a vision, the risen
Lord assures Paul, "No one will attack and harm you." Then almost
immediately Paul is attacked by his opponents who bring him before
the bench of the proconsul Gallio. Gallio, however, has no patience
with intra-Jewish disputes. So Paul is released unharmed.

In today's Gospel, Jesus returns to the theme of his departure.
He tells them that what his disciples will witness as the throes of
death, his suffering and death, are in fact the pangs of birth.

Isaiah used the image of the woman in labor to announce the
arrival of a new day, the day of the Lord (26:16–17; 66:7–10). That
day will dawn when Jesus rises. "On that day" their hearts will rejoice

and all their questions will be answered. But it seems that in some ways even now after the resurrection we are still waiting, our questions unanswered, forced like Paul into an uneasy truce with the world around us. So Easter comes again to tell us that, from the tomb, a Man—the risen Jesus—has been born into the world. That joy no one can take from us.

FIRST READING
Acts 18:9–18

I have many people in this city.

A reading from the Acts of the Apostles

One night while Paul was in Corinth, the Lord said to him in a vision, "Do not be afraid. Go on speaking, and do not be silent, for I am with you. No one will attack and harm you, for I have many people in this city." He settled there for a year and a half and taught the word of God among them.

But when Gallio was proconsul of Achaia, the Jews rose up together against Paul and brought him to the tribunal, saying, "This man is inducing people to worship God contrary to the law." When Paul was about to reply, Gallio spoke to the Jews, "If it were a matter of some crime or malicious fraud, I should with reason hear the complaint of you Jews; but since it is a question of arguments over doctrine and titles and your own law, see to it yourselves. I do not wish to be a judge of such matters." And he drove them away from the tribunal. They all seized Sosthenes, the synagogue official, and beat him in full view of the tribunal. But none of this was of concern to Gallio.

Paul remained for quite some time, and after saying farewell to the brothers he sailed for Syria, together with Priscilla and Aquila. At Cenchreae he had shaved his head because he had taken a vow.

The word of the Lord.

Responsorial Psalm   Ps 47:2–3, 4–5, 6–7

R. God is king of all the earth.

All you peoples, clap your hands,
  shout to God with cries of gladness,
For the LORD, the Most High, the awesome,
  is the great king over all the earth.

R. God is king of all the earth.

He brings people under us;
  nations under our feet.
He chooses for us our inheritance,
  the glory of Jacob, whom he loves.

R. God is king of all the earth.

God mounts his throne amid shouts of joy;
  the LORD, amid trumpet blasts.
Sing praise to God, sing praise;
  sing praise to our king, sing praise.

R. God is king of all the earth.

Or: **R. Alleluia.**

Alleluia, alleluia See Lk 24:46, 26
Christ had to suffer and to rise from the dead,
and so enter into his glory.
Alleluia, alleluia

GOSPEL   Jn 16:20–23
No one will take your joy away from you.

A reading from the holy Gospel according to John

Jesus said to his disciples: "Amen, amen, I say to you, you will weep and mourn, while the world rejoices; you will grieve, but your grief will become joy. When a woman is in labor, she is in anguish because her hour has arrived; but when she has given birth to a child, she no longer remembers the pain because of her joy that a child has been born into the world. So you also are now in anguish. But I will see you again, and your hearts will rejoice, and no one will take your joy away from you. On that day you will not question me about anything. Amen, amen, I say to you, whatever you ask the Father in my name he will give you."

The Gospel of the Lord.

Liturgy of the Eucharist, *p. 897.*

Prayer over the Gifts

Pray, brethren...

Lord,
accept these gifts from your family.
May we hold fast to the life you have given us
and come to the eternal gifts you promise.
We ask this in the name of Jesus the Lord.

If the Ascension has been celebrated on Thursday of this week:
Preface of Ascension I–II, *p. 947.*

If the Ascension is celebrated on the Seventh Sunday of Easter:
Preface of Easter II–V, *pp. 945–946.*

Communion Antiphon

Christ our Lord was put to death for our sins; and he rose again to make us worthy of life, alleluia.   (Rom 4:25)

Prayer after Communion

Let us pray.

Pause for silent prayer, if this has not preceded.

Lord,
watch over those you have saved in Christ.
May we who are redeemed by his suffering and death
always rejoice in his resurrection,
for he is Lord for ever and ever.

Saturday

Entrance Antiphon

You are a people God claims as his own, to praise him who called you out of darkness into his marvelous light, alleluia.

(1 Pt 2:9)

Opening Prayer

Father,
at your Son's ascension into heaven
you promised to send the Holy Spirit
on your apostles.
You filled them with heavenly wisdom:
fill us also with the gift of your Spirit.

Grant this through our Lord Jesus Christ, your Son,
who lives and reigns with you and the Holy Spirit,
one God, for ever and ever.

In places where the Ascension is celebrated on the Seventh Sunday of Easter, the following Opening Prayer is said:

Lord,
teach us to know you better
by doing good to others.
Help us to grow in your love
and come to understand the eternal mystery
of Christ's death and resurrection.

We ask this through our Lord Jesus Christ, your Son,
who lives and reigns with you and the Holy Spirit,
one God, for ever and ever.

TODAY'S LIVING WORD

Today's first reading introduces Apollos, the impassioned and eloquent Jew from Alexandria, who was "an authority on the scriptures" and "had been instructed in the Way of the Lord...although he knew only the baptism of John." Where he received his instruction in the new way is a mystery. Alexandria was a cosmopolitan city and a center of learning, but the beginnings of the Church there are not known. Given that the Old Testament had been translated from Hebrew into Greek in Alexandria (from ca. 200 B.C.E.), Apollos' knowledge of the Scriptures is not surprising. In Ephesus and later in Corinth, he distinguished himself by his competence in "establishing from the scriptures that the Messiah is Jesus."

Luke in Luke-Acts often refers to the Christian use of the Scriptures. One role of the Paraclete in John was to make intelligible what Jesus had said "in figures of speech" and what he had done in his earthly life by referring it back to the Scriptures. In John's view, this activity of the Spirit enabled Christians like Apollos to show that Jesus was the fulfillment of all that the Scriptures had promised.

FIRST READING   Acts 18:23–28

Apollos established from the Scriptures that the Christ is Jesus.

A reading from the Acts of the Apostles

After staying in Antioch some time, Paul left and traveled in orderly sequence through the Galatian country and Phrygia, bringing strength to all the disciples.

A Jew named Apollos, a native of Alexandria, an eloquent speaker, arrived in Ephesus. He was an authority on the Scriptures. He had been instructed in the Way of the Lord and, with ardent spirit, spoke and taught accurately about Jesus, although he knew only the baptism of John. He began to speak boldly in the synagogue; but when Priscilla and Aquila heard him, they took him aside and explained to him the Way of God more accurately. And when he wanted to cross to Achaia, the brothers encouraged him and wrote to the disciples there to welcome him. After his arrival he gave great assistance to those who had come to believe through grace. He vigorously refuted

the Jews in public, establishing from the Scriptures that the
Christ is Jesus.

The word of the Lord.

Responsorial Psalm

Ps 47:2-3, 8-9, 10

R. **God is king of all the earth.**

All you peoples, clap your hands;
  shout to God with cries of gladness.
For the LORD, the Most High, the awesome,
  is the great king over all the earth.

R. **God is king of all the earth.**

For king of all the earth is God;
  sing hymns of praise.
God reigns over the nations,
  God sits upon his holy throne.

R. **God is king of all the earth.**

The princes of the peoples are gathered together
  with the people of the God of Abraham.
For God's are the guardians of the earth;
  he is supreme.

R. **God is king of all the earth.**

Or: R. **Alleluia.**

Alleluia, alleluia Jn 16:28
I came from the Father and have come into the world;
now I am leaving the world and going back to the Father.
Alleluia, alleluia

GOSPEL

Jn 16:23b-28

My Father loves you because you have loved me and believed in me.

A reading from the holy Gospel according to John

Jesus said to his disciples: "Amen, amen, I say to you, whatever
you ask the Father in my name he will give you. Until now

you have not asked anything in my name; ask and you will receive, so that your joy may be complete.

"I have told you this in figures of speech. The hour is coming when I will no longer speak to you in figures but I will tell you clearly about the Father. On that day you will ask in my name, and I do not tell you that I will ask the Father for you. For the Father himself loves you, because you have loved me and have come to believe that I came from God. I came from the Father and have come into the world. Now I am leaving the world and going back to the Father."

The Gospel of the Lord.

Liturgy of the Eucharist, *p. 897.*

Prayer over the Gifts

Pray, brethren...

Merciful Lord,
make holy these gifts,
and let our spiritual sacrifice
make us an everlasting gift to you.

We ask this in the name of Jesus the Lord.

If the Ascension has been celebrated on Thursday of this week:
  Preface of Ascension I–II, *p. 947.*

If the Ascension is celebrated on the Seventh Sunday of Easter:
  Preface of Easter II–V, *pp. 945–946.*

Communion Antiphon

Father, I want the men you have given me to be with me where I am, so that they may see the glory you have given me, alleluia.
(Jn 17:24)

Prayer after Communion

Let us pray.

Pause for silent prayer, if this has not preceded.

Lord,
may this eucharist,
which we have celebrated in memory of your Son,
help us to grow in love.

We ask this in the name of Jesus the Lord.

SEVENTH WEEK OF EASTER
Monday

Entrance Antiphon

**You will receive power when the Holy Spirit comes upon you.
You will be my witnesses to all the world, alleluia.**   (Acts 1:8)

Opening Prayer

Lord,
send the power of your Holy Spirit upon us
that we may remain faithful
and do your will in our daily lives.

We ask this through our Lord Jesus Christ, your Son,
who lives and reigns with you and the Holy Spirit,
one God, for ever and ever.

TODAY'S LIVING WORD

Both of today's readings contain examples of incomplete confessions of faith. In Acts, Paul meets disciples who were baptized with the baptism of John, intended only to prepare the way for "the stronger One" who would baptize with the Holy Spirit (cf. Lk 3:15–16). As Luke Timothy Johnson remarks, "The fact that John apparently has disciples twenty years after his death in places as far from the Jordan as Alexandria (Apollos) and Ephesus, supports the portrait of John as an important religious figure in his own right."* The disciples, who had never even heard of the Holy Spirit, receive the Spirit's gifts.

Thinking they finally understand his words, the disciples of Jesus make a partial confession of faith in him. Like Peter at Caesarea Philippi (cf. Mk 8:27–30 and par.), they profess their belief that he has come from God, but they have not yet reckoned with the manner of his return to the Father. His hour is still coming, and it will usher in their hour as well. With a view to this—the loneliness of their hour—Jesus assures them, "I have conquered the world."

* *The Acts of the Apostles,* Sacra Pagina 5 (Collegeville: Liturgical Press, 1992), p. 338.

FIRST READING

Acts 19:1–8

Did you receive the Holy Spirit when you became believers?

A reading from the Acts of the Apostles

While Apollos was in Corinth, Paul traveled through the interior of the country and down to Ephesus where he found some disciples. He said to them, "Did you receive the Holy Spirit when you became believers?" They answered him, "We have never even heard that there is a Holy Spirit." He said, "How were you baptized?" They replied, "With the baptism of John." Paul then said, "John baptized with a baptism of repentance, telling the people to believe in the one who was to come after him, that is, in Jesus." When they heard this, they were baptized in the name of the Lord Jesus. And when Paul laid his hands on them, the Holy Spirit came upon them, and they spoke in tongues and prophesied. Altogether there were about twelve men.

He entered the synagogue, and for three months debated boldly with persuasive arguments about the Kingdom of God.

The word of the Lord.

Responsorial Psalm

Ps 68:2 –3ab, 4 – 5acd, 6–7ab

R. Sing to God, O kingdoms of the earth.

God arises; his enemies are scattered,
  and those who hate him flee before him.
As smoke is driven away, so are they driven;
  as wax melts before the fire.

R. Sing to God, O kingdoms of the earth.

But the just rejoice and exult before God;
  they are glad and rejoice.
Sing to God, chant praise to his name;
  whose name is the LORD.

R. Sing to God, O kingdoms of the earth.

The father of orphans and the defender of widows
  is God in his holy dwelling.
God gives a home to the forsaken;
  he leads forth prisoners to prosperity.

R. Sing to God, O kingdoms of the earth.

Or: **R. Alleluia.**

> **Alleluia, alleluia**   Col 3:1
> If then you were raised with Christ,
> seek what is above,
> where Christ is seated at the right hand of God.
> **Alleluia, alleluia**

GOSPEL

Jn 16:29 – 33

Take courage, I have conquered the world.

A reading from the holy Gospel according to John

The disciples said to Jesus, "Now you are talking plainly, and not in any figure of speech. Now we realize that you know everything and that you do not need to have anyone question you. Because of this we believe that you came from God." Jesus answered them, "Do you believe now? Behold, the hour is coming and has arrived when each of you will be scattered

Liturgy of the Eucharist, *p. 897.*

Prayer over the Gifts

Pray, brethren...

Father,
accept the prayers and offerings of your people
and bring us to the glory of heaven,
where Jesus is Lord for ever and ever.

Preface of Ascension I–II, *p. 947.*

Communion Antiphon

The Lord says, the Holy Spirit whom the Father will send in
my name will teach you all things, and remind you of all I have
said to you, alleluia.
(Jn 14:26)

Prayer after Communion

Let us pray.

Pause for silent prayer, if this has not preceded.

Lord,
may this eucharist,
which we have celebrated in memory of your Son,
help us to grow in love.
We ask this in the name of Jesus the Lord.

Wednesday

Entrance Antiphon

All nations, clap your hands. Shout with a voice of joy to God,
alleluia.
(Ps 46:2)

Opening Prayer

God of mercy,
unite your Church in the Holy Spirit

that we may serve you with all our hearts
and work together with unselfish love.

Grant this through our Lord Jesus Christ, your Son,
who lives and reigns with you and the Holy Spirit,
one God, for ever and ever.

TODAY'S LIVING WORD

Commentators often note that the prayer of Jesus resembles the prayer he taught his disciples. Today's excerpt has at least three points of contact with the Lord's Prayer. Jesus addresses God as Father, as he taught his disciples to do. He calls upon the Father's holy name and petitions the Father to deliver his disciples from the evil one.

Paul's prayer in Acts also echoes the prayer of Jesus. As both men prepare to leave those entrusted to their care, they voice their pastoral concerns. They worry that those they so carefully guarded will come to harm, that some may be lost (Jesus) or go astray (Paul). They recognize the grave dangers that threaten their communities, that "the world hated them" (Jesus), that "savage wolves...will not spare the flock" (Paul). So they pray. Jesus asks the Father to *"consecrate* them in the truth. Your *word* is truth"; and Paul commends them "to God and to that gracious *word* of his that can...give you the inheritance among all who are *consecrated."* For Jesus and for Paul, safety in a hostile world lies in being holy.

FIRST READING
Acts 20:28–38

I commend you to God who has the power to build you up
and to give you an inheritance.

A reading from the Acts of the Apostles

At Miletus, Paul spoke to the presbyters of the Church of Ephesus: "Keep watch over yourselves and over the whole flock of which the Holy Spirit has appointed you overseers, in which you tend the Church of God that he acquired with his own Blood. I know that after my departure savage wolves will come among you, and they will not spare the flock. And from your own group, men will come forward perverting the truth to draw the disciples away after them. So be vigilant and remember that for three years, night and day, I unceasingly admonished each of you with tears. And now I commend you to God and to that gracious word of his that can build you up and give you the inheritance among all who are consecrated. I have never wanted anyone's silver or gold or clothing. You know well that these very hands have served my needs and my companions. In every way I have shown you that by hard work of that sort we must help the weak, and keep in mind the words of the Lord Jesus who himself said, 'It is more blessed to give than to receive.'"

When he had finished speaking he knelt down and prayed with them all. They were all weeping loudly as they threw their arms around Paul and kissed him, for they were deeply distressed that he had said that they would never see his face again. Then they escorted him to the ship.

The word of the Lord.

Responsorial Psalm

Ps 68:29–30, 33–35a, 35bc–36ab

R. **Sing to God, O kingdoms of the earth.**

Show forth, O God, your power,
  the power, O God, with which you took our part;
For your temple in Jerusalem
  let the kings bring you gifts.

R. **Sing to God, O kingdoms of the earth.**

You kingdoms of the earth, sing to God,
  chant praise to the Lord
  who rides on the heights of the ancient heavens.
Behold, his voice resounds, the voice of power:
  "Confess the power of God!"

R. **Sing to God, O kingdoms of the earth.**

Over Israel is his majesty;
  his power is in the skies.
Awesome in his sanctuary is God, the God of Israel;
  he gives power and strength to his people.

R. Sing to God, O kingdoms of the earth.

Or: **R. Alleluia.**

> Alleluia, alleluia   See Jn 17:17b, 17a
> Your word, O Lord, is truth;
>   consecrate us in the truth.
> Alleluia, alleluia

GOSPEL

Jn 17:11b–19

May they be one just as we are one.

A reading from the holy Gospel according to John

Lifting up his eyes to heaven, Jesus prayed, saying: "Holy Father, keep them in your name that you have given me, so that they may be one just as we are one. When I was with them I protected them in your name that you gave me, and I guarded them, and none of them was lost except the son of destruction, in order that the Scripture might be fulfilled. But now I am coming to you. I speak this in the world so that they may share my joy completely. I gave them your word, and the world hated them, because they do not belong to the world any more than I belong to the world. I do not ask that you take them out of the world but that you keep them from the Evil One. They do not belong to the world any more than I belong to the world. Consecrate them in the truth. Your word is truth. As you sent me into the world, so I sent them into the world. And I consecrate myself for them, so that they also may be consecrated in truth."

The Gospel of the Lord.

Liturgy of the Eucharist, *p. 897.*

Prayer over the Gifts

Pray, brethren...

Lord,
accept this offering we make at your command.
May these sacred mysteries by which we worship you
bring your salvation to perfection within us.

We ask this in the name of Jesus the Lord.

Preface of Ascension I–II, *p. 947.*

Communion Antiphon

The Lord says: When the Holy Spirit comes to you, the Spirit whom I shall send, the Spirit of truth who proceeds from the Father, he will bear witness to me, and you also will be my witnesses, alleluia.   (Jn 15:26–27)

Prayer after Communion

Let us pray.

Pause for silent prayer, if this has not preceded.

Lord,
may our participation in the eucharist
increase your life in us,
cleanse us from sin,
and make us increasingly worthy
of this holy sacrament.

We ask this through Christ our Lord.

Thursday

Entrance Antiphon

Let us come to God's presence with confidence, because we will find mercy, and strength when we need it, alleluia.

(Heb 4:16)

Opening Prayer

Father,
let your Spirit come upon us with power
to fill us with his gifts.
May he make our hearts pleasing to you,
and ready to do your will.

We ask this through our Lord Jesus Christ, your Son,
who lives and reigns with you and the Holy Spirit,
one God, for ever and ever.

TODAY'S LIVING WORD

At first glance, it may seem that in today's reading Paul is using a clever ploy to extricate himself from a tight spot. However, a closer look shows Paul speaking the simple truth. He is being tried precisely for his hope in the resurrection of the dead, of which the risen Jesus is the firstfruits (cf. 1 Cor 15:20). Paul never shrinks from preaching the Gospel in its entirety. Only this time the ensuing debate between the Sadducees, who do not believe in resurrection, and the Pharisees, who do, works to his advantage.

It is entertaining to read about the exploits of Paul. It is more daunting to reflect on the prayer of Jesus, which in today's Gospel reaches beyond his immediate circle to include all of us in his oneness with the Father. For John, says James McPolin, communion with God means inclusion in the community within God, through which in turn life in human community is radically changed.*

* *John*, New Testament Message 6, 4th ed. (Wilmington: Michael Glazier, Inc., 1986), p. 228.

FIRST READING
Acts 22:30; 23:6–11

You must bear witness in Rome.

A reading from the Acts of the Apostles

Wishing to determine the truth about why Paul was being accused by the Jews, the commander freed him and ordered the chief priests and the whole Sanhedrin to convene. Then he brought Paul down and made him stand before them.

Paul was aware that some were Sadducees and some Pharisees, so he called out before the Sanhedrin, "My brothers, I am a Pharisee, the son of Pharisees; I am on trial for hope in the resurrection of the dead." When he said this, a dispute broke out between the Pharisees and Sadducees, and the group became divided. For the Sadducees say that there is no resurrection or angels or spirits, while the Pharisees acknowledge all three. A great uproar occurred, and some scribes belonging to the Pharisee party stood up and sharply argued, "We find nothing wrong with this man. Suppose a spirit or an angel has spoken to him?" The dispute was so serious that the commander, afraid that Paul would be torn to pieces by them, ordered his troops to go down and rescue Paul from their midst and take him into the compound. The following night the Lord stood by him and said, "Take courage. For just as you have borne witness to my cause in Jerusalem, so you must also bear witness in Rome."

The word of the Lord.

Responsorial Psalm   Ps 16:1–2a and 5, 7–8, 9–10, 11

R. Keep me safe, O God; you are my hope.

Keep me, O God, for in you I take refuge;
    I say to the LORD, "My Lord are you."
O LORD, my allotted portion and my cup,
    you it is who hold fast my lot.

R. Keep me safe, O God; you are my hope.

I bless the LORD who counsels me;
    even in the night my heart exhorts me.
I set the LORD ever before me;
    with him at my right hand I shall not be disturbed.

R. Keep me safe, O God; you are my hope.

Therefore my heart is glad and my soul rejoices,
   my body, too, abides in confidence;
Because you will not abandon my soul to the nether world,
   nor will you suffer your faithful one to undergo corruption.

R. Keep me safe, O God; you are my hope.

You will show me the path to life,
   fullness of joys in your presence,
   the delights at your right hand forever.

R. Keep me safe, O God; you are my hope.

Or: **R. Alleluia.**

> **Alleluia, alleluia** Jn 17:21
> May they all be one as you, Father, are in me and I in you,
> that the world may believe that you sent me, says the Lord.
> **Alleluia, alleluia**

GOSPEL

Jn 17:20–26

May they all be one.

A reading from the holy Gospel according to John

Lifting up his eyes to heaven, Jesus prayed saying: "I pray not only for these, but also for those who will believe in me through their word, so that they may all be one, as you, Father, are in me and I in you, that they also may be in us, that the world may believe that you sent me. And I have given them the glory you gave me, so that they may be one, as we are one, I in them and you in me, that they may be brought to perfection as one, that the world may know that you sent me, and that you loved them even as you loved me. Father, they are your gift to me. I wish that where I am they also may be with me, that they may see my glory that you gave me, because you loved me before the foundation of the world. Righteous Father, the world also does not know you, but I know you, and they know that you sent me. I made known to them your name and I will make it known, that the love with which you loved me may be in them and I in them."

The Gospel of the Lord.

Liturgy of the Eucharist, *p. 897.*

Prayer over the Gifts

Pray, brethren...

Merciful Lord,
make holy these gifts,
and let our spiritual sacrifice
make us an everlasting gift to you.

We ask this in the name of Jesus the Lord.

Preface of Ascension I–II, *p. 947.*

Communion Antiphon

This is the word of Jesus: It is best for me to leave you; be-cause if I do not go, the Spirit will not come to you, alleluia.

(Jn 16:7)

Prayer after Communion

Let us pray.

Pause for silent prayer, if this has not preceded.

Lord,
renew us by the mysteries we have shared.
Help us to know you
and prepare us for the gifts of the Spirit.

We ask this through Christ our Lord.

Friday

Entrance Antiphon

Christ loved us and has washed away our sins with his blood, and has made us a kingdom of priests to serve his God and Father, alleluia.
(Rv 1:5–6)

Opening Prayer

Father,
in glorifying Christ and sending us your Spirit,
you open the way to eternal life.
May our sharing in this gift increase our love
and make our faith grow stronger.

Grant this through our Lord Jesus Christ, your Son,
who lives and reigns with you and the Holy Spirit,
one God, for ever and ever.

TODAY'S LIVING WORD

Today's readings foreshadow the deaths of Paul and Peter respectively. In the account from Acts, the Roman procurator Festus refers Paul's case to King Agrippa II and his sister, Bernice—for their entertainment as much as anything else. Jesus had told his disciples that they would be paraded "before kings and governors because of my name" (Lk 21:12) and so it is with Paul, in Jerusalem now and later in Rome before the emperor.

The appendix of John's Gospel describes Jesus asking a chastened Peter three times to profess his love for him. To each assurance of Peter's love, Jesus responds with the command, "Feed my lambs…. Tend my sheep…. Feed my sheep." Peter will be shepherd of the flock, the followers of Jesus. Since, as Jesus taught, "A good shepherd lays down his life for the sheep" (Jn 10:11), there follows a prophecy indicating to Peter "by what kind of death he would glorify God."

FIRST READING

Acts 25:13b – 21

Jesus was dead, whom Paul claimed to be alive.

A reading from the Acts of the Apostles

King Agrippa and Bernice arrived in Caesarea on a visit to Festus. Since they spent several days there, Festus referred Paul's case to the king, saying, "There is a man here left in custody by Felix. When I was in Jerusalem the chief priests and the elders of the Jews brought charges against him and demanded his condemnation. I answered them that it was not Roman practice to hand over an accused person before he has faced his accusers and had the opportunity to defend himself against their charge. So when they came together here, I made no delay; the next day I took my seat on the tribunal and ordered the man to be brought in. His accusers stood around him, but did not charge him with any of the crimes I suspected. Instead they had some issues with him about their own religion and about a certain Jesus who had died but who Paul claimed was alive. Since I was at a loss how to investigate this controversy, I asked if he were willing to go to Jerusalem and there stand trial on these charges. And when Paul appealed that he be held in custody for the Emperor's decision, I ordered him held until I could send him to Caesar."

The word of the Lord.

Responsorial Psalm

Ps 103:1–2, 11–12, 19–20ab

R. The Lord has established his throne in heaven.

Bless the Lord, O my soul;
  and all my being, bless his holy name.
Bless the Lord, O my soul,
  and forget not all his benefits.

R. The Lord has established his throne in heaven.

For as the heavens are high above the earth,
  so surpassing is his kindness toward those who fear him.
As far as the east is from the west,
  so far has he put our transgressions from us.

R. The Lord has established his throne in heaven.

The LORD has established his throne in heaven,
  and his kingdom rules over all.
Bless the LORD, all you his angels,
  you mighty in strength, who do his bidding.

R. The Lord has established his throne in heaven.

Or: **R. Alleluia.**

> **Alleluia, alleluia**   Jn 14:26
> The Holy Spirit will teach you everything
> and remind you of all I told you.
> **Alleluia, alleluia**

GOSPEL   Jn 21:15 –19

Feed my lambs, feed my sheep.

A reading from the holy Gospel according to John

After Jesus had revealed himself to his disciples and eaten
breakfast with them, he said to Simon Peter, "Simon, son of
John, do you love me more than these?" Simon Peter answered
him, "Yes, Lord, you know that I love you." Jesus said to him,
"Feed my lambs." He then said to Simon Peter a second time,
"Simon, son of John, do you love me?" Simon Peter answered
him, "Yes, Lord, you know that I love you." He said to him,
"Tend my sheep." He said to him the third time, "Simon, son
of John, do you love me?" Peter was distressed that he had
said to him a third time, "Do you love me?" and he said to
him, "Lord, you know everything; you know that I love you."

Jesus said to him, "Feed my sheep. Amen, amen, I say to you, when you were younger, you used to dress yourself and go where you wanted; but when you grow old, you will stretch out your hands, and someone else will dress you and lead you where you do not want to go." He said this signifying by what kind of death he would glorify God. And when he had said this, he said to him, "Follow me."

The Gospel of the Lord.

Liturgy of the Eucharist, *p. 897.*

Prayer over the Gifts

Pray, brethren...

Father of love and mercy,
we place our offering before you.
Send your Holy Spirit to cleanse our lives
so that our gifts may be acceptable.

We ask this through Christ our Lord.

Preface of Ascension I–II, *p. 947.*

Communion Antiphon

When the Spirit of truth comes, says the Lord, he will lead you to the whole truth, alleluia. (Jn 16:13)

Prayer after Communion

Let us pray.

Pause for silent prayer, if this has not preceded.

God our Father,
the eucharist is our bread of life
and the sacrament of our forgiveness.
May our sharing in this mystery
bring us to eternal life,
where Jesus is Lord for ever and ever.

Saturday
Mass in the Morning

Entrance Antiphon

The disciples were constantly at prayer together, with Mary the mother of Jesus, the other women, and the brothers of Jesus, alleluia.
(Acts 1:14)

Opening Prayer

Almighty Father,
let the love we have celebrated in this Easter season
be put into practice in our daily lives.

We ask this through our Lord Jesus Christ, your Son,
who lives and reigns with you and the Holy Spirit,
one God, for ever and ever.

TODAY'S LIVING WORD

Today's reading from Acts finds Paul in Rome, under house arrest. But though he is chained like a common criminal, the word of God is not chained (cf. 2 Tm 2:9). He spends his days preaching "the Kingdom of God" and teaching "about the Lord Jesus Christ."

As the end of today's Gospel attests, behind the Fourth Gospel stands the unnamed disciple "whom Jesus loved," the hero of the Johannine community. He appears in the second half of the Gospel, always in juxtaposition with Peter. So it is not surprising to find him here. When Peter asks, "What about him?" Jesus answers enigmatically, "What if I want him to remain until I come?" What does this mean, if not that the beloved disciple is not going to die? Raymond Brown suggests that the answer lies in the disciple's "dual nature." As an actual person, the beloved disciple must have died in due course. But as the perfect disciple, embodying all who are loved by Jesus because they love him and keep his commandments, he must remain until Jesus returns.* The Church must never be without him.

* *A Risen Christ in Eastertime* (Collegeville: Liturgical Press, 1991), p. 95.

FIRST READING

Acts 28:16 – 20, 30 – 31

Paul remained at Rome, proclaiming the Kingdom of God.

A reading from the Acts of the Apostles

When he entered Rome, Paul was allowed to live by himself, with the soldier who was guarding him.

Three days later he called together the leaders of the Jews. When they had gathered he said to them, "My brothers, although I had done nothing against our people or our ancestral customs, I was handed over to the Romans as a prisoner from Jerusalem. After trying my case the Romans wanted to release me, because they found nothing against me deserving the death penalty. But when the Jews objected, I was obliged to appeal to Caesar, even though I had no accusation to make against my own nation. This is the reason, then, I have requested to see you and to speak with you, for it is on account of the hope of Israel that I wear these chains."

He remained for two full years in his lodgings. He received all who came to him, and with complete assurance and without hindrance he proclaimed the Kingdom of God and taught about the Lord Jesus Christ.

The word of the Lord.

Responsorial Psalm

Ps 11:4, 5 and 7

R. The just will gaze on your face, O Lord.

The LORD is in his holy temple;
  the LORD's throne is in heaven.
His eyes behold,
  his searching glance is on mankind.

R. The just will gaze on your face, O Lord.

The LORD searches the just and the wicked;

the lover of violence he hates.
For the LORD is just, he loves just deeds;
  the upright shall see his face.

R. The just will gaze on your face, O Lord.

Or: **R. Alleluia.**

Alleluia, alleluia Jn 16:7, 13
I will send to you the Spirit of truth, says the Lord;
he will guide you to all truth.
Alleluia, alleluia

GOSPEL

Jn 21:20 – 25

*This is the disciple who has written these things
and his testimony is true.*

A reading from the conclusion of the holy Gospel according to John

Peter turned and saw the disciple following whom Jesus loved, the one who had also reclined upon his chest during the supper and had said, "Master, who is the one who will betray you?" When Peter saw him, he said to Jesus, "Lord, what about him?" Jesus said to him, "What if I want him to remain until I come? What concern is it of yours? You follow me." So the word spread among the brothers that that disciple would not die. But Jesus had not told him that he would not die, just "What if I want him to remain until I come? What concern is it of yours?"

It is this disciple who testifies to these things and has written them, and we know that his testimony is true. There are also many other things that Jesus did, but if these were to be described individually, I do not think the whole world would contain the books that would be written.

The Gospel of the Lord.

Liturgy of the Eucharist, *p. 897.*

Prayer over the Gifts

Pray, brethren...

Lord,
may the coming of the Holy Spirit
prepare us to receive these holy sacraments,
for he is our forgiveness.

We ask this in the name of Jesus the Lord.

Preface of Ascension I–II, *p. 947.*

Communion Antiphon

The Lord says: The Holy Spirit will give glory to me, because he takes my words from me and will hand them on to you, alleluia.

(Jn 16:14)

Prayer after Communion

Let us pray.

Pause for silent prayer, if this has not preceded.

Father of mercy,
hear our prayers
that we may leave our former selves behind
and serve you with holy and renewed hearts.

Grant this through Christ our Lord.

For the VIGIL MASS OF PENTECOST, *see the* **Vatican II Sunday Missal,** *p. 544.*

THE ORDER OF MASS

**Lord, by your cross and resurrection
you have set us free.
You are the Savior of the world.**

INTRODUCTORY RITES

Acts of prayer and penitence prepare us to meet Christ as he comes in Word and Sacrament. We gather as a worshiping community to celebrate our unity with him and with one another in faith.

ENTRANCE SONG

Joined together as Christ's people, we open the celebration by raising our voices in praise of God who is present among us. This song should deepen our unity as it introduces the Mass we celebrate today.

After the people have assembled, the priest and the ministers go to the altar while the entrance song is being sung.

> *If there is no singing at the entrance, the antiphon in the missal is recited either by the people, by some of them, or by a reader. (Turn to the Proper of the day for the* **Entrance Antiphon.** *For the page number of the Proper of the day, see the* **Calendars,** *on pages 12–25 and 26–41.) Otherwise, it is said by the priest after the greeting.*

When the priest comes to the altar, he makes the customary reverence with the ministers, kisses the altar and (if incense is used) incenses it. Then, with the ministers, he goes to the chair.

GREETING

After the entrance song, the priest and the faithful remain standing and make the sign of the cross, as the priest says:

> Priest: In the name of the Father, and of the Son,
> and of the Holy Spirit.
>
> People: **Amen.**

The priest welcomes us in the name of the Lord. We show our union with God, our neighbor, and the priest by a united response to his greeting.

> **a**
>
> Priest: The grace of our Lord Jesus Christ and the
> love of God and the fellowship of the Holy
> Spirit be with you all.
>
> People: **And also with you.**

b	Priest:	The grace and peace of God our Father and the Lord Jesus Christ be with you.
	People:	**Blessed be God, the Father of our Lord Jesus Christ.**
		or:
		And also with you.
c	Priest:	The Lord be with you.
	People:	**And also with you.**
	[Bishop:	Peace be with you.
	People:	**And also with you.]**

The priest, deacon, or other suitable minister may very briefly introduce the Mass of the day.

A. The rite of blessing and sprinkling holy water may be celebrated in all churches and chapels at all Sunday Masses celebrated on Sunday or on Saturday evening.

Or

B. The penitential rite follows.

Or

C. If the Mass is preceded by some part of the liturgy of the hours, the **Penitential Rite** is omitted, and the **Kyrie** may be omitted.

RITE OF BLESSING AND SPRINKLING HOLY WATER

When this rite is celebrated it takes the place of the **Penitential Rite** at the beginning of Mass. The **Kyrie** is also omitted.

After greeting the people the priest remains standing at his chair. A vessel containing the water to be blessed is placed before him. Facing the people, he invites them to pray, using these or similar words:

> Dear friends,
> this water will be used
> to remind us of our baptism.
> Let us ask God to bless ✠ it,
> and to keep us faithful
> to the Spirit he has given us.

After a brief silence, he joins his hands and continues:

a

God our Father,
your gift of water
brings life and freshness to the earth;
it washes away our sins
and brings us eternal life.

We ask you now to bless ✠ this water,
and to give us your protection on this day
which you have made your own.

Renew the living spring of your life within us
and protect us in spirit and body,
that we may be free from sin
and come into your presence
to receive your gift of salvation.

We ask this through Christ our Lord.

Or:

b

Lord God almighty,
creator of all life,
of body and soul,
we ask you to bless ✠ this water:
as we use it in faith
forgive our sins
and save us from all illness
and the power of evil.

Lord,
in your mercy
give us living water,
always springing up as a fountain of salvation:
free us, body and soul, from every danger,
and admit us to your presence
in purity of heart.

Grant this through Christ our Lord.

Or (during the Easter season):

Lord God almighty,
hear the prayers of your people:
we celebrate our creation and redemption.
Hear our prayers and bless ✠ this water
which gives fruitfulness to the fields,
and refreshment and cleansing to man.
You chose water to show your goodness
when you led your people to freedom
through the Red Sea
and satisfied their thirst in the desert
with water from the rock.
Water was the symbol used by the prophets
to foretell your new covenant with man.
You made the water of baptism holy
by Christ's baptism in the Jordan:
by it you give us a new birth
and renew us in holiness.
May this water remind us of our baptism
and let us share the joy
of all who have been baptized at Easter.

We ask this through Christ our Lord.

Where it is customary, salt may be mixed with the holy water. The priest
blesses the salt, saying:

Almighty God,
we ask you to bless ✠ this salt
as once you blessed the salt scattered over the water
by the prophet Elisha.
Wherever this salt and water are sprinkled,
drive away the power of evil,
and protect us always
by the presence of your Holy Spirit.

Grant this through Christ our Lord.

Then he pours the salt into the water in silence.

Taking the sprinkler, the priest sprinkles himself and his ministers, then the rest of the clergy and people. He may move through the church for the sprinkling of the people. Meanwhile, an antiphon or another appropriate song is sung.

When he returns to his place and the song is finished, the priest faces the people, and with joined hands, says:

> May almighty God cleanse us of our sins,
> and through the eucharist we celebrate
> make us worthy to sit at his table
> in his heavenly kingdom.

People: **Amen.**

When it is prescribed, the **Gloria** is then sung or said, p. 892.

 **B** PENITENTIAL RITE

Before we hear God's word, we acknowledge our sins humbly, ask for mercy, and accept his pardon.

After the introduction to the day's Mass, the priest invites the people to recall their sins and to repent of them in silence. He may use these or similar words:

a As we prepare to celebrate the mystery of Christ's love, let us acknowledge our failures and ask the Lord for pardon and strength.

b Coming together as God's family, with confidence let us ask the Father's forgiveness, for he is full of gentleness and compassion.

c My brothers and sisters, to prepare ourselves to celebrate the sacred mysteries, let us call to mind our sins.

A pause for silent reflection follows.

After the silence, one of the following three forms is chosen:

a

All say: **I confess to almighty God,**
and to you, my brothers and sisters,
that I have sinned through my own fault

They strike their breast:

in my thoughts and in my words,
in what I have done,
and in what I have failed to do;
and I ask blessed Mary, ever virgin,
all the angels and saints,
and you, my brothers and sisters,
to pray for me to the Lord our God.

The priest says the absolution:

Priest: May almighty God have mercy on us,
forgive us our sins,
and bring us to everlasting life.
People: **Amen.**

b

Priest: Lord, we have sinned against you:
Lord, have mercy.
People: **Lord, have mercy.**
Priest: Lord, show us your mercy and love.
People: **And grant us your salvation.**

The priest says the absolution:

Priest: May almighty God have mercy on us,
forgive us our sins,
and bring us to everlasting life.
People: **Amen.**

c The priest (or other suitable minister) makes the following or other invocations. The people's response is in **bold print**.

i

You were sent to heal the contrite:
Lord, have mercy. **Lord, have mercy.**

You came to call sinners:
Christ, have mercy. **Christ, have mercy.**

You plead for us at the right hand of the Father:
Lord, have mercy **Lord, have mercy.**

ii

Lord Jesus, you came to gather the nations into the
peace of God's kingdom:
Lord, have mercy. **Lord, have mercy.**

You come in word and sacrament to strengthen us in
holiness:
Christ, have mercy. **Christ, have mercy.**

You will come in glory with salvation for your people:
Lord, have mercy. **Lord, have mercy.**

iii

Lord Jesus, you are mighty God and Prince of peace:
Lord, have mercy. **Lord, have mercy.**

Lord Jesus, you are Son of God and Son of Mary:
Christ, have mercy. **Christ, have mercy.**

Lord Jesus, you are Word made flesh and splendor of
the Father:
Lord, have mercy. **Lord, have mercy.**

iv

Lord Jesus, you came to reconcile us to one another and
to the Father:
Lord, have mercy. **Lord, have mercy.**

Lord Jesus, you heal the wounds of sin and division:
Christ, have mercy. **Christ, have mercy.**

Lord Jesus, you intercede for us with your Father:
Lord, have mercy. **Lord, have mercy.**

v

You raise the dead to life in the Spirit:
Lord, have mercy.   **Lord, have mercy.**
You bring pardon and peace to the sinner:
Christ, have mercy.   **Christ, have mercy.**
You bring light to those in darkness:
Lord, have mercy.   **Lord, have mercy.**

vi

Lord Jesus, you raise us to new life:
Lord, have mercy.   **Lord, have mercy.**
Lord Jesus, you forgive us our sins:
Christ, have mercy.   **Christ, have mercy.**
Lord Jesus, you feed us with your body and blood:
Lord, have mercy.   **Lord, have mercy.**

vii

Lord Jesus, you have shown us the way to the Father:
Lord, have mercy.   **Lord, have mercy.**
Lord Jesus, you have given us the consolation
   of the truth:
Christ, have mercy.   **Christ, have mercy.**
Lord Jesus, you are the Good Shepherd,
   leading us into everlasting life:
Lord, have mercy.   **Lord, have mercy.**

viii

Lord Jesus, you healed the sick:
Lord, have mercy.   **Lord, have mercy.**
Lord Jesus, you forgave sinners:
Christ, have mercy.   **Christ, have mercy.**
Lord Jesus, you give us yourself to heal us and
   bring us strength:
Lord, have mercy.   **Lord, have mercy.**

At the end of each of the above options, the priest says the absolution:

May almighty God have mercy on us,
   forgive us our sins,
   and bring us to everlasting life.

The people respond: **Amen.**

KYRIE

The invocations, LORD, HAVE MERCY, follow, unless they have already been used in one of the forms of the act of penance.

V. Lord, have mercy.　　　　**R. Lord, have mercy.**
V. Christ, have mercy.　　　**R. Christ, have mercy.**
V. Lord, have mercy.　　　　**R. Lord, have mercy.**

GLORIA

As the Church assembled in the Spirit, we praise and pray to the Father and the Lamb.

This hymn is said or sung on Sundays outside Advent and Lent, on solemnities and feasts, and in solemn local celebrations.

Glory to God in the highest,
　　　and peace to his people on earth.

Lord God, heavenly King,
almighty God and Father,
　　　we worship you, we give you thanks,
　　　　we praise you for your glory.

Lord Jesus Christ, only Son of the Father,
Lord God, Lamb of God,
you take away the sin of the world:
　　　have mercy on us;
you are seated at the right hand of the Father:
　　　receive our prayer.

For you alone are the Holy One,
you alone are the Lord,
you alone are the Most High,
　　　Jesus Christ,
　　　　with the Holy Spirit,
　　　　in the glory of God the Father. Amen.

OPENING PRAYER

The priest invites us to pray silently for a moment and then, in our name, expresses the theme of the day's celebration and petitions God the Father through the mediation of Christ in the Holy Spirit.

Priest: **Let us pray.**

Priest and people pray silently for a while.

Turn to the **Opening Prayer** *in the Proper of the day.*

Then the priest extends his hands and sings or says the opening prayer, at the end of which the people respond: **Amen.**

LITURGY OF THE WORD

The proclamation of God's Word is always centered on Christ, present through his Word. Old Testament writings prepare for him; New Testament books speak of him directly. All of Scripture calls us to believe once more and to follow. After the reading we reflect upon God's words and respond to them.

Turn to the **Liturgy of the Word** *in the Proper of the day. For the page number of the Proper of the day, see the* **Calendars,** *on pages 12–25 and 26–41.*

FIRST READING

The reader goes to the lectern for the first reading. All sit and listen. To indicate the end, the reader adds: THE WORD OF THE LORD. All respond: **Thanks be to God.**

RESPONSORIAL PSALM

The cantor sings or recites the psalm, and the people respond.

SECOND READING

When there is a second reading, it is read at the lectern as before. To indicate the end, the reader adds: THE WORD OF THE LORD. All respond: **Thanks be to God.**

ALLELUIA OR GOSPEL ACCLAMATION

Jesus will speak to us in the gospel. We rise now out of respect and prepare for his message with the alleluia.

The alleluia or other chant follows. It is to be omitted if not sung.

GOSPEL

Meanwhile, if incense is used, the priest puts some in the censer. Then the deacon who is to proclaim the gospel bows to the priest and in a low voice asks his blessing:

> Father, give me your blessing.

The priest says in a low voice:

> The Lord be in your heart and on your lips that you may worthily proclaim his gospel. In the name of the Father, and of the Son, ✠ and of the Holy Spirit.

The deacon answers: Amen.

If there is no deacon, the priest bows before the altar and says inaudibly:

> Almighty God, cleanse my heart and my lips that I may worthily proclaim your gospel.

Then the deacon (or the priest) goes to the lectern. He may be accompanied by ministers with incense and candles. He sings or says:

> The Lord be with you.

> People: **And also with you.**

Deacon (or priest):

> A reading from the holy gospel according to N.

He makes the sign of the cross on the book, and then on his forehead, lips, and breast. The people respond:

> People: **Glory to you, Lord.**

Then, if the incense is used, the deacon (or priest) incenses the book, and proclaims the gospel.

At the end of the gospel, the deacon (or priest) adds:

The gospel of the Lord.

All respond: **Praise to you, Lord Jesus Christ.**

Then he kisses the book, saying inaudibly:

May the words of the gospel wipe away our sins.

HOMILY

God's word is spoken again in the homily. The Holy Spirit speaking through the lips of the preacher explains and applies today's biblical readings to the needs of this particular congregation. He calls us to respond to Christ through the life we lead.

A homily shall be given on all Sundays and holy days of obligation; it is recommended for other days.

PROFESSION OF FAITH

As a people we express our acceptance of God's message in the Scriptures and homily. We summarize our faith by proclaiming a creed handed down from the early Church.

After the homily, the profession of faith is said on Sundays and solemnities; it may also be said in solemn local celebrations.

We believe in one God,
the Father, the Almighty,
maker of heaven and earth,
of all that is seen and unseen.

We believe in one Lord, Jesus Christ,
the only Son of God,
eternally begotten of the Father,
God from God, Light from Light,
true God from true God,

begotten, not made, one in Being with the Father.
Through him all things were made.
For us men and for our salvation
he came down from heaven:

All bow during these two lines:

by the power of the Holy Spirit
he was born of the Virgin Mary, and became
man.

For our sake he was crucified under Pontius Pilate;
he suffered, died and was buried.
On the third day he rose again
in fulfillment of the Scriptures;
he ascended into heaven
and is seated at the right hand of the Father.
He will come again in glory to judge the living and
the dead,
and his kingdom will have no end.

We believe in the Holy Spirit, the Lord, the giver of life,
who proceeds from the Father and the Son.
With the Father and the Son he is worshiped and
glorified.
He has spoken through the Prophets.
We believe in one holy catholic and apostolic
Church.
We acknowledge one baptism for the forgiveness of
sins.
We look for the resurrection of the dead,
and the life of the world to come. Amen.

GENERAL INTERCESSIONS

*As a priestly people we unite with one another to pray for today's
needs in the Church and the world.*

Then follow the general intercessions (prayer of the faithful). The priest presides at the prayer. With a brief introduction, he invites the people to pray; after the intentions he says the concluding prayer.

It is desirable that the intentions be announced by the deacon, cantor, or other person.

LITURGY OF THE EUCHARIST

Made ready by reflection on God's Word, we enter now into the eucharistic sacrifice itself, the Supper of the Lord. We celebrate the memorial which the Lord instituted at his Last Supper. We are God's new people, the redeemed brothers and sisters of Christ, gathered by him around his table. We are here to bless God and to receive the gift of Jesus' body and blood so that our faith and life may be transformed.

PREPARATION OF THE ALTAR AND THE GIFTS

The bread and wine for the Eucharist, with our gifts for the Church and the poor, are gathered and brought to the altar. We prepare our hearts by song or in silence as the Lord's table is being set.

After the liturgy of the word, the offertory song is begun. Meanwhile the ministers place the corporal, the purificator, the chalice, and the missal on the altar.

Sufficient hosts (and wine) for the communion of the faithful are to be prepared. It is most important that the faithful should receive the body of the Lord in hosts consecrated at the same Mass and should share the cup when it is permitted. Communion is thus a clearer sign of sharing in the sacrifice which is actually taking place.

It is desirable that the participation of the faithful be expressed by members of the congregation bringing up the bread and wine for the celebration of the eucharist or other gifts for the needs of the Church and the poor.

The priest, standing at the altar, takes the paten with the bread and, holding it slightly raised above the altar, says inaudibly:

> Blessed are you, Lord, God of all creation.
> Through your goodness we have this bread to offer,
> which earth has given and human hands have made.
> It will become for us the bread of life.

Then he places the paten with the bread on the corporal.

If no offertory song is sung, the priest may say the preceding words in an audible voice; then the people may respond:

Blessed be God forever.

The deacon (or the priest) pours wine and a little water into the chalice, saying inaudibly:

> By the mystery of this water and wine may we come to share in the divinity of Christ, who humbled himself to share in our humanity.

Then the priest takes the chalice, and, holding it slightly raised above the altar, says inaudibly:

> Blessed are you, Lord, God of all creation.
> Through your goodness we have this wine to offer,
> fruit of the vine and work of human hands.
> It will become our spiritual drink.

Then he places the chalice on the corporal.

If no offertory song is sung, the priest may say the preceding words in an audible voice; then the people may respond:

Blessed be God for ever.

The priest bows and says inaudibly:

> Lord God, we ask you to receive us and be pleased with the sacrifice we offer you with humble and contrite hearts.

He may now incense the offerings and the altar. Afterwards the deacon or a minister incenses the priest and people.

Next the priest stands at the side of the altar and washes his hands, saying inaudibly:

> Lord, wash away my iniquity; cleanse me from my sin.

Standing at the center of the altar, facing the people, he extends and then joins his hands, saying:

> Pray, brethren, that our sacrifice
> may be acceptable to God, the almighty
> Father.

People: **May the Lord accept the sacrifice at your
hands
for the praise and glory of his name,
for our good and the good of all his
Church.**

PRAYER OVER THE GIFTS

*The priest, speaking in our name, asks the Father to bless and accept
these gifts.*

> *Turn to the* **Prayer over the Gifts** *in the Proper of the day.*

With hands extended, the priest sings or says the prayer over the gifts, at the
end of which the people respond:

Amen.

EUCHARISTIC PRAYER

*We begin the eucharistic service of praise and thanksgiving, the cen-
ter of the entire celebration, the central prayer of worship. At the
priest's invitation we lift our hearts to God and unite with him in the
words he addresses to the Father through Jesus Christ. Together we
join Christ in his sacrifice, celebrating his memorial in the holy meal
and acknowledging with him the wonderful works of God in our lives.*

The priest begins the eucharistic prayer. With hands extended he sings or
says:

Priest: The Lord be with you.
People: **And also with you.**
Priest: Lift up your hearts.
People: **We lift them up to the Lord.**
Priest: Let us give thanks to the Lord our God.
People: **It is right to give him thanks and praise.**

The priest continues the preface with hands extended.

The following alphabetical list of **Prefaces** *is for quick reference.*

ACCLAMATION

At the end of the preface, he joins his hands, and, together with the people, concludes it by singing or saying aloud:

Holy, holy, holy Lord, God of power and might,
heaven and earth are full of your glory.
    Hosanna in the highest.
Blessed is he who comes in the name of the Lord.
    Hosanna in the highest.

EUCHARISTIC PRAYER I
(ROMAN CANON)

[Praise to the Father]

Priest:

We come to you, Father,
with praise and thanksgiving,
through Jesus Christ your Son.
Through him we ask you to accept and bless
these gifts we offer you in sacrifice.

[Intercessions: For the Church]

We offer them for your holy catholic Church,
watch over it, Lord, and guide it;
grant it peace and unity throughout the world.
We offer them for N. our Pope,
for N. our bishop,
and for all who hold and teach the catholic faith
that comes to us from the apostles.

Remember, Lord, your people,
especially those for whom we now pray, N. and N.
Remember all of us gathered here before you.
You know how firmly we believe in you
and dedicate ourselves to you.
We offer you this sacrifice of praise
for ourselves and those who are dear to us.
We pray to you, our living and true God,
for our well-being and redemption.

[In Communion with the Saints]

In union with the whole Church
we honor Mary,
the ever-virgin mother of Jesus Christ our Lord and God.
† We honor Joseph, her husband,
the apostles and martyrs

Peter and Paul, Andrew,
>[James, John, Thomas,
>James, Philip,
>Bartholomew, Matthew, Simon and Jude;
>we honor Linus, Cletus, Clement, Sixtus,
>Cornelius, Cyprian, Lawrence, Chrysogonus,
>John and Paul, Cosmas and Damian]

and all the saints.
May their merits and prayers
gain us your constant help and protection.
>[Through Christ our Lord. Amen.]

SPECIAL FORM of In union with the whole Church
(Communicantes)

Christmas and during the Octave

In union with the whole Church
we celebrate that day (night)
when Mary without loss of her
   virginity
gave the world its savior.
We honor Mary,
the ever-virgin mother of Jesus
   Christ our Lord and God. †

Epiphany

In union with the whole Church
we celebrate that day
when your only Son,
sharing your eternal glory,
showed himself in a human body.
We honor Mary,
the ever-virgin mother of Jesus
   Christ our Lord and God. †

Holy Thursday

In union with the whole Church
we celebrate that day
when Jesus Christ, our Lord,
was betrayed for us.
We honor Mary,
the ever-virgin mother of Jesus
   Christ our Lord and God. †

From the Easter Vigil to the Saturday before the Second Sunday of Easter Inclusive

In union with the whole Church
we celebrate that day (night)
when Jesus Christ, our Lord,
rose from the dead in his human body.
We honor Mary,
the ever-virgin mother of Jesus Christ
   our Lord and God. †

Ascension

In union with the whole Church
we celebrate that day
when your only Son, our Lord,
took his place with you
and raised our frail human nature
   to glory.
We honor Mary,
the ever-virgin mother of Jesus Christ
   our Lord and God. †

Pentecost

In union with the whole Church
we celebrate the day of Pentecost
when the Holy Spirit appeared to
   the apostles
in the form of countless tongues.
We honor Mary,
the ever-virgin mother of Jesus Christ
   our Lord and God. †

Father, accept this offering
from your whole family.
Grant us your peace in this life,
save us from final damnation,
and count us among those you have chosen.
[Through Christ our Lord. Amen.]

Bless and approve our offering;
make it acceptable to you,
an offering in spirit and in truth.
Let it become for us
the body and blood of Jesus Christ,
your only Son, our Lord.
[Through Christ our Lord. Amen.]

[The Lord's Supper]

The day before he suffered*
he took bread into his sacred hands
and looking up to heaven,
to you, his almighty Father,
he gave you thanks and praise.
He broke the bread,
gave it to his disciples, and said:

**Take this, all of you, and eat it:
this is my body which will be given up for you.**

SPECIAL FORM of Father, accept this offering (Hanc igitur)

Holy Thursday
Father, accept this offering
from your whole family
in memory of the day when Jesus
    Christ, our Lord,
gave the mysteries of his body and
    blood
for his disciples to celebrate.
Grant us...

*Holy Thursday
The day before he suffered
to save us and all men, that is
    today,...

**From the Easter Vigil to the Second
Sunday of Easter Inclusive**
Father, accept this offering
from your whole family
and from those born into the new life
of water and the Holy Spirit,
with all their sins forgiven.
Grant us...

When supper was ended,
he took the cup.
Again he gave you thanks and praise,
gave the cup to his disciples, and said:

Take this, all of you, and drink from it:
this is the cup of my blood,
the blood of the new and everlasting covenant.

It will be shed for you and for all
so that sins may be forgiven.
Do this in memory of me.

[Memorial Acclamation]

Let us proclaim the mystery of faith:

People with the celebrant and concelebrants:

a
Christ has died,
Christ is risen,
Christ will come again.

b
Dying you destroyed our death,
rising you restored our life.
Lord Jesus, come in glory.

c
When we eat this bread and drink this cup,
we proclaim your death, Lord Jesus,
until you come in glory.

d
Lord, by your cross and resurrection
you have set us free.
You are the Savior of the world.

[The Memorial Prayer]

Priest:

Father, we celebrate the memory of Christ, your Son.
We, your people and your ministers,

recall his passion,
his resurrection from the dead,
and his ascension into glory;
and from the many gifts you have given us
we offer to you, God of glory and majesty,
this holy and perfect sacrifice:
the bread of life
and the cup of eternal salvation.

Look with favor on these offerings
and accept them as once you accepted
the gifts of your servant Abel,
the sacrifice of Abraham, our father in faith,
and the bread and wine offered by your priest Melchisedech.

Almighty God,
we pray that your angel may take this sacrifice
to your altar in heaven.
Then, as we receive from this altar
the sacred body and blood of your Son,
let us be filled with every grace and blessing.
    [Through Christ our Lord. Amen.]

[Commemoration of the Dead]

Remember, Lord, those who have died
and have gone before us marked with the sign of faith,
especially those for whom we now pray, N. and N.
May these, and all who sleep in Christ,
find in your presence
light, happiness, and peace.
    [Through Christ our Lord. Amen.]

For ourselves, too, we ask
some share in the fellowship of your apostles and martyrs,
with John the Baptist, Stephen, Matthias, Barnabas,

[Ignatius, Alexander, Marcellinus, Peter,
Felicity, Perpetua, Agatha, Lucy,
Agnes, Cecilia, Anastasia]

and all the saints.

Though we are sinners,
we trust in your mercy and love.
Do not consider what we truly deserve,
but grant us your forgiveness.

Through Christ our Lord
you give us all these gifts.
You fill them with life and goodness,
you bless them and make them holy.

[Concluding Doxology]

Through him,
with him,
in him,
in the unity of the Holy Spirit,
all glory and honor is yours,
almighty Father,
for ever and ever.

The people respond:

Amen.

For the **Communion Rite** *and the* **Our Father,** *turn to p. 930.*

EUCHARISTIC PRAYER II

Priest:	The Lord be with you.
People:	**And also with you.**
Priest:	Lift up your hearts.
People:	**We lift them up to the Lord.**
Priest:	Let us give thanks to the Lord our God.
People:	**It is right to give him thanks and praise.**

[Praise to the Father]

Priest: Father, it is our duty and our salvation,
always and everywhere
to give you thanks
through your beloved Son, Jesus Christ.

He is the Word through whom you made the
    universe,
the Savior you sent to redeem us.
By the power of the Holy Spirit
he took flesh and was born of the Virgin Mary.

For our sake he opened his arms on the cross;
he put an end to death
and revealed the resurrection.
In this he fulfilled your will
and won for you a holy people.

And so we join the angels and the saints
in proclaiming your glory
as we say:

All: **Holy, holy, holy Lord, God of power and might,
heaven and earth are full of your glory.**
        Hosanna in the highest.
**Blessed is he who comes in the name of the
    Lord.**
        Hosanna in the highest.

[Invocation of the Holy Spirit]

Priest:

Lord, you are holy indeed,
the fountain of all holiness.
Let your Spirit come upon these gifts to make them holy,
so that they may become for us
the body and blood of our Lord Jesus Christ.

[The Lord's Supper]

Before he was given up to death,
a death he freely accepted,
he took bread and gave you thanks.
He broke the bread,
gave it to his disciples, and said:

Take this, all of you, and eat it:
this is my body which will be given up for you.

When supper was ended, he took the cup.
Again he gave you thanks and praise,
gave the cup to his disciples, and said:

Take this, all of you, and drink from it:
this is the cup of my blood,
the blood of the new and everlasting covenant.
It will be shed for you and for all
so that sins may be forgiven.
Do this in memory of me.

[Memorial Acclamation]

Let us proclaim the mystery of faith:

People with celebrant and concelebrants:

Christ has died,
Christ is risen,
Christ will come again.

b
Dying you destroyed our death,
rising you restored our life.
Lord Jesus, come in glory.

c
When we eat this bread and drink this cup,
we proclaim your death, Lord Jesus,
until you come in glory.

d
Lord, by your cross and resurrection
you have set us free.
You are the Savior of the world.

[The Memorial Prayer]

Priest:

In memory of his death and resurrection,
we offer you, Father, this life-giving bread,
this saving cup.
We thank you for counting us worthy
to stand in your presence and serve you.

[Invocation of the Holy Spirit]

May all of us who share in the body and blood of Christ
be brought together in unity by the Holy Spirit.

[Intercessions: For the Church]

Lord, remember your Church throughout the world;
make us grow in love,
together with N. our Pope,
N. our bishop, and all the clergy. *

[For the Dead]

In Masses for the dead the following may be added:
Remember N., whom you have called from this life.
In baptism he (she) died with Christ:
may he (she) also share his resurrection.

Remember our brothers and sisters
who have gone to their rest
in the hope of rising again;
bring them and all the departed
into the light of your presence.

[In Communion with the Saints]

Have mercy on us all;
make us worthy to share eternal life
with Mary, the virgin Mother of God,
with the apostles, and with all the saints
who have done your will throughout the ages.
May we praise you in union with them,
and give you glory
through your Son, Jesus Christ.

[Concluding Doxology]

Through him,
with him,
in him,
in the unity of the Holy Spirit,
all glory and honor is yours,
almighty Father,
for ever and ever.

The people respond:

Amen.

For the **Communion Rite** *and the* **Our Father,** *turn to p. 930.*

EUCHARISTIC PRAYER III

[Praise to the Father]

Priest:

Father, you are holy indeed,
and all creation rightly gives you praise.
All life, all holiness comes from you
through your Son, Jesus Christ our Lord,
by the working of the Holy Spirit.
From age to age you gather a people to yourself,
so that from east to west
a perfect offering may be made
to the glory of your name.

[Invocation of the Holy Spirit]

And so, Father, we bring you these gifts.
We ask you to make them holy by the power of your Spirit,
that they may become the body and blood
of your Son, our Lord Jesus Christ,
at whose command we celebrate this eucharist.

[The Lord's Supper]

On the night he was betrayed,
he took bread and gave you thanks and praise.
He broke the bread, gave it to his disciples, and said:

Take this, all of you, and eat it:
this is my body which will be given up for you.

When supper was ended, he took the cup.
Again he gave you thanks and praise,
gave the cup to his disciples, and said:

Take this, all of you, and drink from it:
this is the cup of my blood,

the blood of the new and everlasting covenant.
It will be shed for you and for all
so that sins may be forgiven.
Do this in memory of me.

[Memorial Acclamation]

Let us proclaim the mystery of faith:

People with celebrant and concelebrants:

a **Christ has died,**
Christ is risen,
Christ will come again.

b **Dying you destroyed our death,**
rising you restored our life.
Lord Jesus, come in glory.

c **When we eat this bread and drink this cup,**
we proclaim your death, Lord Jesus,
until you come in glory.

d **Lord, by your cross and resurrection**
you have set us free.
You are the Savior of the world.

[The Memorial Prayer]

Priest:

Father, calling to mind the death your Son endured for
  our salvation,
his glorious resurrection and ascension into heaven,
and ready to greet him when he comes again,
we offer you in thanksgiving this holy and living sacrifice.

Look with favor on your Church's offering,
and see the Victim whose death has reconciled us to yourself.

[Invocation of the Holy Spirit]

Grant that we, who are nourished by his body and blood,
may be filled with his Holy Spirit,
and become one body, one spirit in Christ.

[Intercessions: In Communion with the Saints]

May he make us an everlasting gift to you
and enable us to share in the inheritance of your saints,
with Mary, the virgin Mother of God;
with the apostles, the martyrs,
(Saint N.—the saint of the day or the patron saint) and all
    your saints,
on whose constant intercession we rely for help.

[For the Church]

Lord, may this sacrifice,
which has made our peace with you,
advance the peace and salvation of all the world.
Strengthen in faith and love your pilgrim Church on earth;
your servant, Pope N., our bishop N.,
and all the bishops,
with the clergy and the entire people your Son has gained
    for you.
Father, hear the prayers of the family you have gathered here
    before you.
In mercy and love unite all your children wherever they
    may be.*

[For the Dead]

Welcome into your kingdom our departed brothers and
    sisters,
and all who have left this world in your friendship.
We hope to enjoy for ever the vision of your glory,
through Christ our Lord, from whom all good things come.

[Concluding Doxology]

Through him,
with him,
in him,
in the unity of the Holy Spirit,
all glory and honor is yours,
almighty Father,
for ever and ever.

The people respond:

Amen.

For the **Communion Rite** *and the* **Our Father,** *turn to p. 930.*

---

*When this eucharistic prayer is used in Masses for the dead, the following may be said:

Remember N.
In baptism he (she) died with Christ:
may he (she) also share his resurrection,
when Christ will raise our mortal bodies
and make them like his own in glory.

Welcome into your kingdom our departed brothers and
    sisters,
and all who have left this world in your friendship.
There we hope to share in your glory
when every tear will be wiped away.
On that day we shall see you, our God, as you are.

We shall become like you
and praise you for ever through Christ our Lord,
from whom all good things come.

Through him....

EUCHARISTIC PRAYER IV

Priest: The Lord be with you.
People: **And also with you.**
Priest: Lift up your hearts.
People: **We lift them up to the Lord.**
Priest: Let us give thanks to the Lord our God.
People: **It is right to give him thanks and praise.**

[Praise to the Father]

Priest: Father in heaven,
          it is right that we should give you thanks and
              glory:
          you are the one God, living and true.
          Through all eternity you live in unapproachable
              light.
          Source of life and goodness, you have created all
              things,
          to fill your creatures with every blessing
          and lead all men to the joyful vision of your light.
          Countless hosts of angels stand before you to do
              your will;
          they look upon your splendor
          and praise you, night and day.
          United with them,
          and in the name of every creature under heaven,
          we too praise your glory as we say:

All: **Holy, holy, holy Lord, God of power and might,
          heaven and earth are full of your glory.
              Hosanna in the highest.
          Blessed is he who comes in the name of the
                  Lord.
              Hosanna in the highest.**

[Praise to the Father]

Priest:

Father, we acknowledge your greatness:
all your actions show your wisdom and love.
You formed man in your own likeness
and set him over the whole world
to serve you, his creator,
and to rule over all creatures.
Even when he disobeyed you and lost your friendship
you did not abandon him to the power of death,
but helped all men to seek and find you.
Again and again you offered a covenant to man,
and through the prophets taught him to hope for salvation.
Father, you so loved the world
that in the fullness of time you sent your only Son to be
    our Savior.

He was conceived through the power of the Holy Spirit,
and born of the Virgin Mary,
a man like us in all things but sin.
To the poor he proclaimed the good news of salvation,
to prisoners, freedom,
and to those in sorrow, joy.
In fulfillment of your will
he gave himself up to death;
but by rising from the dead,
he destroyed death and restored life.
And that we might live no longer for ourselves but for him,
he sent the Holy Spirit from you, Father,
as his first gift to those who believe,
to complete his work on earth
and bring us the fullness of grace.

[Invocation of the Holy Spirit]

Father, may this Holy Spirit sanctify these offerings.
Let them become the body and blood of Jesus Christ
    our Lord
as we celebrate the great mystery
which he left us as an everlasting covenant.

[The Lord's Supper]

He always loved those who were his own in the world.
When the time came for him to be glorified by you, his
    heavenly Father,
he showed the depth of his love.
While they were at supper,
he took the bread, said the blessing, broke the bread
and gave it to his disciples, saying:

Take this, all of you, and eat it:
this is my body which will be given up for you.

In the same way, he took the cup, filled with wine.
He gave you thanks, and giving the cup to his disciples, said:

Take this, all of you, and drink from it:
this is the cup of my blood,
the blood of the new and everlasting covenant.
It will be shed for you and for all
so that sins may be forgiven.
Do this in memory of me.

Let us proclaim the mystery of faith:

People with celebrant and concelebrants:

Christ has died,
Christ is risen,
Christ will come again.

b
Dying you destroyed our death,
rising you restored our life.
Lord Jesus, come in glory.

c
When we eat this bread and drink this cup,
we proclaim your death, Lord Jesus,
until you come in glory.

d
Lord, by your cross and resurrection
you have set us free.
You are the Savior of the world.

[The Memorial Prayer]

Priest:

Father, we now celebrate this memorial of our redemption.
We recall Christ's death, his descent among the dead,
his resurrection, and his ascension to your right hand;
and, looking forward to his coming in glory,
we offer you his body and blood,
the acceptable sacrifice
which brings salvation to the whole world.

Lord, look upon this sacrifice which you have given to
   your Church;
and by your Holy Spirit, gather all who share this one bread
   and one cup
into the one body of Christ, a living sacrifice of praise.

[Intercessions: For the Church]

Lord, remember those for whom we offer this sacrifice,
especially N. our Pope,
N. our bishop, and bishops and clergy everywhere.

Remember those who take part in this offering,
those here present and all your people,
and all who seek you with a sincere heart.

[For the Dead]

Remember those who have died in the peace of Christ
and all the dead whose faith is known to you alone.

[In Communion with the Saints]

Father, in your mercy grant also to us, your children,
to enter into our heavenly inheritance
in the company of the Virgin Mary, the Mother of God,
and your apostles and saints.
Then, in your kingdom, freed from the corruption of sin
    and death,
we shall sing your glory with every creature through Christ
    our Lord,
through whom you give us everything that is good.

[Concluding Doxology]

Through him,
with him,
in him,
in the unity of the Holy Spirit,
all glory and honor is yours,
almighty Father,
for ever and ever.

The people respond:

Amen.

For the **Communion Rite** *and the* **Our Father,** *turn to p. 930.*

EUCHARISTIC PRAYER
FOR MASSES OF RECONCILIATION I

Priest: The Lord be with you.
People: **And also with you.**
Priest: Lift up your hearts.
People: **We lift them up to the Lord.**
Priest: Let us give thanks to the Lord our God.
People: **It is right to give him thanks and praise.**

Father, all-powerful and ever-living God,
we do well always and everywhere to give you
    thanks and praise.

You never cease to call us to a new and more
    abundant life.
God of love and mercy, you are always ready to
    forgive;
we are sinners, and you invite us to trust in your
    mercy.

Time and time again we broke your covenant,
but you did not abandon us.
Instead, through your Son, Jesus our Lord,
you bound yourself even more closely to the
    human family
by a bond that can never be broken.

Now is the time
for your people to turn back to you
and to be renewed in Christ your Son,
a time of grace and reconciliation.
You invite us
to serve the family of mankind

by opening our hearts
to the fullness of your Holy Spirit.

In wonder and gratitude,
we join our voices with the choirs of heaven
to proclaim the power of your love
and to sing of our salvation in Christ:

All: **Holy, holy, holy Lord, God of power and might,
heaven and earth are full of your glory.
Hosanna in the highest.
Blessed is he who comes in the name of the
Lord.
Hosanna in the highest.**

Priest:
Father,
from the beginning of time
you have always done what is good for man
so that we may be holy as you are holy.

Look with kindness on your people
gathered here before you:
send forth the power of your Spirit
so that these gifts may become for us
the body and blood of your beloved Son, Jesus the Christ,
in whom we have become your sons and daughters.

When we were lost
and could not find the way to you,
you loved us more than ever:
Jesus, your Son, innocent and without sin,
gave himself into our hands and was nailed to a cross.
Yet before he stretched out his arms between heaven and earth
in the everlasting sign of your covenant,
he desired to celebrate the Paschal feast
in the company of his disciples.

While they were at supper,
he took bread and gave you thanks and praise.
He broke the bread, gave it to his disciples, and said:

Take this, all of you, and eat it:
this is my body which will be given up for you.

At the end of the meal,
knowing that he was to reconcile all things in himself
by the blood of his cross,
he took the cup, filled with wine.
Again he gave you thanks,
handed the cup to his friends, and said:

Take this, all of you, and drink from it:
this is the cup of my blood,
the blood of the new and everlasting covenant.
It will be shed for you and for all
so that sins may be forgiven.
Do this in memory of me.

Let us proclaim the mystery of faith:

People with celebrant and concelebrants:

a **Christ has died,**
Christ is risen,
Christ will come again.

b **Dying you destroyed our death,**
rising you restored our life.
Lord Jesus, come in glory.

c **When we eat this bread and drink this cup,**
we proclaim your death, Lord Jesus,
until you come in glory.

d **Lord, by your cross and resurrection**
you have set us free.
You are the savior of the world.

Priest:

We do this in memory of Jesus Christ,
our Passover and our lasting peace.
We celebrate his death and resurrection
and look for the coming of that day
when he will return to give us the fullness of joy.
Therefore we offer you, God ever faithful and true,
the sacrifice which restores man to your friendship.

Father,
look with love
on those you have called
to share in the one sacrifice of Christ.
By the power of your Holy Spirit
make them one body,
healed of all division.

Keep us all
in communion of mind and heart
with N., our Pope, and N., our bishop.
Help us to work together
for the coming of your kingdom,
until at last we stand in your presence
to share the life of the saints,
in the company of the Virgin Mary and the apostles,
and of our departed brothers and sisters
whom we commend to your mercy.

Then, freed from every shadow of death,
we shall take our place in the new creation
and give you thanks with Christ, our risen Lord.

Through him,
with him,
in him,
in the unity of the Holy Spirit,
all glory and honor is yours,
almighty Father,
for ever and ever.

The people respond:

Amen.

For the **Communion Rite** *and the* **Our Father,** *turn to p. 930.*

EUCHARISTIC PRAYER
FOR MASSES OF RECONCILIATION II

Priest: The Lord be with you.

People: **And also with you.**

Priest: Lift up your hearts.

People: **We lift them up to the Lord.**

Priest: Let us give thanks to the Lord our God.

People: **It is right to give him thanks and praise.**

Priest: Father, all-powerful and ever-living God,
we praise and thank you through Jesus Christ
          our Lord
for your presence and action in the world.

In the midst of conflict and division,
we know it is you
who turn our minds to thoughts of peace.
Your Spirit changes our hearts:
enemies begin to speak to one another,
those who were estranged join hands in friendship,
and nations seek the way of peace together.

Your Spirit is at work
when understanding puts an end to strife,
when hatred is quenched by mercy,
and vengeance gives way to forgiveness.

For this we should never cease
to thank and praise you.
We join with all the choirs of heaven
as they sing for ever to your glory:

All: **Holy, holy, holy Lord, God of power and might,
heaven and earth are full of your glory.**

Hosanna in the highest.
Blessed is he who comes in the name of the
Lord.
Hosanna in the highest.

Priest:

God of power and might,
we praise you through your Son, Jesus Christ,
who comes in your name.
He is the Word that brings salvation.
He is the hand you stretch out to sinners.
He is the way that leads to your peace.

God our Father,
we had wandered far from you,
but through your Son you have brought us back.
You gave him up to death
so that we might turn again to you
and find our way to one another.

Therefore we celebrate the reconciliation
Christ has gained for us.

We ask you to sanctify these gifts
by the power of your Spirit,
as we now fulfill your Son's command.

While he was at supper
on the night before he died for us,
he took bread in his hands,
and gave you thanks and praise.
He broke the bread,
gave it to his disciples, and said:

Take this, all of you, and eat it:
this is my body which will be given up for you.

At the end of the meal he took the cup.
Again he praised you for your goodness,
gave the cup to his disciples, and said:

Take this, all of you, and drink from it:
this is the cup of my blood,
the blood of the new and everlasting covenant.
It will be shed for you and for all
so that sins may be forgiven.
Do this in memory of me.

Let us proclaim the mystery of faith:

People with celebrant and concelebrants:

a
Christ has died,
Christ is risen,
Christ will come again.

b
Dying you destroyed our death,
rising you restored our life.
Lord Jesus, come in glory.

c
When we eat this bread and drink this cup,
we proclaim your death, Lord Jesus,
until you come in glory.

d
Lord, by your cross and resurrection
you have set us free.
You are the savior of the world.

Priest:

Lord our God,
your Son has entrusted to us
this pledge of his love.
We celebrate the memory of his death and resurrection
and bring you the gift you have given us,
the sacrifice of reconciliation.

Therefore, we ask you, Father,
to accept us, together with your Son.
Fill us with his Spirit
through our sharing in this meal.
May he take away all that divides us.

May this Spirit keep us always in communion
with N., our Pope, N., our bishop,
with all the bishops and all your people.
Father, make your Church throughout the world
a sign of unity and an instrument of your peace.

You have gathered us here
around the table of your Son,
in fellowship with the Virgin Mary, Mother of God, and all
   the saints.

In that new world where the fullness of your peace will be
   revealed,
gather people of every race, language, and way of life
to share in the one eternal banquet
with Jesus Christ the Lord.

Through him,
with him,
in him,
in the unity of the Holy Spirit,
all glory and honor is yours,
almighty Father,
for ever and ever.

The people respond:

Amen.

COMMUNION RITE

To prepare for the paschal meal, to welcome the Lord, we pray for forgiveness and exchange a sign of peace. Before eating Christ's body and drinking his blood, we must be one with him and with all our brothers and sisters in the Church.

LORD'S PRAYER

Priest:

a Let us pray with confidence to the Father
in the words our Savior gave us.

b Jesus taught us to call God our Father,
and so we have the courage to say:

c Let us ask our Father to forgive our sins
and to bring us to forgive those who sin against us.

d Let us pray for the coming of the kingdom
as Jesus taught us.

Priest and people:

**Our Father, who art in heaven,
hallowed be thy name;
thy kingdom come;
thy will be done on earth as it is in heaven.
Give us this day our daily bread;
and forgive us our trespasses
as we forgive those who trespass against us;
and lead us not into temptation,
but deliver us from evil.**

With hands extended, the priest continues alone:

Deliver us, Lord, from every evil,
and grant us peace in our day.
In your mercy keep us free from sin
and protect us from all anxiety
as we wait in joyful hope
for the coming of our Savior, Jesus Christ.

DOXOLOGY

People: **For the kingdom, the power and the glory are yours, now and for ever.**

SIGN OF PEACE

The Church is a community of Christians joined by the Spirit in love. It needs to express, deepen, and restore its peaceful unity before eating the one body of the Lord and drinking from the one cup of salvation. We do this by a sign of peace.

The priest, with hands extended, says aloud:

> Lord Jesus Christ, you said to your apostles:
> I leave you peace, my peace I give you.
> Look not on our sins, but on the faith of
>   your Church,
>   and grant us the peace and unity of your
>   kingdom
> where you live for ever and ever.

People: **Amen.**

Priest: The peace of the Lord be with you always.

People: **And also with you.**

Then the deacon (or the priest) may add:

> Let us offer each other the sign of peace.

All make an appropriate sign of peace, according to local custom.

BREAKING OF THE BREAD

Christians are gathered for the "breaking of the bread," another name for the Mass. In communion, though many, we are made one body in the one bread, which is Christ.

The following is sung or said:

> **Lamb of God, you take away the sins of the world:**
> **have mercy on us.**

**Lamb of God, you take away the sins of the world:
have mercy on us.
Lamb of God, you take away the sins of the world:
grant us peace.**

This may be repeated until the breaking of the bread is finished, but the last phrase is always GRANT US PEACE.

Meanwhile, the priest takes the host and breaks it over the paten. He places a small piece in the chalice, saying inaudibly:

May this mingling of the body and blood of our Lord Jesus Christ bring eternal life to us who receive it.

Private Preparation of the Priest

Then the priest joins his hands and says inaudibly:

Lord Jesus Christ, Son of the living God, by the will of the Father and the work of the Holy Spirit your death brought life to the world. By your holy body and blood free me from all my sins and from every evil. Keep me faithful to your teaching, and never let me be parted from you.

or:

Lord Jesus Christ, with faith in your love and mercy I eat your body and drink your blood. Let it not bring me condemnation, but health in mind and body.

COMMUNION

We pray in silence and then voice words of humility and hope as our final preparation before meeting Christ in the Eucharist.

Priest:

This is the Lamb of God
who takes away the sins of the world.
Happy are those who are called to his supper.

He adds, once only, with the people:

**Lord, I am not worthy to receive you,
but only say the word and I shall be healed.**

Facing the altar, the priest says inaudibly:

May the body of Christ bring me to everlasting life.

He reverently consumes the body of Christ. Then he takes the chalice and says inaudibly:

May the blood of Christ bring me to everlasting life.

He reverently drinks the blood of Christ.

After this he takes the paten or other vessel and goes to the communicants. He takes a host for each one, raises it a little, and shows it, saying:

The body of Christ.

The communicant answers:

Amen.

and receives communion.

The sign of communion is more complete when given under both kinds, since the sign of the eucharistic meal appears more clearly. The intention of Christ that the new and eternal covenant be ratified in his blood is better expressed, as is the relation of the eucharistic banquet to the heavenly banquet.

When he presents the chalice, the priest or deacon says:

The blood of Christ.

The communicant answers:

Amen.

and drinks it.

COMMUNION SONG

While the priest receives the body of Christ, the communion song is begun.

> If there is no singing, the antiphon in the Missal is recited either by the people, by some of them, or by a reader. Otherwise the priest himself says it after he receives communion and before he gives communion to the congregation. *(Turn to the* **Communion Antiphon** *in the Proper of the day.)*

The vessels are cleansed by the priest or deacon or acolyte after the communion or after Mass, if possible at the side table.

Meanwhile he says inaudibly:

Lord, may I receive these gifts in purity of heart.
May they bring me healing and strength, now and for ever.

PERIOD OF SILENCE OR SONG OF PRAISE

Then the priest may return to the chair. A period of silence may now be observed, or a psalm or song of praise may be sung.

PRAYER AFTER COMMUNION

The priest prays in our name that we may live the life of faith since we have been strengthened by Christ himself. Our Amen makes his prayer our own.

Then, standing at the chair or at the altar, the priest sings or says:

Priest: **Let us pray.**

Turn to the **Prayer after Communion** *in the Proper of the day.*

Priest and people pray in silence for a while, unless a period of silence has already been observed. Then the priest extends his hands and sings or says the prayer after communion, at the end of which the people respond: **Amen.**

CONCLUDING RITE

We have heard God's Word and eaten the body of Christ. Now it is time for us to leave, to do good works, to praise and bless the Lord in our daily lives.

If there are any brief announcements, they are made at this time.

GREETING

The rite of dismissal takes place.

Priest: **The Lord be with you.**
People: **And also with you.**

BLESSING

Simple form

a

Priest: May almighty God bless you,
the Father, and the Son, ✠ and the Holy
Spirit.

People: **Amen.**

On certain days or occasions another more solemn form of blessing or prayer over the people may be used as the rubrics direct.

Solemn blessing

Deacon: Bow your heads and pray for God's blessing.

Texts of all the **Solemn Blessings** *are given on pp. 966–976.*

b

The priest always concludes the solemn blessing by adding:

May almighty God bless you,
the Father, and the Son, ✠ and the Holy
Spirit.

People: **Amen.**

Prayer over the people

Texts of all **Prayers over the People** *are given on pp. 977–982.*

After the prayer over the people, the priest always adds:

c

And may the blessing of almighty God,
the Father, and the Son, ✠ and the Holy
Spirit,
come upon you and remain with you for
ever.

People: **Amen.**

DISMISSAL

The dismissal sends each member of the congregation to do good works,
praising and blessing the Lord.

Deacon (or Priest):

a   Go in the peace of Christ.

b   The Mass is ended, go in peace.

c   Go in peace to love and serve the Lord.

People: **Thanks be to God.**

If any liturgical service follows immediately, the rite of dismissal is
omitted.

PREFACES

ADVENT I

The two comings of Christ

This preface is said in the Masses of the season from the first Sunday of Advent to December 16 and in other Masses celebrated during this period which have no preface of their own.

Father, all-powerful and ever-living God,
we do well always and everywhere to give you thanks
through Jesus Christ our Lord.

When he humbled himself to come among us as a man,
he fulfilled the plan you formed long ago
and opened for us the way to salvation.

Now we watch for the day,
hoping that the salvation promised us will be ours
when Christ our Lord will come again in his glory.

And so, with all the choirs of angels in heaven
we proclaim your glory
and join in their unending hymn of praise:
Holy, holy, holy Lord..., *p. 901.*

ADVENT II

Waiting for the two comings of Christ

This preface is said in the Masses of the season from December 17 to December 24 inclusive and in other Masses celebrated during this period which have no preface of their own.

Father, all-powerful and ever-living God,
we do well always and everywhere to give you thanks
through Jesus Christ our Lord.

His future coming was proclaimed by all the prophets.
The virgin mother bore him in her womb
with love beyond all telling.
John the Baptist was his herald
and made him known when at last he came.

937

In his love Christ has filled us with joy
as we prepare to celebrate his birth,
so that when he comes he may find us watching in prayer,
our hearts filled with wonder and praise.

And so, with all the choirs of angels in heaven
we proclaim your glory
and join in their unending hymn of praise:

Holy, holy, holy Lord..., *p. 901.*

CHRISTMAS I

Christ the Light

This preface is said in Masses of Christmas and its octave; in Masses within the Christmas octave even if they have their own preface, with the exception of Masses with a proper preface of the divine mysteries or Persons; and on weekdays of the Christmas season.

Father, all-powerful and ever-living God,
we do well always and everywhere to give you thanks
through Jesus Christ our Lord.

In the wonder of the incarnation
your eternal Word has brought to the eyes of faith
a new and radiant vision of your glory.
In him we see our God made visible
and so are caught up in love of the God we cannot see.

And so, with all the choirs of angels in heaven
we proclaim your glory
and join in their unending hymn of praise:

Holy, holy, holy Lord..., *p. 901.*

CHRISTMAS II

Christ restores unity to all creation

This preface is said in Masses of Christmas and its octave; in Masses within the Christmas octave even if they have their own preface, with the exception of Masses with a proper preface of the divine mysteries or Persons; and on weekdays of the Christmas season.

Father, all-powerful and ever-living God,
we do well always and everywhere to give you thanks
through Jesus Christ our Lord.

Today you fill our hearts with joy
as we recognize in Christ the revelation of your love.
No eye can see his glory as our God,
yet now he is seen as one like us.

Christ is your Son before all ages,
yet now he is born in time.
He has come to lift up all things to himself,
to restore unity to creation,
and to lead mankind from exile into your heavenly kingdom.

With all the angels of heaven
we sing our joyful hymn of praise:

Holy, holy, holy Lord..., *p. 901.*

CHRISTMAS III

Divine and human exchange in the incarnation of the Word

*This preface is said in Masses of Christmas and its octave; in Masses
within the Christmas octave even if they have their own preface, with the
exception of Masses with a proper preface of the divine mysteries or Persons; and on weekdays of the Christmas season.*

Father, all-powerful and ever-living God,
we do well always and everywhere to give you thanks
through Jesus Christ our Lord.

Today in him a new light has dawned upon the world:
God has become one with man,
and man has become one again with God.
Your eternal Word has taken upon himself our human weakness,
giving our mortal nature immortal value.
So marvelous is this oneness between God and man
that in Christ man restores to man the gift of everlasting life.

In our joy we sing to your glory
with all the choirs of angels:

Holy, holy, holy Lord..., *p. 901.*

EPIPHANY

Christ the light of the nations

The preface is said in Masses on Epiphany. It may be said, as may the Christmas prefaces, on the days between Epiphany and the Baptism of the Lord.

Father, all-powerful and ever-living God,
we do well always and everywhere to give you thanks.

Today you revealed in Christ your eternal plan of salvation
and showed him as the light of all peoples.
Now that his glory has shone among us
you have renewed humanity in his immortal image.

Now, with angels and archangels,
and the whole company of heaven,
we sing the unending hymn of your praise:

Holy, holy, holy Lord…, *p. 901.*

LENT I

The spiritual meaning of Lent

This preface is said in the Masses of Lent, especially on Sundays which have no preface of their own.

Father, all-powerful and ever-living God,
we do well always and everywhere to give you thanks
through Jesus Christ our Lord.

Each year you give us this joyful season
when we prepare to celebrate the paschal mystery
with mind and heart renewed.
You give us a spirit of loving reverence for you, our Father,
and of willing service to our neighbor.

As we recall the great events that gave us new life in Christ,
you bring the image of your Son to perfection within us.

Now, with angels and archangels,
and the whole company of heaven

we sing the unending hymn of your praise:

Holy, holy, holy Lord..., *p. 901.*

LENT II

The spirit of penance

This preface is said in the Masses of Lent, especially on Sundays which have no preface of their own.

Father, all-powerful and ever-living God,
we do well always and everywhere to give you thanks.

This great season of grace is your gift to your family
to renew us in spirit.
You give us strength to purify our hearts,
to control our desires,
and so to serve you in freedom.
You teach us how to live in this passing world,
with our heart set on the world that will never end.

Now, with all the saints and angels,
we praise you for ever:

Holy, holy, holy Lord..., *p. 901.*

LENT III

The fruits of self-denial

This preface is said in the Masses of Lent, especially on Sundays which have no preface of their own.

Father, all-powerful and ever-living God,
we do well always and everywhere to give you thanks.

You ask us to express our thanks by self-denial.
We are to master our sinfulness and conquer our pride.
We are to show to those in need your goodness to ourselves.

Now, with all the saints and angels,
we praise you for ever:

Holy, holy, holy Lord..., *p. 901.*

LENT IV

The reward of fasting

This preface is said in the Masses of Lent, especially on Sundays which have no preface of their own.

Father, all-powerful and ever-living God,
we do well always and everywhere to give you thanks.

Through our observance of Lent
you correct our faults and raise our minds to you,
you help us grow in holiness,
and offer us the reward of everlasting life
through Jesus Christ our Lord.

Through him the angels and all the choirs of heaven
worship in awe before your presence.
May our voices be one with theirs
as they sing with joy the hymn of your glory:

Holy, holy, holy Lord…, *p. 901.*

PASSION OF THE LORD I

The power of the cross

This preface is said during the fifth week of Lent and in Masses of the mysteries of the cross and the passion of the Lord.

Father, all-powerful and ever-living God,
we do well always and everywhere to give you thanks.

The suffering and death of your Son
brought life to the whole world,
moving our hearts to praise your glory.
The power of the cross reveals your judgment on this world
and the kingship of Christ crucified.

We praise you, Lord,
with all the angels and saints in their song of joy:

Holy, holy, holy Lord…, *p. 901.*

PASSION OF THE LORD II

The victory of the passion

This preface is said on Monday, Tuesday, and Wednesday of Holy Week.

Father, all-powerful and ever-living God,
we do well always and everywhere to give you thanks
through Jesus Christ our Lord.

The days of his life-giving death and glorious resurrection
   are approaching.
This is the hour when he triumphed over Satan's pride,
the time when we celebrate the great event of our redemption.

Through Christ
the angels of heaven offer their prayer of adoration
as they rejoice in your presence for ever.
May our voices be one with theirs
in their triumphant hymn of praise:

Holy, holy, holy Lord..., *p. 901.*

PRIESTHOOD (CHRISM MASS)

The priesthood and the ministry of priests

This preface is said in the chrism Mass on Holy Thursday.

Father, all-powerful and ever-living God,
we do well always and everywhere to give you thanks.

By your Holy Spirit
you anointed your only Son
High Priest of the new and eternal covenant.
With wisdom and love you have planned
that this one priesthood should continue in the Church.

Christ gives the dignity of a royal priesthood
to the people he has made his own.
From these, with a brother's love,
he chooses men to share his sacred ministry
by the laying on of hands.

He appoints them to renew in his name
the sacrifice of our redemption
as they set before your family his paschal meal.
He calls them to lead your holy people in love,
nourish them by your word,
and strengthen them through the sacraments.

Father, they are to give their lives in your service
and for the salvation of your people
as they strive to grow in the likeness of Christ
and honor you by their courageous witness of faith and love.

We praise you, Lord, with all the angels and saints
in their song of joy:
Holy, holy, holy Lord..., *p. 901.*

EASTER I

The paschal mystery

*This preface is said in the Masses of the Easter Vigil and Easter Sunday
and during the octave.*

Father, all-powerful and ever-living God,
we do well always and everywhere to give you thanks
through Jesus Christ our Lord.

We praise you with greater joy than ever
on this Easter night (day) (in this Easter season),
when Christ became our paschal sacrifice.

He is the true Lamb who took away the sins of the world.
By dying he destroyed our death;
by rising he restored our life.

And so, with all the choirs of angels in heaven
we proclaim your glory
and join in their unending hymn of praise:
Holy, holy, holy Lord..., *p. 901.*

EASTER II

New life in Christ

This preface is said during the Easter season.

Father, all-powerful and ever-living God,
we do well always and everywhere to give you thanks
through Jesus Christ our Lord.

We praise you with greater joy than ever in this Easter season,
when Christ became our paschal sacrifice.

He has made us children of the light,
rising to new and everlasting life.
He has opened the gates of heaven
to receive his faithful people.
His death is our ransom from death;
his resurrection is our rising to life.

The joy of the resurrection renews the whole world,
while the choirs of heaven sing for ever to your glory:
Holy, holy, holy Lord..., *p. 901.*

EASTER III

Christ lives and intercedes for us for ever

This preface is said during the Easter season.

Father, all-powerful and ever-living God,
we do well always and everywhere to give you thanks
through Jesus Christ our Lord.

We praise you with greater joy than ever in this Easter season,
when Christ became our paschal sacrifice.

He is still our priest,
our advocate who always pleads our cause.
Christ is the victim who dies no more,
the Lamb, once slain, who lives for ever.

The joy of the resurrection renews the whole world,

while the choirs of heaven sing for ever to your glory:

Holy, holy, holy Lord..., *p. 901.*

EASTER IV

The restoration of the universe through the paschal mystery

This preface is said during the Easter season.

Father, all-powerful and ever-living God,
we do well always and everywhere to give you thanks
through Jesus Christ our Lord.

We praise you with greater joy than ever in this Easter season,
when Christ became our paschal sacrifice.

In him a new age has dawned,
the long reign of sin is ended,
a broken world has been renewed,
and man is once again made whole.

The joy of the resurrection renews the whole world,
while the choirs of heaven sing for ever to your glory:

Holy, holy, holy Lord..., *p. 901.*

EASTER V

Christ is priest and victim

This preface is said during the Easter season.

Father, all-powerful and ever-living God,
we do well always and everywhere to give you thanks
through Jesus Christ our Lord.

We praise you with greater joy than ever in this Easter season,
when Christ became our paschal sacrifice.

As he offered his body on the cross,
his perfect sacrifice fulfilled all others.
As he gave himself into your hands for our salvation,
he showed himself to be the priest, the altar, and the lamb of
    sacrifice.

The joy of the resurrection renews the whole world,
while the choirs of heaven sing for ever to your glory:
Holy, holy, holy Lord…, *p. 901.*

ASCENSION I
The mystery of the ascension

This preface is said on the Ascension in all Masses which have no preface of their own, from the Ascension to the Saturday before Pentecost inclusive.

Father, all-powerful and ever-living God,
we do well always and everywhere to give you thanks.

[Today] the Lord Jesus, the king of glory,
the conqueror of sin and death,
ascended into heaven while the angels sang his praises.

Christ, the mediator between God and man,
judge of the world and Lord of all,
has passed beyond our sight,
not to abandon us but to be our hope.
Christ is the beginning, the head of the Church;
where he has gone, we hope to follow.

The joy of the resurrection and ascension renews the whole world,
while the choirs of heaven sing for ever to your glory:
Holy, holy, holy Lord…, *p. 901.*

ASCENSION II
The mystery of the ascension

This preface is said on the Ascension and in all Masses which have no preface of their own, from the Ascension to the Saturday before Pentecost inclusive.

Father, all-powerful and ever-living God,
we do well always and everywhere to give you thanks
through Jesus Christ our Lord.

In his risen body he plainly showed himself to his disciples
and was taken up to heaven in their sight
to claim for us a share in his divine life.

And so, with all the choirs of angels in heaven
we proclaim your glory
and join in their unending hymn of praise:

Holy, holy, holy Lord…, *p. 901.*

WEEKDAYS I
All things made one in Christ

This preface is said in Masses which have no preface of their own, unless they call for a seasonal preface.

Father, all-powerful and ever-living God,
we do well always and everywhere to give you thanks
through Jesus Christ our Lord.

In him you have renewed all things
and you have given us all a share in his riches.

Though his nature was divine,
he stripped himself of glory
and by shedding his blood on the cross
he brought his peace to the world.

Therefore he was exalted above all creation
and became the source of eternal life
to all who serve him.

And so, with all the choirs of angels in heaven
we proclaim your glory
and join in their unending hymn of praise:

Holy, holy, holy Lord…, *p. 901.*

WEEKDAYS II
Salvation through Christ

This preface is said in Masses which have no preface of their own, unless they call for a seasonal preface.

Father, all-powerful and ever-living God,
we do well always and everywhere to give you thanks.

In love you created man,

in justice you condemned him,
but in mercy you redeemed him,
through Jesus Christ our Lord.

Through him the angels and all the choirs of heaven
worship in awe before your presence.
May our voices be one with theirs
as they sing with joy
the hymn of your glory:

Holy, holy, holy Lord..., *p. 901.*

WEEKDAYS III

The praise of God in creation
and through the conversion of man

This preface is said in Masses which have no preface of their own, unless they call for a seasonal preface.

Father, all-powerful and ever-living God,
we do well always and everywhere to give you thanks.

Through your beloved Son
you created our human family.
Through him you restored us to your likeness.

Therefore it is your right
to receive the obedience of all creation,
the praise of the Church on earth,
the thanksgiving of your saints in heaven.

We too rejoice with the angels
as we proclaim your glory for ever:

Holy, holy, holy Lord..., *p. 901.*

WEEKDAYS IV

Praise of God is his gift

This preface is said in Masses which have no preface of their own, unless they call for a seasonal preface.

Father, all-powerful and ever-living God,

we do well always and everywhere to give you thanks.

You have no need of our praise,
yet our desire to thank you is itself your gift.
Our prayer of thanksgiving adds nothing to your greatness,
but makes us grow in your grace,
through Jesus Christ our Lord.

In our joy we sing to your glory
with all the choirs of angels:

Holy, holy, holy Lord…, *p. 901.*

WEEKDAYS V

The mystery of Christ is proclaimed

This preface is said in Masses which have no preface of their own, unless they call for a seasonal preface.

Father, all-powerful and ever-living God,
we do well always and everywhere to give you thanks
through Jesus Christ our Lord.

With love we celebrate his death.
With living faith we proclaim his resurrection.
With unwavering hope we await his return in glory.

Now, with the saints and all the angels
we praise you for ever:

Holy, holy, holy Lord…, *p. 901.*

WEEKDAYS VI

Salvation in Christ

This preface, taken from Eucharistic Prayer II, is said in Masses which have no preface of their own, unless they call for a seasonal preface.

Father, all-powerful and ever-living God,
we do well always and everywhere to give you thanks
through your beloved Son, Jesus Christ.

He is the Word through whom you made the universe,
the Savior you sent to redeem us.
By the power of the Holy Spirit

he took flesh and was born of the Virgin Mary.

For our sake he opened his arms on the cross;
he put an end to death
and revealed the resurrection.
In this he fulfilled your will
and won for you a holy people.

And so we join the angels and the saints
in proclaiming your glory:

Holy, holy, holy Lord…, *p. 901.*

SACRED HEART

The boundless love of Christ

This preface is said in Masses of the Sacred Heart.

Father, all-powerful and ever-living God,
we do well always and everywhere to give you thanks
through Jesus Christ our Lord.

Lifted high on the cross,
Christ gave his life for us,
so much did he love us.
From his wounded side flowed blood and water,
the fountain of sacramental life in the Church.
To his open heart the Savior invites all men,
to draw water in joy from the springs of salvation.

Now, with all the saints and angels,
we praise you for ever:

Holy, holy, holy Lord…, *p. 901.*

DEDICATION OF A CHURCH I

Anniversary of the Dedication
A. Celebration in the Dedicated Church

The mystery of God's temple, which is the Church

Father, all-powerful and ever-living God,
we do well always and everywhere to give you thanks.

We thank you now for this house of prayer
in which you bless your family
as we come to you on pilgrimage.

Here you reveal your presence
by sacramental signs,
and make us one with you
through the unseen bond of grace.
Here you build your temple of living stones,
and bring the Church to its full stature
as the body of Christ throughout the world,
to reach its perfection at last
in the heavenly city of Jerusalem,
which is the vision of your peace.

In communion with all the angels and saints
we bless and praise your greatness
in the temple of your glory:

Holy, holy, holy Lord…, *p. 901.*

DEDICATION OF A CHURCH II

Anniversary of the Dedication
B. Celebration in Other Churches

The mystery of the Church, the bride of Christ and the temple of the Spirit

Father, all-powerful and ever-living God,
we do well always and everywhere to give you thanks.

Your house is a house of prayer,
and your presence makes it a place of blessing.
You give us grace upon grace
to build the temple of your Spirit,
creating its beauty from the holiness of our lives.

Your house of prayer
is also the promise of the Church in heaven.
Here your love is always at work,
preparing the Church on earth

for its heavenly glory
as the sinless bride of Christ,
the joyful mother of a great company of saints.

Now, with the saints and all the angels
we praise you for ever:

Holy, holy, holy Lord…, *p. 901.*

BLESSED VIRGIN MARY I
Motherhood of Mary

This preface is said in Masses of the Blessed Virgin Mary, with the mention of the particular celebration, as indicated in the individual Masses.

Father, all-powerful and ever-living God,
we do well always and everywhere to give you thanks
(as we celebrate…of the Blessed Virgin Mary).
(as we honor the Blessed Virgin Mary).

Through the power of the Holy Spirit,
she became the virgin mother of your only Son,
our Lord Jesus Christ,
who is for ever the light of the world.

Through him the choirs of angels
and all the powers of heaven
praise and worship your glory.
May our voices blend with theirs
as we join in their unending hymn:

Holy, holy, holy Lord…, *p. 901.*

BLESSED VIRGIN MARY II
The Church echoes Mary's song of praise

This preface is said in Masses of the Blessed Virgin Mary.

Father, all-powerful and ever-living God,
we do well always and everywhere to give you thanks,
and to praise you for your gifts

as we contemplate your saints in glory.

In celebrating the memory of the Blessed Virgin Mary,
it is our special joy to echo her song of thanksgiving.
What wonders you have worked throughout the world.
All generations have shared the greatness of your love.
When you looked on Mary your lowly servant,
you raised her to be the mother of Jesus Christ, your Son, our Lord,
the savior of all mankind.

Through him the angels of heaven
offer their prayer of adoration
as they rejoice in your presence for ever.
May our voices be one with theirs
in their triumphant hymn of praise:

Holy, holy, holy Lord..., *p. 901.*

ANGELS

The glory of God in the angels

This preface is said in Masses of the angels.

Father, all-powerful and ever-living God,
we do well always and everywhere to give you thanks.

In praising your faithful angels and archangels,
we also praise your glory,
for in honoring them, we honor you, their creator.
Their splendor shows us your greatness,
which surpasses in goodness the whole of creation.

Through Christ our Lord
the great army of angels rejoices in your glory.
In adoration and joy
we make their hymn of praise our own:

Holy, holy, holy Lord..., *p. 901.*

JOHN THE BAPTIST

The mission of John the Baptist

This preface is said in Masses of Saint John the Baptist.

Father, all-powerful and ever-living God,
we do well always and everywhere to give you thanks
through Jesus Christ our Lord.

We praise your greatness
as we honor the prophet
who prepared the way before your Son.
You set John the Baptist apart from other men,
marking him out with special favor.
His birth brought great rejoicing:
even in the womb he leapt for joy,
so near was man's salvation.

You chose John the Baptist from all the prophets
to show the world its redeemer,
the lamb of sacrifice.
He baptized Christ, the giver of baptism,
in the waters made holy by the one who was baptized.
You found John worthy of a martyr's death,
his last and greatest act of witness to your Son.

In our unending joy we echo on earth
the song of the angels in heaven
as they praise your glory for ever:
Holy, holy, holy Lord…, *p. 901.*

JOSEPH, HUSBAND OF MARY

The mission of Saint Joseph

This preface is said in Masses of Saint Joseph.

Father, all-powerful and ever-living God,
we do well always and everywhere to give you thanks
as we honor Saint Joseph.

He is that just man,
that wise and loyal servant,
whom you placed at the head of your family.
With a husband's love he cherished Mary,
the virgin Mother of God.

With fatherly care he watched over Jesus Christ your Son,
conceived by the power of the Holy Spirit.

Through Christ the choirs of angels
and all the powers of heaven
praise and worship your glory.
May our voices blend with theirs
as we join in their unending hymn:

Holy, holy, holy Lord..., *p. 901.*

APOSTLES I

The apostles are shepherds of God's people

This preface is said in Masses of the Apostles, especially of Saint Peter and Saint Paul.

Father, all-powerful and ever-living God,
we do well always and everywhere to give you thanks.

You are the eternal Shepherd
who never leaves his flock untended.
Through the apostles
you watch over us and protect us always.
You made them shepherds of the flock
to share in the work of your Son,
and from their place in heaven they guide us still.

And so, with all the choirs of angels in heaven
we proclaim your glory
and join in their unending hymn of praise:

Holy, holy, holy Lord..., *p. 901.*

APOSTLES II

Apostolic foundation and witness

This preface is said in Masses of the apostles and evangelists.

Father, all-powerful and ever-living God,
we do well always and everywhere to give you thanks.

You founded your Church on the apostles
to stand firm for ever

as the sign on earth of your infinite holiness
and as the living gospel for all men to hear.

With steadfast love
we sing your unending praise:
we join with the hosts of heaven
in their triumphant song:
Holy, holy, holy Lord..., *p. 901.*

MARTYRS

The sign and example of martyrdom

This preface is said on the solemnities and feasts of martyrs. It may also be said on the memorials of martyrs.

Father, all-powerful and ever-living God,
we do well always and everywhere to give you thanks.

Your holy martyr N. followed the example of Christ,
and gave his (her) life for the glory of your name.
His (her) death reveals your power
shining through our human weakness.
You choose the weak and make them strong
in bearing witness to you,
through Jesus Christ our Lord.

In our unending joy we echo on earth
the song of the angels in heaven
as they praise your glory for ever:
Holy, holy, holy Lord..., *p. 901.*

PASTORS

The presence of shepherds in the Church

This preface is said on the solemnities and feasts of pastors. It may also be said on the memorials of pastors.

Father, all-powerful and ever-living God,
we do well always and everywhere to give you thanks.

You give the Church this feast in honor of Saint N.;
you inspire us by his holy life,

instruct us by his preaching,
and give us your protection in answer to his prayers.

We join the angels and the saints
as they sing their unending hymn of praise:

Holy, holy, holy Lord…, *p. 901.*

VIRGINS AND RELIGIOUS

The sign of a life consecrated to God

This preface is said on the solemnities and feasts of virgins and religious. It may also be said on the memorials of virgins and religious.

Father, all-powerful and ever-living God,
we do well always and everywhere to give you thanks.

Today we honor your saints
who consecrated their lives to Christ
for the sake of the kingdom of heaven.
What love you show us
as you recall mankind to its innocence,
and invite us to taste on earth
the gifts of the world to come!

Now, with the saints and all the angels
we praise you for ever:

Holy, holy, holy Lord…, *p. 901.*

HOLY MEN AND WOMEN I

The glory of the saints

This preface is said in Masses of all saints, patrons, and titulars of churches, and on the solemnities and feasts of saints which have no preface of their own. It may also be said on the memorials of saints.

Father, all-powerful and ever-living God,
we do well always and everywhere to give you thanks.

You are glorified in your saints,
for their glory is the crowning of your gifts.
In their lives on earth
you give us an example.

In our communion with them,
you give us their friendship.
In their prayer for the Church
you give us strength and protection.
This great company of witnesses spurs us on to victory,
to share their prize of everlasting glory,
through Jesus Christ our Lord.

With angels and archangels
and the whole company of saints
we sing our unending hymn of praise:
Holy, holy, holy Lord..., *p. 901.*

HOLY MEN AND WOMEN II

The activity of the saints

This preface is said in Masses of all saints, patrons, and titulars of churches, and on the solemnities and feasts which have no preface of their own. It may also be said on the memorials of saints.

Father, all-powerful and ever-living God,
we do well always and everywhere to give you thanks.

You renew the Church in every age
by raising up men and women outstanding in holiness,
living witnesses of your unchanging love.
They inspire us by their heroic lives,
and help us by their constant prayers
to be the living sign of your saving power.

We praise you, Lord, with all the angels and saints
in their song of joy:
Holy, holy, holy Lord..., *p. 901.*

MARRIAGE I

The dignity of the marriage bond

Father, all-powerful and ever-living God,
we do well always and everywhere to give you thanks.

By this sacrament your grace unites man and woman

in an unbreakable bond of love and peace.

You have designed the chaste love of husband and wife
for the increase both of the human family
and of your own family born in baptism.

You are the loving Father of the world of nature;
you are the loving Father of the new creation of grace.
In Christian marriage you bring together the two orders of creation:
nature's gift of children enriches the world
and your grace enriches also your Church.

Through Christ the choirs of angels
and all the saints
praise and worship your glory.
May our voices blend with theirs
as we join in their unending hymn:

Holy, holy, holy Lord..., *p. 901.*

MARRIAGE II

The great sacrament of marriage

Father, all-powerful and ever-living God,
we do well always and everywhere to give you thanks
through Jesus Christ our Lord.

Through him you entered into a new covenant with your people.
You restored man to grace in the saving mystery of redemption.
You gave him a share in the divine life
through his union with Christ.
You made him an heir of Christ's eternal glory.

This outpouring of love in the new covenant of grace
is symbolized in the marriage covenant
that seals the love of husband and wife
and reflects your divine plan of love.

And so, with the angels and all the saints in heaven
we proclaim your glory
and join in their unending hymn of praise:

Holy, holy, holy Lord..., *p. 901.*

MARRIAGE III

Marriage, a sign of God's love

Father, all-powerful and ever-living God,
we do well always and everywhere to give you thanks.

You created man in love to share your divine life.
We see his high destiny in the love of husband and wife,
which bears the imprint of your own divine love.

Love is man's origin,
love is his constant calling,
love is his fulfillment in heaven.

The love of man and woman
is made holy in the sacrament of marriage,
and becomes the mirror of your everlasting love.

Through Christ the choirs of angels
and all the saints
praise and worship your glory.
May our voices blend with theirs
as we join in their unending hymn:
Holy, holy, holy Lord..., *p. 901.*

CHRISTIAN DEATH I

The hope of rising in Christ

This preface is said in Masses for the dead.

Father, all-powerful and ever-living God,
we do well always and everywhere to give you thanks
through Jesus Christ our Lord.

In him, who rose from the dead,
our hope of resurrection dawned.
The sadness of death gives way
to the bright promise of immortality.

Lord, for your faithful people life is changed, not ended.
When the body of our earthly dwelling lies in death
we gain an everlasting dwelling place in heaven.

And so, with all the choirs of angels in heaven
we proclaim your glory
and join in their unending hymn of praise:
Holy, holy, holy Lord..., *p. 901.*

CHRISTIAN DEATH II

Christ's death, our life

This preface is said in Masses for the dead.

Father, all-powerful and ever-living God,
we do well always and everywhere to give you thanks
through Jesus Christ our Lord.

He chose to die
that he might free all men from dying.
He gave his life
that we might live to you alone for ever.

In our joy we sing to your glory
with all the choirs of angels:
Holy, holy, holy Lord..., *p. 901.*

CHRISTIAN DEATH III

Christ, salvation and life

This preface is said in Masses for the dead.

Father, all-powerful and ever-living God,
we do well always and everywhere to give you thanks
through Jesus Christ our Lord.

In him the world is saved,
man is reborn,
and the dead rise again to life.

Through Christ the angels of heaven
offer their prayer of adoration
as they rejoice in your presence for ever.
May our voices be one with theirs
in their triumphant hymn of praise:
Holy, holy, holy Lord..., *p. 901.*

CHRISTIAN DEATH IV

From earthly life to heaven's glory

This preface is said in Masses for the dead.

Father, all-powerful and ever-living God,
we do well always and everywhere to give you thanks.

By your power you bring us to birth.
By your providence you rule our lives.
By your command you free us at last from sin
as we return to the dust from which we came.
Through the saving death of your Son
we rise at your word to the glory of the resurrection.

Now we join the angels and the saints
as they sing their unending hymn of praise:
Holy, holy, holy Lord…, *p. 901.*

CHRISTIAN DEATH V

Our resurrection through Christ's victory

This preface is said in Masses for the dead.

Father, all-powerful and ever-living God,
we do well always and everywhere to give you thanks
through Jesus Christ our Lord.

Death is the just reward for our sins,
yet, when at last we die,
your loving kindness calls us back to life
in company with Christ,
whose victory is our redemption.

Our hearts are joyful,
for we have seen your salvation,
and now with the angels and saints
we praise you for ever:
Holy, holy, holy Lord…, *p. 901.*

[In the dioceses of the United States]

INDEPENDENCE DAY
AND OTHER CIVIC OBSERVANCES I

Father, all-powerful and ever-living God,
we do well to sing your praise for ever,
and to give you thanks in all we do
through Jesus Christ our Lord.

He spoke to men a message of peace
and taught us to live as brothers.
His message took form in the vision of our fathers
as they fashioned a nation
where men might live as one.
This message lives on in our midst
as a task for men today
and a promise for tomorrow.

We thank you, Father, for your blessings in the past
and for all that, with your help, we must yet achieve.
And so, with hearts full of love,
we join the angels today and every day of our lives,
to sing your glory in a hymn of endless praise:

Holy, holy, holy Lord…, *p. 901.*

[In the dioceses of the United States]

INDEPENDENCE DAY
AND OTHER CIVIC OBSERVANCES II

Father, all-powerful and ever-living God,
we praise your oneness and truth.

We praise you as the God of creation,
as the Father of Jesus, the Savior of mankind,
in whose image we seek to live.
He loved the children of the lands he walked
and enriched them with his witness of justice and truth.
He lived and died that we might be reborn in the Spirit
and filled with love of all men.

And so, with hearts full of love,

we join the angels, today and every day of our lives,
to sing your glory in a hymn of endless praise:
Holy, holy, holy Lord…, *p. 901.*

[In the dioceses of the United States]
THANKSGIVING DAY

Father, we do well to join all creation,
in heaven and on earth,
in praising you, our mighty God
through Jesus Christ our Lord.

You made man to your own image
and set him over all creation.
Once you chose a people
and gave them a destiny
and, when you brought them out of bondage to freedom,
they carried with them the promise
that all men would be blessed
and all men could be free.

What the prophets pledged
was fulfilled in Jesus Christ,
your Son and our saving Lord.
It has come to pass in every generation
for all men who have believed that Jesus
by his death and resurrection
gave them a new freedom in his Spirit.

It happened to our fathers,
who came to this land as if out of the desert
into a place of promise and hope.

It happens to us still, in our time,
as you lead all men through your Church
to the blessed vision of peace.

And so, with hearts full of love,
we join the angels, today and every day of our lives,
to sing your glory in a hymn of endless praise:
Holy, holy, holy Lord…, *p. 901.*

SOLEMN BLESSINGS

The following blessings may be used, at the discretion of the priest, at the end of Mass, or after the liturgy of the word, the office, and the celebration of the sacraments.

The deacon, or in his absence, the priest himself, gives the invitation: BOW YOUR HEADS AND PRAY FOR GOD'S BLESSING. Another form of invitation may be used. Then the priest extends his hands over the people while he says or sings the blessings. All respond: **Amen.**

I. Celebrations During the Proper of Seasons

1. ADVENT

You believe that the Son of God once came to us;
you look for him to come again.
May his coming bring you the light of his holiness
and free you with his blessing.
R. Amen.

May God make you steadfast in faith,
joyful in hope, and untiring in love
all the days of your life.
R. Amen.

You rejoice that our Redeemer came to live with us as man.
When he comes again in glory,
may he reward you with endless life.
R. Amen.

May almighty God bless you,
the Father, and the Son, ✠ and the Holy Spirit.
R. Amen.

2. CHRISTMAS

When he came to us as a man,
the Son of God scattered the darkness of this world
and filled this holy night (day) with his glory.
May the God of infinite goodness

scatter the darkness of sin
and brighten your hearts with holiness.
R. Amen.

God sent his angels to shepherds
to herald the great joy of our Savior's birth.
May he fill you with joy
and make you heralds of his gospel.
R. Amen.

When the Word became man,
earth was joined to heaven.
May he give you his peace and good will,
and fellowship with all the heavenly host.
R. Amen.

May almighty God bless you,
the Father, and the Son, ✠ and the Holy Spirit.
R. Amen.

3. BEGINNING OF THE NEW YEAR

Every good gift comes from the Father of light.
May he grant you his grace and every blessing,
and keep you safe throughout the coming year.
R. Amen.

May he grant you unwavering faith,
constant hope, and love that endures to the end.
R. Amen.

May he order your days and work in his peace,
hear your every prayer,
and lead you to everlasting life and joy.
R. Amen.

May almighty God bless you,
the Father, and the Son, ✠ and the Holy Spirit.
R. Amen.

4. EPIPHANY

God has called you out of darkness
into his wonderful light.
May you experience his kindness and blessings,
and be strong in faith, in hope, and in love.

R. Amen.

Because you are followers of Christ,
who appeared on this day as a light shining in darkness,
may he make you a light to all your sisters and brothers.

R. Amen.

The wise men followed the star,
and found Christ who is light from light.
May you too find the Lord
when your pilgrimage is ended.

R. Amen.

May almighty God bless you,
the Father, and the Son, ✠ and the Holy Spirit.

R. Amen.

5. PASSION OF THE LORD

The Father of mercies has given us an example of unselfish love
in the sufferings of his only Son.
Through your service of God and neighbor
may you receive his countless blessings.

R. Amen.

You believe that by his dying
Christ destroyed death for ever.
May he give you everlasting life.

R. Amen.

He humbled himself for our sakes.
May you follow his example
and share in his resurrection.

R. Amen.

May almighty God bless you,
the Father, and the Son, ✠ and the Holy Spirit.
R. Amen.

6. EASTER VIGIL AND EASTER SUNDAY

May almighty God bless you on this solemn feast of Easter,
and may he protect you against all sin.
R. Amen.

Through the resurrection of his Son
God has granted us healing.
May he fulfill his promises,
and bless you with eternal life.
R. Amen.

You have mourned for Christ's sufferings;
now you celebrate the joy of his resurrection.
May you come with joy to the feast which lasts for ever.
R. Amen.

May almighty God bless you,
the Father, and the Son, ✠ and the Holy Spirit.
R. Amen.

7. EASTER SEASON

Through the resurrection of his Son
God has redeemed you and made you his children.
May he bless you with joy.
R. Amen.

The Redeemer has given you lasting freedom.
May you inherit his everlasting life.
R. Amen.

By faith you rose with him in baptism.
May your lives be holy,
so that you will be united with him for ever.
R. Amen.

May almighty God bless you,
the Father, and the Son, ✠ and the Holy Spirit.
R. Amen.

8. ASCENSION

May almighty God bless you on this day
when his only Son ascended into heaven
to prepare a place for you.
R. Amen.

After his resurrection, Christ was seen by his disciples.
When he appears as a judge
may you be pleasing for ever in his sight.
R. Amen.

You believe that Jesus has taken his seat in majesty
at the right hand of the Father.
May you have the joy of experiencing
that he is also with you to the end of time,
according to his promise.
R. Amen.

May almighty God bless you,
the Father, and the Son, ✠ and the Holy Spirit.
R. Amen.

9. HOLY SPIRIT

(This day) the Father of light
has enlightened the minds of the disciples
by the outpouring of the Holy Spirit.
May he bless you
and give you the gifts of the Spirit for ever.
R. Amen.

May that fire which hovered over the disciples
as tongues of flame
burn out all evil from your hearts
and make them glow with pure light.
R. Amen.

God inspired speech in different tongues
to proclaim one faith.
May he strengthen your faith
and fulfill your hope of seeing him face to face.
R. Amen.

May almighty God bless you,
the Father, and the Son, ✠ and the Holy Spirit.
R. Amen.

10. ORDINARY TIME I

Blessing of Aaron (Num 6:24–26)

May the Lord bless you and keep you.
R. Amen.

May his face shine upon you,
and be gracious to you.
R. Amen.

May he look upon you with kindness,
and give you his peace.
R. Amen.

May almighty God bless you,
the Father, and the Son, ✠ and the Holy Spirit.
R. Amen.

11. ORDINARY TIME II

(Phil 4:7)

May the peace of God
which is beyond all understanding
keep your hearts and minds
in the knowledge and love of God
and of his Son, our Lord Jesus Christ.
R. Amen.

May almighty God bless you,
the Father, and the Son, ✠ and the Holy Spirit.
R. Amen.

12. ORDINARY TIME III

May almighty God bless you in his mercy,
and make you always aware of his saving wisdom.
R. Amen.

May he strengthen your faith with proofs of his love,
so that you will persevere in good works.
R. Amen.

May he direct your steps to himself,
and show you how to walk in charity and peace.
R. Amen.

May almighty God bless you,
the Father, and the Son, ✠ and the Holy Spirit.
R. Amen.

13. ORDINARY TIME IV

May the God of all consolation
bless you in every way
and grant you peace all the days of your life.
R. Amen.

May he free you from all anxiety
and strengthen your hearts in his love.
R. Amen.

May he enrich you with his gifts of faith, hope, and love,
so that what you do in this life
will bring you to the happiness of everlasting life.
R. Amen.

May almighty God bless you,
the Father, and the Son, ✠ and the Holy Spirit.
R. Amen.

14. ORDINARY TIME V

May almighty God keep you from all harm
and bless you with every good gift.
R. Amen.

May he set his Word in your heart
and fill you with lasting joy.
R. Amen.

May you walk in his ways,
always knowing what is right and good,
until you enter your heavenly inheritance.
R. Amen.

May almighty God bless you,
the Father, and the Son, ✠ and the Holy Spirit.
R. Amen.

II. Celebrations of Saints

15. BLESSED VIRGIN MARY

Born of the Blessed Virgin Mary,
the Son of God redeemed mankind.
May he enrich you with his blessings.
R. Amen.

You received the author of life through Mary.
May you always rejoice in her loving care.
R. Amen.

You have come to rejoice at Mary's feast.
May you be filled with the joys of the Spirit
and the gifts of your eternal home.
R. Amen.

May almighty God bless you,
the Father, and the Son, ✠ and the Holy Spirit.
R. Amen.

16. PETER AND PAUL

The Lord has set you firm within his Church,
which he built upon the rock of Peter's faith.
May he bless you with a faith that never falters.
R. Amen.

The Lord has given you knowledge of the faith
through the labors and preaching of St. Paul.
May his example inspire you to lead others to Christ
by the manner of your life.
R. Amen.

May the keys of Peter, and the words of Paul,
their undying witness and their prayers,
lead you to the joy of that eternal home
which Peter gained by his cross, and Paul by the sword.
R. Amen.

May almighty God bless you,
the Father, and the Son, ✠ and the Holy Spirit.
R. Amen.

17. APOSTLES

May God who founded his Church upon the apostles
bless you through the prayers of St. N. (and St. N.).
R. Amen.

May God inspire you to follow the example of the apostles,
and give witness to the truth before all men.
R. Amen.

The teaching of the apostles has strengthened your faith.
May their prayers lead you
to your true and eternal home.
R. Amen.

May almighty God bless you,
the Father, and the Son, ✠ and the Holy Spirit.
R. Amen.

18. ALL SAINTS

God is the glory and joy of all his saints,
whose memory we celebrate today.
May his blessing be with you always.
R. Amen.

May the prayers of the saints deliver you from present evil.
May their example of holy living
turn your thoughts to service of God and neighbor.
R. Amen.

God's holy Church rejoices that her saints
have reached their heavenly goal,
and are in lasting peace.
May you come to share all the joys of our Father's house.
R. Amen.

May almighty God bless you,
the Father, and the Son, ✠ and the Holy Spirit.
R. Amen.

III. Other Blessings

19. DEDICATION OF A CHURCH

The Lord of earth and heaven
has assembled you before him this day
to dedicate this house of prayer
(to recall the dedication of this church).
May he fill you with the blessings of heaven.
R. Amen.

God the Father wills that all his children
scattered throughout the world
become one family in his Son.
May he make you his temple,
the dwelling-place of his Holy Spirit.
R. Amen.

May God free you from every bond of sin,
dwell within you and give you joy.
May you live with him for ever
in the company of all his saints.
R. Amen.

May almighty God bless you,
the Father, and the Son, ✠ and the Holy Spirit.
R. Amen.

20. THE DEAD

In his great love,
the God of all consolation gave man the gift of life.
May he bless you with faith
in the resurrection of his Son,
and with the hope of rising to new life.
R. Amen.

To us who are alive
may he grant forgiveness,
and to all who have died
a place of light and peace.
R. Amen.

As you believe that Jesus rose from the dead,
so may you live with him for ever in joy.
R. Amen.

May almighty God bless you,
the Father, and the Son, ✠ and the Holy Spirit.
R. Amen.

PRAYERS OVER THE PEOPLE

The following prayers may be used, at the discretion of the priest, at the end of Mass, or after the liturgy of the word, the office, and the celebration of the sacraments.

The deacon, or in his absence the priest himself, gives the invitation: BOW YOUR HEADS AND PRAY FOR GOD'S BLESSING. Another form of invitation may be used. Then the priest extends his hands over the people while he says or sings the prayer. All respond: **Amen.**

After the prayer, the priest always adds:

And may the blessing of almighty God,
the Father, and the Son, ✠ and the Holy Spirit,
come upon you and remain with you for ever.
All respond: **Amen.**

1.

Lord,
have mercy on your people.
Grant us in this life the good things
that lead to the everlasting life you prepare for us.
We ask this through Christ our Lord.

2.

Lord,
grant your people your protection and grace.
Give them health of mind and body,
perfect love for one another,
and make them always faithful to you.
Grant this through Christ our Lord.

3.

Lord,
may all Christian people both know and cherish
the heavenly gifts they have received.
We ask this in the name of Jesus the Lord.

4.

Lord,
bless your people and make them holy
so that avoiding evil,
they may find in you the fulfillment of their longing.
We ask this through Christ our Lord.

5.

Lord,
bless and strengthen your people.
May they remain faithful to you
and always rejoice in your mercy.
We ask this in the name of Jesus the Lord.

6.

Lord,
you care for your people even when they stray.
Grant us a complete change of heart,
so that we may follow you with greater fidelity.
Grant this through Christ our Lord.

7.

Lord,
send your light upon your family.
May they continue to enjoy your favor
and devote themselves to doing good.
We ask this through Christ our Lord.

8.

Lord,
we rejoice that you are our creator and ruler.
As we call upon your generosity,
renew and keep us in your love.
Grant this through Christ our Lord.

9.

Lord,
we pray for your people who believe in you.
May they enjoy the gift of your love,
share it with others,
and spread it everywhere.
We ask this in the name of Jesus the Lord.

10.

Lord,
bless your people who hope for your mercy.
Grant that they may receive
the things they ask for at your prompting.
Grant this through Christ our Lord.

11.

Lord,
bless us with your heavenly gifts,
and in your mercy make us ready to do your will.
We ask this through Christ our Lord.

12.

Lord,
protect your people always,
that they may be free from every evil
and serve you with all their hearts.
We ask this through Christ our Lord.

13.

Lord,
help your people to seek you with all their hearts
and to deserve what you promise.
Grant this through Christ our Lord.

14.

Father,
help your people to rejoice in the mystery of redemption
and to win its reward.
We ask this in the name of Jesus the Lord.

15.

Lord,
have pity on your people;
help them each day to avoid what displeases you
and grant that they may serve you with joy.
We ask this through Christ our Lord.

16.

Lord,
care for your people and purify them.
Console them in this life
and bring them to the life to come.
We ask this in the name of Jesus the Lord.

17.

Father,
look with love upon your people,
the love which our Lord Jesus Christ showed us
when he delivered himself to evil men
and suffered the agony of the cross,
for he is Lord for ever.

18.

Lord,
grant that your faithful people
may continually desire to relive the mystery of the eucharist
and so be reborn to lead a new life.
We ask this through Christ our Lord.

19.

Lord God,
in your great mercy,
enrich your people with your grace
and strengthen them by your blessing
so that they may praise you always.
Grant this through Christ our Lord.

20.

May God bless you with every good gift from on high.
May he keep you pure and holy in his sight at all times.
May he bestow riches of his grace upon you,
bring you the good news of salvation,
and always fill you with love for all men.
We ask this through Christ our Lord.

21.

Lord,
make us pure in mind and body,
that we will avoid all evil pleasures
and always delight in you.
We ask this in the name of Jesus the Lord.

22.

Lord,
bless your people and fill them with zeal.
Strengthen them by your love to do your will.
We ask this through Christ our Lord.

23.

Lord,
come, live in your people
and strengthen them by your grace.

Help them to remain close to you in prayer
and give them a true love for one another.
Grant this through Christ our Lord.

24.

Father,
look kindly on your children who put their trust in you;
bless them and keep them from all harm,
strengthen them against the attacks of the devil.
May they never offend you
but seek to love you in all they do.
We ask this through Christ our Lord.

FEASTS OF SAINTS

25.

God our Father,
may all Christian people rejoice in the glory of your saints.
Give us fellowship with them
and unending joy in your kingdom.
We ask this in the name of Jesus the Lord.

26.

Lord,
you have given us many friends in heaven.
Through their prayers we are confident
that you will watch over us always
and fill our hearts with your love.
Grant this through Christ our Lord.

For TRINITY SUNDAY, *see* **Vatican II Sunday Missal,** p. 569
For CORPUS CHRISTI *(in U.S.A., Sunday after Trinity Sunday), see* **Vatican II Sunday Missal,** p. 580.

Friday after the Second Sunday after Pentecost
THE SOLEMNITY OF THE
MOST SACRED HEART OF JESUS

Entrance Antiphon

The thoughts of his heart last through every generation, that he will rescue them from death and feed them in time of famine.

(Ps 32:11, 19)

Opening Prayer

Let us pray

[that we will respond to the love of Christ]

Pause for silent prayer

Father,
we rejoice in the gifts of love
we have received from the heart
of Jesus your Son.
Open our hearts to share his life
and continue to bless us with his love.

We ask this through our Lord Jesus Christ, your Son,
who lives and reigns with you and the Holy Spirit,
one God, for ever and ever.

Or:

Let us pray

[that the love of Christ's heart
may touch the world with healing peace]

Pause for silent prayer

Father,
we have wounded the heart of Jesus your Son,

983

but he brings us forgiveness and grace.
Help us to prove our grateful love
and make amends for our sins.

We ask this through our Lord Jesus Christ, your Son,
who lives and reigns with you and the Holy Spirit,
one God, for ever and ever.

Alternative Opening Prayer

Let us pray
   [that the love of Christ's heart
   may touch the world with healing peace]

Pause for silent prayer

Father,
we honor the heart of your Son
broken by man's cruelty,
yet symbol of love's triumph,
pledge of all that man is called to be.
Teach us to see Christ in the lives we touch,
to offer him living worship
by love-filled service to our brothers and sisters.

We ask this through Christ our Lord.

Liturgy of the Word: *for A cycle, see below; for B cycle, turn to p. 987; for C cycle, turn to p. 991.*

TODAY'S LIVING WORD

"Everything God wanted to tell us about himself and about his love he placed in the Heart of Jesus. We find ourselves before an inscrutable mystery. In Jesus' Heart we read the eternal divine plan of the world's salvation. It is a plan of love.

"Christ loves us and reveals his Heart to us as the fount of life and holiness, the source of our redemption…. Jesus is the source; from him divine life in us finds its beginning. To have this life, we need only approach him and remain in him. And what is this life if not the beginning of human holiness, the holiness which is in God and which we can reach with the help of grace?" (Pope John Paul II).

A

2005, 2008, 2011, 2014, 2017, 2020, 2023

FIRST READING   Dt 7:6–11

The Lord set his heart on you and chose you.

A reading from the Book of Deuteronomy

Moses said to the people: "You are a people sacred to the LORD, your God; he has chosen you from all the nations on the face of the earth to be a people peculiarly his own. It was not because you are the largest of all nations that the LORD set his heart on you and chose you, for you are really the smallest of all nations. It was because the LORD loved you and because of his fidelity to the oath he had sworn to your fathers, that he brought you out with his strong hand from the place of slavery, and ransomed you from the hand of Pharaoh, king of Egypt. Understand, then, that the LORD, your God, is God indeed, the faithful God who keeps his merciful covenant down to the thousandth generation toward those who love him and keep his commandments, but who repays with destruction the person who hates him; he does not dally with such a one, but makes him personally pay for it. You shall therefore carefully observe the commandments, the statutes and the decrees which I enjoin on you today."

The word of the Lord.

Responsorial Psalm   Ps 103:1–2, 3–4, 6–7, 8, 10

R. The Lord's kindness is everlasting to those who fear him.

Bless the LORD, O my soul;
  all my being, bless his holy name.
Bless the LORD, O my soul,
  and forget not all his benefits.

R. The Lord's kindness is everlasting to those who fear him.

He pardons all your iniquities,
  heals all your ills,
He redeems your life from destruction,
  crowns you with kindness and compassion.

R. The Lord's kindness is everlasting to those who fear him.

Merciful and gracious is the LORD,
  slow to anger and abounding in kindness.
Not according to our sins does he deal with us,
  nor does he requite us according to our crimes.

R. The Lord's kindness is everlasting to those who fear him.

SECOND READING
1 Jn 4:7–16

If we love one another, God remains in us.

A reading from the first Letter of Saint John

Beloved, let us love one another, because love is of God; everyone who loves is begotten by God and knows God. Whoever is without love does not know God, for God is love. In this way the love of God was revealed to us: God sent his only-begotten Son into the world so that we might have life through him. In this is love: not that we have loved God, but that he loved us and sent his Son as expiation for our sins. Beloved, if God so loved us, we also must love one another. No one has ever seen God. Yet, if we love one another, God remains in us, and his love is brought to perfection in us.

This is how we know that we remain in him and he in us, that he has given us of his Spirit. Moreover, we have seen and testify that the Father sent his Son as savior of the world. Whoever acknowledges that Jesus is the Son of God, God remains in him and he in God. We have come to know and to believe in the love God has for us.

God is love, and whoever remains in love remains in God and God in him.

The word of the Lord.

> **Alleluia, alleluia**   Mt 11:29ab
> Take my yoke upon you, says the Lord;
> And learn from me, for I am meek and humble of heart.
> **Alleluia, alleluia**

GOSPEL

Mt 11:25–30

*Although you have hidden these things from the
wise and the learned, you have revealed them to the childlike.*

A reading from the holy Gospel according to Matthew

At that time Jesus exclaimed: "I give praise to you, Father, Lord of heaven and earth, for although you have hidden these things from the wise and the learned you have revealed them to the childlike. Yes, Father, such has been your gracious will. All things have been handed over to me by my Father. No one knows the Son except the Father, and no one knows the Father except the Son and anyone to whom the Son wishes to reveal him.

"Come to me, all you who labor and are burdened, and I will give you rest. Take my yoke upon you and learn from me, for I am meek and humble of heart; and you will find rest for yourselves. For my yoke is easy, and my burden light."

The Gospel of the Lord.

Liturgy of the Eucharist, *p. 897;* **Prayer over the Gifts,** *p. 994.*

B

2003, 2006, 2009, 2012, 2015, 2018, 2021

FIRST READING

Hos 11:1, 3–4, 8c–9

My heart is overwhelmed.

A reading from the Book of the Prophet Hosea

Thus says the LORD:
When Israel was a child I loved him,
    out of Egypt I called my son.
Yet it was I who taught Ephraim to walk,
    who took them in my arms;
I drew them with human cords,
    with bands of love;
I fostered them like one
    who raises an infant to his cheeks;
Yet, though I stooped to feed my child,
    they did not know that I was their healer.

My heart is overwhelmed,
    my pity is stirred.
I will not give vent to my blazing anger,
    I will not destroy Ephraim again;
For I am God and not man,
    the Holy One present among you;
    I will not let the flames consume you.

The word of the Lord.

Responsorial Psalm

Is 12:2 – 3, 4, 5 – 6

**R. You will draw water joyfully from the springs of
salvation.**

God indeed is my savior;
    I am confident and unafraid.
My strength and my courage is the LORD,
    and he has been my savior.
With joy you will draw water
    at the fountain of salvation.

**R. You will draw water joyfully from the springs of
salvation.**

Give thanks to the L ORD, acclaim his name;
  among the nations make known his deeds,
  proclaim how exalted is his name.

**R. You will draw water joyfully from the springs of
    salvation**

Sing praise to the L ORD for his glorious achievement;
  let this be known throughout all the earth.
Shout with exultation, O city of Zion,
  for great in your midst
  is the Holy One of Israel!

**R. You will draw water joyfully from the springs of
    salvation.**

SECOND READING
Eph 3:8–12, 14–19

To know the love of Christ which surpasses knowledge.

A reading from the Letter of Saint Paul to the Ephesians

Brothers and sisters:

To me, the very least of all the holy ones, this grace was given,
to preach to the Gentiles the inscrutable riches of Christ, and
to bring to light for all what is the plan of the mystery hidden
from ages past in God who created all things, so that the
manifold wisdom of God might now be made known through
the Church to the principalities and authorities in the heavens.
This was according to the eternal purpose that he accomplished
in Christ Jesus our Lord, in whom we have boldness of speech
and confidence of access through faith in him.

For this reason I kneel before the Father, from whom every
family in heaven and on earth is named, that he may grant
you in accord with the riches of his glory to be strengthened
with power through his Spirit in the inner self, and that Christ
may dwell in your hearts through faith; that you, rooted and

grounded in love, may have strength to comprehend with all the holy ones what is the breadth and length and height and depth, and to know the love of Christ that surpasses knowledge, so that you may be filled with all the fullness of God.

The word of the Lord.

> **Alleluia, alleluia**
> Take my yoke upon you, says the Lord;
> And learn from me, for I am meek and humble of heart.   Mt 11:29ab

Or:

> God first loved us
> And sent his Son as expiation for our sins.   1 Jn 4:10b
> **Alleluia, alleluia**

GOSPEL   Jn 19:31–37

One soldier thrust his lance into his side,
and immediately blood and water flowed out.

A reading from the holy Gospel according to John

Since it was preparation day, in order that the bodies might not remain on the cross on the sabbath, for the sabbath day of that week was a solemn one, the Jews asked Pilate that their legs be broken and they be taken down. So the soldiers came and broke the legs of the first and then of the other one who was crucified with Jesus. But when they came to Jesus and saw that he was already dead, they did not break his legs, but one soldier thrust his lance into his side, and immediately blood and water flowed out. An eyewitness has testified, and his testimony is true; he knows that he is speaking the truth, so that you also may come to believe. For this happened so that the scripture passage might be fulfilled:

Not a bone of it will be broken.

And again another passage says:

They will look upon him whom they have pierced.

The Gospel of the Lord.

Liturgy of the Eucharist, *p. 897;* **Prayer over the Gifts,** *p. 994.*

C

2004, 2007, 2010, 2013, 2016, 2019, 2022

FIRST READING   Ez 34:11–16

As a shepherd tends his flock, so will I tend my sheep.

A reading from the Book of the Prophet Ezekiel

Thus says the Lord GOD: I myself will look after and tend my sheep. As a shepherd tends his flock when he finds himself among his scattered sheep, so will I tend my sheep. I will rescue them from every place where they were scattered when it was cloudy and dark. I will lead them out from among the peoples and gather them from the foreign lands; I will bring them back to their own country and pasture them upon the mountains of Israel in the land's ravines and all its inhabited places. In good pastures will I pasture them, and on the mountain heights of Israel shall be their grazing ground. There they shall lie down on good grazing ground, and in rich pastures shall they be pastured on the mountains of Israel. I myself will pasture my sheep; I myself will give them rest, says the Lord GOD. The lost I will seek out, the strayed I will bring back, the injured I will bind up, the sick I will heal, but the sleek and the strong I will destroy, shepherding them rightly.

The word of the Lord.

Responsorial Psalm

Ps 23:1–3a, 3b–4, 5, 6

R. The Lord is my shepherd; there is nothing I shall want.

The LORD is my shepherd; I shall not want.
  In verdant pastures he gives me repose;
Beside restful waters he leads me;
  he refreshes my soul.

R. The Lord is my shepherd; there is nothing I shall want.

He guides me in right paths
  For his name's sake.
Even though I walk in the dark valley
  I fear no evil; for you are at my side
With your rod and your staff
  that give me courage.

R. The Lord is my shepherd; there is nothing I shall want.

You spread the table before me
  in the sight of my foes;
You anoint my head with oil;
  my cup overflows.

R. The Lord is my shepherd; there is nothing I shall want.

Only goodness and kindness follow me
  all the days of my life;
And I shall dwell in the house of the LORD
  for years to come.

R. The Lord is my shepherd; there is nothing I shall want.

SECOND READING

Rom 5:5b–11

God proves his love for us.

A reading from the Letter of Saint Paul to the Romans

Brothers and sisters:

The love of God has been poured out into our hearts through the holy Spirit that has been given to us. For Christ, while we were still helpless, died at the appointed time for the ungodly.

Indeed, only with difficulty does one die for a just person, though perhaps for a good person one might even find courage to die. But God proves his love for us in that while we were still sinners Christ died for us. How much more then, since we are now justified by his blood, will we be saved through him from the wrath. Indeed, if, while we were enemies, we were reconciled to God through the death of his Son, how much more, once reconciled, will we be saved by his life. Not only that, but we also boast of God through our Lord Jesus Christ, through whom we have now received reconciliation.

The word of the Lord.

Alleluia, alleluia
Take my yoke upon you, says the Lord;
And learn from me, for I am meek and humble of heart.   Mt 11:29ab

Or:

I am the good shepherd, says the Lord;
I know my sheep, and mine know me.   Jn 10:14
Alleluia, alleluia

GOSPEL   Lk 15:3–7
Rejoice with me because I have found my lost sheep.

A reading from the holy Gospel according to Luke

Jesus addressed this parable to the Pharisees and scribes: "What man among you having a hundred sheep and losing one of them would not leave the ninety-nine in the desert and go after the lost one until he finds it? And when he does find it, he sets it on his shoulders with great joy and, upon his arrival home, he calls together his friends and neighbors and says to them, 'Rejoice with me because I have found my lost sheep.' I tell you, in just the same way there will be more joy in heaven over one sinner who repents than over ninety-nine righteous people who have no need of repentance."

The Gospel of the Lord.

Liturgy of the Eucharist, *p. 897;* **Prayer over the Gifts** *follows.*

Prayer over the Gifts

Pray, brethren...

Lord,
look on the heart of Christ your Son
filled with love for us.
Because of his love
accept our eucharist and forgive our sins.

Grant this through Christ our Lord

Preface of the Sacred Heart, *p. 951.*

Communion Antiphon

The Lord says: If anyone is thirsty, let him come to me; whoever believes in me, let him drink. Streams of living water shall flow out from within him. (Jn 7:37–38)

Or:

One of the soldiers pierced Jesus' side with a lance, and at once there flowed out blood and water. (Jn 19:34)

Prayer after Communion

Let us pray.

Pause for silent prayer, if this has not preceded.

Father,
may this sacrament fill us with love.
Draw us closer to Christ your Son
and help us to recognize him in others.

We ask this in the name of Jesus the Lord.

Ordinary Time

See **Liturgical Calendar,** *pp. 26–41, for the Week in Ordinary Time proper to the Mass of the day.*

For the Sixth Week in Ordinary Time, turn to p. 392; Seventh Week, p. 421; Eighth Week, p. 452; Ninth Week, p. 482.

For a more detailed explanation of **Ordinary Time,** *turn to p. 233.*

TENTH WEEK IN ORDINARY TIME

The **Antiphons and Prayers** *may be the following, or may be chosen from any of the other 33 weeks in Ordinary Time (refer to Liturgical Calendar, pp. 26–41).*

The **Liturgy of the Word** *varies: for Monday, see p. 997; Tuesday, p. 1002; Wednesday, p. 1006; Thursday, p. 1011; Friday, p. 1016; Saturday, p. 1020.*

Entrance Antiphon

The Lord is my light and my salvation. Who shall frighten me? The Lord is the defender of my life. Who shall make me tremble?

(Ps 27:1–2)

Opening Prayer

Let us pray
   [for the guidance of the Holy Spirit]

Pause for silent prayer.

God of wisdom and love,
source of all good,
send your Spirit to teach us your truth
and guide our actions
in your way of peace.

We ask this through our Lord Jesus Christ, your Son,
who lives and reigns with you and the Holy Spirit,
one God, for ever and ever.

Alternative Opening Prayer

Let us pray
[to our Father
who calls us to freedom in Jesus his Son]

Pause for silent prayer.

Father in heaven,
words cannot measure the boundaries of love
for those born to new life in Christ Jesus.
Raise us beyond the limits this world imposes,
so that we may be free to love as Christ teaches
and find our joy in your glory.
We ask this through Christ our Lord.

Prayer over the Gifts

Pray, brethren...

Lord,
look with love on our service.
Accept the gifts we bring
and help us grow in Christian love.

Grant this through Christ our Lord.

Preface of Weekdays in Ordinary Time I–VI, *pp. 948–950.*

Communion Antiphon

I can rely on the Lord; I can always turn to him for shelter. It
was he who gave me my freedom. My God, you are always there
to help me! (Ps 18:3)

Or:

God is love, and he who lives in love, lives in God, and God
in him. (1 Jn 4:16)

Prayer after Communion

Let us pray.

Pause for silent prayer, if this has not preceded.

Lord,
may your healing love
turn us from sin
and keep us on the way that leads to you.
We ask this in the name of Jesus the Lord.

Monday

Antiphons and Prayers, *p. 995;* **Liturgy of the Word** *for Year I (odd years) follows; Year II (even years), p. 999.*

TODAY'S LIVING WORD

Matthew's version of the Beatitudes of Jesus emphasizes their thoroughly Jewish character. In form and in content, each one echoes the Hebrew Scriptures, with the difference that Jesus' Beatitudes are eschatological. They announce happiness in the future, when the reign of God inaugurated by Jesus will be fully realized. As Daniel Harrington explains, "the Beatitudes function not as 'entrance requirements' but rather as...an appropriate eschatological reward" for the meek and the merciful, the pure of heart and the makers of peace.* Jesus says that the reign of God belongs to such as these.

Consolation is the theme of all three of today's readings. Paul assures the Corinthians that "the God of all encouragement" will comfort them, for they share in the sufferings of Christ. God comforts Elijah the Tishbite, one of the few faithful servants of God left in Israel during the reign of Ahab and Jezebel, and miraculously provides him with bread and meat in the Wadi Cherith. The Beatitudes of Jesus console the poor and the persecuted by promising them abundant life in God's kingdom.

The Gospel of Matthew, Sacra Pagina 1 (Collegeville: Liturgical Press, 1991), p. 83.

FIRST READING

2 Cor 1:1–7

*God encourages us that we ourselves may be able
to encourage those who are in any affliction.*

A reading from the beginning of the second Letter of Saint Paul
to the Corinthians

Paul, an Apostle of Christ Jesus by the will of God, and Timothy
our brother, to the Church of God that is at Corinth, with all
the holy ones throughout Achaia: grace to you and peace from
God our Father and the Lord Jesus Christ.

Blessed be the God and Father of our Lord Jesus Christ, the
Father of compassion and the God of all encouragement, who
encourages us in our every affliction, so that we may be able
to encourage those who are in any affliction with the encouragement with which we ourselves are encouraged by God. For
as Christ's sufferings overflow to us, so through Christ does
our encouragement also overflow. If we are afflicted, it is for
your encouragement and salvation; if we are encouraged, it is
for your encouragement, which enables you to endure the same
sufferings that we suffer. Our hope for you is firm, for we know
that as you share in the sufferings, you also share in the
encouragement.

The word of the Lord.

Responsorial Psalm

Ps 34:2–3, 4–5, 6–7, 8–9

R. **Taste and see the goodness of the Lord.**

I will bless the LORD at all times;
   his praise shall be ever in my mouth.
Let my soul glory in the LORD;
   the lowly will hear me and be glad.

R. Taste and see the goodness of the Lord.

Glorify the LORD with me,
  let us together extol his name.
I sought the LORD, and he answered me
  and delivered me from all my fears.

R. Taste and see the goodness of the Lord.

Look to him that you may be radiant with joy,
  and your faces may not blush with shame.
When the poor one called out, the LORD heard,
  and from all his distress he saved him.

R. Taste and see the goodness of the Lord.

The angel of the LORD encamps
  around those who fear him, and delivers them.
Taste and see how good the LORD is;
  blessed the man who takes refuge in him.

R. Taste and see the goodness of the Lord.

Alleluia Verse *and* **Gospel,** *p. 1000f.*

Year II

FIRST READING

1 Kgs 17:1–6

Elijah stands before the LORD God of Israel.

A reading from the first Book of Kings

Elijah the Tishbite, from Tishbe in Gilead, said to Ahab: "As the LORD, the God of Israel, lives, whom I serve, during these years there shall be no dew or rain except at my word." The LORD then said to Elijah: "Leave here, go east and hide in the Wadi Cherith, east of the Jordan. You shall drink of the stream, and I have commanded ravens to feed you there." So he left and did as the LORD had commanded. He went and remained by the Wadi Cherith, east of the Jordan. Ravens brought him bread and meat in the morning, and bread and meat in the evening, and he drank from the stream.

The word of the Lord.

Responsorial Psalm

Ps 121:1bc–2, 3–4, 5–6, 7–8

R. Our help is from the Lord, who made heaven and earth.

I lift up my eyes toward the mountains;
  whence shall help come to me?
My help is from the LORD,
  who made heaven and earth.

R. Our help is from the Lord, who made heaven and earth.

May he not suffer your foot to slip;
  may he slumber not who guards you:
Indeed he neither slumbers nor sleeps,
  the guardian of Israel.

R. Our help is from the Lord, who made heaven and earth.

The LORD is your guardian; the LORD is your shade;
  he is beside you at your right hand.
The sun shall not harm you by day,
  nor the moon by night.

R. Our help is from the Lord, who made heaven and earth.

The LORD will guard you from all evil;
  he will guard your life.
The LORD will guard your coming and your going,
  both now and forever.

R. Our help is from the Lord, who made heaven and earth.

Alleluia, alleluia Mt 5:12a
  Rejoice and be glad;
  for your reward will be great in heaven.
Alleluia, alleluia

Years I and II

GOSPEL

Mt 5:1–12

Blessed are the poor in spirit.

A reading from the holy Gospel according to Matthew

When Jesus saw the crowds, he went up the mountain, and after he had sat down, his disciples came to him. He began to teach them, saying:

"Blessed are the poor in spirit,
   for theirs is the Kingdom of heaven.
Blessed are they who mourn,
   for they will be comforted.
Blessed are the meek,
   for they will inherit the land.
Blessed are they who hunger and thirst for righteousness,
   for they will be satisfied.
Blessed are the merciful,
   for they will be shown mercy.
Blessed are the clean of heart,
   for they will see God.
Blessed are the peacemakers,
   for they will be called children of God.
Blessed are they who are persecuted for the sake of
      righteousness,
   for theirs is the Kingdom of heaven.

Blessed are you when they insult you and persecute you and utter every kind of evil against you falsely because of me. Rejoice and be glad, for your reward will be great in heaven. Thus they persecuted the prophets who were before you."
The Gospel of the Lord.

Liturgy of the Eucharist, *p. 897;* **Prayer over the Gifts,** *p. 996.*

Tuesday

Antiphons and Prayers, *p. 995;* **Liturgy of the Word** *for Year I (odd years) follows; Year II (even years), p. 1004.*

TODAY'S LIVING WORD

The sayings of Jesus that Matthew records in today's Gospel are biblically based. In the Hebrew Bible, salt is used as a metaphor in a number of different senses. But combining light with the city on a hill unmistakably alludes to Isaiah 2 (cf. also Micah 4). There the prophet speaks of the days to come, when all the nations shall stream to the mountain of the Lord's house that towers above the hills, to be instructed in God's ways. Therefore, he calls the house of Jacob to "walk in the light of the Lord!"

Jesus' message is clear. Just as the miracle Elijah worked invited a Sidonian widow to recognize the power of Israel's God, and just as God intended faithful Israel to be a beckoning light to the nations, so must we who follow Jesus incite others to praise God our heavenly Father by our good works. As Paul would say, it is for this that God has anointed us, sealed us and deposited the Spirit in our hearts.

Year I

FIRST READING

2 Cor 1:18–22

Jesus was not yes and no, but yes has always been in him.

A reading from the second Letter of Saint Paul to the Corinthians

Brothers and sisters:

As God is faithful, our word to you is not "yes" and "no." For the Son of God, Jesus Christ, who was proclaimed to you by us, Silvanus and Timothy and me, was not "yes" and "no," but "yes" has been in him. For however many are the promises of God, their Yes is in him; therefore, the Amen from us also goes through him to God for glory. But the one who gives us security with you in Christ and who anointed us is God; he has also put his seal upon us and given the Spirit in our hearts as a first installment.

The word of the Lord.

Responsorial Psalm
Ps 119:129, 130, 131, 132, 133, 135

R. Lord, let your face shine on me.

Wonderful are your decrees;
  therefore I observe them.

R. Lord, let your face shine on me.

The revelation of your words sheds light,
  gives understanding to the simple.

R. Lord, let your face shine on me.

I gasp with open mouth
  in my yearning for your commands.

R. Lord, let your face shine on me.

Turn to me in pity
  as you turn to those who love your name.

R. Lord, let your face shine on me.

Steady my footsteps according to your promise,
  and let no iniquity rule over me.

R. Lord, let your face shine on me.

Let your countenance shine upon your servant,
  and teach me your statutes.

R. Lord, let your face shine on me.

Alleluia Verse *and* **Gospel,** *p. 1005.*

Year II

FIRST READING   1 Kgs 17:7–16

> *The jar of flour shall not go empty,*
> *as the LORD had foretold through Elijah.*

A reading from the first Book of Kings

The brook near where Elijah was hiding ran dry, because no rain had fallen in the land. So the LORD said to Elijah: "Move on to Zarephath of Sidon and stay there. I have designated a widow there to provide for you." He left and went to Zarephath. As he arrived at the entrance of the city, a widow was gathering sticks there; he called out to her, "Please bring me a small cupful of water to drink." She left to get it, and he called out after her, "Please bring along a bit of bread." She answered, "As the LORD, your God, lives, I have nothing baked; there is only a handful of flour in my jar and a little oil in my jug. Just now I was collecting a couple of sticks, to go in and prepare something for myself and my son; when we have eaten it, we shall die." Elijah said to her, "Do not be afraid. Go and do as you propose. But first make me a little cake and bring it to me. Then you can prepare something for yourself and your son. For the LORD, the God of Israel, says, 'The jar of flour shall not go empty, nor the jug of oil run dry, until the day when the LORD sends rain upon the earth.'" She left and did as Elijah had said. She was able to eat for a year, and Elijah and her son as well; the jar of flour did not go empty, nor the jug of oil run dry, as the LORD had foretold through Elijah.

The word of the Lord.

Responsorial Psalm   Ps 4:2–3, 4–5, 7b–8

R. Lord, let your face shine on us.

When I call, answer me, O my just God,
  you who relieve me when I am in distress;
  Have pity on me, and hear my prayer!
Men of rank, how long will you be dull of heart?
  Why do you love what is vain and seek after falsehood?

  R. Lord, let your face shine on us.

Know that the LORD does wonders for his faithful one;
  the LORD will hear me when I call upon him.
Tremble, and sin not;
  reflect, upon your beds, in silence.

  R. Lord, let your face shine on us.

O LORD, let the light of your countenance shine upon us!
You put gladness into my heart,
  more than when grain and wine abound.

  R. Lord, let your face shine on us.

  Alleluia, alleluia Mt 5:16
  Let your light shine before others
  that they may see your good deeds
    and glorify your heavenly Father.
  Alleluia, alleluia

Years I and II

GOSPEL   Mt 5:13 –16
  You are the light of the world.

A reading from the holy Gospel according to Matthew

Jesus said to his disciples: "You are the salt of the earth. But if salt loses its taste, with what can it be seasoned? It is no longer good for anything but to be thrown out and trampled underfoot. You are the light of the world. A city set on a mountain cannot be hidden. Nor do they light a lamp and then put it under a bushel basket; it is set on a lampstand, where it gives light to all

in the house. Just so, your light must shine before others, that they may see your good deeds and glorify your heavenly Father."
The Gospel of the Lord.

Liturgy of the Eucharist, *p. 897;* **Prayer over the Gifts,** *p. 996.*

Wednesday

Antiphons and Prayers, *p. 995;* **Liturgy of the Word** *for Year I (odd years) follows; Year II (even years), p. 1008.*

TODAY'S LIVING WORD

The somewhat complicated distinction that Paul makes in 2 Corinthians (chap. 3) between the surpassing glory of the new covenant and the fading glory of the former one may be misleading. He seems to say that the new covenant has rendered the Mosaic law obsolete. But scholars are not so sure he meant that. For our purposes, it is enough to note the force of Jesus' own words, reported by Matthew in today's Gospel: "Until heaven and earth pass away, not the smallest letter…will pass from the law."

Paul's main concern in 2 Corinthians (chap. 3) is to defend his ministry as an apostle. His credentials have been challenged and he responds by affirming that his qualifications come from God alone. In the contest on Mount Carmel, Elijah challenges the prophets of Baal to give proof of their credentials, and his success shows him to be the true prophet of the Lord who alone is God. As for us, Jesus tells us that whatever credibility we have as followers of Christ lies in our fulfilling God's commands and teaching others to do so too.

Year I

FIRST READING   2 Cor 3:4 –11
He has qualified us as ministers of a new covenant,
not of the letter but of spirit.

A reading from the second Letter of Saint Paul to the Corinthians

Brothers and sisters:

Such confidence we have through Christ toward God. Not that of ourselves we are qualified to take credit for anything as coming from us; rather, our qualification comes from God, who has indeed qualified us as ministers of a new covenant, not of letter but of spirit; for the letter brings death, but the Spirit gives life.

Now if the ministry of death, carved in letters on stone, was so glorious that the children of Israel could not look intently at the face of Moses because of its glory that was going to fade, how much more will the ministry of the Spirit be glorious? For if the ministry of condemnation was glorious, the ministry of righteousness will abound much more in glory. Indeed, what was endowed with glory has come to have no glory in this respect because of the glory that surpasses it. For if what was going to fade was glorious, how much more will what endures be glorious.

The word of the Lord.

Responsorial Psalm

Ps 99:5, 6, 7, 8, 9

R. Holy is the Lord our God.

Extol the LORD, our God,
  and worship at his footstool;
  holy is he!

R. Holy is the Lord our God.

Moses and Aaron were among his priests,
  and Samuel, among those who called upon his name;
  they called upon the LORD, and he answered them.

R. Holy is the Lord our God.

From the pillar of cloud he spoke to them;
  they heard his decrees and the law he gave them.

R. Holy is the Lord our God.

O LORD, our God, you answered them;
a forgiving God you were to them,
though requiting their misdeeds.

R. Holy is the Lord our God.

Extol the LORD, our God,
and worship at his holy mountain;
for holy is the LORD, our God.

R. Holy is the Lord our God.

Alleluia Verse *and* **Gospel,** *p. 1010f.*

Year II

FIRST READING   1 Kgs 18:20–39

Let it be known this day that you, LORD, are God.

A reading from the first Book of Kings

Ahab sent to all the children of Israel and had the prophets assemble on Mount Carmel.

Elijah appealed to all the people and said, "How long will you straddle the issue? If the LORD is God, follow him; if Baal, follow him." The people, however, did not answer him. So Elijah said to the people, "I am the only surviving prophet of the LORD, and there are four hundred and fifty prophets of Baal. Give us two young bulls. Let them choose one, cut it into pieces, and place it on the wood, but start no fire. I shall prepare the other and place it on the wood, but shall start no fire. You shall call on your gods, and I will call on the LORD. The God who answers with fire is God." All the people answered, "Agreed!"

Elijah then said to the prophets of Baal, "Choose one young bull and prepare it first, for there are more of you. Call upon your gods, but do not start the fire." Taking the young bull that was turned over to them, they prepared it and called on Baal from morning to noon, saying, "Answer us, Baal!" But there was no sound, and no one answering. And they hopped around the altar they had prepared. When it was noon, Elijah taunted them: "Call louder, for he is a god and may be meditating, or may have retired, or may be on a journey. Perhaps he is asleep and must be awakened." They called out louder and slashed themselves with swords and spears, as was their custom, until blood gushed over them. Noon passed and they remained in a prophetic state until the time for offering sacrifice. But there was not a sound; no one answered, and no one was listening.

Then Elijah said to all the people, "Come here to me." When the people had done so, he repaired the altar of the LORD that had been destroyed. He took twelve stones, for the number of tribes of the sons of Jacob, to whom the LORD had said, "Your name shall be Israel." He built an altar in honor of the LORD with the stones, and made a trench around the altar large enough for two measures of grain. When he had arranged the wood, he cut up the young bull and laid it on the wood. "Fill four jars with water," he said, "and pour it over the burnt offering and over the wood." "Do it again," he said, and they did it again. "Do it a third time," he said, and they did it a third time. The water flowed around the altar, and the trench was filled with the water.

At the time for offering sacrifice, the prophet Elijah came forward and said, "LORD, God of Abraham, Isaac, and Israel, let it be known this day that you are God in Israel and that I am your servant and have done all these things by your command. Answer me, LORD! Answer me, that this people may know

that you, LORD, are God and that you have brought them back
to their senses." The LORD's fire came down and consumed the
burnt offering, wood, stones, and dust, and it lapped up the
water in the trench. Seeing this, all the people fell prostrate
and said, "The LORD is God! The LORD is God!"

The word of the Lord.

Responsorial Psalm
Ps 16:1b–2ab, 4, 5ab and 8, 11

R. **Keep me safe, O God; you are my hope.**

Keep me, O God, for in you I take refuge;
  I say to the LORD, "My Lord are you."

R. **Keep me safe, O God; you are my hope.**

They multiply their sorrows
  who court other gods.
Blood libations to them I will not pour out,
  nor will I take their names upon my lips.

R. **Keep me safe, O God; you are my hope.**

O LORD, my allotted portion and cup,
  you it is who hold fast my lot.
I set the LORD ever before me;
  with him at my right hand I shall not be disturbed.

R. **Keep me safe, O God; you are my hope.**

You will show me the path to life,
  fullness of joys in your presence,
  the delights at your right hand forever.

R. **Keep me safe, O God; you are my hope.**

Alleluia, alleluia Ps 25:4b, 5a
Teach me your paths, my God,
and guide me in your truth.
Alleluia, alleluia

Years I and II

GOSPEL

Mt 5:17–19

I have come not to abolish the law, but to fulfill it.

A reading from the holy Gospel according to Matthew

Jesus said to his disciples: "Do not think that I have come to abolish the law or the prophets. I have come not to abolish but to fulfill. Amen, I say to you, until heaven and earth pass away, not the smallest letter or the smallest part of a letter will pass from the law, until all things have taken place. Therefore, whoever breaks one of the least of these commandments and teaches others to do so will be called least in the Kingdom of heaven. But whoever obeys and teaches these commandments will be called greatest in the Kingdom of heaven."

The Gospel of the Lord.

Liturgy of the Eucharist, *p. 897;* **Prayer over the Gifts,** *p. 996.*

Thursday

Antiphons and Prayers, *p. 995;* **Liturgy of the Word** *for Year I (odd years) follows; Year II (even years), p. 1013.*

TODAY'S LIVING WORD

Jesus does not claim that his teaching is superior to Jewish tradition in the law and the prophets; rather, he calls his followers to a superior observance of that tradition. Their holiness must surpass that of the scribes and Pharisees. He explains what he means in a series of "antitheses," or contrasts, all structured in the same way: "You have heard.... But I say to you...." In each case, Jesus' interpretation of a given law cuts to its core, the better to expose its meaning and to express it in practical terms. In today's reading, for example, he recognizes that anger and abuse often lie at the root of murder, and so he prohibits these behaviors as well. But Jesus' teaching is more than prohibition; he underscores the overriding importance of reconciliation too.

Reconciliation characterizes the ministry of Elijah and Paul as well. Elijah's whole life is spent calling Israel and its royal house, as in today's selection, to return to the Lord their God. Paul works to remove the veil that keeps his people and all peoples from knowing "the glory of God on the face of [Jesus] Christ."

Year I

FIRST READING

2 Cor 3:15—4:1, 3–6

*God has shone in our hearts to bring to light
the knowledge of the glory of God.*

A reading from the second Letter of Saint Paul to the Corinthians

Brothers and sisters:

To this day, whenever Moses is read, a veil lies over the hearts of the children of Israel, but whenever a person turns to the Lord the veil is removed. Now the Lord is the Spirit and where the Spirit of the Lord is, there is freedom. All of us, gazing with unveiled face on the glory of the Lord, are being transformed into the same image from glory to glory, as from the Lord who is the Spirit.

Therefore, since we have this ministry through the mercy shown us, we are not discouraged. And even though our Gospel is veiled, it is veiled for those who are perishing, in whose case the god of this age has blinded the minds of the unbelievers, so that they may not see the light of the Gospel of the glory of Christ, who is the image of God. For we do not preach ourselves but Jesus Christ as Lord, and ourselves as your slaves for the sake of Jesus. For God who said, *Let light shine out of darkness,* has shone in our hearts to bring to light the knowledge of the glory of God on the face of Jesus Christ.

The word of the Lord.

Responsorial Psalm

Ps 85:9ab and 10, 11–12, 13–14

R. The glory of the Lord will dwell in our land.

I will hear what God proclaims;
    the LORD—for he proclaims peace to his people.
Near indeed is his salvation to those who fear him,
    glory dwelling in our land.

R. The glory of the Lord will dwell in our land.

Kindness and truth shall meet;
    justice and peace shall kiss.
Truth shall spring out of the earth,
    and justice shall look down from heaven.

R. The glory of the Lord will dwell in our land.

The LORD himself will give his benefits;
    our land shall yield its increase.
Justice shall walk before him,
    and salvation, along the way of his steps.

R. The glory of the Lord will dwell in our land.

Alleluia Verse *and* **Gospel, p. 1015.**

Year II

FIRST READING

1 Kgs 18:41–46

Elijah prayed and the sky gave rain (Jas 5:18).

A reading from the first Book of Kings

Elijah said to Ahab, "Go up, eat and drink, for there is the sound of a heavy rain." So Ahab went up to eat and drink, while Elijah climbed to the top of Carmel, crouched down to the earth, and put his head between his knees. "Climb up and look out to sea," he directed his servant, who went up and looked, but reported, "There is nothing." Seven times he said, "Go, look again!" And the seventh time the youth reported, "There is a cloud as small as a man's hand rising from the sea." Elijah said, "Go and say to Ahab, 'Harness up and leave the mountain before the rain stops you.'" In a trice the sky grew dark with clouds and wind, and a heavy rain fell. Ahab mounted his chariot and made for Jezreel. But the hand of the LORD was on Elijah, who girded up his clothing and ran before Ahab as far as the approaches to Jezreel.

The word of the Lord.

Responsorial Psalm   Ps 65:10, 11, 12–13

R. It is right to praise you in Zion, O God.

You have visited the land and watered it;
    greatly have you enriched it.
God's watercourses are filled;
    you have prepared the grain.

R. It is right to praise you in Zion, O God.

Thus have you prepared the land:
    drenching its furrows, breaking up its clods,
Softening it with showers,
    blessing its yield.

R. It is right to praise you in Zion, O God.

You have crowned the year with your bounty,
    and your paths overflow with a rich harvest;
The untilled meadows overflow with it,
    and rejoicing clothes the hills.

R. It is right to praise you in Zion, O God.

Alleluia, alleluia Jn 13:34
I give you a new commandment:
love one another as I have loved you.
Alleluia, alleluia

Years I and II

GOSPEL
Mt 5:20 – 26

Whoever is angry with his brother will be liable to judgment.

A reading from the holy Gospel according to Matthew

Jesus said to his disciples: "I tell you, unless your righteousness surpasses that of the scribes and Pharisees, you will not enter into the Kingdom of heaven.

"You have heard that it was said to your ancestors, *You shall not kill; and whoever kills will be liable to judgment.* But I say to you, whoever is angry with his brother will be liable to judgment, and whoever says to his brother, 'Raqa,' will be answerable to the Sanhedrin, and whoever says, 'You fool,' will be liable to fiery Gehenna. Therefore, if you bring your gift to the altar, and there recall that your brother has anything against you, leave your gift there at the altar, go first and be reconciled with your brother, and then come and offer your gift. Settle with your opponent quickly while on the way to court with him. Otherwise your opponent will hand you over to the judge, and the judge will hand you over to the guard, and you will be thrown into prison. Amen, I say to you, you will not be released until you have paid the last penny."

The Gospel of the Lord.

Liturgy of the Eucharist, *p. 897;* **Prayer over the Gifts,** *p. 996.*

Friday

Antiphons and Prayers, *p. 995;* **Liturgy of the Word** *for Year I (odd years) follows; Year II (even years), p. 1018.*

TODAY'S LIVING WORD

In today's Gospel, Jesus continues to interpret the law and the prophets. He says that as anger lies at the root of murder, so lust lies at the root of adultery, adding a stern warning: "If your right hand causes you to sin, cut it off and throw it away!" The urgency and the intimacy of his language betray his intimate knowledge of our frail and fallen humanity. After all, he is our brother. Paul too knows all about human frailty. "We are afflicted in every way," he writes to the Corinthians. And in 1 Kings the prophet Elijah, having been "constantly…given up to death," as Paul might say, finally gains the safety of Mount Horeb (Sinai) only to have God send him back into the fray.

Elijah, Paul, and the human Jesus were all "earthen vessels" like us. Through them and through us the power of God is revealed. So like them, we must often seek out the mountain, that place of prayer, where God speaks in "a tiny whispering sound."

Year I

FIRST READING
2 Cor 4:7–15

He who raised the Lord Jesus will raise us also with Jesus.

A reading from the second Letter of Saint Paul to the Corinthians

Brothers and sisters:

We hold this treasure in earthen vessels, that the surpassing power may be of God and not from us. We are afflicted in every way, but not constrained; perplexed, but not driven to despair; persecuted, but not abandoned; struck down, but not destroyed; always carrying about in the Body the dying of Jesus, so that the life of Jesus may also be manifested in our body. For we who live are constantly being given up to death for the sake of Jesus, so that the life of Jesus may be manifested in our mortal flesh.

So death is at work in us, but life in you. Since, then, we have the same spirit of faith, according to what is written, "I believed, therefore I spoke," we too believe and therefore speak, knowing that the one who raised the Lord Jesus will raise us also with Jesus and place us with you in his presence. Everything indeed is for you, so that the grace bestowed in abundance on more and more people may cause the thanksgiving to overflow for the glory of God.

The word of the Lord.

Responsorial Psalm
Ps 116:10–11, 15–16, 17–18

R. To you, Lord, I will offer a sacrifice of praise.

I believed, even when I said,
  "I am greatly afflicted";
I said in my alarm,
  "No man is dependable."

R. To you, Lord, I will offer a sacrifice of praise.

Precious in the eyes of the LORD
  is the death of his faithful ones.
O LORD, I am your servant;
  I am your servant, the son of your handmaid;
  you have loosed my bonds.

R. To you, Lord, I will offer a sacrifice of praise.

To you will I offer sacrifice of thanksgiving,
  and I will call upon the name of the LORD.
My vows to the LORD I will pay
  in the presence of all his people.

R. To you, Lord, I will offer a sacrifice of praise.

Or: **R. Alleluia.**

Alleluia Verse *and* **Gospel,** *p. 1019.*

Year II

FIRST READING
1 Kgs 19:9a, 11–16

Stand on the mountain before the LORD.

A reading from the first Book of Kings

At the mountain of God, Horeb, Elijah came to a cave, where he took shelter. But the word of the LORD came to him, "Go outside and stand on the mountain before the LORD; the LORD will be passing by." A strong and heavy wind was rending the mountains and crushing rocks before the LORD—but the LORD was not in the wind. After the wind there was an earthquake—but the LORD was not in the earthquake. After the earthquake there was fire—but the LORD was not in the fire. After the fire there was a tiny whispering sound. When he heard this, Elijah hid his face in his cloak and went and stood at the entrance of the cave. A voice said to him, "Elijah, why are you here?" He replied, "I have been most zealous for the LORD, the God of hosts. But the children of Israel have forsaken your covenant, torn down your altars, and put your prophets to the sword. I alone am left, and they seek to take my life." The LORD said to him, "Go, take the road back to the desert near Damascus. When you arrive, you shall anoint Hazael as king of Aram. Then you shall anoint Jehu, son of Nimshi, as king of Israel, and Elisha, son of Shaphat of Abel-meholah, as prophet to succeed you."

The word of the Lord.

Responsorial Psalm

Ps 27:7–8a, 8b–9abc, 13–14

R. I long to see your face, O Lord.

Hear, O LORD, the sound of my call;
   have pity on me, and answer me.
Of you my heart speaks; you my glance seeks.

R. I long to see your face, O Lord.

Your presence, O LORD, I seek.
Hide not your face from me;
   do not in anger repel your servant.
You are my helper: cast me not off.

R. I long to see your face, O Lord.

I believe that I shall see the bounty of the LORD
   in the land of the living.
Wait for the LORD with courage;
   be stouthearted, and wait for the LORD.

R. I long to see your face, O Lord.

> **Alleluia, alleluia** Phil 2:15d, 16a
> Shine like lights in the world,
> as you hold on to the word of life.
> **Alleluia, alleluia**

Years I and II

GOSPEL

Mt 5:27–32

*Everyone who looks at a woman with lust
has already committed adultery with her in his heart.*

A reading from the holy Gospel according to Matthew

Jesus said to his disciples: "You have heard that it was said, *You shall not commit adultery.* But I say to you, everyone who looks at a woman with lust has already committed adultery with her in his heart. If your right eye causes you to sin, tear it out and throw it away. It is better for you to lose one of your members than to have your whole body thrown into Gehenna.

And if your right hand causes you to sin, cut it off and throw it away. It is better for you to lose one of your members than to have your whole body go into Gehenna.

"It was also said, *Whoever divorces his wife must give her a bill of divorce.* But I say to you, whoever divorces his wife (unless the marriage is unlawful) causes her to commit adultery, and whoever marries a divorced woman commits adultery."

The Gospel of the Lord.

Liturgy of the Eucharist, *p. 897;* **Prayer over the Gifts,** *p. 996.*

Saturday

Antiphons and Prayers, *p. 995;* **Liturgy of the Word** *for Year I (odd years) follows; Year II (even years), p. 1022.*

TODAY'S LIVING WORD

In this Gospel, Jesus may seem to be abolishing the commandment against swearing; in fact, he is challenging his hearers to a radical and rigorous living of it. This is what it means to "fulfill" the law, that is, to bring it to its fullest expression. Some have argued that Jesus is presenting an ideal beyond the reach of all but the most heroic. But that misses the point. According to Joachim Jeremias, the Sermon on the Mount in Matthew was a catechism for newly baptized Christians. Therefore, he says, "it was preceded by conversion, by a being overpowered by the Good News."* The rigorous, radical way of life that Jesus outlined is intended for those who are already, in Paul's words, "in Christ…a new creation." Thus reconciled with God, they are able to live a new life.

The brief episode from 1 Kings describes the call of Elisha. He is quite literally "overpowered" by Elijah and compelled to leave everything and follow him. In the same way, the love of Christ impels us to live no longer for ourselves, but for him.

* *The Sermon on the Mount,* trans. Norman Perrin, Facet Books—Biblical Series 2 (Philadelphia: Fortress Press, 1963), p. 23.

Year I

FIRST READING   2 Cor 5:14 – 21

For our sake, he made him to be sin who did not know sin.

A reading from the second Letter of Saint Paul to the Corinthians

Brothers and sisters:

The love of Christ impels us, once we have come to the conviction that one died for all; therefore, all have died. He indeed died for all, so that those who live might no longer live for themselves but for him who for their sake died and was raised.

Consequently, from now on we regard no one according to the flesh; even if we once knew Christ according to the flesh, yet now we know him so no longer. So whoever is in Christ is a new creation: the old things have passed away; behold, new things have come. And all this is from God, who has reconciled us to himself through Christ and given us the ministry of reconciliation, namely, God was reconciling the world to himself in Christ, not counting their trespasses against them and entrusting to us the message of reconciliation. So we are ambassadors for Christ, as if God were appealing through us. We implore you on behalf of Christ, be reconciled to God. For our sake he made him to be sin who did not know sin, so that we might become the righteousness of God in him.

The word of the Lord.

Responsorial Psalm   Ps 103:1–2, 3–4, 9–10, 11–12

R. The Lord is kind and merciful.

Bless the LORD, O my soul;
  and all my being, bless his holy name.

Bless the LORD, O my soul,
  and forget not all his benefits.

R. The Lord is kind and merciful.

He pardons all your iniquities,
  he heals all your ills.
He redeems your life from destruction,
  he crowns you with kindness and compassion.

R. The Lord is kind and merciful.

He will not always chide,
  nor does he keep his wrath forever.
Not according to our sins does he deal with us,
  nor does he requite us according to our crimes.

R. The Lord is kind and merciful.

For as the heavens are high above the earth,
  so surpassing is his kindness toward those who fear him.
As far as the east is from the west,
  so far has he put our transgressions from us.

R. The Lord is kind and merciful.

Alleluia Verse *and* **Gospel**, *p. 1023.*

Year II

FIRST READING   1 Kgs 19:19–21

Then Elisha left and followed Elijah.

A reading from the first Book of Kings

Elijah set out, and came upon Elisha, son of Shaphat, as he was plowing with twelve yoke of oxen; he was following the twelfth. Elijah went over to him and threw his cloak over him. Elisha left the oxen, ran after Elijah, and said, "Please, let me kiss my father and mother goodbye, and I will follow you." Elijah answered, "Go back! Have I done anything to you?"

Elisha left him and, taking the yoke of oxen, slaughtered them; he used the plowing equipment for fuel to boil their flesh, and gave it to his people to eat. Then he left and followed Elijah as his attendant.

The word of the Lord.

Responsorial Psalm
Ps 16:1b–2a and 5, 7–8, 9–10

R. You are my inheritance, O Lord.

Keep me, O God, for in you I take refuge;
  I say to the LORD, "My Lord are you."
O LORD, my allotted portion and my cup,
  you it is who hold fast my lot.

R. You are my inheritance, O Lord.

I bless the LORD who counsels me;
  even in the night my heart exhorts me.
I set the LORD ever before me;
  with him at my right hand I shall not be disturbed.

R. You are my inheritance, O Lord.

Therefore my heart is glad and my soul rejoices,
  my body, too, abides in confidence;
Because you will not abandon my soul to the nether world,
  nor will you suffer your faithful one to undergo corruption.

R. You are my inheritance, O Lord.

Alleluia, alleluia Ps 119:36a, 29b
Incline my heart, O God, to your decrees;
and favor me with your law.
Alleluia, alleluia

Years I and II

GOSPEL   Mt 5:33–37

I say to you, do not swear at all.

A reading from the holy Gospel according to Matthew

Jesus said to his disciples: "You have heard that it was said to your ancestors, *Do not take a false oath, but make good to the Lord all that you vow.* But I say to you, do not swear at all; not by heaven, for it is God's throne; nor by the earth, for it is his footstool; nor by Jerusalem, for it is the city of the great King. Do not swear by your head, for you cannot make a single hair white or black. Let your 'Yes' mean 'Yes,' and your 'No' mean 'No.' Anything more is from the Evil One."

The Gospel of the Lord.

Liturgy of the Eucharist, *p. 897;* **Prayer over the Gifts,** *p. 996.*

ELEVENTH WEEK IN ORDINARY TIME

The **Antiphons and Prayers** *may be the following, or may be chosen from any of the other 33 weeks in Ordinary Time (refer to Liturgical Calendar, pp. 26–41).*

The **Liturgy of the Word** *varies: for Monday, see p. 1026; Tuesday, p. 1031; Wednesday, p. 1035; Thursday, p. 1040; Friday, p. 1046; Saturday, p. 1051.*

Entrance Antiphon

Lord, hear my voice when I call to you. You are my help; do not cast me off, do not desert me, my Savior God.   (Ps 27:7, 9)

Opening Prayer

Let us pray

[for the grace to follow Christ more closely]

Pause for silent prayer.

Almighty God,
our hope and our strength,
without you we falter.
Help us to follow Christ
and to live according to your will.

We ask this through our Lord Jesus Christ, your Son,
who lives and reigns with you and the Holy Spirit,
one God, for ever and ever.

Alternative Opening Prayer

Let us pray
   [to the Father
     whose love gives us strength to follow his Son]
       Pause for silent prayer.

God our Father,
we rejoice in the faith that draws us together,
aware that selfishness can drive us apart.
Let your encouragement be our constant strength.
Keep us one in the love that has sealed our lives,
help us to live as one family
the gospel we profess.
We ask this through Christ our Lord.

Prayer over the Gifts

Pray, brethren...
Lord God,
in this bread and wine
you give us food for body and spirit.
May the eucharist renew our strength
and bring us health of mind and body.
We ask this in the name of Jesus the Lord.

Preface of Weekdays in Ordinary Time I–VI, *pp. 948–950.*

Communion Antiphon

**One thing I seek: to dwell in the house of the Lord all the days
of my life.** (Ps 27:4)

Or:

Father, keep in your name those you have given me, that they may be one as we are one, says the Lord.   (Jn 17:11)

Prayer after Communion

Let us pray.

Pause for silent prayer, if this has not preceded.

Lord,
may this eucharist
accomplish in your Church
the unity and peace it signifies.

Grant this through Christ our Lord.

Monday

Antiphons and Prayers, *p. 1024;* **Liturgy of the Word** *for Year I (odd years) follows; Year II (even years), p. 1028.*

TODAY'S LIVING WORD

At first glance, Naboth's refusal of King Ahab's offer seems to contradict the spirit that Jesus urges upon his hearers in today's Gospel. But it is only a seeming contradiction. The teaching of Jesus did not oppose the law of Israel, but sought only to fulfill it. The "law of retaliation" which he cites in today's reading, for example, can be found in Exodus 21, Leviticus 24, and Deuteronomy 19. The purpose of the law was to prevent the escalation of violence. Far from abolishing the law, Jesus proposes another way of accomplishing the same goal. Ahab's offer to purchase Naboth's vineyard, however, was a violation of Israel's law. Leviticus 25 prohibited the sale of ancestral lands, "for the land is mine," says God, "and you are but aliens who have become my tenants."

On the other hand, Paul exemplifies Jesus' teaching by always acting with patient endurance in the face of violence. Armed only with the "weapons of righteousness," he not only endures but enriches many.

Year I

FIRST READING
2 Cor 6:1–10

In everything we commend ourselves as ministers of God.

A reading from the second Letter of Saint Paul to the Corinthians

Brothers and sisters:

As your fellow workers, we appeal to you not to receive the grace of God in vain. For he says:

> *In an acceptable time I heard you,*
> *and on the day of salvation I helped you.*

Behold, now is a very acceptable time; behold, now is the day of salvation. We cause no one to stumble in anything, in order that no fault may be found with our ministry; on the contrary, in everything we commend ourselves as ministers of God, through much endurance, in afflictions, hardships, constraints, beatings, imprisonments, riots, labors, vigils, fasts; by purity, knowledge, patience, kindness, in the Holy Spirit, in unfeigned love, in truthful speech, in the power of God; with weapons of righteousness at the right and at the left; through glory and dishonor, insult and praise. We are treated as deceivers and yet are truthful; as unrecognized and yet acknowledged; as dying and behold we live; as chastised and yet not put to death; as sorrowful yet always rejoicing; as poor yet enriching many; as having nothing and yet possessing all things.

The word of the Lord.

Responsorial Psalm
Ps 98:1, 2b, 3ab, 3cd – 4

R. The Lord has made known his salvation.

Sing to the LORD a new song,
  for he has done wondrous deeds;

His right hand has won victory for him,
  his holy arm.

  R. The Lord has made known his salvation.

In the sight of the nations he has revealed his justice.
He has remembered his kindness and his faithfulness
  toward the house of Israel.

  R. The Lord has made known his salvation.

All the ends of the earth have seen
  the salvation by our God.
Sing joyfully to the LORD, all you lands;
  break into song; sing praise.

  R. The Lord has made known his salvation.

  Alleluia Verse *and* **Gospel,** *p. 1030.*

Year II

FIRST READING   1 Kgs 21:1-16

Naboth has been stoned to death.

A reading from the first Book of Kings

Naboth the Jezreelite had a vineyard in Jezreel next to the palace
of Ahab, king of Samaria. Ahab said to Naboth, "Give me your
vineyard to be my vegetable garden, since it is close by, next
to my house. I will give you a better vineyard in exchange, or,
if you prefer, I will give you its value in money." Naboth answered him, "The LORD forbid that I should give you my ancestral heritage." Ahab went home disturbed and angry at the
answer Naboth the Jezreelite had made to him: "I will not give
you my ancestral heritage." Lying down on his bed, he turned
away from food and would not eat.

His wife Jezebel came to him and said to him, "Why are you so angry that you will not eat?" He answered her, "Because I spoke to Naboth the Jezreelite and said to him, 'Sell me your vineyard, or, if you prefer, I will give you a vineyard in exchange.' But he refused to let me have his vineyard." His wife Jezebel said to him, "A fine ruler over Israel you are indeed! Get up. Eat and be cheerful. I will obtain the vineyard of Naboth the Jezreelite for you."

So she wrote letters in Ahab's name and, having sealed them with his seal, sent them to the elders and to the nobles who lived in the same city with Naboth. This is what she wrote in the letters: "Proclaim a fast and set Naboth at the head of the people. Next, get two scoundrels to face him and accuse him of having cursed God and king. Then take him out and stone him to death." His fellow citizens—the elders and nobles who dwelt in his city—did as Jezebel had ordered them in writing, through the letters she had sent them. They proclaimed a fast and placed Naboth at the head of the people. Two scoundrels came in and confronted him with the accusation, "Naboth has cursed God and king." And they led him out of the city and stoned him to death. Then they sent the information to Jezebel that Naboth had been stoned to death.

When Jezebel learned that Naboth had been stoned to death, she said to Ahab, "Go on, take possession of the vineyard of Naboth the Jezreelite that he refused to sell you, because Naboth is not alive, but dead." On hearing that Naboth was dead, Ahab started off on his way down to the vineyard of Naboth the Jezreelite, to take possession of it.

The word of the Lord.

Responsorial Psalm

Ps 5:2–3ab, 4b–6a, 6b–7

R. Lord, listen to my groaning.

Hearken to my words, O LORD,
  attend to my sighing.
Heed my call for help,
  my king and my God!

R. Lord, listen to my groaning.

At dawn I bring my plea expectantly before you.
For you, O God, delight not in wickedness;
  no evil man remains with you;
  the arrogant may not stand in your sight.

R. Lord, listen to my groaning.

You hate all evildoers.
  You destroy all who speak falsehood;
The bloodthirsty and the deceitful
  the LORD abhors.

R. Lord, listen to my groaning.

Alleluia, alleluia   Ps 119:105
A lamp to my feet is your word,
  a light to my path.
Alleluia, alleluia

Years I and II

GOSPEL

Mt 5:38–42

But I say to you, offer no resistance to one who is evil.

A reading from the holy Gospel according to Matthew

Jesus said to his disciples: "You have heard that it was said, *An eye for an eye and a tooth for a tooth.* But I say to you, offer no resistance to one who is evil. When someone strikes you on your right cheek, turn the other one to him as well. If anyone wants to go to law with you over your tunic, hand him your cloak as well. Should anyone press you into service for one mile, go with him for two miles. Give to the one who asks of you, and do not turn your back on one who wants to borrow." The Gospel of the Lord.

Liturgy of the Eucharist, *p. 897;* **Prayer over the Gifts,** *p. 1025.*

Tuesday

Antiphons and Prayers, *p. 1024;* **Liturgy of the Word** *for Year I (odd years) follows; Year II (even years), p. 1033.*

TODAY'S LIVING WORD

The "law of retaliation" fully operates in today's reading from 1 Kings. God sends Elijah to confront and condemn Ahab for the murder of Naboth. Ahab will suffer the same fate as Naboth, even to the goriest detail. Yet sincere repentance wins Ahab a reprieve. The destruction of his house is postponed to the next generation. Thus do we see that the God of Israel is indeed the God of Jesus, the heavenly Father who makes the sun to rise and the rain to fall on the bad and the good, the just and the unjust. This is the "wealth of generosity" that Paul wants to inspire in the Corinthian community as well. To that end, he holds up the example of the churches of Macedonia whose generous donation to the collection spills over from their total self-donation to God.

Totality is the key to the last verse of the Gospel reading, which tells us to be perfect, "as your heavenly Father is perfect." The Hebrew Bible never describes God as "perfect." The word here points rather to God's wholeness revealed in his surpassing and sometimes surprising generosity. It is this we are called to imitate.

Year I

FIRST READING   2 Cor 8:1–9

Christ became poor for your sake.

A reading from the second Letter of Saint Paul to the Corinthians

We want you to know, brothers and sisters, of the grace of God that has been given to the churches of Macedonia, for in a severe test of affliction, the abundance of their joy and their profound poverty overflowed in a wealth of generosity on their part. For according to their means, I can testify, and beyond their means, spontaneously, they begged us insistently for the favor of taking part in the service to the holy ones, and this, not as we expected, but they gave themselves first to the Lord and to us through the will of God, so that we urged Titus that, as he had already begun, he should also complete for you this gracious act also. Now as you excel in every respect, in faith, discourse, knowledge, all earnestness, and in the love we have for you, may you excel in this gracious act also.

I say this not by way of command, but to test the genuineness of your love by your concern for others. For you know the gracious act of our Lord Jesus Christ, that for your sake he became poor although he was rich, so that by his poverty you might become rich.

The word of the Lord.

Responsorial Psalm   Ps 146:2, 5–6ab, 6c–7, 8–9a

R. Praise the Lord, my soul!

Praise the LORD, my soul!
  I will praise the LORD all my life;
  I will sing praise to my God while I live.

R. Praise the Lord, my soul!

Blessed he whose help is the God of Jacob,
  whose hope is in the LORD, his God,
Who made heaven and earth,
  the sea and all that is in them.

R. Praise the Lord, my soul!

Who keeps faith forever,
  secures justice for the oppressed,
  gives food to the hungry.
The LORD sets captives free.

R. Praise the Lord, my soul!

The LORD gives sight to the blind.
The LORD raises up those who were bowed down;
  the LORD loves the just.
The LORD protects strangers.

R. Praise the Lord, my soul!

Or: **R. Alleluia.**

Alleluia Verse *and* **Gospel,** *p. 1035.*

Year II

FIRST READING   1 Kgs 21:17–29

You have provoked me by leading Israel into sin.

A reading from the first Book of Kings

After the death of Naboth the LORD said to Elijah the Tishbite:
"Start down to meet Ahab, king of Israel, who rules in Samaria.
He will be in the vineyard of Naboth, of which he has come to
take possession. This is what you shall tell him, 'The LORD
says: After murdering, do you also take possession? For this,
the LORD says: In the place where the dogs licked up the blood
of Naboth, the dogs shall lick up your blood, too.'" Ahab said
to Elijah, "Have you found me out, my enemy?" "Yes," he
answered. "Because you have given yourself up to doing evil
in the LORD's sight, I am bringing evil upon you: I will destroy
you and will cut off every male in Ahab's line, whether slave

or freeman, in Israel. I will make your house like that of Jeroboam, son of Nebat, and like that of Baasha, son of Ahijah, because of how you have provoked me by leading Israel into sin." (Against Jezebel, too, the LORD declared, "The dogs shall devour Jezebel in the district of Jezreel.") "When one of Ahab's line dies in the city, dogs will devour him; when one of them dies in the field, the birds of the sky will devour him." Indeed, no one gave himself up to the doing of evil in the sight of the LORD as did Ahab, urged on by his wife Jezebel. He became completely abominable by following idols, just as the Amorites had done, whom the LORD drove out before the children of Israel.

When Ahab heard these words, he tore his garments and put on sackcloth over his bare flesh. He fasted, slept in the sackcloth, and went about subdued. Then the LORD said to Elijah the Tishbite, "Have you seen that Ahab has humbled himself before me? Since he has humbled himself before me, I will not bring the evil in his time. I will bring the evil upon his house during the reign of his son."

The word of the Lord.

Responsorial Psalm
Ps 51:3–4, 5–6ab, 11 and 16

R. Be merciful, O Lord, for we have sinned.

Have mercy on me, O God, in your goodness;
   in the greatness of your compassion wipe out my offense.
Thoroughly wash me from my guilt
   and of my sin cleanse me.

R. Be merciful, O Lord, for we have sinned.

For I acknowledge my offense,
   and my sin is before me always:
"Against you only have I sinned,
   and done what is evil in your sight."

R. Be merciful, O Lord, for we have sinned.

Turn away your face from my sins,
  and blot out all my guilt.
Free me from blood guilt, O God, my saving God;
  then my tongue shall revel in your justice.

R. Be merciful, O Lord, for we have sinned.

Alleluia, alleluia   Jn 13:34
I give you a new commandment:
love one another as I have loved you.
Alleluia, alleluia

Years I and II

GOSPEL   Mt 5:43 – 48

Love your enemies.

A reading from the holy Gospel according to Matthew

Jesus said to his disciples: "You have heard that it was said, *You shall love your neighbor and hate your enemy.* But I say to you, love your enemies and pray for those who persecute you, that you may be children of your heavenly Father, for he makes his sun rise on the bad and the good, and causes rain to fall on the just and the unjust. For if you love those who love you, what recompense will you have? Do not the tax collectors do the same? And if you greet your brothers only, what is unusual about that? Do not the pagans do the same? So be perfect, just as your heavenly Father is perfect."

The Gospel of the Lord.

Liturgy of the Eucharist, *p. 897;* **Prayer over the Gifts,** *p. 1025.*

Wednesday

Antiphons and Prayers, *p. 1024;* **Liturgy of the Word** *for Year I (odd years) follows; Year II (even years), p. 1037.*

TODAY'S LIVING WORD

In today's Gospel, taken from the Sermon on the Mount, Jesus comments on three acts of traditional Jewish piety—almsgiving, prayer, and fasting. The fact that Matthew has preserved these sayings of Jesus indicates that Christians also practiced these religious acts. As he touches on each one in turn, Jesus cautions against making any one of these private acts of piety into a self-serving public display. To do so is to forfeit any reward from the heavenly Father. In 2 Corinthians Paul is especially concerned with the practice of almsgiving. He writes to encourage everyone to give "without sadness or compulsion," confident that the Father who sees in secret will repay.

The reading from 2 Kings may help us to appreciate how private prayer may be richly repaid. It describes the powerful and empowering religious experience of Elisha. Leaving the fifty guild prophets on the other side of the Jordan, Elisha learns the secret of Elijah's power and returns with the prophet's mantle and a double portion of his spirit.

Year I

FIRST READING

2 Cor 9:6–11

God loves a cheerful giver.

A reading from the second Letter of Saint Paul to the Corinthians

Brothers and sisters, consider this: whoever sows sparingly will also reap sparingly, and whoever sows bountifully will also reap bountifully. Each must do as already determined, without sadness or compulsion, for God loves a cheerful giver. Moreover, God is able to make every grace abundant for you, so that in all things, always having all you need, you may have an abundance for every good work. As it is written:

He scatters abroad, he gives to the poor;
his righteousness endures forever.

The one who supplies seed to the sower and bread for food will supply and multiply your seed and increase the harvest of your righteousness.

You are being enriched in every way for all generosity, which through us produces thanksgiving to God.

The word of the Lord.

Responsorial Psalm

Ps 112:1bc – 2, 3 – 4, 9

R. Blessed the man who fears the Lord.

Blessed the man who fears the Lord,
 who greatly delights in his commands.
His posterity shall be mighty upon the earth;
 the upright generation shall be blessed.

R. Blessed the man who fears the Lord.

Wealth and riches shall be in his house;
 his generosity shall endure forever.
Light shines through the darkness for the upright;
 he is gracious and merciful and just.

R. Blessed the man who fears the Lord.

Lavishly he gives to the poor;
 his generosity shall endure forever;
 his horn shall be exalted in glory.

R. Blessed the man who fears the Lord.

Or: **R. Alleluia.**

Alleluia Verse *and* **Gospel,** *p. 1039.*

Year II

FIRST READING

2 Kgs 2:1, 6 – 14

A flaming chariot came between them, and Elijah went up to heaven.

A reading from the second Book of Kings

When the LORD was about to take Elijah up to heaven in a whirlwind, he and Elisha were on their way from Gilgal. Elijah said to Elisha, "Please stay here; the LORD has sent me on to the Jordan." "As the LORD lives, and as you yourself live, I will not leave you," Elisha replied. And so the two went on together. Fifty of the guild prophets followed and when the two stopped at the Jordan, they stood facing them at a distance. Elijah took his mantle, rolled it up and struck the water, which divided, and both crossed over on dry ground.

When they had crossed over, Elijah said to Elisha, "Ask for whatever I may do for you, before I am taken from you." Elisha answered, "May I receive a double portion of your spirit." "You have asked something that is not easy," Elijah replied. "Still, if you see me taken up from you, your wish will be granted; otherwise not." As they walked on conversing, a flaming chariot and flaming horses came between them, and Elijah went up to heaven in a whirlwind. When Elisha saw it happen he cried out, "My father! my father! Israel's chariots and drivers!" But when he could no longer see him, Elisha gripped his own garment and tore it in two.

Then he picked up Elijah's mantle that had fallen from him, and went back and stood at the bank of the Jordan. Wielding the mantle that had fallen from Elijah, Elisha struck the water in his turn and said, "Where is the LORD, the God of Elijah?" When Elisha struck the water it divided and he crossed over. The word of the Lord.

Responsorial Psalm

Ps 31:20, 21, 24

R. Let your hearts take comfort, all who hope in the Lord.

How great is the goodness, O LORD,
  which you have in store for those who fear you,
And which, toward those who take refuge in you,
  you show in the sight of the children of men.

  R. Let your hearts take comfort, all who hope in the Lord.

You hide them in the shelter of your presence
  from the plottings of men;
You screen them within your abode
  from the strife of tongues.

  R. Let your hearts take comfort, all who hope in the Lord.

Love the LORD, all you his faithful ones!
  The LORD keeps those who are constant,
  but more than requites those who act proudly.

  R. Let your hearts take comfort, all who hope in the Lord.

    Alleluia, alleluia   Jn 14:23
    Whoever loves me will keep my word,
    and my Father will love him
    and we will come to him.
    Alleluia, alleluia

Years I and II

GOSPEL   Mt 6:1–6, 16–18

    And your Father who sees what is hidden will repay you.

A reading from the holy Gospel according to Matthew

Jesus said to his disciples: "Take care not to perform righteous deeds in order that people may see them; otherwise, you will have no recompense from your heavenly Father. When you give alms, do not blow a trumpet before you, as the hypocrites do in the synagogues and in the streets to win the praise of others. Amen, I say to you, they have received their reward. But when you give alms, do not let your left hand know what your right is doing, so that your almsgiving may be secret. And your Father who sees in secret will repay you.

"When you pray, do not be like the hypocrites, who love to stand and pray in the synagogues and on street corners so that others may see them. Amen, I say to you, they have received their reward. But when you pray, go to your inner room, close the door, and pray to your Father in secret. And your Father who sees in secret will repay you.

"When you fast, do not look gloomy like the hypocrites. They neglect their appearance, so that they may appear to others to be fasting. Amen, I say to you, they have received their reward. But when you fast, anoint your head and wash your face, so that you may not appear to others to be fasting, except to your Father who is hidden. And your Father who sees what is hidden will repay you."

The Gospel of the Lord.

Liturgy of the Eucharist, *p. 897;* **Prayer over the Gifts,** *p. 1025.*

Thursday

Antiphons and Prayers, *p. 1024;* **Liturgy of the Word** *for Year I (odd years) follows; Year II (even years), p. 1043.*

TODAY'S LIVING WORD

The relationship between Elijah and Elisha, celebrated by Sirach in today's reading, was Luke's model for the relationship between Jesus and his followers. As Elisha stood watching Elijah being taken up to heaven, the disciples watched the Ascension of Jesus. And as Elisha received a double portion of Elijah's spirit, the disciples on Pentecost received the Spirit of their risen Lord. Thus it was that they came to share his passion and his power. Although he was not there on the day of Pentecost, the same fiery zeal filled Paul who made the Gospel of God revealed in Christ Jesus his unceasing boast. The new *Catechism* tells us that when we pray the first three petitions of the Our Father, we too are seized by "the burning desire...of the beloved Son for his Father's glory" (n. 2804).

The first three petitions of the Our Father are summed up in the central one: "Thy Kingdom come." All three long for the reign of God to come in its fullness. To pray for this is to ask the Father to bring to completion the saving work begun in Christ.

"This is how you are to pray," says Jesus.

Year I

FIRST READING

2 Cor 11:1–11

I preached the Gospel of God to you without charge.

A reading from the second Letter of Saint Paul to the Corinthians

Brothers and sisters:

If only you would put up with a little foolishness from me! Please put up with me. For I am jealous of you with the jealousy of God, since I betrothed you to one husband to present you as a chaste virgin to Christ. But I am afraid that, as the serpent deceived Eve by his cunning, your thoughts may be corrupted from a sincere and pure commitment to Christ. For if someone comes and preaches another Jesus than the one we preached, or if you receive a different spirit from the one you received or a different gospel from the one you accepted, you put up with it well enough. For I think that I am not in any way inferior to these "superapostles." Even if I am untrained in speaking, I am not so in knowledge; in every way we have made this plain to you in all things.

Did I make a mistake when I humbled myself so that you might be exalted, because I preached the Gospel of God to you without charge? I plundered other churches by accepting from them in order to minister to you. And when I was with you and in need, I did not burden anyone, for the brothers who came from Macedonia supplied my needs. So I refrained and will refrain from burdening you in any way. By the truth of Christ in me, this boast of mine shall not be silenced in the regions of Achaia. And why? Because I do not love you? God knows I do!

The word of the Lord.

Responsorial Psalm

Ps 111:1b–2, 3–4, 7–8

R. Your works, O Lord, are justice and truth.

I will give thanks to the LORD with all my heart
  in the company and assembly of the just.
Great are the works of the LORD,
  exquisite in all their delights.

R. Your works, O Lord, are justice and truth.

Majesty and glory are his work,
  and his justice endures forever.
He has won renown for his wondrous deeds;
  gracious and merciful is the LORD.

R. Your works, O Lord, are justice and truth.

The works of his hands are faithful and just;
  sure are all his precepts,
Reliable forever and ever,
  wrought in truth and equity.

R. Your works, O Lord, are justice and truth.

Or: **R. Alleluia.**

Alleluia Verse *and* **Gospel,** p. 1045.

Year II

FIRST READING

Sir 48:1–14

Elijah was enveloped in a whirlwind,
and Elisha was filled with the twofold portion of his spirit.

A reading from the Book of Sirach

Like a fire there appeared the prophet Elijah
    whose words were as a flaming furnace.
Their staff of bread he shattered,
    in his zeal he reduced them to straits;
By the Lord's word he shut up the heavens
    and three times brought down fire.
How awesome are you, Elijah, in your wondrous deeds!
    Whose glory is equal to yours?
You brought a dead man back to life
    from the nether world, by the will of the LORD.
You sent kings down to destruction,
    and easily broke their power into pieces.
You brought down nobles, from their beds of sickness.
You heard threats at Sinai,
    at Horeb avenging judgments.
You anointed kings who should inflict vengeance,
    and a prophet as your successor.
You were taken aloft in a whirlwind of fire,
    in a chariot with fiery horses.
You were destined, it is written, in time to come
    to put an end to wrath before the day of the LORD,
To turn back the hearts of fathers toward their sons,
    and to re-establish the tribes of Jacob.

Blessed is he who shall have seen you
And who falls asleep in your friendship.
For we live only in our life,
    but after death our name will not be such.
    O Elijah, enveloped in the whirlwind!

Then Elisha, filled with the twofold portion of his spirit,
    wrought many marvels by his mere word.
During his lifetime he feared no one,
    nor was any man able to intimidate his will.
Nothing was beyond his power;
    beneath him flesh was brought back into life.
In life he performed wonders,
    and after death, marvelous deeds.

The word of the Lord.

Responsorial Psalm

Ps 97:1–2, 3–4, 5–6, 7

R. Rejoice in the Lord, you just!

The LORD is king; let the earth rejoice;
    let the many isles be glad.
Clouds and darkness are round about him,
    justice and judgment are the foundation of his throne.

R. Rejoice in the Lord, you just!

Fire goes before him
    and consumes his foes round about.
His lightnings illumine the world;
    the earth sees and trembles.

R. Rejoice in the Lord, you just!

The mountains melt like wax before the LORD,
    before the Lord of all the earth.
The heavens proclaim his justice,
    and all peoples see his glory.

R. Rejoice in the Lord, you just!

All who worship graven things are put to shame,
   who glory in the things of nought;
   all gods are prostrate before him.

R. Rejoice in the Lord, you just!

> **Alleluia, alleluia**   Rom 8:15bc
> You have received a spirit of adoption as sons
> through which we cry: Abba! Father!
> **Alleluia, alleluia**

Years I and II

GOSPEL

Mt 6:7–15

This is how you are to pray.

A reading from the holy Gospel according to Matthew

Jesus said to his disciples: "In praying, do not babble like the pagans, who think that they will be heard because of their many words. Do not be like them. Your Father knows what you need before you ask him.

   "This is how you are to pray:

'Our Father who art in heaven,
   hallowed be thy name,
   thy Kingdom come,
thy will be done,
   on earth as it is in heaven.
Give us this day our daily bread;
   and forgive us our trespasses,
   as we forgive those who trespass against us;
   and lead us not into temptation,
   but deliver us from evil.'

"If you forgive others their transgressions, your heavenly Father will forgive you. But if you do not forgive others, neither will your Father forgive your transgressions."
The Gospel of the Lord.

Liturgy of the Eucharist, *p. 897;* **Prayer over the Gifts,** *p. 1025.*

Friday

Antiphons and Prayers, *p. 1024;* **Liturgy of the Word** *for Year I (odd years) follows; Year II (even years), p. 1048.*

TODAY'S LIVING WORD

In today's selection the author of 2 Kings concludes the story of Ahab. The promised destruction of Ahab's house, punishment for the murder of Naboth, was deferred until his children succeeded him. Athalia, Ahab's daughter, ruled the land of Judah for six years. Then in the seventh year Jehoiada the priest made a clean sweep of the royal house. For the people of Judah, his action was a defining moment. Not only did he return Ahaziah's son to power, but he renewed the people's covenant with God as well. Thus, having recovered their heavenly treasure, they were able to reorder their hearts. "All the people...rejoiced and the city was quiet."

In the Gospel for today Jesus, like Jehoiada, calls his disciples to clarify their vision and values too. He reminds them that what they cherish will determine what they choose. Second Corinthians shows Paul as living proof of that. This catalog of Paul's sufferings in the service of the Gospel is truly remarkable. Only a man whose "eye is sound," who sees everything in the light of Christ, could bear such hardships and more.

Year I

FIRST READING   2 Cor 11:18, 21–30

Apart from these things, there is the daily pressure upon me of my anxiety for all the churches.

A reading from the second Letter of Saint Paul to the Corinthians

Brothers and sisters:

Since many boast according to the flesh, I too will boast. To my shame I say that we were too weak!

But what anyone dares to boast of (I am speaking in foolishness) I also dare. Are they Hebrews? So am I. Are they children of Israel? So am I. Are they descendants of Abraham? So am I. Are they ministers of Christ? (I am talking like an insane person). I am still more, with far greater labors, far more imprisonments, far worse beatings, and numerous brushes with death. Five times at the hands of the Jews I received forty lashes minus one. Three times I was beaten with rods, once I was stoned, three times I was shipwrecked, I passed a night and a day on the deep; on frequent journeys, in dangers from rivers, dangers from robbers, dangers from my own race, dangers from Gentiles, dangers in the city, dangers in the wilderness, dangers at sea, dangers among false brothers; in toil and hardship, through many sleepless nights, through hunger and thirst, through frequent fastings, through cold and exposure. And apart from these things, there is the daily pressure upon me of my anxiety for all the churches. Who is weak, and I am not weak? Who is led to sin, and I am not indignant?

If I must boast, I will boast of the things that show my weakness.

The word of the Lord.

Responsorial Psalm

Ps 34:2–3, 4–5, 6–7

R. From all their distress God rescues the just.

I will bless the LORD at all times;
  his praise shall be ever in my mouth.

Let my soul glory in the Lord;
  the lowly will hear me and be glad.

  R. From all their distress God rescues the just.

Glorify the Lord with me,
  let us together extol his name.
I sought the Lord, and he answered me
  and delivered me from all my fears.

  R. From all their distress God rescues the just.

Look to him that you may be radiant with joy,
  and your faces may not blush with shame.
When the poor one called out, the Lord heard,
  and from all his distress he saved him.

  R. From all their distress God rescues the just.

  Alleluia Verse *and* **Gospel,** *p. 1050f.*

Year II

FIRST READING   2 Kgs 11:1–4, 9–18, 20

They anointed him and shouted: "Long live the king!"

A reading from the second Book of Kings

When Athaliah, the mother of Ahaziah, saw that her son was dead, she began to kill off the whole royal family. But Jehosheba, daughter of King Jehoram and sister of Ahaziah, took Joash, his son, and spirited him away, along with his nurse, from the bedroom where the princes were about to be slain. She concealed him from Athaliah, and so he did not die. For six years he remained hidden in the temple of the Lord, while Athaliah ruled the land.

But in the seventh year, Jehoiada summoned the captains of the Carians and of the guards. He had them come to him in the temple of the LORD, exacted from them a sworn commitment, and then showed them the king's son.

The captains did just as Jehoiada the priest commanded. Each one with his men, both those going on duty for the sabbath and those going off duty that week, came to Jehoiada the priest. He gave the captains King David's spears and shields, which were in the temple of the LORD. And the guards, with drawn weapons, lined up from the southern to the northern limit of the enclosure, surrounding the altar and the temple on the king's behalf. Then Jehoiada led out the king's son and put the crown and the insignia upon him. They proclaimed him king and anointed him, clapping their hands and shouting, "Long live the king!"

Athaliah heard the noise made by the people, and appeared before them in the temple of the LORD. When she saw the king standing by the pillar, as was the custom, and the captains and trumpeters near him, with all the people of the land rejoicing and blowing trumpets, she tore her garments and cried out, "Treason, treason!" Then Jehoiada the priest instructed the captains in command of the force: "Bring her outside through the ranks. If anyone follows her," he added, "let him die by the sword." He had given orders that she should not be slain in the temple of the LORD. She was led out forcibly to the horse gate of the royal palace, where she was put to death.

Then Jehoiada made a covenant between the LORD as one party and the king and the people as the other, by which they would be the LORD's people; and another covenant, between the king and the people. Thereupon all the people of the land went to the temple of Baal and demolished it. They shattered its altars and images completely, and slew Mattan, the priest of Baal, before the altars. Jehoiada appointed a detachment for the temple of the LORD. All the people of the land rejoiced and the city was quiet, now that Athaliah had been slain with the sword at the royal palace.

The word of the Lord.

Responsorial Psalm
Ps 132:11, 12, 13–14, 17–18

R. The Lord has chosen Zion for his dwelling.

The LORD swore to David
  a firm promise from which he will not withdraw:
"Your own offspring
  I will set upon your throne."

R. The Lord has chosen Zion for his dwelling.

"If your sons keep my covenant
  and the decrees which I shall teach them,
Their sons, too, forever
  shall sit upon your throne."

R. The Lord has chosen Zion for his dwelling.

For the LORD has chosen Zion;
  he prefers her for his dwelling.
"Zion is my resting place forever;
  in her will I dwell, for I prefer her."

R. The Lord has chosen Zion for his dwelling.

"In her will I make a horn to sprout forth for David;
  I will place a lamp for my anointed.
His enemies I will clothe with shame,
  but upon him my crown shall shine."

R. The Lord has chosen Zion for his dwelling.

Alleluia, alleluia   Mt 5:3
Blessed are the poor in spirit;
  for theirs is the Kingdom of heaven.
Alleluia, alleluia

Years I and II

GOSPEL   Mt 6:19–23

For where your treasure is, there also will your heart be.

A reading from the holy Gospel according to Matthew

Jesus said to his disciples: "Do not store up for yourselves treasures on earth, where moth and decay destroy, and thieves break in and steal. But store up treasures in heaven, where neither moth nor decay destroys, nor thieves break in and steal. For where your treasure is, there also will your heart be.

"The lamp of the body is the eye. If your eye is sound, your whole body will be filled with light; but if your eye is bad, your whole body will be in darkness. And if the light in you is darkness, how great will the darkness be."

The Gospel of the Lord.

Liturgy of the Eucharist, *p. 897;* **Prayer over the Gifts,** *p. 1025.*

Saturday

Antiphons and Prayers, *p. 1024;* **Liturgy of the Word** *for Year I (odd years) follows; Year II (even years), p. 1053.*

TODAY'S LIVING WORD

"No one can serve two masters," Jesus declares in today's Gospel. "He will either hate one and love the other, or be devoted to one and despise the other." The short story from 2 Chronicles is a case in point. Torn between their priest and the princes of Judah, Joash and his people forsook the God of their fathers, ignored God's prophets, and slew Jehoiada's son, Zechariah, in the temple court.

The word "mammon," sometimes rendered as "money," may be the key to Jesus' meaning. It is derived from the Hebrew *'mn*, which means "trust." Jesus' words raise precisely that issue: in whom or in what will we put our trust? There is no doubt of Paul's answer. Trusting the power of God, whose grace is always enough, he boasts of his weaknesses. He says, "I am content with weaknesses, insults, hardships, persecutions, and constraints, for the sake of Christ." Are we?

Year I

FIRST READING

2 Cor 12:1–10

I will rather boast most gladly of my weaknesses.

A reading from the second Letter of Saint Paul to the Corinthians

Brothers and sisters:

I must boast; not that it is profitable, but I will go on to visions and revelations of the Lord. I know a man in Christ who, fourteen years ago (whether in the body or out of the body I do not know, God knows), was caught up to the third heaven. And I know that this man (whether in the body or out of the body I do not know, God knows) was caught up into Paradise and heard ineffable things, which no one may utter. About this man I will boast, but about myself I will not boast, except about my weaknesses. Although if I should wish to boast, I would not be foolish, for I would be telling the truth. But I refrain, so that no one may think more of me than what he sees in me or hears from me because of the abundance of the revelations. Therefore, that I might not become too elated, a thorn in the flesh was given to me, an angel of Satan, to beat me, to keep me from being too elated. Three times I begged the Lord about this, that it might leave me, but he said to me, "My grace is sufficient for you, for power is made perfect in weakness." I will rather boast most gladly of my weaknesses, in order that the power of Christ may dwell with me. Therefore, I am content with weaknesses, insults, hardships, persecutions, and constraints, for the sake of Christ; for when I am weak, then I am strong.

The word of the Lord.

Responsorial Psalm

Ps 34:8–9, 10–11, 12–13

R. Taste and see the goodness of the Lord.

The angel of the LORD encamps
  around those who fear him, and delivers them.
Taste and see how good the LORD is;
  blessed the man who takes refuge in him.

R. Taste and see the goodness of the Lord.

Fear the LORD, you his holy ones,
  for nought is lacking to those who fear him.
The great grow poor and hungry;
  but those who seek the LORD want for no good thing.

R. Taste and see the goodness of the Lord.

Come, children, hear me;
  I will teach you the fear of the LORD.
Which of you desires life,
  and takes delight in prosperous days?

R. Taste and see the goodness of the Lord.

Alleluia Verse *and* **Gospel,** *p. 1055.*

Year II

FIRST READING

2 Chr 24:17–25

*They murdered Zechariah between the sanctuary
and the altar (Mt 23:35).*

A reading from the second Book of Chronicles

After the death of Jehoiada, the princes of Judah came and paid homage to King Joash, and the king then listened to them. They forsook the temple of the LORD, the God of their fathers, and began to serve the sacred poles and the idols; and because of this crime of theirs, wrath came upon Judah and Jerusalem. Although prophets were sent to them to convert them to the Lord, the people would not listen to their warnings. Then the Spirit of God possessed Zechariah, son of Jehoiada the priest. He took his stand above the people and said to them: "God says, 'Why are you transgressing the Lord's commands, so that you cannot prosper? Because you have abandoned the Lord, he has abandoned you.'" But they conspired against him, and at the king's order they stoned him to death in the court of the Lord's temple. Thus King Joash was unmindful of the devotion shown him by Jehoiada, Zechariah's father, and slew his son. And as Zechariah was dying, he said, "May the Lord see and avenge."

At the turn of the year a force of Arameans came up against Joash. They invaded Judah and Jerusalem, did away with all the princes of the people, and sent all their spoil to the king of Damascus. Though the Aramean force came with few men, the Lord surrendered a very large force into their power, because Judah had abandoned the Lord, the God of their fathers. So punishment was meted out to Joash. After the Arameans had departed from him, leaving him in grievous suffering, his servants conspired against him because of the murder of the son of Jehoiada the priest. He was buried in the City of David, but not in the tombs of the kings.

The word of the Lord.

Responsorial Psalm
Ps 89:4 – 5, 29 – 30, 31 – 32, 33 – 34

R. For ever I will maintain my love for my servant.

"I have made a covenant with my chosen one,
  I have sworn to David my servant:

Forever will I confirm your posterity
  and establish your throne for all generations."

R. For ever I will maintain my love for my servant.

"Forever I will maintain my kindness toward him,
  and my covenant with him stands firm.
I will make his posterity endure forever
  and his throne as the days of heaven."

R. For ever I will maintain my love for my servant.

"If his sons forsake my law
  and walk not according to my ordinances,
If they violate my statutes
  and keep not my commands."

R. For ever I will maintain my love for my servant.

"I will punish their crime with a rod
  and their guilt with stripes.
Yet my mercy I will not take from him,
  nor will I belie my faithfulness."

R. For ever I will maintain my love for my servant.

  Alleluia, alleluia   2 Cor 8:9
  Jesus Christ became poor although he was rich,
  so that by his poverty you might become rich.
  Alleluia, alleluia

Years I and II

GOSPEL   Mt 6:24 – 34
        Do not worry about tomorrow.

A reading from the holy Gospel according to Matthew

Jesus said to his disciples: "No one can serve two masters. He
will either hate one and love the other, or be devoted to one
and despise the other. You cannot serve God and mammon.

  "Therefore I tell you, do not worry about your life, what
you will eat or drink, or about your body, what you will wear.

Is not life more than food and the body more than clothing? Look at the birds in the sky; they do not sow or reap, they gather nothing into barns, yet your heavenly Father feeds them. Are not you more important than they? Can any of you by worrying add a single moment to your life-span? Why are you anxious about clothes? Learn from the way the wild flowers grow. They do not work or spin. But I tell you that not even Solomon in all his splendor was clothed like one of them. If God so clothes the grass of the field, which grows today and is thrown into the oven tomorrow, will he not much more provide for you, O you of little faith? So do not worry and say, 'What are we to eat?' or 'What are we to drink?' or 'What are we to wear?' All these things the pagans seek. Your heavenly Father knows that you need them all. But seek first the Kingdom of God and his righteousness, and all these things will be given you besides. Do not worry about tomorrow; tomorrow will take care of itself. Sufficient for a day is its own evil."

The Gospel of the Lord.

Liturgy of the Eucharist, *p. 897;* **Prayer over the Gifts,** *p. 1025.*

TWELFTH WEEK IN ORDINARY TIME

The **Antiphons and Prayers** *may be the following, or may be chosen from any of the other 33 weeks in Ordinary Time (refer to Liturgical Calendar, pp. 26–41).*

The **Liturgy of the Word** *varies: for Monday, see p. 1058; Tuesday, p. 1063; Wednesday, p. 1068; Thursday, p. 1073; Friday, p. 1079; Saturday, p. 1084.*

Entrance Antiphon

God is the strength of his people. In him, we his chosen live in safety. Save us, Lord, who share in your life, and give us your blessing; be our shepherd for ever.   (Ps 28:8–9)

Opening Prayer

Let us pray
   [that we may grow
   in the love of God]
      Pause for silent prayer.

Father,
guide and protector of your people,
grant us an unfailing respect for your name,
and keep us always in your love.

Grant this through our Lord Jesus Christ, your Son,
Who lives and reigns with you and the Holy Spirit,
one God, for ever and ever.

Alternative Opening Prayer

Let us pray
   [to God whose fatherly love keeps us safe]
      Pause for silent prayer.

God of the universe,
we worship you as Lord.
God, ever close to us,
we rejoice to call you Father.
From this world's uncertainty we look to your covenant.
Keep us one in your peace, secure in your love.

We ask this through Christ our Lord.

Prayer over the Gifts

Pray, brethren...

Lord,
receive our offering,
and may this sacrifice of praise
purify us in mind and heart
and make us always eager to serve you.

We ask this in the name of Jesus the Lord.

Communion Antiphon

The eyes of all look to you, O Lord, and you give them food in
due season.   (Ps 145:15)

Or:

I am the Good Shepherd; I give my life for my sheep, says
the Lord.   (Jn 10:11, 15)

Prayer after Communion

Let us pray.
Pause for silent prayer, if this has not preceded.

Lord,
you give us the body and blood of your Son
to renew your life within us.
In your mercy, assure our redemption
and bring us to the eternal life
we celebrate in this eucharist.

We ask this through Christ our Lord.

Monday

Antiphons and Prayers, *p. 1056;* **Liturgy of the Word** *for Year I (odd
years) follows; Year II (even years), p. 1060.*

TODAY'S LIVING WORD

The gift promised to Abram in the reading from Genesis is
forfeited by Israel in the selection from 2 Kings. Unlike Abram who
"went as the Lord directed him," the Israelites went their own way,
rejecting "the covenant which [God] had made with their fathers."
So "in his great anger," God condemned them to the cruel tyranny
of Assyria. God's anger here, as elsewhere in the Bible, gives God's
judgment an emotional force which is difficult for us to bear. But as
Abraham Heschel explains, in the Bible divine anger signifies God's
care, and divine judgment springs from God's desire to save.* That
is why biblical people, though fully aware of the terrifying reality of
God's anger, came not only to tolerate it but to trust it.

The biblical image of God as judge, impatient with human hypocrisy, underlies Jesus' warning against passing judgment in today's Gospel. Jesus tells us that God *alone* is judge, and this God will pass on us the verdict we so glibly pass on others.

* *The Prophets,* vol. 1 (New York: Harper & Row, 1962), pp. 59–78.

Year I

FIRST READING

Gn 12:1–9

Abraham went as the LORD directed him.

A reading from the Book of Genesis

The LORD said to Abram: "Go forth from the land of your kinsfolk and from your father's house to a land that I will show you.

"I will make of you a great nation,
 and I will bless you;
I will make your name great,
 so that you will be a blessing
I will bless those who bless you
 and curse those who curse you.
All the communities of the earth
 shall find blessing in you."

Abram went as the LORD directed him, and Lot went with him. Abram was seventy-five years old when he left Haran. Abram took his wife, Sarai, his brother's son Lot, all the possessions that they had accumulated, and the persons they had acquired in Haran, and they set out for the land of Canaan. When they came to the land of Canaan, Abram passed through the land as far as the sacred place at Shechem, by the terebinth of Moreh. (The Canaanites were then in the land.)

The LORD appeared to Abram and said, "To your descendants I will give this land." So Abram built an altar there to the LORD who had appeared to him. From there he moved on to the hill country east of Bethel, pitching his tent with Bethel to the west and Ai to the east. He built an altar there to the LORD and invoked the LORD by name. Then Abram journeyed on by stages to the Negeb.

The word of the Lord.

Responsorial Psalm

Ps 33:12–13, 18–19, 20 and 22

R. Blessed the people the Lord has chosen to be his own.

Blessed the nation whose God is the LORD,
  the people he has chosen for his own inheritance.
From heaven the LORD looks down;
  he sees all mankind.

R. Blessed the people the Lord has chosen to be his own.

See, the eyes of the LORD are upon those who fear him,
  upon those who hope for his kindness,
To deliver them from death
  and preserve them in spite of famine.

R. Blessed the people the Lord has chosen to be his own.

Our soul waits for the LORD,
  who is our help and our shield.
May your kindness, O LORD, be upon us
  who have put our hope in you.

R. Blessed the people the Lord has chosen to be his own.

Alleluia Verse *and* **Gospel,** *p. 1062.*

Year II

FIRST READING

2 Kgs 17:5–8, 13–15a, 18

In his great anger against Israel,
the LORD put them away out of his sight.
Only the tribe of Judah was left.

A reading from the second Book of Kings

Shalmaneser, king of Assyria, occupied the whole land and attacked Samaria, which he besieged for three years. In the ninth year of Hoshea, king of Israel the king of Assyria took Samaria, and deported the children of Israel to Assyria, setting them in Halah, at the Habor, a river of Gozan, and the cities of the Medes.

This came about because the children of Israel sinned against the LORD, their God, who had brought them up from the land of Egypt, from under the domination of Pharaoh, king of Egypt, and because they venerated other gods. They followed the rites of the nations whom the LORD had cleared out of the way of the children of Israel and the kings of Israel whom they set up.

And though the LORD warned Israel and Judah by every prophet and seer, "Give up your evil ways and keep my commandments and statutes, in accordance with the entire law which I enjoined on your fathers and which I sent you by my servants the prophets," they did not listen, but were as stiff-necked as their fathers, who had not believed in the LORD, their God. They rejected his statutes, the covenant which he had made with their fathers, and the warnings which he had given them, till, in his great anger against Israel, the LORD put them away out of his sight. Only the tribe of Judah was left.

The word of the Lord.

Responsorial Psalm
Ps 60:3, 4 – 5, 12 – 13

R. Help us with your right hand, O Lord, and answer us.

O God, you have rejected us and broken our defenses;
  you have been angry; rally us!

R. Help us with your right hand, O Lord, and answer us.

You have rocked the country and split it open;
  repair the cracks in it, for it is tottering.
You have made your people feel hardships;
  you have given us stupefying wine.

R. Help us with your right hand, O Lord, and answer us.

Have not you, O God, rejected us,
  so that you go not forth, O God, with our armies?
Give us aid against the foe,
  for worthless is the help of men.

R. Help us with your right hand, O Lord, and answer us.

Alleluia, alleluia Heb 4:12
The word of God is living and effective,
  able to discern reflections and thoughts of the heart.
Alleluia, alleluia

Years I and II

GOSPEL   Mt 7:1–5

Remove the wooden beam from your eye first.

A reading from the holy Gospel according to Matthew

Jesus said to his disciples: "Stop judging, that you may not be judged. For as you judge, so will you be judged, and the measure with which you measure will be measured out to you. Why do you notice the splinter in your brother's eye, but do not perceive the wooden beam in your own eye? How can you say to your brother, 'Let me remove that splinter from your eye,' while the wooden beam is in your eye? You hypocrite, remove the wooden beam from your eye first; then you will see clearly to remove the splinter from your brother's eye."

The Gospel of the Lord.

Liturgy of the Eucharist, *p. 897;* **Prayer over the Gifts,** *p. 1057.*

Tuesday

Antiphons and Prayers, *p. 1056;* **Liturgy of the Word** *for Year I (odd years) follows; Year II (even years), p. 1065.*

TODAY'S LIVING WORD

The sayings of Jesus in today's passage from Matthew seem to comment on the two first readings. Jesus' summary of "the Law and the Prophets" is reminiscent of a well-known story about Hillel, a rabbi who died when Jesus was about ten years old. A scoffer once asked Hillel if he could teach him the whole Torah while he stood on one foot. Hillel replied, "What is hateful to you do not do to your neighbor; that is the whole Torah; go and study it." In the view of both Hillel and Jesus, Abraham's treatment of Lot in today's reading from Genesis anticipates the Golden Rule and so fulfills the Torah.

Jesus goes on, calling his hearers to "enter through the narrow gate...that leads to life." The notion of the two ways or two gates, as Jesus puts it here, is also found in the Hebrew Scriptures. In Deuteronomy 31, for example, Moses sets before his people life and death, blessing and curse, and urges them to "choose life." Hezekiah faces this choice in the reading from 2 Kings: to take the path of least resistance by submitting to Assyria's demands or to take the less-traveled road of trust in the living God.

Year I

FIRST READING

Gn 13:2, 5 –18

Let there be no strife between you and me, for we are brothers.

A reading from the Book of Genesis

Abram was very rich in livestock, silver, and gold.

Lot, who went with Abram, also had flocks and herds and tents, so that the land could not support them if they stayed together; their possessions were so great that they could not dwell together. There were quarrels between the herdsmen of

Abram's livestock and those of Lot's. (At this time the Canaanites and the Perizzites were occupying the land.)

So Abram said to Lot: "Let there be no strife between you and me, or between your herdsmen and mine, for we are kinsmen. Is not the whole land at your disposal? Please separate from me. If you prefer the left, I will go to the right; if you prefer the right, I will go to the left." Lot looked about and saw how well watered the whole Jordan Plain was as far as Zoar, like the LORD's own garden, or like Egypt. (This was before the LORD had destroyed Sodom and Gomorrah.) Lot, therefore, chose for himself the whole Jordan Plain and set out eastward. Thus they separated from each other; Abram stayed in the land of Canaan, while Lot settled among the cities of the Plain, pitching his tents near Sodom. Now the inhabitants of Sodom were very wicked in the sins they committed against the LORD.

After Lot had left, the LORD said to Abram: "Look about you, and from where you are, gaze to the north and south, east and west; all the land that you see I will give to you and your descendants forever. I will make your descendants like the dust of the earth; if anyone could count the dust of the earth, your descendants too might be counted. Set forth and walk about in the land, through its length and breadth, for to you I will give it." Abram moved his tents and went on to settle near the terebinth of Mamre, which is at Hebron. There he built an altar to the LORD.

The word of the Lord.

Responsorial Psalm

R. He who does justice will live in the presence of the Lord.

He who walks blamelessly and does justice;
　who thinks the truth in his heart
　and slanders not with his tongue.

R. He who does justice will live in the presence of the Lord.

Who harms not his fellow man,
　nor takes up a reproach against his neighbor;
By whom the reprobate is despised,
　while he honors those who fear the LORD.

R. He who does justice will live in the presence of the Lord.

Who lends not his money at usury
　and accepts no bribe against the innocent.
He who does these things
　shall never be disturbed.

R. He who does justice will live in the presence of the Lord.

Alleluia Verse *and* **Gospel,** *p. 1067.*

Year II

FIRST READING　　　　　　　2 Kgs 19:9b–11, 14–21, 31–35a, 36

*I will shield and save this city for my own sake and
for the sake of my servant David.*

A reading from the second Book of Kings

Sennacherib, king of Assyria, sent envoys to Hezekiah with
this message: "Thus shall you say to Hezekiah, king of Judah:
'Do not let your God on whom you rely deceive you by saying
that Jerusalem will not be handed over to the king of Assyria.
You have heard what the kings of Assyria have done to all
other countries: they doomed them! Will you, then, be saved?'"

　　Hezekiah took the letter from the hand of the messengers
and read it; then he went up to the temple of the LORD, and

spreading it out before him, he prayed in the LORD's presence: "O LORD, God of Israel, enthroned upon the cherubim! You alone are God over all the kingdoms of the earth. You have made the heavens and the earth. Incline your ear, O LORD, and listen! Open your eyes, O LORD, and see! Hear the words of Sennacherib which he sent to taunt the living God. Truly, O LORD, the kings of Assyria have laid waste the nations and their lands, and cast their gods into the fire; they destroyed them because they were not gods, but the work of human hands, wood and stone. Therefore, O LORD, our God, save us from the power of this man, that all the kingdoms of the earth may know that you alone, O LORD, are God."

Then Isaiah, son of Amoz, sent this message to Hezekiah: "Thus says the LORD, the God of Israel, in answer to your prayer for help against Sennacherib, king of Assyria: I have listened! This is the word the LORD has spoken concerning him:

"'She despises you, laughs you to scorn,
    the virgin daughter Zion!
Behind you she wags her head,
    daughter Jerusalem.

"'For out of Jerusalem shall come a remnant,
    and from Mount Zion, survivors.
The zeal of the LORD of hosts shall do this.'

"Therefore, thus says the LORD concerning the king of Assyria: 'He shall not reach this city, nor shoot an arrow at it, nor come before it with a shield, nor cast up siege-works against it. He shall return by the same way he came, without entering the city, says the LORD. I will shield and save this city for my own sake, and for the sake of my servant David.'"

That night the angel of the Lord went forth and struck down one hundred and eighty-five thousand men in the Assyrian camp. So Sennacherib, the king of Assyria, broke camp, and went back home to Nineveh.

The word of the Lord.

Responsorial Psalm
Ps 48:2 –3ab, 3cd –4, 10 –11

R. God upholds his city for ever.

Great is the Lord and wholly to be praised
  in the city of our God.
His holy mountain, fairest of heights,
  is the joy of all the earth.

R. God upholds his city for ever.

Mount Zion, "the recesses of the North,"
  is the city of the great King.
God is with her castles;
  renowned is he as a stronghold.

R. God upholds his city for ever.

O God, we ponder your mercy
  within your temple.
As your name, O God, so also your praise
  reaches to the ends of the earth.
Of justice your right hand is full.

R. God upholds his city for ever.

Alleluia, alleluia Jn 8:12
I am the light of the world, says the Lord;
whoever follows me will have the light of life.
Alleluia, alleluia

Years I and II

GOSPEL
Mt 7:6, 12 –14
Do to others whatever you would have them do to you.

A reading from the holy Gospel according to Matthew

Jesus said to his disciples: "Do not give what is holy to dogs, or throw your pearls before swine, lest they trample them underfoot, and turn and tear you to pieces.

"Do to others whatever you would have them do to you. This is the Law and the Prophets.

"Enter through the narrow gate; for the gate is wide and the road broad that leads to destruction, and those who enter through it are many. How narrow the gate and constricted the road that leads to life. And those who find it are few."

The Gospel of the Lord.

Liturgy of the Eucharist, *p. 897;* **Prayer over the Gifts,** *p. 1057.*

Wednesday

Antiphons and Prayers, *p. 1056;* **Liturgy of the Word** *for Year I (odd years) follows; Year II (even years), p. 1071.*

TODAY'S LIVING WORD

Today's two first readings take up the theme of covenant. In Genesis, God "cuts" a covenant with Abraham in a ritual that seems strange to us, but is attested to in Jeremiah 34. In 2 Kings the people of Judah, having recovered "the book of the law" that was lost when the temple was desecrated during the reign of a previous king, renew their covenant with God. These stories convey two aspects of covenant. God's covenant with Abraham underscores the graciousness of God, who here goes so far as to assume the obligations of the covenant by passing like a flaming torch between the animals. The account from 2 Kings, on the other hand, focuses on the covenant obligations that fall upon the people. These are contained in the book of the law, which scholars believe to be a version of Deuteronomy. The sayings of Jesus in today's Gospel stress this point too.

Jesus declares that false prophets are known not by their words but by their deeds. For prophets, as for all God's people then and now, covenant fidelity consists in keeping God's statutes and decrees with their whole hearts and souls.

Year I

FIRST READING

Gn 15:1–12, 17–18

Abraham believed God, and it was credited to him as right-eousness (Rom 4:3b), and the Lord made a covenant with him.

A reading from the Book of Genesis

The word of the Lord came to Abram in a vision:

"Fear not, Abram!
I am your shield;
I will make your reward very great."

But Abram said, "O Lord GOD, what good will your gifts be, if I keep on being childless and have as my heir the steward of my house, Eliezer?" Abram continued, "See, you have given me no offspring, and so one of my servants will be my heir." Then the word of the LORD came to him: "No, that one shall not be your heir; your own issue shall be your heir." He took him outside and said: "Look up at the sky and count the stars, if you can. Just so," he added, "shall your descendants be." Abram put his faith in the LORD, who credited it to him as an act of righteousness.

He then said to him, "I am the LORD who brought you from Ur of the Chaldeans to give you this land as a possession." "O Lord GOD," he asked, "how am I to know that I shall possess it?" He answered him, "Bring me a three-year-old heifer, a three-year-old she-goat, a three-year-old ram, a turtledove, and a young pigeon." Abram brought him all these, split them in two, and placed each half opposite the other; but the birds he did not cut up. Birds of prey swooped down on the carcasses, but Abram stayed with them. As the sun was about to set, a trance fell upon Abram, and a deep, terrifying darkness enveloped him.

When the sun had set and it was dark, there appeared a smoking fire pot and a flaming torch, which passed between those pieces. It was on that occasion that the Lord made a covenant with Abram, saying: "To your descendants I give this land, from the Wadi of Egypt to the Great River the Euphrates."
The word of the Lord.

Responsorial Psalm

Ps 105:1–2, 3–4, 6–7, 8–9

R. The Lord remembers his covenant for ever.

Give thanks to the Lord, invoke his name;
  make known among the nations his deeds.
Sing to him, sing his praise,
  proclaim all his wondrous deeds.

R. The Lord remembers his covenant for ever.

Glory in his holy name;
  rejoice, O hearts that seek the Lord!
Look to the Lord in his strength;
  seek to serve him constantly.

R. The Lord remembers his covenant for ever.

You descendants of Abraham, his servants,
  sons of Jacob, his chosen ones!
He, the Lord, is our God;
  throughout the earth his judgments prevail.

R. The Lord remembers his covenant for ever.

He remembers forever his covenant
  which he made binding for a thousand generations—
Which he entered into with Abraham
  and by his oath to Isaac.

R. The Lord remembers his covenant for ever.

Or: **R. Alleluia.**

Alleluia Verse *and* **Gospel,** *p. 1073.*

Year II

FIRST READING
2 Kgs 22:8–13; 23:1–3

*The king had the book that had been found
in the temple read out to them,
and he made a covenant before the Lord.*

A reading from the second Book of Kings

The high priest Hilkiah informed the scribe Shaphan, "I have found the book of the law in the temple of the Lord." Hilkiah gave the book to Shaphan, who read it. Then the scribe Shaphan went to the king and reported, "Your servants have smelted down the metals available in the temple and have consigned them to the master workmen in the temple of the Lord." The scribe Shaphan also informed the king that the priest Hilkiah had given him a book, and then read it aloud to the king. When the king heard the contents of the book of the law, he tore his garments and issued this command to Hilkiah the priest, Ahikam, son of Shaphan, Achbor, son of Micaiah, the scribe Shaphan, and the king's servant Asaiah: "Go, consult the Lord for me, for the people, for all Judah, about the stipulations of this book that has been found, for the anger of the Lord has been set furiously ablaze against us, because our fathers did not obey the stipulations of this book, nor fulfill our written obligations."

The king then had all the elders of Judah and of Jerusalem summoned together before him. The king went up to the temple of the Lord with all the men of Judah and all the inhabitants of

Jerusalem: priests, prophets, and all the people, small and great. He had the entire contents of the book of the covenant that had been found in the temple of the LORD, read out to them. Standing by the column, the king made a covenant before the LORD that they would follow him and observe his ordinances, statutes and decrees with their whole hearts and souls, thus reviving the terms of the covenant which were written in this book. And all the people stood as participants in the covenant.

The word of the Lord.

Responsorial Psalm
Ps 119:33, 34, 35, 36, 37, 40

R. Teach me the way of your decrees, O Lord.

Instruct me, O LORD, in the way of your statutes,
    that I may exactly observe them.

R. Teach me the way of your decrees, O Lord.

Give me discernment, that I may observe your law
    and keep it with all my heart.

R. Teach me the way of your decrees, O Lord.

Lead me in the path of your commands,
    for in it I delight.

R. Teach me the way of your decrees, O Lord.

Incline my heart to your decrees
    and not to gain.

R. Teach me the way of your decrees, O Lord.

Turn away my eyes from seeing what is vain:
    by your way give me life.

R. Teach me the way of your decrees, O Lord.

Behold, I long for your precepts;
    in your justice give me life.

R. Teach me the way of your decrees, O Lord.

Alleluia, alleluia Jn 15:4a, 5b
Remain in me, as I remain in you, says the Lord;
whoever remains in me will bear much fruit.
Alleluia, alleluia

Years I and II

GOSPEL   Mt 7:15–20

By their fruits you will know them.

A reading from the holy Gospel according to Matthew

Jesus said to his disciples: "Beware of false prophets, who come to you in sheep's clothing, but underneath are ravenous wolves. By their fruits you will know them. Do people pick grapes from thornbushes, or figs from thistles? Just so, every good tree bears good fruit, and a rotten tree bears bad fruit. A good tree cannot bear bad fruit, nor can a rotten tree bear good fruit. Every tree that does not bear good fruit will be cut down and thrown into the fire. So by their fruits you will know them."

The Gospel of the Lord.

Liturgy of the Eucharist, *p. 897;* **Prayer over the Gifts,** *p. 1057.*

Thursday

Antiphons and Prayers, *p. 1056;* **Liturgy of the Word** *for Year I (odd years) follows; Year II (even years), p. 1076.*

TODAY'S LIVING WORD

In today's two first readings, Sarai and Jehoiachin are both tragically conditioned by the world in which they find themselves. Sarai's abuse of Hagar is deplorable, but Sarai is the product of a patriarchal society in which a woman's worth was determined by her ability to bear male heirs for her husband. She is caught in what Megan McKenna describes as "an interlocking set of oppressions" that pit one woman against the other.* The young king Jehoiachin "did evil in the sight of the Lord," but Jehoiachin is the end of a long line of unscrupulous kings and queens who routinely ignored the warnings of God's prophets. He is heir to a royal house that was built "on sandy ground." So it will collapse, completely ruined. This is not to excuse either Sarai or Jehoiachin, but only to observe, as the poet did, "how much we are the world we wander in."

We are no different. Born and raised in a Christian culture, we easily cry out, "Lord, Lord." But Jesus demands more. It is not enough to hear his words but we must put them into practice, with raised consciousness and renewed heart.

* *Not Counting Women and Children* (Maryknoll: Orbis Books, 1994), p. 185.

Year I

FIRST READING   Gn 16:1–12, 15–16 or 16:6b–12,15–16

Hagar bore Abram a son and he called him Ishmael.

A reading from the Book of Genesis

Long form follows; for short form omit what is in brackets.

[Abram's wife Sarai had borne him no children. She had, however, an Egyptian maidservant named Hagar. Sarai said to Abram: "The LORD has kept me from bearing children. Have intercourse, then, with my maid; perhaps I shall have sons through her." Abram heeded Sarai's request. Thus, after Abram had lived ten years in the land of Canaan, his wife Sarai took her maid, Hagar the Egyptian, and gave her to her husband Abram to be his concubine. He had intercourse with her, and she became pregnant. When she became aware of her pregnancy, she looked on her mistress with disdain. So Sarai said to Abram: "You are responsible for this outrage against me. I myself gave my maid to your embrace; but ever since she became aware of her pregnancy, she has been looking on me with disdain. May the LORD decide between you and me!"] Abram told Sarai: "Your maid is in your power. Do to her whatever you please." Sarai then abused her so much that Hagar ran away from her.

The LORD's messenger found her by a spring in the wilderness, the spring on the road to Shur, and he asked, "Hagar, maid of Sarai, where have you come from and where are you going?" She answered, "I am running away from my mistress, Sarai." But the LORD's messenger told her: "Go back to your mistress and submit to her abusive treatment. I will make your descendants so numerous," added the LORD's messenger, "that they will be too many to count. Besides," the LORD's messenger said to her:

"You are now pregnant and shall bear a son;
	you shall name him Ishmael,
For the LORD has heard you,
	God has answered you.

This one shall be a wild ass of a man,
	his hand against everyone,
	and everyone's hand against him;
In opposition to all his kin
	shall he encamp."

Hagar bore Abram a son, and Abram named the son whom Hagar bore him Ishmael. Abram was eighty-six years old when Hagar bore him Ishmael.

The word of the Lord.

Responsorial Psalm
Ps 106:1b–2, 3–4a, 4b–5

R. Give thanks to the Lord, for he is good.

Give thanks to the LORD, for he is good,
  for his mercy endures forever.
Who can tell the mighty deeds of the LORD,
  or proclaim all his praises?

R. Give thanks to the Lord, for he is good.

Blessed are they who observe what is right,
  who do always what is just.
Remember us, O LORD, as you favor your people.

R. Give thanks to the Lord, for he is good.

Visit me with your saving help,
that I may see the prosperity of your chosen ones,
  rejoice in the joy of your people,
  and glory with your inheritance.

R. Give thanks to the Lord, for he is good.

Or: **R. Alleluia.**

Alleluia Verse *and* **Gospel,** *p. 1078.*

Year II

FIRST READING   2 Kgs 24:8–17

*The king of Babylon also led captive to Babylon Jehoiachin
and the chief men of the land.*

A reading from the second Book of Kings

Jehoiachin was eighteen years old when he began to reign,
and he reigned three months in Jerusalem. His mother's name
was Nehushta, daughter of Elnathan of Jerusalem. He did evil
in the sight of the LORD, just as his forebears had done.

At that time the officials of Nebuchadnezzar, king of
Babylon, attacked Jerusalem, and the city came under siege.
Nebuchadnezzar, king of Babylon, himself arrived at the city
while his servants were besieging it. Then Jehoiachin, king of

Judah, together with his mother, his ministers, officers, and functionaries, surrendered to the king of Babylon, who, in the eighth year of his reign, took him captive. And he carried off all the treasures of the temple of the LORD and those of the palace, and broke up all the gold utensils that Solomon, king of Israel, had provided in the temple of the LORD, as the LORD had foretold. He deported all Jerusalem: all the officers and men of the army, ten thousand in number, and all the craftsmen and smiths. None were left among the people of the land except the poor. He deported Jehoiachin to Babylon, and also led captive from Jerusalem to Babylon the king's mother and wives, his functionaries, and the chief men of the land. The king of Babylon also led captive to Babylon all seven thousand men of the army, and a thousand craftsmen and smiths, all of them trained soldiers. In place of Jehoiachin, the king of Babylon appointed his uncle Mattaniah king, and changed his name to Zedekiah.

The word of the Lord.

Responsorial Psalm

Ps 79:1b–2, 3–5, 8, 9

R. For the glory of your name, O Lord, deliver us.

O God, the nations have come into your inheritance;
  they have defiled your holy temple,
  they have laid Jerusalem in ruins.
They have given the corpses of your servants
  as food to the birds of heaven,
  the flesh of your faithful ones to the beasts of the earth.

R. For the glory of your name, O Lord, deliver us.

They have poured out their blood like water
  round about Jerusalem,
  and there is no one to bury them.
We have become the reproach of our neighbors,

the scorn and derision of those around us.
O Lord, how long? Will you be angry forever?
  Will your jealousy burn like fire?

    R. For the glory of your name, O Lord, deliver us.

Remember not against us the iniquities of the past;
  may your compassion quickly come to us,
  for we are brought very low.

    R. For the glory of your name, O Lord, deliver us.

Help us, O God our savior,
  because of the glory of your name;
Deliver us and pardon our sins
  for your name's sake.

    R. For the glory of your name, O Lord, deliver us.

    Alleluia, alleluia   Jn 14:23
    Whoever loves me will keep my word,
    and my Father will love him
    and we will come to him.
    Alleluia, alleluia

Years I and II

GOSPEL   Mt 7:21–29

The house built on rock and the house built on sand.

A reading from the holy Gospel according to Matthew

Jesus said to his disciples: "Not everyone who says to me, 'Lord, Lord,' will enter the Kingdom of heaven, but only the one who does the will of my Father in heaven. Many will say to me on that day, 'Lord, Lord, did we not prophesy in your name? Did we not drive out demons in your name? Did we not do mighty deeds in your name?' Then I will declare to them solemnly, 'I never knew you. Depart from me, you evildoers.'

"Everyone who listens to these words of mine and acts on them will be like a wise man who built his house on rock. The rain fell, the floods came, and the winds blew and buffeted the house. But it did not collapse; it had been set solidly on rock. And everyone who listens to these words of mine but does not act on them will be like a fool who built his house on sand. The rain fell, the floods came, and the winds blew and buffeted the house. And it collapsed and was completely ruined."

When Jesus finished these words, the crowds were astonished at his teaching, for he taught them as one having authority, and not as their scribes.

The Gospel of the Lord.

Liturgy of the Eucharist, *p. 897;* **Prayer over the Gifts,** *p. 1057.*

Friday

Antiphons and Prayers, *p. 1056;* **Liturgy of the Word** *for Year I (odd years) follows; Year II (even years), p. 1081.*

TODAY'S LIVING WORD

In today's Gospel a leper approaches Jesus and asks to be cured. In response, Jesus shows himself as powerful in deed as he has been in word, having just concluded the Sermon on the Mount. Just as he insisted in the Sermon that he had not come to abolish the law and the prophets, so here he sends the leper to the priest to fulfill the requirement of the law as set forth in Leviticus 14. Clearly Matthew wants us to see Jesus as a true son of Abraham, a faithful Jew who walks blamelessly in God's presence.

Sadly, the same cannot be said of Zedekiah in the reading from 2 Kings. Zedekiah was Jehoiachin's uncle, whom the Babylonians installed as king after Jehoiachin and his entourage were led into captivity. But Zedekiah would not heed the word of the Lord spoken through the prophet Jeremiah. Had he done so, he would have died in peace. Once again divine judgment is accomplished in the history of God's people. Only this time, the agent of God is not Assyria but Babylon. The temple is burned, the city walls torn down, and fifty years of exile begin.

Year I

FIRST READING   Gn 17:1, 9–10, 15–22

Every male among you shall be circumcised:
thus is my covenant with you. Sarah shall bear you a son.

A reading from the Book of Genesis

When Abram was ninety-nine years old, the LORD appeared to him and said: "I am God the Almighty. Walk in my presence and be blameless."

God also said to Abraham: "On your part, you and your descendants after you must keep my covenant throughout the ages. This is my covenant with you and your descendants after you that you must keep: every male among you shall be circumcised."

God further said to Abraham: "As for your wife Sarai, do not call her Sarai; her name shall be Sarah. I will bless her, and I will give you a son by her. Him also will I bless; he shall give rise to nations, and rulers of peoples shall issue from him." Abraham prostrated himself and laughed as he said to himself, "Can a child be born to a man who is a hundred years old? Or can Sarah give birth at ninety?" Then Abraham said to God, "Let but Ishmael live on by your favor!" God replied: "Nevertheless, your wife Sarah is to bear you a son, and you shall call him Isaac. I will maintain my covenant with him as an everlasting pact, to be his God and the God of his descendants after him. As for Ishmael, I am heeding you: I hereby bless him. I will make him fertile and will multiply him exceedingly. He shall become the father of twelve chieftains, and I will make of him a great nation. But my covenant I will maintain with Isaac, whom Sarah shall bear to you by this time next year." When he had finished speaking with him, God departed from Abraham.

The word of the Lord.

Responsorial Psalm

Ps 128:1–2, 3, 4–5

R. See how the Lord blesses those who fear him.

Blessed are you who fear the LORD,
 who walk in his ways!
For you shall eat the fruit of your handiwork;
 blessed shall you be, and favored.

R. See how the Lord blesses those who fear him.

Your wife shall be like a fruitful vine
 in the recesses of your home;
Your children like olive plants
 around your table.

R. See how the Lord blesses those who fear him.

Behold, thus is the man blessed
 who fears the LORD.
The LORD bless you from Zion:
 may you see the prosperity of Jerusalem
 all the days of your life.

R. See how the Lord blesses those who fear him.

Alleluia Verse *and* **Gospel,** p. 1083.

Year II

FIRST READING

2 Kgs 25:1–12

Thus was Judah exiled from her land (2 Kgs 25:21).

A reading from the second Book of Kings

In the tenth month of the ninth year of Zedekiah's reign, on the tenth day of the month, Nebuchadnezzar, king of Babylon, and his whole army advanced against Jerusalem, encamped around it, and built siege walls on every side. The siege of the city continued until the eleventh year of Zedekiah. On the ninth day of the fourth month, when famine had gripped the city, and the people had no more bread, the city walls were breached. Then the king and all the soldiers left the city by night through the gate between the two walls that was near the king's garden. Since the Chaldeans had the city surrounded, they went in the direction of the Arabah. But the Chaldean army pursued the king and overtook him in the desert near Jericho, abandoned by his whole army.

The king was therefore arrested and brought to Riblah to the king of Babylon, who pronounced sentence on him. He had Zedekiah's sons slain before his eyes. Then he blinded Zedekiah, bound him with fetters, and had him brought to Babylon.

On the seventh day of the fifth month (this was in the nineteenth year of Nebuchadnezzar, king of Babylon), Nebuzaradan, captain of the bodyguard, came to Jerusalem as the representative of the king of Babylon. He burned the house of the LORD, the palace of the king, and all the houses of Jerusalem; every large building was destroyed by fire. Then the Chaldean troops who were with the captain of the guard tore down the walls that surrounded Jerusalem.

Then Nebuzaradan, captain of the guard, led into exile the last of the people remaining in the city, and those who had deserted to the king of Babylon, and the last of the artisans. But some of the country's poor, Nebuzaradan, captain of the guard, left behind as vinedressers and farmers.

The word of the Lord.

Responsorial Psalm

Ps 137:1–2, 3, 4–5, 6

R. Let my tongue be silenced, if I ever forget you!

By the streams of Babylon
  we sat and wept
    when we remembered Zion.
On the aspens of that land
  we hung up our harps.

R. Let my tongue be silenced, if I ever forget you!

Though there our captors asked of us
  the lyrics of our songs,
And our despoilers urged us to be joyous:
  "Sing for us the songs of Zion!"

R. Let my tongue be silenced, if I ever forget you!

How could we sing a song of the LORD
  in a foreign land?
If I forget you, Jerusalem,
  may my right hand be forgotten!

R. Let my tongue be silenced, if I ever forget you!

May my tongue cleave to my palate
  if I remember you not,
If I place not Jerusalem
  ahead of my joy.

R. Let my tongue be silenced, if I ever forget you!

Alleluia, alleluia   Mt 8:17
Christ took away our infirmities
and bore our diseases.
Alleluia, alleluia

Years I and II

GOSPEL

Mt 8:1–4

If you wish, you can make me clean.

A reading from the holy Gospel according to Matthew

When Jesus came down from the mountain, great crowds followed him. And then a leper approached, did him homage, and said, "Lord, if you wish, you can make me clean." He stretched out his hand, touched him, and said, "I will do it. Be made clean." His leprosy was cleansed immediately. Then Jesus said to him, "See that you tell no one, but go show yourself to the priest, and offer the gift that Moses prescribed; that will be proof for them."

The Gospel of the Lord.

Liturgy of the Eucharist, *p. 897;* **Prayer over the Gifts,** *p. 1057.*

Saturday

Antiphons and Prayers, *p. 1056;* **Liturgy of the Word** *for Year I (odd years) follows; Year II (even years), p. 1087.*

TODAY'S LIVING WORD

All three of today's readings are child-centered. In the passage from Genesis Abraham's three visitors announce that Sarah will bear a child. In the poem from Lamentations, the laughter of Sarah is answered by the tears of the mothers of Jerusalem, whose children faint from hunger and breathe their last in their arms. And in the Gospel, a centurion asks Jesus to cure his servant boy. Although the passages are not at all alike, an air of expectancy pervades all three. Sarah, the desperate women of Jerusalem, and the centurion all wait on the power of God to do for them what they cannot do for themselves—to bring new life to the barren womb, the ravaged city, the sick child.

Jesus commends the centurion's words: "I too am a man subject to authority," which is to say, "I know power when I see it." So must we, for recognition of God's power, revealed in Jesus, admits us from east and west to the table with Abraham in the kingdom of God.

FIRST READING

Gn 18:1–15

Is anything too marvelous for the LORD to do?
I will surely return to you and Sarah will then have a son.

A reading from the Book of Genesis

The LORD appeared to Abraham by the Terebinth of Mamre, as Abraham sat in the entrance of his tent, while the day was growing hot. Looking up, he saw three men standing nearby. When he saw them, he ran from the entrance of the tent to greet them; and bowing to the ground, he said: "Sir, if I may ask you this favor, please do not go on past your servant. Let some water be brought, that you may bathe your feet, and then rest yourselves under the tree. Now that you have come this close to your servant, let me bring you a little food, that you may refresh yourselves; and afterward you may go on your way." The men replied, "Very well, do as you have said."

Abraham hastened into the tent and told Sarah, "Quick, three measures of fine flour! Knead it and make rolls." He ran to the herd, picked out a tender, choice steer, and gave it to a servant, who quickly prepared it. Then Abraham got some curds and milk, as well as the steer that had been prepared, and set these before them; and he waited on them under the tree while they ate.

They asked him, "Where is your wife Sarah?" He replied, "There in the tent." One of them said, "I will surely return to you about this time next year, and Sarah will then have a son." Sarah was listening at the entrance of the tent, just behind him. Now Abraham and Sarah were old, advanced in years, and Sarah had stopped having her womanly periods. So Sarah laughed to herself and said, "Now that I am so withered and my husband is so old, am I still to have sexual pleasure?" But the LORD said to Abraham: "Why did Sarah laugh and say, 'Shall I really bear a child, old as I am?' Is anything too marvelous for the LORD to do? At the appointed time, about this time next year, I will return to you, and Sarah will have a son." Because she was afraid, Sarah dissembled, saying, "I didn't laugh." But he replied, "Yes you did."

The word of the Lord.

Responsorial Psalm   Lk 1:46–47, 48–49, 50 and 53, 54–55

R. The Lord has remembered his mercy.

"My soul proclaims the greatness of the Lord,
  my spirit rejoices in God my Savior."

R. The Lord has remembered his mercy.

"For he has looked with favor on his lowly servant.
From this day all generations will call me blessed:
  the Almighty has done great things for me,
  and holy is his Name."

R. The Lord has remembered his mercy.

"He has mercy on those who fear him
  in every generation.
He has filled the hungry with good things,
  and the rich he has sent away empty."

R. The Lord has remembered his mercy.

"He has come to the help of his servant Israel
  for he has remembered his promise of mercy,

"The promise he made to our fathers,
    to Abraham and his children for ever."

R. The Lord has remembered his mercy.

Alleluia Verse *and* **Gospel,** *p. 1089f.*

Year II

FIRST READING   Lam 2:2, 10 –14, 18 –19

Cry out to the Lord over the fortresses of the daughter Zion.

A reading from the Book of Lamentations

The Lord has consumed without pity
    all the dwellings of Jacob;
He has torn down in his anger
    the fortresses of daughter Judah;
He has brought to the ground in dishonor
    her king and her princes.

On the ground in silence sit
    the old men of daughter Zion;
They strew dust on their heads
    and gird themselves with sackcloth;
The maidens of Jerusalem
    bow their heads to the ground.

Worn out from weeping are my eyes,
    within me all is in ferment;
My gall is poured out on the ground
    because of the downfall of the daughter of my people,
As child and infant faint away
    in the open spaces of the town.

In vain they ask their mothers,
    "Where is the grain?"
As they faint away like the wounded
    in the streets of the city,
And breathe their last
    in their mothers' arms.

To what can I liken or compare you,
    O daughter Jerusalem?
What example can I show you for your comfort,
    virgin daughter Zion?
For great as the sea is your downfall;
    who can heal you?

Your prophets had for you
    false and specious visions;
They did not lay bare your guilt,
    to avert your fate;
They beheld for you in vision
    false and misleading portents.

Cry out to the Lord;
    moan, O daughter Zion!
Let your tears flow like a torrent
    day and night;
Let there be no respite for you,
    no repose for your eyes.

Rise up, shrill in the night,
    at the beginning of every watch;
Pour out your heart like water
    in the presence of the Lord;
Lift up your hands to him
    for the lives of your little ones

Who faint from hunger
    at the corner of every street.

The word of the Lord.

Responsorial Psalm
Ps 74:1b–2, 3 – 5, 6–7, 20–21

R. Lord, forget not the souls of your poor ones.

Why, O God, have you cast us off forever?
  Why does your anger smolder against the sheep of your pasture?
Remember your flock which you built up of old,
  the tribe you redeemed as your inheritance,
  Mount Zion, where you took up your abode.

R. Lord, forget not the souls of your poor ones.

Turn your steps toward the utter ruins;
  toward all the damage the enemy has done in the sanctuary.
Your foes roar triumphantly in your shrine;
  they have set up their tokens of victory.
They are like men coming up with axes to a clump of trees.

R. Lord, forget not the souls of your poor ones.

With chisel and hammer they hack at all the paneling of the
    sanctuary.
They set your sanctuary on fire;
  the place where your name abides they have razed and profaned.

R. Lord, forget not the souls of your poor ones.

Look to your covenant,
  for the hiding places in the land and the plains are full of
    violence.
May the humble not retire in confusion;
  may the afflicted and the poor praise your name.

R. Lord, forget not the souls of your poor ones.

Alleluia, alleluia Mt 8:17
Christ took away our infirmities
and bore our diseases.
Alleluia, alleluia

Years I and II

GOSPEL

Mt 8:5 –17

Many will come from east and west and
will recline with Abraham, Isaac and Jacob.

A reading from the holy Gospel according to Matthew

When Jesus entered Capernaum, a centurion approached him and appealed to him, saying, "Lord, my servant is lying at home paralyzed, suffering dreadfully." He said to him, "I will come and cure him." The centurion said in reply, "Lord, I am not worthy to have you enter under my roof; only say the word and my servant will be healed. For I too am a man subject to authority, with soldiers subject to me. And I say to one, 'Go,' and he goes; and to another, 'Come here,' and he comes; and to my slave, 'Do this,' and he does it." When Jesus heard this, he was amazed and said to those following him, "Amen, I say to you, in no one in Israel have I found such faith. I say to you, many will come from the east and the west, and will recline with Abraham, Isaac, and Jacob at the banquet in the Kingdom of heaven, but the children of the Kingdom will be driven out into the outer darkness, where there will be wailing and grinding of teeth." And Jesus said to the centurion, "You may go; as you have believed, let it be done for you." And at that very hour his servant was healed.

Jesus entered the house of Peter, and saw his mother-in-law lying in bed with a fever. He touched her hand, the fever left her, and she rose and waited on him.

When it was evening, they brought him many who were possessed by demons, and he drove out the spirits by a word and cured all the sick, to fulfill what had been said by Isaiah the prophet:

> He took away our infirmities
> and bore our diseases.

The Gospel of the Lord.

Liturgy of the Eucharist, *p. 897;* **Prayer over the Gifts,** *p. 1057.*

THIRTEENTH WEEK IN ORDINARY TIME

The **Antiphons and Prayers** *may be the following, or may be chosen from any of the other 33 weeks in Ordinary Time (refer to Liturgical Calendar, pp. 26–41).*

The **Liturgy of the Word** *varies: for Monday, see p. 1093; Tuesday, p. 1098; Wednesday, p. 1104; Thursday, p. 1109; Friday, p. 1114; Saturday, p. 1120.*

Entrance Antiphon

All nations, clap your hands. Shout with a voice of joy to God.
(Ps 47:2)

Opening Prayer

Let us pray
[that Christ may be our light]

Pause for silent prayer.

Father,
you call your children
to walk in the light of Christ.
Free us from darkness
and keep us in the radiance of your truth.

We ask this through our Lord Jesus Christ, your Son,
who lives and reigns with you and the Holy Spirit,
one God, for ever and ever.

Alternative Opening Prayer

Let us pray

[for the strength to reject the darkness of sin]

Pause for silent prayer.

Father in heaven,
the light of Jesus
has scattered the darkness of hatred and sin.
Called to that light
we ask for your guidance.
Form our lives in your truth, our hearts in your love.

We ask this through Christ our Lord.

Prayer over the Gifts

Pray, brethren...

Lord God,
through the sacraments
you give us the power of your grace.
May this eucharist
help us to serve you faithfully.

We ask this in the name of Jesus the Lord.

Preface of Weekdays in Ordinary Time I–VI, *pp. 948–950.*

Communion Antiphon

O, bless the Lord, my soul, and all that is within me bless his
holy name.   (Ps 103:1)

Prayer after Communion

Let us pray.

Pause for silent prayer, if this has not preceded.

Lord,
may this sacrifice and communion
give us a share in your life

and help us bring your love to the world.

Grant this through Christ our Lord.

Monday

Antiphons and Prayers, *p. 1091;* **Liturgy of the Word** *for Year I (odd years) follows; Year II (even years), p. 1096.*

TODAY'S LIVING WORD

Divine judgment appears in both of today's first readings. In Genesis, the Lord visits the cities of Sodom and Gomorrah to determine if their actions correspond to the outcry against them, while the prophecy of Amos announces a day of judgment for "three crimes of Israel, and for four." In both, the Lord God is understood to be "the judge of all the world." Abraham's conversation with God probes and proves the justice of the divine judge. As judge, God is as anxious as Abraham to distinguish between the innocent and the guilty, so the bargaining is pressed to its natural limit. Abraham, who has been called to father a people who keep the way of the Lord by doing what is just, learns that the judge of all the world does indeed act justly.

The excerpt from Matthew's Gospel includes a hard saying about discipleship. Scholars agree that the words of Jesus—"Let the dead bury their dead"—are a "hyperbole," a deliberate exaggeration intended to shock. Jesus means that even the solemn obligation of burying the dead must yield to the demands of true discipleship.

Year I

FIRST READING   Gn 18:16–33

Will you sweep away the innocent with the guilty?

A reading from the Book of Genesis

Abraham and the men who had visited him by the Terebinth of Mamre set out from there and looked down toward Sodom; Abraham was walking with them, to see them on their way.

The LORD reflected: "Shall I hide from Abraham what I am about to do, now that he is to become a great and populous nation, and all the nations of the earth are to find blessing in him? Indeed, I have singled him out that he may direct his children and his household after him to keep the way of the LORD by doing what is right and just, so that the LORD may carry into effect for Abraham the promises he made about him." Then the LORD said: "The outcry against Sodom and Gomorrah is so great, and their sin so grave, that I must go down and see whether or not their actions fully correspond to the cry against them that comes to me. I mean to find out."

While the two men walked on farther toward Sodom, the LORD remained standing before Abraham. Then Abraham drew nearer to him and said: "Will you sweep away the innocent with the guilty? Suppose there were fifty innocent people in the city; would you wipe out the place, rather than spare it for the sake of the fifty innocent people within it? Far be it from you to do such a thing, to make the innocent die with the guilty, so that the innocent and the guilty would be treated alike! Should not the judge of all the world act with justice?" The LORD replied, "If I find fifty innocent people in the city of Sodom, I will spare the whole place for their sake." Abraham spoke up again: "See how I am presuming to speak to my Lord, though I am but dust and ashes! What if there are five less than fifty innocent people? Will you destroy the whole city because of those five?" He answered, "I will not destroy it if I find forty-five there." But Abraham persisted, saying, "What if only forty are found there?" He replied, "I will forbear doing it for the sake of forty." Then Abraham said, "Let not my Lord grow impatient if I go on. What if only thirty are found there?" He replied, "I will forbear doing it if I can find but thirty there."

Still Abraham went on, "Since I have thus dared to speak to my Lord, what if there are no more than twenty?" He answered, "I will not destroy it for the sake of the twenty." But he still persisted: "Please, let not my Lord grow angry if I speak up this last time. What if there are at least ten there?" He replied, "For the sake of those ten, I will not destroy it."

The LORD departed as soon as he had finished speaking with Abraham, and Abraham returned home.

The word of the Lord.

Responsorial Psalm

Ps 103:1b–2, 3–4, 8–9, 10–11

R. The Lord is kind and merciful.

Bless the LORD, O my soul;
  and all my being, bless his holy name.
Bless the LORD, O my soul,
  and forget not all his benefits.

R. The Lord is kind and merciful.

He pardons all your iniquities,
  he heals all your ills.
He redeems your life from destruction,
  he crowns you with kindness and compassion.

R. The Lord is kind and merciful.

Merciful and gracious is the LORD,
  slow to anger and abounding in kindness.
He will not always chide,
  nor does he keep his wrath forever.

R. The Lord is kind and merciful.

Not according to our sins does he deal with us,
  nor does he requite us according to our crimes.
For as the heavens are high above the earth,
  so surpassing is his kindness toward those who fear him.

R. The Lord is kind and merciful.

Alleluia Verse *and* **Gospel,** *p. 1098.*

FIRST READING
Am 2:6–10, 13–16

They trample the heads of the weak into the dust of the earth.

A reading from the Book of the Prophet Amos

Thus says the LORD:

For three crimes of Israel, and for four,
    I will not revoke my word;
Because they sell the just man for silver,
    and the poor man for a pair of sandals.
They trample the heads of the weak
    into the dust of the earth,
    and force the lowly out of the way.
Son and father go to the same prostitute,
    profaning my holy name.
Upon garments taken in pledge
    they recline beside any altar;
And the wine of those who have been fined
    they drink in the house of their god.

Yet it was I who destroyed the Amorites before them,
    who were as tall as the cedars,
    and as strong as the oak trees.
I destroyed their fruit above,
    and their roots beneath.
It was I who brought you up from the land of Egypt,
    and who led you through the desert for forty years,
    to occupy the land of the Amorites.

Beware, I will crush you into the ground
    as a wagon crushes when laden with sheaves.
Flight shall perish from the swift,

and the strong man shall not retain his strength;
The warrior shall not save his life,
    nor the bowman stand his ground;
The swift of foot shall not escape,
    nor the horseman save his life.
And the most stouthearted of warriors
    shall flee naked on that day, says the LORD.

The word of the Lord.

Responsorial Psalm

Ps 50:16bc–17, 18–19, 20–21, 22–23

  R. Remember this, you who never think of God.

"Why do you recite my statutes,
  and profess my covenant with your mouth,
Though you hate discipline
  and cast my words behind you?"

  R. Remember this, you who never think of God.

"When you see a thief, you keep pace with him,
  and with adulterers you throw in your lot.
To your mouth you give free rein for evil,
  you harness your tongue to deceit."

  R. Remember this, you who never think of God.

"You sit speaking against your brother;
  against your mother's son you spread rumors.
When you do these things, shall I be deaf to it?
  Or do you think that I am like yourself?
  I will correct you by drawing them up before your eyes."

  R. Remember this, you who never think of God.

"Consider this, you who forget God,
  lest I rend you and there be no one to rescue you.
He that offers praise as a sacrifice glorifies me;
  and to him that goes the right way I will show the salvation
    of God."

  R. Remember this, you who never think of God.

Alleluia, alleluia   Ps 95:8
If today you hear his voice,
harden not your hearts.
Alleluia, alleluia

Years I and II

GOSPEL   Mt 8:18–22

Follow me.

A reading from the holy Gospel according to Matthew

When Jesus saw a crowd around him, he gave orders to cross to the other shore. A scribe approached and said to him, "Teacher, I will follow you wherever you go." Jesus answered him, "Foxes have dens and birds of the sky have nests, but the Son of Man has nowhere to rest his head." Another of his disciples said to him, "Lord, let me go first and bury my father." But Jesus answered him, "Follow me, and let the dead bury their dead."

The Gospel of the Lord.

Liturgy of the Eucharist, *p. 897;* **Prayer over the Gifts,** *p. 1092.*

Tuesday

Antiphons and Prayers, *p. 1093;* **Liturgy of the Word** *for Year I (odd years) follows; Year II (even years), p. 1101.*

TODAY'S LIVING WORD

The two first readings present two sides of divine election. God's choice of Abraham meant blessing not only for himself, but for everyone associated with him. Lot is a good example. As we hear in today's reading, God spared Lot and his family because of Abraham. But with God's choice of Abraham and his descendants came the responsibility of keeping God's commandments. When they failed to do so, as at the time of Amos the prophet, the people of Israel were not spared the fury of God's wrath, despite their being God's chosen people. "You alone have I favored, more than all the families of the earth," says the Lord, "therefore I will punish you for all your crimes." Clearly, divine favor was not divine favoritism.

Today's Gospel depicts the familiar scene of Jesus calming the storm, a story found in Mark and Luke as well. One distinctive feature of Matthew's version is Jesus' addressing his disciples as *oligopistoi*, "little-faiths." They have some faith, but not always enough. They are like us. So like them we pray, "Lord, save us!"

Year I

FIRST READING

Gn 19:15–29

*The Lord God rained down sulphurous fire
upon Sodom and Gomorrah.*

A reading from the Book of Genesis

As dawn was breaking, the angels urged Lot on, saying, "On your way! Take with you your wife and your two daughters who are here, or you will be swept away in the punishment of Sodom." When he hesitated, the men, by the Lord's mercy, seized his hand and the hands of his wife and his two daughters and led them to safety outside the city. As soon as they had been brought outside, he was told: "Flee for your life! Don't look back or stop anywhere on the Plain. Get off to the hills at once, or you will be swept away." "Oh, no, my lord!" Lot replied, "You have already thought enough of your servant to do me the great kindness of intervening to save my life. But I cannot flee to the hills to keep the disaster from overtaking me, and so I shall die. Look, this town ahead is near enough to escape to. It's only a small place. Let me flee there—it's a small place, is it not?—that my life may be saved." "Well, then," he replied, "I will also grant you the favor you now ask. I will not overthrow the town you speak of. Hurry, escape there! I cannot do anything until you arrive there." That is why the town is called Zoar.

The sun was just rising over the earth as Lot arrived in Zoar; at the same time the LORD rained down sulphurous fire upon Sodom and Gomorrah from the LORD out of heaven. He overthrew those cities and the whole Plain, together with the inhabitants of the cities and the produce of the soil. But Lot's wife looked back, and she was turned into a pillar of salt.

Early the next morning Abraham went to the place where he had stood in the LORD's presence. As he looked down toward Sodom and Gomorrah and the whole region of the Plain, he saw dense smoke over the land rising like fumes from a furnace.

Thus it came to pass: when God destroyed the Cities of the Plain, he was mindful of Abraham by sending Lot away from the upheaval by which God overthrew the cities where Lot had been living.

The word of the Lord.

Responsorial Psalm
Ps 26:2–3, 9–10, 11–12

R. **O Lord, your mercy is before my eyes.**

Search me, O LORD, and try me;
  test my soul and my heart.
For your mercy is before my eyes,
  and I walk in your truth.

R. **O Lord, your mercy is before my eyes.**

Gather not my soul with those of sinners,
  nor with men of blood my life.

On their hands are crimes,
   and their right hands are full of bribes.

   R. O Lord, your mercy is before my eyes.

But I walk in integrity;
   redeem me, and have mercy on me.
My foot stands on level ground;
   in the assemblies I will bless the LORD.

   R. O Lord, your mercy is before my eyes.

   Alleluia Verse *and* **Gospel,** *p. 1103.*

Year II

FIRST READING   Am 3:1–8; 4:11–12

   The Lord GOD speaks—who will not prophesy!

A reading from the Book of the Prophet Amos

Hear this word, O children of Israel, that the LORD pronounces
over you, over the whole family that I brought up from the
land of Egypt:

   You alone have I favored,
      more than all the families of the earth;
   Therefore I will punish you
      for all your crimes.

   Do two walk together
      unless they have agreed?
   Does a lion roar in the forest
      when it has no prey?
   Does a young lion cry out from its den
      unless it has seized something?
   Is a bird brought to earth by a snare

when there is no lure for it?
Does a snare spring up from the ground
     without catching anything?
If the trumpet sounds in a city,
     will the people not be frightened?
If evil befalls a city,
     has not the Lord caused it?
Indeed, the Lord God does nothing
     without revealing his plan
     to his servants, the prophets.

The lion roars—
     who will not be afraid!
The Lord God speaks—
     who will not prophesy!

I brought upon you such upheaval
     as when God overthrew Sodom and Gomorrah:
     you were like a brand plucked from the fire;
Yet you returned not to me,
     says the Lord.

So now I will deal with you in my own way, O Israel!
     and since I will deal thus with you,
     prepare to meet your God, O Israel.

The word of the Lord.

Responsorial Psalm   Ps 5:4b–6a, 6b–7, 8

R. Lead me in your justice, Lord.

At dawn I bring my plea expectantly before you.
For you, O God, delight not in wickedness;
   no evil man remains with you;
   the arrogant may not stand in your sight.

R. Lead me in your justice, Lord.

You hate all evildoers;
  you destroy all who speak falsehood;
The bloodthirsty and the deceitful
  the LORD abhors.

R. Lead me in your justice, Lord.

But I, because of your abundant mercy,
  will enter your house;
I will worship at your holy temple
  in fear of you, O LORD.

R. Lead me in your justice, Lord.

> **Alleluia, alleluia**   Ps 130:5
> I trust in the LORD;
>   my soul trusts in his word.
> **Alleluia, alleluia**

Years I and II

GOSPEL   Mt 8:23–27

Jesus rebuked the winds and the sea, and there was great calm.

A reading from the holy Gospel according to Matthew

As Jesus got into a boat, his disciples followed him. Suddenly a violent storm came up on the sea, so that the boat was being swamped by waves; but he was asleep. They came and woke him, saying, "Lord, save us! We are perishing!" He said to them, "Why are you terrified, O you of little faith?" Then he got up, rebuked the winds and the sea, and there was great calm. The men were amazed and said, "What sort of man is this, whom even the winds and the sea obey?"

The Gospel of the Lord.

Liturgy of the Eucharist, *p. 897;* **Prayer over the Gifts,** *p. 1092.*

Wednesday

Antiphons and Prayers, *p. 1091;* **Liturgy of the Word** *for Year I (odd years) follows; Year II (even years), p. 1106.*

TODAY'S LIVING WORD

The story from Genesis and the words of Amos stand in a jarring juxtaposition. Sarah's jealousy and Hagar's banishment strangely seem to be condoned by God, the same God who condemns the sacrifices of Israel, asking only that "justice surge like water, and goodness like an unfailing stream." The key may be to borrow Matthew's strategy in today's Gospel. As Matthew retells the story of the Gerasene demoniac which he took from Mark, he makes several changes—for example, he sums up Mark's detailed description of the demoniac's behavior before the exorcism and omits altogether his request to follow Jesus after it. These changes keep the story focused on Jesus.

In the same way we must keep our eyes on God when we read the story of Hagar. God's command, not Sarah's contempt, controls the action of the story. "Do not be distressed about the boy or about your slave woman," God tells Abraham. Then God acts to vindicate both women—Sarah, through whose child Abraham's line will continue, and Hagar, whose son too will be made a great nation.

Year I

FIRST READING

Gn 21:5, 8 – 20a

*No son of that slave is going to share
the inheritance with my son Isaac!*

A reading from the Book of Genesis

Abraham was a hundred years old when his son Isaac was born to him. Isaac grew, and on the day of the child's weaning Abraham held a great feast.

Sarah noticed the son whom Hagar the Egyptian had borne to Abraham playing with her son Isaac; so she demanded of Abraham: "Drive out that slave and her son! No son of that slave is going to share the inheritance with my son Isaac!" Abraham was greatly distressed, especially on account of his son Ishmael. But God said to Abraham: "Do not be distressed about the boy or about your slave woman. Heed the demands of Sarah, no matter what she is asking of you; for it is through Isaac that descendants shall bear your name. As for the son of the slave woman, I will make a great nation of him also, since he too is your offspring."

Early the next morning Abraham got some bread and a skin of water and gave them to Hagar. Then, placing the child on her back, he sent her away. As she roamed aimlessly in the wilderness of Beer-sheba, the water in the skin was used up. So she put the child down under a shrub, and then went and sat down opposite him, about a bowshot away; for she said to herself, "Let me not watch to see the child die." As she sat opposite Ishmael, he began to cry. God heard the boy's cry, and God's messenger called to Hagar from heaven: "What is the matter, Hagar? Don't be afraid; God has heard the boy's cry in this plight of his. Arise, lift up the boy and hold him by the hand; for I will make of him a great nation." Then God opened her eyes, and she saw a well of water. She went and filled the skin with water, and then let the boy drink.

God was with the boy as he grew up.

The word of the Lord.

Responsorial Psalm

Ps 34:7–8, 10–11, 12–13

R. The Lord hears the cry of the poor.

When the poor one called out, the Lord heard,
  and from all his distress he saved him.
The angel of the Lord encamps
  around those who fear him, and delivers them.

R. The Lord hears the cry of the poor.

Fear the Lord, you his holy ones,
  for nought is lacking to those who fear him.
The great grow poor and hungry;
  but those who seek the Lord want for no good thing.

R. The Lord hears the cry of the poor.

Come, children, hear me;
  I will teach you the fear of the Lord.
Which of you desires life,
  and takes delight in prosperous days?

R. The Lord hears the cry of the poor.

Alleluia Verse *and* **Gospel,** *p. 1108.*

Year II

FIRST READING
Am 5:14–15, 21–24

Away with your noisy songs!
Let justice surge like an unfailing stream.

A reading from the Book of the Prophet Amos

Seek good and not evil,
  that you may live;
Then truly will the Lord, the God of hosts,
  be with you as you claim!
Hate evil and love good,
  and let justice prevail at the gate;
Then it may be that the Lord, the God of hosts,
  will have pity on the remnant of Joseph.

I hate, I spurn your feasts, says the LORD,
>   I take no pleasure in your solemnities;
Your cereal offerings I will not accept,
>   nor consider your stall-fed peace offerings.
Away with your noisy songs!
>   I will not listen to the melodies of your harps.
But if you would offer me burnt offerings,
>   then let justice surge like water,
>   and goodness like an unfailing stream.

The word of the Lord.

Responsorial Psalm
Ps 50:7, 8–9, 10–11, 12–13, 16bc–17

> **R. To the upright I will show the saving power of God.**

"Hear, my people, and I will speak;
>   Israel, I will testify against you;
>   God, your God, am I."

> **R. To the upright I will show the saving power of God.**

"Not for your sacrifices do I rebuke you,
>   for your burnt offerings are before me always.
I take from your house no bullock,
>   no goats out of your fold."

> **R. To the upright I will show the saving power of God.**

"For mine are all the animals of the forests,
>   beasts by the thousand on my mountains.
I know all the birds of the air,
>   and whatever stirs in the plains, belongs to me."

> **R. To the upright I will show the saving power of God.**

"If I were hungry, I should not tell you,
>   for mine are the world and its fullness.
Do I eat the flesh of strong bulls,
>   or is the blood of goats my drink?"

R. To the upright I will show the saving power of God.

"Why do you recite my statutes,
  and profess my covenant with your mouth,
Though you hate discipline
  and cast my words behind you?"

R. To the upright I will show the saving power of God.

> **Alleluia, alleluia**   Jas 1:18
> The Father willed to give us birth by the word of truth
> that we may be a kind of firstfruits of his creatures.
> **Alleluia, alleluia**

Years I and II

GOSPEL   Mt 8:28–34

Have you come here to torment us before the appointed time?

A reading from the holy Gospel according to Matthew

When Jesus came to the territory of the Gadarenes, two demoniacs who were coming from the tombs met him. They were so savage that no one could travel by that road. They cried out, "What have you to do with us, Son of God? Have you come here to torment us before the appointed time?" Some distance away a herd of many swine was feeding. The demons pleaded with him, "If you drive us out, send us into the herd of swine." And he said to them, "Go then!" They came out and entered the swine, and the whole herd rushed down the steep bank into the sea where they drowned. The swineherds ran away, and when they came to the town they reported everything, including what had happened to the demoniacs. Thereupon the whole town came out to meet Jesus, and when they saw him they begged him to leave their district.

The Gospel of the Lord.

Liturgy of the Eucharist, *p. 897;* **Prayer over the Gifts,** *p. 1092.*

Thursday

Antiphons and Prayers, *p. 1091;* **Liturgy of the Word** *for Year I (odd years) follows; Year II (even years), p. 1112.*

Today's Living Word

Controversy swirls around Amos and Jesus in today's readings. The words of Amos threaten the priest of Bethel, who tells Jeroboam, "The country cannot endure all his words." Similarly, Jesus' words trouble some scribes. "This man is blaspheming," they think. Amos responds by recounting the story of how God took him from his flocks and his sycamore trees to be a prophet. Jesus answers by healing the paralytic. "Which is easier to say?" he asks. By dramatizing his power over sickness, he raises the possibility at least that he also has power over sin. Even his critics are awed.

In the Bible, testing proves the faith of God's people. As he reads the story of the testing of Abraham, Sean McEvenue finds that it tests the reader as well. The author's narrative technique aims "directly at making readers participants in the story."* With Abraham, we are challenged to trust God absolutely and to learn again that God will provide.

* "The Elohist at Work," *Interpretation and Bible* (Collegeville: Liturgical Press, 1994), p. 131.

Year I

FIRST READING   Gn 22:1b–19

The sacrifice of Abraham, our father in faith.

A reading from the Book of Genesis

God put Abraham to the test. He called to him, "Abraham!" "Here I am," he replied. Then God said: "Take your son Isaac, your only one, whom you love, and go to the land of Moriah. There you shall offer him up as a burnt offering on a height that I will point out to you." Early the next morning Abraham saddled his donkey, took with him his son Isaac, and two of

R. The judgments of the Lord are true, and all of them are just.

Alleluia, alleluia   2 Cor 5:19
God was reconciling the world to himself in Christ
and entrusting to us the message of reconciliation.
Alleluia, alleluia

Years I and II

GOSPEL   Mt 9:1–8

They glorified God who had given such authority to men.

A reading from the holy Gospel according to Matthew

After entering a boat, Jesus made the crossing, and came into his own town. And there people brought to him a paralytic lying on a stretcher. When Jesus saw their faith, he said to the paralytic, "Courage, child, your sins are forgiven." At that, some of the scribes said to themselves, "This man is blaspheming." Jesus knew what they were thinking, and said, "Why do you harbor evil thoughts? Which is easier, to say, 'Your sins are forgiven,' or to say, 'Rise and walk'? But that you may know that the Son of Man has authority on earth to forgive sins"—he then said to the paralytic, "Rise, pick up your stretcher, and go home." He rose and went home. When the crowds saw this they were struck with awe and glorified God who had given such authority to men.

The Gospel of the Lord.

Liturgy of the Eucharist, *p. 897;* **Prayer over the Gifts,** *p. 1092.*

Friday

Antiphons and Prayers, *p. 1091;* **Liturgy of the Word** *for Year I (odd years) follows; Year II (even years), p. 1117.*

TODAY'S LIVING WORD

Today's Gospel finds Jesus once again at odds with the Pharisees who object to his eating with sinners. When reading such conflict stories, we must remember Jesus' close association with the Pharisees. Some scholars believe that the Pharisees so strongly criticized Jesus' table fellowship because he sometimes also ate with them. Even the quote from Hosea, chapter 6, that Matthew has added to the punch line of this story, "I desire mercy, not sacrifice," is not intended to depict Jesus against the Jews. As Matthew certainly knew after the temple was destroyed in 70 C.E., the rabbis themselves read this passage to mean that works of mercy could replace temple sacrifice as a way of attaining forgiveness of sins. In today's reading, Abraham's last task is to insure that Isaac will continue his father's journey without ever turning back. Jesus and the Pharisees wanted this for all Israel; they simply disagreed on how to achieve it.

Amos also proclaimed the message that God wants mercy, not sacrifice. As mercy defined the mission of Jesus, who came to call sinners, so must it describe our lives as his disciples.

Year I

FIRST READING
Gn 23:1–4, 19; 24:1–8, 62–67

*In his love for Rebekah, Isaac found solace after the death
of his mother Sarah.*

A reading from the Book of Genesis

The span of Sarah's life was one hundred and twenty-seven years. She died in Kiriatharba (that is, Hebron) in the land of Canaan, and Abraham performed the customary mourning rites for her. Then he left the side of his dead one and addressed the Hittites: "Although I am a resident alien among you, sell me from your holdings a piece of property for a burial ground, that I may bury my dead wife."

After the transaction, Abraham buried his wife Sarah in the cave of the field of Machpelah, facing Mamre (that is, Hebron) in the land of Canaan.

Abraham had now reached a ripe old age, and the LORD had blessed him in every way. Abraham said to the senior servant of his household, who had charge of all his possessions: "Put your hand under my thigh, and I will make you swear by the LORD, the God of heaven and the God of earth, that you will not procure a wife for my son from the daughters of the Canaanites among whom I live, but that you will go to my own land and to my kindred to get a wife for my son Isaac." The servant asked him: "What if the woman is unwilling to follow me to this land? Should I then take your son back to the land from which you migrated?" "Never take my son back there for any reason," Abraham told him. "The LORD, the God of heaven, who took me from my father's house and the land of my kin, and who confirmed by oath the promise he then made to me, 'I will give this land to your descendants'—he will send his messenger before you, and you will obtain a wife for my son there. If the woman is unwilling to follow you, you will be released from this oath. But never take my son back there!"

A long time later, Isaac went to live in the region of the Negeb. One day toward evening he went out...in the field, and as he looked around, he noticed that camels were approaching. Rebekah, too, was looking about, and when she saw him, she alighted from her camel and asked the servant, "Who is the man out there, walking through the fields toward us?" "That is my master," replied the servant. Then she covered herself with her veil.

The servant recounted to Isaac all the things he had done. Then Isaac took Rebekah into his tent; he married her, and thus she became his wife. In his love for her, Isaac found solace after the death of his mother Sarah.

The word of the Lord.

Responsorial Psalm

Ps 106:1b–2, 3–4a, 4b–5

R. Give thanks to the Lord, for he is good.

Give thanks to the LORD, for he is good,
  for his mercy endures forever.
Who can tell the mighty deeds of the LORD,
  or proclaim all his praises?

R. Give thanks to the Lord, for he is good.

Blessed are they who observe what is right,
  who do always what is just.
Remember us, O LORD, as you favor your people.

R. Give thanks to the Lord, for he is good.

Visit me with your saving help,
That I may see the prosperity of your chosen ones,
  rejoice in the joy of your people,
  and glory with your inheritance.

R. Give thanks to the Lord, for he is good.

Alleluia Verse *and* **Gospel,** *p. 1119f.*

Year II

FIRST READING

Am 8:4–6, 9–12

*I will send famine upon the land:
not a famine of bread or thirst for water,
but for hearing the word of the LORD.*

A reading from the Book of the Prophet Amos

Hear this, you who trample upon the needy
    and destroy the poor of the land!
"When will the new moon be over," you ask,
    "that we may sell our grain,
    and the sabbath, that we may display the wheat?"
We will diminish the containers for measuring,
    add to the weights,
    and fix our scales for cheating!
We will buy the lowly man for silver,
    and the poor man for a pair of sandals;
    even the refuse of the wheat we will sell!"

On that day, says the Lord GOD,
    I will make the sun set at midday
    and cover the earth with darkness in broad daylight.
I will turn your feasts into mourning
    and all your songs into lamentations.
I will cover the loins of all with sackcloth
    and make every head bald.
I will make them mourn as for an only son,
    and bring their day to a bitter end.

Yes, days are coming, says the Lord GOD,
    when I will send famine upon the land:
Not a famine of bread, or thirst for water,
    but for hearing the word of the LORD.
Then shall they wander from sea to sea
    and rove from the north to the east
In search of the word of the LORD,
    but they shall not find it.
The word of the Lord.

Responsorial Psalm

Ps 119:2, 10, 20, 30, 40, 131

> **R. One does not live by bread alone, but by every word that comes from the mouth of God.**

Blessed are they who observe his decrees,
  who seek him with all their heart.

> **R. One does not live by bread alone, but by every word that comes from the mouth of God.**

With all my heart I seek you;
  let me not stray from your commands.

> **R. One does not live by bread alone, but by every word that comes from the mouth of God.**

My soul is consumed with longing
  for your ordinances at all times.

> **R. One does not live by bread alone, but by every word that comes from the mouth of God.**

The way of truth I have chosen;
  I have set your ordinances before me.

> **R. One does not live by bread alone, but by every word that comes from the mouth of God.**

Behold, I long for your precepts;
  in your justice give me life.

> **R. One does not live by bread alone, but by every word that comes from the mouth of God.**

I gasp with open mouth
  in my yearning for your commands.

> **R. One does not live by bread alone, but by every word that comes from the mouth of God.**

> **Alleluia, alleluia**   Mt 11:28
> Come to me, all you who labor and are burdened,
> and I will give you rest, says the Lord.
> **Alleluia, alleluia**

GOSPEL   Mt 9:9–13

Those who are well do not need a physician;
I desire mercy, not sacrifice.

A reading from the holy Gospel according to Matthew

As Jesus passed by, he saw a man named Matthew sitting at the customs post. He said to him, "Follow me." And he got up and followed him. While he was at table in his house, many tax collectors and sinners came and sat with Jesus and his disciples. The Pharisees saw this and said to his disciples, "Why does your teacher eat with tax collectors and sinners?" He heard this and said, "Those who are well do not need a physician, but the sick do. Go and learn the meaning of the words, *I desire mercy, not sacrifice.* I did not come to call the righteous but sinners." The Gospel of the Lord.

Liturgy of the Eucharist, *p. 897;* **Prayer over the Gifts,** *p. 1092.*

Saturday

Antiphons and Prayers, *p. 1091;* **Liturgy of the Word** *for Year I (odd years) follows; Year II (even years), p. 1123.*

TODAY'S LIVING WORD

In the Bible blessing means fullness of life. This theme holds together today's three readings. In the passage from Genesis "the fertility of the earth" shows forth God's blessing as it yields an "abundance of grain and wine." The prophecy of Amos also expresses that same abundant life in agricultural terms: "The plowman shall overtake the reaper, and the vintager, him who sows the seed." In the Gospel, however, Jesus prefers wedding imagery to talk about the blessings that accompany the arrival of God's reign in him and his ministry.

These passages also show that God's blessing often comes in unexpected ways. Rebekah orchestrates Jacob's deception of Isaac to deprive Esau of his birthright. Yet, far from passing a moral judgment on mother and son, the author acknowledges that God is not bound by the conventional arrangement that gave preference to the firstborn son. Similarly in the Gospel, Jesus, speaking in parables, declares that in him God is again blessing Israel in a new way that shakes up and shatters old categories and conventions.

Year I

FIRST READING

Gn 27:1–5, 15–29

Jacob displaced his brother and usurped his blessing (Gn 27:36).

A reading from the Book of Genesis

When Isaac was so old that his eyesight had failed him, he called his older son Esau and said to him, "Son!" "Yes father!" he replied. Isaac then said, "As you can see, I am so old that I may now die at any time. Take your gear, therefore—your quiver and bow—and go out into the country to hunt some game for me. With your catch prepare an appetizing dish for me, such as I like, and bring it to me to eat, so that I may give you my special blessing before I die."

Rebekah had been listening while Isaac was speaking to his son Esau. So, when Esau went out into the country to hunt some game for his father, Rebekah [then] took the best clothes of her older son Esau that she had in the house, and gave them to her younger son Jacob to wear; and with the skins of the kids she covered up his hands and the hairless parts of his neck. Then she handed her son Jacob the appetizing dish and the bread she had prepared.

Bringing them to his father, Jacob said, "Father!" "Yes?" replied Isaac. "Which of my sons are you?" Jacob answered his father: "I am Esau, your first-born. I did as you told me. Please sit up and eat some of my game, so that you may give me your special blessing." But Isaac asked, "How did you succeed so quickly, son?" He answered, "The LORD, your God, let things turn out well with me." Isaac then said to Jacob, "Come closer, son, that I may feel you, to learn whether you really are my son Esau or not." So Jacob moved up closer to his father. When Isaac felt him, he said, "Although the voice is Jacob's, the hands are Esau's." (He failed to identify him because his hands were hairy, like those of his brother Esau; so in the end he gave him his blessing.) Again he asked Jacob, "Are you really my son Esau?" "Certainly," Jacob replied. Then Isaac said, "Serve me your game, son, that I may eat of it and then give you my blessing." Jacob served it to him, and Isaac ate; he brought him wine, and he drank. Finally his father Isaac said to Jacob, "Come closer, son, and kiss me." As Jacob went up and kissed him, Isaac smelled the fragrance of his clothes. With that, he blessed him saying,

"Ah, the fragrance of my son
    is like the fragrance of a field
    that the LORD has blessed!

"May God give to you
    of the dew of the heavens
And of the fertility of the earth
    abundance of grain and wine.

"Let peoples serve you,
    and nations pay you homage;
Be master of your brothers,
    and may your mother's sons bow down to you.

Cursed be those who curse you,
and blessed be those who bless you."

The word of the Lord.

Responsorial Psalm

Ps 135:1b–2, 3–4, 5–6

R. Praise the Lord for the Lord is good!

Praise the name of the LORD;
  Praise, you servants of the LORD
Who stand in the house of the LORD,
  in the courts of the house of our God.

R. Praise the Lord for the Lord is good!

Praise the LORD, for the LORD is good;
  sing praise to his name, which we love;
For the LORD has chosen Jacob for himself,
  Israel for his own possession.

R. Praise the Lord for the Lord is good!

For I know that the LORD is great;
  our LORD is greater than all gods.
All that the LORD wills he does
  in heaven and on earth,
  in the seas and in all the deeps.

R. Praise the Lord for the Lord is good!

Or: **R. Alleluia.**

Alleluia Verse *and* **Gospel**, *p. 1125.*

Year II

FIRST READING

Am 9:11–15

*I will bring about the restoration of my people Israel;
I will plant them upon their own ground.*

A reading from the Book of the Prophet Amos

Thus says the LORD:
On that day I will raise up
    the fallen hut of David;
I will wall up its breaches,
    raise up its ruins,
    and rebuild it as in the days of old,
That they may conquer what is left of Edom
    and all the nations that shall bear my name,
    say I, the LORD, who will do this.
Yes, days are coming,
    says the LORD,
When the plowman shall overtake the reaper,
    and the vintager, him who sows the seed;
The juice of grapes shall drip down the mountains,
    and all the hills shall run with it.
I will bring about the restoration of my people Israel;
    they shall rebuild and inhabit their ruined cities,
Plant vineyards and drink the wine,
    set out gardens and eat the fruits.
I will plant them upon their own ground;
    never again shall they be plucked
From the land I have given them,
    say I, the LORD, your God.
The word of the Lord.

Responsorial Psalm
Ps 85:9ab and 10, 11–12, 13–14

R. The Lord speaks of peace to his people.

I will hear what God proclaims;
    the LORD—for he proclaims peace to his people.

Near indeed is his salvation to those who fear him,
  glory dwelling in our land.

R. The Lord speaks of peace to his people.

Kindness and truth shall meet;
  justice and peace shall kiss.
Truth shall spring out of the earth,
  and justice shall look down from heaven.

R. The Lord speaks of peace to his people.

The LORD himself will give his benefits;
  our land shall yield its increase.
Justice shall walk before him,
  and salvation, along the way of his steps.

R. The Lord speaks of peace to his people.

> **Alleluia, alleluia**   Jn 10:27
> My sheep hear my voice, says the Lord;
> I know them, and they follow me.
> **Alleluia, alleluia**

Years I and II

GOSPEL   Mt 9:14–17

*Can the wedding guests mourn as long
as the bridegroom is with them?*

A reading from the holy Gospel according to Matthew

The disciples of John approached Jesus and said, "Why do we
and the Pharisees fast much, but your disciples do not fast?"
Jesus answered them, "Can the wedding guests mourn as long
as the bridegroom is with them? The days will come when the
bridegroom is taken away from them, and then they will fast.
No one patches an old cloak with a piece of unshrunken cloth,
for its fullness pulls away from the cloak and the tear gets
worse. People do not put new wine into old wineskins. Other-

wise the skins burst, the wine spills out, and the skins are ruined. Rather, they pour new wine into fresh wineskins, and both are preserved."

The Gospel of the Lord.

Liturgy of the Eucharist, *p. 897;* **Prayer over the Gifts,** *p. 1092.*

FOURTEENTH WEEK IN ORDINARY TIME

The **Antiphons and Prayers** *may be the following, or may be chosen from any of the other 33 weeks in Ordinary Time (refer to Liturgical Calendar, pp. 26–41).*

The **Liturgy of the Word** *varies: for Monday, see p. 1128; Tuesday, p. 1133; Wednesday, p. 1138; Thursday, p. 1143; Friday, p. 1148; Saturday, p. 1153.*

Entrance Antiphon

Within your temple, we ponder your loving kindness, O God. As your name, so also your praise reaches to the ends of the earth; your right hand is filled with justice. (Ps 48:10–11)

Opening Prayer

Let us pray
[for forgiveness
through the grace of Jesus Christ]

Pause for silent prayer.

Father,
through the obedience of Jesus,
your servant and your Son,
you raised a fallen world.
Free us from sin
and bring us the joy that lasts for ever.

We ask this through our Lord Jesus Christ, your Son,
who lives and reigns with you and the Holy Spirit,
one God, for ever and ever.

Alternative Opening Prayer

Let us pray
  [for greater willingness
  to serve God and our fellow man]

Pause for silent prayer.

Father,
in the rising of your Son
death gives birth to a new life.
The sufferings he endured restored hope to a fallen world.
Let sin never ensnare us
with empty promises of passing joy.
Make us one with you always,
so that our joy may be holy,
and our love may give life.

We ask this through Christ our Lord.

Prayer over the Gifts

Pray, brethren...

Lord,
let this offering to the glory of your name
purify us and bring us closer to eternal life.

We ask this in the name of Jesus the Lord.

Preface of Weekdays in Ordinary Time I–VI, *pp. 948–950.*

Communion Antiphon

Taste and see the goodness of the Lord; blessed is he who hopes in God. (Ps 34:9)

Or:

Come to me, all you that labor and are burdened, and I will give you rest, says the Lord. (Mt 11:28)

Prayer after Communion

Let us pray.

Pause for silent prayer, if this has not preceded.

Lord,
may we never fail to praise you
for the fullness of life and salvation
you give us in this eucharist.

We ask this through Christ our Lord.

Monday

Antiphons and Prayers, *p. 1126;* **Liturgy of the Word** *for Year I (odd years) follows; Year II (even years), p. 1130.*

TODAY'S LIVING WORD

Today's two first readings speak of a sacred place, a place where human beings come close to the living God. Genesis speaks of Jacob's so-called "ladder" with the messengers of God "going up and down on it." The ladder connects earth and heaven, suggesting "open lines" of communication between the two. In Hosea, the desert to which God draws Israel is the place of espousal, where God speaks and Israel responds "as in the days of her youth." More striking still is the content of God's speech in both selections. To Jacob God says, "Know that I am with you; I will protect you wherever you go." And to the people of Israel, God's words are a pledge of everlasting love.

In the two miracles retold in today's Gospel, the person of Jesus is the sacred place where a synagogue leader and an ailing woman come into contact with the living God. Here again there is movement in two directions. The synagogue leader wants Jesus to touch his daughter; the ailing woman wants to touch Jesus. As the new *Catechism* says, this is the dynamic of prayer, where God's desire and ours intersect (n. 2560).

FIRST READING   Gn 28:10–22a

Jacob had a dream: a stairway rested on the ground and God's
messengers were going up and down on it and the LORD was speaking.

A reading from the Book of Genesis

Jacob departed from Beer-sheba and proceeded toward Haran.
When he came upon a certain shrine, as the sun had already
set, he stopped there for the night. Taking one of the stones at
the shrine, he put it under his head and lay down to sleep at
that spot. Then he had a dream: a stairway rested on the ground,
with its top reaching to the heavens; and God's messengers
were going up and down on it. And there was the LORD standing
beside him and saying: "I, the LORD, am the God of your
forefather Abraham and the God of Isaac; the land on which
you are lying I will give to you and your descendants. These
shall be as plentiful as the dust of the earth, and through them
you shall spread out east and west, north and south. In you and
your descendants all the nations of the earth shall find blessing.
Know that I am with you; I will protect you wherever you go,
and bring you back to this land. I will never leave you until I
have done what I promised you."

When Jacob awoke from his sleep, he exclaimed, "Truly,
the LORD is in this spot, although I did not know it!" In solemn
wonder he cried out: "How awesome is this shrine! This is
nothing else but an abode of God, and that is the gateway to
heaven!" Early the next morning Jacob took the stone that he
had put under his head, set it up as a memorial stone, and poured

oil on top of it. He called the site Bethel, whereas the former name of the town had been Luz.

Jacob then made this vow: "If God remains with me, to protect me on this journey I am making and to give me enough bread to eat and clothing to wear, and I come back safe to my father's house, the LORD shall be my God. This stone that I have set up as a memorial stone shall be God's abode."

The word of the Lord.

Responsorial Psalm   Ps 91:1–2, 3–4, 14–15ab

R. In you, my God, I place my trust.

You who dwell in the shelter of the Most High,
  who abide in the shadow of the Almighty,
Say to the LORD, "My refuge and my fortress,
  my God, in whom I trust."

R. In you, my God, I place my trust.

For he will rescue you from the snare of the fowler,
  from the destroying pestilence.
With his pinions he will cover you,
  and under his wings you shall take refuge.

R. In you, my God, I place my trust.

Because he clings to me, I will deliver him;
  I will set him on high because he acknowledges my name.
He shall call upon me, and I will answer him;
  I will be with him in distress.

R. In you, my God, I place my trust.

Alleluia Verse *and* **Gospel,** *p. 1132.*

Year II

FIRST READING   Hos 2:16, 17c–18, 21–22

I will espouse you to me forever.

A reading from the Book of the Prophet Hosea

Thus says the LORD:
I will allure her;
  I will lead her into the desert
  and speak to her heart.
She shall respond there as in the days of her youth,
  when she came up from the land of Egypt.

    On that day, says the LORD,
She shall call me "My husband,"
  and never again "My baal."

I will espouse you to me forever:
  I will espouse you in right and in justice,
  in love and in mercy;
I will espouse you in fidelity,
  and you shall know the LORD.

The word of the Lord.

Responsorial Psalm

Ps 145:2–3, 4–5, 6–7, 8–9

  R. The Lord is gracious and merciful.

Every day will I bless you,
  and I will praise your name forever and ever.
Great is the LORD and highly to be praised;
  his greatness is unsearchable.

  R. The Lord is gracious and merciful.

Generation after generation praises your works
  and proclaims your might.
They speak of the splendor of your glorious majesty
  and tell of your wondrous works.

  R. The Lord is gracious and merciful.

They discourse of the power of your terrible deeds
  and declare your greatness.

They publish the fame of your abundant goodness
  and joyfully sing of your justice.

  R. **The Lord is gracious and merciful.**

The LORD is gracious and merciful,
  slow to anger and of great kindness.
The LORD is good to all
  and compassionate toward all his works.

  R. **The Lord is gracious and merciful.**

> **Alleluia, alleluia**   See 2 Tm 1:10
> Our Savior Jesus Christ has destroyed death
> and brought life to light through the Gospel.
> **Alleluia, alleluia**

Years I and II

GOSPEL   Mt 9:18–26

My daughter has just died, but come and she will live.

A reading from the holy Gospel according to Matthew

While Jesus was speaking, an official came forward, knelt down
before him, and said, "My daughter has just died. But come,
lay your hand on her, and she will live." Jesus rose and followed
him, and so did his disciples. A woman suffering hemorrhages
for twelve years came up behind him and touched the tassel
on his cloak. She said to herself, "If only I can touch his cloak,
I shall be cured." Jesus turned around and saw her, and said,
"Courage, daughter! Your faith has saved you." And from that
hour the woman was cured.

  When Jesus arrived at the official's house and saw the flute
players and the crowd who were making a commotion, he said,
"Go away! The girl is not dead but sleeping." And they ridiculed
him. When the crowd was put out, he came and took her by

the hand, and the little girl arose. And news of this spread throughout all that land.

The Gospel of the Lord.

Liturgy of the Eucharist, *p. 897;* **Prayer over the Gifts,** *p. 1127.*

Tuesday

Antiphons and Prayers, *p. 1126;* **Liturgy of the Word** *for Year I (odd years) follows; Year II (even years), p. 1135.*

TODAY'S LIVING WORD

The story of Jacob's struggle with God, one of today's first readings, is variously interpreted. The *Catechism of the Catholic Church* sees it as "the symbol of prayer as a battle of faith" (n. 2573). All the readings for today deal with this battle. An irony underlies the idolatry of Israel which Hosea so strenuously condemns: when they "made many altars to expiate sin," he says, their "altars became occasions of sin." Hosea did not condemn the altars but the lack of discernment of the people who used them. Similarly in the Gospel, the mixed reaction to Jesus' healing of the demoniac who was also mute suggests the necessary struggle that Jesus' ministry precipitated among his people.

The spiritual life is a mysterious battle, demanding a daily, disciplined discernment, lest our altars become occasions of sin. Struggling with God is a costly grace. It may mean many dark nights of wrestling with beings divine and human. But from this battle we emerge as "wounded healers," like Jacob who goes limping to meet his long lost brother.

Year I

FIRST READING

Gn 32:23–33

You shall be spoken of as Israel,
because you have contended with God and have prevailed.

A reading from the Book of Genesis

In the course of the night, Jacob arose, took his two wives, with the two maidservants and his eleven children, and crossed the ford of the Jabbok. After he had taken them across the stream and had brought over all his possessions, Jacob was left there alone. Then some man wrestled with him until the break of dawn. When the man saw that he could not prevail over him, he struck Jacob's hip at its socket, so that the hip socket was wrenched as they wrestled. The man then said, "Let me go, for it is daybreak." But Jacob said, "I will not let you go until you bless me." The man asked, "What is your name?" He answered, "Jacob." Then the man said, "You shall no longer be spoken of as Jacob, but as Israel, because you have contended with divine and human beings and have prevailed." Jacob then asked him, "Do tell me your name, please." He answered, "Why should you want to know my name?" With that, he bade him farewell. Jacob named the place Peniel, "Because I have seen God face to face," he said, "yet my life has been spared."

At sunrise, as he left Penuel, Jacob limped along because of his hip. That is why, to this day, the children of Israel do not eat the sciatic muscle that is on the hip socket, inasmuch as Jacob's hip socket was struck at the sciatic muscle.

The word of the Lord.

Responsorial Psalm
Ps 17:1b, 2–3, 6–7ab, 8b and 15

R. In justice, I shall behold your face, O Lord.

Hear, O LORD, a just suit;
    attend to my outcry;
    hearken to my prayer from lips without deceit.

R. In justice, I shall behold your face, O Lord.

From you let my judgment come;
  your eyes behold what is right.
Though you test my heart, searching it in the night,
  though you try me with fire, you shall find no malice in me.

R. In justice, I shall behold your face, O Lord.

I call upon you, for you will answer me, O God;
  incline your ear to me; hear my word.
Show your wondrous mercies,
  O savior of those who flee from their foes.

R. In justice, I shall behold your face, O Lord.

Hide me in the shadow of your wings.
I in justice shall behold your face;
  on waking, I shall be content in your presence.

R. In justice, I shall behold your face, O Lord.

Alleluia Verse *and* **Gospel,** *p. 1137.*

Year II

FIRST READING

Hos 8:4 – 7, 11–13

When they sow the wind, they shall reap the whirlwind.

A reading from the Book of the Prophet Hosea

Thus says the LORD:
They made kings in Israel, but not by my authority;
  they established princes, but without my approval.
With their silver and gold they made
  idols for themselves, to their own destruction.
Cast away your calf, O Samaria!
  my wrath is kindled against them;
How long will they be unable to attain
  innocence in Israel?

The work of an artisan,
  no god at all,
Destined for the flames—
  such is the calf of Samaria!

When they sow the wind,
  they shall reap the whirlwind;
The stalk of grain that forms no ear
  can yield no flour;
Even if it could,
  strangers would swallow it.

When Ephraim made many altars to expiate sin,
  his altars became occasions of sin.
Though I write for him my many ordinances,
  they are considered as a stranger's.
Though they offer sacrifice,
  immolate flesh and eat it,
  the LORD is not pleased with them.
He shall still remember their guilt
  and punish their sins;
  they shall return to Egypt.

The word of the Lord.

Responsorial Psalm   Ps 115:3–4, 5–6, 7ab–8, 9–10

  R. The house of Israel trusts in the Lord.

Our God is in heaven;
  whatever he wills, he does.
Their idols are silver and gold,
  the handiwork of men.

  R. The house of Israel trusts in the Lord.

They have mouths but speak not;
  they have eyes but see not;
They have ears but hear not;
  they have noses but smell not.

R. The house of Israel trusts in the Lord.

They have hands but feel not;
  they have feet but walk not.
Their makers shall be like them,
  everyone that trusts in them.

R. The house of Israel trusts in the Lord.

Or: **R. Alleluia.**

> **Alleluia, alleluia**   Jn 10:14
> I am the good shepherd, says the Lord;
> I know my sheep, and mine know me.
> **Alleluia, alleluia**

Years I and II

GOSPEL   Mt 9:32–38

The harvest is abundant but the laborers are few.

A reading from the holy Gospel according to Matthew

A demoniac who could not speak was brought to Jesus, and
when the demon was driven out the mute man spoke. The
crowds were amazed and said, "Nothing like this has ever been
seen in Israel." But the Pharisees said, "He drives out demons
by the prince of demons."

    Jesus went around to all the towns and villages, teaching in
their synagogues, proclaiming the Gospel of the Kingdom, and
curing every disease and illness. At the sight of the crowds,
his heart was moved with pity for them because they were
troubled and abandoned, like sheep without a shepherd. Then

he said to his disciples, "The harvest is abundant but the laborers
are few; so ask the master of the harvest to send out laborers
for his harvest."

The Gospel of the Lord.

Liturgy of the Eucharist, *p. 897;* **Prayer over the Gifts,** *p. 1127.*

Wednesday

Antiphons and Prayers, *p. 1126;* **Liturgy of the Word** *for Year I (odd
years) follows; Year II (even years), p. 1140.*

TODAY'S LIVING WORD

Agricultural motifs figure in all three of today's readings. The
Genesis text is a much abridged version of the story of Joseph and
his brothers. A famine brings Jacob's sons to Egypt and leads to their
eventual reconciliation with Joseph. Hosea uses agricultural imagery
to reinforce his claim that God controls fertility, not the Baals. In the
Gospel, Jesus directs his newly-named apostles to "the lost sheep of
the house of Israel." In all three passages God is at work, however
imperceptibly, to create new opportunities.

In Genesis the poignant self-recriminations that his brothers make
in his hearing move Joseph, "a God-fearing man," not to revenge
but to a reconciliation that will mean prosperity for his brothers.
The words Hosea addresses to Israel are as much a summons as a
sentence. They are motivated by God's hope that Israel might once
again sow justice and reap piety. Jesus' instructions to the Twelve
make it clear that the good news of God's reign is to be proclaimed,
first and foremost, to all Israel.

Year I

FIRST READING   Gn 41:55–57; 42:5–7a, 17–24a

Alas, we are being punished because of our brother.

A reading from the Book of Genesis

When hunger came to be felt throughout the land of Egypt and the people cried to Pharaoh for bread, Pharaoh directed all the Egyptians to go to Joseph and do whatever he told them. When the famine had spread throughout the land, Joseph opened all the cities that had grain and rationed it to the Egyptians, since the famine had gripped the land of Egypt. In fact, all the world came to Joseph to obtain rations of grain, for famine had gripped the whole world.

The sons of Israel were among those who came to procure rations.

It was Joseph, as governor of the country, who dispensed the rations to all the people. When Joseph's brothers came and knelt down before him with their faces to the ground, he recognized them as soon as he saw them. But Joseph concealed his own identity from them and spoke sternly to them.

With that, he locked them up in the guardhouse for three days. On the third day Joseph said to his brothers: "Do this, and you shall live; for I am a God-fearing man. If you have been honest, only one of your brothers need be confined in this prison, while the rest of you may go and take home provisions for your starving families. But you must come back to me with your youngest brother. Your words will thus be verified, and you will not die." To this they agreed. To one another, however, they said: "Alas, we are being punished because of our brother. We saw the anguish of his heart when he pleaded with us, yet we paid no heed; that is why this anguish has now come upon us." Reuben broke in, "Did I not tell you not to do wrong to the boy? But you would not listen! Now comes the reckoning for his blood." The brothers did not know, of course, that Joseph understood what they said, since he spoke with them through an interpreter. But turning away from them, he wept.

The word of the Lord.

Responsorial Psalm

Ps 33:2–3, 10–11, 18–19

R. **Lord, let your mercy be on us,**
   as we place our trust in you.

Give thanks to the LORD on the harp;
   with the ten-stringed lyre chant his praises.
Sing to him a new song;
   pluck the strings skillfully, with shouts of gladness.

R. **Lord, let your mercy be on us,**
   as we place our trust in you.

The LORD brings to nought the plans of nations;
   he foils the designs of peoples.
But the plan of the LORD stands forever;
   the design of his heart, through all generations.

R. **Lord, let your mercy be on us,**
   as we place our trust in you..

But see, the eyes of the LORD are upon those who fear him,
   upon those who hope for his kindness,
To deliver them from death
   and preserve them in spite of famine.

R. **Lord, let your mercy be on us,**
   as we place our trust in you.

Alleluia Verse *and* **Gospel,** *p. 1142.*

Year II

FIRST READING

Hos 10:1–3, 7–8, 12

It is time to seek the LORD.

A reading from the Book of the Prophet Hosea

Israel is a luxuriant vine
    whose fruit matches its growth.
The more abundant his fruit,
    the more altars he built;
The more productive his land,
    the more sacred pillars he set up.
Their heart is false,
    now they pay for their guilt;
God shall break down their altars
    and destroy their sacred pillars.
If they would say,
    "We have no king"—
Since they do not fear the LORD,
    what can the king do for them?

The king of Samaria shall disappear,
    like foam upon the waters.
The high places of Aven shall be destroyed,
    the sin of Israel;
    thorns and thistles shall overgrow their altars.
Then they shall cry out to the mountains, "Cover us!"
    and to the hills, "Fall upon us!"

"Sow for yourselves justice,
    reap the fruit of piety;
break up for yourselves a new field,
    for it is time to seek the LORD,
    till he come and rain down justice upon you."
The word of the Lord.

Responsorial Psalm

Ps 105:2–3, 4–5, 6–7

    R. **Seek always the face of the Lord.**

Sing to him, sing his praise,
  proclaim all his wondrous deeds.
Glory in his holy name;
  rejoice, O hearts that seek the LORD!

R. Seek always the face of the Lord.

Look to the LORD in his strength;
  seek to serve him constantly.
Recall the wondrous deeds that he has wrought,
  his portents, and the judgments he has uttered.

R. Seek always the face of the Lord.

You descendants of Abraham, his servants,
  sons of Jacob, his chosen ones!
He, the LORD, is our God;
  throughout the earth his judgments prevail.

R. Seek always the face of the Lord.

Or: **R. Alleluia.**

> **Alleluia, alleluia**   Mk 1:15
> The Kingdom of God is at hand:
> repent and believe in the Gospel.
> **Alleluia, alleluia**

Years I and II

GOSPEL   Mt 10:1–7

Go rather to the lost sheep of the house of Israel.

A reading from the holy Gospel according to Matthew

Jesus summoned his Twelve disciples and gave them authority over unclean spirits to drive them out and to cure every disease and every illness. The names of the Twelve Apostles are these: first, Simon called Peter, and his brother Andrew; James, the son of Zebedee, and his brother John; Philip and Bartholomew, Thomas and Matthew the tax collector; James, the son of

Alphaeus, and Thaddeus; Simon the Cananean, and Judas Iscariot who betrayed Jesus.

Jesus sent out these Twelve after instructing them thus, "Do not go into pagan territory or enter a Samaritan town. Go rather to the lost sheep of the house of Israel. As you go, make this proclamation: 'The Kingdom of heaven is at hand.'" The Gospel of the Lord.

Liturgy of the Eucharist, p. 897; **Prayer over the Gifts,** p. 1127.

Thursday

Antiphons and Prayers, p. 1126; **Liturgy of the Word** for Year I (odd years) follows; Year II (even years), p. 1146.

TODAY'S LIVING WORD

The two first readings for today paint powerful pictures of parental love. The climax of the story of Joseph and his brothers—Joseph's self-disclosure—is preceded by Judah's moving speech. Dramatically, he pleads with Joseph to spare Benjamin for the sake of Jacob, their father, who dotes on his youngest child. It is a plea for Jacob's life, for he has warned Judah that the loss of Benjamin would send his "white head down to the nether world in grief." In the passage from Hosea, God is the doting parent whose heart is overwhelmed at the thought of Ephraim's destruction. McCarthy and Murphy in their article on Hosea in *The New Jerome Biblical Commentary* call this passage "one of the high points of the...revelation of God's nature" in the Hebrew Scriptures.*

Against this background, today's Gospel exhorts all who are sent to do what Jesus did. They must "cure the sick, raise the dead, cleanse lepers, drive out demons," all with a view to making present in the world the patient, pitying love of God the Father.

* Dennis McCarthy and Roland Murphy, "Hosea," *The New Jerome Biblical Commentary*, ed. Raymond E. Brown, SS, Joseph A. Fitzmyer, SJ, Roland E. Murphy, O. Carm. (Englewood Cliffs: Prentice Hall, 1990), p. 226.

Year II

FIRST READING   Hos 11:1–4, 8e–9

My heart is overwhelmed.

A reading from the Book of the Prophet Hosea

Thus says the LORD:
When Israel was a child I loved him,
    out of Egypt I called my son.
The more I called them,
    the farther they went from me,
Sacrificing to the Baals
    and burning incense to idols.
Yet it was I who taught Ephraim to walk,
    who took them in my arms;
I drew them with human cords,
    with bands of love;
I fostered them like one
    who raises an infant to his cheeks;
Yet, though I stooped to feed my child,
    they did not know that I was their healer.

My heart is overwhelmed,
    my pity is stirred.
I will not give vent to my blazing anger,
    I will not destroy Ephraim again;
For I am God and not man,
    the Holy One present among you;
I will not let the flames consume you.
The word of the Lord.

Responsorial Psalm   Ps 80:2ac and 3b, 15–16
    R. Let us see your face, Lord, and we shall be saved.

O shepherd of Israel, hearken.
From your throne upon the cherubim, shine forth.
Rouse your power.

R. Let us see your face, Lord, and we shall be saved.

Once again, O LORD of hosts,
   look down from heaven, and see:
Take care of this vine,
   and protect what your right hand has planted,
   the son of man whom you yourself made strong.

R. Let us see your face, Lord, and we shall be saved.

Alleluia, alleluia   Mk 1:15
The Kingdom of God is at hand:
repent and believe in the Gospel.
Alleluia, alleluia

Years I and II

GOSPEL
                                                Mt 10:7–15
Without cost you have received; without cost you are to give.

A reading from the holy Gospel according to Matthew

Jesus said to his Apostles: "As you go, make this proclamation: 'The Kingdom of heaven is at hand.' Cure the sick, raise the dead, cleanse the lepers, drive out demons. Without cost you have received; without cost you are to give. Do not take gold or silver or copper for your belts; no sack for the journey, or a second tunic, or sandals, or walking stick. The laborer deserves his keep. Whatever town or village you enter, look for a worthy person in it, and stay there until you leave. As you enter a house, wish it peace. If the house is worthy, let your peace come upon it; if not, let your peace return to you. Whoever will not receive you or listen to your words—go outside that house or town and shake the dust from your feet. Amen, I say to you, it will be more tolerable for the land of Sodom and Gomorrah on the day of judgment than for that town."

The Gospel of the Lord.

Liturgy of the Eucharist, *p. 897;* **Prayer over the Gifts,** *p. 1127.*

Friday

Antiphons and Prayers, *p. 1126;* **Liturgy of the Word** *for Year I (odd years) follows; Year II (even years), p. 1150.*

TODAY'S LIVING WORD

All three of today's readings sound the theme of divine reassurance. On his way to Egypt, Jacob (Israel) stops at Beer-sheba where God speaks to him in a vision: "Do not be afraid to go down to Egypt, for there I will make you a great nation." The prophecy of Hosea concludes with divine reassurance that, though he has collapsed through his guilt, Ephraim (Israel, the people this time) will prosper once more, for God's wrath will turn away from them. In the Gospel, Jesus sends his disciples out "like sheep in the midst of wolves." They will be tried by rulers and kings but they must not worry about their defense. For just as the God of his father will go down to Egypt with Jacob, so will the Spirit of their Father speak for the disciples of Jesus.

In Matthew's arrangement of Jesus' words in today's Gospel, signs of God's future—such as the gift of the Spirit, the division of families— appear as present realities. Already the Gospel divides family members, and the Spirit must defend disciples persecuted for their faith. For Matthew, God's future has already arrived.

Year I

FIRST READING

Gn 46:1–7, 28–30

At last I can die, now that I have seen for myself that Joseph is still alive.

A reading from the Book of Genesis

Israel set out with all that was his. When he arrived at Beer-sheba, he offered sacrifices to the God of his father Isaac. There God, speaking to Israel in a vision by night, called, "Jacob! Jacob!" He answered, "Here I am." Then he said: "I am God, the God of your father. Do not be afraid to go down to Egypt, for there I will make you a great nation. Not only will I go down to Egypt with you; I will also bring you back here, after Joseph has closed your eyes."

So Jacob departed from Beer-sheba, and the sons of Israel put their father and their wives and children on the wagons that Pharaoh had sent for his transport. They took with them their livestock and the possessions they had acquired in the land of Canaan. Thus Jacob and all his descendants migrated to Egypt. His sons and his grandsons, his daughters and his granddaughters —all his descendants—he took with him to Egypt.

Israel had sent Judah ahead to Joseph, so that he might meet him in Goshen. On his arrival in the region of Goshen, Joseph hitched the horses to his chariot and rode to meet his father Israel in Goshen. As soon as Joseph saw him, he flung himself on his neck and wept a long time in his arms. And Israel said to Joseph, "At last I can die, now that I have seen for myself that Joseph is still alive."

The word of the Lord.

Responsorial Psalm   Ps 37:3–4, 18–19, 27–28, 39–40

R. The salvation of the just comes from the Lord.

Trust in the LORD and do good,
   that you may dwell in the land and be fed in security.
Take delight in the LORD,
   and he will grant you your heart's requests.

R. The salvation of the just comes from the Lord.

The LORD watches over the lives of the wholehearted;
  their inheritance lasts forever.
They are not put to shame in an evil time;
  in days of famine they have plenty.

R. The salvation of the just comes from the Lord.

Turn from evil and do good,
  that you may abide forever;
For the LORD loves what is right,
  and forsakes not his faithful ones.

R. The salvation of the just comes from the Lord.

The salvation of the just is from the LORD;
  he is their refuge in time of distress.
And the LORD helps them and delivers them;
  he delivers them from the wicked and saves them,
  because they take refuge in him.

R. The salvation of the just comes from the Lord.

Alleluia Verse *and* **Gospel,** *p. 1152.*

Year II

FIRST READING

Hos 14:2–10

We shall say no more "Our god" to the work of our hands.

A reading from the Book of the Prophet Hosea

    Thus says the LORD:
Return, O Israel, to the LORD, your God;
  you have collapsed through your guilt.
Take with you words,
  and return to the LORD;
Say to him, "Forgive all iniquity,
  and receive what is good, that we may render

as offerings the bullocks from our stalls.
Assyria will not save us,
    nor shall we have horses to mount;
We shall say no more, 'Our god,'
    to the work of our hands;
    for in you the orphan finds compassion."
I will heal their defection, says the LORD,
    I will love them freely;
    for my wrath is turned away from them.
I will be like the dew for Israel:
    he shall blossom like the lily;
He shall strike root like the Lebanon cedar,
    and put forth his shoots.
His splendor shall be like the olive tree
    and his fragrance like the Lebanon cedar.
Again they shall dwell in his shade
    and raise grain;
They shall blossom like the vine,
    and his fame shall be like the wine of Lebanon.

Ephraim! What more has he to do with idols?
    I have humbled him, but I will prosper him.
"I am like a verdant cypress tree"—
    because of me you bear fruit!

Let him who is wise understand these things;
    let him who is prudent know them.
Straight are the paths of the LORD,
    in them the just walk,
    but sinners stumble in them.
The word of the Lord.

Responsorial Psalm
Ps 51:3 – 4, 8 – 9, 12 – 13, 14 and 17

R. My mouth will declare your praise.

Have mercy on me, O God, in your goodness;
  in the greatness of your compassion wipe out my offense.
Thoroughly wash me from my guilt
  and of my sin cleanse me.

R. My mouth will declare your praise.

Behold, you are pleased with sincerity of heart,
  and in my inmost being you teach me wisdom.
Cleanse me of sin with hyssop, that I may be purified;
  wash me, and I shall be whiter than snow.

R. My mouth will declare your praise.

A clean heart create for me, O God,
  and a steadfast spirit renew within me.
Cast me not out from your presence,
  and your Holy Spirit take not from me.

R. My mouth will declare your praise.

Give me back the joy of your salvation,
  and a willing spirit sustain in me.
O Lord, open my lips,
  and my mouth shall proclaim your praise.

R. My mouth will declare your praise.

Alleluia, alleluia   Jn 16:13a; 14:26d
When the Spirit of truth comes,
he will guide you to all truth
and remind you of all I told you.
Alleluia, alleluia

Years I and II

GOSPEL
Mt 10:16 – 23

For it will not be you who speak,
but the Spirit of your Father speaking through you.

A reading from the holy Gospel according to Matthew

Jesus said to his Apostles: "Behold, I am sending you like sheep in the midst of wolves; so be shrewd as serpents and simple as doves. But beware of men, for they will hand you over to courts and scourge you in their synagogues, and you will be led before governors and kings for my sake as a witness before them and the pagans. When they hand you over, do not worry about how you are to speak or what you are to say. You will be given at that moment what you are to say. For it will not be you who speak but the Spirit of your Father speaking through you. Brother will hand over brother to death, and the father his child; children will rise up against parents and have them put to death. You will be hated by all because of my name, but whoever endures to the end will be saved. When they persecute you in one town, flee to another. Amen, I say to you, you will not finish the towns of Israel before the Son of Man comes."

The Gospel of the Lord.

Liturgy of the Eucharist, *p. 897;* **Prayer over the Gifts,** *p. 1127.*

Saturday

Antiphons and Prayers, *p. 1126;* **Liturgy of the Word** *for Year I (odd years) follows; Year II (even years), p. 1156.*

TODAY'S LIVING WORD

All three readings today call our attention to God's holiness. In the Bible holiness is not static perfection but the total and dynamic otherness of God. It is dramatically displayed in today's account of Isaiah's call. Here God's holiness is acclaimed by seraphim and accompanied by earthquake and smoke, elements that usually attend the manifestation of God. Isaiah knows that in the presence of such holiness, a sinful human being is doomed. In the Gospel, Jesus urges his disciples not to fear human beings, but God who alone is Lord of life. Such fear of God recognizes that only God is God.

The story of Joseph offers a practical example of the biblical fear of God, experienced by Isaiah and expressed in Jesus' teaching. After the death of their father, Joseph's brothers fear that he may now want to kill them, so they beg his forgiveness. Joseph's answer acknowledges that there is one God, only one. "Can I take the place of God?" he asks. Thus he shows himself to be a God-fearing man.

Year I

FIRST READING
Gn 49:29 – 32; 50:15 – 26a

God will surely take care of you and lead you out of this land.

A reading from the Book of Genesis

Jacob gave his sons this charge: "Since I am about to be taken to my people, bury me with my fathers in the cave that lies in the field of Ephron the Hittite, the cave in the field of Machpelah, facing on Mamre, in the land of Canaan, the field that Abraham bought from Ephron the Hittite for a burial ground. There Abraham and his wife Sarah are buried, and so are Isaac and his wife Rebekah, and there, too, I buried Leah—the field and the cave in it that had been purchased from the Hittites."

Now that their father was dead, Joseph's brothers became fearful and thought, "Suppose Joseph has been nursing a grudge against us and now plans to pay us back in full for all the wrong we did him!" So they approached Joseph and said: "Before your father died, he gave us these instructions: 'You shall say to Joseph, Jacob begs you to forgive the criminal wrongdoing of your brothers, who treated you so cruelly.' Please, therefore, forgive the crime that we, the servants of your father's God, committed." When they spoke these words to him, Joseph broke into tears. Then his brothers proceeded to fling themselves down before him and said, "Let us be your slaves!" But Joseph replied to them: "Have no fear. Can I take the place of God? Even though you meant harm to me, God meant it for good, to achieve his present end, the survival of many people. Therefore have no fear. I will provide for you and for your children." By thus speaking kindly to them, he reassured them.

Joseph remained in Egypt, together with his father's family. He lived a hundred and ten years. He saw Ephraim's children to the third generation, and the children of Manasseh's son Machir were also born on Joseph's knees.

Joseph said to his brothers: "I am about to die. God will surely take care of you and lead you out of this land to the land that he promised on oath to Abraham, Isaac and Jacob." Then, putting the sons of Israel under oath, he continued, "When God thus takes care of you, you must bring my bones up with you from this place." Joseph died at the age of a hundred and ten. The word of the Lord.

Responsorial Psalm

Ps 105:1–2, 3–4, 6–7

R. Be glad you lowly ones; may your hearts be glad!

Give thanks to the LORD, invoke his name;
    make known among the nations his deeds.
Sing to him, sing his praise,
    proclaim all his wondrous deeds.

R. Be glad you lowly ones; may your hearts be glad!

Glory in his holy name;
    rejoice, O hearts that seek the LORD!
Look to the LORD in his strength;
    seek to serve him constantly.

R. Be glad you lowly ones; may your hearts be glad!

You descendants of Abraham, his servants,
  sons of Jacob, his chosen ones!
He, the LORD, is our God;
  throughout the earth his judgments prevail.

R. Be glad you lowly ones; may your hearts be glad!

Alleluia Verse *and* **Gospel,** *p. 1157.*

Year II

FIRST READING   Is 6:1–8

I am a man of unclean lips;
yet my eyes have seen the King, the LORD of hosts!

A reading from the Book of the Prophet Isaiah

In the year King Uzziah died, I saw the Lord seated on a high
and lofty throne, with the train of his garment filling the temple.
Seraphim were stationed above; each of them had six wings:
with two they veiled their faces, with two they veiled their
feet, and with two they hovered aloft.

They cried one to the other, "Holy, holy, holy is the LORD of
hosts! All the earth is filled with his glory!" At the sound of
that cry, the frame of the door shook and the house was filled
with smoke.

Then I said, "Woe is me, I am doomed! For I am a man of
unclean lips, living among a people of unclean lips; yet my
eyes have seen the King, the LORD of hosts!" Then one of the
seraphim flew to me, holding an ember that he had taken with
tongs from the altar.

He touched my mouth with it and said, "See, now that
this has touched your lips, your wickedness is removed, your
sin purged."

Then I heard the voice of the Lord saying, "Whom shall I send? Who will go for us?" "Here I am," I said; "send me!"

The word of the Lord.

Responsorial Psalm
Ps 93:1ab, 1cd – 2, 5

R. The Lord is king; he is robed in majesty.

The LORD is king, in splendor robed;
  robed is the LORD and girt about with strength.

R. The Lord is king; he is robed in majesty.

And he has made the world firm,
  not to be moved.
Your throne stands firm from of old;
  from everlasting you are, O LORD.

R. The Lord is king; he is robed in majesty.

Your decrees are worthy of trust indeed:
  holiness befits your house,
O LORD, for length of days.

R. The Lord is king; he is robed in majesty.

Alleluia, alleluia   1 Pt 4:14
If you are insulted for the name of Christ, blessed are you,
for the Spirit of God rests upon you.
Alleluia, alleluia

Years I and II

GOSPEL
Mt 10:24 – 33

Do not be afraid of those who kill the body.

A reading from the holy Gospel according to Matthew

Jesus said to his Apostles: "No disciple is above his teacher, no slave above his master. It is enough for the disciple that he become like his teacher, for the slave that he become like his master. If they have called the master of the house Beelzebul, how much more those of his household!

"Therefore do not be afraid of them. Nothing is concealed that will not be revealed, nor secret that will not be known. What I say to you in the darkness, speak in the light; what you hear whispered, proclaim on the housetops. And do not be afraid of those who kill the body but cannot kill the soul; rather, be afraid of the one who can destroy both soul and body in Gehenna. Are not two sparrows sold for a small coin? Yet not one of them falls to the ground without your Father's knowledge. Even all the hairs of your head are counted. So do not be afraid; you are worth more than many sparrows. Everyone who acknowledges me before others I will acknowledge before my heavenly Father. But whoever denies me before others, I will deny before my heavenly Father."

The Gospel of the Lord.

Liturgy of the Eucharist, *p. 897;* **Prayer over the Gifts,** *p. 1127.*

FIFTEENTH WEEK IN ORDINARY TIME

The **Antiphons and Prayers** *may be the following, or may be chosen from any of the other 33 weeks in Ordinary Time (refer to Liturgical Calendar, pp. 26–41).*

The **Liturgy of the Word** *varies: for Monday, see p. 1160; Tuesday, p. 1166; Wednesday, p. 1171; Thursday, p. 1176; Friday, p. 1181; Saturday, p. 1186.*

Entrance Antiphon

In my justice I shall see your face, O Lord; when your glory appears, my joy will be full.   (Ps 17:15)

Opening Prayer

Let us pray
  [that the gospel may be our rule of life]

Pause for silent prayer.

God our Father,
your light of truth
guides us to the way of Christ.
May all who follow him
reject what is contrary to the gospel.

We ask this through our Lord Jesus Christ, your Son,
who lives and reigns with you and the Holy Spirit,
one God, for ever and ever.

Alternative Opening Prayer

Let us pray
  [to be faithful to the light we have received,
  to the name we bear]

Pause for silent prayer.

Father,
let the light of your truth
guide us to your kingdom
through a world filled with lights contrary to your own.
Christian is the name and the gospel we glory in.
May your love make us what you have called us to be.

We ask this through Christ our Lord.

Prayer over the Gifts

Pray, brethren...

Lord,
accept the gifts of your Church.

May this eucharist
help us grow in holiness and faith.

We ask this in the name of Jesus the Lord.

Preface of Weekdays in Ordinary Time I–VI, *pp. 948–950.*

Communion Antiphon

The sparrow even finds a home, the swallow finds a nest wherein to place her young, near to your altars, Lord of hosts, my King, my God! How happy they who dwell in your house! For ever they are praising you.   (Ps 84:4–5)

Or:

Whoever eats my flesh and drinks my blood will live in me and I in him, says the Lord.   (Jn 6:57)

Prayer after Communion

Let us pray.

Pause for silent prayer, if this has not preceded.

Lord,
by our sharing in the mystery of this eucharist,
let your saving love grow within us.

Grant this through Christ our Lord.

Monday

Antiphons and Prayers, *p. 1158;* **Liturgy of the Word** *for Year I (odd years) follows; Year II (even years), p. 1163.*

TODAY'S LIVING WORD

"The one sent by a man is as the man himself." This Jewish legal principle stands behind Jesus' words in today's Gospel: "Whoever receives you receives me, and whoever receives me receives the one who sent me." This saying uncovers the deepest meaning of Christian mission. The Christian missionary is to make Christ present as Christ makes God present in the world.

The identity of the one sent to represent Christ gives a key to the other two readings. He or she is "one of these little ones." In other words, acceptance or rejection of Christ is signified by one's treatment of the lowly. They are his representatives. This is the sense of the passage from Isaiah as well. God tells the people that true worship lies in hearing the orphan's plea and defending the widow, the lowly who are God's agents among us. Finally, the words of Isaiah and Jesus both reflect the touchstone of Jewish law recalled in the reading from Exodus: for you were once slaves in Egypt.

Year I

FIRST READING   Ex 1:8–14, 22

Come, let us deal shrewdly with them to stop their increase.

A reading from the Book of Exodus

A new king, who knew nothing of Joseph, came to power in Egypt. He said to his subjects, "Look how numerous and powerful the people of the children of Israel are growing, more so than we ourselves! Come, let us deal shrewdly with them to stop their increase; otherwise, in time of war they too may join our enemies to fight against us, and so leave our country."

Accordingly, taskmasters were set over the children of Israel to oppress them with forced labor. Thus they had to build for Pharaoh the supply cities of Pithom and Raamses. Yet the more they were oppressed, the more they multiplied and spread. The Egyptians, then, dreaded the children of Israel and reduced them to cruel slavery, making life bitter for them with hard work in mortar and brick and all kinds of field work—the whole cruel fate of slaves.

Pharaoh then commanded all his subjects, "Throw into the river every boy that is born to the Hebrews, but you may let all the girls live."

The word of the Lord.

Responsorial Psalm
Ps 124:1b–3, 4–6, 7–8

R. Our help is in the name of the Lord.

Had not the LORD been with us—
  let Israel say, had not the LORD been with us—
When men rose up against us,
  then would they have swallowed us alive,
When their fury was inflamed against us.

R. Our help is in the name of the Lord.

Then would the waters have overwhelmed us;
The torrent would have swept over us;
  over us then would have swept
  the raging waters.
Blessed be the LORD, who did not leave us
  a prey to their teeth.

R. Our help is in the name of the Lord.

We were rescued like a bird
  from the fowlers' snare;
Broken was the snare,
  and we were freed.
Our help is in the name of the LORD,
  who made heaven and earth.

R. Our help is in the name of the Lord.

Alleluia Verse *and* **Gospel,** *p. 1164f.*

Year II

FIRST READING   Is 1:10–17

Wash yourselves clean!
Put away your misdeeds from before my eyes.

A reading from the Book of the Prophet Isaiah

Hear the word of the LORD,
　　princes of Sodom!
Listen to the instruction of our God,
　　people of Gomorrah!
What care I for the number of your sacrifices?
　　says the LORD.
I have had enough of whole-burnt rams
　　and fat of fatlings;
In the blood of calves, lambs and goats
　　I find no pleasure.

When you come in to visit me,
　　who asks these things of you?
Trample my courts no more!
　　Bring no more worthless offerings;
　　your incense is loathsome to me.
New moon and sabbath, calling of assemblies,
　　octaves with wickedness: these I cannot bear.
Your new moons and festivals I detest;
　　they weigh me down, I tire of the load.
When you spread out your hands,
　　I close my eyes to you;
Though you pray the more,
　　I will not listen.

Your hands are full of blood!
    Wash yourselves clean!
Put away your misdeeds from before my eyes;
    cease doing evil; learn to do good.
Make justice your aim: redress the wronged,
    hear the orphan's plea, defend the widow.

The word of the Lord.

Responsorial Psalm

Ps 50:8–9, 16bc–17, 21 and 23

R. To the upright I will show the saving power of God.

"Not for your sacrifices do I rebuke you,
    for your burnt offerings are before me always.
I take from your house no bullock,
    no goats out of your fold."

R. To the upright I will show the saving power of God.

"Why do you recite my statutes,
    and profess my covenant with your mouth,
Though you hate discipline
    and cast my words behind you?"

R. To the upright I will show the saving power of God.

"When you do these things, shall I be deaf to it?
    Or do you think that I am like yourself?
I will correct you by drawing them up before your eyes.
He that offers praise as a sacrifice glorifies me;
    and to him that goes the right way I will show the salvation of God."

R. To the upright I will show the saving power of God.

     Alleluia, alleluia   Mt 5:10
     Blessed are they who are persecuted
       for the sake of righteousness,
     for theirs is the Kingdom of heaven.
     Alleluia, alleluia

Years I and II

GOSPEL   Mt 10:34 — 11:1

I have come to bring not peace, but the sword.

A reading from the holy Gospel according to Matthew

Jesus said to his Apostles: "Do not think that I have come to bring peace upon the earth. I have come to bring not peace but the sword. For I have come to set

a man against his father,
   a daughter against her mother,
and a daughter-in-law against her mother-in-law;
   and one's enemies will be those of his household.

"Whoever loves father or mother more than me is not worthy of me, and whoever loves son or daughter more than me is not worthy of me; and whoever does not take up his cross and follow after me is not worthy of me. Whoever finds his life will lose it, and whoever loses his life for my sake will find it.

"Whoever receives you receives me, and whoever receives me receives the one who sent me. Whoever receives a prophet because he is a prophet will receive a prophet's reward, and whoever receives a righteous man because he is righteous will receive a righteous man's reward. And whoever gives only a cup of cold water to one of these little ones to drink because he is a disciple—amen, I say to you, he will surely not lose his reward."

When Jesus finished giving these commands to his Twelve disciples, he went away from that place to teach and to preach in their towns.

The Gospel of the Lord.

Liturgy of the Eucharist, *p. 897;* **Prayer over the Gifts,** *p. 1159.*

Tuesday

Antiphons and Prayers, *p. 1158;* **Liturgy of the Word** *for Year I (odd years) follows; Year II (even years), p. 1168.*

TODAY'S LIVING WORD

Fear is a moving force in the two first readings. Fear of Pharaoh makes a fugitive of Moses, and fear of the Syro-Ephraimite alliance causes the heart of King Ahaz and the hearts of his people to tremble, "as the trees of the forest tremble in the wind." In both situations faith in God is lacking. Moses has not yet met the God of his father, and Ahaz lacks the courage that Isaiah urges upon him.

The last line of the reading from Isaiah—"Unless your faith is firm you shall not be firm!"—is a bridge to the Gospel reading. This verse is a play on words, using two forms of the same verb, *aman,* which means "to be firm" and is the root of our word "amen." This verb is used often of the house of David whose throne, God has promised, shall stand firm forever. But such a privilege, Isaiah tells Ahaz, requires faith to be effective. Jesus says much the same thing to Capernaum and the neighboring towns. They have been privileged to see his miracles, but they have failed to respond with firm faith. So they, like the house of David, will be liable to judgment.

Year I

FIRST READING

Ex 2:1–15a

She called him Moses for she said, "I drew him out of the water." After Moses had grown up, he visited his people.

A reading from the Book of Exodus

A certain man of the house of Levi married a Levite woman, who conceived and bore a son. Seeing that he was a goodly child, she hid him for three months. When she could hide him no longer, she took a papyrus basket, daubed it with bitumen and pitch, and putting the child in it, placed it among the reeds on the river bank. His sister stationed herself at a distance to find out what would happen to him.

Pharaoh's daughter came down to the river to bathe, while her maids walked along the river bank. Noticing the basket among the reeds, she sent her handmaid to fetch it. On opening it, she looked, and lo, there was a baby boy, crying! She was moved with pity for him and said, "It is one of the Hebrews' children." Then his sister asked Pharaoh's daughter, "Shall I go and call one of the Hebrew women to nurse the child for you?" "Yes, do so," she answered. So the maiden went and called the child's own mother. Pharaoh's daughter said to her, "Take this child and nurse it for me, and I will repay you." The woman therefore took the child and nursed it. When the child grew, she brought him to Pharaoh's daughter, who adopted him as her son and called him Moses; for she said, "I drew him out of the water.

On one occasion, after Moses had grown up, when he visited his kinsmen and witnessed their forced labor, he saw an Egyptian striking a Hebrew, one of his own kinsmen. Looking about and seeing no one, he slew the Egyptian and hid him in the sand. The next day he went out again, and now two Hebrews were fighting! So he asked the culprit, "Why are you striking your fellow Hebrew?" But the culprit replied, "Who has appointed you ruler and judge over us? Are you thinking of killing me as you killed the Egyptian?" Then Moses became afraid and thought, "The affair must certainly be known."

Pharaoh, too, heard of the affair and sought to put Moses to death. But Moses fled from him and stayed in the land of Midian. The word of the Lord.

Responsorial Psalm

R. Turn to the Lord in your need, and you will live.

I am sunk in the abysmal swamp
  where there is no foothold;
I have reached the watery depths;
  the flood overwhelms me.

R. Turn to the Lord in your need, and you will live.

But I pray to you, O LORD,
  for the time of your favor, O God!
In your great kindness answer me
  with your constant help.

R. Turn to the Lord in your need, and you will live.

But I am afflicted and in pain;
  let your saving help, O God, protect me;
I will praise the name of God in song,
  and I will glorify him with thanksgiving.

R. Turn to the Lord in your need, and you will live.

"See, you lowly ones, and be glad;
  you who seek God, may your hearts revive!
For the LORD hears the poor,
  and his own who are in bonds he spurns not."

R. Turn to the Lord in your need, and you will live.

Alleluia Verse *and* **Gospel,** *p. 1170.*

Year II

FIRST READING

Unless your faith is firm, you shall not be firm!

A reading from the Book of the Prophet Isaiah

In the days of Ahaz, king of Judah, son of Jotham, son of Uzziah,
Rezin, king of Aram, and Pekah, king of Israel, son of Remaliah,

went up to attack Jerusalem, but they were not able to conquer it. When word came to the house of David that Aram was encamped in Ephraim, the heart of the king and the heart of the people trembled, as the trees of the forest tremble in the wind.

Then the LORD said to Isaiah: Go out to meet Ahaz, you and your son Shear-jashub, at the end of the conduit of the upper pool, on the highway of the fuller's field, and say to him: Take care you remain tranquil and do not fear; let not your courage fail before these two stumps of smoldering brands the blazing anger of Rezin and the Arameans, and of the son Remaliah, because of the mischief that Aram, Ephraim and the son of Remaliah, plots against you, saying, "Let us go up and tear Judah asunder, make it our own by force, and appoint the son of Tabeel king there."

Thus says the LORD:
> This shall not stand, it shall not be!
> Damascus is the capital of Aram,
>   and Rezin is the head of Damascus;
> Samaria is the capital of Ephraim,
>   and Remaliah's son the head of Samaria.
> But within sixty years and five,
>   Ephraim shall be crushed, no longer a nation.
> Unless your faith is firm
>   you shall not be firm!

The word of the Lord.

Responsorial Psalm

Ps 48:2 –3a, 3b–4, 5 – 6, 7 – 8

R. God upholds his city for ever.

Great is the LORD and wholly to be praised
   in the city of our God.

His holy mountain, fairest of heights,
  is the joy of all the earth.

R. God upholds his city for ever.

Mount Zion, "the recesses of the North,"
  is the city of the great King.
God is with her castles;
  renowned is he as a stronghold.

R. God upholds his city for ever.

For lo! the kings assemble,
  they come on together;
They also see, and at once are stunned,
  terrified, routed.

R. God upholds his city for ever.

Quaking seizes them there;
  anguish, like a woman's in labor,
As though a wind from the east
  were shattering ships of Tarshish.

R. God upholds his city for ever.

Alleluia, alleluia Ps 95:8
If today you hear his voice,
harden not your hearts.
Alleluia, alleluia

Years I and II

GOSPEL   Mt 11:20–24

*It will be more tolerable for Tyre and Sidon
and for the land of Sodom on the day of judgment than for you.*

A reading from the holy Gospel according to Matthew

Jesus began to reproach the towns where most of his mighty
deeds had been done, since they had not repented. "Woe to

you, Chorazin! Woe to you, Bethsaida! For if the mighty deeds done in your midst had been done in Tyre and Sidon, they would long ago have repented in sackcloth and ashes. But I tell you, it will be more tolerable for Tyre and Sidon on the day of judgment than for you. And as for you, Capernaum:

Will you be exalted to heaven?
You will go down to the netherworld.

For if the mighty deeds done in your midst had been done in Sodom, it would have remained until this day. But I tell you, it will be more tolerable for the land of Sodom on the day of judgment than for you."

The Gospel of the Lord.

Liturgy of the Eucharist, *p. 897;* **Prayer over the Gifts,** *p. 1159.*

Wednesday

Antiphons and Prayers, *p. 1158;* **Liturgy of the Word** *for Year I (odd years) follows; Year II (even years), p. 1173.*

TODAY'S LIVING WORD

Taken together, the two first readings are a study in contrasts. Both Moses in the passage from Exodus, and Assyria in the prophecy of Isaiah, are chosen to be God's instruments. God sends both against "an impious nation." But what a difference in their response! The overweening pride of Assyria as it boasts, "By my own power I have done it," sharply contrasts with the meekness of Moses who protests, "Who am I that I should go to Pharaoh and lead the children of Israel out of Egypt?" As Jesus proclaims in the Gospel, God is revealed to the meek like Moses, "to the childlike."

The conclusion of today's Gospel selection depicts Jesus as the Son who knows the Father and makes the Father known. In a sense, Jesus too is God's instrument, God's servant as well as God's Son, sent to reveal the Father who is "Lord of heaven and earth." Like Moses, Jesus too acknowledges with thankful praise, "All things have been handed over to me by my Father."

Year I

FIRST READING

Ex 3:1–6, 9–12

The angel of the LORD appeared to Moses in the burning bush.

A reading from the Book of Exodus

Moses was tending the flock of his father-in-law Jethro, the priest of Midian. Leading the flock across the desert, he came to Horeb, the mountain of God. There an angel of the LORD appeared to him in fire flaming out of a bush. As he looked on, he was surprised to see that the bush, though on fire, was not consumed. So Moses decided, "I must go over to look at this remarkable sight, and see why the bush is not burned."

When the LORD saw him coming over to look at it more closely, God called out to him from the bush, "Moses! Moses!" He answered, "Here I am." God said, "Come no nearer! Remove the sandals from your feet, for the place where you stand is holy ground. I am the God of your father," he continued, "the God of Abraham, the God of Isaac, the God of Jacob. The cry of the children of Israel has reached me, and I have truly noted that the Egyptians are oppressing them. Come, now! I will send you to Pharaoh to lead my people, the children of Israel, out of Egypt."

But Moses said to God, "Who am I that I should go to Pharaoh and lead the children of Israel out of Egypt?" He answered, "I will be with you; and this shall be your proof that it is I who have sent you: when you bring my people out of Egypt, you will worship God on this very mountain."

The word of the Lord.

Responsional Psalm

Ps 103:1b–2, 3–4, 6–7

R. The Lord is kind and merciful.

Bless the LORD, O my soul;
   and all my being, bless his holy name.
Bless the LORD, O my soul,
   and forget not all his benefits.

R. The Lord is kind and merciful.

He pardons all your iniquities,
   he heals all your ills.
He redeems your life from destruction,
   he crowns you with kindness and compassion.

R. The Lord is kind and merciful.

The LORD secures justice
   and the rights of all the oppressed.
He has made known his ways to Moses,
   and his deeds to the children of Israel.

R. The Lord is kind and merciful.

Alleluia Verse *and* **Gospel,** *p. 1175.*

Year II

FIRST READING   Is 10:5–7, 13b–16

   Will the axe boast against the one who hews with it?

A reading from the Book of the Prophet Isaiah

   Thus says the LORD:
Woe to Assyria! My rod in anger,
   my staff in wrath.

Against an impious nation I send him,
    and against a people under my wrath I order him
To seize plunder, carry off loot,
    and tread them down like the mud of the streets.
But this is not what he intends,
    nor does he have this in mind;
Rather, it is in his heart to destroy,
    to make an end of nations not a few.

    For he says:
"By my own power I have done it,
    and by my wisdom, for I am shrewd.
I have moved the boundaries of peoples,
    their treasures I have pillaged,
    and, like a giant, I have put down the enthroned.
My hand has seized like a nest
    the riches of nations;
As one takes eggs left alone,
    so I took in all the earth;
No one fluttered a wing,
    or opened a mouth, or chirped!"

Will the axe boast against him who hews with it?
    Will the saw exalt itself above him who wields it?
As if a rod could sway him who lifts it,
    or a staff him who is not wood!
Therefore the Lord, the LORD of hosts,
    will send among his fat ones leanness,
And instead of his glory there will be kindling
    like the kindling of fire.
The word of the Lord.

Responsorial Psalm

Ps 94:5–6, 7–8, 9–10, 14–15

R. The Lord will not abandon his people.

Your people, O LORD, they trample down,
  your inheritance they afflict.
Widow and stranger they slay,
  the fatherless they murder.

R. The Lord will not abandon his people.

And they say, "The LORD sees not;
  the God of Jacob perceives not."
Understand, you senseless ones among the people;
  and, you fools, when will you be wise?

R. The Lord will not abandon his people.

Shall he who shaped the ear not hear?
  or he who formed the eye not see?
Shall he who instructs nations not chastise,
  he who teaches men knowledge?

R. The Lord will not abandon his people.

For the LORD will not cast off his people,
  nor abandon his inheritance;
But judgment shall again be with justice,
  and all the upright of heart shall follow it.

R. The Lord will not abandon his people.

Alleluia, alleluia Mt 11:25
Blessed are you, Father, Lord of heaven and earth,
you have revealed to little ones the mysteries of the Kingdom.
Alleluia, alleluia

Years I and II

GOSPEL

Mt 11:25–27

*Although you have hidden these things from the wise and the
learned you have revealed them to the childlike.*

A reading from the holy Gospel according to Matthew

At that time Jesus exclaimed: "I give praise to you, Father, Lord of heaven and earth, for although you have hidden these things from the wise and the learned you have revealed them to the childlike. Yes, Father, such has been your gracious will. All things have been handed over to me by my Father. No one knows the Son except the Father, and no one knows the Father except the Son and anyone to whom the Son wishes to reveal him."

The Gospel of the Lord.

Liturgy of the Eucharist, *p. 897;* **Prayer over the Gifts,** *p. 1159.*

Thursday

Antiphons and Prayers, *p. 1158;* **Liturgy of the Word** *for Year I (odd years) follows; Year II (even years), p. 1179.*

TODAY'S LIVING WORD

Both the reading from Exodus and the selection from Matthew offer rest to the weary. Indeed, the invitation Jesus extends to his disciples is very much like the invitation God extends to the Israelites through Moses. It is a promise of rest—of release from oppression and fruitless toil. Jesus describes this rest as a "yoke" and this word, often used to refer to the law of Moses, links the two invitations. What is promised here is not cheap grace. The people of God will find rest in the land "flowing with milk and honey" by keeping God's commandments, just as the disciples of Jesus find refreshment by conforming to the likeness of Christ, who is "meek and humble of heart." As Matthew says, this is the lighter, more liberating yoke.

The passage from Isaiah is a psalm of lament. It is the prayer of the man or woman who looks back contritely on days of fruitless labor—"We conceived and writhed in pain, giving birth to wind" —and longs now, with confidence, for the salvation that only God can give.

Year I

FIRST READING   Ex 3:13 – 20

I AM WHO AM. I AM has sent me to you.

A reading from the Book of Exodus

Moses, hearing the voice of the LORD from the burning bush, said to him, "When I go to the children of Israel and say to them, 'The God of your fathers has sent me to you,' if they ask me, 'What is his name?' what am I to tell them?" God replied, "I am who am." Then he added, "This is what you shall tell the children of Israel: I AM sent me to you."

God spoke further to Moses, "Thus shall you say to the children of Israel: The LORD, the God of your fathers, the God of Abraham, the God of Isaac, the God of Jacob, has sent me to you.

"This is my name forever;
     this my title for all generations."

"Go and assemble the elders of Israel, and tell them: The LORD, the God of your fathers, the God of Abraham, Isaac, and Jacob, has appeared to me and said: I am concerned about you and about the way you are being treated in Egypt; so I have decided to lead you up out of the misery of Egypt into the land of the Canaanites, Hittites, Amorites, Perizzites, Hivites, and Jebusites, a land flowing with milk and honey.

"Thus they will heed your message. Then you and the elders of Israel shall go to the king of Egypt and say to him: The LORD, the God of the Hebrews, has sent us word. Permit us, then, to go a three-days' journey in the desert, that we may offer sacrifice to the LORD, our God.

"Yet I know that the king of Egypt will not allow you to go unless he is forced. I will stretch out my hand, therefore, and smite Egypt by doing all kinds of wondrous deeds there. After that he will send you away."

The word of the Lord.

Responsorial Psalm
Ps 105:1 and 5, 8–9, 24–25, 26–27

R. **The Lord remembers his covenant for ever.**

Give thanks to the LORD, invoke his name;
  make known among the nations his deeds.
Recall the wondrous deeds that he has wrought,
  his portents, and the judgments he has uttered.

R. **The Lord remembers his covenant for ever.**

He remembers forever his covenant
  which he made binding for a thousand generations—
Which he entered into with Abraham
  and by his oath to Isaac.

R. **The Lord remembers his covenant for ever.**

He greatly increased his people
  and made them stronger than their foes,
Whose hearts he changed, so that they hated his people,
  and dealt deceitfully with his servants.

R. **The Lord remembers his covenant for ever.**

He sent Moses his servant;
  Aaron, whom he had chosen.
They wrought his signs among them,
  and wonders in the land of Ham.

R. **The Lord remembers his covenant for ever.**

Or: R. **Alleluia.**

Alleluia Verse *and* **Gospel,** *p. 1180f.*

Year II

FIRST READING   Is 26:7–9, 12, 16–19

Awake and sing, you who lie in the dust.

A reading from the Book of the Prophet Isaiah

The way of the just is smooth;
  the path of the just you make level.
Yes, for your way and your judgments, O LORD,
  we look to you;
Your name and your title
  are the desire of our souls.
My soul yearns for you in the night,
  yes, my spirit within me keeps vigil for you;
When your judgment dawns upon the earth,
  the world's inhabitants learn justice.
O LORD, you mete out peace to us,
  for it is you who have accomplished all we have done.

O LORD, oppressed by your punishment,
  we cried out in anguish under your chastising.
As a woman about to give birth
  writhes and cries out in her pains,
  so were we in your presence, O LORD.
We conceived and writhed in pain,
  giving birth to wind;
Salvation we have not achieved for the earth,
  the inhabitants of the world cannot bring it forth.
But your dead shall live, their corpses shall rise;
  awake and sing, you who lie in the dust.

For your dew is a dew of light,
and the land of shades gives birth.

The word of the Lord.

Responsorial Psalm

Ps 102:13–14ab and 15, 16–18, 19–21

R. From heaven the Lord looks down on the earth.

You, O LORD, abide forever,
and your name through all generations.
You will arise and have mercy on Zion,
for it is time to pity her.
For her stones are dear to your servants,
and her dust moves them to pity.

R. From heaven the Lord looks down on the earth.

The nations shall revere your name, O LORD,
and all the kings of the earth your glory,
When the LORD has rebuilt Zion
and appeared in his glory;
When he has regarded the prayer of the destitute,
and not despised their prayer.

R. From heaven the Lord looks down on the earth.

Let this be written for the generation to come,
and let his future creatures praise the LORD:
"The LORD looked down from his holy height,
from heaven he beheld the earth,
To hear the groaning of the prisoners,
to release those doomed to die."

R. From heaven the Lord looks down on the earth.

> **Alleluia, alleluia**   Mt 11:28
> Come to me, all you who labor and are burdened,
> and I will give you rest, says the Lord.
> **Alleluia, alleluia**

Years I and II

GOSPEL   Mt 11:28–30

I am meek and humble of heart.

A reading from the holy Gospel according to Matthew

Jesus said: "Come to me, all you who labor and are burdened, and I will give you rest. Take my yoke upon you and learn from me, for I am meek and humble of heart; and you will find rest for yourselves. For my yoke is easy, and my burden light."

The Gospel of the Lord.

Liturgy of the Eucharist, *p. 897;* **Prayer over the Gifts,** *p. 1159.*

Friday

Antiphons and Prayers, *p. 1158;* **Liturgy of the Word** *for Year I (odd years) follows; Year II (even years), p. 1184.*

TODAY'S LIVING WORD

Today's two Old Testament readings depict the saving work of God. The selection from Exodus recounts "the Passover of the Lord," when God devastated the Egyptians and delivered the Israelites from their oppression. The story from Isaiah retells Hezekiah's recovery from a mortal illness by the grace of God who heard his prayer and saw his tears.

Today's Gospel attests to Jesus' liberal view of Sabbath law. By recalling the example of David and the exception made for the priests, Jesus seems to say that although the Pharisees sharply criticize his view, it has a precedent in Jewish Scripture. However marginal, he remains a Jew. But even more important, by referring to the text of Hosea—"I desire mercy, not sacrifice"—Jesus, as Lord of the Sabbath, seems to suggest that Sabbath is best kept by practicing compassion and so imitating the saving work of God.

FIRST READING   Ex 11:10—12:14

It shall be slaughtered during the evening twilight.
Seeing the blood, I will pass over you.

A reading from the Book of Exodus

Although Moses and Aaron performed various wonders in Pharaoh's presence, the LORD made Pharaoh obstinate, and he would not let the children of Israel leave his land.

The LORD said to Moses and Aaron in the land of Egypt, "This month shall stand at the head of your calendar; you shall reckon it the first month of the year. Tell the whole community of Israel: On the tenth of this month every one of your families must procure for itself a lamb, one apiece for each household. If a family is too small for a whole lamb, it shall join the nearest household in procuring one and shall share in the lamb in proportion to the number of persons who partake of it. The lamb must be a year-old male and without blemish. You may take it from either the sheep or the goats. You shall keep it until the fourteenth day of this month, and then, with the whole assembly of Israel present, it shall be slaughtered during the evening twilight. They shall take some of its blood and apply it to the two doorposts and the lintel of every house in which they partake of the lamb. That same night they shall eat its roasted flesh with unleavened bread and bitter herbs. It shall not be eaten raw or boiled, but roasted whole, with its head and shanks and inner organs. None of it must be kept beyond the next morning; whatever is left over in the morning shall be burned up.

"This is how you are to eat it: with your loins girt, sandals on your feet and your staff in hand, you shall eat like those who are in flight. It is the Passover of the LORD. For on this same night I will go through Egypt, striking down every first born of the land, both man and beast, and executing judgment on all the gods of Egypt—I, the LORD! But the blood will mark the houses where you are. Seeing the blood, I will pass over you; thus, when I strike the land of Egypt, no destructive blow will come upon you.

"This day shall be a memorial feast for you, which all your generations shall celebrate with pilgrimage to the LORD, as a perpetual institution."

The word of the Lord.

Responsorial Psalm

Ps 116:12–13, 15 and 16bc, 17–18

R.   **I will take the cup of salvation,
      and call on the name of the Lord.**

How shall I make a return to the LORD
   for all the good he has done for me?
The cup of salvation I will take up,
   and I will call upon the name of the LORD.

R.   **I will take the cup of salvation,
      and call on the name of the Lord.**

Precious in the eyes of the LORD
   is the death of his faithful ones.
I am your servant, the son of your handmaid;
   you have loosed my bonds.

R.   **I will take the cup of salvation,
      and call on the name of the Lord.**

To you will I offer sacrifice of thanksgiving,
   and I will call upon the name of the LORD.
My vows to the LORD I will pay
   in the presence of all his people.

R.   **I will take the cup of salvation,
      and call on the name of the Lord.**

Alleluia Verse *and* **Gospel,** *p. 1185.*

Year II

FIRST READING

Is 38:1–6, 21–22, 7–8

I have heard your prayer and seen your tears.

A reading from the Book of the Prophet Isaiah

When Hezekiah was mortally ill, the prophet Isaiah, son of Amoz, came and said to him: "Thus says the LORD: Put your house in order, for you are about to die; you shall not recover." Then Hezekiah turned his face to the wall and prayed to the LORD:

"O LORD, remember how faithfully and wholeheartedly I conducted myself in your presence, doing what was pleasing to you!" And Hezekiah wept bitterly.

Then the word of the LORD came to Isaiah: "Go, tell Hezekiah: Thus says the LORD, the God of your father David: I have heard your prayer and seen your tears. I will heal you: in three days you shall go up to the LORD's temple; I will add fifteen years to your life. I will rescue you and this city from the hand of the king of Assyria; I will be a shield to this city."

Isaiah then ordered a poultice of figs to be taken and applied to the boil, that he might recover. Then Hezekiah asked, "What is the sign that I shall go up to the temple of the LORD?"

Isaiah answered: "This will be the sign for you from the LORD that he will do what he has promised: See, I will make the shadow cast by the sun on the stairway to the terrace of Ahaz go back the ten steps it has advanced." So the sun came back the ten steps it had advanced.

The word of the Lord.

Responsorial Psalm

Is 38:10, 11, 12abcd, 16

R. You saved my life, O Lord; I shall not die.

Once I said,
 "In the noontime of life I must depart!
To the gates of the nether world I shall be consigned
 for the rest of my years."

R. You saved my life, O Lord; I shall not die.

I said, "I shall see the LORD no more
 in the land of the living.
No longer shall I behold my fellow men
 among those who dwell in the world."

R. You saved my life, O Lord; I shall not die.

My dwelling, like a shepherd's tent,
 is struck down and borne away from me;
You have folded up my life, like a weaver
 who severs the last thread.

R. You saved my life, O Lord; I shall not die.

Those live whom the LORD protects;
 yours is the life of my spirit.
You have given me health and life.

R. You saved my life, O Lord; I shall not die.

  Alleluia, alleluia   Jn 10:27
  My sheep hear my voice, says the Lord,
  I know them, and they follow me.
  Alleluia, alleluia

Years I and II

GOSPEL   Mt 12:1–8

The Son of Man is Lord of the sabbath.

A reading from the holy Gospel according to Matthew

Jesus was going through a field of grain on the sabbath. His disciples were hungry and began to pick the heads of grain and eat them. When the Pharisees saw this, they said to him,

"See, your disciples are doing what is unlawful to do on the sabbath." He said to the them, "Have you not read what David did when he and his companions were hungry, how he went into the house of God and ate the bread of offering, which neither he nor his companions but only the priests could lawfully eat? Or have you not read in the law that on the sabbath the priests serving in the temple violate the sabbath and are innocent? I say to you, something greater than the temple is here. If you knew what this meant, *I desire mercy, not sacrifice*, you would not have condemned these innocent men. For the Son of Man is Lord of the sabbath."

The Gospel of the Lord.

Liturgy of the Eucharist, *p. 897;* **Prayer over the Gifts,** *p. 1159.*

Saturday

Antiphons and Prayers, *p. 1158;* **Liturgy of the Word** *for Year I (odd years) follows; Year II (even years), p. 1188.*

TODAY'S LIVING WORD

The two first readings present two contrasting images—one of imminent triumph, the other of impending tragedy. The Exodus reading describes the triumphal march of the Israelites when the Lord "led them out of the land of Egypt." Micah's prophecy, however, proclaims punishment for these people who are now oppressing one another, after having escaped oppression in Egypt. The prophet knows that rampant injustice has already led to the downfall of Samaria; he announces the same tragic end for Judah. On that day, he warns, they will not "walk with head high, for it will be a time of evil."

In today's Gospel, Matthew uses the words of another prophet to shed light on the activity of Jesus. Scholars tell us that these words were originally addressed to the people of Judah in exile in Babylon, and the servant is a symbol of the chosen people. Isaiah promises that they will again triumph, not by war but by a way of life that "will proclaim justice to the Gentiles." Many years later, Matthew saw in the ministry of Jesus the fullest realization of that vocation of God's people.

Year I

FIRST READING

Ex 12:37–42

*This was a night of vigil for the Lord
as he led them out of the land of Egypt.*

A reading from the Book of Exodus

The children of Israel set out from Rameses for Succoth, about six hundred thousand men on foot, not counting the little ones. A crowd of mixed ancestry also went up with them, besides their livestock, very numerous flocks and herds. Since the dough they had brought out of Egypt was not leavened, they baked it into unleavened loaves. They had rushed out of Egypt and had no opportunity even to prepare food for the journey.

The time the children of Israel had stayed in Egypt was four hundred and thirty years. At the end of four hundred and thirty years, all the hosts of the Lord left the land of Egypt on this very date. This was a night of vigil for the Lord, as he led them out of the land of Egypt; so on this same night all the children of Israel must keep a vigil for the Lord throughout their generations.

The word of the Lord.

Responsorial Psalm

Ps 136:1 and 23–24, 10–12, 13–15

R. His mercy endures forever.

Give thanks to the Lord, for he is good,
  for his mercy endures forever;
Who remembered us in our abjection,

for his mercy endures forever;
And freed us from our foes,
   for his mercy endures forever.

   R. His mercy endures forever.

Who smote the Egyptians in their first-born,
   for his mercy endures forever;
And brought out Israel from their midst,
   for his mercy endures forever;
With a mighty hand and an outstretched arm,
   for his mercy endures forever.

   R. His mercy endures forever.

Who split the Red Sea in twain,
   for his mercy endures forever;
And led Israel through its midst,
   for his mercy endures forever;
But swept Pharaoh and his army into the Red Sea,
   for his mercy endures forever.

   R. His mercy endures forever.

   Or: **R. Alleluia.**

   Alleluia Verse *and* **Gospel,** *p. 1190.*

Year II

FIRST READING   Mi 2:1–5

   They covet fields, and seize them; houses, and they take them.

A reading from the Book of the Prophet Micah

Woe to those who plan iniquity,
      and work out evil on their couches;
In the morning light they accomplish it
      when it lies within their power.
They covet fields, and seize them;

houses, and they take them;
They cheat an owner of his house,
    a man of his inheritance.
        Therefore thus says the LORD:
Behold, I am planning against this race an evil
    from which you shall not withdraw your necks;
Nor shall you walk with head high,
    for it will be a time of evil.

On that day a satire shall be sung over you,
    and there shall be a plaintive chant:
"Our ruin is complete,
    our fields are portioned out among our captors,
The fields of my people are measured out,
    and no one can get them back!"
Thus you shall have no one
    to mark out boundaries by lot
    in the assembly of the LORD.
The word of the Lord.

Responsorial Psalm

Ps 10:1–2, 3–4, 7–8, 14

R. Do not forget the poor, O Lord!

Why, O LORD, do you stand aloof?
    Why hide in times of distress?
Proudly the wicked harass the afflicted,
    who are caught in the devices the wicked have contrived.

R. Do not forget the poor, O Lord!

For the wicked man glories in his greed,
    and the covetous blasphemes, sets the LORD at nought.
The wicked man boasts, "He will not avenge it";
    "There is no God," sums up his thoughts.

R. Do not forget the poor, O Lord!

His mouth is full of cursing, guile and deceit;
  under his tongue are mischief and iniquity.
He lurks in ambush near the villages;
  in hiding he murders the innocent;
  his eyes spy upon the unfortunate.

R. Do not forget the poor, O Lord!

You do see, for you behold misery and sorrow,
  taking them in your hands.
On you the unfortunate man depends;
  of the fatherless you are the helper.

R. Do not forget the poor, O Lord!

Alleluia, alleluia 2 Cor 5:19
God was reconciling the world to himself in Christ,
and entrusting to us the message of reconciliation.
Alleluia, alleluia

Years I and II

GOSPEL   Mt 12:14–21

He warned them not to make him known
to fulfill what had been spoken.

A reading from the holy Gospel according to Matthew

The Pharisees went out and took counsel against Jesus to put
him to death.

When Jesus realized this, he withdrew from that place. Many
people followed him, and he cured them all, but he warned
them not to make him known. This was to fulfill what had
been spoken through Isaiah the prophet:

Behold, my servant whom I have chosen,
  my beloved in whom I delight;
I shall place my Spirit upon him,

and he will proclaim justice to the Gentiles.
He will not contend or cry out,
  nor will anyone hear his voice in the streets.
A bruised reed he will not break,
  a smoldering wick he will not quench,
until he brings justice to victory.
  And in his name the Gentiles will hope.

The Gospel of the Lord.

Liturgy of the Eucharist, *p. 897;* **Prayer over the Gifts,** *p. 1159.*

SIXTEENTH WEEK IN ORDINARY TIME

The **Antiphons and Prayers** *may be the following, or may be chosen from any of the other 33 weeks in Ordinary Time (refer to Liturgical Calendar, pp. 26–41).*

The **Liturgy of the Word** *varies: for Monday, see p. 1193; Tuesday, p. 1198; Wednesday, p. 1203; Thursday, p. 1208; Friday, p. 1214; Saturday, p. 1219.*

Entrance Antiphon

God himself is my help. The Lord upholds my life. I will offer you a willing sacrifice; I will praise your name, O Lord, for its goodness.
(Ps 54:6, 8)

Opening Prayer

Let us pray
  [to be kept faithful in the service of God]
    Pause for silent prayer.

Lord,
be merciful to your people.
Fill us with your gifts
and make us always eager to serve you
in faith, hope, and love.

Grant this through our Lord Jesus Christ, your Son,
who lives and reigns with you and the Holy Spirit,
one God, for ever and ever.

Alternative Opening Prayer

Let us pray
  [that God will continue to bless us
  with his compassion and love]

  Pause for silent prayer.

Father,
let the gift of your life
continue to grow in us,
drawing us from death to faith, hope, and love.
Keep us alive in Christ Jesus.
Keep us watchful in prayer
and true to his teaching
till your glory is revealed in us.

Grant this through Christ our Lord.

Prayer over the Gifts

Pray, brethren...
Lord,
bring us closer to salvation
through these gifts which we bring in your honor.
Accept the perfect sacrifice you have given us,
bless it as you blessed the gifts of Abel.

We ask this through Christ our Lord.

Preface of Weekdays in Ordinary Time I–VI, *pp. 948–950.*

Communion Antiphon

  The Lord keeps in our minds the wonderful things he has done.
He is compassion and love; he always provides for his faithful.

(Ps 111:4–5)

Or:

I stand at the door and knock, says the Lord. If anyone hears my voice and opens the door, I will come in and sit down to supper with him, and he with me. (Rv 3:20)

Prayer after Communion

Let us pray.

Pause for silent prayer, if this has not preceded.

Merciful Father,
may these mysteries
give us new purpose
and bring us to a new life in you.

We ask this in the name of Jesus the Lord.

Monday

Antiphons and Prayers, *p. 1191;* **Liturgy of the Word** *for Year I (odd years) follows; Year II (even years), p. 1196.*

TODAY'S LIVING WORD

Today's readings deal with the identity of God as Lord. God declares that in the crossing of the sea, "the Egyptians shall know that I am the Lord." Not only the Egyptians, but the Israelites too will find in this event an authenticating sign that indeed the Lord God is fighting for them. The passage from Micah indicts the people for their failure to remember this sign.

In the Gospel Matthew depicts scribes and Pharisees asking for a similar authenticating sign from Jesus. But Jesus says that God will not give them a sign except the sign of Jonah, which for Matthew has a double meaning. On the one hand, it points to the death and resurrection of Jesus, the confirming sign par excellence that he is Lord. On the other hand, it likens Jesus to Jonah, just as the concluding verses liken him to Solomon. But the comparison is ironic: people respond positively to the preaching of Jonah and the wisdom of Solomon, but negatively to the ministry of Jesus who is greater than either Solomon or Jonah.

Year I

FIRST READING   Ex 14:5–18

*They will know that I am the Lord
when I receive glory through Pharaoh.*

A reading from the Book of Exodus

When it was reported to the king of Egypt that the people had fled, Pharaoh and his servants changed their minds about them. They exclaimed, "What have we done! Why, we have released Israel from our service!" So Pharaoh made his chariots ready and mustered his soldiers—six hundred first-class chariots and all the other chariots of Egypt, with warriors on them all. So obstinate had the Lord made Pharaoh that he pursued the children of Israel even while they were marching away in triumph. The Egyptians, then, pursued them; Pharaoh's whole army, his horses, chariots and charioteers, caught up with them as they lay encamped by the sea, at Pi-hahiroth, in front of Baal-zephon.

Pharaoh was already near when the children of Israel looked up and saw that the Egyptians were on the march in pursuit of them. In great fright they cried out to the Lord. And they complained to Moses, "Were there no burial places in Egypt that you had to bring us out here to die in the desert? Why did you do this to us? Why did you bring us out of Egypt? Did we not tell you this in Egypt, when we said, 'Leave us alone. Let us serve the Egyptians'? Far better for us to be the slaves of the Egyptians than to die in the desert." But Moses answered the people, "Fear not! Stand your ground, and you will see the victory the Lord will win for you today. These Egyptians whom you see today you will never see again. The LORD himself will fight for you; you have only to keep still."

Then the LORD said to Moses, "Why are you crying out to me? Tell the children of Israel to go forward. And you, lift up your staff and, with hand outstretched over the sea, split the sea in two, that the children of Israel may pass through it on dry land. But I will make the Egyptians so obstinate that they will go in after them. Then I will receive glory through Pharaoh and all his army, his chariots and charioteers. The Egyptians shall know that I am the LORD, when I receive glory through Pharaoh and his chariots and charioteers."

The word of the Lord.

Responsorial Psalm

Ex 15:1bc–2, 3–4, 5–6

R. Let us sing to the Lord; he has covered himself in glory.

I will sing to the LORD, for he is gloriously triumphant;
  horse and chariot he has cast into the sea.
My strength and my courage is the LORD,
  and he has been my savior.
He is my God, I praise him;
  the God of my father, I extol him.

R. Let us sing to the Lord; he has covered himself in glory.

The LORD is a warrior,
  LORD is his name!
Pharaoh's chariots and army he hurled into the sea;
  the elite of his officers were submerged in the Red Sea.

R. Let us sing to the Lord; he has covered himself in glory.

The flood waters covered them,
  they sank into the depths like a stone.
Your right hand, O LORD, magnificent in power,
  your right hand, O LORD, has shattered the enemy.

R. Let us sing to the Lord; he has covered himself in glory.

Alleluia Verse *and* **Gospel,** *p. 1197f.*

Year II

FIRST READING

Mi 6:1–4, 6–8

You have been told, O man, what the LORD requires of you.

A reading from the Book of the Prophet Micah

Hear what the LORD says:
Arise, present your plea before the mountains,
    and let the hills hear your voice!
Hear, O mountains, the plea of the LORD,
    pay attention, O foundations of the earth!
For the LORD has a plea against his people,
    and he enters into trial with Israel.

O my people, what have I done to you,
    or how have I wearied you? Answer me!
For I brought you up from the land of Egypt,
    from the place of slavery I released you;
and I sent before you Moses,
    Aaron, and Miriam.

With what shall I come before the LORD,
    and bow before God most high?
Shall I come before him with burnt offerings,
    with calves a year old?
Will the LORD be pleased with thousands of rams,
    with myriad streams of oil?
Shall I give my first-born for my crime,
    the fruit of my body for the sin of my soul?

You have been told, O man, what is good,
    and what the LORD requires of you:
Only to do the right and to love goodness,
    and to walk humbly with your God.

The word of the Lord.

Responsional Psalm   Ps 50:5–6, 8–9, 16bc–17, 21 and 23

R. To the upright I will show the saving power of God.

"Gather my faithful ones before me,
  those who have made a covenant with me by sacrifice."
And the heavens proclaim his justice;
  for God himself is the judge.

R. To the upright I will show the saving power of God.

"Not for your sacrifices do I rebuke you,
  for your burnt offerings are before me always.
I take from your house no bullock,
  no goats out of your fold."

R. To the upright I will show the saving power of God.

"Why do you recite my statutes,
  and profess my covenant with your mouth,
Though you hate discipline
  and cast my words behind you?"

R. To the upright I will show the saving power of God.

"When you do these things, shall I be deaf to it?
  Or do you think that I am like yourself?
  I will correct you by drawing them up before your eyes.
He that offers praise as a sacrifice glorifies me;
  and to him that goes the right way I will show the salvation of God."

R. To the upright I will show the saving power of God.

   Alleluia, alleluia   Ps 95:8
   If today you hear his voice,
   harden not your hearts.
   Alleluia, alleluia

Years I and II

GOSPEL   Mt 12:38–42

At the judgment the queen of the south
will arise with this generation and condemn it.

A reading from the holy Gospel according to Matthew

Some of the scribes and Pharisees said to Jesus, "Teacher, we wish to see a sign from you." He said to them in reply, "An evil and unfaithful generation seeks a sign, but no sign will be given it except the sign of Jonah the prophet. Just as Jonah was in the belly of the whale three days and three nights, so will the Son of Man be in the heart of the earth three days and three nights. At the judgment, the men of Nineveh will arise with this generation and condemn it, because they repented at the preaching of Jonah; and there is something greater than Jonah here. At the judgment the queen of the south will arise with this generation and condemn it, because she came from the ends of the earth to hear the wisdom of Solomon; and there is something greater than Solomon here."

The Gospel of the Lord.

Liturgy of the Eucharist, *p. 897;* **Prayer over the Gifts,** *p. 1192.*

Tuesday

Antiphons and Prayers, *p. 1191;* **Liturgy of the Word** *for Year I (odd years) follows; Year II (even years), p. 1201.*

TODAY'S LIVING WORD

If the theme of yesterday's Gospel was the identity of Jesus, authenticated by the sign of Jonah, the theme of today's reading is the identity of Jesus' family. The two first readings provide the link. The passage from Exodus recounts the awesome demonstration of God's power at the crossing of the sea, the authenticating sign that the God of Israel is Lord of all. The prayer of the prophet Micah invokes this memory, asking God to act powerfully once again: "As in the days when you came from the land of Egypt, show us wonderful signs."

In the Gospel, however, Jesus asks us as his followers for a sign. Pointing to his disciples—then and now—he says that doing the will of his heavenly Father is the authenticating sign of membership in his family.

Year I

FIRST READING
Ex 14:21—15:1

The children of Israel marched into the midst of the sea on dry land.

A reading from the Book of Exodus

Moses stretched out his hand over the sea, and the LORD swept the sea with a strong east wind throughout the night and so turned it into dry land. When the water was thus divided, the children of Israel marched into the midst of the sea on dry land, with the water like a wall to their right and to their left.

The Egyptians followed in pursuit; all Pharaoh's horses and chariots and charioteers went after them right into the midst of the sea. In the night watch just before dawn the LORD cast through the column of the fiery cloud upon the Egyptian force a glance that threw it into a panic; and he so clogged their chariot wheels that they could hardly drive. With that the Egyptians sounded the retreat before Israel, because the LORD was fighting for them against the Egyptians.

Then the LORD told Moses, "Stretch out your hand over the sea, that the water may flow back upon the Egyptians, upon their chariots and their charioteers." So Moses stretched out his hand over the sea, and at dawn the sea flowed back to its normal depth. The Egyptians were fleeing head on toward the sea, when the LORD hurled them into its midst. As the water flowed back, it covered the chariots and the charioteers of Pharaoh's whole army that had followed the children of Israel into the sea. Not a single one of them escaped. But the children of Israel had marched on dry land through the midst of the sea, with the water like a wall to their right and to their left. Thus the LORD saved Israel on that day from the power of the Egyptians. When Israel saw the Egyptians lying dead on the seashore and beheld the great power that the LORD had shown against the Egyptians, they feared the LORD and believed in him and in his servant Moses.

Then Moses and the children of Israel sang this song to the LORD:

I will sing to the LORD, for he is gloriously triumphant;
horse and chariot he has cast into the sea.

The word of the Lord.

Responsorial Psalm   Ex 15:8–9, 10 and 12, 17

R. Let us sing to the Lord; he has covered himself in glory.

At the breath of your anger the waters piled up,
  the flowing waters stood like a mound,
  the flood waters congealed in the midst of the sea.
The enemy boasted, "I will pursue and overtake them;
  I will divide the spoils and have my fill of them;
  I will draw my sword; my hand shall despoil them!"

R. Let us sing to the Lord; he has covered himself in glory.

When your wind blew, the sea covered them;
  like lead they sank in the mighty waters.

When you stretched out your right hand,
the earth swallowed them!

R. Let us sing to the Lord; he has covered himself in glory.

And you brought them in and planted them on the mountain of
your inheritance—
the place where you made your seat, O Lord,
the sanctuary, O Lord, which your hands established.

R. Let us sing to the Lord; he has covered himself in glory.

Alleluia Verse *and* **Gospel,** *p. 1202f.*

Year II

FIRST READING   Mi 7:14–15, 18–20

He will cast into the depths of the sea all our sins.

A reading from the Book of the Prophet Micah

Shepherd your people with your staff,
the flock of your inheritance,
That dwells apart in a woodland,
in the midst of Carmel.
Let them feed in Bashan and Gilead,
as in the days of old;
As in the days when you came from the land of Egypt,
show us wonderful signs.

Who is there like you, the God who removes guilt
and pardons sin for the remnant of his inheritance;
Who does not persist in anger forever,
but delights rather in clemency,
And will again have compassion on us,
treading underfoot our guilt?

You will cast into the depths of the sea
all our sins;
You will show faithfulness to Jacob,
and grace to Abraham,
As you have sworn to our fathers
from days of old.

The word of the Lord.

Responsorial Psalm

Ps 85:2–4, 5–6, 7–8

R. Lord, show us your mercy and love.

You have favored, O LORD, your land;
you have brought back the captives of Jacob.
You have forgiven the guilt of your people;
you have covered all their sins.
You have withdrawn all your wrath;
you have revoked your burning anger.

R. Lord, show us your mercy and love.

Restore us, O God our savior,
and abandon your displeasure against us.
Will you be ever angry with us,
prolonging your anger to all generations?

R. Lord, show us your mercy and love.

Will you not instead give us life;
and shall not your people rejoice in you?
Show us, O LORD, your kindness,
and grant us your salvation.

R. Lord, show us your mercy and love.

Alleluia, alleluia Jn 14:23
Whoever loves me will keep my word,
and my Father will love him
and we will come to him.
Alleluia, alleluia

Years I and II

GOSPEL   Mt 12:46–50

Stretching out his hands toward his disciples, he said,
"Here are my mother and my brothers."

A reading from the holy Gospel according to Matthew

While Jesus was speaking to the crowds, his mother and his brothers appeared outside, wishing to speak with him. Someone told him, "Your mother and your brothers are standing outside, asking to speak with you." But he said in reply to the one who told him, "Who is my mother? Who are my brothers?" And stretching out his hand toward his disciples, he said, "Here are my mother and my brothers. For whoever does the will of my heavenly Father is my brother, and sister, and mother." The Gospel of the Lord.

Liturgy of the Eucharist, *p. 897;* **Prayer over the Gifts,** *p. 1192.*

Wednesday

Antiphons and Prayers, *p. 1191;* **Liturgy of the Word** *for Year I (odd years) follows; Year II (even years), p. 1206.*

TODAY'S LIVING WORD

Today's Gospel parable primarily concerns the seed, not the sower. The action of the story, which would have been so familiar to Galilean farmers, traces the "mission" of the seed. It meets with resistance and reversal of all kinds, yet still yields a rich harvest. Since the seed in the story is the word of God, the parable is a profession of faith in the power of God's word to overcome every obstacle.

The parable sheds light on the two first readings. Jeremiah is called and commissioned to speak the word of God, "to root up and to tear down...to build and to plant." In his career as a prophet, he will come to know all too well the resistance and reversals that so often greet the seed of God's word. The grumbling of the Israelites in the reading from Exodus reminds us of the unpromising condition of the soil in the parable—the human condition, which only the grace of God can make ready to receive God's word.

Year I

FIRST READING Ex 16:1– 5, 9 –15
I will rain down bread from heaven for you.

A reading from the Book of Exodus

The children of Israel set out from Elim, and came into the desert of Sin, which is between Elim and Sinai, on the fifteenth day of the second month after their departure from the land of Egypt. Here in the desert the whole assembly of the children of Israel grumbled against Moses and Aaron. The children of Israel said to them, "Would that we had died at the Lord's hand in the land of Egypt, as we sat by our fleshpots and ate our fill of bread! But you had to lead us into this desert to make the whole community die of famine!"

Then the Lord said to Moses, "I will now rain down bread from heaven for you. Each day the people are to go out and gather their daily portion; thus will I test them, to see whether they follow my instructions or not. On the sixth day, however, when they prepare what they bring in, let it be twice as much as they gather on the other days."

Then Moses said to Aaron, "Tell the whole congregation of the children of Israel: Present yourselves before the Lord, for he has heard your grumbling." When Aaron announced this to the whole assembly of the children of Israel, they turned toward the desert, and lo, the glory of the LORD appeared in the cloud! The LORD spoke to Moses and said, "I have heard the grumbling of the children of Israel. Tell them: In the evening twilight you shall eat flesh, and in the morning you shall have your fill of bread, so that you may know that I, the LORD, am your God."

In the evening quail came up and covered the camp. In the morning a dew lay all about the camp, and when the dew evaporated, there on the surface of the desert were fine flakes like hoarfrost on the ground. On seeing it, the children of Israel asked one another, "What is this?" for they did not know what it was. But Moses told them, "This is the bread which the LORD has given you to eat."

The word of the Lord.

Responsorial Psalm
Ps 78:18–19, 23–24, 25–26, 27–28

R. The Lord gave them bread from heaven.

They tempted God in their hearts
  by demanding the food they craved.
Yes, they spoke against God, saying,
  "Can God spread a table in the desert?"

R. The Lord gave them bread from heaven.

Yet he commanded the skies above
  and the doors of heaven he opened;
He rained manna upon them for food
  and gave them heavenly bread.

R. The Lord gave them bread from heaven.

Man ate the bread of angels,
  food he sent them in abundance.
He stirred up the east wind in the heavens,
  and by his power brought on the south wind.

R. The Lord gave them bread from heaven.

And he rained meat upon them like dust,
  and, like the sand of the sea, winged fowl,
Which fell in the midst of their camp
  round about their tents.

R. The Lord gave them bread from heaven.

Alleluia Verse *and* Gospel, *p. 1207f.*

Year II

FIRST READING   Jer 1:1, 4–10

A prophet to the nations I appointed you.

A reading from the beginning of the Book of the Prophet Jeremiah

The words of Jeremiah, son of Hilkiah, of a priestly family in
Anathoth, in the land of Benjamin.

The word of the LORD came to me thus:

  Before I formed you in the womb I knew you,
    before you were born I dedicated you,
    a prophet to the nations I appointed you.
  "Ah, Lord GOD!" I said,
    "I know not how to speak; I am too young."

  But the LORD answered me,
  Say not, "I am too young."
    To whomever I send you, you shall go;
    whatever I command you, you shall speak.
  Have no fear before them,
    because I am with you to deliver you, says the LORD.

Then the LORD extended his hand and touched my mouth,
saying,

  See, I place my words in your mouth!
    This day I set you

over nations and over kingdoms,
To root up and to tear down,
to destroy and to demolish,
to build and to plant.

The word of the Lord.

Responsorial Psalm

Ps 71:1–2, 3–4a, 5–6ab, 15 and 17

R. I will sing of your salvation.

In you, O LORD, I take refuge;
let me never be put to shame.
In your justice rescue me, and deliver me;
incline your ear to me, and save me.

R. I will sing of your salvation.

Be my rock of refuge,
a stronghold to give me safety,
for you are my rock and my fortress.
O my God, rescue me from the hand of the wicked.

R. I will sing of your salvation.

For you are my hope, O Lord;
my trust, O God, from my youth.
On you I depend from birth;
from my mother's womb you are my strength.

R. I will sing of your salvation.

My mouth shall declare your justice,
day by day your salvation.
O God, you have taught me from my youth,
and till the present I proclaim your wondrous deeds.

R. I will sing of your salvation.

Alleluia, alleluia
The seed is the word of God, Christ is the sower;
all who come to him will live for ever.
Alleluia, alleluia

GOSPEL   Mt 13:1–9

The seed produced grain a hundredfold.

A reading from the holy Gospel according to Matthew

On that day, Jesus went out of the house and sat down by the sea. Such large crowds gathered around him that he got into a boat and sat down, and the whole crowd stood along the shore. And he spoke to them at length in parables, saying: "A sower went out to sow. And as he sowed, some seed fell on the path, and birds came and ate it up. Some fell on rocky ground, where it had little soil. It sprang up at once because the soil was not deep, and when the sun rose it was scorched, and it withered for lack of roots. Some seed fell among thorns, and the thorns grew up and choked it. But some seed fell on rich soil, and produced fruit, a hundred or sixty or thirtyfold. Whoever has ears ought to hear."

The Gospel of the Lord.

Liturgy of the Eucharist, *p. 897;* **Prayer over the Gifts,** *p. 1192.*

Thursday

Antiphons and Prayers, *p. 1191;* **Liturgy of the Word** *for Year I (odd years) follows; Year II (even years), p. 1211.*

TODAY'S LIVING WORD

Their covenant with God on Sinai, described in the account from Exodus, fashioned Israel into the people of God. Thus they became, in the words of Jeremiah, "the first fruits of [God's] harvest." Throughout their subsequent history, the people often debated the question: what constitutes membership in the community of God's people? This is the context of Matthew's Gospel.

The Christians for whom Matthew wrote were convinced that belonging to the people of God meant believing in Jesus as Messiah and Lord. They agonized over the question of why so many of their fellow Jews rejected the Gospel. In today's reading Jesus tells his disciples that God has given them a privileged insight into the mysteries of God's reign. So they are more blessed than the prophets and saints before them. As for those who do not hear or understand, their refusal is part of God's plan too. For us, living in other times, today's Gospel may invite us to recognize and to reflect upon the inscrutable mystery of God's choice of Israel and of us.

Year I

FIRST READING
Ex 19:1–2, 9–11, 16–20b

The LORD descended on Mount Sinai before the eyes of all the people.

A reading from the Book of Exodus

In the third month after their departure from the land of Egypt, on its first day, the children of Israel came to the desert of Sinai. After the journey from Rephidim to the desert of Sinai, they pitched camp.

While Israel was encamped here in front of the mountain, the LORD told Moses, "I am coming to you in a dense cloud, so that when the people hear me speaking with you, they may always have faith in you also." When Moses, then, had reported to the LORD the response of the people, the LORD added, "Go to the people and have them sanctify themselves today and tomorrow. Make them wash their garments and be ready for the third day; for on the third day the LORD will come down on Mount Sinai before the eyes of all the people."

On the morning of the third day there were peals of thunder and lightning, and a heavy cloud over the mountain, and a very loud trumpet blast, so that all the people in the camp trembled. But Moses led the people out of the camp to meet God, and they stationed themselves at the foot of the mountain. Mount Sinai was all wrapped in smoke, for the LORD came down upon it in fire. The smoke rose from it as though from a furnace, and the whole mountain trembled violently. The trumpet blast grew louder and louder, while Moses was speaking and God answering him with thunder.

When the LORD came down to the top of Mount Sinai, he summoned Moses to the top of the mountain.

The word of the Lord.

Responsorial Psalm   Dn 3:52, 53, 54, 55, 56

R. Glory and praise for ever!

"Blessed are you, O Lord, the God of our fathers,
    praiseworthy and exalted above all forever;
And blessed is your holy and glorious name,
    praiseworthy and exalted above all for all ages."

R. Glory and praise for ever!

"Blessed are you in the temple of your holy glory,
    praiseworthy and glorious above all forever."

R. Glory and praise for ever!

"Blessed are you on the throne of your Kingdom,
    praiseworthy and exalted above all forever."

R. Glory and praise for ever!

"Blessed are you who look into the depths
    from your throne upon the cherubim,
    praiseworthy and exalted above all forever."

R. Glory and praise for ever!

"Blessed are you in the firmament of heaven,
  praiseworthy and glorious forever."

R. Glory and praise for ever!

Alleluia Verse *and* Gospel, *p. 1212f.*

Year II

FIRST READING

Jer 2:1–3, 7–8, 12–13

They have forsaken me, the source of living waters;
they have dug themselves broken cisterns.

A reading from the Book of the Prophet Jeremiah

This word of the LORD came to me: Go, cry out this message
for Jerusalem to hear!

I remember the devotion of your youth,
  how you loved me as a bride,
Following me in the desert,
  in a land unsown.
Sacred to the LORD was Israel,
  the first fruits of his harvest;
Should any presume to partake of them,
  evil would befall them, says the LORD.

When I brought you into the garden land
  to eat its goodly fruits,
You entered and defiled my land,
  you made my heritage loathsome.
The priests asked not,
  "Where is the LORD?"
Those who dealt with the law knew me not:

the shepherds rebelled against me.
The prophets prophesied by Baal,
    and went after useless idols.

Be amazed at this, O heavens,
    and shudder with sheer horror, says the LORD.
Two evils have my people done:
    they have forsaken me, the source of living waters;
They have dug themselves cisterns,
    broken cisterns, that hold no water.

The word of the Lord.

Responsorial Psalm

Ps 36:6 – 7ab, 8 – 9, 10 –11

R. With you is the fountain of life, O Lord.

O LORD, your mercy reaches to heaven;
    your faithfulness, to the clouds.
Your justice is like the mountains of God;
    your judgments, like the mighty deep.

R. With you is the fountain of life, O Lord.

How precious is your mercy, O God!
    The children of men take refuge in the shadow of your wings.
They have their fill of the prime gifts of your house;
    from your delightful stream you give them to drink.

R. With you is the fountain of life, O Lord.

For with you is the fountain of life,
    and in your light we see light.
Keep up your mercy toward your friends,
    your just defense of the upright of heart.

R. With you is the fountain of life, O Lord.

Alleluia, alleluia   See Mt 11:25
Blessed are you, Father, Lord of heaven and earth;
    you have revealed to little ones the mysteries of the Kingdom.
Alleluia, alleluia

Years I and II

GOSPEL   Mt 13:10–17

Because knowledge of the mysteries
of the Kingdom of heaven has been granted to you,
but to them it has not been granted.

A reading from the holy Gospel according to Matthew

The disciples approached Jesus and said, "Why do you speak to the crowd in parables?" He said to them in reply, "Because knowledge of the mysteries of the Kingdom of heaven has been granted to you, but to them it has not been granted. To anyone who has, more will be given and he will grow rich; from anyone who has not, even what he has will be taken away. This is why I speak to them in parables, because *they look but do not see and hear but do not listen or understand.* Isaiah's prophecy is fulfilled in them, which says:

> *You shall indeed hear but not understand,*
> *   you shall indeed look but never see.*
> *Gross is the heart of this people,*
> *   they will hardly hear with their ears,*
> *   they have closed their eyes,*
> *   lest they see with their eyes*
> *   and hear with their ears*
> *and understand with their hearts and be converted*
> *   and I heal them.*

"But blessed are your eyes, because they see, and your ears, because they hear. Amen, I say to you, many prophets and righteous people longed to see what you see but did not see it, and to hear what you hear but did not hear it."

The Gospel of the Lord.

Liturgy of the Eucharist, *p. 897;* **Prayer over the Gifts,** *p. 1192.*

Friday

Antiphons and Prayers, *p. 1191;* **Liturgy of the Word** *for Year I (odd years) follows; Year II (even years), p. 1216.*

TODAY'S LIVING WORD

Most scholars agree that the interpretation of the parable of the sower found in today's Gospel is the work of the early Church. Note how the focus has shifted from the seed to the soil. The passage warns us, as it did the first Christians, against all those things that may threaten the life of faith.

All three of today's readings are also examples of how the teaching of the Scriptures developed. The passage from Exodus is the earliest version of the decalogue, the Ten Commandments. These words of God not only undergird the whole law of Israel, but they also undergo development as they are handed down to a generation in changed circumstances (cf. Dt 5:6–21). The text from Jeremiah announces a development in which the Jerusalem temple will replace the Ark of the Covenant as the Lord's throne. The Gospel shows how even the parables of Jesus were developed in new directions to speak to the needs of the early Church.

Year I

FIRST READING   Ex 20:1–17

The law was given through Moses.

A reading from the Book of Exodus

In those days: God delivered all these commandments:

"I, the LORD, am your God, who brought you out of the land of Egypt, that place of slavery. You shall not have other gods besides me. You shall not carve idols for yourselves in the shape of anything in the sky above or on the earth below or in the waters beneath the earth; you shall not bow down before them or worship them. For I, the LORD, your God, am a jealous God, inflicting punishment for their fathers' wickedness on the children of those who hate me, down to the third and fourth generation; but bestowing mercy down to the thousandth generation on the children of those who love me and keep my commandments.

"You shall not take the name of the LORD, your God, in vain. For the LORD will not leave unpunished him who takes his name in vain.

"Remember to keep holy the sabbath day. Six days you may labor and do all your work, but the seventh day is the sabbath of the LORD, your God. No work may be done then either by you, or your son or daughter, or your male or female slave, or your beast, or by the alien who lives with you. In six days the LORD made the heavens and the earth, the sea and all that is in them; but on the seventh day he rested. That is why the LORD has blessed the sabbath day and made it holy.

"Honor your father and your mother, that you may have a long life in the land which the LORD, your God, is giving you.

"You shall not kill.

"You shall not commit adultery.

"You shall not steal.

"You shall not bear false witness against your neighbor.

"You shall not covet your neighbor's house. You shall not covet your neighbor's wife, nor his male or female slave, nor his ox or ass, nor anything else that belongs to him."

The word of the Lord.

Responsorial Psalm

Ps 19:8, 9, 10, 11

R. Lord, you have the words of everlasting life.

The law of the LORD is perfect,
  refreshing the soul;
The decree of the LORD is trustworthy,
  giving wisdom to the simple.

R. Lord, you have the words of everlasting life.

The precepts of the LORD are right,
  rejoicing the heart;
The command of the LORD is clear,
  enlightening the eye.

R. Lord, you have the words of everlasting life.

The fear of the LORD is pure,
  enduring forever;
The ordinances of the LORD are true,
  all of them just.

R. Lord, you have the words of everlasting life.

They are more precious than gold,
  than a heap of purest gold;
Sweeter also than syrup
  or honey from the comb.

R. Lord, you have the words of everlasting life.

Alleluia Verse *and* **Gospel,** *p. 1218.*

Year II

FIRST READING

Jer 3:14–17

*I will appoint over you shepherds after my own heart;
all nations will be gathered together at Jerusalem.*

A reading from the Book of the Prophet Jeremiah

Return, rebellious children, says the LORD,
  for I am your Master;

I will take you, one from a city, two from a clan,
    and bring you to Zion.
I will appoint over you shepherds after my own heart,
    who will shepherd you wisely and prudently.
When you multiply and become fruitful in the land,
    says the LORD,
They will in those days no longer say,
    "The ark of the covenant of the LORD!"
They will no longer think of it, or remember it,
    or miss it, or make another.

At that time they will call Jerusalem the LORD's throne; there
all nations will be gathered together to honor the name of the
LORD at Jerusalem, and they will walk no longer in their
hardhearted wickedness.

The word of the Lord.

Responsorial Psalm

Jer 31:10, 11–12abcd, 13

R. The Lord will guard us as a shepherd guards his flock.

Hear the word of the LORD, O nations,
    proclaim it on distant isles, and say:
He who scattered Israel, now gathers them together,
    he guards them as a shepherd his flock.

R. The Lord will guard us as a shepherd guards his flock.

The LORD shall ransom Jacob,
    he shall redeem him from the hand of his conqueror.
Shouting, they shall mount the heights of Zion,
    they shall come streaming to the LORD's blessings:
The grain, the wine, and the oil,
    the sheep and the oxen.

R. The Lord will guard us as a shepherd guards his flock.

Then the virgins shall make merry and dance,
  and young men and old as well.
I will turn their mourning into joy,
  I will console and gladden them after their sorrows.

R. The Lord will guard us as a shepherd guards his flock.

Alleluia, alleluia   See Lk 8:15
Blessed are they who have kept the word with a generous heart
and yield a harvest through perseverance.
Alleluia, alleluia

Years I and II

GOSPEL   Mt 13:18–23
The one who hears the word and understands it will bear much fruit.

A reading from the holy Gospel according to Matthew

Jesus said to his disciples: "Hear the parable of the sower. The
seed sown on the path is the one who hears the word of the
Kingdom without understanding it, and the Evil One comes
and steals away what was sown in his heart. The seed sown on
rocky ground is the one who hears the word and receives it at
once with joy. But he has no root and lasts only for a time.
When some tribulation or persecution comes because of the
word, he immediately falls away. The seed sown among thorns
is the one who hears the word, but then worldly anxiety and
the lure of riches choke the word and it bears no fruit. But the
seed sown on rich soil is the one who hears the word and understands it, who indeed bears fruit and yields a hundred or sixty
or thirtyfold."

The Gospel of the Lord.

Liturgy of the Eucharist, *p. 897;* **Prayer over the Gifts,** *p. 1192.*

Saturday

Antiphons and Prayers, *p. 1193;* **Liturgy of the Word** *for Year I (odd years) follows; Year II (even years), p. 1220.*

TODAY'S LIVING WORD

All three readings for today share a concern for faithful living. In the passage from Exodus, all twelve tribes of Israel formally ratify their covenant with God, committing themselves to observe all the ordinances and words of the Lord contained in the book of the covenant. In the selection from Jeremiah, the prophet reminds God's people of their covenant obligations by paraphrasing the Ten Commandments: "Are you to steal and murder, commit adultery and perjury, burn incense to Baal, go after strange gods…?"

With the realism characteristic of Jesus' parables, the Gospel story recognizes that those who live faithfully in this world often do so surrounded by those who do not. But the Sower of the good seed, who is also the Lord of the harvest, trusts that the wheat can withstand the weeds and be the stronger for it.

Year I

FIRST READING

Ex 24:3–8

This is the blood of the covenant that the LORD has made with you.

A reading from the Book of Exodus

When Moses came to the people and related all the words and ordinances of the LORD, they all answered with one voice, "We will do everything that the LORD has told us." Moses then wrote down all the words of the LORD and, rising early the next day, he erected at the foot of the mountain an altar and twelve pillars for the twelve tribes of Israel. Then, having sent certain young men of the children of Israel to offer burnt offerings and sacrifice young bulls as peace offerings to the LORD, Moses took half of the blood and put it in large bowls; the other half he splashed on the altar. Taking the book of the covenant, he read it aloud to the people, who answered, "All that the L ORD has said, we will heed and do." Then he took the blood and sprinkled it on the people, saying, "This is the blood of the covenant that the L ORD has made with you in accordance with all these words of his."

The word of the Lord.

Responsorial Psalm

Ps 50:1b–2, 5–6, 14–15

R. Offer to God a sacrifice of praise.

God the L ORD has spoken and summoned the earth,
   from the rising of the sun to its setting.
From Zion, perfect in beauty,
   God shines forth.

R. Offer to God a sacrifice of praise.

"Gather my faithful ones before me,
   those who have made a covenant with me by sacrifice."
And the heavens proclaim his justice;
   for God himself is the judge.

R. Offer to God a sacrifice of praise.

"Offer to God praise as your sacrifice
   and fulfill your vows to the Most High;
Then call upon me in time of distress;
   I will rescue you, and you shall glorify me."

R. Offer to God a sacrifice of praise.

   Alleluia Verse *and* **Gospel,** *p. 1222.*

Alleluia Verse *and* **Gospel,** *p. 1222.*

Year II

FIRST READING

Jer 7:1–11

*Has this house which bears my name
become in your eyes a den of thieves?*

A reading from the Book of the Prophet Jeremiah

The following message came to Jeremiah from the LORD: Stand at the gate of the house of the LORD, and there proclaim this message: Hear the word of the LORD, all you of Judah who enter these gates to worship the LORD! Thus says the LORD of hosts, the God of Israel: Reform your ways and your deeds, so that I may remain with you in this place. Put not your trust in the deceitful words: "This is the temple of the LORD! The temple of the LORD! The temple of the LORD!" Only if you thoroughly reform your ways and your deeds; if each of you deals justly with his neighbor; if you no longer oppress the resident alien, the orphan, and the widow; if you no longer shed innocent blood in this place, or follow strange gods to your own harm, will I remain with you in this place, in the land I gave your fathers long ago and forever.

But here you are, putting your trust in deceitful words to your own loss! Are you to steal and murder, commit adultery and perjury, burn incense to Baal, go after strange gods that you know not, and yet come to stand before me in this house which bears my name, and say: "We are safe; we can commit all these abominations again"? Has this house which bears my name become in your eyes a den of thieves? I too see what is being done, says the LORD.

The word of the Lord.

Responsorial Psalm Ps 84:3, 4, 5 – 6a and 8a, 11

R. How lovely is your dwelling place, Lord, mighty God!

My soul yearns and pines
  for the courts of the LORD.
My heart and my flesh
  cry out for the living God.

R. How lovely is your dwelling place, Lord, mighty God!

Even the sparrow finds a home,
   and the swallow a nest
   in which she puts her young—
Your altars, O LORD of hosts,
   my king and my God!

R. How lovely is your dwelling place, Lord, mighty God!

Blessed they who dwell in your house!
   continually they praise you.
Blessed the men whose strength you are!
They go from strength to strength.

R. How lovely is your dwelling place, Lord, mighty God!

I had rather one day in your courts
   than a thousand elsewhere;
I had rather lie at the threshold of the house of my God
   than dwell in the tents of the wicked.

R. How lovely is your dwelling place, Lord, mighty God!

Alleluia, alleluia   Jas 1:21bc
Humbly welcome the word that has been planted in you
and is able to save your souls.
Alleluia, alleluia

Years I and II

GOSPEL   Mt 13:24 – 30

Let them grow together until harvest.

A reading from the holy Gospel according to Matthew

Jesus proposed a parable to the crowds. "The Kingdom of
heaven may be likened to a man who sowed good seed in his
field. While everyone was asleep his enemy came and sowed
weeds all through the wheat, and then went off. When the crop
grew and bore fruit, the weeds appeared as well. The slaves of

the householder came to him and said, 'Master, did you not sow good seed in your field? Where have the weeds come from?' He answered, 'An enemy has done this.' His slaves said to him, 'Do you want us to go and pull them up?' He replied, 'No, if you pull up the weeds you might uproot the wheat along with them. Let them grow together until harvest; then at harvest time I will say to the harvesters, "First collect the weeds and tie them in bundles for burning; but gather the wheat into my barn."'"

The Gospel of the Lord.

Liturgy of the Eucharist, *p. 897;* **Prayer over the Gifts,** *p. 1192.*

SEVENTEENTH WEEK IN ORDINARY TIME

The **Antiphons and Prayers** *may be the following, or may be chosen from any of the other 33 weeks in Ordinary Time (refer to Liturgical Calendar, pp. 26–41).*

The **Liturgy of the Word** *varies: for Monday, see p. 1225; Tuesday, p. 1230; Wednesday, p. 1235; Thursday, p. 1240; Friday, p. 1244; Saturday, p. 1249.*

Entrance Antiphon

God is in his holy dwelling; he will give a home to the lonely, he gives power and strength to his people.   (Ps 68:6–7, 36)

Opening Prayer

Let us pray
  [that we will make good use of the gifts
  that God has given us]

  Pause for silent prayer.

God our Father and protector,
without you nothing is holy,

nothing has value.
Guide us to everlasting life
by helping us to use wisely
the blessings you have given to the world.

We ask this through our Lord Jesus Christ, your Son,
who lives and reigns with you and the Holy Spirit,
one God, for ever and ever.

Alternative Opening Prayer

Let us pray
[for the faith to recognize God's presence
in our world]

Pause for silent prayer.

God our Father,
open our eyes to see your hand at work
in the splendor of creation,
in the beauty of human life.
Touched by your hand our world is holy.
Help us to cherish the gifts that surround us,
to share your blessings with our brothers and sisters,
and to experience the joy of life in your presence.

We ask this through Christ our Lord.

Prayer over the Gifts

Pray, brethren...

Lord,
receive these offerings
chosen from your many gifts.
May these mysteries make us holy
and lead us to eternal joy.

Grant this through Christ our Lord.

Preface of Weekdays in Ordinary Time I–VI, *pp. 948–950.*

Communion Antiphon

O bless the Lord, my soul, and remember all his kindness.

(Ps 103:2)

Or:

Happy are those who show mercy; mercy shall be theirs. Happy are the poor of heart, for they shall see God.   (Mt 5:7– 8)

Prayer after Communion

Let us pray.

Pause for silent prayer, if this has not preceded.

Lord,
we receive the sacrament
which celebrates the memory
of the death and resurrection of Christ your Son.
May this gift bring us closer to our eternal salvation.
We ask this through Christ our Lord.

Monday

Antiphons and Prayers, *p. 1223;* **Liturgy of the Word** *for Year I (odd years) follows; Year II (even years), p. 1228.*

Today's Living Word

In the two first readings, Moses and Jeremiah are given similar roles to play: both are moved to identify sympathetically with God and with God's people. According to the *Catechism,* Moses' sympathy with God, as well as with his people, makes him "the most striking example of intercessory prayer…[who] 'stands in the breach' before God in order to save the people" (nn. 2574, 2577). Today's reading from Exodus is one example. In the passage from Jeremiah, the rotted loincloth is more than an image of destruction. By being made to wear the loincloth, Jeremiah comes symbolically to share God's own intimate attachment to "the whole house of Israel and the whole house of Judah."

To grasp the message of the parables in today's Gospel also requires imaginative identification. In both, a humble agent (the seed) and a hidden activity (the yeast) yield impressive results. Jesus invites us imaginatively to take on the humble, hidden work of providing sheltering presence and nourishing bread in and for the world.

Year I

FIRST READING   Ex 32:15–24, 30–34

This people has indeed committed a grave sin,
in making a god of gold for themselves.

A reading from the Book of Exodus

Moses turned and came down the mountain with the two tablets of the commandments in his hands, tablets that were written on both sides, front and back; tablets that were made by God, having inscriptions on them that were engraved by God himself. Now, when Joshua heard the noise of the people shouting, he said to Moses, "That sounds like a battle in the camp." But Moses answered, "It does not sound like cries of victory, nor does it sound like cries of defeat; the sounds that I hear are cries of revelry." As he drew near the camp, he saw the calf and the dancing. With that, Moses' wrath flared up, so that he threw the tablets down and broke them on the base of the mountain. Taking the calf they had made, he fused it in the fire and then ground it down to powder, which he scattered on the water and made the children of Israel drink.

Moses asked Aaron, "What did this people ever do to you that you should lead them into so grave a sin?" Aaron replied, "Let not my lord be angry. You know well enough how prone the people are to evil. They said to me, 'Make us a god to be our leader; as for the man Moses who brought us out of the land of

Egypt, we do not know what has happened to him.' So I told them, 'Let anyone who has gold jewelry take it off.' They gave it to me, and I threw it into the fire, and this calf came out."

On the next day Moses said to the people, "You have committed a grave sin. I will go up to the LORD, then; perhaps I may be able to make atonement for your sin." So Moses went back to the LORD and said, "Ah, this people has indeed committed a grave sin in making a god of gold for themselves! If you would only forgive their sin! If you will not, then strike me out of the book that you have written." The LORD answered, "Him only who has sinned against me will I strike out of my book. Now, go and lead the people to the place I have told you. My angel will go before you. When it is time for me to punish, I will punish them for their sin."

The word of the Lord.

Responsorial Psalm
Ps 106:19–20, 21–22, 23

R. Give thanks to the Lord, for he is good.

Our fathers made a calf in Horeb
  and adored a molten image;
They exchanged their glory
  for the image of a grass-eating bullock.

R. Give thanks to the Lord, for he is good.

They forgot the God who had saved them,
  who had done great deeds in Egypt,
Wondrous deeds in the land of Ham,
  terrible things at the Red Sea.

R. Give thanks to the Lord, for he is good.

Then he spoke of exterminating them,
  but Moses, his chosen one,
Withstood him in the breach
  to turn back his destructive wrath.

R. Give thanks to the Lord, for he is good.

Alleluia Verse *and* **Gospel,** *p. 1229.*

Year II

FIRST READING

Jer 13:1–11

This people shall be like a loincloth which is good for nothing.

A reading from the Book of the Prophet Jeremiah

The LORD said to me: Go buy yourself a linen loincloth; wear it on your loins, but do not put it in water. I bought the loincloth, as the LORD commanded, and put it on. A second time the word of the LORD came to me thus: Take the loincloth which you bought and are wearing, and go now to the Parath; there hide it in a cleft of the rock. Obedient to the LORD's command, I went to the Parath and buried the loincloth. After a long interval, the LORD said to me: Go now to the Parath and fetch the loincloth which I told you to hide there. Again I went to the Parath, sought out and took the loincloth from the place where I had hid it. But it was rotted, good for nothing! Then the message came to me from the LORD: Thus says the LORD: So also I will allow the pride of Judah to rot, the great pride of Jerusalem. This wicked people who refuse to obey my words, who walk in the stubbornness of their hearts, and follow strange gods to serve and adore them, shall be like this loincloth which is good for nothing. For, as close as the loincloth clings to a man's loins, so had I made the whole house of Israel and the whole house of Judah cling to me, says the LORD; to be my people, my renown, my praise, my beauty. But they did not listen.

The word of the Lord.

Responsorial Psalm

Dt 32:18–19, 20, 21

R. You have forgotten God who gave you birth.

You were unmindful of the Rock that begot you,
  You forgot the God who gave you birth.
When the LORD saw this, he was filled with loathing
  and anger toward his sons and daughters.

R. You have forgotten God who gave you birth.

"I will hide my face from them," he said,
  "and see what will then become of them.
What a fickle race they are,
  sons with no loyalty in them!"

R. You have forgotten God who gave you birth.

"Since they have provoked me with their 'no-god'
  and angered me with their vain idols,
I will provoke them with a 'no-people';
  with a foolish nation I will anger them."

R. You have forgotten God who gave you birth.

Alleluia, alleluia   Jas 1:18
The Father willed to give us birth by the word of truth
that we may be a kind of firstfruits of his creatures.
Alleluia, alleluia

Years I and II

GOSPEL

Mt 13:31–35

The mustard seed becomes a large bush and
the birds of the sky come and dwell in its branches.

A reading from the holy Gospel according to Matthew

Jesus proposed a parable to the crowds. "The Kingdom of heaven is like a mustard seed that a person took and sowed in a field. It is the smallest of all the seeds, yet when full-grown it is the largest of plants. It becomes a large bush, and the *birds of the sky come and dwell in its branches.*"

He spoke to them another parable. "The Kingdom of heaven is like yeast that a woman took and mixed with three measures of wheat flour until the whole batch was leavened."

All these things Jesus spoke to the crowds in parables. He spoke to them only in parables, to fulfill what had been said through the prophet:

> *I will open my mouth in parables,*
> *I will announce what has lain hidden from the*
> *foundation of the world.*

The Gospel of the Lord.

Liturgy of the Eucharist, *p. 897;* **Prayer over the Gifts,** *p. 1224.*

Tuesday

Antiphons and Prayers, *p. 1223;* **Liturgy of the Word** *for Year I (odd years) follows; Year II (even years), p. 1233.*

TODAY'S LIVING WORD

Again in today's Gospel we hear the early Church's interpretation of a parable of Jesus—the parable of the wheat and the weeds. Note the shift in emphasis: the parable urges patience; the interpretation stresses punishment.

Without denying punishment, patience dominates the two first readings. In the text from Exodus, which the *Catechism* considers pivotal, "God hears Moses' prayer of intercession and agrees to walk in the midst of an unfaithful people" (n. 210). Thus does God's name express God's patience: "The Lord, the Lord, a merciful and gracious God, slow to anger and rich in kindness and fidelity, continuing his kindness for a thousand generations, and forgiving wickedness and crime and sin" (cf. n. 211). Jeremiah's lament in the midst of the double calamity of drought and war also appeals to the divine patience promised by God's name: "For your name's sake spurn us not."

Year I

FIRST READING

Ex 33:7–11; 34:5b–9, 28

The Lord spoke to Moses face to face.

A reading from the Book of Exodus

The tent, which was called the meeting tent, Moses used to pitch at some distance away, outside the camp. Anyone who wished to consult the Lord would go to this meeting tent outside the camp. Whenever Moses went out to the tent, the people would all rise and stand at the entrance of their own tents, watching Moses until he entered the tent. As Moses entered the tent, the column of cloud would come down and stand at its entrance while the Lord spoke with Moses. On seeing the column of cloud stand at the entrance of the tent, all the people would rise and worship at the entrance of their own tents. The Lord used to speak to Moses face to face, as one man speaks to another. Moses would then return to the camp, but his young assistant, Joshua, son of Nun, would not move out of the tent.

Moses stood there with the Lord and proclaimed his name, "Lord." Thus the Lord passed before him and cried out, "The Lord, the Lord, a merciful and gracious God, slow to anger and rich in kindness and fidelity, continuing his kindness for a thousand generations, and forgiving wickedness and crime and sin; yet not declaring the guilty guiltless, but punishing children and grandchildren to the third and fourth generation for their fathers' wickedness!" Moses at once bowed down to the ground in worship. Then he said, "If I find favor with you, O Lord, do come along in our company. This is indeed a stiff-necked people; yet pardon our wickedness and sins, and receive us as your own."

So Moses stayed there with the LORD for forty days and forty nights, without eating any food or drinking any water, and he wrote on the tablets the words of the covenant, the ten commandments.

The word of the Lord.

Responsorial Psalm

Ps 103:6–7, 8–9, 10–11, 12–13

R. The Lord is kind and merciful.

The LORD secures justice
  and the rights of all the oppressed.
He has made known his ways to Moses,
  and his deeds to the children of Israel.

R. The Lord is kind and merciful.

Merciful and gracious is the LORD,
  slow to anger and abounding in kindness.
He will not always chide,
  nor does he keep his wrath forever.

R. The Lord is kind and merciful.

Not according to our sins does he deal with us,
  nor does he requite us according to our crimes.
For as the heavens are high above the earth,
  so surpassing is his kindness toward those who fear him.

R. The Lord is kind and merciful.

As far as the east is from the west,
  so far has he put our transgressions from us.
As a father has compassion on his children,
  so the LORD has compassion on those who fear him.

R. The Lord is kind and merciful.

Alleluia Verse *and* **Gospel,** *p. 1234.*

Year II

FIRST READING Jer 14:17–22

Remember, Lord, your covenant with us and break it not.

A reading from the Book of the Prophet Jeremiah

Let my eyes stream with tears
  day and night, without rest,
Over the great destruction which overwhelms
  the virgin daughter of my people,
  over her incurable wound.
If I walk out into the field,
  look! those slain by the sword;
If I enter the city,
  look! those consumed by hunger.
Even the prophet and the priest
  forage in a land they know not.

Have you cast Judah off completely?
  Is Zion loathsome to you?
Why have you struck us a blow
  that cannot be healed?
We wait for peace, to no avail;
  for a time of healing, but terror comes instead.
We recognize, O LORD, our wickedness,
  the guilt of our fathers;
  that we have sinned against you.
For your name's sake spurn us not,
  disgrace not the throne of your glory;
  remember your covenant with us, and break it not.
Among the nations' idols is there any that gives rain?

Or can the mere heavens send showers?
Is it not you alone, O LORD,
our God, to whom we look?
You alone have done all these things.

The word of the Lord.

Responsorial Psalm

Ps 79:8, 9, 11 and 13

R. For the glory of your name, O Lord, deliver us.

Remember not against us the iniquities of the past;
may your compassion quickly come to us,
for we are brought very low.

R. For the glory of your name, O Lord, deliver us.

Help us, O God our savior,
because of the glory of your name;
Deliver us and pardon our sins
for your name's sake.

R. For the glory of your name, O Lord, deliver us.

Let the prisoners' sighing come before you;
with your great power free those doomed to death.
Then we, your people and the sheep of your pasture,
will give thanks to you forever;
through all generations we will declare your praise.

R. For the glory of your name, O Lord, deliver us.

Alleluia, alleluia
The seed is the word of God, Christ is the sower;
all who come to him will live for ever.
Alleluia, alleluia

Years I and II

GOSPEL

Mt 13:36–43

*Just as the weeds are collected now and burned up with fire,
so will it be at the end of the age.*

A reading from the holy Gospel according to Matthew

Jesus dismissed the crowds and went into the house. His disciples approached him and said, "Explain to us the parable of the weeds in the field." He said in reply, "He who sows good seed is the Son of Man, the field is the world, the good seed the children of the Kingdom. The weeds are the children of the Evil One, and the enemy who sows them is the Devil. The harvest is the end of the age, and the harvesters are angels. Just as weeds are collected and burned up with fire, so will it be at the end of the age. The Son of Man will send his angels, and they will collect out of his Kingdom all who cause others to sin and all evildoers. They will throw them into the fiery furnace, where there will be wailing and grinding of teeth. Then the righteous will shine like the sun in the Kingdom of their Father. Whoever has ears ought to hear."

The Gospel of the Lord.

Liturgy of the Eucharist, *p. 897;* **Prayer over the Gifts,** *p. 1224.*

Wednesday

Antiphons and Prayers, *p. 1223;* **Liturgy of the Word** *for Year I (odd years) follows; Year II (even years), p. 1237.*

TODAY'S LIVING WORD

Today's three readings recall a phrase from Paul that assesses the cost of discipleship: "For this momentary light affliction is producing for us an eternal weight of glory beyond all comparison" (2 Cor 4:17). In the Exodus text the radiance of Moses' face signals his share, as God's faithful friend and servant, in God's unfading glory. The autobiographical passage from Jeremiah reveals his struggle under the weight of God's hand. Yet a glorious future awaits him too: "If you bring forth the precious without the vile, you shall be my mouthpiece," God says, adding, "For I am with you, to deliver and rescue you."

The two short parables in today's Gospel cast Paul's statement in story form. When the treasure and the pearl are discovered, they relativize the value of everything else. Both men eagerly sell all that they have in order to secure them. With these stories Jesus invites us into the company of Moses, Jeremiah and Paul, the company of those who have glimpsed God's glory and gladly give all to attain it.

Year I

FIRST READING   Ex 34:29–35

Seeing the face of Moses, they were afraid to come near him.

A reading from the Book of Exodus

As Moses came down from Mount Sinai with the two tablets of the commandments in his hands, he did not know that the skin of his face had become radiant while he conversed with the Lord. When Aaron, then, and the other children of Israel saw Moses and noticed how radiant the skin of his face had become, they were afraid to come near him. Only after Moses called to them did Aaron and all the rulers of the community come back to him. Moses then spoke to them. Later on, all the children of Israel came up to him, and he enjoined on them all that the Lord had told him on Mount Sinai. When he finished speaking with them, he put a veil over his face. Whenever Moses entered the presence of the Lord to converse with him, he removed the veil until he came out again. On coming out, he would tell the children of Israel all that had been commanded. Then the children of Israel would see that the skin of Moses' face was radiant; so he would again put the veil over his face until he went in to converse with the Lord.

The word of the Lord.

Responsorial Psalm

Ps 99:5, 6, 7, 9

R. Holy is the Lord our God.

Extol the LORD, our God,
and worship at his footstool;
holy is he!

R. Holy is the Lord our God.

Moses and Aaron were among his priests,
and Samuel, among those who called upon his name;
they called upon the LORD, and he answered them.

R. Holy is the Lord our God.

From the pillar of cloud he spoke to them;
they heard his decrees and the law he gave them.

R. Holy is the Lord our God.

Extol the LORD, our God,
and worship at his holy mountain;
for holy is the LORD, our God.

R. Holy is the Lord our God.

Alleluia Verse *and* **Gospel,** *p. 1239.*

Year II

FIRST READING

Jer 15:10, 16 – 21

*Why is my pain continuous?—If you repent,
you shall stand in my presence.*

A reading from the Book of the Prophet Jeremiah

Woe to me, mother, that you gave me birth!
a man of strife and contention to all the land!
I neither borrow nor lend,
yet all curse me.
When I found your words, I devoured them;
they became my joy and the happiness of my heart,

Because I bore your name,
    O Lord, God of hosts.
I did not sit celebrating
    in the circle of merrymakers;
Under the weight of your hand I sat alone
    because you filled me with indignation.
Why is my pain continuous,
    my wound incurable, refusing to be healed?
You have indeed become for me a treacherous brook,
    whose waters do not abide!
      Thus the Lord answered me:
If you repent, so that I restore you,
    in my presence you shall stand;
If you bring forth the precious without the vile,
    you shall be my mouthpiece.
Then it shall be they who turn to you,
    and you shall not turn to them;
And I will make you toward this people
    a solid wall of brass.
Though they fight against you,
    they shall not prevail,
For I am with you,
    to deliver and rescue you, says the Lord.
I will free you from the hand of the wicked,
    and rescue you from the grasp of the violent.

The word of the Lord.

Responsorial Psalm
Ps 59:2–3, 4, 10–11, 17, 18

    R. God is my refuge on the day of distress.

Rescue me from my enemies, O my God;
  from my adversaries defend me.

Rescue me from evildoers;
   from bloodthirsty men save me.

R. God is my refuge on the day of distress.

For behold, they lie in wait for my life;
   mighty men come together against me,
Not for any offense or sin of mine, O LORD.

R. God is my refuge on the day of distress.

O my strength! for you I watch;
   for you, O God, are my stronghold,
As for my God, may his mercy go before me;
   may he show me the fall of my foes.

R. God is my refuge on the day of distress.

But I will sing of your strength
   and revel at dawn in your mercy;
You have been my stronghold,
   my refuge in the day of distress.

R. God is my refuge on the day of distress.

O my strength! your praise will I sing;
   for you, O God, are my stronghold,
   my merciful God!

R. God is my refuge on the day of distress.

Alleluia, alleluia Jn 15:15b
I call you my friends, says the Lord,
   for I have made known to you all that the Father has told me.
Alleluia, alleluia

Years I and II

GOSPEL   Mt 13:44 – 46

He sells all he has and buys that field.

A reading from the holy Gospel according to Matthew

Jesus said to his disciples: "The Kingdom of heaven is like a treasure buried in a field, which a person finds and hides again, and out of joy goes and sells all that he has and buys that field. Again, the Kingdom of heaven is like a merchant searching for fine pearls. When he finds a pearl of great price, he goes and sells all that he has and buys it."

The Gospel of the Lord.

Liturgy of the Eucharist, *p. 897;* **Prayer over the Gifts,** *p. 1224.*

Thursday

Antiphons and Prayers, *p. 1223;* **Liturgy of the Word** *for Year I (odd years) follows; Year II (even years), p. 1242.*

TODAY'S LIVING WORD

Each of today's readings discloses a different facet of God's dealings with people. Through the symbols of the Dwelling, the cloud by day and the fire by night, the Exodus text describes God's active presence with the house of Israel "in all the stages of their journey." The episode retold by Jeremiah depicts God as a potter, patient and painstaking in re-forming the work of his hands. The parable of the net returns to a familiar theme in Matthew, the theme of God as judge at the end of the world when "angels will go out and separate the wicked from the righteous."

Some think that the concluding verses of today's Gospel describe Matthew himself, a learned scribe. Be that as it may, the householder who values both the new and the old is a model for all of us who want to be wise in the ways of God with us.

Year I

FIRST READING   Ex 40:16–21, 34–38

The cloud covered the meeting tent and the glory of the LORD filled the Dwelling.

A reading from the Book of Exodus

Moses did exactly as the Lord had commanded him. On the first day of the first month of the second year the Dwelling was erected. It was Moses who erected the Dwelling. He placed its pedestals, set up its boards, put in its bars, and set up its columns. He spread the tent over the Dwelling and put the covering on top of the tent, as the Lord had commanded him. He took the commandments and put them in the ark; he placed poles alongside the ark and set the propitiatory upon it. He brought the ark into the Dwelling and hung the curtain veil, thus screening off the ark of the commandments, as the Lord had commanded him.

Then the cloud covered the meeting tent, and the glory of the Lord filled the Dwelling. Moses could not enter the meeting tent, because the cloud settled down upon it and the glory of the Lord filled the Dwelling. Whenever the cloud rose from the Dwelling, the children of Israel would set out on their journey. But if the cloud did not lift, they would not go forward; only when it lifted did they go forward. In the daytime the cloud of the Lord was seen over the Dwelling; whereas at night, fire was seen in the cloud by the whole house of Israel in all the stages of their journey.

The word of the Lord.

Responsorial Psalm

Ps 84:3, 4, 5–6a and 8a, 11

R. How lovely is your dwelling place, O Lord, mighty God!

My soul yearns and pines
  for the courts of the Lord.
My heart and my flesh
  cry out for the living God.

R. How lovely is your dwelling place, O Lord, mighty God!

Even the sparrow finds a home,
  and the swallow a nest
  in which she puts her young—
Your altars, O LORD of hosts,
  my king and my God!

  R. How lovely is your dwelling place, O Lord, mighty God!

Blessed they who dwell in your house!
  continually they praise you.
Blessed the men whose strength you are!
They go from strength to strength.

  R. How lovely is your dwelling place, O Lord, mighty God!

I had rather one day in your courts
  than a thousand elsewhere;
I had rather lie at the threshold of the house of my God
  than dwell in the tents of the wicked.

  R. How lovely is your dwelling place, O Lord, mighty God!

  Alleluia Verse *and* **Gospel**, *p. 1243.*

Year II

FIRST READING   Jer 18:1–6

Like the clay in the hand of the potter,
so are you in my hand, house of Israel.

A reading from the Book of the Prophet Jeremiah

This word came to Jeremiah from the LORD: Rise up, be off to
the potter's house; there I will give you my message. I went
down to the potter's house and there he was, working at the
wheel. Whenever the object of clay which he was making
turned out badly in his hand, he tried again, making of the clay
another object of whatever sort he pleased. Then the word of
the LORD came to me: Can I not do to you, house of Israel, as

this potter has done? says the LORD. Indeed, like clay in the hand of the potter, so are you in my hand, house of Israel.

The word of the Lord.

Responsorial Psalm

Ps 146:1b–2, 3–4, 5–6ab

R. Blessed is he whose help is the God of Jacob.

Praise the LORD, O my soul;
  I will praise the LORD all my life;
  I will sing praise to my God while I live.

R. Blessed is he whose help is the God of Jacob.

Put not your trust in princes,
  in the sons of men, in whom there is no salvation.
When his spirit departs he returns to his earth;
  on that day his plans perish.

R. Blessed is he whose help is the God of Jacob.

Blessed he whose help is the God of Jacob,
  whose hope is in the LORD, his God.
Who made heaven and earth,
  the sea and all that is in them.

R. Blessed is he whose help is the God of Jacob.

Or: **R. Alleluia.**

Alleluia, alleluia See Acts 16:14b
Open our hearts, O Lord,
to listen to the words of your Son.
Alleluia, alleluia

Years I and II

GOSPEL Mt 13:47–53

They put what is good into buckets, what is bad they throw away.

A reading from the holy Gospel according to Matthew

Jesus said to the disciples: "The Kingdom of heaven is like a net thrown into the sea, which collects fish of every kind. When it is full they haul it ashore and sit down to put what is good into buckets. What is bad they throw away. Thus it will be at the end of the age. The angels will go out and separate the wicked from the righteous and throw them into the fiery furnace, where there will be wailing and grinding of teeth.

"Do you understand all these things?" They answered, "Yes." And he replied, "Then every scribe who has been instructed in the Kingdom of heaven is like the head of a household who brings from his storeroom both the new and the old." When Jesus finished these parables, he went away from there.

The Gospel of the Lord.

Liturgy of the Eucharist, *p. 897;* **Prayer over the Gifts,** *p. 1224.*

Friday

Antiphons and Prayers, *p. 1223;* **Liturgy of the Word** *for Year I (odd years) follows; Year II (even years), p. 1247.*

TODAY'S LIVING WORD

Today's readings show us Jeremiah and Jesus as two prophets found to be too much for those to whom they are sent. The people of Judah react angrily to the words of Jeremiah, refusing to heed his warning of impending doom. The amazement of the people of Nazareth gives way to incredulity as they reflect on Jesus' roots in their village. "Is he not the carpenter's son? Is not his mother named Mary...?" Consequently, having rejected the prophet's words, the house of Judah will fall. The temple will be destroyed and the city devastated. Similarly, the lack of faith among the people in his native place will mean that Jesus cannot work many miracles there. These stories may cause us to wonder if we too fail to hear the words of God-sent prophets because they are too fearsome or too familiar.

Participation in liturgy is one way of remaining attuned to God's word. The text from Leviticus is a schedule of feasts, Israel's liturgical calendar. In these festivals, God commands the attention of the people and calls them to acknowledge that the Lord alone is God. There is no other.

Year I

FIRST READING

Lv 23:1, 4–11, 15–16, 27, 34b–37

These are the festivals of the LORD on which you shall proclaim a sacred assembly.

A reading from the Book of Leviticus

The LORD said to Moses, "These are the festivals of the LORD which you shall celebrate at their proper time with a sacred assembly. The Passover of the LORD falls on the fourteenth day of the first month, at the evening twilight. The fifteenth day of this month is the LORD's feast of Unleavened Bread. For seven days you shall eat unleavened bread. On the first of these days you shall hold a sacred assembly and do no sort of work. On each of the seven days you shall offer an oblation to the LORD. Then on the seventh day you shall again hold a sacred assembly and do no sort of work."

The LORD said to Moses, "Speak to the children of Israel and tell them: When you come into the land which I am giving you, and reap your harvest, you shall bring a sheaf of the first fruits of your harvest to the priest, who shall wave the sheaf before the LORD that it may be acceptable for you. On the day after the sabbath the priest shall do this.

"Beginning with the day after the sabbath, the day on which you bring the wave-offering sheaf, you shall count seven full weeks, and then on the day after the seventh week, the fiftieth day, you shall present the new cereal offering to the LORD.

"The tenth of this seventh month is the Day of Atonement, when you shall hold a sacred assembly and mortify yourselves and offer an oblation to the LORD.

"The fifteenth day of this seventh month is the LORD's feast of Booths, which shall continue for seven days. On the first day there shall be a sacred assembly, and you shall do no sort of work. For seven days you shall offer an oblation to the LORD, and on the eighth day you shall again hold a sacred assembly and offer an oblation to the LORD. On that solemn closing you shall do no sort of work.

"These, therefore, are the festivals of the LORD on which you shall proclaim a sacred assembly, and offer as an oblation to the LORD burnt offerings and cereal offerings, sacrifices and libations, as prescribed for each day."

The word of the Lord.

Responsorial Psalm   Ps 81:3–4, 5–6, 10–11ab

R. Sing with joy to God our help.

Take up a melody, and sound the timbrel,
  the pleasant harp and the lyre.
Blow the trumpet at the new moon,
  at the full moon, on our solemn feast.

R. Sing with joy to God our help.

For it is a statute in Israel,
  an ordinance of the God of Jacob,
Who made it a decree for Joseph
  when he came forth from the land of Egypt.

R. Sing with joy to God our help.

There shall be no strange god among you
  nor shall you worship any alien god.
I, the LORD, am your God
  who led you forth from the land of Egypt.

R. Sing with joy to God our help.

Alleluia Verse *and* **Gospel,** *p. 1248f.*

Year II

FIRST READING

Jer 26:1–9

All the people gathered about Jeremiah in the house of the LORD.

A reading from the Book of the Prophet Jeremiah

In the beginning of the reign of Jehoiakim, son of Josiah, king
of Judah, this message came from the LORD: Thus says the
LORD: Stand in the court of the house of the LORD and speak to
the people of all the cities of Judah who come to worship in
the house of the LORD; whatever I command you, tell them,
and omit nothing. Perhaps they will listen and turn back, each
from his evil way, so that I may repent of the evil I have planned
to inflict upon them for their evil deeds. Say to them: Thus
says the LORD: If you disobey me, not living according to the
law I placed before you and not listening to the words of my
servants the prophets, whom I send you constantly though you
do not obey them, I will treat this house like Shiloh, and make
this the city to which all the nations of the earth shall refer
when cursing another.

Now the priests, the prophets, and all the people heard
Jeremiah speak these words in the house of the LORD. When
Jeremiah finished speaking all that the LORD bade him speak

to all the people, the priests and prophets laid hold of him, crying, "You must be put to death! Why do you prophesy in the name of the LORD: 'This house shall be like Shiloh,' and 'This city shall be desolate and deserted'?" And all the people gathered about Jeremiah in the house of the LORD.

The word of the Lord.

Responsorial Psalm

Ps 69:5, 8–10, 14

R. Lord, in your great love, answer me.

Those outnumber the hairs of my head
    who hate me without cause.
Too many for my strength
    are they who wrongfully are my enemies.
    Must I restore what I did not steal?

R. Lord, in your great love, answer me.

Since for your sake I bear insult,
    and shame covers my face.
I have become an outcast to my brothers,
    a stranger to my mother's sons,
Because zeal for your house consumes me,
    and the insults of those who blaspheme you fall upon me.

R. Lord, in your great love, answer me.

But I pray to you, O LORD,
    for the time of your favor, O God!
In your great kindness answer me
    with your constant help.

R. Lord, in your great love, answer me.

Alleluia, alleluia   1 Pt 1:25
The word of the Lord remains forever;
    this is the word that has been proclaimed to you.
Alleluia, alleluia

Years I and II

GOSPEL   Mt 13:54–58

Is he not the carpenter's son?
Where did this man get such wisdom and mighty deeds?

A reading from the holy Gospel according to Matthew

Jesus came to his native place and taught the people in their synagogue. They were astonished and said, "Where did this man get such wisdom and mighty deeds? Is he not the carpenter's son? Is not his mother named Mary and his brothers James, Joseph, Simon, and Judas? Are not his sisters all with us? Where did this man get all this?" And they took offense at him. But Jesus said to them, "A prophet is not without honor except in his native place and in his own house." And he did not work many mighty deeds there because of their lack of faith.

The Gospel of the Lord.

Liturgy of the Eucharist, *p. 897;* **Prayer over the Gifts,** *p. 1224.*

Saturday

Antiphons and Prayers, *p. 1223;* **Liturgy of the Word** *for Year I (odd years) follows; Year II (even years), p. 1252.*

TODAY'S LIVING WORD

Today's reading from Leviticus established in Israel the observance of Jubilee. This fiftieth year, announced on the Day of Atonement *(Yom Kippur),* was to be a sacred time, "proclaiming liberty in the land for all its inhabitants." The text outlines the goals of the Jubilee year as human liberation (releasing captives and so curbing the institution of slavery), economic liberation (restoring land to its original owner and so controlling the distribution of wealth), and ecological liberation (respecting the earth and the animals on it by allowing them to rest and replenish themselves). Scholars do not know if the Jubilee was ever actually implemented in Israel. But in time it came to symbolize that day when God's reign would be finally, fully revealed.

Throughout the ages prophets have announced this "year of favor from the Lord, a day of vindication by our God" (Is 61:2; cf. Lk 4:19). Confronting powerful, political regimes, they have risked all by speaking "in the name of the Lord, our God." This is the witness of Jeremiah and of John the Baptizer in today's readings.

Year I

FIRST READING
Lv 25:1, 8–17

In the year of the jubilee you shall return, everyone of you, to your own property.

A reading from the Book of Leviticus

The LORD said to Moses on Mount Sinai, "Seven weeks of years shall you count—seven times seven years—so that the seven cycles amount to forty-nine years. Then, on the tenth day of the seventh month, let the trumpet resound; on this, the Day of Atonement, the trumpet blast shall re-echo throughout your land. This fiftieth year you shall make sacred by proclaiming liberty in the land for all its inhabitants. It shall be a jubilee for you, when every one of you shall return to his own property, every one to his own family estate. In this fiftieth year, your year of jubilee, you shall not sow, nor shall you reap the after-growth or pick the grapes from the untrimmed vines. Since this is the jubilee, which shall be sacred for you, you may not eat of its produce, except as taken directly from the field.

"In this year of jubilee, then, every one of you shall return to his own property. Therefore, when you sell any land to your neighbor or buy any from him, do not deal unfairly. On the basis of the number of years since the last jubilee shall you purchase the land from your neighbor; and so also, on the basis of the number of years for crops, shall he sell it to you. When the years are many, the price shall be so much the more; when the years are few, the price shall be so much the less. For it is really the number of crops that he sells you. Do not deal unfairly, then; but stand in fear of your God. I, the LORD, am your God."

The word of the Lord.

Responsorial Psalm

Ps 67:2–3, 5, 7–8

R. O God, let all the nations praise you!

May God have pity on us and bless us;
  may he let his face shine upon us.
So may your way be known upon earth;
  among all nations, your salvation.

R. O God, let all the nations praise you!

May the nations be glad and exult
  because you rule the peoples in equity;
  the nations on the earth you guide.

R. O God, let all the nations praise you!

The earth has yielded its fruits;
  God, our God, has blessed us.
May God bless us,
  and may all the ends of the earth fear him!

R. O God, let all the nations praise you!

Alleluia Verse *and* **Gospel,** *p. 1253.*

Year II

FIRST READING   Jer 26:11–16, 24

For in truth it was the LORD who sent me to you,
to speak all these things for you to hear.

A reading from the Book of the Prophet Jeremiah

The priests and prophets said to the princes and to all the people, "This man deserves death; he has prophesied against this city, as you have heard with your own ears." Jeremiah gave this answer to the princes and all the people: "It was the LORD who sent me to prophesy against this house and city all that you have heard. Now, therefore, reform your ways and your deeds; listen to the voice of the LORD your God, so that the LORD will repent of the evil with which he threatens you. As for me, I am in your hands; do with me what you think good and right. But mark well: if you put me to death, it is innocent blood you bring on yourselves, on this city and its citizens. For in truth it was the LORD who sent me to you, to speak all these things for you to hear."

Thereupon the princes and all the people said to the priests and the prophets, "This man does not deserve death; it is in the name of the LORD, our God, that he speaks to us."

So Ahikam, son of Shaphan, protected Jeremiah, so that he was not handed over to the people to be put to death.

The word of the Lord.

Responsorial Psalm   Ps 69:15–16, 30–31, 33–34

R. Lord, in your great love, answer me.

Rescue me out of the mire; may I not sink!
    may I be rescued from my foes,

and from the watery depths.
Let not the flood-waters overwhelm me,
  nor the abyss swallow me up,
  nor the pit close its mouth over me.

R. Lord, in your great love, answer me.

But I am afflicted and in pain;
  let your saving help, O God, protect me.
I will praise the name of God in song,
  and I will glorify him with thanksgiving.

R. Lord, in your great love, answer me.

"See, you lowly ones, and be glad;
  you who seek God, may your hearts revive!
For the LORD hears the poor,
  and his own who are in bonds he spurns not."

R. Lord, in your great love, answer me.

   Alleluia, alleluia   Mt 5:10
   Blessed are they who are persecuted
      for the sake of righteousness
   for theirs is the Kingdom of heaven.
   Alleluia, alleluia

Years I and II

GOSPEL   Mt 14:1–12

Herod had John beheaded; John's disciples came and told Jesus.

A reading from the holy Gospel according to Matthew

Herod the tetrarch heard of the reputation of Jesus and said to
his servants, "This man is John the Baptist. He has been raised
from the dead; that is why mighty powers are at work in him."

   Now Herod had arrested John, bound him, and put him in
prison on account of Herodias, the wife of his brother Philip,
for John had said to him, "It is not lawful for you to have her."

Although he wanted to kill him, he feared the people, for they regarded him as a prophet. But at a birthday celebration for Herod, the daughter of Herodias performed a dance before the guests and delighted Herod so much that he swore to give her whatever she might ask for. Prompted by her mother, she said, "Give me here on a platter the head of John the Baptist." The king was distressed, but because of his oaths and the guests who were present, he ordered that it be given, and he had John beheaded in the prison. His head was brought in on a platter and given to the girl, who took it to her mother. His disciples came and took away the corpse and buried him; and they went and told Jesus.

The Gospel of the Lord.

Liturgy of the Eucharist, *p. 897;* **Prayer over the Gifts,** *p. 1224.*

EIGHTEENTH WEEK IN ORDINARY TIME

The **Antiphons and Prayers** *may be the following, or may be chosen from any of the other 33 weeks in Ordinary Time (refer to Liturgical Calendar, pp. 26–41).*

The **Liturgy of the Word** *varies: for Monday, see p. 1256; Tuesday, p. 1262; Wednesday, p. 1269; Thursday, p. 1274; Friday, p. 1279; Saturday, p. 1284.*

Entrance Antiphon

God, come to my help. Lord, quickly give me assistance. You are the one who helps me and sets me free: Lord, do not be long in coming. (Ps 70:2, 6)

Opening Prayer

Let us pray

[for the gift of God's forgiveness and love]

Pause for silent prayer.

Father of everlasting goodness,
our origin and guide,
be close to us
and hear the prayers of all who praise you.
Forgive our sins and restore us to life.
Keep us safe in your love.

Grant this through our Lord Jesus Christ, your Son,
who lives and reigns with you and the Holy Spirit,
one God, for ever and ever.

Alternative Opening Prayer

Let us pray
[to the Father whose kindness never fails]

> *Pause for silent prayer.*

God our Father,
gifts without measure flow from your goodness
to bring us your peace.
Our life is your gift.
Guide our life's journey,
for only your love makes us whole.
Keep us strong in your love.

We ask this through Christ our Lord.

Prayer over the Gifts

Pray, brethren...

Merciful Lord,
make holy these gifts,
and let our spiritual sacrifice
make us an everlasting gift to you.

We ask this in the name of Jesus the Lord.

Preface of Weekdays in Ordinary Time I–VI, *pp. 948–950.*

Communion Antiphon

You gave us bread from heaven, Lord: a sweet-tasting bread that was very good to eat.   (Wis 16:20)

Or:

The Lord says: I am the bread of life. A man who comes to me will not go away hungry, and no one who believes in me will thirst.
                    (Jn 6:35)

Prayer after Communion

Let us pray.

   Pause for silent prayer, if this has not preceded.

Lord,
you give us the strength of new life
by the gift of the eucharist.
Protect us with your love
and prepare us for eternal redemption.

We ask this through Christ our Lord.

Monday

Antiphons and Prayers, *p. 1254;* **Liturgy of the Word** *for Year I (odd years) follows; Year II (even years), p. 1258.*

TODAY'S LIVING WORD

It is easy to see a connection between the passage from Numbers and Matthew's account of the multiplication of the loaves. The setting of Jesus' miracle is "a deserted place," recalling another desert where God provided manna for the Israelites to eat. In today's reading from Numbers, the people demand meat as well. Some scholars interpret the fish mentioned in the story of the multiplication of the loaves as a reference to the quail with which God will answer the people's request. The quail, after all, came from the sea (Nm 11:31).

All three readings for today draw attention to those who are the mediators of God's providence. Each in his own way experiences the burden of caring for God's needy people. Moses is most direct:

"I cannot carry all this people by myself," he complains, "they are too heavy for me." Jeremiah is forced to compete with the false prophet Hananiah, whose empty promise of peace better suits God's people in denial. Even the disciples of Jesus want to dismiss the hungry crowds. His own resources depleted, each one must trust the unbounded resourcefulness of God to provide bread even in the desert.

Year I

FIRST READING   Nm 11:4b–15

I cannot carry all this people by myself.

A reading from the Book of Numbers

The children of Israel lamented, "Would that we had meat for food! We remember the fish we used to eat without cost in Egypt, and the cucumbers, the melons, the leeks, the onions, and the garlic. But now we are famished; we see nothing before us but this manna."

Manna was like coriander seed and had the color of resin. When they had gone about and gathered it up, the people would grind it between millstones or pound it in a mortar, then cook it in a pot and make it into loaves, which tasted like cakes made with oil. At night, when the dew fell upon the camp, the manna also fell.

When Moses heard the people, family after family, crying at the entrance of their tents, so that the LORD became very angry, he was grieved. "Why do you treat your servant so badly?" Moses asked the LORD. "Why are you so displeased with me that you burden me with all this people? Was it I who conceived all this people? Or was it I who gave them birth, that you tell me to carry them at my bosom, like a foster father carrying an infant, to the land you have promised under oath to their fathers?

Where can I get meat to give to all this people? For they are crying to me, 'Give us meat for our food.' I cannot carry all this people by myself, for they are too heavy for me. If this is the way you will deal with me, then please do me the favor of killing me at once, so that I need no longer face this distress." The word of the Lord.

Responsorial Psalm   Ps 81:12–13, 14–15, 16–17

R. Sing with joy to God our help.

"My people heard not my voice,
    and Israel obeyed me not;
So I gave them up to the hardness of their hearts;
    they walked according to their own counsels."

R. Sing with joy to God our help.

"If only my people would hear me,
    and Israel walk in my ways,
Quickly would I humble their enemies;
    against their foes I would turn my hand."

R. Sing with joy to God our help.

"Those who hated the LORD would seek to flatter me,
    but their fate would endure forever,
While Israel I would feed with the best of wheat,
    and with honey from the rock I would fill them."

R. Sing with joy to God our help.

Alleluia Verse *and* **Gospel,** *p. 1261.*

Year II

FIRST READING   Jer 28:1–17

The LORD has not sent you,
and you have raised false confidence in this people.

A reading from the Book of the Prophet Jeremiah

In the beginning of the reign of Zedekiah, king of Judah, in the fifth month of the fourth year, the prophet Hananiah, son of Azzur, from Gibeon, said to me in the house of the LORD in the presence of the priests and all the people: "Thus says the LORD of hosts, the God of Israel: 'I will break the yoke of the king of Babylon. Within two years I will restore to this place all the vessels of the temple of the LORD which Nebuchadnezzar, king of Babylon, took away from this place to Babylon. And I will bring back to this place Jeconiah, son of Jehoiakim, king of Judah, and all the exiles of Judah who went to Babylon,' says the LORD, 'for I will break the yoke of the king of Babylon.'"

The prophet Jeremiah answered the prophet Hananiah in the presence of the priests and all the people assembled in the house of the LORD, and said: Amen! thus may the LORD do! May he fulfill the things you have prophesied by bringing the vessels of the house of the LORD and all the exiles back from Babylon to this place! But now, listen to what I am about to state in your hearing and the hearing of all the people. From of old, the prophets who were before you and me prophesied war, woe, and pestilence against many lands and mighty kingdoms. But the prophet who prophesies peace is recognized as truly sent by the LORD only when his prophetic prediction is fulfilled.

Thereupon the prophet Hananiah took the yoke from the neck of the prophet Jeremiah and broke it, and said in the presence of all the people: "Thus says the LORD: 'Even so, within two years I will break the yoke of Nebuchadnezzar, king of Babylon, from off the neck of all the nations.'" At that, the prophet Jeremiah went away.

Some time after the prophet Hananiah had broken the yoke from off the neck of the prophet Jeremiah, The word of the Lord came to Jeremiah: Go tell Hananiah this: Thus says the

LORD: By breaking a wooden yoke, you forge an iron yoke! For thus says the LORD of hosts, the God of Israel: A yoke of iron I will place on the necks of all these nations serving Nebuchadnezzar, king of Babylon, and they shall serve him; even the beasts of the field I give him.

To the prophet Hananiah the prophet Jeremiah said: Hear this, Hananiah! The LORD has not sent you, and you have raised false confidence in this people. For this, says the LORD, I will dispatch you from the face of the earth; this very year you shall die, because you have preached rebellion against the LORD. That same year, in the seventh month, Hananiah the prophet died.

The word of the Lord.

Responsorial Psalm

Ps 119:29, 43, 79, 80, 95, 102

> **R. Lord, teach me your statutes.**

Remove from me the way of falsehood,
  and favor me with your law.

> **R. Lord, teach me your statutes.**

Take not the word of truth from my mouth,
  for in your ordinances is my hope.

> **R. Lord, teach me your statutes.**

Let those turn to me who fear you
  and acknowledge your decrees.

> **R. Lord, teach me your statutes.**

Let my heart be perfect in your statutes,
  that I be not put to shame.

> **R. Lord, teach me your statutes.**

Sinners wait to destroy me,
  but I pay heed to your decrees.

R. Lord, teach me your statutes.

From your ordinances I turn not away,
   for you have instructed me.

R. Lord, teach me your statutes.

Alleluia, alleluia   Mt 4:4
One does not live on bread alone,
but on every word that comes forth from the mouth of God.
Alleluia, alleluia

Years I and II

GOSPEL   Mt 14:13 – 21

In Cycle A, when the Gospel below is read on the preceding Sunday, Matthew
14:22–36 is read on Monday as below, p. 1267.

*Looking up to heaven, he said the blessing and gave the loaves
   to the disciples, who in turn gave them to the crowds.*

A reading from the holy Gospel according to Matthew

When Jesus heard of the death of John the Baptist, he withdrew
in a boat to a deserted place by himself. The crowds heard of
this and followed him on foot from their towns. When he
disembarked and saw the vast crowd, his heart was moved
with pity for them, and he cured their sick. When it was evening, the disciples approached him and said, "This is a deserted
place and it is already late; dismiss the crowds so that they can
go to the villages and buy food for themselves." He said to
them, "There is no need for them to go away; give them some
food yourselves." But they said to him, "Five loaves and two
fish are all we have here." Then he said, "Bring them here to
me," and he ordered the crowds to sit down on the grass. Taking
the five loaves and the two fish, and looking up to heaven, he
said the blessing, broke the loaves, and gave them to the dis-

ciples, who in turn gave them to the crowds. They all ate and were satisfied, and they picked up the fragments left over—twelve wicker baskets full. Those who ate were about five thousand men, not counting women and children.

The Gospel of the Lord.

Liturgy of the Eucharist, *p. 897;* **Prayer over the Gifts,** *p. 1255.*

Tuesday

Antiphons and Prayers, *p. 1254;* **Liturgy of the Word** *for Year I (odd years) follows; Year II (even years), p. 1265.*

TODAY'S LIVING WORD

Today's Gospel makes a profound Christological statement. In the story of Jesus walking on water, Matthew depicts Jesus doing what only God can do: "He alone stretches out the heavens and treads upon the crests of the sea" (Jb 9:8). When his terrified disciples cry out, Jesus' answer echoes the divine name: "It is I." Finally, the power of Jesus is revealed in his fully restoring people to wholeness. This is the same divine power announced by Jeremiah. Note the repetition of "I" as the prophet declares God's intention to restore the tents of Jacob.

In the Gospel, Peter is a little like Aaron and Miriam in the text from Numbers. They fail to appreciate Moses' status as God's servant, and he fails to appreciate Jesus' status as God's Son. They want to do what Moses does; he wants to do what Jesus does. All are brought up short.

Critics have rightly noted the unequal treatment of Miriam in the text from Numbers. Other scholars have pointed out the unfair depiction of the Pharisees as blind leaders in the alternative Gospel selection. It is important to realize that both of these cases reflect the historical conditioning of human writers and not the judgment of God.

Year I

FIRST READING   Nm 12:1–13

Not so with my servant Moses!
Why, then, did you not fear to speak against him?

A reading from the Book of Numbers

Miriam and Aaron spoke against Moses on the pretext of the marriage he had contracted with a Cushite woman. They complained, "Is it through Moses alone that the LORD speaks? Does he not speak through us also?" And the LORD heard this. Now, Moses himself was by far the meekest man on the face of the earth. So at once the LORD said to Moses and Aaron and Miriam, "Come out, you three, to the meeting tent." And the three of them went. Then the LORD came down in the column of cloud, and standing at the entrance of the tent, called Aaron and Miriam. When both came forward, he said, "Now listen to the words of the LORD:

> Should there be a prophet among you,
>> in visions will I reveal myself to him,
>> in dreams will I speak to him;
> not so with my servant Moses!
> Throughout my house he bears my trust:
>> face to face I speak to him;
>> plainly and not in riddles.
> The presence of the LORD he beholds.

Why, then, did you not fear to speak against my servant Moses?"

So angry was the LORD against them that when he departed, and the cloud withdrew from the tent, there was Miriam, a snow-white leper! When Aaron turned and saw her a leper, he said to Moses, "Ah, my lord! Please do not charge us with the sin that we have foolishly committed! Let her not thus be like the stillborn babe that comes forth from its mother's womb with its flesh half consumed." Then Moses cried to the LORD, "Please, not this! Pray, heal her!"

The word of the Lord.

Responsorial Psalm

Ps 51:3–4, 5–6ab, 6cd–7, 12–13

R. Be merciful, O Lord, for we have sinned.

Have mercy on me, O God, in your goodness;
   in the greatness of your compassion wipe out my offense.
Thoroughly wash me from my guilt
   and of my sin cleanse me.

R. Be merciful, O Lord, for we have sinned.

For I acknowledge my offense;
   and my sin is before me always:
"Against you only have I sinned;
   and done what is evil in your sight."

R. Be merciful, O Lord, for we have sinned.

That you may be justified in your sentence,
   vindicated when you condemn.
Indeed, in guilt was I born,
   and in sin my mother conceived me.

R. Be merciful, O Lord, for we have sinned.

A clean heart create for me, O God,
   and a steadfast spirit renew within me.
Cast me not off from your presence,
   and your Holy Spirit take not from me.

R. Be merciful, O Lord, for we have sinned.

Alleluia Verse *and* Gospel, *p. 1267.*

Year II

FIRST READING   Jer 30:1–2, 12–15, 18–22

Because of your numerous sins, I have done this to you.
See! I will restore the tents of Jacob.

A reading from the Book of the Prophet Jeremiah

The following message came to Jeremiah from the LORD: For
thus says the LORD, the God of Israel: Write all the words I
have spoken to you in a book.

> For thus says the LORD:
> Incurable is your wound,
>   grievous your bruise;
> There is none to plead your cause,
>   no remedy for your running sore,
>   no healing for you.
> All your lovers have forgotten you,
>   they do not seek you.
> I struck you as an enemy would strike,
>   punished you cruelly;
> Why cry out over your wound?
>   your pain is without relief.
> Because of your great guilt,
>   your numerous sins,
>   I have done this to you.

> Thus says the LORD:
> See! I will restore the tents of Jacob,
>   his dwellings I will pity;
> City shall be rebuilt upon hill,
>   and palace restored as it was.

From them will resound songs of praise,
>   the laughter of happy men.
I will make them not few, but many;
>   they will not be tiny, for I will glorify them.
His sons shall be as of old,
>   his assembly before me shall stand firm;
>   I will punish all his oppressors.
His leader shall be one of his own,
>   and his rulers shall come from his kin.
When I summon him, he shall approach me;
>   how else should one take the deadly risk
>   of approaching me? says the LORD.
You shall be my people,
>   and I will be your God.

The word of the Lord.

Responsorial Psalm

Ps 102:16–18, 19–21, 29 and 22–23

**R. The Lord will build up Zion again,
and appear in all his glory.**

The nations shall revere your name, O LORD,
>   and all the kings of the earth your glory,
When the LORD has rebuilt Zion
>   and appeared in his glory;
When he has regarded the prayer of the destitute,
>   and not despised their prayer.

**R. The Lord will build up Zion again,
and appear in all his glory.**

Let this be written for the generation to come,
>   and let his future creatures praise the LORD:
"The LORD looked down from his holy height,
>   from heaven he beheld the earth,

To hear the groaning of the prisoners,
  to release those doomed to die."

**R. The Lord will build up Zion again,
  and appear in all his glory.**

The children of your servants shall abide,
  and their posterity shall continue in your presence,
That the name of the LORD may be declared on Zion;
  and his praise, in Jerusalem,
When the peoples gather together
  and the kingdoms, to serve the LORD.

**R. The Lord will build up Zion again,
  and appear in all his glory.**

Alleluia, alleluia   Jn 1:49b
Rabbi, you are the Son of God;
you are the King of Israel.
Alleluia, alleluia

Years I and II

GOSPEL   Mt 14:22–36

Command me to come to you on the water.

A reading from the holy Gospel according to Matthew

Jesus made the disciples get into a boat and precede him to the
other side of the sea, while he dismissed the crowds. After
doing so, he went up on the mountain by himself to pray. When
it was evening he was there alone. Meanwhile the boat, already
a few miles offshore, was being tossed about by the waves, for
the wind was against it. During the fourth watch of the night,
he came toward them, walking on the sea. When the disciples
saw him walking on the sea they were terrified. "It is a ghost,"
they said, and they cried out in fear. At once Jesus spoke to
them, "Take courage, it is I; do not be afraid." Peter said to

him in reply, "Lord, if it is you, command me to come to you on the water." He said, "Come." Peter got out of the boat and began to walk on the water toward Jesus. But when he saw how strong the wind was he became frightened; and, beginning to sink, he cried out, "Lord, save me!" Immediately Jesus stretched out his hand and caught him, and said to him, "O you of little faith, why did you doubt?" After they got into the boat, the wind died down. Those who were in the boat did him homage, saying, "Truly, you are the Son of God."

After making the crossing, they came to land at Gennesaret. When the men of that place recognized him, they sent word to all the surrounding country. People brought to him all those who were sick and begged him that they might touch only the tassel on his cloak, and as many as touched it were healed.

The Gospel of the Lord.

Liturgy of the Eucharist, *p. 897;* **Prayer over the Gifts,** *p. 1255.*

Or:

GOSPEL   Mt 15:1–2, 10–14

The following text may be substituted, especially in Cycle A when the above Gospel is read on Monday.

Every plant that my heavenly Father has not planted will be uprooted.

A reading from the holy Gospel according to Matthew

Some Pharisees and scribes came to Jesus from Jerusalem and said, "Why do your disciples break the tradition of the elders? They do not wash their hands when they eat a meal." He summoned the crowd and said to them, "Hear and understand. It is not what enters one's mouth that defiles the man; but what

comes out of the mouth is what defiles one." Then his disciples approached and said to him, "Do you know that the Pharisees took offense when they heard what you said?" He said in reply, "Every plant that my heavenly Father has not planted will be uprooted. Let them alone; they are blind guides of the blind. If a blind man leads a blind man, both will fall into a pit."
The Gospel of the Lord.

Liturgy of the Eucharist, *p. 897;* **Prayer over the Gifts,** *p. 1255.*

Wednesday

Antiphons and Prayers, *p. 1254;* **Liturgy of the Word** *for Year I (odd years) follows; Year II (even years), p. 1272.*

TODAY'S LIVING WORD

In today's Gospel we find Matthew taking a story from Mark and making it his own. In his commentary on Matthew, Daniel Harrington explains how Matthew has heightened the theme of prayer in his version of this story. Where Mark simply relates that the desperate woman begged Jesus to cast the demon out of her daughter, Matthew reports her words. She speaks three times. The first two times her words are prayers: "Have pity on me, Lord, Son of David!" and "Lord, help me!" In the end, Jesus himself remarks on her great faith. In this way, Harrington says, Matthew portrays this woman as a "model of praying faith."* In today's episode from Numbers, the Israelite community lacks precisely this—praying faith.

The poem from Jeremiah makes an important point about the power of prayer. It is not praying faith that causes miracles to happen—like the cure of the woman's daughter or the restoration of the tribes of Israel. It is rather the mercy of God who loves us, all of us, "with age-old love."

* *The Gospel of Matthew,* Sacra Pagina 1 (Collegeville: Liturgical Press, 1991), p. 236.

FIRST READING   Nm 13:1–2, 25 —14:1, 26a–29a, 34–35

They despised the desirable land (Ps 106:24).

A reading from the Book of Numbers

The LORD said to Moses [in the desert of Paran,] "Send men to reconnoiter the land of Canaan, which I am giving the children of Israel. You shall send one man from each ancestral tribe, all of them princes."

After reconnoitering the land for forty days they returned, met Moses and Aaron and the whole congregation of the children of Israel in the desert of Paran at Kadesh, made a report to them all, and showed the fruit of the country to the whole congregation. They told Moses: "We went into the land to which you sent us. It does indeed flow with milk and honey, and here is its fruit. However, the people who are living in the land are fierce, and the towns are fortified and very strong. Besides, we saw descendants of the Anakim there. Amalekites live in the region of the Negeb; Hittites, Jebusites, and Amorites dwell in the highlands, and Canaanites along the seacoast and the banks of the Jordan."

Caleb, however, to quiet the people toward Moses, said, "We ought to go up and seize the land, for we can certainly do so." But the men who had gone up with him said, "We cannot attack these people; they are too strong for us." So they spread discouraging reports among the children of Israel about the land they had scouted, saying, "The land that we explored is a country that consumes its inhabitants. And all the people we saw there are huge, veritable giants (the Anakim were a race of giants); we felt like mere grasshoppers, and so we must have seemed to them."

At this, the whole community broke out with loud cries, and even in the night the people wailed.

The LORD said to Moses and Aaron: "How long will this wicked assembly grumble against me? I have heard the grumblings of the children of Israel against me. Tell them: By my life, says the LORD, I will do to you just what I have heard you say. Here in the desert shall your dead bodies fall. Forty days you spent in scouting the land; forty years shall you suffer for your crimes: one year for each day. Thus you will realize what it means to oppose me. I, the LORD, have sworn to do this to all this wicked assembly that conspired against me: here in the desert they shall die to the last man."

The word of the Lord.

Responsial Psalm
Ps 106:6–7ab, 13–14, 21–22, 23

R. **Remember us, O Lord, as you favor your people.**

We have sinned, we and our fathers;
  we have committed crimes; we have done wrong.
Our fathers in Egypt
  considered not your wonders.

R. **Remember us, O Lord, as you favor your people.**

But soon they forgot his works;
  they waited not for his counsel.
They gave way to craving in the desert
  and tempted God in the wilderness.

R. **Remember us, O Lord, as you favor your people.**

They forgot the God who had saved them,
  who had done great deeds in Egypt,
Wondrous deeds in the land of Ham,
  terrible things at the Red Sea.

R. Remember us, O Lord, as you favor your people.

Then he spoke of exterminating them,
   but Moses, his chosen one,
Withstood him in the breach
   to turn back his destructive wrath.

R. Remember us, O Lord, as you favor your people.

Alleluia Verse *and* **Gospel,** *p. 1273f.*

Year II

FIRST READING   Jer 31:1–7

With age-old love I have loved you.

A reading from the Book of the Prophet Jeremiah

At that time, says the LORD,
   I will be the God of all the tribes of Israel,
      and they shall be my people.
         Thus says the LORD:
The people that escaped the sword
   have found favor in the desert.
As Israel comes forward to be given his rest,
   the LORD appears to him from afar:
With age-old love I have loved you;
   so I have kept my mercy toward you.
Again I will restore you, and you shall be rebuilt,
   O virgin Israel;
Carrying your festive tambourines,
   you shall go forth dancing with the merrymakers.
Again you shall plant vineyards
   on the mountains of Samaria;
      those who plant them shall enjoy the fruits.
Yes, a day will come when the watchmen

will call out on Mount Ephraim:
"Rise up, let us go to Zion,
to the LORD, our God."

For thus says the LORD:
Shout with joy for Jacob,
exult at the head of the nations;
proclaim your praise and say:
The LORD has delivered his people,
the remnant of Israel.

The word of the Lord.

Responsorial Psalm

Jer 31:10, 11–12ab, 13

R. The Lord will guard us as a shepherd guards his flock.

Hear the word of the LORD, O nations,
proclaim it on distant isles, and say:
He who scattered Israel, now gathers them together,
he guards them as a shepherd his flock.

R. The Lord will guard us as a shepherd guards his flock.

The LORD shall ransom Jacob,
he shall redeem him from the hand of his conqueror.
Shouting, they shall mount the heights of Zion,
they shall come streaming to the LORD's blessings.

R. The Lord will guard us as a shepherd guards his flock.

Then the virgins shall make merry and dance,
and young men and old as well.
I will turn their mourning into joy.
I will console and gladden them after their sorrows.

R. The Lord will guard us as a shepherd guards his flock.

Alleluia, alleluia Lk 7:16
A great prophet has arisen in our midst
and God has visited his people.
Alleluia, alleluia

Years I and II

GOSPEL   Mt 15: 21–28

O woman, great is your faith!

A reading from the holy Gospel according to Matthew

At that time Jesus withdrew to the region of Tyre and Sidon. And behold, a Canaanite woman of that district came and called out, "Have pity on me, Lord, Son of David! My daughter is tormented by a demon." But he did not say a word in answer to her. His disciples came and asked him, "Send her away, for she keeps calling out after us." He said in reply, "I was sent only to the lost sheep of the house of Israel." But the woman came and did him homage, saying, "Lord, help me." He said in reply, "It is not right to take the food of the children and throw it to the dogs." She said, "Please, Lord, for even the dogs eat the scraps that fall from the table of their masters." Then Jesus said to her in reply, "O woman, great is your faith! Let it be done for you as you wish." And her daughter was healed from that hour.

The Gospel of the Lord.

Liturgy of the Eucharist, *p. 897;* **Prayer over the Gifts***, p. 1255.*

Thursday

Antiphons and Prayers, *p. 1254;* **Liturgy of the Word** *for Year I (odd years) follows; Year II (even years), p. 1277.*

TODAY'S LIVING WORD

The image of the rock links the reading from Numbers to today's Gospel. In both texts the rock ensures the community's survival. From the rock God gives the people water to drink; on the rock who is Peter, Jesus will build his Church. But in both texts the rock also becomes a stumbling block. For Moses and Aaron it is an occasion of sin, and Peter becomes for Jesus the instrument of Satan. Although the exact nature of their sin is unclear, Moses and Aaron's angry outburst obscures the holiness of God who is acting to save. Similarly, Peter's own inadequate interpretation of messiahship obscures God's saving plan and tempts Jesus to trip and fall. Like all of us at times, Moses, Aaron, and Peter are "little-faiths," in Matthew's favorite phrase.

Jeremiah offers hope to them and to us. The newness of the new covenant lies in a new capacity on the part of God's people, from least to greatest, to know the Lord who remembers their sin no more.

Year I

FIRST READING

Nm 20:1–13

Water gushed out in abundance.

A reading from the Book of Numbers

The whole congregation of the children of Israel arrived in the desert of Zin in the first month, and the people settled at Kadesh. It was here that Miriam died, and here that she was buried.

As the community had no water, they held a council against Moses and Aaron. The people contended with Moses, exclaiming, "Would that we too had perished with our kinsmen in the LORD's presence! Why have you brought the LORD's assembly into this desert where we and our livestock are dying? Why did you lead us out of Egypt, only to bring us to this wretched place which has neither grain nor figs nor vines nor pomegranates? Here there is not even water to drink!" But Moses and Aaron went away from the assembly to the entrance of the meeting tent, where they fell prostrate.

Then the glory of the LORD appeared to them, and the LORD said to Moses, "Take your staff and assemble the community, you and your brother Aaron, and in their presence order the rock to yield its waters. From the rock you shall bring forth water for the congregation and their livestock to drink." So Moses took his staff from its place before the LORD, as he was ordered. He and Aaron assembled the community in front of the rock, where he said to them, "Listen to me, you rebels! Are we to bring water for you out of this rock?" Then, raising his hand, Moses struck the rock twice with his staff, and water gushed out in abundance for the people and their livestock to drink. But the LORD said to Moses and Aaron, "Because you were not faithful to me in showing forth my sanctity before the children of Israel, you shall not lead this community into the land I will give them."

These are the waters of Meribah, where the children of Israel contended against the LORD, and where the LORD revealed his sanctity among them.

The word of the Lord.

Responsional Psalm

Ps 95:1–2, 6–7, 8–9

R. If today you hear his voice, harden not your hearts.

Come, let us sing joyfully to the LORD;
   let us acclaim the Rock of our salvation.
Let us come into his presence with thanksgiving;
   let us joyfully sing psalms to him.

R. If today you hear his voice, harden not your hearts.

Come, let us bow down in worship;
   let us kneel before the LORD who made us.
For he is our God,
   and we are the people he shepherds, the flock he guides.

R. If today you hear his voice, harden not your hearts.

Oh, that today you would hear his voice:
"Harden not your hearts as at Meribah,
as in the day of Massah in the desert,
Where your fathers tested me;
they tested me though they had seen my works."

R. If today you hear his voice, harden not your hearts.

Alleluia Verse *and* **Gospel,** *p. 1278.*

Year II

FIRST READING

Jer 31:31–34

The days are coming when I will make a new covenant
with the house of Israel and I will remember their sin no more.

A reading from the Book of the Prophet Jeremiah

The days are coming, says the LORD,
when I will make a new covenant with the house of
Israel
and the house of Judah.
It will not be like the covenant I made with their fathers:
the day I took them by the hand
to lead them forth from the land of Egypt;
for they broke my covenant,
and I had to show myself their master, says the LORD.
But this is the covenant that I will make
with the house of Israel after those days, says the LORD.
I will place my law within them, and write it upon their hearts;
I will be their God, and they shall be my people.
No longer will they have need to teach their friends and relatives
how to know the LORD.
All, from least to greatest, shall know me, says the LORD,

for I will forgive their evildoing and remember their sin
no more.

The word of the Lord.

Responsorial Psalm
Ps 51:12–13, 14–15, 18–19

R. Create a clean heart in me, O God.

A clean heart create for me, O God,
  and a steadfast spirit renew within me.
Cast me not out from your presence,
  and your Holy Spirit take not from me.

R. Create a clean heart in me, O God.

Give me back the joy of your salvation,
  and a willing spirit sustain in me.
I will teach transgressors your ways,
  and sinners shall return to you.

R. Create a clean heart in me, O God.

For you are not pleased with sacrifices;
  should I offer a burnt offering, you would not accept it.
My sacrifice, O God, is a contrite spirit;
  a heart contrite and humbled, O God, you will not spurn.

R. Create a clean heart in me, O God.

Alleluia, alleluia Mt 16:18
You are Peter, and upon this rock I will build my Church,
and the gates of the netherworld shall not prevail against it.
Alleluia, alleluia

Years I and II

GOSPEL
Mt 16:13–23

You are Peter, I will give you the keys to the Kingdom of heaven.

A reading from the holy Gospel according to Matthew

Jesus went into the region of Caesarea Philippi and he asked his disciples, "Who do people say that the Son of Man is?" They replied, "Some say John the Baptist, others Elijah, still others Jeremiah or one of the prophets." He said to them, "But who do you say that I am?" Simon Peter said in reply, "You are the Christ, the Son of the living God." Jesus said to him in reply, "Blessed are you, Simon son of Jonah. For flesh and blood has not revealed this to you, but my heavenly Father. And so I say to you, you are Peter, and upon this rock I will build my Church, and the gates of the netherworld shall not prevail against it. I will give you the keys to the Kingdom of heaven. Whatever you bind on earth shall be bound in heaven; and whatever you loose on earth shall be loosed in heaven." Then he strictly ordered his disciples to tell no one that he was the Christ.

From that time on, Jesus began to show his disciples that he must go to Jerusalem and suffer greatly from the elders, the chief priests, and the scribes, and be killed and on the third day be raised. Then Peter took Jesus aside and began to rebuke him, "God forbid, Lord! No such thing shall ever happen to you." He turned and said to Peter, "Get behind me, Satan! You are an obstacle to me. You are thinking not as God does, but as human beings do."

The Gospel of the Lord.

Liturgy of the Eucharist, *p. 897;* **Prayer over the Gifts,** *p. 1255.*

Friday

Antiphons and Prayers, *p. 1254;* **Liturgy of the Word** *for Year I (odd years) follows; Year II (even years), p. 1282.*

You led your people like a flock
    under the care of Moses and Aaron.

R. I remember the deeds of the Lord.

Alleluia Verse *and* **Gospel,** *p. 1283.*

Year II

FIRST READING   Na 2:1, 3; 3:1–3, 6–7

Woe to the city of blood!

A reading from the Book of the Prophet Nahum

See, upon the mountains there advances
    the bearer of good news,
        announcing peace!
Celebrate your feasts, O Judah,
    fulfill your vows!
For nevermore shall you be invaded
    by the scoundrel; he is completely destroyed.
The LORD will restore the vine of Jacob,
    the pride of Israel,
Though ravagers have ravaged them
    and ruined the tendrils.

Woe to the bloody city, all lies,
    full of plunder, whose looting never stops!
The crack of the whip, the rumbling sounds of wheels;
    horses a-gallop, chariots bounding,
Cavalry charging, the flame of the sword, the flash of the spear,
    the many slain, the heaping corpses,
        the endless bodies to stumble upon!
I will cast filth upon you,

disgrace you and put you to shame;
Till everyone who sees you runs from you, saying,
    "Nineveh is destroyed; who can pity her?
   Where can one find any to console her?"
The word of the Lord.

Responsional Psalm

Dt 32:35cd–36ab, 39abcd, 41

  R. It is I who deal death and give life.

Close at hand is the day of their disaster,
  and their doom is rushing upon them!
Surely, the LORD shall do justice for his people;
  on his servants he shall have pity.

  R. It is I who deal death and give life.

"Learn then that I, I alone, am God,
  and there is no god besides me.
It is I who bring both death and life,
  I who inflict wounds and heal them."

  R. It is I who deal death and give life.

I will sharpen my flashing sword,
  and my hand shall lay hold of my quiver,
"With vengeance I will repay my foes
 and requite those who hate me."

  R. It is I who deal death and give life.

    Alleluia, alleluia   Mt 5:10
    Blessed are they who are persecuted for the sake of righteousness;
    for theirs is the Kingdom of heaven.
    Alleluia, alleluia

Years I and II

GOSPEL

Mt 16:24–28

What can one give in exchange for one's life?

A reading from the holy Gospel according to Matthew

Jesus said to his disciples, "Whoever wishes to come after me must deny himself, take up his cross, and follow me. For whoever wishes to save his life will lose it, but whoever loses his life for my sake will find it. What profit would there be for one to gain the whole world and forfeit his life? Or what can one give in exchange for his life? For the Son of Man will come with his angels in his Father's glory, and then he will repay each according to his conduct. Amen, I say to you, there are some standing here who will not taste death until they see the Son of Man coming in his Kingdom."

The Gospel of the Lord.

Liturgy of the Eucharist, *p. 897;* **Prayer over the Gifts,** *p. 1255.*

Saturday

Antiphons and Prayers, *p. 1254;* **Liturgy of the Word** *for Year I (odd years) follows; Year II (even years), p. 1286.*

TODAY'S LIVING WORD

Each of today's three readings is a statement about faith. The text from Deuteronomy contains the principal profession of faith of the Jewish people, the *Shema*. It begins with the words, "Hear, O Israel! The Lord is our God, the Lord alone!" The verses that follow describe how totally their faith in the one God must pervade the life of this people. When the word of the Lord finally comes to the prophet Habakkuk in a time of national crisis, it tells him, "The just man, because of his faith, shall live." In such times, faith must be sturdy and steadfast.

Today's Gospel is also a statement about faith. Here again Matthew adapts a story from Mark. In Mark this story focuses on the faith of the boy's father; in Matthew it focuses on the little faith of Jesus' disciples. When they wonder why they could not expel the demon, Jesus answers, "Because of your little faith." Then he goes on to tell them and us what even a little faith can do, even if only "the size of a mustard seed."

Year I

FIRST READING

Dt 6:4–13

You shall love the LORD, your God, with all your heart.

A reading from the Book of Deuteronomy

Moses said to the people: "Hear, O Israel! The LORD is our God, the LORD alone! Therefore, you shall love the LORD, your God, with all your heart, and with all your soul, and with all your strength. Take to heart these words which I enjoin on you today. Drill them into your children. Speak of them at home and abroad, whether you are busy or at rest. Bind them at your wrist as a sign and let them be as a pendant on your forehead. Write them on the doorposts of your houses and on your gates.

"When the LORD, your God, brings you into the land which he swore to your fathers: Abraham, Isaac and Jacob, that he would give you, a land with fine, large cities that you did not build, with houses full of goods of all sorts that you did not garner, with cisterns that you did not dig, with vineyards and olive groves that you did not plant; and when, therefore, you eat your fill, take care not to forget the LORD, who brought you out of the land of Egypt, that place of slavery. The LORD, your God, shall you fear; him shall you serve, and by his name shall you swear."

The word of the Lord.

Responsorial Psalm

Ps 18:2–3a, 3bc–4, 47 and 51

R. I love you, Lord, my strength.

I love you, O Lord, my strength,
  O Lord, my rock, my fortress, my deliverer.

R. I love you, Lord, my strength.

My God, my rock of refuge,
  my shield, the horn of my salvation, my stronghold!
Praised be the Lord, I exclaim!
  And I am safe from my enemies.

R. I love you, Lord, my strength.

The Lord live! And blessed be my Rock!
  Extolled be God my savior!
You who gave great victories to your king,
  and showed kindness to your anointed,
  to David and his posterity forever.

R. I love you, Lord, my strength.

Alleluia Verse *and* **Gospel,** *p. 1288.*

Year II

FIRST READING   Hab 1:12 —2:4

The just, because of their faith, shall live.

A reading from the Book of the Prophet Habakkuk

Are you not from eternity, O Lord,
  my holy God, immortal?
O Lord, you have marked him for judgment,
  O Rock, you have readied him punishment!
Too pure are your eyes to look upon evil,
  and the sight of misery you cannot endure.
Why, then, do you gaze on the faithless in silence
  while the wicked man devours
  one more just than himself?
You have made man like the fish of the sea,

like creeping things without a ruler.
He brings them all up with his hook,
 he hauls them away with his net,
He gathers them in his seine;
 and so he rejoices and exults.
Therefore he sacrifices to his net,
 and burns incense to his seine;
for thanks to them his portion is generous,
 and his repast sumptuous.
Shall he, then, keep on brandishing his sword
 to slay peoples without mercy?

I will stand at my guard post,
 and station myself upon the rampart,
And keep watch to see what he will say to me,
 and what answer he will give to my complaint.

Then the LORD answered me and said:
 Write down the vision
Clearly upon the tablets,
 so that one can read it readily.
For the vision still has its time,
 presses on to fulfillment, and will not disappoint;
If it delays, wait for it,
 it will surely come, it will not be late.
The rash man has no integrity;
 but the just man, because of his faith, shall live.
The word of the Lord.

Responsorial Psalm

Ps 9:8–9, 10–11, 12–13

R. You forsake not those who seek you, O Lord.

The LORD sits enthroned forever;
 he has set up his throne for judgment.

He judges the world with justice;
   he governs the peoples with equity.

   R. You forsake not those who seek you, O Lord.

The LORD is a stronghold for the oppressed,
   a stronghold in times of distress.
They trust in you who cherish your name,
   for you forsake not those who seek you, O LORD.

   R. You forsake not those who seek you, O Lord.

Sing praise to the LORD enthroned in Zion;
   proclaim among the nations his deeds;
For the avenger of blood has remembered;
   he has not forgotten the cry of the poor.

   R. You forsake not those who seek you, O Lord.

   Alleluia, alleluia   See 2 Tm 1:10
   Our Savior Jesus Christ has destroyed death
   and brought life to light through the Gospel.
   Alleluia, alleluia

Years I and II

GOSPEL   Mt 17:14–20

If you have faith, nothing will be impossible for you.

A reading from the holy Gospel according to Matthew

A man came up to Jesus, knelt down before him, and said,
"Lord, have pity on my son, who is a lunatic and suffers severely; often he falls into fire, and often into water. I brought
him to your disciples, but they could not cure him." Jesus said
in reply, "O faithless and perverse generation, how long will I
be with you? How long will I endure you? Bring the boy here to
me." Jesus rebuked him and the demon came out of him, and
from that hour the boy was cured. Then the disciples ap-

proached Jesus in private and said, "Why could we not drive it out?" He said to them, "Because of your little faith. Amen, I say to you, if you have faith the size of a mustard seed, you will say to this mountain, 'Move from here to there,' and it will move. Nothing will be impossible for you."

The Gospel of the Lord.

Liturgy of the Eucharist, *p. 897;* **Prayer over the Gifts,** *p. 1255.*

NINETEENTH WEEK IN ORDINARY TIME

The **Antiphons and Prayers** *may be the following, or may be chosen from any of the other 33 weeks in Ordinary Time (refer to Liturgical Calendar, pp. 26–41).*

The **Liturgy of the Word** *varies: for Monday, see p. 1291; Tuesday, p. 1296; Wednesday, p. 1300; Thursday, p. 1305; Friday, p. 1311; Saturday, p. 1318.*

Entrance Antiphon

Lord, be true to your covenant, forget not the life of your poor ones for ever. Rise up, O God, and defend your cause; do not ignore the shouts of your enemies. (Ps 74:20, 19, 22, 23)

Opening Prayer

Let us pray
[in the Spirit
that we may grow in the love of God]

Pause for silent prayer.

Almighty and ever-living God,
your Spirit made us your children,
confident to call you Father.
Increase your Spirit within us
and bring us to our promised inheritance.

Grant this through our Lord Jesus Christ, your Son,
who lives and reigns with you and the Holy Spirit,
one God, for ever and ever.

Alternative Opening Prayer

Let us pray
[that through us
others may find the way to life in Christ]

Pause for silent prayer.

Father,
we come, reborn in the Spirit,
to celebrate our sonship in the Lord Jesus Christ.
Touch our hearts,
help them grow toward the life you have promised.
Touch our lives,
make them signs of your love for all men.

Grant this through Christ our Lord.

Prayer over the Gifts

Pray, brethren...

God of power,
giver of the gifts we bring,
accept the offering of your Church
and make it the sacrament of our salvation.

We ask this through Christ our Lord.

Preface of Weekdays in Ordinary Time I–VI, *pp. 948–950.*

Communion Antiphon

Praise the Lord, Jerusalem; he feeds you with the finest wheat.

(Ps 148:12, 14)

Or:

The bread I shall give is my flesh for the life of the world, says the Lord. (Jn 6:51)

Prayer after Communion

Let us pray.

Pause for silent prayer, if this has not preceded.

Lord,
may the eucharist you give us
bring us to salvation
and keep us faithful to the light of your truth.

We ask this in the name of Jesus the Lord.

Monday

Antiphons and Prayers, *p. 1289;* **Liturgy of the Word** *for Year I (odd years) follows; Year II (even years), p. 1293.*

TODAY'S LIVING WORD

The selections from Deuteronomy and Ezekiel bear witness to "the God of gods, the Lord of lords, the great God, mighty and awesome," who is the glory of Israel. In Deuteronomy that glory is revealed in the "great and terrible things" God did in order to secure the freedom and the future of Israel. In Ezekiel the glory of God appears in human likeness resplendent with fire and with electrum—an alloy of silver and gold.

By comparison the Gospel story seems very prosaic. Yet even in this somewhat mundane exchange about paying taxes, we catch a glimpse of God's glory. When Jesus asks Peter whether the kings of the world take tribute from their sons *(huiōn* in Greek) or from strangers, he makes a profound claim. The tax in question was levied on Jews for the upkeep of the temple. Jesus' question and the expected answer from Peter imply that Jesus is exempt from paying this tax for the maintenance of God's house because he is the Son of God.

Year I

FIRST READING

Dt 10:12–22

Circumcise your hearts. Befriend the alien,
for you were once aliens yourselves.

A reading from the Book of Deuteronomy

Moses said to the people: "And now, Israel, what does the LORD, your God, ask of you but to fear the LORD, your God, and follow his ways exactly, to love and serve the LORD, your God, with all your heart and all your soul, to keep the commandments and statutes of the LORD which I enjoin on you today for your own good? Think! The heavens, even the highest heavens, belong to the LORD, your God, as well as the earth and everything on it. Yet in his love for your fathers the LORD was so attached to them as to choose you, their descendants, in preference to all other peoples, as indeed he has now done. Circumcise your hearts, therefore, and be no longer stiff-necked. For the LORD, your God, is the God of gods, the LORD of lords, the great God, mighty and awesome, who has no favorites, accepts no bribes; who executes justice for the orphan and the widow, and befriends the alien, feeding and clothing him. So you too must befriend the alien, for you were once aliens yourselves in the land of Egypt. The LORD, your God, shall you fear, and him shall you serve; hold fast to him and swear by his name. He is your glory, he, your God, who has done for you those great and terrible things which your own eyes have seen. Your ancestors went down to Egypt seventy strong, and now the LORD, your God, has made you as numerous as the stars of the sky."

The word of the Lord.

Responsorial Psalm

Ps 147:12–13, 14–15, 19–20

R. **Praise the Lord, Jerusalem.**

Glorify the LORD, O Jerusalem;
  praise your God, O Zion.
For he has strengthened the bars of your gates;
  he has blessed your children within you.

R. **Praise the Lord, Jerusalem.**

He has granted peace in your borders;
  with the best of wheat he fills you.
He sends forth his command to the earth;
  swiftly runs his word!

R. **Praise the Lord, Jerusalem.**

He has proclaimed his word to Jacob,
  his statutes and his ordinances to Israel.
He has not done thus for any other nation;
  his ordinances he has not made known to them. Alleluia.

R. **Praise the Lord, Jerusalem.**

Alleluia Verse *and* **Gospel**, *p. 1295.*

Year II

FIRST READING

Ez 1:2–5, 24–28c

Such was the vision of the likeness of the glory of the LORD.

A reading from the Book of the Prophet Ezekiel

On the fifth day of the fourth month of the fifth year, that is, of King Jehoiachin's exile, The word of the LORD came to the priest Ezekiel, the son of Buzi, in the land of the Chaldeans by the river Chebar.—There the hand of the LORD came upon me.

As I looked, a stormwind came from the North, a huge cloud with flashing fire enveloped in brightness, from the midst of which (the midst of the fire) something gleamed like electrum. Within it were figures resembling four living creatures that looked like this: their form was human.

Then I heard the sound of their wings, like the roaring of mighty waters, like the voice of the Almighty. When they moved, the sound of the tumult was like the din of an army. And when they stood still, they lowered their wings.

Above the firmament over their heads something like a throne could be seen, looking like sapphire. Upon it was seated, up above, one who had the appearance of a man. Upward from what resembled his waist I saw what gleamed like electrum; downward from what resembled his waist I saw what looked like fire; he was surrounded with splendor. Like the bow which appears in the clouds on a rainy day was the splendor that surrounded him. Such was the vision of the likeness of the glory of the LORD.

The word of the Lord.

Responsorial Psalm

Ps 148:1–2, 11–12, 13, 14

R. Heaven and earth are filled with your glory.

Praise the LORD from the heavens;
  praise him in the heights;
Praise him, all you his angels;
  praise him, all you his hosts.

R. Heaven and earth are filled with your glory.

Let the kings of the earth and all peoples,
  the princes and all the judges of the earth,
Young men too, and maidens,
  old men and boys,

R. Heaven and earth are filled with your glory.

Praise the name of the LORD,
  for his name alone is exalted;
His majesty is above earth and heaven.

R. Heaven and earth are filled with your glory.

And he has lifted up the horn of his people.
Be this his praise from all his faithful ones,
  from the children of Israel, the people close to him.
  Alleluia.

R. Heaven and earth are filled with your glory.

Or: **R. Alleluia.**

Alleluia, alleluia   See 2 Thes 2:14
God has called you through the Gospel
to possess the glory of our Lord Jesus Christ.
Alleluia, alleluia

Years I and II

GOSPEL   Mt 17:22–27
They will kill him and he will be raised.
The subjects are exempt from the tax.

A reading from the holy Gospel according to Matthew

As Jesus and his disciples were gathering in Galilee, Jesus
said to them, "The Son of Man is to be handed over to men,
and they will kill him, and he will be raised on the third day."
And they were overwhelmed with grief.

   When they came to Capernaum, the collectors of the temple
tax approached Peter and said, "Does not your teacher pay the
temple tax?" "Yes," he said. When he came into the house, before he had time to speak, Jesus asked him, "What is your
opinion, Simon? From whom do the kings of the earth take
tolls or census tax? From their subjects or from foreigners?"

When he said, "From foreigners," Jesus said to him, "Then the subjects are exempt. But that we may not offend them, go to the sea, drop in a hook, and take the first fish that comes up. Open its mouth and you will find a coin worth twice the temple tax. Give that to them for me and for you."

The Gospel of the Lord.

Liturgy of the Eucharist, *p. 897;* **Prayer over the Gifts,** *p. 1290.*

Tuesday

Antiphons and Prayers, *p. 1289;* **Liturgy of the Word** *for Year I (odd years) follows;* **Year II** *(even years), p. 1298.*

TODAY'S LIVING WORD

In all three of today's readings servants of God and of God's people are being commissioned. In every case, they are urged to internalize the saving will of God. As Moses' successor, Joshua will lead Israel on the last stage of their journey, bringing them into the promised land. Moses tells him that he will only be able to do this if he trusts that God marches before him and his people. Ezekiel is called to speak God's word to the rebellious house of Israel, and is required literally to ingest that word, taking it in and making it his own word of "lamentation and wailing and woe."

Today's Gospel is from Matthew 18, which contains Jesus' instructions to those who will one day lead his Church. Clearly, concern for the "little ones," the most vulnerable members of the community, is of paramount importance. Why? The parable gives the answer: because the heavenly Father, the Good Shepherd, wills that not "one of these little ones be lost."

Year I

FIRST READING   Dt 31:1–8

Be brave and steadfast,
for you must bring this people into the land.

A reading from the Book of Deuteronomy

When Moses had finished speaking to all Israel, he said to them, "I am now one hundred and twenty years old and am no longer able to move about freely; besides, the LORD has told me that I shall not cross this Jordan. It is the LORD, your God, who will cross before you; he will destroy these nations before you, that you may supplant them. It is Joshua who will cross before you, as the LORD promised. The LORD will deal with them just as he dealt with Sihon and Og, the kings of the Amorites whom he destroyed, and with their country. When, therefore, the LORD delivers them up to you, you must deal with them exactly as I have ordered you. Be brave and steadfast; have no fear or dread of them, for it is the LORD, your God, who marches with you; he will never fail you or forsake you."

Then Moses summoned Joshua and in the presence of all Israel said to him, "Be brave and steadfast, for you must bring this people into the land which the LORD swore to their fathers he would give them; you must put them in possession of their heritage. It is the LORD who marches before you; he will be with you and will never fail you or forsake you. So do not fear or be dismayed."

The word of the Lord.

Responsorial Psalm

Dt 32:3–4ab, 7, 8, 9 and 12

R. The portion of the Lord is his people.

For I will sing the LORD's renown.
  Oh, proclaim the greatness of our God!
The Rock—how faultless are his deeds,
  how right all his ways!

R. The portion of the Lord is his people.

Think back on the days of old,
    reflect on the years of age upon age.
Ask your father and he will inform you,
    ask your elders and they will tell you.

    R. The portion of the Lord is his people.

When the Most High assigned the nations their heritage,
    when he parceled out the descendants of Adam,
He set up the boundaries of the peoples
    after the number of the sons of Israel.

    R. The portion of the Lord is his people.

While the LORD's own portion was Jacob,
    his hereditary share was Israel.
The LORD alone was their leader,
    no strange god was with him.

    R. The portion of the Lord is his people.

    Alleluia Verse *and* **Gospel,** *p. 1299f.*

Year II

FIRST READING
Ez 2:8—3:4

He fed me with this scroll, and it was as sweet as honey in my mouth.

A reading from the Book of the Prophet Ezekiel

The Lord GOD said to me: As for you, son of man, obey me when I speak to you: be not rebellious like this house of rebellion, but open your mouth and eat what I shall give you.

    It was then I saw a hand stretched out to me, in which was a written scroll which he unrolled before me. It was covered with writing front and back, and written on it was: Lamentation and wailing and woe!

    He said to me: Son of man, eat what is before you; eat this scroll, then go, speak to the house of Israel. So I opened my mouth and he gave me the scroll to eat. Son of man, he then said to me, feed your belly and fill your stomach with this scroll I am giving you. I ate it, and it was as sweet as honey in my mouth. He said: Son of man, go now to the house of Israel, and speak my words to them.

The word of the Lord.

Responsorial Psalm   Ps 119:14, 24, 72, 103, 111, 131

R. How sweet to my taste is your promise!

In the way of your decrees I rejoice,
  as much as in all riches.

R. How sweet to my taste is your promise!

Yes, your decrees are my delight;
  they are my counselors.

R. How sweet to my taste is your promise!

The law of your mouth is to me more precious
  than thousands of gold and silver pieces.

R. How sweet to my taste is your promise!

How sweet to my palate are your promises,
  sweeter than honey to my mouth!

R. How sweet to my taste is your promise!

Your decrees are my inheritance forever;
  the joy of my heart they are.

R. How sweet to my taste is your promise!

I gasp with open mouth,
  in my yearning for your commands.

R. How sweet to my taste is your promise!

> **Alleluia, alleluia** Mt 11:29ab
> Take my yoke upon you and learn from me,
> for I am meek and humble of heart.
> **Alleluia, alleluia**

Years I and II

GOSPEL   Mt 18:1–5, 10, 12–14

See that you do not despise one of these little ones.

A reading from the holy Gospel according to Matthew

The disciples approached Jesus and said, "Who is the greatest in the Kingdom of heaven?" He called a child over, placed it in their midst, and said, "Amen, I say to you, unless you turn and become like children, you will not enter the Kingdom of heaven. Whoever becomes humble like this child is the greatest in the Kingdom of heaven. And whoever receives one child such as this in my name receives me.

"See that you do not despise one of these little ones, for I say to you that their angels in heaven always look upon the face of my heavenly Father. What is your opinion? If a man has a hundred sheep and one of them goes astray, will he not leave the ninety-nine in the hills and go in search of the stray? And if he finds it, amen, I say to you, he rejoices more over it than over the ninety-nine that did not stray. In just the same way, it is not the will of your heavenly Father that one of these little ones be lost."

The Gospel of the Lord.

Liturgy of the Eucharist, *p. 897;* **Prayer over the Gifts,** *p. 1290.*

Wednesday

Antiphons and Prayers, *p. 1289;* **Liturgy of the Word** *for Year I (odd years) follows; Year II (even years), p. 1303.*

TODAY'S LIVING WORD

The powerful presence of God links all three readings today. In each one, the same divine presence is symbolized in a different way. In the passage from Deuteronomy, the powerful presence of God descends on Joshua as he is filled with the *spirit* of wisdom. In the vision of Ezekiel, the powerful presence of God is *glory,* and it departs from the Jerusalem temple because of "all the abominations that are practiced within it." In the Gospel selection, Jesus' *name* conveys the reality of God's powerful presence.

Today's Gospel is also of interest for what it tells us about life in the church of Matthew. Clearly, that community of Christians found it necessary at times to deal firmly and forcefully with its sinful members. The three-step process outlined in these verses counsels confrontation, intervention and excommunication as a last resort. But the most important aspect for us to note is that the community takes this action while united in prayer, assuring them of God's powerful presence.

Year I

FIRST READING

Dt 34:1–12

There Moses died as the Lord had said,
and since then no prophet has arisen in Israel like him.

A reading from the Book of Deuteronomy

Moses went up from the plains of Moab to Mount Nebo, the headland of Pisgah which faces Jericho, and the Lord showed him all the land—Gilead, and as far as Dan, all Naphtali, the land of Ephraim and Manasseh, all the land of Judah as far as the Western Sea, the Negeb, the circuit of the Jordan with the lowlands at Jericho, city of palms, and as far as Zoar. The Lord then said to him, "This is the land which I swore to Abraham, Isaac, and Jacob that I would give to their descendants. I have let you feast your eyes upon it, but you shall not cross over." So there, in the land of Moab, Moses, the servant of the Lord, died as the Lord had said; and he was buried in the ravine opposite Beth-peor in the land of Moab, but to this day no one knows the place of his burial. Moses was one hundred and twenty years old when he died, yet his eyes were undimmed and his vigor unabated. For thirty days the children of Israel wept for Moses in the plains of Moab, till they had completed the period of grief and mourning for Moses.

Now Joshua, son of Nun, was filled with the spirit of wisdom, since Moses had laid his hands upon him; and so the children of Israel gave him their obedience, thus carrying out the LORD's command to Moses.

Since then no prophet has arisen in Israel like Moses, whom the LORD knew face to face. He had no equal in all the signs and wonders the LORD sent him to perform in the land of Egypt against Pharaoh and all his servants and against all his land, and for the might and the terrifying power that Moses exhibited in the sight of all Israel.

The word of the Lord.

Responsorial Psalm

Ps 66:1–3a, 5 and 8, 16–17

R. Blessed be God who filled my soul with fire!

Shout joyfully to God, all the earth;
    sing praise to the glory of his name;
    proclaim his glorious praise.
Say to God: "How tremendous are your deeds!"

R. Blessed be God who filled my soul with fire!

Come and see the works of God,
    his tremendous deeds among the children of Adam.
Bless our God, you peoples;
    loudly sound his praise.

R. Blessed be God who filled my soul with fire!

Hear now, all you who fear God, while I declare
    what he has done for me.

When I appealed to him in words,
  praise was on the tip of my tongue.

R. Blessed be God who filled my soul with fire!

Alleluia Verse *and* **Gospel,** *p. 1304f.*

Year II

FIRST READING   Ez 9:1–7; 10:18–22

*Mark a "Thau" on the foreheads of those who moan and groan
over all the abominations in Jerusalem.*

A reading from the Book of the Prophet Ezekiel

The LORD cried loud for me to hear: Come, you scourges of
the city! With that I saw six men coming from the direction of
the upper gate which faces the north, each with a destroying
weapon in his hand. In their midst was a man dressed in linen,
with a writer's case at his waist. They entered and stood beside
the bronze altar. Then he called to the man dressed in linen
with the writer's case at his waist, saying to him: Pass through
the city, through Jerusalem, and mark a "Thau" on the foreheads
of those who moan and groan over all the abominations that
are practiced within it. To the others I heard the LORD say: Pass
through the city after him and strike! Do not look on them
with pity nor show any mercy! Old men, youths and maidens,
women and children—wipe them out! But do not touch any
marked with the "Thau"; begin at my sanctuary. So they began
with the men, the elders, who were in front of the temple. Defile
the temple, he said to them, and fill the courts with the slain;
then go out and strike in the city.

Then the glory of the LORD left the threshold of the temple
and rested upon the cherubim. These lifted their wings, and I

saw them rise from the earth, the wheels rising along with them. They stood at the entrance of the eastern gate of the LORD's house, and the glory of the God of Israel was up above them. Then the cherubim lifted their wings, and the wheels went along with them, while up above them was the glory of the God of Israel.

The word of the Lord.

Responsorial Psalm

Ps 113:1–2, 3–4, 5–6

R. **The glory of the Lord is higher than the skies.**

Praise, you servants of the LORD,
  praise the name of the LORD.
Blessed be the name of the LORD
  both now and forever.

R. **The glory of the Lord is higher than the skies.**

From the rising to the setting of the sun
  is the name of the LORD to be praised.
High above all nations is the LORD;
  above the heavens is his glory.

R. **The glory of the Lord is higher than the skies.**

Who is like the LORD, our God, who is enthroned on high,
  and looks upon the heavens and the earth below?

R. **The glory of the Lord is higher than the skies.**

Or: R. **Alleluia.**

Alleluia, alleluia 2 Cor 5:19
God was reconciling the world to himself in Christ,
and entrusting to us the message of reconciliation.
Alleluia, alleluia

Years I and II

GOSPEL   Mt 18:15–20

If your brother listens to you, you have won him over.

A reading from the holy Gospel according to Matthew

Jesus said to his disciples: "If your brother sins against you, go and tell him his fault between you and him alone. If he listens to you, you have won over your brother. If he does not listen, take one or two others along with you, so that every fact may be established on the testimony of two or three witnesses. If he refuses to listen to them, tell the Church. If he refuses to listen even to the Church, then treat him as you would a Gentile or a tax collector. Amen, I say to you, whatever you bind on earth shall be bound in heaven, and whatever you loose on earth shall be loosed in heaven. Again, amen, I say to you, if two of you agree on earth about anything for which they are to pray, it shall be granted to them by my heavenly Father. For where two or three are gathered together in my name, there am I in the midst of them."

The Gospel of the Lord.

Liturgy of the Eucharist, *p. 897;* **Prayer over the Gifts,** *p. 1290.*

Thursday

Antiphons and Prayers, *p. 1289;* **Liturgy of the Word** *for Year I (odd years) follows; Year II (even years), p. 1308.*

Today's Living Word

Each of the three readings for today presents a sign and urges us to heed it. The Israelites' long journey from Egypt to the promised land began with the crossing of the Red Sea and ends, in today's excerpt from Joshua, with the crossing of the Jordan River. "This," Joshua tells the people, "is how you will know that there is a living God in your midst." It is a sign that God is with them. The prophet Ezekiel lives among a rebellious people, who "have eyes to see but do not see, and ears to hear but do not hear." Ezekiel's charade is a sign for these people about the exile that will soon befall them.

In the Gospel Jesus answers Peter's question—"How often must I forgive?… Seven times?"—with a numerical sign. "Not seven times," he says, but "seventy-seven times," an unlimited number. The parable drives the point home: if God places no limit on forgiveness, neither can we. Let the one who has ears hear.

Year I

FIRST READING
Jos 3:7–10a, 11, 13–17

The ark of the covenant of the LORD will precede you into the Jordan.

A reading from the Book of Joshua

The LORD said to Joshua, "Today I will begin to exalt you in the sight of all Israel, that they may know I am with you, as I was with Moses. Now command the priests carrying the ark of the covenant to come to a halt in the Jordan when you reach the edge of the waters."

So Joshua said to the children of Israel, "Come here and listen to the words of the LORD, your God. This is how you will know that there is a living God in your midst, who at your approach will dispossess the Canaanites. The ark of the covenant of the LORD of the whole earth will precede you into the Jordan. When the soles of the feet of the priests carrying the ark of the LORD, the Lord of the whole earth, touch the water of the Jordan, it will cease to flow; for the water flowing down from upstream will halt in a solid bank."

The people struck their tents to cross the Jordan, with the priests carrying the ark of the covenant ahead of them. No sooner had these priestly bearers of the ark waded into the waters at the edge of the Jordan, which overflows all its banks during the entire season of the harvest, than the waters flowing from upstream halted, backing up in a solid mass for a very great distance indeed, from Adam, a city in the direction of Zarethan; while those flowing downstream toward the Salt Sea of the Arabah disappeared entirely. Thus the people crossed over opposite Jericho. While all Israel crossed over on dry ground, the priests carrying the ark of the covenant of the LORD remained motionless on dry ground in the bed of the Jordan until the whole nation had completed the passage.

The word of the Lord.

Responsorial Psalm

Ps 114:1–2, 3–4, 5–6

R. Alleluia!

When Israel came forth from Egypt,
  the house of Jacob from a people of alien tongue,
Judah became his sanctuary,
  Israel his domain.

R. Alleluia!

The sea beheld and fled;
  Jordan turned back.
The mountains skipped like rams,
  the hills like the lambs of the flock.

R. Alleluia!

Why is it, O sea, that you flee?
  O Jordan, that you turn back?
You mountains, that you skip like rams?
  You hills, like the lambs of the flock?

R. Alleluia!

Alleluia Verse *and* **Gospel,** *p. 1309.*

FIRST READING   Ez 12:1–12

You shall bring out your baggage like an exile
in the daytime while they are looking on.

A reading from the Book of the Prophet Ezekiel

The word of the LORD came to me: Son of man, you live in the
midst of a rebellious house; they have eyes to see but do not
see, and ears to hear but do not hear, for they are a rebellious
house. Now, son of man, during the day while they are looking
on, prepare your baggage as though for exile, and again while
they are looking on, migrate from where you live to another
place; perhaps they will see that they are a rebellious house.
You shall bring out your baggage like an exile in the daytime
while they are looking on; in the evening, again while they are
looking on, you shall go out like one of those driven into exile;
while they look on, dig a hole in the wall and pass through it;
while they look on, shoulder the burden and set out in the darkness; cover your face that you may not see the land, for I have
made you a sign for the house of Israel.

I did as I was told. During the day I brought out my baggage
as though it were that of an exile, and at evening I dug a hole
through the wall with my hand and, while they looked on, set
out in the darkness, shouldering my burden.

Then, in the morning, the word of the LORD came to me:
Son of man, did not the house of Israel, that rebellious house,
ask you what you were doing? Tell them: Thus says the Lord
GOD: This oracle concerns Jerusalem and the whole house of
Israel within it. I am a sign for you: as I have done, so shall it
be done to them; as captives they shall go into exile. The prince
who is among them shall shoulder his burden and set out in

darkness, going through a hole he has dug out in the wall, and covering his face lest he be seen by anyone.

The word of the Lord.

Responsorial Psalm

Ps 78:56–57, 58–59, 61–62

R. **Do not forget the works of the Lord!**

They tempted and rebelled against God the Most High,
  and kept not his decrees.
They turned back and were faithless like their fathers;
  they recoiled like a treacherous bow.

R. **Do not forget the works of the Lord!**

They angered him with their high places
  and with their idols roused his jealousy.
God heard and was enraged
  and utterly rejected Israel.

R. **Do not forget the works of the Lord!**

And he surrendered his strength into captivity,
  his glory in the hands of the foe.
He abandoned his people to the sword
  and was enraged against his inheritance.

R. **Do not forget the works of the Lord!**

Alleluia, alleluia Ps 119:135
Let your countenance shine upon your servant
and teach me your statutes.
Alleluia, alleluia

Years I and II

GOSPEL

Mt 18:21—19:1

I say to you, not seven times but seventy-seven times.

A reading from the holy Gospel according to Matthew

Peter approached Jesus and asked him, "Lord, if my brother sins against me, how often must I forgive him? As many as seven times?" Jesus answered, "I say to you, not seven times but seventy-seven times. That is why the Kingdom of heaven may be likened to a king who decided to settle accounts with his servants. When he began the accounting, a debtor was brought before him who owed him a huge amount. Since he had no way of paying it back, his master ordered him to be sold, along with his wife, his children, and all his property, in payment of the debt. At that, the servant fell down, did him homage, and said, 'Be patient with me, and I will pay you back in full.' Moved with compassion the master of that servant let him go and forgave him the loan. When that servant had left, he found one of his fellow servants who owed him a much smaller amount. He seized him and started to choke him, demanding, 'Pay back what you owe.' Falling to his knees, his fellow servant begged him, 'Be patient with me, and I will pay you back.' But he refused. Instead, he had the fellow servant put in prison until he paid back the debt. Now when his fellow servants saw what had happened, they were deeply disturbed, and went to their master and reported the whole affair. His master summoned him and said to him, 'You wicked servant! I forgave you your entire debt because you begged me to. Should you not have had pity on your fellow servant, as I had pity on you?' Then in anger his master handed him over to the torturers until he should pay back the whole debt. So will my heavenly Father do to you, unless each of you forgives his brother from his heart."

When Jesus finished these words, he left Galilee and went to the district of Judea across the Jordan.

The Gospel of the Lord.

Liturgy of the Eucharist, *p. 897;* **Prayer over the Gifts,** *p. 1290.*

Friday

Antiphons and Prayers, *p. 1289;* **Liturgy of the Word** *for Year I (odd years) follows; Year II (even years), p. 1314.*

TODAY'S LIVING WORD

In each of today's readings three different sacred writers employ the same basic strategy in order to proclaim God's will and purpose. That strategy is to recount God's gracious deeds of the past in order to call God's people in the present to grateful, graceful living. In the two first readings, the recital of God's past favors is the historical prologue that culminates in a renewal of the covenant. Joshua presides at such a covenant renewal ceremony at Shechem, where he prepares the tribes of Israel to take possession of the promised land. Ezekiel uses an allegory to relate God's graciousness to Israel from the beginning and to announce an everlasting covenant. In the Gospel Jesus appeals to God's past activity as Creator in order to support his prohibition of divorce.

The disciples' astonished response to Jesus' teaching on divorce leads him to make a still more startling statement on celibacy. Just as marriage must be understood with reference to God's creative activity in the past, celibacy must be understood with a view to God's saving activity in the future, that is, the kingdom which is at hand.

Year I

FIRST READING Jos 24:1–13

I brought your father Abraham from the region beyond the River; led you out of Egypt, I brought you to your land.

A reading from the Book of Joshua

Joshua gathered together all the tribes of Israel at Shechem, summoning their elders, their leaders, their judges and their officers. When they stood in ranks before God, Joshua addressed all the people: "Thus says the LORD, the God of Israel: In times past your fathers, down to Terah, father of Abraham and Nahor, dwelt beyond the River and served other gods. But I brought your father Abraham from the region beyond the River and led him through the entire land of Canaan. I made his descendants numerous, and gave him Isaac. To Isaac I gave Jacob and Esau. To Esau I assigned the mountain region of Seir in which to settle, while Jacob and his children went down to Egypt.

"Then I sent Moses and Aaron, and smote Egypt with the prodigies which I wrought in her midst. Afterward I led you out of Egypt, and when you reached the sea, the Egyptians pursued your fathers to the Red Sea with chariots and horsemen. Because they cried out to the LORD, he put darkness between your people and the Egyptians, upon whom he brought the sea so that it engulfed them. After you witnessed what I did to Egypt, and dwelt a long time in the desert, I brought you into the land of the Amorites who lived east of the Jordan. They fought against you, but I delivered them into your power. You took possession of their land, and I destroyed them, the two kings of the Amorites, before you. Then Balak, son of Zippor, king of Moab, prepared to war against Israel. He summoned Balaam, son of Beor, to curse you; but I would not listen to Balaam. On the contrary, he had to bless you, and I saved you from him. Once you crossed the Jordan and came to Jericho, the men of Jericho fought against you, but I delivered them also into your power. And I sent the hornets ahead of you that drove them (the Amorites, Perizzites, Canaanites, Hittites, Girgashites, Hivites and Jebusites) out of your way; it was not your sword or your bow.

"I gave you a land that you had not tilled and cities that you had not built, to dwell in; you have eaten of vineyards and olive groves which you did not plant."

The word of the Lord.

Responsorial Psalm
Ps 136:1–3, 16–18, 21–22 and 24

R. His mercy endures forever.

Give thanks to the LORD, for he is good,
 for his mercy endures forever;
Give thanks to the God of gods,
 for his mercy endures forever;
Give thanks to the LORD of lords,
 for his mercy endures forever.

R. His mercy endures forever.

Who led his people through the wilderness,
 for his mercy endures forever;
Who smote great kings,
 for his mercy endures forever;
And slew powerful kings,
 for his mercy endures forever.

R. His mercy endures forever.

And made their land a heritage,
 for his mercy endures forever;
The heritage of Israel his servant,
 for his mercy endures forever;
And freed us from our foes,
 for his mercy endures forever.

R. His mercy endures forever.

Alleluia Verse *and* **Gospel,** *p. 1316f.*

Year II

FIRST READING   Ez 16:1–15, 60, 63

You are perfect because of my splendor
which I bestowed on you; you became a harlot.

A reading from the Book of the Prophet Ezekiel
Long Form

The word of the LORD came to me: Son of man, make known to Jerusalem her abominations. Thus says the Lord GOD to Jerusalem: By origin and birth you are of the land of Canaan; your father was an Amorite and your mother a Hittite. As for your birth, the day you were born your navel cord was not cut; you were neither washed with water nor anointed, nor were you rubbed with salt, nor swathed in swaddling clothes. No one looked on you with pity or compassion to do any of these things for you. Rather, you were thrown out on the ground as something loathsome, the day you were born.

Then I passed by and saw you weltering in your blood. I said to you: Live in your blood and grow like a plant in the field. You grew and developed, you came to the age of puberty; your breasts were formed, your hair had grown, but you were still stark naked. Again I passed by you and saw that you were now old enough for love. So I spread the corner of my cloak over you to cover your nakedness; I swore an oath to you and entered into a covenant with you; you became mine, says the Lord GOD. Then I bathed you with water, washed away your blood, and anointed you with oil. I clothed you with an embroidered gown, put sandals of fine leather on your feet; I gave you a fine linen sash and silk robes to wear. I adorned you with jewelry: I put bracelets on your arms, a necklace about your neck, a ring in your nose, pendants in your ears, and a glorious diadem upon your head. Thus you were adorned with gold and silver; your garments were of fine linen, silk, and embroidered cloth. Fine flour, honey, and oil were your food. You were exceedingly beautiful, with the dignity of a queen. You were renowned among the nations for your beauty, perfect as it was, because of my splendor which I had bestowed on you, says the Lord GOD.

But you were captivated by your own beauty, you used your renown to make yourself a harlot, and you lavished your harlotry on every passer-by, whose own you became.

Yet I will remember the covenant I made with you when you were a girl, and I will set up an everlasting covenant with you, that you may remember and be covered with confusion, and that you may be utterly silenced for shame when I pardon you for all you have done, says the Lord GOD.

The word of the Lord.

Or:

FIRST READING

Ez 16:59–63

*I will remember the covenant I made with you
and you will be ashamed.*

A reading from the Book of the Prophet Ezekiel

Short Form

Thus says the LORD: I will deal with you according to what you have done, you who despised your oath, breaking a covenant. Yet I will remember the covenant I made with you when you were a girl, and I will set up an everlasting covenant with you. Then you shall remember your conduct and be ashamed when I take your sisters, those older and younger than you, and give them to you as daughters, even though I am not bound by my covenant with you. For I will re-establish my covenant with you, that you may know that I am the LORD, that you may remember and be covered with confusion, and that you may be utterly silenced for shame when I pardon you for all you have done, says the Lord GOD.

The word of the Lord.

Responsorial Psalm

Is 12:2–3, 4bcd, 5–6

R. **You have turned from your anger.**

God indeed is my savior;
  I am confident and unafraid.
My strength and my courage is the LORD,
  and he has been my savior.
With joy you will draw water
  at the fountain of salvation.

R. **You have turned from your anger.**

Give thanks to the LORD, acclaim his name;
  among the nations make known his deeds,
  proclaim how exalted is his name.

R. **You have turned from your anger.**

Sing praise to the LORD for his glorious achievement;
  let this be known throughout all the earth.
Shout with exultation, O city of Zion,
  for great in your midst
  is the Holy One of Israel!

R. **You have turned from your anger.**

Alleluia, alleluia   See 1 Thes 2:13
Receive the word of God, not as the word of men,
but, as it truly is, the word of God.
Alleluia, alleluia

Years I and II

GOSPEL

Mt 19:3–12

Because of the hardness of your hearts Moses allowed you to divorce your wives, but from the beginning it was not so.

A reading from the holy Gospel according to Matthew

Some Pharisees approached Jesus, and tested him, saying, "Is it lawful for a man to divorce his wife for any cause whatever?" He said in reply, "Have you not read that from the beginning the Creator *made them male and female* and said, *For this reason a man shall leave his father and mother and be joined to his wife, and the two shall become one flesh?* So they are no longer two, but one flesh. Therefore, what God has joined together, man must not separate." They said to him, "Then why did Moses command that the man give the woman a bill of divorce and dismiss her?" He said to them, "Because of the hardness of your hearts Moses allowed you to divorce your wives, but from the beginning it was not so. I say to you, whoever divorces his wife (unless the marriage is unlawful) and marries another commits adultery." His disciples said to him, "If that is the case of a man with his wife, it is better not to marry." He answered, "Not all can accept this word, but only those to whom that is granted. Some are incapable of marriage because they were born so; some, because they were made so by others; some, because they have renounced marriage for the sake of the Kingdom of heaven. Whoever can accept this ought to accept it."

The Gospel of the Lord.

Liturgy of the Eucharist, *p. 897;* **Prayer over the Gifts,** *p. 1290.*

Saturday

Antiphons and Prayers, *p. 1289;* **Liturgy of the Word** *for Year I (odd years) follows; Year II (even years), p. 1320.*

TODAY'S LIVING WORD

Some element of family life figures in all of today's readings. Joshua confronts the house of Israel with a decision: Whom will they serve in the land they are about to occupy? "As for me and my household," he declares, "we will serve the Lord." In the Gospel Jesus welcomes children, saying that the kingdom of God belongs to them. Both to choose God and to cherish children are positive family values.

Ezekiel too has something to say about relationships within the family. Citing the proverb, "Fathers have eaten green grapes, thus their children's teeth are on edge," God announces the reversal of conventional wisdom. No longer will the sins of their parents be visited upon children; each will he held responsible for his or her own sin. Translated into today's terms, this new teaching says that, however dysfunctional a family system may be, individual family members are always free to make for themselves a new heart and a new spirit, and, by the grace of God, to return and live.

Year I

FIRST READING   Jos 24:14–29

Decide today whom you will serve.

A reading from the Book of Joshua

Joshua gathered together all the tribes of Israel at Shechem, and addressed them, saying: "Fear the LORD and serve him completely and sincerely. Cast out the gods your fathers served beyond the River and in Egypt, and serve the LORD. If it does not please you to serve the LORD, decide today whom you will serve, the gods your fathers served beyond the River or the gods of the Amorites in whose country you are dwelling. As for me and my household, we will serve the LORD."

But the people answered, "Far be it from us to forsake the LORD for the service of other gods. For it was the LORD, our God, who brought us and our fathers up out of the land of Egypt, out of a state of slavery. He performed those great miracles before our very eyes and protected us along our entire journey and among all the peoples through whom we passed. At our approach the LORD drove out all the peoples, including the Amorites who dwelt in the land. Therefore we also will serve the LORD, for he is our God."

Joshua in turn said to the people, "You may not be able to serve the LORD, for he is a holy God; he is a jealous God who will not forgive your transgressions or your sins. If, after the good he has done for you, you forsake the LORD and serve strange gods, he will do evil to you and destroy you."

But the people answered Joshua, "We will still serve the LORD." Joshua therefore said to the people, "You are your own witnesses that you have chosen to serve the LORD." They replied, "We are, indeed!" Joshua continued: "Now, therefore, put away the strange gods that are among you and turn your hearts to the LORD, the God of Israel." Then the people promised Joshua, "We will serve the LORD, our God, and obey his voice."

So Joshua made a covenant with the people that day and made statutes and ordinances for them at Shechem, which he recorded in the book of the law of God. Then he took a large stone and set it up there under the oak that was in the sanctuary of the LORD. And Joshua said to all the people, "This stone shall be our witness, for it has heard all the words which the LORD spoke to us. It shall be a witness against you, should you wish to deny your God." Then Joshua dismissed the people, each to his own heritage.

After these events, Joshua, son of Nun, servant of the LORD, died at the age of a hundred and ten.

The word of the Lord.

Responsorial Psalm
Ps 16:1–2a and 5, 7–8, 11

R. You are my inheritance, O Lord.

Keep me, O God, for in you I take refuge;
  I say to the LORD, "My Lord are you."
O LORD, my allotted portion and my cup,
  you it is who hold fast my lot.

R. You are my inheritance, O Lord.

I bless the LORD who counsels me;
  even in the night my heart exhorts me.
I set the LORD ever before me;
  with him at my right hand I shall not be disturbed.

R. You are my inheritance, O Lord.

You will show me the path to life,
  fullness of joys in your presence,
  the delights at your right hand forever.

R. You are my inheritance, O Lord.

Alleluia Verse *and* **Gospel**, *p. 1322.*

Year II

FIRST READING
Ez 18:1–10, 13b, 30–32

I will judge you according to your ways.

A reading from the Book of the Prophet Ezekiel

The word of the LORD came to me: Son of man, what is the meaning of this proverb that you recite in the land of Israel:

"Fathers have eaten green grapes,
     thus their children's teeth are on edge"?

As I live, says the Lord GOD: I swear that there shall no longer be anyone among you who will repeat this proverb in Israel. For all lives are mine; the life of the father is like the life of the son, both are mine; only the one who sins shall die.

If a man is virtuous—if he does what is right and just, if he does not eat on the mountains, nor raise his eyes to the idols of the house of Israel; if he does not defile his neighbor's wife, nor have relations with a woman in her menstrual period; if he oppresses no one, gives back the pledge received for a debt, commits no robbery; if he gives food to the hungry and clothes the naked; if he does not lend at interest nor exact usury; if he holds off from evildoing, judges fairly between a man and his opponent; if he lives by my statutes and is careful to observe my ordinances, that man is virtuous—he shall surely live, says the Lord GOD.

But if he begets a son who is a thief, a murderer, or lends at interest and exacts usury—this son certainly shall not live. Because he practiced all these abominations, he shall surely die; his death shall be his own fault.

Therefore I will judge you, house of Israel, each one according to his ways, says the Lord GOD. Turn and be converted from all your crimes, that they may be no cause of guilt for you. Cast away from you all the crimes you have committed, and make for yourselves a new heart and a new spirit. Why should you die, O house of Israel? For I have no pleasure in the death of anyone who dies, says the Lord GOD. Return and live!

The word of the Lord.

Responsorial Psalm
Ps 51:12–13, 14–15, 18–19

R. Create a clean heart in me, O God.

A clean heart create for me, O God;
  and a steadfast spirit renew within me.
Cast me not out from your presence,
  and your Holy Spirit take not from me.

R. Create a clean heart in me, O God.

Give me back the joy of your salvation,
  and a willing spirit sustain in me.
I will teach transgressors your ways,
  and sinners shall return to you.

R. Create a clean heart in me, O God.

For you are not pleased with sacrifices;
  should I offer a burnt offering, you would not accept it.
My sacrifice, O God, is a contrite spirit;
  a heart contrite and humbled, O God, you will not spurn.

R. Create a clean heart in me, O God.

Alleluia, alleluia See Mt 11:25
Blessed are you, Father, Lord of heaven and earth;
you have revealed to little ones the mysteries of the Kingdom.
Alleluia, alleluia

Years I and II

GOSPEL
Mt 19:13–15

Let the children come to me, and do not prevent them;
  for the Kingdom of heaven belongs to such as these.

A reading from the holy Gospel according to Matthew

Children were brought to Jesus that he might lay his hands on
them and pray. The disciples rebuked them, but Jesus said,
"Let the children come to me, and do not prevent them; for the

Kingdom of heaven belongs to such as these." After he placed his hands on them, he went away.

The Gospel of the Lord.

Liturgy of the Eucharist, *p. 897;* **Prayer over the Gifts,** *p. 1290.*

TWENTIETH WEEK IN ORDINARY TIME

The **Antiphons and Prayers** *may be the following, or may be chosen from any of the other 33 weeks in Ordinary Time (refer to Liturgical Calendar, pp. 26–41).*

The **Liturgy of the Word** *varies: for Monday, see p. 1325; Tuesday, p. 1330; Wednesday, p. 1335; Thursday, p. 1341; Friday, p. 1346; Saturday, p. 1351.*

Entrance Antiphon

God, our protector, keep us in mind; always give strength to your people. For if we can be with you even one day, it is better than a thousand without you. (Ps 84:10–11)

Opening Prayer

Let us pray

[that the love of God
may raise us beyond what we see
to the unseen glory of his kingdom]

Pause for silent prayer.

God our Father,
may we love you in all things and above all things
and reach the joy you have prepared for us
beyond all our imagining.

We ask this through our Lord Jesus Christ, your Son,
who lives and reigns with you and the Holy Spirit,
one God, for ever and ever.

Alternative Opening Prayer

Let us pray
 [with humility and persistence]

   Pause for silent prayer.

Almighty God, ever-loving Father,
your care extends beyond the boundaries of race and nation
to the hearts of all who live.
May the walls, which prejudice raises between us,
crumble beneath the shadow of your outstretched arm.

We ask this through Christ our Lord.

Prayer over the Gifts

Pray, brethren...

Lord,
accept our sacrifice
as a holy exchange of gifts.
By offering what you have given us
may we receive the gift of yourself.

We ask this in the name of Jesus the Lord.

Preface of Weekdays in Ordinary Time I–VI, *pp. 948–950.*

Communion Antiphon

   With the Lord there is mercy, and fullness of redemption.
                                                    (Ps 130:7)

Or:

   **I am the living bread from heaven, says the Lord; if anyone
   eats this bread he will live for ever.**   (Jn 6:51)

Prayer after Communion

Let us pray.
   Pause for silent prayer, if this has not preceded.
God of mercy,

by this sacrament you make us one with Christ.
By becoming more like him on earth,
may we come to share his glory in heaven,
where he lives and reigns for ever and ever.

Monday

Antiphons and Prayers, *p. 1323;* **Liturgy of the Word** *for Year I (odd years) follows; Year II (even years), p. 1327.*

TODAY'S LIVING WORD

Matthew alone of all the Gospel writers describes the rich man who approaches Jesus as young. Perhaps he wants us to read Jesus' word, rendered here as "to be perfect," as "to be mature" instead. That is one meaning of the Greek *teleios*. In this light, Jesus is inviting the rich young man not so much to give up but to grow up by dedicating himself totally to God. The two first readings offer a negative and a positive illustration of such total dedication.

The passage from Judges depicts the chronic instability of the Israelites during the period before the monarchy. "They were quick to stray from the way their fathers had taken, and did not follow their example of obedience to the commandments of the Lord." The selection from Ezekiel, however, reveals the maturity of the prophet's faith. His dedication to the word of God strips him not of mere material things but of the delight of his eyes, his wife, and even of the comfort of mourning her loss. Such is the cost of true discipleship.

Year I

FIRST READING   Jgs 2:11–19

When the Lord raised up judges, they did not listen.

A reading from the Book of Judges

The children of Israel offended the LORD by serving the Baals.
Abandoning the LORD, the God of their fathers, who led them

out of the land of Egypt, they followed the other gods of the various nations around them, and by their worship of these gods provoked the LORD.

Because they had thus abandoned him and served Baal and the Ashtaroth, the anger of the LORD flared up against Israel, and he delivered them over to plunderers who despoiled them. He allowed them to fall into the power of their enemies round about whom they were no longer able to withstand. Whatever they undertook, the LORD turned into disaster for them, as in his warning he had sworn he would do, till they were in great distress. Even when the LORD raised up judges to deliver them from the power of their despoilers, they did not listen to their judges, but abandoned themselves to the worship of other gods. They were quick to stray from the way their fathers had taken, and did not follow their example of obedience to the commandments of the LORD. Whenever the LORD raised up judges for them, he would be with the judge and save them from the power of their enemies as long as the judge lived; it was thus the LORD took pity on their distressful cries of affliction under their oppressors. But when the judge died, they would relapse and do worse than their ancestors, following other gods in service and worship, relinquishing none of their evil practices or stubborn conduct.

The word of the Lord.

Responsorial Psalm   Ps 106:34–35, 36–37, 39–40, 43ab and 44

R. Remember us, O Lord, as you favor your people.

They did not exterminate the peoples,
   as the LORD had commanded them,
But mingled with the nations
   and learned their works.

R. Remember us, O Lord, as you favor your people.

They served their idols,
  which became a snare for them.
They sacrificed their sons
  and their daughters to demons.

R. Remember us, O Lord, as you favor your people.

They became defiled by their works,
  and wanton in their crimes.
And the LORD grew angry with his people,
  and abhorred his inheritance.

R. Remember us, O Lord, as you favor your people.

Many times did he rescue them,
  but they embittered him with their counsels.
Yet he had regard for their affliction
  when he heard their cry.

R. Remember us, O Lord, as you favor your people.

Alleluia Verse *and* **Gospel,** *p. 1329.*

Year II

FIRST READING

Ez 24:15–23

*Ezekiel shall be a sign for you: all that he did
you shall do when it happens.*

A reading from the Book of the Prophet Ezekiel

The word of the LORD came to me: Son of man, by a sudden
blow I am taking away from you the delight of your eyes, but
do not mourn or weep or shed any tears. Groan in silence,
make no lament for the dead, bind on your turban, put your
sandals on your feet, do not cover your beard, and do not eat
the customary bread. That evening my wife died, and the next
morning I did as I had been commanded. Then the people asked

me, "Will you not tell us what all these things that you are doing mean for us?" I therefore spoke to the people that morning, saying to them: Thus the word of the LORD came to me: Say to the house of Israel: Thus says the Lord GOD: I will now desecrate my sanctuary, the stronghold of your pride, the delight of your eyes, the desire of your soul. The sons and daughters you left behind shall fall by the sword. Ezekiel shall be a sign for you: all that he did you shall do when it happens. Thus you shall know that I am the LORD. You shall do as I have done, not covering your beards nor eating the customary bread. Your turbans shall remain on your heads, your sandals on your feet. You shall not mourn or weep, but you shall rot away because of your sins and groan one to another.

The word of the Lord.

Responsorial Psalm
Dt 32:18–19, 20, 21

R. You have forgotten God who gave you birth.

You were unmindful of the Rock that begot you.
  You forgot the God who gave you birth.
When the LORD saw this, he was filled with loathing
  and anger toward his sons and daughters.

R. You have forgotten God who gave you birth.

"I will hide my face from them," he said,
  "and see what will then become of them.
What a fickle race they are,
  sons with no loyalty in them!"

R. You have forgotten God who gave you birth.

"Since they have provoked me with their 'no-god'
  and angered me with their vain idols,

I will provoke them with a 'no-people';
  with a foolish nation I will anger them."

R. You have forgotten God who gave you birth.

Alleluia, alleluia Mt 5:3
Blessed are the poor in spirit;
for theirs is the Kingdom of heaven.
Alleluia, alleluia

Years I and II

GOSPEL   Mt 19:16–22

*If you wish to be perfect, go, sell what you have
and you will have treasure in heaven.*

A reading from the holy Gospel according to Matthew

A young man approached Jesus and said, "Teacher, what good must I do to gain eternal life?" He answered him, "Why do you ask me about the good? There is only One who is good. If you wish to enter into life, keep the commandments." He asked him, "Which ones?" And Jesus replied, *"You shall not kill; you shall not commit adultery; you shall not steal; you shall not bear false witness; honor your father and your mother; and you shall love your neighbor as yourself."* The young man said to him, "All of these I have observed. What do I still lack?" Jesus said to him, "If you wish to be perfect, go, sell what you have and give to the poor, and you will have treasure in heaven. Then come, follow me." When the young man heard this statement, he went away sad, for he had many possessions.

The Gospel of the Lord.

Liturgy of the Eucharist, *p. 897;* **Prayer over the Gifts,** *p. 1324.*

Tuesday

Antiphons and Prayers, *p. 1323;* **Liturgy of the Word** *for Year I (odd years) follows; Year II (even years), p. 1332.*

TODAY'S LIVING WORD

Today's readings present a study in contrast: the call of Gideon described in the Book of Judges, and the arrogance of the king of Tyre, mocked in the prophecy of Ezekiel. Gideon frankly acknowledges that he is the least important in his father's house. Ironically, it is he who will save Israel from the power of Midian, because God will be with him and nothing is impossible with God. The king of Tyre, on the other hand, is haughty of heart. "A god am I!" he boasts. His overweening pride will be his downfall.

Ezekiel says that the heart of the king of Tyre has grown haughty from his riches. So does wealth corrupt even the best of us. Jesus draws this lesson from the refusal of the rich young man. As John Meier puts it in his commentary on Matthew, "The young man cannot measure up to [the standard of Jesus], because he possesses great riches, or rather, they possess him."*

* *Matthew,* New Testament Message 3, 5th ed. (Wilmington: Michael Glazier, Inc., 1986), p. 220.

Year I

FIRST READING   Jgs 6:11–24a

Go and save Israel; it is I who send you.

A reading from the Book of Judges

The angel of the LORD came and sat under the terebinth in Ophrah that belonged to Joash the Abiezrite. While his son Gideon was beating out wheat in the wine press to save it from the Midianites, the angel of the LORD appeared to him and said, "The LORD is with you, O champion!" Gideon said to him, "My Lord, if the LORD is with us, why has all this happened to us? Where are his wondrous deeds of which our fathers told us when they said, 'Did not the LORD bring us up from Egypt?' For now the LORD has abandoned us and has delivered us into the power of Midian." The LORD turned to him and said, "Go with the strength you have and save Israel from the power of Midian. It is I who send you." But Gideon answered him, "Please, my lord, how can I save Israel? My family is the lowliest in Manasseh, and I am the most insignificant in my father's house." "I shall be with you," the LORD said to him, "and you will cut down Midian to the last man." Gideon answered him, "If I find favor with you, give me a sign that you are speaking with me. Do not depart from here, I pray you, until I come back to you and bring out my offering and set it before you." He answered, "I will await your return."

So Gideon went off and prepared a kid and a measure of flour in the form of unleavened cakes. Putting the meat in a basket and the broth in a pot, he brought them out to him under the terebinth and presented them. The angel of God said to him, "Take the meat and unleavened cakes and lay them on this rock; then pour out the broth." When he had done so, the angel of the LORD stretched out the tip of the staff he held, and touched the meat and unleavened cakes. Thereupon a fire came up from the rock that consumed the meat and unleavened cakes, and the angel of the LORD disappeared from sight. Gideon, now aware that it had been the angel of the LORD, said, "Alas, Lord GOD, that I have seen the angel of the LORD face to face!" The LORD answered him, "Be calm, do not fear. You shall not die." So Gideon built there an altar to the LORD and called it Yahweh-shalom.

The word of the Lord.

Responsorial Psalm

Ps 85:9, 11–12, 13–14

R. The Lord speaks of peace to his people.

I will hear what God proclaims;
  the LORD—for he proclaims peace
To his people, and to his faithful ones,
  and to those who put in him their hope.

R. The Lord speaks of peace to his people.

Kindness and truth shall meet;
  justice and peace shall kiss.
Truth shall spring out of the earth,
  and justice shall look down from heaven.

R. The Lord speaks of peace to his people.

The LORD himself will give his benefits;
  our land shall yield its increase.
Justice shall walk before him,
  and salvation, along the way of his steps.

R. The Lord speaks of peace to his people.

Alleluia Verse *and* **Gospel,** *p. 1334.*

Year II

FIRST READING

Ez 28:1–10

You are a mortal and not God,
however you may think yourself like a god.

A reading from the Book of the Prophet Ezekiel

The word of the LORD came to me: Son of man, say to the prince of Tyre: Thus says the Lord GOD:

Because you are haughty of heart,
    you say, "A god am I!
I occupy a godly throne

in the heart of the sea!"—
And yet you are a man, and not a god,
    however you may think yourself like a god.
Oh yes, you are wiser than Daniel,
    there is no secret that is beyond you.
By your wisdom and your intelligence
    you have made riches for yourself;
You have put gold and silver
    into your treasuries.
By your great wisdom applied to your trading
    you have heaped up your riches;
    your heart has grown haughty from your riches—
    therefore thus says the Lord GOD:
Because you have thought yourself
    to have the mind of a god,
Therefore I will bring against you
    foreigners, the most barbarous of nations.
They shall draw their swords
    against your beauteous wisdom,
    they shall run them through your splendid apparel.
They shall thrust you down to the pit, there to die
    a bloodied corpse, in the heart of the sea.
Will you then say, "I am a god!"
    when you face your murderers?
No, you are man, not a god,
    handed over to those who will slay you.
You shall die the death of the uncircumcised
    at the hands of foreigners,
    for I have spoken, says the Lord GOD.

The word of the Lord.

Responsorial Psalm

Dt 32:26–27ab, 27cd–28, 30, 35cd–36ab

R. It is I who deal death and give life.

"I would have said, 'I will make an end of them
  and blot out their name from men's memories,'
Had I not feared the insolence of their enemies,
  feared that these foes would mistakenly boast."

R. It is I who deal death and give life.

" 'Our own hand won the victory;
  the LORD had nothing to do with it.' "
For they are a people devoid of reason,
  having no understanding.

R. It is I who deal death and give life.

"How could one man rout a thousand,
  or two men put ten thousand to flight,
Unless it was because their Rock sold them
  and the LORD delivered them up?"

R. It is I who deal death and give life.

Close at hand is the day of their disaster,
  and their doom is rushing upon them!
Surely, the LORD shall do justice for his people;
  on his servants he shall have pity.

R. It is I who deal death and give life.

Alleluia, alleluia   2 Cor 8:9
Jesus Christ became poor although he was rich
so that by his poverty you might become rich.
Alleluia, alleluia

Years I and II

GOSPEL   Mt 19:23–30

*It is easier for a camel to pass through the eye of a needle
than for one who is rich to enter the Kingdom of God.*

A reading from the holy Gospel according to Matthew

Jesus said to his disciples: "Amen, I say to you, it will be hard for one who is rich to enter the Kingdom of heaven. Again I say to you, it is easier for a camel to pass through the eye of a needle than for one who is rich to enter the Kingdom of God." When the disciples heard this, they were greatly astonished and said, "Who then can be saved?" Jesus looked at them and said, "For men this is impossible, but for God all things are possible." Then Peter said to him in reply, "We have given up everything and followed you. What will there be for us?" Jesus said to them, "Amen, I say to you that you who have followed me, in the new age, when the Son of Man is seated on his throne of glory, will yourselves sit on twelve thrones, judging the twelve tribes of Israel. And everyone who has given up houses or brothers or sisters or father or mother or children or lands for the sake of my name will receive a hundred times more, and will inherit eternal life. But many who are first will be last, and the last will be first."

The Gospel of the Lord.

Liturgy of the Eucharist, *p. 897;* **Prayer over the Gifts,** *p. 1324.*

Wednesday

Antiphons and Prayers, *p. 1323;* **Liturgy of the Word** *for Year I (odd years) follows; Year II (even years), p. 1338.*

TODAY'S LIVING WORD

Today's readings offer us a literary feast: a fable, an extended metaphor and a parable. The two first readings denounce bad kings and kingship itself. The fable of Jotham is an old antimonarchical tradition. The only tree willing to reign over the other trees is no tree at all. The buckthorn is bramble, too close to the ground to cast a shadow, so close that it causes fire to spread. Rulers in the Ancient Near East described themselves as the shepherds of their people. Ezekiel extends the metaphor as he indicts the kings of Israel who have given God's sheep over to pillage, leaving them "scattered over the whole earth, with no one to look after them."

The owner of the vineyard in Jesus' parable might be described as a good shepherd. The generosity he extends to the workers hired late in the day is simple justice, as the Bible defines it. It honors the claims of the relationship that exists between an employer and his workers. That may not be good business sense, but it is good shepherding, says the Lord.

Year I

FIRST READING

Jgs 9:6–15

It is said: The king will reign over us,
when the LORD God reigns among you (1 Sm 12:12).

A reading from the Book of Judges

All the citizens of Shechem and all Beth-millo came together and proceeded to make Abimelech king by the terebinth at the memorial pillar in Shechem.

When this was reported to him, Jotham went to the top of Mount Gerizim and, standing there, cried out to them in a loud voice: "Hear me, citizens of Shechem, that God may then hear you! Once the trees went to anoint a king over themselves. So they said to the olive tree, 'Reign over us.' But the olive tree answered them, 'Must I give up my rich oil, whereby men and gods are honored, and go to wave over the trees?' Then the trees said to the fig tree, 'Come; you reign over us!' But the fig tree answered them, 'Must I give up my sweetness and my good fruit, and go to wave over the trees?' Then the trees said to the vine, 'Come you, and reign over us.' But the vine answered them, 'Must I give up my wine that cheers gods and men, and go to wave over the trees?' Then all the trees said to the buckthorn, 'Come; you reign over us!' But the buckthorn replied to the trees, 'If you wish to anoint me king over you in good faith, come and take refuge in my shadow. Otherwise, let fire come from the buckthorn and devour the cedars of Lebanon.'"

The word of the Lord.

Responsorial Psalm

Ps 21:2-3, 4-5, 6-7

R. Lord, in your strength the king is glad.

O LORD, in your strength the king is glad;
 in your victory how greatly he rejoices!
You have granted him his heart's desire;
 you refused not the wish of his lips.

R. Lord, in your strength the king is glad.

For you welcomed him with goodly blessings,
 you placed on his head a crown of pure gold.
He asked life of you: you gave him
 length of days forever and ever.

R. Lord, in your strength the king is glad.

Great is his glory in your victory;
 majesty and splendor you conferred upon him.
You made him a blessing forever,
 you gladdened him with the joy of your face.

R. Lord, in your strength the king is glad.

Alleluia Verse *and* **Gospel**, p. 1339f.

FIRST READING

Ez 34:1–11

*I will save my sheep, that they may no longer
be food for their mouths.*

A reading from the Book of the Prophet Ezekiel

The word of the Lord came to me: Son of man, prophesy against the shepherds of Israel, in these words prophesy to them to the shepherds: Thus says the Lord GOD: Woe to the shepherds of Israel who have been pasturing themselves! Should not shepherds, rather, pasture sheep? You have fed off their milk, worn their wool, and slaughtered the fatlings, but the sheep you have not pastured. You did not strengthen the weak nor heal the sick nor bind up the injured. You did not bring back the strayed nor seek the lost, but you lorded it over them harshly and brutally. So they were scattered for the lack of a shepherd, and became food for all the wild beasts. My sheep were scattered and wandered over all the mountains and high hills; my sheep were scattered over the whole earth, with no one to look after them or to search for them.

Therefore, shepherds, hear the word of the LORD: As I live, says the Lord GOD, because my sheep have been given over to pillage, and because my sheep have become food for every wild beast, for lack of a shepherd; because my shepherds did not look after my sheep, but pastured themselves and did not pasture my sheep; because of this, shepherds, hear the word of the LORD: Thus says the Lord GOD: I swear I am coming against these shepherds. I will claim my sheep from them and put a stop to their shepherding my sheep so that they may no longer pasture themselves. I will save my sheep, that they may no longer be food for their mouths.

For thus says the Lord GOD: I myself will look after and tend my sheep.

The word of the Lord.

Responsorial Psalm

Ps 23:1–3a, 3b–4, 5, 6

R. The Lord is my shepherd; there is nothing I shall want.

The LORD is my shepherd; I shall not want.
  In verdant pastures he gives me repose;
Beside restful waters he leads me;
  he refreshes my soul.

R. The Lord is my shepherd; there is nothing I shall want.

He guides me in right paths
  for his name's sake.
Even though I walk in the dark valley
  I fear no evil; for you are at my side
With your rod and your staff
  that give me courage.

R. The Lord is my shepherd; there is nothing I shall want.

You spread the table before me
  in the sight of my foes;
You anoint my head with oil;
  my cup overflows.

R. The Lord is my shepherd; there is nothing I shall want.

Only goodness and kindness will follow me
  all the days of my life;
And I shall dwell in the house of the LORD
  for years to come.

R. The Lord is my shepherd; there is nothing I shall want.

Alleluia, alleluia Heb 4:12
  The word of God is living and effective,
  able to discern the reflections and thoughts of the heart.
Alleluia, alleluia

GOSPEL   Mt 20:1–16

Are you envious because I am generous?

A reading from the holy Gospel according to Matthew

Jesus told his disciples this parable: "The Kingdom of heaven is like a landowner who went out at dawn to hire laborers for his vineyard. After agreeing with them for the usual daily wage, he sent them into his vineyard. Going out about nine o'clock, he saw others standing idle in the marketplace, and he said to them, 'You too go into my vineyard, and I will give you what is just.' So they went off. And he went out again around noon, and around three o'clock, and did likewise. Going out about five o'clock, he found others standing around, and said to them, 'Why do you stand here idle all day?' They answered, 'Because no one has hired us.' He said to them, 'You too go into my vineyard.' When it was evening the owner of the vineyard said to his foreman, 'Summon the laborers and give them their pay, beginning with the last and ending with the first.' When those who had started about five o'clock came, each received the usual daily wage. So when the first came, they thought that they would receive more, but each of them also got the usual wage. And on receiving it they grumbled against the landowner, saying, 'These last ones worked only one hour, and you have made them equal to us, who bore the day's burden and the heat.' He said to one of them in reply, 'My friend, I am not cheating you. Did you not agree with me for the usual daily wage? Take what is yours and go. What if I wish to give this last one the same as you? Or am I not free to do as I wish with

my own money? Are you envious because I am generous?'
Thus, the last will be first, and the first will be last."
The Gospel of the Lord.

Liturgy of the Eucharist, *p. 897;* **Prayer over the Gifts,** *p. 1324.*

Thursday

Antiphons and Prayers, *p. 1323;* **Liturgy of the Word** *for Year I (odd years) follows; Year II (even years), p. 1343.*

TODAY'S LIVING WORD

The theme of missed opportunity runs through all of today's readings. The story of Jephthah begins with the words, "The spirit of the Lord came upon Jephthah." Unbidden, God acts in Jephthah, assuring him of victory. But for Jephthah God's grace is not enough; he wants a guarantee. So he makes a foolish, faithless vow and his triumph turns into tragedy. The parable of the wedding feast in Matthew is aimed at the Jewish leaders. Their violent refusal of the king's double invitation will have dire consequences. But it will create an opportunity for those along the byways. Yet Matthew warns that grace is not a guarantee even for them. The wedding garment symbolizes a life responsive to God's grace. Seized by grace, we must act in faith on the gift we have received.

Ezekiel addresses his words to the people of God exiled in Babylon. They are there because of a missed opportunity: they defiled their land, God's gift, "by their conduct and deeds" (36:17). But the prophet offers hope of another opportunity not because of their good behavior, but because of God's good name.

Year I

FIRST READING   Jgs 11:29–39a

*I shall offer whoever comes out of the doors
of my house as a burnt offering.*

A reading from the Book of Judges

The Spirit of the LORD came upon Jephthah. He passed through Gilead and Manasseh, and through Mizpah-Gilead as well, and from there he went on to the Ammonites. Jephthah made a vow to the LORD. "If you deliver the Ammonites into my power," he said, "whoever comes out of the doors of my house to meet me when I return in triumph from the Ammonites shall belong to the LORD. I shall offer him up as a burnt offering."

Jephthah then went on to the Ammonites to fight against them, and the LORD delivered them into his power, so that he inflicted a severe defeat on them, from Aroer to the approach of Minnith (twenty cities in all) and as far as Abel-keramim. Thus were the Ammonites brought into subjection by the children of Israel. When Jephthah returned to his house in Mizpah, it was his daughter who came forth, playing the tambourines and dancing. She was an only child: he had neither son nor daughter besides her. When he saw her, he rent his garments and said, "Alas, daughter, you have struck me down and brought calamity upon me. For I have made a vow to the LORD and I cannot retract." She replied, "Father, you have made a vow to the LORD. Do with me as you have vowed, because the LORD has wrought vengeance for you on your enemies the Ammonites." Then she said to her father, "Let me have this favor. Spare me for two months, that I may go off down the mountains to mourn my virginity with my companions." "Go," he replied, and sent her away for two months. So she departed with her companions and mourned her virginity on the mountains. At the end of the two months she returned to her father, who did to her as he had vowed.

The word of the Lord.

Responsorial Psalm

Ps 40:5, 7–8a, 8b–9, 10

R. Here I am, Lord; I come to do your will.

Blessed the man who makes the LORD his trust;
  who turns not to idolatry
  or to those who stray after falsehood.

R. Here I am, Lord; I come to do your will.

Sacrifice or oblation you wished not,
  but ears open to obedience you gave me.
Burnt offerings or sin-offerings you sought not;
  then said I, "Behold I come."

R. Here I am, Lord; I come to do your will.

"In the written scroll it is prescribed for me.
To do your will, O my God, is my delight,
  and your law is within my heart!"

R. Here I am, Lord; I come to do your will.

I announced your justice in the vast assembly;
  I did not restrain my lips, as you, O LORD, know.

R. Here I am, Lord; I come to do your will.

Alleluia Verse *and* **Gospel,** *p. 1345.*

Year II

FIRST READING

Ez 36:23–28

I will give you a new heart and place a new spirit within you.

A reading from the Book of the Prophet Ezekiel

Thus says the LORD: I will prove the holiness of my great name,
profaned among the nations, in whose midst you have profaned
it. Thus the nations shall know that I am the LORD, says the
Lord GOD, when in their sight I prove my holiness through
you. For I will take you away from among the nations, gather

you from all the foreign lands, and bring you back to your own land. I will sprinkle clean water upon you to cleanse you from all your impurities, and from all your idols I will cleanse you. I will give you a new heart and place a new spirit within you, taking from your bodies your stony hearts and giving you natural hearts. I will put my spirit within you and make you live by my statutes, careful to observe my decrees. You shall live in the land I gave your ancestors; you shall be my people, and I will be your God.

The word of the Lord.

Responsorial Psalm

Ps 51:12–13, 14–15, 18–19

R. I will pour clean water on you and wash away
all your sins.

A clean heart create for me, O God,
    and a steadfast spirit renew within me.
Cast me not out from your presence,
    and your Holy Spirit take not from me.

R. I will pour clean water on you and wash away
all your sins.

Give me back the joy of your salvation,
    and a willing spirit sustain in me.
I will teach transgressors your ways,
    and sinners shall return to you.

R. I will pour clean water on you and wash away
all your sins.

For you are not pleased with sacrifices;
    should I offer a burnt offering, you would not accept it.
My sacrifice, O God, is a contrite spirit;
    a heart contrite and humbled, O God, you will not spurn.

R. I will pour clean water on you and wash away
all your sins.

Alleluia, alleluia   Ps 95:8
If today you hear his voice,
harden not your hearts.
Alleluia, alleluia

Years I and II

GOSPEL   Mt 22:1–14

Invite to the wedding feast whomever you find.

A reading from the holy Gospel according to Matthew

Jesus again in reply spoke to the chief priests and the elders of
the people in parables saying, "The Kingdom of heaven may
be likened to a king who gave a wedding feast for his son. He
dispatched his servants to summon the invited guests to the
feast, but they refused to come. A second time he sent other
servants, saying, 'Tell those invited: "Behold, I have prepared
my banquet, my calves and fattened cattle are killed, and
everything is ready; come to the feast." Some ignored the invitation and went away, one to his farm, another to his business.
The rest laid hold of his servants, mistreated them, and killed
them. The king was enraged and sent his troops, destroyed
those murderers, and burned their city. Then the king said to
his servants, 'The feast is ready, but those who were invited
were not worthy to come. Go out, therefore, into the main roads
and invite to the feast whomever you find.' The servants went
out into the streets and gathered all they found, bad and good
alike, and the hall was filled with guests. But when the king
came in to meet the guests he saw a man there not dressed in a
wedding garment. He said to him, 'My friend, how is it that
you came in here without a wedding garment?' But he was
reduced to silence. Then the king said to his attendants, 'Bind

his hands and feet, and cast him into the darkness outside, where
there will be wailing and grinding of teeth.' Many are invited,
but few are chosen."

The Gospel of the Lord.

Liturgy of the Eucharist, *p. 897;* **Prayer over the Gifts,** *p. 1324.*

Friday

Antiphons and Prayers, *p. 1323;* **Liturgy of the Word** *for Year I (odd years) follows; Year II (even years), p. 1348.*

TODAY'S LIVING WORD

The rabbis counted 613 commandments in the Torah. Teachers,
however, often summarized the commandments to make them easier
to learn and to live, as Jesus does in today's Gospel. He says that the
whole law can be summed up in two commandments: love of God,
as prescribed in Deuteronomy 6:5, and love of neighbor, as in
Leviticus 19:18. While Jewish rabbis routinely emphasized love of
God or love of neighbor as basic, Jesus may have been the first to
combine the two commandments. Clearly he means to say that true
love of God—covenant fidelity—is expressed concretely in love of
neighbor.

The story of Ruth illustrates the teaching of Jesus. She proves her
loyalty to the God of Israel in the practical love she extends to Naomi.
Ezekiel's vision of the dry bones, on the other hand, demonstrates
that God's own creative fidelity makes possible the covenant fidelity
required of us. It is God who opens our graves, God who gives us
the spirit that we may live and love as God wills.

Year I

FIRST READING   Ru 1:1, 3–6, 14b–16, 22

*Naomi returned with the Moabite
daughter-in-law, Ruth, to Bethlehem.*

A reading from the beginning of the Book of Ruth

Once in the time of the judges there was a famine in the land; so a man from Bethlehem of Judah departed with his wife and two sons to reside on the plateau of Moab. Elimelech, the husband of Naomi, died, and she was left with her two sons, who married Moabite women, one named Orpah, the other Ruth. When they had lived there about ten years, both Mahlon and Chilion died also, and the woman was left with neither her two sons nor her husband. She then made ready to go back from the plateau of Moab because word reached her there that the LORD had visited his people and given them food.

Orpah kissed her mother-in-law good-bye, but Ruth stayed with her.

Naomi said, "See now! Your sister-in-law has gone back to her people and her god. Go back after your sister-in-law!" But Ruth said, "Do not ask me to abandon or forsake you! For wherever you go, I will go, wherever you lodge I will lodge, your people shall be my people, and your God my God."

Thus it was that Naomi returned with the Moabite daughter-in-law, Ruth, who accompanied her back from the plateau of Moab. They arrived in Bethlehem at the beginning of the barley harvest.

The word of the Lord.

Responsorial Psalm

Ps 146:5–6ab, 6c–7, 8–9a, 9bc–10

R. Praise the Lord, my soul!

Blessed is he whose help is the God of Jacob,
  whose hope is in the LORD, his God,
Who made heaven and earth,
  the sea and all that is in them.

R. Praise the Lord, my soul!

The Lord keeps faith forever,
  secures justice for the oppressed,
  gives food to the hungry.
The Lord sets captives free.

R. Praise the Lord, my soul!

The Lord gives sight to the blind.
The Lord raises up those who were bowed down;
  The Lord loves the just.
The Lord protects strangers.

R. Praise the Lord, my soul!

The fatherless and the widow he sustains,
  but the way of the wicked he thwarts.
The Lord shall reign forever;
  your God, O Zion, through all generations. Alleluia.

R. Praise the Lord, my soul!

Alleluia Verse and **Gospel**, p. 1350.

Year II

FIRST READING   Ez 37:1–14

Dry bones, hear the word of the Lord.
I will bring you back from your graves, O my people Israel.

A reading from the Book of the Prophet Ezekiel

The hand of the Lord came upon me, and led me out in the
Spirit of the Lord and set me in the center of the plain, which
was now filled with bones. He made me walk among the bones
in every direction so that I saw how many they were on the
surface of the plain. How dry they were! He asked me: Son of
man, can these bones come to life? I answered, "Lord God,
you alone know that." Then he said to me: Prophesy over these
bones, and say to them: Dry bones, hear the word of the Lord!

Thus says the Lord GOD to these bones: See! I will bring spirit into you, that you may come to life. I will put sinews upon you, make flesh grow over you, cover you with skin, and put spirit in you so that you may come to life and know that I am the LORD. I prophesied as I had been told, and even as I was prophesying I heard a noise; it was a rattling as the bones came together, bone joining bone. I saw the sinews and the flesh come upon them, and the skin cover them, but there was no spirit in them. Then the LORD said to me: Prophesy to the spirit, prophesy, son of man, and say to the spirit: Thus says the Lord GOD: From the four winds come, O spirit, and breathe into these slain that they may come to life. I prophesied as he told me, and the spirit came into them; they came alive and stood upright, a vast army. Then he said to me: Son of man, these bones are the whole house of Israel. They have been saying, "Our bones are dried up, our hope is lost, and we are cut off." Therefore, prophesy and say to them: Thus says the Lord GOD: O my people, I will open your graves and have you rise from them, and bring you back to the land of Israel. Then you shall know that I am the LORD, when I open your graves and have you rise from them, O my people! I will put my spirit in you that you may live, and I will settle you upon your land; thus you shall know that I am the LORD. I have promised, and I will do it, says the LORD.

The word of the Lord.

Responsorial Psalm

Ps 107:2–3, 4–5, 6–7, 8–9

R. Give thanks to the Lord; his love is everlasting.

Let the redeemed of the LORD say,
  those whom he has redeemed from the hand of the foe
And gathered from the lands,
  from the east and the west, from the north and the south.

R. Give thanks to the Lord; his love is everlasting.

They went astray in the desert wilderness;
  the way to an inhabited city they did not find.
Hungry and thirsty,
  their life was wasting away within them.

R. Give thanks to the Lord; his love is everlasting.

They cried to the LORD in their distress;
  from their straits he rescued them.
And he led them by a direct way
  to reach an inhabited city.

R. Give thanks to the Lord; his love is everlasting.

Let them give thanks to the LORD for his mercy
  and his wondrous deeds to the children of men,
Because he satisfied the longing soul
  and filled the hungry soul with good things.

R. Give thanks to the Lord; his love is everlasting.

Alleluia, alleluia Ps 25:4b, 5a
Teach me your paths, my God,
  guide me in your truth.
Alleluia, alleluia

Years I and II

GOSPEL   Mt 22:34–40

*You shall love the Lord, your God, with all your heart
and your neighbor as yourself.*

A reading from the holy Gospel according to Matthew

When the Pharisees heard that Jesus had silenced the Sadducees, they gathered together, and one of them, a scholar of the law, tested him by asking, "Teacher, which commandment in the law is the greatest?" He said to him, "You shall love the Lord, your God, with all your heart, with all your soul, and with all your mind. This is the greatest and the first commandment. The second is like it: You shall love your neighbor as yourself. The whole law and the prophets depend on these two commandments."

The Gospel of the Lord.

Liturgy of the Eucharist, *p. 897;* **Prayer over the Gifts,** *p. 1324.*

Saturday

Antiphons and Prayers, *p. 1323;* **Liturgy of the Word** *for Year I (odd years) follows; Year II (even years), p. 1354.*

TODAY'S LIVING WORD

Each Gospel writer recounted the story of Jesus with a view to the pastoral needs of his particular church. Recognizing this is a key to understanding today's selection from Matthew. At first glance the passage seems to contradict itself. On the one hand, Jesus acknowledges the authority of Moses' successors and urges his hearers to "do and observe all things whatsoever they tell you." On the other hand, he accuses them of hypocrisy and warns against doing what they do. This seeming contradiction reflects Matthew's dual aim: to depict Jesus as he was, an observant Jew, and at the same time to discredit the Jewish rivals of his church and those Christian leaders who are already imitating them.

The two first readings uncover the deep truth hidden in today's Gospel. Both point to God's choice of Israel, a choice signified in Ezekiel by the restoration of the temple. The same divine choice is evident in the person of Jesus. Jesus "did not just happen to be a Jew," writes Eugene Fisher, "he could only have been born a Jew."* Therefore, we Christians are all, like Ruth, foreigners who have found refuge in the house of Israel.

* Dr. Eugene J. Fisher and Rabbi Leon Klenicki, eds., *"Basic Jewish and Christian Beliefs in Dialogue: Covenant,"* Understanding the Jewish Experience (Education Department, USCC, and Interfaith Affairs, ADL), p. 3.

FIRST READING

Ru 2:1–3, 8–11; 4:13–17

The LORD has not failed to provide you today with an heir.
He was the father of Jesse, the father of David.

A reading from the Book of Ruth

Naomi had a prominent kinsman named Boaz, of the clan of her husband Elimelech. Ruth the Moabite said to Naomi, "Let me go and glean ears of grain in the field of anyone who will allow me that favor." Naomi said to her, "Go, my daughter," and she went. The field she entered to glean after the harvesters happened to be the section belonging to Boaz of the clan of Elimelech.

Boaz said to Ruth, "Listen, my daughter! Do not go to glean in anyone else's field; you are not to leave here. Stay here with my women servants. Watch to see which field is to be harvested, and follow them; I have commanded the young men to do you no harm. When you are thirsty, you may go and drink from the vessels the young men have filled." Casting herself prostrate upon the ground, Ruth said to him, "Why should I, a foreigner, be favored with your notice?" Boaz answered her: "I have had a complete account of what you have done for your mother-in-law after your husband's death; you have left your father and your mother and the land of your birth, and have come to a people whom you did not know previously."

Boaz took Ruth. When they came together as man and wife, the LORD enabled her to conceive and she bore a son. Then the women said to Naomi, "Blessed is the LORD who has not failed to provide you today with an heir! May he become famous in

Israel! He will be your comfort and the support of your old age, for his mother is the daughter-in-law who loves you. She is worth more to you than seven sons!" Naomi took the child, placed him on her lap, and became his nurse. And the neighbor women gave him his name, at the news that a grandson had been born to Naomi. They called him Obed. He was the father of Jesse, the father of David.

The word of the Lord.

Responsorial Psalm
Ps 128:1b–2, 3, 4, 5

R. See how the Lord blesses those who fear him.

Blessed are you who fear the LORD,
    who walk in his ways!
For you shall eat the fruit of your handiwork;
    blessed shall you be, and favored.

R. See how the Lord blesses those who fear him.

You wife shall be like a fruitful vine
    in the recesses of your home;
Your children like olive plants
    around your table.

R. See how the Lord blesses those who fear him.

Behold, thus is the man blessed
    who fears the LORD.

R. See how the Lord blesses those who fear him.

The LORD bless you from Zion:
    may you see the prosperity of Jerusalem
    all the days of your life.

R. See how the Lord blesses those who fear him.

Alleluia Verse *and* **Gospel,** *p. 1355.*

FIRST READING   Ez 43:1–7ab

The glory of God entered the temple.

A reading from the Book of the Prophet Ezekiel

The angel led me to the gate which faces the east, and there I saw the glory of the God of Israel coming from the east. I heard a sound like the roaring of many waters, and the earth shone with his glory. The vision was like that which I had seen when he came to destroy the city, and like that which I had seen by the river Chebar. I fell prone as the glory of the LORD entered the temple by way of the gate which faces the east, but spirit lifted me up and brought me to the inner court. And I saw that the temple was filled with the glory of the LORD. Then I heard someone speaking to me from the temple, while the man stood beside me. The voice said to me: Son of man, this is where my throne shall be, this is where I will set the soles of my feet; here I will dwell among the children of Israel forever.

The word of the Lord.

Responsorial Psalm   Ps 85:9ab and 10, 11–12, 13–14

R. **The glory of the Lord will dwell in our land.**

I will hear what God proclaims;
    the LORD—for he proclaims peace.
Near indeed is his salvation to those who fear him,
    glory dwelling in our land.

R. **The glory of the Lord will dwell in our land.**

Kindness and truth shall meet;
    justice and peace shall kiss.
Truth shall spring out of the earth,
    and justice shall look down from heaven.

R. **The glory of the Lord will dwell in our land.**

The LORD himself will give his benefits;
  our land shall yield its increase.
Justice shall walk before him,
  and salvation, along the way of his steps.

R. The glory of the Lord will dwell in our land.

Alleluia, alleluia Mt 23:9b, 10b
You have but one Father in heaven;
you have but one master, the Christ.
Alleluia, alleluia

Years I and II

GOSPEL   Mt 23:1–12

They preach but they do not practice.

A reading from the holy Gospel according to Matthew

Jesus spoke to the crowds and to his disciples, saying, "The scribes and the Pharisees have taken their seat on the chair of Moses. Therefore, do and observe all things whatsoever they tell you, but do not follow their example. For they preach but they do not practice. They tie up heavy burdens hard to carry and lay them on people's shoulders, but they will not lift a finger to move them. All their works are performed to be seen. They widen their phylacteries and lengthen their tassels. They love places of honor at banquets, seats of honor in synagogues, greetings in marketplaces, and the salutation 'Rabbi.' As for you, do not be called 'Rabbi.' You have but one teacher, and you are all brothers. Call no one on earth your father; you have but one Father in heaven. Do not be called 'Master'; you have but one master, the Christ. The greatest among you must be your servant. Whoever exalts himself will be humbled; but whoever humbles himself will be exalted."

The Gospel of the Lord.

Liturgy of the Eucharist, *p. 897;* **Prayer over the Gifts,** *p. 1324.*

TWENTY-FIRST WEEK IN ORDINARY TIME

The **Antiphons and Prayers** *may be the following, or may be chosen from any of the other 33 weeks in Ordinary Time (refer to Liturgical Calendar, pp. 26–41).*

The **Liturgy of the Word** *varies: for Monday, see p. 1358; Tuesday, p. 1362; Wednesday, p. 1366; Thursday, p. 1370; Friday, p. 1374; Saturday, p. 1379.*

Entrance Antiphon

Listen, Lord, and answer me. Save your servant who trusts in you. I call to you all day long; have mercy on me, O Lord.

(Ps 86:1–3)

Opening Prayer

Let us pray

[that God will make us one in mind and heart]

Pause for silent prayer.

Father,
help us to seek the values
that will bring us lasting joy in this changing world.
In our desire for what you promise
make us one in mind and heart.

Grant this through our Lord Jesus Christ, your Son,
who lives and reigns with you and the Holy Spirit,
one God, for ever and ever.

Alternative Opening Prayer

Let us pray

[with minds fixed on eternal truth]

Pause for silent prayer.

Lord our God,
all truth is from you,
and you alone bring oneness of heart.
Give your people the joy
of hearing your word in every sound

and of longing for your presence more than for life itself.
May all the attractions of a changing world
serve only to bring us
the peace of your kingdom which this world does not give.

Grant this through Christ our Lord.

Prayer over the Gifts

Pray, brethren...

Merciful God,
the perfect sacrifice of Jesus Christ
made us your people.
In your love,
grant peace and unity to your Church.

We ask this through Christ our Lord.

Preface of Weekdays in Ordinary Time I–VI, *pp. 948–950.*

Communion Antiphon

Lord, the earth is filled with your gift from heaven; man grows bread from earth, and wine to cheer his heart.   (Ps 104:13–15)

Or:

The Lord says: The man who eats my flesh and drinks my blood will live for ever; I shall raise him to life on the last day.

(Jn 6:54)

Prayer after Communion

Let us pray.

Pause for silent prayer, if this has not preceded.

Lord,
may this eucharist increase within us
the healing power of your love.
May it guide and direct our efforts
to please you in all things.

We ask this in the name of Jesus the Lord.

Monday

Antiphons and Prayers, *p. 1356;* **Liturgy of the Word** *for Year I (odd years) follows; Year II (even years), p. 1360.*

TODAY'S LIVING WORD

The first readings for today from 1 and 2 Thessalonians and the selection from Matthew's Gospel reflect the experience of two early Christian communities in different times and circumstances. Both 1 and 2 Thessalonians address a church founded by Paul. The passage from 1 Thessalonians makes it evident that they are Gentiles (non-Jews) who have become followers of Jesus. There Paul describes them as having "turned to God from idols," and 2 Thessalonians adds that they have been constant and faithful in persecution and trial. While Paul commends the Thessalonians, Matthew's Jesus condemns the Pharisees and scribes. Matthew is writing for a Christian-Jewish group engaged in a bitter rivalry with a rabbinic-Jewish group. These are the "scribes and Pharisees" accused in today's woes of stopping their fellow Jews from embracing the Gospel of Jesus. It is in this sense that Matthew says they "lock the kingdom of heaven before human beings."

These glimpses into the life of the early Church keep us mindful of the variety of religious experiences that, by the power of the Spirit, were the beginnings of the Church.

Year I

FIRST READING

1 Thes 1:1–5, 8b–10

You turned to God from idols to await his Son,
whom he raised from the dead.

A reading from the beginning of the first Letter of Saint Paul to the Thessalonians

Paul, Silvanus, and Timothy to the Church of the Thessalonians in God the Father and the Lord Jesus Christ: grace to you and peace.

We give thanks to God always for all of you, remembering you in our prayers, unceasingly calling to mind your work of faith and labor of love and endurance in hope of our Lord Jesus Christ, before our God and Father, knowing, brothers and sisters loved by God, how you were chosen. For our Gospel did not come to you in word alone, but also in power and in the Holy Spirit and with much conviction. You know what sort of people we were among you for your sake. In every place your faith in God has gone forth, so that we have no need to say anything. For they themselves openly declare about us what sort of reception we had among you, and how you turned to God from idols to serve the living and true God and to await his Son from heaven, whom he raised from the dead, Jesus, who delivers us from the coming wrath.

The word of the Lord.

Responsorial Psalm
Ps 149:1b–2, 3–4, 5–6a and 9b

R. The Lord takes delight in his people.

Sing to the LORD a new song
   of praise in the assembly of the faithful.
Let Israel be glad in their maker,
   let the children of Zion rejoice in their king.

R. The Lord takes delight in his people.

Let them praise his name in the festive dance,
   let them sing praise to him with timbrel and harp.
For the LORD loves his people,
   and he adorns the lowly with victory.

R. The Lord takes delight in his people.

Let the faithful exult in glory;
   let them sing for joy upon their couches;

Let the high praises of God be in their throats.
This is the glory of all his faithful. Alleluia!

R. The Lord takes delight in his people.

Or: **R. Alleluia.**

Alleluia Verse and **Gospel**, p. 1361.

Year II

FIRST READING   2 Thes 1:1–5, 11–12

*May the name of our Lord Jesus be glorified in you
and you in him.*

A reading from the beginning of the second Letter of Saint Paul
to the Thessalonians

Paul, Silvanus, and Timothy to the Church of the Thessalonians
in God our Father and the Lord Jesus Christ: grace to you and
peace from God our Father and the Lord Jesus Christ.

We ought to thank God always for you, brothers and sisters,
as is fitting, because your faith flourishes ever more, and the
love of every one of you for one another grows ever greater.
Accordingly, we ourselves boast of you in the churches of God
regarding your endurance and faith in all your persecutions
and the afflictions you endure.

This is evidence of the just judgment of God, so that you
may be considered worthy of the Kingdom of God for which
you are suffering.

We always pray for you, that our God may make you worthy
of his calling and powerfully bring to fulfillment every good
purpose and every effort of faith, that the name of our Lord
Jesus may be glorified in you, and you in him, in accord with
the grace of our God and Lord Jesus Christ.

The word of the Lord.

Responsorial Psalm

Ps 96:1–2a, 2b–3, 4–5

R. Proclaim God's marvelous deeds to all the nations.

Sing to the LORD a new song;
  sing to the LORD, all you lands.
Sing to the LORD; bless his name.

R. Proclaim God's marvelous deeds to all the nations.

Announce his salvation, day after day.
Tell his glory among the nations;
  among all peoples, his wondrous deeds.

R. Proclaim God's marvelous deeds to all the nations.

For great is the LORD and highly to be praised;
  awesome is he, beyond all gods.
For all the gods of the nations are things of nought,
  but the LORD made the heavens.

R. Proclaim God's marvelous deeds to all the nations.

Alleluia, alleluia Jn 10:27
My sheep hear my voice, says the Lord;
I know them, and they follow me.
Alleluia, alleluia

Years I and II

GOSPEL

Mt 23:13–22

Woe to you, blind guides.

A reading from the holy Gospel according to Matthew

Jesus said to the crowds and to his disciples: "Woe to you, scribes and Pharisees, you hypocrites. You lock the Kingdom of heaven before men. You do not enter yourselves, nor do you allow entrance to those trying to enter.

"Woe to you, scribes and Pharisees, you hypocrites. You traverse sea and land to make one convert, and when that happens you make him a child of Gehenna twice as much as yourselves.

"Woe to you, blind guides, who say, 'If one swears by the temple, it means nothing, but if one swears by the gold of the temple, one is obligated.' Blind fools, which is greater, the gold, or the temple that made the gold sacred? And you say, 'If one swears by the altar, it means nothing, but if one swears by the gift on the altar, one is obligated.' You blind ones, which is greater, the gift, or the altar that makes the gift sacred? One who swears by the altar swears by it and all that is upon it; one who swears by the temple swears by it and by him who dwells in it; one who swears by heaven swears by the throne of God and by him who is seated on it."

The Gospel of the Lord.

Liturgy of the Eucharist, *p. 897;* **Prayer over the Gifts,** *p. 1357.*

Tuesday

Antiphons and Prayers, *p. 1356;* **Liturgy of the Word** *for Year I (odd years) follows; Year II (even years), p. 1364.*

TODAY'S LIVING WORD

Today's Gospel is taken from Matthew 23, which is an example of religious polemic. Polemic is a verbal attack on one's opponents, characterized by harsh denunciation, gross exaggeration, mockery, sarcasm, etc. In today's selection, Matthew ridicules the values of his Jewish rivals. He says they "strain out the gnat and swallow the camel" (an unclean animal, no less!). Note, however, that he does not say that tithes on mint and herbs and seed should not be paid; only that the weightier matters of Jewish law—justice and mercy and faith—should be given priority.

The distinction Matthew makes between the inside and the outside is also made in both first readings. Both warn Christians against being moved by flattering words (1 Thes) or disquieting rumors (2 Thes). These things that come from outside may be deceptive. Rather, they must take their stand on what is inside, holding fast to the traditions they have received from those like Paul, whose hearts have been tested by God, "who judges our hearts," and found true.

Year I

FIRST READING   1 Thes 2:1–8

*We were determined to share with you
not only the Gospel of God, but our very selves as well.*

A reading from the first Letter of Saint Paul to the Thessalonians

You yourselves know, brothers and sisters, that our reception among you was not without effect. Rather, after we had suffered and been insolently treated, as you know, in Philippi, we drew courage through our God to speak to you the Gospel of God with much struggle. Our exhortation was not from delusion or impure motives, nor did it work through deception. But as we were judged worthy by God to be entrusted with the Gospel, that is how we speak, not as trying to please men, but rather God, who judges our hearts. Nor, indeed, did we ever appear with flattering speech, as you know, or with a pretext for greed —God is witness—nor did we seek praise from men, either from you or from others, although we were able to impose our weight as Apostles of Christ. Rather, we were gentle among you, as a nursing mother cares for her children. With such affection for you, we were determined to share with you not only the Gospel of God, but our very selves as well, so dearly beloved had you become to us.

The word of the Lord.

Responsorial Psalm   Ps 139:1–3, 4–6

R. **You have searched me and you know me, Lord.**

O LORD, you have probed me and you know me;
  you know when I sit and when I stand;
  you understand my thoughts from afar.
My journeys and my rest you scrutinize,
  with all my ways you are familiar.

R. You have searched me and you know me, Lord.

Even before a word is on my tongue,
  behold, O LORD, you know the whole of it.
Behind me and before, you hem me in
  and rest your hand upon me.
Such knowledge is too wonderful for me;
  too lofty for me to attain.

R. You have searched me and you know me, Lord.

Alleluia Verse *and* **Gospel,** *p. 1365.*

Year II

FIRST READING
2 Thes 2:1–3a, 14–17

Hold fast to the traditions that you were taught.

A reading from the second Letter of Saint Paul to the Thessalonians

We ask you, brothers and sisters, with regard to the coming of our Lord Jesus Christ and our assembling with him, not to be shaken out of your minds suddenly, or to be alarmed either by a "spirit," or by an oral statement, or by a letter allegedly from us to the effect that the day of the Lord is at hand. Let no one deceive you in any way.

To this end he has also called you through our Gospel to possess the glory of our Lord Jesus Christ. Therefore, brothers and sisters, stand firm and hold fast to the traditions that you were taught, either by an oral statement or by a letter of ours.

May our Lord Jesus Christ himself and God our Father, who has loved us and given us everlasting encouragement and good hope through his grace, encourage your hearts and strengthen them in every good deed and word.

The word of the Lord.

Responsorial Psalm

Ps 96:10, 11–12, 13

R. **The Lord comes to judge the earth.**

Say among the nations: The LORD is king.
He has made the world firm, not to be moved;
  he governs the peoples with equity.

R. **The Lord comes to judge the earth.**

Let the heavens be glad and the earth rejoice;
  let the sea and what fills it resound;
  let the plains be joyful and all that is in them!
Then shall all the trees of the forest exult.

R. **The Lord comes to judge the earth.**

Before the LORD, for he comes;
  for he comes to rule the earth.
He shall rule the world with justice
  and the peoples with his constancy.

R. **The Lord comes to judge the earth.**

Alleluia, alleluia   Heb 4:12
The word of God is living and effective,
able to discern reflections and thoughts of the heart.
Alleluia, alleluia

Years I and II

GOSPEL

Mt 23:23–26

But these you should have done, without neglecting the others.

A reading from the holy Gospel according to Matthew

Jesus said: "Woe to you, scribes and Pharisees, you hypocrites. You pay tithes of mint and dill and cummin, and have neglected the weightier things of the law: judgment and mercy and fidelity. But these you should have done, without neglecting the others. Blind guides, who strain out the gnat and swallow the camel!

"Woe to you, scribes and Pharisees, you hypocrites. You cleanse the outside of cup and dish, but inside they are full of plunder and self-indulgence. Blind Pharisee, cleanse first the inside of the cup, so that the outside also may be clean."
The Gospel of the Lord.

Liturgy of the Eucharist, *p. 897;* **Prayer over the Gifts,** *p. 1357.*

Wednesday

Antiphons and Prayers, *p. 1356;* **Liturgy of the Word** *for Year I (odd years) follows; Year II (even years), p. 1368.*

Today's Living Word

Religious polemic reaches a climax in today's Gospel as Matthew's Jesus accuses the scribes and Pharisees of being "the children of those who murdered the prophets." Then with the words, "now fill up what your ancestors measured out," he seems to point to their murder of him and of his disciples. Surely this is Matthew's intent: to condemn his opponents and consign them, a "brood of vipers," to the judgment of Gehenna (23:33). However distasteful we may find such language, it is a standard feature in the Dead Sea Scrolls and other Jewish and Greco-Roman writings, as well as in the Gospels.

Historically, the polemic of Matthew in passages like today's has been used to caricature and condemn Jews and Judaism. It is imperative, therefore, that when Christians read the Gospels they take into account the historical context in which they were written and the literary conventions they employ. Only thus will we, like Paul's Thessalonians, receive their message "not as a human word but, as it truly is, the word of God."

Year I

FIRST READING

1 Thes 2:9–13

Working night and day we proclaimed to you the Gospel of God.

A reading from the first Letter of Saint Paul to the Thessalonians

You recall, brothers and sisters, our toil and drudgery. Working night and day in order not to burden any of you, we proclaimed to you the Gospel of God. You are witnesses, and so is God, how devoutly and justly and blamelessly we behaved toward you believers. As you know, we treated each one of you as a father treats his children, exhorting and encouraging you and insisting that you walk in a manner worthy of the God who calls you into his Kingdom and glory.

And for this reason we too give thanks to God unceasingly, that, in receiving the word of God from hearing us, you received it not as the word of men, but as it truly is, the word of God, which is now at work in you who believe.

The word of the Lord.

Responsorial Psalm

Ps 139:7–8, 9–10, 11–12ab

R. You have searched me and you know me, Lord.

Where can I go from your spirit?
  From your presence where can I flee?
If I go up to the heavens, you are there;
  if I sink to the nether world, you are present there.

R. You have searched me and you know me, Lord.

If I take the wings of the dawn,
  if I settle at the farthest limits of the sea,
Even there your hand shall guide me,
  and your right hand hold me fast.

R. You have searched me and you know me, Lord.

If I say, "Surely the darkness shall hide me,
  and night shall be my light"—
For you darkness itself is not dark,
  and night shines as the day.

R. You have searched me and you know me, Lord.

Alleluia Verse *and* **Gospel,** *p. 1369.*

Year II

FIRST READING

2 Thes 3:6–10, 16–18

If anyone is unwilling to work, neither should that one eat.

A reading from the second Letter of Saint Paul to the Thessalonians

We instruct you, brothers and sisters, in the name of our Lord
Jesus Christ, to shun any brother who walks in a disorderly
way and not according to the tradition they received from us.
For you know how one must imitate us. For we did not act in
a disorderly way among you, nor did we eat food received free
from anyone. On the contrary, in toil and drudgery, night and
day we worked, so as not to burden any of you. Not that we do
not have the right. Rather, we wanted to present ourselves as a
model for you, so that you might imitate us. In fact, when we
were with you, we instructed you that if anyone was unwilling
to work, neither should that one eat.

May the Lord of peace himself give you peace at all times
and in every way. The Lord be with all of you.

This greeting is in my own hand, Paul's. This is the sign in
every letter; this is how I write. The grace of our Lord Jesus
Christ be with all of you.

The word of the Lord.

Responsorial Psalm

Ps 128:1–2, 4–5

R. Blessed are those who fear the Lord.

Blessed are you who fear the LORD,
    who walk in his ways!
For you shall eat the fruit of your handiwork;
    blessed shall you be, and favored.

R. Blessed are those who fear the Lord.

Behold, thus is the man blessed
    who fears the LORD.
The LORD bless you from Zion:
    may you see the prosperity of Jerusalem
    all the days of your life.

R. Blessed are those who fear the Lord.

Alleluia, alleluia   1 Jn 2:5
Whoever keeps the word of Christ,
    the love of God is truly perfected in him.
Alleluia, alleluia

Years I and II

GOSPEL

Mt 23:27–32

You are the children of those who murdered the prophets.

A reading from the holy Gospel according to Matthew

Jesus said, "Woe to you, scribes and Pharisees, you hypocrites. You are like whitewashed tombs, which appear beautiful on the outside, but inside are full of dead men's bones and every kind of filth. Even so, on the outside you appear righteous, but inside you are filled with hypocrisy and evildoing.

"Woe to you, scribes and Pharisees, you hypocrites. You build the tombs of the prophets and adorn the memorials of the righteous, and you say, 'If we had lived in the days of our ancestors, we would not have joined them in shedding the prophets'

blood.' Thus you bear witness against yourselves that you are
the children of those who murdered the prophets; now fill up
what your ancestors measured out!"

The Gospel of the Lord.

Liturgy of the Eucharist, *p. 897;* **Prayer over the Gifts,** *p. 1357.*

Thursday

Antiphons and Prayers, *p. 1356;* **Liturgy of the Word** *for Year I (odd
years) follows; Year II (even years), p. 1372.*

TODAY'S LIVING WORD

All three of today's readings resonate with the theme of Christian
apocalyptic, the expectation of Christ's Second Coming. The Gospel
praises the faithful, farsighted servant who is always ready to receive
the Son of Man, who will come when least expected. In both letters Paul exhorts his churches to the same fidelity. He prays that
they may be strong and blameless "at the coming of our Lord Jesus
with all his holy ones" (1 Thes), that is, "on the day of our Lord Jesus
[Christ]" (1 Cor).

In the Gospel parable, the delay of the Second Coming becomes
the occasion for the worthless servant to abuse his fellow servants.
The warning is especially urgent for us, to whom the Lord's return
seems so long delayed. A delay of two thousand years naturally
gives rise to doubt that may lead to dissolution. We must, therefore,
resolve to stay awake and stand firm in the knowledge that "God is
faithful." As we watch and wait, we must let our love "for one another
and for all" overflow.

Year I

FIRST READING   1 Thes 3:7–13

*May the Lord make you increase
and abound in love for one another and for all.*

A reading from the first Letter of Saint Paul to the Thessalonians

We have been reassured about you, brothers and sisters, in our every distress and affliction, through your faith. For we now live, if you stand firm in the Lord.

What thanksgiving, then, can we render to God for you, for all the joy we feel on your account before our God? Night and day we pray beyond measure to see you in person and to remedy the deficiencies of your faith. Now may God himself, our Father, and our Lord Jesus direct our way to you, and may the Lord make you increase and abound in love for one another and for all, just as we have for you, so as to strengthen your hearts, to be blameless in holiness before our God and Father at the coming of our Lord Jesus with all his holy ones. Amen.
The word of the Lord.

Responsorial Psalm

Ps 90:3–5a, 12–13, 14 and 17

R. Fill us with your love, O Lord, and we will sing for joy!

You turn man back to dust,
  saying, "Return, O children of men."
For a thousand years in your sight
  are as yesterday, now that it is past,
  or as a watch of the night.

R. Fill us with your love, O Lord, and we will sing for joy!

Teach us to number our days aright,
  that we may gain wisdom of heart.
Return, O LORD! How long?
  Have pity on your servants!

R. Fill us with your love, O Lord, and we will sing for joy!

Fill us at daybreak with your kindness,
  that we may shout for joy and gladness all our days.
And may the gracious care of the LORD our God be ours;

prosper the work of our hands for us!
Prosper the work of our hands!

R. Fill us with your love, O Lord, and we will sing for joy!

Alleluia Verse *and* **Gospel,** *p. 1373.*

Year II

FIRST READING   1 Cor 1:1–9

In him you were enriched in every way.

A reading from the beginning of the first Letter of Saint Paul
to the Corinthians

Paul, called to be an Apostle of Christ Jesus by the will of
God, and Sosthenes our brother, to the Church of God that is
in Corinth, to you who have been sanctified in Christ Jesus,
called to be holy, with all those everywhere who call upon the
name of our Lord Jesus Christ, their Lord and ours. Grace to
you and peace from God our Father and the Lord Jesus Christ.

I give thanks to my God always on your account for the
grace of God bestowed on you in Christ Jesus, that in him you
were enriched in every way, with all discourse and all knowledge, as the testimony to Christ was confirmed among you, so
that you are not lacking in any spiritual gift as you wait for the
revelation of our Lord Jesus Christ. He will keep you firm to
the end, irreproachable on the day of our Lord Jesus Christ.
God is faithful, and by him you were called to fellowship with
his Son, Jesus Christ our Lord.

The word of the Lord.

Responsorial Psalm   Ps 145:2–3, 4–5, 6–7

R. I will praise your name for ever, Lord.

Every day will I bless you,
  and I will praise your name forever and ever.

Great is the LORD and highly to be praised;
  his greatness is unsearchable.

R. I will praise your name for ever, Lord.

Generation after generation praises your works
  and proclaims your might.
They speak of the splendor of your glorious majesty
  and tell of your wondrous works.

R. I will praise your name for ever, Lord.

They discourse of the power of your terrible deeds
  and declare your greatness.
They publish the fame of your abundant goodness
  and joyfully sing of your justice.

R. I will praise your name for ever, Lord.

Alleluia, alleluia   Mt 24:42a, 44
Stay awake!
For you do not know when the Son of Man will come.
Alleluia, alleluia

Years I and II

GOSPEL   Mt 24:42–51

Stay awake!

A reading from the holy Gospel according to Matthew

Jesus said to his disciples: "Stay awake! For you do not know
on which day your Lord will come. Be sure of this: if the master
of the house had known the hour of night when the thief was
coming, he would have stayed awake and not let his house be
broken into. So too, you also must be prepared, for at an hour
you do not expect, the Son of Man will come.

   "Who, then, is the faithful and prudent servant, whom the
master has put in charge of his household to distribute to them
their food at the proper time? Blessed is that servant whom his

master on his arrival finds doing so. Amen, I say to you, he will put him in charge of all his property. But if that wicked servant says to himself, 'My master is long delayed,' and begins to beat his fellow servants, and eat and drink with drunkards, the servant's master will come on an unexpected day and at an unknown hour and will punish him severely and assign him a place with the hypocrites, where there will be wailing and grinding of teeth."

The Gospel of the Lord.

Liturgy of the Eucharist, *p. 897;* **Prayer over the Gifts,** *p. 1357.*

Friday

Antiphons and Prayers, *p. 1356;* **Liturgy of the Word** *for Year I (odd years) follows; Year II (even years), p. 1376.*

TODAY'S LIVING WORD

Today's parable, found only in Matthew, again calls us to vigilance in view of the Lord's return. "You know neither the day nor the hour." The unpreparedness of the foolish is severely punished. Their cry—"Lord, Lord!"—reminds us of the earlier words of Jesus: "Not everyone who says to me, 'Lord, Lord,' will enter the kingdom of heaven, but only the one who does the will of my Father in heaven" (Mt 7:21). The foolish lack the "oil" of good works; they fail to do the Father's will. Thus Paul instructs the Thessalonians as well. He tells them God wills that they grow in holiness and that they abstain from immorality.

Matthew's parable also makes a massive Christological claim. In the Old Testament, God is the Bridegroom of Israel. In this parable, however, Jesus is the Bridegroom whose return must be awaited in joyful hope. He is the wisdom of God who causes the foolish of this world to stumble.

Year I

FIRST READING

1 Thes 4:1–8

This is the will of God, your holiness.

A reading from the first Letter of Saint Paul to the Thessalonians

Brothers and sisters, we earnestly ask and exhort you in the Lord Jesus that, as you received from us how you should conduct yourselves to please God—and as you are conducting yourselves—you do so even more. For you know what instructions we gave you through the Lord Jesus.

This is the will of God, your holiness: that you refrain from immorality, that each of you know how to acquire a wife for himself in holiness and honor, not in lustful passion as do the Gentiles who do not know God; not to take advantage of or exploit a brother or sister in this matter, for the Lord is an avenger in all these things, as we told you before and solemnly affirmed. For God did not call us to impurity but to holiness. Therefore, whoever disregards this, disregards not a human being but God, who also gives his Holy Spirit to you.

The word of the Lord.

Responsorial Psalm

Ps 97:1 and 2b, 5–6, 10, 11–12

R. Rejoice in the Lord, you just!

The LORD is king; let the earth rejoice;
  let the many isles be glad.
  Justice and judgment are the foundation of his throne.

R. Rejoice in the Lord, you just!

The mountains melt like wax before the LORD,
  before the LORD of all the earth.
The heavens proclaim his justice,
  and all peoples see his glory.

R. Rejoice in the Lord, you just!

The LORD loves those who hate evil;
  he guards the lives of his faithful ones;
  from the hand of the wicked he delivers them.

R. Rejoice in the Lord, you just!

Light dawns for the just;
  and gladness, for the upright of heart.
Be glad in the LORD, you just,
  and give thanks to his holy name.

R. Rejoice in the Lord, you just!

Alleluia Verse and **Gospel**, p. 1377f.

Year II

FIRST READING

1 Cor 1:17–25

We proclaim Christ crucified, foolishness to Gentiles,
but to those who are called, the wisdom of God.

A reading from the first Letter of Saint Paul to the Corinthians

Brothers and sisters:
Christ did not send me to baptize but to preach the Gospel,
and not with the wisdom of human eloquence, so that the cross
of Christ might not be emptied of its meaning.

The message of the cross is foolishness to those who are
perishing, but to us who are being saved it is the power of
God. For it is written:

I will destroy the wisdom of the wise,
  and the learning of the learned I will set aside.

Where is the wise one? Where is the scribe? Where is the
debater of this age? Has not God made the wisdom of the world
foolish? For since in the wisdom of God the world did not

come to know God through wisdom, it was the will of God through the foolishness of the proclamation to save those who have faith. For Jews demand signs and Greeks look for wisdom, but we proclaim Christ crucified, a stumbling block to Jews and foolishness to Gentiles, but to those who are called, Jews and Greeks alike, Christ the power of God and the wisdom of God. For the foolishness of God is wiser than human wisdom, and the weakness of God is stronger than human strength.

The word of the Lord.

Responsorial Psalm
Ps 33:1–2, 4–5, 10–11

R. The earth is full of the goodness of the Lord.

Exult, you just, in the LORD;
  praise from the upright is fitting.
Give thanks to the LORD on the harp;
  with the ten-stringed lyre chant his praises.

R. The earth is full of the goodness of the Lord.

For upright is the word of the LORD,
  and all his works are trustworthy.
He loves justice and right;
  of the kindness of the LORD the earth is full.

R. The earth is full of the goodness of the Lord.

The LORD brings to nought the plans of nations;
  he foils the designs of peoples.
But the plan of the LORD stands forever;
  the design of his heart, through all generations.

R. The earth is full of the goodness of the Lord.

Alleluia, alleluia Lk 21:36
Be vigilant at all times and pray,
  that you may have the strength to stand before the Son of Man.
Alleluia, alleluia

Years I and II

GOSPEL   Mt 25:1–13

Behold, the bridegroom! Come out to meet him!

A reading from the holy Gospel according to Matthew

Jesus told his disciples this parable: "The Kingdom of heaven will be like ten virgins who took their lamps and went out to meet the bridegroom. Five of them were foolish and five were wise. The foolish ones, when taking their lamps, brought no oil with them, but the wise brought flasks of oil with their lamps. Since the bridegroom was long delayed, they all became drowsy and fell asleep. At midnight, there was a cry, 'Behold, the bridegroom! Come out to meet him!' Then all those virgins got up and trimmed their lamps. The foolish ones said to the wise, 'Give us some of your oil, for our lamps are going out.' But the wise ones replied, 'No, for there may not be enough for us and you. Go instead to the merchants and buy some for yourselves.' While they went off to buy it, the bridegroom came and those who were ready went into the wedding feast with him. Then the door was locked. Afterwards the other virgins came and said, 'Lord, Lord, open the door for us!' But he said in reply, 'Amen, I say to you, I do not know you.' Therefore, stay awake, for you know neither the day nor the hour."

The Gospel of the Lord.

Liturgy of the Eucharist, *p. 897;* **Prayer over the Gifts,** *p. 1357.*

Saturday

Antiphons and Prayers, *p. 1356;* **Liturgy of the Word** *for Year I (odd years) follows; Year II (even years), p. 1380.*

TODAY'S LIVING WORD

Today's Gospel is another parable about the return of the Son of Man. This one further explains what preparedness for Christ's Second Coming entails. It requires positive, productive activity, utilizing the gifts God has entrusted to us according to our abilities. That the two "good and faithful" servants both receive the same reward indicates that the quality of their activity is what counts, not the quantity of their achievement. Such committed, creative activity in response to God's grace enables "the foolish of the world to shame the wise," as Paul tells the Corinthians, and "the weak of the world to shame the strong." Similarly, Paul urges the Thessalonians to work, recognizing the danger of inactivity, as does the parable.

Because this passage uses three times the Greek word for "hand over," the root of the word for tradition, some commentators find in this parable a critique of those who "bury" religious tradition, refusing the risk of developing it. Matthew's Christian Jews may have thought this way about the rabbinic Jews with whom they were in conflict.

Year I

FIRST READING

1 Thes 4:9–11

You have been taught by God to love one another.

A reading from the first Letter of Saint Paul to the Thessalonians

Brothers and sisters:

On the subject of fraternal charity you have no need for anyone to write you, for you yourselves have been taught by God to love one another. Indeed, you do this for all the brothers throughout Macedonia. Nevertheless we urge you, brothers and sisters, to progress even more, and to aspire to live a tranquil

life, to mind your own affairs, and to work with your own
hands, as we instructed you.

The word of the Lord.

Responsorial Psalm

Ps 98:1, 7–8, 9

R. The Lord comes to rule the earth with justice.

Sing to the LORD a new song,
  for he has done wondrous deeds;
His right hand has won victory for him,
  his holy arm.

R. The Lord comes to rule the earth with justice.

Let the sea and what fills it resound,
  the world and those who dwell in it;
Let the rivers clap their hands,
  the mountains shout with them for joy.

R. The Lord comes to rule the earth with justice.

Before the LORD, for he comes,
  for he comes to rule the earth;
He will rule the world with justice
  and the peoples with equity.

R. The Lord comes to rule the earth with justice.

Alleluia Verse *and* **Gospel,** *p. 1381f.*

Year II

FIRST READING

1 Cor 1:26–31

God chose the weak of the world.

A reading from the first Letter of Saint Paul to the Corinthians

Consider your own calling, brothers and sisters. Not many of
you were wise by human standards, not many were powerful,
not many were of noble birth. Rather, God chose the foolish of

the world to shame the wise, and God chose the weak of the world to shame the strong, and God chose the lowly and despised of the world, those who count for nothing, to reduce to nothing those who are something, so that no human being might boast before God. It is due to him that you are in Christ Jesus, who became for us wisdom from God, as well as righteousness, sanctification, and redemption, so that, as it is written, *Whoever boasts, should boast in the Lord.*

The word of the Lord.

Responsorial Psalm

Ps 33:12–13, 18–19, 20–21

R. Blessed the people the Lord has chosen to be his own.

Blessed the nation whose God is the LORD,
  the people he has chosen for his own inheritance.
From heaven the LORD looks down;
  he sees all mankind.

R. Blessed the people the Lord has chosen to be his own.

But see, the eyes of the LORD are upon those who fear him,
  upon those who hope for his kindness,
To deliver them from death
  and preserve them in spite of famine.

R. Blessed the people the Lord has chosen to be his own.

Our soul waits for the LORD,
  who is our help and our shield,
For in him our hearts rejoice;
  in his holy name we trust.

R. Blessed the people the Lord has chosen to be his own.

Alleluia, alleluia Jn 13:34
I give you a new commandment:
love one another as I have loved you.
Alleluia, alleluia

Years I and II

GOSPEL   Mt 25:14–30

*Since you have been faithful in small matters,
come, share your master's joy.*

A reading from the holy Gospel according to Matthew

Jesus told his disciples this parable: "A man going on a journey called in his servants and entrusted his possessions to them. To one he gave five talents; to another, two; to a third, one— to each according to his ability. Then he went away. Immediately the one who received five talents went and traded with them, and made another five. Likewise, the one who received two made another two. But the man who received one went off and dug a hole in the ground and buried his master's money. After a long time the master of those servants came back and settled accounts with them. The one who had received five talents came forward bringing the additional five. He said, 'Master, you gave me five talents. See, I have made five more.' His master said to him, 'Well done, my good and faithful servant. Since you were faithful in small matters, I will give you great responsibilities. Come, share your master's joy.' Then the one who had received two talents also came forward and said, 'Master, you gave me two talents. See, I have made two more.' His master said to him, 'Well done, my good and faithful servant. Since you were faithful in small matters, I will give you great responsibilities. Come, share your master's joy.' Then the one who had received the one talent came forward and said, 'Master, I knew you were a demanding person, harvesting where you did not plant and gathering where you did not scatter; so out of fear I went off and buried your talent in the ground.

Here it is back.' His master said to him in reply, 'You wicked, lazy servant! So you knew that I harvest where I did not plant and gather where I did not scatter? Should you not then have put my money in the bank so that I could have got it back with interest on my return? Now then! Take the talent from him and give it to the one with ten. For to everyone who has, more will be given and he will grow rich; but from the one who has not, even what he has will be taken away. And throw this useless servant into the darkness outside, where there will be wailing and grinding of teeth.'"

The Gospel of the Lord.

Liturgy of the Eucharist, *p. 897;* **Prayer over the Gifts,** *p. 1357.*

TWENTY-SECOND WEEK IN ORDINARY TIME

The **Antiphons and Prayers** *may be the following, or may be chosen from any of the other 33 weeks in Ordinary Time (refer to Liturgical Calendar, pp. 26–41).*

The **Liturgy of the Word** *varies: for Monday, see p. 1385; Tuesday, p. 1390; Wednesday, p. 1395; Thursday, p. 1399; Friday, p. 1403; Saturday, p. 1407.*

Entrance Antiphon

I call to you all day long, have mercy on me, O Lord. You are good and forgiving, full of love for all who call to you.

(Ps 86:3, 5)

Opening Prayer

Let us pray

[that God will increase our faith
and bring to perfection the gifts he has given us]

Pause for silent prayer.

Almighty God,
every good thing comes from you.
Fill our hearts with love for you,
increase our faith,
and by your constant care
protect the good you have given us.
We ask this through our Lord Jesus Christ, your Son,
who lives and reigns with you and the Holy Spirit,
one God, for ever and ever.

Alternative Opening Prayer

Let us pray
    [to God who forgives all who call upon him]

> *Pause for silent prayer.*

Lord God of power and might,
nothing is good which is against your will,
and all is of value which comes from your hand.
Place in our hearts a desire to please you
and fill our minds with insight into love,
so that every thought may grow in wisdom
and all our efforts may be filled with your peace.

We ask this through Christ our Lord.

Prayer over the Gifts

Pray, brethren...

Lord,
may this holy offering
bring us your blessing
and accomplish within us
its promise of salvation.
Grant this through Christ our Lord.

Preface of Weekdays in Ordinary Time I–VI, pp. 948–950.

Communion Antiphon

O Lord, how great is the depth of the kindness which you have shown to those who love you.

(Ps 31:20)

Or:

Happy the peacemakers; they shall be called sons of God. Happy are they who suffer persecution for justice; the kingdom of heaven is theirs.

(Mt 5:9–10)

Prayer after Communion

Let us pray.

Pause for silent prayer, if this has not preceded.

Lord,
you renew us at your table with the bread of life.
May this food strengthen us in love
and help us to serve you in each other.
We ask this in the name of Jesus the Lord.

Monday

Antiphons and Prayers, p. 1383; Liturgy of the Word *for Year I (odd years) follows; Year II (even years), p. 1387.*

TODAY'S LIVING WORD

Both Jesus in the selection from Luke and Paul in 1 Corinthians present themselves as coming in the power of the Spirit. That power designates both men as prophets. The Gospel passage is particularly significant because it stands at the very beginning of Jesus' career and is the key to all that follows. Luke's Jesus will be a prophetic Messiah. Anointed by the Spirit, he will announce good news to the powerless and the poor—not socioeconomic reform, but spiritual release from sin and death, as Paul explains to the Thessalonians. Furthermore, as Jesus' references to the prophets Elijah and Elisha indicate, his messianic mission will extend beyond the boundaries of Israel to all the nations.

Today's Gospel clarifies the distinctive nature of Jesus' messiahship. As announced by Isaiah and expected by the Jews, the Messiah was to undertake a secular mission within the national boundaries of Israel. The spiritual messiahship of Jesus represented a transformation of the Jewish understanding. Therefore, it is unjust to condemn the Jews for not accepting Jesus as Messiah.

Year I

FIRST READING

1 Thes 4:13–18

God, through Jesus, will bring with him
those who have fallen asleep.

A reading from the first Letter of Saint Paul to the Thessalonians

We do not want you to be unaware, brothers and sisters, about those who have fallen asleep, so that you may not grieve like the rest, who have no hope. For if we believe that Jesus died and rose, so too will God, through Jesus, bring with him those who have fallen asleep. Indeed, we tell you this, on the word of the Lord, that we who are alive, who are left until the coming of the Lord, will surely not precede those who have fallen asleep. For the Lord himself, with a word of command, with the voice of an archangel and with the trumpet of God, will come down from heaven, and the dead in Christ will rise first. Then we who are alive, who are left, will be caught up together with them in the clouds to meet the Lord in the air. Thus we shall always be with the Lord. Therefore, console one another with these words.

The word of the Lord.

Responsorial Psalm

Ps 96:1 and 3, 4–5, 11–12, 13

R. The Lord comes to judge the earth.

Sing to the LORD a new song;
 sing to the LORD, all you lands.
Tell his glory among the nations;
 among all peoples, his wondrous deeds.

R. The Lord comes to judge the earth.

For great is the LORD and highly to be praised;
 awesome is he, beyond all gods.
For all the gods of the nations are things of nought,
 but the LORD made the heavens.

R. The Lord comes to judge the earth.

Let the heavens be glad and the earth rejoice;
 let the sea and what fills it resound;
 let the plains be joyful and all that is in them!
Then shall all the trees of the forest exult.

R. The Lord comes to judge the earth.

Before the LORD, for he comes;
 for he comes to rule the earth.
He shall rule the world with justice
 and the peoples with his constancy.

R. The Lord comes to judge the earth.

Alleluia Verse *and* **Gospel,** *p. 1389.*

Year II

FIRST READING

1 Cor 2:1–5

I came to you proclaiming Jesus Christ, and him crucified.

A reading from the first Letter of Saint Paul to the Corinthians

When I came to you, brothers and sisters, proclaiming the mystery of God, I did not come with sublimity of words or of wisdom. For I resolved to know nothing while I was with you except Jesus Christ, and him crucified. I came to you in weakness and fear and much trembling, and my message and my proclamation were not with persuasive words of wisdom, but with a demonstration of spirit and power, so that your faith might rest not on human wisdom but on the power of God.

The word of the Lord.

Responsorial Psalm

Ps 119:97, 98, 99, 100, 101, 102

R. Lord, I love your commands.

How I love your law, O LORD!
  It is my meditation all the day.

R. Lord, I love your commands.

Your command has made me wiser than my enemies,
  for it is ever with me.

R. Lord, I love your commands.

I have more understanding than all my teachers
  when your decrees are my meditation.

R. Lord, I love your commands.

I have more discernment than the elders,
  because I observe your precepts.

R. Lord, I love your commands.

From every evil way I withhold my feet,
  that I may keep your words.

R. Lord, I love your commands.

From your ordinances I turn not away,
  for you have instructed me.

R. Lord, I love your commands.

Alleluia, alleluia See Lk 4:18
The Spirit of the Lord is upon me;
he has sent me to bring glad tidings to the poor.
Alleluia, alleluia

Years I and II

GOSPEL   Lk 4:16–30

*He has sent me to bring glad tidings to the poor.
No prophet is accepted in his own native place.*

A reading from the holy Gospel according to Luke

Jesus came to Nazareth, where he had grown up, and went according to his custom into the synagogue on the sabbath day. He stood up to read and was handed a scroll of the prophet Isaiah. He unrolled the scroll and found the passage where it was written:

> *The Spirit of the Lord is upon me,*
>   *because he has anointed me*
>   *to bring glad tidings to the poor.*
> *He has sent me to proclaim liberty to captives*
>   *and recovery of sight to the blind,*
>   *to let the oppressed go free,*
> *and to proclaim a year acceptable to the Lord.*

Rolling up the scroll, he handed it back to the attendant and sat down, and the eyes of all in the synagogue looked intently at him. He said to them, "Today this Scripture passage is fulfilled in your hearing." And all spoke highly of him and were amazed at the gracious words that came from his mouth. They also asked, "Is this not the son of Joseph?" He said to them, "Surely you will quote me this proverb, 'Physician, cure yourself,' and say, 'Do here in your native place the things that we heard were done in Capernaum.' " And he said, "Amen, I say to you, no prophet is accepted in his own native place. Indeed, I tell you, there were many widows in Israel in the days of Elijah when the sky was closed for three and a half years and a severe famine spread over the entire land. It was to none of these that Elijah was sent, but only to a widow in Zarephath in the land of Sidon. Again, there were many lepers in Israel during the time of Elisha the prophet; yet not one of them was cleansed, but only Naaman the Syrian." When the people in the synagogue heard this, they were all filled with fury. They rose up, drove him out of the town, and led him to the brow of the hill on which their town had been built, to hurl him down headlong. But he passed through the midst of them and went away.

The Gospel of the Lord.

Liturgy of the Eucharist, *p. 897;* **Prayer over the Gifts,** *p. 1384.*

Tuesday

Antiphons and Prayers, *p. 1383;* **Liturgy of the Word** *for Year I (odd years) follows; Year II (even years), p. 1392.*

Today's Living Word

The first full day of Jesus' ministry in Capernaum, described in today's Gospel, bears witness to his anointing by the Spirit. The close connection between the words and works of Jesus identifies him as the "prophet like Moses," a messianic figure whose coming was announced in Deuteronomy: "I will raise up for them a prophet like you," God told Moses, "and will put my words into his mouth" (18:18). So the people are spellbound by Jesus' teaching, "because he spoke with authority." Just as Moses had no equal in "the terrifying power that [he] exhibited in the sight of all Israel" (Dt 34:12), even so does the power of Jesus over the unclean spirits strike all who see it with astonishment.

The two first readings explore the ramifications of Jesus' prophetic ministry for all who follow him. Through him we have received the very Spirit of God (1 Cor) and with him we will live forever, "children of the light and children of the day" (1 Thes).

Year I

FIRST READING
1 Thes 5:1–6, 9–11

Jesus Christ died for us so that we may live together with him.

A reading from the first Letter of Saint Paul to the Thessalonians

Concerning times and seasons, brothers and sisters, you have no need for anything to be written to you. For you yourselves know very well that the day of the Lord will come like a thief at night. When people are saying, "Peace and security," then sudden disaster comes upon them, like labor pains upon a pregnant woman, and they will not escape.

But you, brothers and sisters, are not in darkness, for that day to overtake you like a thief. For all of you are children of the light and children of the day. We are not of the night or of darkness. Therefore, let us not sleep as the rest do, but let us stay alert and sober. For God did not destine us for wrath, but to gain salvation through our Lord Jesus Christ, who died for us, so that whether we are awake or asleep we may live together with him. Therefore, encourage one another and build one another up, as indeed you do.

The word of the Lord.

Responsorial Psalm
Ps 27:1, 4, 13–14

R. **I believe that I shall see the good things of the Lord in the land of the living.**

The LORD is my light and my salvation;
  whom should I fear?
The LORD is my life's refuge;
  of whom should I be afraid?

R. I believe that I shall see the good things of the Lord
   in the land of the living.

One thing I ask of the LORD;
  this I seek:
To dwell in the house of the LORD
  all the days of my life,
That I may gaze on the loveliness of the LORD
  and contemplate his temple.

R. I believe that I shall see the good things of the Lord
   in the land of the living.

I believe that I shall see the bounty of the LORD
  in the land of the living.
Wait for the LORD with courage;
  be stouthearted, and wait for the LORD.

R. I believe that I shall see the good things of the Lord
   in the land of the living.

Alleluia Verse and **Gospel,** p. 1394.

Year II

FIRST READING   1 Cor 2:10b–16

Natural persons do not accept what pertains to the Spirit of God:
spiritual persons, however, can judge everything.

A reading from the first Letter of Saint Paul to the Corinthians

Brothers and sisters:

The Spirit scrutinizes everything, even the depths of God.
Among men, who knows what pertains to the man except his

spirit that is within? Similarly, no one knows what pertains to God except the Spirit of God. We have not received the spirit of the world but the Spirit who is from God, so that we may understand the things freely given us by God. And we speak about them not with words taught by human wisdom, but with words taught by the Spirit, describing spiritual realities in spiritual terms.

Now the natural man does not accept what pertains to the Spirit of God, for to him it is foolishness, and he cannot understand it, because it is judged spiritually. The one who is spiritual, however, can judge everything but is not subject to judgment by anyone.

For "who has known the mind of the Lord, so as to counsel him?" But we have the mind of Christ.

The word of the Lord.

Responsorial Psalm   Ps 145:8–9, 10–11, 12–13ab, 13cd–14

R. The Lord is just in all his ways.

The LORD is gracious and merciful,
    slow to anger and of great kindness.
The LORD is good to all
    and compassionate toward all his works.

R. The Lord is just in all his ways.

Let all your works give you thanks, O LORD,
    and let your faithful ones bless you.
Let them discourse of the glory of your Kingdom
    and speak of your might.

R. The Lord is just in all his ways.

Making known to men your might
    and the glorious splendor of your Kingdom.

Your Kingdom is a Kingdom for all ages,
and your dominion endures through all generations.

R. The Lord is just in all his ways.

The LORD is faithful in all his words
and holy in all his works.
The LORD lifts up all who are falling
and raises up all who are bowed down.

R. The Lord is just in all his ways.

Alleluia, alleluia   Lk 7:16
A great prophet has arisen in our midst
and God has visited his people.
Alleluia, alleluia

Years I and II

GOSPEL   Lk 4:31–37

I know who you are—the Holy One of God!

A reading from the holy Gospel according to Luke

Jesus went down to Capernaum, a town of Galilee. He taught
them on the sabbath, and they were astonished at his teaching
because he spoke with authority. In the synagogue there was a
man with the spirit of an unclean demon, and he cried out in a
loud voice, "What have you to do with us, Jesus of Nazareth?
Have you come to destroy us? I know who you are—the Holy
One of God!" Jesus rebuked him and said, "Be quiet! Come
out of him!" Then the demon threw the man down in front of
them and came out of him without doing him any harm. They
were all amazed and said to one another, "What is there about
his word? For with authority and power he commands the unclean spirits, and they come out." And news of him spread
everywhere in the surrounding region.

The Gospel of the Lord.

Liturgy of the Eucharist, *p. 1383;* **Prayer over the Gifts,** *p. 1384.*

Wednesday

Antiphons and Prayers, *p. 1383;* **Liturgy of the Word** *for Year I (odd years) follows; Year II (even years), p. 1396.*

TODAY'S LIVING WORD

Today's selection from the Gospel of Luke contains Jesus' mission statement: "To the other towns also I must proclaim the good news of the Kingdom of God, because for this purpose I have been sent." Later Jesus will send the Twelve to continue his mission: "He summoned the Twelve and gave them power and authority over all demons and to cure diseases, and he sent them to proclaim the kingdom of God…" (9:1–2). The two first readings for today attest to the spread of the Gospel, which they describe in agricultural terms. Writing to the Corinthians, Paul compares the word of the Gospel to seed, as Jesus did. Paul planted it and Apollos watered it, but it grows by the power of God alone. That seed has borne fruit among the Colossians as well and it continues to grow in their midst "just as in the whole world it is bearing fruit and growing."

Like Epaphras, Apollos, and Paul, other faithful ministers of Christ and co-workers with God have proclaimed the word and planted the seed among us. We pray that, by the power of God, it will bear fruit in our faith and love and hope.

Year I

FIRST READING

Col 1:1–8

The Gospel has come to you just as in the whole world.

A reading from the beginning of the Letter of Saint Paul to the Colossians

Paul, an Apostle of Christ Jesus by the will of God, and Timothy our brother, to the holy ones and faithful brothers and sisters in Christ in Colossae: grace to you and peace from God our Father.

We always give thanks to God, the Father of our Lord Jesus Christ, when we pray for you, for we have heard of your faith in Christ Jesus and the love that you have for all the holy ones because of the hope reserved for you in heaven. Of this you have already heard through the word of truth, the Gospel, that has come to you. Just as in the whole world it is bearing fruit and growing, so also among you, from the day you heard it and came to know the grace of God in truth, as you learned it from Epaphras our beloved fellow slave, who is a trustworthy minister of Christ on your behalf and who also told us of your love in the Spirit.

The word of the Lord.

Responsorial Psalm

Ps 52:10, 11

R. **I trust in the mercy of God for ever.**

I, like a green olive tree
   in the house of God,
Trust in the mercy of God
   forever and ever.

R. **I trust in the mercy of God for ever.**

I will thank you always for what you have done,
   and proclaim the goodness of your name
   before your faithful ones.

R. **I trust in the mercy of God for ever.**

Alleluia Verse and **Gospel,** *p. 1398.*

Year II

FIRST READING

1 Cor 3:1–9

We are God's co-workers; you are God's field, God's building.

A reading from the first Letter of Saint Paul to the Corinthians

Brothers and sisters, I could not talk to you as spiritual people, but as fleshly people, as infants in Christ. I fed you milk, not solid food, because you were unable to take it. Indeed, you are still not able, even now, for you are still of the flesh. While there is jealousy and rivalry among you, are you not of the flesh, and walking according to the manner of man? Whenever someone says, "I belong to Paul," and another, "I belong to Apollos," are you not merely men?

What is Apollos, after all, and what is Paul? Ministers through whom you became believers, just as the Lord assigned each one. I planted, Apollos watered, but God caused the growth. Therefore, neither the one who plants nor the one who waters is anything, but only God, who causes the growth. He who plants and he who waters are one, and each will receive wages in proportion to his labor. For we are God's co-workers; you are God's field, God's building.

The word of the Lord.

Responsorial Psalm

Ps 33:12–13, 14–15, 20–21

R. Blessed the people the Lord has chosen to be his own.

Blessed the nation whose God is the Lord,
 the people he has chosen for his own inheritance.
From heaven the Lord looks down;
 he sees all mankind.

R. Blessed the people the Lord has chosen to be his own.

From his fixed throne he beholds
 all who dwell on the earth,
He who fashioned the heart of each,
 he who knows all their works.

R. Blessed the people the Lord has chosen to be his own.

Our soul waits for the LORD,
  who is our help and our shield,
For in him our hearts rejoice;
  in his holy name we trust.

R. Blessed the people the Lord has chosen to be his own.

Alleluia, alleluia   Lk 4:18
The Lord sent me to bring glad tidings to the poor
and to proclaim liberty to captives.
Alleluia, alleluia

Years I and II

GOSPEL   Lk 4:38–44

*To the other towns also I must proclaim the good news
of the Kingdom of God, because for this purpose I have been sent.*

A reading from the holy Gospel according to Luke

After Jesus left the synagogue, he entered the house of Simon.
Simon's mother-in-law was afflicted with a severe fever, and
they interceded with him about her. He stood over her, rebuked
the fever, and it left her. She got up immediately and waited
on them.

  At sunset, all who had people sick with various diseases
brought them to him. He laid his hands on each of them and
cured them. And demons also came out from many, shouting,
"You are the Son of God." But he rebuked them and did not
allow them to speak because they knew that he was the Christ.

  At daybreak, Jesus left and went to a deserted place. The
crowds went looking for him, and when they came to him,
they tried to prevent him from leaving them. But he said to
them, "To the other towns also I must proclaim the good news
of the Kingdom of God, because for this purpose I have been
sent." And he was preaching in the synagogues of Judea.

The Gospel of the Lord.

Liturgy of the Eucharist, *p. 897;* **Prayer over the Gifts,** *p. 1384.*

Thursday

Antiphons and Prayers, *p. 1383;* **Liturgy of the Word** *for Year I (odd years) follows; Year II (even years), p. 1401.*

TODAY'S LIVING WORD

Unlike Mark and Matthew, Luke delays the call of the disciples until the ministry of Jesus is well underway. When Jesus does call them, in today's Gospel, the focus falls on Simon Peter. This brief encounter reveals much about Peter. First, he is a fisherman full of bluster that causes him here as elsewhere to object to Jesus' command. Peter is also a sinner who recognizes his unworthiness in the presence of the Lord. He is a leader too, whose contagious amazement seizes his shipmates as well as James and John, Zebedee's sons. Finally, he is a follower of Jesus, and will realize in his life as a disciple the prayer of Colossians, to "walk in a manner worthy of the Lord, so as to be fully pleasing, in every good work bearing fruit and growing in the knowledge of God, strengthened with every power, in accord with his glorious might, for all endurance and patience, with joy."

"Put out into deep water," Jesus tells Peter who, on second thought, does just that. A fool in the eyes of the world, he leaves everything only to find that everything is his, for he is Christ's and Christ is God's.

Year I

FIRST READING   Col 1:9–14

God delivered us from the power of darkness and transferred us to the Kingdom of his beloved Son.

A reading from the Letter of Saint Paul to the Colossians

Brothers and sisters:

From the day we heard about you, we do not cease praying for you and asking that you may be filled with the knowledge of

Who can ascend the mountain of the Lord?
  or who may stand in his holy place?
He whose hands are sinless, whose heart is clean,
  who desires not what is vain.

R. To the Lord belongs the earth and all that fills it.

He shall receive a blessing from the Lord,
  a reward from God his savior.
Such is the race that seeks for him,
  that seeks the face of the God of Jacob.

R. To the Lord belongs the earth and all that fills it.

Alleluia, alleluia Mt 4:19
Come after me, says the Lord,
and I will make you fishers of men.
Alleluia, alleluia

Years I and II

GOSPEL Lk 5:1-11
They left everything and followed Jesus.
A reading from the holy Gospel according to Luke

While the crowd was pressing in on Jesus and listening to the word of God, he was standing by the Lake of Gennesaret. He saw two boats there alongside the lake; the fishermen had disembarked and were washing their nets. Getting into one of the boats, the one belonging to Simon, he asked him to put out a short distance from the shore. Then he sat down and taught the crowds from the boat. After he had finished speaking, he said to Simon, "Put out into deep water and lower your nets for a catch." Simon said in reply, "Master, we have worked hard all night and have caught nothing, but at your command I will lower the nets." When they had done this, they caught a great number of fish and their nets were tearing. They signaled to their partners in the other boat to come to help them. They came and filled both boats so that the boats were in danger of sinking. When Simon Peter saw this, he fell at the knees of Jesus and said, "Depart from me, Lord, for I am a sinful man." For astonishment at the catch of fish they had made seized him and all those with him, and likewise James and John, the sons of Zebedee, who were partners of Simon. Jesus said to Simon, "Do not be afraid; from now on you will be catching men." When they brought their boats to the shore, they left everything and followed him.

The Gospel of the Lord.

Liturgy of the Eucharist, *p. 897;* **Prayer over the Gifts,** *p. 1384.*

Friday

Antiphons and Prayers, *p. 1383;* **Liturgy of the Word** *for Year I (odd years) follows; Year II (even years), p. 1405.*

TODAY'S LIVING WORD

Like Paul in 1 Corinthians, Jesus in today's reading from Luke comes under judgment. His opponents complain that his disciples, unlike those of John the Baptist, do not observe the traditional forms of piety such as fasting. Jesus answers in a parable, likening his teaching to a new coat and to new wine. He says it is so new that it is incompatible with the old ways and will require new forms of piety.

Today's reading from Colossians very fully expresses the newness of the revelation of Jesus. These verses are part of an early Christian hymn presenting Christ as the "image" of God. The claim that Genesis makes for all of us—that we are made in God's image—is here applied to Jesus in a unique way. As "the firstborn of all creation," he is the one through whom the world was created. As "the firstborn from the dead," he is the one through whom the world was recreated, that is, reconciled to God through the blood of his cross.

Year I

FIRST READING
Col 1:15–20

In him were created all things.

A reading from the Letter of Saint Paul to the Colossians

Brothers and sisters:

Christ Jesus is the image of the invisible God, the firstborn of all creation. For in him were created all things in heaven and on earth, the visible and the invisible, whether thrones or dominions or principalities or powers; all things were created through him and for him. He is before all things, and in him all things hold together. He is the head of the Body, the Church. He is the beginning, the firstborn from the dead, that in all things he himself might be preeminent. For in him all the fullness was pleased to dwell, and through him to reconcile all things for him, making peace by the Blood of his cross through him, whether those on earth or those in heaven.

The word of the Lord.

Responsorial Psalm
Ps 100:1b–2, 3, 4, 5

R. **Come with joy into the presence of the Lord.**

Sing joyfully to the LORD, all you lands;
   serve the LORD with gladness;
   come before him with joyful song.

R. **Come with joy into the presence of the Lord.**

Know that the LORD is God;
  he made us, his we are;
  his people, the flock he tends.

  R. Come with joy into the presence of the Lord.

Enter his gates with thanksgiving,
  his courts with praise;
Give thanks to him; bless his name.

  R. Come with joy into the presence of the Lord.

For he is good,
  the LORD, whose kindness endures forever,
  and his faithfulness, to all generations.

  R. Come with joy into the presence of the Lord.

  Alleluia Verse *and* **Gospel,** *p. 1406f.*

Year II

FIRST READING
1 Cor 4:1–5

The Lord will manifest the motives of our hearts.

A reading from the first Letter of Saint Paul to the Corinthians

Brothers and sisters:

Thus should one regard us: as servants of Christ and stewards of the mysteries of God. Now it is of course required of stewards that they be found trustworthy. It does not concern me in the least that I be judged by you or any human tribunal; I do not even pass judgment on myself; I am not conscious of anything against me, but I do not thereby stand acquitted; the one who judges me is the Lord. Therefore, do not make any judgment before the appointed time, until the Lord comes, for he will bring to light what is hidden in darkness and will manifest the motives of our hearts, and then everyone will receive praise from God.

The word of the Lord.

Responsorial Psalm

Ps 37:3–4, 5–6, 27–28, 39–40

R. **The salvation of the just comes from the Lord.**

Trust in the LORD and do good,
    that you may dwell in the land and be fed in security.
Take delight in the LORD,
    and he will grant you your heart's requests.

R. **The salvation of the just comes from the Lord.**

Commit to the LORD your way;
    trust in him, and he will act.
He will make justice dawn for you like the light;
    bright as the noonday shall be your vindication.

R. **The salvation of the just comes from the Lord.**

Turn from evil and do good,
    that you may abide forever;
For the LORD loves what is right,
    and forsakes not his faithful ones.
Criminals are destroyed
    and the posterity of the wicked is cut off.

R. **The salvation of the just comes from the Lord.**

The salvation of the just is from the LORD;
    he is their refuge in time of distress.
And the LORD helps them and delivers them;
    he delivers them from the wicked and saves them,
    because they take refuge in him.

R. **The salvation of the just comes from the Lord.**

Alleluia, alleluia   Jn 8:12
    I am the light of the world, says the Lord;
    whoever follows me will have the light of life.
Alleluia, alleluia

Years I and II

GOSPEL
Lk 5:33–39

When the bridegroom is taken away from them, then they will fast.

A reading from the holy Gospel according to Luke

The scribes and Pharisees said to Jesus, "The disciples of John the Baptist fast often and offer prayers, and the disciples of the Pharisees do the same; but yours eat and drink." Jesus answered them, "Can you make the wedding guests fast while the bridegroom is with them? But the days will come, and when the bridegroom is taken away from them, then they will fast in those days." And he also told them a parable. "No one tears a piece from a new cloak to patch an old one. Otherwise, he will tear the new and the piece from it will not match the old cloak. Likewise, no one pours new wine into old wineskins. Otherwise, the new wine will burst the skins, and it will be spilled, and the skins will be ruined. Rather, new wine must be poured into fresh wineskins. And no one who has been drinking old wine desires new, for he says, 'The old is good.' "

The Gospel of the Lord.

Liturgy of the Eucharist, *p. 897;* **Prayer over the Gifts,** *p. 1384.*

Saturday

Antiphons and Prayers, *p. 1383;* **Liturgy of the Word** *for Year I (odd years) follows; Year II (even years), p. 1409.*

TODAY'S LIVING WORD

Today's Gospel is the familiar story of Jesus' disciples plucking heads of grain on the Sabbath. Luke has taken the story from Mark and trimmed it to fit the scheme of his Gospel. Like Mark, Luke reports Jesus' answer to his critics as an allusion to the story of David. But where in Mark's account Jesus says that David entered God's house and ate the bread, Luke adds the word *took*. In Luke's version, then David *took (labōn)* the bread and *gave (edōken)* it to his friends. "He went into the house of God, *took* the bread of offering, which only the priests could lawfully eat, ate of it, and *shared* it with his companions." Thus he anticipates the action of Jesus at the Last Supper (cf. 22:19) and gives the story a eucharistic flavor. In the Eucharist we savor and celebrate the achievement of Jesus that Paul explains to the Colossians. Like them, we too were once alienated from God, but now we also know the reconciliation that Christ has achieved for us "in his fleshly body."

In 1 Corinthians Paul describes at what cost and under what conditions he and his fellow apostles labor, entrusted with the ministry of reconciliation. He does so not to shame us, but to show us the gratitude we owe to our fathers and mothers in Christ.

Year I

FIRST READING   Col 1:21–23

*Christ has now reconciled you to present you holy
and unblemished before him.*

A reading from the Letter of Saint Paul to the Colossians

Brothers and sisters:

You once were alienated and hostile in mind because of evil deeds; God has now reconciled you in the fleshly Body of Christ through his death, to present you holy, without blemish, and irreproachable before him, provided that you persevere in the faith, firmly grounded, stable, and not shifting from the hope of the Gospel that you heard, which has been preached to every creature under heaven, of which I, Paul, am a minister.

The word of the Lord.

Responsorial Psalm

Ps 54:3 – 4, 6 and 8

R. God himself is my help.

O God, by your name save me,
 and by your might defend my cause.
O God, hear my prayer;
 hearken to the words of my mouth.

R. God himself is my help.

Behold, God is my helper;
 the Lord sustains my life.
Freely will I offer you sacrifice;
 I will praise your name, O LORD, for its goodness.

R. God himself is my help.

Alleluia Verse *and* **Gospel,** *p. 1411.*

Year II

FIRST READING

1 Cor 4:6b–15

We go hungry and thirsty and we are poorly clad.

A reading from the first Letter of Saint Paul to the Corinthians

Brothers and sisters:

Learn from myself and Apollos not to go beyond what is written, so that none of you will be inflated with pride in favor of one person over against another. Who confers distinction upon you? What do you possess that you have not received? But if you have received it, why are you boasting as if you did not receive it? You are already satisfied; you have already grown rich; you have become kings without us! Indeed, I wish that you had become kings, so that we also might become kings with you.

For as I see it, God has exhibited us Apostles as the last of all, like people sentenced to death, since we have become a spectacle to the world, to angels and men alike. We are fools on Christ's account, but you are wise in Christ; we are weak, but you are strong; you are held in honor, but we in disrepute. To this very hour we go hungry and thirsty, we are poorly clad and roughly treated, we wander about homeless and we toil, working with our own hands. When ridiculed, we bless; when persecuted, we endure; when slandered, we respond gently. We have become like the world's rubbish, the scum of all, to this very moment.

I am writing you this not to shame you, but to admonish you as my beloved children. Even if you should have countless guides to Christ, yet you do not have many fathers, for I became your father in Christ Jesus through the Gospel.

The word of the Lord.

Responsorial Psalm

Ps 145:17–18, 19–20, 21

R. The Lord is near to all who call upon him.

The LORD is just in all his ways
   and holy in all his works.
The LORD is near to all who call upon him,
   to all who call upon him in truth.

R. The Lord is near to all who call upon him.

He fulfills the desire of those who fear him,
   he hears their cry and saves them.
The LORD keeps all who love him,
   but all the wicked he will destroy.

R. The Lord is near to all who call upon him.

May my mouth speak the praise of the LORD,
   and may all flesh bless his holy name forever and ever.

R. The Lord is near to all who call upon him.

Alleluia, alleluia Jn 14:6
I am the way and the truth and the life, says the Lord;
no one comes to the Father except through me.
Alleluia, alleluia

Years I and II

GOSPEL   Lk 6:1–5

Why are you doing what is unlawful on the sabbath?

A reading from the holy Gospel according to Luke

While Jesus was going through a field of grain on a sabbath, his disciples were picking the heads of grain, rubbing them in their hands, and eating them. Some Pharisees said, "Why are you doing what is unlawful on the sabbath?" Jesus said to them in reply, "Have you not read what David did when he and those who were with him were hungry? How he went into the house of God, took the bread of offering, which only the priests could lawfully eat, ate of it, and shared it with his companions?" Then he said to them, "The Son of Man is lord of the sabbath."

The Gospel of the Lord.

Liturgy of the Eucharist, *p. 897;* **Prayer over the Gifts,** *p. 1383.*

TWENTY-THIRD WEEK IN ORDINARY TIME

The **Antiphons and Prayers** *may be the following, or may be chosen from any of the other 33 weeks in Ordinary Time (refer to Liturgical Calendar, pp. 26–41).*

The **Liturgy of the Word** *varies: for Monday, see p. 1413; Tuesday, p. 1418; Wednesday, p. 1422; Thursday, p. 1427; Friday, p. 1432; Saturday, p. 1436.*

Entrance Antiphon

Lord, you are just, and the judgments you make are right. Show mercy when you judge me, your servant.

(Ps 119:137, 124)

Opening Prayer

Let us pray

[that we may realize the freedom God has given us
in making us his sons and daughters]

Pause for silent prayer.

God our Father,
you redeem us
and make us your children in Christ.
Look upon us,
give us true freedom
and bring us to the inheritance you promised.

Grant this through our Lord Jesus Christ, your Son,
who lives and reigns with you and the Holy Spirit,
one God, for ever and ever.

Alternative Opening Prayer

Let us pray

[to our just and merciful God]

Pause for silent prayer.

Lord our God,
in you justice and mercy meet.
With unparalleled love you have saved us from death
and drawn us into the circle of your life.
Open our eyes to the wonders this life sets before us,
that we may serve you free from fear
and address you as God our Father.
We ask this in the name of Jesus the Lord.

Prayer over the Gifts

Pray, brethren...

God of peace and love,
may our offering bring you true worship
and make us one with you.

Grant this through Christ our Lord.

Preface of Weekdays in Ordinary Time I–VI, *pp. 948–950.*

Communion Antiphon

Like a deer that longs for running streams, my soul longs for
you, my God. My soul is thirsting for the living God.

(Ps 42:2–3)

Or:

I am the light of the world, says the Lord; the man who follows me will have the light of life.

(Jn 8:12)

Prayer after Communion

Let us pray.

Pause for silent prayer, if this has not preceded.

Lord,
your word and your sacrament
give us food and life.
May this gift of your Son
lead us to share his life for ever.
We ask this through Christ our Lord.

Monday

Antiphons and Prayers, *p. 1412;* **Liturgy of the Word** *for Year I (odd
years) follows; Year II (even years), p. 1415.*

TODAY'S LIVING WORD

The Lucan reading for today again retells a story from Mark.
Scholars note that Luke has softened Mark's portrayal of the Pharisees.

In Mark this story ends with the Pharisees plotting to destroy Jesus, while here they discuss what to do about Jesus. The story's effect impresses on the reader the high priority Jesus placed, not just on human life (the Pharisees would have agreed with him about that), but on human need. In Colossians, the priority of the person becomes a theological insight. Paul makes clear that the core of his message is not a principle nor a precept, but a person—the person of Jesus Christ. In light of this revelation, the priority of every person can be seen.

First Corinthians demonstrates just how difficult it is to live the mystery of God revealed in Christ. Some at Corinth have mistaken the priority of the person to mean that they can ignore social mores, in this case against incest. Paul offers a corrective. They must clean house, as Jews do at Passover, and rid themselves of the old yeast (a symbol of evil). They must make of themselves fresh dough, unleavened bread.

I am the light of the world, says the Lord; the man who follows me will have the light of life. (Jn 8:12)

Year I

FIRST READING

Col 1:24 —2:3

*I am a minister of the Church to bring to completion
the mystery hidden from ages past.*

A reading from the Letter of Saint Paul to the Colossians

Brothers and sisters:

I rejoice in my sufferings for your sake, and in my flesh I am filling up what is lacking in the afflictions of Christ on behalf of his Body, which is the Church, of which I am a minister in accordance with God's stewardship given to me to bring to completion for you the word of God, the mystery hidden from ages and from generations past. But now it has been manifested to his holy ones, to whom God chose to make known the riches of the glory of this mystery among the Gentiles; it is Christ in you, the hope for glory. It is he whom we proclaim, admonish-

ing everyone and teaching everyone with all wisdom, that we
may present everyone perfect in Christ. For this I labor and
struggle, in accord with the exercise of his power working
within me.

For I want you to know how great a struggle I am having
for you and for those in Laodicea and all who have not seen
me face to face, that their hearts may be encouraged as they
are brought together in love, to have all the richness of assured
understanding, for the knowledge of the mystery of God, Christ,
in whom are hidden all the treasures of wisdom and knowledge.
The word of the Lord.

Responsorial Psalm

Ps 62:6-7, 9

R. In God is my safety and my glory.

Only in God be at rest, my soul,
  for from him comes my hope.
He only is my rock and my salvation,
  my stronghold; I shall not be disturbed.

R. In God is my safety and my glory.

Trust in him at all times, O my people!
  Pour out your hearts before him;
  God is our refuge!

R. In God is my safety and my glory.

Alleluia Verse *and* **Gospel,** *p. 1417.*

Year II

FIRST READING

1 Cor 5:1-8

*Clean out the old yeast; for our Paschal Lamb,
Christ, has been sacrificed.*

A reading from the first Letter of Saint Paul to the Corinthians

Brothers and sisters:

It is widely reported that there is immorality among you, and immorality of a kind not found even among pagans—a man living with his father's wife. And you are inflated with pride. Should you not rather have been sorrowful? The one who did this deed should be expelled from your midst. I, for my part, although absent in body but present in spirit, have already, as if present, pronounced judgment on the one who has committed this deed, in the name of our Lord Jesus: when you have gathered together and I am with you in spirit with the power of the Lord Jesus, you are to deliver this man to Satan for the destruction of his flesh, so that his spirit may be saved on the day of the Lord.

Your boasting is not appropriate. Do you not know that a little yeast leavens all the dough? Clear out the old yeast, so that you may become a fresh batch of dough, inasmuch as you are unleavened. For our Paschal Lamb, Christ, has been sacrificed. Therefore, let us celebrate the feast, not with the old yeast, the yeast of malice and wickedness, but with the unleavened bread of sincerity and truth.

The word of the Lord.

Responsorial Psalm

Ps 5:5–6, 7, 12

R. Lead me in your justice, Lord.

For you, O God, delight not in wickedness;
  no evil man remains with you;
  the arrogant may not stand in your sight.
You hate all evildoers.

R. Lead me in your justice, Lord.

You destroy all who speak falsehood;
The bloodthirsty and the deceitful
  the LORD abhors.

R. Lead me in your justice, Lord.

But let all who take refuge in you
  be glad and exult forever.
Protect them, that you may be the joy
  of those who love your name.

R. Lead me in your justice, Lord.

Alleluia, alleluia   Jn 10:27
My sheep hear my voice, says the Lord;
I know them, and they follow me.
Alleluia, alleluia

Years I and II

GOSPEL   Lk 6:6–11

*The scribes and the Pharisees watched him closely
to see if he would cure on the sabbath.*

A reading from the holy Gospel according to Luke

On a certain sabbath Jesus went into the synagogue and taught,
and there was a man there whose right hand was withered.
The scribes and the Pharisees watched him closely to see if he
would cure on the sabbath so that they might discover a reason
to accuse him. But he realized their intentions and said to the
man with the withered hand, "Come up and stand before us."
And he rose and stood there. Then Jesus said to them, "I ask
you, is it lawful to do good on the sabbath rather than to do
evil, to save life rather than to destroy it?" Looking around at
them all, he then said to him, "Stretch out your hand." He did
so and his hand was restored. But they became enraged and
discussed together what they might do to Jesus.
The Gospel of the Lord.

Liturgy of the Eucharist, *p. 897;* **Prayer over the Gifts,** *p. 1413.*

Tuesday

Antiphons and Prayers, *p. 1412;* **Liturgy of the Word** *for Year I (odd years) follows; Year II (even years), p. 1420.*

TODAY'S LIVING WORD

Today's selection from Colossians returns to the high Christology of the hymn that opened this letter. In Christ "dwells the whole fullness of the deity bodily." Yet even as he waxes poetic, Paul warns, "See to it that no one captivate you with an empty, seductive philosophy." The best protection against error is to be grounded in Christ, "established in the faith as *you were taught.*" In a more prosaic passage Paul warns the Christians in Corinth against bringing lawsuits against each other in pagan courts of law. He urges them instead to bring their cases to their duly designated fellow Christians, who are destined by God to "judge the world."

Both of today's first readings attest to the Church's need for authoritative teachers and guides. In today's Gospel, Jesus takes the first step toward providing for that need. He selects twelve men from among his followers to be his apostles. Later he will assign to them the dominion the Father has assigned to him. "In my kingdom," he will tell them, "you will sit on thrones judging the twelve tribes of Israel" (22:29–30).

Year I

FIRST READING

Col 2:6–15

God brought you to life along with Christ having forgiven us all our transgressions.

A reading from the Letter of Saint Paul to the Colossians

Brothers and sisters:

As you received Christ Jesus the Lord, walk in him, rooted in him and built upon him and established in the faith as you were taught, abounding in thanksgiving. See to it that no one captivate you with an empty, seductive philosophy according to the tradition of men, according to the elemental powers of the world and not according to Christ.

For in him dwells the whole fullness of the deity bodily, and you share in this fullness in him, who is the head of every principality and power. In him you were also circumcised with a circumcision not administered by hand, by stripping off the carnal body, with the circumcision of Christ. You were buried with him in baptism, in which you were also raised with him through faith in the power of God, who raised him from the dead. And even when you were dead in transgressions and the uncircumcision of your flesh, he brought you to life along with him, having forgiven us all our transgressions; obliterating the bond against us, with its legal claims, which was opposed to us, he also removed it from our midst, nailing it to the cross; despoiling the principalities and the powers, he made a public spectacle of them, leading them away in triumph by it.
The word of the Lord.

Responsorial Psalm

Ps 145:1b–2, 8–9, 10–11

R. **The Lord is compassionate toward all his works.**

I will extol you, O my God and King,
  and I will bless your name forever and ever.
Every day will I bless you,
  and I will praise your name forever and ever.

R. **The Lord is compassionate toward all his works.**

The LORD is gracious and merciful,
  slow to anger and of great kindness.

The LORD is good to all
 and compassionate toward all his works.

R. The Lord is compassionate toward all his works.

Let all your works give you thanks, O LORD,
 and let your faithful ones bless you.
Let them discourse of the glory of your Kingdom
 and speak of your might.

R. The Lord is compassionate toward all his works.

Alleluia Verse *and* **Gospel,** *p. 1421f.*

Year II

FIRST READING   1 Cor 6:1–11

*A believer goes to court against a believer
and that before unbelievers.*

A reading from the first Letter of Saint Paul to the Corinthians

Brothers and sisters:
How can any one of you with a case against another dare to
bring it to the unjust for judgment instead of to the holy ones?
Do you not know that the holy ones will judge the world? If
the world is to be judged by you, are you unqualified for the
lowest law courts? Do you not know that we will judge angels?
Then why not everyday matters? If, therefore, you have courts
for everyday matters, do you seat as judges people of no
standing in the Church? I say this to shame you. Can it be that
there is not one among you wise enough to be able to settle a
case between brothers? But rather brother goes to court against
brother, and that before unbelievers?

   Now indeed then it is, in any case, a failure on your part
that you have lawsuits against one another. Why not rather put
up with injustice? Why not rather let yourselves be cheated?

Instead, you inflict injustice and cheat, and this to brothers. Do you not know that the unjust will not inherit the Kingdom of God? Do not be deceived; neither fornicators nor idolaters nor adulterers nor boy prostitutes nor sodomites nor thieves nor the greedy nor drunkards nor slanderers nor robbers will inherit the Kingdom of God. That is what some of you used to be; but now you have had yourselves washed, you were sanctified, you were justified in the name of the Lord Jesus Christ and in the Spirit of our God.

The word of the Lord.

Responsorial Psalm
Ps 149:1b–2, 3–4, 5–6a and 9b

R. The Lord takes delight in his people.

Sing to the Lord a new song
of praise in the assembly of the faithful.
Let Israel be glad in their maker,
let the children of Zion rejoice in their king.

R. The Lord takes delight in his people.

Let them praise his name in the festive dance,
let them sing praise to him with timbrel and harp.
For the Lord loves his people,
and he adorns the lowly with victory.

R. The Lord takes delight in his people.

Let the faithful exult in glory;
let them sing for joy upon their couches;
Let the high praises of God be in their throats.
This is the glory of all his faithful. Alleluia.

R. The Lord takes delight in his people.

Alleluia, alleluia   See Jn 15:16
I chose you from the world,
that you may go and bear fruit that will last, says the Lord.
Alleluia, alleluia

Years I and II

GOSPEL   Lk 6:12–19

He spent the night in prayer. He chose Twelve,
whom he also named Apostles.

A reading from the holy Gospel according to Luke

Jesus departed to the mountain to pray, and he spent the night in prayer to God. When day came, he called his disciples to himself, and from them he chose Twelve, whom he also named Apostles: Simon, whom he named Peter, and his brother Andrew, James, John, Philip, Bartholomew, Matthew, Thomas, James the son of Alphaeus, Simon who was called a Zealot, and Judas the son of James, and Judas Iscariot, who became a traitor.

And he came down with them and stood on a stretch of level ground. A great crowd of his disciples and a large number of the people from all Judea and Jerusalem and the coastal region of Tyre and Sidon came to hear him and to be healed of their diseases; and even those who were tormented by unclean spirits were cured. Everyone in the crowd sought to touch him because power came forth from him and healed them all.

The Gospel of the Lord.

Liturgy of the Eucharist, *p. 897;* **Prayer over the Gifts,** *p. 1413.*

Wednesday

Antiphons and Prayers, *p. 1412;* **Liturgy of the Word** *for Year I (odd years) follows; Year II (even years), p. 1425.*

TODAY'S LIVING WORD

All three of today's readings reflect a distinctly apocalyptic perspective. They all have as their horizon the "what is above," to which Christians have already been raised "with Christ." Yet there is nothing "other-worldly" about these readings. The Beatitudes of Jesus are addressed to those who are living now in poverty, hunger and grief. They know firsthand the emptiness of the present age and set their hearts on the promised future, the reign of God already theirs, but "hidden with Christ in God." This perspective underlies Paul's teaching too. He tells the Colossians to "think of what is above, not of what is on earth" and the Corinthians that "the time is running out…[let] those buying [act] as not owning, those using the world as not using it fully. For the world in its present form is passing away."

Luke does not spiritualize the Beatitudes as Matthew does. He intends the materially poor, not the "poor in spirit." In this way his Gospel comforts the afflicted and, at the same time, afflicts the comfortable.

Year I

FIRST READING   Col 3:1–11

You have died with Christ; put to death, then,
the parts of you that are earthly.

A reading from the Letter of Saint Paul to the Colossians

Brothers and sisters:

If you were raised with Christ, seek what is above, where Christ is seated at the right hand of God. Think of what is above, not of what is on earth. For you have died, and your life is hidden with Christ in God. When Christ your life appears, then you too will appear with him in glory.

Put to death, then, the parts of you that are earthly: immorality, impurity, passion, evil desire, and the greed that is idolatry. Because of these the wrath of God is coming upon the disobedient. By these you too once conducted yourselves, when you lived in that way. But now you must put them all away: anger, fury, malice, slander, and obscene language out of your mouths. Stop lying to one another, since you have taken off the old self with its practices and have put on the new self, which is being renewed, for knowledge, in the image of its creator. Here there is not Greek and Jew, circumcision and uncircumcision, barbarian, Scythian, slave, free; but Christ is all and in all.

The word of the Lord.

Responsorial Psalm

Ps 145:2–3, 10–11, 12–13ab

R. The Lord is compassionate toward all his works.

Every day will I bless you,
    and I will praise your name forever and ever.
Great is the LORD and highly to be praised;
    his greatness is unsearchable.

R. The Lord is compassionate toward all his works.

Let all your works give you thanks, O LORD,
    and let your faithful ones bless you.
Let them discourse of the glory of your Kingdom
    and speak of your might.

R. The Lord is compassionate toward all his works.

Making known to men your might
    and the glorious splendor of your Kingdom.
Your Kingdom is a Kingdom for all ages,
    and your dominion endures through all generations.

R. The Lord is compassionate toward all his works.

Alleluia Verse *and* **Gospel,** *p. 1426.*

Year II

FIRST READING   1 Cor 7:25–31

Are you bound to a wife? Do not seek a separation.
Are you free of a wife? Then, do not look for a wife.

A reading from the first Letter of Saint Paul to the Corinthians

Brothers and sisters:

In regard to virgins, I have no commandment from the Lord, but I give my opinion as one who by the Lord's mercy is trustworthy. So this is what I think best because of the present distress: that it is a good thing for a person to remain as he is. Are you bound to a wife? Do not seek a separation. Are you free of a wife? Then do not look for a wife. If you marry, however, you do not sin, nor does an unmarried woman sin if she marries; but such people will experience affliction in their earthly life, and I would like to spare you that.

I tell you, brothers, the time is running out. From now on, let those having wives act as not having them, those weeping as not weeping, those rejoicing as not rejoicing, those buying as not owning, those using the world as not using it fully. For the world in its present form is passing away.

The word of the Lord.

Responsorial Psalm   Ps 45:11–12, 14–15, 16–17

R. Listen to me, daughter; see and bend your ear.

Hear, O daughter, and see; turn your ear,
  forget your people and your father's house.
So shall the king desire your beauty;
  for he is your lord, and you must worship him.

R. Listen to me, daughter; see and bend your ear.

All glorious is the king's daughter as she enters;
  her raiment is threaded with spun gold.
In embroidered apparel she is borne in to the king;
  behind her the virgins of her train are brought to you.

R. Listen to me, daughter; see and bend your ear.

They are borne in with gladness and joy;
  they enter the palace of the king.
The place of your fathers your sons shall have;
  you shall make them princes through all the land.

R. Listen to me, daughter; see and bend your ear.

Alleluia, alleluia   Lk 6:23ab
Rejoice and leap for joy!
Your reward will be great in heaven.
Alleluia, alleluia

Years I and II

GOSPEL   Lk 6:20–26

Blessed are you who are poor. Woe to you who are rich.

A reading from the holy Gospel according to Luke

Raising his eyes toward his disciples Jesus said:

"Blessed are you who are poor,
  for the Kingdom of God is yours.
Blessed are you who are now hungry,
  for you will be satisfied.
Blessed are you who are now weeping,
  for you will laugh.
Blessed are you when people hate you,
  and when they exclude and insult you,
  and denounce your name as evil
  on account of the Son of Man.

Rejoice and leap for joy on that day! Behold, your reward will be great in heaven. For their ancestors treated the prophets in the same way.

> But woe to you who are rich,
>> for you have received your consolation.
> But woe to you who are filled now,
>> for you will be hungry.
> Woe to you who laugh now,
>> for you will grieve and weep.
> Woe to you when all speak well of you,
>> for their ancestors treated the false prophets in this way."

The Gospel of the Lord.

Liturgy of the Eucharist, *p. 897;* **Prayer over the Gifts,** *p. 1413.*

Thursday

Antiphons and Prayers, *p. 1412;* **Liturgy of the Word** *for Year I (odd years) follows; Year II (even years), p. 1429.*

TODAY'S LIVING WORD

A number of points from today's Gospel deserve attention as it puts forth the practical demands of the law of love. First, love here is not a noun but a verb; it is described by a series of action words: "do good...bless...pray....," Also, this love must be given even if one is not loved in return. Luke's version says it twice: "Love your enemies, do good to those who hate you." In this it goes beyond the ancient norm of reciprocity. In fact, the criterion for such love is not, "Do to others what you would have them do to you," but do to others *what God would do,* who "himself is kind to the ungrateful and the wicked." This principle of the imitation of God originates in

Israel's covenant with God who commanded, "Be holy, for I, the Lord, your God, am holy" (Lv 19:2).

The way the Colossians are addressed recalls the covenant context of the law of love. They must love because they are "God's chosen ones." Paul tells the Corinthians that such love surpasses knowledge for it "builds up," like God who builds us up into the body of Christ.

Year I

FIRST READING   Col 3:12–17

Put on love, that is, the bond of perfection.

A reading from the Letter of Saint Paul to the Colossians

Brothers and sisters:

Put on, as God's chosen ones, holy and beloved, heartfelt compassion, kindness, humility, gentleness, and patience, bearing with one another and forgiving one another, if one has a grievance against another; as the Lord has forgiven you, so must you also do. And over all these put on love, that is, the bond of perfection. And let the peace of Christ control your hearts, the peace into which you were also called in one Body. And be thankful. Let the word of Christ dwell in you richly, as in all wisdom you teach and admonish one another, singing psalms, hymns, and spiritual songs with gratitude in your hearts to God. And whatever you do, in word or in deed, do everything in the name of the Lord Jesus, giving thanks to God the Father through him.

The word of the Lord.

Responsorial Psalm   Ps 150:1b–2, 3–4, 5–6

R. Let everything that breathes praise the Lord!

Praise the LORD in his sanctuary,
  praise him in the firmament of his strength.
Praise him for his mighty deeds,
  praise him for his sovereign majesty.

R. Let everything that breathes praise the Lord!

Praise him with the blast of the trumpet,
  praise him with lyre and harp,
Praise him with timbrel and dance,
  praise him with strings and pipe.

R. Let everything that breathes praise the Lord!

Praise him with sounding cymbals,
  praise him with clanging cymbals.
Let everything that has breath
  praise the LORD! Alleluia.

R. Let everything that breathes praise the Lord!

Alleluia Verse *and* **Gospel,** *p. 1431.*

_____

Year II

FIRST READING   1 Cor 8:1b–7, 11–13

*When you sin against your brothers, weak as they are,
you are sinning against Christ.*

A reading from the first Letter of Saint Paul to the Corinthians

Brothers and sisters:

Knowledge inflates with pride, but love builds up. If anyone
supposes he knows something, he does not yet know as he
ought to know. But if one loves God, one is known by him.

So about the eating of meat sacrificed to idols: we know
that *there is no idol in the world,* and that *there is no God but*

one. Indeed, even though there are so-called gods in heaven and on earth (there are, to be sure, many "gods" and many "lords"), yet for us there is

> one God, the Father,
>> from whom all things are and for whom we exist,
> and one Lord, Jesus Christ,
>> through whom all things are and through whom we exist.

But not all have this knowledge. There are some who have been so used to idolatry up until now that, when they eat meat sacrificed to idols, their conscience, which is weak, is defiled.

Thus, through your knowledge, the weak person is brought to destruction, the brother for whom Christ died. When you sin in this way against your brothers and wound their consciences, weak as they are, you are sinning against Christ. Therefore, if food causes my brother to sin, I will never eat meat again, so that I may not cause my brother to sin.

The word of the Lord.

Responsorial Psalm

Ps 139:1b–3, 13–14ab, 23–24

R. Guide me, Lord, along the everlasting way.

O LORD, you have probed me and you know me;
  you know when I sit and when I stand;
  you understand my thoughts from afar.
My journeys and my rest you scrutinize,
  with all my ways you are familiar.

R. Guide me, Lord, along the everlasting way.

Truly you have formed my inmost being;
  you knit me in my mother's womb.
I give you thanks that I am fearfully, wonderfully made;
  wonderful are your works.

R. Guide me, Lord, along the everlasting way.

Probe me, O God, and know my heart;
 try me, and know my thoughts;
See if my way is crooked,
 and lead me in the way of old.

R. Guide me, Lord, along the everlasting way.

> **Alleluia, alleluia** 1 Jn 4:12
> If we love one another,
> God remains in us,
> and his love is brought to perfection in us.
> **Alleluia, alleluia**

Years I and II

GOSPEL   Lk 6:27–38

Be merciful, just as your Father is merciful.

A reading from the holy Gospel according to Luke

Jesus said to his disciples: "To you who hear I say, love your enemies, do good to those who hate you, bless those who curse you, pray for those who mistreat you. To the person who strikes you on one cheek, offer the other one as well, and from the person who takes your cloak, do not withhold even your tunic. Give to everyone who asks of you, and from the one who takes what is yours do not demand it back. Do to others as you would have them do to you. For if you love those who love you, what credit is that to you? Even sinners love those who love them. And if you do good to those who do good to you, what credit is that to you? Even sinners do the same. If you lend money to those from whom you expect repayment, what credit is that to you? Even sinners lend to sinners, and get back the same amount. But rather, love your enemies and do good to them, and lend expecting nothing back; then your reward will be great and you will be children of the Most High, for he himself is kind to the ungrateful and the wicked. Be merciful, just as also your Father is merciful.

"Stop judging and you will not be judged. Stop condemning and you will not be condemned. Forgive and you will be forgiven. Give and gifts will be given to you; a good measure, packed together, shaken down, and overflowing, will be poured into your lap. For the measure with which you measure will in return be measured out to you."

The Gospel of the Lord.

Liturgy of the Eucharist, *p. 897;* **Prayer over the Gifts,** *p. 1413.*

Friday

Antiphons and Prayers, *p. 1412;* **Liturgy of the Word** *for Year I (odd years) follows; Year II (even years), p. 1434.*

TODAY'S LIVING WORD

An athletic quality marks the commitment that today's three readings require of Christians. In 1 Timothy we learn that Paul has been strengthened for Christian service by the grace of the Lord Jesus granted him in abundance. The selection from 1 Corinthians shows the robustness of Paul's faith. He does all that he does for the sake of the Gospel in the hope of sharing its blessings. In Luke Jesus teaches that only strenuous self-criticism—removing the plank from one's own eye—enables one to guide others without falling into a ditch.

First Corinthians develops the metaphor as Paul compares the Christian to the athlete in the stadium. He says that a competitor must "run so as to win!" To that end he submits to a rigorous discipline, never losing sight of the finish line. As was the custom among the rabbis, Paul then argues from the lighter to the weightier matter:

if athletes do this "to win a perishable crown," how much more should we to win an imperishable crown.

Year I

FIRST READING

1 Tm 1:1–2, 12–14

I was once a blasphemer, but I have been mercifully treated.

A reading from the beginning of the first Letter of Saint Paul to Timothy

Paul, an Apostle of Christ Jesus by command of God our savior and of Christ Jesus our hope, to Timothy, my true child in faith: grace, mercy, and peace from God the Father and Christ Jesus our Lord.

I am grateful to him who has strengthened me, Christ Jesus our Lord, because he considered me trustworthy in appointing me to the ministry. I was once a blasphemer and a persecutor and an arrogant man, but I have been mercifully treated because I acted out of ignorance in my unbelief. Indeed, the grace of our Lord has been abundant, along with the faith and love that are in Christ Jesus.

The word of the Lord.

Responsional Psalm

Ps 16:1b–2a and 5, 7–8, 11

R. You are my inheritance, O Lord.

Keep me, O God, for in you I take refuge;
  I say to the LORD, "My Lord are you."
O LORD, my allotted portion and my cup,
  you it is who hold fast my lot.

R. You are my inheritance, O Lord.

I bless the LORD who counsels me;
  even in the night my heart exhorts me.

I set the LORD ever before me;
  with him at my right hand I shall not be disturbed.

  R. You are my inheritance, O Lord.

You will show me the path to life,
  fullness of joys in your presence,
  the delights at your right hand forever.

  R. You are my inheritance, O Lord.

  Alleluia Verse *and* **Gospel,** *p. 1435f.*

Year II

FIRST READING   1 Cor 9:16–19, 22b–27

  I have become all things to all, to save at least some.

A reading from the first Letter of Saint Paul to the Corinthians

Brothers and sisters:

If I preach the Gospel, this is no reason for me to boast, for an obligation has been imposed on me, and woe to me if I do not preach it! If I do so willingly, I have a recompense, but if unwillingly, then I have been entrusted with a stewardship. What then is my recompense? That, when I preach, I offer the Gospel free of charge so as not to make full use of my right in the Gospel.

Although I am free in regard to all, I have made myself a slave to all so as to win over as many as possible. I have become all things to all, to save at least some. All this I do for the sake of the Gospel, so that I too may have a share in it.

Do you not know that the runners in the stadium all run in the race, but only one wins the prize? Run so as to win. Every athlete exercises discipline in every way. They do it to win a perishable crown, but we an imperishable one. Thus I do not run aimlessly; I do not fight as if I were shadowboxing. No, I drive my body and train it, for fear that, after having preached to others, I myself should be disqualified.

The word of the Lord.

Responsorial Psalm

Ps 84:3, 4, 5–6, 12

R. **How lovely is your dwelling place, Lord, mighty God!**

My soul yearns and pines
  for the courts of the LORD.
My heart and my flesh
  cry out for the living God.

R. **How lovely is your dwelling place, Lord, mighty God!**

Even the sparrow finds a home,
  and the swallow a nest
  in which she puts her young—
Your altars, O LORD of hosts,
  my king and my God!

R. **How lovely is your dwelling place, Lord, mighty God!**

Blessed they who dwell in your house!
  continually they praise you.
Blessed the men whose strength you are!
  their hearts are set upon the pilgrimage.

R. **How lovely is your dwelling place, Lord, mighty God!**

For a sun and a shield is the LORD God;
  grace and glory he bestows;
The LORD withholds no good thing
  from those who walk in sincerity.

R. **How lovely is your dwelling place, Lord, mighty God!**

Alleluia, alleluia   See Jn 17:17b, 17a
  Your word, O Lord, is truth;
  consecrate us in the truth.
Alleluia, alleluia

Years I and II

GOSPEL
Lk 6:39–42

Can a blind person guide a blind person?

A reading from the holy Gospel according to Luke

Jesus told his disciples a parable: "Can a blind person guide a blind person? Will not both fall into a pit? No disciple is superior to the teacher; but when fully trained, every disciple will be like his teacher. Why do you notice the splinter in your brother's eye, but do not perceive the wooden beam in your own? How can you say to your brother, 'Brother, let me remove that splinter in your eye,' when you do not even notice the wooden beam in your own eye? You hypocrite! Remove the wooden beam from your eye first; then you will see clearly to remove the splinter in your brother's eye."

The Gospel of the Lord.

Liturgy of the Eucharist, *p. 897;* **Prayer over the Gifts,** *p. 1413.*

Saturday

Antiphons and Prayers, *p. 1412;* **Liturgy of the Word** *for Year I (odd years) follows; Year II (even years), p. 1438.*

TODAY'S LIVING WORD

Today's Gospel concludes the Sermon on the Plain and gives us a succinct message: practice what Jesus preaches. "Why do you call me, 'Lord, Lord,' but not do what I command?" he asks. "I will show you what someone is like who comes to me, listens to my words, and acts on them." This message is introduced by one parable about trees and illustrated by another about houses. As a good tree is known by its yield, so is the patience of Christ revealed in the exemplary life of Paul, according to 1 Timothy.

In the excerpt from 1 Corinthians, Paul expresses concern that that community is being built like a house without a solid foundation. Some in Corinth profess faith in Christ by partaking of the Lord's table, but at the same time practice idol worship by participating in pagan temple meals. Thus, their common union with idols and idolators threatens the communion of the one body of Christ.

Year I

FIRST READING

1 Tm 1:15–17

Christ Jesus came into the world to save sinners.

A reading from the first Letter of Saint Paul to Timothy

Beloved:

This saying is trustworthy and deserves full acceptance: Christ Jesus came into the world to save sinners. Of these I am the foremost. But for that reason I was mercifully treated, so that in me, as the foremost, Christ Jesus might display all his patience as an example for those who would come to believe in him for everlasting life. To the king of ages, incorruptible, invisible, the only God, honor and glory forever and ever. Amen.

The word of the Lord.

Responsorial Psalm

Ps 113:1b–2, 3–4, 5 and 6–7

R. **Blessed be the name of the Lord for ever.**

Praise, you servants of the LORD,
  praise the name of the LORD.
Blessed be the name of the LORD
  both now and forever.

R. **Blessed be the name of the Lord for ever.**

From the rising to the setting of the sun
  is the name of the LORD to be praised.
High above all nations is the LORD;
  above the heavens is his glory.

R. Blessed be the name of the Lord for ever.

Who is like the LORD, our God,
  and looks upon the heavens and the earth below?
He raises up the lowly from the dust;
  from the dunghill he lifts up the poor.

R. Blessed be the name of the Lord for ever.

Alleluia Verse *and* **Gospel**, *p. 1439.*

Year II

FIRST READING

1 Cor 10:14 – 22

We, though many, are one Body,
for we all partake of the one bread.

A reading from the first Letter of Saint Paul to the Corinthians

My beloved ones, avoid idolatry. I am speaking as to sensible people; judge for yourselves what I am saying. The cup of blessing that we bless, is it not a participation in the Blood of Christ? The bread that we break, is it not a participation in the Body of Christ? Because the loaf of bread is one, we, though many, are one Body, for we all partake of the one loaf.

Look at Israel according to the flesh; are not those who eat the sacrifices participants in the altar? So what am I saying? That meat sacrificed to idols is anything? Or that an idol is anything? No, I mean that what they sacrifice, they sacrifice to demons, not to God, and I do not want you to become participants with demons. You cannot drink the cup of the Lord and also the cup of demons. You cannot partake of the table of the Lord and of the table of demons. Or are we provoking the Lord to jealous anger? Are we stronger than him?

The word of the Lord.

Responsorial Psalm

Ps 116:12–13, 17–18

R. To you, Lord, I will offer a sacrifice of praise.

How shall I make a return to the LORD
  for all the good he has done for me?
The cup of salvation I will take up,
  and I will call upon the name of the LORD.

R. To you, Lord, I will offer a sacrifice of praise.

To you will I offer sacrifice of thanksgiving,
  and I will call upon the name of the LORD.
My vows to the LORD I will pay
  in the presence of all his people.

R. To you, Lord, I will offer a sacrifice of praise.

Alleluia, alleluia Jn 14:23
Whoever loves me will keep my word,
and my Father will love him,
and we will come to him.
Alleluia, alleluia

Years I and II

GOSPEL

Lk 6:43–49

*Why do you call me, "Lord, Lord,"
but do not do what I command?*

A reading from the holy Gospel according to Luke

Jesus said to his disciples: "A good tree does not bear rotten fruit, nor does a rotten tree bear good fruit. For every tree is known by its own fruit. For people do not pick figs from thornbushes, nor do they gather grapes from brambles. A good person out of the store of goodness in his heart produces good, but an evil person out of a store of evil produces evil; for from the fullness of the heart the mouth speaks.

"Why do you call me, 'Lord, Lord,' but not do what I command? I will show you what someone is like who comes to me, listens to my words, and acts on them. That one is like a man building a house, who dug deeply and laid the foundation on rock; when the flood came, the river burst against that house but could not shake it because it had been well built. But the one who listens and does not act is like a person who built a house on the ground without a foundation. When the river burst against it, it collapsed at once and was completely destroyed." The Gospel of the Lord.

Liturgy of the Eucharist, *p. 897;* **Prayer over the Gifts,** *p. 1413.*

TWENTY-FOURTH WEEK IN ORDINARY TIME

The **Antiphons and Prayers** *may be the following, or may be chosen from any of the other 33 weeks in Ordinary Time (refer to Liturgical Calendar, pp. 26–41).*

The **Liturgy of the Word** *varies: for Monday, see p. 1442; Tuesday, p. 1447; Wednesday, p. 1451; Thursday, p. 1456; Friday, p. 1460; Saturday, p. 1465.*

Entrance Antiphon

Give peace, Lord, to those who wait for you and your prophets will proclaim you as you deserve. Hear the prayers of your servant and of your people Israel. (See Sir 36:15–16)

Opening Prayer

Let us pray

[that God will keep us faithful in his service]

Pause for silent prayer.

Almighty God,
our creator and guide,
may we serve you with all our heart
and know your forgiveness in our lives.

We ask this through our Lord Jesus Christ, your Son,
who lives and reigns with you and the Holy Spirit,
one God, for ever and ever.

Alternative Opening Prayer

Let us pray
   [for the peace which is born of faith and hope]

Pause for silent prayer.

Father in heaven, Creator of all,
look down upon your people in their moments of need,
for you alone are the source of our peace.
Bring us to the dignity which distinguishes the poor in spirit
and show us how great is the call to serve,
that we may share in the peace of Christ
who offered his life in the service of all.

We ask this through Christ our Lord.

Prayer over the Gifts

Pray, brethren...
Lord,
hear the prayers of your people
and receive our gifts.
May the worship of each one here
bring salvation to all.

Grant this through Christ our Lord.

Preface of Weekdays in Ordinary Time I–VI, *pp. 948–950.*

Communion Antiphon

O God, how much we value your mercy! All mankind can gather under your protection. (Ps 36:8)

Or:

The cup that we bless is a communion with the blood of Christ; and the bread that we break is a communion with the body of the Lord. (See 1 Cor 10:16)

Prayer after Communion

Let us pray.

Pause for silent prayer, if this has not preceded.

Lord,
may the eucharist you have given us
influence our thoughts and actions.
May your Spirit guide and direct us in your way.

We ask this in the name of Jesus the Lord.

Monday

Antiphons and Prayers, *p. 1440;* **Liturgy of the Word** *for Year I (odd years) follows; Year II (even years), p. 1444.*

TODAY'S LIVING WORD

In Luke's Gospel, Jesus, the messianic prophet, began his ministry by announcing that his mission was to all nations. He did this by alluding to the work of two earlier prophets: Elijah who was sent to a widow of Zarephath, and Elisha who healed the Syrian Naaman (cf. 4:25, 27). The miracle retold in today's Gospel is meant to remind us of the cure of Naaman the leper (cf. 2 Kgs 5). Like the centurion in today's story, Naaman too was a Gentile military officer. Just as the Jewish elders petition Jesus on behalf of the centurion, so did a Jewish girl tell Naaman about Elisha. Thus, like the cure of Naaman himself, the cure of the centurion's servant makes it known "that there is a prophet in Israel" (2 Kgs 5:15) and that the God of Israel, as Paul writes to Timothy, "wills everyone to be saved and to come to knowledge of the truth."

Today's excerpt from 1 Timothy ends with the wish that all might be free from dissension. Dissension characterizes the Corinthians when they assemble for the Lord's Supper. Paul invokes the sacred tradition of the Last Supper for their instruction.

Year I

FIRST READING
1 Tm 2:1–8

I ask that prayers be offered for everyone to God who wills everyone to be saved.

A reading from the first Letter of Saint Paul to Timothy

Beloved:

First of all, I ask that supplications, prayers, petitions, and thanksgivings be offered for everyone, for kings and for all in authority, that we may lead a quiet and tranquil life in all devotion and dignity. This is good and pleasing to God our savior, who wills everyone to be saved and to come to knowledge of the truth.

> For there is one God.
> There is also one mediator between God and men,
> the man Christ Jesus,
> who gave himself as ransom for all.

This was the testimony at the proper time. For this I was appointed preacher and Apostle (I am speaking the truth, I am not lying), teacher of the Gentiles in faith and truth.

It is my wish, then, that in every place the men should pray, lifting up holy hands, without anger or argument.

The word of the Lord.

Responsorial Psalm

Ps 28:2, 7, 8–9

R. Blessed be the Lord, for he has heard my prayer.

Hear the sound of my pleading, when I cry to you,
  lifting up my hands toward your holy shrine.

R. Blessed be the Lord, for he has heard my prayer.

The LORD is my strength and my shield.
In him my heart trusts, and I find help;
  then my heart exults, and with my song I give him thanks.

R. Blessed be the Lord, for he has heard my prayer.

The LORD is the strength of his people,
  the saving refuge of his anointed.
Save your people, and bless your inheritance;
  feed them, and carry them forever!

R. Blessed be the Lord, for he has heard my prayer.

Alleluia Verse *and* **Gospel,** *p. 1446.*

Year II

FIRST READING

1 Cor 11:17–26, 33

If there are divisions among you,
then you do not eat the Lord's supper.

A reading from the first Letter of Saint Paul to the Corinthians

Brothers and sisters:

In giving this instruction, I do not praise the fact that your meetings are doing more harm than good. First of all, I hear that when you meet as a Church there are divisions among you, and to a degree I believe it; there have to be factions among you in order that also those who are approved among you may become known. When you meet in one place, then, it is not to eat the Lord's supper, for in eating, each one goes ahead with his own supper, and one goes hungry while another gets drunk.

Do you not have houses in which you can eat and drink? Or do you show contempt for the Church of God and make those who have nothing feel ashamed? What can I say to you? Shall I praise you? In this matter I do not praise you.

For I received from the Lord what I also handed on to you, that the Lord Jesus, on the night he was handed over, took bread and, after he had given thanks, broke it and said, "This is my Body that is for you. Do this in remembrance of me." In the same way also the cup, after supper, saying, "This cup is the new covenant in my Blood. Do this, as often as you drink it, in remembrance of me." For as often as you eat this bread and drink the cup, you proclaim the death of the Lord until he comes.

Therefore, my brothers and sisters, when you come together to eat, wait for one another.

The word of the Lord.

Responsorial Psalm

Ps 40:7 – 8a, 8b – 9, 10, 17

R. Proclaim the death of the Lord until he comes again.

Sacrifice or oblation you wished not,
  but ears open to obedience you gave me.
Burnt offerings or sin-offerings you sought not;
  then said I, "Behold I come."

R. Proclaim the death of the Lord until he comes again.

"In the written scroll it is prescribed for me,
To do your will, O my God, is my delight,
  and your law is within my heart!"

R. Proclaim the death of the Lord until he comes again.

I announced your justice in the vast assembly;
  I did not restrain my lips, as you, O LORD, know.

R. Proclaim the death of the Lord until he comes again.

May all who seek you
  exult and be glad in you
And may those who love your salvation
  say ever, "The LORD be glorified."

R. Proclaim the death of the Lord until he comes again.

Alleluia, alleluia Jn 3:16
God so loved the world that he gave his only-begotten Son,
  so that everyone who believes in him might have eternal life.
Alleluia, alleluia

Years I and II

GOSPEL   Lk 7:1–10
Not even in Israel have I found such faith.

A reading from the holy Gospel according to Luke

When Jesus had finished all his words to the people, he entered
Capernaum. A centurion there had a slave who was ill and
about to die, and he was valuable to him. When he heard about
Jesus, he sent elders of the Jews to him, asking him to come
and save the life of his slave. They approached Jesus and
strongly urged him to come, saying, "He deserves to have you
do this for him, for he loves our nation and he built the
synagogue for us." And Jesus went with them, but when he
was only a short distance from the house, the centurion sent
friends to tell him, "Lord, do not trouble yourself, for I am not
worthy to have you enter under my roof. Therefore, I did not
consider myself worthy to come to you; but say the word and
let my servant be healed. For I too am a person subject to authority, with soldiers subject to me. And I say to one, Go, and
he goes; and to another, Come here, and he comes; and to my
slave, Do this, and he does it." When Jesus heard this he was
amazed at him and, turning, said to the crowd following him,

"I tell you, not even in Israel have I found such faith." When the messengers returned to the house, they found the slave in good health.

The Gospel of the Lord.

Liturgy of the Eucharist, *p. 897;* **Prayer over the Gifts,** *p. 1441.*

Tuesday

Antiphons and Prayers, *p. 1440;* **Liturgy of the Word** *for Year I (odd years) follows; Year II (even years), p. 1449.*

TODAY'S LIVING WORD

Today's Gospel miracle is reminiscent of Elijah's raising of the son of the widow of Zarephath (cf. 1 Kgs 17). Because of this miracle, Jesus is acclaimed as a prophet and his ministry acknowledged as a visitation, a biblical term for God's intervention in history.

The two first readings are both concerned about various roles within the Church. First Corinthians lists charismatic roles, that is, they derive from the gifts of the one Spirit whom all Christians receive at baptism. That the first three are numbered—"first, apostles; second, prophets; third, teachers"—indicates their importance in the foundation of the Church. The others ensure the body's continued growth and vitality. First Timothy, written some time after 1 Corinthians, attests to a development in the Church's infrastructure. Roles are no longer charismatic now, and so personal qualifications must determine who may serve as a bishop or a deacon. Yet, in both letters, what finally matters is that the Church be a credible witness to the good news that "God has visited his people."

Year I

FIRST READING

1 Tm 3:1–13

*The bishop must be irreproachable;
similarly, deacons must hold fast to the mystery of the faith
with a clear conscience.*

A reading from the first Letter of Saint Paul to Timothy

Beloved, this saying is trustworthy: whoever aspires to the office of bishop desires a noble task. Therefore, a bishop must be irreproachable, married only once, temperate, self-controlled, decent, hospitable, able to teach, not a drunkard, not aggressive, but gentle, not contentious, not a lover of money. He must manage his own household well, keeping his children under control with perfect dignity; for if a man does not know how to manage his own household, how can he take care of the Church of God? He should not be a recent convert, so that he may not become conceited and thus incur the Devil's punishment. He must also have a good reputation among outsiders, so that he may not fall into disgrace, the Devil's trap.

Similarly, deacons must be dignified, not deceitful, not addicted to drink, not greedy for sordid gain, holding fast to the mystery of the faith with a clear conscience. Moreover, they should be tested first; then, if there is nothing against them, let them serve as deacons. Women, similarly, should be dignified, not slanderers, but temperate and faithful in everything. Deacons may be married only once and must manage their children and their households well. Thus those who serve well as deacons gain good standing and much confidence in their faith in Christ Jesus.

The word of the Lord.

Responsorial Psalm

Ps 101:1b–2ab, 2cd–3ab, 5, 6

R. I will walk with blameless heart.

Of mercy and judgment I will sing;
  to you, O LORD, I will sing praise.
I will persevere in the way of integrity;
  when will you come to me?

R. I will walk with blameless heart.

I will walk with blameless heart,
  within my house;
I will not set before my eyes
  any base thing.

R. I will walk with blameless heart.

Whoever slanders his neighbor in secret,
  him will I destroy.
The man of haughty eyes and puffed-up heart
  I will not endure.

R. I will walk with blameless heart.

My eyes are upon the faithful of the land,
  that they may dwell with me.
He who walks in the way of integrity
  shall be in my service.

R. I will walk with blameless heart.

Alleluia Verse *and* **Gospel,** *p. 1450f.*

___

Year II

FIRST READING   1 Cor 12:12 –14, 27 –31a

Now you are Christ's Body, and individually parts of it.

A reading from the first Letter of Saint Paul to the Corinthians

Brothers and sisters:

As a body is one though it has many parts, and all the parts of
the body, though many, are one body, so also Christ. For in
one Spirit we were all baptized into one Body, whether Jews
or Greeks, slaves or free persons, and we were all given to
drink of one Spirit.

  Now the body is not a single part, but many.

  Now you are Christ's Body, and individually parts of it.

Some people God has designated in the Church to be, first, Apostles; second, prophets; third, teachers; then, mighty deeds; then gifts of healing, assistance, administration, and varieties of tongues. Are all Apostles? Are all prophets? Are all teachers? Do all work mighty deeds? Do all have gifts of healing? Do all speak in tongues? Do all interpret? Strive eagerly for the greatest spiritual gifts.

The word of the Lord.

Responsorial Psalm

Ps 100:1b–2, 3, 4, 5

R. We are his people: the sheep of his flock.

Sing joyfully to the LORD, all you lands;
  serve the LORD with gladness;
  come before him with joyful song.

R. We are his people: the sheep of his flock.

Know that the LORD is God;
  he made us, his we are;
  his people, the flock he tends.

R. We are his people: the sheep of his flock.

Enter his gates with thanksgiving,
  his courts with praise;
Give thanks to him; bless his name.

R. We are his people: the sheep of his flock.

For he is good, the LORD,
  whose kindness endures forever,
  and his faithfulness, to all generations.

R. We are his people: the sheep of his flock.

Alleluia, alleluia Lk 7:16
  A great prophet has arisen in our midst
  and God has visited his people.
Alleluia, alleluia

Years I and II

GOSPEL   Lk 7:11–17

Young man, I tell you, arise!

A reading from the holy Gospel according to Luke

Jesus journeyed to a city called Nain, and his disciples and a large crowd accompanied him. As he drew near to the gate of the city, a man who had died was being carried out, the only son of his mother, and she was a widow. A large crowd from the city was with her. When the Lord saw her, he was moved with pity for her and said to her, "Do not weep." He stepped forward and touched the coffin; at this the bearers halted, and he said, "Young man, I tell you, arise!" The dead man sat up and began to speak, and Jesus gave him to his mother. Fear seized them all, and they glorified God, exclaiming, "A great prophet has arisen in our midst," and "God has visited his people." This report about him spread through the whole of Judea and in all the surrounding region.

The Gospel of the Lord.

Liturgy of the Eucharist, *p. 897;* **Prayer over the Gifts,** *p. 1441.*

Wednesday

Antiphons and Prayers, *p. 1440;* **Liturgy of the Word** *for Year I (odd years) follows; Year II (even years), p. 1453.*

TODAY'S LIVING WORD

In today's Gospel Jesus uses a saying from the wisdom tradition of his people to characterize the men of his generation who lack seriousness and sincerity. They are noisy children who do not know what they want and so spend the day teasing and taunting each other. Similarly, Paul depicts the Corinthians as childish for quibbling and quarreling over spiritual gifts, when all the time they lack the one gift that surpasses all others.

The excerpt from 1 Timothy, on the other hand, is a monument to the seriousness and sincerity of the mature Paul. He urges Timothy to conduct himself in a manner that befits "the household of God, which is the church of the living God, the pillar and foundation of truth." That truth he sums up in an early creed tracing the career of Jesus, from his being "manifested in the flesh" to his resurrection "in the spirit" and his ascension among the angels. It continues as a call, to Timothy and to us, to commit ourselves to preaching Christ among the Gentiles so that he may be "believed in throughout the world."

Year I

FIRST READING   1 Tm 3:14–16

Undeniably great is the mystery of devotion.

A reading from the first Letter of Saint Paul to Timothy

Beloved:

I am writing you, although I hope to visit you soon. But if I should be delayed, you should know how to behave in the household of God, which is the Church of the living God, the pillar and foundation of truth. Undeniably great is the mystery of devotion,

> Who was manifested in the flesh,
> vindicated in the spirit,
> seen by angels,
> proclaimed to the Gentiles,
> believed in throughout the world,
> taken up in glory.

The word of the Lord.

Responsorial Psalm

Ps 111:1–2, 3–4, 5–6

R. How great are the works of the Lord!

I will give thanks to the LORD with all my heart
  in the company and assembly of the just.
Great are the works of the LORD,
  exquisite in all their delights.

R. How great are the works of the Lord!

Majesty and glory are his work,
  and his justice endures forever.
He has won renown for his wondrous deeds;
  gracious and merciful is the LORD.

R. How great are the works of the Lord!

He has given food to those who fear him;
  he will forever be mindful of his covenant.
He has made known to his people the power of his works,
  giving them the inheritance of the nations.

R. How great are the works of the Lord!

Alleluia Verse *and* **Gospel,** *p. 1455.*

Year II

FIRST READING

1 Cor 12:31—13:13

So faith, hope, love remain, these three;
but the greatest of these is love.

A reading from the first Letter of Saint Paul to the Corinthians

Brothers and sisters:
Strive eagerly for the greatest spiritual gifts.

But I shall show you a still more excellent way.

If I speak in human and angelic tongues but do not have love, I am a resounding gong or a clashing cymbal. And if I have the gift of prophecy and comprehend all mysteries and all knowledge; if I have all faith so as to move mountains, but do not have love, I am nothing. If I give away everything I own, and if I hand my body over so that I may boast but do not have love, I gain nothing.

Love is patient, love is kind. It is not jealous, love is not pompous, it is not inflated, it is not rude, it does not seek its own interests, it is not quick-tempered, it does not brood over injury, it does not rejoice over wrongdoing but rejoices with the truth. It bears all things, believes all things, hopes all things, endures all things.

Love never fails. If there are prophecies, they will be brought to nothing; if tongues, they will cease; if knowledge, it will be brought to nothing. For we know partially and we prophesy partially, but when the perfect comes, the partial will pass away. When I was a child, I used to talk as a child, think as a child, reason as a child; when I became a man, I put aside childish things. At present we see indistinctly, as in a mirror, but then face to face. At present I know partially; then I shall know fully, as I am fully known. So faith, hope, love remain, these three; but the greatest of these is love.

The word of the Lord.

Responsorial Psalm
Ps 33:2 – 3, 4 – 5, 12 and 22

R. **Blessed the people the Lord has chosen to be his own.**

Give thanks to the LORD on the harp;
  with the ten-stringed lyre chant his praises.
Sing to him a new song;
  pluck the strings skillfully, with shouts of gladness.

R. **Blessed the people the Lord has chosen to be his own.**

For upright is the word of the LORD,
  and all his works are trustworthy.

He loves justice and right;
  of the kindness of the LORD the earth is full.

R. Blessed the people the Lord has chosen to be his own.

Blessed the nation whose God is the LORD,
  the people he has chosen for his own inheritance.
May your kindness, O LORD, be upon us
  who have put our hope in you.

R. Blessed the people the Lord has chosen to be his own.

Alleluia, alleluia See Jn 6:63c, 68c
  Your words, Lord, are Spirit and life,
  you have the words of everlasting life.
Alleluia, alleluia

Years I and II

GOSPEL   Lk 7:31– 35

We played the flute for you, but you did not dance.
We sang a dirge, but you did not weep.

A reading from the holy Gospel according to Luke

Jesus said to the crowds: "To what shall I compare the people
of this generation? What are they like? They are like children
who sit in the marketplace and call to one another,

  'We played the flute for you, but you did not dance.
    We sang a dirge, but you did not weep.'

For John the Baptist came neither eating food nor drinking
wine, and you said, 'He is possessed by a demon.' The Son of
Man came eating and drinking and you said, 'Look, he is a
glutton and a drunkard, a friend of tax collectors and sinners.'
But wisdom is vindicated by all her children."

The Gospel of the Lord.

Liturgy of the Eucharist, *p. 897;* **Prayer over the Gifts,** *p. 1441.*

Thursday

Antiphons and Prayers, *p. 1440;* **Liturgy of the Word** *for Year I (odd years) follows; Year II (even years), p. 1457.*

Today's Living Word

Today's Gospel finds Jesus at the table of a Pharisee. Some scholars note that the Pharisee here, and elsewhere in Luke, may represent Christians in Luke's church who would prefer more rigid standards for admission to the table fellowship of the community. This Pharisee is given an object lesson on the nature of salvation. The parable of the two debtors provides the key to the story. The woman's great love, concretely expressed by her generous actions, proves that God has forgiven her many sins; her faith has saved her and set her feet on the path of peace (cf. 1:77, 79). Conversely, the Pharisee's failure to show love for Jesus proves that his sins are not forgiven. Not only does the prophet Jesus read people's hearts; he reveals them as well (cf. 2:35).

It is easy to read Paul's heart in the two first readings. He tells the Corinthians that hard work, in response to God's grace, has characterized his own ministry as an apostle. He urges such work upon Timothy with the promise, "for by doing so you will save both yourself and those who listen to you."

Year I

FIRST READING

1 Tm 4:12–16

Attend to yourself and to your teaching;
you will save both yourself and those who listen to you.

A reading from the first Letter of Saint Paul to Timothy

Beloved:
Let no one have contempt for your youth, but set an example for those who believe, in speech, conduct, love, faith, and purity. Until I arrive, attend to the reading, exhortation, and teaching. Do not neglect the gift you have, which was conferred on you

through the prophetic word with the imposition of hands by the presbyterate. Be diligent in these matters, be absorbed in them, so that your progress may be evident to everyone. Attend to yourself and to your teaching; persevere in both tasks, for by doing so you will save both yourself and those who listen to you.

The word of the Lord.

Responsorial Psalm

Ps 111:7 – 8, 9, 10

   R. How great are the works of the Lord!

The works of his hands are faithful and just;
   sure are all his precepts,
Reliable forever and ever,
   wrought in truth and equity.

   R. How great are the works of the Lord!

He has sent deliverance to his people;
   he has ratified his covenant forever;
   holy and awesome is his name.

   R. How great are the works of the Lord!

The fear of the LORD is the beginning of wisdom;
   prudent are all who live by it.
   His praise endures forever.

   R. How great are the works of the Lord!

Alleluia Verse *and* **Gospel**, *p. 1459.*

Year II

FIRST READING

1 Cor 15:1–11

So we preach and so you believed.

A reading from the first Letter of Saint Paul to the Corinthians

I am reminding you, brothers and sisters, of the Gospel I preached to you, which you indeed received and in which you also stand. Through it you are also being saved, if you hold fast to the word I preached to you, unless you believed in vain. For I handed on to you as of first importance what I also received: that Christ died for our sins in accordance with the Scriptures; that he was buried; that he was raised on the third day in accordance with the Scriptures; that he appeared to Cephas, then to the Twelve. After that, he appeared to more than five hundred brothers at once, most of whom are still living, though some have fallen asleep. After that he appeared to James, then to all the Apostles. Last of all, as to one born abnormally, he appeared to me. For I am the least of the Apostles, not fit to be called an Apostle, because I persecuted the Church of God. But by the grace of God I am what I am, and his grace to me has not been ineffective. Indeed, I have toiled harder than all of them; not I, however, but the grace of God that is with me. Therefore, whether it be I or they, so we preach and so you believed.

The word of the Lord.

Responsorial Psalm
Ps 118:1b–2, 16ab–17, 28

R. Give thanks to the Lord, for he is good.

Give thanks to the Lord, for he is good,
  for his mercy endures forever.
Let the house of Israel say,
  "His mercy endures forever."

R. Give thanks to the Lord, for he is good.

"The right hand of the Lord is exalted;
  the right hand of the Lord has struck with power."
I shall not die, but live,
  and declare the works of the Lord.

R. Give thanks to the Lord, for he is good.

You are my God, and I give thanks to you;
  O my God, I extol you.

R. Give thanks to the Lord, for he is good.

Alleluia, alleluia Mt 11:28
Come to me, all you who labor and are burdened,
and I will give you rest, says the Lord.
Alleluia, alleluia

Years I and II

GOSPEL   Lk 7:36–50

Her many sins have been forgiven;
hence, she has shown great love.

A reading from the holy Gospel according to Luke

A certain Pharisee invited Jesus to dine with him, and he
entered the Pharisee's house and reclined at table. Now there
was a sinful woman in the city who learned that he was at
table in the house of the Pharisee. Bringing an alabaster flask
of ointment, she stood behind him at his feet weeping and began to bathe his feet with her tears. Then she wiped them with
her hair, kissed them, and anointed them with the ointment.
When the Pharisee who had invited him saw this he said to
himself, "If this man were a prophet, he would know who and
what sort of woman this is who is touching him, that she is a
sinner." Jesus said to him in reply, "Simon, I have something
to say to you." "Tell me, teacher," he said. "Two people were
in debt to a certain creditor; one owed five hundred days' wages
and the other owed fifty. Since they were unable to repay the
debt, he forgave it for both. Which of them will love him
more?" Simon said in reply, "The one, I suppose, whose larger
debt was forgiven." He said to him, "You have judged rightly."

Then he turned to the woman and said to Simon, "Do you see this woman? When I entered your house, you did not give me water for my feet, but she has bathed them with her tears and wiped with her hair. You did not give me a kiss, but she has not ceased kissing my feet since the time I entered. You did not anoint my head with oil, but she anointed my feet with ointment. So I tell you, her many sins have been forgiven; hence, she has shown great love. But the one to whom little is forgiven, loves little." He said to her, "Your sins are forgiven." The others at table said to themselves, "Who is this who even forgives sins?" But he said to the woman, "Your faith has saved you; go in peace."

The Gospel of the Lord.

Liturgy of the Eucharist, p. 897; **Prayer over the Gifts,** p. 1441.

Friday

Antiphons and Prayers, p. 1440; **Liturgy of the Word** for Year I (odd years) follows; Year II (even years), p. 1463.

TODAY'S LIVING WORD

Today's Gospel—all of three verses—is a film clip, a preview of the early Christian community that Luke will depict in Acts: devoted to the teaching of the apostles and sharing their property and possessions (cf. 2:42, 45). With 1 Corinthians we fast-forward to a church in the mid-50s C.E. Some in Corinth are denying the bodily resurrection of Jesus and Paul writes to say, "If Christ has not been raised, your faith is vain." This is the "religious teaching" that a church leader writing in Paul's name promotes in 1 Timothy, a letter that most scholars date some 50 years after the Corinthian correspondence.

Today's selection is taken from 1 Corinthian 15, the earliest commentary we have on the resurrection of Jesus. We find the key to how Paul understood the central mystery of our faith in the last line of today's reading: "Christ has been raised from the dead, the firstfruits of those who have fallen asleep." The resurrection of Jesus is so important because it reveals what awaits us all. This is what 1 Timothy means when it tells us to "lay hold of eternal life, to which you were called."

Year I

FIRST READING

1 Tm 6:2c–12

But you, man of God, pursue righteousness.

A reading from the first Letter of Saint Paul to Timothy

Beloved:

Teach and urge these things. Whoever teaches something different and does not agree with the sound words of our Lord Jesus Christ and the religious teaching is conceited, understanding nothing, and has a morbid disposition for arguments and verbal disputes. From these come envy, rivalry, insults, evil suspicions, and mutual friction among people with corrupted minds, who are deprived of the truth, supposing religion to be a means of gain. Indeed, religion with contentment is a great gain. For we brought nothing into the world, just as we shall not be able to take anything out of it. If we have food and clothing, we shall be content with that. Those who want to be rich are falling into temptation and into a trap and into many foolish and harmful desires, which plunge them into ruin and destruction. For the love of money is the root of all evils, and some people in their desire for it have strayed from the faith and have pierced themselves with many pains.

But you, man of God, avoid all this. Instead, pursue righteousness, devotion, faith, love, patience, and gentleness. Compete well for the faith. Lay hold of eternal life, to which you were called when you made the noble confession in the presence of many witnesses.

The word of the Lord.

Responsorial Psalm

Ps 49:6–7, 8–10, 17–18, 19–20

> R. Blessed the poor in spirit;
>   the Kingdom of heaven is theirs!

Why should I fear in evil days
  when my wicked ensnarers ring me round?
They trust in their wealth;
  the abundance of their riches is their boast.

> R. Blessed the poor in spirit;
>   the Kingdom of heaven is theirs!

Yet in no way can a man redeem himself,
  or pay his own ransom to God;
Too high is the price to redeem one's life; he would never have
    enough
  to remain alive always and not see destruction.

> R. Blessed the poor in spirit;
>   the Kingdom of heaven is theirs!

Fear not when a man grows rich,
  when the wealth of his house becomes great,
For when he dies, he shall take none of it;
  his wealth shall not follow him down.

> R. Blessed the poor in spirit;
>   the Kingdom of heaven is theirs!

Though in his lifetime he counted himself blessed,
  "They will praise you for doing well for yourself,"
He shall join the circle of his forebears
  who shall never more see light.

> R. Blessed the poor in spirit;
>   the Kingdom of heaven is theirs!

Alleluia Verse *and* **Gospel,** *p. 1464.*

Year II

FIRST READING
1 Cor 15:12–20

If Christ has not been raised, your faith is vain.

A reading from the first Letter of Saint Paul to the Corinthians

Brothers and sisters:

If Christ is preached as raised from the dead, how can some among you say there is no resurrection of the dead? If there is no resurrection of the dead, then neither has Christ been raised. And if Christ has not been raised, then empty too is our preaching; empty, too, your faith. Then we are also false witnesses to God, because we testified against God that he raised Christ, whom he did not raise if in fact the dead are not raised. For if the dead are not raised, neither has Christ been raised, and if Christ has not been raised, your faith is vain; you are still in your sins. Then those who have fallen asleep in Christ have perished. If for this life only we have hoped in Christ, we are the most pitiable people of all.

But now Christ has been raised from the dead, the firstfruits of those who have fallen asleep.

The word of the Lord.

Responsorial Psalm
Ps 17:1bcd, 6–7, 8b and 15

R. Lord, when your glory appears, my joy will be full.

Hear, O Lord, a just suit;
    attend to my outcry;
    hearken to my prayer from lips without deceit.

R. Lord, when your glory appears, my joy will be full.

I call upon you, for you will answer me, O God;
    incline your ear to me; hear my word.
Show your wondrous mercies,

O savior of those who flee
from their foes to refuge at your right hand.

R. Lord, when your glory appears, my joy will be full.

Hide me in the shadow of your wings,
But I in justice shall behold your face;
on waking, I shall be content in your presence.

R. Lord, when your glory appears, my joy will be full.

Alleluia, alleluia   See Mt 11:25
Blessed are you, Father, Lord of heaven and earth;
you have revealed to little ones the mysteries of the Kingdom.
Alleluia, alleluia

Years I and II

GOSPEL   Lk 8:1–3

Accompanying them were some women,
who provided for them out of their resources.

A reading from the holy Gospel according to Luke

Jesus journeyed from one town and village to another, preaching and proclaiming the good news of the Kingdom of God. Accompanying him were the Twelve and some women who had been cured of evil spirits and infirmities, Mary, called Magdalene, from whom seven demons had gone out, Joanna, the wife of Herod's steward Chuza, Susanna, and many others who provided for them out of their resources.

The Gospel of the Lord.

Liturgy of the Eucharist, *p. 897;* **Prayer over the Gifts,** *p. 1441.*

Saturday

Antiphons and Prayers, *p. 1440;* **Liturgy of the Word** *for Year I (odd years) follows; Year II (even years), p. 1466.*

TODAY'S LIVING WORD

In Luke's account the parable of the seed is a comment on the stages of Christian life. Those on the footpath are almost Christians; they hear the word of God but never come to "believe and be saved." Those on rocky ground are Christians who welcome the word of God with joy, but whose fervor fades when they are tested. Those among the briars do make some progress, but they are kept from maturing as Christians by the pressures and the pleasures of life. Thus it is possible at any stage to lose or to let go of the word of God. Only those who hold on to it, "with a generous and good heart," bear fruit. That is why Paul charges Timothy to keep God's word "without stain or reproach until the appearance of our Lord Jesus Christ."

In 1 Corinthians Paul uses the image of the seed to explain what the resurrected body is like. The physical body of the dead is sown in the earth, like seed, and raised up a spiritual body. The image of the seed allows Paul to make the point that it is the same body though radically changed.

Year I

FIRST READING   1 Tm 6:13–16

*Keep the commandment without stain or reproach
until the appearance of our Lord Jesus Christ.*

A reading from the first Letter of Saint Paul to Timothy

Beloved:

I charge you before God, who gives life to all things, and before Christ Jesus, who gave testimony under Pontius Pilate for the noble confession, to keep the commandment without stain or reproach until the appearance of our Lord Jesus Christ that the blessed and only ruler will make manifest at the proper time, the King of kings and Lord of lords, who alone has immortality,

who dwells in unapproachable light, and whom no human being has seen or can see. To him be honor and eternal power. Amen.
The word of the Lord.

Responsorial Psalm

Ps 100:1b–2, 3, 4, 5

R. Come with joy into the presence of the Lord.

Sing joyfully to the LORD, all you lands;
  serve the LORD with gladness;
  come before him with joyful song.

R. Come with joy into the presence of the Lord.

Know that the LORD is God;
  he made us, his we are;
  his people, the flock he tends.

R. Come with joy into the presence of the Lord.

Enter his gates with thanksgiving,
  his courts with praise;
Give thanks to him; bless his name.

R. Come with joy into the presence of the Lord.

For he is good:
  the LORD, whose kindness endures forever,
  and his faithfulness, to all generations.

R. Come with joy into the presence of the Lord.

Alleluia Verse *and* **Gospel,** *p. 1468.*

Year II

FIRST READING

1 Cor 15:35–37, 42–49

It is sown corruptible; it is raised incorruptible.

A reading from the first Letter of Saint Paul to the Corinthians

Brothers and sisters:
Someone may say, "How are the dead raised? With what kind of body will they come back?"

You fool! What you sow is not brought to life unless it dies. And what you sow is not the body that is to be but a bare kernel of wheat, perhaps, or of some other kind.

So also is the resurrection of the dead. It is sown corruptible; it is raised incorruptible. It is sown dishonorable; it is raised glorious. It is sown weak; it is raised powerful. It is sown a natural body; it is raised a spiritual body. If there is a natural body, there is also a spiritual one.

So, too, it is written, "The first man, Adam, became a living being," the last Adam a life-giving spirit. But the spiritual was not first; rather the natural and then the spiritual. The first man was from the earth, earthly; the second man, from heaven. As was the earthly one, so also are the earthly, and as is the heavenly one, so also are the heavenly. Just as we have borne the image of the earthly one, we shall also bear the image of the heavenly one.

The word of the Lord.

Responsorial Psalm

Ps 56:10c–12, 13–14

**R. I will walk in the presence of God,
in the light of the living.**

Now I know that God is with me.
In God, in whose promise I glory,
in God I trust without fear;
what can flesh do against me?

**R. I will walk in the presence of God,
in the light of the living.**

I am bound, O God, by vows to you;
your thank offerings I will fulfill.
For you have rescued me from death,
my feet, too, from stumbling;
that I may walk before God in the light of the living.

R. **I will walk in the presence of God,
in the light of the living.**

Alleluia, alleluia See Lk 8:15
Blessed are they who have kept the word with a generous heart
and yield a harvest through perseverance.
Alleluia, alleluia

Years I and II

GOSPEL   Lk 8:4–15

*As for the seed that fell on rich soil,
they are the ones who embrace the word and bear
much fruit through perseverance.*

A reading from the holy Gospel according to Luke

When a large crowd gathered, with people from one town after another journeying to Jesus, he spoke in a parable. "A sower went out to sow his seed. And as he sowed, some seed fell on the path and was trampled, and the birds of the sky ate it up. Some seed fell on rocky ground, and when it grew, it withered for lack of moisture. Some seed fell among thorns, and the thorns grew with it and choked it. And some seed fell on good soil, and when it grew, it produced fruit a hundredfold." After saying this, he called out, "Whoever has ears to hear ought to hear."

Then his disciples asked him what the meaning of this parable might be. He answered, "Knowledge of the mysteries of the Kingdom of God has been granted to you; but to the rest, they are made known through parables so that they may look but not see, and hear but not understand.

"This is the meaning of the parable. The seed is the word of God. Those on the path are the ones who have heard, but the Devil comes and takes away the word from their hearts that they may not believe and be saved. Those on rocky ground are the ones who, when they hear, receive the word with joy, but they have no root; they believe only for a time and fall away in time of temptation. As for the seed that fell among thorns, they are the ones who have heard, but as they go along, they are choked by the anxieties and riches and pleasures of life, and they fail to produce mature fruit. But as for the seed that fell on rich soil, they are the ones who, when they have heard the word, embrace it with a generous and good heart, and bear fruit through perseverance."

The Gospel of the Lord

Liturgy of the Eucharist, *p. 897;* **Prayer over the Gifts,** *p. 1441.*

TWENTY-FIFTH WEEK IN ORDINARY TIME

The **Antiphons and Prayers** *may be the following, or may be chosen from any of the other 33 weeks in Ordinary Time (refer to Liturgical Calendar, pp. 26–41).*

The **Liturgy of the Word** *varies: for Monday, see p. 1471; Tuesday, p. 1475; Wednesday, p. 1480; Thursday, p. 1484; Friday, p. 1489; Saturday, p. 1494.*

Entrance Antiphon

I am the Savior of all people, says the Lord. Whatever their troubles, I will answer their cry, and I will always be their Lord.

Opening Prayer

Let us pray

[that we will grow in the love of God and of one another]

Pause for silent prayer.

Father,
guide us, as you guide creation
according to your law of love.
May we love one another
and come to perfection
in the eternal life prepared for us.

Grant this through our Lord Jesus Christ, your Son,
who lives and reigns with you and the Holy Spirit,
one God, for ever and ever.

Alternative Opening Prayer

Let us pray
[to the Lord who is a God of love to all peoples]
Pause for silent prayer.

Father in heaven,
the perfection of justice is found in your love
and all mankind is in need of your law.
Help us to find this love in each other
that justice may be attained
through obedience to your law.

We ask this through Christ our Lord.

Prayer over the Gifts

Pray, brethren...

Lord,
may these gifts which we now offer
to show our belief and our love
be pleasing to you.
May they become for us
the eucharist of Jesus Christ your Son,
who is Lord for ever and ever.

Preface of Weekdays in Ordinary Time I–VI, *pp. 948–950.*

Communion Antiphon

You have laid down your precepts to be faithfully kept. May
my footsteps be firm in keeping your commands.   (Ps 119:4–5)

Or:

I am the Good Shepherd, says the Lord; I know my sheep and mine know me.
(Jn 10:14)

Prayer after Communion

Let us pray.

Pause for silent prayer, if this has not preceded.

Lord,
help us with your kindness.
Make us strong through the eucharist.
May we put into action
the saving mystery we celebrate.
We ask this in the name of Jesus the Lord.

Monday

Antiphons and Prayers, *p. 1469;* **Liturgy of the Word** *for Year I (odd years) follows; Year II (even years), p. 1473.*

TODAY'S LIVING WORD

One of today's first readings is taken from the Book of Proverbs, which is an example of "wisdom literature." Wisdom here is not esoteric knowledge but the common sense that allows individuals and communities to conduct themselves reasonably and responsibly. Such wisdom is not learned by reading books but by reflecting on one's lived experience. Often it is captured in pithy sayings, easy to remember and to pass on. The selection for today collects five of these sayings about being a good neighbor. In today's Gospel, Jesus also resorts to proverbial wisdom to impress on his disciples that the word of God they have heard from him must be shared with others.

Today's other first reading, from the Book of Ezra, records a momentous event. The edict of Cyrus the King of Persia marks the end of the Babylonian exile. This news is greeted with a proverb in the responsorial psalm: "Those that sow in tears shall reap rejoicing" (Ps 126).

FIRST READING

Ezr 1:1–6

*Those who are any part of God's people, let them go up
and build the house of the LORD in Jerusalem.*

A reading from the beginning of the Book of Ezra

In the first year of Cyrus, king of Persia, in order to fulfill the
word of the LORD spoken by Jeremiah, the LORD inspired King
Cyrus of Persia to issue this proclamation throughout his
kingdom, both by word of mouth and in writing: "Thus says
Cyrus, king of Persia: 'All the kingdoms of the earth the LORD,
the God of heaven, has given to me, and he has also charged
me to build him a house in Jerusalem, which is in Judah. Therefore, whoever among you belongs to any part of his people,
let him go up, and may his God be with him! Let everyone
who has survived, in whatever place he may have dwelt, be
assisted by the people of that place with silver, gold, goods,
and cattle, together with free-will offerings for the house of
God in Jerusalem.'"

Then the family heads of Judah and Benjamin and the priests
and Levites—everyone, that is, whom God had inspired to do
so—prepared to go up to build the house of the LORD in Jerusalem. All their neighbors gave them help in every way, with
silver, gold, goods, and cattle, and with many precious gifts
besides all their free-will offerings.

The word of the Lord.

Responsorial Psalm

Ps 126:1b–2ab, 2cd–3, 4–5, 6

R. **The Lord has done marvels for us.**

When the LORD brought back the captives of Zion,
 we were like men dreaming.

Then our mouth was filled with laughter,
  and our tongue with rejoicing.

> **R. The Lord has done marvels for us.**

Then they said among the nations,
  "The LORD has done great things for them."
The LORD has done great things for us;
  we are glad indeed.

> **R. The Lord has done marvels for us.**

Restore our fortunes, O LORD,
  like the torrents in the southern desert.
Those that sow in tears
  shall reap rejoicing.

> **R. The Lord has done marvels for us.**

Although they go forth weeping,
  carrying the seed to be sown,
They shall come back rejoicing,
  carrying their sheaves.

> **R. The Lord has done marvels for us.**

Alleluia Verse *and* **Gospel,** *p. 1474f.*

FIRST READING   **Year II**

Prv 3:27–34

The curse of the LORD is on the house of the wicked.

A reading from the Book of Proverbs

Refuse no one the good on which he has a claim
  when it is in your power to do it for him.
Say not to your neighbor, "Go, and come again,
  tomorrow I will give," when you can give at once.
Plot no evil against your neighbor,
  against one who lives at peace with you.
Quarrel not with a man without cause,
  · with one who has done you no harm.

Envy not the lawless man
    and choose none of his ways:
To the Lᴏʀᴅ the perverse one is an abomination,
    but with the upright is his friendship.

The curse of the Lᴏʀᴅ is on the house of the wicked,
    but the dwelling of the just he blesses;
When dealing with the arrogant, he is stern,
    but to the humble he shows kindness.

The word of the Lord.

Responsorial Psalm

Ps 15:2–3a, 3bc–4ab, 5

R. The just one shall live on your holy mountain, O Lord.

He who walks blamelessly and does justice;
    who thinks the truth in his heart
    and slanders not with his tongue.

R. The just one shall live on your holy mountain, O Lord.

Who harms not his fellow man,
    nor takes up a reproach against his neighbor;
By whom the reprobate is despised,
    while he honors those who fear the Lᴏʀᴅ.

R. The just one shall live on your holy mountain, O Lord.

Who lends not his money at usury
    and accepts no bribe against the innocent.
He who does these things
    shall never be disturbed.

R. The just one shall live on your holy mountain, O Lord.

Alleluia, alleluia Mt 5:16
Let your light shine before others,
that they may see your good deeds and glorify
    your heavenly Father.
Alleluia, alleluia

Years I and II

GOSPEL   Lk 8:16–18

A lamp is placed on a lampstand
so that those who enter may see the light.

A reading from the holy Gospel according to Luke

Jesus said to the crowd: "No one who lights a lamp conceals it with a vessel or sets it under a bed; rather, he places it on a lampstand so that those who enter may see the light. For there is nothing hidden that will not become visible, and nothing secret that will not be known and come to light. Take care, then, how you hear. To anyone who has, more will be given, and from the one who has not, even what he seems to have will be taken away."

The Gospel of the Lord.

Liturgy of the Eucharist, *p. 897;* **Prayer over the Gifts,** *p. 1470.*

Tuesday

Antiphons and Prayers, *p. 1469;* **Liturgy of the Word** *for Year I (odd years) follows; Year II (even years), p. 1478.*

TODAY'S LIVING WORD

Today's reading from Ezra reports that the Jews returned from exile have completed the house of God, which the Persians subsidized and the prophets Haggai and Zechariah supported. Finally, "the children of Israel...celebrated the dedication of this house of God with joy." So the service of God resumed in Jerusalem, as "prescribed in the book of Moses." Echoing earlier prophets, the selection from Proverbs says this about worship in God's house: "To do what is right and just is more acceptable to the Lord than sacrifice." This is not a rejection of sacrifice, but a reminder of the overriding importance of keeping God's commandments.

Similarly, in today's Gospel Jesus declares that membership in his house consists in hearing the word of God and acting on it. In Luke's version, the passage takes on a Marian flavor, for Luke has presented Mary from the beginning as the handmaid of the Lord, who hears the word of God and does it (cf. 1:38).

Year I

FIRST READING   Ezr 6:7–8, 12b, 14–20

They completed the temple of God, and ate the Passover.

A reading from the Book of Ezra

King Darius issued an order to the officials of West-of-Euphrates: "Let the governor and the elders of the Jews continue the work on that house of God; they are to rebuild it on its former site. I also issue this decree concerning your dealing with these elders of the Jews in the rebuilding of that house of God: From the royal revenue, the taxes of West-of-Euphrates, let these men be repaid for their expenses, in full and without delay. I, Darius, have issued this decree; let it be carefully executed."

The elders of the Jews continued to make progress in the building, supported by the message of the prophets, Haggai and Zechariah, son of Iddo. They finished the building according to the command of the God of Israel and the decrees of Cyrus and Darius and of Artaxerxes, king of Persia. They completed this house on the third day of the month Adar, in the sixth year of the reign of King Darius. The children of Israel—priests, Levites, and the other returned exiles—celebrated the dedication of this house of God with joy. For the dedication of this house of God, they offered one hundred bulls, two hundred rams, and four hundred lambs, together with twelve he-goats as a sin-offering for all Israel, in keeping with the number of the tribes of Israel. Finally, they set up the priests in their classes and the Levites in their divisions for the service of God in Jerusalem, as is prescribed in the book of Moses.

The exiles kept the Passover on the fourteenth day of the first month. The Levites, every one of whom had purified himself for the occasion, sacrificed the Passover for the rest of the exiles, for their brethren the priests, and for themselves. The word of the Lord.

Responsorial Psalm

Ps 122:1–2, 3–4ab, 4cd–5

R. Let us go rejoicing to the house of the Lord.

I rejoiced because they said to me,
    "We will go up to the house of the LORD."
And now we have set foot
    within your gates, O Jerusalem.

R. Let us go rejoicing to the house of the Lord.

Jerusalem, built as a city
    with compact unity.
To it the tribes go up,
    the tribes of the LORD.

R. Let us go rejoicing to the house of the Lord.

According to the decree for Israel,
    to give thanks to the name of the LORD.
In it are set up judgment seats,
    seats for the house of David.

R. Let us go rejoicing to the house of the Lord.

Alleluia Verse *and* **Gospel,** *p. 1479.*

Year II

FIRST READING
Prv 21:1–6, 10–13

Various proverbs.

A reading from the Book of Proverbs

Like a stream is the king's heart in the hand of the LORD;
    wherever it pleases him, he directs it.

All the ways of a man may be right in his own eyes,
    but it is the LORD who proves hearts.

To do what is right and just
    is more acceptable to the LORD than sacrifice.

Haughty eyes and a proud heart—
    the tillage of the wicked is sin.

The plans of the diligent are sure of profit,
    but all rash haste leads certainly to poverty.

Whoever makes a fortune by a lying tongue
    is chasing a bubble over deadly snares.

The soul of the wicked man desires evil;
    his neighbor finds no pity in his eyes.

When the arrogant man is punished, the simple are the wiser;
    when the wise man is instructed, he gains knowledge.

The just man appraises the house of the wicked:
    there is one who brings down the wicked to ruin.

He who shuts his ear to the cry of the poor
    will himself also call and not be heard.

The word of the Lord.

Responsorial Psalm
Ps 119:1, 27, 30, 34, 35, 44

    R. Guide me, Lord, in the way of your commands.

Blessed are they whose way is blameless,
  who walk in the law of the LORD.

> **R. Guide me, Lord, in the way of your commands.**

Make me understand the way of your precepts,
  and I will meditate on your wondrous deeds.

> **R. Guide me, Lord, in the way of your commands.**

The way of truth I have chosen;
  I have set your ordinances before me.

> **R. Guide me, Lord, in the way of your commands.**

Give me discernment, that I may observe your law
  and keep it with all my heart.

> **R. Guide me, Lord, in the way of your commands.**

Lead me in the path of your commands,
  for in it I delight.

> **R. Guide me, Lord, in the way of your commands.**

And I will keep your law continually,
  forever and ever.

> **R. Guide me, Lord, in the way of your commands.**

> **Alleluia, alleluia**   Lk 11:28
> Blessed are those who hear the word of God
> and observe it.
> **Alleluia, alleluia**

Years I and II

GOSPEL   Lk 8:19–21

*My mother and my brothers are those
who hear the word of God and act on it.*

A reading from the holy Gospel according to Luke

The mother of Jesus and his brothers came to him but were
unable to join him because of the crowd. He was told, "Your
mother and your brothers are standing outside and they wish

to see you." He said to them in reply, "My mother and my brothers are those who hear the word of God and act on it."

The Gospel of the Lord.

Liturgy of the Eucharist, *p. 897;* **Prayer over the Gifts,** *p. 1470.*

Wednesday

Antiphons and Prayers, *p. 1469;* **Liturgy of the Word** *for Year I (odd years) follows; Year II (even years), p. 1482.*

TODAY'S LIVING WORD

In today's Gospel Jesus sends the Twelve to spread the good news, as he himself has been doing, that is, by combining preaching and healing. The text emphasizes that they are to take only the barest necessities and to depend for the rest on God's providence. In this they are like Agur, the wise man, whose words are recorded in today's reading from Proverbs. He asks only for truth and the little food he needs to live.

In a way the Twelve are also like the priest-scribe Ezra, who journeyed from Babylon to bring the book of the law of God to the Jews who had returned from exile. His message was not always well received, and the conditions he found in Jerusalem greatly disturbed him. Today's selection is his prayer of lament at the sin of his people, his "testimony against them," as it were. Yet his prayer ends in gratitude to God for not abandoning Israel, but rather giving them "new life" to build the house of God and begin afresh.

Year I

FIRST READING   Ezr 9:5–9

In our servitude our God has not abandoned us.

A reading from the Book of Ezra

At the time of the evening sacrifice, I, Ezra, rose in my wretchedness, and with cloak and mantle torn I fell on my knees, stretching out my hands to the LORD, my God.

I said: "My God, I am too ashamed and confounded to raise my face to you, O my God, for our wicked deeds are heaped up above our heads and our guilt reaches up to heaven. From the time of our fathers even to this day great has been our guilt, and for our wicked deeds we have been delivered up, we and our kings and our priests, to the will of the kings of foreign lands, to the sword, to captivity, to pillage, and to disgrace, as is the case today.

"And now, but a short time ago, mercy came to us from the LORD, our God, who left us a remnant and gave us a stake in his holy place; thus our God has brightened our eyes and given us relief in our servitude. For slaves we are, but in our servitude our God has not abandoned us; rather, he has turned the good will of the kings of Persia toward us. Thus he has given us new life to raise again the house of our God and restore its ruins, and has granted us a fence in Judah and Jerusalem."

The word of the Lord.

Responsorial Psalm   Tb 13:2, 3–4a, 4befghn, 7–8

R. **Blessed be God, who lives for ever.**

He scourges and then has mercy;
  he casts down to the depths of the nether world,
  and he brings up from the great abyss.
No one can escape his hand.

R. **Blessed be God, who lives for ever.**

Praise him, you children of Israel, before the Gentiles,
  for though he has scattered you among them,
  he has shown you his greatness even there.

R. **Blessed be God, who lives for ever.**

So now consider what he has done for you,
  and praise him with full voice.
Bless the Lord of righteousness,
  and exalt the King of ages.

R. Blessed be God, who lives for ever.

In the land of my exile I praise him
  and show his power and majesty to a sinful nation.

R. Blessed be God, who lives for ever.

Bless the Lord, all you his chosen ones,
  and may all of you praise his majesty.
Celebrate days of gladness, and give him praise.

R. Blessed be God, who lives for ever.

Alleluia Verse *and* **Gospel,** *p. 1483.*

Year II

FIRST READING

Prv 30:5–9

Give me neither poverty nor riches;
provide me only with the food I need.

A reading from the Book of Proverbs

Every word of God is tested;
  he is a shield to those who take refuge in him.
Add nothing to his words,
    lest he reprove you, and you will be exposed as a
      deceiver.
Two things I ask of you,
    deny them not to me before I die:
Put falsehood and lying far from me,
    give me neither poverty nor riches;
    provide me only with the food I need;
Lest, being full, I deny you,
    saying, "Who is the LORD?"
Or, being in want, I steal,
    and profane the name of my God.

The word of the Lord.

Responsorial Psalm

Ps 119:29, 72, 89, 101, 104, 163

R. Your word, O Lord, is a lamp for my feet.

Remove from me the way of falsehood,
and favor me with your law.

R. Your word, O Lord, is a lamp for my feet.

The law of your mouth is to me more precious
than thousands of gold and silver pieces.

R. Your word, O Lord, is a lamp for my feet.

Your word, O Lord, endures forever;
it is firm as the heavens.

R. Your word, O Lord, is a lamp for my feet.

From every evil way I withhold my feet,
that I may keep your words.

R. Your word, O Lord, is a lamp for my feet.

Through your precepts I gain discernment;
therefore I hate every false way.

R. Your word, O Lord, is a lamp for my feet.

Falsehood I hate and abhor;
your law I love.

R. Your word, O Lord, is a lamp for my feet.

Alleluia, alleluia Mk 1:15
The Kingdom of God is at hand;
repent and believe in the Gospel.
Alleluia, alleluia

Years I and II

GOSPEL

Lk 9:1–6

He sent them to proclaim the Kingdom of God and to heal the sick.

A reading from the holy Gospel according to Luke

Jesus summoned the Twelve and gave them power and authority over all demons and to cure diseases, and he sent them to proclaim the Kingdom of God and to heal the sick. He said to them, "Take nothing for the journey, neither walking stick, nor sack, nor food, nor money, and let no one take a second tunic. Whatever house you enter, stay there and leave from there. And as for those who do not welcome you, when you leave that town, shake the dust from your feet in testimony against them." Then they set out and went from village to village proclaiming the good news and curing diseases everywhere. The Gospel of the Lord.

Liturgy of the Eucharist, *p. 897;* **Prayer over the Gifts,** *p. 1470.*

Thursday

Antiphons and Prayers, *p. 1469;* **Liturgy of the Word** *for Year I (odd years) follows; Year II (even years), p. 1486.*

TODAY'S LIVING WORD

Each of today's readings seems to say something about priorities. The prophet Haggai calls the Jews who have returned from exile in Babylon to consider their ways: "You have sown much, but have brought in little; you have eaten, but have not been satisfied." The reason? They did not make rebuilding the house of God their priority. They dwell in paneled houses, while God's house lies in ruins. Thomas a Kempis, who wrote the Imitation of Christ, thought that Qoheleth's totally negative portrayal of life was "the highest wisdom," since it assessed all things as vain and futile, giving sole priority to the service of God.

In the brief selection from Luke, Herod finds himself confused and confounded by Jesus. His past actions are called into question, such as the beheading of John the Baptist. He faces an insecure future. "Who then is this?" he wonders. The answer could reorder all his priorities and reorient his whole life. But then, it could simply satisfy his curiosity and serve his political ambition. He has a choice, and so do we.

Year I

FIRST READING

Hg 1:1-8

Build the house that I may take pleasure in it.

A reading from the beginning of the Book of the Prophet Haggai

On the first day of the sixth month in the second year of King Darius, The word of the LORD came through the prophet Haggai to the governor of Judah, Zerubbabel, son of Shealtiel, and to the high priest Joshua, son of Jehozadak:

Thus says the LORD of hosts: This people says: "The time has not yet come to rebuild the house of the LORD." (Then this word of the LORD came through Haggai, the prophet:) Is it time for you to dwell in your own paneled houses, while this house lies in ruins?

> Now thus says the LORD of hosts:
> Consider your ways!
> You have sown much, but have brought in little;
> you have eaten, but have not been satisfied;
> You have drunk, but have not been exhilarated;
> have clothed yourselves, but not been warmed;
> And whoever earned wages
> earned them for a bag with holes in it.
>
> Thus says the LORD of hosts:
> Consider your ways!
> Go up into the hill country;
> bring timber, and build the house
> That I may take pleasure in it
> and receive my glory, says the LORD.

The word of the Lord.

Responsorial Psalm

Ps 149:1b–2, 3–4, 5–6a and 9b

R. The Lord takes delight in his people.

Sing to the LORD a new song
  of praise in the assembly of the faithful.
Let Israel be glad in their maker,
  let the children of Zion rejoice in their king.

R. The Lord takes delight in his people.

Let them praise his name in the festive dance,
  let them sing praise to him with timbrel and harp.
For the LORD loves his people,
  and he adorns the lowly with victory.

R. The Lord takes delight in his people.

Let the faithful exult in glory;
  let them sing for joy upon their couches;
Let the high praises of God be in their throats.
  This is the glory of all his faithful. Alleluia.

R. The Lord takes delight in his people.

Alleluia Verse *and* **Gospel,** *p. 1488.*

FIRST READING

Year II

Eccl 1:2–11

Nothing is new under the sun.

A reading from the Book of Ecclesiastes

Vanity of vanities, says Qoheleth,
  vanity of vanities! All things are vanity!
What profit has man from all the labor
  which he toils at under the sun?
One generation passes and another comes,
  but the world forever stays.

The sun rises and the sun goes down;
>   then it presses on to the place where it rises.
Blowing now toward the south, then toward the north,
>   the wind turns again and again, resuming its rounds.
All rivers go to the sea,
>   yet never does the sea become full.
To the place where they go,
>   the rivers keep on going.
All speech is labored;
>   there is nothing one can say.
The eye is not satisfied with seeing
>   nor is the ear satisfied with hearing.

What has been, that will be; what has been done, that will be done. Nothing is new under the sun. Even the thing of which we say, "See, this is new!" has already existed in the ages that preceded us. There is no remembrance of the men of old; nor of those to come will there be any remembrance among those who come after them.

The word of the Lord.

Responsorial Psalm

Ps 90:3-4, 5-6, 12-13, 14 and 17bc

R. In every age, O Lord, you have been our refuge.

You turn man back to dust,
>   saying, "Return, O children of men."
For a thousand years in your sight
>   are as yesterday, now that it is past,
>   or as a watch of the night.

R. In every age, O Lord, you have been our refuge.

You make an end of them in their sleep;
>   the next morning they are like the changing grass,

Which at dawn springs up anew,
  but by evening wilts and fades.

R. In every age, O Lord, you have been our refuge.

Teach us to number our days aright,
  that we may gain wisdom of heart.
Return, O LORD! How long?
  Have pity on your servants!

R. In every age, O Lord, you have been our refuge.

Fill us at daybreak with your kindness,
  that we may shout for joy and gladness all our days.
Prosper the work of our hands for us!
Prosper the work of our hands!

R. In every age, O Lord, you have been our refuge.

Alleluia, alleluia Jn 14:6
I am the way and the truth and the life, says the Lord;
  no one comes to the Father except through me.
Alleluia, alleluia

Years I and II

GOSPEL

Lk 9:7-9

John I beheaded. Who then is this about whom I hear such things?

A reading from the holy Gospel according to Luke

Herod the tetrarch heard about all that was happening, and he was greatly perplexed because some were saying, "John has been raised from the dead"; others were saying, "Elijah has appeared"; still others, "One of the ancient prophets has arisen." But Herod said, "John I beheaded. Who then is this about whom I hear such things?" And he kept trying to see him.

The Gospel of the Lord.

Liturgy of the Eucharist, *p. 897;* **Prayer over the Gifts,** *p. 1470.*

Friday

Antiphons and Prayers, *p. 1469;* **Liturgy of the Word** *for Year I (odd years) follows; Year II (even years), p. 1491.*

TODAY'S LIVING WORD

Today's readings confirm the popular wisdom that tells us not to judge a book by its cover. The temple built by the Jews who returned from exile lacked the glory of Solomon's temple. In today's reading, God speaks through Haggai to reassure the people: "I [not you] will fill this house with glory." In other words, the true glory of God's house will consist not in external trappings of silver and gold, but in the continuing presence of God. Similarly, in today's well-known excerpt from Ecclesiastes, Qoheleth suggests that a person's external achievement, the fruit of one's labor, does not determine one's true worth. Rather, "the timeless" that God has put into the human heart gives worth to every person.

In today's Gospel, Peter confers on Jesus the familiar title "the Christ of God." But Jesus immediately qualifies Peter's answer by predicting the suffering and death he must endure. Thus he cautions Peter and all who would be disciples: even messiahship does not consist in external achievements, but in hearing God's word and doing it.

Year I

FIRST READING

Hg 2:1–9

One moment yet and I will fill this house with glory.

A reading from the Book of the Prophet Haggai

In the second year of King Darius, on the twenty-first day of the seventh month, the word of the LORD came through the prophet Haggai: Tell this to the governor of Judah, Zerubbabel, son of Shealtiel, and to the high priest Joshua, son of Jehozadak, and to the remnant of the people:

Who is left among you
    that saw this house in its former glory?
And how do you see it now?
    Does it not seem like nothing in your eyes?
But now take courage, Zerubbabel, says the LORD,
    and take courage, Joshua, high priest,
        son of Jehozadak,
And take courage, all you people of the land,
    says the LORD, and work!
    For I am with you, says the LORD of hosts.
This is the pact that I made with you
    when you came out of Egypt,
And my spirit continues in your midst;
    do not fear!
    For thus says the LORD of hosts:
One moment yet, a little while,
    and I will shake the heavens and the earth,
        the sea and the dry land.
I will shake all the nations,
    and the treasures of all the nations will come in,
And I will fill this house with glory,
    says the LORD of hosts.
Mine is the silver and mine the gold,
    says the LORD of hosts.
Greater will be the future glory of this house
    than the former, says the LORD of hosts;
And in this place I will give you peace,
    says the LORD of hosts!
The word of the Lord.

Responsorial Psalm

Ps 43:1, 2, 3, 4

R. Hope in God; I will praise him, my savior and my God.

Do me justice, O God, and fight my fight
   against a faithless people;
   from the deceitful and impious man rescue me.

R. Hope in God; I will praise him, my savior and my God.

For you, O God, are my strength.
   Why do you keep me so far away?
Why must I go about in mourning,
   with the enemy oppressing me?

R. Hope in God; I will praise him, my savior and my God.

Send forth your light and your fidelity;
   they shall lead me on
And bring me to your holy mountain,
   to your dwelling-place.

R. Hope in God; I will praise him, my savior and my God.

Then will I go in to the altar of God,
   the God of my gladness and joy;
Then will I give you thanks upon the harp,
   O God, my God!

R. Hope in God; I will praise him, my savior and my God.

Alleluia Verse *and* **Gospel,** *p. 1493.*

Year II

FIRST READING

Eccl 3:1–11

There is a time for everything under the heavens.

A reading from the Book of Ecclesiastes

There is an appointed time for everything,
   and a time for every thing under the heavens.

A time to be born, and a time to die;
    a time to plant, and a time to uproot the plant.
A time to kill, and a time to heal;
    a time to tear down, and a time to build.
A time to weep, and a time to laugh;
    a time to mourn, and a time to dance.
A time to scatter stones, and a time to gather them;
    a time to embrace, and a time to be far from embraces.
A time to seek, and a time to lose;
    a time to keep, and a time to cast away.
A time to rend, and a time to sew;
    a time to be silent, and a time to speak.
A time to love, and a time to hate;
    a time of war, and a time of peace.

What advantage has the worker from his toil? I have considered the task that God has appointed for the sons of men to be busied about. He has made everything appropriate to its time, and has put the timeless into their hearts, without man's ever discovering, from beginning to end, the work which God has done.

The word of the Lord.

Responsorial Psalm

Ps 144:1b and 2abc, 3–4

R. **Blessed be the Lord, my Rock!**

Blessed be the LORD, my rock,
    my mercy and my fortress,
    my stronghold, my deliverer,
My shield, in whom I trust.

R. Blessed be the Lord, my Rock!

LORD, what is man, that you notice him;
 the son of man, that you take thought of him?
Man is like a breath;
 his days, like a passing shadow.

R. Blessed be the Lord, my Rock!

Alleluia, alleluia   Mk 10:45
The Son of Man came to serve
and to give his life as a ransom for many.
Alleluia, alleluia

Years I and II

GOSPEL   Lk 9:18–22

You are the Christ of God.
The Son of Man must suffer greatly.

A reading from the holy Gospel according to Luke

Once when Jesus was praying in solitude, and the disciples
were with him, he asked them, "Who do the crowds say that I
am?" They said in reply, "John the Baptist; others, Elijah; still
others, 'One of the ancient prophets has arisen.'" Then he said
to them, "But who do you say that I am?" Peter said in reply,
"The Christ of God." He rebuked them and directed them not
to tell this to anyone.

He said, "The Son of Man must suffer greatly and be rejected
by the elders, the chief priests, and the scribes, and be killed
and on the third day be raised."

The Gospel of the Lord.

Liturgy of the Eucharist, *p. 897;* **Prayer over the Gifts,** *p. 1470.*

Saturday

Antiphons and Prayers, *p. 1469;* **Liturgy of the Word** *for Year I (odd years) follows; Year II (even years), p. 1496.*

TODAY'S LIVING WORD

In today's Gospel the disciples, afraid to question, cannot or will not grasp the reality of impending death. But Qoheleth, who boldly questions everything, confronts it squarely. In the first reading he presents old age allegorically: the idle "grinders" are the few teeth left in the mouth of an old person; the closed "doors to the street" are his deaf ears; the bloom of the almond is his white hair; etc. The poem ends with four images: the snapped silver cord, the broken golden bowl, the shattered pitcher, and the broken pulley. Thus "the life breath returns to God who gave it." This is death, and the disciples fail to understand that even Jesus will not be spared.

The vision of the prophet Zechariah proclaims the future glory of Jerusalem. This city teeming with human beings and animals will not need walls for protection, for God "will be for her an encircling wall of fire...the glory in her midst." This vision meant for returning exiles is a symbol of resurrection—of the power of God to raise what is dead to new life.

Year I

FIRST READING

Zec 2:5–9, 14–15a

See, I am coming to dwell among you.

A reading from the Book of the Prophet Zechariah

I, Zechariah, raised my eyes and looked: there was a man with a measuring line in his hand. I asked, "Where are you going?" He answered, "To measure Jerusalem, to see how great is its width and how great its length."

When the angel who spoke with me advanced, and another angel came out to meet him and said to him, "Run, tell this to that young man: People will live in Jerusalem as though in open country, because of the multitude of men and beasts in her midst. But I will be for her an encircling wall of fire, says the LORD, and I will be the glory in her midst."

Sing and rejoice, O daughter Zion! See, I am coming to dwell among you, says the LORD. Many nations shall join themselves to the LORD on that day, and they shall be his people and he will dwell among you.

The word of the Lord.

Responsorial Psalm

Jer 31:10, 11–12ab, 13

R. The Lord will guard us as a shepherd guards his flock.

Hear the word of the LORD, O nations,
  proclaim it on distant isles, and say:
He who scattered Israel, now gathers them together,
  he guards them as a shepherd guards his flock.

R. The Lord will guard us as a shepherd guards his flock.

The LORD shall ransom Jacob,
  he shall redeem him from the hand of his conqueror.
Shouting, they shall mount the heights of Zion,
  they shall come streaming to the LORD's blessings.

R. The Lord will guard us as a shepherd guards his flock.

Then the virgins shall make merry and dance,
  and young men and old as well.
I will turn their mourning into joy,
  I will console and gladden them after their sorrows.

R. The Lord will guard us as a shepherd guards his flock.

Alleluia Verse *and* **Gospel,** *p. 1498.*

FIRST READING

Eccl 11:9—12:8

Remember your Creator in the days of your youth,
before the dust returns to the earth, and the life breath
returns to God.

A reading from the Book of Ecclesiastes

Rejoice, O young man, while you are young
    and let your heart be glad in the days of your youth.
Follow the ways of your heart,
    the vision of your eyes;
Yet understand that as regards all this
    God will bring you to judgment.
Ward off grief from your heart
    and put away trouble from your presence,
        though the dawn of youth is fleeting.

Remember your Creator in the days of your youth,
    before the evil days come
And the years approach of which you will say,
    I have no pleasure in them;
Before the sun is darkened,
    and the light, and the moon, and the stars,
    while the clouds return after the rain;
When the guardians of the house tremble,
    and the strong men are bent,
And the grinders are idle because they are few,
    and they who look through the windows grow blind;
When the doors to the street are shut,
    and the sound of the mill is low;

When one waits for the chirp of a bird,
    but all the daughters of song are suppressed;
And one fears heights,
    and perils in the street;
When the almond tree blooms,
    and the locust grows sluggish
    and the caper berry is without effect,
Because man goes to his lasting home,
    and mourners go about the streets;
Before the silver cord is snapped
    and the golden bowl is broken,
And the pitcher is shattered at the spring,
    and the broken pulley falls into the well,
And the dust returns to the earth as it once was,
    and the life breath returns to God who gave it.

Vanity of vanities, says Qoheleth,
    all things are vanity!

The word of the Lord.

Responsorial Psalm

Ps 90:3–4, 5–6, 12–13, 14 and 17

R. In every age, O Lord, you have been our refuge.

You turn man back to dust,
    saying, "Return, O children of men."
For a thousand years in your sight
    are as yesterday, now that it is past,
    or as a watch of the night.

R. In every age, O Lord, you have been our refuge.

You make an end of them in their sleep;
    the next morning they are like the changing grass,
Which at dawn springs up anew,
    but by evening wilts and fades.

R. In every age, O Lord, you have been our refuge.

Teach us to number our days aright,
  that we may gain wisdom of heart.
Return, O LORD! How long?
  Have pity on your servants!

R. In every age, O Lord, you have been our refuge.

Fill us at daybreak with your kindness,
  that we may shout for joy and gladness all our days.
And may the gracious care of the Lord our God be ours;
  prosper the work of our hands for us!
  Prosper the work of our hands!

R. In every age, O Lord, you have been our refuge.

> **Alleluia, alleluia**   See 2 Tm 1:10
> Our Savior Christ Jesus destroyed death
> and brought life to light through the Gospel.
> **Alleluia, alleluia**

Years I and II

GOSPEL   Lk 9:43b–45

The Son of Man is to be handed over to men.
They were afraid to ask him about this saying.

A reading from the holy Gospel according to Luke

While they were all amazed at his every deed, Jesus said to his disciples, "Pay attention to what I am telling you. The Son of Man is to be handed over to men." But they did not understand this saying; its meaning was hidden from them so that they should not understand it, and they were afraid to ask him about this saying.

The Gospel of the Lord.

Liturgy of the Eucharist, *p. 897;* **Prayer over the Gifts,** *p. 1470.*

TWENTY-SIXTH WEEK IN ORDINARY TIME

The **Antiphons and Prayers** *may be the following, or may be chosen from any of the other 33 weeks in Ordinary Time (refer to Liturgical Calendar, pp. 26–41).*

The **Liturgy of the Word** *varies: for Monday, see p. 1501; Tuesday, p. 1506; Wednesday, p. 1511; Thursday, p. 1516; Friday, p. 1521; Saturday, p. 1526.*

Entrance Antiphon

O Lord, you had just cause to judge men as you did: because we sinned against you and disobeyed your will. But now show us your greatness of heart, and treat us with your unbounded kindness.

(Dn 3:31, 29, 30, 43, 42)

Opening Prayer

Let us pray
[for God's forgiveness and for the happiness it brings]

Pause for silent prayer.

Father,
you show your almighty power
in your mercy and forgiveness.
Continue to fill us with your gifts of love.
Help us to hurry toward the eternal life you promise
and come to share in the joys of your kingdom.

Grant this through our Lord Jesus Christ, your Son,
who lives and reigns with you and the Holy Spirit,
one God, for ever and ever.

Alternative Opening Prayer

Let us pray
[for the peace of the kingdom
which we have been promised]

Pause for silent prayer.

Father of our Lord Jesus Christ,
in your unbounded mercy
you have revealed the beauty of your power
through your constant forgiveness of our sins.
May the power of this love be in our hearts
to bring your pardon and your kingdom to all we meet.

We ask this through Christ our Lord.

Prayer over the Gifts

Pray, brethren...

God of mercy,
accept our offering
and make it a source of blessing for us.

We ask this in the name of Jesus the Lord.

Preface of Weekdays in Ordinary Time I–VI, *pp. 948–950.*

Communion Antiphon

O Lord, remember the words you spoke to me, your servant,
which made me live in hope and consoled me when I was downcast. (Ps 119:49–50)

Or:

This is how we know what love is: Christ gave up his life
for us; and we too must give up our lives for our brothers.

(1 Jn 3:16)

Prayer after Communion

Let us pray.

Pause for silent prayer, if this has not preceded.

Lord,
may this eucharist
in which we proclaim the death of Christ

bring us salvation
and make us one with him in glory,
for he is Lord for ever and ever.

Monday

Antiphons and Prayers, *p. 1499;* **Liturgy of the Word** *for Year I (odd years) follows; Year II (even years), p. 1503.*

TODAY'S LIVING WORD

The concept of the name figures in some way in all of today's readings. The Gospel reworks the familiar saying of Jesus about the little child. In Luke, however, it is not so much an exhortation to be humble as an explanation of what it means to be sent. Jesus tells the disciples that being sent in his name *(epi to onomati)* makes even the least among them great. In Zechariah's prophecy, the presence of God in Jerusalem confers a new name on that city. It shall now "be called the faithful city and…the holy mountain." Finally, Job's testing is to determine if he is worthy to bear the name that God has given him, "my servant Job." And he is. In all his trials, he does not blaspheme, but blesses the name of the Lord.

Like Job and like Jerusalem, so we who have been baptized in the name of Jesus must strive to be worthy of that name "that is above every name" (Phil 2:9).

Year I

FIRST READING
Zec 8:1–8

*I will rescue my people from the land of the rising sun,
and from the land of the setting sun.*

A reading from the Book of the Prophet Zechariah

This word of the LORD of hosts came:

Thus says the LORD of hosts:

I am intensely jealous for Zion,
stirred to jealous wrath for her.

Thus says the LORD:
I will return to Zion,
and I will dwell within Jerusalem;
Jerusalem shall be called the faithful city,
and the mountain of the LORD of hosts,
the holy mountain.

Thus says the LORD of hosts: Old men and old women, each with staff in hand because of old age, shall again sit in the streets of Jerusalem. The city shall be filled with boys and girls playing in its streets. Thus says the LORD of hosts: Even if this should seem impossible in the eyes of the remnant of this people, shall it in those days be impossible in my eyes also, says the LORD of hosts? Thus says the LORD of hosts: Lo, I will rescue my people from the land of the rising sun, and from the land of the setting sun. I will bring them back to dwell within Jerusalem. They shall be my people, and I will be their God, with faithfulness and justice.

The word of the Lord.

Responsorial Psalm

Ps 102:16–18, 19–21, 2 and 22–23

R. The Lord will build up Zion again, and appear
   in all his glory.

The nations shall revere your name, O LORD,
   and all the kings of the earth your glory,
When the LORD has rebuilt Zion
   and appeared in his glory;
When he has regarded the prayer of the destitute,
   and not despised their prayer.

R. The Lord will build up Zion again, and appear
   in all his glory.

Let this be written for the generation to come,
   and let his future creatures praise the LORD:

"The LORD looked down from his holy height,
from heaven he beheld the earth,
To hear the groaning of the prisoners,
to release those doomed to die."

**R. The Lord will build up Zion again, and appear
in all his glory.**

The children of your servants shall abide,
and their posterity shall continue in your presence.
That the name of the LORD may be declared in Zion;
and his praise, in Jerusalem,
When the peoples gather together,
and the kingdoms, to serve the LORD.

**R. The Lord will build up Zion again, and appear
in all his glory.**

Alleluia Verse *and* **Gospel,** p. 1505.

Year II

FIRST READING

Jb 1:6–22

*The LORD gave and the LORD has taken away;
blessed be the name of the LORD!*

A reading from the Book of Job

One day, when the angels of God came to present themselves before the LORD, Satan also came among them. And the LORD said to Satan, "Whence do you come?" Then Satan answered the LORD and said, "From roaming the earth and patrolling it." And the LORD said to Satan, "Have you noticed my servant Job, and that there is no one on earth like him, blameless and upright, fearing God and avoiding evil?" But Satan answered the LORD and said, "Is it for nothing that Job is God-fearing? Have you not surrounded him and his family and all that he has with your protection? You have blessed the work of his hands, and his livestock are spread over the land. But now put forth your hand and touch anything that he has, and surely he will blaspheme you to your face." And the LORD said to Satan, "Behold, all that he has is in your power; only do not lay a hand upon his person." So Satan went forth from the presence of the LORD.

And so one day, while his sons and his daughters were eating and drinking wine in the house of their eldest brother, a messenger came to Job and said, "The oxen were ploughing and the asses grazing beside them, and the Sabeans carried them off in a raid. They put the herdsmen to the sword, and I alone have escaped to tell you." While he was yet speaking, another came and said, "Lightning has fallen from heaven and struck the sheep and their shepherds and consumed them; and I alone have escaped to tell you." While he was yet speaking, another messenger came and said, "The Chaldeans formed three columns, seized the camels, carried them off, and put those tending them to the sword, and I alone have escaped to tell you." While he was yet speaking, another came and said, "Your sons and daughters were eating and drinking wine in the house of their eldest brother, when suddenly a great wind came across the desert and smote the four corners of the house. It fell upon the young people and they are dead; and I alone have escaped to tell you." Then Job began to tear his cloak and cut off his hair. He cast himself prostrate upon the ground, and said,

"Naked I came forth from my mother's womb,
and naked shall I go back again.
The LORD gave and the LORD has taken away;
blessed be the name of the LORD!"

In all this Job did not sin, nor did he say anything disrespectful of God.

The word of the Lord.

Responsorial Psalm

Ps 17:1bcd, 2–3, 6–7

R. Incline your ear to me and hear my word.

Hear, O LORD, a just suit;
  attend to my outcry;
  hearken to my prayer from lips without deceit.

R. Incline your ear to me and hear my word.

From you let my judgment come;
  your eyes behold what is right.
Though you test my heart, searching it in the night,
  though you try me with fire, you shall find no malice in me.

R. Incline your ear to me and hear my word.

I call upon you, for you will answer me, O God;
  incline your ear to me; hear my word.
Show your wondrous mercies,
  O savior of those who flee
  from their foes to refuge at your right hand.

R. Incline your ear to me and hear my word.

Alleluia, alleluia Mk 10:45
The Son of Man came to serve
and to give his life as a ransom for many.
Alleluia, alleluia

Years I and II

GOSPEL

Lk 9:46–50

*The one who is least among all of you
is the one who is the greatest.*

A reading from the holy Gospel according to Luke

An argument arose among the disciples about which of them
was the greatest. Jesus realized the intention of their hearts
and took a child and placed it by his side and said to them,
"Whoever receives this child in my name receives me, and

whoever receives me receives the one who sent me. For the one who is least among all of you is the one who is the greatest."

Then John said in reply, "Master, we saw someone casting out demons in your name and we tried to prevent him because he does not follow in our company." Jesus said to him, "Do not prevent him, for whoever is not against you is for you." The Gospel of the Lord.

Liturgy of the Eucharist, p. 897; **Prayer over the Gifts**, p. 1500.

Tuesday

Antiphons and Prayers, p. 1499; **Liturgy of the Word** for Year I (odd years) follows; Year II (even years), p. 1508.

TODAY'S LIVING WORD

Today's Gospel uses an expression often found in Ezekiel that means literally "to harden one's face." This is the posture of Job as he mounts his verbal attack against the God who has hemmed him in. Cursing his day, he will finally come into the presence of God, who will answer from the heart of the storm. It is the posture of Jesus too as he resolutely determines to go to Jerusalem. For Luke, Jesus' journey to Jerusalem, where he will be taken up from this world, is an image of the Christian life. Like the first disciples, we are all called to journey faithfully with Jesus along the road to Jerusalem, by way of the cross, into the presence of God.

The prophet Zechariah looks to the time when many peoples and nations will firmly resolve to go to Jerusalem. He says that in those days, people of every nationality and of every language will take hold of every Jew—and, we would say, of every follower of Jesus the Jew—and beg, "Let us go with you, for we have heard that God is with you."

FIRST READING   Zec 8:20–23

Many peoples shall come to seek the LORD in Jerusalem.

A reading from the Book of the Prophet Zechariah

Thus says the LORD of hosts: There shall yet come peoples, the inhabitants of many cities; and the inhabitants of one city shall approach those of another, and say, "Come! let us go to implore the favor of the LORD"; and, "I too will go to seek the LORD." Many peoples and strong nations shall come to seek the LORD of hosts in Jerusalem and to implore the favor of the LORD. Thus says the LORD of hosts: In those days ten men of every nationality, speaking different tongues, shall take hold, yes, take hold of every Jew by the edge of his garment and say,

"Let us go with you, for we have heard that God is with you."

The word of the Lord.

Responsorial Psalm   Ps 87:1b–3, 4–5, 6–7

R. God is with us.

His foundation upon the holy mountains
    the LORD loves:
The gates of Zion,
    more than any dwelling of Jacob.
Glorious things are said of you,
    O city of God!

R. God is with us.

I tell of Egypt and Babylon
    among those that know the LORD;
Of Philistia, Tyre, Ethiopia:
    "This man was born there."
And of Zion they shall say:

"One and all were born in her;
And he who has established her
is the Most High LORD."

R. God is with us.

They shall note, when the peoples are enrolled:
"This man was born there."
And all shall sing, in their festive dance:
"My home is within you."

R. God is with us.

Alleluia Verse *and* **Gospel,** *p. 1510.*

Year II

FIRST READING

Jb 3:1–3, 11–17, 20–23

Why is light given to the toilers?

A reading from the Book of Job

Job opened his mouth and cursed his day. Job spoke out and said:

Perish the day on which I was born,
the night when they said, "The child is a boy!"

Why did I not perish at birth,
come forth from the womb and expire?

Or why was I not buried away like an untimely birth,
like babes that have never seen the light?

Wherefore did the knees receive me?
or why did I suck at the breasts?

For then I should have lain down and been tranquil;
had I slept, I should then have been at rest

With kings and counselors of the earth
who built where now there are ruins

Or with princes who had gold
  and filled their houses with silver.
There the wicked cease from troubling,
  there the weary are at rest.
Why is light given to the toilers,
  and life to the bitter in spirit?
They wait for death and it comes not;
  they search for it rather than for hidden treasures,
Rejoice in it exultingly,
  and are glad when they reach the grave:
Those whose path is hidden from them,
  and whom God has hemmed in!

The word of the Lord.

Responsorial Psalm

Ps 88:2–3, 4–5, 6, 7–8

R. Let my prayer come before you, Lord.

O LORD, my God, by day I cry out;
  at night I clamor in your presence.
Let my prayer come before you;
  incline your ear to my call for help.

R. Let my prayer come before you, Lord.

For my soul is surfeited with troubles
  and my life draws near to the nether world.
I am numbered with those who go down into the pit;
  I am a man without strength.

R. Let my prayer come before you, Lord.

My couch is among the dead,
  like the slain who lie in the grave,
Whom you remember no longer
  and who are cut off from your care.

R. Let my prayer come before you, Lord.

You have plunged me into the bottom of the pit,
  into the dark abyss.
Upon me your wrath lies heavy,
  and with all your billows you overwhelm me.

  R. Let my prayer come before you, Lord.

> **Alleluia, alleluia**   Mk 10:45
> The Son of Man came to serve
> and to give his life as a ransom for many.
> **Alleluia, alleluia**

Years I and II

GOSPEL   Lk 9:51–56

He resolutely determined to journey to Jerusalem.

A reading from the holy Gospel according to Luke

When the days for Jesus to be taken up were fulfilled, he resolutely determined to journey to Jerusalem, and he sent messengers ahead of him. On the way they entered a Samaritan village to prepare for his reception there, but they would not welcome him because the destination of his journey was Jerusalem. When the disciples James and John saw this they asked, "Lord, do you want us to call down fire from heaven to consume them?" Jesus turned and rebuked them, and they journeyed to another village.

The Gospel of the Lord.

Liturgy of the Eucharist, *p. 897;* **Prayer over the Gifts,** *p. 1500.*

Wednesday

Antiphons and Prayers, *p. 1499;* **Liturgy of the Word** *for Year I (odd years) follows; Year II (even years), p. 1513.*

TODAY'S LIVING WORD

In today's Gospel Luke continues to portray Jesus as a messianic prophet. Already we have seen that like Ezekiel, Jesus the Son of Man hardens his face to go to Jerusalem (21:7–8), where he will be "taken up" to heaven like Elijah (2 Kgs 2:1). In today's selection, the request a would-be follower makes of Jesus reminds us of the request that Elisha made of Elijah, except that where Elisha asks to bid farewell to his father and mother (1 Kgs 19:19–21), the man in the Gospel asks to bury his father. Elisha is allowed to fulfill his filial duty; the would-be disciple is not. There is something greater than Elijah here. The demands of discipleship supersede all other duties.

Like Jesus, Nehemiah in today's reading also sets his face to Jerusalem. He is determined to go there, "to the city of my ancestors' graves, to rebuild it." On the other hand, Job deliberates. He wants to sue God, but has little hope of winning his case, since the defendant would also be the judge! Even he must bow—and beg—before the awesome otherness of God.

Year I

FIRST READING

Neh 2:1–8

If it please the king, send me to the city of my ancestors and I will rebuild it.

A reading from the Book of Nehemiah

In the month Nisan of the twentieth year of King Artaxerxes, when the wine was in my charge, I took some and offered it to the king. As I had never before been sad in his presence, the king asked me, "Why do you look sad? If you are not sick, you must be sad at heart." Though I was seized with great fear, I answered the king: "May the king live forever! How could I not look sad when the city where my ancestors are buried lies in ruins, and its gates have been eaten out by fire?" The king asked me, "What is it, then, that you wish?" I prayed to the God of heaven and then answered the king: "If it please the king, and if your servant is deserving of your favor, send me to Judah, to the city of my ancestors' graves, to rebuild it." Then the king, and the queen seated beside him, asked me how long my journey would take and when I would return. I set a date that was acceptable to him, and the king agreed that I might go.

I asked the king further: "If it please the king, let letters be given to me for the governors of West-of-Euphrates, that they may afford me safe-conduct until I arrive in Judah; also a letter for Asaph, the keeper of the royal park, that he may give me wood for timbering the gates of the temple-citadel and for the city wall and the house that I shall occupy." The king granted my requests, for the favoring hand of my God was upon me. The word of the Lord.

Responsorial Psalm

Ps 137:1–2, 3, 4–5, 6

R. Let my tongue be silenced if I ever forget you!

By the streams of Babylon
  we sat and wept
  when we remembered Zion.
On the aspens of that land
  we hung up our harps.

R. Let my tongue be silenced if I ever forget you!

Though there our captors asked of us
  the lyrics of our songs,
And our despoilers urged us to be joyous:
  "Sing for us the songs of Zion!"

R. Let my tongue be silenced if I ever forget you!

How could we sing a song of the LORD
  in a foreign land?
If I forget you, Jerusalem,
  may my right hand be forgotten!

R. Let my tongue be silenced if I ever forget you!

May my tongue cleave to my palate
  if I remember you not,
If I place not Jerusalem
  ahead of my joy.

R. Let my tongue be silenced if I ever forget you!

Alleluia Verse *and* **Gospel,** *p. 1515.*

Year II

FIRST READING   Jb 9:1–12, 14–16

How can one be justified before God?

A reading from the Book of Job

Job answered his friends and said:

  I know well that it is so;
      but how can a man be justified before God?
  Should one wish to contend with him,
      he could not answer him once in a thousand times.
  God is wise in heart and mighty in strength;
      who has withstood him and remained unscathed?
  He removes the mountains before they know it;
      he overturns them in his anger.
  He shakes the earth out of its place,
      and the pillars beneath it tremble.
  He commands the sun, and it rises not;
      he seals up the stars.

He alone stretches out the heavens
  and treads upon the crests of the sea.
He made the Bear and Orion,
  the Pleiades and the constellations of the south;
He does great things past finding out,
  marvelous things beyond reckoning.

Should he come near me, I see him not;
  should he pass by, I am not aware of him;
Should he seize me forcibly, who can say him nay?
  Who can say to him, "What are you doing?"

How much less shall I give him any answer,
  or choose out arguments against him!
Even though I were right, I could not answer him,
  but should rather beg for what was due me.
If I appealed to him and he answered my call,
  I could not believe that he would hearken
    to my words.

The word of the Lord.

Responsorial Psalm

Ps 88:10bc–11, 12–13, 14–15

R. Let my prayer come before you, Lord.

Daily I call upon you, O LORD;
  to you I stretch out my hands.
Will you work wonders for the dead?
  Will the shades arise to give you thanks?

R. Let my prayer come before you, Lord.

Do they declare your mercy in the grave,
  your faithfulness among those who have perished?
Are your wonders made known in the darkness,
  or your justice in the land of oblivion?

R. Let my prayer come before you, Lord.

But I, O LORD, cry out to you;
 with my morning prayer I wait upon you.
Why, O LORD, do you reject me;
 why hide from me your face?

R. Let my prayer come before you, Lord.

Alleluia, alleluia   Phil 3:8–9
I consider all things so much rubbish
that I may gain Christ and be found in him.
Alleluia, alleluia

Years I and II

GOSPEL   Lk 9:57–62

I will follow you wherever you go.

A reading from the holy Gospel according to Luke

As Jesus and his disciples were proceeding on their journey,
someone said to him, "I will follow you wherever you go."
Jesus answered him, "Foxes have dens and birds of the sky
have nests, but the Son of Man has nowhere to rest his head."
And to another he said, "Follow me." But he replied, "Lord,
let me go first and bury my father." But he answered him, "Let
the dead bury their dead. But you, go and proclaim the Kingdom
of God." And another said, "I will follow you, Lord, but first
let me say farewell to my family at home." Jesus answered
him, "No one who sets a hand to the plow and looks to what
was left behind is fit for the Kingdom of God."
The Gospel of the Lord.

Liturgy of the Eucharist, *p. 897;* **Prayer over the Gifts,** *p. 1500.*

Thursday

Antiphons and Prayers, *p. 1499;* **Liturgy of the Word** *for Year I (odd years) follows; Year II (even years), p. 1518.*

TODAY'S LIVING WORD

Today's selections from Nehemiah and from Luke both concern the proclamation of God's word. In the first reading, Ezra brings the book of the law of God to the whole people gathered in the liturgical assembly. He not only reads from the book, but interprets what is read so that all can understand the word of the Lord. The people weep in repentance, but he tells them this is good news, adding, "Rejoicing in the Lord must be your strength." In the Gospel, Jesus sends the seventy-two to bring to all the nations of the world (cf. Gn 10) the good news that "the Kingdom of God is at hand." They are not only to preach, but to interpret their message by healing the sick as well. This too is good news for those who receive it, but judgment for those who refuse.

Even Job is the bearer of good news in today's reading. "I know that my Vindicator lives," he declares and, although commentators disagree as to who this *go 'el* is, there is no doubt that Job hopes against hope that he will be vindicated. As Karl Barth used to say, "The good news is that the bad news is not the last word."

Year I

FIRST READING   Neh 8:1–4a, 5–6, 7b–12

Ezra opened the book of the law, blessed the LORD,
and all the people answered, Amen! Amen!

A reading from the Book of Nehemiah

The whole people gathered as one in the open space before the Water Gate, and they called upon Ezra the scribe to bring forth the book of the law of Moses which the LORD prescribed for Israel. On the first day of the seventh month, therefore, Ezra the priest brought the law before the assembly, which consisted of men, women, and those children old enough to understand. Standing at one end of the open place that was before the Water Gate, he read out of the book from daybreak until midday, in the presence of the men, the women, and those children old enough to understand; and all the people listened attentively to the book of the law. Ezra the scribe stood on a wooden platform that had been made for the occasion. He opened the scroll so that all the people might see it (for he was standing higher up than any of the people); and, as he opened it, all the people rose. Ezra blessed the LORD, the great God, and all the people, their hands raised high, answered, "Amen, amen!" Then they bowed down and prostrated themselves before the LORD, their faces to the ground. As the people remained in their places, Ezra read plainly from the book of the law of God, interpreting it so that all could understand what was read. Then Nehemiah, that is, His Excellency, and Ezra the priest-scribe and the Levites who were instructing the people said to all the people: "Today is holy to the LORD your God. Do not be sad, and do not weep"——for all the people were weeping as they heard the words of the law. He said further: "Go, eat rich foods and drink sweet drinks, and allot portions to those who had nothing prepared; for today is holy to our LORD. Do not be saddened this day, for rejoicing in the LORD must be your strength!" And the Levites quieted all the people, saying, "Hush, for today is holy, and you must not be saddened." Then all the people went to eat and drink, to distribute portions, and to celebrate with great joy, for they understood the words that had been expounded to them.

The word of the Lord.

Responsorial Psalm

Ps 19:8, 9, 10, 11

R. The precepts of the Lord give joy to the heart.

The law of the LORD is perfect,
  refreshing the soul;
The decree of the LORD is trustworthy,
  giving wisdom to the simple.

R. The precepts of the Lord give joy to the heart.

The precepts of the LORD are right,
  rejoicing the heart;
The command of the LORD is clear,
  enlightening the eye;

R. The precepts of the Lord give joy to the heart.

The fear of the LORD is pure,
  enduring forever;
The ordinances of the LORD are true,
  all of them just.

R. The precepts of the Lord give joy to the heart.

They are more precious than gold,
  than a heap of purest gold;
Sweeter also than syrup
  or honey from the comb.

R. The precepts of the Lord give joy to the heart.

Alleluia Verse *and* **Gospel,** *p. 1520.*

Year II

FIRST READING

Jb 19:21–27

I know that my Vindicator lives.

A reading from the Book of Job

Job said:

> Pity me, pity me, O you my friends,
>   for the hand of God has struck me!

Why do you hound me as though you were divine,
  and insatiably prey upon me?

Oh, would that my words were written down!
  Would that they were inscribed in a record:
That with an iron chisel and with lead
  they were cut in the rock forever!
But as for me, I know that my Vindicator lives,
  and that he will at last stand forth upon the dust;
Whom I myself shall see:
  my own eyes, not another's, shall behold him,
And from my flesh I shall see God;
  my inmost being is consumed with longing.

The word of the Lord.

Responsorial Psalm

Ps 27:7–8a, 8b–9abc, 13–14

**R. I believe that I shall see the good things of the Lord
  in the land of the living.**

Hear, O LORD, the sound of my call;
  have pity on me, and answer me.
Of you my heart speaks; you my glance seeks.

**R. I believe that I shall see the good things of the Lord
  in the land of the living.**

Your presence, O LORD, I seek.
Hide not your face from me;
  do not in anger repel your servant.
You are my helper: cast me not off.

**R. I believe that I shall see the good things of the Lord
  in the land of the living.**

I believe that I shall see the bounty of the LORD
  in the land of the living.
Wait for the LORD with courage;
  be stouthearted, and wait for the LORD.

**R. I believe that I shall see the good things of the Lord
in the land of the living.**

Alleluia, alleluia Mk 1:15
The Kingdom of God is at hand;
repent and believe in the Gospel.
Alleluia, alleluia

Years I and II

GOSPEL   Lk 10:1–12
Your peace will rest on him.

A reading from the holy Gospel according to Luke

Jesus appointed seventy-two other disciples whom he sent
ahead of him in pairs to every town and place he intended to
visit. He said to them, "The harvest is abundant but the laborers are few; so ask the master of the harvest to send out
laborers for his harvest. Go on your way; behold, I am sending
you like lambs among wolves. Carry no money bag, no sack,
no sandals; and greet no one along the way. Into whatever house
you enter, first say, 'Peace to this household.' If a peaceful
person lives there, your peace will rest on him; but if not, it
will return to you. Stay in the same house and eat and drink
what is offered to you, for the laborer deserves his payment.
Do not move about from one house to another. Whatever town
you enter and they welcome you, eat what is set before you,
cure the sick in it and say to them, 'The Kingdom of God is at
hand for you.' Whatever town you enter and they do not receive
you, go out into the streets and say, 'The dust of your town
that clings to our feet, even that we shake off against you.' Yet
know this: the Kingdom of God is at hand. I tell you, it will be
more tolerable for Sodom on that day than for that town."

The Gospel of the Lord.

Liturgy of the Eucharist, *p. 897;* **Prayer over the Gifts**, *p. 1500.*

Friday

Antiphons and Prayers, *p. 1499;* **Liturgy of the Word** *for Year I (odd years) follows; Year II (even years), p. 1523.*

TODAY'S LIVING WORD

All three of today's readings announce dire consequences for the wicked, who fail to hear or to heed the word of God. The passage from Baruch is a penitential prayer, a confession of sin that spans "the time [when] the Lord led our ancestors out of the land of Egypt until the present day," that is, the time of the exile in Babylon. He says that evil clings to them because "we have been disobedient to the Lord...and only too ready to disregard his voice." In Job, the command of the Lord is heard and heeded by the morning that at dawn colors the earth "as though it were a garment," but withholds light from sinners and shatters their pride, shaking them from the surface of the earth. In the Gospel, Jesus says that the same fate will befall Chorazin, Bethsaida, and Capernaum. They will "go down to the netherworld" because they have rejected the word of life.

The readings call us in turn to heed those whom Jesus has sent to speak his word to us. To hear him is to hear him, and the One who sent him.

Year I

FIRST READING

Bar 1:15–22

We have sinned in the Lord's sight and disobeyed him.

A reading from the Book of the Prophet Baruch

During the Babylonian captivity, the exiles prayed: "Justice is with the Lord, our God; and we today are flushed with shame, we men of Judah and citizens of Jerusalem, that we, with our kings and rulers and priests and prophets, and with our ancestors, have sinned in the Lord's sight and disobeyed him. We have neither heeded the voice of the Lord, our God, nor followed the precepts which the Lord set before us. From the time the Lord led our ancestors out of the land of Egypt until the present day, we have been disobedient to the Lord, our God, and only too ready to disregard his voice. And the evils and the curse that the Lord enjoined upon Moses, his servant, at the time he led our ancestors forth from the land of Egypt to give us the land flowing with milk and honey, cling to us even today. For we did not heed the voice of the Lord, our God, in all the words of the prophets whom he sent us, but each one of us went off after the devices of his own wicked heart, served other gods, and did evil in the sight of the Lord, our God."

The word of the Lord.

Responsional Psalm

Ps 79:1b–2, 3–5, 8, 9

R. For the glory of your name, O Lord, deliver us.

O God, the nations have come into your inheritance;
   they have defiled your holy temple,
   they have laid Jerusalem in ruins.
They have given the corpses of your servants
   as food to the birds of heaven,
   the flesh of your faithful ones to the beasts of the earth.

R. For the glory of your name, O Lord, deliver us.

They have poured out their blood like water
   round about Jerusalem,
   and there is no one to bury them.
We have become the reproach of our neighbors,
   the scorn and derision of those around us.
O LORD, how long? Will you be angry forever?
   Will your jealousy burn like fire?

R. For the glory of your name, O Lord, deliver us.

Remember not against us the iniquities of the past;
   may your compassion quickly come to us,
   for we are brought very low.

R. For the glory of your name, O Lord, deliver us.

Help us, O God our savior,
  because of the glory of your name;
Deliver us and pardon our sins
  for your name's sake.

R. For the glory of your name, O Lord, deliver us.

Alleluia Verse *and* **Gospel,** *p. 1525.*

Year II

FIRST READING   Jb 38:1, 12 – 21; 40:3–5

*Have you ever in your lifetime commanded the morning
and entered into the sources of the sea?*

A reading from the Book of Job

The LORD addressed Job out of the storm and said:

Have you ever in your lifetime commanded the morning
    and shown the dawn its place
For taking hold of the ends of the earth,
    till the wicked are shaken from its surface?
The earth is changed as is clay by the seal,
    and dyed as though it were a garment;
But from the wicked the light is withheld,
    and the arm of pride is shattered.

Have you entered into the sources of the sea,
    or walked about in the depths of the abyss?
Have the gates of death been shown to you,
    or have you seen the gates of darkness?
Have you comprehended the breadth of the earth?
    Tell me, if you know all:

Which is the way to the dwelling place of light,
    and where is the abode of darkness,
That you may take them to their boundaries
    and set them on their homeward paths?
You know, because you were born before them,
    and the number of your years is great!

Then Job answered the LORD and said:

Behold, I am of little account; what can I answer you?
    I put my hand over my mouth.
Though I have spoken once, I will not do so again;
    though twice, I will do so no more.

The word of the Lord.

Responsorial Psalm

Ps 139:1–3, 7–8, 9–10, 13–14ab

R. Guide me, Lord, along the everlasting way.

O LORD, you have probed me and you know me;
    you know when I sit and when I stand;
    you understand my thoughts from afar.
My journeys and my rest you scrutinize,
    with all my ways you are familiar.

R. Guide me, Lord, along the everlasting way.

Where can I go from your spirit?
    From your presence where can I flee?
If I go up to the heavens, you are there;
    if I sink to the nether world, you are present there.

R. Guide me, Lord, along the everlasting way.

If I take the wings of the dawn,
    if I settle at the farthest limits of the sea,
Even there your hand shall guide me,
    and your right hand hold me fast.

R. Guide me, Lord, along the everlasting way.

Truly you have formed my inmost being;
 you knit me in my mother's womb.
I give you thanks that I am fearfully, wonderfully made;
 wonderful are your works.

R. Guide me, Lord, along the everlasting way.

Alleluia, alleluia Ps 95:8
If today you hear his voice,
harden not your hearts.
Alleluia, alleluia

Years I and II

GOSPEL   Lk 10:13–16

Whoever rejects me rejects the one who sent me.

A reading from the holy Gospel according to Luke

Jesus said to them, "Woe to you, Chorazin! Woe to you, Bethsaida! For if the mighty deeds done in your midst had been done in Tyre and Sidon, they would long ago have repented, sitting in sackcloth and ashes. But it will be more tolerable for Tyre and Sidon at the judgment than for you. And as for you, Capernaum, 'Will you be exalted to heaven? You will go down to the netherworld.' Whoever listens to you listens to me. Whoever rejects you rejects me. And whoever rejects me rejects the one who sent me."

The Gospel of the Lord.

Liturgy of the Eucharist, *p. 897;* **Prayer over the Gifts,** *p. 1500.*

Saturday

Antiphons and Prayers, *p. 1499;* **Liturgy of the Word** *for Year I (odd years) follows; Year II (even years), p. 1528.*

TODAY'S LIVING WORD

Each of today's readings promises a happy ending. The passage from Baruch depicts the city of Jerusalem as a widow bereft of her children, who have been taken into exile because of their sins. Framing her lament are the prophet's words of reassurance: "Fear not," he tells the people, "for he who has brought disaster upon you will, in saving you, bring you back enduring joy." The Book of Job also ends on a happy note in the other first reading for today. Once bereft of his children like Jerusalem, Job is given back in his last days the joy of his earlier ones, and more.

The return of the seventy-two disciples, after their first foray into the mission field, fills Jesus with joy in today's Gospel. He rejoices in God's victory over Satan and in the part his own disciples have played in it. The joy of Jesus here is *agalliasis,* that is, joy that originates, not in the self, but in the Spirit. It is grateful praise, the enduring joy that God evokes in saving us.

Year I

FIRST READING

Bar 4:5–12, 27–29

*He who brought disaster upon you will bring you back
enduring joy.*

A reading from the Book of the Prophet Baruch

Fear not, my people!

Remember, Israel,

You were sold to the nations

not for your destruction;

It was because you angered God

that you were handed over to your foes.

For you provoked your Maker
  with sacrifices to demons, to no-gods;
You forsook the Eternal God who nourished you,
  and you grieved Jerusalem who fostered you.
She indeed saw coming upon you
  the anger of God; and she said:

"Hear, you neighbors of Zion!
  God has brought great mourning upon me,
For I have seen the captivity
  that the Eternal God has brought
  upon my sons and daughters.
With joy I fostered them;
  but with mourning and lament I let them go.
Let no one gloat over me, a widow,
  bereft of many:
For the sins of my children I am left desolate,
  because they turned from the law of God.

Fear not, my children; call out to God!
  He who brought this upon you will remember you.
As your hearts have been disposed to stray from God,
  turn now ten times the more to seek him;
For he who has brought disaster upon you
  will, in saving you, bring you back enduring joy."
The word of the Lord.

Responsorial Psalm

Ps 69:33–35, 36–37

R. The Lord listens to the poor.
"See, you lowly ones, and be glad;
  you who seek God, may your hearts revive!

For the LORD hears the poor,
    and his own who are in bonds he spurns not.
Let the heavens and the earth praise him,
    the seas and whatever moves in them!"

   R. The Lord listens to the poor.

For God will save Zion
    and rebuild the cities of Judah.
They shall dwell in the land and own it,
    and the descendants of his servants shall inherit it,
    and those who love his name shall inhabit it.

   R. The Lord listens to the poor.

   Alleluia Verse *and* **Gospel,** *p. 1530.*

_____

                                                  Year II

FIRST READING   Jb 42:1–3, 5–6, 12–17

   But now my eye has seen you and I disown what I have said.

A reading from the Book of Job

Job answered the LORD and said:

    I know that you can do all things,
        and that no purpose of yours can be hindered.
    I have dealt with great things that I do not understand;
        things too wonderful for me, which I cannot know.
    I had heard of you by word of mouth,
        but now my eye has seen you.
    Therefore I disown what I have said,
        and repent in dust and ashes.

    Thus the LORD blessed the latter days of Job more than his
earlier ones. For he had fourteen thousand sheep, six thousand
camels, a thousand yoke of oxen, and a thousand she-asses.

And he had seven sons and three daughters, of whom he called the first Jemimah, the second Keziah, and the third Keren-happuch. In all the land no other women were as beautiful as the daughters of Job; and their father gave them an inheritance along with their brothers. After this, Job lived a hundred and forty years; and he saw his children, his grandchildren, and even his great-grandchildren. Then Job died, old and full of years.

The word of the Lord.

Responsorial Psalm
Ps 119:66, 71, 75, 91, 125, 130

R. Lord, let your face shine on me.

Teach me wisdom and knowledge,
 for in your commands I trust.

R. Lord, let your face shine on me.

It is good for me that I have been afflicted,
 that I may learn your statutes.

R. Lord, let your face shine on me.

I know, O LORD, that your ordinances are just,
 and in your faithfulness you have afflicted me.

R. Lord, let your face shine on me.

According to your ordinances they still stand firm:
 all things serve you.

R. Lord, let your face shine on me.

I am your servant; give me discernment
 that I may know your decrees.

R. Lord, let your face shine on me.

The revelation of your words sheds light,
 giving understanding to the simple.

R. Lord, let your face shine on me.

Alleluia, alleluia See Mt 11:25
Blessed are you, Father, Lord of heaven and earth,
you have revealed to little ones the mysteries of the Kingdom.
Alleluia, alleluia

Years I and II

GOSPEL   Lk 10:17–24

Rejoice because your names are written in heaven.

A reading from the holy Gospel according to Luke

The seventy-two disciples returned rejoicing and said to Jesus,
"Lord, even the demons are subject to us because of your
name." Jesus said, "I have observed Satan fall like lightning
from the sky. Behold, I have given you the power 'to tread
upon serpents' and scorpions and upon the full force of the
enemy and nothing will harm you. Nevertheless, do not rejoice
because the spirits are subject to you, but rejoice because your
names are written in heaven."

At that very moment he rejoiced in the Holy Spirit and said,
"I give you praise, Father, Lord of heaven and earth, for
although you have hidden these things from the wise and the
learned you have revealed them to the childlike. Yes, Father,
such has been your gracious will. All things have been handed
over to me by my Father. No one knows who the Son is except
the Father, and who the Father is except the Son and anyone to
whom the Son wishes to reveal him."

Turning to the disciples in private he said, "Blessed are the
eyes that see what you see. For I say to you, many prophets
and kings desired to see what you see, but did not see it, and to
hear what you hear, but did not hear it."

The Gospel of the Lord.

Liturgy of the Eucharist, *p. 897;* **Prayer over the Gifts,** *p. 1500.*

TWENTY-SEVENTH WEEK
IN ORDINARY TIME

The **Antiphons and Prayers** *may be the following, or may be chosen from any of the other 33 weeks in Ordinary Time (refer to Liturgical Calendar, pp. 26–41).*

The **Liturgy of the Word** *varies: for Monday, see p. 1533; Tuesday, p. 1538; Wednesday, p. 1543; Thursday, p. 1547; Friday, p. 1552; Saturday, p. 1557.*

Entrance Antiphon

O Lord, you have given everything its place in the world, and no one can make it otherwise. For it is your creation, the heavens and the earth and the stars: you are the Lord of all.

(Est 13:9, 10–11)

Opening Prayer

Let us pray
[that God will forgive our failings
and bring us peace]

Pause for silent prayer.

Father,
your love for us
surpasses all our hopes and desires.
Forgive our failings,
keep us in your peace
and lead us in the way of salvation.
We ask this through our Lord Jesus Christ, your Son,
who lives and reigns with you and the Holy Spirit,
one God, for ever and ever.

Alternative Opening Prayer

Let us pray
[before the face of God,
in trusting faith]

Pause for silent prayer.

Almighty and eternal God,
Father of the world to come,
your goodness is beyond what our spirit can touch
and your strength is more than the mind can bear.
Lead us to seek beyond our reach
and give us the courage to stand before your truth.

We ask this through Christ our Lord.

Prayer over the Gifts

Pray, brethren...

Father,
receive these gifts
which our Lord Jesus Christ
has asked us to offer in his memory.
May our obedient service
bring us to the fullness of your redemption.

We ask this in the name of Jesus the Lord.

Preface of Weekdays in Ordinary Time I–VI, *pp. 948–950.*

Communion Antiphon

The Lord is good to those who hope in him, to those who are
searching for his love.   (Lam 3:25)

Or:

Because there is one bread, we, though many, are one body, for
we all share in the one loaf and in the one cup.   (See 1 Cor 10:17)

Prayer after Communion

Let us pray.

Pause for silent prayer, if this has not preceded.

Almighty God,
let the eucharist we share
fill us with your life.

May the love of Christ
which we celebrate here
touch our lives and lead us to you.

We ask this in the name of Jesus the Lord.

Monday

Antiphons and Prayers, *p. 1531;* **Liturgy of the Word** *for Year I (odd years) follows; Year II (even years), p. 1536.*

TODAY'S LIVING WORD

The story of Jonah and the parable of the Good Samaritan both share an element of surprise. Commanded by God to preach to the Ninevites, a people the Israelites hated for their cruelty to the nations they conquered, Jonah makes for Tarshish. While he sleeps in the hold of the ship, a violent storm threatens to destroy him and everyone else aboard. The crew soon discovers that Jonah's flight from God has placed them in peril. But the unexpected humanity of these pagan sailors surprises the reader. They throw Jonah into the sea with great reluctance and only as a last resort. Similarly in the parable of Jesus, the surprise lies in the unexpected humanity of the hated Samaritan. Both stories aim to shock their hearers into new ways of seeing and acting.

Paul based his entire apostolate on this new way of seeing and acting. He proclaimed to the Galatians the Gospel he received as a revelation from Jesus Christ: that salvation is possible for all human beings who actively love God and neighbor.

Year I

FIRST READING
Jon 1:1—2:1-2, 11

But Jonah made ready to flee away from the LORD.

A reading from the beginning of the Book of the Prophet Jonah

This is the word of the LORD that came to Jonah, son of Amittai:

"Set out for the great city of Nineveh, and preach against

it; their wickedness has come up before me." But Jonah made ready to flee to Tarshish away from the LORD. He went down to Joppa, found a ship going to Tarshish, paid the fare, and went aboard to journey with them to Tarshish, away from the LORD.

The LORD, however, hurled a violent wind upon the sea, and in the furious tempest that arose the ship was on the point of breaking up. Then the mariners became frightened and each one cried to his god. To lighten the ship for themselves, they threw its cargo into the sea. Meanwhile, Jonah had gone down into the hold of the ship, and lay there fast asleep. The captain came to him and said, "What are you doing asleep? Rise up, call upon your God! Perhaps God will be mindful of us so that we may not perish."

Then they said to one another, "Come, let us cast lots to find out on whose account we have met with this misfortune." So they cast lots, and thus singled out Jonah. "Tell us," they said, "what is your business? Where do you come from? What is your country, and to what people do you belong?" Jonah answered them, "I am a Hebrew, I worship the LORD, the God of heaven, who made the sea and the dry land."

Now the men were seized with great fear and said to him, "How could you do such a thing!"—They knew that he was fleeing from the LORD, because he had told them.—They asked, "What shall we do with you, that the sea may quiet down for us?" For the sea was growing more and more turbulent. Jonah said to them, "Pick me up and throw me into the sea, that it may quiet down for you; since I know it is because of me that this violent storm has come upon you."

Still the men rowed hard to regain the land, but they could not, for the sea grew ever more turbulent. Then they cried to the LORD: "We beseech you, O LORD, let us not perish for taking this man's life; do not charge us with shedding innocent blood, for you, Lord, have done as you saw fit." Then they took Jonah and threw him into the sea, and the sea's raging abated. Struck with great fear of the Lord, the men offered sacrifice and made vows to him.

But the Lord sent a large fish, that swallowed Jonah; and Jonah remained in the belly of the fish three days and three nights. From the belly of the fish Jonah prayed to the Lord, his God. Then the Lord commanded the fish to spew Jonah upon the shore.

The word of the Lord.

Responsorial Psalm
Jon 2:3, 4, 5, 8

R. You will rescue my life from the pit, O Lord.

Out of my distress I called to the Lord,
  and he answered me;
From the midst of the nether world I cried for help,
  and you heard my voice.

R. You will rescue my life from the pit, O Lord.

For you cast me into the deep, into the heart of the sea,
  and the flood enveloped me;
All your breakers and your billows
  passed over me.

R. You will rescue my life from the pit, O Lord.

Then I said, "I am banished from your sight!
  yet would I again look upon your holy temple."

R. You will rescue my life from the pit, O Lord.

When my soul fainted within me,
  I remembered the Lord;
My prayer reached you
  in your holy temple.

R. You will rescue my life from the pit, O Lord.

Alleluia Verse *and* **Gospel,** *p. 1537.*

FIRST READING

Gal 1:6–12

*The Gospel preached by me is not of human origin
but through a revelation of Jesus Christ.*

A reading from the Letter of Saint Paul to the Galatians

Brothers and sisters:

I am amazed that you are so quickly forsaking the one who called you by the grace of Christ for a different gospel (not that there is another). But there are some who are disturbing you and wish to pervert the Gospel of Christ. But even if we or an angel from heaven should preach to you a gospel other than the one that we preached to you, let that one be accursed! As we have said before, and now I say again, if anyone preaches to you a gospel other than the one that you received, let that one be accursed!

Am I now currying favor with human beings or God? Or am I seeking to please people? If I were still trying to please people, I would not be a slave of Christ.

Now I want you to know, brothers and sisters, that the Gospel preached by me is not of human origin. For I did not receive it from a human being, nor was I taught it, but it came through a revelation of Jesus Christ.

The word of the Lord.

Responsorial Psalm

Ps 111:1b–2, 7–8, 9 and 10c

R. **The Lord will remember his covenant for ever.**

I will give thanks to the LORD with all my heart
　in the company and assembly of the just.
Great are the works of the LORD,
　exquisite in all their delights.

R. **The Lord will remember his covenant for ever.**

The works of his hands are faithful and just;
  sure are all his precepts,
Reliable forever and ever,
  wrought in truth and equity.

R. The Lord will remember his covenant for ever.

He has sent deliverance to his people;
  he has ratified his covenant forever;
  holy and awesome is his name.
His praise endures forever.

R. The Lord will remember his covenant for ever.

Or: **R. Alleluia.**

> **Alleluia, alleluia** Jn 13:34
> I give you a new commandment:
> love one another as I have loved you.
> **Alleluia, alleluia**

Years I and II

GOSPEL   Lk 10:25–37

Who is my neighbor?

A reading from the holy Gospel according to Luke

There was a scholar of the law who stood up to test Jesus and said, "Teacher, what must I do to inherit eternal life?" Jesus said to him, "What is written in the law? How do you read it?" He said in reply, "You shall love the Lord, your God, with all your heart, with all your being, with all your strength, and with all your mind, and your neighbor as yourself." He replied to him, "You have answered correctly; do this and you will live."

But because he wished to justify himself, he said to Jesus, "And who is my neighbor?" Jesus replied, "A man fell victim to robbers as he went down from Jerusalem to Jericho. They stripped and beat him and went off leaving him half-dead. A priest happened to be going down that road, but when he saw him, he passed by on the opposite side. Likewise a Levite came to the place, and when he saw him, he passed by on the opposite side. But a Samaritan traveler who came upon him was moved with compassion at the sight. He approached the victim, poured oil and wine over his wounds and bandaged them. Then he lifted him up on his own animal, took him to an inn, and cared for him. The next day he took out two silver coins and gave them to the innkeeper with the instruction, 'Take care of him. If you spend more than what I have given you, I shall repay you on my way back.' Which of these three, in your opinion, was neighbor to the robbers' victim?" He answered, "The one who treated him with mercy." Jesus said to him, "Go and do likewise."

The Gospel of the Lord.

Liturgy of the Eucharist, *p. 897;* **Prayer over the Gifts,** *p. 1532.*

Tuesday

Antiphons and Prayers, *p. 1531;* **Liturgy of the Word** *for Year I (odd years) follows; Year II (even years), p. 1541.*

TODAY'S LIVING WORD

The theme of repentance marks the two first readings for today. The selection from Jonah describes the conversion of Nineveh. Like everything else in this humorous book, this too is told with deliberate exaggeration. This "enormously large" city experiences a total repentance that extends to all, great and small, man and beast alike. Such repentance moves God to repent as well and Nineveh is spared. The excerpt from Galatians relates the conversion of Paul. The text deliberately emphasizes the totality that seems to have characterized Paul, such as his persecution of the Church "beyond measure" because he was "even more a zealot" as a fervent Jew. But such totality must have attracted the grace of God, for Paul is called to spread the Gospel among the Gentiles.

Today's Gospel is a lesson on hospitality. Jesus teaches Martha that the one thing hospitality requires is wholly attending to the guest, as Mary is doing. Yet this may teach us about repentance too. The conversion required of most of us is not dramatic, like Nineveh's or Paul's. It may only require that we learn to give our undivided attention to the Guest who already dwells in our anxious and busy hearts.

Year I

FIRST READING   Jon 3:1–10

The Ninevites turned from their evil way and God
repented of the evil he had threatened.

A reading from the Book of the Prophet Jonah

The word of the LORD came to Jonah a second time: "Set out for the great city of Nineveh, and announce to it the message that I will tell you." So Jonah made ready and went to Nineveh, according to the LORD's bidding. Now Nineveh was an enormously large city; it took three days to go through it. Jonah began his journey through the city, and had gone but a single day's walk announcing, "Forty days more and Nineveh shall be destroyed," when the people of Nineveh believed God; they proclaimed a fast and all of them, great and small, put on sackcloth.

When the news reached the king of Nineveh, he rose from his throne, laid aside his robe, covered himself with sackcloth, and sat in the ashes. Then he had this proclaimed throughout Nineveh, by decree of the king and his nobles: "Neither man nor beast, neither cattle nor sheep, shall taste anything; they shall not eat, nor shall they drink water. Man and beast shall be covered with sackcloth and call loudly to God; every man shall turn from his evil way and from the violence he has in hand. Who knows, God may relent and forgive, and withhold his blazing wrath, so that we shall not perish." When God saw by their actions how they turned from their evil way, he repented of the evil that he had threatened to do to them; he did not carry it out.

The word of the Lord.

Responsorial Psalm

Ps 130:1b–2, 3–4ab, 7–8

R. **If you, O Lord, mark iniquities, who can stand?**

Out of the depths I cry to you, O LORD;
  LORD, hear my voice!
Let your ears be attentive
  to my voice in supplication.

R. **If you, O Lord, mark iniquities, who can stand?**

If you, O LORD, mark iniquities,
  LORD, who can stand?
But with you is forgiveness,
  that you may be revered.

R. **If you, O Lord, mark iniquities, who can stand?**

Let Israel wait for the LORD,
For with the LORD is kindness
  and with him is plenteous redemption;
And he will redeem Israel
  from all their iniquities.

R. **If you, O Lord, mark iniquities, who can stand?**

Alleluia Verse *and* **Gospel,** *p. 1542.*

Year II

FIRST READING

Gal 1:13–24

God was pleased to reveal his Son to me,
so that I might proclaim him to the Gentiles.

A reading from the Letter of Saint Paul to the Galatians

Brothers and sisters:

You heard of my former way of life in Judaism, how I persecuted the Church of God beyond measure and tried to destroy it, and progressed in Judaism beyond many of my contemporaries among my race, since I was even more a zealot for my ancestral traditions. But when he, who from my mother's womb had set me apart and called me through his grace, was pleased to reveal his Son to me, so that I might proclaim him to the Gentiles, I did not immediately consult flesh and blood, nor did I go up to Jerusalem to those who were Apostles before me; rather, I went into Arabia and then returned to Damascus.

Then after three years I went up to Jerusalem to confer with Cephas and remained with him for fifteen days. But I did not see any other of the Apostles, only James the brother of the Lord. (As to what I am writing to you, behold, before God, I am not lying.) Then I went into the regions of Syria and Cilicia. And I was unknown personally to the churches of Judea that are in Christ; they only kept hearing that "the one who once was persecuting us is now preaching the faith he once tried to destroy." So they glorified God because of me.

The word of the Lord.

Responsorial Psalm

Ps 139:1b–3, 13–14ab, 14c–15

R. **Guide me, Lord, along the everlasting way.**

O LORD, you have probed me and you know me;
  you know when I sit and when I stand;
  you understand my thoughts from afar.
My journeys and my rest you scrutinize,
  with all my ways you are familiar.

R. Guide me, Lord, along the everlasting way.

Truly you have formed my inmost being;
  you knit me in my mother's womb.
I give you thanks that I am fearfully, wonderfully made;
  wonderful are your works.

R. Guide me, Lord, along the everlasting way.

My soul also you knew full well;
  nor was my frame unknown to you
When I was made in secret,
  when I was fashioned in the depths of the earth.

R. Guide me, Lord, along the everlasting way.

Alleluia, alleluia Lk 11:28
Blessed are those who hear the word of God
and observe it.
Alleluia, alleluia

Years I and II

GOSPEL Lk 10:38–42

Martha welcomed him into her house.
Mary has chosen the better part.

A reading from the holy Gospel according to Luke

Jesus entered a village where a woman whose name was Martha
welcomed him. She had a sister named Mary who sat beside
the Lord at his feet listening to him speak. Martha, burdened
with much serving, came to him and said, "Lord, do you not
care that my sister has left me by myself to do the serving?
Tell her to help me." The Lord said to her in reply, "Martha,

Martha, you are anxious and worried about many things. There is need of only one thing. Mary has chosen the better part and it will not be taken from her."
The Gospel of the Lord.

Liturgy of the Eucharist, *p. 897;* **Prayer over the Gifts,** *p. 1532.*

Wednesday

Antiphons and Prayers, *p. 1531;* **Liturgy of the Word** *for Year I (odd years) follows; Year II (even years), p. 1545.*

TODAY'S LIVING WORD

The prayer that Jesus teaches his disciples in today's Gospel is typically Jewish. The first two petitions of the Lord's Prayer—"hallowed be your name / your Kingdom come"— are paralleled in the Jewish prayer called the *kaddish*. It begins, "Magnified and sanctified be his great Name," and goes on, "May he establish his kingdom during your life and during your days and during the life of all the house of Israel." The Jewishness of Jesus gives us a key to understand the controversy Paul reports in today's passage from Galatians. The first followers of Jesus were Jews, like him. Their mission was limited to the Jews, like Jesus' mission during his earthly life. Paul's mission to the Gentiles challenged the nascent Church to make an imaginative leap of faith in a new direction. It would require an education of the heart.

The Book of Jonah describes the education of Jonah's heart. Jonah seems unable to imagine God's desire to save all people, even Ninevites. Loving and losing the gourd plant gives Jonah an inkling of God's love for all and of God's reluctance to lose any.

Year I

FIRST READING
Jon 4:1–11

You are concerned over a plant.
And should I not be concerned over Nineveh, the great city?

A reading from the Book of the Prophet Jonah

Jonah was greatly displeased and became angry that God did not carry out the evil he threatened against Nineveh. He prayed, "I beseech you, LORD, is not this what I said while I was still in my own country? This is why I fled at first to Tarshish. I knew that you are a gracious and merciful God, slow to anger, rich in clemency, loathe to punish. And now, LORD, please take my life from me; for it is better for me to die than to live." But the LORD asked, "Have you reason to be angry?"

Jonah then left the city for a place to the east of it, where he built himself a hut and waited under it in the shade, to see what would happen to the city. And when the LORD God provided a gourd plant that grew up over Jonah's head, giving shade that relieved him of any discomfort, Jonah was very happy over the plant. But the next morning at dawn God sent a worm that attacked the plant, so that it withered. And when the sun arose, God sent a burning east wind; and the sun beat upon Jonah's head till he became faint. Then Jonah asked for death, saying, "I would be better off dead than alive."

But God said to Jonah, "Have you reason to be angry over the plant?" "I have reason to be angry," Jonah answered, "angry enough to die." Then the LORD said, "You are concerned over the plant which cost you no labor and which you did not raise; it came up in one night and in one night it perished. And should I not be concerned over Nineveh, the great city, in which there are more than a hundred and twenty thousand persons who cannot distinguish their right hand from their left, not to mention the many cattle?"

The word of the Lord.

Responsorial Psalm

Ps 86:3–4, 5–6, 9–10

R. Lord, you are merciful and gracious.

Have mercy on me, O Lord,
  for to you I call all the day.
Gladden the soul of your servant,
  for to you, O Lord, I lift up my soul.

R. Lord, you are merciful and gracious.

For you, O Lord, are good and forgiving,
  abounding in kindness to all who call upon you.
Hearken, O Lord, to my prayer
  and attend to the sound of my pleading.

R. Lord, you are merciful and gracious.

All the nations you have made shall come
  and worship you, O Lord,
  and glorify your name.
For you are great, and you do wondrous deeds;
  you alone are God.

R. Lord, you are merciful and gracious.

Alleluia Verse *and* **Gospel,** *p. 1547.*

Year II

FIRST READING

Gal 2:1–2, 7–14

They recognized the grace bestowed upon me.

A reading from the Letter of Saint Paul to the Galatians

Brothers and sisters:

After fourteen years I again went up to Jerusalem with Barnabas, taking Titus along also. I went up in accord with a revelation, and I presented to them the Gospel that I preach to the Gentiles—but privately to those of repute—so that I might not be running, or have run, in vain. On the contrary, when they saw that I had been entrusted with the Gospel to the uncircumcised, just as Peter to the circumcised, for the one who worked in Peter for an apostolate to the circumcised worked also in me for the Gentiles, and when they recognized the grace bestowed upon me, James and Cephas and John, who were reputed to be pillars, gave me and Barnabas their right hands in partnership, that we should go to the Gentiles and they to the circumcised. Only, we were to be mindful of the poor, which is the very thing I was eager to do.

And when Cephas came to Antioch, I opposed him to his face because he clearly was wrong. For, until some people came from James, he used to eat with the Gentiles; but when they came, he began to draw back and separated himself, because he was afraid of the circumcised. And the rest of the Jews acted hypocritically along with him, with the result that even Barnabas was carried away by their hypocrisy. But when I saw that they were not on the right road in line with the truth of the Gospel, I said to Cephas in front of all, "If you, though a Jew, are living like a Gentile and not like a Jew, how can you compel the Gentiles to live like Jews?"

The word of the Lord.

Responsorial Psalm
Ps 117:1bc, 2

R. Go out to all the world, and tell the Good News.

Praise the Lord, all you nations,
  glorify him, all you peoples!

R. Go out to all the world, and tell the Good News.

For steadfast is his kindness toward us,
  and the fidelity of the Lord endures forever.

R. Go out to all the world, and tell the Good News.

Alleluia, alleluia   Rom 8:15bc
You have received a spirit of adoption as sons
through which we cry: Abba! Father!
Alleluia, alleluia

Years I and II

GOSPEL   Lk 11:1–4

Lord, teach us to pray.

A reading from the holy Gospel according to Luke

Jesus was praying in a certain place, and when he had finished, one of his disciples said to him, "Lord, teach us to pray just as John taught his disciples." He said to them, "When you pray, say:

> Father, hallowed be your name,
>> your Kingdom come.
>> Give us each day our daily bread
>> and forgive us our sins
>> for we ourselves forgive everyone in debt to us,
>> and do not subject us to the final test."

The Gospel of the Lord.

Liturgy of the Eucharist, *p. 897;* **Prayer over the Gifts,** *p. 1532.*

Thursday

Antiphons and Prayers, *p. 1531;* **Liturgy of the Word** *for Year I (odd years) follows; Year II (even years), p. 1550.*

TODAY'S LIVING WORD

Both the prophet we know as Malachi and the Apostle Paul are addressing recalcitrant members of their respective communities in today's two first readings. The prophet speaks to a post-exilic community of Jews, some of whom are struggling with the age-old question of why the wicked prosper. Disgruntled, they declare they have nothing to gain by keeping God's command. Malachi distinguishes between these scoffers and those who fear God, who alone are designated as God's "special possession." Paul scolds the Gentile Christians of Galatia for succumbing to the influence of "Judaizers"—those who believed that Gentile converts should observe Mosaic law. He distinguishes between the Gospel he preached and the other gospel on the basis of their experience of the Spirit. "Does, then, the one who supplies the Spirit to you…do so from works of the law or from faith in what you heard?"

Like Paul, today's Gospel suggests that God gives us the Holy Spirit not to acknowledge our works, but to answer our fervent, faithful prayer.

Year I

FIRST READING

Mal 3:13–20b

The day is coming, blazing like an oven.

A reading from the Book of the Prophet Malachi

You have defied me in word, says the LORD,
    yet you ask, "What have we spoken against you?"
You have said, "It is vain to serve God,
    and what do we profit by keeping his command,
And going about in penitential dress
    in awe of the LORD of hosts?
Rather must we call the proud blessed;
    for indeed evildoers prosper,
    and even tempt God with impunity."
Then they who fear the LORD spoke with one another,
    and the LORD listened attentively;
And a record book was written before him
    of those who fear the LORD and trust in his name.

And they shall be mine, says the LORD of hosts,
> my own special possession, on the day I take action.

And I will have compassion on them,
> as a man has compassion on his son who serves him.

Then you will again see the distinction
> between the just and the wicked;

Between the one who serves God,
> and the one who does not serve him.

For lo, the day is coming, blazing like an oven,
> when all the proud and all evildoers will be stubble,

And the day that is coming will set them on fire,
> leaving them neither root nor branch,
> > says the LORD of hosts.

But for you who fear my name, there will arise
> the sun of justice with its healing rays.

The word of the Lord.

Responsorial Psalm

Ps 1:1–2, 3, 4 and 6

R. Blessed are they who hope in the Lord.

Blessed the man who follows not
> the counsel of the wicked
Nor walks in the way of sinners,
> nor sits in the company of the insolent,
But delights in the law of the LORD
> and meditates on his law day and night.

R. Blessed are they who hope in the Lord.

He is like a tree
> planted near running water,
That yields its fruit in due season,
> and whose leaves never fade.
> Whatever he does, prospers.

R. Blessed are they who hope in the Lord.

Not so the wicked, not so;
   they are like chaff which the wind drives away.
For the LORD watches over the way of the just,
   but the way of the wicked vanishes.

R. Blessed are they who hope in the Lord.

Alleluia Verse *and* **Gospel,** *p. 1551.*

Year II

FIRST READING

Gal 3:1–5

Did you receive the Spirit from works of the law,
or from faith in what you heard?

A reading from the Letter of Saint Paul to the Galatians

O stupid Galatians! Who has bewitched you, before whose eyes Jesus Christ was publicly portrayed as crucified? I want to learn only this from you: did you receive the Spirit from works of the law, or from faith in what you heard? Are you so stupid? After beginning with the Spirit, are you now ending with the flesh? Did you experience so many things in vain?— if indeed it was in vain. Does, then, the one who supplies the Spirit to you and works mighty deeds among you do so from works of the law or from faith in what you heard?

The word of the Lord.

Responsorial Psalm

Lk 1:69–70, 71–72, 73–75

R. Blessed be the Lord, the God of Israel;
   he has come to his people.

He has raised up for us a mighty savior,
   born of the house of his servant David.

R. Blessed be the Lord, the God of Israel;
   he has come to his people.

Through his holy prophets he promised of old
  that he would save us from our enemies,
  from the hands of all who hate us.

  R. Blessed be the Lord, the God of Israel;
    he has come to his people.

He promised to show mercy to our fathers
  and to remember his holy covenant.

  R. Blessed be the Lord, the God of Israel;
    he has come to his people.

This was the oath he swore to our father Abraham:
  to set us free from the hands of our enemies,
  free to worship him without fear,
  holy and righteous in his sight
  all the days of our life.

  R. Blessed be the Lord, the God of Israel;
    he has come to his people.

    Alleluia, alleluia See Acts 16:14b
    Open our hearts, O Lord,
    to listen to the words of your Son.
    Alleluia, alleluia

Years I and II

GOSPEL
                                  Lk 11:5–13

Ask and you will receive.

A reading from the holy Gospel according to Luke

Jesus said to his disciples: "Suppose one of you has a friend to whom he goes at midnight and says, 'Friend, lend me three loaves of bread, for a friend of mine has arrived at my house from a journey and I have nothing to offer him,' and he says in reply from within, 'Do not bother me; the door has already been locked and my children and I are already in bed. I cannot get up to give you anything.' I tell you, if he does not get up to give him the loaves because of their friendship, he will get up to give him whatever he needs because of his persistence.

"And I tell you, ask and you will receive; seek and you will find; knock and the door will be opened to you. For everyone who asks, receives; and the one who seeks, finds; and to the one who knocks, the door will be opened. What father among you would hand his son a snake when he asks for a fish? Or hand him a scorpion when he asks for an egg? If you then, who are wicked, know how to give good gifts to your children, how much more will the Father in heaven give the Holy Spirit to those who ask him?"

The Gospel of the Lord.

Liturgy of the Eucharist, *p. 897;* **Prayer over the Gifts,** *p. 1532.*

Friday

Antiphons and Prayers, *p. 1531;* **Liturgy of the Word** *for Year I (odd years) follows; Year II (even years), p. 1554.*

TODAY'S LIVING WORD

The two first readings for today are both difficult passages. The excerpt from Joel is part of a communal lament, a special liturgy during a natural disaster when a plague of locusts devastates the land. They (the locusts) are the vast army, "a people numerous and mighty," who overspread the mountains like dawn. But this dawn brings darkness, not light, and it portends the day of the Lord. In the selection from Galatians, Paul marshals no less than five passages from the Hebrew Bible in order to support his argument: the righteousness of Abraham consisted in faith and not in the works of the law.

Like Paul, Jesus too makes his argument with the help of the Hebrew Bible. "If it is by the finger of God that [I] drive out demons," he says, "then the Kingdom of God has come upon you." This alludes to Moses, who "by the finger of God" bested Pharaoh's magicians (cf. Ex 8:19). Here again Luke presents Jesus as a prophetic Messiah, powerful in deed as in word.

Year I

FIRST READING

Jl 1:13–15; 2:1–2

The day of the LORD is coming, a day of darkness and of gloom.

A reading from the Book of the Prophet Joel

Gird yourselves and weep, O priests!
   wail, O ministers of the altar!
Come, spend the night in sackcloth,
   O ministers of my God!
The house of your God is deprived
   of offering and libation.
Proclaim a fast,
   call an assembly;
Gather the elders,
   all who dwell in the land,
Into the house of the LORD, your God,
   and cry to the LORD!

Alas, the day!
   for near is the day of the LORD,
   and it comes as ruin from the Almighty.
Blow the trumpet in Zion,
   sound the alarm on my holy mountain!
Let all who dwell in the land tremble,
   for the day of the LORD is coming;
Yes, it is near, a day of darkness and of gloom,
   a day of clouds and somberness!
Like dawn spreading over the mountains,
   a people numerous and mighty!

Their like has not been from of old,
   nor will it be after them,
      even to the years of distant generations.

The word of the Lord.

Responsorial Psalm

Ps 9:2–3, 6 and 16, 8–9

R. The Lord will judge the world with justice.

I will give thanks to you, O LORD, with all my heart;
   I will declare all your wondrous deeds.
I will be glad and exult in you;
   I will sing praise to your name, Most High.

R. The Lord will judge the world with justice.

You rebuked the nations and destroyed the wicked;
   their name you blotted out forever and ever.
The nations are sunk in the pit they have made;
   in the snare they set, their foot is caught.

R. The Lord will judge the world with justice.

But the LORD sits enthroned forever;
   he has set up his throne for judgment.
He judges the world with justice;
   he governs the peoples with equity.

R. The Lord will judge the world with justice.

Alleluia Verse *and* **Gospel,** p. 1556.

Year II

FIRST READING

Gal 3:7–14

*Those who have faith are blessed along with Abraham
who had faith.*

A reading from the Letter of Saint Paul to the Galatians

Brothers and sisters:

Realize that it is those who have faith who are children of
Abraham. Scripture, which saw in advance that God would

justify the Gentiles by faith, foretold the good news to Abraham, saying, *Through you shall all the nations be blessed.* Consequently, those who have faith are blessed along with Abraham who had faith. For all who depend on works of the law are under a curse; for it is written, *Cursed be everyone who does not persevere in doing all the things written in the book of the law.* And that no one is justified before God by the law is clear, for *the one who is righteous by faith will live.* But the law does not depend on faith; rather, *the one who does these things will live by them.* Christ ransomed us from the curse of the law by becoming a curse for us, for it is written, *Cursed be everyone who hangs on a tree,* that the blessing of Abraham might be extended to the Gentiles through Christ Jesus, so that we might receive the promise of the Spirit through faith.

The word of the Lord.

Responsorial Psalm

Ps 111:1b–2, 3–4, 5–6

R. The Lord will remember his covenant for ever.

I will give thanks to the LORD with all my heart
  in the company and assembly of the just.
Great are the works of the LORD,
  exquisite in all their delights.

R. The Lord will remember his covenant for ever.

Majesty and glory are his work,
  and his justice endures forever.
He has won renown for his wondrous deeds;
  gracious and merciful is the LORD.

R. The Lord will remember his covenant for ever.

He has given food to those who fear him;
  he will forever be mindful of his covenant.

He has made known to his people the power of his works,
  giving them the inheritance of the nations.

R. The Lord will remember his covenant for ever.

> **Alleluia, alleluia** Jn 12:31b–32
> The prince of this world will now be cast out,
> and when I am lifted up from the earth
> I will draw all to myself, says the Lord.
> **Alleluia, alleluia**

Years I and II

GOSPEL Lk 11:15–26

If it is by the finger of God that I drive out demons,
then the Kingdom of God has come upon you.

A reading from the holy Gospel according to Luke

When Jesus had driven out a demon, some of the crowd said:
"By the power of Beelzebul, the prince of demons, he drives
out demons." Others, to test him, asked him for a sign from
heaven. But he knew their thoughts and said to them, "Every
kingdom divided against itself will be laid waste and house
will fall against house. And if Satan is divided against himself,
how will his kingdom stand? For you say that it is by Beelzebul that I drive out demons. If I, then, drive out demons by
Beelzebul, by whom do your own people drive them out?
Therefore they will be your judges. But if it is by the finger of
God that I drive out demons, then the Kingdom of God has
come upon you. When a strong man fully armed guards his
palace, his possessions are safe. But when one stronger than
he attacks and overcomes him, he takes away the armor on
which he relied and distributes the spoils. Whoever is not with
me is against me, and whoever does not gather with me scatters.

"When an unclean spirit goes out of someone, it roams through arid regions searching for rest but, finding none, it says, 'I shall return to my home from which I came.' But upon returning, it finds it swept clean and put in order. Then it goes and brings back seven other spirits more wicked than itself who move in and dwell there, and the last condition of that man is worse than the first."

The Gospel of the Lord.

Liturgy of the Eucharist, *p. 897;* **Prayer over the Gifts,** *p. 1532.*

Saturday

Antiphons and Prayers, *p. 1531;* **Liturgy of the Word** *for Year I (odd years) follows; Year II (even years), p. 1560.*

Today's Living Word

Today's Gospel, all of two verses, is unique to Luke and is important for what it tells us about Mary. A woman declares the mother of Jesus blessed for the privilege of being his biological parent. Jesus replies with a second beatitude that, in spite of the English translation, does not discount the first one. As Raymond Brown et al. explain in their book, *Mary in the New Testament,* the word *menoun,* rendered here as "rather," can also mean "yes, but even more."* Without denying Mary's unique privilege, Jesus declares her even more blessed for having heard the word of God and kept it. His mother is a model disciple. Marian devotion has often used the city of Jerusalem as an image of Mary. Today's reading from Joel explains why, for God's presence within her makes both Jerusalem and Mary holy—full of grace.

The selection from Galatians extends our reflection on Mary. Faith and baptism in Christ Jesus make us children of God, but of Mary too, that daughter of Abraham who inherited all that was promised.

* Raymond E. Brown, Karl P. Donfried, et al. eds., "Mary in the Gospel of Luke and the Acts of the Apostles," *Mary in the New Testament* (New York: Paulist Press, 1978), p. 171.

FIRST READING   Jl 4:12–21

Apply the sickle, for the harvest is ripe.

A reading from the Book of the Prophet Joel

Thus says the LORD:

Let the nations bestir themselves and come up
        to the Valley of Jehoshaphat;
For there will I sit in judgment
        upon all the neighboring nations.

Apply the sickle,
        for the harvest is ripe;
Come and tread,
        for the wine press is full;
The vats overflow,
        for great is their malice.
Crowd upon crowd
        in the valley of decision;
For near is the day of the LORD
        in the valley of decision.
Sun and moon are darkened,
        and the stars withhold their brightness.
The LORD roars from Zion,
        and from Jerusalem raises his voice;
The heavens and the earth quake,
        but the LORD is a refuge to his people,
        a stronghold to the children of Israel.
Then shall you know that I, the LORD, am your God,
        dwelling on Zion, my holy mountain;
Jerusalem shall be holy,

and strangers shall pass through her no more.
And then, on that day,
    the mountains shall drip new wine,
    and the hills shall flow with milk;
And the channels of Judah
    shall flow with water:
A fountain shall issue from the house of the LORD,
    to water the Valley of Shittim.
Egypt shall be a waste,
    and Edom a desert waste,
Because of violence done to the people of Judah,
    because they shed innocent blood in their land.
But Judah shall abide forever,
    and Jerusalem for all generations.
I will avenge their blood,
    and not leave it unpunished.
    The LORD dwells in Zion.

The word of the Lord.

Responsorial Psalm

Ps 97:1–2, 5–6, 11–12

R. Rejoice in the Lord, you just!

The LORD is king; let the earth rejoice;
    let the many isles be glad.
Clouds and darkness are round about him,
    justice and judgment are the foundation of his throne.

R. Rejoice in the Lord, you just!

The mountains melt like wax before the LORD,
    before the LORD of all the earth.
The heavens proclaim his justice,
    and all peoples see his glory.

R. Rejoice in the Lord, you just!

Light dawns for the just;
  and gladness, for the upright of heart.
Be glad in the LORD, you just,
  and give thanks to his holy name.

R. Rejoice in the Lord, you just!

Alleluia Verse *and* **Gospel,** *p. 1561.*

Year II

FIRST READING   Gal 3:22–29

Through faith you are all children of God.

A reading from the Letter of Saint Paul to the Galatians

Brothers and sisters:
Scripture confined all things under the power of sin, that
through faith in Jesus Christ the promise might be given to
those who believe.

Before faith came, we were held in custody under law, confined for the faith that was to be revealed. Consequently, the
law was our disciplinarian for Christ, that we might be justified
by faith. But now that faith has come, we are no longer under
a disciplinarian. For through faith you are all children of God
in Christ Jesus. For all of you who were baptized into Christ
have clothed yourselves with Christ. There is neither Jew nor
Greek, there is neither slave nor free person, there is not male
and female; for you are all one in Christ Jesus. And if you belong to Christ, then you are Abraham's descendants, heirs
according to the promise.

The word of the Lord.

Responsorial Psalm   Ps 105:2–3, 4–5, 6–7

  R. The Lord remembers his covenant for ever.

Sing to him, sing his praise,
  proclaim all his wondrous deeds.
Glory in his holy name;
  rejoice, O hearts that seek the LORD!

R. The Lord remembers his covenant for ever.

Look to the LORD in his strength;
  seek to serve him constantly.
Recall the wondrous deeds that he has wrought,
  his portents, and the judgments he has uttered.

R. The Lord remembers his covenant for ever.

You descendants of Abraham, his servants,
  sons of Jacob, his chosen ones!
He, the LORD, is our God;
  throughout the earth his judgments prevail.

R. The Lord remembers his covenant for ever.

Or: **R. Alleluia.**

> **Alleluia, alleluia** Lk 11:28
> Blessed are those who hear the word of God
> and observe it.
> **Alleluia, alleluia**

Years I and II

GOSPEL   Lk 11:27–28
Blessed is the womb that carried you.
Rather, blessed are those who hear the word of God and observe it.

A reading from the holy Gospel according to Luke

While Jesus was speaking, a woman from the crowd called out and said to him, "Blessed is the womb that carried you and the breasts at which you nursed." He replied, "Rather, blessed are those who hear the word of God and observe it."

The Gospel of the Lord.

Liturgy of the Eucharist, *p. 897;* **Prayer over the Gifts,** *p. 1532.*

TWENTY-EIGHTH WEEK
IN ORDINARY TIME

The **Antiphons and Prayers** *may be the following, or may be chosen from any of the other 33 weeks in Ordinary Time (refer to Liturgical Calendar, pp. 26–41).*

The **Liturgy of the Word** *varies: for Monday, see p. 1564; Tuesday, p. 1568; Wednesday, p. 1572; Thursday, p. 1576; Friday, p. 1580; Saturday, p. 1584.*

Entrance Antiphon

If you, O Lord, laid bare our guilt, who could endure it? But you are forgiving, God of Israel.   (Ps 130:3–4)

Opening Prayer

Let us pray
   [that God will help us to love one another]
         Pause for silent prayer.

Lord,
our help and guide,
make your love the foundation of our lives.
May our love for you express itself
in our eagerness to do good for others.

Grant this through our Lord Jesus Christ, your Son,
who lives and reigns with you and the Holy Spirit,
one God, for ever and ever.

Alternative Opening Prayer

Let us pray
   [in quiet for the grace of sincerity]
         Pause for silent prayer.

Father in heaven,
the hand of your loving kindness

powerfully yet gently guides all the moments of our day.
Go before us in our pilgrimage of life,
anticipate our needs and prevent our falling.
Send your Spirit to unite us in faith,
that sharing in your service,
we may rejoice in your presence.
We ask this through Christ our Lord.

Prayer over the Gifts

Pray, brethren...

Lord,
accept the prayers and gifts
we offer in faith and love.
May this eucharist bring us to your glory.
We ask this in the name of Jesus the Lord.

Preface of Weekdays in Ordinary Time I–VI, *pp. 948–950.*

Communion Antiphon

The rich suffer want and go hungry, but nothing shall be lacking to those who fear the Lord. (Ps 34:11)

Or:

When the Lord is revealed we shall be like him, for we shall see him as he is. (1 Jn 3:2)

Prayer after Communion

Let us pray.

Pause for silent prayer, if this has not preceded.

Almighty Father,
may the body and blood of your Son
give us a share in his life,
for he is Lord for ever and ever.

Monday

Antiphons and Prayers, *p. 1562;* **Liturgy of the Word** *for Year I (odd years) follows; Year II (even years), p. 1566.*

TODAY'S LIVING WORD

The sayings of Jesus in today's Gospel and the allegory of Paul in the letter to the Galatians both make the same claim: the revelation of God in Jesus is greater than Jonah, greater than Solomon, and even greater than Moses and the covenant he mediated. On the lips of Jesus and Paul, both of them Jews, such claims did not abrogate the sign of Jonah, or the wisdom of Solomon or the law of Moses. They simply affirmed that the revelation of Jesus surpassed that of Jonah and Solomon and Moses, surpassed without superseding it, that is, without making it now obsolete. The Hebrew Scriptures remained divine revelation, the word of God, for Jesus and Paul as they do for us.

The Gospel Paul proclaimed is summed up in the opening of Paul's letter to the Romans. It is thoroughly Christocentric. Designating the risen Jesus as "Son of God in power," God identified him as the Messiah. The "Gospel of God" is that, in Jesus and through him, the messianic age of freedom and fullness of life has dawned.

Year I

FIRST READING

Rom 1:1-7

Through Christ Jesus we have received the grace of apostleship, to bring about the obedience of faith among the Gentiles.

A reading from the beginning of the Letter of Saint Paul to the Romans

Paul, a slave of Christ Jesus, called to be an Apostle and set apart for the Gospel of God, which he promised previously through his prophets in the holy Scriptures, the Gospel about his Son, descended from David according to the flesh, but established as Son of God in power according to the Spirit of holiness through resurrection from the dead, Jesus Christ our Lord. Through him we have received the grace of apostleship, to bring about the obedience of faith, for the sake of his name, among all the Gentiles, among whom are you also, who are called to belong to Jesus Christ; to all the beloved of God in Rome, called to be holy. Grace to you and peace from God our Father and the Lord Jesus Christ.

The word of the Lord.

Responsorial Psalm

Ps 98:1bcde, 2–3ab, 3cd–4

R. **The Lord has made known his salvation.**

Sing to the LORD a new song,
  for he has done wondrous deeds;
His right hand has won victory for him,
  his holy arm.

R. **The Lord has made known his salvation.**

The LORD has made his salvation known:
  in the sight of the nations he has revealed his justice.
He has remembered his kindness and his faithfulness
  toward the house of Israel.

R. **The Lord has made known his salvation.**

All the ends of the earth have seen
  the salvation by our God.
Sing joyfully to the LORD, all you lands;
  break into song; sing praise.

R. **The Lord has made known his salvation.**

Alleluia Verse *and* **Gospel,** *p. 1567.*

Year II

FIRST READING
Gal 4:22–24, 26–27, 31—5:1

We are children not of the slave woman but of the freeborn woman.

A reading from the Letter of Saint Paul to the Galatians

Brothers and sisters:

It is written that Abraham had two sons, one by the slave woman and the other by the freeborn woman. The son of the slave woman was born naturally, the son of the freeborn through a promise. Now this is an allegory. These women represent two covenants. One was from Mount Sinai, bearing children for slavery; this is Hagar. But the Jerusalem above is freeborn, and she is our mother. For it is written:

> *Rejoice, you barren one who bore no children;*
>   *break forth and shout, you who were not in labor;*
> *for more numerous are the children of the deserted one*
>   *than of her who has a husband.*

Therefore, brothers and sisters, we are children not of the slave woman but of the freeborn woman.

For freedom Christ set us free; so stand firm and do not submit again to the yoke of slavery.

The word of the Lord.

Responsorial Psalm
Ps 113:1b–2, 3–4, 5a and 6–7

R. Blessed be the name of the Lord forever.

Praise, you servants of the LORD,
    praise the name of the LORD.
Blessed be the name of the LORD
    both now and forever.

R. Blessed be the name of the Lord forever.

From the rising to the setting of the sun
  is the name of the LORD to be praised.
High above all nations is the LORD;
  above the heavens is his glory.

R. Blessed be the name of the Lord forever.

Who is like the LORD, our God,
  who looks upon the heavens and the earth below?
He raises up the lowly from the dust;
  from the dunghill he lifts up the poor.

R. Blessed be the name of the Lord forever.

Or: **R. Alleluia, alleluia.**

Alleluia, alleluia Ps 95:8
If today you hear his voice,
harden not your hearts.
Alleluia, alleluia

Years I and II

GOSPEL   Lk 11:29-32

This generation seeks a sign,
but no sign will be given it, except the sign of Jonah.

A reading from the holy Gospel according to Luke

While still more people gathered in the crowd, Jesus said to
them, "This generation is an evil generation; it seeks a sign,
but no sign will be given it, except the sign of Jonah. Just as
Jonah became a sign to the Ninevites, so will the Son of Man
be to this generation. At the judgment the queen of the south
will rise with the men of this generation and she will condemn
them, because she came from the ends of the earth to hear the
wisdom of Solomon, and there is something greater than
Solomon here. At the judgment the men of Nineveh will arise

with this generation and condemn it, because at the preaching of Jonah they repented, and there is something greater than Jonah here."

The Gospel of the Lord.

Liturgy of the Eucharist, *p. 897;* **Prayer over the Gifts,** *p. 1563.*

Tuesday

Antiphons and Prayers, *p. 1562;* **Liturgy of the Word** *for Year I (odd years) follows; Year II (even years), p. 1570.*

TODAY'S LIVING WORD

In today's reading from Romans, Paul condemns as fools those godless people who resist the knowledge of God accessible to all who have eyes to see the world God has made. Paul says that such folly is inexcusable. Similarly, in today's Gospel, Jesus indicts as fools those Pharisees who care more about external observances than about internal dispositions.

Along the same lines, Paul insists in Galatians that we have been set free, not by external observance of the law, but by the internal disposition of faith in Christ. He says this is all that matters: "only faith working through love." This may be the sense of Jesus' concluding remark as well. "Give alms," he tells the Pharisees, "and behold, everything will be clean for you." In other words, not ritual washing but love—caring concretely for the needs of others—makes one clean before God.

Year I

FIRST READING

Rom 1:16–25

Although they knew God they did not accord him glory as God.

A reading from the Letter of Saint Paul to the Romans

Brothers and sisters:

I am not ashamed of the Gospel. It is the power of God for the salvation of everyone who believes: for Jew first, and then Greek. For in it is revealed the righteousness of God from faith to faith; as it is written, "The one who is righteous by faith will live."

The wrath of God is indeed being revealed from heaven against every impiety and wickedness of those who suppress the truth by their wickedness. For what can be known about God is evident to them, because God made it evident to them. Ever since the creation of the world, his invisible attributes of eternal power and divinity have been able to be understood and perceived in what he has made. As a result, they have no excuse; for although they knew God they did not accord him glory as God or give him thanks. Instead, they became vain in their reasoning, and their senseless minds were darkened. While claiming to be wise, they became fools and exchanged the glory of the immortal God for the likeness of an image of mortal man or of birds or of four-legged animals or of snakes.

Therefore, God handed them over to impurity through the lusts of their hearts for the mutual degradation of their bodies. They exchanged the truth of God for a lie and revered and worshiped the creature rather than the creator, who is blessed forever. Amen.

The word of the Lord.

Responsional Psalm

Ps 19:2–3, 4–5

R. **The heavens proclaim the glory of God.**

The heavens declare the glory of God,
and the firmament proclaims his handiwork.
Day pours out the word to day,
and night to night imparts knowledge.

R. **The heavens proclaim the glory of God.**

Not a word nor a discourse
  whose voice is not heard;
Through all the earth their voice resounds,
  and to the ends of the world, their message.

R. The heavens proclaim the glory of God.

   Alleluia Verse *and* **Gospel,** *p. 1571.*

                                                                    Year II

FIRST READING   Gal 5:1–6

   Neither circumcision nor uncircumcision counts for
      anything, but only faith working through love.

A reading from the Letter of Saint Paul to the Galatians

Brothers and sisters:
For freedom Christ set us free; so stand firm and do not submit
again to the yoke of slavery.

   It is I, Paul, who am telling you that if you have yourselves
circumcised, Christ will be of no benefit to you. Once again I
declare to every man who has himself circumcised that he is
bound to observe the entire law. You are separated from Christ,
you who are trying to be justified by law; you have fallen from
grace. For through the Spirit, by faith, we await the hope of
righteousness. For in Christ Jesus, neither circumcision nor
uncircumcision counts for anything, but only faith working
through love.

The word of the Lord.

Responsorial Psalm   Ps 119:41, 43, 44, 45, 47, 48

   R. Let your mercy come to me, O Lord.

Let your mercy come to me, O LORD,
  your salvation according to your promise.

R. Let your mercy come to me, O Lord.

Take not the word of truth from my mouth,
  for in your ordinances is my hope.

R. Let your mercy come to me, O Lord.

And I will keep your law continually,
  forever and ever.

R. Let your mercy come to me, O Lord.

And I will walk at liberty,
  because I seek your precepts.

R. Let your mercy come to me, O Lord.

And I will delight in your commands,
  which I love.

R. Let your mercy come to me, O Lord.

And I will lift up my hands to your commands
  and meditate on your statutes.

R. Let your mercy come to me, O Lord.

Alleluia, alleluia   Heb 4:12
The word of God is living and effective,
  able to discern reflections and thoughts of the heart.
Alleluia, alleluia

Years I and II

GOSPEL   Lk 11:37–41

Give alms and behold, everything will be clean for you.

A reading from the holy Gospel according to Luke

After Jesus had spoken, a Pharisee invited him to dine at his home. He entered and reclined at table to eat. The Pharisee was amazed to see that he did not observe the prescribed washing before the meal. The Lord said to him, "Oh you Pharisees! Although you cleanse the outside of the cup and the dish, inside you are filled with plunder and evil. You fools!

Did not the maker of the outside also make the inside? But as to what is within, give alms, and behold, everything will be clean for you."

The Gospel of the Lord.

Liturgy of the Eucharist, *p. 897;* **Prayer over the Gifts,** *p. 1563.*

Wednesday

Antiphons and Prayers, *p. 1562;* **Liturgy of the Word** *for Year I (odd years) follows; Year II (even years), p. 1574.*

TODAY'S LIVING WORD

Paul's diatribe in today's selection from Romans might be directed to the Pharisees and lawyers in today's Gospel as well. Those who lord their authority over others, those who lay impossible burdens on others, those who judge others will not escape the just judgment of God, who has no favorites.

Although he does not overlook the works of the flesh (unredeemed humanity), Paul concludes his letter to the Galatians on a more positive note, listing the fruits of the Spirit. He calls these "fruits" rather than "works" in order to show that they are not human achievements, but the result of belonging to Christ and living by the Spirit. For Paul morality is not characterized by virtue, but by vitality; it comes from sharing the risen life of Jesus the Christ. Not surprisingly, the hallmark of life in the Spirit is love (agape), a term which includes both love of God and love of others.

Year I

FIRST READING   Rom 2:1–11

God will repay each according to his works,
Jew first and then Greek.

A reading from the Letter of Saint Paul to the Romans

You, O man, are without excuse, every one of you who passes judgment. For by the standard by which you judge another you condemn yourself, since you, the judge, do the very same things. We know that the judgment of God on those who do such things is true. Do you suppose, then, you who judge those who engage in such things and yet do them yourself, that you will escape the judgment of God? Or do you hold his priceless kindness, forbearance, and patience in low esteem, unaware that the kindness of God would lead you to repentance? By your stubbornness and impenitent heart, you are storing up wrath for yourself for the day of wrath and revelation of the just judgment of God, who will repay everyone according to his works, eternal life to those who seek glory, honor, and immortality through perseverance in good works, but wrath and fury to those who selfishly disobey the truth and obey wickedness. Yes, affliction and distress will come upon everyone who does evil, Jew first and then Greek. But there will be glory, honor, and peace for everyone who does good, Jew first and then Greek. There is no partiality with God.

The word of the Lord.

Responsorial Psalm

Ps 62:2–3, 6–7, 9

R. Lord, you give back to everyone according to his works.

Only in God is my soul at rest;
  from him comes my salvation.
He only is my rock and my salvation,
  my stronghold; I shall not be disturbed at all.

R. Lord, you give back to everyone according to his works.

Only in God be at rest, my soul,
  for from him comes my hope.
He only is my rock and my salvation,
  my stronghold; I shall not be disturbed.

R. Lord, you give back to everyone according to his works.

Trust in him at all times, O my people!
  Pour out your hearts before him;
  God is our refuge!

R. Lord, you give back to everyone according to his works.

Alleluia Verse and **Gospel,** *p. 1575.*

Year II

FIRST READING

Gal 5:18–25

*Those who belong to Christ Jesus have crucified
their flesh with its passions and desires.*

A reading from the Letter of Saint Paul to the Galatians

Brothers and sisters:

If you are guided by the Spirit, you are not under the law. Now the works of the flesh are obvious: immorality, impurity, licentiousness, idolatry, sorcery, hatreds, rivalry, jealousy, outbursts of fury, acts of selfishness, dissensions, factions, occasions of envy, drinking bouts, orgies, and the like. I warn you, as I warned you before, that those who do such things will not inherit the Kingdom of God. In contrast, the fruit of the Spirit is love, joy, peace, patience, kindness, generosity, faithfulness, gentleness, self-control. Against such there is no law. Now those who belong to Christ Jesus have crucified their flesh with its passions and desires. If we live in the Spirit, let us also follow the Spirit.

The word of the Lord.

Responsorial Psalm

Ps 1:1–2, 3, 4 and 6

R. Those who follow you, Lord, will have the light of life.

Blessed the man who follows not
  the counsel of the wicked

Nor walks in the way of sinners,
  nor sits in the company of the insolent,
But delights in the law of the LORD
  and meditates on his law day and night.

R. Those who follow you, Lord, will have the light of life.

He is like a tree
  planted near running water,
That yields its fruit in due season,
  and whose leaves never fade.
  Whatever he does, prospers.

R. Those who follow you, Lord, will have the light of life.

Not so the wicked, not so;
  they are like chaff which the wind drives away.
For the LORD watches over the way of the just,
  but the way of the wicked vanishes.

R. Those who follow you, Lord, will have the light of life.

Alleluia, alleluia Jn 10:27
My sheep hear my voice, says the Lord;
I know them, and they follow me.
Alleluia, alleluia

Years I and II

GOSPEL Lk 11:42–46
Woe to you Pharisees! Woe also to you scholars of the law!

A reading from the holy Gospel according to Luke

The Lord said: "Woe to you Pharisees! You pay tithes of mint and of rue and of every garden herb, but you pay no attention to judgment and to love for God. These you should have done, without overlooking the others. Woe to you Pharisees! You love the seat of honor in synagogues and greetings in marketplaces. Woe to you! You are like unseen graves over which people unknowingly walk."

Then one of the scholars of the law said to him in reply, "Teacher, by saying this you are insulting us too." And he said, "Woe also to you scholars of the law! You impose on people burdens hard to carry, but you yourselves do not lift one finger to touch them."

The Gospel of the Lord.

Liturgy of the Eucharist, *p. 897;* **Prayer over the Gifts,** *p. 1563.*

Thursday

Antiphons and Prayers, *p. 1562;* **Liturgy of the Word** *for Year I (odd years) follows; Year II (even years), p. 1578.*

TODAY'S LIVING WORD

Today's readings must be understood in light of their respective literary forms: a diatribe in Romans, a Jewish prayer form in Ephesians, and polemic in the Gospel. A diatribe is a sustained scholarly discussion with an imaginary opponent. In today's text from Romans, Paul wants to persuade a Jewish opponent that if justification is by faith and not by the works of the law, then it is open to all, and Jews no longer have grounds for boasting. Polemic is a verbal attack on one's opponents who are routinely depicted with gross exaggeration. In today's Gospel, Jesus' prophetic criticism of certain Pharisees and lawyers has been exaggerated by the bitter rivalry that raged between the early Church and the Jewish community.

The letter to the Ephesians is happily free of the hostility that tore Christianity from its Jewish roots. It opens with a prayer modeled on the Jewish blessing *(berakah)*. This positive appropriation of a Jewish prayer form is echoed in the new *Catechism*. It describes blessing as the human response to God's gifts. "Because God blesses, the human heart can in return bless the One who is the source of every blessing" (n. 2626).

Year I

FIRST READING

Rom 3:21–30

A person is justified by faith apart from works of the law.

A reading from the Letter of Saint Paul to the Romans

Brothers and sisters:

Now the righteousness of God has been manifested apart from the law, though testified to by the law and the prophets, the righteousness of God through faith in Jesus Christ for all who believe. For there is no distinction; all have sinned and are deprived of the glory of God. They are justified freely by his grace through the redemption in Christ Jesus, whom God set forth as an expiation, through faith, by his Blood, to prove his righteousness because of the forgiveness of sins previously committed, through the forbearance of God—to prove his righteousness in the present time, that he might be righteous and justify the one who has faith in Jesus.

What occasion is there then for boasting? It is ruled out. On what principle, that of works? No, rather on the principle of faith. For we consider that a person is justified by faith apart from works of the law. Does God belong to Jews alone? Does he not belong to Gentiles, too? Yes, also to Gentiles, for God is one and will justify the circumcised on the basis of faith and the uncircumcised through faith.

The word of the Lord.

Responsorial Psalm

Ps 130:1b–2, 3–4, 5–6ab

R. **With the Lord there is mercy, and fullness of redemption.**

Out of the depths I cry to you, O LORD;
  LORD, hear my voice!
Let your ears be attentive
  to my voice in supplication.

R. With the Lord there is mercy, and fullness of redemption.

If you, O Lord, mark iniquities,
  Lord, who can stand?
But with you is forgiveness,
  that you may be revered.

R. With the Lord there is mercy, and fullness of redemption.

I trust in the Lord;
  my soul trusts in his word.
My soul waits for the Lord
  more than sentinels wait for the dawn.

R. With the Lord there is mercy, and fullness of redemption.

Alleluia Verse *and* **Gospel,** *p. 1579f.*

Year II

FIRST READING   Eph 1:1–10

God chose us in Christ, before the foundation of the world.

A reading from the beginning of the Letter of Saint Paul to the Ephesians

Paul, an Apostle of Christ Jesus by the will of God, to the holy ones who are in Ephesus and faithful in Christ Jesus: grace to you and peace from God our Father and the Lord Jesus Christ.

Blessed be the God and Father of our Lord Jesus Christ, who has blessed us in Christ with every spiritual blessing in the heavens, as he chose us in him, before the foundation of the world, to be holy and without blemish before him. In love he destined us for adoption to himself through Jesus Christ, in accord with the favor of his will, for the praise of the glory of his grace that he granted us in the beloved.

In Christ we have redemption by his Blood, the forgiveness of transgressions, in accord with the riches of his grace that he lavished upon us. In all wisdom and insight, he has made known to us the mystery of his will in accord with his favor that he set forth in him as a plan for the fullness of times, to sum up all things in Christ, in heaven and on earth.

The word of the Lord.

Responsorial Psalm

Ps 98:1, 2–3ab, 3cd–4, 5–6

R. The Lord has made known his salvation.

Sing to the LORD a new song,
  for he has done wondrous deeds;
His right hand has won victory for him,
  his holy arm.

R. The Lord has made known his salvation.

The LORD has made his salvation known:
  in the sight of the nations he has revealed his justice.
He has remembered his kindness and his faithfulness
  toward the house of Israel.

R. The Lord has made known his salvation.

All the ends of the earth have seen
  the salvation by our God.
Sing joyfully to the LORD, all you lands;
  break into song; sing praise.

R. The Lord has made known his salvation.

Sing praise to the LORD with the harp,
  with the harp and melodious song.
With trumpets and the sound of the horn
  sing joyfully before the King, the LORD.

R. The Lord has made known his salvation.

> **Alleluia, alleluia**   Jn 14:6
> I am the way and the truth and the life, says the Lord;
> no one comes to the Father except through me.
> **Alleluia, alleluia**

Years I and II

GOSPEL   Lk 11:47–54

The blood of the prophets is required,
from the blood of Abel to the blood of Zechariah.

A reading from the holy Gospel according to Luke

The Lord said: "Woe to you who build the memorials of the prophets whom your fathers killed. Consequently, you bear witness and give consent to the deeds of your ancestors, for they killed them and you do the building. Therefore, the wisdom of God said, 'I will send to them prophets and Apostles; some of them they will kill and persecute' in order that this generation might be charged with the blood of all the prophets shed since the foundation of the world, from the blood of Abel to the blood of Zechariah who died between the altar and the temple building. Yes, I tell you, this generation will be charged with their blood! Woe to you, scholars of the law! You have taken away the key of knowledge. You yourselves did not enter and you stopped those trying to enter." When Jesus left, the scribes and Pharisees began to act with hostility toward him and to interrogate him about many things, for they were plotting to catch him at something he might say.

The Gospel of the Lord.

Liturgy of the Eucharist, *p. 897;* **Prayer over the Gifts,** *p. 1563.*

Friday

Antiphons and Prayers, *p. 1562;* **Liturgy of the Word** *for Year I (odd years) follows; Year II (even years), p. 1582.*

TODAY'S LIVING WORD

In today's selection from Romans, Paul returns to a familiar theme. He argues that Abraham is the father of all the uncircumcised (the

Gentiles) who are justified by faith, since according to the Scripture Abraham was justified by believing God, long before circumcision was decreed. Thus Paul firmly grounds his Gospel in the long history of God's people, recorded in the Hebrew Scriptures. Many scholars read the letter to the Ephesians as a synthesis of Paul's thought. Today's passage seems to generalize from his argument in Romans. Here in Ephesians, the concept of divine election—God's choice of Israel, first revealed in the call of Abraham—is taken over from the Hebrew Scriptures. Christians now are "chosen" by God to receive a promised "inheritance."

Today's Gospel makes it clear that divine election is a costly grace. Jesus prepares his friends and followers for the real possibility of persecution. But he assures them, and us as well, that in the eyes of God we are worth more than many sparrows.

Year I

FIRST READING

Rom 4:1–8

Abraham believed God, and it was credited to him as righteousness.

A reading from the Letter of Saint Paul to the Romans

Brothers and sisters:

What can we say that Abraham found, our ancestor according to the flesh? Indeed, if Abraham was justified on the basis of his works, he has reason to boast; but this was not so in the sight of God. For what does the Scripture say? *Abraham believed God, and it was credited to him as righteousness.* A worker's wage is credited not as a gift, but as something due. But when one does not work, yet believes in the one who justifies the ungodly, his faith is credited as righteousness. So also David declares the blessedness of the person to whom God credits righteousness apart from works:

> *Blessed are they whose iniquities are forgiven*
>   *and whose sins are covered.*
> *Blessed is the man whose sin the Lord does not record.*

The word of the Lord.

Responsorial Psalm

Ps 32:1b–2, 5, 11

**R. I turn to you, Lord, in time of trouble,
   and you fill me with the joy of salvation.**

Blessed is he whose fault is taken away,
  whose sin is covered.
Blessed the man to whom the Lord imputes not guilt,
  in whose spirit there is no guile.

**R. I turn to you, Lord, in time of trouble,
   and you fill me with the joy of salvation.**

Then I acknowledged my sin to you,
  my guilt I covered not.
I said, "I confess my faults to the Lord,"
  and you took away the guilt of my sin.

**R. I turn to you, Lord, in time of trouble,
   and you fill me with the joy of salvation.**

Be glad in the Lord and rejoice, you just;
  exult, all you upright of heart.

**R. I turn to you, Lord, in time of trouble,
   and you fill me with the joy of salvation.**

Alleluia Verse *and Gospel, p. 1583.*

Year II

FIRST READING

Eph 1:11–14

We first hoped in Christ, and you were sealed with the Holy Spirit.

A reading from the Letter of Saint Paul to the Ephesians

Brothers and sisters:

In Christ we were also chosen, destined in accord with the purpose of the One who accomplishes all things according to the intention of his will, so that we might exist for the praise of his glory, we who first hoped in Christ. In him you also, who have heard the word of truth, the Gospel of your salvation, and have believed in him, were sealed with the promised Holy Spirit, which is the first installment of our inheritance toward redemption as God's possession, to the praise of his glory.

The word of the Lord.

Responsional Psalm — Ps 33:1–2, 4–5, 12–13

R. **Blessed the people the Lord has chosen to be his own.**

Exult, you just, in the LORD;
  praise from the upright is fitting.
Give thanks to the LORD on the harp;
  with the ten-stringed lyre chant his praises.

R. **Blessed the people the Lord has chosen to be his own.**

For upright is the word of the LORD,
  and all his works are trustworthy.
He loves justice and right;
  of the kindness of the LORD the earth is full.

R. **Blessed the people the Lord has chosen to be his own.**

Blessed the nation whose God is the LORD,
  the people he has chosen for his own inheritance.
From heaven the LORD looks down;
  he sees all mankind.

R. **Blessed the people the Lord has chosen to be his own.**

Alleluia, alleluia Ps 33:22
May your kindness, O LORD, be upon us;
who have put our hope in you.
Alleluia, alleluia

Years I and II

GOSPEL

Lk 12:1–7

Even the hairs of your head have all been counted.

A reading from the holy Gospel according to Luke

At that time: So many people were crowding together that they were trampling one another underfoot. Jesus began to speak, first to his disciples, "Beware of the leaven—that is, the hypocrisy—of the Pharisees.

"There is nothing concealed that will not be revealed, nor secret that will not be known. Therefore whatever you have said in the darkness will be heard in the light, and what you have whispered behind closed doors will be proclaimed on the housetops. I tell you, my friends, do not be afraid of those who kill the body but after that can do no more. I shall show you whom to fear. Be afraid of the one who after killing has the power to cast into Gehenna; yes, I tell you, be afraid of that one. Are not five sparrows sold for two small coins? Yet not one of them has escaped the notice of God. Even the hairs of your head have all been counted. Do not be afraid. You are worth more than many sparrows."

The Gospel of the Lord.

Liturgy of the Eucharist, *p. 897;* **Prayer over the Gifts,** *p. 1563.*

Saturday

Antiphons and Prayers, *p. 1562;* **Liturgy of the Word** *for Year I (odd years) follows; Year II (even years), p. 1586.*

TODAY'S LIVING WORD

In today's reading Paul tells the Romans that all "depends on faith, so that it may be a gift." The author of the Letter to the Ephesians, having heard of that community's faith, gives thanks for the way in which God's grace—"the surpassing greatness of his power for us who believe"—has manifested itself in them and through them.

The vision of Ephesians is triumphant. The Gospel, however, envisions a different scenario. The promised triumph, "before the angels of God" at the judgment, will depend on the disciples' uncompromising loyalty to the Son of Man when they are brought before the judges of this world. But even here those who live by faith in the God "who gives life to the dead" are assured of God's grace. Jesus says, "Do not worry about how or what your defense will be or about what you are to say. For the Holy Spirit will teach you at that moment what you should say."

Year I

FIRST READING

Rom 4:13, 16–18

Abraham believed, hoping against hope.

A reading from the Letter of Saint Paul to the Romans

Brothers and sisters:

It was not through the law that the promise was made to Abraham and his descendants that he would inherit the world, but through the righteousness that comes from faith. For this reason, it depends on faith, so that it may be a gift, and the promise may be guaranteed to all his descendants, not to those who only adhere to the law but to those who follow the faith of Abraham, who is the father of all of us, as it is written, *I have made you father of many nations.* He is our father in the sight of God, in whom he believed, who gives life to the dead and calls into being what does not exist. He believed, hoping against hope, that he would become *the father of many nations,* according to what was said, *Thus shall your descendants be.* The word of the Lord.

Responsorial Psalm

Ps 105:6–7, 8–9, 42–43

R. The Lord remembers his covenant for ever.

You descendants of Abraham, his servants,
  sons of Jacob, his chosen ones!
He, the LORD, is our God;
  throughout the earth his judgments prevail.

R. The Lord remembers his covenant for ever.

He remembers forever his covenant
  which he made binding for a thousand generations—
Which he entered into with Abraham
  and by his oath to Isaac.

R. The Lord remembers his covenant for ever.

For he remembered his holy word
  to his servant Abraham.
And he led forth his people with joy;
  with shouts of joy, his chosen ones.

R. The Lord remembers his covenant for ever.

Alleluia Verse and **Gospel,** *p. 1588.*

Year II

FIRST READING

Eph 1:15–23

He gave Christ as head over all things
to the Church, which is his Body.

A reading from the Letter of Saint Paul to the Ephesians

Brothers and sisters:

Hearing of your faith in the Lord Jesus and of your love for all the holy ones, I do not cease giving thanks for you, remembering you in my prayers, that the God of our Lord Jesus Christ, the Father of glory, may give you a spirit of wisdom and revelation resulting in knowledge of him. May the eyes of your hearts be enlightened, that you may know what is the hope that belongs to his call, what are the riches of glory in his inheritance among the holy ones, and what is the surpassing greatness of his power for us who believe, in accord with the exercise of his great might, which he worked in Christ, raising him from the dead and seating him at his right hand in the heavens, far above every principality, authority, power, and dominion, and every name that is named not only in this age but also in the one to come. And he put all things beneath his feet and gave him as head over all things to the Church, which is his Body, the fullness of the one who fills all things in every way.

The word of the Lord.

Responsorial Psalm

Ps 8:2–3ab, 4–5, 6–7

R. **You have given your Son rule over the works of your hands.**

O LORD, our LORD,
  how glorious is your name over all the earth!
  You have exalted your majesty above the heavens.
Out of the mouths of babes and sucklings
  you have fashioned praise because of your foes.

R. **You have given your Son rule over the works of your hands.**

When I behold your heavens, the work of your fingers,
  the moon and the stars which you set in place—
What is man that you should be mindful of him,
  or the son of man that you should care for him?

R. **You have given your Son rule over the works of your hands.**

You have made him little less than the angels,
  and crowned him with glory and honor.

You have given him rule over the works of your hands,
  putting all things under his feet.

**R. You have given your Son rule over the works of your
  hands.**

Alleluia, alleluia Jn 15:26b, 27a
The Spirit of truth will testify to me, says the Lord,
and you also will testify.
Alleluia, alleluia

Years I and II

GOSPEL   Lk 12:8–12

*The Holy Spirit will teach you at that
moment what you should say.*

A reading from the holy Gospel according to Luke

Jesus said to his disciples: "I tell you, everyone who acknowledges me before others the Son of Man will acknowledge
before the angels of God. But whoever denies me before others
will be denied before the angels of God.

"Everyone who speaks a word against the Son of Man will
be forgiven, but the one who blasphemes against the Holy Spirit
will not be forgiven. When they take you before synagogues
and before rulers and authorities, do not worry about how
or what your defense will be or about what you are to say.
For the Holy Spirit will teach you at that moment what you
should say."

The Gospel of the Lord.

Liturgy of the Eucharist, *p. 897;* **Prayer over the Gifts,** *p. 1563.*

TWENTY-NINTH WEEK IN ORDINARY TIME

*The **Antiphons and Prayers** may be the following, or may be chosen from any of the other 33 weeks in Ordinary Time (refer to Liturgical Calendar, pp. 26–41).*

*The **Liturgy of the Word** varies: for Monday, see p. 1591; Tuesday, p. 1595; Wednesday, p. 1599; Thursday, p. 1604; Friday, p. 1608; Saturday, p. 1612.*

Entrance Antiphon

I call upon you, God, for you will answer me; bend your ear and hear my prayer. Guard me as the pupil of your eye; hide me in the shade of your wings. (Ps 17:6, 8)

Opening Prayer

Let us pray
    [for the gift of simplicity and joy
    in our service of God and man]
        Pause for silent prayer.

Almighty and ever-living God,
our source of power and inspiration,
give us strength and joy
in serving you as followers of Christ,
who lives and reigns with you and the Holy Spirit,
one God, for ever and ever.

Alternative Opening Prayer

Let us pray
    [to the Lord who bends close to hear our prayer]
        Pause for silent prayer.

Lord our God, Father of all,
you guard us under the shadow of your wings

and search into the depths of our hearts.
Remove the blindness that cannot know you
and relieve the fear that would hide us from your sight.

We ask this through Christ our Lord.

Prayer over the Gifts

Pray, brethren...

Lord God,
may the gifts we offer
bring us your love and forgiveness
and give us freedom to serve you with our lives.

We ask this in the name of Jesus the Lord.

Preface of Weekdays in Ordinary Time I–VI, *pp. 948–950.*

Communion Antiphon

See how the eyes of the Lord are on those who fear him, on those who hope in his love, that he may rescue them from death and feed them in time of famine. (Ps 33:18–19)

Or:

The Son of Man came to give his life as a ransom for many. (Mk 10:45)

Prayer after Communion

Let us pray.
Pause for silent prayer, if this has not preceded.

Lord,
may this eucharist help us to remain faithful.
May it teach us the way to eternal life.

Grant this through Christ our Lord.

Monday

Antiphons and Prayers, *p. 1589;* **Liturgy of the Word** *for Year I (odd years) follows; Year II (even years), p. 1593.*

Today's Living Word

Commenting on today's Gospel, Luke Timothy Johnson notes how astutely Luke has grasped the function of possessions in human life.* Luke seems to know that greed expresses fear, a massive insecurity that seeks to secure life with many possessions. The only way to dispel such fear is to recognize that life is a gift from the living God, a gift that no amount of material possessions can gain or guarantee. The man in the parable is a fool because he thinks that having insured his many possessions, he has secured his life "for many years."

For Paul writing to the Romans, Abraham is the paradigm of the person of faith who accepts God's promise of life as a gift, never questioning or doubting it and never trying to secure it by his own power or possessions. Such faith relies rather on what Ephesians describes as "the immeasurable riches of [God's] grace in his kindness to us in Christ Jesus."

* *The Gospel of Luke,* Sacra Pagina 3 (Collegeville: Liturgical Press, 1991), p. 201.

Year I

FIRST READING

Rom 4:20–25

It was written for us when it says that our faith in God will be counted.

A reading from the Letter of Saint Paul to the Romans

Brothers and sisters:

Abraham did not doubt God's promise in unbelief; rather, he was empowered by faith and gave glory to God and was fully convinced that what God had promised he was also able to do. That is why *it was credited to him as righteousness.* But it was not for him alone that it was written that *it was credited to him;* it was also for us, to whom it will be credited, who believe in the one who raised Jesus our Lord from the dead, who was handed over for our transgressions and was raised for our justification.

The word of the Lord.

Responsorial Psalm

Lk 1:69–70, 71–72, 73–75

R. **Blessed be the Lord, the God of Israel;
he has come to his people.**

He has come to his people and set them free.
He has raised up for us a mighty savior,
  born of the house of his servant David.

R. **Blessed be the Lord, the God of Israel;
he has come to his people.**

Through his holy prophets he promised of old
  that he would save us from our enemies,
  from the hands of all who hate us.
He promised to show mercy to our fathers
  and to remember his holy covenant.

R. **Blessed be the Lord, the God of Israel;
he has come to his people.**

This was the oath he swore to our father Abraham:
  to set us free from the hands of our enemies,
  free to worship him without fear,
  holy and righteous in his sight all the days of our life.

R. **Blessed be the Lord, the God of Israel;
he has come to his people.**

Alleluia Verse *and* **Gospel,** *p. 1594.*

Year II

FIRST READING

Eph 2:1–10

*God brought us to life with Christ
and seated us with him in the heavens.*

A reading from the Letter of Saint Paul to the Ephesians

Brothers and sisters:

You were dead in your transgressions and sins in which you once lived following the age of this world, following the ruler of the power of the air, the spirit that is now at work in the disobedient. All of us once lived among them in the desires of our flesh, following the wishes of the flesh and the impulses, and we were by nature children of wrath, like the rest. But God, who is rich in mercy, because of the great love he had for us, even when we were dead in our transgressions, brought us to life with Christ (by grace you have been saved), raised us up with him, and seated us with him in the heavens in Christ Jesus, that in the ages to come he might show the immeasurable riches of his grace in his kindness to us in Christ Jesus. For by grace you have been saved through faith, and this is not from you; it is the gift of God; it is not from works, so no one may boast. For we are his handiwork, created in Christ Jesus for good works that God has prepared in advance, that we should live in them.

The word of the Lord.

Responsorial Psalm

Ps 100:1b–2, 3, 4ab, 4c–5

R. **The Lord made us, we belong to him.**

Sing joyfully to the LORD all you lands;
 serve the LORD with gladness;
 come before him with joyful song.

R. The Lord made us, we belong to him.

Know that the LORD is God;
  he made us, his we are;
  his people, the flock he tends.

R. The Lord made us, we belong to him.

Enter his gates with thanksgiving,
  his courts with praise.

R. The Lord made us, we belong to him.

Give thanks to him; bless his name, for he is good:
  the LORD, whose kindness endures forever,
  and his faithfulness, to all generations.

R. The Lord made us, we belong to him.

> **Alleluia, alleluia** Mt 5:3
> Blessed are the poor in spirit;
> for theirs is the Kingdom of heaven.
> **Alleluia, alleluia**

Years I and II

GOSPEL   Lk 12:13–21

And the things you have prepared, to whom will they belong?

A reading from the holy Gospel according to Luke

Someone in the crowd said to Jesus, "Teacher, tell my brother to share the inheritance with me." He replied to him, "Friend, who appointed me as your judge and arbitrator?" Then he said to the crowd, "Take care to guard against all greed, for though one may be rich, one's life does not consist of possessions."

Then he told them a parable. "There was a rich man whose land produced a bountiful harvest. He asked himself, 'What shall I do, for I do not have space to store my harvest?' And he said, 'This is what I shall do: I shall tear down my barns and build larger ones. There I shall store all my grain and other goods and I shall say to myself, "Now as for you, you have so many good things stored up for many years, rest, eat, drink, be merry!"' But God said to him, 'You fool, this night your life will be demanded of you; and the things you have prepared, to whom will they belong?' Thus will it be for the one who stores up treasure for himself but is not rich in what matters to God."

The Gospel of the Lord.

Liturgy of the Eucharist, *p. 897;* **Prayer over the Gifts,** *p. 1590.*

Tuesday

Antiphons and Prayers, *p. 1589;* **Liturgy of the Word** *for Year I (odd years) follows; Year II (even years), p. 1597.*

TODAY'S LIVING WORD

In today's Gospel Luke gives particular force to the familiar exhortation to wait and watch for the Master's return. In Luke's version the Master, finding his servants wide-awake, "will gird himself, have them recline at table, and proceed to wait on them." This striking image points in two directions. It looks ahead to the Last Supper where Jesus will declare, "I am among you as the one who serves" (22:27). It also looks back, as does the reading from Romans, to suggest a contrast with Adam. The haughtiness of Adam, who overreached himself in his desire to be like a god, is redeemed by the humility of Jesus, who makes himself the servant of all. Or as Paul puts it, "Just as through the disobedience of one man the many were made sinners, so, through the obedience of the one the many will be made righteous."

The letter to the Ephesians today picks up this strain and proclaims what the obedience of Christ has achieved for us. He has not only reconciled us to God but to one another, making us, in himself, one new humanity.

FIRST READING
Rom 5:12, 15b, 17–19, 20b–21

If by the transgressions of one person death came to reign, how much more will those who receive grace come to reign in life.

A reading from the Letter of Saint Paul to the Romans

Brothers and sisters:
Through one man sin entered the world, and through sin, death, and thus death came to all men, inasmuch as all sinned.

If by that one person's transgression the many died, how much more did the grace of God and the gracious gift of the one man Jesus Christ overflow for the many. For if, by the transgression of the one, death came to reign through that one, how much more will those who receive the abundance of grace and the gift of justification come to reign in life through the one Jesus Christ. In conclusion, just as through one transgression condemnation came upon all, so, through one righteous act acquittal and life came to all. For just as through the disobedience of one man the many were made sinners, so, through the obedience of the one the many will be made righteous. Where sin increased, grace overflowed all the more, so that, as sin reigned in death, grace also might reign through justification for eternal life through Jesus Christ our Lord.

The word of the Lord.

Responsorial Psalm
Ps 40:7–8a, 8b–9, 10, 17

R. Here I am, Lord; I come to do your will.

Sacrifice or oblation you wished not,
    but ears open to obedience you gave me.
Burnt offerings or sin-offerings you sought not;
    then said I, "Behold I come."

R. Here I am, Lord; I come to do your will.

"In the written scroll it is prescribed for me,
To do your will, O my God, is my delight,
   and your law is within my heart!"

R. Here I am, Lord; I come to do your will.

I announced your justice in the vast assembly;
   I did not restrain my lips, as you, O LORD, know.

R. Here I am, Lord; I come to do your will.

May all who seek you
   exult and be glad in you,
And may those who love your salvation
   say ever, "The LORD be glorified."

R. Here I am, Lord; I come to do your will.

Alleluia Verse *and* **Gospel,** *p. 1599.*

Year II

FIRST READING

Eph 2:12–22

He is our peace; he made both one.

A reading from the Letter of Saint Paul to the Ephesians

Brothers and sisters:

You were at that time without Christ, alienated from the community of Israel and strangers to the covenants of promise, without hope and without God in the world. But now in Christ Jesus you who once were far off have become near by the Blood of Christ.

For he is our peace, he made both one and broke down the dividing wall of enmity, through his Flesh, abolishing the law with its commandments and legal claims, that he might create in himself one new person in place of the two, thus establishing peace, and might reconcile both with God, in one Body, through the cross, putting that enmity to death by it. He came and preached peace to you who were far off and peace to those who were near, for through him we both have access in one Spirit to the Father.

So then you are no longer strangers and sojourners, but you are fellow citizens with the holy ones and members of the household of God, built upon the foundation of the Apostles and prophets, with Christ Jesus himself as the capstone. Through him the whole structure is held together and grows into a temple sacred in the Lord; in him you also are being built together into a dwelling place of God in the Spirit.

The word of the Lord.

Responsorial Psalm

Ps 85:9ab–10, 11–12, 13–14

R. The Lord speaks of peace to his people.

I will hear what God proclaims;
  the LORD—for he proclaims peace.
Near indeed is his salvation to those who fear him,
  glory dwelling in our land.

R. The Lord speaks of peace to his people.

Kindness and truth shall meet;
  justice and peace shall kiss.
Truth shall spring out of the earth,
  and justice shall look down from heaven.

R. The Lord speaks of peace to his people.

The LORD himself will give his benefits;
  our land shall yield its increase.
Justice shall walk before him,
  and salvation, along the way of his steps.

R. The Lord speaks of peace to his people.

Alleluia, alleluia Lk 21:36
Be vigilant at all times and pray
that you may have the strength to stand before the Son of Man.
Alleluia, alleluia

Years I and II

GOSPEL
Lk 12:35–38

*Blessed are those servants whom the master
finds vigilant on his arrival.*

A reading from the holy Gospel according to Luke

Jesus said to his disciples: "Gird your loins and light your lamps and be like servants who await their master's return from a wedding, ready to open immediately when he comes and knocks. Blessed are those servants whom the master finds vigilant on his arrival. Amen, I say to you, he will gird himself, have them recline at table, and proceed to wait on them. And should he come in the second or third watch and find them prepared in this way, blessed are those servants."

The Gospel of the Lord.

Liturgy of the Eucharist, *p. 897;* **Prayer over the Gifts,** *p. 1590.*

Wednesday

Antiphons and Prayers, *p. 1589;* **Liturgy of the Word** *for Year I (odd years) follows; Year II (even years), p. 1601.*

TODAY'S LIVING WORD

Peter's question in today's Gospel alerts us that this parable of Jesus is meant not only for the Twelve, but also for all who will succeed them as leaders in the household of God. To appreciate the force of Jesus' teaching, it is important to remember that the steward who is set over the other servants remains himself subject to the authority of the Master. In other words, the leader is also a servant, a slave. His position is not a privilege. Rather it is a test and a trust—a test of how well he knows the Master's wishes and a sacred trust that will require of him a greater degree of accountability. To him especially Paul's words in Romans apply: "If you present yourselves to someone as obedient slaves, you are slaves of the one you obey."

In today's selection from Ephesians, Paul shows himself mindful of the ministry that God has entrusted to him. He claims as well to know his Master's wishes, "the mystery" to make Gentiles as well as Jews sharers of the promise, and he commits himself responsibly and unreservedly to it.

Year I

FIRST READING   Rom 6:12–18

Present yourselves to God as raised from the dead to life.

A reading from the Letter of Saint Paul to the Romans

Brothers and sisters:

Sin must not reign over your mortal bodies so that you obey their desires. And do not present the parts of your bodies to sin as weapons for wickedness, but present yourselves to God as raised from the dead to life and the parts of your bodies to God as weapons for righteousness. For sin is not to have any power over you, since you are not under the law but under grace.

What then? Shall we sin because we are not under the law but under grace? Of course not! Do you not know that if you present yourselves to someone as obedient slaves, you are slaves of the one you obey, either of sin, which leads to death, or of obedience, which leads to righteousness? But thanks be to God that, although you were once slaves of sin, you have become obedient from the heart to the pattern of teaching to which you were entrusted. Freed from sin, you have become slaves of righteousness.

The word of the Lord.

Responsorial Psalm

Ps 124:1b–3, 4–6, 7–8

R. Our help is in the name of the Lord.

Had not the LORD been with us,
　let Israel say, had not the LORD been with us—
When men rose up against us,
　then would they have swallowed us alive;
When their fury was inflamed against us.

R. Our help is in the name of the Lord.

Then would the waters have overwhelmed us;
The torrent would have swept over us;
　over us then would have swept the raging waters.
Blessed be the LORD, who did not leave us
　a prey to their teeth.

R. Our help is in the name of the Lord.

We were rescued like a bird
　from the fowlers' snare;
Broken was the snare,
　and we were freed.
Our help is in the name of the LORD,
　who made heaven and earth.

R. Our help is in the name of the Lord.

Alleluia Verse *and* **Gospel,** *p. 1603.*

Year II

FIRST READING

Eph 3:2–12

The mystery of Christ has now been revealed
and the Gentiles are coheirs in the promise.

A reading from the Letter of Saint Paul to the Ephesians

Brothers and sisters:

You have heard of the stewardship of God's grace that was given to me for your benefit, namely, that the mystery was made known to me by revelation, as I have written briefly earlier. When you read this you can understand my insight into the mystery of Christ, which was not made known to human beings in other generations as it has now been revealed to his holy Apostles and prophets by the Spirit, that the Gentiles are coheirs, members of the same Body, and copartners in the promise in Christ Jesus through the Gospel.

Of this I became a minister by the gift of God's grace that was granted me in accord with the exercise of his power. To me, the very least of all the holy ones, this grace was given, to preach to the Gentiles the inscrutable riches of Christ, and to bring to light for all what is the plan of the mystery hidden from ages past in God who created all things, so that the manifold wisdom of God might now be made known through the Church to the principalities and authorities in the heavens. This was according to the eternal purpose that he accomplished in Christ Jesus our Lord, in whom we have boldness of speech and confidence of access through faith in him.

The word of the Lord.

Responsorial Psalm

Is 12:2–3, 4bcd, 5–6

R. **You will draw water joyfully from the springs of salvation.**

God indeed is my savior;
  I am confident and unafraid.
My strength and my courage is the LORD,
  and he has been my savior.

With joy you will draw water
  at the fountain of salvation.

> **R. You will draw water joyfully from the springs
>   of salvation.**

Give thanks to the LORD, acclaim his name;
  among the nations make known his deeds,
  proclaim how exalted is his name.

> **R. You will draw water joyfully from the springs
>   of salvation.**

Sing praise to the LORD for his glorious achievement;
  let this be known throughout all the earth.
Shout with exultation, O city of Zion,
  for great in your midst
  is the Holy One of Israel!

> **R. You will draw water joyfully from the springs
>   of salvation.**

Alleluia, alleluia Mt 24:42a, 44
Stay awake!
For you do not know when the Son of Man will come.
Alleluia, alleluia

Years I and II

GOSPEL Lk 12:39–48

Much will be required of the person entrusted with much.

A reading from the holy Gospel according to Luke

Jesus said to his disciples: "Be sure of this: if the master of the house had known the hour when the thief was coming, he would not have let his house be broken into. You also must be prepared, for at an hour you do not expect, the Son of Man will come."

Then Peter said, "Lord, is this parable meant for us or for everyone?" And the Lord replied, "Who, then, is the faithful and prudent steward whom the master will put in charge of his servants to distribute the food allowance at the proper time? Blessed is that servant whom his master on arrival finds doing so. Truly, I say to you, he will put him in charge of all his property. But if that servant says to himself, 'My master is delayed in coming,' and begins to beat the menservants and the maidservants, to eat and drink and get drunk, then that servant's master will come on an unexpected day and at an unknown hour and will punish the servant severely and assign him a place with the unfaithful. That servant who knew his master's will but did not make preparations nor act in accord with his will shall be beaten severely; and the servant who was ignorant of his master's will but acted in a way deserving of a severe beating shall be beaten only lightly. Much will be required of the person entrusted with much, and still more will be demanded of the person entrusted with more."

The Gospel of the Lord.

Liturgy of the Eucharist, *p. 897;* **Prayer over the Gifts,** *p. 1590.*

Thursday

Antiphons and Prayers, *p. 1589;* **Liturgy of the Word** *for Year I (odd years) follows; Year II (even years), p. 1606.*

TODAY'S LIVING WORD

In today's selection from Luke, Jesus the messianic prophet is like Elijah who called down fire on the earth (cf. 1 Kgs 18:38). But is it the fire of judgment, as in the story of Elijah, or the fire of the Spirit? Similarly, Jesus says he has a baptism to undergo. But is he referring to his death or to the descent of the Holy Spirit? These sayings are ambiguous. It is not ambiguous, however, that the God revealed in Jesus, the same God revealed through Elijah on Mt.

Carmel, demands a decision, a decision that may sever the closest family ties. Simeon had prophesied this (cf. 2:35), and Jesus himself now proclaims it.

In today's reading, Paul hints at the critical decision that the Christians at Rome have made. He reminds them of how they were once the slaves of sin; now they must be "slaves to righteousness." The same is implied of the Ephesians. Their decision Paul credits to their being "strengthened with power through his Spirit." That same power is at work in us too, enabling us, in turn, to decide to let the love of Christ be the root and foundation of our lives.

Year I

FIRST READING

Rom 6:19–23

Now you have been freed from sin
and have been become slaves of God.

A reading from the Letter of Saint Paul to the Romans

Brothers and sisters:

I am speaking in human terms because of the weakness of your nature. For just as you presented the parts of your bodies as slaves to impurity and to lawlessness for lawlessness, so now present them as slaves to righteousness for sanctification. For when you were slaves of sin, you were free from righteousness. But what profit did you get then from the things of which you are now ashamed? For the end of those things is death. But now that you have been freed from sin and have become slaves of God, the benefit that you have leads to sanctification, and its end is eternal life. For the wages of sin is death, but the gift of God is eternal life in Christ Jesus our Lord.

The word of the Lord.

Responsorial Psalm

Ps 1:1–2, 3, 4 and 6

R. Blessed are they who hope in the Lord.

Blessed the man who follows not
  the counsel of the wicked
Nor walks in the way of sinners,
  nor sits in the company of the insolent,
But delights in the law of the LORD
  and meditates on his law day and night.

R. Blessed are they who hope in the Lord.

He is like a tree
  planted near running water,
That yields its fruit in due season,
  and whose leaves never fade.
  Whatever he does, prospers.

R. Blessed are they who hope in the Lord.

Not so the wicked, not so;
  they are like chaff which the wind drives away.
For the LORD watches over the way of the just,
  but the way of the wicked vanishes.

R. Blessed are they who hope in the Lord.

Alleluia Verse *and* **Gospel,** *p. 1608.*

Year II

FIRST READING

Eph 3:14–21

Rooted and grounded in love,
you may be filled with the fullness of God.

A reading from the Letter of Saint Paul to the Ephesians

Brothers and sisters:

I kneel before the Father, from whom every family in heaven
and on earth is named, that he may grant you in accord with
the riches of his glory to be strengthened with power through

his Spirit in the inner self, and that Christ may dwell in your hearts through faith; that you, rooted and grounded in love, may have strength to comprehend with all the holy ones what is the breadth and length and height and depth, and to know the love of Christ that surpasses knowledge, so that you may be filled with all the fullness of God.

Now to him who is able to accomplish far more than all we ask or imagine, by the power at work within us, to him be glory in the Church and in Christ Jesus to all generations, forever and ever. Amen.

The word of the Lord.

Responsorial Psalm

Ps 33:1–2, 4–5, 11–12, 18–19

R. The earth is full of the goodness of the Lord.

Exult, you just, in the Lord;
  praise from the upright is fitting.
Give thanks to the Lord on the harp;
  with the ten-stringed lyre chant his praises.

R. The earth is full of the goodness of the Lord.

For upright is the word of the Lord,
  and all his works are trustworthy.
He loves justice and right;
  of the kindness of the Lord the earth is full.

R. The earth is full of the goodness of the Lord.

But the plan of the Lord stands forever;
  the design of his heart, through all generations.
Blessed the nation whose God is the Lord,
  the people he has chosen for his own inheritance.

R. The earth is full of the goodness of the Lord.

But see, the eyes of the Lord are upon those who fear him,
  upon those who hope for his kindness,
To deliver them from death
  and preserve them in spite of famine.

R. **The earth is full of the goodness of the Lord.**

Alleluia, alleluia   Phil 3:8–9
I consider all things so much rubbish
that I may gain Christ and be found in him.
Alleluia, alleluia

Years I and II

GOSPEL   Lk 12:49–53
I have not come to establish peace but division.

A reading from the holy Gospel according to Luke

Jesus said to his disciples: "I have come to set the earth on fire, and how I wish it were already blazing! There is a baptism with which I must be baptized, and how great is my anguish until it is accomplished! Do you think that I have come to establish peace on the earth? No, I tell you, but rather division. From now on a household of five will be divided, three against two and two against three; a father will be divided against his son and a son against his father, a mother against her daughter and a daughter against her mother, a mother-in-law against her daughter-in-law and a daughter-in-law against her mother-in-law."

The Gospel of the Lord.

Liturgy of the Eucharist, *p. 897;* **Prayer over the Gifts,** *p. 1590.*

Friday

Antiphons and Prayers, *p. 1589;* **Liturgy of the Word** *for Year I (odd years) follows; Year II (even years), p. 1610.*

TODAY'S LIVING WORD

The need to discern the present time and to decide for Jesus is reiterated in today's Gospel reading—with two added features. First,

Jesus insists that each one must make this decision for himself or herself. "Why do you not judge for yourselves what is right?" he asks. The short parable that concludes the reading makes the second point. In Matthew, this parable is part of a lesson in the Sermon on the Mount on how Jesus' followers should deal with one another. In Luke, however, the setting is Jesus' journey to Jerusalem. Here the opponent is not a fellow Christian, but Jesus himself who urges all he meets to decide, that is, "to settle the matter on the way."

The two first readings for today illustrate the challenge of this decision. The law of sin that Paul describes in Romans, that centrifugal pull away from the law of God, makes impossible a decision that would recenter the whole of life, impossible except for the grace of God. Grace also makes it possible for us, as well as for the Ephesians, to live lives worthy of the calling we have received.

Year I

FIRST READING

Rom 7:18–25a

Who will deliver me from this mortal body?

A reading from the Letter of Saint Paul to the Romans

Brothers and sisters:

I know that good does not dwell in me, that is, in my flesh. The willing is ready at hand, but doing the good is not. For I do not do the good I want, but I do the evil I do not want. Now if I do what I do not want, it is no longer I who do it, but sin that dwells in me. So, then, I discover the principle that when I want to do right, evil is at hand. For I take delight in the law of God, in my inner self, but I see in my members another principle at war with the law of my mind, taking me captive to the law of sin that dwells in my members. Miserable one that I am! Who will deliver me from this mortal body? Thanks be to God through Jesus Christ our Lord.

The word of the Lord.

Responsorial Psalm

Ps 119:66, 68, 76, 77, 93, 94

R. Lord, teach me your statutes.

Teach me wisdom and knowledge,
  for in your commands I trust.

R. Lord, teach me your statutes.

You are good and bountiful;
  teach me your statutes.

R. Lord, teach me your statutes.

Let your kindness comfort me
  according to your promise to your servants.

R. Lord, teach me your statutes.

Let your compassion come to me that I may live,
  for your law is my delight.

R. Lord, teach me your statutes.

Never will I forget your precepts,
  for through them you give me life.

R. Lord, teach me your statutes.

I am yours; save me,
  for I have sought your precepts.

R. Lord, teach me your statutes.

Alleluia Verse *and* **Gospel**, *p. 1611f.*

Year II

FIRST READING

Eph 4:1–6

There is one Body, one Lord, one faith, one baptism.

A reading from the Letter of Saint Paul to the Ephesians

Brothers and sisters:

I, a prisoner for the Lord, urge you to live in a manner worthy of the call you have received, with all humility and gentleness, with patience, bearing with one another through love, striving to preserve the unity of the spirit through the bond of peace; one Body and one Spirit, as you were also called to the one hope of your call; one Lord, one faith, one baptism; one God and Father of all, who is over all and through all and in all.

The word of the Lord.

Responsorial Psalm
Ps 24:1–2, 3–4ab, 5–6

R. **Lord, this is the people that longs to see your face.**

The Lord's are the earth and its fullness;
  the world and those who dwell in it.
For he founded it upon the seas
  and established it upon the rivers.

R. **Lord, this is the people that longs to see your face.**

Who can ascend the mountain of the Lord?
  or who may stand in his holy place?
He whose hands are sinless, whose heart is clean,
  who desires not what is vain.

R. **Lord, this is the people that longs to see your face.**

He shall receive a blessing from the Lord,
  a reward from God his savior.
Such is the race that seeks for him,
  that seeks the face of the God of Jacob.

R. **Lord, this is the people that longs to see your face.**

Alleluia, alleluia See Mt 11:25
Blessed are you, Father, Lord of heaven and earth;
  you have revealed to little ones the mysteries of the Kingdom.
Alleluia, alleluia

Years I and II

GOSPEL   Lk 12:54–59

You know how to interpret the appearance of the earth and sky;
why do you not know how to interpret the present time?

A reading from the holy Gospel according to Luke

Jesus said to the crowds, "When you see a cloud rising in the west you say immediately that it is going to rain—and so it does; and when you notice that the wind is blowing from the south you say that it is going to be hot—and so it is. You hypocrites! You know how to interpret the appearance of the earth and the sky; why do you not know how to interpret the present time?

"Why do you not judge for yourselves what is right? If you are to go with your opponent before a magistrate, make an effort to settle the matter on the way; otherwise your opponent will turn you over to the judge, and the judge hand you over to the constable, and the constable throw you into prison. I say to you, you will not be released until you have paid the last penny."

The Gospel of the Lord.

Liturgy of the Eucharist, *p. 897;* **Prayer over the Gifts,** *p. 1590.*

Saturday

Antiphons and Prayers, *p. 1589;* **Liturgy of the Word** *for Year I (odd years) follows; Year II (even years), p. 1615.*

TODAY'S LIVING WORD

Paul exhorts the Ephesians that they may no longer be children. Today's Gospel is surely not for children. It begins with two reports only found in Luke of sudden and violent death, which Jesus turns into dire warnings for his listeners. "If you do not repent, you will all perish as they did!" Since we cannot secure our lives, death is always near for all of us, so we must not postpone repentance.

Although Luke's version of the parable of the fig tree suggests that a little more time has been given, without repentance the end remains the same. If the fig tree does not bear fruit, it will surely be cut down.

For Paul, as for Luke, repentance is not simply turning away from sin, but turning toward Jesus in faith. He tells the Romans, "Now there is no condemnation for those who are in Christ Jesus," that is, for those in whom the Spirit of God dwells. The Spirit gives to each and every one of us gifts that enable us to do the truth in love and so grow, as one body, to the full maturity of Christ our head.

Year I

FIRST READING

Rom 8:1–11

The Spirit of the one who raised Jesus from the dead dwells in you.

A reading from the Letter of Saint Paul to the Romans

Brothers and sisters:

Now there is no condemnation for those who are in Christ Jesus. For the law of the spirit of life in Christ Jesus has freed you from the law of sin and death. For what the law, weakened by the flesh, was powerless to do, this God has done: by sending his own Son in the likeness of sinful flesh and for the sake of sin, he condemned sin in the flesh, so that the righteous decree of the law might be fulfilled in us, who live not according to the flesh but according to the spirit. For those who live according to the flesh are concerned with the things of the flesh, but those who live according to the spirit with the things of the spirit. The concern of the flesh is death, but the concern of the spirit is life and peace. For the concern of the flesh is hostility toward God; it does not submit to the law of God, nor can it; and those who are in the flesh cannot please God. But you are not in the flesh; on the contrary, you are in the spirit, if only the Spirit of God dwells in you. Whoever does not have the Spirit of Christ does not belong to him. But if Christ is in you, although the body is dead because of sin, the spirit is alive because of righteousness. If the Spirit of the one who raised Jesus from the dead dwells in you, the one who raised Christ from the dead will give life to your mortal bodies also, through his Spirit that dwells in you.

The word of the Lord.

Responsorial Psalm

Ps 24:1b–2, 3–4ab, 5–6

R. Lord, this is the people that longs to see your face.

The LORD's are the earth and its fullness;
    the world and those who dwell in it.
For he founded it upon the seas
    and established it upon the rivers.

R. Lord, this is the people that longs to see your face.

Who can ascend the mountain of the LORD?
    or who may stand in his holy place?
He whose hands are sinless, whose heart is clean,
    who desires not what is vain.

R. Lord, this is the people that longs to see your face.

He shall receive a blessing from the LORD,
    a reward from God his savior.
Such is the race that seeks for him,
    that seeks the face of the God of Jacob.

R. Lord, this is the people that longs to see your face.

Alleluia Verse *and* Gospel, *p. 1616.*

Year II

FIRST READING

Eph 4:7–16

Christ is the head from whom the whole Body grows and builds itself up in love.

A reading from the Letter of Saint Paul to the Ephesians

Brothers and sisters:

Grace was given to each of us according to the measure of Christ's gift. Therefore, it says:

> *He ascended on high and took prisoners captive;*
>   *he gave gifts to men.*

What does "he ascended" mean except that he also descended into the lower regions of the earth? The one who descended is also the one who ascended far above all the heavens, that he might fill all things.

And he gave some as Apostles, others as prophets, others as evangelists, others as pastors and teachers, to equip the holy ones for the work of ministry, for building up the Body of Christ, until we all attain to the unity of faith and knowledge of the Son of God, to mature manhood to the extent of the full stature of Christ, so that we may no longer be infants, tossed by waves and swept along by every wind of teaching arising from human trickery, from their cunning in the interests of deceitful scheming. Rather, living the truth in love, we should grow in every way into him who is the head, Christ, from whom the whole Body, joined and held together by every supporting ligament, with the proper functioning of each part, brings about the Body's growth and builds itself up in love.

The word of the Lord.

Responsorial Psalm

Ps 122:1–2, 3–4ab, 4cd–5

R. Let us go rejoicing to the house of the Lord.

I rejoiced because they said to me,
  "We will go up to the house of the Lord."
And now we have set foot
  within your gates, O Jerusalem.

R. Let us go rejoicing to the house of the Lord.

Jerusalem, built as a city
  with compact unity.
To it the tribes go up,
  the tribes of the Lord.

R. Let us go rejoicing to the house of the Lord.

According to the decree for Israel,
  to give thanks to the name of the Lord.
In it are set up judgment seats,
  seats for the house of David.

R. Let us go rejoicing to the house of the Lord.

Alleluia, alleluia Ez 33:11
  I take no pleasure in the death of the wicked man,
    says the Lord,
  but rather in his conversion that he may live.
Alleluia, alleluia

Years I and II

GOSPEL

Lk 13:1–9

If you do not repent, you will all perish as they did!

A reading from the holy Gospel according to Luke

Some people told Jesus about the Galileans whose blood Pilate had mingled with the blood of their sacrifices. He said to them in reply, "Do you think that because these Galileans suffered in this way they were greater sinners than all other Galileans?

By no means! But I tell you, if you do not repent, you will all perish as they did! Or those eighteen people who were killed when the tower at Siloam fell on them—do you think they were more guilty than everyone else who lived in Jerusalem? By no means! But I tell you, if you do not repent, you will all perish as they did!"

And he told them this parable: "There once was a person who had a fig tree planted in his orchard, and when he came in search of fruit on it but found none, he said to the gardener, 'For three years now I have come in search of fruit on this fig tree but have found none. So cut it down. Why should it exhaust the soil?' He said to him in reply, 'Sir, leave it for this year also, and I shall cultivate the ground around it and fertilize it; it may bear fruit in the future. If not you can cut it down.'"
The Gospel of the Lord.

Liturgy of the Eucharist, *p. 897;* **Prayer over the Gifts,** *p. 1590.*

THIRTIETH WEEK IN ORDINARY TIME

The **Antiphons and Prayers** *may be the following, or may be chosen from any of the other 33 weeks in Ordinary Time (refer to Liturgical Calendar, pp. 26–41).*

The **Liturgy of the Word** *varies: for Monday, see p. 1619; Tuesday, p. 1624; Wednesday, p. 1628; Thursday, p. 1632; Friday, p. 1637; Saturday, p. 1641.*

Entrance Antiphon

Let hearts rejoice who search for the Lord. Seek the Lord and his strength, seek always the face of the Lord. (Ps 105:3–4)

Opening Prayer

Let us pray

[for the strength to do God's will]

Pause for silent prayer.

Almighty and ever-living God,
strengthen our faith, hope, and love.
May we do with loving hearts
what you ask of us
and come to share the life you promise.

We ask this through our Lord Jesus Christ, your Son,
who lives and reigns with you and the Holy Spirit,
one God, for ever and ever.

Alternative Opening Prayer

Let us pray
   [in humble hope for salvation]

   Pause for silent prayer.

Praised be you, God and Father of our Lord Jesus Christ.
There is no power for good
which does not come from your covenant,
and no promise to hope in,
that your love has not offered.
Strengthen our faith to accept your covenant
and give us the love to carry out your command.

We ask this through Christ our Lord.

Prayer over the Gifts

Pray, brethren...

Lord God of power and might,
receive the gifts we offer
and let our service give you glory.

Grant this through Christ our Lord.

Preface of Weekdays in Ordinary Time I–VI, *pp. 948–950.*

ING

Communion Antiphon

We will rejoice at the victory of God and make our boast in his great name.
(Ps 20:6)

Or:

Christ loved us and gave himself up for us as a fragrant offering to God.
(Eph 5:2)

Prayer after Communion

Let us pray.

Pause for silent prayer, if this has not preceded.

Lord,
bring to perfection within us
the communion we share in this sacrament.
May our celebration have an effect in our lives.

We ask this in the name of Jesus the Lord.

Monday

Antiphons and Prayers, *p. 1617;* **Liturgy of the Word** *for Year I (odd years) follows; Year II (even years), p. 1621.*

Today's Living Word

At first glance today's Gospel seems like just another controversy over sabbath regulations. But a closer look takes us to the heart of Jesus' ministry. The messianic prophet, who came "to proclaim liberty to captives" (Lk 4:18), releases a woman from bondage and restores her dignity as a daughter of Abraham. "She at once stood up straight and glorified God." Furthermore, as Jesus himself argues, his action is not in conflict but in continuity with the meaning of sabbath. The sabbath was to be a day of rest and release from the bondage of hard labor, for beasts of burden as well as for human beings, for women as well as for men.

For Paul, as we have seen, to be a daughter or a son of Abraham is to be by faith an adopted child of God. In today's reading, Paul tells the Romans that no less than God's Spirit testifies to our adoption, and that adoption secures our inheritance with Christ. To this, the passage from Ephesians adds an ethical note: as children of God, we must also "be imitators of God," loving others as Christ has loved us.

Year I

FIRST READING

Rom 8:12–17

You have received a spirit of adoption through which we cry, Abba, Father!

A reading from the Letter of Saint Paul to the Romans

Brothers and sisters:
We are not debtors to the flesh, to live according to the flesh. For if you live according to the flesh, you will die, but if by the spirit you put to death the deeds of the body, you will live.

For those who are led by the Spirit of God are sons of God. For you did not receive a spirit of slavery to fall back into fear, but you received a spirit of adoption, through which we cry, "*Abba*, Father!" The Spirit himself bears witness with our spirit that we are children of God, and if children, then heirs, heirs of God and joint heirs with Christ, if only we suffer with him so that we may also be glorified with him.

The word of the Lord.

Responsorial Psalm

Ps 68:2 and 4, 6–7ab, 20–21

R. Our God is the God of salvation.

God arises; his enemies are scattered,
    and those who hate him flee before him.

But the just rejoice and exult before God;
  they are glad and rejoice.

R. Our God is the God of salvation.

The father of orphans and the defender of widows
  is God in his holy dwelling.
God gives a home to the forsaken;
  he leads forth prisoners to prosperity.

R. Our God is the God of salvation.

Blessed day by day be the Lord,
  who bears our burdens; God, who is our salvation.
God is a saving God for us;
  the LORD, my Lord, controls the passageways of death.

R. Our God is the God of salvation.

Alleluia Verse *and* **Gospel,** *p. 1623.*

Year II

FIRST READING
Eph 4:32—5:8

Walk in love, just as Christ.

A reading from the Letter of Saint Paul to the Ephesians

Brothers and sisters:
Be kind to one another, compassionate, forgiving one another
as God has forgiven you in Christ.

Be imitators of God, as beloved children, and live in love,
as Christ loved us and handed himself over for us as a
sacrificial offering to God for a fragrant aroma. Immorality or
any impurity or greed must not even be mentioned among
you, as is fitting among holy ones, no obscenity or silly or
suggestive talk, which is out of place, but instead, thanksgiving. Be sure of this, that no immoral or impure or greedy per-

son, that is, an idolater, has any inheritance in the Kingdom of Christ and of God.

Let no one deceive you with empty arguments, for because of these things the wrath of God is coming upon the disobedient. So do not be associated with them. For you were once darkness, but now you are light in the Lord. Live as children of light.

The word of the Lord.

Responsorial Psalm
Ps 1:1–2, 3, 4 and 6

R. Behave like God as his very dear children.

Blessed the man who follows not
   the counsel of the wicked
Nor walks in the way of sinners,
   nor sits in the company of the insolent,
But delights in the law of the LORD
   and meditates on his law day and night.

R. Behave like God as his very dear children.

He is like a tree
   planted near running water,
That yields its fruit in due season,
   and whose leaves never fade.
   Whatever he does, prospers.

R. Behave like God as his very dear children.

Not so the wicked, not so;
   they are like chaff which the wind drives away.
For the LORD watches over the way of the just,
   but the way of the wicked vanishes.

R. Behave like God as his very dear children.

Alleluia, alleluia Jn 17:17b, 17a
   Your word, O Lord, is truth;
   consecrate us in the truth.
Alleluia, alleluia

Years I and II

GOSPEL

Lk 13:10–17

This daughter of Abraham, ought she not to have been set free on the sabbath day?

A reading from the holy Gospel according to Luke

Jesus was teaching in a synagogue on the sabbath. And a woman was there who for eighteen years had been crippled by a spirit; she was bent over, completely incapable of standing erect. When Jesus saw her, he called to her and said, "Woman, you are set free of your infirmity." He laid his hands on her, and she at once stood up straight and glorified God. But the leader of the synagogue, indignant that Jesus had cured on the sabbath, said to the crowd in reply, "There are six days when work should be done. Come on those days to be cured, not on the sabbath day." The Lord said to him in reply, "Hypocrites! Does not each one of you on the sabbath untie his ox or his ass from the manger and lead it out for watering? This daughter of Abraham, whom Satan has bound for eighteen years now, ought she not to have been set free on the sabbath day from this bondage?" When he said this, all his adversaries were humiliated; and the whole crowd rejoiced at all the splendid deeds done by him.

The Gospel of the Lord.

Liturgy of the Eucharist, *p. 897;* **Prayer over the Gifts,** *p. 1618.*

Tuesday

Antiphons and Prayers, *p. 1617;* **Liturgy of the Word** *for Year I (odd years) follows; Year II (even years), p. 1626.*

TODAY'S LIVING WORD

Today's selection from Ephesians is an example of a household code. Household codes sought to order the roles and relationships in Roman households between husbands and wives, parents and children, masters and slaves. Christian writers sometimes adapted these codes, as in today's reading. Here it emphasizes the husband's obligation to love his wife. Although the implied lack of equality between the two may offend our modern sensibilities, the requirement that Christian husbands love their wives "as Christ loved the church" would, in fact, ensure that women be treated with respect. Luke often attests to Jesus' equal treatment of men and women. In today's Gospel, for example, a parable about a man is paired with a matching parable about a woman.

In the twin parables of Jesus, the mustard seed and the yeast are metaphors for the action of the Spirit that Paul describes in the excerpt from Romans. Together with all creation, we who have the Spirit "groan within ourselves" as we await the quiet revolution that the power of God is working within us.

Year I

FIRST READING

Rom 8:18–25

Creation awaits with eager expectation the
revelation of the children of God.

A reading from the Letter of Saint Paul to the Romans

Brothers and sisters:

I consider that the sufferings of this present time are as nothing compared with the glory to be revealed for us. For creation awaits with eager expectation the revelation of the children of

God; for creation was made subject to futility, not of its own accord but because of the one who subjected it, in hope that creation itself would be set free from slavery to corruption and share in the glorious freedom of the children of God. We know that all creation is groaning in labor pains even until now; and not only that, but we ourselves, who have the firstfruits of the Spirit, we also groan within ourselves as we wait for adoption, the redemption of our bodies. For in hope we were saved. Now hope that sees for itself is not hope. For who hopes for what one sees? But if we hope for what we do not see, we wait with endurance.

The word of the Lord.

Responsorial Psalm

Ps 126:1b–2ab, 2cd–3, 4–5, 6

R. **The Lord has done marvels for us.**

When the LORD brought back the captives of Zion,
  we were like men dreaming.
Then our mouth was filled with laughter,
  and our tongue with rejoicing.

R. **The Lord has done marvels for us.**

Then they said among the nations,
  "The LORD has done great things for them."
The LORD has done great things for us;
  we are glad indeed.

R. **The Lord has done marvels for us.**

Restore our fortunes, O LORD,
  like the torrents in the southern desert.
Those that sow in tears
  shall reap rejoicing.

R. **The Lord has done marvels for us.**

Although they go forth weeping,
  carrying the seed to be sown,

They shall come back rejoicing,
  carrying their sheaves.

R. The Lord has done marvels for us.

Alleluia Verse *and* **Gospel,** *p. 1627f.*

FIRST READING

Eph 5:21–33

*This is a great mystery, but I speak in reference
to Christ and the Church.*

A reading from the Letter of Saint Paul to the Ephesians

Brothers and sisters:

Be subordinate to one another out of reverence for Christ. Wives should be subordinate to their husbands as to the Lord. For the husband is head of his wife just as Christ is head of the Church, he himself the savior of the Body. As the Church is subordinate to Christ, so wives should be subordinate to their husbands in everything. Husbands, love your wives, even as Christ loved the Church and handed himself over for her to sanctify her, cleansing her by the bath of water with the word, that he might present to himself the Church in splendor, without spot or wrinkle or any such thing, that she might be holy and without blemish. So also husbands should love their wives as their own bodies. He who loves his wife loves himself. For no one hates his own flesh but rather nourishes and cherishes it, even as Christ does the Church, because we are members of his Body.

*For this reason a man shall leave his father
  and his mother*

and be joined to his wife,
   and the two shall become one flesh.

This is a great mystery, but I speak in reference to Christ and the Church. In any case, each one of you should love his wife as himself, and the wife should respect her husband.

The word of the Lord.

Responsorial Psalm

Ps 128:1–2, 3, 4–5

R. Blessed are those who fear the Lord.

Blessed are you who fear the LORD,
   who walk in his ways!
For you shall eat the fruit of your handiwork;
   blessed shall you be, and favored.

R. Blessed are those who fear the Lord.

Your wife shall be like a fruitful vine
   in the recesses of your home;
Your children like olive plants
   around your table.

R. Blessed are those who fear the Lord.

Behold, thus is the man blessed
   who fears the LORD.
The LORD bless you from Zion:
   may you see the prosperity of Jerusalem
   all the days of your life.

R. Blessed are those who fear the Lord.

Alleluia, alleluia See Mt 11:25
   Blessed are you, Father, Lord of heaven and earth;
   you have revealed to little ones the mysteries of the Kingdom.
Alleluia, alleluia

Years I and II

GOSPEL   Lk 13:18–21

When it was fully grown, it became a large bush.

A reading from the holy Gospel according to Luke

Jesus said, "What is the Kingdom of God like? To what can I compare it? It is like a mustard seed that a man took and planted in the garden. When it was fully grown, it became a large bush and *the birds of the sky dwelt in its branches.*"

Again he said, "To what shall I compare the Kingdom of God? It is like yeast that a woman took and mixed in with three measures of wheat flour until the whole batch of dough was leavened."

The Gospel of the Lord.

Liturgy of the Eucharist, *p. 897;* **Prayer over the Gifts,** *p. 1618.*

Wednesday

Antiphons and Prayers, *p. 1617;* **Liturgy of the Word** *for Year I (odd years) follows; Year II (even years), p. 1630.*

TODAY'S LIVING WORD

As often happens in the Gospels, Jesus turns the question of an interested bystander into a dire warning as he goes about his work en route to Jerusalem. Grammatically, the question does not read, "Will only a few people *be saved?*" in the future, but "Are only a few people *being saved?*" (*sōzomenoi*) here and now. In answer, Jesus warns that occasionally sharing his table or listening to his teaching does not satisfy the demands of true discipleship, a rigorous rite of passage through a notoriously "narrow gate."

Jesus' answer evokes an image from the Hebrew prophets, who often described the messianic age as a banquet where scattered Israel would be assembled from east and west, from north and south.

Here Jesus, the messianic prophet, warns those who rely on cheap grace that they may not be admitted. The household code from Ephesians issues the same warning to Christian masters who are called, with their slaves, to the same heavenly table of the one Master, for "with him there is no partiality." And Paul reminds the Romans that the Spirit groans within them, like hunger pains, for the promised banquet of eternal life.

Year I

FIRST READING
Rom 8:26–30

All things work to the good for those who love God.

A reading from the Letter of Saint Paul to the Romans

Brothers and sisters:

The Spirit comes to the aid of our weakness; for we do not know how to pray as we ought, but the Spirit himself intercedes with inexpressible groanings. And the one who searches hearts knows what is the intention of the Spirit, because he intercedes for the holy ones according to God's will.

We know that all things work for good for those who love God, who are called according to his purpose. For those he foreknew he also predestined to be conformed to the image of his Son, so that he might be the firstborn among many brothers. And those he predestined he also called; and those he called he also justified; and those he justified he also glorified.

The word of the Lord.

Responsorial Psalm
Ps 13:4–5, 6

R. My hope, O Lord, is in your mercy.

Look, answer me, O Lord, my God!
Give light to my eyes that I may not sleep in death

lest my enemy say, "I have overcome him";
lest my foes rejoice at my downfall.

R. My hope, O Lord, is in your mercy.

Though I trusted in your mercy,
Let my heart rejoice in your salvation;
let me sing of the LORD, "He has been good to me."

R. My hope, O Lord, is in your mercy.

Alleluia Verse *and* **Gospel,** *p. 1631.*

Year II

FIRST READING   Eph 6:1–9

Willingly serving the Lord and not human beings.

A reading from the Letter of Saint Paul to the Ephesians

Children, obey your parents in the Lord, for this is right. *Honor your father and mother.* This is the first commandment with a promise, *that it may go well with you and that you may have a long life on earth.* Fathers, do not provoke your children to anger, but bring them up with the training and instruction of the Lord.

Slaves, be obedient to your human masters with fear and trembling, in sincerity of heart, as to Christ, not only when being watched, as currying favor, but as slaves of Christ, doing the will of God from the heart, willingly serving the Lord and not men, knowing that each will be requited from the Lord for whatever good he does, whether he is slave or free. Masters, act in the same way towards them, and stop bullying, knowing that both they and you have a Master in heaven and that with him there is no partiality.

The word of the Lord.

Responsorial Psalm Ps 145:10–11, 12–13ab, 13cd–14

R. The Lord is faithful in all his words.

Let all your works give you thanks, O LORD,
  and let your faithful ones bless you.
Let them discourse of the glory of your Kingdom
  and speak of your might.

R. The Lord is faithful in all his words.

Making known to men your might
  and the glorious splendor of your Kingdom.
Your Kingdom is a Kingdom for all ages,
  and your dominion endures through all generations.

R. The Lord is faithful in all his words.

The LORD is faithful in all his words
  and holy in all his works.
The LORD lifts up all who are falling
  and raises up all who are bowed down.

R. The Lord is faithful in all his words.

> **Alleluia, alleluia** See 2 Thes 2:14
> God has called us through the Gospel
> to possess the glory of our Lord Jesus Christ.
> **Alleluia, alleluia**

Years I and II

GOSPEL Lk 13:22–30

*And people will come from the east and the west and will
recline at the table in the Kingdom of God.*

A reading from the holy Gospel according to Luke

Jesus passed through towns and villages, teaching as he went
and making his way to Jerusalem. Someone asked him,
"Lord, will only a few people be saved?" He answered them,
"Strive to enter through the narrow gate, for many, I tell you,

will attempt to enter but will not be strong enough. After the master of the house has arisen and locked the door, then will you stand outside knocking and saying, 'Lord, open the door for us.' He will say to you in reply, 'I do not know where you are from.' And you will say, 'We ate and drank in your company and you taught in our streets.' Then he will say to you, 'I do not know where you are from. Depart from me, all you evildoers!' And there will be wailing and grinding of teeth when you see Abraham, Isaac, and Jacob and all the prophets in the Kingdom of God and you yourselves cast out. And people will come from the east and the west and from the north and the south and will recline at table in the Kingdom of God. For behold, some are last who will be first, and some are first who will be last."

The Gospel of the Lord.

Liturgy of the Eucharist, *p. 897;* **Prayer over the Gifts,** *p. 1618.*

Thursday

Antiphons and Prayers, *p. 1617;* **Liturgy of the Word** *for Year I (odd years) follows; Year II (even years), p. 1634.*

TODAY'S LIVING WORD

Taken together today's three readings constitute something of a call to arms. In the Gospel, Jesus the messianic prophet ignores the warning of the Pharisees and renews his resolve to go to Jerusalem, "for it is impossible that a prophet should die outside of Jerusalem." In the selection from Romans, Christians who, like Jesus, "are being slain all the day," declare that "in all these things we conquer overwhelmingly" because of the love of Christ. The conclusion of the letter to the Ephesians calls all Christians to "put on the armor of God"— the belt of truth, the breastplate of justice, the footgear of zeal for peace, the shield of faith, the helmet of salvation and the sword of the word of God.

The conviction of all holy warriors that God is with them and for them underlies all the readings. So Ephesians counsels constant prayer "for all the holy ones," while Paul tells the Romans that nothing can separate us from the love of God. In the Gospel, Jesus offers that same love to Jerusalem in the biblical image of the mother bird who, gathering her young under her wings, keeps them safe.

Year I

FIRST READING

Rom 8:31b–39

Nor any other creature will be able to separate us from the love of God in Christ Jesus our Lord.

A reading from the Letter of Saint Paul to the Romans

Brothers and sisters:

If God is for us, who can be against us? He did not spare his own Son but handed him over for us all, how will he not also give us everything else along with him? Who will bring a charge against God's chosen ones? It is God who acquits us. Who will condemn? It is Christ Jesus who died, rather, was raised, who also is at the right hand of God, who indeed intercedes for us. What will separate us from the love of Christ? Will anguish, or distress, or persecution, or famine, or nakedness, or peril, or the sword? As it is written:

> *For your sake we are being slain all the day;*
> *we are looked upon as sheep to be slaughtered.*

No, in all these things we conquer overwhelmingly through him who loved us. For I am convinced that neither death, nor life, nor angels, nor principalities, nor present things, nor future things, nor powers, nor height, nor depth, nor any other creature will be able to separate us from the love of God in Christ Jesus our Lord.

The word of the Lord.

Responsorial Psalm

Ps 109:21–22, 26–27, 30–31

R. Save me, O Lord, in your mercy.

Do you, O GOD, my Lord, deal kindly with me for your name's
   sake;
  in your generous mercy rescue me;
For I am wretched and poor,
  and my heart is pierced within me.

R. Save me, O Lord, in your mercy.

Help me, O LORD, my God;
  save me, in your mercy,
And let them know that this is your hand;
  that you, O LORD, have done this.

R. Save me, O Lord, in your mercy.

I will speak my thanks earnestly to the LORD,
  and in the midst of the throng I will praise him,
For he stood at the right hand of the poor man,
  to save him from those who would condemn his soul.

R. Save me, O Lord, in your mercy.

Alleluia Verse *and* **Gospel,** *p. 1636.*

Year II

FIRST READING

Eph 6:10–20

Put on the armor of God, that you may be able,
having done everything, to hold your ground.

A reading from the Letter of Saint Paul to the Ephesians

Brothers and sisters:

Draw your strength from the Lord and from his mighty power.

Put on the armor of God so that you may be able to stand firm against the tactics of the Devil. For our struggle is not with flesh and blood but with the principalities, with the powers, with the world rulers of this present darkness, with the evil spirits in the heavens. Therefore, put on the armor of God, that you may be able to resist on the evil day and, having done everything, to hold your ground. So stand fast with your loins girded in truth, clothed with righteousness as a breastplate, and your feet shod in readiness for the Gospel of peace. In all circumstances, hold faith as a shield, to quench all the flaming arrows of the Evil One. And take the helmet of salvation and the sword of the Spirit, which is the word of God.

With all prayer and supplication, pray at every opportunity in the Spirit. To that end, be watchful with all perseverance and supplication for all the holy ones and also for me, that speech may be given me to open my mouth, to make known with boldness the mystery of the Gospel for which I am an ambassador in chains, so that I may have the courage to speak as I must.

The word of the Lord.

Responsorial Psalm

Ps 144:1b, 2, 9–10

R. **Blessed be the Lord, my Rock!**

Blessed be the LORD, my rock,
   who trains my hands for battle, my fingers for war.

R. **Blessed be the Lord, my Rock!**

My mercy and my fortress,
   my stronghold, my deliverer,
My shield, in whom I trust,
   who subdues my people under me.

R. **Blessed be the Lord, my Rock!**

O God, I will sing a new song to you;
  with a ten-stringed lyre I will chant your praise,
You who give victory to kings,
  and deliver David, your servant from the evil sword.

R. Blessed be the Lord, my Rock!

> **Alleluia, alleluia**   See Lk 19:38; 2:14
> Blessed is the king who comes in the name of the Lord.
> Glory to God in the highest and on earth peace to those on
>   whom his favor rests.
> **Alleluia, alleluia**

Years I and II

GOSPEL   Lk 13:31–35

It is impossible that a prophet should die outside of Jerusalem.

A reading from the holy Gospel according to Luke

Some Pharisees came to Jesus and said, "Go away, leave this area because Herod wants to kill you." He replied, "Go and tell that fox, 'Behold, I cast out demons and I perform healings today and tomorrow, and on the third day I accomplish my purpose. Yet I must continue on my way today, tomorrow, and the following day, for it is impossible that a prophet should die outside of Jerusalem.'

"Jerusalem, Jerusalem, you who kill the prophets and stone those sent to you, how many times I yearned to gather your children together as a hen gathers her brood under her wings, but you were unwilling! Behold, your house will be abandoned. But I tell you, you will not see me until the time comes when you say, *Blessed is he who comes in the name of the Lord.*"
The Gospel of the Lord.

Liturgy of the Eucharist, *p. 897;* **Prayer over the Gifts,** *p. 1618.*

Friday

Antiphons and Prayers, *p. 1617;* **Liturgy of the Word** *for Year I (odd years) follows; Year II (even years), p. 1638.*

TODAY'S LIVING WORD

The two first readings for today uncover two sides of Paul's concern as a Christian missionary. In Romans 9—11, Paul takes up the difficult question of God's plan for the Jews, while in Philippians he writes to his first foundation among the Greeks. As apostle to the Gentiles, Paul had a vested interest in the faith development of his non-Jewish converts. That interest met with a generous response among the Philippians, who made themselves sharers in Paul's work by giving him material support. The Letter to the Philippians was written in part as a thank-you note to these Christians whom Paul held dear. As a Jew, however, Paul also had a vested interest in the destiny of his brothers, his kinsmen the Israelites, whose refusal of the Gospel of Jesus caused him heartfelt grief.

This concern of Paul's runs through much of the New Testament. Today's Gospel dramatizes the controversy that Jesus' ministry created among the Jews. In this story the hostile scrutiny of Jesus by his opponents and their ominous silence prepare us for their eventual rejection of him.

Year I

FIRST READING

Rom 9:1–5

*I could wish that I were accused
for the sake of my own people.*

A reading from the Letter of Saint Paul to the Romans

Brothers and sisters:

I speak the truth in Christ, I do not lie; my conscience joins with the Holy Spirit in bearing me witness that I have great sorrow and constant anguish in my heart. For I could wish that

I myself were accursed and cut off from Christ for the sake of my own people, my kindred according to the flesh. They are children of Israel; theirs the adoption, the glory, the covenants, the giving of the law, the worship, and the promises; theirs the patriarchs, and from them, according to the flesh, is the Christ, who is over all, God blessed forever. Amen.

The word of the Lord.

Responsorial Psalm

Ps 147:12–13, 14–15, 19–20

R. Praise the Lord, Jerusalem.

Glorify the LORD, O Jerusalem;
  praise your God, O Zion.
For he has strengthened the bars of your gates;
  he has blessed your children within you.

R. Praise the Lord, Jerusalem.

He has granted peace in your borders;
  with the best of wheat he fills you.
He sends forth his command to the earth;
  swiftly runs his word!

R. Praise the Lord, Jerusalem.

He has proclaimed his word to Jacob,
  his statutes and his ordinances to Israel.
He has not done thus for any other nation;
  his ordinances he has not made known to them. Alleluia.

R. Praise the Lord, Jerusalem.

Alleluia Verse and **Gospel**, p. 1640.

Year II

FIRST READING

Phil 1:1–11

The one who began a good work in you will continue to complete it until the day of Christ Jesus.

A reading from the beginning of the Letter of Saint Paul to the Philippians

Paul and Timothy, slaves of Christ Jesus, to all the holy ones in Christ Jesus who are in Philippi, with the bishops and deacons: grace to you and peace from God our Father and the Lord Jesus Christ.

I give thanks to my God at every remembrance of you, praying always with joy in my every prayer for all of you, because of your partnership for the Gospel from the first day until now. I am confident of this, that the one who began a good work in you will continue to complete it until the day of Christ Jesus. It is right that I should think this way about all of you, because I hold you in my heart, you who are all partners with me in grace, both in my imprisonment and in the defense and confirmation of the Gospel. For God is my witness, how I long for all of you with the affection of Christ Jesus. And this is my prayer: that your love may increase ever more and more in knowledge and every kind of perception, to discern what is of value, so that you may be pure and blameless for the day of Christ, filled with the fruit of righteousness that comes through Jesus Christ for the glory and praise of God.

The word of the Lord.

Responsorial Psalm

Ps 111:1–2, 3–4, 5–6

R. **How great are the works of the Lord!**

I will give thanks to the LORD with all my heart
   in the company and assembly of the just.
Great are the works of the LORD,
   exquisite in all their delights.

R. **How great are the works of the Lord!**

Majesty and glory are his work,
   and his justice endures forever.

He has won renown for his wondrous deeds;
  gracious and merciful is the LORD.

  R. How great are the works of the Lord!

He has given food to those who fear him;
  he will forever be mindful of his covenant.
He has made known to his people the power of his works,
  giving them the inheritance of the nations.

  R. How great are the works of the Lord!

  Or: **R. Alleluia.**

> **Alleluia, alleluia** Jn 10:27
> My sheep hear my voice, says the Lord;
> I know them, and they follow me.
> **Alleluia, alleluia**

Years I and II

GOSPEL   Lk 14:1–6

Who among you, if your son or ox falls into a cistern,
would not immediately pull him out on the sabbath day?

A reading from the holy Gospel according to Luke

On a sabbath Jesus went to dine at the home of one of the
leading Pharisees, and the people there were observing him
carefully. In front of him there was a man suffering from dropsy.
Jesus spoke to the scholars of the law and Pharisees in reply,
asking, "Is it lawful to cure on the sabbath or not?" But they
kept silent; so he took the man and, after he had healed him,
dismissed him. Then he said to them "Who among you, if your
son or ox falls into a cistern, would not immediately pull him
out on the sabbath day?" But they were unable to answer his
question.

The Gospel of the Lord.

Liturgy of the Eucharist, *p. 897;* **Prayer over the Gifts,** *p. 1618.*

Saturday

Antiphons and Prayers, *p. 1617;* **Liturgy of the Word** *for Year I (odd years) follows; Year II (even years), p. 1643.*

TODAY'S LIVING WORD

The ancient world was as preoccupied as ours with social status. Conventional wisdom advised guests to seek the last places, "for it is better that you be told, 'Come up closer!' than that you be humbled before the prince" (Prv 25:7). In today's Gospel, Jesus seems to say the same thing, until the punch line: "For everyone who exalts himself will be humbled, but the one who humbles himself will be exalted." The use of the passive voice here is a biblical way of indicating God's action, that is, everyone who exalts himself shall be humbled *by God,* and he who humbles himself shall be exalted *by God,* who does not defer to our social arrangements.

In the Letter to the Romans, Paul warns Christians not to make the mistake of exalting themselves over and against the Jews. For the Jews are God's beloved, he says, the chosen people of God, whose gifts and whose call are irrevocable. In the Letter to the Philippians, Paul, imprisoned for preaching the Gospel, trusts that he will never be put to shame for his hope, but that Christ will be exalted through him, and he with Christ.

Year I

FIRST READING

Rom 11:1–2a, 11–12, 25–29

If their transgression is enrichment for the world,
how much more their full number.

A reading from the Letter of Saint Paul to the Romans

Brothers and sisters:

I ask, then, has God rejected his people? Of course not! For I too am a child of Israel, a descendant of Abraham, of the tribe of Benjamin. God has not rejected his people whom he foreknew. Do you not know what the Scripture says about Elijah, how he pleads with God against Israel?

Hence I ask, did they stumble so as to fall? Of course not! But through their transgression salvation has come to the Gentiles, so as to make them jealous. Now if their transgression is enrichment for the world, and if their diminished number is enrichment for the Gentiles, how much more their full number.

I do not want you to be unaware of this mystery, brothers and sisters, so that you will not become wise in your own estimation: a hardening has come upon Israel in part, until the full number of the Gentiles comes in, and thus all Israel will be saved, as it is written:

> *The deliverer will come out of Zion,*
>   *he will turn away godlessness from Jacob;*
> *and this is my covenant with them*
>   *when I take away their sins.*

In respect to the Gospel, they are enemies on your account; but in respect to election, they are beloved because of the patriarch. For the gifts and the call of God are irrevocable.

The word of the Lord.

Responsorial Psalm

Ps 94:12–13a, 14–15, 17–18

R. The Lord will not abandon his people.

Blessed the man whom you instruct, O LORD,
   whom by your law you teach,
Giving him rest from evil days.

R. The Lord will not abandon his people.

For the LORD will not cast off his people,
   nor abandon his inheritance;
But judgment shall again be with justice,
   and all the upright of heart shall follow it.

R. The Lord will not abandon his people.

Were not the LORD my help,
  my soul would soon dwell in the silent grave.
When I say, "My foot is slipping,"
  your mercy, O LORD, sustains me.

R. The Lord will not abandon his people.

Alleluia Verse *and* **Gospel**, *p. 1644.*

Year II

FIRST READING   Phil 1:18b–26

For to me life is Christ, and death is gain.

A reading from the Letter of Saint Paul to the Philippians

Brothers and sisters:

As long as in every way, whether in pretense or in truth, Christ is being proclaimed, and in that I rejoice.

Indeed I shall continue to rejoice, for I know that this will result in deliverance for me through your prayers and support from the Spirit of Jesus Christ. My eager expectation and hope is that I shall not be put to shame in any way, but that with all boldness, now as always, Christ will be magnified in my body, whether by life or by death. For to me life is Christ, and death is gain. If I go on living in the flesh, that means fruitful labor for me. And I do not know which I shall choose. I am caught between the two. I long to depart this life and be with Christ, for that is far better. Yet that I remain in the flesh is more necessary for your benefit. And this I know with confidence, that I shall remain and continue in the service of all of you for your progress and joy in the faith, so that your boasting in Christ Jesus may abound on account of me when I come to you again.

The word of the Lord.

Responsorial Psalm

Ps 42:2, 3, 5cdef

R. My soul is thirsting for the living God.

As the hind longs for the running waters,
  so my soul longs for you, O God.

R. My soul is thirsting for the living God.

Athirst is my soul for God, the living God.
  When shall I go and behold the face of God?

R. My soul is thirsting for the living God.

I went with the throng
  and led them in procession to the house of God.
Amid loud cries of joy and thanksgiving,
  with the multitude keeping festival.

R. My soul is thirsting for the living God.

Alleluia, alleluia Mt 11:29ab
  Take my yoke upon you and learn from me,
  for I am meek and humble of heart.
Alleluia, alleluia

Years I and II

GOSPEL   Lk 14:1, 7–11

Everyone who exalts himself will be humbled,
  but the one who humbles himself will be exalted.

A reading from the holy Gospel according to Luke

On a sabbath Jesus went to dine at the home of one of the leading Pharisees, and the people there were observing him carefully.

He told a parable to those who had been invited, noticing how they were choosing the places of honor at the table. "When you are invited by someone to a wedding banquet, do not recline at table in the place of honor. A more distinguished guest than you may have been invited by him, and the host who invited both of you may approach you and say, 'Give your place to this man,' and then you would proceed with embarrassment to take the lowest place. Rather, when you are invited, go and take the lowest place so that when the host comes to you he may say, 'My friend, move up to a higher position.' Then you will enjoy the esteem of your companions at the table. For everyone who exalts himself will be humbled, but the one who humbles himself will be exalted."

The Gospel of the Lord.

Liturgy of the Eucharist, *p. 897;* **Prayer over the Gifts,** *p. 1618.*

THIRTY-FIRST WEEK IN ORDINARY TIME

The **Antiphons and Prayers** *may be the following, or may be chosen from any of the other 33 weeks in Ordinary Time (refer to Liturgical Calendar, pp. 26–41).*

The **Liturgy of the Word** *varies: for Monday, see p. 1647; Tuesday, p. 1651; Wednesday, p. 1655; Thursday, p. 1660; Friday, p. 1664; Saturday, p. 1669.*

Entrance Antiphon

Do not abandon me, Lord. My God, do not go away from me! Hurry to help me, Lord, my Savior. (Ps 38:22–23)

Opening Prayer

Let us pray
[that our lives will reflect our faith]

Pause for silent prayer.

God of power and mercy,
only with your help
can we offer you fitting service and praise.
May we live the faith we profess
and trust your promise of eternal life.

Grant this through our Lord Jesus Christ, your Son,
who lives and reigns with you and the Holy Spirit,
one God, for ever and ever.

Alternative Opening Prayer

Let us pray
  [in the presence of God,
   the source of every good]

  Pause for silent prayer.

Father in heaven, God of power and Lord of mercy,
from whose fullness we have received,
direct our steps in our everyday efforts.
May the changing moods of the human heart
and the limits which our failings impose on hope
never blind us to you, source of every good.
Faith gives us the promise of peace
and makes known the demands of love.
Remove the selfishness that blurs our faith.

Grant this through Christ our Lord.

Prayer over the Gifts

Pray, brethren...

God of mercy,
may we offer a pure sacrifice
for the forgiveness of our sins.

We ask this through Christ our Lord.

  Preface of Weekdays in Ordinary Time I–VI, *pp. 948–950.*

Communion Antiphon

  **Lord, you will show me the path of life and fill me with joy in
your presence.** (Ps 16:11)

Or:

As the living Father sent me, and I live because of the Father, so he who eats my flesh and drinks my blood will live because of me.

(Jn 6:57)

Prayer after Communion

Let us pray.

Pause for silent prayer, if this has not preceded.

Lord,
you give us new hope in this eucharist.
May the power of your love
continue its saving work among us
and bring us to the joy you promise.
We ask this in the name of Jesus the Lord.

Monday

Antiphons and Prayers, *p. 1645;* **Liturgy of the Word** *for Year I (odd years) follows; Year II (even years), p. 1649.*

TODAY'S LIVING WORD

In the social world of Luke's Jesus, like our own, generosity to others was governed by the law of reciprocity, that is, by others' ability to repay the gift or return the favor. In today's Gospel, Jesus challenges this conventional code of behavior. He says instead that we should invite precisely those who cannot reciprocate, those whom God would invite and *is inviting* to the banquet of the king-dom through the ministry of Jesus—the poor, the lame, the blind (cf. 7:22). Here again Jesus makes imitation of God the norm for Christian behavior. Paul does too in the letter to the Philippians, when he instructs them always to place the interests of others above their own self-interest.

Reciprocity also figures in today's selection from Romans. Paul marvels at God's generosity, the depth of God's riches, and he asks, "Who has given him anything that he may be repaid?"

FIRST READING   Rom 11:29–36

God delivered all to disobedience,
that he might have mercy upon all.

A reading from the Letter of Saint Paul to the Romans

Brothers and sisters:

The gifts and the call of God are irrevocable.

Just as you once disobeyed God but have now received mercy because of their disobedience, so they have now disobeyed in order that, by virtue of the mercy shown to you, they too may now receive mercy. For God delivered all to disobedience, that he might have mercy upon all.

Oh, the depth of the riches and wisdom and knowledge of God! How inscrutable are his judgments and how unsearchable his ways!

> For who has known the mind of the Lord
>   or who has been his counselor?
> Or who has given him anything
>   that he may be repaid?

For from him and through him and for him are all things. To God be glory forever. Amen.

The word of the Lord.

Responsorial Psalm   Ps 69:30–31, 33–34, 36

R. Lord, in your great love, answer me.

But I am afflicted and in pain;
    let your saving help, O God, protect me.
I will praise the name of God in song,
    and I will glorify him with thanksgiving.

R. Lord, in your great love, answer me.

"See, you lowly ones, and be glad;
  you who seek God, may your hearts revive!
For the LORD hears the poor,
  and his own who are in bonds he spurns not."

R. Lord, in your great love, answer me.

For God will save Zion
  and rebuild the cities of Judah.
They shall dwell in the land and own it,
  and the descendants of his servants shall inherit it,
  and those who love his name shall inhabit it.

R. Lord, in your great love, answer me.

Alleluia Verse *and* **Gospel,** *p. 1650.*

Year II

FIRST READING

Phil 2:1–4

Complete my joy by being of the same mind.

A reading from the Letter of Saint Paul to the Philippians

Brothers and sisters:

If there is any encouragement in Christ, any solace in love, any participation in the Spirit, any compassion and mercy, complete my joy by being of the same mind, with the same love, united in heart, thinking one thing. Do nothing out of selfishness or out of vainglory; rather, humbly regard others as more important than yourselves, each looking out not for his own interests, but also everyone for those of others.

The word of the Lord.

Responsorial Psalm

Ps 131:1bcde, 2, 3

R. In you, O Lord, I have found my peace.

O LORD, my heart is not proud,
  nor are my eyes haughty;

I busy not myself with great things,
   nor with things too sublime for me.

   R. In you, O Lord, I have found my peace.

Nay rather, I have stilled and quieted
   my soul like a weaned child.
Like a weaned child on its mother's lap,
   so is my soul within me.

   R. In you, O Lord, I have found my peace.

O Israel, hope in the LORD,
   both now and forever.

   R. In you, O Lord, I have found my peace.

   Alleluia, alleluia   Jn 8:31b–32
   If you remain in my word, you will truly be my disciples,
   and you will know the truth, says the Lord.
   Alleluia, alleluia

Years I and II

GOSPEL   Lk 14:12–14

Do not invite your friends,
but those who are poor and crippled.

A reading from the holy Gospel according to Luke

On a sabbath Jesus went to dine at the home of one of the
leading Pharisees. He said to the host who invited him, "When
you hold a lunch or a dinner, do not invite your friends or your
brothers or sisters or your relatives or your wealthy neighbors,
in case they may invite you back and you have repayment.
Rather, when you hold a banquet, invite the poor, the crippled,
the lame, the blind; blessed indeed will you be because of their
inability to repay you. For you will be repaid at the resurrection
of the righteous."

The Gospel of the Lord.

   Liturgy of the Eucharist, *p. 897;* **Prayer over the Gifts,** *p. 1646.*

Tuesday

Antiphons and Prayers, *p. 1645;* **Liturgy of the Word** *for Year I (odd years) follows; Year II (even years), p. 1653.*

TODAY'S LIVING WORD

In today's Gospel a casual comment by an invited guest becomes the occasion for a parable of reversal. Jesus speaks not to second or to support the guest's exclamation—"Blessed is the one who will dine in the Kingdom of God"—but to challenge his assumption. Who will eat bread in God's kingdom? Not the invited guests, as it turns out. They are too busy with their own affairs, with their investments and their intimate relationships. Their excuses betray their self-interest. How different the attitude of Christ, portrayed in the hymn in Philippians. "He emptied himself, taking the form of a slave, coming in human likeness."

Paul tells the Romans that self-emptying, not self-interest, must characterize the attitude of Christians as well. They must be disinterested in their service of others and place whatever gifts they may have at the disposal of others, showing "the same regard for one another."

Year I

FIRST READING

Rom 12:5–16ab

We are individually parts of one another.

A reading from the Letter of Saint Paul to the Romans

Brothers and sisters:

We, though many, are one Body in Christ and individually parts of one another. Since we have gifts that differ according to the grace given to us, let us exercise them: if prophecy, in proportion to the faith; if ministry, in ministering; if one is a teacher, in teaching; if one exhorts, in exhortation; if one contributes, in generosity; if one is over others, with diligence; if one does acts of mercy, with cheerfulness.

Let love be sincere; hate what is evil, hold on to what is good; love one another with mutual affection; anticipate one another in showing honor. Do not grow slack in zeal, be fervent in spirit, serve the Lord. Rejoice in hope, endure in affliction, persevere in prayer. Contribute to the needs of the holy ones, exercise hospitality. Bless those who persecute you, bless and do not curse them. Rejoice with those who rejoice, weep with those who weep. Have the same regard for one another; do not be haughty but associate with the lowly.

The word of the Lord.

Responsorial Psalm

Ps 131:1bcde, 2, 3

R. **In you, O Lord, I have found my peace.**

O LORD, my heart is not proud,
  nor are my eyes haughty;
I busy not myself with great things,
  nor with things too sublime for me.

R. **In you, O Lord, I have found my peace.**

Nay rather, I have stilled and quieted
  my soul like a weaned child.
Like a weaned child on its mother's lap,
  so is my soul within me.

R. **In you, O Lord, I have found my peace.**

O Israel, hope in the LORD,
  both now and forever.

R. **In you, O Lord, I have found my peace.**

Alleluia Verse *and* **Gospel**, *p. 1654.*

Year II

FIRST READING

Phil 2:5–11

He emptied himself and because of this, God exalted him.

A reading from the Letter of Saint Paul to the Philippians

Brothers and sisters:

Have among yourselves the same attitude that is also yours in Christ Jesus,

> Who, though he was in the form of God,
>> did not regard equality with God
>>> something to be grasped.
>> Rather, he emptied himself,
>> taking the form of a slave,
>> coming in human likeness;
>> and, found human in appearance,
>> he humbled himself,
>> becoming obedient to death,
>>> even death on a cross.
> Because of this, God greatly exalted him
>> and bestowed on him the name
>> that is above every name,
>> that at the name of Jesus
>> every knee should bend,
>> of those in heaven and on earth and under the earth,
>> and every tongue confess that
>> Jesus Christ is Lord,
>> to the glory of God the Father.

The word of the Lord.

Responsorial Psalm

Ps 22:26b–27, 28–30ab, 30e, 31–32

R. I will praise you, Lord, in the assembly of your people.

I will fulfill my vows before those who fear him.
The lowly shall eat their fill;
  they who seek the LORD shall praise him:
  "May your hearts be ever merry!"

R. I will praise you, Lord, in the assembly of your people.

All the ends of the earth
  shall remember and turn to the LORD;
All the families of the nations
  shall bow down before him.

R. I will praise you, Lord, in the assembly of your people.

For dominion is the LORD's,
  and he rules the nations.
To him alone shall bow down
  all who sleep in the earth.

R. I will praise you, Lord, in the assembly of your people.

To him my soul shall live;
  my descendants shall serve him.
Let the coming generation be told of the LORD
  that they may proclaim to a people yet to be born
  the justice he has shown.

R. I will praise you, Lord, in the assembly of your people.

Alleluia, alleluia   Mt 11:28
Come to me, all you who labor and are burdened,
and I will give you rest, says the Lord.
Alleluia, alleluia

Years I and II

GOSPEL   Lk 14:15–24

*Go out quickly into highways and hedgerows and make
people come in that my home may be filled.*

A reading from the holy Gospel according to Luke

One of those at table with Jesus said to him, "Blessed is the
one who will dine in the Kingdom of God." He replied to him,

"A man gave a great dinner to which he invited many. When the time for the dinner came, he dispatched his servant to say to those invited, 'Come, everything is now ready.' But one by one, they all began to excuse themselves. The first said to him, 'I have purchased a field and must go to examine it; I ask you, consider me excused.' And another said, 'I have purchased five yoke of oxen and am on my way to evaluate them; I ask you, consider me excused.' And another said, 'I have just married a woman, and therefore I cannot come.' The servant went and reported this to his master. Then the master of the house in a rage commanded his servant, 'Go out quickly into the streets and alleys of the town and bring in here the poor and the crippled, the blind and the lame.' The servant reported, 'Sir, your orders have been carried out and still there is room.' The master then ordered the servant, 'Go out to the highways and hedgerows and make people come in that my home may be filled. For, I tell you, none of those men who were invited will taste my dinner.'"

The Gospel of the Lord.

Liturgy of the Eucharist, *p. 897;* **Prayer over the Gifts,** *p. 1646.*

Wednesday

Antiphons and Prayers, *p. 1645;* **Liturgy of the Word** *for Year I (odd years) follows; Year II (even years), p. 1657.*

TODAY'S LIVING WORD

In today's Gospel, Jesus reiterates the conditions for discipleship. Luke's version is particularly harsh. He uses the Greek verb *misein*, meaning "hate." However, the saying does not dictate what one should feel as a family member, but what one must do as a follower of Jesus. Discipleship demands a total commitment. Therefore, it is a decision that must be carefully considered, like building a tower or going to war. For in the end it may require renouncing all possessions, relinquishing family ties, and taking up one's cross.

Paul's total commitment as a disciple of Christ is evident in the excerpt from his Letter to the Philippians. There is no doubt that he will finish the race and complete the work he has begun, by the grace of God. He says he is ready to be "poured out as a libation." This outpouring, the essence of discipleship, expresses itself concretely in love of others, as Paul writes to the Romans. Such love not only fulfills the law; it finishes the life project which is the following of Christ.

Year I

FIRST READING

Rom 13:8–10

Love is the fulfillment of the law.

A reading from the Letter of Saint Paul to the Romans

Brothers and sisters:
Owe nothing to anyone, except to love one another; for the one who loves another has fulfilled the law. The commandments, *You shall not commit adultery; you shall not kill; you shall not steal; you shall not covet,* and whatever other commandment there may be, are summed up in this saying, namely, *You shall love your neighbor as yourself.* Love does no evil to the neighbor; hence, love is the fulfillment of the law.
The word of the Lord.

Responsorial Psalm

Ps 112:1b–2, 4–5, 9

R. **Blessed the man who is gracious and lends to those in need.**

Blessed the man who fears the LORD,
   who greatly delights in his commands.

His posterity shall be mighty upon the earth;
  the upright generation shall be blessed.

  R. Blessed the man who is gracious and lends to those in need.

He dawns through the darkness, a light for the upright;
  he is gracious and merciful and just.
Well for the man who is gracious and lends,
  who conducts his affairs with justice.

  R. Blessed the man who is gracious and lends to those in need.

Lavishly he gives to the poor;
  his generosity shall endure forever;
  his horn shall be exalted in glory.

  R. Blessed the man who is gracious and lends to those in need.

  Or: **R. Alleluia.**

  Alleluia Verse *and* **Gospel,** *p. 1658.*

Year II

FIRST READING
Phil 2:12–18

*Work out your salvation. For God is the one
who works in you both to desire and to work.*

A reading from the Letter of Saint Paul to the Philippians

My beloved, obedient as you have always been, not only when
I am present but all the more now when I am absent, work out
your salvation with fear and trembling. For God is the one
who, for his good purpose, works in you both to desire and to
work. Do everything without grumbling or questioning, that
you may be blameless and innocent, children of God without
blemish in the midst of a crooked and perverse generation,
among whom you shine like lights in the world, as you hold
on to the word of life, so that my boast for the day of Christ
may be that I did not run in vain or labor in vain. But, even if

I am poured out as a libation upon the sacrificial service of your faith, I rejoice and share my joy with all of you. In the same way you also should rejoice and share your joy with me.
The word of the Lord.

Responsorial Psalm

Ps 27:1, 4, 13–14

R. The Lord is my light and my salvation.

The LORD is my light and my salvation;
  whom should I fear?
The LORD is my life's refuge;
  of whom should I be afraid?

R. The Lord is my light and my salvation.

One thing I ask of the LORD;
  this I seek:
To dwell in the house of the LORD
  all the days of my life,
That I may gaze on the loveliness of the LORD
  and contemplate his temple.

R. The Lord is my light and my salvation.

I believe that I shall see the bounty of the LORD
  in the land of the living.
Wait for the LORD with courage;
  be stouthearted, and wait for the LORD.

R. The Lord is my light and my salvation.

Alleluia, alleluia 1 Pt 4:14
If you are insulted for the name of Christ, blessed are you,
for the Spirit of God rests upon you.
Alleluia, alleluia

Years I and II

GOSPEL
Lk 14:25–33

*Everyone of you who does not renounce all his
possessions cannot be my disciple.*

A reading from the holy Gospel according to Luke

Great crowds were traveling with Jesus, and he turned and addressed them, "If anyone comes to me without hating his father and mother, wife and children, brothers and sisters, and even his own life, he cannot be my disciple. Whoever does not carry his own cross and come after me cannot be my disciple. Which of you wishing to construct a tower does not first sit down and calculate the cost to see if there is enough for its completion? Otherwise, after laying the foundation and finding himself unable to finish the work the onlookers should laugh at him and say, 'This one began to build but did not have the resources to finish.' Or what king marching into battle would not first sit down and decide whether with ten thousand troops he can successfully oppose another king advancing upon him with twenty thousand troops? But if not, while he is still far away, he will send a delegation to ask for peace terms. In the same way, everyone of you who does not renounce all his possessions cannot be my disciple."

The Gospel of the Lord.

Liturgy of the Eucharist, *p. 897;* **Prayer over the Gifts,** *p. 1646.*

Thursday

Antiphons and Prayers, *p. 1645;* **Liturgy of the Word** *for Year I (odd years) follows; Year II (even years), p. 1662.*

TODAY'S LIVING WORD

Today's reading from Romans seems to comment on the setting of the Gospel for today. "Why then do you judge your brother or sister?" Paul asks. "Why do you look down on your brother or sister?" Jesus addresses two parables to those who are doing just that by criticizing him for welcoming sinners. The parables are a matched set: a male example is paired with a female example to depict God's desire to save. In both stories something small and insignificant is lost; a single sheep, a paltry sum seem altogether unworthy of the seeking ("until he finds it") and the celebrating that follows. Yet Jesus says, "there will be rejoicing among the angels of God over one sinner who repents." So it seems, to return to Paul, that the Master to whom we belong in life and in death is determined and diligent in seeking the lost, even if they are the least.

And that is good news, as Paul declares to the Philippians. His own life is a case in point. All those things he once considered gain he reassessed as loss when he was found by the Lord Jesus Christ.

Year I

FIRST READING   Rom 14:7–12

Whether we live or die, we are the Lord's.

A reading from the Letter of Saint Paul to the Romans

Brothers and sisters:
None of us lives for oneself, and no one dies for oneself. For if we live, we live for the Lord, and if we die, we die for the Lord; so then, whether we live or die, we are the Lord's. For this is why Christ died and came to life, that he might be Lord of both the dead and the living. Why then do you judge your

brother or sister? Or you, why do you look down on your brother or sister? For we shall all stand before the judgment seat of God; for it is written:

> As I live, says the Lord, every knee shall bend before me,
> and every tongue shall give praise to God.

So then each of us shall give an account of himself to God.

The word of the Lord.

Responsorial Psalm

Ps 27:1bcde, 4, 13–14

R. I believe that I shall see the good things of the Lord in the land of the living.

The LORD is my light and my salvation;
 whom should I fear?
The LORD is my life's refuge;
 of whom should I be afraid?

R. I believe that I shall see the good things of the Lord in the land of the living.

One thing I ask of the LORD;
 this I seek:
To dwell in the house of the LORD
 all the days of my life,
That I may gaze on the loveliness of the LORD
 and contemplate his temple.

R. I believe that I shall see the good things of the Lord in the land of the living.

I believe that I shall see the bounty of the LORD
 in the land of the living.
Wait for the LORD with courage;
 be stouthearted, and wait for the LORD.

R. I believe that I shall see the good things of the Lord in the land of the living.

Alleluia Verse *and* **Gospel,** *p. 1663.*

Year II

FIRST READING   Phil 3:3–8a

But whatever gains I had, I even consider as a loss,
because of Christ.

A reading from the Letter of Saint Paul to the Philippians

Brothers and sisters:

We are the circumcision, we who worship through the Spirit
of God, who boast in Christ Jesus and do not put our confidence
in flesh, although I myself have grounds for confidence even
in the flesh.

If anyone else thinks he can be confident in flesh, all the
more can I. Circumcised on the eighth day, of the race of Israel,
of the tribe of Benjamin, a Hebrew of Hebrew parentage, in
observance of the law a Pharisee, in zeal I persecuted the
Church, in righteousness based on the law I was blameless.

But whatever gains I had, these I have come to consider a
loss because of Christ. More than that, I even consider everything as a loss because of the supreme good of knowing Christ
Jesus my Lord.

The word of the Lord.

Responsorial Psalm   Ps 105:2–3, 4–5, 6–7

R. Let hearts rejoice who search for the Lord.

Sing to him, sing his praise,
    proclaim all his wondrous deeds.
Glory in his holy name;
    rejoice, O hearts that seek the LORD!

R. Let hearts rejoice who search for the Lord.

Look to the LORD in his strength;
    seek to serve him constantly.

Recall the wondrous deeds that he has wrought,
 his portents, and the judgments he has uttered.

R. Let hearts rejoice who search for the Lord.

You descendants of Abraham, his servants,
 sons of Jacob, his chosen ones!
He, the LORD, is our God;
 throughout the earth his judgments prevail.

R. Let hearts rejoice who search for the Lord.

Or: **R. Alleluia.**

> **Alleluia, alleluia** Mt 11:28
> Come to me, all you who labor and are burdened,
> and I will give you rest, says the Lord.
> **Alleluia, alleluia**

Years I and II

GOSPEL

Lk 15:1–10

There will be more joy in heaven over one sinner who repents.

A reading from the holy Gospel according to Luke

The tax collectors and sinners were all drawing near to listen to Jesus, but the Pharisees and scribes began to complain, saying, "This man welcomes sinners and eats with them." So Jesus addressed this parable to them. "What man among you having a hundred sheep and losing one of them would not leave the ninety-nine in the desert and go after the lost one until he finds it? And when he does find it, he sets it on his shoulders with great joy and, upon his arrival home, he calls together his friends and neighbors and says to them, 'Rejoice with me because I have found my lost sheep.' I tell you, in just the same way there will be more joy in heaven over one sinner who repents than over ninety-nine righteous people who have no need of repentance.

"Or what woman having ten coins and losing one would not light a lamp and sweep the house, searching carefully until she finds it? And when she does find it, she calls together her friends and neighbors and says to them, 'Rejoice with me because I have found the coin that I lost.' In just the same way, I tell you, there will be rejoicing among the angels of God over one sinner who repents."

The Gospel of the Lord.

Liturgy of the Eucharist, *p. 897;* **Prayer over the Gifts,** *p. 1646.*

Friday

Antiphons and Prayers, *p. 1645;* **Liturgy of the Word** *for Year I (odd years) follows; Year II (even years), p. 1666.*

TODAY'S LIVING WORD

Today's Gospel seems to affront our moral sensibilities. Is Jesus really presenting the devious manager of the parable as an example? Yes, but for what he does, not how he does it. Because the accounting methods of Jesus' day are not well known to us, it is impossible for us to understand exactly what the manager did to extricate himself from his predicament. Did he reduce the actual amount owed? Or the interest hidden in the principal? Or did he forego his commission? Yet the point is not his action, but his reaction. His employer's demand for an audit precipitates a crisis for the manager. He shows initiative as he realistically assesses his situation and resourcefully acts to save himself. He is commended for responding boldly and decisively in crisis. Jesus urges this mode of action on his hearers, for whom his ministry precipitates a crisis of a different kind—one that is not "of this world."

The two first readings, both from Paul, give us "snapshots" of a man who responded boldly and decisively in crisis throughout his whole life. He is worthy of imitation.

Year I

FIRST READING   Rom 15:14–21

A minister of Christ Jesus to the Gentiles, so that
the offering up of the Gentiles may be acceptable.

A reading from the Letter of Saint Paul to the Romans

I myself am convinced about you, my brothers and sisters,
that you yourselves are full of goodness, filled with all knowledge, and able to admonish one another. But I have written to
you rather boldly in some respects to remind you, because of
the grace given me by God to be a minister of Christ Jesus to
the Gentiles in performing the priestly service of the Gospel
of God, so that the offering up of the Gentiles may be acceptable, sanctified by the Holy Spirit. In Christ Jesus, then, I have
reason to boast in what pertains to God. For I will not dare
to speak of anything except what Christ has accomplished through me to lead the Gentiles to obedience by word and
deed, by the power of signs and wonders, by the power of the
Spirit of God, so that from Jerusalem all the way around to
Illyricum I have finished preaching the Gospel of Christ. Thus
I aspire to proclaim the Gospel not where Christ has already
been named, so that I do not build on another's foundation,
but as it is written:

   Those who have never been told of him shall see,
   and those who have never heard of him shall understand.

The word of the Lord.

Responsorial Psalm   Ps 98:1, 2–3ab, 3cd–4

   R. The Lord has revealed to the nations his saving power.

Sing to the LORD a new song,
  for he has done wondrous deeds;
His right hand has won victory for him,
  his holy arm.

  R. **The Lord has revealed to the nations his saving power.**

The LORD has made his salvation known:
  in the sight of the nations he has revealed his justice.
He has remembered his kindness and his faithfulness
  toward the house of Israel.

  R. **The Lord has revealed to the nations his saving power.**

All the ends of the earth have seen
  the salvation by our God.
Sing joyfully to the LORD, all you lands;
  break into song; sing praise.

  R. **The Lord has revealed to the nations his saving power.**

  Alleluia Verse *and* **Gospel,** *p. 1667f.*

Year II

FIRST READING   Phil 3:17—4:1

*We await a savior who will change our lowly body
to conform with his glorified Body.*

A reading from the Letter of Saint Paul to the Philippians

Join with others in being imitators of me, brothers and sisters,
and observe those who thus conduct themselves according to
the model you have in us. For many, as I have often told you
and now tell you even in tears, conduct themselves as enemies
of the cross of Christ. Their end is destruction. Their God is
their stomach; their glory is in their "shame." Their minds are
occupied with earthly things. But our citizenship is in heaven,

and from it we also await a savior, the Lord Jesus Christ. He will change our lowly body to conform with his glorified Body by the power that enables him also to bring all things into subjection to himself.

Therefore, my brothers and sisters, whom I love and long for, my joy and crown, in this way stand firm in the Lord, beloved.

The word of the Lord.

Responsorial Psalm

Ps 122:1–2, 3–4ab, 4cd–5

R. Let us go rejoicing to the house of the Lord.

I rejoiced because they said to me,
  "We will go up to the house of the LORD."
And now we have set foot
  within your gates, O Jerusalem.

R. Let us go rejoicing to the house of the Lord.

Jerusalem, built as a city
  with compact unity.
To it the tribes go up,
  the tribes of the LORD.

R. Let us go rejoicing to the house of the Lord.

According to the decree for Israel,
  to give thanks to the name of the LORD.
In it are set up judgment seats,
  seats for the house of David.

R. Let us go rejoicing to the house of the Lord.

    Alleluia, alleluia   1 Jn 2:5
    Whoever keeps the word of Christ,
    the love of God is truly perfected in him.
    Alleluia, alleluia

Years I and II

GOSPEL   Lk 16:1–8

For the children of this world are more prudent in dealing
with their own generation than are the children of light.

A reading from the holy Gospel according to Luke

Jesus said to his disciples, "A rich man had a steward who was reported to him for squandering his property. He summoned him and said, 'What is this I hear about you? Prepare a full account of your stewardship, because you can no longer be my steward.' The steward said to himself, 'What shall I do, now that my master is taking the position of steward away from me? I am not strong enough to dig and I am ashamed to beg. I know what I shall do so that, when I am removed from the stewardship, they may welcome me into their homes.' He called in his master's debtors one by one. To the first he said, 'How much do you owe my master?' He replied, 'One hundred measures of olive oil.' He said to him, 'Here is your promissory note. Sit down and quickly write one for fifty.' Then to another he said, 'And you, how much do you owe?' He replied, 'One hundred measures of wheat.' He said to him, 'Here is your promissory note; write one for eighty.' And the master commended that dishonest steward for acting prudently. For the children of this world are more prudent in dealing with their own generation than the children of light."

The Gospel of the Lord.

Liturgy of the Eucharist, *p. 897;* **Prayer over the Gifts,** *p. 1646.*

Saturday

Antiphons and Prayers, *p. 1645;* **Liturgy of the Word** *for Year I (odd years) follows; Year II (even years), p. 1671.*

TODAY'S LIVING WORD

Luke has appended many sayings to the parable of the devious manager, which indicates the early Church found it as difficult to understand as we do. The parable's main point was to call for a decisive response to the crisis precipitated by Jesus' ministry. Although the parable itself was not directly concerned with the ethics of the manager, Luke knew that ethical obligations do devolve upon those who recognize the arrival of God's kingdom in the ministry of Jesus. Taken as a whole, all these sayings about managing money tell us that how we handle money says much about what is in our hearts. It should be noted that the generalization about Pharisees being avaricious is Luke's bias. Almsgiving was a cornerstone of the ethics of the rabbis.

The reading from Philippians shows us Paul's attitude toward money. Thanking them for their financial support, he tells them that he has learned to live in poverty and in plenty by finding his strength in Christ. He most appreciates not their gift but what it signifies, a share in his ministry which redounds to the glory of God. In the same way in Romans, he acknowledges all his fellow workers in the service of Christ.

Year I

FIRST READING

Rom 16:3–9, 16, 22–27

Greet one another with a holy kiss.

A reading from the Letter of Saint Paul to the Romans

Brothers and sisters:

Greet Prisca and Aquila, my co-workers in Christ Jesus, who risked their necks for my life, to whom not only I am grateful but also all the churches of the Gentiles; greet also the Church at their house. Greet my beloved Epaenetus, who was the firstfruits in Asia for Christ. Greet Mary, who has worked hard for you. Greet Andronicus and Junia, my relatives and my fellow prisoners; they are prominent among the Apostles and they were in Christ before me. Greet Ampliatus, my beloved in the Lord. Greet Urbanus, our co-worker in Christ, and my beloved Stachys. Greet one another with a holy kiss. All the churches of Christ greet you.

I, Tertius, the writer of this letter, greet you in the Lord. Gaius, who is host to me and to the whole Church, greets you. Erastus, the city treasurer, and our brother Quartus greet you.

Now to him who can strengthen you, according to my Gospel and the proclamation of Jesus Christ, according to the revelation of the mystery kept secret for long ages but now manifested through the prophetic writings and, according to the command of the eternal God, made known to all nations to bring about the obedience of faith, to the only wise God, through Jesus Christ be glory forever and ever. Amen.

The word of the Lord.

Responsorial Psalm

Ps 145:2–3, 4–5, 10–11

R. I will praise your name for ever, Lord.

Every day will I bless you,
  and I will praise your name forever and ever.
Great is the LORD and highly to be praised;
  his greatness is unsearchable.

R. I will praise your name for ever, Lord.

Generation after generation praises your works
  and proclaims your might.

They speak of the splendor of your glorious majesty
   and tell of your wondrous works.

   R. I will praise your name for ever, Lord.

Let all your works give you thanks, O LORD,
   and let your faithful ones bless you.
Let them discourse of the glory of your Kingdom
   and speak of your might.

   R. I will praise your name for ever, Lord.

   Alleluia Verse *and* **Gospel,** *p. 1672f.*

Year II

FIRST READING

Phil 4:10–19

I have the strength for everything through him who empowers me.

A reading from the Letter of Saint Paul to the Philippians

Brothers and sisters:
I rejoice greatly in the Lord that now at last you revived your
concern for me. You were, of course, concerned about me but
lacked an opportunity. Not that I say this because of need, for
I have learned, in whatever situation I find myself, to be self-
sufficient. I know indeed how to live in humble circumstances;
I know also how to live with abundance. In every circumstance
and in all things I have learned the secret of being well fed and
of going hungry, of living in abundance and of being in need.
I have the strength for everything through him who empowers
me. Still, it was kind of you to share in my distress.

   You Philippians indeed know that at the beginning of the
Gospel, when I left Macedonia, not a single church shared with
me in an account of giving and receiving, except you alone.
For even when I was at Thessalonica you sent me something

for my needs, not only once but more than once. It is not that I am eager for the gift; rather, I am eager for the profit that accrues to your account. I have received full payment and I abound. I am very well supplied because of what I received from you through Epaphroditus, "a fragrant aroma," an acceptable sacrifice, pleasing to God. My God will fully supply whatever you need, in accord with his glorious riches in Christ Jesus.

The word of the Lord.

Responsorial Psalm

Ps 112:1b–2, 5–6, 8a and 9

R. Blessed the man who fears the Lord.

Blessed the man who fears the LORD,
  who greatly delights in his commands.
His posterity shall be mighty upon the earth;
  the upright generation shall be blessed.

R. Blessed the man who fears the Lord.

Well for the man who is gracious and lends,
  who conducts his affairs with justice;
He shall never be moved;
  the just one shall be in everlasting remembrance.

R. Blessed the man who fears the Lord.

His heart is steadfast; he shall not fear.
Lavishly he gives to the poor;
  his generosity shall endure forever;
  his horn shall be exalted in glory.

R. Blessed the man who fears the Lord.

Or: **R. Alleluia.**

Alleluia, alleluia 2 Cor 8:9
Jesus Christ became poor although he was rich,
  so that by his poverty you might become rich.
Alleluia, alleluia

Years I and II

GOSPEL

Lk 16:9–15

If, therefore, you are not trustworthy with dishonest wealth,
who will trust you with true wealth?

A reading from the holy Gospel according to Luke

Jesus said to his disciples: "I tell you, make friends for yourselves with dishonest wealth, so that when it fails, you will be welcomed into eternal dwellings. The person who is trustworthy in very small matters is also trustworthy in great ones; and the person who is dishonest in very small matters is also dishonest in great ones. If, therefore, you are not trustworthy with dishonest wealth, who will trust you with true wealth? If you are not trustworthy with what belongs to another, who will give you what is yours? No servant can serve two masters. He will either hate one and love the other, or be devoted to one and despise the other. You cannot serve God and mammon."

The Pharisees, who loved money, heard all these things and sneered at him. And he said to them, "You justify yourselves in the sight of others, but God knows your hearts; for what is of human esteem is an abomination in the sight of God."

The Gospel of the Lord.

Liturgy of the Eucharist, *p. 897;* **Prayer over the Gifts,** *p. 1646.*

THIRTY-SECOND WEEK IN ORDINARY TIME

The **Antiphons and Prayers** *may be the following, or may be chosen from any of the other 33 weeks in Ordinary Time (refer to Liturgical Calendar, pp. 26–41).*

The **Liturgy of the Word** *varies: for Monday, see p. 1676; Tuesday, p. 1680; Wednesday, p. 1685; Thursday, p. 1689; Friday, p. 1694; Saturday, p. 1699.*

Entrance Antiphon

Let my prayer come before you, Lord; listen, and answer me.
(Ps 88:3)

Opening Prayer

Let us pray
[for health of mind and body]

Pause for silent prayer.

God of power and mercy,
protect us from all harm.
Give us freedom of spirit
and health in mind and body
to do your work on earth.

We ask this through our Lord Jesus Christ, your Son,
who lives and reigns with you and the Holy Spirit,
one God, for ever and ever.

Alternative Opening Prayer

Let us pray
[that our prayer rise like incense
in the presence of God]

Pause for silent prayer.

Almighty Father,
strong is your justice and great is your mercy.
Protect us in the burdens and challenges of life.
Shield our minds from the distortion of pride

and enfold our desire with the beauty of truth.
Help us to become more aware of your loving design
so that we may more willingly give our lives in service to all.

We ask this through Christ our Lord.

Prayer over the Gifts

Pray, brethren...

God of mercy,
in this eucharist we proclaim the death of the Lord.
Accept the gifts we present
and help us follow him with love,
for he is Lord for ever and ever.

Preface of Weekdays in Ordinary Time I–VI, *pp. 948–950.*

Communion Antiphon

The Lord is my shepherd; there is nothing I shall want. In green pastures he gives me rest, he leads me beside the waters of peace.
(Ps 23:1–2)

Or:

The disciples recognized the Lord Jesus in the breaking of bread.
(Lk 24:35)

Prayer after Communion

Let us pray.

Pause for silent prayer, if this has not preceded.

Lord,
we thank you for the nourishment you give us
through your holy gift.
Pour out your Spirit upon us
and in the strength of this food from heaven
keep us single-minded in your service.

We ask this in the name of Jesus the Lord.

Monday

Antiphons and Prayers, *p. 1674;* **Liturgy of the Word** *for Year I (odd years) follows; Year II (even years), p. 1678.*

TODAY'S LIVING WORD

All the readings for today speak to the need for discipline. The selection from the Book of Wisdom exhorts those in authority to "love justice." The vital principle that will enable them to act justly is none other than "the holy Spirit of discipline" which "flees deceit... withdraws from senseless counsels" and roundly rebukes injustice. The excerpt from the Letter to Titus also concerns those who wield authority. It says that presbyters must know how to discipline their children, and bishops must be self-disciplined. In today's Gospel, Jesus continues to teach the daily demands of Christian life. Here again disciplined vigilance—"Be on your guard" —will enable his disciples not to give scandal and to forgive as unstintingly as God does.

As though in response to Jesus' teaching, the disciples pray, "Increase our faith." Perhaps that should be our prayer too as we, in turn, undertake the daily discipline of following Christ.

Year I

FIRST READING   Wis 1:1–7

Wisdom is a kindly spirit,
the Spirit of the Lord fills the world.

A reading from the beginning of the Book of Wisdom

Love justice, you who judge the earth;
    think of the Lord in goodness,
    and seek him in integrity of heart;
Because he is found by those who test him not,
    and he manifests himself to those who do not disbelieve
        him.
For perverse counsels separate a man from God,

and his power, put to the proof, rebukes the foolhardy;
Because into a soul that plots evil, wisdom enters not,
    nor dwells she in a body under debt of sin.
For the holy Spirit of discipline flees deceit
    and withdraws from senseless counsels;
    and when injustice occurs it is rebuked.
For wisdom is a kindly spirit,
    yet she acquits not the blasphemer of his guilty lips;
Because God is the witness of his inmost self
    and the sure observer of his heart
    and the listener to his tongue.
For the Spirit of the Lord fills the world,
    is all-embracing, and knows what man says.

The word of the Lord.

Responsorial Psalm

Ps 139:1b–3, 4–6, 7–8, 9–10

R. Guide me, Lord, along the everlasting way.

O LORD, you have probed me and you know me;
  you know when I sit and when I stand;
  you understand my thoughts from afar.
My journeys and my rest you scrutinize,
  with all my ways you are familiar.

R. Guide me, Lord, along the everlasting way.

Even before a word is on my tongue,
  behold, O LORD, you know the whole of it.
Behind me and before, you hem me in
  and rest your hand upon me.
Such knowledge is too wonderful for me;
  too lofty for me to attain.

R. Guide me, Lord, along the everlasting way.

Where can I go from your spirit?
  From your presence where can I flee?

If I go up to the heavens, you are there;
  if I sink to the nether world, you are present there.

R. Guide me, Lord, along the everlasting way.

If I take the wings of the dawn,
  if I settle at the farthest limits of the sea,
Even there your hand shall guide me,
  and your right hand hold me fast.

R. Guide me, Lord, along the everlasting way.

Alleluia Verse *and* **Gospel,** *p. 1679.*

Year II

FIRST READING

Appoint presbyters in every town, as I directed you.

A reading from the beginning of the Letter of Saint Paul to Titus

Paul, a slave of God and Apostle of Jesus Christ for the sake of the faith of God's chosen ones and the recognition of religious truth, in the hope of eternal life that God, who does not lie, promised before time began, who indeed at the proper time revealed his word in the proclamation with which I was entrusted by the command of God our savior, to Titus, my true child in our common faith: grace and peace from God the Father and Christ Jesus our savior.

  For this reason I left you in Crete so that you might set right what remains to be done and appoint presbyters in every town, as I directed you, on condition that a man be blameless, married only once, with believing children who are not accused of licentiousness or rebellious. For a bishop as God's steward must be blameless, not arrogant, not irritable, not a drunkard, not aggressive, not greedy for sordid gain, but hospitable, a lover of goodness, temperate, just, holy, and self-controlled, holding fast to the true message as taught so that he will be able both to exhort with sound doctrine and to refute opponents. The word of the Lord.

Responsorial Psalm

Ps 24:1b–2, 3–4ab, 5–6

R. Lord, this is the people that longs to see your face.

The LORD's are the earth and its fullness;
  the world and those who dwell in it.
For he founded it upon the seas
  and established it upon the rivers.

R. Lord, this is the people that longs to see your face.

Who can ascend the mountain of the LORD?
  or who may stand in his holy place?
He whose hands are sinless, whose heart is clean,
  who desires not what is vain.

R. Lord, this is the people that longs to see your face.

He shall receive a blessing from the LORD,
  a reward from God his savior.
Such is the race that seeks for him,
  that seeks the face of the God of Jacob.

R. Lord, this is the people that longs to see your face.

Alleluia, alleluia Phil 2:15d, 16a
Shine like lights in the world,
  as you hold on to the word of life.
Alleluia, alleluia

Years I and II

GOSPEL

Lk 17:1–6

*If your brother wrongs you seven times in one day, and returns
to you seven times saying, "I am sorry," you should forgive him.*

A reading from the holy Gospel according to Luke

Jesus said to his disciples, "Things that cause sin will inevitably occur, but woe to the one through whom they occur. It would be better for him if a millstone were put around his neck and he be thrown into the sea than for him to cause one of these little ones to sin. Be on your guard! If your brother sins, rebuke him; and if he repents, forgive him. And if he wrongs you seven times in one day and returns to you seven times saying, 'I am sorry,' you should forgive him."

And the Apostles said to the Lord, "Increase our faith." The Lord replied, "If you have faith the size of a mustard seed, you would say to this mulberry tree, 'Be uprooted and planted in the sea,' and it would obey you."

The Gospel of the Lord.

Liturgy of the Eucharist, *p. 897;* **Prayer over the Gifts,** *p. 1675.*

Tuesday

Antiphons and Prayers, *p. 1674;* **Liturgy of the Word** *for Year I (odd years) follows; Year II (even years), p. 1682.*

TODAY'S LIVING WORD

In today's Gospel Jesus concludes his instruction on discipleship with a homey example. He points out that there is nothing particularly heroic in going the hard way with him. He tells the disciples, "When you have done all you have been commanded"—relativizing family ties and renouncing all possessions (Lk 14:26, 33), avoiding scandal and forgiving whenever asked (Lk 17:2, 3–4)—"say, 'We are unprofitable servants. We have done what we were obliged to do.'"

Those words may seem somewhat deflating to us who so often falter as we follow in Jesus' steps. The reason may be, as the Book of Wisdom explains, that sin has distorted the image of God in us, though not destroyed it. Discipleship restores to us the dignity God willed for us in the beginning. As the Letter to Titus puts it, the grace of God revealed in Christ is "training us to reject godless ways and worldly desires and to live temperately, justly, and devoutly" as we await the appearance of God's glory.

Year I

FIRST READING

Wis 2:23—3:9

In the view of the foolish they seemed to be dead,
but they are in peace.

A reading from the Book of Wisdom

God formed man to be imperishable;
  the image of his own nature he made them.
But by the envy of the Devil, death entered the world,
  and they who are in his possession experience it.

But the souls of the just are in the hand of God,
  and no torment shall touch them.
They seemed, in the view of the foolish, to be dead;
  and their passing away was thought an affliction
  and their going forth from us, utter destruction.
But they are in peace.
For if before men, indeed, they be punished,
  yet is their hope full of immortality;
Chastised a little, they shall be greatly blessed,
  because God tried them
  and found them worthy of himself.
As gold in the furnace, he proved them,
  and as sacrificial offerings he took them to himself.
In the time of their visitation they shall shine,
  and shall dart about as sparks through stubble;
They shall judge nations and rule over peoples,
  and the Lord shall be their King forever.
Those who trust in him shall understand truth,
  and the faithful shall abide with him in love:

Because grace and mercy are with his holy ones,
  and his care is with his elect.

The word of the Lord.

Responsorial Psalm

Ps 34:2–3, 16–17, 18–19

R. I will bless the Lord at all times.

I will bless the LORD at all times;
  his praise shall be ever in my mouth.
Let my soul glory in the LORD;
  the lowly will hear me and be glad.

  R. I will bless the Lord at all times.

The LORD has eyes for the just,
  and ears for their cry.
The LORD confronts the evildoers,
  to destroy remembrance of them from the earth.

  R. I will bless the Lord at all times.

When the just cry out, the LORD hears them,
  and from all their distress he rescues them.
The LORD is close to the brokenhearted;
  and those who are crushed in spirit he saves.

  R. I will bless the Lord at all times.

  Alleluia Verse *and* **Gospel,** *p. 1684.*

Year II

FIRST READING

Ti 2:1–8, 11–14

We live devoutly in this age, as we await the blessed hope,
the appearance of our savior Jesus Christ.

A reading from the Letter of Saint Paul to Titus

Beloved:
You must say what is consistent with sound doctrine, namely,
that older men should be temperate, dignified, self-controlled,

sound in faith, love, and endurance. Similarly, older women should be reverent in their behavior, not slanderers, not addicted to drink, teaching what is good, so that they may train younger women to love their husbands and children, to be self-controlled, chaste, good homemakers, under the control of their husbands, so that the word of God may not be discredited.

Urge the younger men, similarly, to control themselves, showing yourself as a model of good deeds in every respect, with integrity in your teaching, dignity, and sound speech that cannot be criticized, so that the opponent will be put to shame without anything bad to say about us.

For the grace of God has appeared, saving all and training us to reject godless ways and worldly desires and to live temperately, justly, and devoutly in this age, as we await the blessed hope, the appearance of the glory of the great God and of our savior Jesus Christ, who gave himself for us to deliver us from all lawlessness and to cleanse for himself a people as his own, eager to do what is good.

The word of the Lord.

Responsorial Psalm
Ps 37:3-4, 8 and 23, 27 and 29

R. The salvation of the just comes from the Lord.

Trust in the LORD and do good,
   that you may dwell in the land and be fed in security.
Take delight in the LORD,
   and he will grant you your heart's requests.

R. The salvation of the just comes from the Lord.

The LORD watches over the lives of the wholehearted;
   their inheritance lasts forever.
By the LORD are the steps of a man made firm,
   and he approves his way.

R. The salvation of the just comes from the Lord.

Turn from evil and do good,
 that you may abide forever;
The just shall possess the land
 and dwell in it forever.

R. The salvation of the just comes from the Lord.

Alleluia, alleluia Jn 14:23
Whoever loves me will keep my word,
and my Father will love him,
and we will come to him.
Alleluia, alleluia

Years I and II

GOSPEL   Lk 17:7-10

*We are unprofitable servants; we have done
what we were obliged to do.*

A reading from the holy Gospel according to Luke

Jesus said to the Apostles: "Who among you would say to your
servant who has just come in from plowing or tending sheep
in the field, 'Come here immediately and take your place at
table'? Would he not rather say to him, 'Prepare something for
me to eat. Put on your apron and wait on me while I eat and
drink. You may eat and drink when I am finished'? Is he grateful
to that servant because he did what was commanded? So should
it be with you. When you have done all you have been commanded, say, 'We are unprofitable servants; we have done what
we were obliged to do.'"

The Gospel of the Lord.

Liturgy of the Eucharist, *p. 897;* **Prayer over the Gifts,** *p. 1675.*

Wednesday

Antiphons and Prayers, *p. 1674;* **Liturgy of the Word** *for Year I (odd years) follows; Year II (even years), p. 1687.*

TODAY'S LIVING WORD

The story of the healing of the ten lepers, found only in Luke, illustrates the teaching of the Book of Wisdom: "The Lord of all shows no partiality." In Jesus' day lepers were outcasts, the least of all people, but God's mercy extended to them too. All ten were made whole. Their faith—even if it was small as mustard seed—was their salvation.

The surprise element in the story lies in the response of the one leper who happened to be a Samaritan. The least of all the lepers, he was not just an outcast but an outsider. Jesus underlined the irony: "Has none but this foreigner returned to give thanks to God?" The Letter to Titus brings home the lesson here. We were all foreigners once, "foolish, disobedient, deluded." We were saved, "through the bath of rebirth and renewal by the Holy Spirit," because of God's mercy. Like the Samaritan, let us realize what has been done for us and give thanks without ceasing.

Year I

FIRST READING   Wis 6:1–11

Hear, kings, that you may learn wisdom.

A reading from the Book of Wisdom

Hear, O kings, and understand;
    learn, you magistrates of the earth's expanse!
Hearken, you who are in power over the multitude
    and lord it over throngs of peoples!
Because authority was given you by the Lord
    and sovereignty by the Most High,

who shall probe your works and scrutinize your
counsels.
Because, though you were ministers of his kingdom, you judged
not rightly,
and did not keep the law,
nor walk according to the will of God,
Terribly and swiftly shall he come against you,
because judgment is stern for the exalted—
For the lowly may be pardoned out of mercy
but the mighty shall be mightily put to the test.
For the Lord of all shows no partiality,
nor does he fear greatness,
Because he himself made the great as well as the small,
and he provides for all alike;
but for those in power a rigorous scrutiny impends.
To you, therefore, O princes, are my words addressed
that you may learn wisdom and that you may not sin.
For those who keep the holy precepts hallowed shall be found
holy,
and those learned in them will have ready a response.
Desire therefore my words;
long for them and you shall be instructed.

The word of the Lord.

Responsorial Psalm
Ps 82:3–4, 6–7

R. Rise up, O God, bring judgment to the earth.

Defend the lowly and the fatherless;
render justice to the afflicted and the destitute.
Rescue the lowly and the poor;
from the hand of the wicked deliver them.

R. Rise up, O God, bring judgment to the earth.

I said: "You are gods,
  all of you sons of the Most High;
yet like men you shall die,
  and fall like any prince."

R. Rise up, O God, bring judgment to the earth.

Alleluia Verse *and* **Gospel,** *p. 1688f.*

Year II

FIRST READING

Ti 3:1–7

For we ourselves were deluded, but because of his mercy, he saved us.

A reading from the Letter of Saint Paul to Titus

Beloved:

Remind them to be under the control of magistrates and authorities, to be obedient, to be open to every good enterprise. They
are to slander no one, to be peaceable, considerate, exercising
all graciousness toward everyone. For we ourselves were once
foolish, disobedient, deluded, slaves to various desires and
pleasures, living in malice and envy, hateful ourselves and hating one another.

  But when the kindness and generous love
    of God our savior appeared,
  not because of any righteous deeds we had done
    but because of his mercy,
  he saved us through the bath of rebirth
    and renewal by the Holy Spirit,
  whom he richly poured out on us
    through Jesus Christ our savior,
  so that we might be justified by his grace
    and become heirs in hope of eternal life.

The word of the Lord.

Responsorial Psalm

Ps 23:1b–3a, 3bc–4, 5, 6

R. The Lord is my shepherd; there is nothing I shall want.

The LORD is my shepherd; I shall not want.
  In verdant pastures he gives me repose;
Beside restful waters he leads me;
  he refreshes my soul.

R. The Lord is my shepherd; there is nothing I shall want.

He guides me in right paths
  for his name's sake.
Even though I walk in the dark valley
  I fear no evil; for you are at my side
With your rod and your staff
  that give me courage.

R. The Lord is my shepherd; there is nothing I shall want.

You spread the table before me
  in the sight of my foes;
You anoint my head with oil;
  my cup overflows.

R. The Lord is my shepherd; there is nothing I shall want.

Only goodness and kindness follow me
  all the days of my life;
And I shall dwell in the house of the LORD
  for years to come.

R. The Lord is my shepherd; there is nothing I shall want.

Alleluia, alleluia   1 Thes 5:18
In all circumstances, give thanks,
  for this is the will of God for you in Christ Jesus.
Alleluia, alleluia

Years I and II

GOSPEL   Lk 17:11–19

Has none but this foreigner returned to give thanks to God?

A reading from the holy Gospel according to Luke

As Jesus continued his journey to Jerusalem, he traveled through Samaria and Galilee. As he was entering a village, ten lepers met him. They stood at a distance from him and raised their voice, saying, "Jesus, Master! Have pity on us!" And when he saw them, he said, "Go show yourselves to the priests." As they were going they were cleansed. And one of them, realizing he had been healed, returned, glorifying God in a loud voice; and he fell at the feet of Jesus and thanked him. He was a Samaritan. Jesus said in reply, "Ten were cleansed, were they not? Where are the other nine? Has none but this foreigner returned to give thanks to God?" Then he said to him, "Stand up and go; your faith has saved you."

The Gospel of the Lord.

Liturgy of the Eucharist, *p. 897;* **Prayer over the Gifts,** *p. 1675.*

Thursday

Antiphons and Prayers, *p. 1674;* **Liturgy of the Word** *for Year I (odd years) follows; Year II (even years), p. 1692.*

Today's Living Word

Scholars often describe the reign of God as "already but not yet," and Jesus' words in today's Gospel may be construed in just this way. He tells the Pharisees that the reign of God is *already* among them; it is being inaugurated by his prophetic activity, his healing and teaching, though they cannot see it. He promises his disciples the day of the Son of Man which they will long to see. But that day is *not yet.* "First...he must suffer greatly and be rejected by this generation." Thus Jesus distinguishes between the arrival of God's kingdom in his ministry and its full realization on that day when the Son of Man lights up the sky.

Some manuscripts substitute "Spirit" for "kingdom" in the Lucan version of the Our Father. Both the Spirit and the kingdom are ways of talking about the pure, pervasive power of God that "renews everything," as the author of Wisdom says. The effect of this power to produce "friends of God" is evidenced in Paul's note to Philemon. He declares that the power of God has transformed Onesimus from a slave to a beloved brother.

Year I

FIRST READING   Wis 7:22b—8:1

For wisdom is the refulgence of eternal light,
the spotless mirror of the power of God.

A reading from the Book of Wisdom

In Wisdom is a spirit
    intelligent, holy, unique,
Manifold, subtle, agile,
    clear, unstained, certain,
Not baneful, loving the good, keen,
    unhampered, beneficent, kindly,
Firm, secure, tranquil,
    all-powerful, all-seeing,
And pervading all spirits,
    though they be intelligent, pure and very subtle.
For Wisdom is mobile beyond all motion,
    and she penetrates and pervades all things by reason of
      her purity.
For she is an aura of the might of God

and a pure effusion of the glory of the Almighty;
  therefore nought that is sullied enters into her.
For she is the refulgence of eternal light,
  the spotless mirror of the power of God,
  the image of his goodness.
And she, who is one, can do all things,
  and renews everything while herself perduring;
And passing into holy souls from age to age,
  she produces friends of God and prophets.
For there is nought God loves, be it not one who dwells
    with Wisdom.
For she is fairer than the sun
  and surpasses every constellation of the stars.
Compared to light, she takes precedence;
  for that, indeed, night supplants,
  but wickedness prevails not over Wisdom.
Indeed, she reaches from end to end mightily
  and governs all things well.

The word of the Lord.

Responsorial Psalm   Ps 119:89, 90, 91, 130, 135, 175

R. Your word is for ever, O Lord.

Your word, O LORD, endures forever;
  it is firm as the heavens.

R. Your word is for ever, O Lord.

Through all generations your truth endures;
  you have established the earth, and it stands firm.

R. Your word is for ever, O Lord.

According to your ordinances they still stand firm:
  all things serve you.

R. **Your word is for ever, O Lord.**

The revelation of your words sheds light,
  giving understanding to the simple.

R. **Your word is for ever, O Lord.**

Let your countenance shine upon your servant,
  and teach me your statutes.

R. **Your word is for ever, O Lord.**

Let my soul live to praise you,
  and may your ordinances help me.

R. **Your word is for ever, O Lord.**

Alleluia Verse *and* **Gospel,** *p. 1694.*

Year II

FIRST READING

Phlm 7–20

*Have him back, no longer as a slave but more
than a slave, a brother, beloved especially to me.*

A reading from the Letter of Saint Paul to Philemon

Beloved:

I have experienced much joy and encouragement from your
love, because the hearts of the holy ones have been refreshed
by you, brother. Therefore, although I have the full right in
Christ to order you to do what is proper, I rather urge you out
of love, being as I am, Paul, an old man, and now also a prisoner
for Christ Jesus. I urge you on behalf of my child Onesimus,
whose father I have become in my imprisonment, who was
once useless to you but is now useful to both you and me. I am
sending him, that is, my own heart, back to you. I should have
liked to retain him for myself, so that he might serve me on
your behalf in my imprisonment for the Gospel, but I did not

want to do anything without your consent, so that the good you do might not be forced but voluntary. Perhaps this is why he was away from you for a while, that you might have him back forever, no longer as a slave but more than a slave, a brother, beloved especially to me, but even more so to you, as a man and in the Lord. So if you regard me as a partner, welcome him as you would me. And if he has done you any injustice or owes you anything, charge it to me. I, Paul, write this in my own hand: I will pay. May I not tell you that you owe me your very self. Yes, brother, may I profit from you in the Lord. Refresh my heart in Christ.

The word of the Lord.

Responsorial Psalm

Ps 146:7, 8–9a, 9bc–10

R. **Blessed is he whose help is the God of Jacob.**

The LORD secures justice for the oppressed,
  gives food to the hungry.
The LORD sets captives free.

R. **Blessed is he whose help is the God of Jacob.**

The LORD gives sight to the blind.
The LORD raises up those who were bowed down;
  the LORD loves the just.
The LORD protects strangers.

R. **Blessed is he whose help is the God of Jacob.**

The fatherless and the widow he sustains,
  but the way of the wicked he thwarts.
The LORD shall reign forever;
  your God, O Zion, through all generations. Alleluia.

R. **Blessed is he whose help is the God of Jacob.**

Or: R. **Alleluia.**

Alleluia, alleluia Jn 15:5
I am the vine, you are the branches, says the Lord:
whoever remains in me and I in him will bear much fruit.
Alleluia, alleluia

Years I and II

GOSPEL   Lk 17:20–25

The Kingdom of God is among you.

A reading from the holy Gospel according to Luke

Asked by the Pharisees when the Kingdom of God would come, Jesus said in reply, "The coming of the Kingdom of God cannot be observed, and no one will announce, 'Look, here it is,' or, 'There it is.' For behold, the Kingdom of God is among you."

Then he said to his disciples, "The days will come when you will long to see one of the days of the Son of Man, but you will not see it. There will be those who will say to you, 'Look, there he is,' or 'Look, here he is.' Do not go off, do not run in pursuit. For just as lightning flashes and lights up the sky from one side to the other, so will the Son of Man be in his day. But first he must suffer greatly and be rejected by this generation." The Gospel of the Lord.

Liturgy of the Eucharist, *p. 897;* **Prayer over the Gifts,** *p. 1675.*

Friday

Antiphons and Prayers, *p. 1674;* **Liturgy of the Word** *for Year I (odd years) follows; Year II (even years), p. 1697.*

TODAY'S LIVING WORD

Luke puts a peculiar twist on the story of Lot's wife in today's Gospel. As the story goes, Lot and his family were fleeing from Sodom and Gomorrah, and, "Lot's wife looked back" (Gn 19:26). In Luke's view, she is an example of those who, having set out with Jesus on the way of salvation, look back at what they have left behind. They are not fit for the kingdom of God (cf. 9:62). So he warns: "Remember the wife of Lot."

Luke appreciates the danger that material possessions pose to salvation. Genesis attests that Lot was a wealthy man, for he and Abram could not live together because they had too many possessions (13:6). Yet Luke does not despise the material world and neither can we. As the author of Wisdom reminds us today, "From the greatness and beauty of created things their original author, by analogy, is seen." As 2 John warns, to deny the sacramentality of the material world is to be deceived by those who would deny the humanity of Jesus, "who do not acknowledge Jesus Christ as coming in the flesh."

Year I

FIRST READING

Wis 13:1–9

For if they so far succeeded in knowledge that they could speculate about the world, how did they not more quickly find its Lord?

A reading from the Book of Wisdom

All men were by nature foolish who were in ignorance of God,
> and who from the good things seen did not succeed in
>> knowing him who is,
> and from studying the works did not discern the artisan;
But either fire, or wind, or the swift air,
> or the circuit of the stars, or the mighty water,
> or the luminaries of heaven, the governors of the world,
>> they considered gods.
Now if out of joy in their beauty they thought them gods,
> let them know how far more excellent is the Lord than
>> these;

for the original source of beauty fashioned them.
Or if they were struck by their might and energy,
    let them from these things realize how much more
        powerful is he who made them.
For from the greatness and the beauty of created things
    their original author, by analogy, is seen.
But yet, for these the blame is less;
For they indeed have gone astray perhaps,
    though they seek God and wish to find him.
For they search busily among his works,
    but are distracted by what they see, because the things
        seen are fair.
But again, not even these are pardonable.
For if they so far succeeded in knowledge
    that they could speculate about the world,
        how did they not more quickly find its Lord?

The word of the Lord.

Responsorial Psalm

Ps 19:2–3, 4–5ab

R. **The heavens proclaim the glory of God.**

The heavens declare the glory of God,
    and the firmament proclaims his handiwork.
Day pours out the word to day,
    and night to night imparts knowledge.

R. **The heavens proclaim the glory of God.**

Not a word nor a discourse
    whose voice is not heard;
Through all the earth their voice resounds,
    and to the ends of the world, their message.

R. **The heavens proclaim the glory of God.**

Alleluia Verse and **Gospel,** p. 1698.

Year II

FIRST READING

2 Jn 4–9

Whoever remains in the teaching has the Father and the Son.

A reading from the second Letter of Saint John

[Chosen Lady:]

I rejoiced greatly to find some of your children walking in the truth just as we were commanded by the Father. But now, Lady, I ask you, not as though I were writing a new commandment but the one we have had from the beginning: let us love one another. For this is love, that we walk according to his commandments; this is the commandment, as you heard from the beginning, in which you should walk.

Many deceivers have gone out into the world, those who do not acknowledge Jesus Christ as coming in the flesh; such is the deceitful one and the antichrist. Look to yourselves that you do not lose what we worked for but may receive a full recompense. Anyone who is so "progressive" as not to remain in the teaching of the Christ does not have God; whoever remains in the teaching has the Father and the Son.

The word of the Lord.

Responsorial Psalm

Ps 119:1, 2, 10, 11, 17, 18

R. **Blessed are they who follow the law of the Lord!**

Blessed are they whose way is blameless,
who walk in the law of the LORD.

R. **Blessed are they who follow the law of the Lord!**

Blessed are they who observe his decrees,
who seek him with all their heart.

R. **Blessed are they who follow the law of the Lord!**

With all my heart I seek you;
  let me not stray from your commands.

R. Blessed are they who follow the law of the Lord!

Within my heart I treasure your promise,
  that I may not sin against you.

R. Blessed are they who follow the law of the Lord!

Be good to your servant, that I may live
  and keep your words.

R. Blessed are they who follow the law of the Lord!

Open my eyes, that I may consider
  the wonders of your law.

R. Blessed are they who follow the law of the Lord!

Alleluia, alleluia   Lk 21:28
Stand erect and raise your heads
because your redemption is at hand.
Alleluia, alleluia

Years I and II

GOSPEL   Lk 17:26–37
So it will be on the day the Son of Man is revealed.

A reading from the holy Gospel according to Luke

Jesus said to his disciples: "As it was in the days of Noah, so it will be in the days of the Son of Man; they were eating and drinking, marrying and giving in marriage up to the day that Noah entered the ark, and the flood came and destroyed them all. Similarly, as it was in the days of Lot: they were eating, drinking, buying, selling, planting, building; on the day when Lot left Sodom, fire and brimstone rained from the sky to destroy them all. So it will be on the day the Son of Man is revealed. On that day, someone who is on the housetop and whose belongings are in the house must not go down to get them, and likewise one in the field must not return to what was left behind. Remember the wife of Lot. Whoever seeks to preserve his life will lose it, but whoever loses it will save it. I tell you, on that night there will be two people in one bed; one will be taken, the other left. And there will be two women grinding meal together; one will be taken, the other left." They said to him in reply, "Where, Lord?" He said to them, "Where the body is, there also the vultures will gather."

The Gospel of the Lord.

Liturgy of the Eucharist, *p. 897;* **Prayer over the Gifts,** *p. 1675.*

Saturday

Antiphons and Prayers, *p. 1674;* **Liturgy of the Word** *for Year I (odd years) follows; Year II (even years), p. 1701.*

TODAY'S LIVING WORD

The parable of the widow and the unjust judge provides comic relief in a discourse full of foreboding about the end-time. Who cannot laugh at an unscrupulous judge who is finally defeated by the nagging of a persistent widow? From this lighter moment Jesus moves to the weightier one: if a corrupt judge can be converted by the cry of a widow, will not the Judge of all the earth "secure the rights of his chosen ones who call out to him day and night?"

The mood of foreboding reasserts itself with the question that concludes the parable: "When the Son of Man comes, will he find faith on earth?" The Book of Wisdom says he will come like "a fierce warrior, into the doomed land, bearing the sharp sword of [God's] inexorable decree." In what does such faith consist? The readings tell us: in Luke, it is the persistence of the widow's prayer; in 3 John, it is the ready welcome one church extends to another; and in Wisdom, it is the boundless praise of those who behold the stupendous wonders of God's saving power.

Year I

FIRST READING
Wis 18:14-16; 19:6-9

*Out of the Red Sea an unimpeded road appeared
and they bounded about like lambs.*

A reading from the Book of Wisdom

When peaceful stillness compassed everything
    and the night in its swift course was half spent,
Your all-powerful word, from heaven's royal throne
    bounded, a fierce warrior, into the doomed land,
    bearing the sharp sword of your inexorable decree.
And as he alighted, he filled every place with death;
    he still reached to heaven, while he stood upon the earth.

For all creation, in its several kinds, was being made over anew,
    serving its natural laws,
    that your children might be preserved unharmed.
The cloud overshadowed their camp;
    and out of what had before been water, dry land was
        seen emerging:
Out of the Red Sea an unimpeded road,
    and a grassy plain out of the mighty flood.
Over this crossed the whole nation sheltered by your hand,
    after they beheld stupendous wonders.
For they ranged about like horses,
    and bounded about like lambs,
    praising you, O Lord! their deliverer.

The word of the Lord.

Responsorial Psalm
Ps 105:2-3, 36-37, 42-43

R. **Remember the marvels the Lord has done!**

Sing to him, sing his praise,
  proclaim all his wondrous deeds.
Glory in his holy name;
  rejoice, O hearts that seek the LORD!

R. Remember the marvels the Lord has done!

Then he struck every first-born throughout their land,
  the first fruits of all their manhood.
And he led them forth laden with silver and gold,
  with not a weakling among their tribes.

R. Remember the marvels the Lord has done!

For he remembered his holy word
  to his servant Abraham.
And he led forth his people with joy;
  with shouts of joy, his chosen ones.

R. Remember the marvels the Lord has done!

Or: **R. Alleluia.**

Alleluia Verse *and* **Gospel,** *p. 1702.*

Year II

FIRST READING   3 Jn 5–8

We ought to support such persons, so that
we may be co-workers in the truth.

A reading from the third Letter of Saint John

Beloved, you are faithful in all you do for the brothers and
sisters, especially for strangers; they have testified to your love
before the Church. Please help them in a way worthy of God
to continue their journey. For they have set out for the sake of
the Name and are accepting nothing from the pagans. Therefore, we ought to support such persons, so that we may be co-
workers in the truth.
The word of the Lord.

Responsorial Psalm   Ps 112:1–2, 3–4, 5–6

R. Blessed the man who fears the Lord.

Blessed the man who fears the LORD,
  who greatly delights in his commands.
His posterity shall be mighty upon the earth;
  the upright generation shall be blessed.

R. Blessed the man who fears the Lord.

Wealth and riches shall be in his house;
  his generosity shall endure forever.
Light shines through the darkness for the upright;
  he is gracious and merciful and just.

R. Blessed the man who fears the Lord.

Well for the man who is gracious and lends,
  who conducts his affairs with justice;
He shall never be moved;
  the just one shall be in everlasting remembrance.

R. Blessed the man who fears the Lord.

Or: **R. Alleluia.**

Alleluia, alleluia   See 2 Thes 2:14
God has called us through the Gospel,
to possess the glory of our Lord Jesus Christ.
Alleluia, alleluia

Years I and II

GOSPEL   Lk 18:1–8

Will not God then secure the rights of his chosen ones
who call out to him day and night?

A reading from the holy Gospel according to Luke

Jesus told his disciples a parable about the necessity for them
to pray always without becoming weary. He said, "There was
a judge in a certain town who neither feared God nor respected
any human being. And a widow in that town used to come to

him and say, 'Render a just decision for me against my adversary.' For a long time the judge was unwilling, but eventually he thought, 'While it is true that I neither fear God nor respect any human being, because this widow keeps bothering me I shall deliver a just decision for her lest she finally come and strike me.'" The Lord said, "Pay attention to what the dishonest judge says. Will not God then secure the rights of his chosen ones who call out to him day and night? Will he be slow to answer them? I tell you, he will see to it that justice is done for them speedily. But when the Son of Man comes, will he find faith on earth?"

The Gospel of the Lord.

Liturgy of the Eucharist, *p. 897;* **Prayer over the Gifts,** *p. 1675.*

THIRTY-THIRD WEEK IN ORDINARY TIME

The **Antiphons and Prayers** *may be the following, or may be chosen from any of the other 33 weeks in Ordinary Time (refer to Liturgical Calendar, pp. 26–41).*

The **Liturgy of the Word** *varies: for Monday, see p. 1705; Tuesday, p. 1710; Wednesday, p. 1716; Thursday, p. 1723; Friday, p. 1728; Saturday, p. 1732.*

Entrance Antiphon

The Lord says: my plans for you are peace and not disaster; when you call to me, I will listen to you, and I will bring you back to the place from which I exiled you. (Jer 29:11, 12, 14)

Opening Prayer

Let us pray

[that God will help us to be faithful]

Pause for silent prayer.

Father of all that is good,

keep us faithful in serving you,
for to serve you is our lasting joy.

We ask this through our Lord Jesus Christ, your Son,
who lives and reigns with you and the Holy Spirit,
one God, for ever and ever.

Alternative Opening Prayer

Let us pray

[with hearts that long for peace]

Pause for silent prayer.

Father in heaven,
ever-living source of all that is good,
from the beginning of time you promised man salvation
through the future coming of your Son, our Lord Jesus
   Christ.
Help us to drink of his truth
and expand our hearts with the joy of his promises,
so that we may serve you in faith and in love
and know for ever the joy of your presence.

We ask this through Christ our Lord.

Prayer over the Gifts

Pray, brethren...

Lord God,
may the gifts we offer
increase our love for you
and bring us to eternal life.

We ask this in the name of Jesus the Lord.

Preface of Weekdays in Ordinary Time I–VI, *pp. 948–950.*

Communion Antiphon

It is good for me to be with the Lord and to put my hope in
him.   (Ps 73:28)

Or:

**I tell you solemnly, whatever you ask for in prayer, believe
that you have received it, and it will be yours, says the Lord.**

(Mk 11:23, 24)

Prayer after Communion

Let us pray.

Pause for silent prayer, if this has not preceded.

Father,
may we grow in love
by the eucharist we have celebrated
in memory of the Lord Jesus,
who is Lord for ever and ever.

Monday

Antiphons and Prayers, *p. 1703;* **Liturgy of the Word** *for Year I (odd
years) follows; Year II (even years), p. 1708.*

TODAY'S LIVING WORD

The historical settings of the two first readings are very much
alike. First Maccabees records the time when the Jewish community
was divided by Hellenization, the introduction of Greek ways among
the Jews by Alexander and his successors. Some were willing enough
to adapt to and even adopt certain Greek customs, while others
resisted. First Maccabees takes the uncompromising view of those
"who preferred to die rather than…to profane the holy covenant."
The Book of Revelation was written at a time when the question of
civic duty under the Romans divided the Christian community. Some
were willing to conform within reasonable limits and show themselves
good citizens, while others resisted. The author of Revelation takes the
uncompromising view, placing him on a collision course with Rome.

In today's reading he commends the church in Ephesus for its
patient endurance, but cautions it too. Their uncompromising stance
toward Rome has cooled their love for one another. The challenges
we face are not so different. Like the blind beggar in the Gospel, we

sit on the side of the road and are often confused by the commotion of the world around us. At those times let us pray, as he did, "Lord, please let me see."

FIRST READING   1 Mc 1:10–15, 41–43, 54–57, 62–63

Terrible affliction was upon Israel.

A reading from the first Book of Maccabees

[From the descendants of Alexander's officers] there sprang a sinful offshoot, Antiochus Epiphanes, son of King Antiochus, once a hostage at Rome. He became king in the year one hundred and thirty-seven of the kingdom of the Greeks.

In those days there appeared in Israel men who were breakers of the law, and they seduced many people, saying: "Let us go and make an alliance with the Gentiles all around us; since we separated from them, many evils have come upon us." The proposal was agreeable; some from among the people promptly went to the king, and he authorized them to introduce the way of living of the Gentiles. Thereupon they built a gymnasium in Jerusalem according to the Gentile custom. They covered over the mark of their circumcision and abandoned the holy covenant; they allied themselves with the Gentiles and sold themselves to wrongdoing.

Then the king wrote to his whole kingdom that all should be one people, each abandoning his particular customs. All the Gentiles conformed to the command of the king, and many children of Israel were in favor of his religion; they sacrificed to idols and profaned the sabbath.

On the fifteenth day of the month Chislev, in the year one hundred and forty-five, the king erected the horrible abomination upon the altar of burnt offerings and in the surrounding cities of Judah they built pagan altars. They also burned incense at the doors of the houses and in the streets. Any scrolls of the law which they found they tore up and burnt. Whoever was found with a scroll of the covenant, and whoever observed the law, was condemned to death by royal decree. But many in Israel were determined and resolved in their hearts not to eat anything unclean; they preferred to die rather than to be defiled with unclean food or to profane the holy covenant; and they did die. Terrible affliction was upon Israel.

The word of the Lord.

Responsorial Psalm
Ps 119:53, 61, 134, 150, 155, 158

R. Give me life, O Lord, and I will do your commands.

Indignation seizes me because of the wicked
who forsake your law.

R. Give me life, O Lord, and I will do your commands.

Though the snares of the wicked are twined about me,
your law I have not forgotten.

R. Give me life, O Lord, and I will do your commands.

Redeem me from the oppression of men,
that I may keep your precepts.

R. Give me life, O Lord, and I will do your commands.

I am attacked by malicious persecutors
who are far from your law.

R. Give me life, O Lord, and I will do your commands.

Far from sinners is salvation,
because they seek not your statutes.

R. Give me life, O Lord, and I will do your commands.

I beheld the apostates with loathing,
  because they kept not to your promise.

R. Give me life, O Lord, and I will do your commands.

Alleluia Verse *and* **Gospel,** *p. 1709f.*

Year II

FIRST READING   Rv 1:1–4; 2:1–5
Realize how far you have fallen and repent.

A reading from the beginning of the Book of Revelation

The revelation of Jesus Christ, which God gave to him, to show
his servants what must happen soon. He made it known by
sending his angel to his servant John, who gives witness to the
word of God and to the testimony of Jesus Christ by reporting
what he saw. Blessed is the one who reads aloud and blessed
are those who listen to this prophetic message and heed what
is written in it, for the appointed time is near.

John, to the seven churches in Asia: grace to you and peace
from him who is and who was and who is to come, and from
the seven spirits before his throne.

I heard the Lord saying to me: "To the angel of the Church
in Ephesus, write this:

" 'The one who holds the seven stars in his right hand and
walks in the midst of the seven gold lampstands says this: "I
know your works, your labor, and your endurance, and that
you cannot tolerate the wicked; you have tested those who call
themselves Apostles but are not, and discovered that they are
impostors. Moreover, you have endurance and have suffered

for my name, and you have not grown weary. Yet I hold this against you: you have lost the love you had at first. Realize how far you have fallen. Repent, and do the works you did at first. Otherwise, I will come to you and remove your lampstand from its place, unless you repent." '"

The word of the Lord.

Responsorial Psalm

Ps 1:1–2, 3, 4 and 6

R. Those who are victorious I will feed from the tree of life.

Blessed the man who follows not
  the counsel of the wicked
Nor walks in the way of sinners,
  nor sits in the company of the insolent,
But delights in the law of the LORD
  and meditates on his law day and night.

R. Those who are victorious I will feed from the tree of life.

He is like a tree
  planted near running water,
That yields its fruit in due season,
  and whose leaves never fade.
  Whatever he does, prospers.

R. Those who are victorious I will feed from the tree of life.

Not so the wicked, not so;
  they are like chaff which the wind drives away.
For the LORD watches over the way of the just,
  but the way of the wicked vanishes.

R. Those who are victorious I will feed from the tree of life.

Alleluia, alleluia Jn 8:12
I am the light of the world, says the Lord;
  whoever follows me will have the light of life.
Alleluia, alleluia

Years I and II

GOSPEL

Lk 18:35–43

What do you want me to do for you? Lord, please let me see.

A reading from the holy Gospel according to Luke

As Jesus approached Jericho a blind man was sitting by the roadside begging, and hearing a crowd going by, he inquired what was happening. They told him, "Jesus of Nazareth is passing by." He shouted, "Jesus, Son of David, have pity on me!" The people walking in front rebuked him, telling him to be silent, but he kept calling out all the more, "Son of David, have pity on me!" Then Jesus stopped and ordered that he be brought to him; and when he came near, Jesus asked him, "What do you want me to do for you?" He replied, "Lord, please let me see." Jesus told him, "Have sight; your faith has saved you." He immediately received his sight and followed him, giving glory to God. When they saw this, all the people gave praise to God.

The Gospel of the Lord.

Liturgy of the Eucharist, *p. 897;* **Prayer over the Gifts,** *p. 1704.*

Tuesday

Antiphons and Prayers, *p. 1703;* **Liturgy of the Word** *for Year I (odd years) follows; Year II (even years), p. 1713.*

TODAY'S LIVING WORD

Today's readings commend two men: Eleazar and Zacchaeus—and condemn two churches: Sardis and Laodicea. At first glance, Eleazar and Zacchaeus seem to be polar opposites: one, a highly respected scribe, the other, a rich and disreputable tax agent. But as their stories show, they are both sons of Abraham. The joy with which they greet the visitation of the Lord in their lives makes them both worthy of this title. The venerable Eleazar submits to the blows of the torturer and says that he suffers "with joy" because of his devotion to the Lord and to the holy laws. Zacchaeus welcomes Jesus with joy and declares himself ready to make full restitution as the law of God requires.

The harsh words addressed to the churches of Sardis and Laodicea in the Book of Revelation are also a visitation of the Lord, not a verdict. "I stand at the door and knock," says the One who searches out the lost. They have only to open wide the door and welcome the salvation that comes to their house.

Year I

FIRST READING

2 Mc 6:18–31

I will leave to the young a noble example of how
to die willingly and generously for the revered and holy laws.

A reading from the second Book of Maccabees

Eleazar, one of the foremost scribes, a man of advanced age and noble appearance, was being forced to open his mouth to eat pork. But preferring a glorious death to a life of defilement, he spat out the meat, and went forward of his own accord to the instrument of torture, as people ought to do who have the courage to reject the food which it is unlawful to taste even for love of life. Those in charge of that unlawful ritual meal took the man aside privately, because of their long acquaintance with him, and urged him to bring meat of his own providing, such as he could legitimately eat, and to pretend to be eating some of the meat of the sacrifice prescribed by the king; in this way he would escape the death penalty, and be treated kindly because of their old friendship with him. But Eleazar made up his mind in a noble manner, worthy of his years, the dignity of his advanced age, the merited distinction of his gray hair, and of the admirable life he had lived from childhood; and so he declared that above all he would be loyal to the holy laws given by God.

He told them to send him at once to the abode of the dead, explaining: "At our age it would be unbecoming to make such a pretense; many young people would think the ninety-year-old Eleazar had gone over to an alien religion. Should I thus pretend for the sake of a brief moment of life, they would be led astray by me, while I would bring shame and dishonor on my old age. Even if, for the time being, I avoid the punishment of men, I shall never, whether alive or dead, escape the hands of the Almighty. Therefore, by manfully giving up my life now, I will prove myself worthy of my old age, and I will leave to the young a noble example of how to die willingly and generously for the revered and holy laws."

Eleazar spoke thus, and went immediately to the instrument of torture. Those who shortly before had been kindly disposed, now became hostile toward him because what he had said seemed to them utter madness. When he was about to die under the blows, he groaned and said: "The Lord in his holy knowledge knows full well that, although I could have escaped death, I am not only enduring terrible pain in my body from this scourging, but also suffering it with joy in my soul because of my devotion to him." This is how he died, leaving in his death a model of courage and an unforgettable example of virtue not only for the young but for the whole nation.

The word of the Lord.

Responsorial Psalm

Ps 3:2–3, 4–5, 6–7

R. The Lord upholds me.

O LORD, how many are my adversaries!
  Many rise up against me!
Many are saying of me,
  "There is no salvation for him in God."

R. The Lord upholds me.

But you, O LORD, are my shield;
  my glory, you lift up my head!
When I call out to the LORD,
  he answers me from his holy mountain.

R. The Lord upholds me.

When I lie down in sleep,
  I wake again, for the LORD sustains me.
I fear not the myriads of people
  arrayed against me on every side.

R. The Lord upholds me.

Alleluia Verse *and* **Gospel,** *p. 1715.*

Year II

FIRST READING

Rv 3:1–6, 14–22

If anyone hears my voice and opens the door,
I will enter his house and dine with him.

A reading from the Book of Revelation

I, John, heard the Lord saying to me: "To the angel of the
Church in Sardis, write this:

" 'The one who has the seven spirits of God and the seven
stars says this: "I know your works, that you have the reputation
of being alive, but you are dead. Be watchful and strengthen

what is left, which is going to die, for I have not found your works complete in the sight of my God. Remember then how you accepted and heard; keep it, and repent. If you are not watchful, I will come like a thief, and you will never know at what hour I will come upon you. However, you have a few people in Sardis who have not soiled their garments; they will walk with me dressed in white, because they are worthy.

" 'The victor will thus be dressed in white, and I will never erase his name from the book of life but will acknowledge his name in the presence of my Father and of his angels.

" 'Whoever has ears ought to hear what the Spirit says to the churches.' "

"To the angel of the Church in Laodicea, write this:

" 'The Amen, the faithful and true witness, the source of God's creation, says this: "I know your works; I know that you are neither cold nor hot. I wish you were either cold or hot. So, because you are lukewarm, neither hot nor cold, I will spit you out of my mouth. For you say, 'I am rich and affluent and have no need of anything,' and yet do not realize that you are wretched, pitiable, poor, blind, and naked. I advise you to buy from me gold refined by fire so that you may be rich, and white garments to put on so that your shameful nakedness may not be exposed, and buy ointment to smear on your eyes so that you may see. Those whom I love, I reprove and chastise. Be earnest, therefore, and repent.

" 'Behold, I stand at the door and knock. If anyone hears my voice and opens the door, then I will enter his house and dine with him, and he with me. I will give the victor the right to sit with me on my throne, as I myself first won the victory and sit with my Father on his throne.

" 'Whoever has ears ought to hear what the Spirit says to the churches.' "

The word of the Lord.

Responsorial Psalm

Ps 15:2–3a, 3bc–4ab, 5

R. **I will seat the victor beside me on my throne.**

He who walks blamelessly and does justice;
  who thinks the truth in his heart
  and slanders not with his tongue.

R. **I will seat the victor beside me on my throne.**

Who harms not his fellow man,
  nor takes up a reproach against his neighbor;
By whom the reprobate is despised,
  while he honors those who fear the LORD.

R. **I will seat the victor beside me on my throne.**

Who lends not his money at usury
  and accepts no bribe against the innocent.
He who does these things
  shall never be disturbed.

R. **I will seat the victor beside me on my throne.**

Alleluia, alleluia 1 Jn 4:10b
God loved us, and sent his Son
as expiation for our sins.
Alleluia, alleluia

Years I and II

GOSPEL

Lk 19:1–10

The Son of Man has come to seek and to save what was lost.

A reading from the holy Gospel according to Luke

At that time Jesus came to Jericho and intended to pass through the town. Now a man there named Zacchaeus, who was a chief tax collector and also a wealthy man, was seeking to see who Jesus was; but he could not see him because of the crowd, for he was short in stature. So he ran ahead and climbed a sycamore tree in order to see Jesus, who was about to pass that way. When he reached the place, Jesus looked up and said, "Zacchaeus, come down quickly, for today I must stay at your house." And he came down quickly and received him with joy. When they saw this, they began to grumble, saying, "He has gone to stay at the house of a sinner." But Zacchaeus stood there and said to the Lord, "Behold, half of my possessions, Lord, I shall give to the poor, and if I have extorted anything from anyone I shall repay it four times over." And Jesus said to him, "Today salvation has come to this house because this man too is a descendant of Abraham. For the Son of Man has come to seek and to save what was lost."

The Gospel of the Lord.

Liturgy of the Eucharist, *p. 897;* **Prayer over the Gifts,** *p. 1704.*

Wednesday

Antiphons and Prayers, *p. 1703;* **Liturgy of the Word** *for Year I (odd years) follows; Year II (even years), p. 1719.*

TODAY'S LIVING WORD

All three of today's readings are shaped in a context of imminent persecution and offer a particular perspective on what is about to befall. The two first readings do this by shifting the point of view from earth to heaven. The brave mother of seven sons in 2 Maccabees encourages her sons to consider the power of God the Creator, the Giver of life. Surely, she reasons, the God who mysteriously "shapes each man's beginning" can and will give back both life and breath to those who defy death in order to keep the law. In the scene from

Revelation, John, a Christian prophet exiled on the island of Patmos for proclaiming God's word (1:9), is taken in vision to the throne of God and shown "what must happen afterwards," the tribulation and the eventual triumph of God.

The perspective of the Gospel is encoded in a parable. Nearing Jerusalem, Jesus interprets what is about to happen there by telling a story about kingship. In the events about to unfold in Jerusalem, he will claim his kingdom and confer it on the Twelve. And "after he had said this, he proceeded on his journey up to Jerusalem."

Year I

FIRST READING   2 Mc 7:1, 20–31

The creator of the universe
will give you back both breath and life.

A reading from the second Book of Maccabees

It happened that seven brothers with their mother were arrested and tortured with whips and scourges by the king, to force them to eat pork in violation of God's law.

Most admirable and worthy of everlasting remembrance was the mother, who saw her seven sons perish in a single day, yet bore it courageously because of her hope in the Lord. Filled with a noble spirit that stirred her womanly heart with manly courage, she exhorted each of them in the language of their ancestors with these words: "I do not know how you came into existence in my womb; it was not I who gave you the breath of life, nor was it I who set in order the elements of which each of you is composed. Therefore, since it is the Creator of the universe who shapes each man's beginning, as he brings about the origin of everything, he, in his mercy, will give you back both breath and life, because you now disregard yourselves for the sake of his law."

Antiochus, suspecting insult in her words, thought he was being ridiculed. As the youngest brother was still alive, the king appealed to him, not with mere words, but with promises on oath, to make him rich and happy if he would abandon his ancestral customs: he would make him his Friend and entrust him with high office. When the youth paid no attention to him at all, the king appealed to the mother, urging her to advise her boy to save his life. After he had urged her for a long time, she went through the motions of persuading her son. In derision of the cruel tyrant, she leaned over close to her son and said in their native language: "Son, have pity on me, who carried you in my womb for nine months, nursed you for three years, brought you up, educated and supported you to your present age. I beg you, child, to look at the heavens and the earth and see all that is in them; then you will know that God did not make them out of existing things; and in the same way the human race came into existence. Do not be afraid of this executioner, but be worthy of your brothers and accept death, so that in the time of mercy I may receive you again with them."

She had scarcely finished speaking when the youth said: "What are you waiting for? I will not obey the king's command. I obey the command of the law given to our fathers through Moses. But you, who have contrived every kind of affliction for the Hebrews, will not escape the hands of God."

The word of the Lord.

Responsorial Psalm
Ps 17:1bcd, 5–6, 8b and 15

R. **Lord, when your glory appears, my joy will be full.**

Hear, O LORD, a just suit;
    attend to my outcry;
    hearken to my prayer from lips without deceit.

R. Lord, when your glory appears, my joy will be full.

My steps have been steadfast in your paths,
  my feet have not faltered.
I call upon you, for you will answer me, O God;
  incline your ear to me; hear my word.

R. Lord, when your glory appears, my joy will be full.

Keep me as the apple of your eye;
  hide me in the shadow of your wings.
But I in justice shall behold your face;
  on waking, I shall be content in your presence.

R. Lord, when your glory appears, my joy will be full.

Alleluia Verse *and* **Gospel,** *p. 1721.*

Year II

FIRST READING   Rv 4:1–11

Holy is the Lord God almighty,
who was, and who is, and who is to come.

A reading from the Book of Revelation

I, John, had a vision of an open door to heaven, and I heard the trumpetlike voice that had spoken to me before, saying, "Come up here and I will show you what must happen afterwards." At once I was caught up in spirit. A throne was there in heaven, and on the throne sat one whose appearance sparkled like jasper and carnelian. Around the throne was a halo as brilliant as an emerald. Surrounding the throne I saw twenty-four other thrones on which twenty-four elders sat, dressed in white garments and with gold crowns on their heads. From the throne came flashes of lightning, rumblings, and peals of thunder. Seven flaming torches burned in front of the throne, which are the seven spirits of God. In front of the throne was something that resembled a sea of glass like crystal.

In the center and around the throne, there were four living creatures covered with eyes in front and in back. The first creature resembled a lion, the second was like a calf, the third had a face like that of a man, and the fourth looked like an eagle in flight. The four living creatures, each of them with six wings, were covered with eyes inside and out. Day and night they do not stop exclaiming:

"Holy, holy, holy is the Lord God almighty,
    who was, and who is, and who is to come."

Whenever the living creatures give glory and honor and thanks to the one who sits on the throne, who lives forever and ever, the twenty-four elders fall down before the one who sits on the throne and worship him, who lives forever and ever. They throw down their crowns before the throne, exclaiming:

"Worthy are you, Lord our God,
    to receive glory and honor and power,
for you created all things;
    because of your will they came to be and were
        created."

The word of the Lord.

Responsorial Psalm
Ps 150:1b–2, 3–4, 5–6

R. Holy, holy, holy Lord, mighty God!

Praise the LORD in his sanctuary,
    praise him in the firmament of his strength.
Praise him for his mighty deeds,
    praise him for his sovereign majesty.

R. Holy, holy, holy Lord, mighty God!

Praise him with the blast of the trumpet,
  praise him with lyre and harp,
Praise him with timbrel and dance,
  praise him with strings and pipe.

R. Holy, holy, holy Lord, mighty God!

Praise him with sounding cymbals,
  praise him with clanging cymbals,
Let everything that has breath
  praise the LORD! Alleluia.

R. Holy, holy, holy Lord, mighty God!

Alleluia, alleluia See Jn 15:16
  I chose you from the world,
  to go and bear fruit that will last, says the Lord.
  Alleluia, alleluia

Years I and II

GOSPEL
                                                    Lk 19:11– 28
    Why did you not put my money in a bank?

A reading from the holy Gospel according to Luke

While people were listening to Jesus speak, he proceeded to
tell a parable because he was near Jerusalem and they thought
that the Kingdom of God would appear there immediately. So
he said, "A nobleman went off to a distant country to obtain
the kingship for himself and then to return. He called ten of
his servants and gave them ten gold coins and told them,
'Engage in trade with these until I return.' His fellow citizens,
however, despised him and sent a delegation after him to
announce, 'We do not want this man to be our king.' But when
he returned after obtaining the kingship, he had the servants
called, to whom he had given the money, to learn what they
had gained by trading. The first came forward and said, 'Sir,

your gold coin has earned ten additional ones.' He replied, 'Well done, good servant! You have been faithful in this very small matter; take charge of ten cities.' Then the second came and reported, 'Your gold coin, sir, has earned five more.' And to this servant too he said, 'You, take charge of five cities.' Then the other servant came and said, 'Sir, here is your gold coin; I kept it stored away in a handkerchief, for I was afraid of you, because you are a demanding man; you take up what you did not lay down and you harvest what you did not plant.' He said to him, 'With your own words I shall condemn you, you wicked servant. You knew I was a demanding man, taking up what I did not lay down and harvesting what I did not plant; why did you not put my money in a bank? Then on my return I would have collected it with interest.' And to those standing by he said, 'Take the gold coin from him and give it to the servant who has ten.' But they said to him, 'Sir, he has ten gold coins.' He replied, 'I tell you, to everyone who has, more will be given, but from the one who has not, even what he has will be taken away. Now as for those enemies of mine who did not want me as their king, bring them here and slay them before me.'"

After he had said this, he proceeded on his journey up to Jerusalem.

The Gospel of the Lord.

Liturgy of the Eucharist, *p. 897;* **Prayer over the Gifts,** *p. 1704.*

Thursday

Antiphons and Prayers, *p. 1703;* **Liturgy of the Word** *for Year I (odd years) follows; Year II (even years), p. 1725.*

TODAY'S LIVING WORD

The prospect of war looms in each of today's three readings. The episode recounted in 1 Maccabees marks the start of the Maccabean revolt against the Greeks. Sparked by the just fury of Mattathias, it will rally those righteous people who are zealous for the law and who stand by the covenant. The scene from Revelation sets the stage for holy war. The divinely appointed leader of this final campaign against the enemies of God and of God's people will be the Lion of the tribe of Judah, the Lamb who was slain, the already victorious risen Lord.

In today's Gospel, Luke's Jesus, the messianic prophet, foresees the fate of the city of Jerusalem at the hands of the Roman army and weeps over it. Having failed to recognize the arrival of the peaceable kingdom in his ministry, which was indeed the time of their visitation, they are now oblivious to their impending doom. "If…you only knew what makes for peace…."

Year I

FIRST READING   1 Mc 2:15–29

We will keep to the covenant of our ancestors.

A reading from the first Book of Maccabees

The officers of the king in charge of enforcing the apostasy came to the city of Modein to organize the sacrifices. Many of Israel joined them, but Mattathias and his sons gathered in a group apart. Then the officers of the king addressed Mattathias: "You are a leader, an honorable and great man in this city, supported by sons and kin. Come now, be the first to obey the king's command, as all the Gentiles and the men of Judah and those who are left in Jerusalem have done. Then you and your sons shall be numbered among the King's Friends, and shall be enriched with silver and gold and many gifts." But Mattathias answered in a loud voice: "Although all the Gentiles in the king's realm obey him, so that each forsakes the religion of his fathers and consents to the king's orders, yet I and my sons and my kin will keep to the covenant of our fathers. God forbid that we should forsake the law and the commandments. We will not obey the words of the king nor depart from our religion in the slightest degree."

As he finished saying these words, a certain Jew came forward in the sight of all to offer sacrifice on the altar in Modein according to the king's order. When Mattathias saw him, he was filled with zeal; his heart was moved and his just fury was aroused; he sprang forward and killed him upon the altar. At the same time, he also killed the messenger of the king who was forcing them to sacrifice, and he tore down the altar. Thus he showed his zeal for the law, just as Phinehas did with Zimri, son of Salu.

Then Mattathias went through the city shouting, "Let everyone who is zealous for the law and who stands by the covenant follow after me!" Thereupon he fled to the mountains with his sons, leaving behind in the city all their possessions. Many who sought to live according to righteousness and religious custom went out into the desert to settle there.

The word of the Lord.

Responsorial Psalm

Ps 50:1b–2, 5–6, 14–15

R. To the upright I will show the saving power of God.

God the LORD has spoken and summoned the earth,
    from the rising of the sun to its setting.

From Zion, perfect in beauty,
  God shines forth.

R. To the upright I will show the saving power of God.

"Gather my faithful ones before me,
  those who have made a covenant with me by sacrifice."
And the heavens proclaim his justice;
  for God himself is the judge.

R. To the upright I will show the saving power of God.

"Offer to God praise as your sacrifice
  and fulfill your vows to the Most High;
Then call upon me in time of distress;
  I will rescue you, and you shall glorify me."

R. To the upright I will show the saving power of God.

Alleluia Verse *and* **Gospel,** *p. 1727.*

Year II

FIRST READING

Rv 5:1–10

*The Lamb that was slain purchased us with
his Blood from every nation.*

A reading from the Book of Revelation

I, John, saw a scroll in the right hand of the one who sat on the throne. It had writing on both sides and was sealed with seven seals. Then I saw a mighty angel who proclaimed in a loud voice, "Who is worthy to open the scroll and break its seals?" But no one in heaven or on earth or under the earth was able to open the scroll or to examine it. I shed many tears because no one was found worthy to open the scroll or to examine it. One of the elders said to me, "Do not weep. The lion of the tribe of Judah, the root of David, has triumphed, enabling him to open the scroll with its seven seals."

Then I saw standing in the midst of the throne and the four living creatures and the elders a Lamb that seemed to have been slain. He had seven horns and seven eyes; these are the seven spirits of God sent out into the whole world. He came and received the scroll from the right hand of the one who sat on the throne. When he took it, the four living creatures and the twenty-four elders fell down before the Lamb. Each of the elders held a harp and gold bowls filled with incense, which are the prayers of the holy ones. They sang a new hymn:

"Worthy are you to receive the scroll
and break open its seals,
for you were slain and with your Blood you purchased for God
those from every tribe and tongue, people and nation.
You made them a kingdom and priests for our God,
and they will reign on earth."

The word of the Lord.

Responsial Psalm
Ps 149:1b–2, 3–4, 5–6a and 9b

R. **The Lamb has made us a kingdom of priests
to serve our God.**

Sing to the LORD a new song
of praise in the assembly of the faithful.
Let Israel be glad in their maker,
let the children of Zion rejoice in their king.

R. **The Lamb has made us a kingdom of priests
to serve our God.**

Let them praise his name in the festive dance,
let them sing praise to him with timbrel and harp.
For the LORD loves his people,
and he adorns the lowly with victory.

R. **The Lamb has made us a kingdom of priests
to serve our God.**

Let the faithful exult in glory;
  let them sing for joy upon their couches;
Let the high praises of God be in their throats.
  This is the glory of all his faithful. Alleluia.

R. **The Lamb has made us a kingdom of priests
to serve our God.**

Or: R. **Alleluia.**

Alleluia, alleluia Ps 95:8
If today you hear his voice,
harden not your hearts.
Alleluia, alleluia

Years I and II

GOSPEL
                                        Lk 19:41–44
If you only knew what makes for peace.

A reading from the holy Gospel according to Luke

As Jesus drew near Jerusalem, he saw the city and wept over
it, saying, "If this day you only knew what makes for peace—
but now it is hidden from your eyes. For the days are coming
upon you when your enemies will raise a palisade against you;
they will encircle you and hem you in on all sides. They will
smash you to the ground and your children within you, and
they will not leave one stone upon another within you because
you did not recognize the time of your visitation."

The Gospel of the Lord.

Liturgy of the Eucharist, *p. 897;* **Prayer over the Gifts,** *p. 1704.*

Friday

Antiphons and Prayers, *p. 1703;* **Liturgy of the Word** *for Year I (odd years) follows; Year II (even years), p. 1730.*

TODAY'S LIVING WORD

The readings from 1 Maccabees and from Luke are both concerned with the dedication of the temple. The Greek king Antiochus IV Epiphanes desecrated the sanctuary by erecting a pagan idol on the altar of holocausts. Therefore, having retaken the temple, Judas and his men restored and rededicated it. This is the origin of the Jewish feast known to us as Hanukkah. In the Gospel, Luke's Jesus is again cast as a prophet. Like the messenger announced by Malachi (cf. 3:1), he comes to the temple. With words from Isaiah (cf. 56:7) and Jeremiah (cf. 7:3–20), he reclaims and, as it were, reconsecrates it for his own teaching. This prophetic gesture divides the people: on one side are the leaders who want to destroy him, and on the other are the people who hang on his every word.

Jesus reclaims the temple not just for his own teaching but for that of the apostles and prophets who will follow him. In the Book of Revelation, John is one of these. Not in the temple in Jerusalem, but from the throne of God in heaven, he is sent to speak God's word, a word not always easy to digest.

Year I

FIRST READING

1 Mc 4:36–37, 52–59

*They celebrated the dedication of the altar
and joyfully offered burnt offerings.*

A reading from the first Book of Maccabees

Judas and his brothers said, "Now that our enemies have been crushed, let us go up to purify the sanctuary and rededicate it." So the whole army assembled, and went up to Mount Zion.

Early in the morning on the twenty-fifth day of the ninth

month, that is, the month of Chislev, in the year one hundred and forty-eight, they arose and offered sacrifice according to the law on the new altar of burnt offerings that they had made. On the anniversary of the day on which the Gentiles had defiled it, on that very day it was reconsecrated with songs, harps, flutes, and cymbals. All the people prostrated themselves and adored and praised Heaven, who had given them success.

For eight days they celebrated the dedication of the altar and joyfully offered burnt offerings and sacrifices of deliverance and praise. They ornamented the facade of the temple with gold crowns and shields; they repaired the gates and the priests' chambers and furnished them with doors. There was great joy among the people now that the disgrace of the Gentiles was removed. Then Judas and his brothers and the entire congregation of Israel decreed that the days of the dedication of the altar should be observed with joy and gladness on the anniversary every year for eight days, from the twenty-fifth day of the month Chislev.

The word of the Lord.

Responsorial Psalm
1 Chr 29:10bcd, 11abc, 11d–12a, 12bcd

R. We praise your glorious name, O mighty God.

"Blessed may you be, O LORD,
God of Israel our father,
from eternity to eternity."

R. We praise your glorious name, O mighty God.

"Yours, O LORD, are grandeur and power,
majesty, splendor, and glory.
For all in heaven and on earth is yours."

R. We praise your glorious name, O mighty God.

"Yours, O LORD, is the sovereignty;
  you are exalted as head over all.
Riches and honor are from you."

R. We praise your glorious name, O mighty God.

"You have dominion over all,
In your hand are power and might;
  it is yours to give grandeur and strength to all."

R. We praise your glorious name, O mighty God.

Alleluia Verse *and* Gospel, *p. 1731.*

Year II

FIRST READING   Rv 10:8–11

I took the small scroll and swallowed it.

A reading from the Book of Revelation

I, John, heard a voice from heaven speak to me. Then the voice
spoke to me and said: "Go, take the scroll that lies open in the
hand of the angel who is standing on the sea and on the land."
So I went up to the angel and told him to give me the small
scroll. He said to me, "Take and swallow it. It will turn your
stomach sour, but in your mouth it will taste as sweet as honey."
I took the small scroll from the angel's hand and swallowed it.
In my mouth it was like sweet honey, but when I had eaten it,
my stomach turned sour. Then someone said to me, "You must
prophesy again about many peoples, nations, tongues, and
kings."

The word of the Lord.

Responsorial Psalm   Ps 119:14, 24, 72, 103, 111, 131

R. How sweet to my taste is your promise!

In the way of your decrees I rejoice,
  as much as in all riches.

R. How sweet to my taste is your promise!

Yes, your decrees are my delight;
  they are my counselors.

R. How sweet to my taste is your promise!

The law of your mouth is to me more precious
  than thousands of gold and silver pieces.

R. How sweet to my taste is your promise!

How sweet to my palate are your promises,
  sweeter than honey to my mouth!

R. How sweet to my taste is your promise!

Your decrees are my inheritance forever;
  the joy of my heart they are.

R. How sweet to my taste is your promise!

I gasp with open mouth
  in my yearning for your commands.

R. How sweet to my taste is your promise!

> **Alleluia, alleluia** Jn 10:27
> My sheep hear my voice, says the Lord;
> I know them, and they follow me.
> **Alleluia, alleluia**

Years I and II

GOSPEL
Lk 19:45–48

You have made it a den of thieves.

A reading from the holy Gospel according to Luke

Jesus entered the temple area and proceeded to drive out those who were selling things, saying to them, "It is written, *My house shall be a house of prayer, but you have made it a den of thieves."* And every day he was teaching in the temple area. The chief priests, the scribes, and the leaders of the people, meanwhile, were seeking to put him to death, but they could find no way to accomplish their purpose because all the people were hanging on his words.

The Gospel of the Lord.

Liturgy of the Eucharist, *p. 897;* **Prayer over the Gifts,** *p. 1704.*

Saturday

Antiphons and Prayers, *p. 1703;* **Liturgy of the Word** *for Year I (odd years) follows; Year II (even years), p. 1735.*

TODAY'S LIVING WORD

First Maccabees reports the death of the Greek King Antiochus, "in bitter grief, in a foreign land," which marks the end of one period of persecution, while John's vision in the Book of Revelation marks the start of another. In the imagery of Revelation, the two witnesses, representing all Christian martyrs, are likened to messianic figures: Joshua and Zerubbabel, "the two olive trees and the two lampstands" (cf. Zec 4:1, 11–14); the prophet Elijah, who had the "power to close up the sky" (cf. 1 Kgs 17:1); and Moses, who had the "power to turn water into blood" (cf. Ex 7:14–23). Having given their testimony, they are martyred. But three and a half days later, they are raised to new life and taken up to heaven in a cloud.

Jesus' answer to the Sadducees, who did not believe in resurrection, provides a basis for the Christian view. God "is not God of the dead, but of the living." Baptism makes us children of the resurrection and so children of God. Therefore, like the two witnesses of Revelation, we must seek to conform to Christ's death, confident that, some day, even our lowly bodies will conform to his glorified one (cf. Phil 3:10, 21).

Year I

FIRST READING

1 Mc 6:1–13

On account of the evils I did in Jerusalem, I am dying in bitter grief.

A reading from the first Book of Maccabees

As King Antiochus was traversing the inland provinces, he heard that in Persia there was a city called Elymais, famous for its wealth in silver and gold, and that its temple was very rich, containing gold helmets, breastplates, and weapons left there by Alexander, son of Philip, king of Macedon, the first king of the Greeks. He went therefore and tried to capture and pillage the city. But he could not do so, because his plan became known to the people of the city who rose up in battle against him. So he retreated and in great dismay withdrew from there to return to Babylon.

While he was in Persia, a messenger brought him news that the armies sent into the land of Judah had been put to flight; that Lysias had gone at first with a strong army and been driven back by the children of Israel; that they had grown strong by reason of the arms, men, and abundant possessions taken from the armies they had destroyed; that they had pulled down the Abomination which he had built upon the altar in Jerusalem; and that they had surrounded with high walls both the sanctuary, as it had been before, and his city of Beth-zur.

When the king heard this news, he was struck with fear and very much shaken. Sick with grief because his designs had failed, he took to his bed. There he remained many days, overwhelmed with sorrow, for he knew he was going to die.

So he called in all his Friends and said to them: "Sleep has departed from my eyes, for my heart is sinking with anxiety. I said to myself: 'Into what tribulation have I come, and in what floods of sorrow am I now! Yet I was kindly and beloved in my rule.' But I now recall the evils I did in Jerusalem, when I carried away all the vessels of gold and silver that were in it, and for no cause gave orders that the inhabitants of Judah be destroyed. I know that this is why these evils have overtaken me; and now I am dying, in bitter grief, in a foreign land." The word of the Lord.

Responsorial Psalm

Ps 9:2–3, 4 and 6, 16 and 19

R. I will rejoice in your salvation, O Lord.

I will give thanks to you, O LORD, with all my heart;
    I will declare all your wondrous deeds.
I will be glad and exult in you;
    I will sing praise to your name, Most High.

R. I will rejoice in your salvation, O Lord.

Because my enemies are turned back,
    overthrown and destroyed before you.
You rebuked the nations and destroyed the wicked;
    their name you blotted out forever and ever.

R. I will rejoice in your salvation, O Lord.

The nations are sunk in the pit they have made;
    in the snare they set, their foot is caught.
For the needy shall not always be forgotten,
    nor shall the hope of the afflicted forever perish.

R. I will rejoice in your salvation, O Lord.

Alleluia Verse *and* **Gospel,** *p. 1736.*

Year II

FIRST READING   Rv 11:4–12

These two prophets tormented the inhabitants of the earth.

A reading from the Book of Revelation

I, John, heard a voice from heaven speak to me: Here are my two witnesses: These are the two olive trees and the two lampstands that stand before the Lord of the earth. If anyone wants to harm them, fire comes out of their mouths and devours their enemies. In this way, anyone wanting to harm them is sure to be slain. They have the power to close up the sky so that no rain can fall during the time of their prophesying. They also have power to turn water into blood and to afflict the earth with any plague as often as they wish.

When they have finished their testimony, the beast that comes up from the abyss will wage war against them and conquer them and kill them. Their corpses will lie in the main street of the great city, which has the symbolic names "Sodom" and "Egypt," where indeed their Lord was crucified. Those from every people, tribe, tongue, and nation will gaze on their corpses for three and a half days, and they will not allow their corpses to be buried. The inhabitants of the earth will gloat over them and be glad and exchange gifts because these two prophets tormented the inhabitants of the earth. But after the three and a half days, a breath of life from God entered them. When they stood on their feet, great fear fell on those who saw them. Then they heard a loud voice from heaven say to them, "Come up here." So they went up to heaven in a cloud as their enemies looked on.

The word of the Lord.

Responsorial Psalm

Ps 144:1, 2, 9–10

R. Blessed be the Lord, my Rock!

Blessed be the LORD, my rock,
  who trains my hands for battle, my fingers for war.

R. Blessed be the Lord, my Rock!

My mercy and my fortress,
  my stronghold, my deliverer,
My shield, in whom I trust,
  who subdues my people under me.

R. Blessed be the Lord, my Rock!

O God, I will sing a new song to you;
  with a ten-stringed lyre I will chant your praise,
You who give victory to kings,
  and deliver David, your servant from the evil sword.

R. Blessed be the Lord, my Rock!

Alleluia, alleluia   See 2 Tm 1:10
Our Savior Jesus Christ has destroyed death
and brought life to light through the Gospel.
Alleluia, alleluia

Years I and II

GOSPEL   Lk 20:27–40

He is not God of the dead, but of the living.

A reading from the holy Gospel according to Luke

Some Sadducees, those who deny that there is a resurrection,
came forward and put this question to Jesus, saying, "Teacher,
Moses wrote for us, *If someone's brother dies leaving a wife
but no child, his brother must take the wife and raise up
descendants for his brother.* Now there were seven brothers;
the first married a woman but died childless. Then the second

and the third married her, and likewise all the seven died childless. Finally the woman also died. Now at the resurrection whose wife will that woman be? For all seven had been married to her." Jesus said to them, "The children of this age marry and remarry; but those who are deemed worthy to attain to the coming age and to the resurrection of the dead neither marry nor are given in marriage. They can no longer die, for they are like angels; and they are the children of God because they are the ones who will rise. That the dead will rise even Moses made known in the passage about the bush, when he called 'Lord' the God of Abraham, the God of Isaac, and the God of Jacob; and he is not God of the dead, but of the living, for to him all are alive." Some of the scribes said in reply, "Teacher, you have answered well." And they no longer dared to ask him anything.

The Gospel of the Lord.

Liturgy of the Eucharist, *p. 897;* **Prayer over the Gifts,** *p. 1704.*

THIRTY-FOURTH OR LAST WEEK IN ORDINARY TIME

The **Antiphons and Prayers** *may be the following, or may be chosen from any of the other 33 weeks in Ordinary Time (refer to Liturgical Calendar, pp. 26–41).*

The **Liturgy of the Word** *varies: for Monday, see p. 1739; Tuesday, p. 1744; Wednesday, p. 1749; Thursday, p. 1754; Friday, p. 1761; Saturday, p. 1766.*

Entrance Antiphon

The Lord speaks of peace to his people, to those who turn to him with all their heart.   (Ps 84:9)

Opening Prayer

Let us pray
[that the Spirit of God
will renew our lives]

Pause for silent prayer.

Lord,
increase our eagerness to do your will
and help us to know the saving power of your love.

Grant this through our Lord Jesus Christ, your Son,
who lives and reigns with you and the Holy Spirit,
one God, for ever and ever.

Prayer over the Gifts

Pray, brethren...

God of love,
may the sacrifice we offer
in obedience to your command
renew our resolution to be faithful to your word.

We ask this through Christ our Lord.

Preface of Weekdays in Ordinary Time I–VI, *pp. 948–950.*

Communion Antiphon

**All you nations, praise the Lord, for steadfast is his kindly
mercy to us.** (Ps 116:1–2)

Or:

I, the Lord, am with you always, until the end of the world.
(Mt 28:20)

Prayer after Communion

Let us pray.

Pause for silent prayer, if this has not preceded.

Almighty God,
in this eucharist

you give us the joy of sharing your life.
Keep us in your presence.
Let us never be separated from you.

We ask this in the name of Jesus the Lord

Monday

Antiphons and Prayers, *p. 1737;* **Liturgy of the Word** *for Year I (odd years) follows; Year II (even years), p. 1742.*

TODAY'S LIVING WORD

Today's readings are all about people who know *who* they are because they know *whose* they are. Daniel and his friends are Israel-ites in the court of the king of Babylon. Still, they resolve not to compromise their identity as God's people: they refuse to risk violat-ing the traditional dietary laws, a distinctive mark of Jewish identity, by eating from the royal table. And their loyalty is rewarded: they not only equal but surpass all their rivals in wisdom. In Revelation, the Lamb stands victorious, surrounded by his hundred and forty-four thousand faithful followers. These are the witnesses (martyrs in Greek) "who follow the Lamb wherever he goes," even to death. The name of God and of the Lamb is inscribed on their foreheads, an indelible identifying mark.

The action of the widow in today's Gospel also speaks of self-possession. In Luke, she stands for those who, having received the promise of the kingdom announced by Jesus, renounce all their possessions. They define themselves not by what they have, but by him in whom they have put their trust.

Year I

FIRST READING   Dn 1:1–6, 8–20

*None were found equal to Daniel,
Hananiah, Mishael, and Azariah.*

A reading from the beginning of the Book of the Prophet Daniel

In the third year of the reign of Jehoiakim, king of Judah, King Nebuchadnezzar of Babylon came and laid siege to Jerusalem. The Lord handed over to him Jehoiakim, king of Judah, and some of the vessels of the temple of God; he carried them off to the land of Shinar, and placed the vessels in the temple treasury of his god.

The king told Ashpenaz, his chief chamberlain, to bring in some of the children of Israel of royal blood and of the nobility, young men without any defect, handsome, intelligent and wise, quick to learn, and prudent in judgment, such as could take their place in the king's palace; they were to be taught the language and literature of the Chaldeans; after three years' training they were to enter the king's service. The king allotted them a daily portion of food and wine from the royal table. Among these were men of Judah: Daniel, Hananiah, Mishael, and Azariah.

But Daniel was resolved not to defile himself with the king's food or wine; so he begged the chief chamberlain to spare him this defilement. Though God had given Daniel the favor and sympathy of the chief chamberlain, he nevertheless said to Daniel, "I am afraid of my lord the king; it is he who allotted your food and drink. If he sees that you look wretched by comparison with the other young men of your age, you will endanger my life with the king." Then Daniel said to the steward whom the chief chamberlain had put in charge of Daniel, Hananiah, Mishael, and Azariah, "Please test your servants for ten days. Give us vegetables to eat and water to drink. Then see how we look in comparison with the other young men who eat from the royal table, and treat your servants according to what you see." He acceded to this request, and tested them for ten days; after ten days they looked healthier and better fed than any of the young men who ate from the royal table. So the steward continued to take away the food and wine they were to receive, and gave them vegetables.

To these four young men God gave knowledge and proficiency in all literature and science, and to Daniel the understanding of all visions and dreams. At the end of the time the king had specified for their preparation, the chief chamberlain brought them before Nebuchadnezzar. When the king had spoken with all of them, none was found equal to Daniel, Hananiah, Mishael, and Azariah; and so they entered the king's service. In any question of wisdom or prudence which the king put to them, he found them ten times better than all the magicians and enchanters in his kingdom.

The word of the Lord.

Responsorial Psalm

Dn 3:52, 53, 54, 55, 56

R. Glory and praise for ever!

"Blessed are you, O Lord, the God of our fathers,
    praiseworthy and exalted above all forever;
And blessed is your holy and glorious name,
    praiseworthy and exalted above all for all ages."

R. Glory and praise for ever!

"Blessed are you in the temple of your holy glory,
    praiseworthy and glorious above all forever."

R. Glory and praise for ever!

"Blessed are you on the throne of your Kingdom,
    praiseworthy and exalted above all forever."

R. Glory and praise for ever!

"Blessed are you who look into the depths
    from your throne upon the cherubim,
    praiseworthy and exalted above all forever."

R. Glory and praise for ever!

"Blessed are you in the firmament of heaven,
   praiseworthy and glorious forever."

R. Glory and praise for ever!

Alleluia Verse *and* **Gospel**, *p. 1743.*

Year II

FIRST READING   Rv 14:1–3, 4b–5

His name and his Father's name are written on their foreheads.

A reading from the Book of Revelation

I, John, looked and there was the Lamb standing on Mount
Zion, and with him a hundred and forty-four thousand who
had his name and his Father's name written on their foreheads.
I heard a sound from heaven like the sound of rushing water or
a loud peal of thunder. The sound I heard was like that of harp-
ists playing their harps. They were singing what seemed to be
a new hymn before the throne, before the four living creatures
and the elders. No one could learn this hymn except the hundred
and forty-four thousand who had been ransomed from the earth.
These are the ones who follow the Lamb wherever he goes.
They have been ransomed as the first fruits of the human race
for God and the Lamb. On their lips no deceit has been found;
they are unblemished.

The word of the Lord.

Responsorial Psalm   Ps 24:1bc–2, 3–4ab, 5–6

R. Lord, this is the people that longs to see your face.

The LORD's are the earth and its fullness;
   the world and those who dwell in it.

For he founded it upon the seas
  and established it upon the rivers.

R. Lord, this is the people that longs to see your face.

Who can ascend the mountain of the LORD?
  or who may stand in his holy place?
He whose hands are sinless, whose heart is clean,
  who desires not what is vain.

R. Lord, this is the people that longs to see your face.

He shall receive a blessing from the LORD,
  a reward from God his savior.
Such is the race that seeks for him,
  that seeks the face of the God of Jacob.

R. Lord, this is the people that longs to see your face.

Alleluia, alleluia Mt 24:42a, 44
Stay awake!
For you do not know when the Son of Man will come.
Alleluia, alleluia

Years I and II

GOSPEL   Lk 21:1–4

He noticed a poor widow putting in two small coins.

A reading from the holy Gospel according to Luke

When Jesus looked up he saw some wealthy people putting their offerings into the treasury and he noticed a poor widow putting in two small coins. He said, "I tell you truly, this poor widow put in more than all the rest; for those others have all made offerings from their surplus wealth, but she, from her poverty, has offered her whole livelihood."

The Gospel of the Lord.

Liturgy of the Eucharist, *p. 897;* **Prayer over the Gifts,** *p. 1738.*

Tuesday

Antiphons and Prayers, *p. 1737;* **Liturgy of the Word** *for Year I (odd years) follows; Year II (even years), p. 1746.*

TODAY'S LIVING WORD

The three readings for today all predict the future. King Nebuchadnezzar's dream becomes a test of Daniel's wisdom. He interprets the four metals that make up the composite statue—gold, silver, bronze, and iron mixed with clay—to correspond to the four kingdoms that ruled Israel from the exile in the sixth century B.C.E. to Hellenization in the second century B.C.E.: the Babylonians, the Medes, the Persians, and the two Greek dynasties (Ptolemies and Seleucids). During the time of the Greeks (when the Book of Daniel was written), he says that God will establish a kingdom—Israel— that will supplant all these others and stand forever. The Gospel is the beginning of Luke's version of Jesus' discourse about the future. He foresees the destruction of the Jerusalem temple by the Romans during the First Jewish Revolt (66–70 C.E.).

The biblical imagery in Revelation makes that prediction of the future a more general prophecy of divine judgment. The first pair of angels harvest the grain (the just) and a second pair harvest the grapes (the unjust) to be thrown into the winepress of God's wrath. The message is clear: all time is in God's hand. "See that you not be deceived."

Year I

FIRST READING
Dn 2:31–45

The God of heaven will set up a kingdom that shall never be destroyed and shall put an end to all these kingdoms.

A reading from the Book of the Prophet Daniel

Daniel said to Nebuchadnezzar: "In your vision, O king, you saw a statue, very large and exceedingly bright, terrifying in appearance as it stood before you. The head of the statue was pure gold, its chest and arms were silver, its belly and thighs bronze, the legs iron, its feet partly iron and partly tile. While you looked at the statue, a stone which was hewn from a mountain without a hand being put to it, struck its iron and tile feet, breaking them in pieces. The iron, tile, bronze, silver, and gold all crumbled at once, fine as the chaff on the threshing floor in summer, and the wind blew them away without leaving a trace. But the stone that struck the statue became a great mountain and filled the whole earth.

"This was the dream; the interpretation we shall also give in the king's presence. You, O king, are the king of kings; to you the God of heaven has given dominion and strength, power and glory; men, wild beasts, and birds of the air, wherever they may dwell, he has handed over to you, making you ruler over them all; you are the head of gold. Another kingdom shall take your place, inferior to yours, then a third kingdom, of bronze, which shall rule over the whole earth. There shall be a fourth kingdom, strong as iron; it shall break in pieces and subdue all these others, just as iron breaks in pieces and crushes everything else. The feet and toes you saw, partly of potter's tile and partly of iron, mean that it shall be a divided kingdom, but yet have some of the hardness of iron. As you saw the iron mixed with clay tile, and the toes partly iron and partly tile, the kingdom shall be partly strong and partly fragile. The iron mixed with clay tile means that they shall seal their alliances by intermarriage, but they shall not stay united, any more than iron mixes with clay. In the lifetime of those kings the God of heaven will set up a kingdom that shall never be destroyed or delivered up to another people; rather, it shall break in pieces all these kingdoms and put an end to them, and it shall stand forever. That is the meaning of the stone you saw hewn from the mountain without a hand being put to it, which broke in pieces the tile, iron, bronze, silver, and gold. The great God has revealed to the king what shall be in the future; this is exactly what you dreamed, and its meaning is sure."

The word of the Lord.

Responsological Psalm

Responsorial Psalm   Dn 3:57, 58, 59, 60, 61

R. Give glory and eternal praise to him.

"Bless the Lord, all you works of the Lord,
   praise and exalt him above all forever."

   R. Give glory and eternal praise to him.

"Angels of the Lord, bless the Lord,
   praise and exalt him above all forever."

   R. Give glory and eternal praise to him.

"You heavens, bless the Lord,
   praise and exalt him above all forever."

   R. Give glory and eternal praise to him.

"All you waters above the heavens, bless the Lord,
   praise and exalt him above all forever."

   R. Give glory and eternal praise to him.

"All you hosts of the Lord, bless the Lord;
   praise and exalt him above all forever."

   R. Give glory and eternal praise to him.

Alleluia Verse *and* **Gospel,** *p. 1748.*

Year II

FIRST READING   Rv 14:14 –19

The time to reap has come,
because the earth's harvest is fully ripe.

A reading from the Book of Revelation

I, John, looked and there was a white cloud, and sitting on the cloud one who looked like a son of man, with a gold crown on his head and a sharp sickle in his hand. Another angel came out of the temple, crying out in a loud voice to the one sitting on the cloud, "Use your sickle and reap the harvest, for the time to reap has come, because the earth's harvest is fully ripe." So the one who was sitting on the cloud swung his sickle over the earth, and the earth was harvested.

Then another angel came out of the temple in heaven who also had a sharp sickle. Then another angel came from the altar, who was in charge of the fire, and cried out in a loud voice to the one who had the sharp sickle, "Use your sharp sickle and cut the clusters from the earth's vines, for its grapes are ripe." So the angel swung his sickle over the earth and cut the earth's vintage. He threw it into the great wine press of God's fury.

The word of the Lord.

Responsorial Psalm
Ps 96:10, 11–12, 13

R. The Lord comes to judge the earth.

Say among the nations: The LORD is king.
He has made the world firm, not to be moved;
  he governs the peoples with equity.

R. The Lord comes to judge the earth.

Let the heavens be glad and the earth rejoice;
  let the sea and what fills it resound;
  let the plains be joyful and all that is in them!
Then shall all the trees of the forest exult.

R. The Lord comes to judge the earth.

Before the LORD, for he comes;
  for he comes to rule the earth.

He shall rule the world with justice
  and the peoples with his constancy.

R. The Lord comes to judge the earth.

Alleluia, alleluia Rv 2:10c
Remain faithful until death,
  and I will give you the crown of life.
Alleluia, alleluia

Years I and II

GOSPEL   Lk 21:5–11
There will not be left a stone upon another stone.

A reading from the holy Gospel according to Luke

While some people were speaking about how the temple was adorned with costly stones and votive offerings, Jesus said, "All that you see here—the days will come when there will not be left a stone upon another stone that will not be thrown down."

Then they asked him, "Teacher, when will this happen? And what sign will there be when all these things are about to happen?" He answered, "See that you not be deceived, for many will come in my name, saying, 'I am he,' and 'The time has come.' Do not follow them! When you hear of wars and insurrections, do not be terrified; for such things must happen first, but it will not immediately be the end." Then he said to them, "Nation will rise against nation, and kingdom against kingdom. There will be powerful earthquakes, famines, and plagues from place to place; and awesome sights and mighty signs will come from the sky."

The Gospel of the Lord.

Liturgy of the Eucharist, *p. 897;* **Prayer over the Gifts,** *p. 1738.*

Wednesday

Antiphons and Prayers, *p. 1737;* **Liturgy of the Word** *for Year I (odd years) follows; Year II (even years), p. 1752.*

TODAY'S LIVING WORD

"The writing is on the wall," as the saying goes, not just in the Book of Daniel, but in all of today's readings. In Daniel, the desecration of the sacred vessels from the Jerusalem temple is answered by an ominous sign. The fingers of a human hand write on the plaster wall three words that announce the end of the Babylonian empire. For as Daniel explains, "the God in whose hand is your life breath …you did not glorify." Similarly, in Revelation the prophet John sees in a vision the seven angels who stand ready to bring the wrath of God to a climax by inflicting the seven final plagues. In the Gospel, not the enemies of God but the followers of Jesus are warned of persecution.

All three readings are sure of God's final victory, but Revelation is most explicit. Its biblical imagery takes us back to the crossing of the Red Sea. Here, however, the victory song of Moses is also the song of the Lamb, taken up by the Christian martyrs. Thus are we assured: "By your perseverance you will secure your lives."

Year I

FIRST READING   Dn 5:1–6, 13–14, 16–17, 23–28

The fingers of a human hand appeared,
writing on the plaster of the wall.

A reading from the Book of the Prophet Daniel

King Belshazzar gave a great banquet for a thousand of his lords, with whom he drank. Under the influence of the wine, he ordered the gold and silver vessels which Nebuchadnezzar, his father, had taken from the temple in Jerusalem, to be brought in so that the king, his lords, his wives and his entertainers might drink from them. When the gold and silver vessels taken from the house of God in Jerusalem had been brought in, and while the king, his lords, his wives and his entertainers were drinking wine from them, they praised their gods of gold and silver, bronze and iron, wood and stone.

Suddenly, opposite the lampstand, the fingers of a human hand appeared, writing on the plaster of the wall in the king's palace. When the king saw the wrist and hand that wrote, his face blanched; his thoughts terrified him, his hip joints shook, and his knees knocked.

Then Daniel was brought into the presence of the king. The king asked him, "Are you the Daniel, the Jewish exile, whom my father, the king, brought from Judah? I have heard that the Spirit of God is in you, that you possess brilliant knowledge and extraordinary wisdom. I have heard that you can interpret dreams and solve difficulties; if you are able to read the writing and tell me what it means, you shall be clothed in purple, wear a gold collar about your neck, and be third in the government of the kingdom."

Daniel answered the king: "You may keep your gifts, or give your presents to someone else; but the writing I will read for you, O king, and tell you what it means. You have rebelled against the Lord of heaven. You had the vessels of his temple brought before you, so that you and your nobles, your wives and your entertainers, might drink wine from them; and you praised the gods of silver and gold, bronze and iron, wood and stone, that neither see nor hear nor have intelligence. But the God in whose hand is your life breath and the whole course of your life, you did not glorify. By him were the wrist and hand sent, and the writing set down.

"This is the writing that was inscribed: MENE, TEKEL, and PERES. These words mean: MENE, God has numbered your kingdom and put an end to it; TEKEL, you have been weighed on the scales and found wanting; PERES, your kingdom has been divided and given to the Medes and Persians."

The word of the Lord.

Responsorial Psalm

Dn 3:62, 63, 64, 65, 66, 67

R. Give glory and eternal praise to him.

"Sun and moon, bless the Lord;
  praise and exalt him above all forever."

R. Give glory and eternal praise to him.

"Stars of heaven, bless the Lord;
  praise and exalt him above all forever."

R. Give glory and eternal praise to him.

"Every shower and dew, bless the Lord;
  praise and exalt him above all forever."

R. Give glory and eternal praise to him.

"All you winds, bless the Lord;
  praise and exalt him above all forever."

R. Give glory and eternal praise to him.

"Fire and heat, bless the Lord;
  praise and exalt him above all forever."

R. Give glory and eternal praise to him.

"Cold and chill, bless the Lord;
  praise and exalt him above all forever."

R. Give glory and eternal praise to him.

Alleluia Verse *and* **Gospel,** *p. 1753.*

Year II

FIRST READING
Rv 15:1–4

They sang the song of Moses and the song of the Lamb.

A reading from the Book of Revelation

I, John, saw in heaven another sign, great and awe-inspiring: seven angels with the seven last plagues, for through them God's fury is accomplished.

Then I saw something like a sea of glass mingled with fire. On the sea of glass were standing those who had won the victory over the beast and its image and the number that signified its name. They were holding God's harps, and they sang the song of Moses, the servant of God, and the song of the Lamb:

> "Great and wonderful are your works,
>   Lord God almighty.
> Just and true are your ways,
>   O king of the nations.
> Who will not fear you, Lord,
>   or glorify your name?
> For you alone are holy.
>   All the nations will come
>   and worship before you,
>   for your righteous acts have been revealed."

The word of the Lord.

Responsorial Psalm
Ps 98:1, 2–3ab, 7–8, 9

R.   Great and wonderful are all your works, Lord, mighty God!

Sing to the LORD a new song,
    for he has done wondrous deeds;

His right hand has won victory for him,
 his holy arm.

R. Great and wonderful are all your works, Lord, mighty God!

The LORD has made his salvation known:
 in the sight of the nations he has revealed his justice.
He has remembered his kindness and his faithfulness
 toward the house of Israel.

R. Great and wonderful are all your works, Lord, mighty God!

Let the sea and what fills it resound,
 the world and those who dwell in it;
Let the rivers clap their hands,
 the mountains shout with them for joy.

R. Great and wonderful are all your works, Lord, mighty God!

Before the LORD, for he comes,
 for he comes to rule the earth;
He will rule the world with justice
 and the peoples with equity.

R. Great and wonderful are all your works, Lord, mighty God!

Alleluia, alleluia Rv 2:10c
Remain faithful until death,
and I will give you the crown of life.
Alleluia, alleluia

Years I and II

GOSPEL   Lk 21:12–19

*You will be hated by all because of my name,
 but not a hair on your head will be destroyed.*

A reading from the holy Gospel according to Luke

Jesus said to the crowd: "They will seize and persecute you,
they will hand you over to the synagogues and to prisons, and

they will have you led before kings and governors because of my name. It will lead to your giving testimony. Remember, you are not to prepare your defense beforehand, for I myself shall give you a wisdom in speaking that all your adversaries will be powerless to resist or refute. You will even be handed over by parents, brothers, relatives, and friends, and they will put some of you to death. You will be hated by all because of my name, but not a hair on your head will be destroyed. By your perseverance you will secure your lives."

The Gospel of the Lord.

Liturgy of the Eucharist, *p. 897;* **Prayer over the Gifts,** *p. 1738.*

Thursday

Antiphons and Prayers, *p. 1737;* **Liturgy of the Word** *for Year I (odd years) follows; Year II (even years), p. 1757.*

TODAY'S LIVING WORD

All three readings today attest to the vindication of God's faithful people. When Daniel's enemies persuade King Darius to outlaw prayer, Daniel continues to pray three times a day as Jewish piety required. His accusers demand that he be thrown into the lion's den, and even the deeply grieved king cannot save him. But the God whom he serves constantly and courageously can and does save him. "For he is the living God, enduring forever." In Revelation, the assembly of heaven rejoices over the fall of Babylon, a code name for the Roman empire. "Salvation, glory and might belong to our God," they sing. "He has avenged the blood of his servants."

Luke's Jesus unfolds the escalating drama of the "time of punishment" when Jerusalem "will be trampled underfoot by the Gentiles." To this he appends a list of the signs of the last days, when earth and heaven will be shaken at the advent of the Son of Man. On that judgment day, fear will yield to joy for God's people, whose salvation is near at hand.

Year I

FIRST READING   Dn 6:12–28

My God has sent his angel and closed the lions' mouths.

A reading from the Book of the Prophet Daniel

Some men rushed into the upper chamber of Daniel's home and found him praying and pleading before his God. Then they went to remind the king about the prohibition: "Did you not decree, O king, that no one is to address a petition to god or man for thirty days, except to you, O king; otherwise he shall be cast into a den of lions?" The king answered them, "The decree is absolute, irrevocable under the Mede and Persian law." To this they replied, "Daniel, the Jewish exile, has paid no attention to you, O king, or to the decree you issued; three times a day he offers his prayer." The king was deeply grieved at this news and he made up his mind to save Daniel; he worked till sunset to rescue him. But these men insisted. They said, "Keep in mind, O king, that under the Mede and Persian law every royal prohibition or decree is irrevocable." So the king ordered Daniel to be brought and cast into the lions' den. To Daniel he said, "May your God, whom you serve so constantly, save you." To forestall any tampering, the king sealed with his own ring and the rings of the lords the stone that had been brought to block the opening of the den.

Then the king returned to his palace for the night; he refused to eat and he dismissed the entertainers. Since sleep was impossible for him, the king rose very early the next morning and hastened to the lions' den. As he drew near, he cried out to Daniel sorrowfully, "O Daniel, servant of the living God, has the God whom you serve so constantly been able to save you from the lions?" Daniel answered the king: "O king, live forever! My God has sent his angel and closed the lions' mouths so that they have not hurt me. For I have been found innocent before him; neither to you have I done any harm, O king!" This gave the king great joy. At his order Daniel was removed from the den, unhurt because he trusted in his God. The king then ordered the men who had accused Daniel, along with their children and their wives, to be cast into the lions' den. Before they reached the bottom of the den, the lions overpowered them and crushed all their bones.

Then King Darius wrote to the nations and peoples of every language, wherever they dwell on the earth: "All peace to you! I decree that throughout my royal domain the God of Daniel is to be reverenced and feared:

> "For he is the living God, enduring forever;
>> his Kingdom shall not be destroyed,
>> and his dominion shall be without end.
> He is a deliverer and savior,
>> working signs and wonders in heaven and on earth,
>> and he delivered Daniel from the lions' power."

The word of the Lord.

Responsorial Psalm
Dn 3:68, 69, 70, 71, 72, 73, 74

R. Give glory and eternal praise to him.

"Dew and rain, bless the Lord;
  praise and exalt him above all forever."

R. Give glory and eternal praise to him.

"Frost and chill, bless the Lord;
  praise and exalt him above all forever."

R. Give glory and eternal praise to him.

"Ice and snow, bless the Lord;
   praise and exalt him above all forever."

R. Give glory and eternal praise to him.

"Nights and days, bless the Lord;
   praise and exalt him above all forever."

R. Give glory and eternal praise to him.

"Light and darkness, bless the Lord;
   praise and exalt him above all forever."

R. Give glory and eternal praise to him.

"Lightnings and clouds, bless the Lord;
   praise and exalt him above all forever."

R. Give glory and eternal praise to him.

"Let the earth bless the Lord,
   praise and exalt him above all forever."

R. Give glory and eternal praise to him.

Alleluia Verse *and* **Gospel,** *p. 1759f.*

Year II

FIRST READING   Rv 18:1–2, 21–23; 19:1–3, 9a

Fallen is Babylon the great.

A reading from the Book of Revelation

I, John, saw another angel coming down from heaven, having
great authority, and the earth became illumined by his splendor.
He cried out in a mighty voice:

   "Fallen, fallen is Babylon the great.
      She has become a haunt for demons.
   She is a cage for every unclean spirit,
      a cage for every unclean bird,
      a cage for every unclean and disgusting beast."

A mighty angel picked up a stone like a huge millstone and threw it into the sea and said:

> "With such force will Babylon the great city
>> be thrown down,
>> and will never be found again.
> No melodies of harpists and musicians,
>> flutists and trumpeters,
>> will ever be heard in you again.
> No craftsmen in any trade
>> will ever be found in you again.
> No sound of the millstone
>> will ever be heard in you again.
> No light from a lamp
>> will ever be seen in you again.
> No voices of bride and groom
>> will ever be heard in you again.
> Because your merchants were the great ones
>> of the world,
>> all nations were led astray by your magic potion."

After this I heard what sounded like the loud voice of a great multitude in heaven, saying:

> "Alleluia!
> Salvation, glory, and might belong to our God,
>> for true and just are his judgments.
> He has condemned the great harlot
>> who corrupted the earth with her harlotry.
> He has avenged on her the blood of his servants."

They said a second time:

> "Alleluia! Smoke will rise from her forever and ever."

Then the angel said to me, "Write this: Blessed are those who have been called to the wedding feast of the Lamb."
The word of the Lord.

Responsorial Psalm

Ps 100:1b–2, 3, 4, 5

> R. Blessed are they who are called
> to the wedding feast of the Lamb.

Sing joyfully to the LORD, all you lands;
  serve the LORD with gladness;
  come before him with joyful song.

> R. Blessed are they who are called
> to the wedding feast of the Lamb.

Know that the LORD is God;
  he made us, his we are;
  his people, the flock he tends.

> R. Blessed are they who are called
> to the wedding feast of the Lamb.

Enter his gates with thanksgiving,
  his courts with praise;
Give thanks to him; bless his name.

> R. Blessed are they who are called
> to the wedding feast of the Lamb.

For he is good:
  the LORD, whose kindness endures forever,
  and his faithfulness, to all generations.

> R. Blessed are they who are called
> to the wedding feast of the Lamb.

> **Alleluia, alleluia** Lk 21:28
> Stand erect and raise your heads
> because your redemption is at hand.
> **Alleluia, alleluia**

Years I and II

GOSPEL   Lk 21:20-28

*Jerusalem will be trampled underfoot by the Gentiles
until the times of the Gentiles are fulfilled.*

A reading from the holy Gospel according to Luke

Jesus said to his disciples: "When you see Jerusalem surrounded by armies, know that its desolation is at hand. Then those in Judea must flee to the mountains. Let those within the city escape from it, and let those in the countryside not enter the city, for these days are the time of punishment when all the Scriptures are fulfilled. Woe to pregnant women and nursing mothers in those days, for a terrible calamity will come upon the earth and a wrathful judgment upon this people. They will fall by the edge of the sword and be taken as captives to all the Gentiles; and Jerusalem will be trampled underfoot by the Gentiles until the times of the Gentiles are fulfilled.

"There will be signs in the sun, the moon, and the stars, and on earth nations will be in dismay, perplexed by the roaring of the sea and the waves. People will die of fright in anticipation of what is coming upon the world, for the powers of the heavens will be shaken. And then they will see the Son of Man coming in a cloud with power and great glory. But when these signs begin to happen, stand erect and raise your heads because your redemption is at hand."

The Gospel of the Lord.

Liturgy of the Eucharist, *p. 897;* **Prayer over the Gifts,** *p. 1738.*

Friday

Antiphons and Prayers, *p. 1737;* **Liturgy of the Word** *for Year I (odd years) follows; Year II (even years), p. 1764.*

TODAY'S LIVING WORD

The passing of time features in all three of today's readings. The vision of Daniel reviews the rise and fall of the four major kingdoms that ruled over God's people from the exile to the time when Daniel was written (second century B.C.E.). The eventual triumph of Israel, in God's good time, is announced when "one like a son of man," a symbol of God's holy ones, receives "dominion, glory, and kingship" from the Ancient One. Revelation introduces the notion of millennium, the "thousand years" when Satan will be chained in the abyss. This passage has evoked much speculation, especially among those who interpret the Bible literally. But Jesus himself warns against such speculation, refusing to give his disciples a timetable for the last days. In today's Gospel he only says that the signs of the arrival of God's kingdom will be as obvious as the change of seasons.

The readings tell us always to know what time it is, not clock and calendar time, but the time of our visitation, when the reign of God draws near—in the events of history, in the mystery of Word and Sacrament, and in the majesty of the Second Coming.

Year I

FIRST READING

Dn 7:2–14

I saw one like a son of man coming, on the clouds of heaven.

A reading from the Book of the Prophet Daniel

In a vision I, Daniel, saw during the night, the four winds of heaven stirred up the great sea, from which emerged four immense beasts, each different from the others. The first was like a lion, but with eagle's wings. While I watched, the wings were plucked; it was raised from the ground to stand on two feet like a man, and given a human mind. The second was like a bear; it was raised up on one side, and among the teeth in its mouth were three tusks. It was given the order, "Up, devour much flesh." After this I looked and saw another beast, like a leopard; on its back were four wings like those of a bird, and it had four heads. To this beast dominion was given. After this, in the visions of the night I saw the fourth beast, different from all the others, terrifying, horrible, and of extraordinary strength; it had great iron teeth with which it devoured and crushed, and what was left it trampled with its feet. I was considering the ten horns it had, when suddenly another, a little horn, sprang out of their midst, and three of the previous horns were torn away to make room for it. This horn had eyes like a man, and a mouth that spoke arrogantly. As I watched,

> Thrones were set up
>> and the Ancient One took his throne.
> His clothing was snow bright,
>> and the hair on his head as white as wool;
> His throne was flames of fire,
>> with wheels of burning fire.
> A surging stream of fire
>> flowed out from where he sat;
> Thousands upon thousands were ministering to him,
>> and myriads upon myriads attended him.

The court was convened, and the books were opened. I watched, then, from the first of the arrogant words which the horn spoke, until the beast was slain and its body thrown into the fire to be burnt up. The other beasts, which also lost their dominion, were granted a prolongation of life for a time and a season. As the visions during the night continued, I saw

One like a son of man coming,
    on the clouds of heaven;
When he reached the Ancient One
    and was presented before him,
He received dominion, glory, and kingship;
    nations and peoples of every language serve him.
His dominion is an everlasting dominion
    that shall not be taken away,
    his kingship shall not be destroyed.

The word of the Lord.

Responsorial Psalm

Dn 3:75, 76, 77, 78, 79, 80, 81

R Give glory and eternal praise to him!

"Mountains and hills, bless the Lord;
  praise and exalt him above all forever."

R. Give glory and eternal praise to him!

"Everything growing from the earth, bless the Lord;
  praise and exalt him above all forever."

R. Give glory and eternal praise to him!

"You springs, bless the Lord;
  praise and exalt him above all forever."

R. Give glory and eternal praise to him!

"Seas and rivers, bless the Lord;
  praise and exalt him above all forever."

R. Give glory and eternal praise to him!

"You dolphins and all water creatures, bless the Lord;
  praise and exalt him above all forever."

R. Give glory and eternal praise to him!

"All you birds of the air, bless the Lord;
  praise and exalt him above all forever."

R. Give glory and eternal praise to him!

"All you beasts, wild and tame, bless the Lord;
  praise and exalt him above all forever."

R. Give glory and eternal praise to him!

Alleluia Verse *and* **Gospel,** *p. 1766.*

Year II

FIRST READING   Rv 20:1–4, 11—21:2

The dead were judged according to their deeds.
I saw a new Jerusalem, coming down out of heaven from God.

A reading from the Book of Revelation

I, John, saw an angel come down from heaven, holding in his hand the key to the abyss and a heavy chain. He seized the dragon, the ancient serpent, which is the Devil or Satan, and tied it up for a thousand years and threw it into the abyss, which he locked over it and sealed, so that it could no longer lead the nations astray until the thousand years are completed. After this, it is to be released for a short time.

Then I saw thrones; those who sat on them were entrusted with judgment. I also saw the souls of those who had been beheaded for their witness to Jesus and for the word of God, and who had not worshiped the beast or its image nor had accepted its mark on their foreheads or hands. They came to life and they reigned with Christ for a thousand years.

Next I saw a large white throne and the one who was sitting on it. The earth and the sky fled from his presence and there was no place for them. I saw the dead, the great and the lowly, standing before the throne, and scrolls were opened. Then another scroll was opened, the book of life. The dead were judged according to their deeds, by what was written in the scrolls. The sea gave up its dead; then Death and Hades gave up their dead. All the dead were judged according to their deeds. Then Death and Hades were thrown into the pool of fire. (This pool of fire is the second death.) Anyone whose name was not found written in the book of life was thrown into the pool of fire.

Then I saw a new heaven and a new earth. The former heaven and the former earth had passed away, and the sea was no more. I also saw the holy city, a new Jerusalem, coming down out of heaven from God, prepared as a bride adorned for her husband.

The word of the Lord.

Responsorial Psalm

Ps 84:3, 4, 5–6a and 8a

R. Here God lives among his people.

My soul yearns and pines
  for the courts of the LORD.
My heart and my flesh
  cry out for the living God.

R. Here God lives among his people.

Even the sparrow finds a home,
  and the swallow a nest
in which she puts her young—
Your altars, O LORD of hosts,
  my king and my God!

R. Here God lives among his people.

Blessed they who dwell in your house!
  continually they praise you.

Blessed the men whose strength you are!
  They go from strength to strength.

R. Here God lives among his people.

Alleluia, alleluia Lk 21:28
Stand erect and raise your heads
because your redemption is at hand.
Alleluia, alleluia

Years I and II

GOSPEL   Lk 21:29–33

*When you see these things happening,
know that the Kingdom of God is near.*

A reading from the holy Gospel according to Luke

Jesus told his disciples a parable. "Consider the fig tree and all the other trees. When their buds burst open, you see for yourselves and know that summer is now near; in the same way, when you see these things happening, know that the Kingdom of God is near. Amen, I say to you, this generation will not pass away until all these things have taken place. Heaven and earth will pass away, but my words will not pass away."

The Gospel of the Lord.

Liturgy of the Eucharist, *p. 897;* **Prayer over the Gifts,** *p. 1738.*

Saturday

Antiphons and Prayers, *p. 1737;* **Liturgy of the Word** *for Year I (odd years) follows; Year II (even years), p. 1769.*

TODAY'S LIVING WORD

Today's two first readings sound a triumphant note. The passage from Daniel is an interpretation of his previous vision of the four beasts. The author is primarily concerned about the fourth beast, the kingdom of the Greek King Antiochus IV, who is oppressing "the holy ones of the Most High, thinking to change the feast days and the law." But his domination will end "by final and absolute destruction," and dominion be given "to the holy people of the Most High." The conclusion of Revelation is a vision of Eden regained. There the trees of life produce fruit and provide healing, the curses of Genesis are reversed, and God's faithful servants "shall reign forever."

Coming after these poetic flights, the Gospel is frankly prosaic. It is a program for Christians like us who have reckoned with the long delay of the triumphant Son of Man. It calls for careful vigilance, constant prayer, and the consistent discipline that keeps us free of dissipation and the distraction of worldly cares. It means being continually on edge but with complete heart's ease, ever ready to stand before the coming Son of Man.

Year I

FIRST READING

Dn 7:15–27

Kingship and domain shall be given to the holy people of the Most High.

A reading from the Book of the Prophet Daniel

I, Daniel, found my spirit anguished within its covering of flesh, and I was terrified by the visions of my mind. I approached one of those present and asked him what all this meant in truth; in answer, he made known to me the meaning of the things: "These four great beasts stand for four kingdoms which shall arise on the earth. But the holy ones of the Most High shall receive the kingship, to possess it forever and ever."

But I wished to make certain about the fourth beast, so very terrible and different from the others, devouring and crushing with its iron teeth and bronze claws, and trampling with its feet what was left; about the ten horns on its head, and the other one that sprang up, before which three horns fell; about the horn with the eyes and the mouth that spoke arrogantly, which appeared greater than its fellows. For, as I watched, that horn made war against the holy ones and was victorious until the Ancient One arrived; judgment was pronounced in favor of the holy ones of the Most High, and the time came when the holy ones possessed the kingdom. He answered me thus:

"The fourth beast shall be a fourth kingdom on earth
    different from all the others;
It shall devour the whole earth,
    beat it down, and crush it.
The ten horns shall be ten kings
    rising out of that kingdom;
    another shall rise up after them,
Different from those before him,
    who shall lay low three kings.
He shall speak against the Most High
    and oppress the holy ones of the Most High,
    thinking to change the feast days and the law.
They shall be handed over to him
    for a year, two years, and a half-year.
But when the court is convened,
    and his power is taken away
    by final and absolute destruction,
Then the kingship and dominion and majesty
    of all the kingdoms under the heavens
    shall be given to the holy people of the Most High,
Whose Kingdom shall be everlasting:
    all dominions shall serve and obey him."

The word of the Lord.

Responsorial Psalm

Dn 3:82, 83, 84, 85, 86, 87

R. Give glory and eternal praise to him.

"You sons of men, bless the Lord;
  praise and exalt him above all forever."

R. Give glory and eternal praise to him.

"O Israel, bless the Lord;
  praise and exalt him above all forever."

R. Give glory and eternal praise to him.

"Priests of the Lord, bless the Lord;
  praise and exalt him above all forever."

R. Give glory and eternal praise to him.

"Servants of the Lord, bless the Lord;
  praise and exalt him above all forever."

R. Give glory and eternal praise to him.

"Spirits and souls of the just, bless the Lord;
  praise and exalt him above all forever."

R. Give glory and eternal praise to him.

"Holy men of humble heart, bless the Lord;
  praise and exalt him above all forever."

R. Give glory and eternal praise to him.

Alleluia Verse *and* **Gospel,** *p. 1771.*

Year II

FIRST READING

Rv 22:1–7

Night will be no more, for the Lord God shall give them light.

A reading from the Book of Revelation

John said: An angel showed me the river of life-giving water,
sparkling like crystal, flowing from the throne of God and of

the Lamb down the middle of the street, On either side of the river grew the tree of life that produces fruit twelve times a year, once each month; the leaves of the trees serve as medicine for the nations. Nothing accursed will be found anymore. The throne of God and of the Lamb will be in it, and his servants will worship him. They will look upon his face, and his name will be on their foreheads. Night will be no more, nor will they need light from lamp or sun, for the Lord God shall give them light, and they shall reign forever and ever.

And he said to me, "These words are trustworthy and true, and the Lord, the God of prophetic spirits, sent his angel to show his servants what must happen soon." "Behold, I am coming soon." Blessed is the one who keeps the prophetic message of this book.

The word of the Lord.

Responsorial Psalm

Ps 95:1–2, 3–5, 6–7ab

R. Marana tha! Come, Lord Jesus!

Come, let us sing joyfully to the LORD;
  let us acclaim the Rock of our salvation.
Let us come into his presence with thanksgiving;
  let us joyfully sing psalms to him.

R. Marana tha! Come, Lord Jesus!

For the LORD is a great God,
  and a great king above all gods;
In his hands are the depths of the earth,
  and the tops of the mountains are his.
His is the sea, for he has made it,
  and the dry land, which his hands have formed.

R. Marana tha! Come, Lord Jesus!

Come, let us bow down in worship;
  let us kneel before the LORD who made us.
For he is our God,
  and we are the people he shepherds, the flock he guides.

R. Marana tha! Come, Lord Jesus!

Alleluia, alleluia Lk 21:36
Be vigilant at all times and pray
that you may have the strength to stand before the Son of Man.
Alleluia, alleluia

Years I and II

GOSPEL   Lk 21:34–36

*Be vigilant that you may have the strength
to escape the tribulations that are imminent.*

A reading from the holy Gospel according to Luke

Jesus said to his disciples: "Beware that your hearts do not become drowsy from carousing and drunkenness and the anxieties of daily life, and that day catch you by surprise like a trap. For that day will assault everyone who lives on the face of the earth. Be vigilant at all times and pray that you have the strength to escape the tribulations that are imminent and to stand before the Son of Man."

The Gospel of the Lord.

Liturgy of the Eucharist, *p. 897;* **Prayer over the Gifts,** *p. 1738.*

Years I and II

GOSPEL

Be vigilant lest your hearts be overcome,
to escape the tribulations that are imminent.

A reading from the holy Gospel according to Luke

Jesus said to his disciples: "Beware that your hearts do not become drowsy from carousing and drunkenness and the anxieties of daily life, and that day catch you by surprise like a trap. For that day will assault everyone who lives on the face of the earth. Be vigilant at all times and pray that you have the strength to escape the tribulations that are imminent and to stand before the Son of Man."

The Gospel of the Lord.

Liturgy of the Eucharist, p. 507/Prayer over the Gifts, p. 738

PROPER OF SAINTS

The saints took the words of Jesus seriously. They believed that they would find happiness by putting those words into practice in their lives. And they realized their truth in everyday experience: despite their trials, moments of darkness, and failures, they already tasted here below the deep joy of communion with Christ. In him they discovered the initial seed, already present in time, of the future glory of God's kingdom.

"This was discovered in particular by Mary Most Holy, who lived in unique communion with the incarnate Word, entrusting herself unreservedly to his saving plan. For this reason she was granted to hear, in anticipation of the 'Sermon on the Mount,' the Beatitude that sums up all the rest: 'Blessed is she who believed that there would be a fulfillment of what was spoken to her from the Lord' (Lk 1:45)" (Pope John Paul II).

Two series of readings are provided for celebrations of the Saints.

1. The Proper of Saints provides the first series for solemnities, feasts, or memorials and particularly when there are proper texts for one or other such celebration. Sometimes in the Proper, however, there is a reference to the most appropriate among the texts in the Commons as the one to be given preference.

2. The Commons of Saints provide the second, more extensive group of readings. There are, first, appropriate texts for the different classes of Saints (martyrs, pastors, virgins, etc.), then numerous texts that deal with holiness in general. These may be freely chosen whenever the Commons are indicated as the source for the choice of readings.

The first concern of a priest celebrating with a congregation is the spiritual benefit of the faithful and he will be careful not to impose his personal preference on them. Above all he will make sure not to omit too often or without sufficient cause the readings assigned for each day in the weekday Lectionary: the Church's desire is that a more lavish table of the word of God be spread before the faithful.

FROM THE INTRODUCTION TO THE REVISED LECTIONARY

JANUARY

For **January 1,** *Octave of Christmas,* SOLEMNITY OF MARY, MOTHER OF GOD, *see* **Vatican II Sunday Missal,** *p. 103.*

January 2

BASIL THE GREAT (330–379) and GREGORY NAZIANZEN (329/30–389/90), bishops and doctors

Memorial

Both Basil and Gregory were born in Asia Minor. They became close friends and studied together in Athens. Both became bishops and important theologians. Basil was an organizer who fought against Arianism; Gregory was more contemplative and poetic. Appointed bishop of the tumultuous See of Constantinople, Gregory soon resigned and ended his days devoutly at Nazianzen.

Antiphons and Prayers: *from the* COMMON OF PASTORS: FOR BISHOPS *(pp. 2170–2175), or* COMMON OF DOCTORS OF THE CHURCH *(pp. 2219–2238), or from the* WEEKDAY MASS, *except:*

Opening Prayer

God our Father,
you inspired the Church
with the example and teaching of your saints Basil and
Gregory.
In humility may we come to know your truth
and put it into action with faith and love.

Grant this through our Lord Jesus Christ, your Son,
who lives and reigns with you and the Holy Spirit,
one God, for ever and ever.

Liturgy of the Word: *from the* COMMON OF PASTORS *(pp. 2188ff.), or* COMMON OF DOCTORS OF THE CHURCH *(pp. 2222ff.), especially Eph 4:1–7, 11–13 (see pp. 2231f.); Ps 23:1b–3a, 4, 5, 6; Mt 23:8–12; or from the* WEEKDAY MASS.

Liturgy of the Eucharist, *p. 897.*

January 4

[In the dioceses of the United States]

ELIZABETH ANN SETON, religious (1774–1821)

Memorial

The first American-born saint, Elizabeth Seton was born into a wealthy Episcopalian family in New York City. She and her husband had five children and after he died, she became a Catholic. In 1809, she started a religious teaching community, the first American Sisters of Charity, and began the Catholic school system. This heroic woman died in 1821 and was canonized on September 14, 1975.

Entrance Antiphon

Praise to the holy woman whose home is built on faithful love and whose pathway leads to God.   (See Prv 14:1–2)

Opening Prayer

Lord God,
you blessed Elizabeth Seton with gifts of grace
as wife and mother, educator and foundress,
so that she might spend her life in service to your people.
Through her example and prayers
may we learn to express our love for you
in love for others.

We ask this through our Lord Jesus Christ, your Son,
who lives and reigns with you and the Holy Spirit,
one God, for ever and ever.

Liturgy of the Word: *from the* COMMON OF HOLY MEN AND WOMEN: FOR RELIGIOUS *(pp. 2273ff.)*, or from the WEEKDAY MASS.

Liturgy of the Eucharist, *p. 897.*

Prayer over the Gifts

Pray, brethren...

Lord,
give to us who offer these gifts at your altar

the same spirit of love that filled St. Elizabeth Seton.
By celebrating this sacred eucharist
with pure minds and loving hearts
may we offer a sacrifice that pleases you,
and brings salvation to us.

Grant this through Christ our Lord.

Communion Antiphon

**I am the living bread from heaven, says the Lord. Whoever
eats this bread will live for ever; the bread I shall give is my flesh
for the life of the world.**   (Jn 6:51)

Prayer after Communion

Let us pray.

Pause for silent prayer, if this has not preceded.

Lord,
we have shared
in the mystery of your love.
May we be strengthened in faith and love for the eucharist
as we recall the example of St. Elizabeth Seton.

We ask this through Christ our Lord.

January 5

[In the dioceses of the United States]

JOHN NEUMANN, bishop (1811–1860)

Memorial

A native of Bohemia, John Neumann came to the United States
where he was ordained as a diocesan priest. He later joined the
Redemptorists and worked tirelessly in the American missions. He
learned twelve languages in order to minister to the various groups
of immigrants. John Neumann became the bishop of Philadelphia
in 1852, during times of Nativist bigotry and difficult growth for the
Church. He was canonized in 1977.

Entrance Antiphon

O Lord, my allotted portion and my cup, you it is who hold fast my lot. For me the measuring lines have fallen on pleasant sites; fair to me indeed is my inheritance. (Ps 16:5–6)

Opening Prayer

Almighty God,
you called St. John Neumann
to a life of service, zeal, and compassion
for the guidance of your people in the new world.
By his prayers
help us to build up the community of the Church
through our dedication to the Christian education of youth
and through the witness of our brotherly love.

Grant this through our Lord Jesus Christ, your Son,
who lives and reigns with you and the Holy Spirit,
one God, for ever and ever.

Liturgy of the Word: *from the* COMMON OF PASTORS *(pp. 2188ff.), or from the* WEEKDAY MASS.

Liturgy of the Eucharist, *p. 897.*

Prayer over the Gifts

Pray, brethren...

Father of mercies,
look upon the gifts
that we present in memory of Christ your Son.
Form us in his likeness
as you formed St. John,
who imitated what he handled
in these holy mysteries.

We ask this in the name of Jesus the Lord.

1778 PROPER OF SAINTS

Communion Antiphon

Everyone who has given up home, brothers or sisters, father or mother, wife or children or property for my sake will receive many times as much and inherit everlasting life. (Mt 19:29)

Prayer after Communion

Let us pray.

Pause for silent prayer, if this has not preceded.

Father of our Lord Jesus Christ,
you have united us with our Redeemer
in this memorial of his death and resurrection.

By the power of this sacrament,
help us to live,
one in spirit and in truth,
in the communion of Christ's body.

Grant this through Christ our Lord.

January 6

[In the dioceses of the United States]

BLESSED ANDRÉ BESSETTE, religious (1845–1937)

Optional Memorial

Born into a poor family in Quebec, André became a Holy Cross brother. With great humility and simplicity he served as a doorkeeper at the College of Notre Dame for 40 years. Intensely devoted to St. Joseph, André obtained funds to build the Oratory of St. Joseph in Montreal. Thousands of people visited the shrine, drawn by Brother André's reputation for holiness and his charismatic gift of healing.

Antiphons and Prayers: *from the* COMMON OF HOLY MEN AND WOMEN *(pp. 2252–2322), or from the* WEEKDAY MASS. *The following is optional:*

Opening Prayer

Lord our God,
friend of the lowly,

you gave your servant, Brother André,
a great devotion to St. Joseph
and a special commitment to the poor and afflicted.
Through his intercession
help us to follow his example of prayer and love
and so come to share with him in your glory.

We ask this through our Lord Jesus Christ, your Son,
who lives and reigns with you and the Holy Spirit,
one God, for ever and ever.

Liturgy of the Word: *from the* COMMON OF HOLY MEN AND WOMEN: FOR RELIGIOUS *(pp. 2273ff.), or from the* WEEKDAY MASS.

Liturgy of the Eucharist, *p. 897.*

January 7
RAYMOND OF PEÑAFORT, priest (1175/80–1275)

Optional Memorial

Born at Peñafort near Barcelona (Spain), Raymond became a priest and professor of philosophy and canon law. He later joined the Dominicans and was a specialist in moral theology and the Sacrament of Reconciliation. Raymond also studied Arabic and the Koran in order to be able to dialogue with Muslims. He wrote the rule for the Order for the Redemption of Captives (to redeem Christian prisoners of the Muslims). The Church declared Raymond a saint in 1601.

Antiphons and Prayers: *from the* COMMON OF PASTORS *(pp. 2170–2218), or from the* WEEKDAY MASS. *The following is optional:*

Opening Prayer

Lord,
you gave St. Raymond the gift of compassion
in his ministry to sinners.
May his prayers free us from the slavery of sin
and help us to love and serve you in liberty.

We ask this through our Lord Jesus Christ, your Son,
who lives and reigns with you and the Holy Spirit,
one God, for ever and ever.

Liturgy of the Word: *from the* COMMON OF PASTORS *(pp. 2188ff.),*
especially 2 Cor 5:14–20; Ps 103:1bc–2, 3–4, 8–9, 13–14, 17–18;
Lk 12:35–40; or from the WEEKDAY MASS.

Liturgy of the Eucharist, *p. 897.*

January 13

HILARY, bishop and doctor (315–367)

Optional Memorial

A native of Poitiers in France, Hilary married and was the father
of a saintly daughter named Abia. Hilary converted to the Christian
faith through his reading of the Scriptures, especially the Prologue
to the Fourth Gospel. As bishop of Poitiers he fought against the Arians, suffered exile, and wrote extensively. Hilary also helped his
friend, St. Martin of Tours, to establish the monastic life in France.

Antiphons and Prayers: *from the* COMMON OF PASTORS: FOR BISHOPS
(pp. 2170–2175, or COMMON OF DOCTORS OF THE CHURCH *(pp. 2219–2238),*
or from the WEEKDAY MASS. *The following is optional:*

Opening Prayer

All-powerful God,
as St. Hilary defended the divinity of Christ your Son,
give us a deeper understanding of this mystery
and help us to profess it in all truth.

Grant this through our Lord Jesus Christ, your Son,
who lives and reigns with you and the Holy Spirit,
one God, for ever and ever.

Liturgy of the Word: *from the* COMMON OF PASTORS *(pp. 2188ff.), or* COMMON
OF DOCTORS OF THE CHURCH *(pp. 2222ff.), especially:*

FIRST READING

1 Jn 2:18–25

Whoever confesses the Son has the Father as well.

A reading from the first Letter of Saint John

Children, it is the last hour; and just as you heard that the antichrist was coming, so now many antichrists have appeared. Thus we know this is the last hour. They went out from us, but they were not really of our number; if they had been, they would have remained with us. Their desertion shows that none of them was of our number. But you have the anointing that comes from the Holy One, and you all have knowledge. I write to you not because you do not know the truth but because you do, and because every lie is alien to the truth. Who is the liar? Whoever denies that Jesus is the Christ. Whoever denies the Father and the Son, this is the antichrist. Anyone who denies the Son does not have the Father, but whoever confesses the Son has the Father as well.

Let what you heard from the beginning remain in you. If what you heard from the beginning remains in you, then you will remain in the Son and in the Father. And this is the promise that he made us: eternal life.

The word of the Lord.

See the Common of Pastors (pp. 2189–2217), for:
  Responsorial Psalm 110:1, 2, 3, 4
  Alleluia Verse Mt 5:16

See the Common of Doctors (p. 2234), for:
  Gospel Mt 5:13–19

  Liturgy of the Eucharist, *p. 897.*

January 17

ANTHONY, abbot (251–356)

Memorial

"If you wish to be perfect, go, sell what you own, give it to the poor, and come, follow me." An orphan named Anthony heard these words proclaimed in his church in Egypt when he was twenty years old. He took them to heart, went into the desert, and lived a profoundly spiritual, disciplined life of penance, prayer, and good works. His example inspired so many followers that Anthony is often called the father of monasticism.

Entrance Antiphon

The just man will flourish like the palm tree. Planted in the courts of God's house, he will grow great like the cedars of Lebanon.
(Ps 91:13–14)

Opening Prayer

Father,
you called St. Anthony
to renounce the world
and serve you in the solitude of the desert.
By his prayers and example,
may we learn to deny ourselves
and to love you above all things.

We ask this through our Lord Jesus Christ, your Son,
who lives and reigns with you and the Holy Spirit,
one God, for ever and ever.

Liturgy of the Word: *from the* COMMON OF HOLY MEN AND WOMEN: FOR RELIGIOUS *(pp. 2273ff.), especially Eph 6:10–13, 18; Ps 16:1–2a and 5, 7–8, 11; or from the* WEEKDAY MASS.

GOSPEL

Mt 19:16–26

If you wish to be perfect, go, sell what you have.

A reading from the holy Gospel according to Matthew

Someone approached Jesus and said, "Teacher, what good must I do to gain eternal life?" Jesus answered him, "Why do you ask me about the good? There is only One who is good. If you wish to enter into life, keep the commandments." He asked him, "Which ones?" And Jesus replied, *"You shall not kill; you shall not commit adultery; you shall not steal; you shall not bear false witness; honor your father and your mother; and you shall love your neighbor as yourself."* The young man said to him, "All of these I have observed. What do I still lack?" Jesus said to him, "If you wish to be perfect, go, sell what you have and give to the poor, and you will have treasure in heaven. Then come, follow me." When the young man heard this statement, he went away sad, for he had many possessions. Then Jesus said to his disciples, "Amen, I say to you, it will be hard for one who is rich to enter the Kingdom of heaven. Again I say to you, it is easier for a camel to pass through the eye of a needle than for one who is rich to enter the Kingdom of God." When the disciples heard this, they were greatly astonished and said, "Who then can be saved?" Jesus looked at them and said, "For men this is impossible, but for God all things are possible."

The Gospel of the Lord.

Liturgy of the Eucharist, *p. 897.*

Prayer over the Gifts

Pray, brethren...

Lord,
accept the sacrifice we offer at your altar
in commemoration of St. Anthony.
May no earthly attractions keep us from loving you.

Grant this through Christ our Lord.

Communion Antiphon

If you wish to be perfect, go, sell what you own, give it all to the poor, then come, follow me.   (Mt 19:21)

Prayer after Communion

Let us pray.

Pause for silent prayer, if this has not preceded.

Lord,
you helped St. Anthony conquer the powers of darkness.
May your sacrament strengthen us
in our struggle with evil.

We ask this in the name of Jesus the Lord.

January 20

FABIAN, pope and martyr (†250)

Optional Memorial

Fabian was pope for 14 years, from 236–250. For the Church these were years of peace, organization, and missionary effort. Selected to become bishop while still a layman, Fabian showed himself to be zealous and wise. His service to the Church ended with the persecution of Decius, during which he died as a martyr.

Antiphons and Prayers: *from the* COMMON OF MARTYRS *(pp. 2128–2169), or* COMMON OF PASTORS: FOR POPES *(pp. 2170–2218), or from the* WEEKDAY MASS. *The following is optional:*

Opening Prayer

God our Father,
glory of your priests,
may the prayers of your martyr Fabian
help us to share his faith
and offer you loving service.

Grant this through our Lord Jesus Christ, your Son,
who lives and reigns with you and the Holy Spirit,
one God, for ever and ever.

Liturgy of the Word: *from the* COMMON OF MARTYRS *(pp. 2147ff.), or* COMMON OF PASTORS: FOR A POPE *(pp. 2188ff.), especially 1 Pt 5:1–4; Ps 40:2 and 4ab, 7–8a, 8b–9, 10; Jn 21:15–17; or from the* WEEKDAY MASS.

Liturgy of the Eucharist, *p. 897.*

Also on January 20

SEBASTIAN, martyr (†288)

Optional Memorial

The severe persecution of Diocletian—the last Roman persecution—began in 300 with a purge of the army. Sebastian, a Christian soldier from Milan, chose Christ over the emperor. The Christians of Rome buried Sebastian's body with honor in the catacombs along the Appian Way.

Antiphons and Prayers: *from the* COMMON OF MARTYRS *(pp. 2128–2169), or from the* WEEKDAY MASS. *The following is optional:*

Opening Prayer

Lord,
fill us with that spirit of courage
which gave your martyr Sebastian
strength to offer his life in faithful witness.
Help us to learn from him to cherish your law
and to obey you rather than men.

We ask this through our Lord Jesus Christ, your Son,
who lives and reigns with you and the Holy Spirit,
one God, for ever and ever.

Liturgy of the Word: *from the* COMMON OF MARTYRS *(pp. 2147ff.), especially 1 Pt 3:14–17; Ps 34:2–3, 4–5, 6–7, 8–9; Mt 10:28–33; or from the* WEEKDAY MASS.

Liturgy of the Eucharist, *p. 897.*

January 21

AGNES, virgin and martyr (†304)

Memorial

The martyrdom of this noble girl, aged between thirteen and fifteen, took place toward the end of Diocletian's persecution. She fearlessly proclaimed her faith and was condemned to death. Because of her heroism, Agnes has been an inspiration since her death. This popular saint is mentioned in the First Eucharistic Prayer.

Antiphons and Prayers: *from the* COMMON OF MARTYRS *(pp. 2128–2169), or the* COMMON OF VIRGINS *(pp. 2238–2252), or from the* WEEKDAY MASS, *except:*

Opening Prayer

Almighty, eternal God,
you choose what the world considers weak
to put the worldly power to shame.
May we who celebrate the birth of St. Agnes into eternal joy
be loyal to the faith she professed.

Grant this through our Lord Jesus Christ, your Son,
who lives and reigns with you and the Holy Spirit,
one God, for ever and ever.

Liturgy of the Word: *from the* COMMON OF MARTYRS *(pp. 2147ff.), or* COMMON OF VIRGINS *(pp. 2244ff.), especially 1 Cor 1:26–31; Ps 23:1b—3a, 4, 5, 6; Mt 13:44–46; or from the* WEEKDAY MASS.

Liturgy of the Eucharist, *p. 897.*

January 22

VINCENT, deacon and martyr (†304)

Optional Memorial

During Diocletian's persecution, the deacon Vincent suffered martyrdom with his bishop, Valerio, in Valencia, Spain. Vincent endured severe torture and willingly gave his life for Christ. This saint reminds us of the noble history of deacons in the early Church, which honored three deacon martyrs: Stephen (Palestine), Lawrence (Rome), and Vincent (Spain).

Antiphons and Prayers: *from the* COMMON OF MARTYRS (*pp. 2128–2169),* *or from the* WEEKDAY MASS. *The following is optional:*

Opening Prayer

Eternal Father,
you gave St. Vincent
the courage to endure torture and death for the gospel:
fill us with your Spirit
and strengthen us in your love.

We ask this through our Lord Jesus Christ, your Son,
who lives and reigns with you and the Holy Spirit,
one God, for ever and ever.

Liturgy of the Word: *from the* COMMON OF MARTYRS *(pp. 2147ff.),* *especially 2 Cor 4:7–15; Ps 34:2–3, 4–5, 6–7, 8–9; Mt 10:17–22; or* *from the* WEEKDAY MASS.

Liturgy of the Eucharist, *p. 897.*

January 24

FRANCIS DE SALES, bishop and doctor (1567–1622)

Memorial

A son of France, Francis lived in the difficult decades following the Protestant Reformation. He became the bishop of Geneva, a center of Calvinism, and related well to Protestants and Catholics. Francis wrote popular books on spiritual guidance, self-discipline, prayer, and kindness. With St. Jane Frances de Chantal, he co-founded the Visitation nuns.

Antiphons and Prayers: *from the* COMMON OF PASTORS: FOR BISHOPS *(pp. 2170–2175), or* COMMON OF DOCTORS OF THE CHURCH *(pp. 2219–2238),* *or from the* WEEKDAY MASS, *except:*

Opening Prayer

Father,
you gave Francis de Sales the spirit of compassion
to befriend all men on the way to salvation.
By his example, lead us to show your gentle love
in the service of our fellow men.

Grant this through our Lord Jesus Christ, your Son,
who lives and reigns with you and the Holy Spirit,
one God, for ever and ever.

Liturgy of the Word: *from the* COMMON OF PASTORS *(pp. 2188ff.), or* COMMON OF DOCTORS OF THE CHURCH *(pp. 2222ff.), especially Eph 3:8–12; Ps 37:3–4, 5–6, 30–31; Jn 15:9–17; or from the* WEEKDAY MASS.

Liturgy of the Eucharist, *p. 897.*

Prayer over the Gifts

Pray, brethren...

Lord,
by this offering
may the divine fire of your Holy Spirit,
which burned in the gentle heart of Francis de Sales,
inspire us with compassion and love.

We ask this through Christ our Lord.

Prayer after Communion

Let us pray.
Pause for silent prayer, if this has not preceded.

Merciful Father,
may the sacrament we have received
help us to imitate Francis de Sales in love and service;
bring us to share with him the glory of heaven.

We ask this in the name of Jesus the Lord.

January 25

CONVERSION OF PAUL, apostle

Feast

The conversion of Saul, persecutor of the Church, was of pivotal importance for the worldwide development of Christianity. Paul was a tireless missionary and the author of important letters contained in the New Testament. His conversion is so significant that it is re-counted three times in the Acts of the Apostles.

Entrance Antiphon

I know whom I have believed. I am sure that he, the just judge, will guard my pledge until the day of judgment.

(2 Tim 1:12; 4:8)

Opening Prayer

God our Father,
you taught the gospel to all the world
through the preaching of Paul your apostle.
May we who celebrate his conversion to the faith
follow him in bearing witness to your truth.

We ask this through our Lord Jesus Christ, your Son,
who lives and reigns with you and the Holy Spirit,
one God, for ever and ever.

The following readings may also be used for a votive Mass of Saint Paul.

FIRST READING

First Option

Acts 22:3–16

Get up and have yourself baptized and your sins washed away, calling upon the name of Jesus.

A reading from the Acts of the Apostles

Paul addressed the people in these words: "I am a Jew, born in Tarsus in Cilicia, but brought up in this city. At the feet of

Gamaliel I was educated strictly in our ancestral law and was zealous for God, just as all of you are today. I persecuted this Way to death, binding both men and women and delivering them to prison. Even the high priest and the whole council of elders can testify on my behalf. For from them I even received letters to the brothers and set out for Damascus to bring back to Jerusalem in chains for punishment those there as well.

"On that journey as I drew near to Damascus, about noon a great light from the sky suddenly shone around me. I fell to the ground and heard a voice saying to me, 'Saul, Saul, why are you persecuting me?' I replied, 'Who are you, sir?' And he said to me, 'I am Jesus the Nazorean whom you are persecuting.' My companions saw the light but did not hear the voice of the one who spoke to me. I asked, 'What shall I do, sir?' The Lord answered me, 'Get up and go into Damascus, and there you will be told about everything appointed for you to do.' Since I could see nothing because of the brightness of that light, I was led by hand by my companions and entered Damascus.

"A certain Ananias, a devout observer of the law, and highly spoken of by all the Jews who lived there, came to me and stood there and said, 'Saul, my brother, regain your sight.' And at that very moment I regained my sight and saw him. Then he said, 'The God of our ancestors designated you to know his will, to see the Righteous One, and to hear the sound of his voice; for you will be his witness before all to what you have seen and heard. Now, why delay? Get up and have yourself baptized and your sins washed away, calling upon his name.'"

The word of the Lord.

Or:

SECOND OPTION

Acts 9:1–22

You will be told what you must do.

A reading from the Acts of the Apostles

Saul, still breathing murderous threats against the disciples of the Lord, went to the high priest and asked him for letters to the synagogues in Damascus, that, if he should find any men or women who belonged to the Way, he might bring them back to Jerusalem in chains. On his journey, as he was nearing Damascus, a light from the sky suddenly flashed around him. He fell to the ground and heard a voice saying to him, "Saul, Saul, why are you persecuting me?" He said, "Who are you, sir?" The reply came, "I am Jesus, whom you are persecuting. Now get up and go into the city and you will be told what you must do." The men who were traveling with him stood speechless, for they heard the voice but could see no one. Saul got up from the ground, but when he opened his eyes he could see nothing; so they led him by the hand and brought him to Damascus. For three days he was unable to see, and he neither ate nor drank.

There was a disciple in Damascus named Ananias, and the Lord said to him in a vision, "Ananias." He answered, "Here I am, Lord." The Lord said to him, "Get up and go to the street called Straight and ask at the house of Judas for a man from Tarsus named Saul. He is there praying, and in a vision he has seen a man named Ananias come in and lay his hands on him, that he may regain his sight." But Ananias replied, "Lord, I have heard from many sources about this man, what evil things he has done to your holy ones in Jerusalem. And here he has authority from the chief priests to imprison all who call upon your name." But the Lord said to him, "Go, for this man is a chosen instrument of mine to carry my name before Gentiles, kings, and children of Israel, and I will show him what he will have to suffer for my name." So Ananias went and entered the house; laying his hands on him, he said, "Saul, my brother, the Lord has sent me, Jesus who appeared to you on the way by which you came, that you may regain your sight and be filled with the Holy Spirit." Immediately things like scales fell from his eyes and he regained his sight. He got up and was baptized, and when he had eaten, he recovered his strength.

He stayed some days with the disciples in Damascus, and he began at once to proclaim Jesus in the synagogues, that he is the Son of God. All who heard him were astounded and said, "Is not this the man who in Jerusalem ravaged those who call upon this name, and came here expressly to take them back in chains to the chief priests?" But Saul grew all the stronger and confounded the Jews who lived in Damascus, proving that this is the Christ.

The word of the Lord.

*See the Common of Pastors (**pp. 2188–2218**), for:*
  Responsorial Psalm 117:1bc, 2
  Alleluia Verse see Jn 15:16

GOSPEL

Mk 16:15–18

Go out to all the world and tell the Good News.

A reading from the holy Gospel according to Mark

Jesus appeared to the Eleven and said to them: "Go into the whole world and proclaim the Gospel to every creature. Whoever believes and is baptized will be saved; whoever does not believe will be condemned. These signs will accompany those who believe: in my name they will drive out demons, they will speak new languages. They will pick up serpents with their hands, and if they drink any deadly thing, it will not harm them. They will lay hands on the sick, and they will recover."

The Gospel of the Lord.

Liturgy of the Eucharist, p. 897.

Prayer over the Gifts

Pray, brethren...

Lord,
may your Spirit who helped Paul the apostle
to preach your power and glory
fill us with the light of faith
as we celebrate this holy eucharist.

We ask this in the name of Jesus the Lord.

Preface of the Apostles I or II, p. 956.

Communion Antiphon

I live by faith in the Son of God, who loved me and sacrificed himself for me.   (Gal 2:20)

Prayer after Communion

Let us pray.

Pause for silent prayer, if this has not preceded.

Lord God,
you filled Paul the apostle
with love for all the churches:
may the sacrament we have received
foster in us this love for your people.

Grant this through Christ our Lord.

January 26

TIMOTHY and TITUS, bishops

Memorial

On this day following the Feast of Paul's Conversion we honor his two close collaborators, Timothy and Titus, who accompanied Paul on some of his apostolic journeys, preached the Gospel and mediated disputes. Although most scholars date the pastoral letters to the end of the first century, the Church uses them today as reminders of their ministry.

Antiphons and Prayers: *from the* COMMON OF PASTORS: FOR BISHOPS *(p. 2170–2175), or from the* WEEKDAY MASS, *except:*

Opening Prayer

God our Father,
you gave your saints Timothy and Titus
the courage and wisdom of the apostles:
may their prayers help us to live holy lives
and lead us to heaven, our true home.

Grant this through our Lord Jesus Christ, your Son,
who lives and reigns with you and the Holy Spirit,
one God, for ever and ever.

Liturgy of the Word: *The first reading for this memorial is proper: from the* COMMON OF PASTORS *(pp. 2188ff); or:*

FIRST READING

FIRST OPTION

2 Tm 1:1–8

I recall your sincere faith.

A reading from the beginning of the second Letter of Saint Paul to Timothy

Paul, an Apostle of Christ Jesus by the will of God for the promise of life in Christ Jesus, to Timothy, my dear child: grace, mercy, and peace from God the Father and Christ Jesus our Lord.

I am grateful to God, whom I worship with a clear conscience as my ancestors did, as I remember you constantly in my prayers, night and day. I yearn to see you again, recalling your tears, so that I may be filled with joy, as I recall your sincere faith that first lived in your grandmother Lois and in your mother Eunice and that I am confident lives also in you.

For this reason, I remind you to stir into flame the gift of God that you have through the imposition of my hands. For God did not give us a spirit of cowardice but rather of power and love and self-control. So do not be ashamed of your testimony to our Lord, nor of me, a prisoner for his sake; but bear your share of hardship for the Gospel with the strength that comes from God.

The word of the Lord.

Or:

SECOND OPTION

Ti 1:1–5

To Titus, my beloved son in a common faith.

A reading from the beginning of the Letter of Saint Paul to Titus

Paul, a slave of God and Apostle of Jesus Christ for the sake of the faith of God's chosen ones and the recognition of religious truth, in the hope of eternal life that God, who does not lie, promised before time began, who indeed at the proper time revealed his word in the proclamation with which I was entrusted by the command of God our savior, to Titus, my true child in our common faith: grace and peace from God the Father and Christ Jesus our savior.

For this reason I left you in Crete so that you might set right what remains to be done and appoint presbyters in every town, as I directed you.

The word of the Lord.

See the Common of Pastors (pp. 2188–2218), for:
Responsorial Psalm 96:1–2a, 2b–3, 7–8a, 10
Alleluia Verse Lk 4:18
Gospel Lk 10:1–9

Liturgy of the Eucharist, *p. 897.*

January 27

ANGELA MERICI, virgin (1474–1540)

Optional Memorial

Wisdom and love are the characteristic virtues of this incomparable educator. Born in northern Italy, she founded the religious family of Ursulines at Brescia in 1516. Angela was especially concerned with the education and Christian formation of girls. To that end, she wrote an adaptable rule, so that the Ursulines could adjust to the needs of the times. She was canonized in 1807.

Antiphons and Prayers: *from the* COMMON OF VIRGINS *(pp. 2238–2252), or* COMMON OF HOLY MEN AND WOMEN: FOR TEACHERS *(pp. 2265–2266), or from the* WEEKDAY MASS. *The following is optional:*

Opening Prayer

Lord,
may St. Angela commend us to your mercy;
may her charity and wisdom help us
to be faithful to your teaching
and to follow it in our lives.

We ask this through our Lord Jesus Christ, your Son,
who lives and reigns with you and the Holy Spirit,
one God, for ever and ever.

Liturgy of the Word: *from the* COMMON OF VIRGINS *(pp. 2244ff.), or* COMMON OF HOLY MEN AND WOMEN: FOR TEACHERS *(pp. 2269ff.), especially* 1 Pt 4:7b–11; Ps 148:1bc–2, 11–13a, 13c–14; Mk 9:34b–37; *or from the* WEEKDAY MASS.

Liturgy of the Eucharist, *p. 897.*

January 28

THOMAS AQUINAS, priest and doctor (1225–1274)

Memorial

This great Dominican teacher, who lived only forty-nine years, is one of the Church's most outstanding theologians. His two *Summas* should not obscure his other biblical, theological, and philosophical writings. Thomas prayed much and dedicated his brilliant talents to investigating the sublime truth of God in the light of faith and the human intellect. On this date, his body was transferred to the Dominican Monastery at Toulouse. Canonized in 1323, he is patron of all Catholic schools and is titled the "Angelic Doctor."

Antiphons and Prayers: *from the* COMMON OF DOCTORS OF THE CHURCH *(pp. 2219–2238), or from the* COMMON OF PASTORS *(pp. 2170–2218), or from the* WEEKDAY MASS, *except:*

Opening Prayer

God our Father,
you made Thomas Aquinas known
for his holiness and learning.
Help us to grow in wisdom by his teaching,
and in holiness by imitating his faith.

Grant this through our Lord Jesus Christ, your Son,
who lives and reigns with you and the Holy Spirit,
one God, for ever and ever.

Liturgy of the Word: *from the* COMMON OF DOCTORS OF THE CHURCH *(pp. 2222ff.), or* COMMON OF PASTORS *(pp. 2188ff.), especially* Wis 7:7–10, 15–16; Ps 119:9, 10, 11, 12, 13, 14; Mt 23:8–12; *or from the* WEEKDAY MASS.

Liturgy of the Eucharist, *p. 897.*

January 31

JOHN BOSCO, priest (1815–1888)

Memorial

In the nineteenth century, the city of Turin in Northern Italy was a growing industrial and political center. But it had hundreds of poor, abandoned boys and girls. The strong personality of Don Bosco came to their aid. A born educator, effective organizer, and prolific writer, he trusted in God and accomplished wonders. He founded the Salesians, religious orders of men and women who care for the young. This "Apostle to Youth" was canonized on Easter of 1934.

Antiphons and Prayers: *from the* COMMON OF PASTORS *(pp. 2170–2218), or from the* COMMON OF HOLY MEN AND WOMEN: FOR TEACHERS *(pp. 2265–2266), or from the* WEEKDAY MASS, *except:*

Opening Prayer

Lord,
you called John Bosco
to be a teacher and father to the young.
Fill us with love like his:
may we give ourselves completely to your service
and to the salvation of mankind.

We ask this through our Lord Jesus Christ, your Son,
who lives and reigns with you and the Holy Spirit,
one God, for ever and ever.

Liturgy of the Word: *from the* COMMON OF PASTORS *(pp. 2188ff.), or* COMMON OF HOLY MEN AND WOMEN: FOR TEACHERS *(pp. 2269ff.), especially Phil 4:4–9; Ps 103:1bc–2, 3–4, 8–9, 13–14, 17–18; Mt 18:1–5; or from the* WEEKDAY MASS.

Liturgy of the Eucharist, *p. 897.*

FEBRUARY

For **February 2,** PRESENTATION OF THE LORD, *see* **Vatican II Sunday Missal,** *p. 1012.*

February 3

BLASE, bishop and martyr (†c. 316)

Optional Memorial

St. Blase was bishop of Sebaste in Armenia (today Turkey). Although we know little about him, it is thought that he was martyred during the persecution of Licinius (320–324). Among the stories about St. Blase is that he cured a young boy choking on a fishbone. This is the origin of the custom of blessing throats on his feast day.

Antiphons and Prayers: *from the* COMMON OF MARTYRS *(pp. 2128–2169), or* COMMON OF PASTORS *(pp. 2170–2218), or from the* WEEKDAY MASS. *The following is optional:*

Opening Prayer

Lord,
hear the prayers of your martyr Blase.
Give us the joy of your peace in this life
and help us to gain the happiness that will never end.

Grant this through our Lord Jesus Christ, your Son,
who lives and reigns with you and the Holy Spirit,
one God, for ever and ever.

Liturgy of the Word: *From the* COMMON OF MARTYRS *(pp. 2147ff.), or* COMMON OF PASTORS *(pp. 2188ff.), especially Rom 5:1–5; Ps 117:1bc, 2; Mk 16:15–20; or from the* WEEKDAY MASS.

Liturgy of the Eucharist, *p. 897.*

Also on February 3

ANSGAR, bishop (801–865)

Optional Memorial

During the Protestant Reformation, the Scandinavian countries as a unit went over to Lutheranism. Today, Catholics in Norway, Sweden, Denmark, and Finland are a scattered, struggling minority. But we should not forget the long Catholic history of those nations or St. Ansgar, their evangelizer. He was a monk of a French abbey. Named bishop and papal legate to all Scandinavian lands, Ansgar worked courageously in the face of discouraging results.

Antiphons and Prayers: *from the* COMMON OF PASTORS: FOR MISSIONARIES, *or* FOR BISHOPS *(p. 2170–2218), or from the* WEEKDAY MASS. *The following is optional:*

Opening Prayer

Father,
you sent St. Ansgar
to bring the light of Christ to many nations.
May his prayers help us
to walk in the light of your truth.

We ask this through our Lord Jesus Christ, your Son,
who lives and reigns with you and the Holy Spirit,
one God, for ever and ever.

Liturgy of the Word: *From the* COMMON OF PASTORS: FOR MISSIONARIES *(pp. 2191ff.), especially Is 52:7–10; Ps 96:1–2a, 2b–3, 7–8, 10; Mk 1:14–20; or from the* WEEKDAY MASS.

Liturgy of the Eucharist, *p. 897.*

February 5

AGATHA, virgin and martyr (†251)

Memorial

The name Agatha in Greek means "good." She was martyred around 251 at Catania in Sicily, during the persecution of Decius.

Although we have few historical details about her life, the accounts of her heroic martyrdom made her a popular saint. The people of Catania often invoked Agatha, especially when Mount Etna was erupting. She is listed in the First Eucharistic Prayer.

Antiphons and Prayers: *from the* COMMON OF VIRGINS *(pp. 2238–2252), or* COMMON OF MARTYRS *(pp. 2128–2169), or from the* WEEKDAY MASS, *except:*

Opening Prayer

Lord,
let your forgiveness be won for us
by the pleading of St. Agatha,
who found favor with you by her chastity
and by her courage in suffering death for the gospel.

Grant this through our Lord Jesus Christ, your Son,
who lives and reigns with you and the Holy Spirit,
one God, for ever and ever.

Liturgy of the Word: *from the* COMMON OF MARTYRS *(pp. 2147ff.), or* COMMON OF VIRGINS *(pp. 2244ff.), especially 1 Cor 1:26–31; Ps 31:3cd–4, 6 and 8ab, 16bc and 17; Lk 9:23–26; or from the* WEEKDAY MASS.

Liturgy of the Eucharist, p. 897.

February 6

PAUL MIKI and COMPANIONS, martyrs
(1564/6–1597)

Memorial

Paul Miki was a Jesuit priest who was crucified in Nagasaki along with 25 other Catholics on February 5, 1597. They were Japanese and Europeans, Jesuits, Franciscans, and lay persons. Their martyrdom, with today's saint encouraging and preaching from his cross, was truly heroic. Canonized in 1862, they are a reminder of the many martyrs and saints of the Far East.

Antiphons and Prayers: *from the* COMMON OF MARTYRS *(pp. 2128–2169), or from the* WEEKDAY MASS, *except:*

Opening Prayer

God our Father,
source of strength for all your saints,
you led Paul Miki and his companions
through the suffering of the cross
to the joy of eternal life.
May their prayers give us the courage
to be loyal until death in professing our faith.

We ask this through our Lord Jesus Christ, your Son,
who lives and reigns with you and the Holy Spirit,
one God, for ever and ever.

Liturgy of the Word: *from the* COMMON OF MARTYRS *(pp. 2147ff.),* *especially Gal 2:19–20; Ps 126:1bc–2ab, 2cd–3, 4–5, 6; Mt 28:16–20;* *or from the* WEEKDAY MASS.

Liturgy of the Eucharist, *p. 897.*

February 8

JEROME EMILIANI (1486–1537)

Optional Memorial

Today's saint was a Venetian soldier who was captured and imprisoned at the age of twenty-five. He converted to Christ while in prison and later dedicated himself to serving the poor. He started the Order of Clerks Regular of Somascha and was heroic in caring for orphans and the sick, especially during the plague. He was canonized in 1767.

Antiphons and Prayers: *from the* COMMON OF HOLY MEN AND WOMEN: FOR TEACHERS *(pp. 2265–2266), or from the* WEEKDAY MASS. *The following is optional:*

Opening Prayer

God of mercy,
you chose Jerome Emiliani
to be a father and friend of orphans.

May his prayers keep us faithful
to the Spirit we have received,
who makes us your children.

Grant this through our Lord Jesus Christ, your Son,
who lives and reigns with you and the Holy Spirit,
one God, for ever and ever.

Liturgy of the Word: *from the* COMMON OF HOLY MEN AND WOMEN: FOR TEACHERS *(pp. 2269ff.), especially Tb 12:6–14a; Ps 34:2–3, 4–5, 6–7, 8–9, 10–11; Mk 10:17–30; or from the* WEEKDAY MASS.

Liturgy of the Eucharist, *p. 897.*

February 10

SCHOLASTICA, virgin (480–547)

Memorial

Scholastica was the twin sister of St. Benedict. She lived in central Italy during difficult times, when armies of Goths and Byzantines crisscrossed the land and repeatedly terrorized the people. Scholastica took up the monastic life and became a beacon of holiness, peace, and strength.

Antiphons and Prayers: *from the* COMMON OF VIRGINS *(pp. 2238–2252), or* COMMON OF HOLY MEN AND WOMEN: FOR RELIGIOUS *(pp.2262–2263), or from the* WEEKDAY MASS, *except:*

Opening Prayer

Lord,
as we recall the memory of St. Scholastica,
we ask that by her example
we may serve you with love
and obtain perfect joy.

Grant this through our Lord Jesus Christ, your Son,
who lives and reigns with you and the Holy Spirit,
one God, for ever and ever.

Liturgy of the Word: *From the* COMMON OF VIRGINS *(pp. 2244ff.), or* COMMON OF HOLY MEN AND WOMEN: FOR RELIGIOUS *(pp. 2271ff.), especially Sg 8:6–7; Ps 148:1bc–2, 11–13a, 13c–14; Lk 10:38–42; or from the* WEEKDAY MASS.

Liturgy of the Eucharist, *p. 897.*

February 11

OUR LADY OF LOURDES

Optional Memorial

Today's feast recalls the dramatic story of Lourdes and its influence on Catholic life. On this day in 1858, in unbelieving, materialistic times, the Immaculate Virgin first appeared to Bernadette Soubirous. Mary referred to herself as the Immaculate Conception, and through Bernadette, called sinners to conversion. Lourdes testifies to the healing power of grace and Mary's motherly concern for us.

Antiphons and Prayers: *from the* COMMON OF THE BLESSED VIRGIN MARY *(pp. 2091–2127), or from the* WEEKDAY MASS. *The following is optional:*

Opening Prayer

God of mercy,
we celebrate the feast of Mary,
the sinless mother of God.
May her prayers help us
to rise above our human weakness.

We ask this through our Lord Jesus Christ, your Son,
who lives and reigns with you and the Holy Spirit,
one God, for ever and ever.

Liturgy of the Word: *from the* COMMON OF THE BLESSED VIRGIN MARY *(pp. 2101ff.), or from the* WEEKDAY MASS.

FIRST READING

Is 66:10–14c

I will send peace to her like a river.

A reading from the Book of the Prophet Isaiah

Rejoice with Jerusalem and be glad because of her,
   all you who love her;

Exult, exult with her,
　　all you who were mourning over her!
Oh, that you may suck fully
　　of the milk of her comfort,
That you may nurse with delight
　　at her abundant breasts!
　　For thus says the LORD:
Lo, I will spread prosperity over her like a river,
　　and the wealth of the nations like an overflowing torrent.
As nurslings, you shall be carried in her arms,
　　and fondled in her lap;
As a mother comforts her child,
　　so will I comfort you;
　　in Jerusalem you shall find your comfort.

When you see this, your heart shall rejoice,
　　and your bodies flourish like the grass;
The LORD's power shall be known to his servants.

The word of the Lord.

See the Common of the Blessed Virgin Mary (pp. 2101–2127), for:
　　Responsorial Psalm Jdt 13:18bcde, 19
　　Alleluia Verse see Lk 1:45
　　Gospel Jn 2:1–11

Liturgy of the Eucharist, *p. 897.*

February 14

CYRIL, monk (827–869) and
METHODIUS, bishop (815–885)

Memorial

These brothers, known as the "Apostles of the Slavs," were born in Greece. They evangelized in Moravia, Bohemia, and Bulgaria. Pope John Paul II named them co-patrons of Europe. In his encyclical, *Slavorum Apostoli,* the pope stressed their successful inculturation of the Gospel and importance as ecumenical figures between East and West.

Antiphons and Prayers: *from the* COMMON OF PASTORS: FOR FOUNDERS OF CHURCHES, *or* FOR MISSIONARIES *(pp. 2180–2187), or from the* WEEKDAY MASS, *except:*

Opening Prayer

Father,
you brought the light of the gospel to the Slavic nations
through St. Cyril and his brother St. Methodius.
Open our hearts to understand your teaching
and help us to become one in faith and praise.

Grant this through our Lord Jesus Christ, your Son,
who lives and reigns with you and the Holy Spirit,
one God, for ever and ever.

Liturgy of the Word: *from the* COMMON OF PASTORS: FOR MISSIONARIES *(pp. 2191ff.), or* COMMON OF HOLY MEN AND WOMEN *(pp. 2269ff.), especially Acts 13:46–49; Ps 117:1bc, 2; Lk 10:1–9; or from the* WEEKDAY MASS.

Liturgy of the Eucharist, *p. 897.*

February 17

SEVEN FOUNDERS OF THE ORDER OF SERVITES (1245–1310)

Optional Memorial

Thirteenth-century Italy saw many remarkable religious developments. Today's memorial recalls how seven businessmen of Florence followed Christ so completely that they together left their city to live as monks in the nearby mountains. They founded the order of Servites of Mary, and were canonized in 1888. On this date in 1310, the last of the seven, Alex Falconieri, died.

Antiphons and Prayers: *from the* COMMON OF HOLY MEN AND WOMEN: FOR RELIGIOUS *(pp. 2260–2263), or from the* WEEKDAY MASS. *The following is optional:*

Opening Prayer

Lord,
fill us with the love
which inspired the seven holy brothers
to honor the mother of God with special devotion
and to lead your people to you.

We ask this through our Lord Jesus Christ, your Son,
who lives and reigns with you and the Holy Spirit,
one God, for ever and ever.

Liturgy of the Word: *from the* COMMON OF HOLY MEN AND WOMEN: FOR
RELIGIOUS *(pp. 2271ff.), especially Rom 8:26–30; Ps 34:2–3, 4–5, 6–7, 8–9,
10–11; Mt 19:27–29; or from the* WEEKDAY MASS.

Liturgy of the Eucharist, *p. 897.*

February 21

PETER DAMIAN, bishop and doctor (1007–1072)

Optional Memorial

Born at Ravenna (Italy), Peter Damian was a professor who became a monk. By his austere life and writings he fought for Church reform. Named a bishop and cardinal, he helped the popes by serving as a papal legate and fighting simony and immorality among the clergy.

Antiphons and Prayers: *from the* COMMON OF DOCTORS OF THE CHURCH
(pp. 2219–2238), or from the COMMON OF PASTORS: FOR BISHOPS *(pp. 2170–2175),
or from the* COMMON OF HOLY MEN AND WOMEN: FOR RELIGIOUS, *(pp. 2260–2263),
or from the* WEEKDAY MASS. *The following is optional:*

Opening Prayer

All-powerful God,
help us to follow the teachings and example of
    Peter Damian.
By making Christ and the service of his Church

the first love of our lives,
may we come to the joys of eternal light,
where he lives and reigns with you and the Holy Spirit,
one God, for ever and ever.

Liturgy of the Word: *from the* COMMON OF DOCTORS OF THE CHURCH
(pp. 2222ff.), or COMMON OF PASTORS *(pp. 2188ff.), or* COMMON OF HOLY MEN
AND WOMEN: FOR RELIGIOUS *(pp. 2271ff.), especially 2 Tm 4:1–5; Ps 16:1–2, 5,
7–8, 11; Jn 15:1–8; or from the* WEEKDAY MASS.

Liturgy of the Eucharist, *p. 897.*

February 22

CHAIR OF PETER, apostle

Feast

This feast dedicated to St. Peter has been celebrated since the
fourth century in Rome to recall how Christ named the Galilean
fisherman the shepherd of his flock. On this day, we meditate on
Peter's special role among the apostles and in the first generation
Church. We also think of the role of Peter's successor, the pope, the
bishop of Rome.

For a votive Mass of Saint Peter the readings are also as follows.

Entrance Antiphon

**The Lord said to Simon Peter: I have prayed that your faith
may not fail; and you in your turn must strengthen your
brothers.** (Lk 22:32)

Opening Prayer

All-powerful Father,
you have built your Church
on the rock of St. Peter's confession of faith.
May nothing divide or weaken
our unity in faith and love.

Grant this through our Lord Jesus Christ, your Son,
who lives and reigns with you and the Holy Spirit,
one God, for ever and ever.

Liturgy of the Word: *from the* COMMON OF PASTORS *(pp. 2188ff.) 1 Pt
5:1–4; Ps 23:1–3a, 4, 5, 6; Mt 16:13–19.*

Liturgy of the Eucharist, *p. 897.*

Prayer over the Gifts

Pray, brethren...

Lord,
accept the prayers and gifts of your Church.
With St. Peter as our shepherd,
keep us true to the faith he taught
and bring us to your eternal kingdom.

We ask this through Christ our Lord.

Preface of the Apostles I *or* **II,** *p. 956*

Communion Antiphon

Peter said: You are the Christ, the Son of the living God. Jesus
answered: You are Peter, the rock on which I will build my
Church.
(Mt 16:16, 18)

Prayer after Communion

Let us pray.

Pause for silent prayer, if this has not preceded.

God our Father,
you have given us the body and blood of Christ
as the food of life.
On this feast of Peter the apostle,
may this communion bring us redemption
and be the sign and source of our unity and peace.

We ask this in the name of Jesus the Lord.

February 23

POLYCARP, bishop and martyr (†155)

Memorial

Today's saint is important for the meaning of tradition in the Church. According to the testimony of St. Irenaeus, Polycarp, the bishop of Smyrna in Asia Minor, was taught by the Apostle John. So he was a link between the apostolic age and the second century. The *Martyrdom of Polycarp* records how, at age eighty-six, he courageously met death through burning in the amphitheatre.

Antiphons and Prayers: *from the* COMMON OF MARTYRS *(pp. 2128–2169), or* COMMON OF PASTORS: FOR BISHOPS *(pp. 2170–2175), or from the* WEEKDAY MASS, *except:*

Opening Prayer

God of all creation,
you gave your bishop Polycarp
the privilege of being counted among the saints
who gave their lives in faithful witness to the gospel.
May his prayers give us the courage
to share with him the cup of suffering
and to rise to eternal glory.

We ask this through our Lord Jesus Christ, your Son,
who lives and reigns with you and the Holy Spirit,
one God, for ever and ever.

Liturgy of the Word: *from the* COMMON OF MARTYRS *(pp. 2147ff.), or* COMMON OF PASTORS, *(pp. 2188ff.), or:*

FIRST READING

Rv 2:8–11

I know your tribulation and poverty.

A reading from the Book of Revelation

"To the angel of the Church in Smyrna, write this:

"'The first and the last, who once died but came to life, says this: "I know your tribulation and poverty, but you are rich. I know the slander of those who claim to be Jews and are not, but rather are members of the assembly of Satan. Do not be afraid of anything that you are going to suffer. Indeed, the Devil will throw some of you into prison, that you may be tested, and you will face an ordeal for ten days. Remain faithful until death, and I will give you the crown of life.

""""Whoever has ears ought to hear what the Spirit says to the churches. The victor shall not be harmed by the second death.""""

The word of the Lord.

*See the Common of Martyrs (**pp. 2147–2169**), for:*
   Responsorial Psalm 31:3cd–4, 6 and 8ab, 16bc and 17
   Alleluia Verse see *Te Deum*
   Gospel Jn 15:18–2

   Liturgy of the Eucharist, *p. 897.*

MARCH

March 3

[In the dioceses of the United States]

KATHARINE DREXEL, virgin (1858–1955)

Optional Memorial

This native of Philadelphia founded the Sisters of the Blessed Sacrament, dedicated to serving Native Americans and African-Americans. Using the substantial funds she had inherited, Katharine established catechetical centers and schools, including Xavier University in New Orleans. Pope John Paul II beatified her in 1988 and canonized her in 2000.

Antiphons and Prayers: *from the* COMMON OF VIRGINS *(pp. 2238–2252), or* COMMON OF HOLY MEN AND WOMEN: FOR RELIGIOUS *(pp. 2260–2263), or from the* WEEKDAY MASS. *The following is optional:*

Opening Prayer

Ever-loving God,
you called St. Katharine Drexel
to teach the message of the Gospel
and to bring the life of the Eucharist
to the African American and Native American peoples.
By her prayers and example,
enable us to work for justice
among the poor and the oppressed,
and keep us undivided in love
in the eucharistic community of your Church.

Grant this through our Lord Jesus Christ, your Son,
who lives and reigns with you and the Holy Spirit,
one God, for ever and ever.

Liturgy of the Word: *from the* COMMON OF VIRGINS *(pp. 2244ff.), or*
COMMON OF HOLY MEN AND WOMEN: FOR RELIGIOUS *(pp. 2271ff.).*

Liturgy of the Eucharist, *p. 897.*

March 4

CASIMIR, prince (1458–1484)

Optional Memorial

Casimir was the son of the King of Poland, who was also Grand Duke of Lithuania. An intelligent and generous young prince, Casimir showed deep concern for national affairs and for the poor. He was devoted to prayer, especially Eucharistic prayer, and had a deep Marian devotion. On this date he died from consumption. He is honored as the patron saint of Poland and Lithuania.

Antiphons and Prayers: *from the* COMMON OF HOLY MEN AND WOMEN
(pp. 2252–2322), or from the WEEKDAY MASS. *The following is optional:*

Opening Prayer

All-powerful God,
to serve you is to reign:

by the prayers of St. Casimir,
help us to serve you in holiness and justice.

Grant this through our Lord Jesus Christ, your Son,
who lives and reigns with you and the Holy Spirit,
one God, for ever and ever.

Liturgy of the Word: *from the* COMMON OF HOLY MEN AND WOMEN *(pp. 2269ff.), especially Phil 3:8–14; Ps 15:2–3ab, 3cd–4ab, 5; Jn 15:9–17; or from the* WEEKDAY MASS.

Liturgy of the Eucharist, *p. 897.*

March 7
PERPETUA and FELICITY, martyrs (†202/3)

Memorial

The martyrdom of these women was a dramatic episode in early Church history. Perpetua, twenty-two years old, was a recently baptized noble woman with a small child. Felicity, a slave, was expecting a child. With shining courage, hand in hand, they faced death from wild beasts and the sword. This took place at Carthage, North Africa, during the persecution of Septimus Severus. *The Passion of Perpetua and Felicitas* provides an eyewitness account of their martyrdom.

Antiphons and Prayers: *from the* COMMON OF MARTYRS *(pp. 2128–2169), or* COMMON OF HOLY MEN AND WOMEN *(pp. 2252–2322), or from the* WEEKDAY MASS, *except:*

Opening Prayer

Father,
your love gave the saints Perpetua and Felicity
courage to suffer a cruel martyrdom.
By their prayers, help us to grow in love of you.

We ask this through our Lord Jesus Christ, your Son,
who lives and reigns with you and the Holy Spirit,
one God, for ever and ever.

Liturgy of the Word: *from the* COMMON OF MARTYRS *(pp. 2147ff.), especially Rom 8:31b–39; Ps 124:2–3, 4–5, 7–8; Mt 10:34–39; or from the* WEEKDAY MASS.

Liturgy of the Eucharist, *p. 897.*

March 8

JOHN OF GOD, religious (1495–1550)

Optional Memorial

Born in Portugal, John Cidade led an adventuresome life in Spain. In his early forties, he was converted after hearing a sermon preached by St. John of Avila. Thereafter he dedicated himself totally to the care of the sick and abandoned, and founded the Order of Brothers Hospitallers of St. John of God. Honored as patron of the sick, he was canonized in 1690.

Antiphons and Prayers: *from the* COMMON OF HOLY MEN AND WOMEN: FOR RELIGIOUS, *or* FOR THOSE WHO WORKED FOR THE UNDERPRIVILEGED *(pp. 2260–2264), or from the* WEEKDAY MASS. *The following is optional:*

Opening Prayer

Father,
you gave John of God
love and compassion for others.
Grant that by doing good for others
we may be counted among the saints in your kingdom.

We ask this through our Lord Jesus Christ, your Son,
who lives and reigns with you and the Holy Spirit,
one God, for ever and ever.

Liturgy of the Word: *from the* COMMON OF HOLY MEN AND WOMEN: FOR RELIGIOUS *(pp. 2271ff.), or* FOR THOSE WHO WORKED FOR THE UNDERPRIVILEGED, *(pp. 2274ff.), especially 1 Jn 3:14–18; Ps 112:1bc–2, 3–4, 5–7a, 7b–8, 9; Mt 25:31–40; or from the* WEEKDAY MASS.

Liturgy of the Eucharist, *p. 897.*

March 9

FRANCES OF ROME, religious (1384–1440)

Optional Memorial

Frances married at an early age and had three children. Each day after doing her domestic work she visited churches and cared for the poor. Even after two of her children died from the plague and her husband was wounded in battle, she courageously continued her social work. She founded a Benedictine Oblate Congregation, which she herself entered after her husband died.

Antiphons and Prayers: *from the* COMMON OF HOLY MEN AND WOMEN: FOR RELIGIOUS *(pp. 2260–2263), or from the* WEEKDAY MASS. *The following is optional:*

Opening Prayer

Merciful Father,
in Frances of Rome
you have given us a unique example of love
in marriage as well as in religious life.
Keep us faithful in your service,
and help us to see and follow you
in all the aspects of life.

We ask this through our Lord Jesus Christ, your Son,
who lives and reigns with you and the Holy Spirit,
one God, for ever and ever.

Liturgy of the Word: *From the* COMMON OF HOLY MEN AND WOMEN *(pp. 2269ff.), especially Prv 31:10–13, 19–20, 30–31; Ps 34:2–3, 4–5, 6–7, 8–9, 10–11; Mt 22:34–40; or from the* WEEKDAY MASS.

Liturgy of the Eucharist, *p. 897.*

March 17

PATRICK, bishop (c. 385–461)

Optional Memorial

Born in Great Britain, Patrick was the son of a permanent deacon. Kidnapped by Irish pirates and enslaved, he later escaped, became a priest, and returned to evangelize the Irish. This Patrick did with much prayer and austerity. As bishop he established the Church in Ireland so successfully that Irish missionaries later became a major force in spreading Catholicism around the world.

Antiphons and Prayers: *from the* COMMON OF PASTORS: FOR MISSIONARIES *or* FOR BISHOPS *(pp. 2170–2218), or from the* WEEKDAY MASS. *The following is optional:*

Opening Prayer

Let us pray
   [that like St. Patrick the missionary
   we will be fearless witnesses
   to the gospel of Jesus Christ]
     Pause for silent prayer.

God our Father,
you sent St. Patrick
to preach your glory to the people of Ireland.
By the help of his prayers,
may all Christians proclaim your love to all men.

Grant this through our Lord Jesus Christ, your Son,
who lives and reigns with you and the Holy Spirit,
one God, for ever and ever.

Alternative Opening Prayer

Let us pray
   [that, like St. Patrick,
   we may be loyal to our faith in Christ]
     Pause for silent prayer.

Father in heaven,
you sent the great bishop Patrick
to the people of Ireland to share his faith
and to spend his life in loving service.

May our lives bear witness
to the faith we profess,

and our love bring others
to the peace and joy of your gospel.
We ask this through Christ our Lord.

Liturgy of the Word: *from the* COMMON OF PASTORS: FOR MISSIONARIES *(pp. 2191ff.), especially 1 Pt 4:7b–11; Ps 96:1–2a, 2b–3, 7–8b, 10; Lk 5:1–11; or from the* WEEKDAY MASS.

Liturgy of the Eucharist, *p. 897.*

March 18

CYRIL OF JERUSALEM, bishop and doctor
(313/15–386/7)

Optional Memorial

Cyril became bishop of Jerusalem around 350 and was forced into exile three times over disputes concerning Arianism. He took part in the Council of Constantinople (381), and he wrote effectively concerning the divinity of Christ and other doctrines. He is best known for his series of catechetical sermons given to those preparing for baptism.

Antiphons and Prayers: *from the* COMMON OF PASTORS: FOR BISHOPS *(pp. 2170–2175), or* COMMON OF DOCTORS OF THE CHURCH *(pp. 2219–2238), or from the* WEEKDAY MASS. *The following is optional:*

Opening Prayer

Father,
through Cyril of Jerusalem
you led your Church to a deeper understanding
of the mysteries of salvation.
Let his prayers help us to know your Son better
and to have eternal life in all its fullness.

We ask this through our Lord Jesus Christ, your Son,
who lives and reigns with you and the Holy Spirit,
one God, for ever and ever.

Liturgy of the Word: *from the* COMMON OF PASTORS *(pp. 2188ff.), or* COMMON OF DOCTORS OF THE CHURCH, *(pp. 2222ff.), especially 1 Jn 5:1–5; Ps 19:8, 9, 10, 11; Jn 15:1–8; or from the* WEEKDAY MASS.

Liturgy of the Eucharist, *p. 897.*

For **March 19,** JOSEPH, HUSBAND OF MARY, *see* **Vatican II Sunday Missal,** *p. 1020.*

March 23

TORIBIO DE MOGROVEJO, bishop
(1538–1606)

Optional Memorial

Today's saint was a heroic, hard-working bishop who did much to organize the Church in Latin America. Born in Spain, he was named archbishop of Lima in 1580. The Latin American missions faced daunting religious, social, and political problems. Turibio began a systematic visitation of his huge diocese to deal with problems and to build up the faith. He used to say: "Jesus Christ did not say 'I am the custom,' but 'I am the Truth.'" He was canonized in 1726.

Antiphons and Prayers: *from the* COMMON OF PASTORS: FOR BISHOPS *(pp. 2170–2175), or from the* WEEKDAY MASS. *The following is optional:*

Opening Prayer

Lord,
through the apostolic work of St. Toribio
and his unwavering love of truth,
you helped your Church to grow.
May your chosen people continue to grow
in faith and holiness.

Grant this through our Lord Jesus Christ, your Son,
who lives and reigns with you and the Holy Spirit,
one God, for ever and ever.

Liturgy of the Word: *from the* COMMON OF PASTORS *(pp.2188ff.), especially* 2 Tm 1:13–14; 2:1–3; Ps 96:1–2a, 2b–3, 7–8c, 10; Mt 9:35–38; *or from the* WEEKDAY MASS.

Liturgy of the Eucharist, *p. 897.*

For **March 25,** THE ANNUNCIATION OF THE LORD, *see* **Vatican II Sunday Missal,** *p. 1025.*

APRIL

April 2
FRANCIS OF PAOLA, hermit (1436–1507)

Optional Memorial

Today's saint was born in Paola, Calabria, in rugged southern Italy. Francis became a hermit at an early age. But his life attracted followers and soon a community developed around him: the Order of Minims (the Littlest Ones). The pope called Francis to Rome and later sent him to France, where he served as spiritual director in the French court and founded many monasteries. An ambassador of spirituality, he died in France on this date, Good Friday of 1507, and was canonized in 1519.

Antiphons and Prayers: *from the* COMMON OF HOLY MEN AND WOMEN: FOR RELIGIOUS *(pp. 2260–2263), or from the* WEEKDAY MASS. *The following is optional:*

Opening Prayer

Father of the lowly,
you raised St. Francis of Paola
to the glory of your saints.
By his example and prayers,
may we come to the rewards
you have promised the humble.

We ask this through our Lord Jesus Christ, your Son,
who lives and reigns with you and the Holy Spirit,
one God, for ever and ever.

Liturgy of the Word: *from the* COMMON OF HOLY MEN AND WOMEN: FOR RELIGIOUS *(pp. 2271ff.), especially Phil 3:8–14; Ps 16:1–2a and 5, 7–8, 11; Lk 12:32–34; or from the* WEEKDAY MASS.

Liturgy of the Eucharist, *p. 897.*

April 4

ISIDORE, bishop and doctor (556–636)

Optional Memorial

Isidore was one of a family of saints. Born in Seville, Spain, he succeeded his brother Leander as bishop of Seville. This great leader rose to the challenges of his day: he evangelized the Visigoths, organized the Church, wrote scholarly works, met pastoral needs, and developed the Mozarabic liturgy. This scholar and pastor was named a Doctor of the Church in 1722.

Antiphons and Prayers: *from the* COMMON OF PASTORS: FOR BISHOPS *(pp. 2170–2175), or* COMMON OF DOCTORS OF THE CHURCH *(pp. 2219–2235), or from the* WEEKDAY MASS. *The following is optional:*

Opening Prayer

Lord,
hear the prayers we offer in commemoration of St. Isidore.
May your Church learn from his teaching
and benefit from his intercession.

Grant this through our Lord Jesus Christ, your Son,
who lives and reigns with you and the Holy Spirit,
one God, for ever and ever.

Liturgy of the Word: *from the* COMMON OF PASTORS *(pp. 2188ff.), or* COMMON OF DOCTORS OF THE CHURCH *(pp. 2222ff.), especially 2 Cor 4:1–2, 5–7; Ps 37:3–4, 5–6, 30–31; Lk 6:43–45; or from the* WEEKDAY MASS.

Liturgy of the Eucharist, *p. 897.*

April 5

VINCENT FERRER, priest (1350–1419)

Optional Memorial

Born in Spain, Vincent entered the Dominicans and until 1390 preached and taught in Valencia. Then, starting at the papal court in Avignon, he began a remarkable mission as a traveling preacher throughout France, Switzerland, and northern Italy. Vincent agonized over the evils of his times: the interminable wars between France and England, the split of the Eastern and Western Churches, and conflicting claims to the papacy. As the "Legate of Christ," he preached ardently and simply. Vincent died at Vannes, France, at the end of a Lenten course of preaching.

Antiphons and Prayers: *from the* COMMON OF PASTORS: FOR MISSIONARIES *(pp. 2170–2218), or from the* WEEKDAY MASS. *The following is optional:*

Opening Prayer

Father,
you called St. Vincent Ferrer
to preach the gospel of the last judgment.
Through his prayers may we come with joy
to meet your Son in the kingdom of heaven,
where he lives and reigns with you and the Holy Spirit,
one God, for ever and ever.

Liturgy of the Word: *from the* COMMON OF PASTORS: FOR MISSIONARIES *(pp. 2191ff.), especially 2 Tm 4:1–5; Ps 40:2, 4, 7–8, 8–9, 10, 11; Lk 12:35–40; or from the* WEEKDAY MASS.

Liturgy of the Eucharist, *p. 897.*

April 7

JOHN BAPTIST DE LA SALLE, priest (1651–1719)

Memorial

Ordained in 1678, John opened a school to educate poor children in Rheims, his city of birth. He favored new teaching methods which were directed toward a practical education and Christian formation. He opened other schools and in 1684 founded a religious community, the Brothers of the Christian Schools. In his later years, he faced great trials and opposition. He died on today's date, Good Friday of 1719, and was canonized in 1900.

Antiphons and Prayers: *from the* COMMON OF PASTORS *(pp. 2170–2218), or* COMMON OF HOLY MEN AND WOMEN: FOR TEACHERS *(pp. 2265–2266), or from the* WEEKDAY MASS, *except:*

Opening Prayer

Father,
you chose St. John Baptist de la Salle
to give young people a Christian education.
Give your Church teachers who will devote themselves
to helping your children grow
as Christian men and women.

We ask this through our Lord Jesus Christ, your Son,
who lives and reigns with you and the Holy Spirit,
one God, for ever and ever.

Liturgy of the Word: *from the* COMMON OF PASTORS *(pp. 2188ff.), or* COMMON OF HOLY MEN AND WOMEN: FOR TEACHERS *(pp. 2269ff.), especially* 2 Tm 1:13–14; 2:1–3; Ps 1:1–2, 3, 4 and 6; Mt 18:1–5; *or from the* WEEKDAY MASS.

Liturgy of the Eucharist, *p. 897.*

April 11

STANISLAUS, bishop and martyr (1030–1079)

Memorial

The patron saint of Poland, Stanislaus became bishop of Kracow in 1072. A good shepherd, he dedicated himself totally to the religious education of the people and the formation of the clergy. He came into conflict with King Boleslaus II and excommunicated him. In retaliation, the king murdered Stanislaus as he was celebrating Mass.

Antiphons and Prayers: *from the* COMMON OF MARTYRS *(pp. 2128–2169), or* COMMON OF PASTORS: FOR BISHOPS *(pp. 2170–2218), or from the* WEEKDAY MASS, *except:*

Opening Prayer

Father,
to honor you, St. Stanislaus faced martyrdom with courage.
Keep us strong and loyal in our faith until death.

Grant this through our Lord Jesus Christ, your Son,
who lives and reigns with you and the Holy Spirit,
one God, for ever and ever.

Liturgy of the Word: *from the* COMMON OF MARTYRS *(pp. 2147ff.), or* COMMON OF PASTORS *(pp. 2188ff.), especially Rv 12:10–12a; Ps 34:2–3, 4–5, 6–7, 8–9; Jn 17:11b–19; or from the* WEEKDAY MASS.

Liturgy of the Eucharist, p. 897.

April 13

MARTIN I, pope and martyr (†655)

Optional Memorial

Born in Italy, Martin was elected pope in 649. He called a council to condemn the heresy of Monothelitism (which denied that Christ had a true human will). In reaction, Emperor Constans II accused the pope of political plotting and had him arrested and brought to Constantinople. Martin was publicly humiliated and exiled to the Crimea. He died there after great sufferings, the last of the martyr popes.

Antiphons and Prayers: *from the* COMMON OF MARTYRS *(pp. 2128–2169), or* COMMON OF PASTORS: FOR POPES *(pp. 2170–2172), or from the* WEEKDAY MASS. *The following is optional:*

Opening Prayer

Merciful God, our Father,
neither hardship, pain, nor the threat of death
could weaken the faith of St. Martin.

Through our faith, give us courage
to endure whatever sufferings the world may inflict upon us.

We ask this through our Lord Jesus Christ, your Son,
who lives and reigns with you and the Holy Spirit,
one God, for ever and ever.

> **Liturgy of the Word:** *from the* COMMON OF MARTYRS *(pp. 2147ff.), or*
> COMMON OF PASTORS: FOR A POPE *(pp. 2188ff.), especially 2 Tm 2:8–13; 3:10–12;
> Ps 126:1bc–2, 2–3, 4–5, 6; Jn 15:18–21; or from the* WEEKDAY MASS.

> **Liturgy of the Eucharist,** *p. 897.*

April 21

ANSELM, bishop and doctor (1033–1109)

Optional Memorial

Today's saint is one of the most significant figures in Church history, a forerunner of medieval thought. Born in northern Italy, Anselm
became a Benedictine and an outstanding teacher of theology at his
monastery in France. In 1093, he was sent to England to become
Archbishop of Canterbury. For his defense of the rights of the Church
against the king, Anselm twice suffered exile. His writings had great
influence and are still read today.

> **Antiphons and Prayers:** *from the* COMMON OF PASTORS: FOR BISHOPS
> *(pp. 2170–2175), or* COMMON OF DOCTORS OF THE CHURCH *(pp. 2219–2238),
> or from the* WEEKDAY MASS. *The following is optional:*

Opening Prayer

Father,
you called St. Anselm
to study and teach the sublime truths you have revealed.
Let your gift of faith come to the aid of our understanding
and open our hearts to your truth.

Grant this through our Lord Jesus Christ, your Son,
who lives and reigns with you and the Holy Spirit,
one God, for ever and ever.

Liturgy of the Word: *from the* COMMON OF PASTORS *(pp. 2188ff.), or* COMMON OF DOCTORS OF THE CHURCH *(pp. 2222ff.), especially Eph 3:14–19; Ps 34:2–3, 4–5, 6–7, 8–9, 10–11; Mt 7:21–29; or from the* WEEKDAY MASS.

Liturgy of the Eucharist, *p. 897.*

April 23

GEORGE, martyr (†c. 303)

Optional Memorial

Few historical details are known about George, the patron saint of England. It is believed he was a soldier who was martyred during the persecution of Diocletian. The legends that grew up around him made him quite popular during the Middle Ages, when the cult of this saint spread through the Near East and into Europe.

Antiphons and Prayers: *from the* COMMON OF MARTYRS *(pp. 2128–2169), or from the* WEEKDAY MASS. *The following is optional:*

Opening Prayer

Lord,

hear the prayers of those who praise your mighty power.

As St. George was ready to follow Christ in suffering and
  death,

so may he be ready to help us in our weakness.

We ask this through our Lord Jesus Christ, your Son,
who lives and reigns with you and the Holy Spirit,
one God, for ever and ever.

Liturgy of the Word: *from the* COMMON OF MARTYRS *(pp. 2147ff.), especially Rv 21:5–7; Ps 126:1bc–2, 2–3, 4–5, 6; Lk 9:23–26; or from the* WEEKDAY MASS.

Liturgy of the Eucharist, *p. 897.*

Also on April 23

ADALBERT, bishop and martyr (956–997)

Optional Memorial

From a noble family in Bohemia, Adalbert became the bishop of Prague. He was twice exiled from his see due to his efforts for Church reform. After spending time in Rome as a monk, he later evangelized in Poland and Prussia, where he was martyred.

Antiphons and Prayers: *from the* COMMON OF MARTYRS *(pp. 2128–2169), or* COMMON OF PASTORS *(pp. 2170–2218), or from the* WEEKDAY MASS.

Liturgy of the Word: *from the* COMMON OF MARTYRS *(pp. 2147ff.), or* COMMON OF PASTORS *(pp. 2188ff.), especially 2 Cor 6:4–10; Ps 31:3cd–4, 6 and 8ab, 16bc and 17; Jn 10:11–16; or from the* WEEKDAY MASS.

Liturgy of the Eucharist, *p. 897.*

April 24

FIDELIS OF SIGMARINGEN, priest and martyr
(1578–1622)

Optional Memorial

This martyr is a witness to the tragic times of the Reformation, when Christians killed Christians in the name of religion. Born in Sigmaringen, Germany, Mark Roy became a Capuchin and changed his name to Fidelis. He showed himself charitable and zealous as superior of different monasteries. Sent on a preaching mission to Calvinists, Fidelis was killed in 1622 by Swiss fanatics. He was canonized in 1746.

Antiphons and Prayers: *from the* COMMON OF MARTYRS *(pp. 2128–2169), or from the* WEEKDAY MASS.

Opening Prayer

Father,
you filled St. Fidelis with the fire of your love
and gave him the privilege of dying
that the faith might live.
Let his prayers keep us firmly grounded in your love,
and help us to come to know the power of Christ's
resurrection.

We ask this through our Lord Jesus Christ, your Son,
who lives and reigns with you and the Holy Spirit,
one God, for ever and ever.

Liturgy of the Word: *from the* COMMON OF MARTYRS *(pp. 2147ff.), or* COMMON OF PASTORS *(pp. 2188ff.), especially Col 1:24–29; Ps 34:2–3, 4–5, 6–7, 8–9; Jn 17:20–26; or from the* WEEKDAY MASS.

Liturgy of the Eucharist, *p. 897.*

April 25

MARK, evangelist

Feast

Mark, or John Mark, was intimately associated with the development of the young Church. Born in Jerusalem, he accompanied Barnabas, Paul, and Peter in their apostolic labors. Mark was a helper to these stronger personalities. According to an ancient tradition, Mark's Gospel reflects his association with Peter. Considered founder of the Church of Alexandria in Egypt, Mark is specially honored by the Coptic Christians of that country.

Entrance Antiphon

Go out to the whole world, and preach the gospel to all creation, alleluia.

(Mk 16:15)

Opening Prayer

Father,
you gave St. Mark
the privilege of proclaiming your gospel.
May we profit by his wisdom
and follow Christ more faithfully.

Grant this through our Lord Jesus Christ, your Son,
who lives and reigns with you and the Holy Spirit,
one God, for ever and ever.

FIRST READING

1 Pt 5:5b–14

Mark, my son, sends you greetings.

A reading from the First Letter of Saint Peter

Beloved:

Clothe yourselves with humility in your dealings with one another, for:

> God opposes the proud
> but bestows favor on the humble.

So humble yourselves under the mighty hand of God, that he may exalt you in due time. Cast all your worries upon him because he cares for you.

Be sober and vigilant. Your opponent the Devil is prowling around like a roaring lion looking for someone to devour. Resist him, steadfast in faith, knowing that your brothers and sisters throughout the world undergo the same sufferings. The God of all grace who called you to his eternal glory through Christ Jesus will himself restore, confirm, strengthen, and establish you after you have suffered a little. To him be dominion forever. Amen.

I write you this briefly through Silvanus, whom I consider a faithful brother, exhorting you and testifying that this is the true grace of God. Remain firm in it. The chosen one at Babylon sends you greeting, as does Mark, my son. Greet one another with a loving kiss. Peace to all of you who are in Christ.

The word of the Lord.

Responsorial Psalm

Ps 89:2–3, 6–7, 16–17

R. For ever I will sing the goodness of the Lord.

The favors of the LORD I will sing forever;
  through all generations my mouth shall proclaim your
    faithfulness.

For you have said, "My kindness is established forever";
   in heaven you have confirmed your faithfulness.

R. For ever I will sing the goodness of the Lord.

The heavens proclaim your wonders, O LORD,
   and your faithfulness, in the assembly of the holy ones.
For who in the skies can rank with the LORD?
   Who is like the LORD among the sons of God?

R. For ever I will sing the goodness of the Lord.

Blessed the people who know the joyful shout;
   in the light of your countenance, O LORD, they walk.
At your name they rejoice all the day,
   and through your justice they are exalted.

R. For ever I will sing the goodness of the Lord.

Or: **R. Alleluia.**

> **Alleluia, alleluia** 1 Cor 1:23a–24b
> We proclaim Christ crucified;
> he is the power of God and the wisdom of God.
> **Alleluia, alleluia**

*See the Common of Pastors (**pp. 2188–2218**), for:*
   Gospel Mk 16:15–20

   Liturgy of the Eucharist, *p. 897.*

Prayer over the Gifts

Pray, brethren...

Lord,
as we offer the sacrifice of praise
on the feast of St. Mark,
we pray that your Church may always be faithful
to the preaching of the gospel.

We ask this through Christ our Lord.

   Preface of the Apostles II, *p. 956.*

Communion Antiphon

I, the Lord, am with you always, until the end of the world, alleluia.
(Mt 28:20)

Prayer after Communion

Let us pray.

Pause for silent prayer, if this has not preceded.

All-powerful God,
may the gifts we have received at this altar
make us holy, and strengthen us
in the faith of the gospel preached by St. Mark.
We ask this in the name of Jesus the Lord.

April 28

PETER CHANEL, priest and martyr (1803–1841)

Optional Memorial

The universal Church today honors the first martyr of Oceania. Born in France, Peter Chanel became a diocesan priest. He served selflessly as an assistant pastor, pastor, and seminary rector. In 1836, he joined the newly formed Society of Mary and was sent to Oceania. Misunderstanding and opposition made his work discouraging, but he found strength in prayer and the Eucharist. Finally, he converted the son of the king of Fotuna in Polynesia, and for that he was martyred.

Antiphons and Prayers: *from the* COMMON OF MARTYRS *(pp. 2128–2169), or* COMMON OF PASTORS: FOR MISSIONARIES *(pp. 2183–2187), or from the* WEEKDAY MASS. *The following is optional:*

Opening Prayer

Father,
you called St. Peter Chanel to work for your Church
and gave him the crown of martyrdom.

May our celebration of Christ's death and resurrection
make us faithful witnesses to the new life he brings,
for he lives and reigns with you and the Holy Spirit,
one God, for ever and ever.

Liturgy of the Word: *from the* COMMON OF MARTYRS *(pp. 2147ff.), or*
COMMON OF PASTORS: FOR MISSIONARIES *(pp. 2191ff.), especially 1 Cor 1:18–25;
Ps 117:1bc, 2; Mk 1:14–20; or from the* WEEKDAY MASS.

Liturgy of the Eucharist, *p. 897.*

Also on April 28

LOUIS MARY DE MONTFORT, priest (1673–1716)

Optional Memorial

Born in Montfort, France, Louis attended the Jesuit College in
Rennes. After ordination he became a hospital chaplain and later
began preaching as a traveling missionary. He founded a congregation of priests, the Missionaries of the Company of Mary, and one
of sisters, the Daughters of Wisdom. His book on Marian consecration, *True Devotion to Mary,* remains popular to this day.

Antiphons and Prayers: *from the* COMMON OF PASTORS: FOR MISSIONARIES
(pp. 2183–2187), or from the WEEKDAY MASS.

Liturgy of the Word: *from the* COMMON OF PASTORS: FOR MISSIONARIES
*(pp. 2191ff.), especially 1 Cor 1:18–25; Ps 40:2 and 4, 7–8a, 8b–9, 10;
Mt 28:16–20; or from the* WEEKDAY MASS.

Liturgy of the Eucharist, *p. 897.*

April 29

CATHERINE OF SIENA, virgin and doctor
(1347–1380)

Memorial

The child of hard-working parents, Catherine showed signs of
unusual sanctity from an early age. She joined the third Order of

Dominicans, became a spiritual guide to many, and influenced public affairs. She encouraged the pope to leave Avignon and return to Rome. A profound mystic, she dictated spiritual writings. She was declared a Doctor of the Church in 1970.

Entrance Antiphon

Here is a wise and faithful virgin who went with lighted lamp to meet her Lord, alleluia.

Opening Prayer

Father,
in meditating on the sufferings of your Son
and in serving your Church,
St. Catherine was filled with the fervor of your love.
By her prayers,
may we share in the mystery of Christ's death
and rejoice in the revelation of his glory,
for he lives and reigns with you and the Holy Spirit,
one God, for ever and ever.

Liturgy of the Word: *from the* COMMON OF VIRGINS *(pp. 2244ff.), especially 1 Jn 1:5–2:2; Ps 103:1–2, 3–4, 8–9, 13–14, 17–18; Mt 11:25–30; or from the* WEEKDAY MASS.

Liturgy of the Eucharist, *p. 897.*

Prayer over the Gifts

Pray, brethren...

Lord,
accept this saving sacrifice
we offer on the feast of St. Catherine.
By following her teaching and example,
may we offer more perfect praise to you.

Grant this through Christ our Lord.

Communion Antiphon

If we walk in the light, as God is in light, there is fellowship among us, and the blood of his Son, Jesus Christ, will cleanse us from all sin, alleluia. (1 Jn 1:7)

Prayer after Communion

Let us pray.

Pause for silent prayer, if this has not preceded.

Lord,
may the eucharist,
which nourished St. Catherine in this life,
bring us eternal life.

We ask this in the name of Jesus the Lord.

April 30

PIUS V, pope (1504–1572)

Optional Memorial

The pontificate of Pius V lasted only six years (1566–1577) but was of great importance. This Dominican pope reformed the Church and carried out the decrees of the Council of Trent. The catechism, breviary, and missal he promulgated set the norm for the Catholic Church until the Second Vatican Council.

Antiphons and Prayers: *from the* COMMON OF PASTORS: FOR POPES *(pp. 2170–2175), or from the* WEEKDAY MASS. *The following is optional:*

Opening Prayer

Father,
you chose St. Pius V as pope of your Church
to protect the faith
and give you more fitting worship.
By his prayers,

help us to celebrate your holy mysteries
with a living faith and an effective love.

We ask this through our Lord Jesus Christ, your Son,
who lives and reigns with you and the Holy Spirit,
one God, for ever and ever.

Liturgy of the Word: *from the* COMMON OF PASTORS: FOR A POPE *(pp. 2188ff.),*
especially 1 Cor 4:1–5; Ps 110:1, 2, 3, 4; Jn 21:15–17; or from the WEEKDAY
MASS.

Liturgy of the Eucharist, *p. 897.*

MAY

May 1

JOSEPH THE WORKER, foster father of Jesus

Feast

The first day of May—"May day"—has long been dedicated to
working people. When he instituted this feast in 1955, Pope Pius XII
expressed hope that it would emphasize the dignity of labor and
bring a spiritual dimension to labor unions and labor legislation. As
Pope John Paul II wrote: "At the workbench where he plied his
trade together with Jesus, Joseph brought human work closer to the
mystery of the redemption" *(Guardian of the Redeemer,* n. 22).

Entrance Antiphon

**Happy are all who fear the Lord and walk in his ways. You
shall enjoy the fruits of your labor, you will prosper and be happy,
alleluia.** (Ps 127:1–2)

Opening Prayer

God our Father,
creator and ruler of the universe,
in every age you call man
to develop and use his gifts for the good of others.
With St. Joseph as our example and guide,

help us to do the work you have asked
and come to the rewards you have promised.

We ask this through our Lord Jesus Christ, your Son,
who lives and reigns with you and the Holy Spirit,
one God, for ever and ever.

The Gospel for this memorial is proper.

FIRST READING

FIRST OPTION

Gn 1:26 — 2:3

Fill the earth and subdue it.

A reading from the Book of Genesis

God said: "Let us make man in our image, after our likeness.
Let them have dominion over the fish of the sea, the birds of
the air, and the cattle, and over all the wild animals and all the
creatures that crawl on the ground."
God created man in his image;
in the divine image he created him;
male and female he created them.

God blessed them, saying: "Be fertile and multiply; fill the
earth and subdue it. Have dominion over the fish of the sea,
the birds of the air, and all the living things that move on the
earth." God also said: "See, I give you every seed-bearing plant
all over the earth and every tree that has seed-bearing fruit on
it to be your food; and to all the animals of the land, all the
birds of the air, and all the living creatures that crawl on the
ground, I give all the green plants for food." And so it happened.
God looked at everything he had made, and he found it very
good. Evening came, and morning followed—the sixth day.

Thus the heavens and the earth and all their array were
completed. Since on the seventh day God was finished with

the work he had been doing, God rested on the seventh day from all the work he had undertaken. So God blessed the seventh day and made it holy, because on it he rested from all the work he had done in creation.

The word of the Lord.

Or:

SECOND OPTION Col 3:14–15, 17, 23–24

> *Whatever you do, do from the heart,*
> *as for the Lord and not for men.*

A reading from the Letter of Saint Paul to the Colossians

Brothers and sisters:

Over all these put on love, that is, the bond of perfection. And let the peace of Christ control your hearts, the peace into which you were also called in one body. And be thankful. And whatever you do, in word or in deed, do everything in the name of the Lord Jesus, giving thanks to God the Father through him.

Whatever you do, do from the heart, as for the Lord and not for men, knowing that you will receive from the Lord the due payment of the inheritance; be slaves of the Lord Christ.

The word of the Lord.

Responsorial Psalm Ps 90:2, 3–4, 12–13, 14 and 16

R. Lord, give success to the work of our hands.

Before the mountains were begotten
  and the earth and the world were brought forth,
  from everlasting to everlasting you are God.

R. Lord, give success to the work of our hands.

You turn men back to dust,
  saying, "Return, O children of men."

For a thousand years in your sight
  are as yesterday, now that it is past,
  or as a watch of the night.

  R. Lord, give success to the work of our hands.

Teach us to number our days aright,
  that we may gain wisdom of heart.
Return, O Lord! How long?
  Have pity on your servants!

  R. Lord, give success to the work of our hands.

Fill us at daybreak with your kindness,
  that we may shout for joy and gladness all our days.
Let your work be seen by your servants
  and your glory by their children.

  R. Lord, give success to the work of our hands.

  Or: **R. Alleluia.**

  Alleluia, alleluia Ps 68:20
  Blessed be the Lord day by day,
  God, our salvation, who bears our burdens.
  Alleluia, alleluia

GOSPEL   Mt 13:54–58

Is he not the carpenter's son?
Where did this man get such wisdom and mighty deeds?

A reading from the holy Gospel according to Matthew

Jesus came to his native place and taught the people in their synagogue. They were astonished and said, "Where did this man get such wisdom and mighty deeds? Is he not the carpenter's son? Is not his mother named Mary and his brothers James, Joseph, Simon, and Judas? Are not his sisters all with us? Where did this man get all this?" And they took offense at him. But Jesus said to them, "A prophet is not without honor except in his native place and in his own house." And he did not work many mighty deeds there because of their lack of faith.

The Gospel of the Lord.

> **Liturgy of the Eucharist,** *p. 897.*

Prayer over the Gifts

Pray, brethren...

Lord God,
fountain of all mercy,
look upon our gifts on this feast of St. Joseph.
Let our sacrifice
become the protection of all who call on you.

We ask this in the name of Jesus the Lord.

> **Preface of Joseph, husband of Mary,** *p.955.*

Communion Antiphon

Let everything you do or say be in the name of the Lord with thanksgiving to God, alleluia.   (Col 3:17)

Prayer after Communion

Let us pray.

> *Pause for silent prayer, if this has not preceded.*

Lord,
hear the prayers of those you nourish in this eucharist.
Inspired by the example of St. Joseph,
may our lives manifest your love;
may we rejoice for ever in your peace.

Grant this through Christ our Lord.

May 2

ATHANASIUS, bishop and doctor (295–373)

Memorial

Athanasius was an important defender of the faith against Arianism. This heresy, which originated from a priest of Alexandria named Arius, denied Christ's divinity and spread widely even after being condemned by the Council of Nicea (325). As bishop of Alexandria for 45 years (328–373), Athanasius suffered exile five times. He remained an intrepid writer and champion of faith in Jesus Christ, true God and true man.

Antiphons and Prayers: *from the* COMMON OF PASTORS: FOR BISHOPS *(pp. 2170–2175), or* COMMON OF DOCTORS OF THE CHURCH *(pp. 2219–2238), or from the* WEEKDAY MASS, *except:*

Opening Prayer

Father,
you raised up St. Athanasius
to be an outstanding defender
of the truth of Christ's divinity.
By his teaching and protection
may we grow in your knowledge and love.

Grant this through our Lord Jesus Christ, your Son,
who lives and reigns with you and the Holy Spirit,
one God, for ever and ever.

Liturgy of the Word: *from the* COMMON OF PASTORS *(pp. 2188ff.), or* COMMON OF DOCTORS OF THE CHURCH *(pp. 2222ff.), especially 1 Jn 5:1–5; Ps 37:3–4, 5–6, 30–31; or from the* WEEKDAY MASS.

GOSPEL

Mt 10:22–25

When they persecute you in one town, flee to another.

A reading from the holy Gospel according to Matthew

Jesus said to the Twelve: "You will be hated by all because of my name, but whoever endures to the end will be saved. When they persecute you in one town, flee to another. Amen, I say to you, you will not finish the towns of Israel before the Son of Man comes. No disciple is above his teacher, no slave above his master. It is enough for the disciple that he become like the teacher, and the slave that he become like the master. If they have called the master of the house Beelzebub, how much more those of his household!"

The Gospel of the Lord.

Liturgy of the Eucharist, *p. 897.*

Prayer over the Gifts

Pray, brethren...

Lord,
look upon the gifts we offer
on the feast of St. Athanasius.
Keep us true to the faith he professed
and let our own witness to your truth
bring us closer to salvation.
We ask this through Christ our Lord.

Prayer after Communion

Let us pray.

Pause for silent prayer, if this has not preceded.

All-powerful God,
we join St. Athanasius in professing our belief
in the true divinity of Christ your Son.
Through this sacrament
may our faith always give us life and protection.
We ask this through Christ our Lord.

May 3

PHILIP and JAMES, apostles

Feast

In Rome, the Church of the Twelve Apostles has relics of these two apostles under its main altar. For this reason they are honored together on this day, the date of the Church's dedication in 565. Philip came from Bethsaida on the shore of the Lake of Galilee. James the Less, son of Alphaeus, is distinguished from the other apostle James, son of Zebedee and brother of John.

Entrance Antiphon

The Lord chose these holy men for their unfeigned love, and gave them eternal glory, alleluia.

Opening Prayer

God our Father,
every year you give us joy
on the festival of the apostles Philip and James.
By the help of their prayers
may we share in the suffering, death, and resurrection
of your only Son
and come to the eternal vision of your glory.

We ask this through our Lord Jesus Christ, your Son,
who lives and reigns with you and the Holy Spirit,
one God, for ever and ever.

FIRST READING

1 Cor 15:1–8

After that he appeared to James, then to all the Apostles.

A reading from the first Letter of Saint Paul to the Corinthians

I am reminding you, brothers and sisters, of the Gospel I preached to you, which you indeed received and in which you also stand. Through it you are also being saved, if you hold fast to the word I preached to you, unless you believed in vain.

For I handed on to you as of first importance what I also received: that Christ died for our sins in accordance with the Scriptures; that he was buried; that he was raised on the third day in accordance with the Scriptures; that he appeared to Cephas, then to the Twelve. After that, he appeared to more than five hundred brothers and sisters at once, most of whom are still living, though some have fallen asleep. After that he appeared to James, then to all the Apostles. Last of all, as to one born abnormally, he appeared to me.

The word of the Lord.

Responsorial Psalm

Ps 19:2–3, 4–5

R. Their message goes out through all the earth.

The heavens declare the glory of God;
  and the firmament proclaims his handiwork.
Day pours out the word to day;
  and night to night imparts knowledge.

R. Their message goes out through all the earth.

Not a word nor a discourse
  whose voice is not heard;
Through all the earth their voice resounds,
  and to the ends of the world, their message.

R. Their message goes out through all the earth.

Or: **R. Alleluia.**

Alleluia, alleluia Jn 14:6b, 9c
I am the way, the truth, and the life, says the Lord;
Philip, whoever has seen me has seen the Father.
Alleluia, alleluia

GOSPEL

Jn 14:6–14

Have I been with you so long and you still do not know me?

A reading from the holy Gospel according to John

Jesus said to Thomas, "I am the way and the truth and the life. No one comes to the Father except through me. If you know me, then you will also know my Father. From now on you do know him and have seen him." Philip said to him, "Master, show us the Father, and that will be enough for us." Jesus said to him, "Have I been with you for so long a time and you still do not know me, Philip? Whoever has seen me has seen the Father. How can you say, 'Show us the Father'? Do you not believe that I am in the Father and the Father is in me? The words that I speak to you I do not speak on my own. The Father who dwells in me is doing his works. Believe me that I am in the Father and the Father is in me, or else, believe because of the works themselves. Amen, amen, I say to you, whoever believes in me will do the works that I do, and will do greater ones than these, because I am going to the Father. And whatever you ask in my name, I will do, so that the Father may be glorified in the Son. If you ask anything of me in my name, I will do it."

The Gospel of the Lord.

Liturgy of the Eucharist, *p. 897.*

Prayer over the Gifts

Pray, brethren...

Lord,
accept our gifts
at this celebration in honor of the apostles Philip and James.
Make our religion pure and undefiled.

We ask this through Christ our Lord.

Preface of the Apostles I *or* **II,** *p.956.*

Communion Antiphon

Lord, let us see the Father, and we shall be content. And Jesus said: Philip, he who sees me, sees the Father, alleluia.

(Jn 14:8–9)

Prayer after Communion

Let us pray.

Pause for silent prayer, if this has not preceded.

Father,
by the holy gifts we have received
free our minds and hearts from sin.
With the apostles Philip and James
may we see you in your Son
and be found worthy to have eternal life.

We ask this through Christ our Lord.

May 10

[In the dioceses of the United States]

BLESSED DAMIEN JOSEPH DE VEUSTER
OF MOLOKA'I, priest (1840–1889)

Optional Memorial

Joseph de Veuster entered the Congregation of the Sacred Hearts of Jesus and Mary in 1860. He left his homeland in Belgium for the missions in Hawaii, where he was ordained. Fr. Damien obtained permission to minister to the lepers on the island of Moloka'i, where he spent the rest of his life. He eventually contracted leprosy but continued his ministry among the lepers until his death.

Antiphons and Prayers: *from the* COMMON OF PASTORS *(pp. 2170–2218), or* COMMON OF HOLY MEN AND WOMEN *(pp. 2252–2322),.; or from the* WEEKDAY MASS.

Liturgy of the Word: *from the* COMMON OF PASTORS *(pp. 2188ff.), or* COMMON OF HOLY MEN AND WOMEN *(pp. 2269ff.).*

Liturgy of the Eucharist, *p. 897.*

May 12

NEREUS and ACHILLEUS, martyrs (†c. 304)

Optional Memorial

A church honoring these two saints was constructed in Rome in the sixth century. Although we know little about them, tradition holds that Nereus and Achilleus were recently baptized soldiers who died courageously for Christ. Their heroic witness inspires us as we live our faith amid the challenges of the modern world.

Antiphons and Prayers: *from the* COMMON OF MARTYRS *(pp.2128–2169), or from the* WEEKDAY MASS. *The following is optional:*

Opening Prayer

Father,
we honor Saints Nereus and Achilleus for their courage
in dying to profess their faith in Christ.
May we experience the help of their prayers
at the throne of your mercy.

Grant this through our Lord Jesus Christ, your Son,
who lives and reigns with you and the Holy Spirit,
one God, for ever and ever.

Liturgy of the Word: *from the* COMMON OF MARTYRS *(pp. 2147ff.), especially Rv 7:9–17; Ps 124:2–3, 4–5, 7–8; Mt 10:17–22; or from the* WEEKDAY MASS.

Liturgy of the Eucharist, *p. 897.*

Also on May 12

PANCRAS, martyr († c. 304)

Optional Memorial

Pancras (or Pancratius) suffered martyrdom during the persecution of Diocletian, perhaps at the same time as Nereus and Achilleus. A boy of only fourteen years, Pancras courageously sacrificed his young life for Jesus Christ. Similar to Agnes, he has been an inspiration to youthful followers of Christ through the centuries.

Antiphons and Prayers: *from the* COMMON OF MARTYRS *(pp. 2128–2169), or from the* WEEKDAY MASS. *The following is optional:*

Opening Prayer

God of mercy,
give your Church joy and confidence
through the prayers of St. Pancras.
Keep us faithful to you
and steadfast in your service.

We ask this through our Lord Jesus Christ, your Son,
who lives and reigns with you and the Holy Spirit,
one God, for ever and ever.

Liturgy of the Word: *from the* COMMON OF MARTYRS *(pp. 2147ff.), especially Rv 19:1, 5–9a; Ps 103:1–2, 3–4, 8–9, 13–14, 17–18; Mt 11:25–30; or from the* WEEKDAY MASS.

Liturgy of the Eucharist, p. 897.

May 14

MATTHIAS, apostle

Feast

We know little about St. Matthias except that he was elected as an apostle to replace Judas. Tradition holds that he was martyred after preaching the Gospel. Today's feast invites us to reflect on the meaning of apostolicity in the Church.

Entrance Antiphon

You have not chosen me; I have chosen you. Go and bear fruit that will last, alleluia.
(Jn 15:16)

Opening Prayer

Father,
you called St. Matthias to share in the mission of the apostles.
By the help of his prayers

may we receive with joy the love you share with us
and be counted among those you have chosen.

We ask this through our Lord Jesus Christ, your Son,
who lives and reigns with you and the Holy Spirit,
one God, for ever and ever.

FIRST READING

Acts 1:15–17, 20–26

*The lot fell upon Matthias, and he was counted
with the Eleven Apostles.*

A reading from the Acts of the Apostles

Peter stood up in the midst of the brothers and sisters (there
was a group of about one hundred and twenty persons in the
one place). He said, "My brothers and sisters, the Scripture
had to be fulfilled which the Holy Spirit spoke beforehand
through the mouth of David, concerning Judas, who was the
guide for those who arrested Jesus. Judas was numbered among
us and was allotted a share in this ministry. For it is written in
the Book of Psalms:

> *Let his encampment become desolate,*
> *and may no one dwell in it.*

and:

> *May another take his office.*

Therefore, it is necessary that one of the men who accompanied
us the whole time the Lord Jesus came and went among us,
beginning from the baptism of John until the day on which he
was taken up from us, become with us a witness to his
resurrection." So they proposed two, Joseph called Barsabbas,
who was also known as Justus, and Matthias. Then they prayed,
"You, Lord, who know the hearts of all, show which one of
these two you have chosen to take the place in this apostolic

ministry from which Judas turned away to go to his own place."
Then they gave lots to them, and the lot fell upon Matthias,
and he was counted with the Eleven Apostles.

The word of the Lord.

Responsorial Psalm

Ps 113:1–2, 3–4, 5–6, 7–8

R. **The Lord will give him a seat with the leaders**
of his people.

Praise, you servants of the LORD,
  praise the name of the LORD.
Blessed be the name of the LORD
  both now and forever.

R. **The Lord will give him a seat with the leaders**
of his people.

From the rising to the setting of the sun
  is the name of the LORD to be praised.
High above all nations is the LORD;
  above the heavens is his glory.

R. **The Lord will give him a seat with the leaders**
of his people.

Who is like the LORD, our God, who is enthroned on high
  and looks upon the heavens and the earth below?

R. **The Lord will give him a seat with the leaders**
of his people.

He raises up the lowly from the dust;
  from the dunghill he lifts up the poor
To set them with princes,
  with the princes of his own people.

R. **The Lord will give him a seat with the leaders**
of his people.

Or: R. **Alleluia.**

Alleluia, alleluia see Jn 15:16
I chose you from the world,
to go and bear fruit that will last, says the Lord.
Alleluia, alleluia

GOSPEL

Jn 15:9–17

I no longer call you slaves; I have called you friends.

A reading from the holy Gospel according to John

Jesus said to his disciples: "As the Father loves me, so I also love you. Remain in my love. If you keep my commandments, you will remain in my love, just as I have kept my Father's commandments and remain in his love.

"I have told you this so that my joy might be in you and your joy might be complete. This is my commandment: love one another as I love you. No one has greater love than this, to lay down one's life for one's friends. You are my friends if you do what I command you. I no longer call you slaves, because a slave does not know what his master is doing. I have called you friends, because I have told you everything I have heard from my Father. It was not you who chose me, but I who chose you and appointed you to go and bear fruit that will remain, so that whatever you ask the Father in my name he may give you. This I command you: love one another."

The Gospel of the Lord.

Liturgy of the Eucharist, *p. 897.*

Prayer over the Gifts

Pray, brethren...
Lord,
accept the gifts your Church offers
on the feast of the apostle, Matthias,

and by this eucharist
strengthen your grace within us.
We ask this through Christ our Lord.

Preface of the Apostles I *or* **II,** *p. 956*

Communion Antiphon

This is my commandment: love one another as I have loved
you.   (Jn 15:12)

Prayer after Communion

Let us pray.

Pause for silent prayer, if this has not preceded.

Lord,
you constantly give life to your people
in this holy eucharist.
By the prayers of the apostle Matthias
prepare us to take our place
among your saints in eternal life.
We ask this through Christ our Lord.

May 15

[In the dioceses of the United States]

ISIDORE, farmer (1070–1130)

Optional Memorial

The United States, with its rural traditions and farm life, today
honors St. Isidore the Farmer. Born at Madrid, Spain, Isidore spent
his life as a farm worker. His wife Maria was also a saint. Isidore
became a legend because of his devotion and miracles. Canonized
in 1622, Isidore is the patron of the National Catholic Rural Life
Conference.

Antiphons and Prayers: *from the* COMMON OF HOLY MEN AND WOMEN
(pp. 2252–2322), or from the WEEKDAY MASS. *The following is optional:*

Opening Prayer

Lord God,
all creation is yours, and you call us to serve you
by caring for the gifts that surround us.
May the example of St. Isidore urge us
to share our food with the hungry
and to work for the salvation of mankind.

We ask this through our Lord Jesus Christ, your Son,
who lives and reigns with you and the Holy Spirit,
one God, for ever and ever.

Liturgy of the Word: *from the* COMMON OF HOLY MEN AND WOMEN
(pp. 2269ff.), or from the WEEKDAY MASS.

Liturgy of the Eucharist, *p. 897.*

May 18

JOHN I, pope and martyr (†526)

Optional Memorial

In his short pontificate (523–526), John convoked the Council of
Orange, fixed the date of Easter, and promoted Roman chant. The
Arian king Theodoric forced John to travel to Constantinople, and
upon his return imprisoned him. John died of starvation at the prison
in Ravenna.

Antiphons and Prayers: *from the* COMMON OF MARTYRS *(pp. 2128–2322),
or from the* COMMON OF PASTORS: FOR POPES *(pp.2170–2175), or from the*
WEEKDAY MASS. *The following is optional:*

Opening Prayer

God our Father,
rewarder of all who believe,
hear our prayers
as we celebrate the martyrdom of Pope John.
Help us to follow him in loyalty to the faith.

Grant this through our Lord Jesus Christ, your Son,
who lives and reigns with you and the Holy Spirit,
one God, for ever and ever.

Liturgy of the Word: *from the* COMMON OF MARTYRS *(pp. 2147ff.), or* COMMON OF PASTORS: FOR A POPE *(pp. 2188ff.), especially Rv 3:14b, 20–22; Ps 23:1–3a, 4, 5, 6; Lk 22:24–30; or from the* WEEKDAY MASS.

Liturgy of the Eucharist, *p. 897.*

May 20

BERNARDINE OF SIENA, priest (1380–1444)

Optional Memorial

Orphaned at a young age, Bernardine became a Franciscan and an itinerant preacher. At that troubled time, Europe was devastated by war, and deep divisions and problems racked the Church. From northern Italy to Rome, Bernardine preached the loving mercy of God and promoted devotion to the Holy Name of Jesus. When he preached, the letters IHS (*Iesus Hominum Salvator*—Jesus, Savior of humanity) were painted on signs and on nearby buildings.

Antiphons and Prayers: *from the* COMMON OF PASTORS: FOR MISSIONARIES *(pp. 2183–2187), or from the* WEEKDAY MASS. *The following is optional:*

Opening Prayer

Father,
you gave St. Bernardine a special love
for the holy name of Jesus.
By the help of his prayers,
may we always be alive with the spirit of your love.

We ask this through our Lord Jesus Christ, your Son,
who lives and reigns with you and the Holy Spirit,
one God, for ever and ever.

Liturgy of the Word: *from the* COMMON OF PASTORS: FOR MISSIONARIES *(pp. 2191ff.), or from the* WEEKDAY MASS.

FIRST READING

Acts 4:8–12

There is no salvation through anyone else.

A reading from the Acts of the Apostles

Peter, filled with the Holy Spirit, answered them: "Leaders of the people and elders: If we are being examined today about a good deed done to a cripple, namely, by what means he was saved, then all of you and all the people of Israel should know that it was in the name of Jesus Christ the Nazorean whom you crucified, whom God raised from the dead; in his name this man stands before you healed. He is the stone rejected by you, the builders, which has become the cornerstone. There is no salvation through anyone else, nor is there any other name under heaven given to the human race by which we are to be saved."

The word of the Lord.

Responsorial Psalm

Ps 40:2, 4, 7–8, 8–9, 10, 11

R. Here am I, Lord; I come to do your will.

I have waited, waited for the LORD,
  and he stooped toward me and heard my cry.
And he put a new song into my mouth,
  a hymn to our God.

R. Here am I, Lord; I come to do your will.

Sacrifice or oblation you wished not,
  but ears open to obedience you gave me.
Burnt offerings or sin-offerings you sought not;
  then said I, "Behold I come."

R. Here am I, Lord; I come to do your will.

"In the written scroll it is prescribed for me,
To do your will, O my God, is my delight,
  and your law is within my heart!"

R. Here am I, Lord; I come to do your will.

I announced your justice in the vast assembly;
  I did not restrain my lips, as you, O LORD, know.

R. Here am I, Lord; I come to do your will.

Your justice I kept not hid within my heart;
  your faithfulness and your salvation I have spoken of;
I have made no secret of your kindness and your truth
  in the vast assembly.

R. Here am I, Lord; I come to do your will.

See the Common of Holy Men and Women (pp. 2269–2322), for:
  Gospel Lk 9:57–62

  Liturgy of the Eucharist, *p. 897.*

May 25

VENERABLE BEDE, priest and doctor (672/3–735)

Optional Memorial

As an Englishman, today's saint is especially honored in English-speaking countries. He was a remarkable Benedictine who combined contemplation and learning. Spending his life in the monastery, Bede wrote much and is considered the Father of English History. Bede is the only Englishman to have been named a Doctor of the Church.

Antiphons and Prayers: *from the* COMMON OF DOCTORS OF THE CHURCH (pp. 2219–2238), *or* COMMON OF HOLY MEN AND WOMEN: FOR RELIGIOUS (pp. 2260–2263), *or from the* WEEKDAY MASS. *The following is optional:*

Opening Prayer

Lord,
you have enlightened your Church
with the learning of St. Bede.
In your love
may your people learn from his wisdom
and benefit from his prayers.

Grant this through our Lord Jesus Christ, your Son,
who lives and reigns with you and the Holy Spirit,
one God, for ever and ever.

Liturgy of the Word: *from the* COMMON OF PASTORS *(pp. 2188ff.), or* COMMON OF DOCTORS OF THE CHURCH *(pp. 2222ff.), especially 1 Cor 2:10b–16; Ps 119:9, 10, 11, 12, 13, 14; Mt 7:21–29; or from the* WEEKDAY MASS.

Liturgy of the Eucharist, *p. 897.*

Also on May 25

GREGORY VII, pope (1020–1085)

Optional Memorial

Gregory was one of the most important popes of the Middle Ages. He lived in turbulent times when ambitious emperors wanted to take over the Church and when the Church itself was divided and weak. As the Benedictine monk Hildebrand, Gregory was active in reforming the Church. As pope (1073–1085) he strove to eliminate simony, lay investiture, and immorality among the clergy. This brought him into conflict with the emperor Henry IV, whom Gregory excommunicated. When Henry tried to depose him and set up an anti-pope, Gregory was forced into exile in Salerno, where he died.

Antiphons and Prayers: *from the* COMMON OF PASTORS: FOR POPES *(pp. 2170–2175), or from the* WEEKDAY MASS. *The following is optional:*

Opening Prayer

Lord,
give your Church
the spirit of courage and love for justice
which distinguished Pope Gregory.
Make us courageous in condemning evil
and free us to pursue justice with love.

We ask this through our Lord Jesus Christ, your Son,
who lives and reigns with you and the Holy Spirit,
one God, for ever and ever.

Liturgy of the Word: *from the* COMMON OF PASTORS: FOR A POPE *(pp. 2188ff.)*, *especially* Acts 20:17–18a, 28–32, 36; Ps 110:1, 2, 3, 4; Mt 16:13–19; *or from the* WEEKDAY MASS.

Liturgy of the Eucharist, *p. 897.*

Also on May 25

MARY MAGDALENE DE PAZZI, virgin (1566–1607)

Optional Memorial

Born in Florence, Italy, Catherine de Pazzi entered a cloistered Carmelite convent at the age of 16 and took the name Mary Magdalene. She overcame profound difficulties, was given special graces of mystical prayer and had ecstasies and revelations. Living in the difficult time after the Reformation, she wrote to Church officials urging them to implement reforms. She was canonized in 1669.

Antiphons and Prayers: *from the* COMMON OF VIRGINS *(pp. 2238–2252), or* COMMON OF HOLY MEN AND WOMEN: FOR RELIGIOUS *(pp. 2260–2263), or from the* WEEKDAY MASS. *The following is optional:*

Opening Prayer

Father,
you love those who give themselves completely to your
  service
and you filled St. Mary Magdalene de Pazzi
with heavenly gifts and the fire of your love.
As we honor her today
may we follow her example of purity and charity.

Grant this through our Lord Jesus Christ, your Son,
who lives and reigns with you and the Holy Spirit,
one God, for ever and ever.

Liturgy of the Word: *from the* COMMON OF VIRGINS *(pp. 2244ff.), or* COMMON OF HOLY MEN AND WOMEN: FOR RELIGIOUS *(pp. 2271ff.), especially* 1 Cor 7:25–35; Ps 148:1–2, 11–13, 13–14; Mk 3:31–35; *or from the* WEEKDAY MASS.

Liturgy of the Eucharist, *p. 897.*

May 26

PHILIP NERI, priest (1515–1595)

Memorial

Today we honor the "saint of joy," the delightful Philip Neri who was gifted with a special sense of humor. Born in Florence, Philip came to Rome at age 26 and never left the Eternal City. Rome, occupied and sacked in 1527, was in pitiable condition. Philip visited the sick and imprisoned, taught children, and heard confessions. He founded the Oratorio of Divine Love—the Oratorian priests. He was canonized in 1622.

Antiphons and Prayers: *from the* COMMON OF PASTORS *(pp. 2170–2218), or* COMMON OF HOLY MEN AND WOMEN: FOR RELIGIOUS *(pp. 2260–2263), or from the* WEEKDAY MASS, *except:*

Opening Prayer

Father,
you continually raise up your faithful
to the glory of holiness.
In your love
kindle in us the fire of the Holy Spirit
who so filled the heart of Philip Neri.

We ask this through our Lord Jesus Christ, your Son,
who lives and reigns with you and the Holy Spirit,
one God, for ever and ever.

Liturgy of the Word: *from the* COMMON OF PASTORS *(pp. 2188ff.), or* COMMON OF HOLY MEN AND WOMEN: FOR RELIGIOUS *(pp. 2271ff.), especially Phil 4:4–9; Ps 34:2–3, 4–5, 6–7, 8–9, 10–11; Jn 17:20–26; or from the* WEEKDAY MASS.

Liturgy of the Eucharist, p. 897.

Prayer over the Gifts

Pray, brethren...

Lord,
help us who offer you this sacrifice of praise

to follow the example of St. Philip.
Keep us always cheerful in our work
for the glory of your name and the good of our neighbor.

Grant this through Christ our Lord.

Prayer after Communion

Let us pray.
Pause for silent prayer, if this has not preceded.

Lord,
strengthen us with the bread of life.
May we always imitate St. Philip
by hungering after this sacrament
in which we find true life.

We ask this in the name of Jesus the Lord.

May 27

AUGUSTINE OF CANTERBURY, bishop († 604/5)

Optional Memorial

In 596, Pope Gregory the Great sent a group of monks as missionaries to the Saxons in England, and appointed Augustine as superior. Despite difficulties, the mission produced excellent results, with many conversions. Augustine became the first Archbishop of Canterbury and organized the Roman Catholic Church in England.

Antiphons and Prayers: *from the* COMMON OF PASTORS: FOR MISSIONARIES *or* FOR BISHOPS *(pp. 2170–2218), or from the* WEEKDAY MASS. *The following is optional:*

Opening Prayer

Father,
by the preaching of St. Augustine of Canterbury,
you led the people of England to the gospel.
May the fruits of his work continue in your Church.

Grant this through our Lord Jesus Christ, your Son,
who lives and reigns with you and the Holy Spirit,
one God, for ever and ever.

Liturgy of the Word: *from the* COMMON OF PASTORS: FOR MISSIONARIES
*(pp. 2191ff.), especially 1 Thes 2:2b–8; Ps 96:1–2a, 2b–3, 7–8a, 10; Mt 9:35–38;
or from the* WEEKDAY MASS.

Liturgy of the Eucharist, *p. 897.*

May 31

VISITATION OF THE BLESSED VIRGIN MARY

Feast

"[In Elizabeth's expression] 'Blessed is she who believed,' we
can therefore rightly find a kind of 'key' which unlocks for us the innermost reality of Mary, whom the angel hailed as 'full of grace.' If
as 'full of grace' she has been eternally present in the mystery of
Christ, through faith she became a sharer in that mystery in
every extension of her earthly journey. She 'advanced in her pilgrimage
of faith' and at the same time, in a discreet yet direct and effective
way, she made present to humanity the mystery of Christ. And she
still continues to do so. Through the mystery of Christ, she too is
present within mankind. Thus through the mystery of the Son the
mystery of the Mother is also made clear" (Pope John Paul II, *Mother
of the Redeemer,* n. 19).

Entrance Antiphon

**Come, all you who fear God, and hear the great things the
Lᴏʀᴅ has done for me.**   (Ps 65:16)

Opening Prayer

Eternal Father,
you inspired the Virgin Mary, mother of your Son,
to visit Elizabeth and assist her in her need.
Keep us open to the working of your Spirit,
and with Mary may we praise you for ever.

We ask this through our Lord Jesus Christ, your Son,
who lives and reigns with you and the Holy Spirit,
one God, for ever and ever.

FIRST READING

FIRST OPTION

Zep 3:14–18a

The King of Israel, the Lord, is in your midst.

A reading from the Book of the Prophet Zephaniah

Shout for joy, O daughter Zion!
Sing joyfully, O Israel!
Be glad and exult with all your heart,
O daughter Jerusalem!
The LORD has removed the judgment against you,
he has turned away your enemies;
The King of Israel, the LORD, is in your midst,
you have no further misfortune to fear.
On that day, it shall be said to Jerusalem:
Fear not, O Zion, be not discouraged!
The LORD, your God, is in your midst,
a mighty savior;
He will rejoice over you with gladness,
and renew you in his love,
He will sing joyfully because of you,
as one sings at festivals.

The word of the Lord.

Or:

SECOND OPTION

Rom 12:9–16

Contribute to the needs of the holy ones, exercise hospitality.

A reading from the Letter of Saint Paul to the Romans

Brothers and sisters:

Let love be sincere; hate what is evil, hold on to what is good; love one another with mutual affection; anticipate one another in showing honor. Do not grow slack in zeal, be fervent in spirit, serve the Lord. Rejoice in hope, endure in affliction, persevere in prayer. Contribute to the needs of the holy ones, exercise hospitality. Bless those who persecute you, bless and do not curse them. Rejoice with those who rejoice, weep with those who weep. Have the same regard for one another; do not be haughty but associate with the lowly; do not be wise in your own estimation.

The word of the Lord.

Responsorial Psalm

Is 12:2–3, 4bcd, 5–6

R. Among you is the great and Holy One of Israel.

God indeed is my savior;
  I am confident and unafraid.
My strength and my courage is the LORD,
  and he has been my savior.
With joy you will draw water
  at the fountain of salvation.

R. Among you is the great and Holy One of Israel.

Give thanks to the LORD, acclaim his name;
  among the nations make known his deeds,
  proclaim how exalted is his name.

R. Among you is the great and Holy One of Israel.

Sing praise to the LORD for his glorious achievement;
  let this be known throughout all the earth.
Shout with exultation, O city of Zion,
  for great in your midst
  is the Holy One of Israel!

R. Among you is the great and Holy One of Israel.

Alleluia, alleluia   See Lk 1:45
Blessed are you, O Virgin Mary, who believed
that what was spoken to you by the Lord would be fulfilled.
Alleluia, alleluia

GOSPEL

Lk 1:39–56

And how does this happen to me,
that the mother of my Lord should come to me?

A reading from the holy Gospel according to Luke

Mary set out and traveled to the hill country in haste to a town
of Judah, where she entered the house of Zechariah and greeted
Elizabeth. When Elizabeth heard Mary's greeting, the infant
leaped in her womb, and Elizabeth, filled with the Holy Spirit, cried out in a loud voice and said, "Most blessed are you
among women, and blessed is the fruit of your womb. And
how does this happen to me, that the mother of my Lord should
come to me? For at the moment the sound of your greeting
reached my ears, the infant in my womb leaped for joy. Blessed
are you who believed that what was spoken to you by the Lord
would be fulfilled."

And Mary said:

"My soul proclaims the greatness of the Lord;
    my spirit rejoices in God my Savior,
        for he has looked with favor on his lowly servant.
From this day all generations will call me blessed:
    the Almighty has done great things for me,
        and holy is his Name.
He has mercy on those who fear him
    in every generation.
He has shown the strength of his arm,
    he has scattered the proud in their conceit.

He has cast down the mighty from their thrones,
    and has lifted up the lowly.
He has filled the hungry with good things,
    and the rich he has sent away empty.
He has come to the help of his servant Israel
    for he has remembered his promise of mercy,
    the promise he made to our fathers,
    to Abraham and his children for ever."

Mary remained with her about three months and then returned to her home.

The Gospel of the Lord.

Liturgy of the Eucharist, *p. 897*.

Prayer over the Gifts

Pray, brethren...

Father,
make our sacrifice acceptable and holy
as you accepted the love of Mary,
the mother of your Son, Jesus Christ,
who is Lord for ever and ever.

Preface of the Blessed Virgin Mary I *or* **II**, *p. 953*.

Communion Antiphon

All generations will call me blessed, for the Almighty has done great things for me. Holy is his name. (Lk 1:48–49)

Prayer after Communion

Let us pray.

Pause for silent prayer, if this has not preceded.

Lord,
let the Church praise you

for the great things you have done for your people.
May we always recognize with joy
the presence of Christ in the eucharist we celebrate,
as John the Baptist hailed the presence
of our Savior in the womb of Mary.
We ask this through Christ our Lord.

SATURDAY FOLLOWING THE SECOND SUNDAY
AFTER PENTECOST OR CORPUS CHRISTI

IMMACULATE HEART OF MARY

Memorial

Devotion to the Immaculate Heart of Mary began as early as the twelfth century. During the seventh century in France, St. John Eudes popularized this devotion along with that of the Sacred Heart devotion. Luke's Gospel twice mentions that Mary "kept all these things in her heart" (Lk 2:51; 2:19), pondering the word of God. The opening prayer for today's Mass speaks of Mary's heart as a home for the Holy Spirit. Mary shows us how to listen to the words the Holy Spirit speaks to us in the depths of our hearts, and to respond in faith.

The Gospel for this memorial is proper.

Entrance Antiphon

My heart rejoices in your saving power. I will sing to the Lord for his goodness to me. (Ps 12:6)

Opening Prayer

Father,
you prepared the heart of the Virgin Mary
to be a fitting home for your Holy Spirit.
By her prayers
may we become a more worthy temple of your glory.

Grant this through our Lord Jesus Christ, your Son,
who lives and reigns with you and the Holy Spirit,
one God, for ever and ever.

Liturgy of the Word: *from the* COMMON OF THE BLESSED VIRGIN MARY *(pp. 2101ff.), especially Is 61:9–11; 1 Sm 2:1, 4–5, 6–7, 8abcd.*

GOSPEL

Lk 2:41–51

Your father and I have been looking for you.

A reading from the holy Gospel according to Luke

Each year Jesus' parents went to Jerusalem for the feast of Passover, and when he was twelve years old, they went up according to festival custom. After they had completed its days, as they were returning, the boy Jesus remained behind in Jerusalem, but his parents did not know it. Thinking that he was in the caravan, they journeyed for a day and looked for him among their relatives and acquaintances, but not finding him, they returned to Jerusalem to look for him. After three days they found him in the temple, sitting in the midst of the teachers, listening to them and asking them questions, and all who heard him were astounded at his understanding and his answers. When his parents saw him, they were astonished, and his mother said to him, "Son, why have you done this to us? Your father and I have been looking for you with great anxiety." And he said to them, "Why were you looking for me? Did you not know that I must be in my Father's house?" But they did not understand what he said to them. He went down with them and came to Nazareth, and was obedient to them; and his mother kept all these things in her heart.

The Gospel of the Lord.

Liturgy of the Eucharist, *p. 897.*

Prayer over the Gifts

Pray, brethren...

Lord,

accept the prayers and gifts we offer
in honor of Mary, the Mother of God.
May they please you
and bring us your help and forgiveness.

We ask this in the name of Jesus the Lord.

Preface of the Blessed Virgin Mary I *or* **II,** *p. 953.*

Communion Antiphon

Mary treasured all these words and pondered them in her heart. (Lk 2:19)

Prayer after Communion

Let us pray.

Pause for silent prayer, if this has not preceded.

Lord,
you have given us the sacrament of eternal redemption.
May we who honor the mother of your Son
rejoice in the abundance of your blessings
and experience the deepening of your life within us.

We ask this in the name of Jesus the Lord.

JUNE

June 1

JUSTIN, martyr (†166)

Memorial

Born in Samaria around A.D. 100, Justin studied various philosophies and was converted to Christ around the age of 30. He taught in Ephesus, opened a catechetical school in Rome, and wrote treatises defending the Christian faith. Justin gave us the most ancient descriptions of the baptismal rite and of the Eucharistic celebration.

He died a heroic martyr's death during the persecution of Marcus Aurelius.

Entrance Antiphon

The wicked tempted me with their fables against your law, but I proclaimed your decrees before kings without fear or shame.

(See Ps 118:85, 46)

Opening Prayer

Father,
through the folly of the cross
you taught St. Justin the sublime wisdom of Jesus Christ.
May we too reject falsehood
and remain loyal to the faith.

We ask this through our Lord Jesus Christ, your Son,
who lives and reigns with you and the Holy Spirit,
one God, for ever and ever.

Liturgy of the Word: *from the* COMMON OF MARTYRS *(pp. 2147ff.), especially 1 Cor 1:18–25; Ps 34:2–3, 4–5, 6–7, 8–9; Mt 5:13–19; or from the* WEEKDAY MASS.

Liturgy of the Eucharist, *p. 897.*

Prayer over the Gifts

Pray, brethren...

Lord,
help us to worship you as we should
when we celebrate these mysteries
which St. Justin vigorously defended.

We ask this in the name of Jesus the Lord.

Communion Antiphon

I resolved that while I was with you I would think of nothing but Jesus Christ and him crucified.

(1 Cor 2:2)

Prayer after Communion

Let us pray.

Pause for silent prayer, if this has not preceded.

Lord,
hear the prayer
of those you renew with spiritual food.
By following the teaching of St. Justin
may we offer constant thanks for the gifts we receive.

Grant this through Christ our Lord.

June 2

MARCELLINUS and PETER, martyrs (†c. 303)

Optional Memorial

These two saints, mentioned in the First Eucharistic Prayer of the Mass, were widely honored in the early Church because of their heroic martyrdom under Diocletian. The catacombs of Marcellinus and Peter, located outside Rome, contain the richest collection of early Christian paintings. In 827, Pope Gregory IV transferred their relics to Germany.

Antiphons and Prayers: *from the* COMMON OF MARTYRS *(pp. 2128–2169), or from the* WEEKDAY MASS. *The following is optional:*

Opening Prayer

Father,
may we benefit from the example
of your martyrs Marcellinus and Peter,
and be supported by their prayers.

Grant this through our Lord Jesus Christ, your Son,
who lives and reigns with you and the Holy Spirit,
one God, for ever and ever.

Liturgy of the Word: *from the* COMMON OF MARTYRS *(pp. 2147ff.), especially 2 Cor 6:4–10; Ps 124:2–3, 4–5, 7b–8; Jn 17:11b–19; or from the* WEEKDAY MASS.

Liturgy of the Eucharist, *p. 897.*

June 3

CHARLES LWANGA and COMPANIONS, martyrs
(†1886–1887)

Memorial

The universal Church today honors 22 African martyrs from Uganda. The first martyrs of sub-Sahara Africa, they died in a persecution similar to those of ancient Rome. Most of them had been baptized for only a short time. Charles Lwanga, chief of the royal pages, was killed with his companions on this date in 1886. Pope Paul VI canonized them in 1964, during the Second Vatican Council.

Antiphons and Prayers: *from the* COMMON OF MARTYRS *(pp. 2128–2169), or from the* WEEKDAY MASS, *except:*

Opening Prayer

Father,
you have made the blood of the martyrs
the seed of Christians.
May the witness of St. Charles and his companions
and their loyalty to Christ in the face of torture
inspire countless men and women
to live the Christian faith.

We ask this through our Lord Jesus Christ, your Son,
who lives and reigns with you and the Holy Spirit,
one God, for ever and ever.

Liturgy of the Word: *from the* COMMON OF MARTYRS *(pp. 2147ff.), especially 2 Mc 7:1–2, 9–14; Ps 124:2–3, 4–5, 7b–8; Mt 5:1–12a; or from the* WEEKDAY MASS.

Liturgy of the Eucharist, *p. 897*.

Prayer over the Gifts

Pray, brethren...

Lord,
accept the gifts we present at your altar.
As you gave your holy martyrs courage to die rather than sin,
help us to give ourselves completely to you.
We ask this in the name of Jesus the Lord.

Prayer after Communion

Let us pray.

Pause for silent prayer, if this has not preceded.

Lord,
at this celebration of the triumph of your martyrs,
we have received the sacraments
which helped them endure their sufferings.
In the midst of our own hardships
may this eucharist keep us steadfast in faith and love.

Grant this through Christ our Lord.

June 5

BONIFACE, bishop and martyr (672/5–754)

Memorial

Boniface, apostle to the Germans, was an Englishman named Wynfrith. He became a Benedictine monk, and in 716 the pope sent him to evangelize the German tribes. Boniface traveled constantly, establishing dioceses and monasteries, including the famous abbey at Fulda. Boniface also labored to reorganize the Church in France. Martyred with 52 companions in 755, Boniface is buried at Fulda.

Antiphons and Prayers: *from the* COMMON OF MARTYRS *(pp. 2128–2169), from the* COMMON OF PASTORS: FOR MISSIONARIES *(pp. 2183–2187), or from the* WEEKDAY MASS, *except:*

Opening Prayer

Lord,
your martyr Boniface
spread the faith by his teaching
and witnessed to it with his blood.
By the help of his prayers
keep us loyal to our faith
and give us the courage to profess it in our lives.

Grant this through our Lord Jesus Christ, your Son,
who lives and reigns with you and the Holy Spirit,
one God, for ever and ever.

Liturgy of the Word: *from the* COMMON OF MARTYRS *(pp. 2147ff.), or* COMMON OF PASTORS: FOR MISSIONARIES *(pp. 2191ff.), especially Acts 26:19–23; Ps 117:1bc, 2; Jn 10:11–16; or from the* WEEKDAY MASS.

Liturgy of the Eucharist, *p. 897.*

June 6

NORBERT, bishop (1080/85–1134)

Optional Memorial

Born in Germany, Norbert led an undisciplined life until he had a dramatic conversion to Christ (1115). He began a life of penance, was ordained a priest, and began preaching to the priests of his day. Norbert then went to a forested area in France called Premontre. There he started a religious order, called the Premonstratensians, dedicated to advancing the holiness of priestly life. Made Archbishop of Magdeburg, Norbert continued his efforts for holiness and renewal in the Church.

Antiphons and Prayers: *from the* COMMON OF PASTORS: FOR BISHOPS *(pp. 2170–2175), or* COMMON OF HOLY MEN AND WOMEN: FOR RELIGIOUS *(pp. 2260–2263), or from the* WEEKDAY MASS. *The following is optional:*

Opening Prayer

Father,
you made the bishop Norbert

an outstanding minister of your Church,
renowned for his preaching and pastoral zeal.
Always grant to your Church faithful shepherds
to lead your people to eternal salvation.

We ask this through our Lord Jesus Christ, your Son,
who lives and reigns with you and the Holy Spirit,
one God, for ever and ever.

Liturgy of the Word: *from the* COMMON OF PASTORS *(pp. 2188ff.), or* COMMON OF HOLY MEN AND WOMEN: FOR RELIGIOUS *(pp. 2271ff.), especially Ez 34:11–16; Ps 23:1–3a, 4, 5, 6; Lk 14:25–33; or from the* WEEKDAY MASS.

Liturgy of the Eucharist, *p. 897.*

June 9

EPHREM, deacon and doctor (306–373)

Optional Memorial

Ephrem was born at Nisibis (now in Turkey). He became a deacon in the Syrian Church. Later transferred to Edessa in Mesopotamia, Ephrem instructed others in theology. He combined contemplation, discipline and catechetical instruction. Ephrem was a poet who used his verse to teach religious truths. He is called the "harp of the Holy Spirit." Ephrem is especially noted for his profound hymns honoring the Blessed Virgin Mary.

Antiphons and Prayers: *from the* COMMON OF DOCTORS OF THE CHURCH *(pp. 2219–2238), or from the* WEEKDAY MASS. *The following is optional:*

Opening Prayer

Lord,
in your love fill our hearts with the Holy Spirit,
who inspired the deacon Ephrem to sing the praise of your
    mysteries
and gave him strength to serve you alone.

Grant this through our Lord Jesus Christ, your Son,
who lives and reigns with you and the Holy Spirit,
one God, for ever and ever.

Liturgy of the Word: *from the* COMMON OF DOCTORS OF THE CHURCH (*pp. 2222ff.*), *especially Col 3:12–17; Ps 37:3–4, 5–6, 30–31; Lk 6:43–45; or from the* WEEKDAY MASS.

Liturgy of the Eucharist, *p. 897.*

June 11

BARNABAS, apostle

Memorial

One of the apostolic men of the New Testament, Barnabas was born in Cyprus and named Joseph. Converted shortly after Pentecost, he gave up all possessions and received the name Barnabas ("son of consolation") because of his helpful, optimistic nature. Barnabas assisted the newly converted Paul and accompanied him for a while on the first missionary journey. Tradition says that Barnabas was martyred in Cyprus during the 60s.

Entrance Antiphon

Blessed are you, St. Barnabas: you were a man of faith filled with the Holy Spirit and counted among the apostles.

(See Acts 11:24)

Opening Prayer

God our Father,
you filled St. Barnabas with faith and the Holy Spirit
and sent him to convert the nations.
Help us to proclaim the gospel by word and deed.

We ask this through our Lord Jesus Christ, your Son,
who lives and reigns with you and the Holy Spirit,
one God, for ever and ever.

FIRST READING

Acts 11:21b–26; 13:1–3

Barnabas was a good man,
filled with the Holy Spirit and with faith.

A reading from the Acts of the Apostles

In those days a great number who believed turned to the Lord. The news about them reached the ears of the Church in Jerusalem, and they sent Barnabas to go to Antioch. When he arrived and saw the grace of God, he rejoiced and encouraged them all to remain faithful to the Lord in firmness of heart, for he was a good man, filled with the Holy Spirit and faith. And a large number of people was added to the Lord. Then he went to Tarsus to look for Saul, and when he had found him he brought him to Antioch. For a whole year they met with the Church and taught a large number of people, and it was in Antioch that the disciples were first called Christians.

Now there were in the Church at Antioch prophets and teachers: Barnabas, Symeon who was called Niger, Lucius of Cyrene, Manaen who was a close friend of Herod the tetrarch, and Saul. While they were worshiping the Lord and fasting, the Holy Spirit said, "Set apart for me Barnabas and Saul for the work to which I have called them." Then, completing their fasting and prayer, they laid hands on them and sent them off. The word of the Lord.

Responsorial Psalm
Ps 98:1, 2–3ab, 3cd–4, 5–6

R. **The Lord has revealed to the nations his saving power.**

Sing to the Lord a new song,
  for he has done wondrous deeds;
His right hand has won victory for him,
  his holy arm.

R. **The Lord has revealed to the nations his saving power.**

The Lord has made his salvation known:
  in the sight of the nations he has revealed his justice.
He has remembered his kindness and his faithfulness
  toward the house of Israel.

R. The Lord has revealed to the nations his saving power.

All the ends of the earth have seen
  the salvation by our God.
Sing joyfully to the LORD, all you lands;
  break into song; sing praise.

R. The Lord has revealed to the nations his saving power.

Sing praise to the LORD with the harp,
  with the harp and melodious song.
With trumpets and the sound of the horn
  sing joyfully before the King, the LORD.

R. The Lord has revealed to the nations his saving power.

Alleluia, alleluia Mt 28:19a, 20b
Go and teach all nations, says the Lord;
I am with you always, until the end of the world.
Alleluia, alleluia

GOSPEL   Mt 10:7–13

Without cost you have received;
without cost you are to give.

A reading from the holy Gospel according to Matthew

Jesus said to the Twelve: "As you go, make this proclamation: 'The Kingdom of heaven is at hand.' Cure the sick, raise the dead, cleanse the lepers, drive out demons. Without cost you have received; without cost you are to give. Do not take gold or silver or copper for your belts; no sack for the journey, or a second tunic, or sandals, or walking stick. The laborer deserves his keep. Whatever town or village you enter, look for a worthy person in it, and stay there until you leave. As you enter a house, wish it peace. If the house is worthy, let your peace come upon it; if not, let your peace return to you."

The Gospel of the Lord.

Liturgy of the Eucharist, *p. 897.*

Prayer over the Gifts

Pray, brethren...

Lord,
bless these gifts we present to you.
May they kindle in us the flame of love
by which St. Barnabas brought the light of the gospel
to the nations.

Grant this through Christ our Lord.

Preface of the Apostles I *or* **II,** *p. 956.*

Communion Antiphon

No longer shall I call you servants, for a servant knows not what his master does. Now I shall call you friends, for I have revealed to you all that I have heard from my Father. (Jn 15:15)

Prayer after Communion

Let us pray.

Pause for silent prayer, if this has not preceded.

Lord,
hear the prayers of those who receive the pledge of eternal
  life
on the feast of St. Barnabas.
May we come to share the salvation
we celebrate in this sacrament.

We ask this in the name of Jesus the Lord.

June 13

ANTHONY OF PADUA, priest and doctor
(1195–1231)

Memorial

Born in Lisbon, Portugal, in 1195 and baptized Fernando, today's saint became an Augustinian priest. Inspired by a group of

Franciscans recently martyred in Morocco, he became a Franciscan himself and took the name Anthony. He preached throughout France and northern Italy, especially against the Cathari heresy (a form of dualism which believed in a good God and an evil one, and rejected marriage). He died at Padua in Italy at age thirty-six.

Antiphons and Prayers: *from the* COMMON OF PASTORS *(pp. 2170–2218), or* COMMON OF DOCTORS OF THE CHURCH *(pp. 2219–2238), or* COMMON OF HOLY MEN AND WOMEN: FOR RELIGIOUS *(pp. 2260–2263), or from the* WEEKDAY MASS, *except:*

Opening Prayer

Almighty God,
you have given St. Anthony to your people
as an outstanding preacher
and a ready helper in time of need.
With his assistance may we follow the gospel of Christ
and know the help of your grace in every difficulty.

Grant this through our Lord Jesus Christ, your Son,
who lives and reigns with you and the Holy Spirit,
one God, for ever and ever.

Liturgy of the Word: *from the* COMMON OF PASTORS *(pp. 2188ff.), or* COMMON OF DOCTORS OF THE CHURCH *(pp. 2222ff.), or* COMMON OF HOLY MEN AND WOMEN: FOR RELIGIOUS *(pp. 2271ff.), especially Is 61:1–3d; Ps 89:2–3, 4–5, 21–22, 25 and 27; Lk 10:1–9; or from the* WEEKDAY MASS.

Liturgy of the Eucharist, *p. 897.*

June 19

ROMUALD, abbot (951/2–1027)

Optional Memorial

Romuald was the son of the Duke of Ravenna. A follower of Benedict but called to the solitary life, he lived as a hermit near Benedictine monasteries so he could join the monks in liturgical prayer. At Comaldi in the Apennine Mountains he founded an order of monks called the Camaldolese. A follower of his could live as a monk or as a hermit joining in liturgical prayer with monks, or as a complete solitary. In 1027, Romuald died in solitude.

Antiphons and Prayers: *from the* COMMON OF HOLY MEN AND WOMEN: FOR RELIGIOUS *(pp. 2260–2263), or from the* WEEKDAY MASS. *The following is optional:*

Opening Prayer

Father,
through St. Romuald
you renewed the life of solitude and prayer in your Church.
By our self-denial as we follow Christ
bring us the joy of heaven.

We ask this through our Lord Jesus Christ, your Son,
who lives and reigns with you and the Holy Spirit,
one God, for ever and ever.

Liturgy of the Word: *from the* COMMON OF HOLY MEN AND WOMEN: FOR RELIGIOUS *(pp. 2271ff.), especially Phil 3:8–14; Ps 131:1bcde, 2, 3; Lk 14:25–33; or from the* WEEKDAY MASS.

Liturgy of the Eucharist, *p. 897.*

June 21

ALOYSIUS GONZAGA, religious (1568–1591)

Memorial

The son of a high dignitary of the Spanish court, Aloysius at age sixteen gave up his hereditary right to be prince of Mantua in Italy. Feeling drawn to the consecrated life, he joined the Jesuits and grew remarkably in holiness. After contracting the plague while tending the sick, Aloysius died at age twenty-three. Canonized in 1726, he was proclaimed "Patron of Youth" by Pope Benedict XIII.

Entrance Antiphon

Who shall climb the mountain of the Lord and stand in his holy place? The innocent man, the pure of heart!

(See Ps 23:4, 3)

Opening Prayer

Father of love,
giver of all good things,
in St. Aloysius you combined remarkable innocence
with the spirit of penance.
By the help of his prayers
may we who have not followed his innocence
follow his example of penance.

Grant this through our Lord Jesus Christ, your Son,
who lives and reigns with you and the Holy Spirit,
one God, for ever and ever.

Liturgy of the Word: *from the* COMMON OF HOLY MEN AND WOMEN: FOR RELIGIOUS *(p. 2271ff.), especially 1 Jn 5:1–5; Ps 16:1–2a and 5, 7–8, 11; Mt 22:34–40; or from the* WEEKDAY MASS.

Liturgy of the Eucharist, *p. 897.*

Prayer over the Gifts

Pray, brethren...

Lord,
help us to follow the example of St. Aloysius
and always come to the eucharist
with hearts free from sin.
By our sharing in this mystery
make us rich in your blessings.

We ask this in the name of Jesus the Lord.

Communion Antiphon

God gave them bread from heaven; men ate the bread of angels. (Ps 77:24–25)

Prayer after Communion

Let us pray.

Pause for silent prayer, if this has not preceded.

Lord,
you have nourished us with the bread of life.
Help us to serve you without sin.
By following the example of St. Aloysius
may we continue to spend our lives in thanksgiving.

We ask this through Christ our Lord.

June 22

PAULINUS OF NOLA, bishop (353/4–431)

Optional Memorial

A native of Bordeaux, France, Paulinus became the Roman consul of the area and acquired vast territories and wealth. He was married and had one son. Desiring a life of evangelical poverty, he gave all of his possessions to the poor, and with his wife, Teresia, moved to Nola, near Naples. In 409 the people of Nola elected him bishop. For twenty-two years Paulinus lived as a model pastor. He helped the poor and encouraged his people during the dangerous times brought on by the decline of the Roman Empire and attacks of the Germanic tribes.

Antiphons and Prayers: *from the* COMMON OF PASTORS: FOR BISHOPS *(pp. 2170–2175), or from the* WEEKDAY MASS. *The following is optional:*

Opening Prayer

Lord,
you made St. Paulinus
renowned for his love of poverty
and concern for his people.
May we who celebrate his witness to the gospel
imitate his example of love for others.

We ask this through our Lord Jesus Christ, your Son,
who lives and reigns with you and the Holy Spirit,
one God, for ever and ever.

Liturgy of the Word: *from the* COMMON OF PASTORS *(pp. 2188ff.), or from the* WEEKDAY MASS.

Liturgy of the Eucharist, *p. 897.*

FIRST READING

2 Cor 8:9 –15

Christ was rich but he became poor for your sake:
to make you rich out of his poverty.

A reading from the second Letter of Saint Paul to the Corinthians

Brothers and sisters:

You know the gracious act of our Lord Jesus Christ, that for your sake he became poor although he was rich, so that by his poverty you might become rich. And I am giving counsel in this matter, for it is appropriate for you who began not only to act but to act willingly last year: complete it now, so that your eager willingness may be matched by your completion of it out of what you have. For if the eagerness is there, it is accep-table according to what one has, not according to what one does not have; not that others should have relief while you are burdened, but that as a matter of equality your surplus at the present time should supply their needs, so that their surplus may also supply your needs, that there may be equality. As it is written:

Whoever had much did not have more,
and whoever had little did not have less.

The word of the Lord.

*See the Common of Pastors (**pp. 2170–2218**), for:*
  Responsorial Psalm 40:2 and 4ab, 7–8a, 8b–9, 10
  Alleluia Verse Mt 5:3

*See the Common of Holy Men and Women (**pp. 2252–2322**), for:*
  Gospel Lk 12:32–34

Liturgy of the Eucharist, *p. 897.*

Also on June 22

JOHN FISHER, bishop and martyr (1469–1535)
and THOMAS MORE, martyr (1477–1535)

Optional Memorial

John Fisher was the lone bishop of England who refused to accept the King of England as head of the Church. Thomas More was a devout layman and lawyer, former chancellor of King Henry VIII, who would not compromise his conscience by signing the oath that Henry demanded. Both saints exemplify the well-educated Christian humanist who combined learning, sense of humor, and profound spirituality. Both were decapitated in the Tower of London. John Fisher, made a cardinal while in the Tower, was martyred on this date in 1535.

Antiphons and Prayers: *from the* COMMON OF MARTYRS *(pp. 2128–2169), or from the* WEEKDAY MASS. *The following is optional:*

Opening Prayer

Father,
you confirm the true faith
with the crown of martyrdom.
May the prayers of Saints John Fisher and Thomas More
give us the courage to proclaim our faith
by the witness of our lives.

Grant this through our Lord Jesus Christ, your Son,
who lives and reigns with you and the Holy Spirit,
one God, for ever and ever.

Liturgy of the Word: *from the* COMMON OF MARTYRS *(pp. 2147ff.), especially 1 Pt 4:12–19; Ps 126:1bc–2ab, 2cd–3, 4–5, 6; Mt 10:34–39; or from the* WEEKDAY MASS.

Liturgy of the Eucharist, *p. 897.*

For **June 24,** BIRTH OF JOHN THE BAPTIST, *see* **Vatican II Sunday Missal,** *Vigil Mass, p. 1030; Mass During the Day, p. 1035.*

June 27

CYRIL OF ALEXANDRIA, bishop and doctor
(370–444)

Optional Memorial

As the patriarch of Alexandria, Cyril played a major role at the Council of Ephesus (431), and battled against the Nestorian heresy. Nestorius split Christ into two persons—one human, one divine—and refused to acknowledge Mary as Mother of God. Under Cyril's leadership, the Council deposed Nestorius and declared Mary to be Theotokos (Mother of God). Cyril holds an important place in the development of Christological and Marian doctrine.

Antiphons and Prayers: *from the* COMMON OF PASTORS: FOR BISHOPS *(pp. 2170–2175), or* COMMON OF DOCTORS OF THE CHURCH *(pp. 2219–2238), or from the* WEEKDAY MASS. *The following is optional:*

Opening Prayer

Father,
the bishop Cyril courageously taught
that Mary was the Mother of God.
May we who cherish this belief
receive salvation through the incarnation of Christ your Son,
who lives and reigns with you and the Holy Spirit,
one God, for ever and ever.

Liturgy of the Word: *from the* COMMON OF PASTORS *(pp. 2188ff.), or* COMMON OF DOCTORS OF THE CHURCH *(pp. 2222ff.), especially 2 Tm 4:1–5; Ps 89:2–3, 4–5, 21–22, 25 and 27; Mt 5:13–19; or from the* WEEKDAY MASS.

Liturgy of the Eucharist, *p. 897.*

June 28

IRENAEUS, bishop and martyr (130–200)

Memorial

Born at Smyrna in Asia Minor, Irenaeus was a student under Polycarp, who had been a disciple of the Apostle John. Irenaeus became a priest in Lyons, France, and later bishop of that city. He wrote important theological expositions to defend the faith against Gnostic heresies, and demonstrated a vigorous missionary spirit.

Antiphons and Prayers: *from the* COMMON OF MARTYRS *(pp. 2128–2169), or* COMMON OF PASTORS: FOR BISHOPS *(pp. 2170–2175), or from the* WEEKDAY MASS, *except:*

Opening Prayer

Father,
you called St. Irenaeus to uphold your truth
and bring peace to your Church.
By his prayers renew us in faith and love
that we may always be intent
on fostering unity and peace.

Grant this through our Lord Jesus Christ, your Son,
who lives and reigns with you and the Holy Spirit,
one God, for ever and ever.

Liturgy of the Word: *from the* COMMON OF MARTYRS *(pp. 2147ff.), or* COMMON OF DOCTORS OF THE CHURCH *(pp. 2222ff.), or from the* WEEKDAY MASS.

FIRST READING   2 Tm 2:22b–26

*A slave of the Lord should be gentle with everyone,
correcting with kindness.*

A reading from the second Letter of Saint Paul to Timothy

Beloved:
Pursue righteousness, faith, love, and peace, along with those who call on the Lord with purity of heart. Avoid foolish and ignorant debates, for you know that they breed quarrels. A slave of the Lord should not quarrel, but should be gentle with everyone, able to teach, tolerant, correcting opponents with kindness. It may be that God will grant them repentance that leads to knowledge of the truth, and that they may return to

their senses out of the Devil's snare, where they are entrapped
by him, for his will.

The word of the Lord.

*See the Common of Doctors (**pp. 2219–2238**), for:*
   Responsorial Psalm   37:3–4, 5–6, 30–31
   Alleluia Verse Jn 15:9b, 5b

*See the Common of Holy Men and Women (**pp. 2252–2322**), for:*
   Gospel Jn 17:20–26

   Liturgy of the Eucharist, *p. 897.*

Prayer over the Gifts

Pray, brethren...

Lord,
as we celebrate the feast of St. Irenaeus
may this eucharist bring you glory,
increase our love of truth,
and help your Church to remain firm in faith and unity.

We ask this in the name of Jesus the Lord.

Prayer after Communion

Let us pray.
       Pause for silent prayer, if this has not preceded.
Lord,
by these holy mysteries increase our faith.
As the holy bishop Irenaeus reached eternal glory
by being faithful until death,
so may we be saved by living our faith.

We ask this through Christ our Lord.

For **June 29,** SOLEMNITY OF PETER AND PAUL, APOSTLES, *see*
Vatican II Sunday Missal, *Vigil Mass, p. 1041; Mass During the Day,
p. 1046.*

June 30

FIRST MARTYRS OF THE CHURCH OF ROME

Optional Memorial

This memorial honors the nameless followers of Christ brutally killed by the depraved Emperor Nero as scapegoats for the fire in Rome. The Roman historian Tacitus and St. Clement of Rome tell of a night of horror (August 15, 64) when in the imperial parks Christians were put into animal skins and hunted, brutally attacked, and made living torches to light the road for Nero's chariot.

Antiphons and Prayers: *from the* COMMON OF MARTYRS *(pp. 2128–2169), or from the* WEEKDAY MASS. *The following is optional:*

Opening Prayer

Father,
you sanctified the Church of Rome
with the blood of its first martyrs.
May we find strength from their courage
and rejoice in their triumph.

We ask this through our Lord Jesus Christ, your Son,
who lives and reigns with you and the Holy Spirit,
one God, for ever and ever.

Liturgy of the Word: *from the* COMMON OF MARTYRS *(pp. 2147ff.), especially Rom 8:31b–39; Ps 124:2–3, 4–5, 7b–8; or from the* WEEKDAY MASS.

GOSPEL

Mt 24:4–13

You will be hated by all nations because of my name.

A reading from the holy Gospel according to Matthew

Jesus said to his disciples: "See that no one deceives you. For many will come in my name, saying, 'I am the Christ,' and they will deceive many. You will hear of wars and reports of wars; see that you are not alarmed, for these things must happen, but it will not yet be the end. Nation will rise against nation, and kingdom against kingdom; there will be famines and earthquakes from place to place. All these are the beginning of the labor pains. Then they will hand you over to persecution, and they will kill you. You will be hated by all nations because of my name. And then many will be led into sin; they will betray and hate one another. Many false prophets will arise and deceive many; and because of the increase of evildoing, the love of many will grow cold. But the one who perseveres to the end will be saved."

The Gospel of the Lord.

Liturgy of the Eucharist, *p. 897.*

JULY

July 1

[In the dioceses of the United States]

BLESSED JUNIPERO SERRA, priest (1713–1784)

Optional Memorial

Born in Mallorca, Spain, José Miguel became a Franciscan priest and a university professor. He felt a desire for missionary work, however, and in 1749 he went to Mexico. From there he later traveled to California, where he established a mission at Monterey-Carmel, which was followed by nine others. Pope John Paul II beatified him in 1988.

Antiphons and Prayers: *from the* COMMON OF PASTORS: FOR MISSIONARIES *(pp. 2183–2187), or* COMMON OF HOLY MEN AND WOMEN: FOR RELIGIOUS *(pp. 2260–2263), or from the* WEEKDAY MASS. *The following is optional:*

Opening Prayer

God most high,
your servant Junipero Serra

brought the gospel of Christ
to the peoples of Mexico and California
and firmly established the Church among them.
By his intercession,
and through the example of his evangelical zeal,
inspire us to be faithful witnesses of Jesus Christ,
who lives and reigns with you and the Holy Spirit,
one God, for ever and ever.

Liturgy of the Word: *from the* COMMON OF PASTORS: FOR MISSIONARIES *(pp. 2191ff.), or* COMMON OF HOLY MEN AND WOMEN: FOR RELIGIOUS *(pp. 2271ff.), or from the* WEEKDAY MASS.

Liturgy of the Eucharist, *p. 897.*

July 3

THOMAS, apostle

Feast

Thomas is famous for doubting Jesus' resurrection, but his unbelief vanished before the risen Christ. Thomas gave us the exclamation of Easter faith: "My Lord and my God!" Apart from the Gospels, nothing certain is known of his life and ministry. The Christians of Malabar (west coast of India) honor Thomas as founder of their Church. The Church of Syria takes its liturgy from St. Thomas and since 232 has honored him on this date.

Entrance Antiphon

You are my God: I will give you praise, O my God, I will extol you, for you are my savior. (Ps 117:28)

Opening Prayer

Almighty Father,
as we honor Thomas the apostle,
let us always experience the help of his prayers.
May we have eternal life by believing in Jesus,

whom Thomas acknowledged as Lord,
for he lives and reigns with you and the Holy Spirit,
one God, for ever and ever.

*See the Common of the Dedication of a Church (**p. 2085**), for:*
  First Reading   Eph 2:19–22

*See the Common of Pastors (**p. 2201**), for:*
  Responsorial Psalm   117:1bc, 2

> **Alleluia, alleluia**   Jn 20:29
> You believe in me, Thomas, because you have seen me,
> says the Lord;
> blessed are those who have not seen, but still believe!
> **Alleluia, alleluia**

GOSPEL

Jn 20:24–29

My Lord and my God!

A reading from the holy Gospel according to John

Thomas, called Didymus, one of the Twelve, was not with them
when Jesus came. So the other disciples said to him, "We have
seen the Lord." But Thomas said to them, "Unless I see the
mark of the nails in his hands and put my finger into the nail-
marks and put my hand into his side, I will not believe." Now
a week later his disciples were again inside and Thomas was
with them. Jesus came, although the doors were locked, and
stood in their midst and said, "Peace be with you." Then he
said to Thomas, "Put your finger here and see my hands, and
bring your hand and put it into my side, and do not be unbelieving, but believe." Thomas answered and said to him,
"My Lord and my God!" Jesus said to him, "Have you come
to believe because you have seen me? Blessed are those who
have not seen and have believed."

The Gospel of the Lord.

  Liturgy of the Eucharist, *p. 897.*

Prayer over the Gifts

Pray, brethren...

Lord,
we offer you our service and we pray:
protect the gifts you have given us
as we offer this sacrifice of praise
on the feast of your apostle Thomas.

We ask this in the name of Jesus the Lord.

Preface of the Apostles I *or* II, p. 956.

Communion Antiphon

Jesus spoke to Thomas: Put your hand here, and see the place
of the nails. Doubt no longer, but believe.   (See Jn 20:27)

Prayer after Communion

Let us pray.

Pause for silent prayer, if this has not preceded.

Father,
in this sacrament we have received
the body and blood of Christ.
With St. Thomas we acknowledge him to be
     our Lord and God.
May we show by our lives that our faith is real.

We ask this through Christ our Lord.

July 4

ELIZABETH OF PORTUGAL, queen (1271–1336)

Optional Memorial

Princess of Aragon and grandniece of St. Elizabeth of Hungary,
today's saint was married at age twelve to King Dionysius of Portugal. Her life was frequently upset by politics and family quarrels,
but kept in balance by deep spirituality, prayer, and charity. As a

widow, she adopted a monastic lifestyle and lived in poverty and obscurity as a Third Order Franciscan. Elizabeth died while trying to settle further family quarrels.

Antiphons and Prayers: *from the* COMMON OF HOLY MEN AND WOMEN: FOR THOSE WHO WORKED FOR THE UNDERPRIVILEGED *(pp. 2263–2264), or from the* WEEKDAY MASS. *The following is optional:*

Opening Prayer

Father of peace and love,
you gave St. Elizabeth the gift of reconciling enemies.
By the help of her prayers
give us the courage to work for peace among men,
that we may be called the sons of God.

We ask this through our Lord Jesus Christ, your Son,
who lives and reigns with you and the Holy Spirit,
one God, for ever and ever.

Liturgy of the Word: *from the* COMMON OF HOLY MEN AND WOMEN: FOR THOSE WHO WORKED FOR THE UNDERPRIVILEGED *(pp. 2280ff.), especially 1 Jn 3:14–18; Ps 112:1–2, 3–4, 5–6, 7–8, 9; Mt 25:31–46; or from the* WEEKDAY MASS.

Liturgy of the Eucharist, *p. 897.*

Also on July 4

INDEPENDENCE DAY
(and for other civic observances)

[In the dioceses of the United States]

Today the United States of America celebrates its anniversary of independence. It is in the best Christian and American tradition to pray for the nation today—to exercise the virtue of patriotism and pray that this may be a nation of peace and justice, one that knows how "to do the right, and to love goodness, and to walk humbly with...God" (Mi 6:8).

Opening Prayer

Let us pray

[for peace and justice and truth
here and in every land]

Pause for silent prayer.

A

God of love, Father of us all,
in wisdom and goodness you guide creation
to fulfillment in Christ your Son.
Open our hearts to the truth of his gospel,
that your peace may rule in our hearts
and your justice guide our lives.

Grant this through our Lord Jesus Christ, your Son,
who lives and reigns with you and the Holy Spirit,
one God, for ever and ever.

B

Father of the family of man,
open our hearts to greater love of your Son.
Let national boundaries not set limits to our concern.
Ward off the pride that comes with worldly wealth and
    power.
Give us the courage to open ourselves in love
to the service of all your people.

Grant this through our Lord Jesus Christ, your Son,
who lives and reigns with you and the Holy Spirit,
one God, for ever and ever.

C

Father of the family of nations,
open our hearts to greater love of your Son.

Grant that the boundaries of nations
will not set limits to our love,
and give us the courage to build a land
that serves you in truth and justice.

Grant this through our Lord Jesus Christ, your Son,
who lives and reigns with you and the Holy Spirit,
one God, for ever and ever.

Liturgy of the Word: *various texts may be selected from the lectionary.*

Prayer over the Gifts

Pray, brethren....

A

God our Father,
you have given us in abundance
that we might give you praise
and serve all your people in love.
Accept these gifts we bring
for the salvation of all the world
and help us to live in love as you have commanded.

We ask this through Christ our Lord.

B

Lord God,
accept these gifts we bring to this altar
and teach us the wisdom of the gospel
which leads to true justice and lasting peace.

We ask this through Christ our Lord.

Preface for Independence Day and Other Civic Observances I *or* **II,** *p. 964.*

Prayer after Communion

Let us pray.

Pause for silent prayer, if this has not preceded.

A

Father,
now that we have shared the body and blood of Christ,
teach us the proper use of your gifts
and true love for our brothers and sisters.

We ask this through Christ our Lord.

B

God our Father,
through the power of this eucharist
keep us constant in the love of your Son.
Help us to play our part in the life of this nation
that its thoughts may be directed toward peace, justice,
and the loving service of all mankind.

We ask this through Christ our Lord.

C

God our Father,
through the food we have received
you bless and sanctify us and the fruit of our toil.
Help us to serve each other in justice and mercy
and share what we have
for the welfare of all men and women.

We ask this through Christ the Lord.

July 5

ANTHONY ZACCARIA, priest (1502–1539)

Optional Memorial

Born at Cremona in northern Italy, today's saint studied medicine before becoming a priest. Even before the Council of Trent, he desired that some priests be neither monks nor mendicants, but live under a rule of life with vows. He founded such a Congregation in Milan. Living at first at the Church of St. Barnabas, they were referred to as the Barnabites. Although Anthony died at the age of 37, his order did much to inspire clergy and to evangelize the people.

Antiphons and Prayers: *from the* COMMON OF PASTORS *(pp. 2170–2218), or* COMMON OF HOLY MEN AND WOMEN: FOR TEACHERS *or* FOR RELIGIOUS *(pp. 2252–2322), or from the* WEEKDAY MASS. *The following is optional:*

Opening Prayer

Lord,
enable us to grasp in the spirit of St. Paul,
the sublime wisdom of Jesus Christ,
the wisdom which inspired St. Anthony Zaccaria
to preach the message of salvation in your Church.

Grant this through our Lord Jesus Christ, your Son,
who lives and reigns with you and the Holy Spirit,
one God, for ever and ever.

Liturgy of the Word: *from the* COMMON OF PASTORS *(pp. 2188ff.), or* COMMON OF HOLY MEN AND WOMEN: FOR TEACHERS *(pp. 2269ff.), or* FOR RELIGIOUS *(pp. 2271ff.), especially 2 Tm 1:13–14; 2:1–3; Ps 1:1–2, 3, 4 and 6; Mk 10:13–16; or from the* WEEKDAY MASS.

Liturgy of the Eucharist, *p. 897.*

July 6

MARIA GORETTI, virgin and martyr (1890–1902)

Optional Memorial

Born into a poor and devout family, Maria had a deep spirit of prayer and worked hard to help her family. When she was only twelve years old, she was stabbed to death as she fought off an attack of a rapist. This took place at Nettuno, near Rome, in the region of the Pontine Marshes. She died forgiving and praying for her assailant, Alexander, who later repented and lived a holy life. Pope Pius XII canonized Maria in 1950, an event attended by her aged mother and Alexander as well.

Antiphons and Prayers: *from the* COMMON OF MARTYRS *(pp. 2168–2169), or* COMMON OF VIRGINS *(pp. 2238–2252), or from the* WEEKDAY MASS. *The following is optional:*

Opening Prayer

Father,
source of innocence and lover of chastity,
you gave St. Maria Goretti the privilege
of offering her life in witness to Christ.
As you gave her the crown of martyrdom,
let her prayers keep us faithful to your teaching.

We ask this through our Lord Jesus Christ, your Son,
who lives and reigns with you and the Holy Spirit,
one God, for ever and ever.

Liturgy of the Word: *from the* COMMON OF MARTYRS *(pp. 2147ff.), or* COMMON OF VIRGINS *(pp. 2244ff.), or from the* WEEKDAY MASS.

FIRST READING   1 Cor 6:13c–15a, 17–20
Your bodies are members of the Body of Christ.

A reading from the first Letter of Saint Paul to the Corinthians

Brothers and sisters:
The body is not for immorality, but for the Lord, and the Lord is for the body; God raised the Lord and will also raise us by his power.

Do you not know that your bodies are members of Christ? Whoever is joined to the Lord becomes one spirit with him.

Avoid immorality. Every other sin a person commits is outside the body, but the immoral person sins against his own body. Do you not know that your body is a temple of the Holy Spirit within you, whom you have from God, and that you are not your own? For you have been purchased at a price. Therefore glorify God in your body.

The word of the Lord.

See the Common of Martyrs (pp. 2156–2168), for:
 Responsorial Psalm 31:3cd–4, 6 and 8ab, 16bc and 17
 Alleluia Verse Jas 1:12
 Gospel Jn 12:24–26

 Liturgy of the Eucharist, *p. 897.*

July 11

BENEDICT, abbot (480–547)

Memorial

Known as the father of Western monasticism, Benedict had a profound influence on the Church and is a patron of Europe. His famous monastic Rule gave birth to a Benedictine tradition that has served both Church and civilization with distinction. Born in central Italy in 480, he studied at Rome before starting a hermit's life at Subiaco. Benedict later founded the celebrated monastery at Cassino. His sister Scholastica is also a canonized saint.

Antiphons and Prayers: *from the* COMMON OF HOLY MEN AND WOMEN: FOR RELIGIOUS *(pp. 2262–2322), or from the* WEEKDAY MASS, *except:*

Opening Prayer

God our Father,
you made St. Benedict an outstanding guide
to teach men how to live in your service.
Grant that by preferring your love to everything else,
we may walk in the way of your commandments.

We ask this through our Lord Jesus Christ, your Son,
who lives and reigns with you and the Holy Spirit,
one God, for ever and ever.

Liturgy of the Word: *from the* COMMON OF HOLY MEN AND WOMEN: FOR
RELIGIOUS *(pp. 2271ff.), or from the* WEEKDAY MASS.

FIRST READING
Prv 2:1–9

Inclining your heart to understanding.

A reading from the Book of Proverbs

My son, if you receive my words
    and treasure my commands,
Turning your ear to wisdom,
    inclining your heart to understanding;
Yes, if you call to intelligence,
    and to understanding raise your voice;
If you seek her like silver,
    and like hidden treasures search her out:
Then will you understand the fear of the LORD;
    the knowledge of God you will find;
For the LORD gives wisdom,
    from his mouth come knowledge and understanding;
He has counsel in store for the upright,
    he is the shield of those who walk honestly,
Guarding the paths of justice,
    protecting the way of his pious ones.
Then you will understand rectitude and justice,
    honesty, every good path.

The word of the Lord.

*See the Common of Holy Men and Women (**pp. 2288–2309**), for:*
    Responsorial Psalm 34:2–3, 4–5, 6–7, 8–9, 10–11

Alleluia Verse Mt 5:3
Gospel Mt 19:27–29

Liturgy of the Eucharist, *p. 897.*

Prayer over the Gifts

Pray, brethren...

Lord,
look kindly on these gifts we present
on the feast of St. Benedict.
By following his example in seeking you,
may we know unity and peace in your service.

Grant this through Christ our Lord.

Prayer after Communion

Let us pray.

Pause for silent prayer, if this has not preceded.

Lord,
hear the prayers of all
who have received this pledge of eternal life.
By following the teaching of St. Benedict,
may we be faithful in doing your work
and in loving our brothers and sisters in true charity.

We ask this in the name of Jesus the Lord.

July 13

HENRY, king (973–1024)

Optional Memorial

Today's remarkable saint was duke of Bavaria and Emperor of
the Holy Roman Empire. A skilled military man and ruler, Henry
was concerned about reform of the Church. He selected able bishops, supported the monastic life, and built churches, including the

Cathedral of Bamberg in Germany. His saintly wife Cunegunda is buried there. Henry was canonized in 1146.

Antiphons and Prayers: *from the* COMMON OF HOLY MEN AND WOMEN *(pp. 2252–2322), or from the* WEEKDAY MASS. *The following is optional:*

Opening Prayer

Lord,
you filled St. Henry with your love
and raised him from the cares of an earthly kingdom
to eternal happiness in heaven.
In the midst of the changes of this world,
may his prayers keep us free from sin
and help us on our way toward you.

Grant this through our Lord Jesus Christ, your Son,
who lives and reigns with you and the Holy Spirit,
one God, for ever and ever.

Liturgy of the Word: *from the* COMMON OF HOLY MEN AND WOMEN *(pp. 2269ff.), especially Mi 6:6–8; Ps 1:1–2, 3, 4 and 6; Mt 7:21–27; or from the* WEEKDAY MASS.

Liturgy of the Eucharist, *p. 897.*

July 14

[In the dioceses of the United States]

BLESSED KATERI TEKAKWITHA, virgin (1656–1680)

Memorial

Ten years after St. Isaac Jogues was martyred in the Mohawk village of Ossernenon (Auriesville, New York), Kateri Tekakwitha, the "Lily of the Mohawks," was born there. Kateri was orphaned by a smallpox epidemic and raised by relatives. The young girl was attracted to Christianity but her family was hostile to it. She asked for baptism nonetheless, but suffered harsh treatment from her family after her conversion. This forced her to move to a Christian village in Canada, where she lived a life of deep prayer and heroic virtue. Pope John Paul II beatified her in 1980.

Antiphons and Prayers: *from the* COMMON OF VIRGINS *(pp. 2238–2252), or from the* WEEKDAY MASS, *except:*

Opening Prayer

Lord God,
you called the virgin, blessed Kateri Tekakwitha,
to shine among the Indian people
as an example of innocence of life.

Through her intercession,
may all peoples of every tribe, tongue, and nation,
having been gathered into your Church,
proclaim your greatness
in one song of praise.

We ask this through our Lord Jesus Christ, your Son,
who lives and reigns with you and the Holy Spirit,
one God, for ever and ever.

Liturgy of the Word: *from the* COMMON OF VIRGINS *(pp. 2244ff.), or from the* WEEKDAY MASS.

July 15

BONAVENTURE, bishop and doctor (1217/18–1274)

Memorial

The "Seraphic Doctor" was endowed with exceptional spiritual and intellectual gifts. Born in northern Italy around 1218, Bonaventure was attracted by the Franciscan ideal early in life. He was an outstanding student and later a professor at the University of Paris, where he taught and wrote profoundly about theology and philosophy. Elected Minister General of the Franciscan Order, Bonaventure was named Cardinal of Albano in 1273. He took part in the Second Ecumenical Council of Lyons—which arranged a short-lived union of the Greek and Latin Churches—and died in Lyons, France, in 1274.

Antiphons and Prayers: *from the* COMMON OF PASTORS: FOR BISHOPS *(pp. 2170–2175), or* COMMON OF DOCTORS OF THE CHURCH *(pp. 2219–2238), or from the* WEEKDAY MASS, *except:*

Opening Prayer

All-powerful Father,
may we who celebrate the feast of St. Bonaventure
always benefit from his wisdom
and follow the example of his love.

Grant this through our Lord Jesus Christ, your Son,
who lives and reigns with you and the Holy Spirit,
one God, for ever and ever.

Liturgy of the Word: *from the* COMMON OF PASTORS *(pp. 2188ff.), or* COMMON OF DOCTORS OF THE CHURCH *(pp. 2222ff.), especially Eph 3:14–19; Ps 119:9, 10, 11, 12, 13, 14; Mt 23:8–12; or from the* WEEKDAY MASS.

Liturgy of the Eucharist, *p. 897.*

July 16

OUR LADY OF MOUNT CARMEL

Optional Memorial

Mount Carmel, a promontory in north Palestine overlooking the Mediterranean, is mentioned in the Bible as a holy place. There, the prophet Elijah defended the purity of faith against the prophets of Baal. Carmel became a dwelling place for Christian hermits during the Crusades. In 1209, the hermits combined to form the Order of Carmel, or Carmelites, dedicated to the Blessed Mother who had lived in contemplation nearby at Nazareth. The Carmelites promoted the life of contemplation and dedication to our Lady. The Scapular Confraternity wears a special cloth to express self-dedication to Mary's service.

Antiphons and Prayers: *from the* COMMON OF THE BLESSED VIRGIN MARY *(pp. 2091–2127), or from the* WEEKDAY MASS. *The following is optional:*

Opening Prayer

Father,
may the prayers of the Virgin Mary protect us
and help us to reach Christ her Son
who lives and reigns with you and the Holy Spirit,
one God, for ever and ever.

> **Liturgy of the Word**: *from the* COMMON OF THE BLESSED VIRGIN MARY *(pp. 2101ff.), especially Zec 2:14–17; Lk 1:46–47, 48–49, 50–51, 52–53, 54–55; Mt 12:46–50; or from the* WEEKDAY MASS.

> **Liturgy of the Eucharist**, *p. 897.*

July 18

CAMILLUS DE LELLIS, priest (1550–1614)

Optional Memorial

Son of a soldier of the Kingdom of Naples, Camillus became a soldier and led an immoral life, until at age twenty-five he came with broken body to the Incurables Hospital in Rome. There, Camillus was converted to Christ and began a life of penance and service to the sick. Though still incurably ill himself, he gathered others to this work and started the Company of Servants of the Sick— the Hospitallers or Camillians. He became a priest, and to the end of his life he lived out the ideal of Christian charity. He was canonized in 1746.

In the United States this memorial is transferred to this date from July 14.

Antiphons and Prayers: *from the* COMMON OF HOLY MEN AND WOMEN: FOR THOSE WHO WORKED FOR THE UNDERPRIVILEGED *(pp. 2263–2264), or from the* WEEKDAY MASS. *The following is optional:*

Opening Prayer

Father,
you gave St. Camillus
a special love for the sick.
Through his prayers inspire us with your grace,

so that by serving you in our brothers and sisters
we may come safely to you at the end of our lives.

We ask this through our Lord Jesus Christ, your Son,
who lives and reigns with you and the Holy Spirit,
one God, for ever and ever.

Liturgy of the Word: *from the* COMMON OF HOLY MEN AND WOMEN:
FOR THOSE WHO WORKED FOR THE UNDERPRIVILEGED *(pp. 2274ff.)*, *especially
1 Jn 3:14–18; Ps 112:1–2, 3–4, 5–7a, 7b–8, 9; Jn 15:9–17; or from the*
WEEKDAY MASS.

Liturgy of the Eucharist, *p. 897.*

July 21

LAWRENCE OF BRINDISI, priest and doctor
(1559–1619)

Optional Memorial

Baptized Julius Caesar Russo at Brindisi in Italy, Lawrence entered the Capuchins and dedicated his many talents to the Church
of that Reformation century. A born orator, he spoke fluent French,
German, Greek, Syriac and Hebrew. As a worker in the Catholic
renewal, he preached throughout central Europe and became papal legate and superior general of the Capuchins. A true son of
St. Francis, he died at Lisbon in simple goodness and was canonized
in 1881.

Antiphons and Prayers: *from the* COMMON OF PASTORS *(pp. 2170–2218),
or* COMMON OF DOCTORS OF THE CHURCH *(pp. 2219–2238), or from the* WEEKDAY
MASS. *The following is optional:*

Opening Prayer

Lord,
for the glory of your name and the salvation of souls
you gave Lawrence of Brindisi
courage and right judgment.

By his prayers,
help us to know what we should do
and give us the courage to do it.

We ask this through our Lord Jesus Christ, your Son,
who lives and reigns with you and the Holy Spirit,
one God, for ever and ever.

   Liturgy of the Word: *from the* COMMON OF PASTORS *(pp. 2188ff.), or*
COMMON OF DOCTORS OF THE CHURCH *(pp. 2222ff.), or from the* WEEKDAY MASS.

See the Common of Pastors (p. 2205), for:
   First Reading 2 Cor 4:1–2, 5–7

Responsorial Psalm

Ps 40:2 and 4ab, 7–8a, 8b–9, 10, 11

   R. Here I am, Lord; I come to do your will.

I have waited, waited for the LORD,
   and he stooped toward me and heard my cry.
And he put a new song into my mouth,
   a hymn to our God.

   R. Here I am, Lord; I come to do your will.

Sacrifice or oblation you wished not,
   but ears open to obedience you gave me.
Burnt offerings or sin-offerings you sought not;
   then said I, "Behold I come."

   R. Here I am, Lord; I come to do your will.

"In the written scroll it is prescribed for me,
To do your will, O my God, is my delight,
   and your law is within my heart!"

   R. Here I am, Lord; I come to do your will.

"I announced your justice in the vast assembly;
   I did not restrain my lips, as you, O LORD, know."

   R. Here I am, Lord; I come to do your will.

"Your justice I kept not hid within my heart;

your faithfulness and your salvation I have spoken of;
I have made no secret of your kindness and your truth
  in the vast assembly."

R. Here I am, Lord; I come to do your will.

> **Alleluia, alleluia**
> The seed is the word of God, Christ the sower;
> all who come to him will live for ever.
> **Alleluia, alleluia**

GOSPEL   Mk 4:1–10, 13–20 or 4:1–9

The sower went out to sow.

A reading from the holy Gospel according to Mark
  Long form follows; for short form omit what is in brackets.

On another occasion, Jesus began to teach by the sea. A very
large crowd gathered around him so that he got into a boat on
the sea and sat down. And the whole crowd was beside the sea
on land. And he taught them at length in parables, and in the
course of his instruction he said to them, "Hear this! A sower
went out to sow. And as he sowed, some seed fell on the path,
and the birds came and ate it up. Other seed fell on rocky ground
where it had little soil. It sprang up at once because the soil
was not deep. And when the sun rose, it was scorched and it
withered for lack of roots. Some seed fell among thorns, and
the thorns grew up and choked it and it produced no grain.
And some seed fell on rich soil and produced fruit. It came up
and grew and yielded thirty, sixty, and a hundredfold." [He
added, "Whoever has ears to hear ought to hear."

  And when he was alone, those present along with the Twelve
questioned him about the parables. Jesus said to them, "Do
you not understand this parable? Then how will you understand
any of the parables? The sower sows the word. These are the

ones on the path where the word is sown. As soon as they hear, Satan comes at once and takes away the word sown in them. And these are the ones sown on rocky ground who, when they hear the word, receive it at once with joy. But they have no roots; they last only for a time. Then when tribulation or persecution comes because of the word, they quickly fall away. Those sown among thorns are another sort. They are the people who hear the word, but worldly anxiety, the lure of riches, and the craving for other things intrude and choke the word, and it bears no fruit. But those sown on rich soil are the ones who hear the word and accept it and bear fruit thirty and sixty and a hundredfold."]

The Gospel of the Lord.

Liturgy of the Eucharist, *p. 897.*

July 22

MARY MAGDALENE

Memorial

Mary of Magdala, from whom Jesus cast seven demons (Mk 16:9), was among the women who assisted Christ and the apostles as they traveled and preached the Good News. This Mary stood at the foot of the cross with the Lord's Mother and John when the other apostles fled. She helped bury the Lord's body, went to complete the burial on Easter morning, and became the first to see the risen Master. The Byzantine Liturgy says Jesus made Mary Magdalene "the apostle to the Apostles."

The Gospel for this memorial is proper.

Entrance Antiphon

The Lord said to Mary Magdalene: Go and tell my brothers that I shall ascend to my Father and your Father, to my God and to your God.

(Jn 20:17)

Opening Prayer

Father,
your Son first entrusted to Mary Magdalene
the joyful news of his resurrection.
By her prayers and example
may we proclaim Christ as our living Lord
and one day see him in glory,
for he lives and reigns with you and the Holy Spirit,
one God, for ever and ever.

FIRST READING   Sg 3:1–4b

I have found him whom my heart loves.

A reading from the Song of Songs

The Bride says:
On my bed at night I sought him
    whom my heart loves—
        I sought him but I did not find him.
I will rise then and go about the city;
    in the streets and crossings I will seek
Him whom my heart loves.
    I sought him but I did not find him.
The watchmen came upon me,
I had hardly left them
    when I found him whom my heart loves.

The word of the Lord.

Or:

2 Cor 5:14–17

*Even if we once knew Christ according to the flesh,
yet now we know him so no longer.*

A reading from the second Letter of Paul to the Corinthians

Brothers and sisters:

The love of Christ impels us, once we have come to the conviction that one died for all; therefore, all have died. He indeed died for all, so that those who live might no longer live for themselves but for him who for their sake died and was raised.

Consequently, from now on we regard no one according to the flesh; even if we once knew Christ according to the flesh, yet now we know him so no longer. So whoever is in Christ is a new creation: the old things have passed away; behold, new things have come.

The word of the Lord.

Responsorial Psalm

Ps 63:2, 3–4, 5–6, 8–9

R. My soul is thirsting for you, O Lord my God.

O God, you are my God whom I seek;
  for you my flesh pines and my soul thirsts
  like the earth, parched, lifeless and without water.

R. My soul is thirsting for you, O Lord my God.

Thus have I gazed toward you in the sanctuary
  to see your power and your glory,
For your kindness is a greater good than life;
  my lips shall glorify you.

R. My soul is thirsting for you, O Lord my God.

Thus will I bless you while I live;
  lifting up my hands, I will call upon your name.
As with the riches of a banquet shall my soul be satisfied,
  and with exultant lips my mouth shall praise you.

R. My soul is thirsting for you, O Lord my God.

You are my help,
  and in the shadow of your wings I shout for joy.
My soul clings fast to you;
  your right hand upholds me.

R. My soul is thirsting for you, O Lord my God.

Alleluia, alleluia
Tell us, Mary, what did you see on the way?
I saw the glory of the risen Christ, I saw his empty tomb.
Alleluia, alleluia

GOSPEL   Jn 20:1–2, 11–18

Woman, why are you weeping?
Whom are you looking for?

A reading from the holy Gospel according to John

On the first day of the week, Mary Magdalene came to the
tomb early in the morning, while it was still dark, and saw the
stone removed from the tomb. So she ran and went to Simon
Peter and to the other disciple whom Jesus loved, and told
them, "They have taken the Lord from the tomb, and we don't
know where they put him."

  Mary stayed outside the tomb weeping. And as she wept,
she bent over into the tomb and saw two angels in white sitting there, one at the head and one at the feet where the Body
of Jesus had been. And they said to her, "Woman, why are you
weeping?" She said to them, "They have taken my Lord, and I
don't know where they laid him." When she had said this, she
turned around and saw Jesus there, but did not know it was
Jesus. Jesus said to her, "Woman, why are you weeping? Whom
are you looking for?" She thought it was the gardener and said
to him, "Sir, if you carried him away, tell me where you laid

him, and I will take him." Jesus said to her, "Mary!" She turned and said to him in Hebrew, "Rabbouni," which means Teacher. Jesus said to her, "Stop holding on to me, for I have not yet ascended to the Father. But go to my brothers and tell them, 'I am going to my Father and your Father, to my God and your God.'" Mary Magdalene went and announced to the disciples, "I have seen the Lord," and then reported what he told her.

The Gospel of the Lord.

Liturgy of the Eucharist, *p. 897.*

Prayer over the Gifts

Pray, brethren...

Lord,
accept the gifts we present in memory of St. Mary
   Magdalene;
her loving worship was accepted by your Son,
who is Lord for ever and ever.

Communion Antiphon

The love of Christ compels us to live not for ourselves but for him who died and rose for us.   (2 Cor 5:14–15)

Prayer after Communion

Let us pray.

Pause for silent prayer, if this has not preceded.

Father,
may the sacrament we have received
fill us with the same faithful love
that kept Mary Magdalene close to Christ,
who is Lord for ever and ever.

BRIDGET, religious (1303–1373)

Optional Memorial

Bridget Persson Gudmarsson belonged by birth and marriage to high Swedish society. A wife and mother of eight children, she and her husband Ulf led a life centered on their family, the Church, and the community. After her husband's death in 1344, Bridget began to receive revelations about the Passion of Jesus Christ and current conditions in the Church and in Europe. In 1350, Bridget came to Rome for the Holy Year, lived there in poverty and prayer, and died in 1373. Bridget's plan for founding the Order of the Holy Savior was carried out by her second oldest daughter, St. Katherine of Sweden. The order is still known today as the Brigittines.

Antiphons and Prayers: *from the* COMMON OF HOLY MEN AND WOMEN *(pp. 2252–2322), or from the* WEEKDAY MASS. *The following is optional:*

Opening Prayer

Lord our God,
you revealed the secrets of heaven to St. Bridget
as she meditated on the suffering and death of your Son.
May your people rejoice in the revelation of your glory.

Grant this through our Lord Jesus Christ, your Son,
who lives and reigns with you and the Holy Spirit,
one God, for ever and ever.

Liturgy of the Word: *from the* COMMON OF HOLY MEN AND WOMEN: FOR RELIGIOUS *(pp. 2271ff.), especially Gal 2:19–20; Ps 34:2–3, 4–5, 6–7, 8–9, 10–11; Jn 15:1–8; or from the* WEEKDAY MASS.

Liturgy of the Eucharist, *p. 897.*

JAMES, apostle

Feast

Son of Zebedee and brother of John the Evangelist and Apostle, James was born at Bethsaida in Galilee. He was present at the special miracles worked by the Lord. The first apostle to die, James was martyred by Herod Agrippa I in 43 or 44 (Acts 12:1–3). Known as James the Greater because of his status, he has been specially honored since the ninth century at Compostela in Spain. From this famous place of pilgrimage, his cult was carried to Latin America, where many cities are named Santiago, after him.

Entrance Antiphon

Walking by the Sea of Galilee, Jesus saw James and John, the sons of Zebedee, mending their nets, and he called them to follow him.
(See Mt 4:18, 21)

Opening Prayer

Almighty Father,
by the martyrdom of St. James
you blessed the work of the early Church.
May his profession of faith
give us courage and his prayers bring us strength.

We ask this through our Lord Jesus Christ, your Son,
who lives and reigns with you and the Holy Spirit,
one God, for ever and ever.

See the Common of Martyrs (**pp. 2158–2165**), *for:*
   First Reading 2 Cor 4:7–15
   Responsorial Psalm 126:1bc–2ab, 2cd–3, 4–5, 6
   Alleluia Verse see Jn 15:16

GOSPEL

Mt 20:20–28

You will drink my chalice.

A reading from the holy Gospel according to Matthew

The mother of the sons of Zebedee approached Jesus with her sons and did him homage, wishing to ask him for something. He said to her, "What do you wish?" She answered him, "Command that these two sons of mine sit, one at your right and the other at your left, in your Kingdom." Jesus said in reply, "You do not know what you are asking. Can you drink the chalice that I am going to drink?" They said to him, "We can." He replied, "My chalice you will indeed drink, but to sit at my right and at my left, this is not mine to give but is for those for whom it has been prepared by my Father." When the ten heard this, they became indignant at the two brothers. But Jesus summoned them and said, "You know that the rulers of the Gentiles lord it over them, and the great ones make their authority over them felt. But it shall not be so among you. Rather, whoever wishes to be great among you shall be your servant; whoever wishes to be first among you shall be your slave. Just so, the Son of Man did not come to be served but to serve and to give his life as a ransom for many."

The Gospel of the Lord.

Liturgy of the Eucharist, p. 897.

Prayer over the Gifts

Pray, brethren...

Lord,
as we honor St. James,
the first apostle to share the cup of suffering and death,
wash away our sins by
the saving passion of your Son,
and make our sacrifice pleasing to you.

We ask this through Christ our Lord.

Preface of the Apostles I or **II,** p. 956.

Communion Antiphon

By sharing the cup of the Lord's suffering, they became the friends of God.
(See Mt 20:22–23)

Prayer after Communion

Let us pray.

Pause for silent prayer, if this has not preceded.

Father,
we have received this holy eucharist with joy
as we celebrate the feast of the apostle James.
Hear his prayers and bring us your help.
We ask this in the name of Jesus the Lord.

July 26

JOACHIM and ANN, parents of Mary

Memorial

An ancient tradition recorded in the Proto-Gospel of St. James, an apocryphal work dating from A.D. 130–150, identifies Mary's parents as Joachim and Ann. In the sixth century a basilica was dedicated to St. Ann at Constantinople. The grandparents of Jesus were honored in Jerusalem, where a Church of St. Ann has existed since the Crusades. Many Catholics have visited Ste Anne de Beaupré in Quebec, where the patroness of Christian mothers is specially reverenced.

Entrance Antiphon

Praised be Joachim and Ann for the child they bore. The Lord gave them the blessing of all the nations.

Opening Prayer

God of our fathers,
you gave Saints Joachim and Ann
the privilege of being the parents of Mary,
the mother of your incarnate Son.
May their prayers help us to attain
the salvation you have promised to your people.

Grant this through our Lord Jesus Christ, your Son,
who lives and reigns with you and the Holy Spirit,
one God, for ever and ever.

FIRST READING

Sir 44:1, 10–15

Their name lives on and on.

A reading from the Book of Sirach

Now will I praise those godly men,
    our ancestors, each in his own time:
These were godly men
    whose virtues have not been forgotten;
Their wealth remains in their families,
    their heritage with their descendants;
Through God's covenant with them their family endures,
    their posterity for their sake.

And for all time their progeny will endure,
    their glory will never be blotted out;
Their bodies are peacefully laid away,
    but their name lives on and on.
At gatherings their wisdom is retold,
    and the assembly proclaims their praise.

The word of the Lord.

Responsorial Psalm

Ps 132:11, 13–14, 17–18

R. God will give him the throne of David, his father.

The LORD swore to David
  a firm promise from which he will not withdraw:
"Your own offspring
  I will set upon your throne."

R. God will give him the throne of David, his father.

For the LORD has chosen Zion;

he prefers her for his dwelling.
"Zion is my resting place forever;
in her will I dwell, for I prefer her."

R. God will give him the throne of David, his father.

"In her will I make a horn to sprout forth for David;
I will place a lamp for my anointed.
His enemies I will clothe with shame,
but upon him my crown shall shine."

R. God will give him the throne of David, his father.

Alleluia, alleluia See Lk 2:25c
They yearned for the comforting of Israel,
and the Holy Spirit rested upon them.
Alleluia, alleluia

GOSPEL

Mt 13:16–17

Many prophets and righteous people longed to see what you see.

A reading from the holy Gospel according to Matthew

Jesus said to his disciples: "Blessed are your eyes, because they see, and your ears, because they hear. Amen, I say to you, many prophets and righteous people longed to see what you see but did not see it, and to hear what you hear but did not hear it."

The Gospel of the Lord.

Liturgy of the Eucharist, *p. 897.*

Prayer over the Gifts

Pray, brethren...

Lord,
receive these gifts as signs of our love
and give us a share in the blessing you promised
to Abraham and his descendants.

We ask this in the name of Jesus the Lord.

Communion Antiphon

They received a blessing from the Lord, and kindness from God their Savior. (See Ps 23:5)

Prayer after Communion

Let us pray.

Pause for silent prayer, if this has not preceded.

Father,
your Son was born as a man
so that men could be born again in you.
As you nourish us with the bread of life,
given only to your sons and daughters,
fill us with the Spirit who makes us your children.

We ask this through Christ our Lord.

July 29

MARTHA

Memorial

Today's saint was the sister of Mary and Lazarus who received the Lord with hospitality into their home in Bethany, not far from Jerusalem. Martha diligently waited on the Lord and with expectant faith beseeched the return of her brother from the dead.

The Gospel for this memorial is proper.

Entrance Antiphon

As Jesus entered a certain village a woman called Martha welcomed him into her house. (Lk 10:38)

Opening Prayer

Father,
your Son honored St. Martha
by coming to her home as a guest.

By her prayers
may we serve Christ in our brothers and sisters
and be welcomed by you into heaven, our true home.

We ask this through our Lord Jesus Christ, your Son,
who lives and reigns with you and the Holy Spirit,
one God, for ever and ever.

Liturgy of the Word: *from the* COMMON OF HOLY MEN AND WOMEN *(pp. 2269ff.), or:*

*See the Common of Holy Men and Women (**pp. 2156–2165**), for:*
First Reading 1 Jn 4:7–16
Responsorial Psalm 34:2–3, 4–5, 6–7, 8–9, 10–11
Alleluia Verse Jn 8:12

GOSPEL

Jn 11:19–27

I have come to believe that you are the Christ, the Son of God.

A reading from the holy Gospel according to John

Many of the Jews had come to Martha and Mary to comfort them about their brother [Lazarus, who had died]. When Martha heard that Jesus was coming, she went to meet him; but Mary sat at home. Martha said to Jesus, "Lord, if you had been here, my brother would not have died. But even now I know that whatever you ask of God, God will give you." Jesus said to her, "Your brother will rise." Martha said to him, "I know he will rise, in the resurrection on the last day." Jesus told her, "I am the resurrection and the life; whoever believes in me, even if he dies, will live, and anyone who lives and believes in me will never die. Do you believe this?" She said to him, "Yes, Lord. I have come to believe that you are the Christ, the Son of God, the one who is coming into the world."

The Gospel of the Lord.

Or:

GOSPEL

Lk 10:38–42

Martha, Martha, you are anxious and worried about many things.

A reading from the holy Gospel according to Luke

Jesus entered a village where a woman whose name was Martha welcomed him. She had a sister named Mary who sat beside the Lord at his feet listening to him speak. Martha, burdened with much serving, came to him and said, "Lord, do you not care that my sister has left me by myself to do the serving? Tell her to help me." The Lord said to her in reply, "Martha, Martha, you are anxious and worried about many things. There is need of only one thing. Mary has chosen the better part and it will not be taken from her."

The Gospel of the Lord.

Liturgy of the Eucharist, *p. 897.*

Prayer over the Gifts

Pray, brethren...

Father,
we praise you for your glory
on the feast of St. Martha.
Accept this service of our worship
as you accepted her love.

Grant this through Christ our Lord.

Communion Antiphon

Martha said to Jesus: You are the Christ, the Son of God, who was to come into the world. (Jn 11:27)

Prayer after Communion

Let us pray.

Pause for silent prayer, if this has not preceded.

Lord,

you have given us the body and blood of your Son
to free us from undue attachment to this passing life.
By following the example of St. Martha,
may we grow in love for you on earth
and rejoice for ever in the vision of your glory in heaven.

We ask this in the name of Jesus the Lord.

July 30

PETER CHRYSOLOGUS, bishop and doctor
(380–451)

Optional Memorial

Called Chrysologus ("golden word") because of his eloquence,
Peter was born near Ravenna in Italy. Elected bishop of Ravenna, he
was an effective, dedicated pastoral leader, especially noted for his
preaching. About 180 of his sermons still exist.

Antiphons and Prayers: *from the* COMMON OF PASTORS: FOR BISHOPS
(pp. 2170–2175), or COMMON OF DOCTORS OF THE CHURCH *(pp. 2219–2238),
or from the* WEEKDAY MASS. *The following is optional:*

Opening Prayer

Father,
you made Peter Chrysologus
an outstanding preacher of your incarnate Word.
May the prayers of St. Peter help us to cherish
the mystery of our salvation
and make its meaning clear in our love for others.

Grant this through our Lord Jesus Christ, your Son,
who lives and reigns with you and the Holy Spirit,
one God, for ever and ever.

Liturgy of the Word: *from the* COMMON OF PASTORS *(pp. 2188ff.), or*
COMMON OF DOCTORS OF THE CHURCH *(pp. 2188ff.), especially Eph 3:8–12;
Ps 119:9, 10, 11, 12, 13, 14; Lk 6:43–45; or from the* WEEKDAY MASS.

Liturgy of the Eucharist, *p. 897.*

IGNATIUS OF LOYOLA, priest (1491–1556)

Memorial

Ignatius, who has had a profound influence on Catholic life, was born at Loyola in the Basque area of Spain. He became a soldier and was wounded in battle. Ignatius turned to Christ during his long recovery. A strong and holy organizer, Ignatius founded the Society of Jesus at Paris in 1534. The Jesuits effectively worked for Church renewal, especially in the missions and in Catholic education. The *Spiritual Exercises* Ignatius developed helped many others to conversion. Ignatius showed unconditional loyalty to the pope. He was canonized in 1622.

Entrance Antiphon

At the name of Jesus every knee must bend, in heaven, on earth, and under the earth; every tongue should proclaim to the glory of God the Father: Jesus Christ is Lord. (Phil 2:10–11)

Opening Prayer

Father,
you gave St. Ignatius of Loyola to your Church
to bring greater glory to your name.
May we follow his example on earth
and share the crown of life in heaven.

We ask this through our Lord Jesus Christ, your Son,
who lives and reigns with you and the Holy Spirit,
one God, for ever and ever.

Liturgy of the Word: *from the* COMMON OF PASTORS *(pp. 2188ff.), or* COMMON OF HOLY MEN AND WOMEN: FOR RELIGIOUS *(pp. 2271ff.), or from the* WEEKDAY MASS, *or:*

FIRST READING

1 Cor 10:31—11:1

Do everything for the glory of God.

A reading from the first Letter of Saint Paul to the Corinthians

Brothers and sisters:

Whether you eat or drink, or whatever you do, do everything for the glory of God. Avoid giving offense, whether to Jews or Greeks or the Church of God, just as I try to please everyone in every way, not seeking my own benefit but that of the many, that they may be saved. Be imitators of me, as I am of Christ.

The word of the Lord.

*See the Common of Holy Men and Women (**pp. 2288–2303**), for:*
  Responsorial Psalm 34:2–3, 4–5, 6–7, 8–9, 10–11
  Alleluia Verse Mt 5:3

GOSPEL

Lk 14:25–33

Everyone of you who does not renounce all his possessions cannot be my disciple.

A reading from the holy Gospel according to Luke

Great crowds were traveling with Jesus, and he turned and addressed them, "If anyone comes to me without hating his father and mother, wife and children, brothers and sisters, and even his own life, he cannot be my disciple. Whoever does not carry his own cross and come after me cannot be my disciple. Which of you wishing to construct a tower does not first sit down and calculate the cost to see if there is enough for its completion? Otherwise, after laying the foundation and finding himself unable to finish the work the onlookers should laugh at him and say, 'This one began to build but did not have the resources to finish.' Or what king marching into battle would not first sit down and decide whether with ten thousand troops he can successfully oppose another king advancing upon him with twenty thousand troops? But if not, while he is still far away, he will send a delegation to ask for peace terms. In the same way, everyone of you who does not renounce all his possessions cannot be my disciple."

The Gospel of the Lord.

Liturgy of the Eucharist, *p. 897.*

Prayer over the Gifts

Pray, brethren...

Lord God,
be pleased with the gifts we present to you
at this celebration in honor of St. Ignatius.
Make us truly holy by this eucharist
which you give us as the source of all holiness.

We ask this in the name of Jesus the Lord.

Communion Antiphon

I have come to bring fire to the earth. How I wish it were already blazing! (Lk 12:49)

Prayer after Communion

Let us pray.

Pause for silent prayer, if this has not preceded.

Lord,
may the sacrifice of thanksgiving
which we have offered on the feast of St. Ignatius
lead us to the eternal praise of your glory.

Grant this through Christ our Lord.

AUGUST

ALPHONSUS LIGUORI, bishop and doctor
(1696–1787)

Memorial

Born near Naples in 1696, Alphonsus earned degrees in civil and canon law. He gave up law to become a priest—an apostle to the poor, an untiring preacher and writer, a merciful confessor. Alphonsus founded the Congregation of the Most Holy Redeemer (Redemptorists) to evangelize the poor. He was an outstanding moral theologian and bishop who worked unceasingly and patiently through many trials. In 1950 he was named patron of moral theologians.

Antiphons and Prayers: *from the* COMMON OF PASTORS: FOR BISHOPS *(pp. 2170–2175), or* COMMON OF DOCTORS OF THE CHURCH *(pp. 2219–2238), or from the* WEEKDAY MASS, *except:*

Opening Prayer

Father,
you constantly build up your Church
by the lives of your saints.
Give us grace to follow St. Alphonsus
in his loving concern for the salvation of men
and so come to share his reward in heaven.

Grant this through our Lord Jesus Christ, your Son,
who lives and reigns with you and the Holy Spirit,
one God, for ever and ever.

Liturgy of the Word: *from the* COMMON OF PASTORS *(pp. 2188ff.), or* COMMON OF DOCTORS OF THE CHURCH *(pp. 2222ff.), or from the* WEEKDAY MASS, *or:*

FIRST READING

Rom 8:1–4

*The law of the spirit of life in Christ Jesus
has set you free from the law of sin and death.*

A reading from the Letter of Saint Paul to the Romans

Brothers and sisters:

Now there is no condemnation for those who are in Christ Jesus. For the law of the spirit of life in Christ Jesus has freed you from the law of sin and death. For what the law, weakened by the flesh, was powerless to do, this God has done: by sending his own Son in the likeness of sinful flesh and for the sake of sin, he condemned sin in the flesh, so that the righteous decree of the law might be fulfilled in us, who live not according to the flesh but according to the spirit.

The word of the Lord.

*See the Common of Doctors (**pp. 2228–2235**), for:*
    Responsorial Psalm 119:9, 10, 11, 12, 13, 14
    Alleluia Verse Mt 5:16
    Gospel Mt 5:13–19

    Liturgy of the Eucharist, *p. 897.*

Prayer over the Gifts

Pray, brethren...

Father,
inflame our hearts with the Spirit of your love
as we present these gifts on the feast of St. Alphonsus,
who dedicated his life to you in the eucharist.

We ask this in the name of Jesus the Lord.

Prayer after Communion

Let us pray.
        Pause for silent prayer, if this has not preceded.

Lord,
you made St. Alphonsus
a faithful minister and preacher of this holy eucharist.

May all who believe in you receive it often
and give you never-ending praise.
We ask this through Christ our Lord.

August 2

EUSEBIUS OF VERCELLI, bishop (c. 315–371)

Optional Memorial

A native of Sardinia, Eusebius went to Rome and was later elected bishop of Vercelli. He strenuously opposed the errors of the Arians, and for this he was exiled from his see. It is thought that he translated the Gospels into Latin.

Antiphons and Prayers: *from the* COMMON OF PASTORS: FOR BISHOPS *(pp. 2170–2175), or from the* WEEKDAY MASS. *The following is optional:*

Opening Prayer

Lord God,
St. Eusebius affirmed the divinity of your Son.
By keeping the faith he taught,
may we come to share the eternal life of Christ,
who lives and reigns with you and the Holy Spirit,
one God, for ever and ever.

Liturgy of the Word: *from the* COMMON OF PASTORS *(pp. 2188ff.), especially 1 Jn 5:1–5; Ps 89:2–3, 4–5, 21–22, 25 and 27; Mt 5:1–12a, or from the* WEEKDAY MASS.

Liturgy of the Eucharist, *p. 897.*

Also on August 2

PETER JULIAN EYMARD, priest (1811–1868)

Optional Memorial

Peter Julian Eymard became a diocesan priest in France and later joined the Marist Order, which had been recently founded. But Eymard became deeply drawn to the idea of developing the Eucharistic life of Catholics. This led him to leave the Marists and start a new congregation of priests and brothers dedicated to his Eucharistic ideals. He later also founded a congregation of sisters. Despite poverty and difficult beginnings, his work succeeded and spread.

Antiphons and Prayers: *from the* COMMON OF PASTORS *(pp. 2170–2218), or from the* COMMON OF HOLY MEN AND WOMEN: FOR RELIGIOUS *(pp. 2260–2263), or from the* WEEKDAY MASS.

Liturgy of the Word: *from the* COMMON OF PASTORS *(pp. 2188ff.), or* COMMON OF HOLY MEN AND WOMEN: FOR RELIGIOUS *(pp. 2271ff.), especially Acts 4:32–35; Ps 34:2–3, 4–5, 6–7, 8–9, 10–11; Jn 15:1–8; or from the* WEEKDAY MASS.

Liturgy of the Eucharist, *p. 897.*

August 4

JOHN VIANNEY, priest (1786–1859)

Memorial

Known as the Curé of Ars, St. John is the beloved patron of parish priests. Born in Lyons, France, he was a "delayed vocation" who had great difficulty with his seminary studies. Sent to Ars, where few people practiced their faith, he transformed the parish by his holiness, preaching, prayer, and penance. People flocked to Ars to confess to this holy pastor, who often spent 16 hours a day in the confessional. After 42 years in Ars, St. John Vianney died on this date. He was canonized in 1925.

Antiphons and Prayers: *from the* COMMON OF PASTORS *(pp. 2170–2218), or from the* WEEKDAY MASS, *except:*

Opening Prayer

Father of mercy,
you made St. John Vianney outstanding
in his priestly zeal and concern for your people.
By his example and prayers,
enable us to win our brothers and sisters

to the love of Christ
and come with them to eternal glory.

We ask this through our Lord Jesus Christ, your Son,
who lives and reigns with you and the Holy Spirit,
one God, for ever and ever.

Liturgy of the Word: *from the* COMMON OF PASTORS *(pp. 2188ff.), especially Ez 3:17–21; Ps 117:1bc, 2; or from the* WEEKDAY MASS, *or the following Gospel.*

Alleluia, alleluia   Lk 4:18
The Lord sent me to bring glad tidings to the poor
and to proclaim liberty to captives.
Alleluia, alleluia

GOSPEL

Mt 9:35—10:1

At the sight of the crowds, his heart was moved with pity for them.

A reading from the holy Gospel according to Matthew

Jesus went around to all the towns and villages, teaching in their synagogues, proclaiming the Gospel of the Kingdom, and curing every disease and illness. At the sight of the crowds, his heart was moved with pity for them because they were troubled and abandoned, like sheep without a shepherd. Then he said to his disciples, "The harvest is abundant but the laborers are few; so ask the master of the harvest to send out laborers for his harvest."

Then he summoned his twelve disciples and gave them authority over unclean spirits to drive them out and to cure every disease and every illness.

The Gospel of the Lord.

Liturgy of the Eucharist, *p. 897.*

August 5

DEDICATION OF THE BASILICA OF SAINT MARY MAJOR

Optional Memorial

One of the four major basilicas in Rome, St. Mary Major was built by Pope Liberius (352–366). It has also been called Our Lady of the Snows, because a medieval legend said a miraculous snowfall in August marked its site. Pope Sixtus III renovated the church twenty years after the Council of Ephesus, which declared belief in Mary as Mother of God. The basilica, dedicated on August 5, 451, represents the homage of the Roman Church to the Blessed Mother. It is called "Major" as the first church in the West in honor of Mary.

Antiphons and Prayers: *from the* COMMON OF THE BLESSED VIRGIN MARY *(pp. 2091–2127), or from the* WEEKDAY MASS. *The following is optional:*

Opening Prayer

Lord,
pardon the sins of your people.
May the prayers of Mary, the mother of your Son,
help to save us,
for by ourselves we cannot please you.
Grant this through our Lord Jesus Christ, your Son,
who lives and reigns with you and the Holy Spirit,
one God, for ever and ever.

Liturgy of the Word: *from the* COMMON OF THE BLESSED VIRGIN MARY *(pp. 2101ff.), especially Rv 21:1–5a; Jdt 13:18bcde, 19; Lk 11:27–28; or from the* WEEKDAY MASS.

Liturgy of the Eucharist, p. 897.

For **August 6,** TRANSFIGURATION, *see* **Vatican II Sunday Missal,** *p. 1053.*

August 7

SIXTUS II, pope and martyr, and COMPANIONS, martyrs (†258)

Optional Memorial

Today we commemorate the most shocking and glorious page in the history of the Roman persecutions. On August 6, 258, the pope was celebrating the Eucharist at the Catacombs of St. Callistus when he and four deacons were arrested and decapitated before the people. Three other deacons were similarly decapitated in that cruel attack launched by the Emperor Valerian against bishops, priests, and deacons.

Antiphons and Prayers: *from the* COMMON OF MARTYRS *(pp. 2128–2169), or from the* WEEKDAY MASS. *The following is optional:*

Opening Prayer

Father,
by the power of the Holy Spirit
you enabled St. Sixtus and his companions to lay down their
　 lives
for your word in witness to Jesus.
Give us the grace to believe in you
and the courage to profess our faith.

We ask this through our Lord Jesus Christ, your Son,
who lives and reigns with you and the Holy Spirit,
one God, for ever and ever.

Liturgy of the Word: *from the* COMMON OF MARTYRS *(pp. 2147ff.), especially Wis 3:1–9; Ps 126:1bc–2ab, 2cd–3, 4–5, 6; Mt 10:28–33; or from the* WEEKDAY MASS.

Liturgy of the Eucharist, *p. 897.*

Also on August 7

CAJETAN, priest (1480–1547)

Optional Memorial

Today's saint is intimately associated with the start of the Catholic Counter Reformation, an effort toward Church renewal and reform in response to the rise of Protestantism. Born in 1480, Cajetan became a prelate of the Roman curia who spent all of his spare time in prayer and serving the poor. With a friend, Fr. Gian Pietro Carafa, he founded an association of priests and laity to live the Gospel. They later formed the Theatines—a religious order of priests totally dedicated to evangelical living, preaching, and renewing the liturgy. Carafa first became a bishop and later Pope Paul IV. Cajetan, superior of the Theatines, was canonized in 1671.

Antiphons and Prayers: *from the* COMMON OF PASTORS *(pp. 2170–2218), or* COMMON OF HOLY MEN AND WOMEN *(pp. 2252–2322), or from the* WEEKDAY MASS. *The following is optional:*

Opening Prayer

Lord,
you helped St. Cajetan
to imitate the apostolic way of life.
By his example and prayers
may we trust in you always
and be faithful in seeking your kingdom.

Grant this through our Lord Jesus Christ, your Son,
who lives and reigns with you and the Holy Spirit,
one God, for ever and ever.

Liturgy of the Word: *from the* COMMON OF PASTORS *(pp. 2188ff.), or* COMMON OF HOLY MEN AND WOMEN: FOR RELIGIOUS *(pp. 2271ff.), especially Sir 2:7–11; Ps 112:1–2, 3–4, 5–6, 7–8, 9; Lk 12:32–34; or from the* WEEKDAY MASS.

Liturgy of the Eucharist, *p. 897.*

August 8

DOMINIC, priest (1170–1221)

Memorial

Dominic de Guzman was born in old Castile, Spain. He became a diocesan priest with thoughts of missionary work in north Europe. But then he saw the dangers of the Cathar or Albigensian heresy sweeping through southern France. Dominic lived and preached in evangelical poverty, gathered others around him and thus founded the Order of Preachers (called the Dominicans). Dominic placed emphasis on preaching and the importance of study. Consumed by work and penance, he died in Bologna on August 6, 1221.

Antiphons and Prayers: *from the* COMMON OF PASTORS *(pp. 2170–2218), or* COMMON OF HOLY MEN AND WOMEN: FOR RELIGIOUS *(pp. 2260–2263), or from the* WEEKDAY MASS, *except:*

Opening Prayer

Lord,
let the holiness and teaching of St. Dominic
come to the aid of your Church.
May he help us now with his prayers
as he once inspired people by his preaching.

We ask this through our Lord Jesus Christ, your Son,
who lives and reigns with you and the Holy Spirit,
one God, for ever and ever.

Liturgy of the Word: *from the* COMMON OF PASTORS: FOR MISSIONARIES *(pp. 2191ff.), or* COMMON OF HOLY MEN AND WOMEN: FOR RELIGIOUS *(pp. 2271ff.), especially 1 Cor 2:1–10a; Ps 96:1–2a, 2b–3, 7–8a, 10; Lk 9:57–62; or from the* WEEKDAY MASS.

Liturgy of the Eucharist, *p. 897.*

Prayer over the Gifts

Pray, brethren...

Lord of mercy,

at the intercession of St. Dominic
hear our prayers,
and by the power of this sacrifice
give us the grace to preach and defend our faith.

Grant this through Christ our Lord.

Prayer after Communion

Let us pray.

Pause for silent prayer, if this has not preceded.

Lord,
may your Church share with a living faith
the power of the sacrament we have received.
As the preaching of St. Dominic helped your Church
   to grow,
may his prayers help us to live for you.

We ask this in the name of Jesus the Lord.

August 10

LAWRENCE, deacon and martyr (†258)

Feast

Lawrence, the most famous of Roman martyrs, was a deacon. Killed four days after Pope Sixtus, Lawrence became famous because of his youth, evangelical love for the poor, courage before his torturers, and sense of humor while dying. Tradition holds that he was roasted to death on a gridiron. A beautiful basilica in honor of St. Lawrence stands in Rome.

Entrance Antiphon

Today let us honor St. Lawrence, who spent himself for the poor of the Church. Thus he merited to suffer martyrdom and to ascend in joy to Jesus Christ the Lord.

Opening Prayer

Father,
you called St. Lawrence to serve you by love
and crowned his life with glorious martyrdom.
Help us to be like him in loving you
and doing your work.

Grant this through our Lord Jesus Christ, your Son,
who lives and reigns with you and the Holy Spirit,
one God, for ever and ever.

FIRST READING   2 Cor 9:6–10

God loves a cheerful giver.

A reading from the second Letter of Saint Paul to the Corinthians

Brothers and sisters:

Whoever sows sparingly will also reap sparingly, and whoever
sows bountifully will also reap bountifully. Each must do as
already determined, without sadness or compulsion, for God
loves a cheerful giver. Moreover, God is able to make every
grace abundant for you, so that in all things, always having all
you need, you may have an abundance for every good work.
As it is written:

> *He scatters abroad, he gives to the poor;*
> *his righteousness endures forever.*

The one who supplies seed to the sower and bread for food
will supply and multiply your seed and increase the harvest of
your righteousness.

The word of the Lord.

See the Common of Holy Men and Women (pp. 2289–2304), for:
  Responsorial Psalm Ps 112:1–2, 5–6, 7–8, 9
  Alleluia Verse Jn 8:12bc

See the Common of Martyrs (p. 2168), for:
  Gospel Jn 12:24–26

Liturgy of the Eucharist, *p. 897.*

Prayer over the Gifts

Pray, brethren...

Lord,
at this celebration in honor of St. Lawrence,
accept the gifts we offer
and let them become a help to our salvation.

We ask this in the name of Jesus the Lord.

Communion Antiphon

**He who serves me, follows me, says the Lord; and where I am,
my servant will also be.** (Jn 12:26)

Prayer after Communion

Let us pray.
Pause for silent prayer, if this has not preceded.

Lord,
we have received your gifts
on this feast of St. Lawrence.
As we offer you our worship in this eucharist,
may we experience the increase of your saving grace.

We ask this through Christ our Lord.

August 11

CLARE, virgin (1193/4–1253)

Memorial

The "little plant of St. Francis," Clare Offreduccio, was born in
Assisi. On Palm Sunday of 1212, at age 18, she escaped from her
wealthy home and received the religious habit from St. Francis. Clare
became the mother and foundress of the Franciscan Second Order,

called the "Poor Clares." She led a life of remarkable discipline, holiness, and poverty, and was canonized in 1255, only two years after her death.

Antiphons and Prayers: *from the* COMMON OF VIRGINS *(pp. 2238–2252), or* COMMON OF HOLY MEN AND WOMEN: FOR RELIGIOUS *(pp. 2260–2263), or from the* WEEKDAY MASS, *except:*

Opening Prayer

God of mercy,
you inspired St. Clare with the love of poverty.
By the help of her prayers
may we follow Christ in poverty of spirit
and come to the joyful vision of your glory
in the kingdom of heaven.

We ask this through our Lord Jesus Christ, your Son,
who lives and reigns with you and the Holy Spirit,
one God, for ever and ever.

Liturgy of the Word: *from the* COMMON OF VIRGINS *(pp. 2244ff.), or* COMMON OF HOLY MEN AND WOMEN: FOR RELIGIOUS *(pp. 2271ff.), especially Phil 3:8–14; Ps 16:1b–2a, 5, 7–8, 11; and the following Gospel, or from the* WEEKDAY MASS.

GOSPEL

Mt 19:27–29

You who have followed me will receive a hundred times more.

A reading from the holy Gospel according to Matthew

Peter said to Jesus, "We have given up everything and followed you. What will there be for us?" Jesus said to them, "Amen, I say to you that you who have followed me, in the new age, when the Son of Man is seated on his throne of glory, will yourselves sit on twelve thrones, judging the twelve tribes of Israel. And everyone who has given up houses or brothers or sisters or father or mother or children or lands for the sake of my name will receive a hundred times more, and will inherit eternal life."

The Gospel of the Lord.

Liturgy of the Eucharist, *p. 897.*

August 13

PONTIAN, pope and martyr, and
HIPPOLYTUS, priest and martyr (†c. 235)

Optional Memorial

Pontian became pope in 230. The Roman Church at that time was divided; the rigorist priest Hippolytus led one faction. In 235 pope and priest were deported into forced labor in Sardinia and there were martyred for their common faith. After the persecution, their bodies were brought back to Rome on this date.

Antiphons and Prayers: *from the* COMMON OF MARTYRS *(pp. 2128–2169), or* COMMON OF PASTORS *(pp. 2170–2218), or from the* WEEKDAY MASS. *The following is optional:*

Opening Prayer

Lord,
may the loyal suffering of your saints, Pontian and
    Hippolytus,
fill us with your love
and make our hearts steadfast in faith.

Grant this through our Lord Jesus Christ, your Son,
who lives and reigns with you and the Holy Spirit,
one God, for ever and ever.

Liturgy of the Word: *from the* COMMON OF MARTYRS *(pp. 2147ff.), or* COMMON OF PASTORS *(pp. 2188ff.), especially 1 Pt 4:12–19; Ps 124:2–3, 4–5, 7–8; Jn 15:18–21; or from the* WEEKDAY MASS.

Liturgy of the Eucharist, *p. 897.*

August 14

MAXIMILIAN MARY KOLBE, priest and martyr
(1894–1941)

Memorial

Born near Lodz, Poland, Raymond Kolbe became a Franciscan priest and took the name Maximilian. He was intensely devoted to the Blessed Virgin Mary, and established an organization called the Militia of Mary Immaculate. He began publishing a monthly magazine that soon had a circulation of over one million copies. After the Nazis invaded Poland, Maximilian was arrested and sent to Auschwitz. He heroically offered his life in place of another man who had been selected for execution. After starving him for two weeks, the Nazis killed him with a lethal injection.

Entrance Antiphon

Come, you whom my Father blessed, says the Lord: I tell you, whatever you did for one of the least of my brothers or sisters, you did for me.   (Mt 25:34, 40)

Opening Prayer

Gracious God,
you filled your priest and martyr,
St. Maximilian Kolbe,
with zeal for souls
and love for his neighbor.
Through the prayer of this devoted servant of Mary
    Immaculate,
grant that in our efforts to serve others for your glory
we too may become like Christ your Son,
who loved his own in the world even to the end,
and now lives and reigns with you and the Holy Spirit,
one God, for ever and ever.

Liturgy of the Word: *from the* COMMON OF MARTYRS *(pp. 2147ff.), or* COMMON OF PASTORS *(pp. 2188ff.), especially Wis 3:1–9 or 1 Jn 3:14–18, with the following response and Gospel, or from the* WEEKDAY MASS.

Responsorial Psalm

Ps 116:10–11, 12–13, 16a c–17

R. **Precious in the eyes of the Lord**
   is the death of his faithful ones.

I believed, even when I said,
"I am greatly afflicted";
I said in my alarm,
"No man is dependable."

R. **Precious in the eyes of the Lord**
   is the death of his faithful ones.

How shall I make a return to the LORD
for all the good he has done for me?
The cup of salvation I will take up,
and I will call upon the name of the LORD.

R. **Precious in the eyes of the Lord**
   is the death of his faithful ones.

O LORD, I am your servant;
you have loosed my bonds.
To you will I offer sacrifice of thanksgiving,
and I will call upon the name of the LORD.

R. **Precious in the eyes of the Lord**
   is the death of his faithful ones.

Alleluia, alleluia   Jn 12:25
If you hate your life in this world,
you will preserve it to life eternal.
Alleluia, alleluia

GOSPEL   Jn 15:12–16

This is my commandment: love one another.

A reading from the holy Gospel according to John

Jesus said to his disciples: "This is my commandment: love one another as I love you. No one has greater love than this, to lay down one's life for one's friends. You are my friends if you do what I command you. I no longer call you slaves, because a slave does not know what his master is doing. I have called you friends, because I have told you everything I have heard from my Father. I was not you who chose me, but I who chose you and appointed you to go and bear fruit that will remain, so that whatever you ask the Father in my name he may give you."

The Gospel of the Lord.

Liturgy of the Eucharist, *p. 897.*

Prayer over the Gifts

Pray, brethren...

We offer these gifts to you, Lord God,
with the prayer that,
inspired by the example of St. Maximilian Kolbe,
we may learn to offer our very lives to you.

We ask this through Christ our Lord.

Communion Antiphon

There is no greater love than this: to lay down one's life for one's friends. (Jn 15:13)

Prayer after Communion

Let us pray.

Pause for silent prayer, if this has not preceded.

Lord Jesus,
renewed by your body and blood,
we pray that the same fire of charity

which St. Maximilian Kolbe drew from this eucharistic
  banquet
may also inflame our hearts
with heroic love for others.

You live and reign for ever and ever.

For **August 15,** ASSUMPTION, *see* **Vatican II Sunday Missal,** *Vigil Mass,*
p. 1059; Mass During the Day, p. 1064.

August 16

STEPHEN OF HUNGARY, king (969/70–1038)

Optional Memorial

Born of the Magyars, Stephen was baptized around 985 by St.
Adalbert of Prague. Stephen succeeded his father as king in 997
and on Christmas of 1000 was crowned "apostolic King of Hungary"
with a crown sent by the pope. Intent on establishing the Church in
Hungary, Stephen invited the Benedictines to help evangelize.
Stephen and his son Emeric were both canonized in 1083.

Antiphons and Prayers: *from the* COMMON OF HOLY MEN AND WOMEN
(pp. 2252–2322), or from the WEEKDAY MASS. *The following is optional:*

Opening Prayer

Almighty Father,
grant that St. Stephen of Hungary,
who fostered the growth of your Church on earth,
may continue to be our powerful helper in heaven.

We ask this through our Lord Jesus Christ, your Son,
who lives and reigns with you and the Holy Spirit,
one God, for ever and ever.

Liturgy of the Word: *from the* COMMON OF HOLY MEN AND WOMEN *(pp.*
2269ff.), especially Dt 6:3–9; Ps 112:1bc–2, 3–4, 5–6, 7–8, 9; Mt 25:14–30;
or from the WEEKDAY MASS.

Liturgy of the Eucharist, *p. 897.*

August 18

[In the dioceses of the United States]

JANE FRANCES DE CHANTAL, religious
(1572–1641)

Optional Memorial

This courageous woman, born in France, was married to the Baron of Chantal. Eight happy years of marriage and six children followed. Her husband was killed accidentally, and in her sorrow she turned to God with total trust. Directed by St. Francis de Sales, Jane became a religious, the foundress of the Visitation Order, and a tireless worker for God.

In the United States this memorial is transferred to this date from December 12.

Antiphons and Prayers: *from the* COMMON OF HOLY MEN AND WOMEN: FOR RELIGIOUS *(pp. 2260–2263), or from the* WEEKDAY MASS. *The following is optional:*

Opening Prayer

Lord,
you chose St. Jane Frances to serve you
both in marriage and in religious life.
By her prayers
help us to be faithful in our vocation
and always to be the light of the world.

We ask this through our Lord Jesus Christ, your Son,
who lives and reigns with you and the Holy Spirit,
one God, for ever and ever.

Liturgy of the Word: *from the* COMMON OF HOLY MEN AND WOMEN: FOR RELIGIOUS *(pp. 2271ff.), especially Prv 31:10–13, 19–20, 30–31; Ps 131:1bcde, 2, 3; Mk 3:31–35; or from the* WEEKDAY MASS.

Liturgy of the Eucharist, *p. 897.*

August 19

JOHN EUDES, priest (1601–1680)

Optional Memorial

Today's saint, born in France, had an outstanding education before his ordination as an Oratorian priest. After years as an effective preacher, he concluded that the best way to bring Christ to the poor was to form educated, zealous priests. So John Eudes founded four seminaries, the Congregation of Jesus and of Mary (the Eudists) to direct seminaries, the Institute of Our Lady of Charity to care for girls, and fostered devotion to the Sacred Heart.

Antiphons and Prayers: *from the* COMMON OF PASTORS *(pp. 2170–2218), or* COMMON OF HOLY MEN AND WOMEN: FOR RELIGIOUS *(pp. 2260–2263), or from the* WEEKDAY MASS. *The following is optional:*

Opening Prayer

Father,
you chose the priest John Eudes
to preach the infinite riches of Christ.
By his teaching and example
help us to know you better
and live faithfully in the light of the gospel.

Grant this through our Lord Jesus Christ, your Son,
who lives and reigns with you and the Holy Spirit,
one God, for ever and ever.

Liturgy of the Word: *from the* COMMON OF PASTORS *(pp. 2188ff.), or* COMMON OF HOLY MEN AND WOMEN *(pp. 2271ff.), especially Eph 3:14–19; Ps 131:1bcde, 2, 3; Mt 11:25–30; or from the* WEEKDAY MASS.

Liturgy of the Eucharist, *p. 897.*

August 20

BERNARD, abbot and doctor (1090–1153)

Memorial

St. Bernard dominated the century in which he lived. He became a Cistercian monk at Clairvaux and was soon named abbot. An outstanding spiritual guide, Bernard encouraged his monks toward holiness and wrote much about the Lord Jesus, spirituality, the Scriptures, and the Blessed Mother. He influenced popes and kings, and traveled throughout Europe to heal divisions in the Church of his day.

Antiphons and Prayers: *from the* COMMON OF DOCTORS OF THE CHURCH *(pp. 2170–2218), or* COMMON OF HOLY MEN AND WOMEN: FOR RELIGIOUS *(pp. 2260–2263), or from the* WEEKDAY MASS, *except:*

Opening Prayer

Heavenly Father,
St. Bernard was filled with zeal for your house
and was a radiant light in your Church.
By his prayers
may we be filled with this spirit of zeal
and walk always as children of light.

We ask this through our Lord Jesus Christ, your Son,
who lives and reigns with you and the Holy Spirit,
one God, for ever and ever.

Liturgy of the Word: *from the* COMMON OF DOCTORS OF THE CHURCH *(pp. 2222ff.), or* COMMON OF HOLY MEN AND WOMEN: FOR RELIGIOUS *(pp. 2271ff.), especially Sir 15:1–6; Ps 119:9, 10, 11, 12, 13, 14; Jn 17:20–26; or from the* WEEKDAY MASS.

Liturgy of the Eucharist, *p. 897.*

Prayer over the Gifts

Pray, brethren...

Lord our God,
may the eucharist we offer
be a sign of unity and peace
as we celebrate the memory of St. Bernard,
who strove in word and deed
to bring harmony to your Church.

We ask this through Christ our Lord.

Prayer after Communion

Let us pray.

Pause for silent prayer, if this has not preceded.

Father,
may the holy food we have received
at this celebration of the feast of St. Bernard
continue your work of salvation in us.
By his example, give us courage,
by his teachings, make us wise,
so that we too may burn with love for your Word,
    Jesus Christ,
who is Lord for ever and ever.

August 21

PIUS X, pope (1835–1914)

Memorial

Born near Venice in 1835, Giuseppe Sarto became successively priest, bishop of Mantua, patriarch of Venice, and pope (1903). He was outstanding for his personal holiness and spirit of poverty. As pope, he initiated liturgical reforms such as allowing reception of First Holy Communion at an earlier age, beginning to codify the Code of Canon Law, and taking strong measures against Modernism. Pius X died as World War I began, and was canonized in 1954.

Antiphons and Prayers: *from the* COMMON OF PASTORS: FOR POPES *(pp. 2170–2173), or from the* WEEKDAY MASS, *except:*

Opening Prayer

Father,
to defend the Catholic faith
and to make all things new in Christ,
you filled St. Pius X
with heavenly wisdom and apostolic courage.
May his example and teaching
lead us to the reward of eternal life.

Grant this through our Lord Jesus Christ, your Son,
who lives and reigns with you and the Holy Spirit,
one God, for ever and ever.

Liturgy of the Word: *from the* COMMON OF PASTORS: FOR A POPE *(pp. 2188ff.),
especially 1 Thes 2:2b–8; Ps 89:2–3, 4–5, 21–22, 25 and 27; Jn 21:15–17; or
from the* WEEKDAY MASS.

Liturgy of the Eucharist, *p. 897.*

Prayer over the Gifts

Pray, brethren...

Lord,
be pleased to accept our offerings.
May we follow the teaching of St. Pius X,
and so come to these mysteries with reverence
and receive them with faith.

We ask this through Christ our Lord.

Prayer after Communion

Let us pray.

Pause for silent prayer, if this has not preceded.

Lord our God,
we honor the memory of St. Pius X
by sharing the bread of heaven.
May it strengthen our faith and unite us in your love.

We ask this in the name of Jesus the Lord.

August 22

QUEENSHIP OF MARY

Memorial

At the end of the Marian Year in 1954, Pope Pius XII established
this feast with his encyclical, *Ad Caeli Reginam*. Mary is Queen be-

cause of her divine maternity and because of her association with Jesus' redemptive mission. Today's feast is linked with that of the Assumption, celebrated eight days earlier, and it highlights Mary's spiritual motherhood in the Church. Her queenship is one of love, exercised in hearts, and reminds us that "if we persevere, we also shall reign with him" (2 Tm 2:12) as members of Christ's "royal priesthood" (1 Pt 2:9). Mary as queen is the eschatological icon of the Church in glory.

Entrance Antiphon

The queen stands at your right hand arrayed in cloth of gold.
(Ps 44:10)

Opening Prayer

Father,
you have given us the mother of your Son
to be our queen and mother.
With the support of her prayers
may we come to share the glory of your children
in the kingdom of heaven.

We ask this through our Lord Jesus Christ, your Son,
who lives and reigns with you and the Holy Spirit,
one God, for ever and ever.

Liturgy of the Word: *from the* COMMON OF THE BLESSED VIRGIN MARY *(pp. 2101ff.), especially Is 9:1–6; Ps 113:1–2, 3–4, 5–6, 7–8; Lk 1:26–38; or from the* WEEKDAY MASS.

Liturgy of the Eucharist, *p. 897.*

Prayer over the Gifts

Pray, brethren...

Lord,
celebrating the feast of the Virgin Mary,
we offer you our gifts and prayers:
may Christ, who offered himself as a perfect sacrifice,

bring mankind the peace and love of your kingdom,
where he lives and reigns for ever and ever.

Preface of the Blessed Virgin Mary I *or* **II,** *p. 953*

Communion Antiphon

**Blessed are you for your firm believing, that the promises of
the Lord would be fulfilled.**
(Lk 1:45)

Prayer after Communion

Let us pray.

Pause for silent prayer, if this has not preceded.

Lord,
we have eaten the bread of heaven.
May we who honor the memory of the Virgin Mary
share one day in your banquet of eternal life.

We ask this in the name of Jesus the Lord.

August 23

ROSE OF LIMA, virgin (1586–1617)

Optional Memorial

Born in Lima, Peru, of Spanish descent, Isabel Flores de Oliva
was called Rose because of her reddish complexion. An intelligent
and efficient girl, she took St. Catherine of Siena as her model. At
15, Rose received the habit of a Third Order Dominican. She lived
at home, leading a humble life of penance and mystical prayer. She
is the first canonized saint of the Americas.

Antiphons and Prayers: *from the* COMMON OF VIRGINS *(pp. 2238–2252),
or* COMMON OF HOLY MEN AND WOMEN *(pp. 2252–2322), or from the* WEEKDAY
MASS. *The following is optional:*

Opening Prayer

God our Father,
for love of you

St. Rose gave up everything
to devote herself to a life of penance.
By the help of her prayers
may we imitate her selfless way of life on earth
and enjoy the fullness of your blessings in heaven.

Grant this through our Lord Jesus Christ, your Son,
who lives and reigns with you and the Holy Spirit,
one God, for ever and ever.

Liturgy of the Word: *from the* COMMON OF VIRGINS *(pp. 2244ff.), or* COMMON OF HOLY MEN AND WOMEN: FOR RELIGIOUS *(pp. 2271ff.), especially 2 Cor 10:17—11:2; Ps 148:1bc–2, 11–13a, 13c–14; Mt 13:44–46; or from the* WEEKDAY MASS.

Liturgy of the Eucharist, *p. 897.*

August 24

BARTHOLOMEW, apostle

Feast

One of the twelve foundation stones of the Church, this apostle was from Cana in Galilee. Because the lists of the Twelve differ, Bartholomew is usually identified with the Nathaniel described in the fourth Gospel. Tradition holds that after the Ascension he preached the Gospel in India or Armenia and suffered martyrdom there.

Entrance Antiphon

Day after day proclaim the salvation of the Lord. Proclaim his glory to all nations. (Ps 95:2–3)

Opening Prayer

Lord,
sustain within us the faith
which made St. Bartholomew ever loyal to Christ.
Let your Church be the sign of salvation
for all the nations of the world.

We ask this through our Lord Jesus Christ, your Son,
who lives and reigns with you and the Holy Spirit,
one God, for ever and ever.

FIRST READING

Rv 21:9–14

I will show you the bride, the wife of the Lamb.

A reading from the Book of Revelation

The angel spoke to me, saying: "Come here. I will show you
the bride, the wife of the Lamb." He took me in spirit to a
great, high mountain and showed me the holy city Jerusalem
coming down out of heaven from God. It gleamed with the
splendor of God. Its radiance was like that of a precious stone,
like jasper, clear as crystal. It had a massive, high wall, with
twelve gates where twelve angels were stationed and on which
names were inscribed, the names of the twelve tribes of the
children of Israel. There were three gates facing east, three
north, three south, and three west. The wall of the city had
twelve courses of stones as its foundation, on which were
inscribed the twelve names of the twelve Apostles of the Lamb.

The word of the Lord.

Responsorial Psalm

Ps 145:10–11, 12–13, 17–18

R. **Your friends make known, O Lord,
the glorious splendor of your Kingdom.**

Let all your works give you thanks, O LORD,
   and let your faithful ones bless you.
Let them discourse of the glory of your Kingdom
   and speak of your might.

R. **Your friends make known, O Lord,
the glorious splendor of your Kingdom.**

Making known to men your might
   and the glorious splendor of your Kingdom.

Your Kingdom is a Kingdom for all ages,
  and your dominion endures through all generations.

  R. **Your friends make known, O Lord,**
      the glorious splendor of your Kingdom.

The Lord is just in all his ways
  and holy in all his works.
The Lord is near to all who call upon him,
  to all who call upon him in truth.

  R. **Your friends make known, O Lord,**
      the glorious splendor of your Kingdom.

  Alleluia, alleluia   Jn 1:49b
  Rabbi, you are the Son of God;
  you are the King of Israel.
  Alleluia, alleluia

GOSPEL   Jn 1:45–51

Here is a true child of Israel.
There is no duplicity in him.

A reading from the holy Gospel according to John

Philip found Nathanael and told him, "We have found the one
about whom Moses wrote in the law, and also the prophets,
Jesus son of Joseph, from Nazareth." But Nathanael said to
him, "Can anything good come from Nazareth?" Philip said to
him, "Come and see." Jesus saw Nathanael coming toward
him and said of him, "Here is a true child of Israel. There is
no duplicity in him." Nathanael said to him, "How do you
know me?" Jesus answered and said to him, "Before Philip
called you, I saw you under the fig tree." Nathanael answered
him, "Rabbi, you are the Son of God; you are the King of
Israel." Jesus answered and said to him, "Do you believe be-

cause I told you that I saw you under the fig tree? You will see greater things than this." And he said to him, "Amen, amen, I say to you, you will see heaven opened and the angels of God ascending and descending on the Son of Man."

The Gospel of the Lord.

Liturgy of the Eucharist, *p. 897.*

Prayer over the Gifts

Pray, brethren...

Lord,
we offer you this sacrifice of praise
on this feast of St. Bartholomew.
May his prayers win us your help.
We ask this in the name of Jesus the Lord.

Preface of the Apostles I *or* **II,** *p. 956.*

Communion Antiphon

I will give you the kingdom that my Father gave to me, and in that kingdom you will eat and drink at my table. (Lk 22:29–30)

Prayer after Communion

Let us pray.

Pause for silent prayer, if this has not preceded.

Lord,
as we celebrate the feast of St. Bartholomew,
we receive the pledge of eternal salvation.
May it help us in this life
and in the life to come.

Grant this through Christ our Lord.

August 25

LOUIS, king (1214–1270)

Optional Memorial

Born in 1214, Louis IX became King of France while quite young. A Franciscan tertiary, he was a model of prayer, kindness, and Christian courtesy. Happily married, Louis cared for the people of France, educated his eleven children, and tried to advance God's kingdom. He knew St. Thomas Aquinas, who taught at the University of Paris. Louis undertook two Crusades to the Holy Land and died, devoutly and ingloriously, near Carthage in Africa.

Antiphons and Prayers: *from the* COMMON OF HOLY MEN AND WOMEN *(pp. 2252–2322), or from the* WEEKDAY MASS. *The following is optional:*

Opening Prayer

Father,
you raised St. Louis
from the cares of earthly rule
to the glory of your heavenly kingdom.
By the help of his prayers
may we come to your eternal kingdom
by our work here on earth.

Grant this through our Lord Jesus Christ, your Son,
who lives and reigns with you and the Holy Spirit,
one God, for ever and ever.

Liturgy of the Word: *from the* COMMON OF HOLY MEN AND WOMEN *(pp. 2269ff.), especially Is 58:6–11; Ps 112:1–2, 3–4, 5–6, 7–8, 9; Mt 22:34–40; or from the* WEEKDAY MASS.

Liturgy of the Eucharist, *p. 897.*

Also on August 25

JOSEPH CALASANZ, priest (1556/7–1648)

Optional Memorial

Born in Aragon, Spain, in 1556, Joseph led the life of a rich young man for 36 years. Converted to Christ, he gave up all possessions to become a priest, zealous for the reform of the Church. Mysteriously attracted to Rome in 1592, he found there his true work—founding free schools for educating all classes. The schools and religious order (the Piarists) flourished in Europe. Joseph's latter years were most difficult. He was canonized in 1767.

Antiphons and Prayers: *from the Common of holy men and women: for teachers, (pp. 2265–2322), or* COMMON OF PASTORS *(pp. 2170–2218), or from the* WEEKDAY MASS. *The following is optional:*

Opening Prayer

Lord,
you blessed St. Joseph Calasanz
with such charity and patience
that he dedicated himself
to the formation of Christian youth.
As we honor this teacher of wisdom
may we follow his example in working for truth.

We ask this through our Lord Jesus Christ, your Son,
who lives and reigns with you and the Holy Spirit,
one God, for ever and ever.

Liturgy of the Word: *from the* COMMON OF PASTORS *(pp. 2188ff.), or* COMMON OF HOLY MEN AND WOMEN: FOR TEACHERS *(pp. 2269ff.), especially 1 Cor 12:31—13:13; Ps 34:2–3, 4–5, 6–7, 8–9, 10–11; Mt 18:1–5; or from the* WEEKDAY MASS.

Liturgy of the Eucharist, *p. 897.*

August 27

MONICA (332–387)

Memorial

Born into a Christian family in Roman Africa, Monica was a young girl when she married Patricius, a non-Christian older man. They had four children, and through Monica's prayer and influence her husband received baptism. Monica poured out tears and prayers to God for the conversion of her oldest son, Augustine. After he was baptized, Monica died peacefully in Ostia, Italy, her mission accomplished.

Antiphons and Prayers: *from the* COMMON OF HOLY MEN AND WOMEN *(pp. 2252–2322), or from the* WEEKDAY MASS, *except:*

Opening Prayer

God of mercy,
comfort of those in sorrow,
the tears of St. Monica moved you
to convert her son St. Augustine to the faith of Christ.
By their prayers, help us to turn from our sins
and to find your loving forgiveness.

Grant this through our Lord Jesus Christ, your Son,
who lives and reigns with you and the Holy Spirit,
one God, for ever and ever.

Liturgy of the Word: *from the* COMMON OF HOLY MEN AND WOMEN *(pp. 2269ff.), especially Sir 26:1–4, 13–16; Ps 131:1bcde, 2, 3; and the following Gospel, or from the* WEEKDAY MASS.

> **Alleluia, alleluia** Jn 8:12
> I am the light of the world, says the Lord;
> whoever follows me will have the light of life.
> **Alleluia, alleluia**

GOSPEL   Lk 7:11–17

> *She bore me in the arms of her prayer,*
> *that you might say to the son of the widow: Young man, I say to*
> *you, arise (Saint Augustine, Confessions, book 6, n. 2).*

A reading from the holy Gospel according to Luke

Jesus journeyed to a city called Nain, and his disciples and a large crowd accompanied him. As he drew near to the gate of the city, a man who had died was being carried out, the only son of his mother, and she was a widow. A large crowd from the city was with her. When the Lord saw her, he was moved with pity for her and said to her, "Do not weep." He stepped forward and touched the coffin; at this the bearers halted, and he said, "Young man, I tell you, arise!" The dead man sat up and began to speak, and Jesus gave him to his mother. Fear seized them all, and they glorified God, exclaiming, "A great prophet has arisen in our midst," and "God has visited his people." This report about him spread through the whole of Judea and in all the surrounding region.

The Gospel of the Lord.

Liturgy of the Eucharist, *p. 897.*

August 28

AUGUSTINE, bishop and doctor
(354–430)

Memorial

This great Doctor of the Church had a most profound effect on Western theology. Before his conversion, Augustine was a Manichaean, lived with a concubine, and fathered a son. Through grace and his mother's prayers, he embraced Christianity and was baptized in Milan by St. Ambrose. Returning to Africa, Augustine led an ascetic life and was elected Bishop of Hippo. He was a totally dedicated pastor for 34 years. By his sermons and prolific writings, he fought errors, explained the faith, and laid the foundations for much of Catholic social teaching and theology. Augustine died as the Vandals besieged Hippo and the Roman world was collapsing. Over the centuries Augustine's *Confessions* have become his most widely read work.

Entrance Antiphon

The Lord opened his mouth in the assembly, and filled him with the spirit of wisdom and understanding, and clothed him in a robe of glory.   (Sir 15:5)

Opening Prayer

Lord,
renew in your Church
the spirit you gave St. Augustine.
Filled with this spirit,
may we thirst for you alone as the fountain of wisdom
and seek you as the source of eternal love.

We ask this through our Lord Jesus Christ, your Son,
who lives and reigns with you and the Holy Spirit,
one God, for ever and ever.

Liturgy of the Word: *from the* COMMON OF PASTORS *(pp. 2188ff.), or* COMMON OF DOCTORS OF THE CHURCH *(pp. 2222ff.), especially 1 Jn 4:7–16; Ps 119:9, 10, 11, 12, 13, 14; Mt 23:8–12; or from the* WEEKDAY MASS.

Liturgy of the Eucharist, *p. 897.*

Prayer over the Gifts

Pray, brethren...

Lord,
as we celebrate the memorial of our salvation,
we pray that this sacrament may be for us
a sign of unity and a bond of love.

We ask this in the name of Jesus the Lord.

Communion Antiphon

Christ is your only teacher: and all of you are brothers.

(Mt 23:10, 8)

Prayer after Communion

Let us pray.

Pause for silent prayer, if this has not preceded.

Lord,
make us holy by our sharing at the table of Christ.

As members of his body,
help us to become what we have received.

Grant this through Christ our Lord.

August 29

BEHEADING OF JOHN THE BAPTIST, martyr

Memorial

John the Baptist, of such importance to Christ, has been special-ly honored throughout Christian history. Today we recall the Baptist's martyrdom—his beheading by Herod of Galilee. John was an ascet-ic and martyr, father of hermits, last of the prophets, forerunner of Christ.

The Gospel for this memorial is proper.

Entrance Antiphon

Lord, I shall expound your law before kings and not fear dis-grace; I shall ponder your decrees, which I have always loved.

(Ps 118:46–47)

Opening Prayer

God our Father,
you called John the Baptist
to be the herald of your Son's birth and death.
As he gave his life in witness to truth and justice,
so may we strive to profess our faith in your gospel.

Grant this through our Lord Jesus Christ, your Son,
who lives and reigns with you and the Holy Spirit,
one God, for ever and ever.

FIRST READING

Jer 1:17–19

Stand up and tell them all that I command you.

A reading from the Book of the Prophet Jeremiah

The word of the LORD came to me thus:
> Gird your loins;
>> stand up and tell them
>> all that I command you.
> Be not crushed on their account,
>> as though I would leave you crushed before them;
> For it is I this day
>> who have made you a fortified city,
> A pillar of iron, a wall of brass,
>> against the whole land:
> Against Judah's kings and princes,
>> against its priests and people.
> They will fight against you, but not prevail over you,
>> for I am with you to deliver you, says the LORD.

The word of the Lord.

Responsorial Psalm

Ps 71:1–2, 3–4a, 5–6ab, 15ab and 17

R. I will sing your salvation.

In you, O LORD, I take refuge;
  let me never be put to shame.
In your justice rescue me, and deliver me;
  incline your ear to me, and save me.

R. I will sing your salvation.

Be my rock of refuge,
  a stronghold to give me safety,
  for you are my rock and my fortress.
O my God, rescue me from the hand of the wicked.

R. I will sing your salvation.

For you are my hope, O LORD;
  my trust, O God, from my youth.
On you I depend from birth;
  from my mother's womb you are my strength.

R. I will sing your salvation.

My mouth shall declare your justice,
  day by day your salvation.
O God, you have taught me from my youth,
  and till the present I proclaim your wondrous deeds.

R. I will sing your salvation.

> **Alleluia, alleluia** Mt 5:10
> Blessed are those who are persecuted for the sake of
>   righteousness,
> for theirs is the Kingdom of heaven.
> **Alleluia, alleluia**

GOSPEL   Mk 6:17–29

*I want you to give me at once on a platter
the head of John the Baptist.*

A reading from the holy Gospel according to Mark

Herod was the one who had John the Baptist arrested and bound
in prison on account of Herodias, the wife of his brother Philip,
whom he had married. John had said to Herod, "It is not lawful for you to have your brother's wife." Herodias harbored a
grudge against him and wanted to kill him but was unable to
do so. Herod feared John, knowing him to be a righteous and
holy man, and kept him in custody. When he heard him speak
he was very much perplexed, yet he liked to listen to him. She
had an opportunity one day when Herod, on his birthday, gave
a banquet for his courtiers, his military officers, and the leading men of Galilee. Herodias' own daughter came in and performed a dance that delighted Herod and his guests. The king
said to the girl, "Ask of me whatever you wish and I will grant
it to you." He even swore many things to her, "I will grant you
whatever you ask of me, even to half of my kingdom." She
went out and said to her mother, "What shall I ask for?" She

replied, "The head of John the Baptist." The girl hurried back to the king's presence and made her request, "I want you to give me at once on a platter the head of John the Baptist." The king was deeply distressed, but because of his oaths and the guests he did not wish to break his word to her. So he promptly dispatched an executioner with orders to bring back his head. He went off and beheaded him in the prison. He brought in the head on a platter and gave it to the girl. The girl in turn gave it to her mother. When his disciples heard about it, they came and took his body and laid it in a tomb.

The Gospel of the Lord.

Liturgy of the Eucharist, *p. 897.*

Prayer over the Gifts

Pray, brethren...

Lord,
by these gifts we offer,
keep us faithful to your way of life,
which John the Baptist preached in the wilderness,
and to which he courageously witnessed
by shedding his blood.
We ask this through Christ our Lord.

Preface of John the Baptist, *p. 954.*

Communion Antiphon

John's answer was: **He must grow greater and I must grow less.**   (Jn 3:27, 30)

Prayer after Communion

Let us pray.

Pause for silent prayer, if this has not preceded.

Lord,
may we who celebrate
the martyrdom of John the Baptist
honor this sacrament of our salvation
and rejoice in the life it brings us.

We ask this in the name of Jesus the Lord.

September

First Monday of September

[In the United States]

LABOR DAY

So that the entire year may be sanctified, liturgical texts are given for Labor Day, which emphasize the duty to work and the dignity of human labor.

Antiphons and Prayers: *may be taken from the* MASS OF ST. JOSEPH THE WORKER, *May 1 (p. 1834).*

Liturgy of the Word: *may be taken from the* MASS OF ST. JOSEPH THE WORKER, *May 1 (pp. 1835ff).*

September 3

GREGORY THE GREAT, pope and doctor (540–604)

Memorial

The son of a Roman senator, Gregory became prefect of Rome and at age 35 entered the Benedictine monastery. He became a deacon, then papal legate to Constantinople, and was elected pope in 590. For 14 years he worked in incomparable fashion—guiding the Church in decadent times, facing the Lombard invasions, sending out missionaries, writing, and advancing the liturgy. Gregorian chant is named after him. His writings were very influential, especially the Pastoral Rule, one of the best guides for pastors ever written.

Antiphons and Prayers: *from the* COMMON OF PASTORS: FOR POPES *(pp. 2170–2173), or* COMMON OF DOCTORS OF THE CHURCH *(pp. 2219–2238), or from the* WEEKDAY MASS, *except:*

Opening Prayer

Father,
you guide your people with kindness
and govern us with love.
By the prayers of St. Gregory
give the spirit of wisdom
to those you have called to lead your Church.
May the growth of your people in holiness
be the eternal joy of our shepherds.

We ask this through our Lord Jesus Christ, your Son,
who lives and reigns with you and the Holy Spirit,
one God, for ever and ever.

Liturgy of the Word: *from the* COMMON OF PASTORS: FOR A POPE *(pp. 2188ff.), or* COMMON OF DOCTORS OF THE CHURCH *(pp.2222ff.), especially 2 Cor 4:1–2, 5–7; Ps 96:1–2a, 2b–3, 7–8, 10; Lk 22:24–30; or from the* WEEKDAY MASS.

Liturgy of the Eucharist, *p. 897.*

Prayer over the Gifts

Pray, brethren...

Lord,
by this sacrifice
you free the world from sin.
As we offer it in memory of St. Gregory,
may it bring us closer to eternal salvation.

Grant this through Christ our Lord.

Prayer after Communion

Let us pray.

Pause for silent prayer, if this has not preceded.

Lord,
at this eucharist you give us Christ to be our living bread.
As we celebrate the feast of St. Gregory,
may we also come to know your truth
and live it in love for others.
We ask this in the name of Jesus the Lord.

September 8

BIRTH OF MARY

Feast

Today's feast originated in Jerusalem around the late fifth century, near a site venerated as Mary's birthplace (the Church of St. Anne). The liturgy invites us to rejoice, for the birth of Mary means that the birth of Jesus, our Savior, is coming near. Mary's birth prepared for the mystery of the redemption. As Pope John Paul II has said, "nobody else can bring us as Mary can into the divine and human dimension of this mystery."

Entrance Antiphon

Let us celebrate with joyful hearts the birth of the Virgin Mary, of whom was born the sun of justice, Christ our Lord.

Opening Prayer

Father of mercy,
give your people help and strength from heaven.
The birth of the Virgin Mary's Son
was the dawn of our salvation.
May this celebration of her birthday
bring us closer to lasting peace.

Grant this through our Lord Jesus Christ, your Son,
who lives and reigns with you and the Holy Spirit,
one God, for ever and ever.

*See the Common of the Blessed Virgin Mary (**pp. 2109–2117**), for:*
   First Reading   Mi 5:1–4a *or* Rom 8:28–30

Responsorial Psalm

Ps 13:6ab, 6c

   R. With delight I rejoice in the Lord.

Though I trusted in your mercy,
   let my heart rejoice in your salvation.

   R. With delight I rejoice in the Lord.

Let me sing of the LORD, "He has been good to me."

   R. With delight I rejoice in the Lord.

   Alleluia, alleluia
   Blessed are you, holy Virgin Mary, deserving of all praise;
   from you rose the sun of justice, Christ our God.
   Alleluia, alleluia

GOSPEL

Mt 1:1–16, 18–23

*For it is through the Holy Spirit
that this child has been conceived in her.*

A reading from the holy Gospel according to Matthew

Long form follows; for short form omit what is in brackets.

[The book of the genealogy of Jesus Christ, the son of David,
the son of Abraham.

   Abraham became the father of Isaac, Isaac the father of
Jacob, Jacob the father of Judah and his brothers. Judah became
the father of Perez and Zerah, whose mother was Tamar. Perez
became the father of Hezron, Hezron the father of Ram, Ram
the father of Amminadab. Amminadab became the father of
Nahshon, Nahshon the father of Salmon, Salmon the father of
Boaz, whose mother was Rahab. Boaz became the father of
Obed, whose mother was Ruth. Obed became the father of
Jesse, Jesse the father of David the king.

David became the father of Solomon, whose mother had been the wife of Uriah. Solomon became the father of Rehoboam, Rehoboam the father of Abijah, Abijah the father of Asaph. Asaph became the father of Jehoshaphat, Jehoshaphat the father of Joram, Joram the father of Uzziah. Uzziah became the father of Jotham, Jotham the father of Ahaz, Ahaz the father of Hezekiah. Hezekiah became the father of Manasseh, Manasseh the father of Amos, Amos the father of Josiah. Josiah became the father of Jechoniah and his brothers at the time of the Babylonian exile.

After the Babylonian exile, Jechoniah became the father of Shealtiel, Shealtiel the father of Zerubbabel, Zerubbabel the father of Abiud. Abiud became the father of Eliakim, Eliakim the father of Azor, Azor the father of Zadok. Zadok became the father of Achim, Achim the father of Eliud, Eliud the father of Eleazar. Eleazar became the father of Matthan, Matthan the father of Jacob, Jacob the father of Joseph, the husband of Mary. Of her was born Jesus who is called the Christ.

Now] this is how the birth of Jesus Christ came about. When his mother Mary was betrothed to Joseph, but before they lived together, she was found with child through the Holy Spirit. Joseph her husband, since he was a righteous man, yet unwilling to expose her to shame, decided to divorce her quietly. Such was his intention when, behold, the angel of the Lord appeared to him in a dream and said, "Joseph, son of David, do not be afraid to take Mary your wife into your home. For it is through the Holy Spirit that this child has been conceived in her. She will bear a son and you are to name him Jesus, because he will save his people from their sins." All this took place to fulfill what the Lord had said through the prophet:

Behold, the virgin shall be with child and bear a son,
and they shall name him Emmanuel,

which means "God is with us."

The Gospel of the Lord.

Liturgy of the Eucharist, *p. 897.*

Prayer over the Gifts

Pray, brethren...

Father,
the birth of Christ your Son
increased the virgin mother's love for you.
May his sharing in our human nature
give us courage in our weakness,
free us from our sins,
and make our offering acceptable.
We ask this in the name of Jesus the Lord.

Preface of the Blessed Virgin Mary I *or* **II,** *p. 953.*

Communion Antiphon

The Virgin shall bear a son, who will save his people from their sins.
                                                                 (Is 7:14; Mt 1:21)

Prayer after Communion

Let us pray.

Pause for silent prayer, if this has not preceded.

Lord,
may your Church,
renewed in this holy eucharist,
be filled with joy at the birth of the Virgin Mary,
who brought the dawn of hope and salvation to the world.
We ask this through Christ our Lord.

September 9

[In the dioceses of the United States]

PETER CLAVER, priest (1580–1654)

Memorial

Born in Spain, Peter Claver vowed to become a missionary in America. Ordained as a Jesuit in Colombia, he spent his life serving the African slaves. Peter would meet slave ships at Cartagena and enter the infested holds to care for the dead, dying, and sick. He instructed and baptized the slaves, and ministered to them on the plantations. Peter Claver, who called himself "the slave of the blacks forever," died on September 8, 1654 and was canonized in 1888.

Antiphons and Prayers: *from the* COMMON OF PASTORS: FOR MISSIONARIES *(pp. 2183–2187), or from the* WEEKDAY MASS, *except:*

Opening Prayer

God of mercy and love,
you offer all peoples
the dignity of sharing in your life.
By the example and prayers of St. Peter Claver,
strengthen us to overcome all racial hatreds
and to love each other as brothers and sisters.

We ask this through our Lord Jesus Christ, your Son,
who lives and reigns with you and the Holy Spirit,
one God, for ever and ever.

Liturgy of the Word: *from the* COMMON OF PASTORS: FOR MISSIONARIES *(pp. 2191ff.), or from the* WEEKDAY MASS.

September 13

JOHN CHRYSOSTOM, bishop and doctor
(344/49–407)

Memorial

This native of Antioch was elected Patriarch of Constantinople in 397. Called "Chrysostom" or "Golden Mouth" because of his eloquent preaching, John was also noted for his writings on the Scriptures. His efforts at Church reform aroused opposition and he suffered exile twice. In present-day Turkey, on the road to exile again, he died of consumption on September 14, 407.

Antiphons and Prayers: *from the* COMMON OF PASTORS: FOR BISHOPS *(pp. 2170–2175), or* COMMON OF DOCTORS OF THE CHURCH *(pp. 2219–2238), or from the* WEEKDAY MASS, *except:*

Opening Prayer

Father,
the strength of all who trust in you,
you made John Chrysostom
renowned for his eloquence
and heroic in his sufferings.
May we learn from his teaching
and gain courage from his patient endurance.

We ask this through our Lord Jesus Christ, your Son,
who lives and reigns with you and the Holy Spirit,
one God, for ever and ever.

Liturgy of the Word: *from the* COMMON OF PASTORS *(pp. 2188ff.), or* COMMON OF DOCTORS OF THE CHURCH *(pp. 2222ff.), especially Eph 4:1–7, 11–13; Ps 40:2 and 4, 7–8a, 8b–9, 10, 11; Mk 4:1–10, 13–20; or from the* WEEKDAY MASS.

Liturgy of the Eucharist, *p. 897.*

Prayer over the Gifts

Pray, brethren...
Lord,
be pleased with this sacrifice we present
in honor of John Chrysostom,
for we gather to praise you as he taught us.

Grant this through Christ our Lord.

Prayer after Communion

Let us pray.

Pause for silent prayer, if this has not preceded.

God of mercy,
may the sacrament we receive
in memory of John Chrysostom
make us strong in your love
and faithful in our witness to your truth.

We ask this in the name of Jesus the Lord.

For **September 14,** THE EXALTATION OF THE HOLY CROSS, *see* **Vatican II Sunday Missal,** *p. 1070.*

September 15

OUR LADY OF SORROWS

Memorial

This feast originated in Germany and was extended to the universal Church by Pope Benedict XIII in 1721. It focuses on the way Mary shared in the sufferings of her Son, Jesus. Commenting on today's two Gospel texts, Pope John Paul II has said: "Simeon's words seem like a second annunciation to Mary, for they tell her of the actual historical situation in which the Son is to accomplish his mission, namely in misunderstanding and sorrow.... At the foot of the cross Mary shares through faith in the shocking mystery of this self-emptying [of Jesus Christ]. This is perhaps the deepest 'kenosis' of faith in human history" (*Mother of the Redeemer,* nn. 16, 18).

The Gospel for this memorial is proper.

Entrance Antiphon

Simeon said to Mary: This child is destined to be a sign which men will reject; he is set for the fall and the rising of many in Israel; and your own soul a sword shall pierce. (Lk 2:34–35)

Opening Prayer

Father,
as your Son was raised on the cross,
his mother Mary stood by him, sharing his sufferings.
May your Church be united with Christ
in his suffering and death
and so come to share in his rising to new life,
where he lives and reigns with you and the Holy Spirit,
one God, for ever and ever.

FIRST READING   Heb 5:7–9

*Christ learned obedience
and became the source of eternal salvation.*

A reading from the Letter to the Hebrews

In the days when Christ was in the flesh, he offered prayers
and supplications with loud cries and tears to the one who was
able to save him from death, and he was heard because of his
reverence. Son though he was, he learned obedience from what
he suffered; and when he was made perfect, he became the
source of eternal salvation for all who obey him.

The word of the Lord.

Responsorial Psalm   Ps 31:2 and 3b, 3cd–4, 5–6, 15–16, 20

  R. **Save me, O Lord, in your kindness.**

In you, O LORD, I take refuge;
  let me never be put to shame.
In your justice rescue me,
  make haste to deliver me!

  R. **Save me, O Lord, in your kindness.**

Be my rock of refuge,
  a stronghold to give me safety.

You are my rock and my fortress;
  for your name's sake you will lead and guide me.

R. Save me, O Lord, in your kindness.

You will free me from the snare they set for me,
  for you are my refuge.
Into your hands I commend my spirit;
  you will redeem me, O LORD, O faithful God.

R. Save me, O Lord, in your kindness.

But my trust is in you, O LORD,
  I say, "You are my God."
In your hands is my destiny; rescue me
  from the clutches of my enemies and my persecutors.

R. Save me, O Lord, in your kindness.

How great is your goodness, O LORD,
  which you have in store for those who fear you,
And which, toward those who take refuge in you,
  you show in the sight of the children of men.

R. Save me, O Lord, in your kindness.

(Optional)

SEQUENCE
Stabat Mater

At the cross her station keeping,
Stood the mournful Mother weeping,
  Close to Jesus to the last.

Through her heart, his sorrow sharing,
All his bitter anguish bearing,
  Now at length the sword had passed.

Oh, how sad and sore distressed
Was that Mother highly blessed
  Of the sole begotten One!

Christ above in torment hangs,
She beneath beholds the pangs
  Of her dying, glorious Son.

Is there one who would not weep,
'Whelmed in miseries so deep,
  Christ's dear Mother to behold?

Can the human heart refrain
From partaking in her pain,
  In that mother's pain untold?

Bruised, derided, cursed, defiled,
She beheld her tender Child,
  All with bloody scourges rent.

For the sins of his own nation
Saw him hang in desolation
  Till his spirit forth he sent.

O sweet Mother! font of love,
Touch my spirit from above,
  Make my heart with yours accord.

Make me feel as you have felt;
Make my soul to glow and melt
  With the love of Christ, my Lord.

Holy Mother, pierce me through,
In my heart each wound renew
  Of my Savior crucified.

Let me share with you his pain,
Who for all our sins was slain,
  Who for me in torments died.

Let me mingle tears with you,
Mourning him who mourned for me,
  All the days that I may live.

By the cross with you to stay,
There with you to weep and pray,
  Is all I ask of you to give.

Virgin of all virgins blest!
Listen to my fond request:
  Let me share your grief divine.

Let me to my latest breath,
In my body bear the death
  Of that dying Son of yours.

Wounded with his every wound,
Steep my soul till it has swooned
  In his very Blood away.

Be to me, O Virgin, nigh,
Lest in flames I burn and die,
  In his awful judgment day.

Christ, when you shall call me hence,
Be your Mother my defense,
  Be your cross my victory.

While my body here decays,
May my soul your goodness praise,
  Safe in heaven eternally.
Amen. (Alleluia)

> **Alleluia, alleluia**
> Blessed are you, O Virgin Mary;
> without dying you won the martyr's crown
> beneath the Cross of the Lord.
> **Alleluia, alleluia**

*See the Common of the Blessed Virgin Mary (**p. 2128**), for:*
  Gospel Jn 19:25–27

Or:

GOSPEL
Lk 2:33–35

And you yourself a sword will pierce.

A reading from the holy Gospel according to Luke

Jesus' father and mother were amazed at what was said about
him; and Simeon blessed them and said to Mary his mother,

"Behold, this child is destined for the fall and rise of many in Israel, and to be a sign that will be contradicted and you yourself a sword will pierce so that the thoughts of many hearts may be revealed."

The Gospel of the Lord.

Liturgy of the Eucharist, *p. 897.*

Prayer over the Gifts

Pray, brethren...

God of mercy,
receive the prayers and gifts we offer
in praise of your name
on this feast of the Virgin Mary.
While she stood beside the cross of Jesus
you gave her to us as our loving mother.

Grant this through Christ our Lord.

Preface of the Blessed Virgin Mary I *or* **II,** *p. 953.*

Communion Antiphon

Be glad to share in the sufferings of Christ! When he comes in glory, you will be filled with joy. (1 Pt 4:13)

Prayer after Communion

Let us pray.
Pause for silent prayer, if this has not preceded.

Lord,
hear the prayers
of those who receive the sacraments of eternal salvation.
As we honor the compassionate love of the Virgin Mary,
may we make up in our own lives
whatever is lacking in the sufferings of Christ
for the good of the Church.
We ask this in the name of Jesus the Lord.

September 16

CORNELIUS, pope and martyr (†253)
and CYPRIAN, bishop and martyr (†258)

Memorial

Today we commemorate two friends in the service of Christ and the Church. Cyprian, Bishop of Carthage, went courageously to his death, which his people witnessed. His martyrdom was almost like a solemn liturgy and developed the faith of the Church of Carthage. To Cornelius he had written earlier, "If God gives one of us the grace to die soon, our friendship will continue before the Lord." Cornelius, pope for a short time (250–253), was exiled and killed for the faith at Civitavecchia in Italy.

Antiphons and Prayers: *from the* COMMON OF MARTYRS *(pp. 2128–2169), or* COMMON OF PASTORS: FOR BISHOPS *(pp. 2170–2175), or from the* WEEKDAY MASS, *except:*

Opening Prayer

God our Father,
in Saints Cornelius and Cyprian
you have given your people an inspiring example
of dedication to the pastoral ministry
and constant witness to Christ in their suffering.
May their prayers and faith give us courage
to work for the unity of your Church.

Grant this through our Lord Jesus Christ, your Son,
who lives and reigns with you and the Holy Spirit,
one God, for ever and ever.

Liturgy of the Word: *from the* COMMON OF MARTYRS *(pp. 2147ff.), or* COMMON OF PASTORS *(pp. 2188ff.), especially 2 Cor 4:7–15; Ps 126:1bc–2ab, 2cd–3, 4–5, 6; Jn 17:11b–19; or from the* WEEKDAY MASS.

Liturgy of the Eucharist, *p. 897.*

Prayer over the Gifts

Pray, brethren...

Lord,
accept the gifts of your people
as we honor the suffering and death
of Saints Cornelius and Cyprian.
The eucharist gave them courage
to offer their lives for Christ.
May it keep us faithful in all our trials.

We ask this through Christ our Lord.

Prayer after Communion

Let us pray.

Pause for silent prayer, if this has not preceded.

Lord,
by the example of your martyrs Cornelius and Cyprian
and by the sacrament we have received,
make us strong in the Spirit
so that we may offer faithful witness
to the truth of your gospel.

We ask this in the name of Jesus the Lord.

September 17

ROBERT BELLARMINE, bishop and doctor
(1542–1621)

Optional Memorial

Robert Bellarmine exemplifies an important aspect of the Society of Jesus: intellectual service to the Church. Born in Italy, he entered the Jesuits at age 18. He taught theology at Louvain and Rome, developed the theological basis for the Catholic Reformation, and became a pastoral bishop and cardinal. His influence on Catholic intellectual life and the Gregorian University in Rome has been extensive. This great theologian also wrote catechisms that were widely used in Europe.

Antiphons and Prayers: *from the* COMMON OF PASTORS: FOR BISHOPS *(pp. 2170–2175), or* COMMON OF DOCTORS OF THE CHURCH *(pp. 2219–2238), or from the* WEEKDAY MASS. *The following is optional:*

Opening Prayer

God our Father,
you gave Robert Bellarmine wisdom and goodness
to defend the faith of your Church.
By his prayers
may we always rejoice in the profession of our faith.

We ask this through our Lord Jesus Christ, your Son,
who lives and reigns with you and the Holy Spirit,
one God, for ever and ever.

Liturgy of the Word: *from the* COMMON OF PASTORS *(pp. 2188ff.), or* COMMON OF DOCTORS OF THE CHURCH *(pp. 2222ff.), especially Wis 7:7–10, 15–16; Ps 19:8, 9, 10, 11; Mt 7:21–29; or from the* WEEKDAY MASS.

Liturgy of the Eucharist, *p. 897.*

September 19

JANUARIUS, bishop and martyr (†305)

Optional Memorial

In 305, this Bishop of Benevento (near Naples in Italy) suffered martyrdom with three deacons, a lector, and two lay people. He became invoked as the protector of Naples, especially at times of danger, as when Vesuvius was erupting. His relics are preserved at Naples. The celebrated "liquefaction of the blood of St. Januarius" has been reported since the thirteenth century.

Antiphons and Prayers: *from the* COMMON OF MARTYRS *(pp. 2128–2169), or* COMMON OF PASTORS: FOR BISHOPS *(pp. 2170–2175), or from the* WEEKDAY MASS. *The following is optional:*

Opening Prayer

God our Father,
enable us who honor the memory of St. Januarius

to share with him the joy of eternal life.

Grant this through our Lord Jesus Christ, your Son,
who lives and reigns with you and the Holy Spirit,
one God, for ever and ever.

Liturgy of the Word: *from the* COMMON OF MARTYRS *(pp. 2147ff.), or*
COMMON OF PASTORS *(pp. 2188ff.), especially Heb 10:32–36; Ps 126:1bc–2ab,
2cd–3, 4–5, 6; Jn 12:24–26; or from the* WEEKDAY MASS.

Liturgy of the Eucharist, p. 897.

September 20

ANDREW KIM TAEGON, priest and martyr, PAUL CHONG HASANG, catechist and martyr, and COMPANIONS, martyrs

Memorial

Today's feast honors a group of 103 martyrs from Korea, who
gave their lives during several persecutions in the 19th century.
Andrew Kim Taegon was the first Korean priest, and Paul Chong
Hasang was a lay missionary. Besides three bishops and seven priests,
the group is composed of heroic lay people of all ages. Pope John
Paul II canonized them in 1984, during a trip to Korea.

Entrance Antiphon

**Let us all rejoice in the Lord, and keep a festival in honor of
Andrew and Paul and their companions. Let us join with the
angels in joyful praise to the Son of God.**

Opening Prayer

O God,
you have created all nations
and you are their salvation.
In the land of Korea your call to Catholic faith
formed a people of adoption,
whose growth you nurtured
by the blood of Andrew, Paul, and their companions.

Through their martyrdom and their intercession
grant us strength that we too may remain faithful to your
    commandments
even until death.

We ask this through our Lord Jesus Christ, your Son,
who lives and reigns with you and the Holy Spirit,
one God, for ever and ever.

Liturgy of the Word: *from the* COMMON OF MARTYRS *(pp. 2147ff.),*
especially Wis 3:1–9, or Rom 8:31b–39; Ps 126:1bc–2ab, 2cd–3, 4–5,
6; Lk 9:23–26; or from the WEEKDAY MASS.

Liturgy of the Eucharist, *p. 897.*

Prayer over the Gifts

Pray, brethren...

All-powerful God,
in your goodness accept these gifts we offer
and through the intercession of your holy martyrs
grant that our own lives will become a sacrifice acceptable
    to you
for the salvation of all the world.

We ask this in the name of Jesus the Lord.

Communion Antiphon

Whoever acknowledges me before the world, I will acknowledge before my Father in heaven.   (Mt 10:32)

Prayer after Communion

Let us pray.

Pause for silent prayer, if this has not preceded.

Lord,
we have been nourished in this celebration of your
    holy martyrs

with the food that gave them strength.
Grant that we too will remain loyal to Christ
and labor in your Church for the salvation of all.
We ask this in the name of Jesus the Lord.

September 21

MATTHEW, apostle and evangelist

Feast

Born at Capernaum and given the name Levi, this tax collector was called by Jesus to be one of the twelve apostles. Tradition holds that he wrote the Gospel in Aramaic. We possess only the canonical Greek Gospel of Matthew, the carefully structured favorite Christian Gospel.

Entrance Antiphon

Go and preach to all nations: baptize them and teach them to observe all that I have commanded you, says the Lord.

(Mt 28:19–20)

Opening Prayer

God of mercy,
you chose a tax collector, St. Matthew,
to share the dignity of the apostles.
By his example and prayers
help us to follow Christ
and remain faithful in your service.

We ask this through our Lord Jesus Christ, your Son,
who lives and reigns with you and the Holy Spirit,
one God, for ever and ever.

FIRST READING   Eph 4:1–7, 11–13

In the work of ministry, in building up the Body of Christ.

A reading from the Letter of Saint Paul to the Ephesians

Brothers and sisters, I, a prisoner for the Lord, urge you to live in a manner worthy of the call you have received, with all humility and gentleness, with patience, bearing with one another through love, striving to preserve the unity of the spirit through the bond of peace: one Body and one Spirit, as you were also called to the one hope of your call; one Lord, one faith, one baptism; one God and Father of all, who is over all and through all and in all.

But grace was given to each of us according to the measure of Christ's gift.

And he gave some as Apostles, others as prophets, others as evangelists, others as pastors and teachers, to equip the holy ones for the work of ministry, for building up the Body of Christ, until we all attain to the unity of faith and knowledge of the Son of God, to mature to manhood, to the extent of the full stature of Christ.

The word of the Lord.

Responsorial Psalm

Ps 19:2–3, 4–5

R. Their message goes out through all the earth.

The heavens declare the glory of God;
  and the firmament proclaims his handiwork.
Day pours out the word to day,
  and night to night imparts knowledge.

R. Their message goes out through all the earth.

Not a word nor a discourse
  whose voice is not heard;
Through all the earth their voice resounds,
  and to the ends of the world, their message.

R. Their message goes out through all the earth.

Alleluia, alleluia See *Te Deum*
We praise you, O God,
we acclaim you as Lord;
the glorious company of Apostles praise you.
Alleluia, alleluia

GOSPEL   Mt 9:9–13

Follow me. And he got up and followed him.

A reading from the holy Gospel according to Matthew

As Jesus passed by, he saw a man named Matthew sitting at
the customs post. He said to him, "Follow me." And he got up
and followed him. While he was at table in his house, many
tax collectors and sinners came and sat with Jesus and his disciples. The Pharisees saw this and said to his disciples, "Why
does your teacher eat with tax collectors and sinners?" He heard
this and said, "Those who are well do not need a physician,
but the sick do. Go and learn the meaning of the words, *I desire
mercy, not sacrifice.* I did not come to call the righteous but
sinners."

The Gospel of the Lord.

Liturgy of the Eucharist, *p. 897.*

Prayer over the Gifts

Pray, brethren...

Lord,
accept the prayers and gifts we present
on this feast of St. Matthew.
Continue to guide us in your love
as you nourished the faith of your Church
by the preaching of the apostles.
We ask this in the name of Jesus the Lord.

Preface of the Apostles I *or* **II,** *p. 956.*

Communion Antiphon

I did not come to call the virtuous, but sinners, says the Lord.
(Mt 9:13)

Prayer after Communion

Let us pray.

Pause for silent prayer, if this has not preceded.

Father,
in this eucharist we have shared the joy of salvation
which St. Matthew knew when he welcomed your Son.
May this food renew us in Christ,
who came to call not the just
but sinners to salvation in his kingdom
where he is Lord for ever and ever.

September 26

COSMAS and DAMIAN, martyrs (†303)

Optional Memorial

Of these two saints we know only that they came from Aleppo
in Syria and led holy lives. At their tomb, devotion flourished and
miracles multiplied. Honored throughout the Mediterranean basin,
they were patrons of a church dedicated by Pope Felix IV in the
ancient Roman forum. The First Eucharistic Prayer mentions them.
Tradition considered them as medical doctors and twins.

Antiphons and Prayers: *from the* COMMON OF MARTYRS *(pp. 2128–2169),
or from the* WEEKDAY MASS. *The following is optional:*

Opening Prayer

Lord,
we honor the memory of Saints Cosmas and Damian.
Accept our grateful praise
for raising them to eternal glory
and for giving us your fatherly care.

We ask this through our Lord Jesus Christ, your Son,
who lives and reigns with you and the Holy Spirit,
one God, for ever and ever.

Liturgy of the Word: *from the* COMMON OF MARTYRS *(pp. 2147ff.),
especially Wis 3:1–9; Ps 126:1bc–2ab, 2cd–3, 4–5, 6; Mt 10:28–33; or
from the* WEEKDAY MASS.

Liturgy of the Eucharist, *p. 897.*

Prayer over the Gifts

Pray, brethren...

Lord,
we who celebrate the death of your holy martyrs
offer you the sacrifice
which gives all martyrdom its meaning.
Be pleased with our praise.

We ask this through Christ our Lord.

Prayer after Communion

Let us pray.

Pause for silent prayer, if this has not preceded.

Lord,
keep your gift ever strong within us.
May the eucharist we receive
in memory of Saints Cosmas and Damian
bring us salvation and peace.

We ask this in the name of Jesus the Lord.

September 27

VINCENT DE PAUL, priest (1581–1660)

Memorial

Today we recall the magnificent life of the "saint of charity," the
totally dedicated "Monsieur Vincent." A parish priest near Paris,

Vincent worked against the physical and moral evils of his time. Galley slaves, abandoned babies, street women, victims of war, and the poor—all came under his mantle of generous care. Together with St. Louise de Marillac, he founded the Daughters of Charity. To develop Christ-like priests he founded the Congregation of the Missions (called Vincentians). The patron of all charitable societies, Vincent de Paul's life and ideal of charity still inspire the Church.

Entrance Antiphon

The Spirit of God is upon me; he has anointed me. He sent me to bring good news to the poor, and to heal the broken-hearted.

(Lk 4:18)

Opening Prayer

God our Father,
you gave Vincent de Paul
the courage and holiness of an apostle
for the well-being of the poor
and the formation of the clergy.
Help us to be zealous in continuing his work.

Grant this through our Lord Jesus Christ, your Son,
who lives and reigns with you and the Holy Spirit,
one God, for ever and ever.

Liturgy of the Word: *from the* COMMON OF PASTORS: FOR MISSIONARIES *(pp. 2191ff.), or* COMMON OF HOLY MEN AND WOMEN: FOR THOSE WHO WORKED FOR THE UNDERPRIVILEGED *(pp. 2274ff.), especially 1 Cor 1:26–31; Ps 112:1bc–2, 3–4, 5–7, 7–8, 9; Mt 9:35–38; or from the* WEEKDAY MASS.

Liturgy of the Eucharist, *p. 897.*

Prayer over the Gifts

Pray, brethren...

Lord,
you helped St. Vincent
to imitate the love he celebrated in these mysteries.

By the power of this sacrifice,
may we also become an acceptable gift to you.
We ask this in the name of Jesus the Lord.

Communion Antiphon

Give praise to the Lord for his kindness, for his wonderful deeds toward men. He has filled the hungry with good things, he has satisfied the thirsty.   (Ps 106:8–9)

Prayer after Communion

Let us pray.

Pause for silent prayer, if this has not preceded.

Lord,
hear the prayers
of those you have renewed with your sacraments from
    heaven.
May the example and prayers of St. Vincent
help us to imitate your Son
in preaching the good news to the poor.
We ask this in the name of Jesus the Lord.

September 28

WENCESLAUS, king and martyr (907/8–929)

Optional Memorial

As the ruling Duke of Bohemia, Wenceslaus was a devout Catholic who showed love for the poor, devotion to Mary, a spirit of penance, and a desire to build up the faith. This provoked opposition, which, with the help of his own brother, led to his assassination in 929. The first Slav to be canonized, Wenceslaus is the patron saint of Bohemia.

Antiphons and Prayers: *from the* COMMON OF MARTYRS *(pp. 2128–2169), or from the* WEEKDAY MASS. *The following is optional:*

Opening Prayer

Lord,
you taught your martyr Wenceslaus
to prefer the kingdom of heaven
to all that the earth has to offer.
May his prayers free us from our self-seeking
and help us to serve you with all our hearts.

We ask this through our Lord Jesus Christ, your Son,
who lives and reigns with you and the Holy Spirit,
one God, for ever and ever.

Liturgy of the Word: *from the* COMMON OF MARTYRS *(pp. 2147ff.),
especially 1 Pt 3:14–17; Ps 126:1bc–2ab, 2cd–3, 4–5, 6; Mt 10:34–39;
or from the* WEEKDAY MASS.

Liturgy of the Eucharist, *p. 897.*

Also on September 28

LAWRENCE RUIZ, martyr,
and COMPANIONS, martyrs (†1637)

Optional Memorial

Lawrence was born in the Philippines and became associated
with the Dominicans. A married man with three children, he fled
the Philippines after being accused of a crime, the circumstances of
which are not clear. He found passage to Japan with some priests,
but they arrived in the midst of an intense persecution of Christians.
Lawrence suffered severe torture and, along with fifteen companions,
gave his life as a martyr in Nagasaki, Japan. Pope John Paul II
canonized them on October 18, 1987.

Antiphons and Prayers: *from the* COMMON OF MARTYRS *(pp. 2128–2169),
or from the* WEEKDAY MASS.

Liturgy of the Word: *from the* COMMON OF MARTYRS *(pp. 2147ff.).*

Liturgy of the Eucharist, *p. 897.*

MICHAEL, GABRIEL, and RAPHAEL, archangels

Feast

Scripture contains many references to angels. Special biblical attention is paid to Michael (protector of the People of God), Gabriel (messenger of the Annunciation to Mary) and Raphael (the healer in the Book of Tobit). Today's date recalls the fifth century dedication of the Basilica of St. Michael the Archangel, located northeast of Rome.

Entrance Antiphon

Bless the Lord, all you his angels, mighty in power, you obey his word and heed the sound of his voice.   (Ps 102:20)

Opening Prayer

God our Father,
in a wonderful way you guide the work of angels and men.
May those who serve you constantly in heaven
keep our lives safe from all harm on earth.

Grant this through our Lord Jesus Christ, your Son,
who lives and reigns with you and the Holy Spirit,
one God, for ever and ever.

FIRST READING

Dn 7:9-10, 13-14

Thousands upon thousands were ministering to him.

A reading from the Book of the Prophet Daniel

As I watched:

Thrones were set up
    and the Ancient One took his throne.
His clothing was bright as snow,
    and the hair on his head as white as wool;
His throne was flames of fire,

with wheels of burning fire.
A surging stream of fire
    flowed out from where he sat;
Thousands upon thousands were ministering to him,
    and myriads upon myriads attended him.

The court was convened, and the books were opened. As
the visions during the night continued, I saw

One like a son of man coming,
    on the clouds of heaven;
When he reached the Ancient One
    and was presented before him,
He received dominion, glory, and kingship;
    nations and peoples of every language serve him.
His dominion is an everlasting dominion
    that shall not be taken away,
    his kingship shall not be destroyed.

The word of the Lord.

Or:

FIRST READING

Rv 12:7–12ab

Michael and his angels battled against the dragon.

A reading from the Book of Revelation

War broke out in heaven; Michael and his angels battled against
the dragon. The dragon and its angels fought back, but they
did not prevail and there was no longer any place for them in
heaven. The huge dragon, the ancient serpent, who is called
the Devil and Satan, who deceived the whole world, was thrown
down to earth, and its angels were thrown down with it.

Then I heard a loud voice in heaven say:

"Now have salvation and power come,
    and the Kingdom of our God
    and the authority of his Anointed.
For the accuser of our brothers is cast out,
    who accuses them before our God day and night.
They conquered him by the Blood of the Lamb
    and by the word of their testimony;
    love for life did not deter them from death.
Therefore, rejoice, you heavens,
    and you who dwell in them."

The word of the Lord.

Responsorial Psalm

Ps 138:1–2ab, 2cde–3, 4–5

R. In the sight of the angels I will sing your praises, Lord.

I will give thanks to you, O LORD, with all my heart,
    for you have heard the words of my mouth;
    in the presence of the angels I will sing your praise;
I will worship at your holy temple
    and give thanks to your name.

R. In the sight of the angels I will sing your praises, Lord.

Because of your kindness and your truth;
    for you have made great above all things
    your name and your promise.
When I called, you answered me;
    you built up strength within me.

R. In the sight of the angels I will sing your praises, Lord.

All the kings of the earth shall give thanks to you, O LORD,
    when they hear the words of your mouth;
And they shall sing of the ways of the LORD:
    "Great is the glory of the LORD."

R. In the sight of the angels I will sing your praises, Lord.

Alleluia, alleluia Ps 103:21
Bless the LORD, all you angels,
you ministers, who do his will.
Alleluia, alleluia

GOSPEL

Jn 1:47–51

*You will see the sky opened and the angels of God
ascending and descending on the Son of Man.*

A reading from the holy Gospel according to John

Jesus saw Nathanael coming toward him and said of him, "Here is a true child of Israel. There is no duplicity in him." Nathanael said to him, "How do you know me?" Jesus answered and said to him, "Before Philip called you, I saw you under the fig tree." Nathanael answered him, "Rabbi, you are the Son of God; you are the King of Israel." Jesus answered and said to him, "Do you believe because I told you that I saw you under the fig tree? You will see greater things than this." And he said to him, "Amen, amen, I say to you, you will see heaven opened and the angels of God ascending and descending on the Son of Man."

The Gospel of the Lord.

Liturgy of the Eucharist, *p. 897.*

Prayer over the Gifts

Pray, brethren...
Lord,
by the ministry of your angels
let our sacrifice of praise come before you.
May it be pleasing to you and helpful to our own salvation.

We ask this through Christ our Lord.

Preface of the Angels, *p. 954.*

Communion Antiphon

In the sight of the angels I will sing your praises, my God.

(Ps 137:1)

Prayer after Communion

Let us pray.

Pause for silent prayer, if this has not preceded.

Lord,
hear the prayers of those you renew with the bread of life.
Made strong by the courage it gives,
and under the watchful care of the angels,
may we advance along the way of salvation.
We ask this in the name of Jesus the Lord.

September 30

JEROME, priest and doctor (c. 347–419/20)

Memorial

Jerome was an outstanding Catholic biblical scholar. After studying in Rome, he received baptism and led an ascetical life. He lived as a hermit in the Holy Land, was ordained a priest, and undertook an intense study of Hebrew. Jerome translated the Bible from the original languages into Latin, called the Vulgate, which became the official text of the Catholic Church. He returned to Bethlehem and spent the next 30 years studying Scripture and living a penitential life. Jerome wrote many commentaries on the Bible and answered Biblical questions from the entire Catholic world.

Entrance Antiphon

The book of the law must be ever on your lips; reflect on it night and day. Observe and do all that it commands: then you will direct your life with understanding.

(Josh 1:8)

Opening Prayer

Father,
you gave St. Jerome delight
in his study of holy scripture.
May your people find in your word
the food of salvation and the fountain of life.

We ask this through our Lord Jesus Christ, your Son,
who lives and reigns with you and the Holy Spirit,
one God, for ever and ever.

Liturgy of the Word: *from the* COMMON OF DOCTORS OF THE CHURCH *(pp. 2222ff.),*
or COMMON OF PASTORS *(pp. 2188ff.), or from the* WEEKDAY MASS, *or:*

FIRST READING
2 Tm 3:14–17

All Scripture is inspired by God and is useful for teaching.

A reading from the second Letter of Saint Paul to Timothy

Beloved:
Remain faithful to what you have learned and believed, because
you know from whom you learned it, and that from infancy
you have known the sacred Scriptures, which are capable of
giving you wisdom for salvation through faith in Christ Jesus.
All Scripture is inspired by God and is useful for teaching, for
refutation, for correction, and for training in righteousness, so
that one who belongs to God may be competent, equipped for
every good work.

The word of the Lord.

See the Common of Doctors **(pp. 2228–2236),** *for:*
   Responsorial Psalm Ps 119:9, 10, 11, 12, 13, 14
   Alleluia Verse see Acts 16:14b
   Gospel Mt 13:47–52

Liturgy of the Eucharist, *p. 897.*

Prayer over the Gifts

Pray, brethren...

Lord,
help us to follow the example of St. Jerome.
In reflecting on your word
may we better prepare ourselves
to offer you this sacrifice of salvation.

We ask this in the name of Jesus the Lord.

Communion Antiphon

When I discovered your teaching, I devoured it. Your words brought me joy and gladness; you have called me your own, O Lord my God.   (Jer 15:16)

Prayer after Communion

Let us pray.

Pause for silent prayer, if this has not preceded.

Lord,
let this holy eucharist we receive
on the feast of St. Jerome
stir up the hearts of all who believe in you.
By studying your sacred teachings,
may we understand the gospel we follow
and come to eternal life.

Grant this through Christ our Lord.

OCTOBER

October 1

THÉRÈSE OF THE CHILD JESUS, virgin and doctor
(1873–1897)

Memorial

Thérèse Martin, the popular "Little Flower of Jesus," obtained special permission to enter the cloistered Carmelites of Lisieux at age 15. She developed a spiritual approach of striving for holiness through her child-like confidence in God's love and mercy known as the "little way." After a period of illness and intense suffering, she died a holy death at the age of 24. The spread of her spiritual teaching grew through her autobiography, *The Story of a Soul.* Canonized in 1925, she was proclaimed a Doctor of the Church in 1997 by Pope John Paul II.

Entrance Antiphon

The Lord nurtured and taught her; he guarded her as the apple of his eye. As the eagle spreads its wings to carry its young, he bore her on his shoulders. The Lord alone was her leader.

(See Dt 32:10–12)

Opening Prayer

God our Father,
you have promised your kingdom
to those who are willing to become like little children.
Help us to follow the way of St. Thérèse with confidence
so that by her prayers
we may come to know your eternal glory.

Grant this through our Lord Jesus Christ, your Son,
who lives and reigns with you and the Holy Spirit,
one God, for ever and ever.

Liturgy of the Word: *from the* COMMON OF VIRGINS *(pp. 2244ff.), or* COMMON OF HOLY MEN AND WOMEN: FOR RELIGIOUS *(pp. 2271ff.), or from the* WEEKDAY MASS, *or:*

FIRST READING

Is 66:10–14c

I will spread prosperity over her like a river.

A reading from the Book of the Prophet Isaiah

Rejoice with Jerusalem and be glad because of her,
    all you who love her;
Exult, exult with her,
    all you who were mourning over her!
Oh, that you may suck fully
    of the milk of her comfort,
That you may nurse with delight
    at her abundant breasts!
    For thus says the LORD:
Lo, I will spread prosperity over her like a river,
    and the wealth of the nations like an overflowing torrent.
As nurslings, you shall be carried in her arms,
    and fondled in her lap;
As a mother comforts her son,
    so will I comfort you;
    in Jerusalem you shall find your comfort.
When you see this, your heart shall rejoice,
    and your bodies flourish like the grass;
The LORD's power shall be known to his servants.

The word of the Lord.

Responsorial Psalm

Ps 131:1bcde, 2, 3

R. In you, Lord, I have found my peace.

O LORD, my heart is not proud,
    nor are my eyes haughty;

I busy not myself with great things,
  nor with things too sublime for me.

  R. In you, Lord, I have found my peace.

Nay rather, I have stilled and quieted
  my soul like a weaned child.
Like a weaned child on its mother's lap,
  so is my soul within me.

  R. In you, Lord, I have found my peace.

O Israel, hope in the LORD,
  both now and forever.

  R. In you, Lord, I have found my peace.

  Alleluia, alleluia   See Mt 11:25
  Blessed are you, Father, Lord of heaven and earth;
  you have revealed to little ones the mysteries of the Kingdom.
  Alleluia, alleluia

GOSPEL   Mt 18:1–4

  *Unless you become like children,
  you will not enter the Kingdom of heaven.*

A reading from the holy Gospel according to Matthew

The disciples approached Jesus and said, "Who is the greatest in the Kingdom of heaven?" He called a child over, placed it in their midst, and said, "Amen, I say to you, unless you turn and become like children, you will not enter the Kingdom of heaven. Whoever humbles himself like this child is the greatest in the Kingdom of heaven."

The Gospel of the Lord.

  Liturgy of the Eucharist, *p. 897.*

Prayer over the Gifts

Pray, brethren...

Lord,

we praise the wonder of your grace in St. Thérèse.
As you were pleased with the witness she offered,
be pleased also to accept this service of ours.

We ask this through Christ our Lord.

Communion Antiphon

Unless you change and become like little children, says the Lord, you shall not enter the kingdom of heaven. (Mt 18:3)

Prayer after Communion

Let us pray.

Pause for silent prayer, if this has not preceded.

Lord,
by the power of your love
St. Thérèse offered herself completely to you
and prayed for the salvation of all mankind.
May the sacraments we have received fill us with love
and bring us forgiveness.

We ask this in the name of Jesus the Lord.

October 2

GUARDIAN ANGELS

Memorial

The Old Testament mentions the Archangel Michael as Guardian of Israel and refers to angels as guarding patriarchs and individuals. Jesus spoke of the angels guarding children. Referring to the angels, the *Catechism of the Catholic Church* says, "From infancy to death human life is surrounded by their watchful care and intercession" (n. 336).

Entrance Antiphon

Bless the Lord, all you angels of the Lord. Sing his glory and praise for ever. (Dn 3:58)

Opening Prayer

God our Father,
in your loving providence
you send your holy angels to watch over us.
Hear our prayers,
defend us always by their protection
and let us share your life with them for ever.

We ask this through our Lord Jesus Christ, your Son,
who lives and reigns with you and the Holy Spirit,
one God, for ever and ever.

FIRST READING

Ex 23:20–23

My angel will go before you.

A reading from the Book of Exodus

Thus says the LORD: "See, I am sending an angel before you,
to guard you on the way and bring you to the place I have prepared. Be attentive to him and heed his voice. Do not rebel
against him, for he will not forgive your sin. My authority
resides in him. If you heed his voice and carry out all I tell
you, I will be an enemy to your enemies and a foe to your foes.

"My angel will go before you and bring you to the Amorites,
Hittites, Perizzites, Canaanites, Hivites, and Jebusites; and I
will wipe them out."

The word of the Lord.

Responsorial Psalm

Ps 91:1–2, 3–4ab, 4c–6, 10–11

R. **The Lord has put angels in charge of you,
to guard you in all your ways.**

You who dwell in the shelter of the Most High,
who abide in the shadow of the Almighty,
Say to the LORD, "My refuge and my fortress,
my God, in whom I trust."

R. **The Lord has put angels in charge of you,**
   to guard you in all your ways.

For he will rescue you from the snare of the fowler,
   from the destroying pestilence.
With his pinions he will cover you,
   and under his wings you shall take refuge.

R. **The Lord has put angels in charge of you,**
   to guard you in all your ways.

His faithfulness is a buckler and a shield.
You shall not fear the terror of the night
   nor the arrow that flies by day;
Nor the pestilence that roams in darkness,
   nor the devastating plague at noon.

R. **The Lord has put angels in charge of you,**
   to guard you in all your ways.

No evil shall befall you,
   nor shall affliction come near your tent,
For to his angels he has given command about you,
   that they guard you in all your ways.

R. **The Lord has put angels in charge of you,**
   to guard you in all your ways.

Alleluia, alleluia Ps 103:21
Bless the LORD, all you angels,
   you ministers, who do his will.
Alleluia, alleluia

GOSPEL   Mt 18:1–5, 10

Their angels in heaven always look upon the face
of my heavenly Father.

A reading from the holy Gospel according to Matthew

The disciples approached Jesus and said, "Who is the greatest in the Kingdom of heaven?" He called a child over, placed it in their midst, and said, "Amen, I say to you, unless you turn and become like children, you will not enter the Kingdom of heaven. Whoever humbles himself like this child is the greatest in the Kingdom of heaven. And whoever receives one child such as this in my name receives me.

"See that you do not despise one of these little ones, for I say to you that their angels in heaven always look upon the face of my heavenly Father."

The Gospel of the Lord.

Liturgy of the Eucharist, *p. 897.*

Prayer over the Gifts

Pray, brethren...

Father,
accept the gifts we bring you
in honor of your holy angels.
Under their constant care,
keep us free from danger in this life
and bring us to the joy of eternal life,
where Jesus is Lord for ever and ever.

Preface of the Angels, *p. 954.*

Communion Antiphon

In the sight of the angels I will sing your praises, my God.

(Ps 137:1)

Prayer after Communion

Let us pray.

Pause for silent prayer, if this has not preceded.

Lord,
you nourish us with the sacraments of eternal life.
By the ministry of your angels
lead us into the way of salvation and peace.

We ask this in the name of Jesus the Lord.

FRANCIS OF ASSISI (1181/82–1226)

Memorial

Called the most Christ-like person since Christ, today's remarkable saint was from a wealthy family in Assisi, Italy. Gifted with a joyful spirit, Francis renounced his father's wealth to become the Little Poor Man of Assisi. An extraordinary person, he attracted many followers (the Franciscans), and by evangelical poverty helped to renew the Church. He received the stigmata toward the end of his life, and died on October 3, 1226.

Entrance Antiphon

Francis, a man of God, left his home and gave away his wealth to become poor and in need. But the Lord cared for him.

Opening Prayer

Father,
you helped St. Francis to reflect the image of Christ
through a life of poverty and humility.
May we follow your Son
by walking in the footsteps of Francis of Assisi,
and by imitating his joyful love.

Grant this through our Lord Jesus Christ, your Son,
who lives and reigns with you and the Holy Spirit,
one God, for ever and ever.

Liturgy of the Word: *from the* COMMON OF HOLY MEN AND WOMEN: FOR RELIGIOUS *(pp. 2271ff.), or from the* WEEKDAY MASS, *or:*

FIRST READING

Gal 6:14–18

Through the cross the world has been crucified.

A reading from the Letter of Saint Paul to the Galatians

Brothers and sisters:

May I never boast except in the cross of our Lord Jesus Christ, through which the world has been crucified to me, and I to the world. For neither does circumcision mean anything, nor does uncircumcision, but only a new creation. Peace and mercy be to all who follow this rule and to the Israel of God.

From now on, let no one make troubles for me; for I bear the marks of Jesus on my body.

The grace of our Lord Jesus Christ be with your spirit, brothers and sisters. Amen.

The word of the Lord.

See the Common of Pastors (pp. 2197), for:
   Responsorial Psalm Ps 16:1b–2a and 5, 7–8, 11
See the Common of Holy Men and Women (pp. 2303–2307), for:
   Alleluia Verse See Mt 11:25
   Gospel Mt 11:25–30

Liturgy of the Eucharist, *p. 897.*

Prayer over the Gifts

Pray, brethren...

Lord,
as we bring you our gifts,
prepare us to celebrate the mystery of the cross,
to which St. Francis adhered with such burning love.

We ask this in the name of Jesus the Lord.

Communion Antiphon

Blessed are the poor in spirit; the kingdom of heaven is theirs!
(Mt 5:3)

Prayer after Communion

Let us pray.
   Pause for silent prayer, if this has not preceded.

Lord,
by the holy eucharist we have celebrated,

help us to imitate
the apostolic love and zeal of St. Francis.
May we who receive your love
share it for the salvation of all mankind.

We ask this through Christ our Lord.

October 6

BRUNO, priest (1035–1101)

Optional Memorial

Born in Cologne, Germany, Bruno was well educated and taught theology for over 25 years. Yearning for a solitary life of penance and contemplation, he joined several companions in a solitary quasi-community life. Bruno settled in the Chartreuse Alps and there founded a contemplative monastic order, the Carthusians. After a brief time as a papal advisor, Bruno returned to his hermitage in Calabria (south Italy). He was canonized in 1514.

Antiphons and Prayers: *from the* COMMON OF PASTORS *(pp. 2170–2218), or* COMMON OF HOLY MEN AND WOMEN: FOR RELIGIOUS *(pp. 2260–2263), or from the* WEEKDAY MASS. *The following is optional:*

Opening Prayer

Father,
you called St. Bruno
to serve you in solitude.
In answer to his prayers
help us to remain faithful to you
amid the changes of this world.

We ask this through our Lord Jesus Christ, your Son,
who lives and reigns with you and the Holy Spirit,
one God, for ever and ever.

Liturgy of the Word: *from the* COMMON OF PASTORS *(pp. 2188ff.), or* COMMON OF HOLY MEN AND WOMEN: FOR RELIGIOUS *(pp. 2271ff.), especially Phil 3:8–14; Ps 1:1–2, 3, 4 and 6; Lk 9:57–62; or from the* WEEKDAY MASS.

Liturgy of the Eucharist, *p. 897.*

Also on October 6

[In the dioceses of the United States]

BLESSED MARIE-ROSE DUROCHER, virgin
(1811–1849)

Optional Memorial

Marie Rose Durocher is especially honored in Canada, her native land. Born into a large family in Quebec, for some years she assisted her brother, a priest, by working in his parish. When the bishop asked her to begin a religious community dedicated to teaching, she founded the Sisters of the Holy Names of Jesus and Mary. During the remaining six years of her life she opened several schools and gave the congregation a solid foundation for future growth.

Antiphons and Prayers: *from the* COMMON OF VIRGINS *(pp. 2238–2252), or* COMMON OF HOLY MEN AND WOMEN: FOR RELIGIOUS *(pp. 2260–2263), or from the* WEEKDAY MASS. *The following is optional:*

Opening Prayer

Lord,
you enkindled in the heart of Blessed Marie Rose Durocher
the flame of ardent charity
and a great desire to collaborate,
as teacher, in the mission of the Church.
Grant us that same active love,
so that, in responding to the needs
of the world today,
we may lead our brothers and sisters
to eternal life.

We ask this through our Lord Jesus Christ, your Son,
who lives and reigns with you and the Holy Spirit,
one God, for ever and ever.

Liturgy of the Word: *from the* COMMON OF VIRGINS *(pp. 2244ff.), or* COMMON OF HOLY MEN AND WOMEN: FOR RELIGIOUS *(pp. 2271ff.), or from the* WEEKDAY MASS.

October 7

OUR LADY OF THE ROSARY

Memorial

Pope St. Pius V established this feast in thanksgiving for the crucial victory of Christian Europe over the Turks at the naval battle of Lepanto (October 7, 1571). The victory was attributed to the Blessed Mother invoked through the Rosary. This Scriptural Marian prayer draws us into meditation on the mysteries of Jesus' life.

Entrance Antiphon

Hail, Mary, full of grace, the Lord is with you; blessed are you among women and blessed is the fruit of your womb.

(Lk 1:28, 42)

Opening Prayer

Lord,
fill our hearts with your love,
and as you revealed to us by an angel
the coming of your Son as man,
so lead us through his suffering and death
to the glory of his resurrection,
who lives and reigns with you and the Holy Spirit,
one God, for ever and ever.

Liturgy of the Word: *from the* COMMON OF THE BLESSED VIRGIN MARY *(pp. 2101ff.), especially Acts 1:12–14; Lk 1:46–47, 48–49, 50–51, 52–53, 54–55; Lk 1:26–38; or from the* WEEKDAY MASS.

Liturgy of the Eucharist, *p. 897.*

Prayer over the Gifts

Pray, brethren...

Lord,
may these gifts we offer in sacrifice transform our lives.
By celebrating the mysteries of your Son,

may we become worthy of the eternal life he promises,
for he is Lord for ever and ever.

Preface of the Blessed Virgin Mary I *or* **II**, *p. 953.*

Communion Antiphon

You shall conceive and bear a Son, and you shall call his name
Jesus.
(Lk 1:31)

Prayer after Communion

Let us pray.

Pause for silent prayer, if this has not preceded.

Lord our God,
in this eucharist we have proclaimed
the death and resurrection of Christ.
Make us partners in his suffering
and lead us to share his happiness
and the glory of eternal life,
where he is Lord for ever and ever.

October 9

DENIS, bishop and martyr,
and COMPANIONS, martyrs (†c. 250)

Optional Memorial

St. Denis is the patron saint of France and, in particular, of Paris
where, as its first bishop, he organized the Church there. He was
martyred in Paris with two clerics during Valerian's persecution. An
abbey and large abbey church were built at his tomb in Paris.

Antiphons and Prayers: *from the* COMMON OF MARTYRS *(pp. 2128–2169),
or from the* WEEKDAY MASS. *The following is optional:*

Opening Prayer

Father,
you sent St. Denis and his companions

to preach your glory to the nations,
and you gave them the strength
to be steadfast in their sufferings for Christ.
Grant that we may learn from their example
to reject the power and wealth of this world
and to brave all earthly trials.

We ask this through our Lord Jesus Christ, your Son,
who lives and reigns with you and the Holy Spirit,
one God, for ever and ever.

Liturgy of the Word: *from the* COMMON OF MARTYRS *(pp. 2147ff.),
especially 2 Cor 6:4–10; Ps 126:1bc–2ab, 2cd–3, 4–5, 6; Mt 5:13–16;
or from the* WEEKDAY MASS.

Liturgy of the Eucharist, *p. 897.*

Also on October 9

JOHN LEONARDI, priest (1541–1609)

Optional Memorial

Born in Tuscany, Italy, John Leonardi became an assistant pharmacist and later a priest. He formed a religious community to teach Catholic doctrine to youths and adults in the confused times of the Reformation. Internal troubles drove him to Rome, where he found the friendship and guidance of St. Philip Neri. Leonardi laid the foundations for the Society for the Propagation of the Faith. He died after helping plague victims, and was canonized in 1938.

Antiphons and Prayers: *from the* COMMON OF PASTORS: FOR MISSIONARIES *(pp. 2183–2187), or* COMMON OF HOLY MEN AND WOMEN: FOR THOSE WHO WORKED FOR THE UNDERPRIVILEGED *(pp. 2263–2264), or from the* WEEKDAY MASS. *The following is optional:*

Opening Prayer

Father,
giver of all good things,
you proclaimed the good news to countless people

through the ministry of St. John Leonardi.
By the help of his prayers
may the true faith continue to grow.

Grant this through our Lord Jesus Christ, your Son,
who lives and reigns with you and the Holy Spirit,
one God, for ever and ever.

Liturgy of the Word: *from the* COMMON OF PASTORS *(pp. 2188ff.), or* COMMON OF HOLY MEN AND WOMEN: FOR THOSE WHO WORKED FOR THE UNDERPRIVILEGED *(pp. 2274ff.), especially 2 Cor 4:1–2, 5–7; Ps 96:1–2, 2–3, 7–8, 10; Lk 5:1–11; or from the* WEEKDAY MASS.

Liturgy of the Eucharist, *p. 897.*

October 14

CALLISTUS I, pope and martyr (†222)

Optional Memorial

In 217 Callistus, a former slave, was ordained deacon to Pope Zephyrinus, and then succeeded him as Pope. Callistus systematized the first official Christian cemetery in Rome, on the Appian Way (the catacombs of St. Callistus), where the popes were buried for a century. Callistus I had to battle several heresies before his martyrdom in 222. His tomb was discovered in Rome in 1960.

Antiphons and Prayers: *from the* COMMON OF MARTYRS *(pp. 2128–2169), or* COMMON OF PASTORS: FOR POPES *(pp. 2170–2173), or from the* WEEKDAY MASS. *The following is optional:*

Opening Prayer

God of mercy,
hear the prayers of your people
that we may be helped by St. Callistus,
whose martyrdom we celebrate with joy.

We ask this through our Lord Jesus Christ, your Son,
who lives and reigns with you and the Holy Spirit,
one God, for ever and ever.

Liturgy of the Word: *from the* COMMON OF MARTYRS *(pp. 2147ff.), or* COMMON OF PASTORS: FOR A POPE *(pp. 2170ff.), especially 1 Pt 5:1–4; Ps 40:2 and 4ab, 7–8a, 8b–9, 10, 11; Lk 22:24–30; or from the* WEEKDAY MASS.

Liturgy of the Eucharist, *p. 897.*

October 15

TERESA OF JESUS, virgin and doctor (1515–1582)

Memorial

Born at Avila, Spain, Teresa entered the Carmelites in 1535. At first, she lived a mediocre religious life, but experienced a profound conversion in 1554. In collaboration with St. John of the Cross, she undertook a reform of the Carmelites. Along the way, she experienced profound mystical revelations along with many difficulties. Teresa composed works of the highest doctrines and mystical theology. She died at age 67, and was named a Doctor of the Church in 1970.

Entrance Antiphon

Like a deer that longs for running streams, my soul longs for you, my God. My soul is thirsting for the living God.

(Ps 41:2–3)

Opening Prayer

Father,
by your Spirit you raised up St. Teresa of Jesus
to show your Church the way to perfection.
May her inspired teaching awaken in us
a longing for true holiness.

Grant this through our Lord Jesus Christ, your Son,
who lives and reigns with you and the Holy Spirit,
one God, for ever and ever.

Liturgy of the Word: *from the* COMMON OF VIRGINS *(pp. 2244ff.), or* COMMON OF HOLY MEN AND WOMEN: FOR RELIGIOUS *(pp. 2271ff.), or from the* WEEKDAY MASS, *or:*

FIRST READING

Rom 8:22–27

The Spirit himself intercedes with inexpressible groanings.

A reading from the Letter of Saint Paul to the Romans

Brothers and sisters:

We know that all creation is groaning in labor pains even until now; and not only that, but we ourselves, who have the firstfruits of the Spirit, we also groan within ourselves as we wait for adoption, the redemption of our bodies. For in hope we were saved. Now hope that sees for itself is not hope. For who hopes for what one sees? But if we hope for what we do not see, we wait with endurance.

In the same way, the Spirit too comes to the aid of our weakness; for we do not know how to pray as we ought, but the Spirit himself intercedes with inexpressible groanings. And the one who searches hearts knows what is the intention of the Spirit, because he intercedes for the holy ones according to God's will.

The word of the Lord.

*See the Common of Doctors (**pp. 2226ff.**), for:*
   Responsorial Psalm Ps 19:8, 9, 10, 11
*See the Common of Holy Men and Women (**pp. 2304–2321**), for:*
   Alleluia Verse Jn 15:9b, 5b
   Gospel Jn 15:1–8

   Liturgy of the Eucharist, *p. 897.*

Prayer over the Gifts

Pray, brethren...

King of heaven,
accept the gifts we bring in your praise,
as you were pleased with St. Teresa's offering
of her life in your service.

We ask this in the name of Jesus the Lord.

Communion Antiphon

For ever I will sing the goodness of the Lord; I will proclaim your faithfulness to all generations. (Ps 88:2)

Prayer after Communion

Let us pray.

Pause for silent prayer, if this has not preceded.

Lord our God,
watch over the family you nourish
with the bread from heaven.
Help us to follow St. Teresa's example
and sing your merciful love for ever.

We ask this through Christ our Lord.

October 16

HEDWIG, religious (1174–1243)

Optional Memorial

A native of Bavaria, Hedwig married Henry I, duke of Silesia and Poland. A devoted mother of seven children, she raised her family in a model way according to the medieval pattern of prayer and penance. She founded a hospital to care for the sick unable to afford medical care. After the deaths of her husband and six of her children, she retired to a convent where she later died. St. Elizabeth of Hungary was her niece.

Antiphons and Prayers: *from the* COMMON OF HOLY MEN AND WOMEN: FOR RELIGIOUS *(pp. 2260–2263), or from the* WEEKDAY MASS. *The following is optional:*

Opening Prayer

All-powerful God,
may the prayers of St. Hedwig bring us your help
and may her life of remarkable humility
be an example to us all.

We ask this through our Lord Jesus Christ, your Son,
who lives and reigns with you and the Holy Spirit,
one God, for ever and ever.

Liturgy of the Word: *from the* COMMON OF HOLY MEN AND WOMEN: FOR RELIGIOUS *(pp. 2271ff.), especially Sir 26:1–4, 13–16; Ps 128:1–2, 3, 4–5; Mk 3:31–35; or from the* WEEKDAY MASS.

Liturgy of the Eucharist, *p. 897.*

Also on October 16

MARGARET MARY ALACOQUE, virgin (1647–1690)

Optional Memorial

Born in 1647 in France, today's saint entered the Visitation convent in Paray-le-Monial at age 24. She received remarkable private revelations concerning the Sacred Heart of Jesus from December 1673 to June 1675. The rich tradition of theology and devotion to the Sacred Heart, so beneficial to Catholic spiritual life, originated with this saint. She died in 1690 and was canonized a saint in 1920.

Anitphons and Prayers: *from the* COMMON OF VIRGINS *(pp. 2238–2252), or the* COMMON OF HOLY MEN AND WOMEN: FOR RELIGIOUS *(pp. 2260–2263).*

Opening Prayer

Lord,
pour out on us the riches of the Spirit
which you bestowed on St. Margaret Mary.
May we come to know the love of Christ,
which surpasses all human understanding,
and be filled with the fullness of God.

Grant this through our Lord Jesus Christ, your Son,
who lives and reigns with you and the Holy Spirit,
one God, for ever and ever.

Liturgy of the Word: *from the* COMMON OF VIRGINS *(pp. 2244ff.), or* COMMON OF HOLY MEN AND WOMEN: FOR RELIGIOUS *(pp. 2271ff.), especially Eph 3:14–19; Ps 23:1b–3a, 4, 5, 6; Mt 11:25–30; or from the* WEEKDAY MASS.

Liturgy of the Eucharist, *p. 897.*

IGNATIUS OF ANTIOCH, bishop and martyr
(†c. 107)

Memorial

Ignatius was bishop of Antioch and suffered martyrdom during the persecution of Trajan. While on his way to Rome, he wrote seven letters to various churches that are an important source of information about Christian life at that time. The Communion antiphon of this Mass is a quote from the sixth of these letters.

Entrance Antiphon

With Christ I am nailed to the cross. I live now not with my own life, but Christ lives within me. I live by faith in the Son of God, who loved me and sacrificed himself for me. (Gal 2:19–20)

Opening Prayer

All-powerful and ever-living God,
you ennoble your Church with the heroic witness of all
who give their lives for Christ.
Grant that the victory of St. Ignatius of Antioch
may bring us your constant help
as it brought him eternal glory.

We ask this through our Lord Jesus Christ, your Son,
who lives and reigns with you and the Holy Spirit,
one God, for ever and ever.

Liturgy of the Word: *from the* COMMON OF MARTYRS *(pp. 2147ff.), or* COMMON OF PASTORS *(pp. 2188ff.), or from the* WEEKDAY MASS, *or:*

FIRST READING

Phil 3:17—4:1

Our citizenship is in heaven.

A reading from the Letter of Saint Paul to the Philippians

Join with others in being imitators of me, brothers and sisters, and observe those who thus conduct themselves according to the model you have in us. For many, as I have often told you and now tell you even in tears, conduct themselves as enemies of the cross of Christ. Their end is destruction. Their God is their stomach; their glory is in their "shame." Their minds are occupied with earthly things. But our citizenship is in heaven, and from it we also await a savior, the Lord Jesus Christ. He will change our lowly body to conform with his glorified Body by the power that enables him also to bring all things into subjection to himself.

Therefore, my brothers and sisters, whom I love and long for, my joy and crown, in this way stand firm in the Lord, beloved.

The word of the Lord.

*See Common of Martyrs (**pp. 2156–2168**), for:*
Responsorial Psalm Ps 34:2–3, 4–5, 6–7, 8–9
Alleluia Verse Jas 1:12
Gospel Jn 12:24–26

Liturgy of the Eucharist, *p. 897.*

Prayer over the Gifts

Pray, brethren...

Lord,
receive our offering
as you accepted St. Ignatius
when he offered himself to you as the wheat of Christ,
formed into pure bread by his death for Christ,
who lives and reigns for ever and ever.

Communion Antiphon

I am the wheat of Christ, ground by the teeth of beasts to become pure bread.

Prayer after Communion

Let us pray.

Pause for silent prayer, if this has not preceded.

Lord,
renew us by the bread of heaven
which we have received on the feast of St. Ignatius.
May it transform us into loyal and true Christians.

Grant this through Christ our Lord.

October 18

LUKE, evangelist

Feast

Born of a gentile family in Antioch, Luke was a cultured man, a medical doctor, and a convert to Christ. An associate of the Apostle Paul, Luke authored the third Gospel and the Acts of the Apostles. These works give us much valuable information about Christ and the early Church.

Entrance Antiphon

How beautiful on the mountains are the feet of the man who brings tidings of peace, joy, and salvation. (Is 52:7)

Opening Prayer

Father,
you chose Luke the evangelist to reveal
by preaching and writing
the mystery of your love for the poor.
Unite in one heart and spirit
all who glory in your name,
and let all nations come to see your salvation.

Grant this through our Lord Jesus Christ, your Son,
who lives and reigns with you and the Holy Spirit,
one God, for ever and ever.

FIRST READING

2 Tm 4:10–17b

Luke is the only one with me.

A reading from the second Letter of Saint Paul to Timothy

Beloved:

Demas, enamored of the present world, deserted me and went to Thessalonica, Crescens to Galatia, and Titus to Dalmatia. Luke is the only one with me. Get Mark and bring him with you, for he is helpful to me in the ministry. I have sent Tychicus to Ephesus. When you come, bring the cloak I left with Carpus in Troas, the papyrus rolls, and especially the parchments.

Alexander the coppersmith did me a great deal of harm; the Lord will repay him according to his deeds. You too be on guard against him, for he has strongly resisted our preaching.

At my first defense no one appeared on my behalf, but everyone deserted me. May it not be held against them! But the Lord stood by me and gave me strength, so that through me the proclamation might be completed and all the Gentiles might hear it.

The word of the Lord.

Responsorial Psalm

Ps 145:10–11, 12–13, 17–18

R. **Your friends make known, O Lord,
the glorious splendor of your Kingdom.**

Let all your works give you thanks, O LORD,
  and let your faithful ones bless you.
Let them discourse of the glory of your Kingdom
  and speak of your might.

R. **Your friends make known, O Lord,
the glorious splendor of your Kingdom.**

Making known to men your might
  and the glorious splendor of your Kingdom.

Your Kingdom is a Kingdom for all ages,
  and your dominion endures through all generations.

> **R. Your friends make known, O Lord,
> the glorious splendor of your Kingdom.**

The LORD is just in all his ways
  and holy in all his works.
The LORD is near to all who call upon him,
  to all who call upon him in truth.

> **R. Your friends make known, O Lord,
> the glorious splendor of your Kingdom.**

Alleluia, alleluia See Jn 15:16
I chose you from the world,
  to go and bear fruit that will last, says the Lord.
Alleluia, alleluia

GOSPEL   Lk 10:1–9

The harvest is abundant but the laborers are few.

A reading from the holy Gospel according to Luke

The Lord Jesus appointed seventy-two disciples whom he sent ahead of him in pairs to every town and place he intended to visit. He said to them, "The harvest is abundant but the laborers are few; so ask the master of the harvest to send out laborers for his harvest. Go on your way; behold, I am sending you like lambs among wolves. Carry no money bag, no sack, no sandals; and greet no one along the way. Into whatever house you enter, first say, 'Peace to this household.' If a peaceful person lives there, your peace will rest on him; but if not, it will return to you. Stay in the same house and eat and drink what is offered to you, for the laborer deserves his payment. Do not move about from one house to another. Whatever town you enter and they welcome you, eat what is set before you, cure the sick in it and say to them, 'The Kingdom of God is at hand for you.'"

The Gospel of the Lord.

Liturgy of the Eucharist, *p. 897.*

Prayer over the Gifts

Pray, brethren...

Father,
may your gifts from heaven free our hearts to serve you.
May the sacrifice we offer on the feast of St. Luke
bring us healing and lead us to eternal glory,
where Jesus is Lord for ever and ever.

Preface of the Apostles II, *p. 956.*

Communion Antiphon

The Lord sent disciples to proclaim to all the towns: the kingdom of God is very near to you.   (See Lk 10:1, 9)

Prayer after Communion

Let us pray.

Pause for silent prayer, if this has not preceded.

All-powerful God,
may the eucharist we have received at your altar
make us holy
and strengthen us in the faith of the gospel
preached by St. Luke.
We ask this in the name of Jesus the Lord.

October 19

[In the dioceses of the United States]

ISAAC JOGUES (1560–1646) and JOHN DE BRÉBEUF (1593–1649), priests and martyrs, and COMPANIONS, martyrs

Memorial

The North American soil is hallowed by the blood of these heroic French martyrs—six Jesuit priests: John de Brébeuf, Isaac Jogues, Noel Chabanel, Anthony Daniel, Charles Garnier, and Gabriel Lalemant; and two lay assistants: René Goupil and Jean de la Lande. Amid great difficulties, they evangelized the native peoples and were martyred between 1624 and 1649—five of them in present Canada and three near Auriesville, New York. A beautiful shrine at Auriesville recalls their martyrdom.

Antiphons and Prayers: *from the* COMMON OF MARTYRS *(pp. 2128–2169), or* COMMON OF PASTORS: FOR MISSIONARIES *(pp. 2183–2187), or from the* WEEKDAY MASS, *except:*

Opening Prayer

Father,
you consecrated the first beginnings
of the faith in North America
by the preaching and martyrdom
of Saints John and Isaac and their companions.
By the help of their prayers
may the Christian faith continue to grow
throughout the world.

We ask this through our Lord Jesus Christ, your Son,
who lives and reigns with you and the Holy Spirit,
one God, for ever and ever.

Liturgy of the Word: *from the* COMMON OF MARTYRS *(pp. 2147ff.), or* COMMON OF PASTORS: FOR MISSIONARIES *(pp. 2191ff.), especially 2 Cor 4:7–15; Ps 126:1bc–2ab, 2cd–3, 4–5, 6; Mt 28:16–20; or from the* WEEKDAY MASS.

Liturgy of the Eucharist, *p. 897.*

Also on October 19

PAUL OF THE CROSS, priest (1694–1775)

Optional Memorial

Born in Italy, Paul Francis Danei labored in commerce and military service, then dedicated his life to meditating on the mystery of Christ's cross and to evangelizing the countryside. In 1720 he became a hermit and later a priest. He founded the Passionists and adopted the name Paul of the Cross. The Passionists developed steadily and in 1771, an order of women was begun.

Entrance Antiphon

I resolved that while I was with you I would think of nothing but Jesus Christ and him crucified.   (1 Cor 2:2)

Opening Prayer

Father,
you gave your priest St. Paul
a special love for the cross of Christ.
May his example inspire us
to embrace our own cross with courage.

Grant this through our Lord Jesus Christ, your Son,
who lives and reigns with you and the Holy Spirit,
one God, for ever and ever.

Liturgy of the Word: *from the* COMMON OF PASTORS *(pp. 2188ff.), or* COMMON OF HOLY MEN AND WOMEN: FOR RELIGIOUS *(pp. 2271ff.), especially 1 Cor 1:18–25; Ps 117:1bc, 2; Mt 16:24–27; or from the* WEEKDAY MASS.

Liturgy of the Eucharist, *p. 897.*

Prayer over the Gifts

Pray, brethren...

All-powerful God,
receive the gifts we offer
in memory of St. Paul of the Cross.

May we who celebrate the mystery
of the Lord's suffering and death
put into effect the self-sacrificing love
we proclaim in this eucharist.

We ask this through Christ our Lord.

Communion Antiphon

We preach a Christ who was crucified; he is the power and the wisdom of God.   (1 Cor 1:23–24)

Prayer after Communion

Let us pray.

Pause for silent prayer, if this has not preceded.

Lord,
in the life of St. Paul
you helped us to understand the mystery of the cross.
May the sacrifice we have offered strengthen us,
keep us faithful to Christ,
and help us to work in the Church
for the salvation of all mankind.

We ask this in the name of Jesus the Lord.

October 23

JOHN OF CAPISTRANO, priest (1386–1456)

Optional Memorial

Today's saint had a remarkable life. Born in Capistrano (Abruzzi) Italy, he was a lawyer and judge before becoming a Franciscan priest. Trained by St. Bernardine of Siena, John preached effectively throughout Italy, France, Germany, Austria, and Poland. He reformed monasteries and opposed errors. Worn out by his tremendous efforts in serving Christ, he died in Croatia and was canonized in 1690.

Antiphons and Prayers: *from the* COMMON OF PASTORS: FOR MISSIONARIES *(pp. 2183–2187), or from the* WEEKDAY MASS. *The following is optional:*

Opening Prayer

Lord,
you raised up St. John of Capistrano
to give your people comfort in their trials.
May your Church enjoy unending peace
and be secure in your protection.

We ask this through our Lord Jesus Christ, your Son,
who lives and reigns with you and the Holy Spirit,
one God, for ever and ever.

Liturgy of the Word: *from the* COMMON OF PASTORS: FOR MISSIONARIES *(pp. 2191ff.), especially 2 Cor 5:14–20; Ps 16:1b–2a and 5, 7–8, 11; Lk 9:57–62; or from the* WEEKDAY MASS.

Liturgy of the Eucharist, *p. 897.*

October 24

ANTHONY MARY CLARET, bishop (1807–1870)

Optional Memorial

Born in Spain, Anthony worked as a weaver before his ordination in 1835. He preached in Spain and the Canary Isles and founded the Missionary Institute of Sons of the Immaculate Heart of Mary (the Claretians). He became Archbishop of Santiago in Cuba (1850–1857), and the confessor to the Queen of Spain. Archbishop Anthony Claret was deeply interested in the Catholic press and the First Vatican Council. After many trials and revolutions, including exile in France, he died peacefully and was canonized in 1950.

Antiphons and Prayers: *from the* COMMON OF PASTORS: FOR MISSIONARIES *or for bishops, (pp. 2170–2187), or from the* WEEKDAY MASS. *The following is optional:*

Opening Prayer

Father,
you endowed Anthony Claret
with the strength of love and patience

to preach the gospel to many nations.
By the help of his prayers
may we work generously for your kingdom
and gain our brothers and sisters for Christ,
who lives and reigns with you and the Holy Spirit,
one God, for ever and ever.

Liturgy of the Word: *from the* COMMON OF PASTORS: FOR MISSIONARIES
*(pp. 2191ff.), especially Is 52:7–10; Ps 96:1–2a, 2b–3, 7–8, 10; Mk 1:14–
20; or from the* WEEKDAY MASS.

Liturgy of the Eucharist, *p. 897.*

October 28

SIMON and JUDE, apostles

Feast

Simon came from Cana and was called "Zealot"—perhaps a
member of the activist political party against Roman occupation of
Judea. Tradition holds he suffered martyrdom after preaching in Egypt
and Persia. The Apostle Jude, called Thaddeus, spoke with Jesus
during the Last Supper (cf. Jn 14:22).

Entrance Antiphon

The Lord chose these holy men for their unfeigned love, and
gave them eternal glory.

Opening Prayer

Father,
you revealed yourself to us
through the preaching of your apostles Simon and Jude.
By their prayers,
give your Church continued growth
and increase the number of those who believe in you.

Grant this through our Lord Jesus Christ, your Son,

who lives and reigns with you and the Holy Spirit,
one God, for ever and ever.

For a votive Mass of Apostles, or of one Apostle, the readings are as follows.

FIRST READING

Eph 2:19–22

> *Through him the whole structure is held together
> and grows into a temple sacred in the Lord.*

A reading from the Letter of Saint Paul to the Ephesians

Brothers and sisters:

You are no longer strangers and sojourners, but you are fellow citizens with the holy ones and members of the household of God, built upon the foundation of the Apostles and prophets, with Christ Jesus himself as the capstone. Through him the whole structure is held together and grows into a temple sacred in the Lord; in him you also are being built together into a dwelling place of God in the Spirit.

The word of the Lord.

Responsorial Psalm

Ps 19:2–3, 4–5

R. Their message goes out through all the earth.

The heavens declare the glory of God,
  and the firmament proclaims his handiwork.
Day pours out the word to day,
  and night to night imparts knowledge.

R. Their message goes out through all the earth.

Not a word nor a discourse
  whose voice is not heard;
Through all the earth their voice resounds,
  and to the ends of the world, their message.

R. Their message goes out through all the earth.

Alleluia, alleluia   See *Te Deum*
We praise you, O God,
we acclaim you as Lord;
the glorious company of Apostles praise you.
Alleluia, alleluia

GOSPEL   Lk 6:12–16

From them Jesus chose Twelve, whom he also named Apostles.

A reading from the holy Gospel according to Luke

Jesus went up to the mountain to pray, and he spent the night
in prayer to God. When day came, he called his disciples to
himself, and from them he chose Twelve, whom he also named
Apostles: Simon, whom he named Peter, and his brother Andrew, James, John, Philip, Bartholomew, Matthew, Thomas,
James the son of Alphaeus, Simon who was called a Zealot,
and Judas the son of James, and Judas Iscariot, who became a
traitor.

The Gospel of the Lord.

Liturgy of the Eucharist, *p. 897.*

Prayer over the Gifts

Pray, brethren...

Lord,
each year we recall the glory
of your apostles Simon and Jude.
Accept our gifts
and prepare us to celebrate these holy mysteries.

We ask this in the name of Jesus the Lord.

Preface of the Apostles I *or* **II,** *p. 956*

Communion Antiphon

If anyone loves me, he will hold to my words, and my Father
will love him, and we will come to him, and make our home with
him.
                                                        (Jn 14:23)

Prayer after Communion

Let us pray.

Pause for silent prayer, if this has not preceded.

Father,
in your Spirit we pray:
may the sacrament we receive today
keep us in your loving care
as we honor the death of Saints Simon and Jude.
We ask this through Christ our Lord.

NOVEMBER

For **November 1,** ALL SAINTS, *see* **Vatican II Sunday Missal,** *p. 1075.*

For **November 2,** ALL SOULS, *see* **Vatican II Sunday Missal,** *p. 1081.*

For other optional readings, see **Masses for the Dead,** *pp. 2407–2458, in this* **Weekday Missal.**

November 3
MARTIN DE PORRES, religious (1579–1639)

Optional Memorial

Martin was born in Lima, Peru, the son of a white Spanish grandee father and a black Panamanian mother. He learned the art of healing as a boy, and when he entered the Dominican Order, he served as infirmarian. He professed his religious vows in 1603. Martin tended the poor who were ill, and was also known for his gentleness with animals. Blessed with extraordinary spiritual gifts, he led a life of profound prayer and penance. He is a patron saint of African-Americans.

Antiphons and Prayers: *from the* COMMON OF HOLY MEN AND WOMEN: FOR RELIGIOUS *(pp. 2260–2263), or from the* WEEKDAY MASS. *The following is optional:*

Opening Prayer

Lord,
you led Martin de Porres by a life of humility
to eternal glory.
May we follow his example
and be exalted with him in the kingdom of heaven.

Grant this through our Lord Jesus Christ, your Son,
who lives and reigns with you and the Holy Spirit,
one God, for ever and ever.

Liturgy of the Word: *from the* COMMON OF HOLY MEN AND WOMEN: FOR
RELIGIOUS *(pp. 2271ff.), especially Phil 4:4–9; Ps 131:1bcde, 2, 3; Mt 22:34–
40; or from the* WEEKDAY MASS.

Liturgy of the Eucharist, *p. 897.*

November 4

CHARLES BORROMEO, bishop (1538–1584)

Memorial

Charles was born near Lago Maggiore in northern Italy, a member of the wealthy Medici family. He became a lawyer and his uncle,
Pope Pius IV, summoned him to Rome and made him a cardinal (although he was still a layman). Charles worked to implement the
Council of Trent and then in 1563 was ordained and named archbishop of Milan. He was an ideal shepherd who dedicated himself
entirely to serving his people, establishing the first seminaries, correcting abuses. He was canonized in 1610.

Antiphons and Prayers: *from the* COMMON OF PASTORS: FOR BISHOPS *(pp.
2170–2175), or from the* WEEKDAY MASS, *except:*

Opening Prayer

Father,
keep in your people the spirit
which filled Charles Borromeo.
Let your Church be continually renewed

and show the image of Christ to the world
by being conformed to his likeness,
who lives and reigns with you and the Holy Spirit,
one God, for ever and ever.

Liturgy of the Word: *from the* COMMON OF PASTORS *(pp. 2188ff.), especially Rom 12:3–13; Ps 89:2–3, 4–5, 21–22, 25 and 27; Jn 10:11–16; or from the* WEEKDAY MASS.

Liturgy of the Eucharist, *p. 897.*

Prayer over the Gifts

Pray, brethren...

Lord,
look with kindness on the gifts we bring to your altar
on this feast of St. Charles.
You made him an example of virtue
and concern for the pastoral ministry.
Through the power of this sacrifice
may we abound in good works.

We ask this through Christ our Lord.

Prayer after Communion

Let us pray.
> *Pause for silent prayer, if this has not preceded.*

Lord,
may the holy mysteries we have received
give us that courage and strength
which made St. Charles faithful in his ministry
and constant in his love.

We ask this in the name of Jesus the Lord.

For **November 9,** THE DEDICATION OF THE LATERAN BASILICA, *see* **Vatican II Sunday Missal,** *p. 1096.*

November 10

LEO THE GREAT, pope and doctor (†461)

Memorial

Elected Pope in 440, Leo I shepherded the Church during most difficult times. He confronted and turned back Attila the Hun (452), witnessed the Vandals' sack of Rome (455), and through it all cared for his people. Fittingly, he has been called Pope Leo the Great.

Antiphons and Prayers: *from the* COMMON OF PASTORS: FOR POPES *(pp. 2170–2173), or* COMMON OF DOCTORS OF THE CHURCH *(pp. 2219–2238), or from the* WEEKDAY MASS, *except:*

Opening Prayer

God our Father,
you will never allow the power of hell
to prevail against your Church,
founded on the rock of the apostle Peter.
Let the prayers of Pope Leo the Great
keep us faithful to your truth
and secure in your peace.

We ask this through our Lord Jesus Christ, your Son,
who lives and reigns with you and the Holy Spirit,
one God, for ever and ever.

Liturgy of the Word: *from the* COMMON OF PASTORS: FOR A POPE *(pp. 2188ff.), or* COMMON OF DOCTORS OF THE CHURCH *(pp. 2222ff.), especially Sir 39:6–10; Ps 37:3–4, 5–6, 30–31; Mt 16:13–19; or from the* WEEKDAY MASS.

Liturgy of the Eucharist, *p. 897.*

Prayer over the Gifts

Pray, brethren...

Lord,
by these gifts we bring,
fill your people with your light.

May your Church continue to grow everywhere
under your guidance
and under the leadership of shepherds pleasing to you.

Grant this through Christ our Lord.

Prayer after Communion

Let us pray.

Pause for silent prayer, if this has not preceded.

Lord,
as you nourish your Church with this holy banquet,
govern it always with your love.
Under your powerful guidance may it grow in freedom
and continue in loyalty to the faith.

We ask this in the name of Jesus the Lord.

November 11

MARTIN OF TOURS, bishop (317–397)

Memorial

A Hungarian raised in Italy, Martin became a Roman soldier and a Christian. He gave away his cloak to a poor man, and later had a vision of Christ as that man. Martin went to Gaul and founded the first monastery in the West. He knew St. Hilary and, in 372, became bishop of Tours. His great work was to convert the pagan countryside.

Entrance Antiphon

I will raise up for myself a faithful priest; he will do what is in my heart and in my mind, says the Lord.   (1 Sm 2:35)

Opening Prayer

Father,
by his life and death
Martin of Tours offered you worship and praise.

Renew in our hearts the power of your love,
so that neither death nor life may separate us from you.

Grant this through our Lord Jesus Christ, your Son,
who lives and reigns with you and the Holy Spirit,
one God, for ever and ever.

Liturgy of the Word: *from the* COMMON OF PASTORS *(pp. 2188ff.), or*
COMMON OF HOLY MEN AND WOMEN: FOR RELIGIOUS *(pp. 2271ff.), especially Is*
61:1–3abcd; Ps 89:2–3, 4–5, 21–22, 25 and 27; and the following Gospel,
or from the WEEKDAY MASS.

Alleluia, alleluia Jn 13:34
I give you a new commandment:
love one another as I have loved you.
Alleluia, alleluia

GOSPEL   Mt 25:31–40

Whatever you did for one of these least brothers of mine,
you did for me.

A reading from the holy Gospel according to Matthew

Jesus said to his disciples: "When the Son of Man comes in
his glory, and all the angels with him, he will sit upon his glorious throne, and all the nations will be assembled before him.
And he will separate them one from another, as a shepherd
separates the sheep from the goats. He will place the sheep on
his right and the goats on his left. Then the king will say to
those on his right, 'Come, you who are blessed by my Father.
Inherit the kingdom prepared for you from the foundation of
the world. For I was hungry and you gave me food, I was thirsty and you gave me drink, a stranger and you welcomed me,
naked and you clothed me, ill and you cared for me, in prison
and you visited me.' Then the righteous will answer him and
say, 'Lord, when did we see you hungry and feed you, or thirs-

ty and give you drink? When did we see you a stranger and welcome you, or naked and clothe you? When did we see you ill or in prison, and visit you?' And the king will say to them in reply, 'Amen, I say to you, whatever you did for one of the least brothers of mine, you did for me.'"

The Gospel of the Lord.

Liturgy of the Eucharist, *p. 897.*

Prayer over the Gifts

Pray, brethren...

Lord God,
bless these gifts we present
on this feast of St. Martin.
May this eucharist help us
in joy and sorrow.

We ask this in the name of Jesus the Lord.

Communion Antiphon

I tell you, anything you did for the least of my brothers, you did for me, says the Lord.   (Mt 25:40)

Prayer after Communion

Let us pray.

Pause for silent prayer, if this has not preceded.

Lord,
you have renewed us with the sacrament of unity:
help us to follow your will in all that we do.
As St. Martin gave himself completely to your service,
may we rejoice in belonging to you.

We ask this through Christ our Lord.

JOSAPHAT, bishop and martyr (1580–1623)

Memorial

Today's saint is a martyr and patron for reunion of the Greek and Latin Churches. Born in the Ukraine as an Orthodox, he became a Catholic and then a monk and priest of the Order of St. Basil. He became archimandrite and later Archbishop of Poloz. A zealous bishop and worker for Christian unity, Josephat was assassinated by enemies in 1623. He was canonized in 1867.

Antiphons and Prayers: *from the* COMMON OF MARTYRS *(pp. 2128–2169), or* COMMON OF PASTORS: FOR BISHOPS *(pp. 2170–2175), or from the* WEEKDAY MASS, *except:*

Opening Prayer

Lord,
fill your Church with the spirit
that gave St. Josaphat courage
to lay down his life for his people.
By his prayers
may your Spirit make us strong
and willing to offer our lives
for our brothers and sisters.

We ask this through our Lord Jesus Christ, your Son,
who lives and reigns with you and the Holy Spirit,
one God, for ever and ever.

Liturgy of the Word: *from the* COMMON OF MARTYRS *(pp. 2147ff.), or* COMMON OF PASTORS *(pp. 2188ff.), especially Eph 4:1–7, 11–13; Ps 1:1–2, 3, 4 and 6; Jn 17:20–26; or from the* WEEKDAY MASS.

Liturgy of the Eucharist, *p. 897.*

Prayer over the Gifts

Pray, brethren...

God of mercy,

pour out your blessing upon these gifts,
and make us strong in the faith
which St. Josaphat professed by shedding his blood.
We ask this in the name of Jesus the Lord.

Prayer after Communion

Let us pray.

Pause for silent prayer, if this has not preceded.

Lord,
may this eucharist we have shared
fill us with your Spirit of courage and peace.
Let the example of St. Josaphat
inspire us to spend our lives
working for the honor and unity of your Church.
Grant this through Christ our Lord.

November 13

[In the dioceses of the United States]

FRANCES XAVIER CABRINI, virgin and religious
(1850–1917)

Memorial

American Catholics have particular devotion to the first canonized United States citizen, "Mother Cabrini." Born in northern Italy,
she was considered too sickly to join the local religious order. In
time she energetically founded the Missionary Sisters of the Sacred
Heart, started several religious houses in Italy and in 1889 came to
New York to help Italian immigrants. Before dying from malaria in
Chicago, Mother Cabrini crossed the Atlantic 30 times and established 67 religious houses with more than 1,500 sisters. She is
buried at Mother Cabrini High School in New York City. She was
canonized in 1946.

Antiphons and Prayers: *from the* COMMON OF VIRGINS *(pp. 2238–2252), or from the* WEEKDAY MASS, *except:*

Opening Prayer

God our Father,
you called Frances Xavier Cabrini from Italy
to serve the immigrants of America.
By her example teach us concern
for the stranger, the sick, and the frustrated.
By her prayers help us to see Christ
in all the men and women we meet.

Grant this through our Lord Jesus Christ, your Son,
who lives and reigns with you and the Holy Spirit,
one God, for ever and ever.

Liturgy of the Word: *from the* COMMON OF VIRGINS *(pp. 2244ff.), or* COMMON OF HOLY MEN AND WOMEN: FOR RELIGIOUS *(pp. 2271ff.), or from the* WEEKDAY MASS.

Liturgy of the Eucharist, *p. 897.*

November 15

ALBERT THE GREAT, bishop and doctor
(1206–1280)

Optional Memorial

Albert was a famous Dominican teacher who taught at Paris and Cologne. His most attentive student in Aristotelian philosophy was St. Thomas Aquinas. Albert became provincial of the Dominicans and then Bishop of Ratisbon, but after two years returned to teaching. He was interested in the natural sciences as well as theology. A profound and holy professor, he died at Cologne and was canonized a saint in 1931. He is patron of scientists and philosophers.

Antiphons and Prayers: *from the* COMMON OF PASTORS: FOR BISHOPS *(pp. 2170–2175), or* COMMON OF DOCTORS OF THE CHURCH *(pp. 2219–2238), or from the* WEEKDAY MASS. *The following is optional:*

Opening Prayer

God our Father,
you endowed St. Albert with the talent
of combining human wisdom with divine faith.
Keep us true to his teachings
that the advance of human knowledge
may deepen our knowledge and love of you.

Grant this through our Lord Jesus Christ, your Son,
who lives and reigns with you and the Holy Spirit,
one God, for ever and ever.

Liturgy of the Word: *from the* COMMON OF PASTORS *(pp. 2188ff.), or* COMMON OF DOCTORS OF THE CHURCH *(pp. 2222ff.), especially Sir 15:1–6; Ps 119:9, 10, 11, 12, 13, 14; Mt 13:47–52; or from the* WEEKDAY MASS.

Liturgy of the Eucharist, *p. 897.*

November 16

MARGARET OF SCOTLAND, queen (1046–1093)

Optional Memorial

Margaret was born in Hungary while her father was in political exile from William the Conqueror. The family returned to England and then to Scotland where she married King Malcolm in 1070. Margaret was an exemplary queen and a mother who was devoted to her husband and eight children. Concerned for religion and social justice, she did much to help the poor of Scotland.

Antiphons and Prayers: *from the* COMMON OF HOLY MEN AND WOMEN: FOR THOSE WHO WORKED FOR THE UNDERPRIVILEGED *(pp. 2263–2264), or from the* WEEKDAY MASS. *The following is optional:*

Opening Prayer

Lord,
you gave St. Margaret of Scotland
a special love for the poor.

Let her example and prayers
help us to become a living sign of your goodness.

We ask this through our Lord Jesus Christ, your Son,
who lives and reigns with you and the Holy Spirit,
one God, for ever and ever.

Liturgy of the Word: *from the* COMMON OF HOLY MEN AND WOMEN: FOR THOSE WHO WORKED FOR THE UNDERPRIVILEGED *(pp. 2274ff.), especially Is 58:6–11; Ps 112:1–2, 3–4, 5–6, 7–8, 9; Jn 15:9–17; or from the* WEEKDAY MASS.

Liturgy of the Eucharist, *p. 897.*

Also on November 16

GERTRUDE, virgin (1256–1302)

Optional Memorial

Born in Saxony, as a child Gertrude was taken to the Benedictine Abbey of Helfta, which was a center of culture and learning. Gertrude studied and wrote all her life. At age 25 she reported special revelations from the Lord and wrote extensively about them. A great mystic of the thirteenth century, Gertrude died on November 17, 1301.

Antiphons and Prayers: *from the* COMMON OF VIRGINS *(pp. 2238–2244), or* COMMON OF HOLY MEN AND WOMEN: FOR RELIGIOUS *(pp. 2260–2263), or from the* WEEKDAY MASS. *The following is optional:*

Opening Prayer

Father,
you filled the heart of St. Gertrude
with the presence of your love.
Bring light into our darkness
and let us experience the joy of your presence
and the power of your grace.

Grant this through our Lord Jesus Christ, your Son,
who lives and reigns with you and the Holy Spirit,
one God, for ever and ever.

Liturgy of the Word: *from the* COMMON OF VIRGINS *(pp. 2244ff.), or* COMMON OF HOLY MEN AND WOMEN: FOR RELIGIOUS *(pp. 2271ff.), especially Eph 3:14–19; Ps 23:1b–3a, 4, 5, 6; Jn 15:1–8; or from the* WEEKDAY MASS.

Liturgy of the Eucharist, *p. 897.*

November 17

ELIZABETH OF HUNGARY, queen and religious
(1207–1231)

Memorial

Born in Hungary in 1207, Elizabeth at 14 was married to Ludwig IV of Thuringia. For the intense Elizabeth it was a happy marriage. The family tried to follow the ideal of Francis of Assisi, then living. As she was expecting their third child Ludwig died in the Crusades. Elizabeth became a Franciscan tertiary, founded a hospital in honor of St. Francis, and dedicated herself totally to the care of the poor. Only 24 when she died, she is the patroness of the Franciscan Third Order and of Catholic Charities.

Antiphons and Prayers: *from the Common of holy men and women: for those who worked for the underprivileged, (pp. 2263–2264), or from the* WEEK-DAY MASS, *except:*

Opening Prayer

Father,
you helped Elizabeth of Hungary
to recognize and honor Christ
in the poor of this world.
Let her prayers help us to serve our brothers and sisters
in time of trouble and need.

We ask this through our Lord Jesus Christ, your Son,
who lives and reigns with you and the Holy Spirit,
one God, for ever and ever.

Liturgy of the Word: *from the* COMMON OF HOLY MEN AND WOMEN: FOR THOSE WHO WORKED FOR THE UNDERPRIVILEGED *(pp. 2274ff.), or* FOR RELIGIOUS, *(pp. 2271ff.), especially 1 Jn 3:14–18; Ps 34:2–3, 4–5, 6–7, 8–9, 10–11; Lk 6:27–38; or from the* WEEKDAY MASS.

Liturgy of the Eucharist, *p. 897.*

November 18

DEDICATION OF THE BASILICAS OF PETER AND PAUL, apostles

Optional Memorial

The tombs in Rome of Peter and Paul have been places of Christian veneration since the second century. Around 330 the Emperor Constantine built a great basilica on the side of the Vatican Hill over the grave of Peter, and shortly afterward a more modest basilica over Paul's tomb. Both basilicas have been rebuilt and stand as magnificent testimonials to the importance and memory of the Princes of the Apostles.

The readings for this memorial are proper.

Entrance Antiphon

You have made them princes over all the earth; they declared your fame to all generations; for ever will the nations declare your praise. (Ps 44:17–18)

Opening Prayer

Lord,
give your Church the protection of the apostles.
From them it first received the faith of Christ.
May they help your Church to grow in your grace
until the end of time.

Grant this through our Lord Jesus Christ, your Son,
who lives and reigns with you and the Holy Spirit,
one God, for ever and ever.

FIRST READING   Acts 28:11–16, 30–31

And thus we came to Rome.

A reading from the Acts of the Apostles

After three months we set sail on a ship that had wintered at the island [of Malta]. It was an Alexandrian ship with the Dioscuri as its figurehead. We put in at Syracuse and stayed there three days, and from there we sailed round the coast and arrived at Rhegium. After a day, a south wind came up and in two days we reached Puteoli. There we found some brothers and were urged to stay with them for seven days. And thus we came to Rome. The brothers from there heard about us and came as far as the Forum of Appius and Three Taverns to meet us. On seeing them, Paul gave thanks to God and took courage. When he entered Rome, Paul was allowed to live by himself, with the soldier who was guarding him.

He remained for two full years in his lodgings. He received all who came to him, and with complete assurance and without hindrance he proclaimed the Kingdom of God and taught about the Lord Jesus Christ.

The word of the Lord.

Responsorial Psalm
Ps 98:1, 2–3ab, 3cd–4, 5–6

R. The Lord has revealed to the nations his saving power.

Sing to the LORD a new song,
  for he has done wondrous deeds;
His right hand has won victory for him,
  his holy arm.

R. The Lord has revealed to the nations his saving power.

The LORD has made his salvation known:
  in the sight of the nations he has revealed his justice.
He has remembered his kindness and his faithfulness
  toward the house of Israel.

R. The Lord has revealed to the nations his saving power.

All the ends of the earth have seen
  the salvation by our God.
Sing joyfully to the LORD, all you lands;
  break into song; sing praise.

R. The Lord has revealed to the nations his saving power.

Sing praise to the LORD with the harp,
  with the harp and melodious song.
With trumpets and the sound of the horn
  sing joyfully before the King, the LORD.

R. The Lord has revealed to the nations his saving power.

Alleluia, alleluia   See *Te Deum*
We praise you, O God,
we acclaim you as Lord;
the glorious company of Apostles praise you.
Alleluia, alleluia

GOSPEL   Mt 14:22–33
Command me to come to you on the water.

A reading from the holy Gospel according to Matthew

After the crowd had eaten their fill, Jesus made the disciples
get into the boat and precede him to the other side, while he
dismissed the crowds. After doing so, he went up on the mountain by himself to pray. When it was evening he was there
alone. Meanwhile the boat, already a few miles offshore, was
being tossed about by the waves, for the wind was against it.
During the fourth watch of the night, he came toward them,
walking on the sea. When the disciples saw him walking on
the sea they were terrified. "It is a ghost," they said, and they
cried out in fear. At once Jesus spoke to them, "Take courage,
it is I; do not be afraid." Peter said to him in reply, "Lord, if it
is you, command me to come to you on the water." He said,
"Come." Peter got out of the boat and began to walk on the
water toward Jesus. But when he saw how strong the wind

was he became frightened; and, beginning to sink, he cried out, "Lord, save me!" Immediately Jesus stretched out his hand and caught him, and said to him, "O you of little faith, why did you doubt?" After they got into the boat, the wind died down. Those who were in the boat did him homage, saying, "Truly, you are the Son of God."

The Gospel of the Lord.

Liturgy of the Eucharist, *p. 897.*

Prayer over the Gifts

Pray, brethren...

Lord,
accept the gift of our worship
and hear our prayers for mercy.
Keep alive in our hearts the truth you gave us
through the ministry of your apostles Peter and Paul.

We ask this through Christ our Lord.

Preface of the Apostles I or II, *p. 956.*

Communion Antiphon

Lord, you have the words of everlasting life, and we believe that you are God's Holy One.   (Jn 6:69–70)

Prayer after Communion

Let us pray.

Pause for silent prayer, if this has not preceded.

Lord,
you have given us bread from heaven.
May this celebration
in memory of your apostles Peter and Paul
bring us the joy of their constant protection.

We ask this in the name of Jesus the Lord.

Also on November 18

[In the dioceses of the United States]

ROSE PHILIPPINE DUCHESNE, virgin (1769–1852)

Optional Memorial

Born in Grenoble, France, Philippine entered the Visitation Order, but the nuns had to disband during the French Revolution. About ten years later she joined a new community, the Religious of the Sacred Heart. Philippine desired to work in the missions, and she was sent to the United States in 1818. She established several foundations in the South and Midwest, especially in New Orleans and Missouri. When she was 72 she realized her dream of working among the Native Americans, who called her "the woman who prays always."

Antiphons and Prayers: *from the* COMMON OF VIRGINS *(pp. 2238–2252), or* COMMON OF HOLY MEN AND WOMEN: FOR RELIGIOUS *(pp. 2260–2263), or from the* WEEKDAY MASS.

Liturgy of the Word: *from the* COMMON OF VIRGINS *(pp. 2244ff.), or* COMMON OF HOLY MEN AND WOMEN: FOR RELIGIOUS *(pp. 2271ff.).*

Liturgy of the Eucharist, *p. 897.*

November 21

PRESENTATION OF MARY

Memorial

A pious tradition, based on the apocryphal Proto-Gospel of James, held that as a child Mary was presented and educated near the Temple in Jerusalem. Although not historical, this story reminds us of how Mary, conceived immaculately, was predestined by God to be the mother of his Son.

Antiphons and Prayers: *from the* COMMON OF THE BLESSED VIRGIN MARY *(pp. 2091–2127), or from the* WEEKDAY MASS, *except:*

Opening Prayer

Eternal Father,
we honor the holiness and glory of the Virgin Mary.
May her prayers bring us
the fullness of your life and love.

We ask this through our Lord Jesus Christ, your Son,
who lives and reigns with you and the Holy Spirit,
one God, for ever and ever.

Liturgy of the Word: *from the* COMMON OF THE BLESSED VIRGIN MARY
*(pp. 2101ff.), especially Zec 2:14–17; Lk 1:46–47, 48–49, 50–51, 52–53,
54–55; Mt 12:46–50.*

Liturgy of the Eucharist, *p. 897.*

November 22

CECILIA, virgin and martyr (second century)

Memorial

A basilica in Rome is dedicated to St. Cecilia. Devotion to her
grew because of a dramatic and popular narrative of her tortures
and death. Though there seems to be some foundation for the
narrative, the details cannot be shown as factual. The story says that
"Cecilia sang in her heart while the musical instruments sounded
for her wedding." Because of this, Cecilia is the patroness of music.

Antiphons and Prayers: *from the* COMMON OF MARTYRS *(pp. 2128–2169),
or* COMMON OF VIRGINS *(pp. 2238–2252), or from the* WEEKDAY MASS, *except:*

Opening Prayer

Lord of mercy,
be close to those who call upon you.
With St. Cecilia to help us
hear and answer our prayers.

Grant this through our Lord Jesus Christ, your Son,
who lives and reigns with you and the Holy Spirit,
one God, for ever and ever.

Liturgy of the Word: *from the* COMMON OF MARTYRS *(pp. 2147ff.), or*
COMMON OF VIRGINS *(pp. 2244ff.), especially Hos 2:16bc, 17cd, 21–22;
Ps 45:11–12, 14–15, 16–17; Mt 25:1–13; or from the* WEEKDAY MASS.

Liturgy of the Eucharist, *p. 897.*

CLEMENT I, pope and martyr (c. 97)

Optional Memorial

After the obscure pontificates of Linus and Cletus, Clement was the first noted successor of Peter as Bishop of Rome. St. Irenaeus states that Clement knew the apostles and was strongly influenced by them. Clement wrote a scripturally based letter to the Corinthians (dated around 95), encouraging them to unity, charity, and holiness. He is believed to have suffered martyrdom.

Antiphons and Prayers: *from the* COMMON OF MARTYRS *(pp. 2128–2169), or* COMMON OF PASTORS: FOR POPES *(pp. 2170–2173), or from the* WEEKDAY MASS. *The following is optional:*

Opening Prayer

All-powerful and ever-living God,
we praise your power and glory
revealed to us in the lives of all your saints.
Give us joy on this feast of St. Clement,
the priest and martyr
who bore witness with his blood to the love he proclaimed
and the gospel he preached.

We ask this through our Lord Jesus Christ, your Son,
who lives and reigns with you and the Holy Spirit,
one God, for ever and ever.

Liturgy of the Word: *from the* COMMON OF MARTYRS *(pp. 2147ff.), or* COMMON OF PASTORS: FOR A POPE *(pp. 2188ff.), especially 1 Pt 5:1–4; Ps 89:2–3, 4–5, 21–22, 25 and 27; Mt 16:13–19; or from the* WEEKDAY MASS.

Liturgy of the Eucharist, *p. 897.*

Also on November 23

COLUMBAN, abbot (543–615)

Optional Memorial

The most famous of Irish monks, Columban was well educated and wanted to be a "pilgrim of God." He traveled to France and founded several well-disciplined monasteries as centers of religion and culture. Because of difficulties, he decided to return to Ireland, but a shipwreck directed him toward Rome and the founding of his final monastery at Bobbio, Italy.

Antiphons and Prayers: *from the* COMMON OF PASTORS: FOR MISSIONARIES *(pp. 2183–2187), or* COMMON OF HOLY MEN AND WOMEN: FOR RELIGIOUS *(pp. 2260–2263), or from the* WEEKDAY MASS. *The following is optional:*

Opening Prayer

Lord,
you called St. Columban to live the monastic life
and to preach the gospel with zeal.
May his prayers and example
help us to seek you above all things
and to work with all our hearts
for the spread of the faith.

Grant this through our Lord Jesus Christ, your Son,
who lives and reigns with you and the Holy Spirit,
one God, for ever and ever.

Liturgy of the Word: *from the* COMMON OF PASTORS: FOR MISSIONARIES *(pp. 2191ff.), or* COMMON OF HOLY MEN AND WOMEN: FOR RELIGIOUS *(pp. 2271ff.), especially Is 52:7–10; Ps 96:1–2a, 2b–3, 7–8a, 10; Lk 9:57–62; or from the* WEEKDAY MASS.

Liturgy of the Eucharist, *p. 897.*

Also on November 23

[In the dioceses of the United States]

BLESSED MIGUEL AGUSTIN PRO, priest and martyr (1891–1927)

Optional Memorial

Miguel Pro was from a deeply Catholic family in Mexico and entered the Jesuits with hopes of becoming a priest. Because the Mexican government was persecuting the Church, he had to leave the country and was ordained in Belgium. Returning to Mexico,

Fr. Pro secretly carried out his priestly ministry despite the persecution. He evaded arrest for several years, but was finally apprehended and put to death. Shortly before his execution he shouted "Viva Cristo Rey!" (Long live Christ the King!)

Antiphons and Prayers: *from the* COMMON OF MARTYRS *(pp. 2128–2169), or* COMMON OF PASTORS *(pp. 2170–2218), or from the* WEEKDAY MASS.

Liturgy of the Word: *from the* COMMON OF MARTYRS *(pp. 2147ff.), or* COMMON OF PASTORS *(pp. 2188ff.).*

Liturgy of the Eucharist, *p. 897.*

November 24

ANDREW DUNG-LAC, priest and martyr, and COMPANIONS, martyrs (†1839)

Optional Memorial

Today the Church honors a group of 117 martyrs of Vietnam. They gave their lives during several persecutions throughout the 18th and 19th centuries. Despite the extreme tortures they had to endure, they heroically witnessed to the faith. Ninety-six of these saints, including the priest Andrew Dung-Lac, were native Vietnamese, and the others were European missionaries.

Antiphons and Prayers: *from the* COMMON OF MARTYRS *(pp. 2128–2169), or from the* WEEKDAY MASS.

Liturgy of the Word: *from the* COMMON OF MARTYRS *(pp. 2147ff.).*

Liturgy of the Eucharist, *p. 897.*

November 30

ANDREW, apostle

Feast

The Church, built on the apostles, has from its beginning honored the Twelve. Probably at one time, each month had an apostle's feast. Andrew of Bethsaida (on the Lake of Galilee) was Peter's brother. Tradition recalls his crucifixion in Greece on an X-shaped cross (St. Andrew's cross).

Entrance Antiphon

By the Sea of Galilee the Lord saw two brothers, Peter and Andrew. He called them; Come and follow me, and I will make you fishers of men.
(See Mt 4:18–19)

Opening Prayer

Lord,
in your kindness hear our petitions.
You called Andrew the apostle
to preach the gospel and guide your Church in faith.
May he always be our friend in your presence
to help us with his prayers.

We ask this through our Lord Jesus Christ, your Son,
who lives and reigns with you and the Holy Spirit,
one God, for ever and ever.

FIRST READING

Rom 10:9–18

Thus faith comes from what is heard,
and what is heard comes through the word of Christ.

A reading from the Letter of Saint Paul to the Romans

Brothers and sisters:

If you confess with your mouth that Jesus is Lord and believe in your heart that God raised him from the dead, you will be saved. For one believes with the heart and so is justified, and one confesses with the mouth and so is saved. The Scripture says, *No one who believes in him will be put to shame.* There is no distinction between Jew and Greek; the same Lord is Lord of all, enriching all who call upon him. *For everyone who calls on the name of the Lord will be saved.*

But how can they call on him in whom they have not believed? And how can they believe in him of whom they have not heard? And how can they hear without someone to preach?

And how can people preach unless they are sent? As it is written, *How beautiful are the feet of those who bring the good news!* But not everyone has heeded the good news; for Isaiah says, *Lord, who has believed what was heard from us?* Thus faith comes from what is heard, and what is heard comes through the word of Christ. But I ask, did they not hear? Certainly they did; for

> *Their voice has gone forth to all the earth,*
> *and their words to the ends of the world.*

The word of the Lord.

Responsorial Psalm

Ps 19:8, 9, 10, 11

R. The judgments of the Lord are true,
and all of them are just.

The law of the LORD is perfect,
  refreshing the soul;
The decree of the LORD is trustworthy,
  giving wisdom to the simple.

R. The judgments of the Lord are true,
and all of them are just.

The precepts of the LORD are right,
  rejoicing the heart;
The command of the LORD is clear,
  enlightening the eye.

R. The judgments of the Lord are true,
and all of them are just.

The fear of the LORD is pure,
  enduring forever;
The ordinances of the LORD are true,
  all of them just.

R. The judgments of the Lord are true,
and all of them are just.

They are more precious than gold,
  than a heap of purest gold;
Sweeter also than syrup
  or honey from the comb.

**R. The judgments of the Lord are true,
     and all of them are just.**

Or: **R. Your words, Lord, are Spirit and life.**

Alleluia, alleluia   Mt 4:19
Come after me, says the Lord,
and I will make you fishers of men.
Alleluia, alleluia

GOSPEL   Mt 4:18–22

Immediately they left their nets and followed him.

A reading from the holy Gospel according to Matthew

As Jesus was walking by the Sea of Galilee, he saw two brothers, Simon who is called Peter, and his brother Andrew, casting a net into the sea; they were fishermen. He said to them, "Come after me, and I will make you fishers of men." At once they left their nets and followed him. He walked along from there and saw two other brothers, James, the son of Zebedee, and his brother John. They were in a boat, with their father Zebedee, mending their nets. He called them, and immediately they left their boat and their father and followed him.
The Gospel of the Lord.

Liturgy of the Eucharist, *p. 897.*

Prayer over the Gifts

Pray, brethren...

All-powerful God,
may these gifts we bring on the feast of St. Andrew

be pleasing to you
and give life to all who receive them.

We ask this in the name of Jesus the Lord.

Preface of the Apostles I *or* **II,** *p. 956.*

Communion Antiphon

Andrew told his brother Simon: We have found the Messiah, the Christ; and he brought him to Jesus. (Jn 1:41–42)

Prayer after Communion

Let us pray.

Pause for silent prayer, if this has not preceded.

Lord,
may the sacrament we have received give us courage
to follow the example of Andrew the apostle.
By sharing in Christ's suffering
may we live with him for ever in glory,
for he is Lord for ever and ever.

Fourth Thursday of November

[In the dioceses of the United States]

THANKSGIVING DAY

Among the finest American traditions is Thanksgiving Day—a day at the end of harvest season when, by national declaration, the citizens as a nation thank God for their blessings. Catholics are fortunate in having a special Votive Mass for Thanksgiving Day.

Opening Prayer

Let us pray

[that our gratitude to God may bear fruit
in loving service to our fellow men and women]

Pause for silent prayer.

Father all-powerful,
your gifts of love are countless
and your goodness infinite.
On Thanksgiving Day we come before you
with gratitude for your kindness:
open our hearts to concern for our fellow men and women,
so that we may share your gifts in loving service.

We ask this through our Lord Jesus Christ, your Son,
who lives and reigns with you and the Holy Spirit,
one God, for ever and ever.

Liturgy of the Word: *various texts may be selected from the lectionary.*

Prayer over the Gifts

Pray, brethren...

God our Father,
from your hand we have received generous gifts
so that we might learn to share your blessings in gratitude.
Accept these gifts of bread and wine,
and let the perfect sacrifice of Jesus
draw us closer to all our brothers and sisters in the family
    of man.

Grant this through Christ our Lord.

Preface for Thanksgiving Day, *p. 965.*

Prayer after Communion

Let us pray.

Pause for silent prayer, if this has not preceded.

Lord God,
in this celebration
we have seen the depths of your love for every man
    and woman

and been reminded of our negligence toward others.
Help us to reach out in love to all your people,
so that we may share with them
the goods of time and eternity.

Grant this through Christ our Lord.

DECEMBER

December 3

FRANCIS XAVIER, priest (1506–1552)

Memorial

Born at Xavier (Navarre), Spain, Francis was one of the first Jesuits. Though suffering from sciatica, he went to preach the Gospel in the unknown Far East. For eleven years, in suffering and prayer, he brought the Gospel to India, Ceylon, and Japan. He fell ill and died at the gates of China at age 46. He was canonized in 1662.

Antiphons and Prayers: *from the* COMMON OF PASTORS: FOR MISSIONARIES *(pp. 2183–2187), or from the* WEEKDAY MASS, *except:*

Opening Prayer

God our Father,
by the preaching of Francis Xavier
you brought many nations to yourself.
Give his zeal for the faith to all who believe in you,
that your Church may rejoice in continued growth
throughout the world.

Grant this through our Lord Jesus Christ, your Son,
who lives and reigns with you and the Holy Spirit,
one God, for ever and ever.

Liturgy of the Word: *from the* COMMON OF PASTORS: FOR MISSIONARIES *(pp. 2191ff.), especially 1 Cor 9:16–19, 22–23; Ps 117:1bc, 2; Mk 16:15–20; or from the* WEEKDAY MASS.

Liturgy of the Eucharist, *p. 897.*

Prayer over the Gifts

Pray, brethren...

Lord,
receive the gifts we bring on the feast of Francis Xavier.
As his zeal for the salvation of mankind
led him to the ends of the earth,
may we be effective witnesses to the gospel
and come with our brothers and sisters
to be with you in the joy of your kingdom.

We ask this through Christ our Lord.

Prayer after Communion

Let us pray.

Pause for silent prayer, if this has not preceded.

Lord God,
may this eucharist fill us with the same love
that inspired Francis Xavier
to work for the salvation of all.
Help us to live in a manner more worthy of our Christian
    calling
and so inherit the promise of eternal life.

We ask this in the name of Jesus the Lord.

December 4

JOHN OF DAMASCUS, priest, religious, and doctor
(c. 675–c. 749)

Optional Memorial

Born at Damascus around 675, John was active in business before becoming a monk. A renowned theologian, he defended the practice of honoring icons of the saints. He is outstanding for his writings about the Blessed Mother. Three homilies he wrote on Mary's Dormition are especially important in tracing the development of the doctrine of the Assumption.

Antiphons and Prayers: *from the* COMMON OF PASTORS *(pp. 2170–2218), or* COMMON OF DOCTORS OF THE CHURCH *(pp. 2219–2238), or from the* WEEKDAY MASS. *The following is optional:*

Opening Prayer

Lord,
may the prayers of St. John Damascene help us,
and may the true faith he taught so well
always be our light and our strength.

We ask this through our Lord Jesus Christ, your Son,
who lives and reigns with you and the Holy Spirit,
one God, for ever and ever.

Liturgy of the Word: *from the* COMMON OF PASTORS *(pp. 2188ff.), or* COMMON OF DOCTORS OF THE CHURCH *(pp. 2222ff.), especially 2 Tm 1:13–14; 2:1–3; Ps 19:8, 9, 10, 11; Mt 25:14–30; or from the* WEEKDAY MASS.

Liturgy of the Eucharist, *p. 897.*

December 6

NICHOLAS, bishop (c. 350)

Optional Memorial

Few saints are as popular as St. Nicholas. Because he is widely venerated in both East and West, he is a patron for ecumenical efforts. Nicholas was bishop of Mira, on the southern coast of Turkey. An ancient tradition indicates he attended the Council of Nicea in 325. Since 1087, his relics have been at Bari, Italy.

Antiphons and Prayers: *from the* COMMON OF PASTORS: FOR BISHOPS *(pp. 2170–2175), or from the* WEEKDAY MASS. *The following is optional:*

Opening Prayer

Father,
hear our prayers for mercy,

and by the help of St. Nicholas
keep us safe from all danger,
and guide us on the way of salvation.

Grant this through our Lord Jesus Christ, your Son,
who lives and reigns with you and the Holy Spirit,
one God, for ever and ever.

Liturgy of the Word: *from the* COMMON OF PASTORS *(pp. 2188ff.), especially Is 6:1–8; Ps 40:2 and 4, 7–8a, 8b–9, 10, 11; Lk 10:1–9; or from the* WEEKDAY MASS.

Liturgy of the Eucharist, *p. 897.*

December 7

AMBROSE, bishop and doctor (339–397)

Memorial

A Roman citizen, Ambrose became the ranking government official in Milan. Ambrose was studying Christianity when the people demanded him as their bishop. He received the sacraments and on this date was ordained bishop. An outstanding pastoral figure and theologian, Ambrose influenced Augustine to embrace Christianity.

Antiphons and Prayers: *from the* COMMON OF PASTORS: FOR BISHOPS *(pp. 2170–2175), or* COMMON OF DOCTORS OF THE CHURCH *(pp. 2219–2238), or from the* WEEKDAY MASS. *The following is optional:*

Opening Prayer

Lord,
you made St. Ambrose
an outstanding teacher of the Catholic faith
and gave him the courage of an apostle.
Raise up in your Church more leaders after your own heart,
to guide us with courage and wisdom.

We ask this through our Lord Jesus Christ, your Son,
who lives and reigns with you and the Holy Spirit,
one God, for ever and ever.

Liturgy of the Word: *from the* COMMON OF PASTORS *(pp. 2188ff.), or* COMMON OF DOCTORS OF THE CHURCH *(pp. 2222ff.), especially Eph 3:8–12; Ps 89:2–3, 4–5, 21–22, 25 and 27; Jn 10:11–16; or from the* WEEKDAY MASS.

Liturgy of the Eucharist, *p. 897.*

Prayer over the Gifts

Pray, brethren...

Lord,
as we celebrate these holy rites,
send your Spirit to give us the light of faith
which guided St. Ambrose to make your glory known.

We ask this in the name of Jesus the Lord.

Prayer after Communion

Let us pray.

Pause for silent prayer, if this has not preceded.

Father,
you have renewed us by the power of this sacrament.
Through the teachings of St. Ambrose,
may we follow your way with courage
and prepare ourselves for the feast of eternal life.

Grant this through Christ our Lord.

For **December 8,** IMMACULATE CONCEPTION OF THE BLESSED VIRGIN MARY, *see* **Vatican II Sunday Missal,** *p. 1101.*

December 9

[In the dioceses of the United States]

JUAN DIEGO, hermit (1474–1548)

Optional Memorial

The story of Our Lady of Guadalupe is intertwined with that of Juan Diego. He was an Amerindian convert who saw the Blessed

Virgin and received her miraculous image on his tilma. He showed great courage in going to the bishop and presenting Mary's request for a church. After it was built, Juan lived nearby and took care of the grounds, received pilgrims to the shrine, and dedicated himself to prayer and works of service.

Antiphons and Prayers: *from the* COMMON OF HOLY MEN AND WOMEN *(pp. 2252–2322), or from the* WEEKDAY MASS.

Liturgy of the Word: *from the* COMMON OF HOLY MEN AND WOMEN *(pp. 2269ff.).*

Liturgy of the Eucharist, *p. 897.*

December 11

DAMASUS I, pope (c. 305–384)

Optional Memorial

Of Spanish descent, Damasus was born in Rome. He became church archivist and preserved records of the still recent persecutions. Elected pope in 366, he was devoted to the Christian martyrs, whose bodies were buried in the catacombs. Damasus encouraged the biblicist St. Jerome, struggled against anti-popes, and guided the Church through a period of difficult growth.

Antiphons and Prayers: *from the* COMMON OF PASTORS: FOR POPES *(pp. 2170–2173), or from the* WEEKDAY MASS. *The following is optional:*

Opening Prayer

Father,
as St. Damasus loved and honored your martyrs,
so may we continue to celebrate their witness for Christ,
who lives and reigns with you and the Holy Spirit,
one God, for ever and ever.

Liturgy of the Word: *from the* COMMON OF PASTORS: FOR A POPE *(pp. 2188ff.), especially Acts 20:17–18a, 28–32, 36; Ps 110:1, 2, 3, 4; Jn 15:9–17; or from the* WEEKDAY MASS.

Liturgy of the Eucharist, *p. 897.*

December 12

[In the dioceses of the United States]

OUR LADY OF GUADALUPE

Feast

The North American continent is honored by the Shrine of Our Lady of Guadalupe near Mexico City. On December 9, 1531, the Blessed Mother appeared to a simple Amerindian convert, Juan Diego. Her picture was miraculously impressed upon his cloak. Our Lady of Guadalupe, Patroness of the Americas, showed herself as a tender and compassionate mother.

Antiphons and Prayers: *from the* COMMON OF THE BLESSED VIRGIN MARY *(pp. 2091–2127), or from the* WEEKDAY MASS, *except:*

Opening Prayer

God of power and mercy,
you blessed the Americas at Tepeyac
with the presence of the Virgin Mary of Guadalupe.
May her prayers help all men and women
to accept each other as brothers and sisters.
Through your justice present in our hearts
may your peace reign in the world.

We ask this through our Lord Jesus Christ, your Son,
who lives and reigns with you and the Holy Spirit,
one God, for ever and ever.

Liturgy of the Word: *from the* COMMON OF THE BLESSED VIRGIN MARY *(pp. 2101ff.), especially Zec 2:14–17 or Rv 11:19a; 12:1–6a, 10ab; Jdt 13:18bcde, 19; Lk 1:26–38 or Lk 1:39–47; or from the* WEEKDAY MASS.

Liturgy of the Eucharist, *p. 897.*

December 13

LUCY, virgin and martyr (†304)

Memorial

This saint has been venerated in Syracuse (Sicily) since the fourth century. She probably suffered martyrdom in the terrible years of

Diocletian's persecution. A popular saint and patroness for those with eye disorders, her name is listed in the First Eucharistic Prayer. The feast of Lucy, whose name means "light," comes during Advent and reminds us of the light of Christ whose birth draws near.

Antiphons and Prayers: *from the* COMMON OF MARTYRS *(pp. 2128–2169), or* COMMON OF VIRGINS *(pp. 2238–2252), or from the* WEEKDAY MASS, *except:*

Opening Prayer

Lord,
give us courage through the prayers of St. Lucy.
As we celebrate her entrance into eternal glory,
we ask to share her happiness in the life to come.

Grant this through our Lord Jesus Christ, your Son,
who lives and reigns with you and the Holy Spirit,
one God, for ever and ever.

Liturgy of the Word: *from the* COMMON OF MARTYRS *(pp. 2147ff.), or* COMMON OF VIRGINS *(pp. 2244ff.), especially 2 Cor 10:17–11:2; Ps 31:3cd–4, 6 and 8ab, 16bc and 17; Mt 25:1–13; or from the* WEEKDAY MASS.

Liturgy of the Eucharist, *p. 897.*

December 14

JOHN OF THE CROSS, priest and doctor (1542–1591)

Memorial

Born near Avila in Spain, John entered the Carmelites in 1563. Shortly after his priestly ordination, he began to collaborate with the remarkable Teresa of Avila in reforming the Carmelites. The renewal brought him many trials. He wrote in masterful fashion about the spiritual life and mystical union with God.

Entrance Antiphon

I should boast of nothing but the cross of our Lord Jesus Christ; through him the world is crucified to me, and I to the world.

(Gal 6:14)

Opening Prayer

Father,
you endowed John of the Cross with a spirit of self-denial
and a love of the cross.
By following his example,
may we come to the eternal vision of your glory.

We ask this through our Lord Jesus Christ, your Son,
who lives and reigns with you and the Holy Spirit,
one God, for ever and ever.

Liturgy of the Word: *from the* COMMON OF PASTORS *(pp. 2188ff.), or* COMMON OF DOCTORS OF THE CHURCH *(pp. 2222ff.), especially 1 Cor 2:1–10a; Ps 37:3–4, 5–6, 30–31; Lk 14:25–33; or from the* WEEKDAY MASS.

Liturgy of the Eucharist, *p. 897.*

Prayer over the Gifts

Pray, brethren...

Almighty Lord,
look upon the gifts we offer
in memory of St. John of the Cross.
May we imitate the love we proclaim
as we celebrate the mystery
of the suffering and death of Christ,
who is Lord for ever and ever.

Communion Antiphon

If anyone wishes to come after me, he must renounce himself, take up his cross, and follow me, says the Lord.   (Mt 16:24)

Prayer after Communion

Let us pray.

Pause for silent prayer, if this has not preceded.

God our Father,
you have shown us the mystery of the cross

in the life of St. John.
May this sacrifice make us strong,
keep us faithful to Christ,
and help us to work in the Church
for the salvation of all mankind.
We ask this in the name of Jesus the Lord.

December 21

PETER CANISIUS, priest and doctor (1521–1597)

Optional Memorial

Peter Canisius, born in Holland, became a Jesuit priest and lived most of his life in Germany. He lived and worked in the tumultuous sixteenth century, and was a major force in the Counter Reformation. Peter was a writer, catechist, preacher, confessor, missionary, papal delegate, and the founder of colleges and seminaries. He wrote a famous "Little Catechism" to teach the faith. Peter Canisius died in a humble assignment and was canonized in 1925.

Antiphons and Prayers: *from the* COMMON OF PASTORS *(pp. 2170–2218), or* COMMON OF DOCTORS OF THE CHURCH *(pp. 2219–2238), or from the* WEEKDAY MASS. *The following is optional:*

Opening Prayer

Lord,
you gave St. Peter Canisius
wisdom and courage to defend the Catholic faith.
By the help of his prayers
may all who seek the truth rejoice in finding you,
and may all who believe in you
be loyal in professing their faith.

Grant this through our Lord Jesus Christ, your Son,
who lives and reigns with you and the Holy Spirit,
one God, for ever and ever.

Liturgy of the Word: *from the* COMMON OF PASTORS *(pp. 2188ff.), or* COMMON OF DOCTORS OF THE CHURCH *(pp. 2222ff.), especially 2 Tm 4:1–5; Ps 40:2 and 4, 7–8a, 8b–9, 10, 11; Mt 5:13–19; or from the* WEEKDAY MASS.

Liturgy of the Eucharist, *p. 897.*

December 23

JOHN OF KANTY, priest (1390–1473)

Optional Memorial

John Wacienga, patron of Poland and Lithuania, was born in 1390 at Kanti, near Kracow, Poland. He studied and lived at the newly founded University of Kracow. During years of devastation, he was outstanding for charity to the poor, pastoral care, and sound theological teaching.

Antiphons and Prayers: *from the* COMMON OF PASTORS *(pp. 2170–2218), or* COMMON OF HOLY MEN AND WOMEN: FOR THOSE WHO WORKED FOR THE UNDER-PRIVILEGED *(pp. 2263–2264), or from the* WEEKDAY MASS. *The following is optional:*

Opening Prayer

Almighty Father,
through the example of John of Kanty
may we grow in the wisdom of the saints.
As we show understanding and kindness to others,
may we receive your forgiveness.

We ask this through our Lord Jesus Christ, your Son,
who lives and reigns with you and the Holy Spirit,
one God, for ever and ever.

Liturgy of the Word: *from the* COMMON OF PASTORS *(pp. 2188ff.), or* COMMON OF HOLY MEN AND WOMEN: THOSE WHO WORKED FOR THE UNDERPRIVI-LEGED *(pp. 2274ff.), especially Jas 2:14–17; Ps 112:1bc–2, 3–4, 5–7, 6–8, 9; Lk 6:27–38; or from the* WEEKDAY MASS.

For **December 26,** ST. STEPHEN, FIRST MARTYR, *see p. 159 in this* **Weekday Missal.**

For **December 27,** ST. JOHN, APOSTLE AND EVANGELIST, *see p. 163 in this* **Weekday Missal.**

For **December 28,** HOLY INNOCENTS, MARTYRS, *see p. 167 in this* **Weekday Missal.**

December 29

THOMAS BECKET, bishop and martyr (1118–1170)

Optional Memorial

Until named archbishop of Canterbury (England) in 1162, Thomas Becket gave no indication of being a courageous and saintly man of the Church. Though an ecclesiastic, he had been chancellor of the nation and friend of King Henry II. As archbishop, however, he defended the Church against the king. During a six-year exile at a Cistercian Monastery in France, Thomas developed a monastic spirituality. He returned to England and was assassinated by the king's men in his own cathedral.

Antiphons and Prayers: *from the* COMMON OF MARTYRS *(pp. 2128–2169), or* COMMON OF PASTORS: FOR BISHOPS *(pp. 2170–2175), or from the* WEEKDAY MASS. *The following is optional:*

Opening Prayer

Almighty God,
you granted the martyr Thomas
the grace to give his life for the cause of justice.
By his prayers
make us willing to renounce for Christ
our life in this world
so that we may find it in heaven.

We ask this through our Lord Jesus Christ, your Son,
who lives and reigns with you and the Holy Spirit,
one God, for ever and ever.

Liturgy of the Word: *from the* COMMON OF MARTYRS *(pp. 2147ff.), or* COMMON OF PASTORS *(pp. 21880ff.), especially 2 Tm 2:8–13; 3:10–12; Ps 34: 2–3, 4–5, 6–7, 8–9; Mt 16:24–27; or from the* WEEKDAY MASS.

Liturgy of the Eucharist, *p. 897.*

December 31

SYLVESTER I, pope (†335)

Optional Memorial

Sylvester became pope in 314, shortly after the Peace of Constantine. Pope for 21 years, he fought Arianism and saw the Church develop in remarkable fashion. He started the basilicas of St. Peter and St. John Lateran. Pope Sylvester is remembered also because his death occurred on the last day of the year in 335. He helps us end the pilgrimage of each civil year.

Antiphons and Prayers: *from the* COMMON OF PASTORS: FOR POPES *(pp. 2170–2173), or from the* WEEKDAY MASS. *The following is optional:*

Opening Prayer

Lord,
help and sustain your people
by the prayers of Pope Sylvester.
Guide us always in this present life
and bring us to the joy that never ends.

We ask this through our Lord Jesus Christ, your Son,
who lives and reigns with you and the Holy Spirit,
one God, for ever and ever.

Liturgy of the Word: *from the* COMMON OF PASTORS: FOR A POPE *(pp. 2188ff.), especially Ez 34:11–16; Ps 23:1–3a, 4, 5, 6; Mt 16:13–19; or from the* WEEKDAY MASS.

COMMONS

Antiphons and Prayers

1. In the individual commons, several Mass formularies, with antiphons and prayers, are arranged for convenience.

The priest, however, may interchange antiphons and prayers of the same common choosing according to the circumstances those texts which seem pastorally appropriate.

In addition, for Masses of memorial, the prayer over the gifts and the prayer after communion may be taken from the weekdays of the current liturgical season as well as from the commons.

2. In the common of martyrs and in the common of holy men and women, all the prayers may be used for men or women with the necessary change of gender.

3. In the individual commons, texts in the singular may be changed to the plural and vice versa.

4. Certain Masses which are given for specific seasons and circumstances should be used for those seasons and circumstances.

5. During the Easter season an alleluia should be added at the end of the entrance and communion antiphons.

For **Optional Antiphons for Solemnities and Feasts**, *turn to p. 2323.*

Liturgy of the Word

On the feasts of the saints, in addition to the texts referred to in individual cases, the readings given in the common of saints may always be selected for pastoral reasons.

Antiphons and Prayers

1. In the individual commons, texts of Masses, together with antiphons and prayers, are arranged for convenience.

The priest, however, may introduce antiphons and prayers from time to time in order to adapt them to the circumstances, or those texts which seem pastorally appropriate.

Instructions for Masses or feasts of the saints, over the antiphons and the prayers of the commons of the same nature, may be taken from the sections of the present handbook section, as well as from the commons.

2. In the Common of Martyrs and in the Common of Holy Men and Women, all the prayers may be used for men or women with the necessary change of gender.

3. In the individual commons, texts in the singular may be changed to the plural and vice versa.

4. Certain Masses which are given for the specific seasons and circumstances should be used for those seasons only and circumstances.

5. During the Easter season, an alleluia should be added to the end of the entrance and communion antiphons.

For Optional Antiphons for Solemnities and Feasts, turn to page 2128.

Liturgy of the Word

On the pages of the annus, in addition to the texts referred to in individual cases, the readings given in the lectionary of saints may always be selected for pastoral reasons.

COMMON OF THE DEDICATION OF A CHURCH

1. On the Day of Dedication

Entrance Antiphon

God in his holy dwelling, God who has gathered us together in his house: he will strengthen and console his people.

Or:

Let us go rejoicing to the house of the Lord. (Ps 122:1)

Opening Prayer

Lord,
fill this place with your presence,
and extend your hand
to all those who call upon you.

May your word here proclaimed
and your sacraments here celebrated
strengthen the hearts of all the faithful.

We ask this through our Lord Jesus Christ, your Son,
who lives and reigns with you and the Holy Spirit,
one God, for ever and ever.

Liturgy of the Word, *pp. 2075–2090.*

Prayer over the Gifts

Lord,
accept the gifts of a rejoicing Church.
May your people,
who are gathered in this sacred place,
arrive at eternal salvation
through the mysteries in which they share.

Grant this through Christ our Lord.

Preface of the Dedication of a Church I, *p. 951.*

Communion Antiphon

My house shall be called a house of prayer, says the Lord: in it all who ask shall receive, all who seek shall find, and all who knock shall have the door opened to them (alleluia).

(See Mt 21:13; Lk 11:10)

Or:

May the children of the Church be like olive branches around the table of the Lord (alleluia). (See Ps 128:3)

Prayer after Communion

Let us pray.

Pause for silent prayer, if this has not preceded.

Lord,
through these gifts
increase the vision of your truth in our minds.
May we always worship you in your holy temple,
and rejoice in your presence with all your saints.

Grant this through Christ our Lord.

2. Anniversary of Dedication
A. IN THE DEDICATED CHURCH

Entrance Antiphon

Greatly to be feared is God in his sanctuary; he, the God of Israel, gives power and strength to his people. Blessed be God!

(Ps 67:36)

Opening Prayer

Father,
each year we recall
the dedication of this church to your service.
Let our worship always be sincere
and help us to find your saving love in this church.

Grant this through our Lord Jesus Christ, your Son,
who lives and reigns with you and the Holy Spirit,
one God, for ever and ever.

Liturgy of the Word, *pp. 2075–2090.*

Prayer over the Gifts

Pray, brethren...

Lord,
as we recall the day you filled this church
with your glory and holiness,
may our lives also become an acceptable offering to you.
Grant this in the name of Jesus the Lord.

Preface of the Dedication of a Church I, *p. 951.*

Communion Antiphon

**You are the temple of God, and God's Spirit dwells in you.
The temple of God is holy; you are that temple.** (1 Cor 3:16–17)

Prayer after Communion

Let us pray.

Pause for silent prayer, if this has not preceded.

Lord,
we know the joy and power of your blessing in our lives.
As we celebrate the dedication of this church,
may we give ourselves once more to your service.

Grant this through Christ our Lord.

B. OUTSIDE THE DEDICATED CHURCH

Entrance Antiphon

**I saw the holy city, new Jerusalem, coming down from God
out of heaven, like a bride adorned in readiness for her husband.**
(Rv 21:2)

Opening Prayer

God our Father,
from living stones, your chosen people,
you built an eternal temple to your glory.
Increase the spiritual gifts you have given to your Church,
so that your faithful people may continue to grow
into the new and eternal Jerusalem.

We ask this through our Lord Jesus Christ, your Son,
who lives and reigns with you and the Holy Spirit,
one God, for ever and ever.

Or:

Father,
you called your people to be your Church.
As we gather together in your name,
may we love, honor, and follow you
to eternal life in the kingdom you promise.

Grant this through our Lord Jesus Christ, your Son,
who lives and reigns with you and the Holy Spirit,
one God, for ever and ever.

Liturgy of the Word, *pp. 2075–2090.*

Prayer over the Gifts

Pray, brethren...

Lord,
receive our gifts.
May we who share this sacrament
experience the life and power it promises,
and hear the answer to our prayers.

We ask this in the name of Jesus the Lord.

Preface of the Dedication of a Church II, *p. 952.*

Communion Antiphon

Like living stones let yourselves be built on Christ as a spiritual house, a holy priesthood. (1 Pt 2:5)

Prayer after Communion

Let us pray.

Pause for silent prayer, if this has not preceded.

Father,
you make your Church on earth
a sign of the new and eternal Jerusalem.
By sharing in this sacrament
may we become the temple of your presence
and the home of your glory.

Grant this in the name of Jesus the Lord.

Liturgy of the Word: Dedication of a Church

READING I   From the Old Testament

Outside the Easter Season

1   1 Kgs 8:22–23, 27–30

May your eyes watch night and day over this temple.

A reading from the first Book of Kings

In those days: Solomon stood before the altar of the LORD in the presence of the whole community of Israel, and stretching forth his hands toward heaven, he said, "LORD, God of Israel, there is no God like you in heaven above or on earth below; you keep your covenant of mercy with your servants who are faithful to you with their whole heart.

"Can it indeed be that God dwells on earth? If the heavens and the highest heavens cannot contain you, how much less this temple which I have built! Look kindly on the prayer and petition of your servant, O LORD, my God, and listen to the cry of supplication I, your servant, utter before you this day. May your eyes watch night and day over this temple, the place where you have decreed you shall be honored; may you heed the prayer which I, your servant, offer in this place. Listen to the petitions of your servant and of your people Israel which they offer in this place. Listen from your heavenly dwelling and grant pardon."

The word of the Lord.

2   2 Chr 5:6–10, 13—6:2

I have truly built a princely house and dwelling,
where you may abide forever.

A reading from the second Book of Chronicles

King Solomon and the entire community of Israel gathered about him before the ark were sacrificing sheep and oxen so numerous that they could not be counted or numbered. The priests brought the ark of the covenant of the LORD to its place beneath the wings of the cherubim in the sanctuary, the holy of holies of the temple. The cherubim had their wings spread out over the place of the ark, sheltering the ark and its poles from above. The poles were long enough so that their ends could be seen from that part of the holy place nearest the sanctuary; however, they could not be seen beyond. The ark has remained there to this day. There was nothing in it but the two tablets which Moses put there on Horeb, the tablets of the covenant which the LORD made with the children of Israel at their departure from Egypt.

When the trumpeters and singers were heard as a single voice praising and giving thanks to the LORD, and when they raised the sound of the trumpets, cymbals and other musical instruments to "give thanks to the LORD, for he is good, for his mercy endures forever," the building of the LORD's temple was filled with a cloud. The priests could not continue to minister because of the cloud, since the LORD's glory filled the house of God.

Then Solomon said: "The LORD intends to dwell in the dark cloud. I have truly built you a princely house and dwelling, where you may abide forever."

The word of the Lord.

3   Is 56:1, 6–7

My house shall be called a house of prayer for all peoples.

A reading from the Book of the Prophet Isaiah

Thus says the LORD:
Observe what is right, do what is just;
    for my salvation is about to come,
    my justice, about to be revealed.

The foreigners who join themselves to the LORD,
    ministering to him,
Loving the name of the LORD,
    and becoming his servants—
All who keep the sabbath free from profanation
    and hold to my covenant,
Them I will bring to my holy mountain

and make joyful in my house of prayer;
Their burnt offerings and sacrifices
    will be acceptable on my altar,
For my house shall be called
    a house of prayer for all peoples.
The word of the Lord.

4   Ez 43:1–2, 3c–7a

The temple was filled with the glory of the LORD.

A reading from the Book of the Prophet Ezekiel

The angel led me to the gate which faces the east, and there
I saw the glory of the God of Israel coming from the east. I
heard a sound like the roaring of many waters, and the earth
shone with his glory. I fell prone as the glory of the LORD
entered the temple by way of the gate which faces the east, but
spirit lifted me up and brought me to the inner court. And I
saw that the temple was filled with the glory of the LORD. Then
I heard someone speaking to me from the temple, while the
man stood beside me. The voice said to me: Son of man, this is
where my throne shall be, this is where I will set the soles of
my feet; here I will dwell among the children of Israel forever.
The word of the Lord.

5   Ez 47:1–2, 8–9, 12

I saw water flowing from the temple,
and all who were touched by it were saved. (See Roman Missal,
antiphon for the blessing and sprinkling of water during the season of Easter).

A reading from the Book of the Prophet Ezekiel

The angel brought me back to the entrance of the temple, and
I saw water flowing out from beneath the threshold of the tem-

ple toward the east, for the façade of the temple was toward the east; the water flowed down from the right side of the temple, south of the altar. He led me outside by the north gate, and around to the outer gate facing the east, where I saw water trickling from the right side. He said to me, "This water flows into the eastern district down upon the Arabah, and empties into the sea, the salt waters, which it makes fresh. Wherever the river flows, every sort of living creature that can multiply shall live, and there shall be abundant fish, for wherever this water comes the sea shall be made fresh. Along both banks of the river, fruit trees of every kind shall grow; their leaves shall not fade, nor their fruit fail. Every month they shall bear fresh fruit, for they shall be watered by the flow from the sanctuary. Their fruit shall serve for food, and their leaves for medicine."

The word of the Lord.

READING I   From the New Testament

During the Easter Season

FIRST OPTION

Acts 7:44–50

The Most High does not dwell in houses made by human hands.

A reading from the Acts of the Apostles

Stephen said to the people, the elders and the scribes: "Our ancestors had the tent of testimony in the desert just as the One who spoke to Moses directed him to make it according to the pattern he had seen. Our ancestors who inherited it brought it with Joshua when they dispossessed the nations that God drove out from before our ancestors, up to the time of David, who found favor in the sight of God and asked that he might find a dwelling place for the house of Jacob. But Solomon built a house for him. Yet the Most High does not dwell in houses made by human hands. As the prophet says:

> The heavens are my throne,
>   the earth is my footstool.
> What kind of house can you build for me?
>   says the Lord,
>   or what is to be my resting place?
> Did not my hand make all these things?"

The word of the Lord.

SECOND OPTION   Rv 21:1–5a

Behold, God's dwelling is with the human race.

A reading from the Book of Revelation

I, John, saw a new heaven and a new earth. The former heaven and the former earth had passed away, and the sea was no more. I also saw the holy city, a new Jerusalem, coming down out of heaven from God, prepared as a bride adorned for her husband. I heard a loud voice from the throne saying, "Behold, God's dwelling is with the human race. He will dwell with them and they will be his people and God himself will always be with them as their God. He will wipe every tear from their eyes, and there shall be no more death or mourning, wailing or pain, for the old order has passed away."

  The One who sat on the throne said, "Behold, I make all things new."

The word of the Lord.

THIRD OPTION

Rv 21:9 –14

I will show you the bride, the wife of the Lamb.

A reading from the Book of Revelation

The angel spoke to me, saying: "Come here. I will show you the bride, the wife of the Lamb." He took me in spirit to a great, high mountain and showed me the holy city Jerusalem coming down out of heaven from God. It gleamed with the splendor of God. Its radiance was like that of a precious stone, like jasper, clear as crystal. It had a massive, high wall, with twelve gates where twelve angels were stationed and on which names were inscribed, the names of the twelve tribes of the children of Israel. There were three gates facing east, three north, three south, and three west. The wall of the city had twelve courses of stones as its foundation, on which were inscribed the twelve names of the twelve Apostles of the Lamb.

The word of the Lord.

Responsorial Psalm

1

1 Chr 29:10, 11, 12

R. We praise your glorious name, O mighty God.

"Blessed may you be, O LORD,
  God of Israel our father,
  from eternity to eternity."

R. We praise your glorious name, O mighty God.

"Yours, O LORD, are grandeur and power,
  majesty, splendor, and glory.
For all in heaven and on earth is yours."

R. We praise your glorious name, O mighty God.

"Yours, O LORD, is the sovereignty;
  you are exalted as head over all.
Riches and honor are from you."

   R. We praise your glorious name, O mighty God.

"You have dominion over all.
In your hands are power and might;
  it is yours to give grandeur and strength to all."

   R. We praise your glorious name, O mighty God.

2   Ps 46:2–3, 5–6, 8–9

   **R. There is a stream whose runlets gladden the city of God,
   the holy dwelling of the Most High!**

God is our refuge and our strength,
  an ever-present help in distress.
Therefore we fear not, though the earth be shaken
  and mountains plunge into the depths of the sea.

   **R. There is a stream whose runlets gladden the city of God,
   the holy dwelling of the Most High!**

There is a stream whose runlets gladden the city of God,
  the holy dwelling of the Most High.
God is in its midst; it shall not be disturbed;
  God will help it at the break of dawn.

   **R. There is a stream whose runlets gladden the city of God,
   the holy dwelling of the Most High!**

The LORD of hosts is with us;
  our stronghold is the God of Jacob.
Come! behold the deeds of the LORD,
  the astounding things he has wrought on earth.

   **R. There is a stream whose runlets gladden the city of God,
   the holy dwelling of the Most High!**

3

Ps 84:3, 4, 5 and 10, 11

R. How lovely is your dwelling-place, Lord, mighty God!

My soul yearns and pines
 for the courts of the LORD.
My heart and my flesh
 cry out for the living God.

R. How lovely is your dwelling-place, Lord, mighty God!

Even the sparrow finds a home,
 and the swallow a nest
 in which she puts her young—
Your altars, O LORD of hosts,
 my king and my God!

R. How lovely is your dwelling-place, Lord, mighty God!

Blessed they who dwell in your house!
 continually they praise you.
O God, behold our shield,
 and look upon the face of your anointed.

R. How lovely is your dwelling-place, Lord, mighty God!

I had rather one day in your courts
 than a thousand elsewhere;
I had rather lie at the threshold of the house of my God
 than dwell in the tents of the wicked.

R. How lovely is your dwelling-place, Lord, mighty God!
Or: **R. Here God lives among his people.**

4

Ps 95:1–2, 3–5, 6–7

R. Let us come before the Lord and praise him.

Come, let us sing joyfully to the LORD;
 let us acclaim the Rock of our salvation.
Let us come into his presence with thanksgiving;
 let us joyfully sing psalms to him.

R. Let us come before the Lord and praise him.

For the LORD is a great God,
  and a great king above all gods;
In his hands are the depths of the earth,
  and the tops of the mountains are his.
His is the sea, for he has made it,
  and the dry land, which his hands have formed.

R. Let us come before the Lord and praise him.

Come, let us bow down in worship;
  let us kneel before the LORD who made us.
For he is our God,
  and we are the people he shepherds, the flock he guides.

R. Let us come before the Lord and praise him.

5

R. Let us go rejoicing to the house of the Lord!

I rejoiced because they said to me,
  "We will go up to the house of the LORD."
And now we have set foot
  within your gates, O Jerusalem.

R. Let us go rejoicing to the house of the Lord!

Jerusalem, built as a city
  with compact unity.
To it the tribes go up,
  the tribes of the LORD.

R. Let us go rejoicing to the house of the Lord!

Because of my relatives and friends
  I will say, "Peace be within you!"
Because of the house of the LORD, our God,
  I will pray for your good.

R. Let us go rejoicing to the house of the Lord!

READING II   From the New Testament

FIRST OPTION   1 Cor 3:9c–11, 16–17

You are God's temple.

A reading from the first Letter of Saint Paul to the Corinthians

Brothers and sisters:

You are God's building.

According to the grace of God given to me, like a wise master builder I laid a foundation, and another is building upon it. But each one must be careful how he builds upon it, for no one can lay a foundation other than the one that is there, namely, Jesus Christ. Do you not know that you are the temple of God, and that the Spirit of God dwells in you? If anyone destroys God's temple, God will destroy that person; for the temple of God, which you are, is holy.

The word of the Lord.

SECOND OPTION   Eph 2:19–22

*Through him the whole structure is held together
and grows into a temple sacred in the Lord.*

A reading from the Letter of Saint Paul to the Ephesians

Brothers and sisters:

You are no longer strangers and sojourners, but you are fellow citizens with the holy ones and members of the household of God, built upon the foundation of the Apostles and prophets, with Christ Jesus himself as the capstone. Through him the whole structure is held together and grows into a temple sacred in the Lord; in him you also are being built together into a dwelling place of God in the Spirit.

The word of the Lord.

THIRD OPTION   Heb 12:18–19, 22–24

You have approached Mount Zion and the city of the living God.

A reading from the Letter to the Hebrews

Brothers and sisters:
You have not approached that which could be touched and a
blazing fire and gloomy darkness and storm and a trumpet blast
and a voice speaking words such that those who heard begged
that no message be further addressed to them. No, you have
approached Mount Zion and the city of the living God, the
heavenly Jerusalem, and countless angels in festal gathering,
and the assembly of the firstborn enrolled in heaven, and God
the judge of all, and the spirits of the just made perfect, and
Jesus, the mediator of a new covenant, and the sprinkled Blood
that speaks more eloquently than that of Abel.

The word of the Lord.

FOURTH OPTION   1 Pt 2:4–9

Like living stones, let yourselves be built into a spiritual house.

A reading from the first Letter of Saint Peter

Beloved:
Come to the Lord, a living stone, rejected by human beings
but chosen and precious in the sight of God, and, like living
stones, let yourselves be built into a spiritual house to be a
holy priesthood to offer spiritual sacrifices acceptable to God
through Jesus Christ. For it says in Scripture:

> *Behold, I am laying a stone in Zion,*
>   *a cornerstone, chosen and precious,*
> *and whoever believes in it shall not be put to shame.*

Therefore, its value is for you who have faith, but for those
without faith:

The stone which the builders rejected
  has become the cornerstone,

and

A stone which will make people stumble,
  and a rock that will make them fall.

They stumble by disobeying the word, as is their destiny.

You are *a chosen race, a royal priesthood, a holy nation, a people of his own, so that you may announce the praises* of him who called you out of darkness into his wonderful light. The word of the Lord.

ALLELUIA VERSE AND VERSE BEFORE THE GOSPEL

1 2 Chr 7:16

I have chosen and consecrated this house, says the Lord,
that my name may be there forever.

2 Is 66:1

"The heavens are my throne, the earth is my footstool,"
  says the LORD;
What kind of house can you build for me?

3 Ez 37:27

My dwelling shall be with them, says the Lord;
I will be their God and they shall be my people.

4 See Mt 7:8

In my house, says the Lord, everyone who asks will
  receive;
The one who seeks, finds; and to the one who knocks,
  the door will be opened.

5 Mt 16:18

You are Peter, and upon this rock I will build my Church,
and the gates of the netherworld shall not prevail against it.

GOSPEL

FIRST OPTION

Mt 16:13–19

You are Peter: I will give you the keys to the Kingdom of heaven.

A reading from the holy Gospel according to Matthew

When Jesus went into the region of Caesarea Philippi he asked his disciples, "Who do people say that the Son of Man is?" They replied, "Some say John the Baptist, others Elijah, still others Jeremiah or one of the prophets." He said to them, "But who do you say that I am?" Simon Peter said in reply, "You are the Christ, the Son of the living God." Jesus said to him in reply, "Blessed are you, Simon son of Jonah. For flesh and blood has not revealed this to you, but my heavenly Father. And so I say to you, you are Peter, and upon this rock I will build my Church, and the gates of the netherworld shall not prevail against it. I will give you the keys to the Kingdom of heaven. Whatever you bind on earth shall be bound in heaven; and whatever you loose on earth shall be loosed in heaven."

The Gospel of the Lord.

SECOND OPTION

Lk 19:1–10

Today salvation has come to this house.

A reading from the holy Gospel according to Luke

At that time, Jesus came to Jericho and intended to pass through the town. Now a man there named Zacchaeus, who was a chief tax collector and also a wealthy man, was seeking to see who Jesus was; but he could not see him because of the crowd, for he was short in stature. So he ran ahead and climbed a sycamore tree in order to see Jesus, who was about to pass that way. When he reached the place, Jesus looked up and said, "Zacchaeus, come down quickly, for today I must stay at your house." And he came down quickly and received him with joy. When they saw this, they began to grumble, saying, "He has gone to stay at the house of a sinner." But Zacchaeus stood there and said to the Lord, "Behold, half of my possessions, Lord, I shall give to the poor, and if I have extorted anything from anyone I shall repay it four times over." And Jesus said to him, "Today salvation has come to this house because this man too is a descendant of Abraham. For the Son of Man has come to seek and to save what was lost."

The Gospel of the Lord.

THIRD OPTION

Jn 2:13–22

Jesus was speaking about the temple of his Body.

A reading from the holy Gospel according to John

Since the Passover of the Jews was near, Jesus went up to Jerusalem. He found in the temple area those who sold oxen, sheep, and doves, as well as the money-changers seated there. He made a whip out of cords and drove them all out of the temple area, with the sheep and oxen, and spilled the coins of the money-changers and overturned their tables, and to those who sold doves he said, "Take these out of here, and stop making my Father's house a marketplace." His disciples recalled the words of Scripture, *Zeal for your house will consume me.* At this the Jews answered and said to him, "What sign can you show us for doing this?" Jesus answered and said to them, "Destroy this temple and in three days I will raise it up." The Jews said, "This temple has been under construction for forty-six years, and you will raise it up in three days?" But he was speaking about the temple of his Body. Therefore, when he was raised from the dead, his disciples remembered that he had said this, and they came to believe the Scripture and the word Jesus had spoken.

The Gospel of the Lord.

FOURTH OPTION   Jn 4:19–24

True worshipers will worship the Father in Spirit and truth.

A reading from the holy Gospel according to John

The Samaritan woman said to Jesus, "Sir, I can see that you are a prophet. Our ancestors worshiped on this mountain; but you people say that the place to worship is in Jerusalem." Jesus said to her, "Believe me, woman, the hour is coming when you will worship the Father neither on this mountain nor in Jerusalem. You people worship what you do not understand; we worship what we understand, because salvation is from the Jews. But the hour is coming, and is now here, when true worshipers will worship the Father in Spirit and truth; and indeed the Father seeks such people to worship him. God is Spirit, and those who worship him must worship in Spirit and truth."

The Gospel of the Lord.

COMMON OF
THE BLESSED VIRGIN MARY

These Masses are also used for the Saturday celebration of the Blessed Virgin Mary and for votive Masses for the Blessed Virgin Mary.

-1-

Entrance Antiphon

Hail, holy Mother! The child to whom you gave birth is the King of heaven and earth for ever. (Sedulius)

Opening Prayer

Lord God,
give to your people the joy
of continual health in mind and body.
With the prayers of the Virgin Mary to help us,
guide us through the sorrows of this life
to eternal happiness in the life to come.

Grant this through our Lord Jesus Christ, your Son,
who lives and reigns with you and the Holy Spirit,
one God, for ever and ever.

Or:

Lord,
take away the sins of your people.
May the prayers of Mary the mother of your Son help us,
for alone and unaided we cannot hope to please you.

We ask this through our Lord Jesus Christ, your Son,
who lives and reigns with you and the Holy Spirit,
one God, for ever and ever.

Liturgy of the Word, *pp. 2101–2127.*

Prayer over the Gifts

Pray, brethren...

Father,
the birth of Christ your Son
deepened the virgin mother's love for you,
and increased her holiness.
May the humanity of Christ
give us courage in our weakness;
may it free us from our sins,
and make our offering acceptable.
We ask this through Christ our Lord.

Preface of the Blessed Virgin Mary I *(feasts or memorials)* or **II** *(votive Masses), p. 953.*

Communion Antiphon

Blessed is the womb of the Virgin Mary; she carried the Son of
the eternal Father.   (See Lk 11:27)

Prayer after Communion

Let us pray.

Pause for silent prayer, if this has not preceded.

Lord,
we rejoice in your sacraments and ask your mercy
as we honor the memory of the Virgin Mary.
May her faith and love
inspire us to serve you more faithfully
in the work of salvation.

Grant this in the name of Jesus the Lord.

-2-

Entrance Antiphon

Blessed are you, Virgin Mary, who carried the creator of all things in your womb; you gave birth to your maker, and remain for ever a virgin.

Opening Prayer

God of mercy,
give us strength.
May we who honor the memory of the Mother of God
rise above our sins and failings
with the help of her prayers.

Grant this through our Lord Jesus Christ, your Son,
who lives and reigns with you and the Holy Spirit,
one God, for ever and ever.

Or:

Lord,
may the prayers of the Virgin Mary
bring us protection from danger
and freedom from sin
that we may come to the joy of your peace.

We ask this through our Lord Jesus Christ, your Son,
who lives and reigns with you and the Holy Spirit,
one God, for ever and ever.

Liturgy of the Word, *pp. 2101–2127.*

Prayer over the Gifts

Pray, brethren...

Lord,
we honor the memory of the mother of your Son.

May the sacrifice we share
make of us an everlasting gift to you.

Grant this through Christ our Lord.

Preface of the Blessed Virgin Mary I *(feasts or memorials)* or **II** *(votive Masses), p. 953.*

Communion Antiphon

The Almighty has done great things for me. Holy is his name.
(Lk 1:49)

Prayer after Communion

Let us pray.

Pause for silent prayer, if this has not preceded.

Lord,
you give us the sacraments of eternal redemption.
May we who honor the memory of the mother of your Son
rejoice in the abundance of your grace
and experience your unfailing help.

We ask this through Christ our Lord.

-3-

Entrance Antiphon

You have been blessed, O Virgin Mary, above all other women on earth by the Lord the most high God; he has so exalted your name that your praises shall never fade from the mouths of men.
(See Jdt 13:23, 25)

Opening Prayer

Lord,
as we honor the glorious memory of the Virgin Mary,
we ask that by the help of her prayers
we too may come to share the fullness of your grace.

Grant this through our Lord Jesus Christ, your Son,
who lives and reigns with you and the Holy Spirit,
one God, for ever and ever.

Or:

Lord Jesus Christ,
you chose the Virgin Mary to be your mother,
a worthy home in which to dwell.
By her prayers keep us from danger
and bring us to the joy of heaven,
where you live and reign with the Father and the Holy Spirit,
one God, for ever and ever.

Liturgy of the Word, *pp. 2101–2127.*

Prayer over the Gifts

Pray, brethren...

Lord,
we bring you our sacrifice of praise
at this celebration in honor of Mary,
    the mother of your Son.
May this holy exchange of gifts
help us on our way to eternal salvation.
We ask this in the name of Jesus the Lord.

Preface of the Blessed Virgin Mary I *(feasts or memorials)* or **II** *(votive Masses), p. 953.*

Communion Antiphon

   All generations will call me blessed, because God has looked
upon his lowly handmaid.   (See Lk 1:48)

Prayer after Communion

Let us pray.

   Pause for silent prayer, if this has not preceded.

Lord,
we eat the bread of heaven.
May we who honor the memory of the Virgin Mary
come one day to your banquet of eternal life.

Grant this through Christ our Lord.

- 4 -

Advent Season

Entrance Antiphon

**Let the clouds rain down the Just One, and the earth bring
forth a Savior.**   (Is 45:8)

Or:

**The angel said to Mary: You have won God's favor. You will
conceive and bear a Son, and he will be called Son of the Most
High.**   (Lk 1:30–32)

Opening Prayer

Father,
in your plan for our salvation
your Word became man,
announced by an angel and born of the Virgin Mary.
May we who believe that she is the Mother of God
receive the help of her prayers.

We ask this through our Lord Jesus Christ, your Son,
who lives and reigns with you and the Holy Spirit,
one God, for ever and ever.

Liturgy of the Word, *pp. 2101–2127.*

Prayer over the Gifts

Pray, brethren...

Lord,
may the power of your Spirit,

which sanctified Mary the Mother of your Son,
make holy the gifts we place upon this altar.

We ask this through Christ our Lord.

Preface of the Blessed Virgin Mary I *(feasts or memorials)* or **II** *(votive Masses)* or **Preface of Advent II,** *p. 953.*

Communion Antiphon

The Virgin is with child and shall bear a son, and she will call him Emmanuel. (Is 7:14)

Prayer after Communion

Let us pray.

Pause for silent prayer, if this has not preceded.

Lord our God,
may the sacraments we receive
show us your forgiveness and love.
May we who honor the mother of your Son
be saved by his coming among us as man
for he is Lord for ever and ever.

-5-

Christmas Season

Entrance Antiphon

Giving birth to the King whose reign is unending, Mary knows the joys of motherhood together with a virgin's honor; none like her before, and there shall be none hereafter.

Or:

O Virgin Mother of God, the universe cannot hold him, and yet, becoming man, he confined himself in your womb.

Opening Prayer

Father,
you gave the human race eternal salvation

through the motherhood of the Virgin Mary.
May we experience the help of her prayers in our lives,
for through her we received the very source of life,
your Son, our Lord Jesus Christ,
who lives and reigns with you and the Holy Spirit,
one God, for ever and ever.

> **Liturgy of the Word,** *pp. 2101–2127.*

Prayer over the Gifts

Pray, brethren...

Lord,
accept our gifts and prayers
and fill our hearts with the light of your Holy Spirit.
Help us to follow the example of the Virgin Mary:
to seek you in all things
and to do your will with gladness.

We ask this in the name of Jesus the Lord.

> **Preface of the Blessed Virgin Mary I** *(feasts or memorials) or* **II** *(votive Masses), p. 953.*

Communion Antiphon

The Word of God became man, and lived among us, full of grace and truth.
(Jn 1:14)

Prayer after Communion

Let us pray.
> *Pause for silent prayer, if this has not preceded.*

Lord,
as we celebrate this feast of the Blessed Virgin Mary,
you renew us with the body and blood of Christ your Son.
May this sacrament give us a share in his life,
for he is Lord for ever and ever.

-6-
Easter Season

Entrance Antiphon

The disciples were constantly at prayer together, with Mary the mother of Jesus, alleluia.
(See Acts 1:14)

Opening Prayer

God our Father,
you give joy to the world
by the resurrection of your Son, our Lord Jesus Christ.
Through the prayers of his mother, the Virgin Mary,
bring us to the happiness of eternal life.

We ask this through our Lord Jesus Christ, your Son,
who lives and reigns with you and the Holy Spirit,
one God, for ever and ever.

Or:

God our Father,
you gave the Holy Spirit to your apostles
as they joined in prayer with Mary, the mother of Jesus.
By the help of her prayers
keep us faithful in your service
and let our words and actions be so inspired
as to being glory to your name.

Grant this through our Lord Jesus Christ, your Son,
who lives and reigns with you and the Holy Spirit,
one God, for ever and ever.

Liturgy of the Word, *pp. 2101–2127.*

Prayer over the Gifts

Pray, brethren...

Father,
as we celebrate the memory of the Virgin Mary,
we offer you our gifts and prayers.
Sustain us by the love of Christ,
who offered himself as a perfect sacrifice on the cross,
and is Lord for ever and ever.

Preface of the Blessed Virgin Mary I *(feasts or memorials)* or **II** *(votive Masses), p. 953.*

Communion Antiphon

Rejoice, virgin mother, for Christ has arisen from his grave, alleluia.

Prayer after Communion

Let us pray.
Pause for silent prayer, if this has not preceded.

Lord,
may this sacrament strengthen the faith in our hearts.
May Mary's Son, Jesus Christ,
whom we proclaim to be God and man,
bring us to eternal life
by the saving power of his resurrection,
for he is Lord for ever and ever.

Other Prayers
for Masses of the Blessed Virgin Mary

Opening Prayer

All-powerful God,
we rejoice in the protection of the holy Virgin Mary.
May her prayers help to free us from all evils here on earth
and lead us to eternal joy in heaven.

Grant this through our Lord Jesus Christ, your Son,
who lives and reigns with you and the Holy Spirit,
one God, for ever and ever.

Liturgy of the Word, *pp. 2101–2127.*

Prayer over the Gifts

Pray, brethren...

Lord,
accept the prayers and gifts we present today
as we honor Mary, the Mother of God.
May they please you
and bring us your forgiveness and help.
We ask this in the name of Jesus the Lord.

Prayer after Communion

Let us pray.

Pause for silent prayer, if this has not preceded.

Lord,
we are renewed with the sacraments of salvation.
May we who celebrate the memory of the Mother of God
come to realize the eternal redemption you promise.

We ask this through Christ our Lord.

Liturgy of the Word: Common of the Blessed Virgin Mary

READING I   From the Old Testament

1

Gn 3:9–15, 20

I will put enmity between your offspring
and the offspring of the woman.

A reading from the Book of Genesis

After the man, Adam, had eaten of the tree, the LORD God called
to the man and asked him, "Where are you?" He answered, "I

heard you in the garden; but I was afraid, because I was naked, so I hid myself." Then he asked, "Who told you that you were naked? You have eaten, then, from the tree of which I had forbidden you to eat!" The man replied, "The woman whom you put here with me—she gave me fruit from the tree, and so I ate it." The LORD God then asked the woman, "Why did you do such a thing?" The woman answered, "The serpent tricked me into it, so I ate it."

Then the LORD God said to the serpent:

"Because you have done this, you shall be banned
    from all the animals
    and from all the wild creatures;
On your belly shall you crawl,
    and dirt shall you eat
    all the days of your life.
I will put enmity between you and the woman,
    and between your offspring and hers;
He will strike at your head,
    while you strike at his heel."

The man called his wife Eve, because she became the mother of all the living.

The word of the Lord.

2

Gn 12:1–7

The Lord spoke to our ancestors,
to Abraham and to his descendants for ever (Lk 1:55).

A reading from the Book of Genesis

The LORD said to Abram: "Go forth from the land of your kinsfolk and from your father's house to a land that I will show you.

"I will make of you a great nation,
  and I will bless you;
I will make your name great,
  so that you will be a blessing.
I will bless those who bless you
  and curse those who curse you.
All the communities of the earth
  shall find blessing in you."

Abram went as the LORD directed him, and Lot went with him. Abram was seventy-five years old when he left Haran. Abram took his wife Sarai, his brother's son Lot, all the possessions that they had accumulated, and the persons they had acquired in Haran, and they set out for the land of Canaan. When they came to the land of Canaan, Abram passed through the land as far as the sacred place at Shechem, by the terebinth of Moreh. (The Canaanites were then in the land.)

The LORD appeared to Abram and said, "To your descendants I will give this land." So Abram built an altar there to the LORD who had appeared to him.

The word of the Lord.

3

2 Sm 7:1–5, 8b–11, 16

*The Lord God will give him the throne of David
his father (Lk 1:32).*

A reading from the second Book of Samuel

When King David was settled in his palace, and the LORD had given him rest from his enemies on every side, he said to Nathan the prophet, "Here I am living in a house of cedar, while the ark of God dwells in a tent!" Nathan answered the king, "Go, do whatever you have in mind, for the LORD is with you." But that night the LORD spoke to Nathan and said: "Go tell my servant David, 'Thus says the LORD: Should you build me a house to dwell in?'

"'It was I who took you from the pasture and from the care of the flock to be commander of my people Israel. I have been with you wherever you went, and I have destroyed all your enemies before you. And I will make you famous like the great ones of the earth. I will fix a place for my people Israel; I will plant them so that they may dwell in their place without further disturbance. Neither shall the wicked continue to afflict them as they did of old, since the time I first appointed judges over my people Israel. I will give you rest from all your enemies. The LORD also reveals to you that he will establish a house for you. Your house and your kingdom shall endure forever before me; your throne shall stand firm forever.'"
The word of the Lord.

4

1 Chr 15:3–4, 15–16; 16:1–2

They brought in the ark of God and set it within the tent which David had pitched for it.

A reading from the first Book of Chronicles

David assembled all Israel in Jerusalem to bring the ark of the LORD to the place which he had prepared for it. David also called together the sons of Aaron and the Levites.

The Levites bore the ark of God on their shoulders with poles, as Moses had ordained according to the word of the LORD.

David commanded the chiefs of the Levites to appoint their brethren as chanters, to play on musical instruments, harps, lyres, and cymbals to make a loud sound of rejoicing.

They brought in the ark of God and set it within the tent which David had pitched for it. Then they offered up burnt offerings and peace offerings to God. When David had finished offering up the burnt offerings and peace offerings, he blessed the people in the name of the LORD.

The word of the Lord.

5

Prv 8:22–31

Mary, seat of Wisdom.

A reading from the Book of Proverbs

The Wisdom of God says:

"The LORD begot me, the first-born of his ways,
　　the forerunner of his prodigies of long ago;
From of old I was poured forth,
　　at the first, before the earth.
When there were no depths I was brought forth,
　　when there were no fountains or springs of water;
Before the mountains were settled into place,
　　before the hills, I was brought forth;
While as yet the earth and fields were not made,
　　nor the first clods of the world.

"When he established the heavens I was there,
　　when he marked out the vault over the face of the deep;
When he made firm the skies above,
　　when he fixed fast the foundations of the earth;
When he set for the sea its limit,
　　so that the waters should not transgress his command;
Then was I beside him as his craftsman,
　　and I was his delight day by day,

Playing before him all the while,
    playing on the surface of his earth;
    and I found delight in the sons of men."
The word of the Lord.

<table>
<tr><td>6</td><td>Sir 24:1–2, 3–4, 8–12, 18–21</td></tr>
</table>

Mary, seat of Wisdom.

A reading from the Book of Sirach

Wisdom sings her own praises and is honored in God,
    before her own people she proclaims her glory;
In the assembly of the Most High she opens her mouth,
    in the presence of his power she declares her worth.

"From the mouth of the Most High I came forth
    the first-born before all creatures.
I made that in the heavens there should arise
    light that never fades
    and mistlike covered the earth.
In the highest heavens did I dwell,
    my throne on a pillar of cloud.

"Then the Creator of all gave me his command,
    and he who formed me chose the spot for my tent,
Saying, 'In Jacob make your dwelling,
    in Israel your inheritance
    and among my chosen put down your roots.'
Before all ages, in the beginning, he created me,
    and through all ages I shall not cease to be.
In the holy tent I ministered before him,
    and in Zion I fixed my abode.

Thus in the chosen city he has given me rest,
     in Jerusalem is my domain.
I have struck root among the glorious people,
     in the portion of the LORD, his heritage
     and in the company of the holy ones do I linger.

"Come to me, all you that yearn for me,
     and be filled with my fruits;
You will remember me as sweeter than honey,
     better to have than the honeycomb
     my memory is unto everlasting generations.
Whoever eats of me will hunger still,
     whoever drinks of me will thirst for more;
Whoever obeys me will not be put to shame,
     whoever serves me will never fail."
The word of the Lord.

7

Is 7:10–14; 8:10

The virgin shall conceive and bear a son.

A reading from the Book of the Prophet Isaiah

The LORD spoke to Ahaz: Ask for a sign from the LORD, your God; let it be deep as the nether world, or high as the sky! But Ahaz answered, "I will not ask! I will not tempt the LORD!" Then Isaiah said: Listen, O house of David! Is it not enough for you to weary people, must you also weary my God? Therefore the Lord himself will give you this sign: the virgin shall conceive, and bear a son, and shall name him Emmanuel which means "God is with us."
The word of the Lord.

8

Is 9:1–6

A son is given us.

A reading from the Book of the Prophet Isaiah

The people who walked in darkness
    have seen a great light;
Upon those who dwelt in the land of gloom
    a light has shone.
You have brought them abundant joy
    and great rejoicing,
As they rejoice before you as at the harvest,
    as people make merry when dividing spoils.
For the yoke that burdened them,
    the pole on their shoulder,
And the rod of their taskmaster
    you have smashed, as on the day of Midian.
For every boot that tramped in battle,
    every cloak rolled in blood,
    will be burned as fuel for flames.

For a child is born to us, a son is given us;
    upon his shoulder dominion rests.
They name him Wonder-Counselor, God-Hero,
    Father-Forever, Prince of Peace.
His dominion is vast
    and forever peaceful,
From David's throne, and over his kingdom,
    which he confirms and sustains
By judgment and justice,
    both now and forever.
The zeal of the LORD of hosts will do this!

The word of the Lord.

9

Is 61:9–11

*I rejoice heartily in the L*ORD.

A reading from the Book of the Prophet Isaiah

Thus says the LORD:
Their descendants shall be renowned among the nations,
    and their offspring among the peoples;
All who see them shall acknowledge them
    as a race the LORD has blessed.

I rejoice heartily in the LORD,
    in my God is the joy of my soul;
For he has clothed me with a robe of salvation,
    and wrapped me in a mantle of justice,
Like a bridegroom adorned with a diadem,
    like a bride bedecked with her jewels.

As the earth brings forth its plants,
    and a garden makes its growth spring up,
So will the Lord GOD make justice and praise
    spring up before all the nations.

The word of the Lord.

10

Mi 5:1–4a

Until the time when she who is to give birth has borne.

A reading from the Book of the Prophet Micah

The LORD says:
You, Bethlehem-Ephrathah,
    too small to be among the clans of Judah,
From you shall come forth for me
    one who is to be ruler in Israel;

Whose origin is from of old,
> from ancient times.

(Therefore the Lord will give them up, until the time
> when she who is to give birth has borne,

And the rest of his brethren shall return
> to the children of Israel.)

He shall stand firm and shepherd his flock
> by the strength of the LORD,
> in the majestic name of the LORD, his God;

And they shall remain, for now his greatness
> shall reach to the ends of the earth;
> he shall be peace.

The word of the Lord.

11   Zec 2:14–17

Rejoice, O daughter Zion! See, I am coming.

A reading from the Book of the Prophet Zechariah

Sing and rejoice, O daughter Zion! See, I am coming to dwell among you, says the LORD. Many nations shall join themselves to the LORD on that day, and they shall be his people, and he will dwell among you, and you shall know that the LORD of hosts has sent me to you. The LORD will possess Judah as his portion in the holy land, and he will again choose Jerusalem. Silence, all mankind, in the presence of the LORD! for he stirs forth from his holy dwelling.

The word of the Lord.

READING I   From the New Testament

During the Easter Season

1

Acts 1:12–14

*All these devoted themselves with one accord
to prayer with Mary, the mother of Jesus.*

A reading from the Acts of the Apostles

After Jesus had been taken up to heaven, the Apostles returned to Jerusalem from the mount called Olivet, which is near Jerusalem, a sabbath day's journey away.

When they entered the city they went to the upper room where they were staying, Peter and John and James and Andrew, Philip and Thomas, Bartholomew and Matthew, James son of Alphaeus, Simon the Zealot, and Judas son of James. All these devoted themselves with one accord to prayer, together with some women, and Mary the mother of Jesus, and his brothers. The word of the Lord.

2

Rv 11:19a; 12:1–6a, 10ab

A great sign appeared in the sky.

A reading from the Book of Revelation

God's temple in heaven was opened, and the ark of his covenant could be seen in the temple.

A great sign appeared in the sky, a woman clothed with the sun, with the moon under her feet, and on her head a crown of twelve stars. She was with child and wailed aloud in pain as she labored to give birth. Then another sign appeared in the sky; it was a huge red dragon, with seven heads and ten horns, and on its heads were seven diadems. Its tail swept away a third of the stars in the sky and hurled them down to the earth. Then the dragon stood before the woman about to give birth, to devour her child when she gave birth. She gave birth to a son, a male child, destined to rule all the nations with an iron rod. Her child was caught up to God and his throne. The woman herself fled into the desert where she had a place prepared by God.

Then I heard a loud voice in heaven say:

"Now have salvation and power come,
and the Kingdom of our God
and the authority of his Anointed."

The word of the Lord.

3   Rv 21:1–5a

*I also saw a new Jerusalem, prepared as a bride
adorned for her husband.*

A reading from the Book of Revelation

I, John, saw a new heaven and a new earth. The former heaven and the former earth had passed away, and the sea was no more. I also saw the holy city, a new Jerusalem, coming down out of heaven from God, prepared as a bride adorned for her husband. I heard a loud voice from the throne saying, "Behold, God's dwelling is with the human race. He will dwell with them and they will be his people and God himself will always be with them as their God. He will wipe every tear from their eyes, and there shall be no more death or mourning, wailing or pain, for the old order has passed away."

The One who sat on the throne said, "Behold, I make all things new."

The word of the Lord.

Responsorial Psalm

1

1 Sm 2:1, 4–5, 6–7, 8abcd

R. My heart exults in the Lord, my Savior.

"My heart exults in the LORD,
  my horn is exalted in my God.
I have swallowed up my enemies;
  I rejoice in my victory."

R. My heart exults in the Lord, my Savior.

"The bows of the mighty are broken,
  while the tottering gird on strength.
The well-fed hire themselves out for bread,
  while the hungry batten on spoil.
The barren wife bears seven sons,
  while the mother of many languishes."

R. My heart exults in the Lord, my Savior.

"The LORD puts to death and gives life;
  he casts down to the nether world;
  he raises up again.
The LORD makes poor and makes rich,
  he humbles, he also exalts."

R. My heart exults in the Lord, my Savior.

"He raises the needy from the dust;
  from the dung heap he lifts up the poor,
To seat them with nobles
  and make a glorious throne their heritage."

R. My heart exults in the Lord, my Savior.

2

Jdt 13:18bcde, 19

R. You are the highest honor of our race.

"Blessed are you, daughter, by the Most High God,
  above all the women on earth;
and blessed be the Lord God,
  the creator of heaven and earth."

R. You are the highest honor of our race.

"Your deed of hope will never be forgotten
  by those who tell of the might of God."

R. You are the highest honor of our race.

---

3 Ps 45:11–12, 14–15, 16–17

R. Listen to me, daughter; see and bend your ear.

Hear, O daughter, and see; turn your ear,
  forget your people and your father's house.
So shall the king desire your beauty;
  for he is your lord, and you must worship him.

R. Listen to me, daughter; see and bend your ear.

All glorious is the king's daughter as she enters;
  her raiment is threaded with spun gold.
In embroidered apparel she is borne in to the king;
  behind her the virgins of her train are brought to you.

R. Listen to me, daughter; see and bend your ear.

They are borne in with gladness and joy;
  they enter the palace of the king.
The place of your fathers your sons shall have;
  you shall make them princes through all the land.

R. Listen to me, daughter; see and bend your ear.

---

4 Ps 113:1b–2, 3–4, 5–6, 7

R. Blessed be the name of the Lord for ever.

Praise, you servants of the Lord,
  praise the name of the Lord.

Blessed be the name of the Lord
  both now and forever.

R. Blessed be the name of the Lord for ever.

From the rising to the setting of the sun
  is the name of the Lord to be praised.
High above all nations is the Lord;
  above the heavens is his glory.

R. Blessed be the name of the Lord for ever.

Who is like the Lord, our God, who is enthroned on high
  and looks upon the heavens and the earth below?

R. Blessed be the name of the Lord for ever.

He raises up the lowly from the dust;
  from the dunghill he lifts up the poor
To seat them with princes,
  with the princes of his own people.

R. Blessed be the name of the Lord for ever.

Or: **R. Alleluia.**

---

5   Lk 1:46–47, 48–49, 50–51, 52–53, 54–55

**R. The Almighty has done great things for me,
    and holy is his Name.**

"My soul proclaims the greatness of the Lord,
  my spirit rejoices in God my Savior."

**R. The Almighty has done great things for me,
    and holy is his Name.**

"For he has looked with favor on his lowly servant.
From this day all generations will call me blessed:
  the Almighty has done great things for me
  and holy is his Name."

**R. The Almighty has done great things for me,
    and holy is his Name.**

"He has mercy on those who fear him
  in every generation.
He has shown the strength of his arm,
  he has scattered the proud in their conceit."

  **R. The Almighty has done great things for me,
      and holy is his Name.**

"He has cast down the mighty from their thrones,
  and has lifted up the lowly.
He has filled the hungry with good things,
  and the rich he has sent away empty."

  **R. The Almighty has done great things for me,
      and holy is his Name.**

"He has come to the help of his servant Israel
  for he has remembered his promise of mercy,
the promise he made to our fathers,
  to Abraham and his children for ever."

  **R. The Almighty has done great things for me,
      and holy is his name.**

  Or: **R. O Blessed Virgin Mary, you carried the Son
      of the eternal Father.**

READING II   From the New Testament

FIRST OPTION   Rom 5:12, 17–19

  Where sin increased, grace overflowed all the more.

A reading from the Letter of Saint Paul to the Romans

Brothers and sisters:
Through one man sin entered the world, and through sin, death,
and thus death came to all men, inasmuch as all sinned.

  For if, by the transgression of the one, death came to reign
through that one, how much more will those who receive the
abundance of grace and of the gift of justification come to reign

in life through the one Jesus Christ. In conclusion, just as through one transgression condemnation came upon all, so, through one righteous act, acquittal and life came to all. For just as through the disobedience of the one man the many were made sinners, so, through the obedience of the one, the many will be made righteous.

The word of the Lord.

SECOND OPTION

Rom 8:28–30

Those he foreknew he also predestined.

A reading from the Letter of Saint Paul to the Romans

Brothers and sisters:

We know that all things work for good for those who love God, who are called according to his purpose. For those he foreknew he also predestined to be conformed to the image of his Son, so that he might be the firstborn among many brothers. And those he predestined he also called; and those he called he also justified; and those he justified he also glorified.

The word of the Lord.

THIRD OPTION

Gal 4:4–7

God sent his Son, born of a woman.

A reading from the Letter of Saint Paul to the Galatians

Brothers and sisters:

When the fullness of time had come, God sent his Son, born of a woman, born under the law, to ransom those under the law, so that we might receive adoption as sons. As proof that you are sons, God sent the spirit of his Son into our hearts, crying out, "Abba, Father!" So you are no longer a slave but a son, and if a son then also an heir, through God.

The word of the Lord.

FOURTH OPTION   Eph 1:3–6, 11–12

God chose us in Christ, before the world began.

A reading from the Letter of Saint Paul to the Ephesians

Blessed be the God and Father of our Lord Jesus Christ, who has blessed us in Christ with every spiritual blessing in the heavens, as he chose us in him, before the foundation of the world, to be holy and without blemish before him. In love he destined us for adoption to himself through Jesus Christ, in accord with the favor of his will, for the praise of the glory of his grace that he granted us in the beloved.

   In him we were also chosen, destined in accord with the purpose of the One who accomplishes all things according to the intention of his will, so that we might exist for the praise of his glory, we who first hoped in Christ.

The word of the Lord.

ALLELUIA VERSE AND VERSE BEFORE THE GOSPEL

1   See Lk 1:28
Hail, Mary, full of grace, the Lord is with you;
blessed are you among women.

2   See Lk 1:45
Blessed are you, O Virgin Mary, who believed
that what was spoken to you by the Lord would be
   fulfilled.

3   See Lk 2:19
Blessed is the Virgin Mary who kept the word of God
and pondered it in her heart.

4   Lk 11:28
Blessed are those who hear the word of God
and observe it.

5 Blessed are you, holy Virgin Mary, deserving of all praise;
from you rose the sun of justice, Christ our God.

6 Blessed are you, O Virgin Mary;
without dying you won the martyr's crown
beneath the Cross of the Lord.

GOSPEL

1

Mt 1:1–16, 18–23

*For it is through the Holy Spirit
that this child has been conceived in her.*

A reading from the holy Gospel according to Matthew

Long form follows; for short form omit what is in brackets.

[The book of the genealogy of Jesus Christ, the son of David,
the son of Abraham.

Abraham became the father of Isaac, Isaac the father of
Jacob, Jacob the father of Judah and his brothers. Judah became
the father of Perez and Zerah, whose mother was Tamar. Perez
became the father of Hezron, Hezron the father of Ram, Ram
the father of Amminadab. Amminadab became the father of
Nahshon, Nahshon the father of Salmon, Salmon the father of
Boaz, whose mother was Rahab. Boaz became the father of
Obed, whose mother was Ruth. Obed became the father of
Jesse, Jesse the father of David the king.

David became the father of Solomon, whose mother had
been the wife of Uriah. Solomon became the father of Rehoboam, Rehoboam the father of Abijah, Abijah the father of
Asaph. Asaph became the father of Jehoshaphat, Jehoshaphat
the father of Joram, Joram the father of Uzziah. Uzziah became

the father of Jotham, Jotham the father of Ahaz, Ahaz the father of Hezekiah. Hezekiah became the father of Manasseh, Manasseh the father of Amos, Amos the father of Josiah. Josiah became the father of Jechoniah and his brothers at the time of the Babylonian exile.

After the Babylonian exile, Jechoniah became the father of Shealtiel, Shealtiel the father of Zerubbabel, Zerubbabel the father of Abiud. Abiud became the father of Eliakim, Eliakim the father of Azor, Azor the father of Zadok. Zadok became the father of Achim, Achim the father of Eliud, Eliud the father of Eleazar. Eleazar became the father of Matthan, Matthan the father of Jacob, Jacob the father of Joseph, the husband of Mary. Of her was born Jesus who is called the Christ.

Now] this is how the birth of Jesus Christ came about. When his mother Mary was betrothed to Joseph, but before they lived together, she was found with child through the Holy Spirit. Joseph her husband, since he was a righteous man, yet unwilling to expose her to shame, decided to divorce her quietly. Such was his intention when, behold, the angel of the Lord appeared to him in a dream and said, "Joseph, son of David, do not be afraid to take Mary your wife into your home. For it is through the Holy Spirit that this child has been conceived in her. She will bear a son and you are to name him Jesus, because he will save his people from their sins." All this took place to fulfill what the Lord had said through the prophet:

Behold, the virgin shall be with child and bear a son,
and they shall name him Emmanuel,

which means "God is with us."

The Gospel of the Lord.

2

Mt 2:13–15, 19–23

Take the child and his mother and flee to Egypt.

A reading from the holy Gospel according to Matthew

When the magi had departed, behold, the angel of the Lord appeared to Joseph in a dream and said, "Rise, take the child and his mother, flee to Egypt, and stay there until I tell you. Herod is going to search for the child to destroy him." Joseph rose and took the child and his mother by night and departed for Egypt. He stayed there until the death of Herod, that what the Lord had said through the prophet might be fulfilled, *Out of Egypt I called my son.*

When Herod had died, behold, the angel of the Lord appeared in a dream to Joseph in Egypt and said, "Rise, take the child and his mother and go to the land of Israel, for those who sought the child's life are dead." He rose, took the child and his mother, and went to the land of Israel. But when he heard that Archelaus was ruling over Judea in place of his father Herod, he was afraid to go back there. And because he had been warned in a dream, he departed for the region of Galilee. He went and dwelt in a town called Nazareth, so that what had been spoken through the prophets might be fulfilled, *He shall be called a Nazorean.*

The Gospel of the Lord.

3

Mt 12:46–50

Stretching out his hand toward his disciples, he said, here are my mother and my brothers.

A reading from the holy Gospel according to Matthew

While Jesus was speaking to the crowds, his mother and his brothers appeared outside, wishing to speak with him. Someone told him, "Your mother and your brothers are standing outside, asking to speak with you." But he said in reply to the one who told him, "Who is my mother? Who are my brothers?" And stretching out his hand toward his disciples, he said, "Here are my mother and my brothers. For whoever does the will of my heavenly Father is my brother, and sister, and mother."

The Gospel of the Lord.

4   Lk 1:26–38

Behold, you will conceive in your womb and bear a son.

A reading from the holy Gospel according to Luke

The angel Gabriel was sent from God to a town of Galilee called Nazareth, to a virgin betrothed to a man named Joseph, of the house of David, and the virgin's name was Mary. And coming to her, he said, "Hail, full of grace! The Lord is with you." But she was greatly troubled at what was said and pondered what sort of greeting this might be. Then the angel said to her, "Do not be afraid, Mary, for you have found favor with God. Behold, you will conceive in your womb and bear a son, and you shall name him Jesus. He will be great and will be called Son of the Most High, and the Lord God will give him the throne of David his father, and he will rule over the house of Jacob forever, and of his Kingdom there will be no end." But Mary said to the angel, "How can this be, since I have no relations with a man?" And the angel said to her in reply, "The Holy Spirit will come upon you, and the power of the Most High will overshadow you. Therefore the child to be born will be called holy, the Son of God. And behold, Elizabeth, your relative, has also conceived a son in her old age, and this is the sixth month for her who was called barren; for nothing will be impossible for God." Mary said, "Behold, I am the handmaid of the Lord. May it be done to me according to your word." Then the angel departed from her.

The Gospel of the Lord.

5

Lk 1:39–47

Blessed is she who believed.

A reading from the holy Gospel according to Luke

Mary set out and traveled to the hill country in haste to a town of Judah, where she entered the house of Zechariah and greeted Elizabeth. When Elizabeth heard Mary's greeting, the infant leaped in her womb, and Elizabeth, filled with the Holy Spirit, cried out in a loud voice and said, "Most blessed are you among women, and blessed is the fruit of your womb. And how does this happen to me, that the mother of my Lord should come to me? For at the moment the sound of your greeting reached my ears, the infant in my womb leaped for joy. Blessed are you who believed that what was spoken to you by the Lord would be fulfilled."

And Mary said:

"My soul proclaims the greatness of the Lord;
     my spirit rejoices in God my savior."

The Gospel of the Lord.

6

Lk 2:1–14

She gave birth to her firstborn son.

A reading from the holy Gospel according to Luke

In those days a decree went out from Caesar Augustus that the whole world should be enrolled. This was the first enrollment, when Quirinius was governor of Syria. So all went to be enrolled, each to his own town. And Joseph too went up from Galilee from the town of Nazareth to Judea, to the city of David that is called Bethlehem, because he was of the house and family of David, to be enrolled with Mary, his betrothed, who was with child. While they were there, the time came for her to have her child, and she gave birth to her firstborn son. She wrapped him in swaddling clothes and laid him in a manger, because there was no room for them in the inn.

Now there were shepherds in that region living in the fields and keeping the night watch over their flock. The angel of the Lord appeared to them and the glory of the Lord shone around them, and they were struck with great fear. The angel said to them, "Do not be afraid; for behold, I proclaim to you good news of great joy that will be for all the people. For today in the city of David a savior has been born for you who is Christ and Lord. And this will be a sign for you: you will find an infant wrapped in swaddling clothes and lying in a manger." And suddenly there was a multitude of the heavenly host with the angel, praising God and saying:

"Glory to God in the highest
and on earth peace to those on whom his favor rests."

The Gospel of the Lord.

7   Lk 2:15b–19

Mary kept all these things, reflecting on them in her heart.

A reading from the holy Gospel according to Luke

The shepherds said to one another, "Let us go, then, to Bethlehem to see this thing that has taken place, which the Lord has made known to us." So they went in haste and found Mary and Joseph and the infant lying in the manger. When they saw this, they made known the message that had been told them about this child. All who heard it were amazed by what had been told them by the shepherds. And Mary kept all these things, reflecting on them in her heart.

The Gospel of the Lord.

8 Lk 2:27–35

You yourself a sword will pierce.

A reading from the holy Gospel according to Luke

Simeon came in the Spirit into the temple; and when the parents brought in the child Jesus to perform the custom of the law in regard to him, he took him into his arms and blessed God, saying:

"Lord, now let your servant go in peace;
  your word has been fulfilled;
my own eyes have seen the salvation
  which you prepared in the sight of every people:
a light to reveal you to the nations
  and the glory of your people Israel."

The child's father and mother were amazed at what was said about him; and Simeon blessed them and said to Mary his mother, "Behold, this child is destined for the fall and rise of many in Israel, and to be a sign that will be contradicted and you yourself a sword will pierce so that the thoughts of many hearts may be revealed."

The Gospel of the Lord.

9   Lk 2:41–52

Your father and I have been looking for you.

A reading from the holy Gospel according to Luke

Each year Jesus' parents went to Jerusalem for the feast of Passover, and when he was twelve years old, they went up according to festival custom. After they had completed its days, as they were returning, the boy Jesus remained behind in Jerusalem, but his parents did not know it. Thinking that he was in the caravan, they journeyed for a day and looked for him among their relatives and acquaintances, but not finding him, they returned to Jerusalem to look for him. After three days they found him in the temple, sitting in the midst of the teachers, listening to them and asking them questions, and all who heard him were astounded at his understanding and his answers. When his parents saw him, they were astonished, and his mother said to him, "Son, why have you done this to us? Your father and I have been looking for you with great anxiety." And he said to them, "Why were you looking for me? Did you not know that I must be in my Father's house?" But they did not understand what he said to them. He went down with them and came to Nazareth, and was obedient to them; and his mother kept all these things in her heart. And Jesus advanced in wisdom and age and favor before God and man.

The Gospel of the Lord.

10   Lk 11:27–28

Blessed is the womb that carried you.

A reading from the holy Gospel according to Luke

While Jesus was speaking, a woman from the crowd called out and said to him, "Blessed is the womb that carried you and

the breasts at which you nursed." He replied, "Rather, blessed are those who hear the word of God and observe it."
The Gospel of the Lord.

11

Jn 2:1–11

The mother of Jesus was there.

A reading from the holy Gospel according to John

There was a wedding in Cana at Galilee, and the mother of Jesus was there. Jesus and his disciples were also invited to the wedding. When the wine ran short, the mother of Jesus said to him, "They have no wine." And Jesus said to her, "Woman, how does your concern affect me? My hour has not yet come." His mother said to the servers, "Do whatever he tells you." Now there were six stone water jars there for Jewish ceremonial washings, each holding twenty to thirty gallons. Jesus told them, "Fill the jars with water." So they filled them to the brim. Then he told them, "Draw some out now and take it to the headwaiter." So they took it. And when the headwaiter tasted the water that had become wine, without knowing where it came from although the servers who had drawn the water knew, the headwaiter called the bridegroom and said to him, "Everyone serves good wine first, and then when people have drunk freely, an inferior one; but you have kept the good wine until now." Jesus did this as the beginning of his signs in Cana in Galilee and so revealed his glory, and his disciples began to believe in him.
The Gospel of the Lord.

12

Behold, your son. Behold, your mother.

A reading from the holy Gospel according to John

Standing by the cross of Jesus were his mother and his mother's sister, Mary the wife of Clopas, and Mary Magdalene. When Jesus saw his mother and the disciple there whom he loved, he said to his mother, "Woman, behold, your son." Then he said to the disciple, "Behold, your mother." And from that hour the disciple took her into his home.

The Gospel of the Lord.

COMMON OF MARTYRS

1. For Several Martyrs, Outside the Easter Season

Entrance Antiphon

The saints are happy in heaven because they followed Christ. They rejoice with him for ever because they shed their blood for love of him.

Opening Prayer

Father,
we celebrate the memory of Saints N. and N.
who died for their faithful witnessing to Christ.
Give us the strength to follow their example,
loyal and faithful to the end.

We ask this through our Lord Jesus Christ, your Son,
who lives and reigns with you and the Holy Spirit,
one God, for ever and ever.

Liturgy of the Word, pp. 2147–2169.

Prayer over the Gifts

Pray, brethren...

Father,
receive the gifts we bring
in memory of your holy martyrs.
Keep us strong in our faith
and in our witness to you.

Grant this through Christ our Lord.

Communion Antiphon

**You are the men who have stood by me faithfully in my trials,
and now I confer a kingdom on you, says the Lord. You will eat
and drink at my table in my kingdom.** (Lk 22:28–30)

Prayer after Communion

Let us pray.

Pause for silent prayer, if this has not preceded.

God our Father,
in your holy martyrs you show us the glory of the cross.
Through this sacrifice, strengthen our resolution
to follow Christ faithfully
and to work in your Church for the salvation of all.

We ask this through Christ our Lord.

2. For Several Martyrs,
Outside the Easter Season

Entrance Antiphon

Many are the sufferings of the just, and from them all the Lord has delivered them; the Lord preserves all their bones, not one of them shall be broken. (Ps 33:20–21)

Opening Prayer

All-powerful, ever-living God,
turn our weakness into strength.
As you gave your martyrs N. and N.
the courage to suffer death for Christ,
give us the courage to live in faithful witness to you.

Grant this through our Lord Jesus Christ, your Son,
who lives and reigns with you and the Holy Spirit,
one God, for ever and ever.

Liturgy of the Word, *pp. 2147–2169.*

Prayer over the Gifts

Pray, brethren...

Lord,
accept the gifts we bring
to celebrate the feast of your martyrs.
May this sacrifice free us from sin
and make our service pleasing to you.

We ask this through Christ our Lord.

Communion Antiphon

No one has greater love, says the Lord, than the man who lays down his life for his friends. (Jn 15:13)

Prayer after Communion

Let us pray.

Pause for silent prayer, if this has not preceded.

Lord,
we eat the bread from heaven
and become one body in Christ.
Never let us be separated from his love
and help us to follow your martyrs N. and N.
by having the courage to overcome all things through Christ,
who loved us all,
and lives and reigns with you for ever and ever.

3. For Several Martyrs,
Outside the Easter Season

Entrance Antiphon

The salvation of the just comes from the Lord. He is their strength in time of need. (Ps 36:39)

Opening Prayer

Lord,
may the victory of your martyrs give us joy.
May their example strengthen our faith,
and their prayers give us renewed courage.

We ask this through our Lord Jesus Christ, your Son,
who lives and reigns with you and the Holy Spirit,
one God, for ever and ever.

Or:

Lord,
hear the prayers of the martyrs N. and N.
and give us courage to bear witness to your truth.

Grant this through our Lord Jesus Christ, your Son,
who lives and reigns with you and the Holy Spirit,
one God, for ever and ever.

Liturgy of the Word, *pp. 2147–2169.*

Prayer over the Gifts

Pray, brethren...

Lord,
accept the gifts of your people
as we honor the suffering and death
of your martyrs N. and N.
As the eucharist gave them strength in persecution
may it keep us faithful in every difficulty.

We ask this through Christ our Lord.

Communion Antiphon

**Whoever loses his life for my sake and the gospel, says the
Lord, will save it.** (Mk 8:35)

Prayer after Communion

Let us pray.

Pause for silent prayer, if this has not preceded.

Lord,
keep this eucharist effective within us.
May the gift we receive
on this feast of the martyrs N. and N.
bring us salvation and peace.

Grant this in the name of Jesus the Lord.

4. For Several Martyrs, Outside the Easter Season

Entrance Antiphon

The Lord will hear the just when they cry out, from all their afflictions he will deliver them. (Ps 33:18)

Opening Prayer

God our Father,
every year you give us the joy
of celebrating this feast of Saints N. and N.
May we who recall their birth to eternal life
imitate their courage in suffering for you.

Grant this through our Lord Jesus Christ, your Son,
who lives and reigns with you and the Holy Spirit,
one God, for ever and ever.

Or:

God our Father,
your generous gift of love
brought Saints N. and N.
to unending glory.
Through the prayers of your martyrs
forgive our sins and free us from every danger.

We ask this through our Lord Jesus Christ, your Son,
who lives and reigns with you and the Holy Spirit,
one God, for ever and ever.

Liturgy of the Word, *pp. 2147–2169.*

Prayer over the Gifts

Pray, brethren...

Lord,
you gave Saints N. and N. the fulfillment of their faith

in the vision of your glory.
May the gifts we bring to honor their memory
gain us your pardon and peace.

We ask this in the name of Jesus the Lord.

Communion Antiphon

We are given over to death for Jesus, that the life of Jesus may be revealed in our dying flesh. (2 Cor 4:11)

Prayer after Communion

Let us pray.

Pause for silent prayer, if this has not preceded.

Lord,
may this food of heaven
bring us a share in the grace
you gave the martyrs N. and N.
From their bitter sufferings
may we learn to become strong
and by patient endurance earn the victory of rejoicing in
    your holiness.

Grant this through Christ our Lord.

5. For Several Martyrs, Outside the Easter Season

Entrance Antiphon

The holy martyrs shed their blood on earth for Christ; there-fore they have received an everlasting reward.

Opening Prayer

Lord,
we honor your martyrs N. and N.
who were faithful to Christ

even to the point of shedding their blood for him.
Increase our own faith and free us from our sins,
and help us to follow their example of love.

We ask this through our Lord Jesus Christ, your Son,
who lives and reigns with you and the Holy Spirit,
one God, for ever and ever.

Liturgy of the Word, *pp. 2147–2169.*

Prayer over the Gifts

Pray, brethren...

Lord,
be pleased with the gifts we bring.
May we who celebrate the mystery of the passion of your Son
make this mystery part of our lives
by the inspiration of the martyrs N. and N.

We ask this through Christ our Lord.

Or:

Lord,
may these gifts which we bring you in sacrifice
to celebrate the victory of Saints N. and N.
fill our hearts with your love
and prepare us for the reward you promise
to those who are faithful.

We ask this in the name of Jesus the Lord.

Communion Antiphon

**Neither death nor life nor anything in all creation can come
between us and Christ's love for us.** (See Rom 8:38–39)

Prayer after Communion

Let us pray.

Pause for silent prayer, if this has not preceded.

Lord,
you give us the body and blood of Christ your only Son
on this feast of your martyrs N. and N.
By being faithful to your love
may we live in you,
receive life from you,
and always be true to your inspiration.

We ask this in the name of Jesus the Lord.

6. For One Martyr, Outside the Easter Season

Entrance Antiphon

**This holy man fought to the death for the law of his God, never
cowed by the threats of the wicked; his house was built on solid
rock.**

Opening Prayer

God of power and mercy,
you gave N., your martyr, victory over pain and suffering.
Strengthen us who celebrate this day of his triumph
and help us to be victorious over the evils that threaten us.

Grant this through our Lord Jesus Christ, your Son,
who lives and reigns with you and the Holy Spirit,
one God, for ever and ever.

Liturgy of the Word, *pp. 2147–2169.*

Prayer over the Gifts

Pray, brethren...
Lord,
bless our offerings and make them holy.
May these gifts fill our hearts

with the love which gave St. N. victory
over all his suffering.

We ask this through Christ our Lord.

Or:

Lord,
accept the gifts we offer in memory of the martyr N.
May they be pleasing to you
as was the shedding of his blood for the faith.

Grant this through Christ our Lord.

Communion Antiphon

**If anyone wishes to come after me, he must renounce himself,
take up his cross, and follow me, says the Lord.**   (Mt 16:24)

Prayer after Communion

Let us pray.

Pause for silent prayer, if this has not preceded.

Lord,
may the mysteries we receive
give us the spiritual courage
which made your martyr N.
faithful in your service and victorious in his suffering.

Grant this in the name of Jesus the Lord.

7. For One Martyr, Outside the Easter Season

Entrance Antiphon

**Here is a true martyr who shed his blood for Christ; his judges
could not shake him by their menaces, and so he won through to
the kingdom of heaven.**

Opening Prayer

All-powerful, ever-living God,
you gave St. N. the courage to witness to the gospel of
    Christ
even to the point of giving his life for it.
By his prayers help us to endure all suffering for love of you
and to seek you with all our hearts,
for you alone are the source of life.

Grant this through our Lord Jesus Christ, your Son,
who lives and reigns with you and the Holy Spirit,
one God, for ever and ever.

Liturgy of the Word, *pp. 2147–2169.*

Prayer over the Gifts

Pray, brethren...

God of love,
pour out your blessing on our gifts
and make our faith strong,
the faith which St. N. professed by shedding his blood.

We ask this through Christ our Lord.

Or:

Lord,
accept these gifts we present in memory of St. N.,
for no temptation could turn him away from you.

We ask this through Christ our Lord.

Communion Antiphon

**I am the vine and you are the branches, says the Lord; he who
lives in me, and I in him, will bear much fruit.** (Jn 15:5)

Prayer after Communion

Let us pray.

Pause for silent prayer, if this has not preceded.

Lord,
we are renewed by the mystery of the eucharist.
By imitating the fidelity of St. N. and by your patience
may we come to share the eternal life you have promised.

We ask this in the name of Jesus the Lord.

8. For Several Martyrs, in the Easter Season

Entrance Antiphon

**Come, you whom my Father has blessed; inherit the kingdom
prepared for you since the foundation of the world, alleluia.**

Opening Prayer

Father,
you gave your martyrs N. and N.
the courage to die in the witness to Christ and the gospel.
By the power of your Holy Spirit,
give us the humility to believe
and the courage to profess the faith
for which they gave their lives.

We ask this through our Lord Jesus Christ, your Son,
who lives and reigns with you and the Holy Spirit,
one God, for ever and ever.

Or:

God our all-powerful Father,
you strengthen our faith
and take away our weakness.

Let the prayers and example of your martyrs N. and N. help us
to share in the passion and resurrection of Christ
and bring us to eternal joy with all your saints.

We ask this through our Lord Jesus Christ, your Son,
who lives and reigns with you and the Holy Spirit,
one God, for ever and ever.

Liturgy of the Word, *pp. 2147–2169.*

Prayer over the Gifts

Pray, brethren...

Lord,
we celebrate the death of your holy martyrs.
May we offer the sacrifice which gives all martyrdom its
    meaning.

Grant this through Christ our Lord.

Communion Antiphon

**Those who are victorious I will feed from the tree of life, which
grows in the paradise of my God, alleluia.** (Rv 2:7)

Prayer after Communion

Let us pray.

Pause for silent prayer, if this has not preceded.

Lord,
at this holy meal
we celebrate the heavenly victory of your martyrs N. and N.
May this bread of life
give us the courage to conquer evil,
so that we may come to share the fruit of the tree of life in
    paradise.

We ask this through Christ our Lord.

9. For Several Martyrs, in the Easter Season

Entrance Antiphon

These are the saints who were victorious in the blood of the Lamb, and in the face of death they did not cling to life; therefore they are reigning with Christ for ever, alleluia.   (Rv 12:11)

Opening Prayer

Lord,
you gave your martyrs N. and N.
the privilege of shedding their blood
for boldly proclaiming the death and resurrection of your Son.
May this celebration of their victory give them honor among
   your people.

We ask this through our Lord Jesus Christ, your Son,
who lives and reigns with you and the Holy Spirit,
one God, for ever and ever.

Liturgy of the Word, *pp. 2147–2169.*

Prayer over the Gifts

Pray, brethren...

Lord,
fill these gifts with the blessing of your Holy Spirit
and fill our hearts with the love
which gave victory to Saints N. and N.
in dying for the faith.

We ask this through Christ our Lord.

Communion Antiphon

If we die with Christ, we shall live with him, and if we are faithful to the end, we shall reign with him, alleluia.

(2 Tim 2:11–12)

Prayer after Communion

Let us pray.

Pause for silent prayer, if this has not preceded.

Lord,
we are renewed by the breaking of one bread
in honor of the martyrs N. and N.
Keep us in your love
and help us to live the new life Christ won for us.

Grant this in the name of Jesus the Lord.

10. For One Martyr, in the Easter Season

Entrance Antiphon

Light for ever will shine on your saints, O Lord, alleluia.

(See 4 Ezr 2:35)

Opening Prayer

God our Father,
you have honored the Church with the victorious witness of
  St. N.,
who died for his faith.
As he imitated the sufferings and death of the Lord,
may we follow in his footsteps and come to eternal joy.

We ask this through our Lord Jesus Christ, your Son,
who lives and reigns with you and the Holy Spirit,
one God, for ever and ever.

Liturgy of the Word, *pp. 2147–2169.*

Prayer over the Gifts

Pray, brethren...

Lord,
accept this offering of praise and peace

in memory of your martyr N.
May it bring us your forgiveness
and inspire us to give you thanks now and for ever.

Grant this in the name of Jesus the Lord.

Communion Antiphon

I tell you solemnly: Unless a grain of wheat falls on the ground and dies, it remains a single grain; but if it dies, it yields a rich harvest, alleluia.
(Jn 12:24–25)

Prayer after Communion

Let us pray.

Pause for silent prayer, if this has not preceded.

Lord,
we receive your gifts from heaven
at this joyful feast.
May we who proclaim at this holy table
the death and resurrection of your Son
come to share his glory with all your holy martyrs.

Grant this through Christ our Lord.

Other Prayers for Martyrs

FOR MISSIONARY MARTYRS

Opening Prayer

God of mercy and love,
through the preaching of your martyrs N. and N.
you brought the good news of Christ
to people who had not known him.
May the prayers of saints N. and N.
make our own faith grow stronger.

We ask this through our Lord Jesus Christ, your Son,
who lives and reigns with you and the Holy Spirit,
one God, for ever and ever.

Liturgy of the Word, *pp. 2147–2169.*

Prayer over the Gifts

Pray, brethren...

Lord,
at this celebration of the eucharist
we honor the suffering and death of your martyrs N. and N.
In offering this sacrifice
may we proclaim the death of your Son
who gave these martyrs courage not only by his words
but also by the example of his own passion,
for he is Lord for ever and ever.

Prayer after Communion

Let us pray.

Pause for silent prayer, if this has not preceded.

Lord,
may we who eat at your holy table
be inspired by the example of Saints N. and N.
May we keep before us the loving sacrifice of your Son,
and come to the unending peace of your kingdom.

We ask this in the name of Jesus the Lord.

FOR A VIRGIN MARTYR

Opening Prayer

God our Father,
you give us joy each year

in honoring the memory of St. N.
May her prayers be a source of help for us,
and may her example of courage and chastity be our
    inspiration.

Grant this through our Lord Jesus Christ, your Son,
who lives and reigns with you and the Holy Spirit,
one God, for ever and ever.

Liturgy of the Word, *pp. 2147–2169.*

Prayer over the Gifts

Pray, brethren...

Lord,
receive our gifts
as you accepted the suffering and death of St. N.
in whose honor we celebrate this eucharist.

We ask this through Christ our Lord.

Prayer after Communion

Let us pray.

Pause for silent prayer, if this has not preceded.

Lord God,
you gave St. N. the crown of eternal joy
because she gave her life
rather than renounce the virginity she had promised
in witness to Christ.
With the courage this eucharist brings
help us to rise out of the bondage of our earthly desires
and attain to the glory of your kingdom.

Grant this through Christ our Lord.

FOR A HOLY WOMAN MARTYR

Opening Prayer

Father,
in our weakness your power reaches perfection.
You gave St. N. the strength
to defeat the power of sin and evil.
May we who celebrate her glory share in her triumph.

We ask this through our Lord Jesus Christ, your Son,
who lives and reigns with you and the Holy Spirit,
one God, for ever and ever.

Liturgy of the Word, *pp. 2147–2169.*

Prayer over the Gifts

Pray, brethren...

Lord,
today we offer this sacrifice in joy
as we recall the victory of St. N.
May we proclaim to others the great things
you have done for us
and rejoice in the constant help of your martyr's prayers.

Grant this through Christ our Lord.

Prayer after Communion

Let us pray.

Pause for silent prayer, if this has not preceded.

Lord,
by this sacrament you give us eternal joys
as we recall the memory of St. N.
May we always embrace the gift of life
we celebrate at this eucharist.

We ask this in the name of Jesus the Lord.

Liturgy of the Word: Common of Martyrs

READING I   From the Old Testament

1

2 Chr 24:18–22

Zechariah was stoned to death in the court of the LORD's temple.

A reading from the second Book of Chronicles

The princes of Judah forsook the temple of the LORD, the God of their fathers, and began to serve the sacred poles and the idols; and because of this crime of theirs, wrath came upon Judah and Jerusalem. Although prophets were sent to them to convert them to the LORD, the people would not listen to their warnings. Then the spirit of God possessed Zechariah, son of Jehoiada the priest. He took his stand above the people and said to them: "God says, 'Why are you transgressing the LORD's commands, so that you cannot prosper? Because you have abandoned the LORD, he has abandoned you.'" But the people conspired against him, and at the king's order they stoned him to death in the court of the LORD's temple. Thus King Joash was unmindful of the devotion shown him by Jehoiada, Zechariah's father, and slew his son. And as he was dying, he said, "May the LORD see and avenge."

The word of the Lord.

2

2 Mc 6:18, 21, 24–31

I am suffering it with joy in my soul because of my devotion to him.

A reading from the second Book of Maccabees

Eleazar, one of the foremost scribes, a man of advanced age and noble appearance, was being forced to open his mouth to eat pork. Those in charge of that unlawful ritual meal took the man aside privately, because of their long acquaintance with him, and urged him to bring meat of his own providing, such as he could legitimately eat, and to pretend to be eating some of the meat of the sacrifice prescribed by the king.

He told them: "At our age it would be unbecoming to make such a pretense; many young men would think the ninety-year-old Eleazar had gone over to an alien religion. Should I thus pretend for the sake of a brief moment of life, they would be led astray by me, while I would bring shame and dishonor on my old age. Even if, for the time being, I avoid the punisment of men, I shall never, whether alive or dead, escape the hands of the Almighty. Therefore, by manfully giving up my life now, I will prove myself worthy of my old age, and I will leave to the young a noble example of how to die willingly and generously for the revered and holy laws."

He spoke thus, and went immediately to the instrument of torture. Those who shortly before had been kindly disposed now became hostile toward him because what he had said seemed to them utter madness. When he was about to die under the blows, he groaned and said: "The LORD in his holy knowledge knows full well that, although I could have escaped death, I am not only enduring terrible pain in my body from this scourging, but also suffering it with joy in my soul because of my devotion to him." This is how he died, leaving in his death a model of courage and an unforgettable example of virtue not only for the young but for the whole nation.

The word of the Lord.

3

2 Mc 7:1–2, 9–14

We are ready to die rather than transgress
the laws of our ancestors.

A reading from the second Book of Maccabees

It happened that seven brothers with their mother were arrested and tortured with whips and scourges by the king, to force them to eat pork in violation of God's law. One of the brothers, speaking for the others, said: "What do you expect to achieve by questioning us? We are ready to die rather than transgress the laws of our ancestors."

At the point of death, the second brother said: "You accursed fiend, you are depriving us of this present life, but the King of the world will raise us up to live again forever. It is for his laws that we are dying."

After him the third suffered their cruel sport. He put out his tongue at once when told to do so, and bravely held out his hands, as he spoke these noble words: "It was from Heaven that I received these; for the sake of his laws I disdain them; from him I hope to receive them again." Even the king and his attendants marveled at the young man's courage, because he regarded his sufferings as nothing.

After he had died, they tortured and maltreated the fourth brother in the same way. When he was near death, he said, "It is my choice to die at the hands of men with the hope God gives of being raised up by him; but for you, there will be no resurrection to life."

The word of the Lord.

4

2 Mc 7:1, 20–23, 27b–29

*This most admirable mother bore it courageously
because of her hope in the LORD.*

A reading from the second Book of Maccabees

It happened that seven brothers with their mother were arrested and tortured with whips and scourges by the king, to force them to eat pork in violation of God's law.

Most admirable and worthy of everlasting remembrance was the mother, who saw her seven sons perish in a single day, yet bore it courageously because of her hope in the LORD. Filled with a noble spirit that stirred her womanly heart with manly courage she exhorted each of them in the language of their forefathers with these words: "I do not know how you came into existence in my womb; it was not I who gave you the breath of life, nor was it I who set in order the elements of which each of you is composed. Therefore, since it is the Creator of the universe who shapes each man's beginning, as he brings about the origin of everything, he, in his mercy, will give you back both breath and life, because you now disregard yourselves for the sake of his law."

"Son, have pity on me, who carried you in my womb for nine months, nursed you for three years, brought you up, educated and supported you to your present age. I beg you, child, to look at the heavens and the earth and see all that is in them; then you will know that God did not make them out of existing things; and in the same way the human race came into existence. Do not be afraid of this executioner, but be worthy of your brothers and accept death, so that in the time of mercy I may receive you again with them."

The word of the Lord.

5

As sacrificial offerings he took them to himself.

A reading from the Book of Wisdom

The souls of the just are in the hand of God,
    and no torment shall touch them.
They seemed, in the view of the foolish, to be dead;
    and their passing away was thought an affliction
    and their going forth from us, utter destruction.
But they are in peace.
For if before men, indeed, they be punished,
    yet is their hope full of immortality;
Chastised a little, they shall be greatly blessed,
    because God tried them
    and found them worthy of himself.
As gold in the furnace, he proved them,
    and as sacrificial offerings he took them to himself.
In the time of their visitation they shall shine,
    and shall dart about as sparks through stubble;
They shall judge nations and rule over peoples,
    and the LORD shall be their King forever.
Those who trust in him shall understand truth,
    and the faithful shall abide with him in love:
Because grace and mercy are with his holy ones,
    and his care is with his elect.

The word of the Lord.

6

You redeemed me, true to the greatness
of your mercy and of your name.

A reading from the Book of Sirach

I give you thanks, O Lord and King;
  I praise you, O God my savior!
I will make known your name,
  for you have been a helper and a protector to me.
You have kept back my body from the pit,
  and from the scourge of a slanderous tongue,
  from lips that went over to falsehood.
And in the sight of those who stood by,
  you have delivered me,
According to the multitude of the mercy of your name,
  and from them that did roar, prepared to devour me,
And from the power of those who sought my life;
  from many a danger you have saved me,
  from flames that hemmed me in on every side;
From the midst of unremitting fire when I was not burnt
  from the deep belly of the nether world;
From deceiving lips and painters of lies,
  from the arrows of dishonest tongues.
My soul was at the point of death,
  my life was nearing the depths of the nether world;
They encompassed me on every side,
    but there was no one to help me,
  I looked for one to sustain me, but could find no one.
But then I remembered the mercies of the LORD,
  his kindness through ages past;

For he saves those who take refuge in him,
    and rescues them from every evil.

The word of the Lord.

READING I   From the New Testament

During the Easter Season

FIRST OPTION

Acts 7:55–60

Lord Jesus, receive my spirit.

A reading from the Acts of the Apostles

Stephen, filled with the Holy Spirit, looked up intently to heaven and saw the glory of God and Jesus standing at the right hand of God, and he said, "Behold, I see the heavens opened and the Son of Man standing at the right hand of God." But they cried out in a loud voice, covered their ears, and rushed upon him together. They threw him out of the city, and began to stone him. The witnesses laid down their cloaks at the feet of a young man named Saul. As they were stoning Stephen, he called out, "Lord Jesus, receive my spirit." Then he fell to his knees and cried out in a loud voice, "Lord, do not hold this sin against them"; and when he said this, he fell asleep.

The word of the Lord.

SECOND OPTION

Rv 7:9–17

These are the ones who have survived the time of great distress.

A reading from the Book of Revelation

I, John, had a vision of a great multitude, which no one could count, from every nation, race, people, and tongue. They stood before the throne and before the Lamb, wearing white robes and holding palm branches in their hands. They cried out in a loud voice:

"Salvation comes from our God, who is seated
     on the throne,
and from the Lamb."

All the angels stood around the throne and around the elders and the four living creatures. They prostrated themselves before the throne, worshiped God, and exclaimed:

"Amen. Blessing and glory, wisdom and thanksgiving,
     honor, power, and might
be to our God forever and ever. Amen."

Then one of the elders spoke up and said to me, "Who are these wearing white robes, and where did they come from?" I said to him, "My lord, you are the one who knows." He said to me, "These are the ones who have survived the time of great distress; they have washed their robes and made them white in the Blood of the Lamb.

"For this reason they stand before God's throne
     and worship him day and night in his temple.
The One who sits on the throne will shelter them.
They will not hunger or thirst anymore,
     nor will the sun or any heat strike them.
For the Lamb who is in the center of the throne
     will shepherd them
and lead them to springs of life-giving water,
     and God will wipe away every tear from their eyes."

The word of the Lord.

THIRD OPTION

Rv 12:10–12a

Love for life did not deter them from death.

A reading from the Book of Revelation

I, John, heard a loud voice in heaven say:

"Now have salvation and power come,
　　and the Kingdom of our God
　　and the authority of his Anointed.
For the accuser of our brothers is cast out,
　　who accuses them before our God day and night.
They conquered him by the Blood of the Lamb
　　and by the word of their testimony;
　　love for life did not deter them from death.
Therefore, rejoice, you heavens,
　　and you who dwell in them."

The word of the Lord.

FOURTH OPTION

Rv 21:5–7

The victor will inherit these gifts.

A reading from the Book of Revelation

The One who was seated on the throne said: "Behold, I make all things new." Then he said, "Write these words down, for they are trustworthy and true." He said to me, "They are accomplished. I am the Alpha and the Omega, the beginning and the end. To the thirsty I will give a gift from the spring of life-giving water. The victor will inherit these gifts, and I shall be his God, and he will be my son."

The word of the Lord.

Responsorial Psalm

Ps 31:3cd –4, 6 and 8ab, 16bc and 17

R. Into your hands, O Lord, I commend my spirit.

Be my rock of refuge,
  a stronghold to give me safety.
You are my rock and my fortress;
  for your name's sake you will lead and guide me.

R. Into your hands, O Lord, I commend my spirit.

Into your hands I commend my spirit;
  you will redeem me, O LORD, O faithful God.
I will rejoice and be glad because of your mercy.

R. Into your hands, O Lord, I commend my spirit.

Rescue me from the clutches of my enemies and my persecutors,
Let your face shine upon your servant;
  save me in your kindness.

R. Into your hands, O Lord, I commend my spirit.

Ps 34:2–3, 4–5, 6–7, 8–9

R. The Lord delivered me from all my fears.

I will bless the LORD at all times;
  his praise shall be ever in my mouth.
Let my soul glory in the LORD;
  the lowly will hear me and be glad.

R. The Lord delivered me from all my fears.

Glorify the LORD with me,
  let us together extol his name.
I sought the LORD, and he answered me
  and delivered me from all my fears.

R. The Lord delivered me from all my fears.

Look to him that you may be radiant with joy,
   and your faces may not blush with shame.
When the afflicted man called out, the LORD heard,
   and from all his distress he saved him.

   R. The Lord delivered me from all my fears.

The angel of the LORD encamps
   around those who fear him, and delivers them.
Taste and see how good the LORD is;
   blessed the man who takes refuge in him.

   R. The Lord delivered me from all my fears.

THIRD OPTION   Ps 124:2–3, 4–5, 7cd–8

   **R. Our soul has been rescued like a bird
      from the fowler's snare.**

Had not the LORD been with us—
When men rose up against us,
   then would they have swallowed us alive
When their fury was inflamed against us.

   **R. Our soul has been rescued like a bird
      from the fowler's snare.**

Then would the waters have overwhelmed us;
The torrent would have swept over us;
   over us then would have swept
   the raging waters.

   **R. Our soul has been rescued like a bird
      from the fowler's snare.**

Broken was the snare,
   and we were freed.
Our help is in the name of the LORD,
   who made heaven and earth.

   **R. Our soul has been rescued like a bird
      from the fowler's snare.**

Fourth Option   Ps 126:1bc–2ab, 2cd–3, 4–5, 6

R. Those who sow in tears shall reap rejoicing.

When the LORD brought back the captives of Zion,
  we were like men dreaming.
Then our mouth was filled with laughter,
  and our tongue with rejoicing.

R. Those who sow in tears shall reap rejoicing.

Then they said among the nations,
  "The LORD has done great things for them."
The LORD has done great things for us;
  we are glad indeed.

R. Those who sow in tears shall reap rejoicing.

Restore our fortunes, O LORD,
  like the torrents in the southern desert.
Those who sow in tears
  shall reap rejoicing.

R. Those who sow in tears shall reap rejoicing.

Although they go forth weeping,
  carrying the seed to be sown,
They shall come back rejoicing,
  carrying their sheaves.

R. Those who sow in tears shall reap rejoicing.

READING II   From the New Testament

1   Rom 5:1–5

We even boast of our afflictions.

A reading from the Letter of Saint Paul to the Romans

Brothers and sisters:
Since we have been justified by faith, we have peace with God
through our Lord Jesus Christ, through whom we have gained
access by faith to this grace in which we stand, and we boast
in hope of the glory of God. Not only that, but we even boast

of our afflictions, knowing that affliction produces endurance, and endurance, proven character, and proven character, hope, and hope does not disappoint, because the love of God has been poured out into our hearts through the Holy Spirit that has been given to us.

The word of the Lord.

2   Rom 8:31b–39

Neither death nor life will be able to separate us
from the love of God.

A reading from the Letter of Saint Paul to the Romans

Brothers and sisters:

If God is for us, who can be against us? He who did not spare his own Son but handed him over for us all, how will he not also give us everything else along with him? Who will bring a charge against God's chosen ones? It is God who acquits us. Who will condemn? Christ Jesus it is who died—or, rather, was raised—who also is at the right hand of God, who indeed intercedes for us. What will separate us from the love of Christ? Will anguish, or distress, or persecution, or famine, or naked-ness, or peril, or the sword? As it is written:

For your sake we are being slain all the day;
we are looked upon as sheep to be slaughtered.

No, in all these things we conquer overwhelmingly through him who loved us. For I am convinced that neither death, nor life, nor angels, nor principalities, nor present things, nor future things, nor powers, nor height, nor depth, nor any other creature will be able to separate us from the love of God in Christ Jesus our Lord.

The word of the Lord.

2 Cor 4:7–15

Always carrying about in the body the dying of Jesus.

A reading from the second Letter of Saint Paul to the Corinthians

Brothers and sisters:

We hold this treasure in earthen vessels, that the surpassing power may be of God and not from us. We are afflicted in every way, but not constrained; perplexed, but not driven to despair; persecuted, but not abandoned; struck down, but not destroyed; always carrying about in the body the dying of Jesus, so that the life of Jesus may also be manifested in our body. For we who live are constantly being given up to death for the sake of Jesus, so that the life of Jesus may be manifested in our mortal flesh.

So death is at work in us, but life in you. Since, then, we have the same spirit of faith, according to what is written, *I believed, therefore I spoke,* we too believe and therefore speak, knowing that the one who raised the Lord Jesus will raise us also with Jesus and place us with you in his presence. Everything indeed is for you, so that the grace bestowed in abundance on more and more people may cause the thanksgiving to overflow for the glory of God.

The word of the Lord.

4

2 Cor 6:4–10

We are treated as dying and behold we live.

A reading from the second Letter of Saint Paul to the Corinthians

Brothers and sisters:

In everything we commend ourselves as ministers of God,

through much endurance, in afflictions, hardships, constraints, beatings, imprisonments, riots, labors, vigils, fasts; by purity, knowledge, patience, kindness, in the Holy Spirit, in unfeigned love, in truthful speech, in the power of God; with weapons of righteousness at the right and at the left; through glory and dishonor, insult and praise. We are treated as deceivers and yet are truthful; as unrecognized and yet acknowledged; as dying and behold we live; as chastised and yet not put to death; as sorrowful yet always rejoicing; as poor yet enriching many; as having nothing and yet possessing all things.

The word of the Lord.

5

2 Tm 2:8–13; 3:10–12

All who want to live religiously in Christ Jesus will be persecuted.

A reading from the second Letter of Saint Paul to Timothy

Beloved:

Remember Jesus Christ, raised from the dead, a descendant of David: such is my Gospel, for which I am suffering, even to the point of chains, like a criminal. But the word of God is not chained. Therefore, I bear with everything for the sake of those who are chosen, so that they too may obtain the salvation that is in Christ Jesus, together with eternal glory. This saying is trustworthy:

If we have died with him
    we shall also live with him;
if we persevere
    we shall also reign with him.
But if we deny him

he will deny us.
If we are unfaithful
    he remains faithful,
    for he cannot deny himself.

You have followed my teaching, way of life, purpose, faith, patience, love, endurance, persecutions, and sufferings, such as happened to me in Antioch, Iconium, and Lystra, persecutions that I endured. Yet from all these things the Lord delivered me. In fact, all who want to live religiously in Christ Jesus will be persecuted.

The word of the Lord.

6

Heb 10:32–36

You endured a great contest of suffering.

A reading from the Letter to the Hebrews

Brothers and sisters:

Remember the days past when, after you had been enlightened, you endured a great contest of suffering. At times you were publicly exposed to abuse and affliction; at other times you associated yourselves with those so treated. You even joined in the sufferings of those in prison and joyfully accepted the confiscation of your property, knowing that you had a better and lasting possession. Therefore, do not throw away your confidence; it will have great recompense. You need endurance to do the will of God and receive what he has promised.

The word of the Lord.

7

Jas 1:2–4, 12

Blessed is the man who perseveres in the face of temptation.

A reading from the Letter of Saint James

Consider it all joy, my brothers and sisters, when you encounter various trials, for you know that the testing of your faith produces perseverance. And let perseverance be perfect, so that you may be perfect and complete, lacking in nothing.

Blessed is the man who perseveres in temptation, for when he has been proved he will receive the crown of life that he promised to those who love him.

The word of the Lord.

8

1 Pt 3:14–17

Do not be afraid or terrified with fear of them.

A reading from the first Letter of Saint Peter

Beloved:

Even if you should suffer because of righteousness, blessed are you. Do not be afraid or terrified with fear of them, but sanctify Christ as Lord in your hearts. Always be ready to give an explanation to anyone who asks you for a reason for your hope, but do it with gentleness and reverence, keeping your conscience clear, so that, when you are maligned, those who defame your good conduct in Christ may themselves be put to shame. For it is better to suffer for doing good, if that be the will of God, than for doing evil.

The word of the Lord.

9   1 Pt 4:12–19

Rejoice to the extent that you share in the sufferings of Christ.

A reading from the first Letter of Saint Peter

Beloved, do not be surprised that a trial by fire is occurring among you, as if something strange were happening to you. But rejoice to the extent that you share in the sufferings of Christ, so that when his glory is revealed you may also rejoice exultantly. If you are insulted for the name of Christ, blessed are you, for the Spirit of glory and of God rests upon you. But let no one among you be made to suffer as a murderer, a thief, an evildoer, or as an intriguer. But whoever is made to suffer as a Christian should not be ashamed but glorify God because of the name. For it is time for the judgment to begin with the household of God; if it begins with us, how will it end for those who fail to obey the Gospel of God?

> *And if the righteous one is barely saved,*
>   *where will the godless and the sinner appear?*

As a result, those who suffer in accord with God's will hand their souls over to a faithful creator as they do good.

The word of the Lord.

10   1 Jn 5:1–5

The victory that conquers the world is our faith.

A reading from the first Letter of Saint John

Beloved:

Everyone who believes that Jesus is the Christ is begotten by God, and everyone who loves the Father loves also the one begotten by him. In this way we know that we love the children of God when we love God and obey his commandments. For the love of God is this, that we keep his commandments. And his commandments are not burdensome, for whoever is begotten by God conquers the world. And the victory that conquers the world is our faith. Who indeed is the victor over the world but the one who believes that Jesus is the Son of God?

The word of the Lord.

ALLELUIA VERSE AND VERSE BEFORE THE GOSPEL

1 Mt 5:10

Blessed are they who are persecuted
for the sake of righteousness,
for theirs is the Kingdom of heaven.

2 Jn 17:19

I consecrate myself for them,
so that they also may be consecrated in the truth.

3 2 Cor 1:3b–4a

Blessed be the Father of compassion
and God of all encouragement,
who encourages us in our every affliction.

4 Jas 1:12

Blessed is the man who perseveres in temptation,
for when he has been proved he will receive the crown
of life.

5 1 Pt 4:14

If you are insulted for the name of Christ, blessed are you,
for the Spirit of God rests upon you.

6 See *Te Deum*

We praise you, O God,
we acclaim you as Lord;
the white-robed army of martyrs praise you.

2166 COMMONS – Common of Martyrs

GOSPEL

Mt 10:17–22

*You will be led before governors and kings for my sake,
as a witness before them and the pagans.*

A reading from the holy Gospel according to Matthew

Jesus said to his Apostles: "Beware of men, for they will hand
you over to courts and scourge you in their synagogues, and
you will be led before governors and kings for my sake as a
witness before them and the pagans. When they hand you over,
do not worry about how you are to speak or what you are to
say. You will be given at that moment what you are to say. For
it will not be you who speak but the Spirit of your Father speaking through you. Brother will hand over brother to death, and
the father his child; children will rise up against parents and
have them put to death. You will be hated by all because of my
name, but whoever endures to the end will be saved."

The Gospel of the Lord.

Mt 10:28–33

Do not be afraid of those who kill the body.

A reading from the holy Gospel according to Matthew

Jesus said to his Apostles: "Do not be afraid of those who kill the
body but cannot kill the soul; rather, be afraid of the one who can
destroy both soul and body in Gehenna. Are not two sparrows
sold for a small coin? Yet not one of them falls to the ground
without your Father's knowledge. Even all the hairs of your head
are counted. So do not be afraid; you are worth more than many
sparrows. Everyone who acknowledges me before others I will

acknowledge before my heavenly Father. But whoever denies me before others, I will deny before my heavenly Father."

The Gospel of the Lord.

3

Mt 10:34–39

I have come to bring not peace but the sword.

A reading from the holy Gospel according to Matthew

Jesus said to his Apostles: "Do not think that I have come to bring peace upon the earth. I have come to bring not peace but the sword. For I have come to set

> a man 'against his father,
>   a daughter against her mother,
> and a daughter-in-law against her mother-in-law;
>   and one's enemies will be those of one's household.'

"Whoever loves father or mother more than me is not worthy of me, and whoever loves son or daughter more than me is not worthy of me; and whoever does not take up his cross and follow after me is not worthy of me. Whoever finds his life will lose it, and whoever loses his life for my sake will find it."

The Gospel of the Lord.

4

Lk 9:23–26

Whoever loses his life for my sake will save it.

A reading from the holy Gospel according to Luke

Jesus said to all, "If anyone wishes to come after me, he must deny himself and take up his cross daily and follow me. For whoever wishes to save his life will lose it, but whoever loses his life for my sake will save it. What profit is there for one to gain the whole world yet lose or forfeit himself? Whoever is ashamed of me and of my words, the Son of Man will be ashamed of when he comes in his glory and in the glory of the Father and of the holy angels."

The Gospel of the Lord.

5   Jn 12:24–26

If a grain of wheat falls to the ground and dies, it produces much fruit.

A reading from the holy Gospel according to John

Jesus said to his disciples: "Amen, amen, I say to you, unless a grain of wheat falls to the ground and dies, it remains just a grain of wheat; but if it dies, it produces much fruit. Whoever loves his life loses it, and whoever hates his life in this world will preserve it for eternal life. Whoever serves me must follow me, and where I am, there also will my servant be. The Father will honor whoever serves me."

The Gospel of the Lord.

6   Jn 15:18–21

If they persecuted me, they will also persecute you.

A reading from the holy Gospel according to John

Jesus said to his disciples: "If the world hates you, realize that it hated me first. If you belonged to the world, the world would love its own; but because you do not belong to the world, and I have chosen you out of the world, the world hates you. Remember the word I spoke to you, 'No slave is greater than his master.' If they persecuted me, they will also persecute you. If they kept my word, they will also keep yours. And they will do all these things to you on account of my name, because they do not know the one who sent me."

The Gospel of the Lord.

7   Jn 17:11b–19

The world hated them.

A reading from the holy Gospel according to John

Lifting his eyes to heaven, Jesus prayed, saying: "Holy Father, keep them in your name that you have given me, so that they may be one just as we are one. When I was with them I protected them in your name that you gave me, and I guarded them, and none of them was lost except the son of destruction, in order that the Scripture might be fulfilled. But now I am coming to you. I speak this in the world so that they may share my joy completely. I gave them your word, and the world hated them, because they do not belong to the world any more than I belong to the world. I do not ask that you take them out of the world but that you keep them from the Evil One. They do not belong to the world any more than I belong to the world. Consecrate them in the truth. Your word is truth. As you sent me into the world, so I sent them into the world. And I consecrate myself for them, so that they also may be consecrated in truth."

The Gospel of the Lord.

COMMON OF PASTORS

1. For Popes or Bishops

Entrance Antiphon

The Lord chose him to be his high priest; he opened his treasures and made him rich in all goodness.

Opening Prayer

(for popes):

All-powerful and ever-living God,
you called St. N. to guide your people
by his word and example.
With him we pray to you:
watch over the pastors of your Church
with the people entrusted to their care,
and lead them to salvation.

We ask this through our Lord Jesus Christ, your Son,
who lives and reigns with you and the Holy Spirit,
one God, for ever and ever.

Or (for bishops):

Father,
you gave St. N. to your Church
as an example of a good shepherd.
May his prayers
help us on our way to eternal life.

Grant this through our Lord Jesus Christ, your Son,
who lives and reigns with you and the Holy Spirit,
one God, for ever and ever.

Liturgy of the Word, *pp. 2188–2218.*

Prayer over the Gifts

Pray, brethren...

Lord,
we offer you this sacrifice of praise
in memory of your saints.
May their prayers keep us from evil
now and in the future

Grant this through Christ our Lord.

Communion Antiphon

The good shepherd gives his life for his sheep. (See Jn 10:11)

Prayer after Communion

Let us pray.

Pause for silent prayer, if this has not preceded.

Lord God,
St. N. loved you
and gave himself completely in the service of your Church.
May the eucharist awaken in us that same love.

We ask this in the name of Jesus the Lord.

2. For Popes or Bishops

Entrance Antiphon

**The Lord sealed a covenant of peace with him, and made him
a prince, bestowing the priestly dignity upon him for ever.**

(See Sir 45:30)

Opening Prayer

(for popes):

Father,
you made St. N. shepherd of the whole Church

and gave to us the witness of his virtue and teaching.
Today as we honor this outstanding bishop,
we ask that our light may shine before men
and that our love for you may be sincere.

Grant this through our Lord Jesus Christ, your Son,
who lives and reigns with you and the Holy Spirit,
one God, for ever and ever.

Or (for bishops):

All-powerful God,
you made St. N. a bishop and leader of the Church
to inspire your people with his teaching and example.
May we give fitting honor to his memory
and always have the assistance of his prayers.

We ask this through our Lord Jesus Christ, your Son,
who lives and reigns with you and the Holy Spirit,
one God, for ever and ever.

Liturgy of the Word, *pp. 2188–2218.*

Prayer over the Gifts

Pray, brethren...

Lord,
may the sacrifice which wipes away the sins of all the world
bring us your forgiveness.
Help us as we offer it
on this yearly feast in honor of St. N.

Grant this through Christ our Lord.

Communion Antiphon

Lord, you know all things: you know that I love you.

(Jn 21:17)

Prayer after Communion

Let us pray.

Pause for silent prayer, if this has not preceded.

Lord God,
let the power of the gifts we receive
on this feast of St. N.
take full effect within us.
May this eucharist bring us your help in this life
and lead us to happiness in the unending life to come.

We ask this through Christ our Lord.

3. For Bishops

Entrance Antiphon

I will look after my sheep, says the Lord, and I will raise up
one shepherd who will pasture them. I, the Lord, will be their
God.   (Ez 34:11, 23–24)

Opening Prayer

All-powerful, ever-living God,
you made St. N. bishop and leader of your people.
May his prayers help to bring us your forgiveness and love.

We ask this through our Lord Jesus Christ, your Son,
who lives and reigns with you and the Holy Spirit,
one God, for ever and ever.

Liturgy of the Word, *pp. 2188 – 2218.*

Prayer over the Gifts

Pray, brethren...

Lord,
accept the gifts we bring to your holy altar

on this feast of St. N.
May our offering bring honor to your name
and pardon to your people.

We ask this through Christ our Lord.

Communion Antiphon

**You have not chosen me; I have chosen you. Go and bear fruit
that will last.** (Jn 15:16)

Prayer after Communion

Let us pray.

Pause for silent prayer, if this has not preceded.

Lord,
may we who receive this sacrament
be inspired by the example of St. N.
May we learn to proclaim what he believed
and put his teaching into action.

We ask this in the name of Jesus the Lord.

4. For Bishops

Entrance Antiphon

**I will raise up for myself a faithful priest; he will do what is in
my heart and in my mind, says the Lord.** (1 Sm 2:35)

Opening Prayer

Lord God,
you counted St. N. among your holy pastors,
renowned for faith and love which conquered evil in this world.
By the help of his prayers
keep us strong in faith and love
and let us come to share his glory.

Grant this through our Lord Jesus Christ, your Son,
who lives and reigns with you and the Holy Spirit,
one God, for ever and ever.

Liturgy of the Word, *pp. 2188–2218.*

Prayer over the Gifts

Pray, brethren...

Lord,
accept the gifts your people offer you
on this feast of St. N.
May these gifts bring us
your help for which we long.

We ask this through Christ our Lord.

Communion Antiphon

I came that men may have life, and have it to the full, says the
Lord. (Jn 10:10)

Prayer after Communion

Let us pray.

Pause for silent prayer, if this has not preceded.

Lord our God,
you give us the holy body and blood
of your Son.
May the salvation we celebrate
be our undying hope.

Grant this through Christ our Lord.

5. For Pastors

Entrance Antiphon

The Spirit of God is upon me; he has anointed me. He sent me
to bring good news to the poor, and to heal the broken-hearted.
(Lk 4:18)

Opening Prayer

God our Father,
in St. (bishop) N. you gave
a light to your faithful people.
You made him a pastor of the Church
to feed your sheep with his word
and to teach them by his example.
Help us by his prayers to keep the faith he taught
and follow the way of life he showed us.

Grant this through our Lord Jesus Christ, your Son,
who lives and reigns with you and the Holy Spirit,
one God, for ever and ever.

Liturgy of the Word, *pp. 2188–2218.*

Prayer over the Gifts

Pray, brethren...

Father of mercy,
we have these gifts to offer in honor of your saints
who bore witness to your mighty power.
May the power of the eucharist
bring us your salvation.

Grant this through Christ our Lord.

Communion Antiphon

I, the Lord, am with you always, until the end of the world.
(Mt 28:20)

Prayer after Communion

Let us pray.

Pause for silent prayer, if this has not preceded.

Lord,
may the mysteries we receive

prepare us for the eternal joys
St. N. won by his faithful ministry.

We ask this in the name of Jesus the Lord.

Or:

All-powerful God,
by our love and worship
may we who share this holy meal
always follow the example of St. N.

Grant this in the name of Jesus the Lord.

6. For Pastors

Entrance Antiphon

**I will give you shepherds after my own heart, and they shall
feed you on knowledge and sound teaching.** (Jer 3:15)

Or:

**Priests of God, bless the Lord; praise God, all you that are
holy and humble of heart.** (Dn 3:84, 87)

Opening Prayer

Lord God,
you gave your Saints (bishops) N. and N.
the spirit of truth and love
to shepherd your people.
May we who honor them on this feast
learn from their example
and be helped by their prayers.

We ask this through our Lord Jesus Christ, your Son,
who lives and reigns with you and the Holy Spirit,
one God, for ever and ever.

Liturgy of the Word, *pp. 2188–2218.*

Prayer over the Gifts

Pray, brethren...

Lord,
accept these gifts from your people.
May the eucharist we offer to your glory
in honor of Saints N. and N.
help us on our way to salvation.

Grant this in the name of Jesus the Lord.

Communion Antiphon

The Son of Man did not come to be served, but to serve, and to give his life as a ransom for many.   (Mt 20:28)

Prayer after Communion

Let us pray.
Pause for silent prayer, if this has not preceded.

Lord,
we receive the bread of heaven
as we honor the memory of your Saints N. and N.
May the eucharist we now celebrate
lead us to eternal joys.

Grant this in the name of Jesus the Lord.

7. For Pastors

Entrance Antiphon

Lord, may your priests be clothed in justice, and your holy ones leap for joy.   (Ps 131:9)

Opening Prayer

All-powerful God,
hear the prayers of Saints N. and N.

Increase your gifts within us
and give us peace in our days.

We ask this through our Lord Jesus Christ, your Son,
who lives and reigns with you and the Holy Spirit,
one God, for ever and ever.

Liturgy of the Word, *pp. 2188–2218.*

Prayer over the Gifts

Pray, brethren...

Lord,
accept the gifts we bring to your altar
in memory of your Saints N. and N.
As you led them to glory through these mysteries,
grant us also your pardon and love.

We ask this in the name of Jesus the Lord.

Communion Antiphon

**Blessed is the servant whom the Lord finds watching when he
comes; truly I tell you, he will set him over all his possessions.**

(Mt 24:46–47)

Or:

**The Lord has put his faithful servant in charge of his house-
hold, to give them their share of bread at the proper time.**

(Lk 12:42)

Prayer after Communion

Let us pray.

Pause for silent prayer, if this has not preceded.

All-powerful God,
by the eucharist we share at your holy table
on this feast of Saints N. and N.
increase our strength of character and love for you.

May we guard from every danger the faith you have given us
and walk always in the way that leads to salvation.

Grant this through Christ our Lord.

8. For Founders of Churches

Entrance Antiphon

**My words that I have put in your mouth, says the Lord, will
never be absent from your lips, and your gifts will be accepted on
my altar.**   (Is 59:21; 56:7)

Opening Prayer

God of mercy,
you gave our fathers the light of faith
through the preaching of St. N.
May we who glory in the Christian name
show in our lives the faith we profess.
We ask this through our Lord Jesus Christ, your Son,
who lives and reigns with you and the Holy Spirit,
one God, for ever and ever.

Or:

Lord,
look upon the family whom your St. (bishop) N. brought to life
with the word of truth
and nourished with the sacrament of life.
By his ministry you gave us the faith;
by his prayers help us grow in love.

Grant this through our Lord Jesus Christ, your Son,
who lives and reigns with you and the Holy Spirit,
one God, for ever and ever.

Liturgy of the Word, *pp. 2188–2218.*

Prayer over the Gifts

Pray, brethren...

Lord,
may the gifts your people bring
in memory of St. N.
bring us your gifts from heaven.
We ask this in the name of Jesus the Lord.

Communion Antiphon

The Son of Man came to give his life as a ransom for many.

(Mk 10:45)

Prayer after Communion

Let us pray.

Pause for silent prayer, if this has not preceded.

Lord,
may this pledge of our eternal salvation
which we receive on this feast of St. N.
be our help now and always.

Grant this through Christ our Lord.

9. For Founders of Churches

Entrance Antiphon

The Lord chose these holy men for their unfeigned love, and gave them eternal glory. The Church has light by their teaching.

Opening Prayer

Lord,
look with love on the church of N.
Through the apostolic zeal of Saints N. and N.
you gave us the beginnings of our faith:
through their prayers keep alive our Christian love.

We ask this through our Lord Jesus Christ, your Son,
who lives and reigns with you and the Holy Spirit,
one God, for ever and ever.

Or:

God,
you called our fathers to the light of the gospel
by the preaching of your bishop N.
By his prayers help us to grow in the love and knowledge
of your Son, our Lord Jesus Christ,
who lives and reigns with you and the Holy Spirit,
one God, for ever and ever.

Liturgy of the Word, *pp. 2188–2218.*

Prayer over the Gifts

Pray, brethren...

Lord,
accept the gifts your people bring
on this feast of Saints N. and N.
Give us purity of heart
and make us pleasing to you.

We ask this through Christ our Lord.

Communion Antiphon

**No longer shall I call you servants, for a servant knows not
what his master does. Now I shall call you friends, for I have
revealed to you all that I have heard from my Father.** (Jn 15:15)

Prayer after Communion

Let us pray.

Pause for silent prayer, if this has not preceded.

Lord,
as we share in your gifts,

we celebrate this feast of Saints N. and N.
We honor the beginnings of our faith
and proclaim your glory in the saints.
May the salvation we receive from your altar
be our unending joy.

Grant this through Christ our Lord.

10. For Missionaries

Entrance Antiphon

These are holy men who became God's friends and glorious heralds of his truth.

Opening Prayer

Father,
through your St. (bishop) N.
you brought those who had no faith
out of darkness into the light of truth.
By the help of his prayers,
keep us strong in our faith
and firm in the hope of the gospel he preached.

Grant this through our Lord Jesus Christ, your Son,
who lives and reigns with you and the Holy Spirit,
one God, for ever and ever.

Or:

All-powerful and ever-living God,
you made this day holy
by welcoming St. N. into the glory of your kingdom.
Keep us true to the faith he professed with untiring zeal,
and help us to bring it to perfection
by acting in love.

We ask this through our Lord Jesus Christ, your Son,
who lives and reigns with you and the Holy Spirit,
one God, for ever and ever.

Liturgy of the Word, *pp. 2188 – 2218.*

Prayer over the Gifts

Pray, brethren...

All-powerful God,
look upon the gifts we bring on this feast
in honor of St. N.
May we who celebrate the mystery of the death of the Lord
imitate the love we celebrate.

We ask this through Christ our Lord.

Communion Antiphon

I will feed my sheep, says the Lord, and give them repose.

(Ez 34:15)

Prayer after Communion

Let us pray.

Pause for silent prayer, if this has not preceded.

Lord,
St. N. worked tirelessly for the faith,
spending his life in its service.
With the power this eucharist gives
make your people strong in the same true faith
and help us to proclaim it everywhere
by all we say and do.

Grant this in the name of Jesus the Lord.

11. For Missionaries

Entrance Antiphon

How beautiful on the mountains are the feet of the man who brings tidings of peace, joy, and salvation. (Is 52:7)

Opening Prayer

Father,
you made your Church grow
through the Christian zeal and apostolic work of St. N.
By the help of his prayers
give your Church continued growth in holiness and faith.

Grant this through our Lord Jesus Christ, your Son,
who lives and reigns with you and the Holy Spirit,
one God, for ever and ever.

Liturgy of the Word, *pp. 2188–2218.*

Prayer over the Gifts

Pray, brethren...

Lord,
be pleased with our prayers
and free us from all guilt.
In your love, wash away our sins
that we may celebrate the mysteries which set us free.

Grant this in the name of Jesus the Lord.

Communion Antiphon

Go out to all the world, and tell the good news: I am with you always, says the Lord. (Mk 16:15; Mt 28:20)

Or:

Live in me and let me live in you, says the Lord; he who lives in me, and I in him, will bear much fruit. (Jn 15:4–5)

Prayer after Communion

Let us pray.

Pause for silent prayer, if this has not preceded.

Lord our God,
by these mysteries help our faith grow to maturity
in the faith the apostles preached and taught, and the faith
    which St. N.
watched over with such care.

We ask this through Christ our Lord.

12. For Missionaries

Entrance Antiphon

**Proclaim his glory among the nations, his marvelous deeds to
all the peoples; great is the Lord and worthy of all praise.**

(Ps 95:3–4)

Opening Prayer

God of mercy,
you gave us St. N. to proclaim the riches of Christ.
by the help of his prayers
may we grow in knowledge of you,
be eager to do good,
and learn to walk before you
by living the truth of the gospel.

Grant this through our Lord Jesus Christ, your Son,
who lives and reigns with you and the Holy Spirit,
one God, for ever and ever.

Or (for martyrs):

All-powerful God,
help us to imitate with steadfast love

the faith of Saints N. and N.
who won the crown of martyrdom
by giving their lives in the service of the gospel.

We ask this through our Lord Jesus Christ, your Son,
who lives and reigns with you and the Holy Spirit,
one God, for ever and ever.

Liturgy of the Word, *pp. 2188–2218.*

Prayer over the Gifts

Pray, brethren...

Lord,
we who honor the memory of St. N.
ask you to send your blessing on these gifts.
By receiving them may we be freed from all guilt
and share in the food from the heavenly table.

We ask this through Christ our Lord.

Communion Antiphon

The Lord sent disciples to proclaim to all the towns: the kingdom of God is very near to you.   (See Lk 10:1, 9)

Prayer after Communion

Let us pray.

Pause for silent prayer, if this has not preceded.

Lord,
let the holy gifts we receive fill us with life
so that we who rejoice in honoring the memory of St. N.
may also benefit from his example of apostolic zeal.

Grant this through Christ our Lord.

Liturgy of the Word: Common of Pastors

READING I   From the Old Testament

Outside the Easter Season

Ex 32:7–14

Then he spoke of exterminating them, but Moses, his chosen one,
withstood him in the breach to turn back his destructive wrath.
(Ps 106:23)

A reading from the Book of Exodus

The LORD said to Moses, "Go down at once to your people, whom you brought out of the land of Egypt, for they have become depraved. They have soon turned aside from the way I pointed out to them, making for themselves a molten calf and worshiping it, sacrificing to it and crying out, 'This is your God, O Israel, who brought you out of the land of Egypt!' I see how stiff-necked this people is," continued the LORD to Moses. "Let me alone, then, that my wrath may blaze up against them to consume them. Then I will make of you a great nation."

But Moses implored the LORD, his God, saying, "Why, O LORD, should your wrath blaze up against your own people, whom you brought out of the land of Egypt with such great power and with so strong a hand? Why should the Egyptians say, 'With evil intent he brought them out, that he might kill them in the mountains and exterminate them from the face of the earth'? Let your blazing wrath die down; relent in punishing your people. Remember your servants Abraham, Isaac, and Israel, and how you swore to them by your own self, saying, 'I will make your descendants as numerous as the stars in the sky; and all this land that I promised, I will give your descendants as their perpetual heritage.'" So the LORD relented in the punishment he had threatened to inflict on his people.

The word of the Lord.

2

Dt 10:8–9

The LORD himself is his heritage.

A reading from the Book of Deuteronomy

Moses summoned all of Israel and said to them: "At that time the LORD set apart the tribe of Levi to carry the ark of the covenant of the LORD, to be in attendance before the LORD and minister to him, and to give blessings in his name, as they have done to this day. For this reason, Levi has no share in the heritage with his brothers; the LORD himself is his heritage, as the LORD, your God, has told him."

The word of the Lord.

3

1 Sm 16:1b, 6–13a

There—anoint him, for this is he!

A reading from the first Book of Samuel

The LORD said to Samuel: "Fill your horn with oil, and be on your way. I am sending you to Jesse of Bethlehem, for I have chosen my king from among his sons."

As Jesse and his sons came to the sacrifice, Samuel looked at Eliab and thought, "Surely the LORD's anointed is here before him." But the LORD said to Samuel: "Do not judge from his appearance or from his lofty stature, because I have rejected him. Not as man sees does God see, because he sees the appearance but the LORD looks into the heart." Then Jesse called Abinadab and presented him before Samuel, who said, "The LORD has not chosen him." Next Jesse presented Shammah, but Samuel said, "The LORD has not chosen this one either." In the same way Jesse presented seven sons before Samuel, but Samuel said to Jesse, "The LORD has not chosen any one of these." Then Samuel asked Jesse, "Are these all the sons you have?" Jesse replied, "There is still the youngest, who is tending the sheep." Samuel said to Jesse, "Send for him; we will not begin the sacrificial banquet until he arrives here." Jesse sent and had the young man brought to them. He was ruddy, a youth handsome to behold and making a splendid appearance. The LORD said, "There—anoint him, for this is he!" Then Samuel, with the horn of oil in hand, anointed him in the midst of his brothers; and from that day on, the spirit of the LORD rushed upon David.

The word of the Lord.

4

Is 6:1–8

Whom shall I send? Who will go for us?

A reading from the Book of the Prophet Isaiah

In the year King Uzziah died, I saw the Lord seated on a high and lofty throne, with the train of his garment filling the temple. Seraphim were stationed above; each of them had six wings with two they veiled their faces, with two they veiled their feet, and with two they hovered aloft.

"Holy, holy, holy is the LORD of hosts!" they cried, one to the other. "All the earth is filled with his glory!" At the sound of that cry, the frame of the door shook and the house was filled with smoke.

Then I said, "Woe is me, I am doomed! For I am a man of unclean lips, living among a people of unclean lips; yet my eyes have seen the King, the Lord of hosts!" Then one of the seraphim flew to me, holding an ember which he had taken with tongs from the altar.

He touched my mouth with it and said, "See, now that this has touched your lips, your wickedness is removed, your sin purged."

Then I heard the voice of the Lord saying, "Whom shall I send? Who will go for us?" "Here I am," I said; "send me!"
The word of the Lord.

FOR MISSIONARIES

5   Is 52:7–10

All the ends of the earth will behold the salvation of our God.

A reading from the Book of the Prophet Isaiah

How beautiful upon the mountains
    are the feet of him who brings glad tidings,
Announcing peace, bearing good news,
    announcing salvation, and saying to Zion,
    "Your God is King!"
Hark! Your sentinels raise a cry,
    together they shout for joy,
For they see directly, before their eyes,
    the Lord restoring Zion.
Break out together in song,
    O ruins of Jerusalem!
For the Lord comforts his people,
    he redeems Jerusalem.
The Lord has bared his holy arm

in the sight of all the nations;
All the ends of the earth will behold
the salvation of our God.

The word of the Lord.

6   Is 61:1–3abcd

The LORD has anointed me;
he has sent me to bring glad tidings to the lowly.

A reading from the Book of the Prophet Isaiah

The spirit of the Lord GOD is upon me,
because the LORD has anointed me;
He has sent me to bring glad tidings to the lowly,
to heal the brokenhearted,
To proclaim liberty to the captives
and release to the prisoners,
To announce a year of favor from the LORD
and a day of vindication by our God,
to comfort all who mourn;
To place on those who mourn in Zion
a diadem instead of ashes,
To give them oil of gladness in place of mourning,
a glorious mantle instead of a listless spirit.

The word of the Lord.

7   Jer 1:4–9

To whomever I send you, you shall go.

A reading from the Book of the Prophet Jeremiah

The word of the LORD came to me thus:

Before I formed you in the womb I knew you,
before you were born I dedicated you,

a prophet to the nations I appointed you.

"Ah, Lord, GOD!" I said,

"I know not how to speak; I am too young."

But the LORD answered me,

Say not, "I am too young."

To whomever I send you, you shall go;

whatever I command you, you shall speak.

Have no fear before them,

because I am with you to deliver you, says the LORD.

Then the LORD extended his hand and touched my mouth, saying,

See, I place my words in your mouth!

The word of the Lord.

8

Ez 3:17–21

I have appointed you a watchman for the house of Israel.

A reading from the Book of the Prophet Ezekiel

The word of the LORD came to me: Son of man, I have appointed you a watchman for the house of Israel. When you hear a word from my mouth, you shall warn them for me.

If I say to the wicked man, You shall surely die; and you do not warn him or speak out to dissuade him from his wicked conduct so that he may live: the wicked man shall die for his sin, but I will hold you responsible for his death. If, on the other hand, you have warned the wicked man, yet he has not turned away from his evil nor from his wicked conduct, then he shall die for his sin, but you shall save your life.

If a virtuous man turns away from virtue and does wrong when I place a stumbling block before him, he shall die. He shall die for his sin, and his virtuous deeds shall not be remembered; but I will hold you responsible for his death if you did not warn him. When, on the other hand, you have warned a virtuous man not to sin, and he has in fact not sinned, he shall surely live because of the warning, and you shall save your own life.

The word of the Lord.

Ez 34:11–16

As a shepherd tends his flock, so will I tend my sheep.

A reading from the Book of the Prophet Ezekiel

Thus says the Lord GOD: I myself will look after and tend my sheep. As a shepherd tends his flock when he finds himself among his scattered sheep, so will I tend my sheep. I will rescue them from every place where they were scattered when it was cloudy and dark. I will lead them out from among the peoples and gather them from the foreign lands; I will bring them back to their own country and pasture them upon the mountains of Israel in the land's ravines and all its inhabited places. In good pastures will I pasture them, and on the mountain heights of Israel shall be their grazing ground. There they shall lie down on good grazing ground, and in rich pastures shall they be pastured on the mountains of Israel. I myself will pasture my sheep; I myself will give them rest, says the Lord GOD. The lost I will seek out, the strayed I will bring back, the injured I will bind up, the sick I will heal, but the sleek and the strong I will destroy, shepherding them rightly.

The word of the Lord.

READING I   From the New Testament

During the Easter Season

FOR MISSIONARIES

1

Acts 13:46 – 49

We now turn to the Gentiles.

A reading from the Acts of the Apostles

Paul and Barnabas spoke out boldly and said, "It was necessary that the word of God be spoken to you first, but since you reject it and condemn yourselves as unworthy of eternal life, we now turn to the Gentiles. For so the Lord has commanded us, *I have made you a light to the Gentiles, that you may be an instrument of salvation to the ends of the earth.*"

The Gentiles were delighted when they heard this and glorified the word of the Lord. All who were destined for eternal life came to believe, and the word of the Lord continued to spread through the whole region.

The word of the Lord.

2

Acts 20:17–18a, 28–32, 36

Keep watch over yourselves and over the whole flock
of which the Holy Spirit has appointed you overseers,
in which you tend the Church of God.

A reading from the Acts of the Apostles

From Miletus Paul had the presbyters of the Church at Ephesus summoned. When they came to him, he addressed them, "Keep watch over yourselves and over the whole flock of which the Holy Spirit has appointed you overseers, in which you tend the Church of God that he acquired with his own Blood. I know that after my departure savage wolves will come among you, and they will not spare the flock. And from your own group, men will come forward perverting the truth to draw the disciples away after them. So be vigilant and remember that for three years, night and day, I unceasingly admonished each of you with tears. And now I commend you to God and to that gracious word of his that can build you up and give you the inheritance among all who are consecrated."

When he had finished speaking he knelt down and prayed with them all.

The word of the Lord.

FOR MISSIONARIES

3   Acts 26:19–23

He would proclaim light both to our people and to the Gentiles.

A reading from the Acts of the Apostles

Paul said: "King Agrippa, I was not disobedient to the heavenly vision. On the contrary, first to those in Damascus and in Jerusalem and throughout the whole country of Judea, and then to the Gentiles, I preached the need to repent and turn to God, and to do works giving evidence of repentance. That is why the Jews seized me when I was in the temple and tried to kill me. But I have enjoyed God's help to this very day, and so I stand here testifying to small and great alike, saying nothing different from what the prophets and Moses foretold, that the Christ must suffer and that, as the first to rise from the dead, he would proclaim light both to our people and to the Gentiles."

The word of the Lord.

Responsorial Psalm

Ps 16:1–2a and 5, 7–8, 11

R. You are my inheritance, O Lord.

Keep me, O God, for in you I take refuge;
  I say to the LORD, "My Lord are you."
O LORD, my allotted portion and my cup,
  you it is who hold fast my lot.

R. You are my inheritance, O Lord.

I bless the LORD who counsels me;
  even in the night my heart exhorts me.
I set the LORD ever before me;
  with him at my right hand I shall not be disturbed.

R. You are my inheritance, O Lord.

You will show me the path to life,
  fullness of joys in your presence,
  the delights at your right hand forever.

R. You are my inheritance, O Lord.

2

Ps 23:1–3a, 4, 5, 6

R. The Lord is my shepherd; there is nothing I shall want.

The LORD is my shepherd; I shall not want.
  In verdant pastures he gives me repose;
Beside restful waters he leads me;
  he refreshes my soul.

R. The Lord is my shepherd; there is nothing I shall want.

Even though I walk in the dark valley
  I fear no evil; for you are at my side
With your rod and your staff
  that give me courage.

R. The Lord is my shepherd; there is nothing I shall want.

You spread the table before me
  in the sight of my foes;
You anoint my head with oil;
  my cup overflows.

R. The Lord is my shepherd; there is nothing I shall want.

Only goodness and kindness follow me
  all the days of my life;
And I shall dwell in the house of the LORD
  for years to come.

R. The Lord is my shepherd; there is nothing I shall want.

3   Ps 40:2 and 4, 7–8a, 8b–9, 10

R. Here I am, Lord; I come to do your will.

I have waited, waited for the LORD,
  and he stooped toward me and heard my cry.
And he put a new song into my mouth,
  a hymn to our God.

R. Here I am, Lord; I come to do your will.

Sacrifice or offering you wished not,
  but ears open to obedience you gave me.
Burnt offerings or sin-offerings you sought not;
  then said I, "Behold I come."

R. Here I am, Lord; I come to do your will.

"In the written scroll it is prescribed for me,
To do your will, O my God, is my delight,
  and your law is within my heart!"

R. Here I am, Lord; I come to do your will.

I announced your justice in the vast assembly;
  I did not restrain my lips, as you, O LORD, know.

R. Here I am, Lord; I come to do your will.

4

Ps 89:2–3, 4–5, 21–22, 25 and 27

R. For ever I will sing the goodness of the Lord.

The favors of the LORD I will sing forever;
  through all generations my mouth
  shall proclaim your faithfulness.
For you have said, "My kindness is established forever";
  in heaven you have confirmed your faithfulness.

R. For ever I will sing the goodness of the Lord.

"I have made a covenant with my chosen one,
  I have sworn to David my servant:
Forever will I confirm your posterity
  and establish your throne for all generations."

R. For ever I will sing the goodness of the Lord.

"I have found David, my servant;
  with my holy oil I have anointed him,
That my hand may be always with him,
  and that my arm may make him strong."

R. For ever I will sing the goodness of the Lord.

"My faithfulness and my mercy shall be with him,
  and through my name shall his horn be exalted.
He shall say of me, 'You are my father,
  my God, the Rock, my savior.'"

R. For ever I will sing the goodness of the Lord.

5

Ps 96:1–2a, 2b–3, 7–8a, 10

R. Proclaim God's marvelous deeds to all the nations.

Sing to the LORD a new song;
  sing to the LORD, all you lands.
Sing to the LORD; bless his name.

R. Proclaim God's marvelous deeds to all the nations.

Announce his salvation, day after day.
Tell his glory among the nations;
   among all peoples, his wondrous deeds.

R. Proclaim God's marvelous deeds to all the nations.

Give to the LORD, you families of nations,
   give to the LORD glory and praise;
   give to the LORD the glory due his name!

R. Proclaim God's marvelous deeds to all the nations.

Say among the nations: The LORD is king.
He has made the world firm, not to be moved;
   he governs the peoples with equity.

R. Proclaim God's marvelous deeds to all the nations.

6
                        Ps 106:19–20, 21–22, 23

R. Remember us, O Lord, as you favor your people.

Our fathers made a calf in Horeb
   and adored a molten image;
They exchanged their glory
   for the image of a grass-eating bullock.

R. Remember us, O Lord, as you favor your people.

They forgot the God who had saved them,
   who had done great deeds in Egypt,
Wondrous deeds in the land of Ham,
   terrible things at the Red Sea.

R. Remember us, O Lord, as you favor your people.

Then he spoke of exterminating them,
   but Moses, his chosen one,
Withstood him in the breach
   to turn back his destructive wrath.

R. Remember us, O Lord, as you favor your people.

7

Ps 110:1, 2, 3, 4

> **R. You are a priest for ever, in the line of Melchizedek.**

The LORD said to my Lord: "Sit at my right hand
   till I make your enemies your footstool."

> **R. You are a priest for ever, in the line of Melchizedek.**

The scepter of your power the LORD will stretch forth from Zion:
   "Rule in the midst of your enemies."

> **R. You are a priest for ever, in the line of Melchizedek.**

"Yours is princely power in the day of your birth, in holy splendor;
   before the daystar, like the dew, I have begotten you."

> **R. You are a priest for ever, in the line of Melchizedek.**

The LORD has sworn, and he will not repent:
   "You are a priest forever, according to the order of Melchizedek."

> **R. You are a priest for ever, in the line of Melchizedek.**

8

Ps 117:1bc, 2

> **R. Go out to all the world and tell the Good News.**

Praise the LORD, all you nations;
   glorify him, all you peoples!

> **R. Go out to all the world, and tell the Good News.**

For steadfast is his kindness toward us,
   and the fidelity of the LORD endures forever.

> **R. Go out to all the world, and tell the Good News.**

> *Or:* **R. Alleluia.**

READING II   From the New Testament

1

Rom 12:3–13

Since we have gifts that differ
according to the grace given to us.

A reading from the Letter of Saint Paul to the Romans

Brothers and sisters:

By the grace given to me I tell everyone among you not to think of himself more highly than one ought to think, but to think soberly, each according to the measure of faith that God has apportioned. For as in one body we have many parts, and all the parts do not have the same function, so we, though many, are one Body in Christ and individually parts of one another. Since we have gifts that differ according to the grace given to us, let us exercise them: if prophecy, in proportion to the faith; if ministry, in ministering; if one is a teacher, in teaching; if one exhorts, in exhortation; if one contributes, in generosity; if one is over others, with diligence; if one does acts of mercy, with cheerfulness.

Let love be sincere; hate what is evil, hold on to what is good; love one another with mutual affection; anticipate one another in showing honor. Do not grow slack in zeal, be fervent in spirit, serve the Lord. Rejoice in hope, endure in affliction, persevere in prayer. Contribute to the needs of the holy ones, exercise hospitality.

The word of the Lord.

FOR MISSIONARIES

2

1 Cor 1:18–25

It was the will of God through the foolishness
of the proclamation to save those who have faith.

A reading from the first Letter of Saint Paul to the Corinthians

Brothers and sisters:

The message of the cross is foolishness to those who are perishing, but to us who are being saved it is the power of God. For it is written:

> *I will destroy the wisdom of the wise,*
> *and the learning of the learned I will set aside.*

Where is the wise one? Where is the scribe? Where is the debater of this age? Has not God made the wisdom of the world foolish? For since in the wisdom of God the world did not come to know God through wisdom, it was the will of God through the foolishness of the proclamation to save those who have faith. For Jews demand signs and Greeks look for wisdom, but we proclaim Christ crucified, a stumbling block to Jews and foolishness to Gentiles, but to those who are called, Jews and Greeks alike, Christ the power of God and the wisdom of God. For the foolishness of God is wiser than human wisdom, and the weakness of God is stronger than human strength.

The word of the Lord.

3

1 Cor 4:1–5

Thus should one regard us: as servants of Christ
and stewards of the mysteries of God.

A reading from the first Letter of Saint Paul to the Corinthians

Brothers and sisters:

Thus should one regard us: as servants of Christ and stewards of the mysteries of God. Now it is of course required of stewards that they be found trustworthy. It does not concern me in the least that I be judged by you or any human tribunal; I do not even pass judgment on myself; I am not conscious of anything against me, but I do not thereby stand acquitted; the one who judges me is the Lord. Therefore do not make any judgment before the appointed time, until the Lord comes, for he will bring to light what is hidden in darkness and will manifest the motives of our hearts, and then everyone will receive praise from God.

The word of the Lord.

4

1 Cor 9:16–19, 22–23

Woe to me if I do not preach it!

A reading from the first Letter of Saint Paul to the Corinthians

Brothers and sisters:

If I preach the Gospel, this is no reason for me to boast, for an obligation has been imposed on me, and woe to me if I do not preach it! If I do so willingly, I have a recompense, but if unwillingly, then I have been entrusted with a stewardship. What then is my recompense? That, when I preach, I offer the Gospel free of charge so as not to make full use of my right in the Gospel.

Although I am free in regard to all, I have made myself a slave to all so as to win over as many as possible. To the weak I became weak, to win over the weak. I have become all things to all, to save at least some. All this I do for the sake of the Gospel, so that I too may have a share in it.

The word of the Lord.

5

2 Cor 3:1–6a

He has indeed qualified us as
ministers of a new covenant.

A reading from the second Letter of Saint Paul to the Corinthians

Brothers and sisters:

Are we beginning to commend ourselves again? Do we need, as some do, letters of recommendation to you or from you? You are our letter, written on our hearts, known and read by all, shown to be a letter of Christ administered by us, written not in ink but by the Spirit of the living God, not on tablets of stone but on tablets that are hearts of flesh.

Such confidence we have through Christ toward God. Not that of ourselves we are qualified to take credit for anything as coming from us; rather, our qualification comes from God, who has indeed qualified us as ministers of a new covenant, not of letter but of spirit.

The word of the Lord.

6

2 Cor 4:1–2, 5–7

We preach Jesus Christ as Lord,
and ourselves as your slaves for the sake of Jesus.

A reading from the second Letter of Saint Paul to the Corinthians

Brothers and sisters:

Since we have this ministry through the mercy shown us, we are not discouraged. Rather, we have renounced shameful, hidden things; not acting deceitfully or falsifying the word of God, but by the open declaration of the truth we commend ourselves to everyone's conscience in the sight of God. For we do not preach ourselves but Jesus Christ as Lord, and ourselves as your slaves for the sake of Jesus. For God who said, *Let light shine out of darkness,* has shone in our hearts to bring to light the knowledge of the glory of God on the face of Jesus Christ.

But we hold this treasure in earthen vessels, that the surpassing power may be of God and not from us.

The word of the Lord.

7   2 Cor 5:14–20

He gave us the ministry of reconciliation.

A reading from the second Letter of Saint Paul to the Corinthians

Brothers and sisters:

The love of Christ impels us, once we have come to the conviction that one died for all; therefore, all have died. He indeed died for all, so that those who live might no longer live for themselves but for him who for their sake died and was raised.

Consequently, from now on we regard no one according to the flesh; even if we once knew Christ according to the flesh, yet now we know him so no longer. So whoever is in Christ is a new creation: the old things have passed away; behold, new things have come. And all this is from God, who has reconciled us to himself through Christ and given us the ministry of reconciliation, namely, God was reconciling the world to himself in Christ, not counting their trespasses against them and entrusting to us the message of reconciliation. So we are ambassadors for Christ, as if God were appealing through us. We implore you on behalf of Christ, be reconciled to God.

The word of the Lord.

8

Eph 4:1–7, 11–13

In the work of ministry, in building up the Body of Christ.

A reading from the Letter of Saint Paul to the Ephesians

Brothers and sisters, I, a prisoner for the Lord, urge you to live in a manner worthy of the call you have received, with all humility and gentleness, with patience, bearing with one another through love, striving to preserve the unity of the spirit through the bond of peace: one Body and one Spirit, as you were also called to the one hope of your call; one Lord, one faith, one baptism; one God and Father of all, who is over all and through all and in all.

But grace was given to each of us according to the measure of Christ's gift.

And he gave some as Apostles, others as prophets, others as evangelists, others as pastors and teachers, to equip the holy ones for the work of ministry, for building up the Body of Christ, until we all attain to the unity of faith and knowledge of the Son of God, to mature to manhood, to the extent of the full stature of Christ.

The word of the Lord.

9

Col 1:24–29

On behalf of his Body, which is the Church, of which I am a minister in accordance with God's stewardship given to me to bring to completion for you the word of God.

A reading from the Letter of Saint Paul to the Colossians

Brothers and sisters:

I rejoice in my sufferings for your sake, and in my flesh I am filling up what is lacking in the afflictions of Christ on behalf of his Body, which is the Church, of which I am a minister in accordance with God's stewardship given to me to bring to completion for you the word of God, the mystery hidden from ages and from generations past. But now it has been manifested to his holy ones, to whom God chose to make known the riches of the glory of this mystery among the Gentiles; it is Christ in you, the hope for glory. It is he whom we proclaim, admonishing everyone and teaching everyone with all wisdom, that we may present everyone perfect in Christ. For this I labor and struggle, in accord with the exercise of his power working within me.

The word of the Lord.

10   1 Thes 2:2b–8

We were determined to share with you not only the Gospel of God but our very selves as well.

A reading from the first Letter of Saint Paul to the Thessalonians

Brothers and sisters:

We drew courage through our God to speak to you the Gospel of God with much struggle. Our exhortation was not from delusion or impure motives, nor did it work through deception. But as we were judged worthy by God to be entrusted with the Gospel, that is how we speak, not as trying to please men, but rather God, who judges our hearts. Nor, indeed, did we ever appear with flattering speech, as you know, or with a pretext for greed—God is witness—nor did we seek praise from men, either from you or from others, although we were able to impose our weight as Apostles of Christ. Rather, we were gentle among you, as a nursing mother cares for her children. With such affection for you, we were determined to share with you not only the Gospel of God, but our very selves as well, so dearly beloved had you become to us.

The word of the Lord.

11

2 Tm 1:13–14; 2:1–3

Guard this rich trust with the help of the
Holy Spirit who dwells within us.

A reading from the second Letter of Saint Paul to Timothy

Beloved:

Take as your norm the sound words that you heard from me, in the faith and love that are in Christ Jesus. Guard this rich trust with the help of the Holy Spirit who dwells within us. So you, my child, be strong in the grace that is in Christ Jesus. And what you heard from me through many witnesses entrust to faithful people who will have the ability to teach others as well. Bear your share of hardship along with me like a good soldier of Christ Jesus.

The word of the Lord.

12

2 Tm 4:1–5

Perform the work of an evangelist, fulfill your ministry.

A reading from the second Letter of Saint Paul to Timothy

Beloved:

I charge you in the presence of God and of Christ Jesus, who will judge the living and the dead, and by his appearing and his kingly power: proclaim the word; be persistent whether it is convenient or inconvenient; convince, reprimand, encourage through all patience and teaching. For the time will come when people will not tolerate sound doctrine but, following their own desires and insatiable curiosity, will accumulate teachers and will stop listening to the truth and will be diverted to myths. But you, be self-possessed in all circumstances; put up with hardship; perform the work of an evangelist; fulfill your ministry.

The word of the Lord.

13   1 Pt 5:1–4

Tend the flock of God in your midst.

A reading from the first Letter of Saint Peter

Beloved:

I exhort the presbyters among you, as a fellow presbyter and witness to the sufferings of Christ and one who has a share in the glory to be revealed. Tend the flock of God in your midst, overseeing it not by constraint but willingly, as God would have it, not for shameful profit but eagerly. Do not lord it over those assigned to you, but be examples to the flock. And when the chief Shepherd is revealed, you will receive the unfading crown of glory.

The word of the Lord.

ALLELUIA VERSE AND VERSE BEFORE THE GOSPEL

1 Mt 23:9b, 10b
You have but one Father in heaven;
you have but one master, the Christ!

2 Mt 28:19a, 20bc
Go, and teach all nations, says the Lord;
I am with you always, until the end of the world.

3 Mk 1:17
Come after me, says the Lord,
and I will make you fishers of men.

4 Lk 4:18

The Lord sent me to bring glad tidings to the poor
and to proclaim liberty to captives.

5 Jn 10:14

I am the good shepherd, says the Lord;
I know my sheep, and mine know me.

6 Jn 15:5

I am the vine, you are the branches, says the Lord:
whoever remains in me and I in him will bear much fruit.

7 Jn 15:15b

I call you my friends, says the Lord,
for I have made known to you
    all that the Father has told me.

8 2 Cor 5:19

God was reconciling the world to himself in Christ,
and entrusting to us the message of reconciliation.

GOSPEL

1

Mt 9:35–38

The harvest is abundant but the laborers are few.

A reading from the holy Gospel according to Matthew

Jesus went around to all the towns and villages, teaching in
their synagogues, proclaiming the Gospel of the Kingdom, and
curing every disease and illness. At the sight of the crowds,
his heart was moved with pity for them because they were
troubled and abandoned, like sheep without a shepherd. Then
he said to his disciples, "The harvest is abundant but the laborers
are few; so ask the master of the harvest to send out laborers
for his harvest."

The Gospel of the Lord.

FOR A POPE

2

Mt 16:13–19

You are Peter, and upon this rock I will build my Church.

A reading from the holy Gospel according to Matthew

Jesus went into the region of Caesarea Philippi and he asked his disciples, "Who do people say that the Son of Man is?" They replied, "Some say John the Baptist, others Elijah, still others Jeremiah or one of the prophets." He said to them, "But who do you say that I am?" Simon Peter said in reply, "You are the Christ, the Son of the living God." Jesus said to him in reply, "Blessed are you, Simon son of Jonah. For flesh and blood has not revealed this to you, but my heavenly Father. And so I say to you, you are Peter, and upon this rock I will build my Church, and the gates of the netherworld shall not prevail against it. I will give you the keys to the Kingdom of heaven. Whatever you bind on earth shall be bound in heaven; and whatever you loose on earth shall be loosed in heaven."

The Gospel of the Lord.

3

Mt 23:8 –12

The greatest among you must be your servant.

A reading from the holy Gospel according to Matthew

Jesus spoke to his disciples: "Do not be called 'Rabbi.' You have but one teacher, and you are all brothers. Call no one on earth your father; you have but one Father in heaven. Do not be called 'Master'; you have but one master, the Christ. The greatest among you must be your servant. Whoever exalts himself will be humbled; but whoever humbles himself will be exalted."

The Gospel of the Lord.

FOR MISSIONARIES

4

Mt 28:16–20

Go, therefore, and make disciples of all nations.

A reading from the holy Gospel according to Matthew

The Eleven disciples went to Galilee, to the mountain to which Jesus had ordered them. When they saw him, they worshiped, but they doubted. Then Jesus approached and said to them, "All power in heaven and on earth has been given to me. Go, therefore, and make disciples of all nations, baptizing them in the name of the Father, and of the Son, and of the Holy Spirit, teaching them to observe all that I have commanded you. And behold, I am with you always, until the end of the age."

The Gospel of the Lord.

5

Mk 1:14–20

I will make you fishers of men.

A reading from the holy Gospel according to Mark

After John had been arrested, Jesus came to Galilee proclaiming the Gospel of God: "This is the time of fulfillment. The Kingdom of God is at hand. Repent, and believe in the Gospel."

As he passed by the Sea of Galilee, he saw Simon and his brother Andrew casting their nets into the sea; they were fishermen. Jesus said to them, "Come after me, and I will make you fishers of men." Then they abandoned their nets and followed him. He walked along a little farther and saw James, the son of Zebedee, and his brother John. They too were in a boat mending their nets. Then he called them. So they left their father Zebedee in the boat along with the hired men and followed him.

The Gospel of the Lord.

FOR MISSIONARIES

6

Mk 16:15–20

*Go into the whole world and
proclaim the Gospel to every creature.*

A reading from the holy Gospel according to Mark

Jesus appeared to the Eleven and said to them: "Go into the whole world and proclaim the Gospel to every creature. Whoever believes and is baptized will be saved; whoever does not believe will be condemned. These signs will accompany those who believe: in my name they will drive out demons, they will speak new languages. They will pick up serpents with their hands, and if they drink any deadly thing, it will not harm them. They will lay hands on the sick, and they will recover."

So then the Lord Jesus, after he spoke to them, was taken up into heaven and took his seat at the right hand of God. But they went forth and preached everywhere, while the Lord worked with them and confirmed the word through accompanying signs.

The Gospel of the Lord.

FOR MISSIONARIES

7

Lk 5:1–11

At your command I will lower the nets.

A reading from the holy Gospel according to Luke

While the crowd was pressing in on Jesus and listening to the word of God, he was standing by the Lake of Gennesaret. He saw two boats there alongside the lake; the fishermen had disembarked and were washing their nets. Getting into one of them, the one belonging to Simon, he asked him to put out a short distance from the shore. Then he sat down and taught the crowds from the boat. After he had finished speaking, he said to Simon, "Put out into deep water and lower your nets for a catch." Simon said in reply, "Master, we have worked hard all night and have caught nothing, but at your command I will lower the nets." When they had done this, they caught a great number of fish and their nets were tearing. They signaled to their partners in the other boat to come to help them. They came and filled both boats so that the boats were in danger of sinking. When Simon Peter saw this, he fell at the knees of Jesus and said, "Depart from me, Lord, for I am a sinful man." For astonishment at the catch of fish they had made seized him and all those with him, and likewise James and John, the sons of Zebedee, who were partners of Simon. Jesus said to Simon, "Do not be afraid; from now on you will be catching men." When they brought their boats to the shore, they left everything and followed him.

The Gospel of the Lord.

8

Lk 10:1–9

The harvest is abundant but the laborers are few.

A reading from the holy Gospel according to Luke

The Lord Jesus appointed seventy-two disciples whom he sent ahead of him in pairs to every town and place he intended to visit. He said to them, "The harvest is abundant but the laborers are few; so ask the master of the harvest to send out laborers for his harvest. Go on your way; behold, I am sending you like lambs among wolves. Carry no money bag, no sack, no sandals; and greet no one along the way. Into whatever house you enter, first say, 'Peace to this household.' If a peaceful person lives there, your peace will rest on him; but if not, it will return to you. Stay in the same house and eat and drink what is offered to you, for the laborer deserves his payment. Do not move about from one house to another. Whatever town you enter and they welcome you, eat what is set before you, cure the sick in it and say to them, 'The Kingdom of God is at hand for you.'"

The Gospel of the Lord.

9   Lk 22:24–30

I confer a kingdom on you,
just as my Father has conferred one on me.

A reading from the holy Gospel according to Luke

An argument broke out among the Apostles about which of them should be regarded as the greatest. Jesus said to them, "The kings of the Gentiles lord it over them and those in author-ity over them are addressed as 'Benefactors'; but among you it shall not be so. Rather, let the greatest among you be as the youngest, and the leader as the servant. For who is greater: the one seated at table or the one who serves? Is it not the one seated at table? I am among you as the one who serves. It is you who have stood by me in my trials; and I confer a king-dom on you, just as my Father has conferred one on me, that you may eat and drink at my table in my Kingdom; and you will sit on thrones judging the twelve tribes of Israel."

The Gospel of the Lord.

10

Jn 10:11–16

A good shepherd lays down his life for the sheep.

A reading from the holy Gospel according to John

Jesus said: "I am the good shepherd. A good shepherd lays down his life for the sheep. A hired man, who is not a shepherd and whose sheep are not his own, sees a wolf coming and leaves the sheep and runs away, and the wolf catches and scatters them. This is because he works for pay and has no concern for the sheep. I am the good shepherd, and I know mine and mine know me, just as the Father knows me and I know the Father; and I will lay down my life for the sheep. I have other sheep that do not belong to this fold. These also I must lead, and they will hear my voice, and there will be one flock, one shepherd."

The Gospel of the Lord.

11

Jn 15:9–17

I no longer call you slaves; I have called you friends.

A reading from the holy Gospel according to John

Jesus said to his disciples: "As the Father loves me, so I also love you. Remain in my love. If you keep my commandments, you will remain in my love, just as I have kept my Father's commandments and remain in his love.

"I have told you this so that my joy might be in you and your joy might be complete. This is my commandment: love one another as I love you. No one has greater love than this, to lay down one's life for one's friends. You are my friends if you do what I command you. I no longer call you slaves, because a slave does not know what his master is doing. I have called you friends, because I have told you everything I have heard from my Father. It was not you who chose me, but I who chose you and appointed you to go and bear fruit that will remain, so that whatever you ask the Father in my name he may give you. This I command you: love one another."

The Gospel of the Lord.

FOR A POPE

12 Jn 21:15–17

Feed my lambs, feed my sheep.

A reading from the holy Gospel according to John

After Jesus had revealed himself to his disciples and eaten breakfast with them, he said to Simon Peter, "Simon, son of John, do you love me more than these?" Simon Peter answered him, "Yes, Lord, you know that I love you." Jesus said to him, "Feed my lambs." He then said to Simon Peter a second time, "Simon, son of John, do you love me?" Simon Peter answered him, "Yes, Lord, you know that I love you." He said to him, "Tend my sheep." He said to him the third time, "Simon, son of John, do you love me?" Peter was distressed that he had said to him a third time, "Do you love me?" and he said to him, "Lord, you know everything; you know that I love you." Jesus said to him, "Feed my sheep."

The Gospel of the Lord.

COMMON OF DOCTORS
OF THE CHURCH

1. Common of Doctors of the Church

Entrance Antiphon

The Lord opened his mouth in the assembly, and filled him with the spirit of wisdom and understanding, and clothed him in a robe of glory. (Sir 15:5)

Or:

The mouth of the just man utters wisdom, and his tongue speaks what is right; the law of his God is in his heart. (Ps 36:30–31)

Opening Prayer

God our Father,
you made your St. (bishop) N. a teacher in your Church.
By the power of the Holy Spirit
establish his teaching in our hearts.
As you give him to us as a patron,
may we have the protection of his prayers.

Grant this through our Lord Jesus Christ, your Son,
who lives and reigns with you and the Holy Spirit,
one God, for ever and ever.

Liturgy of the Word, *pp. 2222–2238.*

Prayer over the Gifts

Pray, brethren…
Lord,
accept our sacrifice on this feast of St. N.,
and following his example

may we give you our praise
and offer you all we have.

Grant this in the name of Jesus the Lord.

Communion Antiphon

**The Lord has put his faithful servant in charge of his house-
hold, to give them their share of bread at the proper time.**

(Lk 12:42)

Prayer after Communion

Let us pray.

Pause for silent prayer, if this has not preceded.

God our Father,
Christ the living bread renews us.
Let Christ our teacher instruct us
that on this feast of St. N.
we may learn your truth
and practice it in love.

We ask this through Christ our Lord.

2. Common of Doctors of the Church

Entrance Antiphon

**The learned will shine like the brilliance of the firmament, and
those who train many in the ways of justice will sparkle like the
stars for all eternity.**

(Dn 12:3)

Or:

**Let the peoples declare the wisdom of the saints and the Church
proclaim their praises; their names shall live for ever.**

(See Sir 44:15, 14)

Opening Prayer

Lord God,
you filled St. N. with heavenly wisdom.
By his (her) help may we remain true to his (her) teaching
and put it into practice.

We ask this through our Lord Jesus Christ, your Son,
who lives and reigns with you and the Holy Spirit,
one God, for ever and ever.

Liturgy of the Word, *pp. 2222–2238.*

Prayer over the Gifts

Pray, brethren...

Lord,
by this celebration,
may your Spirit fill us with the same light of faith
that shines in the teaching of St. N.

We ask this through Christ our Lord.

Communion Antiphon

**We preach a Christ who was crucified; he is the power and the
wisdom of God.**   (1 Cor 1:23–24)

Prayer after Communion

Let us pray.

Pause for silent prayer, if this has not preceded.

Lord,
you renew us with the food of heaven.
May St. N. remain our teacher and example
and keep us thankful for all we have received.

Grant this in the name of Jesus the Lord.

Liturgy of the Word: Common of Doctors of the Church

READING I   From the Old Testament

FIRST OPTION

1 Kgs 3:11–14

I give you a wise and understanding heart.

A reading from the first Book of Kings

The LORD said to Solomon: "Because you have asked for this—not for a long life for yourself, nor for riches, nor for the life of your enemies, but for understanding so that you may know what is right—I do as you requested. I give you a heart so wise and understanding that there has never been anyone like you up to now, and after you there will come no one to equal you. In addition, I give you what you have not asked for, such riches and glory that among kings there is not your like. And if you follow me by keeping my statutes and commandments, as your father David did, I will give you a long life."

The word of the Lord.

SECOND OPTION

Wis 7:7–10, 15–16

Beyond health and comeliness I loved her.

A reading from the Book of Wisdom

I prayed, and prudence was given me;
    I pleaded, and the spirit of wisdom came to me.
I preferred her to scepter and throne,
And deemed riches nothing in comparison with her,
    nor did I liken any priceless gem to her;
Because all gold, in view of her, is a little sand,
    and before her, silver is to be accounted mire.

Beyond health and comeliness I loved her,
And I chose to have her rather than the light,
 because the splendor of her never yields to sleep.
Now God grant I speak suitably
 and value these endowments at their worth:
For he is the guide of Wisdom
 and the director of the wise.
For both we and our words are in his hand,
 as well as all prudence and knowledge of crafts.
The word of the Lord.

THIRD OPTION   Sir 15:1–6

 She will fill him with the spirit of wisdom and understanding.

A reading from the Book of Sirach

He who fears the LORD will do this;
 he who is practiced in the law will come to wisdom.
Motherlike she will meet him,
 like a young bride she will embrace him,
Nourish him with the bread of understanding,
 and give him the water of learning to drink.
He will lean upon her and not fall,
 he will trust in her and not be put to shame.
She will exalt him above his fellows;
 and in the midst of the assembly she will open his mouth
 and fill him with the spirit of wisdom and understanding,
 and clothe him with the robe of glory.
Joy and gladness he will find,
 an everlasting name he will inherit.
The word of the Lord.

Fourth Option

Sir 39:6e–10

He who studies the law of the Most High
will be filled with the spirit of understanding.

A reading from the Book of Sirach

If it pleases the LORD Almighty,
  he who studies the law of the Most High
  will be filled with the spirit of understanding;
He will pour forth his words of wisdom
  and in prayer give thanks to the LORD,
Who will direct his knowledge and his counsel,
  as he meditates upon his mysteries.
He will show the wisdom of what he has learned
  and glory in the law of the LORD's covenant.
Many will praise his understanding;
  his fame can never be effaced;
Unfading will be his memory,
  through all generations his name will live;
Peoples will speak of his wisdom,
  and in assembly sing his praises.

The word of the Lord.

READING I   From the New Testament

During the Easter Season

First Option

Acts 2:14a, 22–24, 32–36

God has made him both Lord and Christ.

A reading from the Acts of the Apostles

On the day of Pentecost, Peter stood up with the Eleven, raised
his voice, and proclaimed to them:

"You who are children of Israel, hear these words. Jesus the Nazorean was a man commended to you by God with mighty deeds, wonders, and signs, which God worked through him in your midst, as you yourselves know. This man, delivered up by the set plan and foreknowledge of God, you killed, using lawless men to crucify him. But God raised him up, releasing him from the throes of death, because it was impossible for him to be held by it.

"God raised this Jesus; of this we are all witnesses. Exalted at the right hand of God, he received the promise of the Holy Spirit from the Father and poured it forth, as you both see and hear. For David did not go up into heaven, but he himself said:

The Lord said to my Lord,
'Sit at my right hand
until I make your enemies your footstool.'

Therefore let the whole house of Israel know for certain that God has made him both Lord and Christ, this Jesus whom you crucified."

The word of the Lord.

SECOND OPTION

Acts 13:26–33

What God promised to our fathers he has brought to
fulfillment by raising up Jesus.

A reading from the Acts of the Apostles

When Paul came to Antioch in Pisidia, he said in the synagogue: "My brothers, sons of the family of Abraham, and those others among you who are God-fearing, to us this word of salvation has been sent. The inhabitants of Jerusalem and their leaders failed to recognize him, and by condemning him they fulfilled the oracles of the prophets that are read sabbath after sabbath. For even though they found no grounds for a death sentence, they asked Pilate to have him put to death, and when they had accomplished all that was written about him, they took him down from the tree and placed him in a tomb. But God raised him from the dead, and for many days he appeared to those who had come up with him from Galilee to Jerusalem. These are now his witnesses before the people. We ourselves are proclaiming this good news to you that what God promised our fathers he has brought to fulfillment for us, their children, by raising up Jesus, as it is written in the second psalm, *You are my Son; this day I have begotten you.*"

The word of the Lord.

Responsorial Psalm

First Option

Ps 19:8, 9, 10, 11

**R. The judgments of the Lord are true,
and all of them are just.**

The law of the Lord is perfect,
  refreshing the soul;
The decree of the Lord is trustworthy,
  giving wisdom to the simple.

**R. The judgments of the Lord are true,
and all of them are just.**

The precepts of the Lord are right,
  rejoicing the heart;
The command of the Lord is clear,
  enlightening the eye.

**R. The judgments of the Lord are true,
and all of them are just.**

The fear of the LORD is pure,
  enduring forever;
The ordinances of the LORD are true,
  all of them just.

**R. The judgments of the Lord are true,
  and all of them are just.**

They are more precious than gold,
  than a heap of purest gold;
Sweeter also than syrup
  or honey from the comb.

**R. The judgments of the Lord are true,
  and all of them are just.**

Or: **R. Your words, Lord, are Spirit and life.**

SECOND OPTION
Ps 37:3–4, 5–6, 30–31

R. The mouth of the just murmurs wisdom.

Trust in the LORD and do good,
  that you may dwell in the land and be fed in security.
Take delight in the LORD,
  and he will grant you your heart's requests.

R. The mouth of the just murmurs wisdom.

Commit to the LORD your way;
  trust in him, and he will act.
He will make justice dawn for you like the light;
  bright as the noonday shall be your vindication.

R. The mouth of the just murmurs wisdom.

The mouth of the just tells of wisdom
  and his tongue utters what is right.
The law of his God is in his heart,
  and his steps do not falter.

R. The mouth of the just murmurs wisdom.

THIRD OPTION   Ps 119:9, 10, 11, 12, 13, 14

  R. Lord, teach me your statutes.

How can a young man be faultless in his way?
  By keeping to your words.

  R. Lord, teach me your statutes.

With all my heart I seek you;
  let me not stray from your commands.

  R. Lord, teach me your statutes.

Within my heart I treasure your promise,
  that I may not sin against you.

  R. Lord, teach me your statutes.

Blessed are you, O LORD;
  teach me your statutes.

  R. Lord, teach me your statutes.

With my lips I declare
  all the ordinances of your mouth.

  R. Lord, teach me your statutes.

In the way of your decrees
  I rejoice as much as in all riches.

  R. Lord, teach me your statutes.

READING II   From the New Testament

1   1 Cor 1:18–25

  *It was the will of God through the foolishness of the
      proclamation to save those who have faith.*

A reading from the first Letter of Saint Paul to the Corinthians

Brothers and sisters:

The message of the cross is foolishness to those who are

perishing, but to us who are being saved it is the power of God. For it is written:

> *I will destroy the wisdom of the wise,*
> *and the learning of the learned I will set aside.*

Where is the wise one? Where is the scribe? Where is the debater of this age? Has not God made the wisdom of the world foolish? For since in the wisdom of God the world did not come to know God through wisdom, it was the will of God through the foolishness of the proclamation to save those who have faith. For Jews demand signs and Greeks look for wisdom, but we proclaim Christ crucified, a stumbling block to Jews and foolishness to Gentiles, but to those who are called, Jews and Greeks alike, Christ the power of God and the wisdom of God. For the foolishness of God is wiser than human wisdom, and the weakness of God is stronger than human strength.

The word of the Lord.

2

1 Cor 2:1–10a

We speak God's wisdom, mysterious, hidden.

A reading from the first Letter of Saint Paul to the Corinthians

When I came to you, brothers and sisters, proclaiming the mystery of God, I did not come with sublimity of words or of wisdom. For I resolved to know nothing while I was with you except Jesus Christ, and him crucified. I came to you in weakness and fear and much trembling, and my message and my proclamation were not with persuasive words of wisdom, but with a demonstration of Spirit and power, so that your faith might rest not on human wisdom but on the power of God.

Yet we speak a wisdom to those who are mature, but not a wisdom of this age, nor of the rulers of this age who are passing away. Rather we speak God's wisdom, mysterious, hidden, which God predetermined before the ages for our glory, and which none of the rulers of this age knew; for, if they had known it, they would not have crucified the Lord of glory. But as it is written:

What eye has not seen, and ear has not heard,
and what has not entered the human heart,
what God has prepared for those who love him,

this God has revealed to us through the Spirit.
The word of the Lord.

3   1 Cor 2:10b–16

But we have the mind of Christ.

A reading from the first Letter of Saint Paul to the Corinthians

Brothers and sisters:
The Spirit scrutinizes everything, even the depths of God. Among men, who knows what pertains to the man except his spirit that is within? Similarly, no one knows what pertains to God except the Spirit of God. We have not received the spirit of the world but the Spirit who is from God, so that we may understand the things freely given us by God. And we speak about them not with words taught by human wisdom, but with words taught by the Spirit, describing spiritual realities in spiritual terms.

Now the natural man does not accept what pertains to the Spirit of God, for to him it is foolishness, and he cannot understand it, because it is judged spiritually. The one who is spiritual, however, can judge everything but is not subject to judgment by anyone.

For *who has known the mind of the Lord, so as to counsel him?*

But we have the mind of Christ.

The word of the Lord.

4

Eph 3:8–12

This grace was given, to preach to the Gentiles the inscrutable riches of Christ.

A reading from the Letter of Saint Paul to the Ephesians

Brothers and sisters:

To me, the very least of all the holy ones, this grace was given, to preach to the Gentiles the inscrutable riches of Christ, and to bring to light for all what is the plan of the mystery hidden from ages past in God who created all things, so that the manifold wisdom of God might now be made known through the Church to the principalities and authorities in the heavens. This was according to the eternal purpose that he accomplished in Christ Jesus our Lord, in whom we have boldness of speech and confidence of access through faith in him.

The word of the Lord.

5

Eph 4:1–7, 11–13

In the work of ministry, in building up the Body of Christ.

A reading from the Letter of Saint Paul to the Ephesians

Brothers and sisters:

I, a prisoner for the Lord, urge you to live in a manner worthy of the call you have received, with all humility and gentleness, with patience, bearing with one another through love, striving to preserve the unity of the Spirit through the bond of peace: one Body and one Spirit, as you were also called to the one hope of your call; one Lord, one faith, one baptism; one God and Father of all, who is over all and through all and in all.

But grace was given to each of us according to the measure of Christ's gift.

And he gave some as Apostles, others as prophets, others as evangelists, others as pastors and teachers, to equip the holy ones for the work of ministry, for building up the Body of Christ, until we all attain to the unity of faith and knowledge of the Son of God, to mature manhood, to the extent of the full stature of Christ.

The word of the Lord.

6   2 Tm 1:13–14; 2:1–3

Guard this rich trust with the help of the Holy Spirit
who dwells within us.

A reading from the second Letter of Saint Paul to Timothy

Beloved:

Take as your norm the sound words that you heard from me, in the faith and love that are in Christ Jesus. Guard this rich trust with the help of the Holy Spirit that dwells within us.

My child, be strong in the grace that is in Christ Jesus. And what you heard from me through many witnesses entrust to faithful people who will have the ability to teach others as well. Bear your share of hardship along with me like a good soldier of Christ Jesus.

The word of the Lord.

7

2 Tm 4:1–5

Perform the work of an evangelist;
fulfill your ministry.

A reading from the second Letter of Saint Paul to Timothy

Beloved:

I charge you in the presence of God and of Christ Jesus, who will judge the living and the dead, and by his appearing and his kingly power: proclaim the word; be persistent whether it is convenient or inconvenient; convince, reprimand, encourage through all patience and teaching. For the time will come when people will not tolerate sound doctrine but, following their own desires and insatiable curiosity, will accumulate teachers and will stop listening to the truth and will be diverted to myths. But you, be self-possessed in all circumstances; put up with hardship; perform the work of an evangelist; fulfill your ministry.

The word of the Lord.

ALLELUIA VERSE AND VERSE BEFORE THE GOSPEL

1 Mt 5:16
Let your light shine before others,
  that they may see your good deeds
    and glorify your heavenly Father.

2 Mt 23:9b, 10b
You have but one Father in heaven.
You have but one master, the Christ.

3 See Jn 6:63c, 68c
Your words, Lord, are Spirit and life;
you have the words of everlasting life.

4 Jn 15:5
I am the vine, you are the branches, says the Lord:
whoever remains in me and I in him will bear much fruit.

5 See Acts 16:14b

Open our hearts, O Lord,
to listen to the words of your Son.

6 1 Cor 1:18

The message about the cross is foolishness to those
who are perishing,
but to us who are being saved it is the power of God.

7 1 Cor 2:7

We speak God's wisdom, mysterious, hidden,
which God predetermined before the ages for our glory.

8 The seed is the word of God, Christ is the sower;
all who come to him will live for ever.

GOSPEL

1   Mt 5:13–19

You are the light of the world.

A reading from the holy Gospel according to Matthew

Jesus said to his disciples: "You are the salt of the earth. But if
salt loses its taste, with what can it be seasoned? It is no longer
good for anything but to be thrown out and trampled underfoot.
You are the light of the world. A city set on a mountain cannot
be hidden. Nor do they light a lamp and then put it under a
bushel basket; it is set on a lampstand, where it gives light to
all in the house. Just so, your light must shine before others,
that they may see your good deeds and glorify your heavenly
Father.

"Do not think that I have come to abolish the law or the
prophets. I have come not abolish but to fulfill. Amen, I say
to you, until heaven and earth pass away, not the smallest letter
or the smallest part of a letter will pass from the law, until all

things have taken place. Therefore, whoever breaks one of the least of these commandments and teaches others to do so will be called least in the Kingdom of heaven. But whoever obeys and teaches these commandments will be called greatest in the Kingdom of heaven."

The Gospel of the Lord.

2

Mt 7:21–29

He taught them as one having authority.

A reading from the holy Gospel according to Matthew

Jesus said to his disciples: "Not everyone who says to me, 'Lord, Lord,' will enter the Kingdom of heaven, but only the one who does the will of my Father in heaven. Many will say to me on that day, 'Lord, Lord, did we not prophesy in your name? Did we not drive out demons in your name? Did we not do mighty deeds in your name?' Then I will declare to them solemnly, 'I never knew you. Depart from me, you evildoers.'

"Everyone who listens to these words of mine and acts on them will be like a wise man who built his house on rock. The rain fell, the floods came, and the winds blew and buffeted the house. But it did not collapse; it had been set solidly on rock. And everyone who listens to these words of mine but does not act on them will be like a fool who built his house on sand. The rain fell, the floods came, and the winds blew and buffeted the house. And it collapsed and was completely ruined."

When Jesus finished these words, the crowds were astonished at his teaching, for he taught them as one having authority, and not as their scribes.

The Gospel of the Lord.

3

Mt 13:47–52

The new and the old.

A reading from the holy Gospel according to Matthew

Jesus said to the crowds: "The Kingdom of heaven is like a net thrown into the sea, which collects fish of every kind. When it is full they haul it ashore and sit down to put what is good into buckets. What is bad they throw away. Thus it will be at the end of the age. The angels will go out and separate the wicked from the righteous and throw them into the fiery furnace, where there will be wailing and grinding of teeth.

"Do you understand all these things?" They answered, "Yes." And he replied, "Then every scribe who has been instructed in the Kingdom of heaven is like the head of a household who brings from his storeroom both the new and the old."

The Gospel of the Lord.

4

Mt 23:8–12

Do not be called "Rabbi."
You have but one teacher, who is Christ.

A reading from the holy Gospel according to Matthew

Jesus said to his disciples: "Do not be called 'Rabbi.' You have but one teacher, and you are all brothers. Call no one on earth your father; you have but one Father in heaven. Do not be called 'Master'; you have but one master, the Christ. The greatest among you must be your servant. Whoever exalts himself will be humbled; whoever humbles himself will be exalted."

The Gospel of the Lord.

5

The sower went out to sow.

A reading from the holy Gospel according to Mark

Long form follows; for short form omit what is in brackets.

On another occasion, Jesus began to teach by the sea. A very large crowd gathered around him so that he got into a boat on the sea and sat down. And the whole crowd was beside the sea on land. And he taught them at length in parables, and in the course of his instruction he said to them, "Hear this! A sower went out to sow. And as he sowed, some seed fell on the path, and the birds came and ate it up. Other seed fell on rocky ground where it had little soil. It sprang up at once because the soil was not deep. And when the sun rose, it was scorched and it withered for lack of roots. Some seed fell among thorns, and the thorns grew up and choked it and it produced no grain. And some seed fell on rich soil and produced fruit. It came up and grew and yielded thirty, sixty, and a hundredfold." He added, "Whoever has ears to hear ought to hear."

[And when he was alone, those present along with the Twelve questioned him about the parables. He said to them, "Do you not understand this parable? Then how will you understand any of the parables? The sower sows the word. These are the ones on the path where the word is sown. As soon as they hear, Satan comes at once and takes away the word sown in them. And these are the ones sown on rocky ground who, when they hear the word, receive it at once with joy. But they have no roots; they last only for a time. Then when tribulation or persecution comes because of the word, they quickly fall away. Those sown among thorns are another sort. They are the people who hear the word, but worldly anxiety, the lure of riches, and the craving for other things intrude and choke the word, and it bears no fruit. But those sown on rich soil are the ones who hear the word and accept it and bear fruit thirty and sixty and a hundredfold."]

The Gospel of the Lord.

6   Lk 6:43–45

From the fullness of the heart the mouth speaks.

A reading from the holy Gospel according to Luke

Jesus said to his disciples: "A good tree does not bear rotten fruit, nor does a rotten tree bear good fruit. For every tree is known by its own fruit. For people do not pick figs from thorn bushes, nor do they gather grapes from brambles. A good person out of the store of goodness in his heart produces good, but an evil person out of a store of evil produces evil; for from the fullness of the heart the mouth speaks."

The Gospel of the Lord.

COMMON OF VIRGINS

1.

Entrance Antiphon

Here is a wise and faithful virgin who went with lighted lamp to meet her Lord.

Opening Prayer

God our Savior,
as we celebrate with joy the memory of the virgin N.,
may we learn from her example of faithfulness and love.

We ask this through our Lord Jesus Christ, your Son,
who lives and reigns with you and the Holy Spirit,
one God, for ever and ever.

Liturgy of the Word, *pp. 2244–2252.*

Prayer over the Gifts

Pray, brethren...

Lord,
we see the wonder of your love
in the life of the virgin N.
and her witness to Christ.
Accept our gifts of praise
and make our offering pleasing to you.

Grant this through Christ our Lord.

Communion Antiphon

The bridegroom is here; let us go out to meet Christ the Lord.

(Mt 25:6)

Prayer after Communion

Let us pray.

Pause for silent prayer, if this has not preceded.

Lord God,
may this eucharist renew our courage and strength.
May we remain close to you, like St. N.,
by accepting in our lives
a share in the suffering of Jesus Christ,
who lives and reigns with you for ever and ever.

2.

Entrance Antiphon

**Let us rejoice and shout for joy, because the Lord of all things
has favored this holy and glorious virgin with his love.**

Opening Prayer

Lord God,
you endowed the virgin N. with gifts from heaven.
By imitating her goodness here on earth
may we come to share her joy in eternal life.

We ask this through our Lord Jesus Christ, your Son,
who lives and reigns with you and the Holy Spirit,
one God, for ever and ever.

Or (for a virgin foundress):

Lord our God,
may the witness of your faithful bride the virgin N.
awaken the fire of divine love in our hearts.
May it inspire other young women to give their lives
to the service of Christ and his Church.

Grant this through our Lord Jesus Christ, your Son,
who lives and reigns with you and the Holy Spirit,
one God, for ever and ever.

Liturgy of the Word, *pp. 2244–2252.*

Prayer over the Gifts

Pray, brethren...

Lord,
may the gifts we bring you
help us follow the example of St. N.
Cleanse us from our earthly way of life,
and teach us to live the new life of your kingdom.

We ask this through Christ our Lord.

Communion Antiphon

The five sensible virgins took flasks of oil as well as their lamps.
At midnight a cry was heard: the bridegroom is here; let us go
out to meet Christ the Lord.   (Mt 25:4, 6)

Prayer after Communion

Let us pray.

Pause for silent prayer, if this has not preceded.

Lord,
may our reception of the body and blood of your Son
keep us from harmful things.
Help us by the example of St. N.
to grow in your love on earth
that we may rejoice for ever in heaven.

We ask this in the name of Jesus the Lord.

3.

Entrance Antiphon

**Come, bride of Christ, and receive the crown, which the Lord
has prepared for you for ever.**

Opening Prayer

Lord,
you have told us that you live for ever
in the hearts of the chaste.
By the prayers of the virgin N.,
help us to live by your grace
and to become a temple of your Spirit.

Grant this through our Lord Jesus Christ, your Son,
who lives and reigns with you and the Holy Spirit,
one God, for ever and ever.

Or:

Lord,
hear the prayers of those who recall the devoted life of the
    virgin N.
Guide us on our way and help us to grow

in love and devotion as long as we live.

We ask this through our Lord Jesus Christ, your Son,
who lives and reigns with you and the Holy Spirit,
one God, for ever and ever.

Liturgy of the Word, pp. 2244–2252.

Prayer over the Gifts

Pray, brethren...

Lord,
receive our worship in memory of N. the virgin.
By this perfect sacrifice
make us grow in unselfish love for you
and for our brothers.

We ask this through Christ our Lord.

Communion Antiphon

**The wise virgin chose the better part for herself, and it shall
not be taken away from her.**   (See Lk 10:42)

Prayer after Communion

Let us pray.

Pause for silent prayer, if this has not preceded.

God of mercy,
we rejoice that on this feast of St. N.
you give us the bread of heaven.
May it bring us pardon for our sins,
health of body,
your grace in this life,
and glory in heaven.

Grant this through Christ our Lord.

4.

Entrance Antiphon

Let virgins praise the name of the Lord, for his name alone is supreme; its majesty outshines both earth and heaven.

(Ps 148:12–14)

Opening Prayer

Lord,
increase in us your gifts of mercy and forgiveness.
May we who rejoice at this celebration
in honor of the virgins N. and N.
receive the joy of sharing eternal life with them.

We ask this through our Lord Jesus Christ, your Son,
who lives and reigns with you and the Holy Spirit,
one God, for ever and ever.

Liturgy of the Word, *pp. 2244–2252.*

Prayer over the Gifts

Pray, brethren...

Lord,
we bring you our gifts and prayers.
We praise your glory on this feast of the virgins N. and N.,
whose witness to Christ was pleasing to you.
Be pleased also with the eucharist we now offer.

Grant this through Christ our Lord.

Communion Antiphon

The bridegroom has come, and the virgins who were ready have gone in with him to the wedding. (Mt 25:10)

Or:

Whoever loves me will be loved by my Father. We shall come to him and make our home with him. (Jn 14:21, 23)

Prayer after Communion

Let us pray.

Pause for silent prayer, if this has not preceded.

Lord,
may the mysteries we receive
on this feast of the virgins N. and N.
keep us alert and ready to welcome your Son at his return,
that he may welcome us to the feast of eternal life.

Grant this through Christ our Lord.

Liturgy of the Word: Common of Virgins

READING I   From the Old Testament

FIRST OPTION   Sg 8:6–7

Stern as death is love.

A reading from the Song of Songs

Set me as a seal on your heart,
    as a seal on your arm;
For stern as death is love,
    relentless as the nether world is devotion;
    its flames are a blazing fire.
Deep waters cannot quench love,
    nor floods sweep it away.
Were one to offer all he owns to purchase love,
    he would be roundly mocked.

The word of the Lord.

SECOND OPTION   Hos 2:16bc, 17cd, 21–22

I will espouse you to me forever.

A reading from the Book of the Prophet Hosea

Thus says the LORD:
I will lead her into the desert
    and speak to her heart.
She shall respond there as in the days of her youth,
    when she came up from the land of Egypt.
I will espouse you to me forever:
    I will espouse you in right and in justice,
    in love and in mercy;
I will espouse you in fidelity,
    and you shall know the LORD.
The word of the Lord.

READING I   From the New Testament

During the Easter Season

FIRST OPTION   Rv 19:1, 5–9a

*Blessed are those who have been
called to the wedding feast of the Lamb.*

A reading from the Book of Revelation

I, John, heard what sounded like the loud voice of a great
multitude in heaven, saying:

    "Alleluia!
    Salvation, glory, and might belong to our God."

A voice coming from the throne said:

    "Praise our God, all you his servants,
    and you who revere him, small and great."

Then I heard something like the sound of a great multitude or the sound of rushing water or mighty peals of thunder, as they said:

"Alleluia!
  The Lord has established his reign,
      our God, the almighty.
  Let us rejoice and be glad
      and give him glory.
  For the wedding day of the Lamb has come,
      his bride has made herself ready.
  She was allowed to wear
      a bright, clean linen garment."

The linen represents the righteous deeds of the holy ones.

Then the angel said to me, "Write this: Blessed are those who have been called to the wedding feast of the Lamb."

The word of the Lord.

SECOND OPTION   Rv 21:1–5a

I saw the new Jerusalem, prepared as a bride
adorned for her husband.

A reading from the Book of Revelation

I, John, saw a new heaven and a new earth. The former heaven and the former earth had passed away, and the sea was no more. I also saw the holy city, a new Jerusalem, coming down out of heaven from God, prepared as a bride adorned for her husband. I heard a loud voice from the throne saying, "Behold, God's dwelling is with the human race. He will dwell with them and they will be his people and God himself will always be with them as their God. He will wipe every tear from their eyes, and there shall be no more death or mourning, wailing or pain, for the old order has passed away."

The One who sat on the throne said, "Behold, I make all things new."

The word of the Lord.

Responsorial Psalm

First Option

Ps 45:11–12, 14–15, 16–17

R. Listen to me, daughter; see and bend your ear.

Hear, O daughter, and see; turn your ear,
  forget your people and your father's house.
So shall the king desire your beauty;
  for he is your lord, and you must worship him.

R. Listen to me, daughter; see and bend your ear.

All glorious is the king's daughter as she enters;
  her raiment is threaded with spun gold.
In embroidered apparel she is borne in to the king;
  behind her the virgins of her train are brought to you.

R. Listen to me, daughter; see and bend your ear.

They are borne in with gladness and joy;
  they enter the palace of the king.
The place of your fathers your sons shall have;
  you shall make them princes through all the land.

R. Listen to me, daughter; see and bend your ear.

Or: **R. The bridegroom is here;
   let us go out to meet Christ the Lord.**

Second Option

Ps 148:1bc–2, 11–12, 13, 14

R. Young men and women, praise the name of the Lord.

Praise the LORD from the heavens;
  praise him in the heights;
Praise him, all you his angels,
  praise him, all you his hosts.

R. Young men and women, praise the name of the Lord.

Let the kings of the earth and all peoples,
  the princes and all the judges of the earth,
Young men, too, and maidens,
  old men and boys,
Praise the name of the LORD,
  for his name alone is exalted.

R. Young men and women, praise the name of the Lord.

His majesty is above earth and heaven.
He has lifted up the horn of his people.
Be this his praise from all his faithful ones;
  from the children of Israel, the people close to him. Alleluia.

R. Young men and women, praise the name of the Lord.

Or: **R. Alleluia.**

READING II   From the New Testament

FIRST OPTION   1 Cor 7:25–35

A virgin is anxious about the things of the Lord.

A reading from the first Letter of Saint Paul to the Corinthians

Brothers and sisters:
In regard to virgins, I have no commandment from the Lord,
but I give my opinion as one who by the Lord's mercy is trustworthy. So this is what I think best because of the present
distress: that it is a good thing for a person to remain as he is.
Are you bound to a wife? Do not seek a separation. Are you
free of a wife? Then do not look for a wife. If you marry,
however, you do not sin, nor does an unmarried woman sin if
she marries; but such people will experience affliction in their
earthly life, and I would like to spare you that.

I tell you, brothers, the time is running out. From now on,
let those having wives act as not having them, those weeping

as not weeping, those rejoicing as not rejoicing, those buying as not owning, those using the world as not using it fully. For the world in its present form is passing away.

I should like you to be free of anxieties. An unmarried man is anxious about the things of the Lord, how he may please the Lord. But a married man is anxious about the things of the world, how he may please his wife, and he is divided. An unmarried woman or a virgin is anxious about the things of the Lord, so that she may be holy in both body and spirit. A married woman, on the other hand, is anxious about the things of the world, how she may please her husband. I am telling you this for your own benefit, not to impose a restraint upon you, but for the sake of propriety and adherence to the Lord without distraction.

The word of the Lord.

SECOND OPTION
2 Cor 10:17—11:2

I betrothed you to one husband,
to present you as a chaste virgin to Christ.

A reading from the second Letter of Saint Paul to the Corinthians

Brothers and sisters:

"Whoever boasts, should boast in the Lord." For it is not the one who recommends himself who is approved, but the one whom the Lord recommends.

If only you would put up with a little foolishness from me! Please put up with me. For I am jealous of you with the jealousy of God, since I betrothed you to one husband to present you as a chaste virgin to Christ.

The word of the Lord.

ALLELUIA VERSE AND VERSE BEFORE THE GOSPEL

1   Jn 14:23
Whoever loves me will keep my word
and my Father will love him,
and we will come to him.

2   This is the wise virgin, whom the Lord found waiting;
at his coming, she went in with him to the wedding feast.

3   Come, bride of Christ, and receive the crown,
which the Lord has prepared for you for ever.

GOSPEL

FIRST OPTION

Mt 19:3–12

For the sake of the Kingdom of heaven.

A reading from the holy Gospel according to Matthew

Some Pharisees approached Jesus, and tested him, saying, "Is it lawful for a man to divorce his wife for any cause whatever?" He said in reply, "Have you not read that from the beginning the Creator *made them male and female* and said, *For this reason a man shall leave his father and mother and be joined to his wife, and the two shall become one flesh'?* So they are no longer two, but one flesh. Therefore, what God has joined together, man must not separate." They said to him, "Then why did Moses command that the man give the woman a bill of divorce and dismiss her?" He said to them, "Because of the hardness of your hearts Moses allowed you to divorce your wives, but from the beginning it was not so. I say to you, who-ever divorces his wife (unless the marriage is unlawful) and marries another commits adultery." His disciples said to him, "If that is the case of a man with his wife, it is better not to marry." He answered, "Not all can accept this word, but only those to whom that is granted. Some are incapable of marriage because they were born so; some, because they were made so by others; some, because they have renounced marriage for the sake of the Kingdom of heaven. Whoever can accept this ought to accept it."

The Gospel of the Lord.

SECOND OPTION
Mt 25:1–13

Behold, the bridegroom! Come out to meet him!

A reading from the holy Gospel according to Matthew

Jesus told his disciples this parable: "The Kingdom of heaven will be like ten virgins who took their lamps and went out to meet the bridegroom. Five of them were foolish and five were wise. The foolish ones, when taking their lamps, brought no oil with them, but the wise brought flasks of oil with their lamps. Since the bridegroom was long delayed, they all became drowsy and fell asleep. At midnight, there was a cry, 'Behold, the bridegroom! Come out to meet him!' Then all those virgins got up and trimmed their lamps. The foolish ones said to the wise, 'Give us some of your oil, for our lamps are going out.' But the wise ones replied, 'No, for there may not be enough for us and you. Go instead to the merchants and buy some for yourselves.' While they went off to buy it, the bridegroom came and those who were ready went into the wedding feast with him. Then the door was locked. Afterwards the other virgins came and said, 'Lord, Lord, open the door for us!' But he said in reply, 'Amen, I say to you, I do not know you.' Therefore, stay awake, for you know neither the day nor the hour."

The Gospel of the Lord.

THIRD OPTION

Lk 10:38–42

Martha welcomed him. Mary has chosen the better part.

A reading from the holy Gospel according to Luke

Jesus entered a village where a woman whose name was Martha welcomed him. She had a sister named Mary who sat beside the Lord at his feet listening to him speak. Martha, burdened with much serving, came to him and said, "Lord, do you not care that my sister has left me by myself to do the serving? Tell her to help me." The Lord said to her in reply, "Martha, Martha, you are anxious and worried about many things. There is need of only one thing. Mary has chosen the better part and it will not be taken from her."

The Gospel of the Lord.

COMMON OF HOLY MEN AND WOMEN

The following Masses, if indicated for a particular rank of saints, are used for saints of that rank. If no indication is given, the Masses may be used for saints of any rank.

1.

Entrance Antiphon

May all your works praise you, Lord, and your saints bless you; they will tell of the glory of your kingdom and proclaim your power. (Ps 144:10–11)

Opening Prayer

Ever-living God,
the signs of your love are manifest

in the honor you give your saints.
May their prayers and their example encourage us
to follow your Son more faithfully.

We ask this through our Lord Jesus Christ, your Son,
who lives and reigns with you and the Holy Spirit,
one God, for ever and ever.

Liturgy of the Word, pp. 2269–2322.

Prayer over the Gifts

Pray, brethren...

Lord,
in your kindness hear our prayers
and the prayers which the saints offer on our behalf.
Watch over us that we may offer fitting service at your altar.

Grant this in the name of Jesus the Lord.

Communion Antiphon

**May the just rejoice as they feast in God's presence, and de-
light in gladness of heart.** (Ps 67:4)

Or:

**Blessed are those servants whom the Lord finds watching when
he comes; truly I tell you, he will seat them at his table and wait
on them.** (Lk 12:37)

Prayer after Communion

Let us pray.

Pause for silent prayer, if this has not preceded.

Father, our comfort and peace,
we have gathered as your family
to praise your name and honor your saints.
Let the sacrament we have received
be the sign and pledge of our salvation.

We ask this through Christ our Lord.

2.

Entrance Antiphon

The just man will rejoice in the Lord and hope in him, and all the upright of heart will be praised.   (Ps 63:11)

Opening Prayer

God our Father,
you alone are holy;
without you nothing is good.
Trusting in the prayers of St. N.
we ask you to help us
to become the holy people you call us to be.
Never let us be found undeserving
of the glory you have prepared for us.

We ask this through our Lord Jesus Christ, your Son,
who lives and reigns with you and the Holy Spirit,
one God, for ever and ever.

Liturgy of the Word, *pp. 2269–2322.*

Prayer over the Gifts

Pray, brethren...

All-powerful God,
may the gifts we present
bring honor to your saints,
and free us from sin in mind and body.

We ask this in the name of Jesus the Lord.

Communion Antiphon

He who serves me, follows me, says the Lord; and where I am, my servant will also be.   (Jn 12:26)

Prayer after Communion

Let us pray.

Pause for silent prayer, if this has not preceded.

Lord,
your sacramental gifts renew us
at this celebration of the birth of your saints to glory.
May the good things you give us
lead us to the joy of your kingdom.

We ask this through Christ our Lord.

3.

Entrance Antiphon

**Lord, your strength gives joy to the just; they greatly delight
in your saving help. You have granted them their heart's desire.**

(Ps 20:2–3)

Opening Prayer

Father,
your saints guide us when in our weakness we tend to stray.
Help us who celebrate the birth of St. N. to glory
grow closer to you by following his (her) example.

We ask this through our Lord Jesus Christ, your Son,
who lives and reigns with you and the Holy Spirit,
one God, for ever and ever.

Liturgy of the Word, *pp. 2269–2322.*

Prayer over the Gifts

Pray, brethren...

Lord,
let the sacrifice we offer

in memory of St. N.
bring to your people the gifts of unity and peace.

Grant this in the name of Jesus the Lord.

Communion Antiphon

If anyone wishes to come after me, he must renounce himself, take up his cross, and follow me, says the Lord. (Mt 16:24)

Prayer after Communion

Let us pray.

Pause for silent prayer, if this has not preceded.

Lord,
may the sacraments we receive
on this feast in honor of N.
give us holiness of mind and body
and bring us into your divine life.

We ask this through Christ our Lord.

4.

Entrance Antiphon

The teaching of truth was in his mouth, and no wrong was found on his lips; he walked with me in peace and justice, and turned many away from wickedness. (Mal 2:6)

Opening Prayer

Merciful Father,
we fail because of our weakness.
Restore us to your love
through the example of your saints.

We ask this through our Lord Jesus Christ, your Son,
who lives and reigns with you and the Holy Spirit,
one God, for ever and ever.

Liturgy of the Word, *pp. 2269–2322.*

Prayer over the Gifts

Pray, brethren...

Lord,
may this sacrifice we share
on the feast of your St. N.
give you praise
and help us on our way to salvation.

Grant this in the name of Jesus the Lord.

Communion Antiphon

Happy are the pure of heart for they shall see God. Happy the peacemakers; they shall be called the sons of God. Happy are they who suffer persecution or justice' sake; the kingdom of heaven is theirs.   (Mt 5:8–10)

Prayer after Communion

Let us pray.

Pause for silent prayer, if this has not preceded.

Lord,
our hunger is satisfied by your holy gift.
May we who have celebrated this eucharist
experience in our lives the salvation which it brings.

We ask this in the name of Jesus the Lord.

5.

Entrance Antiphon

The just man will flourish like the palm tree. Planted in the courts of God's house, he will grow great like the cedars of Lebanon.   (Ps 91:13–14)

Opening Prayer

Lord,
may the prayers of the saints
bring help to your people.
Give to us who celebrate the memory of your saints
a share in their eternal joy.

Grant this through our Lord Jesus Christ, your Son,
who lives and reigns with you and the Holy Spirit,
one God, for ever and ever.

Liturgy of the Word, *pp. 2269–2322.*

Prayer over the Gifts

Pray, brethren...

Lord,
give to us who offer these gifts at your altar
the same spirit of love that filled St. N.
By celebrating this sacred eucharist with pure minds and
loving hearts
may we offer a sacrifice that pleases you,
and brings salvation to us.

Grant this through Christ our Lord.

Communion Antiphon

**Come to me, all you that labor and are burdened, and I will
give you rest, says the Lord.** (Mt 11:28)

Prayer after Communion

Let us pray.
Pause for silent prayer, if this has not preceded.

Lord,
may the sacrament of holy communion which we receive

bring us health and strengthen us
in the light of your truth.
We ask this in the name of Jesus the Lord.

6.

Entrance Antiphon

**Blessed is the man who puts his trust in the Lord; he will be
like a tree planted by the waters, sinking its roots into the moist
earth; he will have nothing to fear in time of drought.**

(Jer 17:7–8)

Opening Prayer

All-powerful God,
help us who celebrate the memory of St. N.
to imitate his (her) way of life.
May the example of your saints
be our challenge to live holier lives.

Grant this through our Lord Jesus Christ, your Son,
who lives and reigns with you and the Holy Spirit,
one God, for ever and ever.

Liturgy of the Word, *pp. 2269–2322.*

Prayer over the Gifts

Pray, brethren...
Lord,
we bring our gifts to your holy altar
on this feast of your saints.
In your mercy let this eucharist
give you glory
and bring us to the fullness of your love.

Grant this through Christ our Lord.

Communion Antiphon

As the Father has loved me, so have I loved you; remain in my love. (Jn 15:9)

Prayer after Communion

Let us pray.

Pause for silent prayer, if this has not preceded.

Lord our God,
may the divine mysteries we celebrate
in memory of your saint
fill us with eternal peace and salvation.

We ask this in the name of Jesus the Lord.

7. For Religious

Entrance Antiphon

The Lord is my inheritance and my cup; he alone will give me my reward. The measuring line has marked a lovely place for me; my inheritance is my great delight. (Ps 15:5–6)

Opening Prayer

Lord God,
you kept St. N. faithful to Christ's pattern of poverty and
    humility.
May his (her) prayers help us to live in fidelity to our calling
and bring us to the perfection you have shown us in your
    Son,
who lives and reigns with you and the Holy Spirit,
one God, for ever and ever.

Or (for an abbot):

Lord,
in your abbot N.
you give an example of the gospel lived to perfection.

Help us to follow him
by keeping before us the things of heaven
amid all the changes of this world.

Grant this through our Lord Jesus Christ, your Son,
who lives and reigns with you and the Holy Spirit,
one God, for ever and ever.

Liturgy of the Word, *pp. 2269–2322.*

Prayer over the Gifts

Pray, brethren...

God of all mercy,
you transformed St. N.
and made him (her) a new creature in your image.
Renew us in the same way
by making our gifts of peace acceptable to you.

We ask this in the name of Jesus the Lord.

Communion Antiphon

**I solemnly tell you: those who have left everything and fol-
lowed me will be repaid a hundredfold and will gain eternal life.**
(See Mt 19:27–29)

Prayer after Communion

Let us pray.

Pause for silent prayer, if this has not preceded.

All-powerful God,
may we who are strengthened by the power of this
    sacrament
learn from the example of St. N.
to seek you above all things
and to live in this world as your new creation.

We ask this through Christ our Lord

8. For Religious

Entrance Antiphon

These are the saints who received blessings from the Lord, a prize from God their Savior. They are the people that long to see his face. (See Ps 23:5–6)

Opening Prayer

God our Father,
you called St. N. to seek your kingdom in this world
by striving to live in perfect charity.
With his (her) prayers to give us courage,
help us to move forward with joyful hearts in the way of
    love.

We ask this through our Lord Jesus Christ, your Son,
who lives and reigns with you and the Holy Spirit,
one God, for ever and ever.

Liturgy of the Word, *pp. 2269–2322.*

Prayer over the Gifts

Pray, brethren...

Lord,
may the gifts we bring to your altar
in memory of St. N.
be acceptable to you.
Free us from the things that keep us from you
and teach us to seek you as our only good.

We ask this through Christ our Lord.

Communion Antiphon

Taste and see the goodness of the Lord; blessed is he who hopes in God. (Ps 33:9)

Prayer after Communion

Let us pray.

Pause for silent prayer, if this has not preceded.

Lord,
by the power of this sacrament and the example of St. N.
guide us always in your love.
May the good work you have begun in us
reach perfection in the day of Christ Jesus
who is Lord for ever and ever.

9. For Those Who Worked for the Underprivileged

Entrance Antiphon

Come, you whom my Father has blessed, says the Lord: I was ill and you comforted me. I tell you, anything you did for one of my brothers, you did for me. (Mt 25:34, 36, 40)

Opening Prayer

Lord God,
you teach us that the commandments of heaven
are summarized in love of you and love of our neighbor.
By following the example of St. N.
in practicing works of charity
may we be counted among the blessed in your kingdom.

Grant this through our Lord Jesus Christ, your Son,
who lives and reigns with you and the Holy Spirit,
one God, for ever and ever.

Liturgy of the Word, *pp. 2269–2322.*

Prayer over the Gifts

Pray, brethren...

Lord,
accept the gifts of your people.
May we who celebrate the love of your Son
also follow the example of your saints
and grow in love for you and for one another.

We ask this through Christ our Lord.

Communion Antiphon

No one has greater love, say the Lord, than the man who lays
down his life for his friends.   (Jn 15:13)

Or:

By the love you have for one another, says the Lord, everyone
will know that you are my disciples.   (Jn 13:35)

Prayer after Communion

Let us pray.

Pause for silent prayer, if this has not preceded.

Lord,
may we who are renewed by these mysteries
follow the example of St. N.
who worshipped you with love
and served your people with generosity.

We ask this through Christ our Lord.

Or:

Lord,
we who receive the sacrament of salvation ask your mercy.
Help us to imitate the love of St. N.
and give to us a share in his (her) glory.

Grant this through Christ our Lord.

10. For Teachers

Entrance Antiphon

Let the children come to me, and do not stop them, says the Lord; to such belongs the kingdom of God. (Mk 10:14)

Or:

The man that keeps these commandments and teaches them, he is the one who will be called great in the kingdom of heaven, says the Lord. (Mt 5:19)

Opening Prayer

Lord God,
you called St. N. to serve you in the Church
by teaching his (her) fellow man the way of salvation.
Inspire us by his (her) example:
help us to follow Christ our teacher,
and lead us to our brothers and sisters in heaven.

We ask this through our Lord Jesus Christ, your Son,
who lives and reigns with you and the Holy Spirit,
one God, for ever and ever.

Liturgy of the Word, *pp. 2269–2322.*

Prayer over the Gifts

Pray, brethren...

Lord,
accept the gifts your people bring
in memory of your saints.
May our sharing in this mystery
help us to live the example of love you give us.

Grant this in the name of Jesus the Lord.

Communion Antiphon

Unless you change, and become like little children, says the Lord, you shall not enter the kingdom of heaven.   (Mt 18:3)

Or:

I am the light of the world, says the Lord; the man who follows me will have the light of life.   (Jn 8:12)

Prayer after Communion

Let us pray.

Pause for silent prayer, if this has not preceded.

All-powerful God,
may this holy meal help us
to follow the example of your saints
by showing in our lives
the light of truth and love for our brothers.

We ask this in the name of Jesus the Lord.

11. For Holy Women

Entrance Antiphon

Honor the woman who fears the Lord. Her sons will bless her, and her husband praise her.   (See Prv 31:30, 28)

Opening Prayer

God our Father,
every year you give us joy on this feast of St. N.
As we honor her memory by this celebration,
may we follow the example of her holy life.

We ask this through our Lord Jesus Christ, your Son,
who lives and reigns with you and the Holy Spirit,
one God, for ever and ever.

Or (for several):

All-powerful God,
may the prayers of Saints N. and N. bring us help from
   heaven
as their lives have already given us an example of holiness.

We ask this through our Lord Jesus Christ, your Son,
who lives and reigns with you and the Holy Spirit,
one God, for ever and ever.

Liturgy of the Word, *pp. 2269–2322.*

Prayer over the Gifts

Pray, brethren...

Lord,
may these gifts we present in memory of St. N.
bring us your forgiveness and salvation.

We ask this in the name of Jesus the Lord.

Communion Antiphon

**The kingdom of heaven is like a merchant in search of fine
pearls; on finding one rare pearl he sells everything he has and
buys it.**   (Mt 13:45–46)

Prayer after Communion

Let us pray.

   Pause for silent prayer, if this has not preceded.

All-powerful God,
fill us with your light and love
by the sacrament we receive on the feast of St. N.
May we burn with love for your kingdom
and let our light shine before men.

We ask this through Christ our Lord.

12. For Holy Women

Entrance Antiphon

**Praise to the holy woman whose home is built on faithful love
and whose pathway leads to God.**   (See Prv 14:1–2)

Opening Prayer

Father,
rewarder of the humble,
you blessed St. N. with charity and patience.
May her prayers help us, and her example inspire us
to carry our cross and to love you always.

We ask this through our Lord Jesus Christ, your Son,
who lives and reigns with you and the Holy Spirit,
one God, for ever and ever.

Or:

Lord,
pour upon us the spirit of wisdom and love
with which you filled our servant St. N.
By serving you as she did,
may we please you with our faith and our actions.

Grant this through our Lord Jesus Christ, your Son,
who lives and reigns with you and the Holy Spirit,
one God, for ever and ever.

Liturgy of the Word, *pp. 2269–2322.*

Prayer over the Gifts

Pray, brethren...

Lord,
receive the gifts your people bring to you
in honor of your saints.

By the eucharist we celebrate
may we progress toward salvation.

Grant this in the name of Jesus the Lord.

Communion Antiphon

**Whoever does the will of my Father in heaven is my brother
and sister and mother, says the Lord.** (Mt 12:50)

Prayer after Communion

Let us pray.

Pause for silent prayer, if this has not preceded.

Lord,
we receive your gifts
at this celebration in honor of St. N.
May they free us from sin
and strengthen us by your grace.

We ask this in the name of Jesus the Lord.

Liturgy of the Word: *Common of Holy Men and Woman*

READING I   From the Old Testament

Gn 12:1–4a

*Go forth from the land of your kinsfolk
and from your father's house.*

A reading from the Book of Genesis

The LORD said to Abram: "Go forth from the land of your kinsfolk
and from your father's house to a land that I will show you.

"I will make of you a great nation,
and I will bless you;

I will make your name great,
    so that you will be a blessing.
I will bless those who bless you and curse those who
    curse you.
  All the communities of the earth
    shall find blessing in you."
  Abram went as the LORD directed him.
The word of the Lord.

2   Lv 19:1–2, 17–18

You shall love your neighbor as yourself.

A reading from the Book of Leviticus

The LORD said to Moses, "Speak to the whole assembly of the children of Israel and tell them: Be holy, for I, the LORD, your God, am holy.

"You shall not bear hatred for your brother in your heart. Though you may have to reprove your fellow citizen, do not incur sin because of him. Take no revenge and cherish no grudge against any of your people. You shall love your neighbor as yourself. I am the LORD."

The word of the Lord.

3   Dt 6:3–9

Love the LORD your God with all your heart.

A reading from the Book of Deuteronomy

Moses said to the people: "Hear, Israel, and be careful to observe these commandments, that you may grow and prosper the more, in keeping with the promise of the LORD, the God of your fathers, to give you a land flowing with milk and honey.

"Hear, O Israel! The LORD is our God, the LORD alone! Therefore, you shall love the LORD, your God, with all your heart, and with all your soul, and with all your strength. Take to heart these words which I enjoin on you today. Drill them into your children. Speak of them at home and abroad, whether you are busy or at rest. Bind them at your wrist as a sign and let them be as a pendant on your forehead. Write them on the doorposts of your houses and on your gates."

The word of the Lord.

FOR RELIGIOUS

4

Dt 10:8–9

The LORD himself is our heritage.

A reading from the Book of Deuteronomy

Moses summoned all of Israel and said to them: "At that time the LORD set apart the tribe of Levi to carry the ark of the covenant of the LORD, to be in attendance before the LORD and minister to him, and to give blessings in his name, as they have done to this day. For this reason, Levi has no share in the heritage with his brothers; the LORD himself is his heritage, as the LORD, your God, has told him."

The word of the Lord.

FOR RELIGIOUS

5

1 Kgs 19:4–9a, 11–15a

Go outside and stand on the mountain before the LORD.

A reading from the first Book of Kings

Elijah went a day's journey into the desert, until he came to a broom tree and sat beneath it. He prayed for death saying:

"This is enough, O LORD! Take my life, for I am no better than my fathers." He lay down and fell asleep under the broom tree, but then an angel touched him and ordered him to get up and eat. He looked and there at his head was a hearth cake and a jug of water. After he ate and drank, he lay down again, but the angel of the LORD came back a second time, touched him, and ordered, "Get up and eat, else the journey will be too long for you!" He got up, ate, and drank; then strengthened by that food, he walked forty days and forty nights to the mountain of God, Horeb.

There he came to a cave, where he took shelter. Then the LORD said to him, "Go outside and stand on the mountain before the LORD; the LORD will be passing by." A strong and heavy wind was rending the mountains and crushing rocks before the LORD—but the LORD was not in the wind. After the wind there was an earthquake—but the LORD was not in the earthquake. After the earthquake there was fire—but the LORD was not in the fire. After the fire there was a tiny whispering sound. When he heard this, Elijah hid his face in his cloak and went and stood at the entrance of the cave. A voice said to him, "Elijah, why are you here?" He replied, "I have been most zealous for the LORD, the God of hosts. But the children of Israel have forsaken your covenant, torn down your altars, and put your prophets to the sword. I alone am left, and they seek to take my life." The LORD said to him, "Go, take the road back to the desert near Damascus."

The word of the Lord.

FOR RELIGIOUS

6

1 Kgs 19:16b, 19–21

Elisha left and followed Elijah.

A reading from the first Book of Kings

The LORD said to Elijah: "You shall anoint Elisha, son of Shaphat of Abel-meholah, as prophet to succeed you."

Elijah set out and came upon Elisha, son of Shaphat, as he was plowing with twelve yoke of oxen; he was following the twelfth. Elijah went over to him and threw his cloak over him. Elisha left the oxen, ran after Elijah, and said, "Please, let me kiss my father and mother goodbye, and I will follow you." Elijah answered, "Go back! Have I done anything to you?" Elisha left him and, taking the yoke of oxen, slaughtered them; he used the plowing equipment for fuel to boil their flesh, and gave it to his people to eat. Then he left and followed Elijah as his attendant.

The word of the Lord.

7

Tb 8:4b–8

Allow us to live together to a happy old age.

A reading from the Book of Tobit

On their wedding night Tobiah arose from bed and said to his wife, "My love, get up. Let us pray and beg our Lord to have mercy on us and to grant us deliverance." She got up, and they started to pray and beg that deliverance might be theirs. He began with these words:

"Blessed are you, O God of our fathers;
praised be your name forever and ever.

Let the heavens and all your creation
  praise you forever.
You made Adam and you gave him his wife Eve
  to be his help and support;
  and from these two the human race descended.
You said, 'It is not good for the man to be alone;
  let us make him a partner like himself.'
Now, Lord, you know that I take this wife of mine
  not because of lust,
  but for a noble purpose.
Call down your mercy on me and on her,
  and allow us to live together to a happy old age."

They said together, "Amen, amen."
The word of the Lord.

FOR THOSE WHO WORKED FOR THE UNDERPRIVILEGED

8   Tb 12:6–14a

*Prayer and fasting are good, but better than either
is almsgiving accompanied by righteousness.*

A reading from the Book of Tobit

The angel Raphael said to Tobit and his son: "Thank God!
Give him the praise and the glory. Before all the living, acknowledge the many good things he has done for you, by
blessing and extolling his name in song. Before all people,
honor and proclaim God's deeds, and do not be slack in praising
him. A king's secret it is prudent to keep, but the works of God
are to be declared and made known. Praise them with due honor.
Do good, and evil will not find its way to you. Prayer and fasting are good, but better than either is almsgiving accompanied

by righteousness. A little with righteousness is better than abundance with wickedness. It is better to give alms than to store up gold; for almsgiving saves one from death and expiates every sin. Those who regularly give alms shall enjoy a full life; but those habitually guilty of sin are their own worst enemies.

"I will now tell you the whole truth; I will conceal nothing at all from you. I have already said to you, 'A king's secret it is prudent to keep, but the works of God are to be made known with due honor.' I can now tell you that when you, Tobit, and Sarah prayed, it was I who presented and read the record of your prayer before the Glory of the Lord; and I did the same thing when you used to bury the dead. When you did not hesitate to get up and leave your dinner in order to go and bury the dead, I was sent to put you to the test."

The word of the Lord.

FOR WIDOWS

9

Jdt 8:2–8

She was a very God-fearing woman.

A reading from the Book of Judith

Judith's husband, Manasseh, of her own tribe and clan, had died at the time of the barley harvest. While he was in the field supervising those who bound the sheaves, he suffered sunstroke; and he died of this illness in Bethulia, his native city. Manasseh was buried with his fathers in the field between Dothan and Balamon. The widowed Judith remained three years and four months at home, where she set up a tent for herself on the roof of her house. She put sackcloth about her loins and wore widow's weeds. She fasted all the days of her widowhood, except sabbath eves and sabbaths, new moon eves and new moons, feastdays and holidays of the house of Israel. She was beautifully formed and lovely to behold.

Her husband, Manasseh, the son of Joseph, the son of Ahitub, the son of Melchis, the son of Eliab, the son of Nathanael, the son of Sarasadai, the son of Simeon, had left her gold and silver, servants and maids, livestock and fields, which she was maintaining. No one had a bad word to say about her, for she was a very God-fearing woman.

The word of the Lord.

10

Est C:1–7, 10

I acted as I did so as not to place
the honor of man above that of God.

A reading from the Book of Esther

Mordecai prayed : "O God of Abraham, God of Isaac, God of Jacob, blessed are you; O Lord God, almighty King, all things are in your power, and there is no one to oppose you in your will to save Israel. You made heaven and earth and every wonderful thing under the heavens. You are LORD of all, and there is no one who can resist you, LORD. You know all things. You know, O LORD, that gladly would I have kissed the soles of Haman's feet for the salvation of Israel. But I acted as I did so as not to place the honor of man above that of God. I will not bow down to anyone but you, my LORD and God. Hear my prayer; have pity on your inheritance and turn our sorrow into joy: thus we shall live to sing praise to your name, O LORD. Do not silence those who praise you."

The word of the Lord.

11

Prv 31:10–13, 19–20, 30–31

The woman who fears the Lord is to be praised.

A reading from the Book of Proverbs

When one finds a worthy wife,
    her value is far beyond pearls.
Her husband, entrusting his heart to her,
    has an unfailing prize.
She brings him good, and not evil,
    all the days of her life.
She obtains wool and flax
    and makes cloth with skillful hands.
She puts her hands to the distaff,
    and her fingers ply the spindle.
She reaches out her hands to the poor,
    and extends her arms to the needy.
Charm is deceptive and beauty fleeting;
    the woman who fears the Lord is to be praised.
Give her a reward of her labors,
    and let her works praise her at the city gates.
The word of the Lord.

12

Sir 2:7–13

You who fear the Lord, believe him, hope in him, love him.

A reading from the Book of Sirach

You who fear the Lord, wait for his mercy,
    turn not away lest you fall.
You who fear the Lord, trust him,
    and your reward will not be lost.
You who fear the Lord, hope for good things,

for lasting joy and mercy.
You who fear the Lord, love him
    and your hearts will be enlightened.
Study the generations long past and understand;
    has anyone hoped in the LORD and been disappointed?
Has anyone persevered in his commandments
      and been forsaken?
    Has anyone called upon him and been rebuffed?
Compassionate and merciful is the LORD;
    he forgives sins, he saves in time of trouble
    and he is a protector to all who seek him in truth.

The word of the Lord.

13   Sir 3:17–24

Humble yourself and you will find favor with God.

A reading from the Book of Sirach

My child, conduct your affairs with humility,
    and you will be loved more than a giver of gifts.
Humble yourself the more, the greater you are,
    and you will find favor with God.
The greater you are,
    the more you must humble yourself in all things,
    and you will find grace before God.
For great is the power of God;
    by the humble he is glorified.
What is too sublime for you, seek not,
    into things beyond your strength search not.
What is committed to you, attend to;
    for it is not necessary for you to see with your eyes
    those things which are hidden.
With what is too much for you meddle not,

when shown things beyond human understanding.
Their own opinion has misled many,
    and false reasoning unbalanced their judgment.
Where the pupil of the eye is missing, there is no light,
    and where there is no knowledge, there is no wisdom.
The word of the Lord.

14

Sir 26:1–4, 13–16

Like the sun rising in the LORD's heavens, the beauty of a
virtuous wife is the radiance of her home.

A reading from the Book of Sirach

Blessed the husband of a good wife,
    twice-lengthened are his days;
A worthy wife brings joy to her husband,
    peaceful and full is his life.
A good wife is a generous gift
    bestowed upon him who fears the LORD;
Be he rich or poor, his heart is content,
    and a smile is ever on his face.

A gracious wife delights her husband,
    her thoughtfulness puts flesh on his bones;
A gift from the LORD is her governed speech,
    and her firm virtue is of surpassing worth.
Choicest of blessings is a modest wife,
    priceless her chaste soul.
A holy and decent woman adds grace upon grace;
    indeed, no price is worthy of her temperate soul.
Like the sun rising in the LORD's heavens,
    the beauty of a virtuous wife is the radiance of her home.
The word of the Lord.

FOR THOSE WHO WORKED FOR THE UNDERPRIVILEGED

15

Is 58:6–11

Share your bread with the hungry.

A reading from the Book of the Prophet Isaiah

Thus says the LORD:
This is the fasting that I wish:
   releasing those bound unjustly,
   untying the thongs of the yoke;
Setting free the oppressed,
   breaking every yoke;
Sharing your bread with the hungry,
   sheltering the oppressed and the homeless;
Clothing the naked when you see them,
   and not turning your back on your own.
Then your light shall break forth like the dawn,
   and your wound shall quickly be healed;
Your vindication shall go before you,
   and the glory of the LORD shall be your rear guard.
Then you shall call, and the LORD will answer,
   you shall cry for help, and he will say: Here I am!
If you remove from your midst oppression,
   false accusation and malicious speech;
If you bestow your bread on the hungry
   and satisfy the afflicted;
Then light shall rise for you in darkness,
   and the gloom shall become for you like midday;
Then the LORD will guide you always
   and give you plenty even on the parched land.
He will renew your strength,

and you shall be like a watered garden,
like a spring whose water never fails.
The word of the Lord.

16

Jer 20:7–9

It becomes like fire burning in my heart.

A reading from the Book of the Prophet Jeremiah

You duped me, O LORD, and I let myself be duped;
you were too strong for me, and you triumphed.
All the day I am an object for laughter;
everyone mocks me.
Whenever I speak, I must cry out,
violence and outrage is my message;
The word of the LORD has brought me
derision and reproach all the day.
I say to myself, I will not mention him,
I will speak in his name no more.
But then it becomes like fire burning in my heart,
imprisoned in my bones;
I grow weary holding it in,
I cannot endure it.
The word of the Lord.

17

Mi 6:6–8

*You have been told, O man,
what the LORD requires of you.*

A reading from the Book of the Prophet Micah

With what shall I come before the LORD,
and bow before God most high?
Shall I come before him with burnt offerings,

with calves a year old?
Will the LORD be pleased with thousands of rams,
    with myriad streams of oil?
Shall I give my first-born for my crime,
    the fruit of my body for the sin of my soul?
You have been told, O man, what is good,
    and what the LORD requires of you:
Only to do the right and to love goodness,
    and to walk humbly with your God.

The word of the Lord.

18
                            Zep 2:3; 3:12–13

But I will leave as a remnant in your midst
a people humble and lowly.

A reading from the Book of the Prophet Zephaniah

Seek the LORD, all you humble of the earth,
    who have observed his law;
Seek justice, seek humility;
    perhaps you may be sheltered
    on the day of the LORD's anger.

But I will leave as a remnant in your midst
    a people humble and lowly,
Who shall take refuge in the name of the Lord:
    the remnant of Israel.
They shall do no wrong
    and speak no lies;
Nor shall there be found in their mouths
    a deceitful tongue;
They shall pasture and couch their flocks
    with none to disturb them.

The word of the Lord.

READING I   From the New Testament

During the Easter Season

FOR RELIGIOUS

FIRST OPTION

Acts 4:32–35

The community of believers was of one heart and mind.

A reading from the Acts of the Apostles

The community of believers was of one heart and mind, and no one claimed that any of his possessions was his own, but they had everything in common. With great power the Apostles bore witness to the resurrection of the Lord Jesus, and great favor was accorded them all. There was no needy person among them, for those who owned property or houses would sell them, bring the proceeds of the sale, and put them at the feet of the Apostles, and they were distributed to each according to need.

The word of the Lord.

SECOND OPTION

Rv 3:14b, 20–22

I will dine with him and he with me.

A reading from the Book of Revelation

"'The Amen, the faithful and true witness, the source of God's creation, says this:

"'"Behold, I stand at the door and knock. If anyone hears my voice and opens the door, then I will enter his house and dine with him, and he with me. I will give the victor the right to sit with me on my throne, as I myself first won the victory and sit with my Father on his throne.

"'"Whoever has ears ought to hear what the Spirit says to the churches."'"

The word of the Lord.

THIRD OPTION

Rv 19:1, 5–9a

*Blessed are those who have been called
to the wedding feast of the Lamb.*

A reading from the Book of Revelation

I, John, heard what sounded like the loud voice of a great multitude in heaven, saying:

"Alleluia!
Salvation, glory, and might belong to our God."

A voice coming from the throne said:

"Praise our God, all you his servants,
and you who revere him, small and great."

Then I heard something like the sound of a great multitude or the sound of rushing water or mighty peals of thunder, as they said:

"Alleluia!
The Lord has established his reign,
our God, the almighty.
Let us rejoice and be glad
and give him glory.
For the wedding day of the Lamb has come,
his bride has made herself ready.
She was allowed to wear
a bright, clean linen garment."

(The linen represents the righteous deeds of the holy ones.)

Then the angel said to me, "Write this: Blessed are those who have been called to the wedding feast of the Lamb."

The word of the Lord.

FOURTH OPTION

Rv 21:5–7

To the thirsty I will give a gift
from the spring of life-giving water.

A reading from the Book of Revelation

The One who was seated on the throne said: "Behold, I make all things new." Then he said, "Write these words down, for they are trustworthy and true." He said to me, "They are accomplished. I am the Alpha and the Omega, the beginning and the end. To the thirsty I will give a gift from the spring of life-giving water. The victor will inherit these gifts, and I shall be his God, and he will be my son."

The word of the Lord.

Responsorial Psalm

 1

Ps 1:1–2, 3, 4 and 6

R. Blessed are they who hope in the Lord.

Blessed the man who follows not
   the counsel of the wicked
Nor walks in the way of sinners,
   nor sits in the company of the insolent,
But delights in the law of the LORD
   and meditates on his law day and night.

R. Blessed are they who hope in the Lord.

He is like a tree
   planted near running water,
That yields its fruit in due season,
   and whose leaves never fade.
   Whatever he does, prospers.

R. Blessed are they who hope in the Lord.

Not so, the wicked, not so;
  they are like chaff which the wind drives away.
For the L{ord} watches over the way of the just,
  but the way of the wicked vanishes.

  R. Blessed are they who hope in the Lord.

  Or: **R. Blessed are they who delight in the law of the Lord.**

  Or: **R. The just will flourish like the palm tree
      in the garden of the Lord.**

2   Ps 15:2–3a, 3bc–4ab, 5

  R. The just one shall live on your holy mountain, O Lord.

He who walks blamelessly and does justice;
  who thinks the truth in his heart
  and slanders not with his tongue.

  R. The just one shall live on your holy mountain, O Lord.

Who harms not his fellow man,
  nor takes up a reproach against his neighbor;
By whom the reprobate is despised,
  while he honors those who fear the L{ord}.

  R. The just one shall live on your holy mountain, O Lord.

Who lends not his money at usury
  and accepts no bribe against the innocent.
He who does these things
  shall never be disturbed.

  R. The just one shall live on your holy mountain, O Lord.

3   Ps 16:1–2ab and 5, 7–8, 11

  R. You are my inheritance, O Lord.

Keep me, O God, for in you I take refuge;
  I say to the L{ord}, "My Lord are you."
O L{ord}, my allotted portion and my cup,
  you it is who hold fast my lot.

R. You are my inheritance, O Lord.

I bless the LORD who counsels me;
  even in the night my heart exhorts me.
I set the LORD ever before me;
  with him at my right hand I shall not be disturbed.

R. You are my inheritance, O Lord.

You will show me the path to life,
  fullness of joys in your presence,
  the delights at your right hand forever.

R. You are my inheritance, O Lord.

4

Ps 23:1–3, 4, 5, 6

R. The Lord is my shepherd; there is nothing I shall want.

The LORD is my shepherd; I shall not want.
  In verdant pastures he gives me repose;
Beside restful waters he leads me;
  he refreshes my soul.
He guides me on right paths
  for his name's sake.

R. The Lord is my shepherd; there is nothing I shall want.

Even though I walk in the dark valley
  I fear no evil; for you are at my side
With your rod and your staff
  that give me courage.

R. The Lord is my shepherd; there is nothing I shall want.

You spread the table before me
  in the sight of my foes;
You anoint my head with oil;
  my cup overflows.

R. The Lord is my shepherd; there is nothing I shall want.

Only goodness and kindness follow me
  all the days of my life;

And I shall dwell in the house of the LORD
  for years to come.

R. The Lord is my shepherd; there is nothing I shall want.

5   Ps 34:2–3, 4–5, 6–7, 8–9, 10–11

R. I will bless the Lord at all times.

I will bless the LORD at all times;
  his praise shall be ever in my mouth.
Let my soul glory in the LORD;
  the lowly will hear and be glad.

R. I will bless the Lord at all times.

Glorify the LORD with me,
  let us together extol his name.
I sought the LORD, and he answered me
  and delivered me from all my fears.

R. I will bless the Lord at all times.

Look to him that you may be radiant with joy,
  and your faces may not blush with shame.
When the poor one called out, the LORD heard,
  and from all his distress he saved him.

R. I will bless the Lord at all times.

The angel of the LORD encamps
  around those who fear him, and delivers them.
Taste and see how good the LORD is;
  blessed the man who takes refuge in him.

R. I will bless the Lord at all times.

Fear the LORD, you his holy ones,
  for nought is lacking to those who fear him.
The great grow poor and hungry;
  but those who seek the LORD want for no good thing.

R. I will bless the Lord at all times.

Or: **R. Taste and see the goodness of the Lord.**

6

Ps 103:1bc–2, 3–4, 8–9, 13–14, 17–18a

R. O, bless the Lord, my soul!

Bless the LORD, O my soul;
  and all my being, bless his holy name.
Bless the LORD, O my soul,
  and forget not all his benefits.

R. O, bless the Lord, my soul!

He pardons all your iniquities,
  he heals all your ills,
He redeems your life from destruction,
  he crowns you with kindness and compassion.

R. O, bless the Lord, my soul!

Merciful and gracious is the LORD,
  slow to anger and abounding in kindness.
He will not always chide,
  nor does he keep his wrath forever.

R. O, bless the Lord, my soul!

As a father has compassion on his children,
  so the LORD has compassion on those who fear him,
For he knows how we are formed;
  he remembers that we are dust.

R. O, bless the Lord, my soul!

But the kindness of the LORD is from eternity
  to eternity toward those who fear him,
And his justice toward his children's children
  among those who keep his covenant.

R. O, bless the Lord, my soul!

7

Ps 112:1–2, 3–4, 5–7a, 7b–8, 9

R. Blessed the man who fears the Lord.

Blessed the man who fears the LORD,
  who greatly delights in his commands.

His posterity shall be mighty upon the earth;
  the upright generation shall be blessed.

R. Blessed the man who fears the Lord.

Wealth and riches shall be in his house;
  his generosity shall endure forever.
Light shines through the darkness for the upright;
  he is gracious and merciful and just.

R. Blessed the man who fears the Lord.

Well for the man who is gracious and lends,
  who conducts his affairs with justice;
He shall never be moved;
  the just one shall be in everlasting remembrance.

R. Blessed the man who fears the Lord.

An evil report he shall not fear;
  his heart is firm, trusting in the LORD.
His heart is steadfast; he shall not fear
  till he looks down upon his foes.

R. Blessed the man who fears the Lord.

Lavishly he gives to the poor,
  his generosity shall endure forever;
his horn shall be exalted in glory.

R. Blessed the man who fears the Lord.

Or: **R. Alleluia.**

8   Ps 128:1–2, 3, 4–5

R. Blessed are those who fear the Lord.

Blessed are you who fear the LORD,
  who walk in his ways!
For you shall eat the fruit of your handiwork;
  blessed shall you be, and favored.

R. Blessed are those who fear the Lord.

Your wife shall be like a fruitful vine
  in the recesses of your home;
Your children like olive plants
  around your table.

R. Blessed are those who fear the Lord.

Behold, thus is the man blessed
  who fears the LORD.
The LORD bless you from Zion:
  may you see the prosperity of Jerusalem
  all the days of your life.

R. Blessed are those who fear the Lord.

9

Ps 131:1bcde, 2, 3

R. In you, Lord, I have found my peace.

O LORD, my heart is not proud,
  nor are my eyes haughty;
I busy not myself with great things,
  nor with things too sublime for me.

R. In you, Lord, I have found my peace.

Nay rather, I have stilled and quieted
  my soul like a weaned child.
Like a weaned child on its mother's lap,
  so is my soul within me.

R. In you, Lord, I have found my peace.

O Israel, hope in the LORD,
  both now and forever.

R. In you, Lord, I have found my peace.

READING II   From the New Testament

Rom 8:26–30

Those he justified he also glorified.

A reading from the Letter of Saint Paul to the Romans

Brothers and sisters:

The Spirit comes to the aid of our weakness; for we do not know how to pray as we ought, but the Spirit himself intercedes with inexpressible groanings. And the one who searches hearts knows what is the intention of the Spirit, because he intercedes for the holy ones according to God's will.

We know that all things work for good for those who love God, who are called according to his purpose. For those he foreknew he also predestined to be conformed to the image of his Son, so that he might be the firstborn among many brothers. And those he predestined he also called; and those he called he also justified; and those he justified he also glorified.

The word of the Lord.

1 Cor 1:26–31

God chose the weak of the world.

A reading from the first Letter of Saint Paul to the Corinthians

Consider your own calling, brothers and sisters. Not many of you were wise by human standards, not many were powerful, not many were of noble birth. Rather, God chose the foolish of the world to shame the wise, and God chose the weak of the world to shame the strong, and God chose the lowly and despised of the world, those who count for nothing, to reduce to nothing those who are something, so that no human being might boast before God. It is due to him that you are in Christ Jesus, who became for us wisdom from God, as well as righteousness, sanctification, and redemption, so that, as it is written, *Whoever boasts, should boast in the Lord.*

The word of the Lord.

3

1 Cor 12:31—13:13 or 13:4–13

Love never fails.

A reading from the first Letter of Saint Paul to the Corinthians

Long form follows; for short form omit what is in brackets.

Brothers and sisters:

[Strive eagerly for the greatest spiritual gifts.

But I shall show you a still more excellent way.

If I speak in human and angelic tongues but do not have love, I am a resounding gong or a clashing cymbal. And if I have the gift of prophecy and comprehend all mysteries and all knowledge; if I have all faith so as to move mountains, but do not have love, I am nothing. If I give away everything I own, and if I hand my body over so that I may boast but do not have love, I gain nothing.]

Love is patient, love is kind. It is not jealous, love is not pompous, it is not inflated, it is not rude, it does not seek its own interests, it is not quick-tempered, it does not brood over injury, it does not rejoice over wrongdoing but rejoices with the truth. It bears all things, believes all things, hopes all things, endures all things.

Love never fails. If there are prophecies, they will be brought to nothing; if tongues, they will cease; if knowledge, it will be brought to nothing. For we know partially and we prophesy partially, but when the perfect comes, the partial will pass away.

When I was a child, I used to talk as a child, think as a child, reason as a child; when I became a man, I put aside childish things. At present we see indistinctly, as in a mirror, but then face to face. At present I know partially; then I shall know fully, as I am fully known. So faith, hope, love remain, these three; but the greatest of these is love.

The word of the Lord.

 4   2 Cor 10:17–11:2

I betrothed you to one husband,
to present you as a chaste virgin to Christ.

A reading from the second Letter of Saint Paul to the Corinthians

Brothers and sisters:
Whoever boasts, should boast in the Lord. For it is not the one who recommends himself who is approved, but the one whom the Lord recommends.

If only you would put up with a little foolishness from me! Please put up with me. For I am jealous of you with the jealousy of God, since I betrothed you to one husband to present you as a chaste virgin to Christ.

The word of the Lord.

 5   Gal 2:19–20

I live, no longer I, but Christ lives in me.

A reading from the Letter of Saint Paul to the Galatians

Brothers and sisters:
Through the law I died to the law, that I might live for God. I have been crucified with Christ; yet I live, no longer I, but Christ lives in me; insofar as I now live in the flesh, I live by

faith in the Son of God who has loved me and given himself up for me.

The word of the Lord.

6

Gal 6:14–16

Through which the world has been
crucified to me and I to the world.

A reading from the Letter of Saint Paul to the Galatians

Brothers and sisters:

May I never boast except in the cross of our Lord Jesus Christ, through which the world has been crucified to me, and I to the world. For neither does circumcision mean anything, nor does uncircumcision, but only a new creation. Peace and mercy be to all who follow this rule and to the Israel of God.

The word of the Lord.

7

Eph 3:14–19

To know the love of Christ which surpasses knowledge.

A reading from the Letter of Saint Paul to the Ephesians

Brothers and sisters:

I kneel before the Father, from whom every family in heaven and on earth is named, that he may grant you in accord with the riches of his glory to be strengthened with power through his Spirit in the inner self, and that Christ may dwell in your hearts through faith; that you, rooted and grounded in love, may have strength to comprehend with all the holy ones what is the breadth and length and height and depth, and to know the love of Christ that surpasses knowledge, so that you may be filled with all the fullness of God.

The word of the Lord.

8   Eph 6:10–13, 18

Put on the armor of God.

A reading from the Letter of Saint Paul to the Ephesians

Brothers and sisters:

Draw your strength from the Lord and from his mighty power. Put on the armor of God so that you may be able to stand firm against the tactics of the Devil. For our struggle is not with flesh and blood but with the principalities, with the powers, with the world rulers of this present darkness, with the evil spirits in the heavens. Therefore, put on the armor of God, that you may be able to resist on the evil day and, having done everything, to hold your ground.

With all prayer and supplication, pray at every opportunity in the Spirit. To that end, be watchful with all perseverance and supplication for all the holy ones.

The word of the Lord.

9   Phil 3:8–14

I continue my pursuit toward the goal, the prize
of God's upward calling, in Christ Jesus.

A reading from the Letter of Saint Paul to the Philippians

Brothers and sisters:

I consider everything as a loss because of the supreme good of knowing Christ Jesus my Lord. For his sake I have accepted the loss of all things and I consider them so much rubbish, that I may gain Christ and be found in him, not having any righteousness of my own based on the law but that which comes through faith in Christ, the righteousness from God, depending on faith to know him and the power of his resurrection and the sharing of his sufferings by being conformed to his death, if somehow I may attain the resurrection from the dead.

It is not that I have already taken hold of it or have already attained perfect maturity, but I continue my pursuit in hope that I may possess it, since I have indeed been taken possession of by Christ Jesus. Brothers and sisters, I for my part do not consider myself to have taken possession. Just one thing: forgetting what lies behind but straining forward to what lies ahead, I continue my pursuit toward the goal, the prize of God's upward calling, in Christ Jesus.

The word of the Lord.

10

Phil 4:4–9

Think about whatever is worthy of praise.

A reading from the Letter of Saint Paul to the Philippians

Brothers and sisters:

Rejoice in the Lord always. I shall say it again: rejoice! Your kindness should be known to all. The Lord is near. Have no anxiety at all, but in everything, by prayer and petition, with thanksgiving, make your requests known to God. Then the peace of God that surpasses all understanding will guard your hearts and minds in Christ Jesus.

Finally, brothers and sisters, whatever is true, whatever is honorable, whatever is just, whatever is pure, whatever is lovely, whatever is gracious, if there is any excellence and if there is anything worthy of praise, think about these things. Keep on doing what you have learned and received and heard and seen in me. Then the God of peace will be with you.

The word of the Lord.

11   Col 3:12–17

Over all these put on love, that is, the bond of perfection.

A reading from the Letter of Saint Paul to the Colossians

Brothers and sisters:

Put on, as God's chosen ones, holy and beloved, heartfelt compassion, kindness, humility, gentleness, and patience, bearing with one another and forgiving one another, if one has a grievance against another; as the Lord has forgiven you, so must you also do. And over all these put on love, that is, the bond of perfection. And let the peace of Christ control your hearts, the peace into which you were also called in one Body. And be thankful. Let the word of Christ dwell in you richly, as in all wisdom you teach and admonish one another, singing psalms, hymns, and spiritual songs with gratitude in your hearts to God. And whatever you do, in word or in deed, do everything in the name of the Lord Jesus, giving thanks to God the Father through him.

The word of the Lord.

FOR WIDOWS

12   1 Tm 5:3–10

The real widow, who is all alone, has set her hope on God.

A reading from the first Letter of Saint Paul to Timothy

Beloved:

Honor widows who are truly widows. But if a widow has children or grandchildren, let these first learn to perform their religious duty to their own family and to make recompense to their parents, for this is pleasing to God. The real widow, who is all alone, has set her hope on God and continues in supplications and prayers night and day. But the one who is self-indulgent is dead while she lives. Command this, so that they may be irreproachable. And whoever does not provide for relatives and especially family members has denied the faith and is worse than an unbeliever.

Let a widow be enrolled if she is not less than sixty years old, married only once, with a reputation for good works, namely, that she has raised children, practiced hospitality, washed the feet of the holy ones, helped those in distress, involved herself in every good work.

The word of the Lord.

13

Jas 2:14–17

Faith of itself, if it does not have works, is dead.

A reading from the Letter of Saint James

What good is it, my brothers and sisters, if someone says he has faith but does not have works? Can that faith save him? If a brother or sister has nothing to wear and has no food for the day, and one of you says to them, "Go in peace, keep warm, and eat well," but you do not give them the necessities of the body, what good is it? So also faith of itself, if it does not have works, is dead.

The word of the Lord.

14

1 Pt 3:1–9

Holy women hoped in God.

A reading from the first Letter of Saint Peter

You wives should be subordinate to your husbands so that, even if some disobey the word, they may be won over without a word by their wives' conduct when they observe your reverent and chaste behavior. Your adornment should not be an external one: braiding the hair, wearing gold jewelry, or dressing in fine clothes, but rather the hidden character of the heart, expressed in the imperishable beauty of a gentle and calm disposition, which is precious in the sight of God. For this is also how the holy women who hoped in God once used to adorn themselves and were subordinate to their husbands; thus Sarah obeyed Abraham, calling him "lord." You are her children when you do what is good and fear no intimidation.

Likewise, you husbands should live with your wives in understanding, showing honor to the weaker female sex, since we are joint heirs of the gift of life, so that your prayers may not be hindered.

Finally, all of you, be of one mind, sympathetic, loving toward one another, compassionate, humble. Do not return evil for evil, or insult for insult; but, on the contrary, a blessing, because to this you were called, that you might inherit a blessing.

The word of the Lord.

 15

1 Pt 4:7b–11

As each one has received a gift,
use it to serve one another.

A reading from the first Letter of Saint Peter

Beloved:

Be serious and sober-minded so that you will be able to pray. Above all, let your love for one another be intense, because love covers a multitude of sins. Be hospitable to one another without complaining. As each one has received a gift, use it to serve one another as good stewards of God's varied grace. Whoever preaches, let it be with the words of God; whoever serves, let it be with the strength that God supplies, so that in all things God may be glorified through Jesus Christ, to whom belong glory and dominion forever and ever. Amen.

The word of the Lord.

FOR THOSE WHO WORKED FOR THE UNDERPRIVILEGED

16

1 Jn 3:14–18

We ought to lay down our lives for our brothers.

A reading from the first Letter of Saint John

Beloved:

We know that we have passed from death to life because we love our brothers. Whoever does not love remains in death. Everyone who hates his brother is a murderer, and you know that anyone who is a murderer does not have eternal life remaining in him. The way we came to know love was that he laid down his life for us; so we ought to lay down our lives for our brothers. If someone who has worldly means sees a brother in need and refuses him compassion, how can the love of God remain in him? Children, let us love not in word or speech but in deed and truth.

The word of the Lord.

17

1 Jn 4:7–16

If we love one another, God remains in us.

A reading from the first Letter of Saint John

Beloved, let us love one another, because love is of God; everyone who loves is begotten by God and knows God. Whoever is without love does not know God, for God is love. In this way the love of God was revealed to us: God sent his only-begotten Son into the world so that we might have life through him. In this is love: not that we have loved God, but that he loved us and sent his Son as expiation for our sins. Beloved, if God so loved us, we also must love one another. No one has ever seen God. Yet, if we love one another, God remains in us, and his love is brought to perfection in us.

This is how we know that we remain in him and he in us, that he has given us of his Spirit. Moreover, we have seen and testify that the Father sent his Son as savior of the world. Whoever acknowledges that Jesus is the Son of God, God remains in him and he in God. We have come to know and to believe in the love God has for us.

God is love, and whoever remains in love remains in God and God in him.

The word of the Lord.

18   1 Jn 5:1–5

The victory that conquers the world is our faith.

A reading from the first Letter of Saint John

Beloved:

Everyone who believes that Jesus is the Christ is begotten by God, and everyone who loves the Father loves also the one begotten by him. In this way we know that we love the children of God when we love God and obey his commandments. For the love of God is this, that we keep his commandments. And his commandments are not burdensome, for whoever is begotten by God conquers the world. And the victory that conquers the world is our faith. Who indeed is the victor over the world but the one who believes that Jesus is the Son of God?

The word of the Lord.

ALLELUIA VERSE AND VERSE BEFORE THE GOSPEL

1 Mt 5:3

Blessed are the poor in spirit;
for theirs is the Kingdom of heaven.

2 Mt 5:6

Blessed are those who hunger and thirst for righteousness,
for they will be satisfied.

3 Mt 5:8

Blessed are the clean of heart,
for they will see God.

4 See Mt 11:25

Blessed are you, Father, Lord of heaven and earth;
you have revealed to little ones the mysteries
   of the Kingdom.

5 Mt 11:28

Come to me, all you who labor and are burdened,
and I will give you rest, says the Lord.

6 Mt 23:11, 12b

The greatest among you must be your servant.
Whoever humbles himself will be exalted.

7 Lk 21:36

Be vigilant at all times
and pray that you may have the strength
   to stand before the Son of Man.

8 Jn 8:12

I am the light of the world, says the Lord;
whoever follows me will have the light of life.

9 Jn 8:31b–32

If you remain in my word, you will truly be my disciples,
and you will know the truth, says the Lord.

10 Jn 13:34

I give you a new commandment:
love one another as I have loved you.

11 Jn 14:23

Whoever loves me will keep my word
and my Father will love him
and we will come to him.

12 Jn 15:4a, 5b

Remain in me, as I remain in you, says the Lord;
whoever remains in me will bear much fruit.

13 Jn 15:9b, 5b

Remain in my love, says the Lord;
whoever remains in me and I in him will bear much fruit.

GOSPEL

1

Mt 5:1–12a

Rejoice and be glad, for your reward will be great in heaven.

A reading from the holy Gospel according to Matthew

When Jesus saw the crowds, he went up the mountain, and
after he had sat down, his disciples came to him. He began to
teach them, saying:

"Blessed are the poor in spirit,
for theirs is the Kingdom of heaven.
Blessed are they who mourn,
for they will be comforted.
Blessed are the meek,
for they will inherit the land.

Blessed are they who hunger and thirst for righteousness,
   for they will be satisfied.
Blessed are the merciful,
   for they will be shown mercy.
Blessed are the clean of heart,
   for they will see God.
Blessed are the peacemakers,
   for they will be called children of God.
Blessed are they who are persecuted for the sake of
   righteousness,
   for theirs is the Kingdom of heaven.

Blessed are you when they insult you and persecute you and utter every kind of evil against you falsely because of me. Rejoice and be glad, for your reward will be great in heaven." The Gospel of the Lord.

2

Mt 5:13–16

You are the light of the world.

A reading from the holy Gospel according to Matthew

Jesus said to his disciples: "You are the salt of the earth. But if salt loses its taste, with what can it be seasoned? It is no longer good for anything but to be thrown out and trampled underfoot. You are the light of the world. A city set on a mountain cannot be hidden. Nor do they light a lamp and then put it under a bushel basket; it is set on a lampstand, where it gives light to all in the house. Just so, your light must shine before others, that they may see your good deeds and glorify your heavenly Father."
The Gospel of the Lord.

3   Mt 7:21–27

The house built on rock and the house built on sand.

A reading from the holy Gospel according to Matthew

Jesus said to his disciples: "Not everyone who says to me, 'Lord, Lord,' will enter the Kingdom of heaven, but only the one who does the will of my Father in heaven. Many will say to me on that day, 'Lord, Lord, did we not prophesy in your name? Did we not drive out demons in your name? Did we not do mighty deeds in your name?' Then I will declare to them solemnly, 'I never knew you. Depart from me, you evildoers.'

"Everyone who listens to these words of mine and acts on them will be like a wise man who built his house on rock. The rain fell, the floods came, and the winds blew and buffeted the house. But it did not collapse; it had been set solidly on rock. And everyone who listens to these words of mine but does not act on them will be like a fool who built his house on sand. The rain fell, the floods came, and the winds blew and buffeted the house. And it collapsed and was completely ruined."

The Gospel of the Lord.

4   Mt 11:25–30

*Although you have hidden these things from the
wise and the learned, you have revealed them to the childlike.*

A reading from the holy Gospel according to Matthew

At that time Jesus exclaimed: "I give praise to you, Father, Lord of heaven and earth, for although you have hidden these things from the wise and the learned you have revealed them to the childlike. Yes, Father, such has been your gracious will. All things have been handed over to me by my Father. No one knows the Son except the Father, and no one knows the Father except the Son and anyone to whom the Son wishes to reveal him.

"Come to me, all you who labor and are burdened, and I will give you rest. Take my yoke upon you and learn from me, for I am meek and humble of heart; and you will find rest for yourselves. For my yoke is easy, and my burden light."

The Gospel of the Lord.

5   Mt 13:44–46

He sells all that he has and buys that field.

A reading from the holy Gospel according to Matthew

Jesus said to the crowds: "The Kingdom of heaven is like a treasure buried in a field, which a person finds and hides again, and out of joy goes and sells all that he has and buys that field. Again, the Kingdom of heaven is like a merchant searching for fine pearls. When he finds a pearl of great price, he goes and sells all that he has and buys it."

The Gospel of the Lord.

6   Mt 16:24–27

Whoever loses his life for my sake will find it.

A reading from the holy Gospel according to Matthew

Jesus said to his disciples, "Whoever wishes to come after me must deny himself, take up his cross, and follow me. For whoever wishes to save his life will lose it, but whoever loses his life for my sake will find it. What profit would there be for one to gain the whole world and forfeit his life? Or what can one give in exchange for his life? For the Son of Man will come with his angels in his Father's glory, and then he will repay each one according to his conduct."

The Gospel of the Lord.

7   Mt 18:1–5

Unless you turn and become like children,
you will not enter the Kingdom of heaven.

A reading from the holy Gospel according to Matthew

The disciples approached Jesus and said, "Who is the greatest in the Kingdom of heaven?" He called a child over, placed it in their midst, and said, "Amen, I say to you, unless you turn and become like children, you will not enter the Kingdom of heaven. Whoever humbles himself like this child is the greatest in the Kingdom of heaven. And whoever receives one child such as this in my name receives me."

The Gospel of the Lord.

FOR RELIGIOUS

8   Mt 19:3–12

For the sake of the Kingdom of heaven.

A reading from the holy Gospel according to Matthew

Some Pharisees approached Jesus and tested him, saying, "Is it lawful for a man to divorce his wife for any cause whatever?" He said in reply, "Have you not read that from the beginning the Creator *made them male and female* and said, *For this reason a man shall leave his father and mother and be joined to his wife, and the two shall become one flesh?* So they are no longer two, but one flesh. Therefore, what God has joined together, man must not separate." They said to him, "Then why did Moses command that the man give the woman a bill of divorce and dismiss her?" He said to them, "Because of the hardness of your hearts Moses allowed you to divorce your wives, but from the beginning it was not so. I say to you, whoever divorces his wife (unless the marriage is unlawful) and marries another commits adultery." His disciples said to him, "If that is the case of a man with his wife, it is better not to marry." He answered, "Not all can accept this word, but only those to whom that is granted. Some are incapable of marriage because they were born so; some, because they were made so by others; some, because they have renounced marriage for the sake of the Kingdom of heaven. Whoever can accept this ought to accept it."

The Gospel of the Lord.

9   Mt 19:27–29

*You who have followed me
will receive a hundred times more.*

A reading from the holy Gospel according to Matthew

Peter said to Jesus, "We have given up everything and followed you. What will there be for us?" Jesus said to them, "Amen, I say to you that you who have followed me, in the new age, when the Son of Man is seated on his throne of glory, will yourselves sit on twelve thrones, judging the twelve tribes of Israel. And everyone who has given up houses or brothers or sisters or father or mother or children or lands for the sake of my name will receive a hundred times more, and will inherit eternal life."

The Gospel of the Lord.

10

Mt 22:34–40

Love the Lord your God and your neighbor as yourself.

A reading from the holy Gospel according to Matthew

When the Pharisees heard that Jesus had silenced the Sadducees, they gathered together, and one of them, a scholar of the law, tested him by asking, "Teacher, which commandment in the law is the greatest?" He said to him, "You shall love the Lord, your God, with all your heart, with all your soul, and with all your mind. This is the greatest and the first commandment. The second is like it: You shall love your neighbor as yourself. The whole law and the prophets depend on these two commandments."

The Gospel of the Lord.

11

Mt 25:1–13

Behold, the bridegroom! Come out to meet him!

A reading from the holy Gospel according to Matthew

Jesus told his disciples this parable: "The Kingdom of heaven will be like ten virgins who took their lamps and went out to meet the bridegroom. Five of them were foolish and five were wise. The foolish ones, when taking their lamps, brought no oil with them, but the wise brought flasks of oil with their lamps. Since the bridegroom was long delayed, they all became drowsy and fell asleep. At midnight, there was a cry, 'Behold, the bridegroom! Come out to meet him!' Then all those virgins got up and trimmed their lamps. The foolish ones said to the wise, 'Give us some of your oil, for our lamps are going out.' But the wise ones replied, 'No, for there may not be enough for us and you. Go instead to the merchants and buy some for yourselves.' While they went off to buy it, the bridegroom came and those who were ready went into the wedding feast with him. Then the door was locked. Afterwards the other virgins came and said, 'Lord, Lord, open the door for us!' But he said in reply, 'Amen, I say to you, I do not know you.' Therefore, stay awake, for you know neither the day nor the hour."

The Gospel of the Lord.

12   Mt 25:14–30 or 25:14–23

Since you were faithful in small matters,
come, share your master's joy.

A reading from the holy Gospel according to Matthew

Long form follows; for short form omit what is in brackets.

Jesus told his disciples this parable: "A man who was going on a journey called in his servants and entrusted his possessions to them. To one he gave five talents; to another, two; to a third, one—to each according to his ability. Then he went away. Immediately the one who received five talents went and traded with them, and made another five. Likewise, the one who received two made another two. But the man who received one went off and dug a hole in the ground and buried his master's money. After a long time the master of those servants came back and settled accounts with them. The one who had received five talents came forward bringing the additional five. He said, 'Master, you gave me five talents. See, I have made five more.' His master said to him, 'Well done, my good and faithful servant. Since you were faithful in small matters, I will give you great responsibilities. Come, share your master's joy.' Then the one who had received two talents also came forward and said, 'Master, you gave me two talents. See, I have made two more.' His master said to him, 'Well done, my good and faithful servant. Since you were faithful in small matters, I will give you great responsibilities. Come, share your master's joy.' [Then the one who had received the one talent came forward and said, 'Master, I knew you were a demanding person, harvesting where you did not plant and gathering where you did not scatter; so out of fear I went off and buried your talent in the ground. Here it is back.' His master said to him in reply, 'You wicked, lazy servant! So you knew that I harvest where I did not plant and gather where I did not scatter? Should you not then have put my money in the bank so that I could have got it back with interest on my return? Now then! Take the talent from him and give it to the one with ten. For to everyone who has more will be given and he will grow rich; but from the one who has not even what he has will be taken away. And throw this useless servant into the darkness outside, where there will be wailing and grinding of teeth.'"]

The Gospel of the Lord.

FOR THOSE WHO WORKED FOR THE UNDERPRIVILEGED

13

Mt 25:31–46 or 25:31–40

Whatever you did for the least of my brothers, you did for me.

A reading from the holy Gospel according to Matthew

Long form follows; for short form omit what is in brackets.

Jesus said to his disciples: "When the Son of Man comes in his glory, and all the angels with him, he will sit upon his glorious throne, and all the nations will be assembled before him. And he will separate them one from another, as a shepherd separates the sheep from the goats. He will place the sheep on his right and the goats on his left. Then the king will say to those on his right, 'Come, you who are blessed by my Father. Inherit the kingdom prepared for you from the foundation of the world. For I was hungry and you gave me food, I was thirsty and you gave me drink, a stranger and you welcomed me, naked and you clothed me, ill and you cared for me, in prison and you visited me.' Then the righteous will answer him and say, 'Lord, when did we see you hungry and feed you, or thirsty and give you drink? When did we see you a stranger and welcome you, or naked and clothe you? When did we see you ill or in prison, and visit you?' And the king will say to them in reply, 'Amen, I say to you, whatever you did for one of the least brothers of mine, you did for me.' [Then he will say to those on his left, 'Depart from me, you accursed, into the eternal fire prepared for the Devil and his angels. For I was hungry and you gave me no food, I was thirsty and you gave me no drink, a stranger and you gave me no welcome, naked and you gave me no clothing, ill and in prison, and you did not care for me.' Then they will answer and say, 'Lord, when did we see you hungry or thirsty or a stranger or naked or ill or in prison, and not minister to your needs?' He will answer them, 'Amen, I say to you, what you did not do for one of these least ones, you did not do for me.' And these will go off to eternal punishment, but the righteous to eternal life."]

The Gospel of the Lord.

14   Mk 3:31–35

Whoever does the will of God
is my brother and sister and mother.

A reading from the holy Gospel according to Mark

The mother of Jesus and his brothers arrived. Standing outside they sent word to him and called him. A crowd seated around him told him, "Your mother and your brothers and your sisters are outside asking for you." But he said to them in reply, "Who are my mother and my brothers?" And looking around at those seated in the circle he said, "Here are my mother and my brothers. For whoever does the will of God is my brother and sister and mother."

The Gospel of the Lord.

FOR TEACHERS

15   Mk 9:34–37

Whoever receives such a child as this, receives me.

A reading from the holy Gospel according to Mark

Jesus' disciples had been discussing among themselves who was the greatest. Then he sat down, called the Twelve, and said to them, "If anyone wishes to be first, he shall be the last of all and the servant of all." Taking a child he placed it in their midst, and putting his arms around it he said to them, "Whoever receives one child such as this in my name, receives me; and whoever receives me, receives not me but the One who sent me."

The Gospel of the Lord.

FOR TEACHERS

16   Mk 10:13–16

Let the children come to me; do not prevent them.

A reading from the holy Gospel according to Mark

People were bringing children to Jesus that he might touch them, but the disciples rebuked them. When Jesus saw this he became indignant and said to them, "Let the children come to me; do not prevent them, for the Kingdom of God belongs to such as these. Amen, I say to you, whoever does not accept the Kingdom of God like a child will not enter it." Then he embraced them and blessed them, placing his hands on them. The Gospel of the Lord.

FOR RELIGIOUS

17   Mk 10:17–30 or 10:17–27

Go, sell what you have, and give to the poor;
then come, follow me.

A reading from the holy Gospel according to Mark

Long form follows; for short form omit what is in brackets.

As Jesus was setting out on a journey, a man ran up, knelt down before him, and asked him, "Good teacher, what must I do to inherit eternal life?" Jesus answered him, "Why do you call me good? No one is good but God alone. You know the commandments: *You shall not kill; you shall not commit adultery; you shall not steal; you shall not bear false witness; you shall not defraud; honor your father and your mother."* He replied and said to him, "Teacher, all of these I have observed from my youth." Jesus, looking at him, loved him and said to him, "You are lacking in one thing. Go, sell what you have, and give to the poor and you will have treasure in heaven; then come, follow me." At that statement his face fell, and he went away sad, for he had many possessions.

Jesus looked around and said to his disciples, "How hard it is for those who have wealth to enter the Kingdom of God!" The disciples were amazed at his words. So Jesus again said to them in reply, "Children, how hard it is to enter the Kingdom of God! It is easier for a camel to pass through the eye of a needle than for one who is rich to enter the Kingdom of God." They were exceedingly astonished and said among themselves, "Then who can be saved?" Jesus looked at them and said, "For men it is impossible, but not for God. All things are possible for God." [Peter began to say to him, "We have given up everything and followed you." Jesus said, "Amen, I say to you, there is no one who has given up house or brothers or sisters or mother or father or children or lands for my sake and for the sake of the Gospel who will not receive a hundred times more now in this present age: houses and brothers and sisters and mothers and children and lands, with persecutions, and eternal life in the age to come."]

The Gospel of the Lord.

18 Lk 6:27–38

Be merciful, just as your Father is merciful.

A reading from the holy Gospel according to Luke

Jesus said to his disciples: "To you who hear I say, love your enemies, do good to those who hate you, bless those who curse you, pray for those who mistreat you. To the person who strikes you on one cheek, offer the other one as well, and from the person who takes your cloak, do not withhold even your tunic. Give to everyone who asks of you, and from the one who takes what is yours do not demand it back. Do to others as you would have them do to you. For if you love those who love you, what credit is that to you? Even sinners love those who love them. And if you do good to those who do good to you, what credit is that to you? Even sinners do the same. If you lend money to those from whom you expect repayment, what credit is that to you? Even sinners lend to sinners, and get back the same amount. But rather, love your enemies and do good to them, and lend expecting nothing back; then your reward will be great and you will be children of the Most High, for he himself is kind to the ungrateful and the wicked. Be merciful, just as also your Father is merciful.

"Stop judging and you will not be judged. Stop condemning and you will not be condemned. Forgive and you will be forgiven. Give and gifts will be given to you; a good measure, packed together, shaken down, and overflowing, will be poured into your lap. For the measure with which you measure will in return be measured out to you."

The Gospel of the Lord.

FOR RELIGIOUS

19

Lk 9:57–62

I will follow you wherever you go.

A reading from the holy Gospel according to Luke

As Jesus and his disciples were proceeding on their journey, someone said to him, "I will follow you wherever you go." Jesus answered him, "Foxes have dens and birds of the sky have nests, but the Son of Man has nowhere to rest his head." And to another he said, "Follow me." But he replied, "Lord, let me go first and bury my father." But he answered him, "Let the dead bury their dead. But you, go and proclaim the Kingdom of God." And another said, "I will follow you, Lord, but first let me say farewell to my family at home." Jesus said to him, "No one who sets a hand to the plow and looks to what was left behind is fit for the Kingdom of God."

The Gospel of the Lord.

20   Lk 10:38–42

Martha welcomed him.
Mary has chosen the better part.

A reading from the holy Gospel according to Luke

Jesus entered a village where a woman whose name was Martha welcomed him. She had a sister named Mary who sat beside the Lord at his feet listening to him speak. Martha, burdened with much serving, came to him and said, "Lord, do you not care that my sister has left me by myself to do the serving? Tell her to help me." The Lord said to her in reply, "Martha, Martha, you are anxious and worried about many things. There is need of only one thing. Mary has chosen the better part and it will not be taken from her."

The Gospel of the Lord.

FOR RELIGIOUS

21   Lk 12:32–34

Your Father is pleased to give you the Kingdom.

A reading from the holy Gospel according to Luke

Jesus said to his disciples: "Do not be afraid any longer, little flock, for your Father is pleased to give you the Kingdom. Sell your belongings and give alms. Provide money bags for yourselves that do not wear out, an inexhaustible treasure in heaven that no thief can reach nor moth destroy. For where your treasure is, there also will your heart be."

The Gospel of the Lord.

22   Lk 12:35–40

You also must be prepared.

A reading from the holy Gospel according to Luke

Jesus said to his disciples: "Gird your loins and light your lamps and be like servants who await their master's return from a wedding, ready to open immediately when he comes and knocks. Blessed are those servants whom the master finds vigilant on his arrival. Amen, I say to you, he will gird himself, have them recline at table, and proceed to wait on them. And should he come in the second or third watch and find them prepared in this way, blessed are those servants. Be sure of this: if the master of the house had known the hour when the thief was coming, he would not have let his house be broken into. You also must be prepared, for at an hour you do not expect, the Son of Man will come."

The Gospel of the Lord.

FOR RELIGIOUS

23   Lk 14:25–33

*Everyone of you who does not renounce all his possessions
cannot be my disciple.*

A reading from the holy Gospel according to Luke

Great crowds were traveling with Jesus, and he turned and addressed them, "If anyone comes to me without hating his father and mother, wife and children, brothers and sisters, and even his own life, he cannot be my disciple. Whoever does not carry his own cross and come after me cannot be my disciple. Which of you wishing to construct a tower does not first sit down and calculate the cost to see if there is enough for its completion? Otherwise, after laying the foundation and finding himself unable to finish the work the onlookers should laugh at him and say, 'This one began to build but did not have the resources to finish.' Or what king marching into battle would not first sit down and decide whether with ten thousand troops he can successfully oppose another king advancing upon him with twenty thousand troops? But if not, while he is still far away, he will send a delegation to ask for peace terms. In the same way, everyone of you who does not renounce all his possessions cannot be my disciple."

The Gospel of the Lord.

24   Jn 15:1–8

Whoever remains in me, and I in him, will bear much fruit.

A reading from the holy Gospel according to John

Jesus said to his disciples: "I am the true vine, and my Father is the vine grower. He takes away every branch in me that does not bear fruit, and everyone that does he prunes so that it bears more fruit. You are already pruned because of the word that I spoke to you. Remain in me, as I remain in you. Just as a branch cannot bear fruit on its own unless it remains on the vine, so neither can you unless you remain in me. I am the vine, you are the branches. Whoever remains in me and I in him will bear much fruit, because without me you can do nothing. Anyone who does not remain in me will be thrown out like a branch and wither; people will gather them and throw them into a fire and they will be burned. If you remain in me and my words remain in you, ask for whatever you want and it will be done for you. By this is my Father glorified, that you bear much fruit and become my disciples."

The Gospel of the Lord.

25   Jn 15:9–17

You are my friends if you do what I command you.

A reading from the holy Gospel according to John

Jesus said to his disciples: "As the Father loves me, so I also love you. Remain in my love. If you keep my commandments, you will remain in my love, just as I have kept my Father's commandments and remain in his love.

"I have told you this so that my joy might be in you and your joy might be complete. This is my commandment: love one another as I love you. No one has greater love than this, to lay down one's life for one's friends. You are my friends if you do what I command you. I no longer call you slaves, because a slave does not know what his master is doing. I have called you friends, because I have told you everything I have heard from my Father. It was not you who chose me, but I who chose you and appointed you to go and bear fruit that will remain, so that whatever you ask the Father in my name he may give you. This I command you: love one another."

The Gospel of the Lord.

26   Jn 17:20–26

I wish that where I am they also may be with me.

A reading from the holy Gospel according to John

Jesus raised his eyes to heaven and said: "Holy Father, I pray not only for these, but also for those who will believe in me through their word, so that they may all be one, as you, Father, are in me and I in you, that they also may be in us, that the world may believe that you sent me. And I have given them the glory you gave me, so that they may be one, as we are one, I in them and you in me, that they may be brought to perfection as one, that the world may know that you sent me, and that you loved them even as you loved me. Father, they are your gift to me. I wish that where I am they also may be with me, that they may see my glory that you gave me, because you loved me before the foundation of the world. Righteous Father, the world also does not know you, but I know you, and they know that you sent me. I made known to them your name and I will make it known, that the love with which you loved me may be in them and I in them."

The Gospel of the Lord.

OPTIONAL ANTIPHONS
FOR SOLEMNITIES AND FEASTS

1

Let us all rejoice in the Lord, and keep a festival in honor of the holy (martyr, pastor) N. Let us join with the angels in joyful praise to the Son of God.

2

Let us all rejoice in the Lord as we honor St. N., our protector. On this day this faithful friend of God entered heaven to reign with Christ for ever.

3

Let us rejoice in celebrating the victory of our patron saint. On earth he proclaimed Christ's love for us. Now Christ leads him to a place of honor before his Father in heaven.

4

Let us rejoice in celebrating the feast of the blessed martyr N. He fought for the law of God on earth; now Christ has granted him an everlasting crown of glory.

5

All his saints and all who fear the Lord, sing your praises to our God; for the Lord our almighty God is King of all creation. Let us rejoice and give him glory.

6

We celebrate the day when blessed N. received his reward; with all the saints he is seated at the heavenly banquet in glory.

FOR THE CONFERRAL
OF THE SACRAMENT OF MARRIAGE

IV. WEDDING MASS

1. For the Celebration of Marriage

When marriage is celebrated during Mass, white vestments are worn and the wedding Mass is used. If the marriage is celebrated on a Sunday or solemnity, the Mass of the day is used with the nuptial blessing and, where appropriate, the special final blessing.

The liturgy of the word relating to the marriage celebration is extremely helpful in emphasizing the meaning of the sacrament and the obligations of marriage. When the wedding Mass may not be used (during the Easter triduum or on Christmas, Epiphany, Ascension, Pentecost, the Body and Blood of Christ, or solemnities which are holy days of obligation) one of the readings for marriage may be chosen. On the Sundays of the Christmas season and on Sundays in ordinary time, in Masses which are not parish Masses, the wedding Mass may be celebrated without change.

When a marriage is celebrated during Advent or other days of penance, the parish priest should advise the couple to take into consideration the special nature of these times.

-A-

Entrance Antiphon

May the Lord send you help from his holy place and from Zion may he watch over you. May he grant you your heart's desire and lend his aid to all your plans. (Ps 19:3, 5)

Opening Prayer

Father,
you have made the bond of marriage
a holy mystery,
a symbol of Christ's love for his Church.

Hear our prayers for N. and N.
With faith in you and in each other
they pledge their love today.
May their lives always bear witness
to the reality of that love.

We ask this through our Lord Jesus Christ, your Son,
who lives and reigns with you and the Holy Spirit,
one God, for ever and ever.

Or:

Father,
when you created mankind
you willed that man and wife should be one.
Bind N. and N.
in the loving union of marriage
and make their love fruitful
so that they may be living witnesses
to your divine love in the world.

We ask this through our Lord Jesus Christ, your Son,
who lives and reigns with you and the Holy Spirit,
one God, for ever and ever.

Liturgy of the Word, *pp. 2339–2361.*

Prayer over the Gifts

Pray, brethren...
Lord,
accept our offering
for this newly-married couple, N. and N.
By your love and providence you have brought them
    together;
now bless them all the days of their married life.

We ask this through Christ our Lord.

2326 RITUAL MASSES – Wedding Mass

Preface of Marriage I, *pp. 959–960.*

When Eucharistic Prayer I is used, the special form of FATHER, ACCEPT THIS OFFERING is said. The words in brackets may be omitted if desired.

Father, accept this offering
from your whole family
and from N. and N., for whom we now pray.
You have brought them to their wedding day:
grant them (the gift and joy of children and)
a long and happy life together.

[Through Christ our Lord. Amen.]

Nuptial Blessing

After the Lord's Prayer, the prayer DELIVER US is omitted. The priest faces the bride and bridegroom and says the following blessing over them.

If one or both of the parties will not be receiving communion, the words in the introduction to the nuptial blessing, THROUGH THE SACRAMENT OF THE BODY AND BLOOD OF CHRIST, may be omitted.

If desired, in the prayer FATHER, BY YOUR POWER, two of the first three paragraphs may be omitted, keeping only the paragraph which corresponds to the reading of the Mass.

In the last paragraph of this prayer, the words in brackets may be omitted whenever circumstances suggest it, for example, if the couple is advanced in years.

With hands joined, the priest says:

My dear friends, let us turn to the Lord and pray
that he will bless with his grace this woman (or N.)
now married in Christ to this man (or N.)
and that (through the sacrament of the body and blood of
     Christ)
he will unite in love the couple he has joined in this holy
     bond.

All pray silently for a short while. Then the priest extends his hands and continues:

Father,
by your power you have made everything out of nothing.
In the beginning you created the universe
and made mankind in your own likeness.

You gave man the constant help of woman
so that man and woman should no longer be two, but one flesh,
and you teach us that what you have united
may never be divided.

Father,
by your plan man and woman are united,
and married life has been established
as the one blessing that was not forfeited by original sin
or washed away in the flood.

Look with love upon this woman, your daughter,
now joined to her husband in marriage.
She asks your blessing.
Give her the grace of love and peace.
May she always follow the example of the holy women
whose praises are sung in the scriptures.

May her husband put his trust in her
and recognize that she is his equal
and the heir with him to the life of grace.
May he always honor her and love her
as Christ loves his bride, the Church.

Father,
keep them always true to your commandments.
Keep them faithful in marriage
and let them be living examples of Christian life.

Give them the strength which comes from the gospel
so that they may be witnesses of Christ to others.
[Bless them with children
and help them to be good parents.

May they live to see their children's children.]
And, after a happy old age,
grant them fullness of life with the saints
in the kingdom of heaven.

We ask this through Christ our Lord.

The Mass continues in the usual way.

Communion Antiphon

Christ loves his Church, and he sacrificed himself for her so that she could become like a holy and untouchable bride.

(See Eph 5:25–27)

Prayer after Communion

Let us pray.

Pause for silent prayer, if this has not preceded.

Lord,
in your love
you have given us this eucharist
to unite us with one another and with you.
As you have made N. and N.
one in this sacrament of marriage
(and in the sharing of the one bread and the one cup),
so now make them one in love for each other.

We ask this through Christ our Lord.

Solemn Blessing

God the eternal Father keep you in love with each other,
so that the peace of Christ may stay with you
and be always in your home. **R. Amen.**

May (your children bless you,)
your friends console you
and all men live in peace with you. **R. Amen.**

May you always bear witness to the love of God in this world
so that the afflicted and the needy
will find in you generous friends
and welcome you into the joys of heaven. **R. Amen.**

May almighty God bless you,
the Father, and the Son, ✠ and the Holy Spirit. **R. Amen.**

-B-

Entrance Antiphon

**Fill us with your love, O Lord, and we will sing for joy all our
days. May the goodness of the Lord be upon us, and give success
to the work of our hands.** (Ps 89:14, 17)

Opening Prayer

Father,
hear our prayers for N. and N.,
who today are united in marriage before you altar.
Give them your blessing,
and strengthen their love for each other.

We ask this through our Lord Jesus Christ, your Son,
who lives and reigns with you and the Holy Spirit,
one God, for ever and ever.

Liturgy of the Word, *pp. 2339–2361.*

Prayer over the Gifts

Pray, brethren...

Lord,
accept the gifts we offer you
on this happy day.
In your fatherly love

watch over and protect N. and N.,
whom you have united in marriage.

We ask this through Christ our Lord.

   Preface of Marriage II, *pp. 959–960.*

When Eucharistic Prayer I is used, the special form of FATHER, ACCEPT THIS
OFFERING is said. The words in brackets may be omitted if desired.

Father, accept this offering
from your whole family
and from N. and N., for whom we now pray.
You have brought them to their wedding day:
grant them (the gift and joy of children and)
a long and happy life together.
[Through Christ our Lord. Amen.]

Nuptial Blessing

After the Lord's Prayer, the prayer DELIVER US is omitted. The priest faces the
bride and bridegroom and says the following blessing over them.

In the prayer HOLY FATHER, either the paragraph, HOLY FATHER, YOU CREATED
MANKIND, or the paragraph, FATHER, TO REVEAL THE PLAN OF YOUR LOVE, may
be omitted, keeping only the paragraph which corresponds to the reading
of the Mass.

With hands joined, the priest says:

Let us pray to the Lord for N. and N.
who come to God's altar at the beginning of their married life
so that they may always be united in love for each other
(as now they share in the body and blood of Christ).

All pray silently for a short while. Then the priest extends his hands and
continues:

Holy Father, you created mankind in your own image
and made man and woman to be joined as husband and wife
in union of body and heart
and so fulfill their mission in this world.

Father,
to reveal the plan of your love,
you made the union of husband and wife
an image of the covenant between you and your people.
In the fulfillment of this sacrament,
the marriage of Christian man and woman
is a sign of the marriage between Christ and the Church.
Father, stretch out your hand, and bless N. and N.

Lord,
grant that as they begin to live this sacrament
they may share with each other the gifts of your love
and become one in heart and mind
as witnesses to your presence in their marriage.
Help them to create a home together
(and give them children to be formed by the gospel
and to have a place in your family).

Give your blessings to N., your daughter,
so that she may be a good wife (and mother),
caring for the home,
faithful in love for her husband,
generous and kind.
Give your blessings to N., your son,
so that he may be a faithful husband
(and a good father).

Father,
grant that as they come together to your table on earth,
so they may one day have the joy of sharing your feast in
  heaven.

We ask this through Christ our Lord.

The Mass continues in the usual way.

2332 RITUAL MASSES – Wedding Mass

Communion Antiphon

I give you a new commandment: love one another as I have loved you, says the Lord.

(Jn 13:34)

Prayer after Communion

Let us pray.

Pause for silent prayer, if this has not preceded.

Lord,
we who have shared the food of your table
pray for our friends N. and N.,
whom you have joined together in marriage.
Keep them close to you always.
May their love for each other
proclaim to all the world
their faith in you.

We ask this through Christ our Lord.

Solemn Blessing

May God, the almighty Father,
give you his joy
and bless you (in your children). **R. Amen.**

May the only Son of God have mercy on you
and help you in good times and in bad. R. Amen.

May the Holy Spirit of God
always fill your hearts with his love. **R. Amen.**

May almighty God bless you,
the Father, and the Son, ✠ and the Holy Spirit. **R. Amen.**

-C-

Entrance Antiphon

Lord, I will bless you day after day, and praise your name for ever; for you are kind to all, and compassionate to all your creatures. (Ps 144:2, 9)

Opening Prayer

Almighty God,
hear our prayers for N. and N.,
who have come here today
to be united in the sacrament of marriage.
Increase their faith in you and in each other,
and through them bless your Church (with Christian
children).
We ask this through our Lord Jesus Christ, your Son,
who lives and reigns with you and the Holy Spirit,
one God, for ever and ever.

Liturgy of the Word, *pp. 2339–2361.*

Prayer over the Gifts

Pray, brethren...

Lord,
hear our prayers
and accept the gifts we offer for N. and N.
Today you have made them one in the sacrament of
   marriage.
May the mystery of Christ's unselfish love,
which we celebrate in this eucharist,
increase their love for you and for each other.

We ask this through Christ our Lord.

Preface of Marriage III, *pp. 959–960.*

When Eucharistic Prayer I is used, the special form of FATHER, ACCEPT THIS OFFERING is said. The words in brackets may be omitted if desired.

Father, accept this offering
from your whole family
and from N. and N., for whom we now pray.
You have brought them to their wedding day:
grant them (the gift and joy of children and)
a long and happy life together.

[Through Christ our Lord. Amen.]

Nuptial Blessing

After the Lord's Prayer, the prayer DELIVER US is omitted. The priest faces the bride and bridegroom and says the following blessing over them:

My dear friends, let us ask God
for his continued blessing upon this bridegroom and his
   bride (or N. and N.).

All pray silently for a short while. Then the priest extends his hands and continues:

Holy Father,
creator of the universe,
maker of man and woman in your own likeness,
source of blessing for married life,
we humbly pray to you for this woman
who today is united with her husband in this sacrament of
   marriage.

May your fullest blessing come upon her and her husband
so that they may together rejoice in your gift of married love
(and enrich your Church with their children).

Lord,
may they both praise you when they are happy
and turn to you in their sorrows.
May they be glad that you help them in their work

and know that you are with them in their need.
May they pray to you in the community of the Church,
and be your witnesses in the world.
May they reach old age in the company of their friends,
and come at last to the kingdom of heaven.

We ask this through Christ our Lord.

The Mass continues in the usual way.

Communion Antiphon

I will bless the Lord at all times, his praise shall be ever on my lips. Taste and see the goodness of the Lord; blessed is he who hopes in God. (Ps 33:1, 9)

Prayer after Communion

Let us pray.

Pause for silent prayer, if this has not preceded.

Almighty God,
may the sacrifice we have offered
and the eucharist we have shared
strengthen the love of N. and N.,
and give us all your fatherly aid.

We ask this through Christ our Lord.

Solemn Blessing

May the Lord Jesus, who was a guest at the wedding in Cana,
bless you and your families and friends. **R. Amen.**

May Jesus, who loved his Church to the end,
always fill your hearts with his love. **R. Amen.**

May he grant that, as you believe in his resurrection,
so you may wait for him in joy and hope. **R. Amen.**

May almighty God bless you,
the Father, and the Son, ✠ and the Holy Spirit. **R. Amen.**

2. The Anniversaries of Marriage

On marriage anniversaries, especially the twenty-fifth and fiftieth anniversaries, the Mass of thanksgiving may be celebrated with the following prayers, if a votive Mass is permitted.

These prayers may also be used if desired at weekday Masses in ordinary time.

A. THE ANNIVERSARY

Opening Prayer

God our Father,
you created man and woman
to love each other
in the bond of marriage.
Bless and strengthen N. and N.
May their marriage become an increasingly more perfect sign
of the union between Christ and his Church.

We ask this through our Lord Jesus Christ, your Son,
who lives and reigns with you and the Holy Spirit,
one God, for ever and ever.

Liturgy of the Word, *pp. 2339–2361.*

Prayer over the Gifts

Pray, brethren...

Father,
the blood and water that flowed
from the wounded heart of Christ your Son
was a sign of the mystery of our rebirth:
accept these gifts we offer in thanksgiving.
Continue to bless the marriage of N. and N.
with all your gifts.

Grant this in the name of Jesus the Lord.

Prayer after Communion

Let us pray.

Pause for silent prayer, if this has not preceded.

Lord,
you give us food and drink from heaven.
Bless N. and N. on their anniversary.
Let their love grow stronger
that they may find within themselves
a greater peace and joy.
Bless their home
that all who come to it in need
may find in it an example of goodness
and a source of comfort.

We ask this through Christ our Lord.

B. THE TWENTY-FIFTH ANNIVERSARY OF MARRIAGE

Opening Prayer

Father,
you have blessed and sustained N. and N.
in the bond of marriage.
Continue to increase their love
throughout the joys and sorrows of life,
and help them to grow in holiness all their days.

Grant this through our Lord Jesus Christ, your Son,
who lives and reigns with you and the Holy Spirit,
one God, for ever and ever.

Liturgy of the Word, *pp. 2339–2361.*

Prayer over the Gifts

Pray, brethren...

Father,

accept these gifts which we offer in thanksgiving for
   N. and N.
May they bring them continued peace and happiness.

We ask this through Christ our Lord.

Prayer after Communion

Let us pray.

Pause for silent prayer, if this has not preceded.

Father,
you bring N. and N. (and their children and friends) together
at the table of your family.
Help them grow in love and unity,
that they may rejoice together
in the wedding feast of heaven.

Grant this through Christ our Lord.

C. THE FIFTIETH ANNIVERSARY OF MARRIAGE

Opening Prayer

God, our Father,
bless N. and N.
We thank you for their long and happy marriage
(for the children they have brought into the world)
and for all the good they have done.
As you blessed the love of their youth,
continue to bless their life together
with gifts of peace and joy.

We ask this through our Lord Jesus Christ, your Son,
who lives and reigns with you and the Holy Spirit,
one God, for ever and ever.

Liturgy of the Word, *pp. 2339–2361.*

Prayer over the Gifts

Pray, brethren...

Lord,
accept the gifts we offer in thanksgiving for N. and N.
With trust in you and in each other
they have shared life together.
Hear their prayers,
and keep them in your peace.
We ask this through Christ our Lord.

Prayer after Communion

Let us pray.

Pause for silent prayer, if this has not preceded.

Lord,
as we gather at the table of your Son,
bless N. and N. on their wedding anniversary.
Watch over them in the coming years,
and after a long and happy life together
bring them to the feast of eternal life.
Grant this through Christ our Lord.

Liturgy of the Word: Marriage

Whenever marriage anniversaries are celebrated on a day when Masses "For
Various Needs and Occasions" are permitted, the readings from the following
section may be used.

READING I   From the Old Testament

Gn 1:26–28, 31a

Male and female he created them.

A reading from the Book of Genesis

Then God said: "Let us make man in our image, after our likeness. Let them have dominion over the fish of the sea, the birds of the air, and the cattle, and over all the wild animals and all the creatures that crawl on the ground."

God created man in his image;
>   in the image of God he created him;
>   male and female he created them.

God blessed them, saying: "Be fertile and multiply; fill the earth and subdue it. Have dominion over the fish of the sea, the birds of the air, and all the living things that move on the earth." God looked at everything he had made, and he found it very good.

The word of the Lord.

2

Gn 2:18–24

The two of them become one body.

A reading from the Book of Genesis

The LORD God said: "It is not good for the man to be alone. I will make a suitable partner for him." So the LORD God formed out of the ground various wild animals and various birds of the air, and he brought them to the man to see what he would call them; whatever the man called each of them would be its name. The man gave names to all the cattle, all the birds of the air, and all wild animals; but none proved to be the suitable partner for the man.

So the LORD God cast a deep sleep on the man, and while he was asleep, he took out one of his ribs and closed up its place with flesh. The LORD God then built up into a woman the rib that he had taken from the man. When he brought her to the man, the man said:

> "This one, at last, is bone of my bones
>   and flesh of my flesh;
> This one shall be called 'woman,'
>   for out of 'her man' this one has been taken."

That is why a man leaves his father and mother and clings to his wife, and the two of them become one body.

The word of the Lord.

---

3   Gn 24:48–51, 58–67

In his love for Rebekah,
Isaac found solace after the death of his mother.

A reading from the Book of Genesis

The servant of Abraham said to Laban: "I bowed down in worship to the LORD, blessing the LORD, the God of my master Abraham, who had led me on the right road to obtain the daughter of my master's kinsman for his son. If, therefore, you have in mind to show true loyalty to my master, let me know; but if not, let me know that, too. I can then proceed accordingly."

Laban and his household said in reply: "This thing comes from the LORD; we can say nothing to you either for or against it. Here is Rebekah, ready for you; take her with you, that she may become the wife of your master's son, as the LORD has said."

So they called Rebekah and asked her, "Do you wish to go

with this man?" She answered, "I do." At this they allowed their sister Rebekah and her nurse to take leave, along with Abraham's servant and his men. Invoking a blessing on Rebekah, they said:

"Sister, may you grow
  into thousands of myriads;
And may your descendants gain possession
  of the gates of their enemies!"

Then Rebekah and her maids started out; they mounted their camels and followed the man. So the servant took Rebekah and went on his way.

Meanwhile Isaac had gone from Beer-lahai-roi and was living in the region of the Negeb. One day toward evening he went out...in the field, and as he looked around, he noticed that camels were approaching. Rebekah, too, was looking about, and when she saw him, she alighted from her camel and asked the servant, "Who is the man out there, walking through the fields toward us?" "That is my master," replied the servant. Then she covered herself with her veil.

The servant recounted to Isaac all the things he had done. Then Isaac took Rebekah into his tent; he married her, and thus she became his wife. In his love for her Isaac found solace after the death of his mother Sarah.

The word of the Lord.

4

Tb 7:6–14

May the Lord of heaven prosper you both.
May he grant you mercy and peace.

A reading from the Book of Tobit

Raphael and Tobiah entered the house of Raguel and greeted him. Raguel sprang up and kissed Tobiah, shedding tears of joy. But when he heard that Tobit had lost his eyesight, he was grieved and wept aloud. He said to Tobiah: "My child, God bless you! You are the son of a noble and good father. But what a terrible misfortune that such a righteous and charitable man should be afflicted with blindness!" He continued to weep in the arms of his kinsman Tobiah. His wife Edna also wept for Tobit; and even their daughter Sarah began to weep.

Afterward, Raguel slaughtered a ram from the flock and gave them a cordial reception. When they had bathed and reclined to eat, Tobiah said to Raphael, "Brother Azariah, ask Raguel to let me marry my kinswoman Sarah." Raguel overheard the words; so he said to the boy: "Eat and drink and be merry tonight, for no man is more entitled to marry my daughter Sarah than you, brother. Besides, not even I have the right to give her to anyone but you, because you are my closest relative. But I will explain the situation to you very frankly. I have given her in marriage to seven men, all of whom were kinsmen of ours, and all died on the very night they approached her. But now, son, eat and drink. I am sure the Lord will look after you both." Tobiah answered, "I will eat or drink nothing until you set aside what belongs to me."

Raguel said to him: "I will do it. She is yours according to the decree of the Book of Moses. Your marriage to her has been decided in heaven! Take your kinswoman from now on you are her love, and she is your beloved. She is yours today and ever after. And tonight, son, may the Lord of heaven prosper you both. May he grant you mercy and peace." Then Raguel called his daughter Sarah, and she came to him. He took her by the hand and gave her to Tobiah with the words: "Take her according to the law. According to the decree written in the Book of Moses she is your wife. Take her and bring her back safely to your father. And may the God of heaven grant both of you peace and prosperity." He then called her mother and told her to bring a scroll, so that he might draw up a marriage contract stating that he gave Sarah to Tobiah as his wife according to the decree of the Mosaic law. Her mother brought the scroll, and he drew up the contract, to which they affixed their seals.

Afterward they began to eat and drink.

The word of the Lord.

5   Tb 8:4b–8

Allow us to live together to a happy old age.

A reading from the Book of Tobit

On their wedding night Tobiah arose from bed and said to his wife, "Sister, get up. Let us pray and beg our Lord to have mercy on us and to grant us deliverance." Sarah got up, and they started to pray and beg that deliverance might be theirs. They began with these words:

"Blessed are you, O God of our fathers;
    praised be your name forever and ever.
Let the heavens and all your creation
    praise you forever.
You made Adam and you gave him his wife Eve
    to be his help and support;
    and from these two the human race descended.

You said, 'It is not good for the man to be alone;
    let us make him a partner like himself.'
Now, Lord, you know that I take this wife of mine
    not because of lust,
    but for a noble purpose.
Call down your mercy on me and on her,
    and allow us to live together to a happy old age."

They said together, "Amen, amen."

The word of the Lord.

6   Prv 31:10–13, 19–20, 30–31

See the Common of Holy Men and Women (p. 2277).

7   Sg 2:8–10, 14, 16a; 8:6–7a

Stern as death is love.

A reading from the Song of Songs

Hark! my lover—here he comes
    springing across the mountains,
    leaping across the hills.
My lover is like a gazelle
    or a young stag.
Here he stands behind our wall,
    gazing through the windows, peering through the
        lattices.
My lover speaks; he says to me,
    "Arise, my beloved, my dove, my beautiful one,
        and come!

"O my dove in the clefts of the rock,
  in the secret recesses of the cliff,
Let me see you,
  let me hear your voice,
For your voice is sweet,
  and you are lovely."

My lover belongs to me and I to him.
  He says to me:

"Set me as a seal on your heart,
  as a seal on your arm;
For stern as death is love,
  relentless as the nether world is devotion;
  its flames are a blazing fire.
Deep waters cannot quench love,
  nor floods sweep it away."

The word of the Lord.

8   Sir 26:1–4, 13–16

See the Common of Holy Men and Women (p. 2279).

9   Jer 31:31–32a, 33–34a

*I will make a new covenant with the house of Israel
and the house of Judah.*

A reading from the Book of the Prophet Jeremiah

The days are coming, says the LORD, when I will make a new covenant with the house of Israel and the house of Judah. It will not be like the covenant I made with their fathers: the day I took them by the hand to lead them forth from the land of Egypt. But this is the covenant which I will make with the house of Israel after those days, says the LORD. I will place my law within them, and write it upon their hearts; I will be their God, and they shall be my people. No longer will they have need to teach their friends and relatives how to know the LORD. All, from least to greatest, shall know me, says the LORD.

The word of the Lord.

READING II   From the New Testament

Rom 8:31b–35, 37–39

What will separate us from the love of Christ?

A reading from the Letter of Saint Paul to the Romans

Brothers and sisters:

If God is for us, who can be against us? He did not spare his own Son but handed him over for us all, how will he not also give us everything else along with him? Who will bring a charge against God's chosen ones? It is God who acquits us. Who will condemn? It is Christ Jesus who died, rather, was raised, who also is at the right hand of God, who indeed intercedes for us. What will separate us from the love of Christ? Will anguish, or distress, or persecution, or famine, or nakedness, or peril, or the sword?

No, in all these things, we conquer overwhelmingly through him who loved us. For I am convinced that neither death, nor life, nor angels, nor principalities, nor present things, nor future things, nor powers, nor height, nor depth, nor any other creature will be able to separate us from the love of God in Christ Jesus our Lord.

The word of the Lord.

2   Rom 12:1–2, 9–18 or 12:1–2, 9–13

Offer your bodies as a living sacrifice, holy and pleasing to God.

A reading from the Letter of Saint Paul to the Romans

Long form follows; for short form omit what is in brackets.

I urge you, brothers and sisters, by the mercies of God, to offer your bodies as a living sacrifice, holy and pleasing to God, your spiritual worship. Do not conform yourselves to this age but be transformed by the renewal of your mind, that you may discern what is the will of God, what is good and pleasing and perfect.

Let love be sincere; hate what is evil, hold on to what is good; love one another with mutual affection; anticipate one another in showing honor. Do not grow slack in zeal, be fervent in spirit, serve the Lord. Rejoice in hope, endure in affliction, persevere in prayer. Contribute to the needs of the holy ones, exercise hospitality. [Bless those who persecute you, bless and do not curse them. Rejoice with those who rejoice, weep with those who weep. Have the same regard for one another; do not be haughty but associate with the lowly; do not be wise in your own estimation. Do not repay anyone evil for evil; be concerned for what is noble in the sight of all. If possible, on your part, live at peace with all.]

The word of the Lord.

3   Rom 15:1b–3a, 5–7, 13

Welcome one another as Christ welcomed you.

A reading from the Letter of Saint Paul to the Romans

Brothers and sisters:

We ought to put up with the failings of the weak and not to

please ourselves; let each of us please our neighbor for the good, for building up. For Christ did not please himself. May the God of endurance and encouragement grant you to think in harmony with one another, in keeping with Christ Jesus, that with one accord you may with one voice glorify the God and Father of our Lord Jesus Christ.

Welcome one another, then, as Christ welcomed you, for the glory of God. May the God of hope fill you with all joy and peace in believing, so that you may abound in hope by the power of the Holy Spirit.

The word of the Lord.

4

1 Cor 6:13c–15a, 17–20

Your body is a temple of the Spirit.
Your bodies are members of the Body of Christ.

A reading from the first Letter of Saint Paul to the Corinthians

Brothers and sisters:

The body is not for immorality, but for the Lord, and the Lord is for the body; God raised the Lord and will also raise us by his power.

Do you not know that your bodies are members of Christ? Whoever is joined to the Lord becomes one spirit with him. Avoid immorality. Every other sin a person commits is outside the body, but the immoral person sins against his own body. Do you not know that your body is a temple of the Holy Spirit within you, whom you have from God, and that you are not your own? For you have been purchased at a price. Therefore glorify God in your body.

The word of the Lord.

5

1 Cor 12:31—13:8a

If I do not have love, I gain nothing.

A reading from the first Letter of Saint Paul to the Corinthians

Brothers and sisters:
Strive eagerly for the greatest spiritual gifts.

But I shall show you a still more excellent way.

If I speak in human and angelic tongues but do not have love, I am a resounding gong or a clashing cymbal. And if I have the gift of prophecy and comprehend all mysteries and all knowledge; if I have all faith so as to move mountains, but do not have love, I am nothing. If I give away everything I own, and if I hand my body over so that I may boast but do not have love, I gain nothing.

Love is patient, love is kind. It is not jealous, is not pompous, it is not inflated, it is not rude, it does not seek its own interests, it is not quick-tempered, it does not brood over injury, it does not rejoice over wrongdoing but rejoices with the truth. It bears all things, believes all things, hopes all things, endures all things.

Love never fails.

The word of the Lord.

6

Eph 5:2a, 21–33 or 5:2a, 25–32

This is a great mystery, but I speak in reference to Christ and the Church.

A reading from the Letter of Saint Paul to the Ephesians

Long form follows; for short form omit what is in brackets.

Brothers and sisters:
Live in love, as Christ loved us and handed himself over for us.

[Be subordinate to one another out of reverence for Christ. Wives should be subordinate to their husbands as to the Lord. For the husband is head of his wife just as Christ is head of the Church, he himself the savior of the body. As the Church is subordinate to Christ, so wives should be subordinate to their husbands in everything.] Husbands, love your wives, even as Christ loved the Church and handed himself over for her to sanctify her, cleansing her by the bath of water with the word, that he might present to himself the Church in splendor, without spot or wrinkle or any such thing, that she might be holy and without blemish. So also husbands should love their wives as their own bodies. He who loves his wife loves himself. For no one hates his own flesh but rather nourishes and cherishes it, even as Christ does the Church, because we are members of his Body.

> *For this reason a man shall leave his father and his mother*
> *and be joined to his wife,*
> *and the two shall become one flesh.*

This is a great mystery, but I speak in reference to Christ and the Church. [In any case, each one of you should love his wife as himself, and the wife should respect her husband.]

The word of the Lord.

---

7   Phil 4:4–9

See the Common of Holy Men and Women (p. 2297).

8   Col 3:12–17

See the Common of Holy Men and Women (p. 2298).

9   Heb 13:1–4a, 5–6b

Let marriage be held in honor by all.

A reading from the Letter to the Hebrews

Brothers and sisters:

Let mutual love continue. Do not neglect hospitality, for through it some have unknowingly entertained angels. Be mindful of prisoners as if sharing their imprisonment, and of the ill-treated as of yourselves, for you also are in the body. Let marriage be honored among all and the marriage bed be kept undefiled. Let your life be free from love of money but be content with what you have, for he has said, *I will never forsake you or abandon you.* Thus we may say with confidence:

> *The Lord is my helper,*
> *and I will not be afraid.*

The word of the Lord.

10   1 Pt 3:1–9

See the Common of Holy Men and Women (p. 2299).

11   1 Jn 3:18–24

Love in deed and in truth

A reading from the first Letter of Saint John

Children, let us love not in word or speech but in deed and truth.

Now this is how we shall know that we belong to the truth and reassure our hearts before him in whatever our hearts condemn, for God is greater than our hearts and knows everything. Beloved, if our hearts do not condemn us, we have confidence in God and receive from him whatever we ask, because we keep his commandments and do what pleases him. And his commandment is this: we should believe in the name of his Son, Jesus Christ, and love one another just as he commanded us. Those who keep his commandments remain in him, and he in them, and the way we know that he remains in us is from the Spirit that he gave us.

The word of the Lord.

12
1 Jn 4:7–12

God is love.

A reading from the first Letter of Saint John

Beloved, let us love one another, because love is of God; everyone who loves is begotten by God and knows God. Whoever is without love does not know God, for God is love. In this way the love of God was revealed to us: God sent his only-begotten Son into the world so that we might have life through him. In this is love: not that we have loved God, but that he loved us and sent his Son as expiation for our sins. Beloved, if God so loved us, we also must love one another. No one has ever seen God. Yet, if we love one another, God remains in us, and his love is brought to perfection in us.

The word of the Lord.

13
Rv 19:1, 5–9a

See the Common of Holy Men and Women (p. 2284).

Responsorial Psalm

1   Ps 33:12 and 18, 20–21, 22

R. The earth is full of the goodness of the Lord.

Blessed the nation whose God is the LORD,
   the people he has chosen for his own inheritance.
But see, the eyes of the LORD are upon those who fear him,
   upon those who hope for his kindness.

   R. The earth is full of the goodness of the Lord.

Our soul waits for the LORD,
   who is our help and our shield,
For in him our hearts rejoice;
   in his holy name we trust.

   R. The earth is full of the goodness of the Lord.

May your kindness, O LORD, be upon us
   who have put our hope in you.

   R. The earth is full of the goodness of the Lord.

2   Ps 34:2–3, 4–5, 6–7, 8–9

R. I will bless the Lord at all times.

Or: **R. Taste and see the goodness of the Lord.**

See the Common of Martys (p. 2288).

3   Ps 103:1–2, 8 and 13, 17–18a

R. The Lord is kind and merciful.

Bless the LORD, O my soul;
   and all my being, bless his holy name.
Bless the LORD, O my soul,
   and forget not all his benefits.

R. The Lord is kind and merciful.

Merciful and gracious is the LORD,
  slow to anger and abounding in kindness.
As a father has compassion on his children,
  so the LORD has compassion on those who fear him.

R. The Lord is kind and merciful.

But the kindness of the LORD is from eternity
  to eternity toward those who fear him,
And his justice towards children's children
  among those who keep his covenant.

R. The Lord is kind and merciful.

Or: **R. The Lord's kindness is everlasting to those who fear
    him.**

4   Ps 112:1bc–2, 3–4, 5–7a, 7b–8, 9

**R. Blessed is the man who greatly delights in the Lord's
    commands.**

Or: **R. Alleluia.**

See the Common of Holy Men and Women (p. 2289).

5   128:1–2, 3, 4–5

R. Blessed are those who fear the Lord.

Or: **R. See how the Lord blesses those who fear him.**

See the Common of Holy Men and Women (p. 2290).

6   145:8–9, 10 and 15, 17–18

R. The Lord is compassionate toward all his works.

The LORD is gracious and merciful,
  slow to anger and of great kindness.

The LORD is good to all
  and compassionate toward all his works.

R. The Lord is compassionate toward all his works.

Let all your works give you thanks, O LORD,
  and let your faithful ones bless you.
The eyes of all look hopefully to you
  and you give them their food in due season.

R. The Lord is compassionate toward all his works.

The LORD is just in all his ways
  and holy in all his works.
The LORD is near to all who call upon him,
  to all who call upon him in truth.

R. The Lord is compassionate toward all his works.

7 148:1–2, 3–4, 9–10, 11–13a, 13c–14a

R. Let all praise the name of the Lord.

Alleluia.
Praise the LORD from the heavens,
  praise him in the heights;
Praise him, all you his angels,
  praise him, all you his hosts.

R. Let all praise the name of the Lord.

Praise him, sun and moon;
  praise him, all you shining stars.
Praise him, you highest heavens,
  and you waters above the heavens.

R. Let all praise the name of the Lord.

You mountains and all you hills,
  you fruit trees and all you cedars;
You wild beasts and all tame animals,
  you creeping things and winged fowl.

R. Let all praise the name of the Lord.

Let the kings of the earth and all peoples,
   the princes and all the judges of the earth,
Young men too, and maidens,
   old men and boys,
Praise the name of the LORD,
   for his name alone is exalted.

 R. Let all praise the name of the Lord.

His majesty is above earth and heaven,
   and he has lifted his horn above the people.

 R. Let all praise the name of the Lord.

 Or: **R. Alleluia.**

ALLELUIA VERSE AND VERSE BEFORE THE GOSPEL

1   1 Jn 4:7b
Everyone who loves is begotten of God and knows God.

2   1 Jn 4:8b, 11
God is love.
If God loved us, we also must love one another.

3   1 Jn 4:12
If we love one another,
God remains in us
and his love is brought to perfection in us.

4   1 Jn 4:16
Whoever remains in love,
remains in God and God in him.

GOSPEL

1   Mt 5:1–12a

See the Common of Holy Men and Women (p. 2304).

2

Mt 5:13–16

See the Common of Holy Men and Women (p. 2305).

3

Mt 7:21, 24–29 or 7:21, 24–25

A wise man built his house on rock.

A reading from the holy Gospel according to Matthew

Long form follows; for short form omit what is in brackets.

Jesus said to his disciples: "Not everyone who says to me, 'Lord, Lord,' will enter the Kingdom of heaven, but only the one who does the will of my Father in heaven.

"Everyone who listens to these words of mine and acts on them will be like a wise man who built his house on rock. The rain fell, the floods came, and the winds blew and buffeted the house. But it did not collapse; it had been set solidly on rock. [And everyone who listens to these words of mine but does not act on them will be like a fool who built his house on sand. The rain fell, the floods came, and the winds blew and buffeted the house. And it collapsed and was completely ruined."

When Jesus finished these words, the crowds were astonished at his teaching, for he taught them as one having authority, and not as their scribes.]

The Gospel of the Lord.

4

Mt 19:3–6

What God has united, man must not separate.

A reading from the holy Gospel according to Matthew

Some Pharisees approached Jesus, and tested him, saying, "Is it lawful for a man to divorce his wife for any cause whatever?" He said in reply, "Have you not read that from the beginning the Creator made them male and female and said, *For this reason a man shall leave his father and mother and be joined to his wife, and the two shall become one flesh?* So they are no longer two, but one flesh. Therefore, what God has joined together, man must not separate."

The Gospel of the Lord.

5

Mt 22:35–40

This is the greatest and the first commandment.
The second is like it.

A reading from the holy Gospel according to Matthew

One of the Pharisees, a scholar of the law, tested Jesus by asking, "Teacher, which commandment in the law is the greatest?" He said to him, "You shall love the Lord, your God, with all your heart, with all your soul, and with all your mind. This is the greatest and the first commandment. The second is like it: You shall love your neighbor as yourself. The whole law and the prophets depend on these two commandments."

The Gospel of the Lord.

6

Mk 10:6–9

They are no longer two, but one flesh.

A reading from the holy Gospel according to Mark

Jesus said: "From the beginning of creation, *God made them male and female. For this reason a man shall leave his father and mother and be joined to his wife, and the two shall become one flesh.* So they are no longer two but one flesh. Therefore what God has joined together, no human being must separate."

The Gospel of the Lord.

7

Jn 2:1–11

See the Common of the Blessed Virgin Mary (p. 2127).

8

John 15:9–12

Remain in my love.

A reading from the holy Gospel according to John

Jesus said to his disciples: "As the Father loves me, so I also love you. Remain in my love. If you keep my commandments, you will remain in my love, just as I have kept my Father's commandments and remain in his love.

"I have told you this so that my joy might be in you and your joy might be complete. This is my commandment: love one another as I love you."

The Gospel of the Lord.

9

Jn 15:12–16

This is my commandment: love one another.

A reading from the holy Gospel according to John

Jesus said to his disciples: "This is my commandment: love one another as I love you. No one has greater love than this, to lay down one's life for one's friends. You are my friends if you do what I command you. I no longer call you slaves, because a slave does not know what his master is doing. I have called you friends, because I have told you everything I have heard from my Father. It was not you who chose me, but I who chose you and appointed you to go and bear fruit that will remain, so that whatever you ask the Father in my name he may give you."

The Gospel of the Lord.

10

That they may be brought to perfection as one.

A reading from the holy Gospel according to John

For long form see the Common of Holy Men and Women (p. 2322).
For short form use Jn 17:20–23 below:

Jesus raised his eyes to heaven and said: "Holy Father, I pray not only for these, but also for those who will believe in me through their word, so that they may all be one, as you, Father, are in me and I in you, that they also may be in us, that the world may believe that you sent me. And I have given them the glory you gave me, so that they may be one, as we are one, I in them and you in me, that they may be brought to perfection as one, that the world may know that you sent me, and that you loved them even as you loved me."

The Gospel of the Lord.

MASSES FOR THE DEAD

1. Although for convenience complete Masses with antiphons and prayers are given, all the texts are interchangeable. This is true especially of the prayers, but the appropriate changes in gender and number should be made.

Similarly, if prayers for funerals or anniversaries are used in other circumstances, the inappropriate words should be omitted.

2. In the Easter season the alleluia at the end of the antiphons may be omitted.

1. FUNERAL MASS

A. OUTSIDE THE EASTER SEASON

Entrance Antiphon

Give them eternal rest, O Lord, and may perpetual light shine on them for ever. (See 4 Ezr 2:34–35)

Opening Prayer

Almighty God, our Father,
we firmly believe that your Son died and rose to life.
We pray for our brother (sister) N.,
who has died in Christ.
Raise him (her) at the last day
to share the glory of the risen Christ,
who lives and reigns with you and the Holy Spirit,
one God, for ever and ever.

Or:

God,
you have called your son (daughter) N. from this life.
Father of all mercy, fulfill his (her) faith and hope in you,
and lead him (her) safely home to heaven,
to be happy with you for ever.

We ask this through our Lord Jesus Christ, your Son,
who lives and reigns with you and the Holy Spirit,
one God, for ever and ever.

Liturgy of the Word, pp. 2407–2445.

Prayer over the Gifts

Pray, brethren...

Lord,
receive the gifts we offer for the salvation of N.
May Christ be merciful in judging our brother (sister) N.
for he (she) believed in Christ
as his (her) Lord and Savior.

We ask this through Christ our Lord.

Preface of Christian Death I–V, pp. 961–963.

Communion Antiphon

**May eternal light shine on them, O Lord, with all your saints
for ever, for you are rich in mercy. Give them eternal rest, O
Lord, and may perpetual light shine on them for ever, for you
are rich in mercy.**   (See 4 Ezr 2:35, 34)

Prayer after Communion

Let us pray.

Pause for silent prayer, if this has not preceded.

Lord God,
your Son Jesus Christ gave us
the sacrament of his body and blood
to guide us on our pilgrim way to your kingdom.
May our brother (sister) N., who shared in the eucharist,
come to the banquet of life Christ has prepared for us.

We ask this through Christ our Lord.

B. OUTSIDE THE EASTER SEASON

Entrance Antiphon

The Lord will open to them the gate of paradise, and they will return to that homeland where there is no death, but only lasting joy.

Opening Prayer

God of mercy,
you are the hope of sinners
and the joy of saints.
We pray for our brother (sister) N.,
whose body we honor with Christian burial.
Give him (her) happiness with your saints,
and raise up his (her) body in glory at the last day
to be in your presence for ever.

Grant this through our Lord Jesus Christ, your Son,
who lives and reigns with you and the Holy Spirit,
one God, for ever and ever.

Liturgy of the Word, *pp. 2407–2445.*

Prayer over the Gifts

Pray, brethren...

Lord,
accept this sacrifice we offer for our brother (sister) N.
on the day of his (her) burial.
May your love cleanse him (her)
from his (her) human weakness
and forgive any sins he (she) may have committed.

We ask this through Christ our Lord.

Preface of Christian Death I–V, *pp. 961–963.*

Communion Antiphon

We are waiting for our Savior, the Lord Jesus Christ; he will transfigure our lowly bodies into copies of his own glorious body.
(Phil 3:20–21)

Prayer after Communion

Let us pray.

Pause for silent prayer, if this has not preceded.

Father, all-powerful God,
we pray for our brother (sister) N.
whom you have called (today) from this world.
May this eucharist cleanse him (her),
forgive his (her) sins,
and raise him (her) up to eternal joy in your presence.

We ask this through Christ our Lord.

C. DURING THE EASTER SEASON

Entrance Antiphon

Just as Jesus died and rose again, so will the Father bring with him those who have died in Jesus. Just as in Adam all men die, so in Christ all will be made alive, alleluia.

(1 Thes 4:14; 1 Cor 15:22)

Opening Prayer

Lord,
hear our prayers.
By raising your Son from the dead,
you have given us faith.
Strengthen our hope that N., our brother (sister),
will share in his resurrection.

We ask this through our Lord Jesus Christ, your Son,
who lives and reigns with you and the Holy Spirit,
one God, for ever and ever.

Liturgy of the Word, *pp. 2407–2445.*

Prayer over the Gifts

Pray, brethren...

Lord,
we are united in this sacrament
by the love of Jesus Christ.
Accept these gifts
and receive our brother (sister) N.
into the glory of your Son,
who is Lord for ever and ever.

Preface of Christian Death I–V, *pp. 961–963.*

Communion Antiphon

**I am the resurrection and the life, says the Lord. If anyone
believes in me, even though he dies, he will live. Anyone who lives
and believes in me, will not die, alleluia.**   (See Jn 11:25–26)

Prayer after Communion

Let us pray.
Pause for silent prayer, if this has not preceded.

Lord God,
may the death and resurrection of Christ
which we celebrate in this eucharist
bring our brother (sister) N. the peace of your eternal home.

We ask this in the name of Jesus the Lord.

D. OTHER PRAYERS FOR A FUNERAL MASS

Opening Prayer

Father, almighty God,
our brother (sister) N.
believed that Christ is the risen Lord.
Release him (her) from sin and grant to him (her) the
   freedom
of your perfect peace.
May our brother (sister) N. be with you
in the glory of your kingdom on the last day.

We ask this through our Lord Jesus Christ, your Son,
who lives and reigns with you and the Holy Spirit,
one God, for ever and ever.

   Liturgy of the Word, *pp. 2407–2445.*

Prayer over the Gifts

Pray, brethren...

All-powerful Father,
may this sacrifice wash away
the sins of our brother (sister) N. in the blood of Christ.
You cleansed him (her) in the waters of baptism.
In your loving mercy grant him (her) pardon and peace.

We ask this in the name of Jesus the Lord.

Prayer after Communion

Let us pray.

   Pause for silent prayer, if this has not preceded.

Lord,
in this sacrament you give us your crucified and risen Son.
Bring to the glory of the resurrection our brother (sister) N.
who has been purified by this holy mystery.

Grant this through Christ our Lord.

2. ANNIVERSARY MASS

A. OUTSIDE THE EASTER SEASON

Entrance Antiphon

God will wipe every tear from their eyes; there will be no more death, no more weeping or pain, for the old order has passed away. (Rv 21:4)

Opening Prayer

Lord God,
you are the glory of believers
and the life of the just.
Your Son redeemed us
by dying and rising to life again.
Our brother (sister) N. was faithful
and believed in our own resurrection.
Give to him (her) the joys and blessings
of the life to come.

We ask this through our Lord Jesus Christ, your Son,
who lives and reigns with you and the Holy Spirit,
one God, for ever and ever.

Liturgy of the Word, *pp. 2407–2445.*

Prayer over the Gifts

Pray, brethren...

Lord,
accept these gifts we offer
for N. our brother (sister).
May they free him (her) from sin
and bring him (her) to the happiness of life in your presence.

We ask this through Christ our Lord.

Preface of Christian Death I–V, *pp. 961–963.*

Communion Antiphon

I am the resurrection and the life, says the Lord. Anyone who believes in me will have eternal life; he will not be condemned but pass from death to life.   (Jn 11:25; 3:36; 5:24)

Prayer after Communion

Let us pray.

Pause for silent prayer, if this has not preceded.

Lord,
you renew our lives by this holy eucharist;
free N. our brother (sister) from sin
and raise him (her) to eternal life.

We ask this in the name of Jesus the Lord.

B. OUTSIDE THE EASTER SEASON

Entrance Antiphon

Lord Jesus, you shed your precious blood for them, so grant them eternal rest.

Opening Prayer

Lord,
we keep the anniversary
of the death (burial) of our brother (sister) N.
Give him (her) the unending joy of your love
in the company of all your saints.

We ask this through our Lord Jesus Christ, your Son,
who lives and reigns with you and the Holy Spirit,
one God, for ever and ever.

Liturgy of the Word, *pp. 2407–2445.*

Prayer over the Gifts

Pray, brethren...

Lord,
as we make this sacrifice of praise
we celebrate the memory of our brother (sister) N.
May this offering of peace
win for him (her) a place with your saints.

We ask this in the name of Jesus the Lord.

Preface of Christian Death I–V, *pp. 961–963.*

Communion Antiphon

Lord, you are our rest after toil, our life after death; grant them eternal rest.

Prayer after Communion

Let us pray.
Pause for silent prayer, if this has not preceded.

Lord,
accept the prayers and gifts
we offer for our brother (sister) N.
May your love and forgiveness free him (her)
from every trace of sin.

We ask this in the name of Jesus the Lord.

C. DURING THE EASTER SEASON

Entrance Antiphon

God, who raised Jesus from the dead, will give new life to our own mortal bodies through his Spirit living in us, alleluia.

(See Rom 8:11)

Opening Prayer

Almighty and merciful God,
may our brother (sister) N. share the victory of Christ
who loved us so much that he died and rose again
     to bring us new life.

We ask this through our Lord Jesus Christ, your Son,
who lives and reigns with you and the Holy Spirit,
one God, for ever and ever.

Liturgy of the Word, *pp. 2407–2445.*

Prayer over the Gifts

Pray, brethren...

God of love,
by this sacrifice
wash away the sins of our brother (sister) N.
in the blood of Jesus Christ.
In your love complete what you began
in the waters of baptism.

Grant this through Christ our Lord.

Preface of Christian Death I–V, *pp. 961–963.*

Communion Antiphon

**I am the living bread from heaven, says the Lord. If anyone
eats this bread he will live for ever; the bread I shall give is my
flesh for the life of the world, alleluia.**   (Jn 6:51–52)

Prayer after Communion

Let us pray.

Pause for silent prayer, if this has not preceded.

Lord,
we celebrate your Son's death for us
and his rising to eternal glory.

May these Easter mysteries free our brother (sister) N.
and bring him (her) to share in the joyful resurrection to
come.
We ask this through Christ our Lord.

D. OTHER PRAYERS ON AN ANNIVERSARY

Opening Prayer

Lord,
may the death of your Son
bring forgiveness to our brother (sister) N.
who prayed for this grace.
May he (she) come into your presence
and rejoice in your glory for ever.

We ask this through our Lord Jesus Christ, your Son,
who lives and reigns with you and the Holy Spirit,
one God, for ever and ever.

Liturgy of the Word, *pp. 2407–2445.*

Prayer over the Gifts

Pray, brethren...

Lord,
may the sacrifice we offer
bring everlasting joy to our brother (sister) N.
who knew you by the light of faith.

We ask this in the name of Jesus the Lord.

Prayer after Communion

Let us pray.
Pause for silent prayer, if this has not preceded.
Lord,
the eucharist we share joins us to your Son

and brings us his life.

May this eucharist free our brother (sister) N.
   from his (her) sins
and lead him (her) to your presence in heaven.

Grant this through Christ our Lord.

E. OTHER PRAYERS ON AN ANNIVERSARY

Opening Prayer

God of mercy,
we keep this anniversary
of the death (burial) of N. our brother (sister).
Give him (her) light, happiness, and peace.

We ask this through our Lord Jesus Christ, your Son,
who lives and reigns with you and the Holy Spirit,
one God, for ever and ever.

Liturgy of the Word, *pp. 2407–2445.*

Prayer over the Gifts

Pray, brethren...

Lord,
accept our prayers and offerings.
Make your son (daughter) N. one with you
in peace and happiness.

We ask this in the name of Jesus the Lord.

Prayer after Communion

Let us pray.
   Pause for silent prayer, if this has not preceded.
Lord,
in your mercy
may this sacrifice we offer

for our brother (sister) N.
free him (her) from his (her) sins
and bring him (her) to the light and happiness
of your kingdom.

We ask this in the name of Jesus the Lord.

3. VARIOUS COMMEMORATIONS

A. FOR ONE PERSON

Entrance Antiphon

The Lord will open to them the gates of paradise, and they will return to that homeland where there is no death, but only lasting joy.

Opening Prayer

Lord God, almighty Father,
you have made the cross for us a sign of strength
and marked us as yours in the sacrament of the resurrection.
Now that you have freed our brother (sister) N. from this
   mortal life
make him (her) one with your saints in heaven.

We ask this through our Lord Jesus Christ, your Son,
who lives and reigns with you and the Holy Spirit,
one God, for ever and ever.

Or:

Lord of mercy,
hear our prayer.
May our brother (sister) N.,
whom you called your son (daughter) on earth,

enter the kingdom of peace and light,
where your saints live in glory.

We ask this through our Lord Jesus Christ, your Son,
who lives and reigns with you and the Holy Spirit,
one God, for ever and ever.

Liturgy of the Word, *pp. 2407–2445.*

Prayer over the Gifts

Pray, brethren...

Lord,
in your mercy
may this sacrifice of praise,
this offering of peace,
bring our brother (sister) N.
to the fullness of risen life.

We ask this through Christ our Lord.

Preface of Christian Death I–V, *pp. 961–963.*

Communion Antiphon

All that the Father gives to me will come to me; the man who comes to me, I shall never turn away. (Jn 6:37)

Prayer after Communion

Let us pray.

Pause for silent prayer, if this has not preceded.

Lord,
you give us life in this sacrament.
May our brother (sister) N. who received life at your table
enter into the everlasting peace and joy of Christ your Son,
who is Lord for ever and ever.

B. FOR ONE PERSON

Entrance Antiphon

I know that my Redeemer lives, and on the last day I shall rise again; in my body I shall look on God, my Savior.

(Jb 19:25–26)

Opening Prayer

Lord,
in your mercy
free our brother (sister) N. from his (her) sins.
As you made him (her) one with Christ here on earth,
raise him (her) to join your saints
in the glory of the resurrection.

We ask this through our Lord Jesus Christ, your Son,
who lives and reigns with you and the Holy Spirit,
one God, for ever and ever.

Liturgy of the Word, *pp. 2407–2445.*

Prayer over the Gifts

Pray, brethren...
Lord,
may this offering help our brother (sister) N.,
for by this sacrifice
you take away the sins of the world.

Grant this in the name of Jesus the Lord.

Preface of Christian Death I–V, *pp. 961–963.*

Communion Antiphon

This is the bread come down from heaven, says the Lord. He who eats this bread will live for ever.   (See Jn 6:50)

Prayer after Communion

Let us pray.

Pause for silent prayer, if this has not preceded.

Lord,
may the sacrifice of your Church
help our brother (sister) N.;
may he (she) who received this sacrament of your mercy
join the saints who are united to Christ,
who is Lord for ever and ever.

C. FOR MORE THAN ONE PERSON OR FOR ALL THE DEAD

Entrance Antiphon

Give them eternal rest, O Lord, and let them share your glory.

Opening Prayer

God, our creator and redeemer,
by your power Christ conquered death
and returned to you in glory.
May all your people who have gone before us in faith
share his victory
and enjoy the vision of your glory for ever,
where Christ lives and reigns with you and the Holy Spirit,
one God, for ever and ever.

Or:

God, our maker and redeemer,
in your mercy hear our prayer.
Grant forgiveness and peace
to our brothers (sisters) N. and N.
who longed for your mercy.

We ask this through our Lord Jesus Christ, your Son,
who lives and reigns with you and the Holy Spirit,
one God, for ever and ever.

Liturgy of the Word, *pp. 2407–2445.*

Prayer over the Gifts

Pray, brethren...

Lord,
receive this sacrifice
for our brothers and sisters.
On earth you gave them the privilege of believing in Christ:
grant them the eternal life promised by that faith.

We ask this through Christ our Lord.

Preface of Christian Death I–V, *pp. 961–963.*

Communion Antiphon

**God sent his only Son into the world so that we could have life
through him.**   (1 Jn 4:9)

Prayer after Communion

Let us pray.

Pause for silent prayer, if this has not preceded.

Lord,
may our sacrifice bring peace and forgiveness
to our brothers and sisters who have died.
Bring the new life given to them in baptism
to the fullness of eternal joy.

We ask through Christ our Lord.

Or:

Lord of mercy,
may our prayer and sacrifice

free our brothers and sisters
and bring them to eternal salvation.
We ask this through Christ our Lord.

D. FOR MORE THAN ONE PERSON OR FOR ALL THE DEAD

Entrance Antiphon

**God loved the world so much, he gave his only Son, that all
who believe in him might not perish, but might have eternal life.**

(Jn 3:16)

Opening Prayer

All-powerful and ever-living God,
you give new life to mankind
and perfect joy to your saints in heaven.
Give our brothers (sister) N. and N. the fullness of freedom
in the kingdom of your glory.

We ask this through our Lord Jesus Christ, your Son,
who lives and reigns with you and the Holy Spirit,
one God, for ever and ever.

Or:

Merciful Lord of the living and the dead,
forgive the sins of our brothers (sisters) N. and N.
for whom we pray.
May they praise you for ever
in the joy of your presence.

Grant this through our Lord Jesus Christ, your Son,
who lives and reigns with you and the Holy Spirit,
one God, for ever and ever.

Liturgy of the Word, *pp. 2407–2445.*

Prayer over the Gifts

Pray, brethren...

Lord,
in your kindness accept these gifts we offer for N. and N.
and for all who sleep in Christ.
May his perfect sacrifice
free them from the power of death
and give them everlasting life.
We ask this through Christ our Lord.

Preface of Christian Death I–V, *pp. 961–963.*

Communion Antiphon

We are waiting for our Savior, the Lord Jesus Christ; he will transfigure our lowly bodies into copies of his own glorious body.
(Phil 3:20–21)

Prayer after Communion

Let us pray.

Pause for silent prayer, if this has not preceded.

All-powerful God,
have mercy upon our brothers and sisters
who have gone before us in faith;
may this eucharist be for us the way to salvation
and for them the means of forgiveness.

We ask this through Christ our Lord.

E. FOR MORE THAN ONE PERSON OR FOR ALL THE DEAD

Entrance Antiphon

Happy are those who have died in the Lord; let them rest from their labors for their good deeds go with them.   (Rev 14:13)

Opening Prayer

God of love,
the peace of heaven is your gift.
Forgive our brothers (sisters) N. and N.
and all who die in Christ
and free them from their sins.
Make them one with Christ
in the glory of his resurrection,
for he lives and reigns with you and the Holy Spirit,
one God, for ever and ever.

Or:

Lord,
have mercy on our brothers (sisters) who have died
May their faith and hope in you be rewarded by eternal life.
We ask this through our Lord Jesus Christ, your Son,
who lives and reigns with you and the Holy Spirit,
one God, for ever and ever.

Liturgy of the Word, *pp. 2407–2445.*

Prayer over the Gifts

Pray, brethren...
Lord,
receive the gifts we offer
to win peace and rest for our brothers and sisters.
By this eucharist, which brings man salvation,
count them among those whom you have freed from death.

We ask this through Christ our Lord.

Preface of Christian Death I–V, *pp. 961–963.*

Communion Antiphon

Grant eternal rest, O Lord, to those in whose memory we receive the body and blood of Christ.

Prayer after Communion

Let us pray.

Pause for silent prayer, if this has not preceded.

Lord,
we receive the sacrament of salvation;
may this eucharist be the sign of your loving care
for your people on earth
and a source of eternal forgiveness
for our departed brothers and sisters.

We ask this in the name of Jesus the Lord.

Or:

Lord,
may our brothers and sisters,
and all who sleep in Christ,
share in the light of eternal life,
the life they came to know
by sharing in this sacrament.

We ask this through Christ our Lord.

VARIOUS PRAYERS FOR THE DEAD

1. FOR A POPE

-A-

Opening Prayer

God our Father,
you reward all who believe in you.
May your servant, N. our Pope, vicar of Peter and shepherd
   of your Church,
who faithfully administered the mysteries of your
   forgiveness and love on earth,
rejoice with you for ever in heaven.

We ask this through our Lord Jesus Christ, your Son,
who lives and reigns with you and the Holy Spirit,
one God, for ever and ever.

Liturgy of the Word, *pp. 2407–2445.*

Prayer over the Gifts

Pray, brethren...

Lord,
by this sacrifice which brings us peace,
give your servant, N. our Pope,
the reward of eternal happiness
and let your mercy win for us
the gift of your life and love.

We ask this through Christ our Lord.

Prayer after Communion

Let us pray.

Pause for silent prayer, if this has not preceded.

Lord,
you renew us with the sacraments of your divine life.
Hear our prayers for your servant, N. our Pope.
You made him the center of the unity of your Church on
    earth,
count him now among the flock of the blessed in your
    kingdom.

Grant this through Christ our Lord.

–B–

Opening Prayer

Father,
in your wise and loving care
you made your servant, N., Pope and teacher of all your
    Church.

He did the work of Christ on earth.
May your Son welcome him to eternal glory,
where he lives and reigns with you and the Holy Spirit,
one God, for ever and ever.

Liturgy of the Word, *pp. 2407–2445.*

Prayer over the Gifts

Pray, brethren...

Lord,
look with kindness on the prayers and gifts of your Church.
By the power of this sacrifice
may your servant N.
whom you appointed high priest of your flock
be counted now among your priests in the life of your kingdom.

We ask this through Christ our Lord.

Prayer after Communion

Let us pray.

Pause for silent prayer, if this has not preceded.

Lord,
hear the prayers of the people you feed
with the gifts of your protection and love.
May your servant N.
who was a faithful minister of your mysteries on earth
praise your goodness for ever in the glory of your saints.

We ask this through Christ our Lord.

- C -

Opening Prayer

Father,
eternal shepherd,

hear the prayers of your people
for your servant, N.,
who governed your Church with love.
In your mercy bring him with the flock entrusted to his care
to the reward you have promised your faithful servants.

We ask this through our Lord Jesus Christ, your Son,
who lives and reigns with you and the Holy Spirit,
one God, for ever and ever.

Liturgy of the Word, *pp. 2407–2445.*

Prayer over the Gifts

Pray, brethren...

Lord,
in your love receive this sacrifice of peace your people offer.
We entrust your servant N., to your mercy with faith and
confidence.
In the human family he was an instrument of your peace and
love.
May he rejoice in those gifts for ever with your saints.

We ask this through Christ our Lord.

Prayer after Communion

Let us pray.
Pause for silent prayer, if this has not preceded.

Lord,
at this meal of eternal life
we ask your mercy for your servant N.
May he rejoice for ever in the possession of that truth
in which he made your people strong by his faith.

We ask this through Christ our Lord.

2. FOR A BISHOP

A. FOR THE DIOCESAN BISHOP

Opening Prayer

All-powerful God,
you made N., your servant,
the guide of your family.
May he enjoy the reward of all his work
and share the eternal joy of his Lord.

We ask this through our Lord Jesus Christ, your Son,
who lives and reigns with you and the Holy Spirit,
one God, for ever and ever.

Liturgy of the Word, *pp. 2407–2445.*

Prayer over the Gifts

Pray, brethren...

Merciful God,
may this sacrifice,
which N. your servant offered during his life
for the salvation of the faithful,
help him now to find pardon and peace.

We ask this through Christ our Lord.

Prayer after Communion

Let us pray.

Pause for silent prayer, if this has not preceded.

Lord,
give your mercy and love to N. your servant.
He hoped in Christ and preached Christ.
By this sacrifice may he share with Christ
the joy of eternal life.

We ask this through Christ our Lord.

B. FOR ANOTHER BISHOP

Opening Prayer

God our Father,
may your servant N., who was our bishop,
rejoice in the fellowship of the successors of the apostles
whose office he shared in this life.

We ask this through our Lord Jesus Christ, your Son,
who lives and reigns with you and the Holy Spirit,
one God, for ever and ever.

Liturgy of the Word, *pp. 2407–2445.*

Prayer over the Gifts

Pray, brethren...

Lord,
accept our offering for N. your servant.
You gave him the dignity of high priesthood in this world.
Let him now share the joy of your saints in the kingdom of
    heaven.

We ask this through Christ our Lord.

Prayer after Communion

Let us pray.

Pause for silent prayer, if this has not preceded.

All-powerful Father, God of mercy,
you have N. your servant
the privilege of doing the work of Christ on earth.
By this sacrifice free him from sin
and bring him to eternal life with Christ in heaven,
who is Lord for ever and ever.

3. FOR A PRIEST

-A-

Opening Prayer

Lord,
you gave N. your servant and priest
the privilege of a holy ministry in this world.
May he rejoice for ever in the glory of your kingdom.

We ask this through our Lord Jesus Christ, your Son,
who lives and reigns with you and the Holy Spirit,
one God, for ever and ever.

Liturgy of the Word, *pp. 2407–2445.*

Prayer over the Gifts

Pray, brethren...

All-powerful God,
by this eucharist may N. your servant and priest
rejoice for ever in the vision of the mysteries
which he faithfully ministered here on earth.

We ask this through Christ our Lord.

Prayer after Communion

Let us pray.

Pause for silent prayer, if this has not preceded.

God of mercy,
we who receive the sacraments of salvation
pray for N. your servant and priest.
You made him a minister of your mysteries on earth.
May he rejoice in the full knowledge of your truth in
    heaven.

We ask through Christ our Lord.

-B-

Opening Prayer

Lord,
hear the prayers we offer for N. your servant and priest.
He faithfully fulfilled his ministry to your name.
May he rejoice for ever in the fellowship of your saints.

We ask this through our Lord Jesus Christ, your Son,
who lives and reigns with you and the Holy Spirit,
one God, for ever and ever.

Liturgy of the Word, *pp. 2407–2445.*

Prayer over the Gifts

Pray, brethren...

Lord God of mercy,
may the sacrifice we offer for N. your servant and priest
bring him forgiveness and life
as once he offered sacrifice to you
in his wholehearted service to your Church.

We ask this through Christ our Lord.

Prayer after Communion

Let us pray.

Pause for silent prayer, if this has not preceded.

Lord,
hear the prayers of those you renew
with the food of life at your holy table.
By the power of this sacrifice
may N. your servant and priest
rejoice in your presence for ever
as he served you faithfully in the Church.

We ask this through Christ our Lord.

4. FOR A DEACON

Opening Prayer

God of mercy,
you gave N. your servant
the privilege of serving your Church.
Bring him now to the joy of eternal life.

We ask this through our Lord Jesus Christ, your Son,
who lives and reigns with you and the Holy Spirit,
one God, for ever and ever.

   Liturgy of the Word, *pp. 2407–2445.*

Prayer over the Gifts

Pray, brethren...

Lord,
be merciful to N. your servant
for whose salvation we offer you this sacrifice.
He ministered during his life to Christ your Son.
May he rise with all your faithful servants to eternal glory.

We ask this through Christ our Lord.

Prayer after Communion

Let us pray.
   Pause for silent prayer, if this has not preceded.

Lord,
you fill us with holy gifts.
Hear our prayers for N. your deacon
whom you counted among the servants of your Church.
By this sacrifice free him from the power of death
and give him a share in the reward you have promised
to all who serve you faithfully.

We ask this through Christ our Lord.

5. FOR A RELIGIOUS

Opening Prayer

All-powerful God,
out of love for Christ and his Church,
N. served you faithfully in the religious life.
May he (she) rejoice at the coming of your glory
and enjoy eternal happiness
with his (her) brothers (sisters) in your kingdom.

We ask this through our Lord Jesus Christ, your Son,
who lives and reigns with you and the Holy Spirit,
one God, for ever and ever.

6. FOR ONE PERSON

-A-

Opening Prayer

Lord,
those who die still live in your presence
and your saints rejoice in complete happiness.
Listen to our prayers for N. your son (daughter)
who has passed from the light of this world,
and bring him (her) to the joy of eternal radiance.

We ask this through our Lord Jesus Christ, your Son,
who lives and reigns with you and the Holy Spirit,
one God, for ever and ever.

Liturgy of the Word, *pp. 2407–2445.*

Prayer over the Gifts

Pray, brethren...

Lord,
be pleased with this sacrifice we offer for N. your servant.

May he (she) find in your presence
the forgiveness he (she) always longed for
and come to praise your glory for ever
in the joyful fellowship of your saints.

We ask this through Christ our Lord.

Prayer after Communion

Let us pray.

Pause for silent prayer, if this has not preceded.

Lord,
we thank you for the holy gifts we receive
and pray for N. our brother (sister).
By the suffering and death of your Son
free him (her) from the bonds of his (her) sins
and bring him (her) to endless joy in your presence.

We ask this through Christ our Lord.

-B-

Opening Prayer

Lord,
may our prayers come before you
and lead N. your servant to eternal joy.
You created him (her) in your image
and made him (her) your son (daughter).
In your mercy now welcome him (her) to a place in your
  kingdom.

We ask this through our Lord Jesus Christ, your Son,
who lives and reigns with you and the Holy Spirit,
one God, for ever and ever.

Liturgy of the Word, *pp. 2407–2445.*

Prayer over the Gifts

Pray, brethren...

Lord,
in your love accept the gifts
we offer in faith for N. your son (daughter).
May the sacrifice you have chosen to be the one source of
    healing for mankind
bring him (her) eternal salvation.

We ask this in the name of Jesus the Lord.

Prayer after Communion

Let us pray.

Pause for silent prayer, if this has not preceded.

Lord,
as you renew us by this sacred food,
free N. our brother (sister) from the power of death
and give him (her) a share in the joyful resurrection of Christ,
who is Lord for ever and ever.

–C–

Opening Prayer

Lord of mercy,
hear our prayers and forgive our brother (sister) N. all his
    (her) sins.
Give him (her) life on the day of resurrection
and peaceful rest in the light of your love.

We ask this through our Lord Jesus Christ, your Son,
who lives and reigns with you and the Holy Spirit,
one God, for ever and ever.

Liturgy of the Word, *pp. 2407–2445.*

2394 MASSES FOR THE DEAD

Prayer over the Gifts

Pray, brethren...

All-powerful and ever-living God,
your Son offered himself to be our bread of life
and poured out his blood to be our cup of salvation.
Have mercy on your servant N.,
and let the eucharist we offer be for him (her) a help to
   salvation.

We ask this through Christ our Lord.

Prayer after Communion

Let us pray.

Pause for silent prayer, if this has not preceded.

Lord,
we have received the pledge of eternal life.
Hear the prayers we offer for your son (daughter) N.
Freed from the limitations of this life,
may he (she) be one with all the redeemed
in the joy of eternal life.

We ask through Christ our Lord.

7. FOR A YOUNG PERSON

Opening Prayer

Lord God,
the days allotted to each of us are in your fatherly care.
Though we are saddened
that our brother (sister) N. was with us for so short a time,
we entrust him (her) to you with confidence.
May he (she) live, radiant and for ever young,
in the happiness of your kingdom.

We ask this through our Lord Jesus Christ, your Son,
who lives and reigns with you and the Holy Spirit,
one God, for ever and ever.

8. FOR ONE WHO WORKED IN THE SERVICE OF THE GOSPEL

Opening Prayer

Lord,
hear our prayers for your son (daughter) N.,
who labored so generously
to bring your gospel to the world.
May he (she) be the more worthy
to share the rewards of your kingdom.

We ask this through our Lord Jesus Christ, your Son,
who lives and reigns with you and the Holy Spirit,
one God, for ever and ever.

9. FOR ONE WHO SUFFERED A LONG ILLNESS

Opening Prayer

Lord God,
in his (her) suffering and long illness
our brother (sister) N. served you faithfully
by imitating the patience of your Son, Jesus Christ.
May he (she) also share in the reward of his glory
where he lives and reigns with you and the Holy Spirit,
one God, for ever and ever.

10. FOR ONE WHO DIED SUDDENLY

Opening Prayer

Lord,
as we mourn the sudden death of our brother (sister) N.,
comfort us with the great power of your love
and strengthen us in our faith
that he (she) is with you for ever.

We ask this through our Lord Jesus Christ, your Son,
who lives and reigns with you and the Holy Spirit,
one God, for ever and ever.

11. FOR SEVERAL PERSONS

-A-

Opening Prayer

Lord,
be merciful to your servants N. and N.
You cleansed them from sin in the fountain of new birth.
Bring them now to the happiness of life in your kingdom.

We ask this through our Lord Jesus Christ, your Son,
who lives and reigns with you and the Holy Spirit,
one God, for ever and ever.

Liturgy of the Word, *pp. 2407–2445.*

Prayer over the Gifts

Pray, brethren...

Lord,
we offer you this sacrifice.
Hear our prayers for N. and N.,

and through this offering
grant our brothers (sisters) your everlasting forgiveness.

We ask this through Christ our Lord.

Prayer after Communion

Let us pray.

Pause for silent prayer, if this has not preceded.

Lord,
we who receive your sacraments
ask your mercy and love.
By sharing in the power of this eucharist
may our brothers (sisters) win forgiveness of their sins,
enter your kingdom,
and praise you for all eternity.

We ask this through Christ our Lord.

-B-

Opening Prayer

Lord,
we entrust to you our brothers (sisters) N. and N.
that they may live with you for ever.
By your merciful love
wash away whatever sins they may have committed in
   human weakness
while they lived on earth.

We ask this through our Lord Jesus Christ, your Son,
who lives and reigns with you and the Holy Spirit,
one God, for ever and ever.

Liturgy of the Word, *pp. 2407–2445.*

Prayer over the Gifts

Pray, brethren...

Lord,
be merciful to your servants N. and N.
for whom we offer you this sacrifice of peace.
They were faithful to you in this life;
reward them with life for ever in your presence.

We ask this through Christ our Lord.

Prayer after Communion

Let us pray.

Pause for silent prayer, if this has not preceded.

All-powerful God,
by the power of this sacrament
give our brothers (sisters) eternal happiness
in the fellowship of the just.

We ask this through Christ our Lord.

-C-

Opening Prayer

All-powerful and ever-living God,
you never refuse mercy to those who call upon you with
    faith.
Be merciful to your servants N. and N.
They left this life believing in your name;
may they be counted among your saints for ever.

We ask this through our Lord Jesus Christ, your Son,
who lives and reigns with you and the Holy Spirit,
one God, for ever and ever.

Liturgy of the Word, *pp. 2407–2445.*

Prayer over the Gifts

Pray, brethren...

Lord God,
as your Son offered himself to you as a living sacrifice,
accept the sacrifice of your Church.
Free your servants N. and N. from all their sins
and lead them to the reward of life without end.
We ask this through Christ our Lord.

Prayer after Communion

Let us pray.

Pause for silent prayer, if this has not preceded.

Father all-powerful, God of mercy,
may the sacraments we receive free us from our sins.
May this sacrifice be our prayer for pardon,
our strength in weakness,
our support in all we do,
and may it be for the living and the dead
the forgiveness of all their sins
and the pledge of eternal redemption.
We ask this through Christ our Lord.

12. FOR A MARRIED COUPLE

Opening Prayer

Lord,
pardon the sins of your servants N. and N.
In this life they were joined in true married love.
Now let the fullness of your own love
unite them for life eternal.

We ask this through our Lord Jesus Christ, your Son,
who lives and reigns with you and the Holy Spirit,
one God, for ever and ever.

Or (for one deceased spouse only):

Lord,
pardon the sins of your servant N.
and watch over him (her) with constant kindness.
In this life they were joined in true married love.
May the fullness of your own love unite them for life
   eternal.

We ask this through our Lord Jesus Christ, your Son,
who lives and reigns with you and the Holy Spirit,
one God, for ever and ever.

13. FOR PARENTS

Opening Prayer

Almighty God,
you command us to honor father and mother.
In your mercy forgive the sins of my (our) parents
and let me (us) one day see them again
in the radiance of eternal joy.

We ask this through our Lord Jesus Christ, your Son,
who lives and reigns with you and the Holy Spirit,
one God, for ever and ever.

Liturgy of the Word, *pp. 2407–2445.*

Prayer over the Gifts

Pray, brethren...

Lord,
receive the sacrifice we offer for my (our) parents.

Give them eternal joy in the land of the living,
and let me (us) join them one day in the happiness of the
   saints.

We ask this through Christ our Lord.

Prayer after Communion

Let us pray.

>*Pause for silent prayer, if this has not preceded.*

Lord,
may this sharing in the sacrament of heaven
win eternal rest and light for my (our) parents
and prepare me (us) to share eternal glory with them.

We ask through Christ our Lord.

14. FOR RELATIVES, FRIENDS, AND BENEFACTORS

Opening Prayer

Father,
source of forgiveness and salvation for all mankind,
hear our prayer.
By the prayers of the ever-virgin Mary,
may our friends, relatives, and benefactors
who have gone from this world
come to share eternal happiness with all your saints.

We ask this through our Lord Jesus Christ, your Son,
who lives and reigns with you and the Holy Spirit,
one God, for ever and ever.

Liturgy of the Word, *pp. 2407–2445.*

Prayer over the Gifts

Pray, brethren...

God of infinite mercy,
hear our prayers
and by this sacrament of our salvation
forgive all the sins of our relatives, friends, and benefactors.

We ask this through Christ our Lord.

Prayer after Communion

Let us pray.

Pause for silent prayer, if this has not preceded.

Father all-powerful, God of mercy,
we have offered you this sacrifice of praise
for our relatives, friends, and benefactors.
By the power of this sacrament
free them from all their sins
and give them the joy of eternal light.

We ask this through Christ our Lord.

FUNERAL MASS OF A BAPTIZED CHILD
-A-

Entrance Antiphon

Come, you whom my Father has blessed; inherit the kingdom prepared for you since the foundation of the world (alleluia).

(Mt 25:34)

Opening Prayer

God of mercy and love,
you called this child to yourself
at the dawn of his (her) life.
By baptism you made him (her) your child

and we believe that he (she) is already in your kingdom.
Hear our prayers
and let us one day share eternal life with him (her).

We ask this through our Lord Jesus Christ, your Son,
who lives and reigns with you and the Holy Spirit,
one God, for ever and ever.

Liturgy of the Word, *pp. 2445–2455.*

Prayer over the Gifts

Pray, brethren...

Lord,
make holy these gifts we offer you.
These parents return to you the child you gave them.
May they have fullness of joy with him (her) in your
    kingdom.

We ask this through Christ our Lord.

Preface of Christian Death I–V, *pp. 961–963.*

Communion Antiphon

**We were baptized with Christ and buried with him in death;
we believe that we shall also come to life with Christ (Easter
season, alleluia).** (See Rom 6:4, 8)

Prayer after Communion

Let us pray.

Pause for silent prayer, if this has not preceded.

Lord,
hear the prayers of those who share in the body and blood of
    your Son.
Comfort those who mourn for this child
and sustain them with the hope of eternal life.

We ask this through Christ our Lord.

B. OTHER PRAYERS

Opening Prayer

God our Father,
you know how much our hearts are saddened
by the death of this child.
As we who live mourn his (her) death
strengthen us in our faith
that he (she) is already at peace in your eternal kingdom.

We ask this through our Lord Jesus Christ, your Son,
who lives and reigns with you and the Holy Spirit,
one God, for ever and ever.

Liturgy of the Word, *pp. 2445–2455.*

Prayer over the Gifts

Pray, brethren...

Father,
receive this sacrifice we offer
as a sign of our love for you,
and comfort us by your merciful love.
We accept what you have asked of us,
for we trust in your wisdom and goodness.

We ask this through Christ our Lord.

Prayer after Communion

Let us pray.

Pause for silent prayer, if this has not preceded.

Lord,
you feed us with the gift of your eucharist.
May we rejoice with this child
at the feast of eternal life in your kingdom.

We ask this through Christ our Lord.

FUNERAL MASS OF A CHILD WHO DIED BEFORE BAPTISM

If a child whom the parents wished to be baptized should die before baptism, the local ordinary, taking into consideration pastoral circumstances, may permit the funeral to be celebrated either in the home of the child or even according to the plan of funeral rites customarily used in the region.

In funerals of this kind there should ordinarily be a liturgy of the word, as describe in the ritual. If at times the celebration of Mass is considered opportune, the following texts should be used.

The doctrine of the necessity of baptism should not be weakened in the catechesis of the faithful.

Entrance Antiphon

God will wipe every tear from their eyes; there will be no more death, no more weeping or pain, for the old order has passed away.   (Rv 21:4)

Opening Prayer

Lord,
listen to the prayers of this family
that has faith in you.
In their sorrow at the death of this child,
may they find hope in your infinite mercy.

We ask this through our Lord Jesus Christ, your Son,
who lives and reigns with you and the Holy Spirit,
one God, for ever and ever.

Or:

Father of all consolation,
from whom nothing is hidden,
you know the faith of these parents
who mourn the death of their child.
May they find comfort in knowing
that he (she) is entrusted to your loving care.

We ask this through our Lord Jesus Christ, your Son,

who lives and reigns with you and the Holy Spirit,
one God, for ever and ever.

Liturgy of the Word, *pp. 2455–2458.*

Prayer over the Gifts

Pray, brethren...

Father,
receive this sacrifice we offer
as a sign of our love for you,
and comfort us by your merciful love.
We accept what you have asked of us,
for we trust in your wisdom and goodness.
We ask this through Christ our Lord.

Preface of Christian Death I–V, *pp. 961–963.*

Communion Antiphon

The Lord has destroyed death for ever; God has wiped away
the tears from every face.   (Is 25:8)

Prayer after Communion

Let us pray.

Pause for silent prayer, if this has not preceded.

Lord,
hear the prayers of those who share in the body and blood of
    your Son.
By these sacred mysteries
you have filled them with the hope of eternal life.
May they be comforted in the sorrows of this present life.

We ask this through Christ our Lord.

Liturgy of the Word: Masses for the Dead

READING I   From the Old Testament

1

2 Mc 12:43–46

He acted in an excellent and noble way
as he had the resurrection of the dead in view.

A reading from the second Book of Maccabees

Judas, the ruler of Israel, took up a collection among all his soldiers, amounting to two thousand silver drachmas, which he sent to Jerusalem to provide for an expiatory sacrifice. In doing this he acted in a very excellent and noble way, inasmuch as he had the resurrection of the dead in view; for if he were not expecting the fallen to rise again, it would have been useless and foolish to pray for them in death. But if he did this with a view to the splendid reward that awaits those who had gone to rest in godliness, it was a holy and pious thought. Thus he made atonement for the dead that they might be freed from this sin.

The word of the Lord.

2

Jb 19:1, 23–27a

I know that my Vindicator lives.

A reading from the Book of Job

Job answered Bildad the Shuhite and said:
Oh, would that my words were written down!
    Would that they were inscribed in a record:
That with an iron chisel and with lead
    they were cut in the rock forever!

But as for me, I know that my Vindicator lives,
and that he will at last stand forth upon the dust;
Whom I myself shall see:
my own eyes, not another's, shall behold him;
And from my flesh I shall see God;
my inmost being is consumed with longing.
The word of the Lord.

3 Wis 3:1–9 or 3:1–6,9

As sacrificial offerings he took them to himself.

A reading from the Book of Wisdom

Long form follows; for short form omit what is in brackets.

The souls of the just are in the hand of God,
and no torment shall touch them.
They seemed, in the view of the foolish, to be dead;
and their passing away was thought an affliction
and their going forth from us, utter destruction.
But they are in peace.
For if before men, indeed they be punished,
yet is their hope full of immortality;
Chastised a little, they shall be greatly blessed,
because God tried them
and found them worthy of himself.
As gold in the furnace, he proved them,
and as sacrificial offerings he took them to himself.
[In the time of their visitation they shall shine,
and shall dart about as sparks through stubble;
They shall judge nations and rule over peoples,
and the LORD shall be their King forever.]

Those who trust in him shall understand truth,
   and the faithful shall abide with him in love:
Because grace and mercy are with his holy ones,
   and his care is with his elect.

The word of the Lord.

4
                                    Wis 4:7–15

An unsullied life, the attainment of old age.

A reading from the Book of Wisdom

The just man, though he die early,
   shall be at rest.
For the age that is honorable comes not
   with the passing of time,
     nor can it be measured in terms of years.
Rather, understanding is the hoary crown for men,
   and an unsullied life, the attainment of old age.
He who pleased God was loved;
   he who lived among sinners was transported—
Snatched away, lest wickedness pervert his mind
   or deceit beguile his soul;
For the witchery of paltry things obscures what is right
   and the whirl of desire transforms the innocent mind.
Having become perfect in a short while,
   he reached the fullness of a long career;
     for his soul was pleasing to the LORD,
   therefore he sped him out of the midst of wickedness.
But the people saw and did not understand,
   nor did they take this into account.

The word of the Lord.

5

Is 25:6a, 7–9

He will destroy death forever.

A reading from the Book of the Prophet Isaiah

On this mountain the LORD of hosts
 will provide for all peoples.
On this mountain he will destroy
 the veil that veils all peoples,
The web that is woven over all nations;
 he will destroy death forever.
The LORD GOD will wipe away
 the tears from all faces;
The reproach of his people he will remove
 from the whole earth; for the LORD has spoken.

 On that day it will be said:
"Behold our God, to whom we looked to save us!
 This is the LORD for whom we looked;
 let us rejoice and be glad that he has saved us!"
The word of the Lord.

6

Lam 3:17–26

It is good to hope in silence for the saving help of the Lord.

A reading from the Book of Lamentations

My soul is deprived of peace,
 I have forgotten what happiness is;
I tell myself my future is lost,
 all that I hoped for from the LORD.
The thought of my homeless poverty
 is wormwood and gall;
Remembering it over and over
 leaves my soul downcast within me.

But I will call this to mind,
  as my reason to have hope:

The favors of the LORD are not exhausted,
  his mercies are not spent;
They are renewed each morning,
  so great is his faithfulness.
My portion is the LORD, says my soul;
  therefore will I hope in him.

Good is the LORD to one who waits for him,
  to the soul that seeks him;
It is good to hope in silence
  for the saving help of the LORD.

The word of the Lord.

7
                                                      Dn 12:1–3

Many of those who sleep in the dust of the earth shall awake.

A reading from the Book of the Prophet Daniel

In those days, I, Daniel, mourned
  and heard this word of the Lord:
At that time there shall arise
  Michael, the great prince,
  guardian of your people;
It shall be a time unsurpassed in distress
  since nations began until that time.
At that time your people shall escape,
  everyone who is found written in the book.

Many of those who sleep in the dust of the earth shall awake;
Some shall live forever,
  others shall be an everlasting horror and disgrace.
But the wise shall shine brightly

like the splendor of the firmament,
And those who lead the many to justice
    shall be like the stars forever.
The word of the Lord.

READING I   From the New Testament

During the Easter Season

1   Acts 10:34–43 or 10:34–36, 42–43

He is the one appointed by God as judge of the living and the dead.

A reading from the Acts of the Apostles

Long form follows; for short form omit what is in brackets.

Peter proceeded to speak, saying: "In truth, I see that God shows no partiality. Rather, in every nation whoever fears him and acts uprightly is acceptable to him. You know the word that he sent to the children of Israel as he proclaimed peace through Jesus Christ, who is Lord of all, [what has happened all over Judea, beginning in Galilee after the baptism that John preached, how God anointed Jesus of Nazareth with the Holy Spirit and power. He went about doing good and healing all those oppressed by the Devil, for God was with him. We are witnesses of all that he did both in the country of the Jews and in Jerusalem. They put him to death by hanging him on a tree. This man God raised on the third day and granted that he be visible, not to all the people, but to us, the witnesses chosen by God in advance, who ate and drank with him after he rose from the dead.] He commissioned us to preach to the people and testify that he is the one appointed by God as judge of the living and the dead. To him all the prophets bear witness, that everyone who believes in him will receive forgiveness of sins through his name."

The word of the Lord.

2

Blessed are the dead who die in the Lord.

A reading from the Book of Revelation

I, John, heard a voice from heaven say, "Write this: Blessed are the dead who die in the Lord from now on." "Yes," said the Spirit, "let them find rest from their labors, for their works accompany them."

The word of the Lord.

3

The dead were judged according to their deeds.

A reading from the Book of Revelation

I, John, saw a large white throne and the one who was sitting on it. The earth and the sky fled from his presence and there was no place for them. I saw the dead, the great and the lowly, standing before the throne, and scrolls were opened. Then another scroll was opened, the book of life. The dead were judged according to their deeds, by what was written in the scrolls. The sea gave up its dead; then Death and Hades gave up their dead. All the dead were judged according to their deeds. Then Death and Hades were thrown into the pool of fire. (This pool of fire is the second death.) Anyone whose name was not found written in the book of life was thrown into the pool of fire.

Then I saw a new heaven and a new earth. The former heaven and the former earth had passed away, and the sea was no more.

The word of the Lord.

4   Rv 21:1–5a, 6b–7

There shall be no more death.

A reading from the Book of Revelation

I, John, saw a new heaven and a new earth. The former heaven and the former earth had passed away, and the sea was no more. I also saw the holy city, a new Jerusalem, coming down out of heaven from God, prepared as a bride adorned for her husband. I heard a loud voice from the throne saying, "Behold, God's dwelling is with the human race. He will dwell with them and they will be his people and God himself will always be with them as their God. He will wipe every tear from their eyes, and there shall be no more death or mourning, wailing or pain, for the old order has passed away."

The One who sat on the throne said, "Behold, I make all things new." I am the Alpha and the Omega, the beginning and the end. To the thirsty I will give a gift from the spring of life-giving water. The victor will inherit these gifts, and I shall be his God, and he will be my son."

The word of the Lord.

Responsorial Psalm

1   Ps 23:1–3, 4, 5, 6

See the Common of Holy Men and Women (p. 2287).

2

Ps 25:6 and 7b, 17–18, 20–21

R. To you, O Lord, I lift my soul.

Remember that your compassion, O LORD,
  and your kindness are from of old.
In your kindness remember me,
  because of your goodness, O LORD

R. To you, O Lord, I lift my soul.

Relieve the troubles of my heart;
  and bring me out of my distress.
Put an end to my affliction and my suffering;
  and take away all my sins.

R. To you, O Lord, I lift my soul.

Preserve my life and rescue me;
  let me not be put to shame, for I take refuge in you.
Let integrity and uprightness preserve me,
  because I wait for you, O LORD.

R. To you, O Lord, I lift my soul.

Or: **R. No one who waits for you, O Lord, will ever be put to
       shame.**

3

Ps 27:1, 4, 7 and 8b and 9a, 13–14

R. The Lord is my light and my salvation.

The LORD is my light and my salvation;
  whom should I fear?
The LORD is my life's refuge;
  of whom should I be afraid?

R. The Lord is my light and my salvation.

One thing I ask of the LORD;
  this I seek:
To dwell in the house of the LORD

all the days of my life,
That I may gaze on the loveliness of the L ORD
and contemplate his temple.

R. The Lord is my light and my salvation.

Hear, O L ORD, the sound of my call;
have pity on me, and answer me.
Your presence, O L ORD, I seek.
Hide not your face from me.

R. The Lord is my light and my salvation.

I believe that I shall see the bounty of the L ORD
in the land of the living.
Wait for the L ORD with courage;
be stouthearted, and wait for the L ORD.

R. The Lord is my light and my salvation.

Or: **R. I believe that I shall see the good things of the Lord
in the land of the living.**

4

Ps 42:2, 3, 5cdef; 43:3, 4, 5

**R. My soul is thirsting for the living God: when shall I see
him face to face.**

As the hind longs for the running waters,
so my soul longs for you, O God.

**R. My soul is thirsting for the living God: when shall I see
him face to face.**

Athirst is my soul for God, the living God.
When shall I go and behold the face of God?

**R. My soul is thirsting for the living God: when shall I see
him face to face.**

I went with the throng and led them in procession
to the house of God.
Amid loud cries of joy and thanksgiving,
with the multitude keeping festival.

**R. My soul is thirsting for the living God: when shall I see
him face to face.**

Send forth your light and your fidelity;
  they shall lead me on
And bring me to your holy mountain,
  to your dwelling-place.

**R. My soul is thirsting for the living God: when shall I see
him face to face.**

Then will I go in to the altar of God,
  the God of my gladness and joy;
Then will I give you thanks upon the harp,
  O God, my God!

**R. My soul is thirsting for the living God: when shall I see
him face to face.**

Why are you so downcast, O my soul?
  Why do you sigh within me?
Hope in God! For I shall again be thanking him,
  in the presence of my savior and my God.

**R. My soul is thirsting for the living God: when shall I see
him face to face.**

5

Ps 63:2, 3–4, 5–6, 8–9

R. My soul is thirsting for you, O Lord my God.

O God, you are my God whom I seek;
  for you my flesh pines and my soul thirsts
  like the earth, parched, lifeless and without water.

R. My soul is thirsting for you, O Lord my God.

Thus have I gazed toward you in the sanctuary
  to see your power and your glory,
For your kindness is a greater good than life;
  my lips shall glorify you.

R. My soul is thirsting for you, O Lord my God.

Thus will I bless you while I live;
   lifting up my hands, I will call upon your name.
As with the riches of a banquet shall my soul be satisfied,
   and with exultant lips my mouth shall praise you.

   R. My soul is thirsting for you, O Lord my God.

You are my help,
   and in the shadow of your wings I shout for joy.
My soul clings fast to you;
   your right hand upholds me.

   R. My soul is thirsting for you, O Lord my God.

6   Ps 103:8 and 10, 13–14, 15–16, 17–18

   R. The Lord is kind and merciful.

Merciful and gracious is the LORD,
   slow to anger, and abounding in kindness.
Not according to our sins does he deal with us,
   nor does he requite us according to our crimes.

   R. The Lord is kind and merciful.

As a father has compassion on his children,
   so the LORD has compassion on those who fear him.
For he knows how we are formed,
   he remembers that we are dust.

   R. The Lord is kind and merciful.

Man's days are like those of grass;
   like a flower of the field he blooms;
The wind sweeps over him and he is gone,
   and his place knows him no more.

   R. The Lord is kind and merciful.

But the kindness of the LORD is from eternity,
   to eternity toward those who fear him,
And his justice toward children's children
   among those who keep his covenant
   and remember to fulfill his precepts.

R. The Lord is kind and merciful.

Or: **R. The salvation of the just comes from the Lord.**

7   Ps 116:5, 6, 10–11, 15–16ac

R. I will walk in the presence of the Lord in the land of the living.

Gracious is the LORD and just;
   yes, our God is merciful.

R. I will walk in the presence of the Lord in the land of the living.

The LORD keeps the little ones;
   I was brought low, and he saved me.

R. I will walk in the presence of the Lord in the land of the living.

I believed, even when I said,
   "I am greatly afflicted";
I said in my alarm,
   "No man is dependable."

R. I will walk in the presence of the Lord in the land of the living.

Precious in the eyes of the LORD
   is the death of his faithful ones.
O LORD, I am your servant,
   you have loosed my bonds.

R. I will walk in the presence of the Lord in the land of the living.

Or: **R. Alleluia.**

8   Ps 122:1–2, 4–5, 6–7, 8–9

R. I rejoiced when I heard them say: let us go to the house of the Lord.

I rejoiced because they said to me,
  "We will go up to the house of the LORD."
And now we have set foot
  within your gates, O Jerusalem.

> **R. I rejoiced when I heard them say: let us go to the house
> of the Lord.**

To it the tribes go up,
  the tribes of the LORD.
According to the decree for Israel,
  to give thanks to the name of the LORD.
In it are set up judgment seats,
  seats for the house of David.

> **R. I rejoiced when I heard them say: let us go to the house
> of the Lord.**

Pray for the peace of Jerusalem!
  May those who love you prosper!
May peace be within your walls,
  prosperity in your buildings.

> **R. I rejoiced when I heard them say: let us go to the house
> of the Lord.**

Because of my relatives and friends
  I will say "Peace be within you!"
Because of the house of the LORD, our God,
  I will pray for your good.

> **R. I rejoiced when I heard them say: let us go to the house
> of the Lord.**

> *Or:* **R. Let us go rejoicing to the house of the Lord.**

9   Ps 130:1–2, 3–4, 5–6ab, 6c–7, 8

> **R. Out of the depths, I cry to you, Lord.**

Out of the depths I cry to you, O LORD;
  LORD, hear my voice!

Let your ears be attentive
 to my voice in supplication.

R. Out of the depths, I cry to you, Lord.

If you, O Lord, mark iniquities,
 Lord, who can stand?
But with you is forgiveness,
 that you may be revered.

R. Out of the depths, I cry to you, Lord.

I trust in the Lord;
 my soul trusts in his word.
My soul waits for the Lord
 more than the sentinels wait for the dawn.

R. Out of the depths, I cry to you, Lord.

More than the sentinels wait for the dawn,
 let Israel wait for the Lord,
For with the Lord is kindness
 and with him is plenteous redemption.

R. Out of the depths, I cry to you, Lord.

And he will redeem Israel
 from all their iniquities.

R. Out of the depths, I cry to you, Lord.

Or: **R. I hope in the Lord, I trust in his word.**

10

Ps 143:1–2, 5–6, 7ab and 8ab, 10

R. O Lord, hear my prayer.

O Lord, hear my prayer;
 hearken to my pleading in your faithfulness;
 in your justice answer me.
And enter not into judgment with your servant,
 for before you no living man is just.

R. O Lord, hear my prayer.

I remember the days of old;
  I meditate on all your doings;
  the works of your hands I ponder.
I stretch out my hands to you;
  my soul thirsts for you like parched land.

R. O Lord, hear my prayer.

Hasten to answer me, O LORD;
  for my spirit fails me.
At dawn let me hear of your mercy,
  for in you I trust.

R. O Lord, hear my prayer.

Teach me to do your will,
  for you are my God.
May your good spirit guide me
  on level ground.

R. O Lord, hear my prayer.

READING II   From the New Testament

Rom 5:5–11

Since we are now justified by his Blood,
we will be saved through him from the wrath.

A reading from the Letter of Saint Paul to the Romans

Brothers and sisters:

Hope does not disappoint, because the love of God has been
poured out into our hearts through the Holy Spirit who has
been given to us. For Christ, while we were still helpless, died
at the appointed time for the ungodly. Indeed, only with
difficulty does one die for a just person, though perhaps for a
good person one might even find courage to die. But God proves
his love for us in that while we were still sinners Christ died

for us. How much more then, since we are now justified by his Blood, will we be saved through him from the wrath. Indeed, if, while we were enemies, we were reconciled to God through the death of his Son, how much more, once reconciled, will we be saved by his life. Not only that, but we also boast of God through our Lord Jesus Christ, through whom we have now received reconciliation.

The word of the Lord.

2

Rom 5:17–21

Where sin increased, grace overflowed all the more.

A reading from the Letter of Saint Paul to the Romans

Brothers and sisters:

If, by the transgression of the one, death came to reign through that one, how much more will those who receive the abundance of grace and of the gift of justification come to reign in life through the one Jesus Christ. In conclusion, just as through one transgression condemnation came upon all, so, through one righteous act, acquittal and life came to all. For just as through the disobedience of the one man the many were made sinners, so through the obedience of the one the many will be made righteous. The law entered in so that transgression might increase but, where sin increased, grace overflowed all the more, so that, as sin reigned in death, grace also might reign through justification for eternal life through Jesus Christ our Lord.

The word of the Lord.

3

Rom 6:3–9 or 6:3–4, 8–9

We too might live in newness of life.

A reading from the Letter of Saint Paul to the Romans

Long form follows; for short form omit what is in brackets.

Brothers and sisters:
Are you unaware that we who were baptized into Christ Jesus were baptized into his death? We were indeed buried with him through baptism into death, so that, just as Christ was raised from the dead by the glory of the Father, we too might live in newness of life.

[For if we have grown into union with him through a death like his, we shall also be united with him in the resurrection. We know that our old self was crucified with him, so that our sinful body might be done away with, that we might no longer be in slavery to sin. For a dead person has been absolved from sin.] If, then, we have died with Christ, we believe that we shall also live with him. We know that Christ, raised from the dead, dies no more; death no longer has power over him.

The word of the Lord.

4

Rom 8:14–23

*We also groan within ourselves as we wait
for adoption, the redemption of our bodies.*

A reading from the Letter of Saint Paul to the Romans

Brothers and sisters:
Those who are led by the Spirit of God are sons of God. For you did not receive a spirit of slavery to fall back into fear, but you received a spirit of adoption, through which we cry, *Abba*, "Father!" The Spirit itself bears witness with our spirit that we are children of God, and if children, then heirs, heirs of God

and joint heirs with Christ, if only we suffer with him so that we may also be glorified with him.

I consider that the sufferings of this present time are as nothing compared with the glory to be revealed for us. For creation awaits with eager expectation the revelation of the children of God; for creation was made subject to futility, not of its own accord but because of the one who subjected it, in hope that creation itself would be set free from slavery to corruption and share in the glorious freedom of the children of God. We know that all creation is groaning in labor pains even until now; and not only that, but we ourselves, who have the firstfruits of the Spirit, we also groan within ourselves as we wait for adoption, the redemption of our bodies.

The word of the Lord.

---

5 Rom 8:31b–35, 37–39

What will separate us from the love of Christ?

A reading from the Letter of Saint Paul to the Romans

Brothers and sisters:

If God is for us, who can be against us? He did not spare his own Son but handed him over for us all, will he not also give us everything else along with him? Who will bring a charge against God's chosen ones? It is God who acquits us. Who will condemn? It is Christ Jesus who died, rather, was raised, who also is at the right hand of God, who indeed intercedes for us. What will separate us from the love of Christ? Will anguish, or distress or persecution, or famine, or nakedness, or peril, or the sword?

No, in all these things, we conquer overwhelmingly through him who loved us. For I am convinced that neither death, nor life, nor angels, nor principalities, nor present things, nor future things, nor powers, nor height, nor depth, nor any other creature will be able to separate us from the love of God in Christ Jesus our Lord.

The word of the Lord.

Rom 14:7–9, 10c –12

Whether we live or die, we are the Lord's.

A reading from the Letter of Saint Paul to the Romans

Brothers and sisters:

No one lives for oneself, and no one dies for oneself. For if we live, we live for the Lord, and if we die, we die for the Lord; so then, whether we live or die, we are the Lord's. For this is why Christ died and came to life, that he might be Lord of both the dead and the living. Why then do you judge your brother? Or you, why do you look down on your brother? For we shall all stand before the judgment seat of God; for it is written:

> As I live, says the Lord, every knee
> shall bend before me,
> and every tongue shall give praise to God.

So then each of us shall give an accounting of himself to God.

The word of the Lord.

7

1 Cor 15:20 – 28 or 15:20 – 23

So too in Christ shall all be brought to life.

A reading from the first Letter of Saint Paul to the Corinthians

Long form follows; for short form omit what is in brackets.

Brothers and sisters:

Christ has been raised from the dead, the firstfruits of those who have fallen asleep. For since death came through a man, the resurrection of the dead came also through man. For just as in Adam all die, so too in Christ shall all be brought to life, but each one in proper order: Christ the firstfruits; then, at his coming, those who belong to Christ; [then comes the end, when he hands over the Kingdom to his God and Father. For he must reign until he has put all his enemies under his feet. The last enemy to be destroyed is death, for "he subjected everything under his feet." But when it says that everything has been subjected, it is clear that it excludes the one who subjected everything to him. When everything is subjected to him, then the Son himself will also be subjected to the one who subjected everything to him, so that God may be all in all.]

The word of the Lord.

8

1 Cor 15:51–57

Death is swallowed up in victory.

A reading from the first Letter of Saint Paul to the Corinthians

Brothers and sisters:

Behold, I tell you a mystery. We shall not all fall asleep, but we will all be changed, in an instant, in the blink of an eye, at the last trumpet. For the trumpet will sound, the dead will be raised incorruptible, and we shall be changed. For that which is corruptible must clothe itself with incorruptibility, and that which is mortal must clothe itself with immortality. And when this which is corruptible clothes itself with incorruptibility and this which is mortal clothes itself with immortality, then the word that is written shall come about:

> *Death is swallowed up in victory.*
> *Where, O death, is your victory?*
> *Where, O death, is your sting?*

The sting of death is sin, and the power of sin is the law. But thanks be to God who gives us the victory through our Lord Jesus Christ.

The word of the Lord.

 9   2 Cor 4:14 – 5:1

What is seen is transitory, but what is unseen is eternal.

A reading from the second Letter of Saint Paul to the Corinthians

Brothers and sisters:

Knowing that the One who raised the Lord Jesus will raise us also with Jesus and place us with you in his presence. Everything indeed is for you, so that the grace bestowed in abundance on more and more people may cause the thanksgiving to overflow for the glory of God. Therefore, we are not discouraged; rather, although our outer self is wasting away, our inner self is being renewed day by day. For this momentary light affliction is producing for us an eternal weight of glory beyond all comparison, as we look not to what is seen but to what is unseen; for what is seen is transitory, but what is unseen is eternal.

For we know that if our earthly dwelling, a tent, should be destroyed, we have a building from God, a dwelling not made with hands, eternal in heaven.

The word of the Lord.

 10   2 Cor 5:1, 6–10

We have a building from God, eternal in heaven.

A reading from the second Letter of Saint Paul to the Corinthians

Brothers and sisters:

We know that if our earthly dwelling, a tent, should be destroyed, we have a building from God, a dwelling not made with hands, eternal in heaven.

We are always courageous, although we know that while we are at home in the body we are away from the Lord, for we walk by faith, not by sight. Yet we are courageous, and we would rather leave the body and go home to the Lord. Therefore, we aspire to please him, whether we are at home or away. For we must all appear before the judgment seat of Christ, so that each may receive recompense, according to what he did in the body, whether good or evil.

The word of the Lord.

11

Phil 3:20–21

He will change our lowly bodies to conform to his glory.

A reading from the Letter of Saint Paul to the Philippians

Brothers and sisters:
Our citizenship is in heaven, and from it we also await a savior, the Lord Jesus Christ. He will change our lowly body to conform with his glorified Body by the power that enables him also to bring all things into subjection to himself.

The word of the Lord.

12

1 Thes 4:13–18

A reading from the first Letter of Saint Paul to the Thessalonians

We do not want you to be unaware, brothers and sisters, about those who have fallen asleep, so that you may not grieve like the rest, who have no hope. For if we believe that Jesus died and rose, so too will God, through Jesus, bring with him those who have fallen asleep. Indeed, we tell you this, on the word of the Lord, that we who are alive, who are left until the coming of the Lord, will surely not precede those who have fallen asleep. For the Lord himself, with a word of command, with the voice of an archangel and with the trumpet of God, will come down from heaven, and the dead in Christ will rise first. Then we who are alive, who are left, will be caught up together with them in the clouds to meet the Lord in the air. Thus we shall always be with the Lord. Therefore, console one another with these words.

The word of the Lord.

13

2 Tm 2:8–13

If we have died with him we shall also live with him.

A reading from the second Letter of Saint Paul to Timothy

Beloved:

Remember Jesus Christ, raised from the dead, a descendant of David: such is my Gospel, for which I am suffering, even to the point of chains, like a criminal. But the word of God is not chained. Therefore, I bear with everything for the sake of those who are chosen, so that they too may obtain the salvation that is in Christ Jesus, together with eternal glory. This saying is trustworthy:

If we have died with him
  we shall also live with him;
if we persevere
  we shall also reign with him.
But if we deny him
  he will deny us.

If we are unfaithful
   he remains faithful,
   for he cannot deny himself.
The word of the Lord.

14   1 Jn 3:1–2

We shall see him as he is.

A reading from the first Letter of Saint John

Beloved:

See what love the Father has bestowed on us that we may be
called the children of God. Yet so we are. The reason the world
does not know us is that it did not know him. Beloved, we are
God's children now; what we shall be has not yet been revealed.
We do know that when it is revealed we shall be like him, for
we shall see him as he is.

The word of the Lord.

15   1 Jn 3:14–16

*We know that we have passed from death to life
because we love our brothers.*

A reading from the first Letter of Saint John

Beloved:

We know that we have passed from death to life because we
love our brothers. Whoever does not love remains in death.
Everyone who hates his brother is a murderer, and you know
that no murderer has eternal life remaining in him. The way
we came to know love was that he laid down his life for us; so
we ought to lay down our lives for our brothers.

The word of the Lord.

ALLELUIA VERSE AND VERSE BEFORE THE GOSPEL

1 See Mt 11:25

Blessed are you, Father, Lord of heaven and earth;
you have revealed to the childlike the mysteries of the
  Kingdom.

2 Mt 25:34

Come, you who are blessed by my Father, says the Lord;
inherit the kingdom prepared for you from the foundation
  of the world.

3 Jn 3:16

God so loved the world that he gave his only-begotten
  Son,
so that everyone who believes in him might have eternal
  life.

4 Jn 6:39

This is the will of my Father, says the Lord,
that I should lose nothing of all that he has given to me,
and that I should raise it up on the last day.

5 Jn 6:40

This is the will of my Father, says the Lord, that everyone
who sees the Son and believes in him may have eternal
  life,
and I shall raise him on the last day.

6 Jn 6:51

I am the living bread that came down from heaven,
  says the Lord;
whoever eats this bread will live forever.

7 Jn 11:25a, 26

I am the resurrection and the life, says the Lord;
whoever believes in me will never die.

8 See Phil 3:20

Our true home is in heaven,
and Jesus Christ, whose return we long for,
will come from heaven to save us.

9   2 Tm 2:11–12a

If we die with Christ, we shall live with him,
and if we persevere we shall also reign with him.

10   Rv 1:5a, 6b

Jesus Christ is the firstborn from the dead;
glory and power be his forever and ever. Amen.

11   Rv 14:13

Blessed are those who have died in the Lord;
let them rest from their labors for their good deeds go
with them.

GOSPEL

1   Mt 5:1–12a

See the Common of Holy Men and Women (p. 2304).

2   Mt 11:25–30

See the Common of Holy Men and Women (p. 2306).

3   Mt 25:1–13

See the Common of Holy Men and Women (p. 2310).

4   Mt 25:31–46

See the Common of Holy Men and Women (p. 2312).

5   Mk 15:33–39; 16:1–6 or 15:33–39

Jesus gave a loud cry and breathed his last.

A reading from the holy Gospel according to Mark

Long form follows; for short form omit what is in brackets.

At noon darkness came over the whole land until three in the
afternoon. And at three o'clock Jesus cried out in a loud voice,

"*Eloi, Eloi, lema sabachthani?*" which is translated, "My God, my God, why have you forsaken me?" Some of the bystanders who heard it said, "Look, he is calling Elijah." One of them ran, soaked a sponge with wine, put it on a reed, and gave it to him to drink, saying, "Wait, let us see if Elijah comes to take him down." Jesus gave a loud cry and breathed his last. The veil of the sanctuary was torn in two from top to bottom. When the centurion who stood facing him saw how he breathed his last he said, "Truly this man was the Son of God!"

[When the sabbath was over, Mary Magdalene, Mary, the mother of James, and Salome bought spices so that they might go and anoint him. Very early when the sun had risen, on the first day of the week, they came to the tomb. They were saying to one another, "Who will roll back the stone for us from the entrance to the tomb?" When they looked up, they saw that the stone had been rolled back; it was very large. On entering the tomb they saw a young man sitting on the right side, clothed in a white robe, and they were utterly amazed. He said to them, "Do not be amazed! You seek Jesus of Nazareth, the crucified. He has been raised; he is not here. Behold the place where they laid him."]

The Gospel of the Lord.

6   Lk 7:11–17

She bore me in the arms of her prayer,
that you might say to the son of the widow: Young man, I say to
you, arise (Saint Augustine, Confessions, book 6, n. 2).

A reading from the holy Gospel according to Luke

Jesus journeyed to a city called Nain, and his disciples and a large crowd accompanied him. As he drew near to the gate of the city, a man who had died was being carried out, the only son of his mother, and she was a widow. A large crowd from the city was with her. When the Lord saw her, he was moved with pity for her and said to her, "Do not weep." He stepped forward and touched the coffin; at this the bearers halted, and he said, "Young man, I tell you, arise!" The dead man sat up and began to speak, and Jesus gave him to his mother. Fear seized them all, and they glorified God, exclaiming, "A great prophet has arisen in our midst," and "God has visited his people." This report about him spread through the whole of Judea and in all the surrounding region.

The Gospel of the Lord.

7   Lk 12:35–40

See the Common of Holy Men and Women (p. 2319).

8   Lk 23:33, 39–43

Today you will be with me in Paradise.

A reading from the holy Gospel according to Luke

When the soldiers came to the place called the Skull, they crucified Jesus and the criminals there, one on his right, the other on his left.

Now one of the criminals hanging there reviled Jesus, saying, "Are you not the Christ? Save yourself and us." The other man, however, rebuking him, said in reply, "Have you no fear of God, for you are subject to the same condemnation? And indeed, we have been condemned justly, for the sentence we received corresponds to our crimes, but this man has done nothing criminal." Then he said, "Jesus, remember me when

you come into your Kingdom." He replied to him, "Amen, I say to you, today you will be with me in Paradise."
The Gospel of the Lord.

9 Lk 23:44–46, 50, 52–53; 24:1–6a or 23:44–46, 50, 52–53

Father, into your hands I commend my spirit.

A reading from the holy Gospel according to Luke

Long form follows; for short form omit what is in brackets.

It was about noon and darkness came over the whole land until three in the afternoon because of an eclipse of the sun. Then the veil of the temple was torn down the middle. Jesus cried out in a loud voice, "Father, into your hands I commend my spirit"; and when he had said this he breathed his last.

Now there was a virtuous and righteous man named Joseph who, though he was a member of the council, went to Pilate and asked for the Body of Jesus. After he had taken the Body down, he wrapped it in a linen cloth and laid him in a rock-hewn tomb in which no one had yet been buried.

[At daybreak on the first day of the week the women took the spices they had prepared and went to the tomb. They found the stone rolled away from the tomb; but when they entered, they did not find the Body of the Lord Jesus. While they were puzzling over this, behold, two men in dazzling garments appeared to them. They were terrified and bowed their faces to the ground. They said to them, "Why do you seek the living one among the dead? He is not here, but he has been raised."]
The Gospel of the Lord.

10

They recognized Jesus in the breaking of the bread.

A reading from the holy Gospel according to Luke

Long form follows; for short form omit what is in brackets.

That very day, the first day of the week, two of Jesus' disciples were going to a village seven miles from Jerusalem called Emmaus, and they were conversing about all the things that had occurred. And it happened that while they were conversing and debating, Jesus himself drew near and walked with them, but their eyes were prevented from recognizing him. [He asked them, "What are you discussing as you walk along?" They stopped, looking downcast. One of them, named Cleopas, said to him in reply, "Are you the only visitor to Jerusalem who does not know of the things that have taken place there in these days?" And he replied to them, "What sort of things?" They said to him, "The things that happened to Jesus the Nazarene, who was a prophet mighty in deed and word before God and all the people, how our chief priests and rulers both handed him over to a sentence of death and crucified him. But we were hoping that he would be the one to redeem Israel; and besides all this, it is now the third day since this took place. Some women from our group, however, have astounded us: they were at the tomb early in the morning and did not find his Body; they came back and reported that they had indeed seen a vision of angels who announced that he was alive. Then some of those with us went to the tomb and found things just as the women had described, but him they did not see." And he said to them, "Oh, how foolish you are! How slow of heart to believe all that the prophets spoke! Was it not necessary that the Christ should suffer these things and enter into his glory?" Then beginning with Moses and all the prophets, he interpreted to them what referred to him in all the Scriptures.] As they approached the village to which they were going, he gave the impression that he was going on farther. But they urged him, "Stay with us, for it is nearly evening and the day is almost over." So he went in to stay with them. And it happened that, while he was with them at table, he took bread, said the blessing, broke it, and gave it to them. With that their eyes were opened and they recognized him, but he vanished from their sight. Then they said to each other, "Were not our hearts burning within us while he spoke to us on the way and opened the Scriptures to us?" So they set out at once and returned to Jerusalem where they found gathered together the Eleven and those with them who were saying, "The Lord has truly been raised and has appeared to Simon!" Then the two recounted what had taken place on the way and how he was made known to them in the breaking of the bread.

The Gospel of the Lord.

11   Jn 5:24 – 29

Whoever hears my word and believes has passed from death to life.

A reading from the holy Gospel according to John

Jesus answered the Jews and said to them: "Amen, amen, I say to you, whoever hears my word and believes in the one who sent me has eternal life and will not come to condemnation, but has passed from death to life. Amen, amen, I say to you, the hour is coming and is now here when the dead will hear the voice of the Son of God, and those who hear will live. For just as the Father has life in himself, so also he gave to the Son the possession of life in himself. And he gave him power to exercise judgment, because he is the Son of Man. Do not be amazed at this, because the hour is coming in which all who are in the tombs will hear his voice and will come out, those who have done good deeds to the resurrection of life, but those who have done wicked deeds to the resurrection of condemnation.

The Gospel of the Lord.

12   Jn 6:37–40

Everyone who sees the Son and
believes in him may have eternal life
and I shall raise him on the last day.

A reading from the holy Gospel according to John

Jesus said to the crowds: "Everything that the Father gives me will come to me, and I will not reject anyone who comes to me, because I came down from heaven not to do my own will but the will of the one who sent me. And this is the will of the one who sent me, that I should not lose anything of what he gave me, but that I should raise it on the last day. For this is the will of my Father, that everyone who sees the Son and believes in him may have eternal life, and I shall raise him on the last day."

The Gospel of the Lord.

13   Jn 6:51–59

Whoever eats this bread will live forever,
and I will raise them up on the last day.

A reading from the holy Gospel according to John

Jesus said to the crowds: "I am the living bread that came down from heaven; whoever eats this bread will live forever; and the bread that I will give is my Flesh for the life of the world."

The Jews quarreled among themselves, saying, "How can this man give us his Flesh to eat?" Jesus said to them, "Amen, amen, I say to you, unless you eat the Flesh of the Son of Man and drink his Blood, you do not have life within you. Whoever eats my Flesh and drinks my Blood has eternal life, and I will raise him on the last day. For my Flesh is true food, and my Blood is true drink. Whoever eats my Flesh and drinks my Blood remains in me and I in him. Just as the living Father sent me and I have life because of the Father, so also the one who feeds on me will have life because of me. This is the bread that came down from heaven. Unlike your ancestors who ate and still died, whoever eats this bread will live forever."

The Gospel of the Lord.

14   Jn 11:17–27 or 11:21–22

I am the resurrection and the life.

A reading from the holy Gospel according to John

Long form follows; for short form omit what is in brackets.

[When Jesus arrived in Bethany, he found that Lazarus had already been in the tomb for four days. Now Bethany was near Jerusalem, only about two miles away. Many of the Jews had come to Martha and Mary to comfort them about their brother. When Martha heard that Jesus was coming, she went to meet him; but Mary sat at home.] Martha said to Jesus, "Lord, if you had been here, my brother would not have died. But even now I know that whatever you ask of God, God will give you." Jesus said to her, "Your brother will rise." Martha said to him, "I know he will rise, in the resurrection on the last day." Jesus told her, "I am the resurrection and the life; whoever believes in me, even if he dies, will live, and everyone who lives and believes in me will never die. Do you believe this?" She said to him, "Yes, Lord. I have come to believe that you are the Christ, the Son of God, the one who is coming into the world." The Gospel of the Lord.

15   Jn 11:32 – 45

Lazarus, come out!

A reading from the holy Gospel according to John

When Mary came to where Jesus was and saw him, she fell at his feet and said to him, "Lord, if you had been here, my brother would not have died." When Jesus saw her weeping and the Jews who had come with her weeping, he became perturbed and deeply troubled, and said, "Where have you laid him?" They said to him, "Sir, come and see." And Jesus wept. So the Jews said, "See how he loved him." But some of them said, "Could not the one who opened the eyes of the blind man have done something so that this man would not have died?"

So Jesus, perturbed again, came to the tomb. It was a cave, and a stone lay across it. Jesus said, "Take away the stone." Martha, the dead man's sister, said to him, "Lord, by now there will be a stench; he has been dead for four days." Jesus said to her, "Did I not tell you that if you believe you will see the glory of God?" So they took away the stone. And Jesus raised his eyes and said, "Father, I thank you for hearing me. I know that you always hear me; but because of the crowd here I have said this, that they may believe that you sent me." And when he had said this, he cried out in a loud voice, "Lazarus, come out!" The dead man came out, tied hand and foot with burial bands, and his face was wrapped in a cloth. So Jesus said to the crowd, "Untie him and let him go."

Now many of the Jews who had come to Mary and seen what he had done began to believe in him.

The Gospel of the Lord.

16   Jn 12:23 – 28 or 12:23 – 26

If it dies, it produces much fruit.

A reading from the holy Gospel according to John

Long form follows; for short form omit what is in brackets.

Jesus said to his disciples: "The hour has come for the Son of Man to be glorified. Amen, amen, I say to you, unless a grain of wheat falls to the ground and dies, it remains just a grain of wheat; but if it dies, it produces much fruit. Whoever loves his life will lose it, and whoever hates his life in this world will preserve it for eternal life. Whoever serves me must follow me, and where I am, there also will my servant be. The Father will honor whoever serves me.

["I am troubled now. Yet what should I say? 'Father, save me from this hour'? But it was for this purpose that I came to this hour. Father, glorify your name." Then a voice came from heaven, "I have glorified it and will glorify it again."]

The Gospel of the Lord.

17   Jn 14:1 – 6

I am the way and the truth and the life.

A reading from the holy Gospel according to John

Jesus said to his disciples: "Do not let your hearts be troubled. You have faith in God; have faith also in me. In my Father's house there are many dwelling places. If there were not, would I have told you that I am going to prepare a place for you? And

if I go and prepare a place for you, I will come back again and take you to myself, so that where I am you also may be. Where I am going you know the way." Thomas said to him, "Master, we do not know where you are going; how can we know the way?" Jesus said to him, "I am the way and the truth and the life. No one comes to the Father except through me."
The Gospel of the Lord.

18   Jn 17:24–26

I wish that where I am they also may be with me.

A reading from the holy Gospel according to John

Jesus raised his eyes to heaven and said:

"Father, those whom you gave me are your gift to me. I wish that where I am they also may be with me, that they may see my glory that you gave me, because you loved me before the foundation of the world. Righteous Father, the world also does not know you, but I know you, and they know that you sent me. I made known to them your name and I will make it known, that the love with which you loved me may be in them and I in them."
The Gospel of the Lord.

19   Jn 19:17–18, 25–39

And bowing his head he handed over his Spirit.

A reading from the holy Gospel according to John

So they took Jesus, and, carrying the cross himself, he went out to what is called the Place of the Skull, in Hebrew, Golgotha. There they crucified him, and with him two others, one on either side, with Jesus in the middle.

Standing by the cross of Jesus were his mother and his mother's sister, Mary the wife of Clopas, and Mary Magdalene. When Jesus saw his mother and the disciple whom he loved, he said to his mother, "Woman, behold, your son." Then he said to the disciple, "Behold, your mother." And from that hour the disciple took her into his home.

After this, aware that everything was now finished, in order that the Scripture might be fulfilled, Jesus said, "I thirst." There was a vessel filled with common wine. So they put a sponge soaked in wine on a sprig of hyssop and put it up to his mouth. When Jesus had taken the wine, he said, "It is finished." And bowing his head, he handed over the Spirit.

Now since it was preparation day, in order that the bodies might not remain on the cross on the sabbath, for the sabbath day of that week was a solemn one, the Jews asked Pilate that their legs be broken and they be taken down. So the soldiers came and broke the legs of the first and then of the other one who was crucified with Jesus. But when they came to Jesus and saw that he was already dead, they did not break his legs, but one soldier thrust his lance into his side, and immediately Blood and water flowed out. An eyewitness has testified, and his testimony is true; he knows that he is speaking the truth, so that you also may come to believe. For this happened so that the Scripture passage might be fulfilled: *Not a bone of it will be broken.* And again another passage says: *They will look upon him whom they have pierced.*

After this, Joseph of Arimathea, secretly a disciple of Jesus for fear of the Jews, asked Pilate if he could remove the Body of Jesus. And Pilate permitted it. So he came and took his Body.

Nicodemus, the one who had first come to him at night, also came bringing a mixture of myrrh and aloes weighing about one hundred pounds.

The Gospel of the Lord.

FUNERALS FOR BAPTIZED CHILDREN

READING I   From the Old Testament

1   Is 25:6a, 7–9

See above reading n. 5 in the first set of Old Testament readings (p. 2410).

2   Lam 3:22–26

It is good to hope in silence for the saving help of the Lord.

A reading from the Book of Lamentations

The favors of the LORD are not exhausted,
    his mercies are not spent;
They are renewed each morning,
    so great is his faithfulness.
My portion is the LORD, says my soul;
    therefore will I hope in him.
Good is the LORD to one who waits for him,
    to the soul that seeks him;
It is good to hope in silence
    for the saving help of the LORD.

The word of the Lord.

READING I From the New Testament

During the Easter Season

1

Rv 7:9–10, 15–17

God will wipe away every tear from their eyes.

A reading from the Book of Revelation

I, John, had a vision of a great multitude, which no one could count, from every nation, race, people, and tongue. They stood before the throne and before the Lamb, wearing white robes and holding palm branches in their hands. They cried out in a loud voice:

"Salvation comes from our God, who is seated on the
    throne,
and from the Lamb.

"For this reason they stand before God's throne
    and worship him day and night in his temple.
    The One who sits on the throne will shelter them.
They will not hunger or thirst anymore,
    nor will the sun or any heat strike them.
For the Lamb who is in the center of the throne
    will shepherd them
    and lead them to springs of life-giving water,
    and God will wipe away every tear from their eyes."

The word of the Lord.

2

Rv 21:1a, 3–5a

There shall be no more death.

A reading from the Book of Revelation

I, John, saw a new heaven and a new earth. I heard a loud voice from the throne saying, "Behold, God's dwelling is with the human race. He will dwell with them and they will be his people and God himself will always be with them as their God. He will wipe away every tear from their eyes, and there shall be no more death or mourning, wailing or pain, for the old order has passed away."

The One who sat on the throne said, "Behold, I make all things new."

The word of the Lord.

Responsorial Psalm

 Ps 23:1–3, 4, 5, 6

R. The Lord is my shepherd; there is nothing I shall want.

The LORD is my shepherd; I shall not want.
  In verdant pastures he gives me repose;
Beside restful waters he leads me;
  he refreshes my soul.
He guides me in right paths
  for his name's sake.

R. The Lord is my shepherd; there is nothing I shall want.

Even though I walk in the dark valley
  I fear no evil; for you are at my side
With your rod and your staff
  that give me courage.

R. The Lord is my shepherd; there is nothing I shall want.

You spread the table before me
  in the sight of my foes;
You anoint my head with oil;
  my cup overflows.

R. The Lord is my shepherd; there is nothing I shall want.

Only goodness and kindness follow me
  all the days of my life;

And I shall dwell in the house of the LORD
  for years to come.

R. The Lord is my shepherd; there is nothing I shall want.

2

Ps 25:4 – 5ab, 6 and 7bc, 20 – 21

R. To you, O Lord, I lift up my soul.

Your ways, O LORD, make known to me;
  teach me your paths,
Guide me in your truth and teach me,
  for you are God my savior.

R. To you, O Lord, I lift up my soul.

Remember that your compassion, O LORD,
  and your kindness are from of old.
In your kindness remember me,
  because of your goodness, O LORD.

R. To you, O Lord, I lift up my soul.

Preserve my life, and rescue me;
  let me not be put to shame, for I take refuge in you.
Let integrity and uprightness preserve me,
  because I wait for you, O LORD.

R. To you, O Lord, I lift up my soul.

3

Ps 42:2, 3, 5cdef; 43:3, 4, 5

**R. My soul is thirsting for the living God: when shall I see
  him face to face.**

As the hind longs for the running waters,
  so my soul longs for you, O God.

**R. My soul is thirsting for the living God: when shall I see
  him face to face.**

Athirst is my soul for God, the living God.
  When shall I go and behold the face of God?

R. My soul is thirsting for the living God: when shall I see him face to face.

I went with the throng
  and led them in procession to the house of God.
Amid loud cries of joy and thanksgiving,
  with the multitude keeping festival.

R. My soul is thirsting for the living God: when shall I see him face to face.

Send forth your light and your fidelity;
  they shall lead me on
And bring me to your holy mountain,
  to your dwelling-place.

R. My soul is thirsting for the living God: when shall I see him face to face.

Then will I go in to the altar of God,
  the God of my gladness and joy;
Then will I give you thanks upon the harp,
  O God, my God!

R. My soul is thirsting for the living God: when shall I see him face to face.

Why are you so downcast, O my soul?
  Why do you sigh within me?
Hope in God! For I shall again be thanking him,
  in the presence of my savior and my God.

R. My soul is thirsting for the living God: when shall I see him face to face.

4   Ps 148:1–2, 11–13a, 13c–14

R. Let all praise the name of the Lord.

Praise the LORD from the heavens,
  praise him in the heights;
Praise him, all you his angels,
  praise him, all you his hosts.

R. Let all praise the name of the Lord.

Let the kings of the earth and all peoples,
  the princes and all the judges of the earth,
Young men too, and maidens,
  old men and boys,
Praise the name of the LORD,
  for his name alone is exalted.

R. Let all praise the name of the Lord.

His majesty is above earth and heaven,
  and he has lifted up the horn of his people.
Be this his praise from all his faithful ones,
  from the children of Israel, the people close to him. Alleluia.

R. Let all praise the name of the Lord.

Or: **R. Alleluia.**

READING II   From the New Testament

1   Rom 6:3 –4, 8 –9

See above New Testament reading n. 3, short form (p. 2424).

2   Rom 14:7–9

Whether we live or die, we are the Lord's.

A reading from the Letter of Saint Paul to the Romans

Brothers and sisters:

No one lives for oneself, and no one dies for oneself. For if we
live, we live for the Lord, and if we die, we die for the Lord; so
then, whether we live or die, we are the Lord's. For this is why
Christ died and came to life, that he might be Lord of both the
dead and the living.

The word of the Lord.

3

1 Cor 15:20 – 23

So too in Christ shall all be brought to life.

A reading from the first Letter of Saint Paul to the Corinthians

Brothers and sisters:

Christ has been raised from the dead, the firstfruits of those who have fallen asleep. For since death came through a man, the resurrection of the dead came also through man. For just as in Adam all die, so too in Christ shall all be brought to life, but each one in proper order: Christ the firstfruits; then, at his coming, those who belong to Christ.

The word of the Lord.

4

Eph 1:3 – 5

He chose us in him, before the foundation of the world, to be holy.

A reading from the Letter of Saint Paul to the Ephesians

Blessed be the God and Father of our Lord Jesus Christ, who has blessed us in Christ with every spiritual blessing in the heavens, as he chose us in him, before the foundation of the world, to be holy and without blemish before him. In love he destined us for adoption to himself through Jesus Christ, in accord with the favor of his will.

The word of the Lord.

5

1 Thes 4:13 –14, 18

We shall be with the Lord forever.

A reading from the first Letter of Saint Paul to the Thessalonians

We do not want you to be unaware, brothers and sisters, about those who have fallen asleep, so that you may not grieve like the rest, who have no hope. For if we believe that Jesus died and rose, so too will God, through Jesus, bring with him those who have fallen asleep. Therefore, console one another with these words.

The word of the Lord.

ALLELUIA VERSE AND VERSE BEFORE THE GOSPEL

1 See Mt 11:25

Blessed are you, Father, Lord of heaven and earth;
you have revealed to the childlike the mysteries of the Kingdom.

2 Jn 6:39

This is the will of my Father, says the Lord,
that I should lose nothing of all that he has given to me,
and that I should raise it up on the last day.

3 2 Cor 1:3b–4a

Blessed be the Father of compassion and God of all encouragement,
who encourages us in our every affliction.

GOSPEL

1 Mt 11:25–30

See the Common of Holy Men and Women (p. 2306).

2 Mk 10:13–16

See the Common of Holy Men and Women (p. 2315).

Jn 6:37–40 or 6:37–39

This is the will of my Father,
that I should not lose anything of what he gave me.

A reading from the holy Gospel according to John

Long form follows; for short form omit what is in brackets.

Jesus said to the crowds: "Everything that the Father gives me will come to me, and I will not reject anyone who comes to me, because I came down from heaven not to do my own will but the will of the one who sent me. And this is the will of the one who sent me, that I should not lose anything of what he gave me, but that I should raise it on the last day. [For this is the will of my Father, that everyone who sees the Son and believes in him may have eternal life, and I shall raise him on the last day."]

The Gospel of the Lord.

4

Jn 6:51–58

(For a child who had already received the Eucharist)

Whoever eats this bread will live forever,
and I will raise him up on the last day.

A reading from the holy Gospel according to John

Jesus said to the Jews: "I am the living bread that came down from heaven; whoever eats this bread will live forever; and the bread that I will give is my Flesh for the life of the world."

The Jews quarreled among themselves, saying, "How can this man give us his Flesh to eat?" Jesus said to them, "Amen, amen, I say to you, unless you eat the Flesh of the Son of Man

and drink his Blood, you do not have life within you. Whoever eats my Flesh and drinks my Blood has eternal life, and I will raise him on the last day. For my Flesh is true food, and my Blood is true drink. Whoever eats my Flesh and drinks my Blood remains in me and I in him. Just as the living Father sent me and I have life because of the Father, so also the one who feeds on me will have life because of me. This is the bread that came down from heaven. Unlike your ancestors who ate and still died, whoever eats this bread will live forever."
The Gospel of the Lord.

5   Jn 11:32–38, 40

If you believe, you will see the glory of God.

A reading from the holy Gospel according to John

When Mary [the sister of Lazarus] came to where Jesus was and saw him, she fell at his feet and said to him, "Lord, if you had been here, my brother would not have died." When Jesus saw her weeping and the Jews who had come with her weeping, he became perturbed and deeply troubled, and said, "Where have you laid him?" They said to him, "Sir, come and see." And Jesus wept. So the Jews said, "See how he loved him." But some of them said, "Could not the one who opened the eyes of the blind man have done something so that this man would not have died?"

So Jesus, perturbed again, came to the tomb. It was a cave, and a stone lay across it. Jesus said to her, "Did I not tell you that if you believe you will see the glory of God?"
The Gospel of the Lord.

6

Jn 19:25–30

Behold, your mother.

A reading from the holy Gospel according to John

Standing by the cross of Jesus were his mother and his mother's sister, Mary the wife of Clopas, and Mary Magdalene. When Jesus saw his mother and the disciple whom he loved he said to his mother, "Woman, behold, your son." Then he said to the disciple, "Behold, your mother." And from that hour the disciple took her into his home.

After this, aware that everything was now finished, in order that the Scripture might be fulfilled, Jesus said, "I thirst." There was a vessel filled with common wine. So they put a sponge soaked in wine on a sprig of hyssop and put it up to his mouth. When Jesus had taken the wine, he said, "It is finished." And bowing his head, he handed over the spirit.

The Gospel of the Lord.

FUNERALS FOR CHILDREN WHO DIED BEFORE BAPTISM

READING I   From the Old Testament

1

Is 25:6a, 7–8

He will destroy death forever.

A reading from the Book of the Prophet Isaiah

On this mountain the LORD of hosts
   will provide for all peoples.

On this mountain he will destroy
    the veil that veils all peoples,
The web that is woven over all nations;
    he will destroy death forever.
The Lord GOD will wipe away
    the tears from all faces.

The word of the Lord.

2   Lam 3:22–26

*See above: Funerals for Baptized Children, Old Testament reading n. 2,
(p. 2445).*

Responsorial Psalm   25:4–5ab, 6 and 7b, 17 and 20

R. To you, O Lord, I lift up my soul.

Your way, O Lord, make known to me;
    teach me your paths.
Guide me in your truth and teach me,
    for you are God my savior.

R. To you, O Lord, I lift up my soul.

Remember that your compassion, O LORD,
    and your kindness are from of old.
In your kindness remember me,
    because of your goodness, O LORD.

R. To you, O Lord, I lift up my soul.

Relieve the troubles of my heart;
    bring me out of my distress.
Preserve my life and rescue me;
    let me not be put to shame, for I take refuge in you.

R. To you, O Lord, I lift up my soul.

ALLELUIA VERSE AND VERSE BEFORE THE GOSPEL

1 2 Cor 1:3b–4a

Blessed be the Father of compassion and God of all encouragement,

who encourages us in our every affliction.

2 Rv 1:5a, 6b

Jesus Christ is the firstborn from the dead;

glory and kingship be his forever and ever. Amen.

GOSPEL

1   Mt 11:25–30

See the Common of Holy Men and Women (p. 2306).

2   Mk 15:33–46

Jesus gave a loud cry and breathed his last.

A reading from the holy Gospel according to Mark

At noon darkness came over the whole land until three in the afternoon. And at three o'clock Jesus cried out in a loud voice, *"Eloi, Eloi, lema sabachthani?"* which is translated, "My God, my God, why have you forsaken me?" Some of the bystanders who heard it said, "Look, he is calling Elijah." One of them ran, soaked a sponge with wine, put it on a reed, and gave it to him to drink, saying, "Wait, let us see if Elijah comes to take him down." Jesus gave a loud cry and breathed his last. The veil of the sanctuary was torn in two from top to bottom. When the centurion who stood facing him saw how he breathed his last he said, "Truly this man was the Son of God!" There were also women looking on from a distance. Among them were Mary Magdalene, Mary the mother of the younger James, and of Joses, and Salome. These women had followed him when he was in Galilee and ministered to him. There were also many other women who had come up with him to Jerusalem.

When it was already evening, since it was the day of preparation, the day before the sabbath, Joseph of Arimathea, a distinguished member of the council, who was himself awaiting the Kingdom of God, came and courageously went to Pilate and asked for the Body of Jesus. Pilate was amazed that he was already dead. He summoned the centurion and asked him if Jesus had already died. And when he learned of it from the centurion, he gave the Body to Joseph. Having bought a linen cloth, he took him down, wrapped him in the linen cloth, and laid him in a tomb that had been hewn out of the rock. Then he rolled a stone against the entrance of the tomb.

The Gospel of the Lord.

3   Jn 19:25–30

See above reading n. 6 (p. 2455).

TREASURY OF PRAYERS

Prayers to God the Father

Father,
Love, spring of living water, we call upon you.
We need your light,
your zest, your freshness.
Melt what is frozen, warm what is tepid,
enlighten what is dark, water what is dry.

Father, make us truly your children,
aware of the eternal source
that gives life to each of us,
in the certainty that in you, there is no end,
but eternal life. Amen.

—*David M. Turoldo,* Revelation of Love

Father,
send the gift of peace into our hearts.
You know our efforts to follow
the trail that Jesus has blazed before us.
Forgive our weakness and infidelity,
so that, reinvigorated by your Spirit of peace,
we may resume our journey with greater courage
until we reach the home where you wait for us. Amen.

—*David M. Turoldo,* Revelation of Love

Prayers to Jesus

Anima Christi

Soul of Christ, make me holy.
Body of Christ, be my salvation.
Blood of Christ, let me drink your wine.
Water flowing from Christ's side, wash me clean.
Passion of Christ, strengthen me.
O Good Jesus, hear my prayer:

Hide me within your wounds
and keep me close to you.
Defend me from all evil;
call me at my death
to the fellowship of your saints
that I may sing your praises with them
for all eternity.

—Traditional

Prayer to Jesus, Divine Master

Jesus Master, you have words of eternal life.
Replace my thoughts with your thoughts,
I want my thinking to be influenced by your teaching;
I want to make decisions according to your standards.
You are the Truth given to me by the Father.
Live in my mind, Jesus Truth!

Your life is the Way—certain, unique, true,
the way of love for the Father,
the way of love for others to the point of total sacrifice.
Grant that I may understand your way.
At every moment, may I follow you,
and may I refuse to follow

every way that is not yours.
What you want, I want; give me your will in place of mine.

Jesus, substitute your heart for my heart.
With your divine life, illumine my life.
You say, *"I am the life."* Therefore, live in me.
May your life be evident in my own living,
just as happened with Saint Paul, who said,
"Christ lives in me."

Live in me, Jesus Master, Way, Truth and Life.
—*Blessed James Alberione, SSP*

Hymn to Christ

Christ of our sufferings,
Christ of our sacrifices,
Christ of our Gethsemane,
Christ of our difficult transformations,
Christ of our faithful service to our neighbor,
Christ of our pilgrimage,
Christ of our community,
Christ our Redeemer,
Christ our Brother! Amen.

—*Pope John Paul II*

Prayers to the Holy Spirit

To the Spirit of Light and Love

May the Holy Spirit,
the Spirit of Pentecost
help you to clarify what is ambiguous,
to give warmth to what is indifferent,

to enlighten what is obscure,
to be before the world
true and generous witnesses of Christ's love,
for no one can live without love.

—*Pope John Paul II*

From a Pentecost Novena

Who are you, sweet light, that fills me
and illumines the darkness of my heart?
You lead me like a mother's hand;
and should you let go of me,
I would not know how to take another step.
You are the space
that embraces my being and buries it in yourself.
You, nearer to me than I to myself
and more interior than my most interior:
Holy Spirit—eternal love!
Holy Spirit—eternal life!
Holy Spirit—ray that penetrates everything!
Holy Spirit—victorious power!
Holy Spirit—God's molding hand!
Holy Spirit—Creator of all!

—*Saint Edith Stein*

Prayers to Mary

Prayer to Mary Immaculate
Patroness of the United States

O Immaculate Mary,
Mother, Teacher, and Queen,
watch over with a loving smile

this nation and its inhabitants.
Your heart welcomes and enfolds all people
in a loving embrace of peace.

You continue to look down upon the earth,
upon the just and the erring,
ever concerned for the salvation of all people.
You remember that Jesus, when dying on the cross,
gave you to us as our Mother,
and inflamed your heart with universal love and care.
Therefore, continue to inspire vocations;
comfort those who labor for the Gospel;
render all hearts docile to the Divine Master.

Through you may all people find in Christ,
the Way, the Truth, and the Life.
May they allow Christ's light to shine upon the world;
and may they always seek the kingdom of God
and his peace and justice.

—Blessed James Alberione, SSP

The Memorare

Remember, O most gracious Virgin Mary,
that never was it known
that anyone who fled to your protection,
implored your help, or sought your intercession,
was left unaided.
Inspired by this confidence,
I fly to you, O Virgin of virgins, my Mother.
To you I come; before you I stand, sinful and sorrowful.
O Mother of the Word Incarnate!
Despise not my petitions,
but in your mercy hear and answer me. Amen.

—Traditional

Pauline
BOOKS & MEDIA

The Daughters of St. Paul operate book and media centers at the following addresses. Visit, call or write the one nearest you today, or find us on the World Wide Web, www.pauline.org